Background on . . .—background information on the topics and/or the people designed to give students a concrete "handle" on the subject.

BACKGROUND ON CHESTER I. BARNARD

Chester Barnard personified the Horatio Alger ideal of a farm boy who made good. Although he never received his degree from Harvard because he lacked a laboratory science course, he has earned a place in history as an eminent management scholar.

Chester I. Barnard. Barnard (1886–1961) became president of New Jersey Bell in 1927. He used his work experiences and his extensive readings in sociology and philosophy to formulate his theories on organizational life. According to Barnard, people come together in formal organizations to achieve things they could not achieve working alone. But as they pursue the organization's goals, they must also satisfy their individual needs. And so Barnard arrived at his central thesis: An enterprise can operate efficiently and survive only when both the organization's goals and the aims and needs of [illegible] working for it are kept in balance.

Here's An Example—real-world examples make lectures lively by illustrating concepts with facts and anecdotes about actual management practices.

THE INTERNATIONAL ENVIRONMENT OF ORGANIZATIONS

HERE'S AN EXAMPLE

Two large corporations, one USA-based and the other Canadian-based, have formed a joint organization called Corporate Networks Operation that will develop and market automated office equipment. Northern Telecom, Ltd. makes telecommunication equipment and Hewlett-Packard Company makes computers and scientific instruments. The joint alliance is viewed as a defense against giant IBM (and its Rolm Corporation subsidiary) and AT&T (with its investments in Ing. C. Olivetti & Co., S.p.A. and Sun Microsystems, Inc.). (*Wall Street Journal*, 5/12/88, p. 13)

The globalization of business is one of the most important changes in the external environment of most organizations. A growing number of companies operate production facilities outside the United States and market their products abroad; even companies with only ostensibly domestic operations face international competition and rely on foreign suppliers. The daily press is filled with reports of trade deficits, calls for protectionism or for free trade, and the latest-breaking news on China, the Soviet Union, and other countries that are experimenting with alternative market mechanisms. Managers can no longer afford to concentrate solely on a domestic point of view. In this section, we will briefly survey a few selected aspects of the international situation that must be classified as aspects of an organization's *environment*. Chapter 24 will be devoted to a full-scale discussion of the nature and nuances of global culture and competition.

New Technology

Class Comments—provide anecdotes or factual data for emphasis

CLASS COMMENT

A one-page advertisement in the *Wall Street Journal*, in May 1988, listing several companies was Ford Motor Company's way of saying "Thanks for the Quality" to its suppliers. Ford's Q1 Preferred Quality Award is a special tribute to those suppliers helping the car company produce the highest quality American cars and trucks. Ford made clear by this advertisement that they recognized the role suppliers take in helping them achieve their goal of Quality Job 1.

Suppliers. Every organization appropriates raw materials, services, energy, equipment, and labor from the environment and uses them to produce its output. What the organization brings in from the environment—and what it *does* with what it brings in—will determine both the quality and the price of its final product, and every organization is therefore dependent upon the suppliers of materials and labor.

Organizations usually deal with suppliers of materials, services, and energy through a purchasing manager or an agent. The purchasing manager has relationships with several competing suppliers, and he or she may choose on occasion to pay a higher unit price in order to keep the organization from becoming overly dependent on

ANNOTATED INSTRUCTOR'S EDITION

MANAGEMENT

ANNOTATED INSTRUCTOR'S EDITION

Mary Coulter
Jack Hill
Gary Yunker

MANAGEMENT

Fourth Edition

James A.F. Stoner
Fordham University

R. Edward Freeman
University of Virginia

Prentice Hall
Englewood Cliffs, New Jersey 07632

Development editor: Ronald S. Librach
Editorial/production supervision: Eleanor Perz
Interior/cover design: Jayne Conte
Cover photo: The Metropolitan Museum of Art/George A. Hearn Fund, 1968
Photo research: Kay Dellosa
Interior art: Network Graphics
Manufacturing buyer: Ed O'Dougherty

A Division of Simon & Schuster
Englewood Cliffs, New Jersey 07632

Printed in the United States of America
10 9 8 7 6 5 4 3 2 1

ISBN 0-13-548884-2

Prentice-Hall International (UK) Limited, *London*
Prentice-Hall of Australia Pty. Limited, *Sydney*
Prentice-Hall Canada Inc., *Toronto*
Prentice-Hall Hispanoamericana, S.A., *Mexico*
Prentice-Hall of India Private Limited, *New Delhi*
Prentice-Hall of Japan, Inc., *Tokyo*
Simon & Schuster Asia Pte. Ltd., *Singapore*
Editora Prentice-Hall do Brasil, Ltda., *Rio de Janeiro*

Contents of the AIE

Preface to the AIE AIE-viii

Introduction to the Instructor's Manual AIE-x

OBJECTIVES OF THE INSTRUCTOR'S MANUAL AIE-x

General Philosophy, Ideas, and Structure of the Text AIE-x

Overall Structure of the Book and Chapter Format AIE-xi

DEVELOPING THE COURSE AIE-xi

Increasing Student Interest in the Study of Management AIE-xi

EXAMPLES OF COURSE POLICIES (CLASSES OF 30–40 STUDENTS) AIE-xii

Grading (Structured) AIE-xii
Grading (Holistic and Subjective) AIE-xii

WRITTEN ASSIGNMENTS: TERM PAPERS AND THEIR ALTERNATIVES AIE-xiii

Term Papers AIE-xiii
Selected Library References for Better Term Papers AIE-xiv
Alternatives to Term Papers AIE-xiv
Improving the Quality of Written Papers AIE-xv

ORAL ASSIGNMENTS AIE-xv

Sample Course Outlines AIE-xvi

Additional Supplementary Aids for the Instructor AIE-xix

Instructor's Resource Package AIE-xix
Supplements Guide AIE-xix
Diploma—Classroom Management System AIE-xix
Test Item File AIE-xx
Telephone Test Preparation Service AIE-xx
Transparency Masters AIE-xx
Color Transparencies AIE-xxi
Lecture Extras AIE-xxi
Videos and Films AIE-xxi

ADDITIONAL SUPPLEMENTS FOR THE STUDENT AIE-xxi

Using Acumen: Educational Version AIE-xxiii

INTRODUCTION AIE-xxiii

What Is *Acumen?* AIE-xxiii

How *Acumen* Measures Self-Concept AIE-xxiv

How Self-Concept Relates to Management Style AIE-xxiv

Interpretation of the Graphic Profile AIE-xxv

Suggested Uses of *Acumen* Results in Relation to the Text AIE-xxvii

Chapter Teaching Guides

Part 1 INTRODUCTION TO MANAGEMENT

1 MANAGING AND MANAGERS AIE-1

2 THE EVOLUTION OF MANAGEMENT THEORY AIE-6

3 THE EXTERNAL ENVIRONMENT OF ORGANIZATIONS AIE-11

4 SOCIAL RESPONSIBILITY AND ETHICS AIE-16

PART 1 CASES AIE-20

Part 2 PLANNING AND DECISION MAKING

5 EFFECTIVE PLANNING AND MANAGEMENT SCIENCE AIE-22

6 PROBLEM SOLVING AND DECISION MAKING AIE-27

7 STRATEGIC PLANNING AND MANAGEMENT AIE-32

8 STRATEGY IMPLEMENTATION AIE-37

PART 2 CASE AIE-41

Part 3 ORGANIZING FOR STABILITY AND CHANGE

9 DIVISION OF WORK, ORGANIZATIONAL STRUCTURE, AND COORDINATION AIE-43

10 AUTHORITY, DELEGATION, AND DECENTRALIZATION AIE-48

11 HUMAN RESOURCE MANAGEMENT AIE-53

12 MANAGING ORGANIZATIONAL CHANGE AND DEVELOPMENT AIE-58

13 MANAGING ORGANIZATIONAL CONFLICT AND CREATIVITY AIE-63

PART 3 CASES AIE-67

Part 4 LEADING

14 MOTIVATION, PERFORMANCE, AND SATISFACTION AIE-69

15 LEADERSHIP AIE-74

16 GROUPS AND COMMITTEES AIE-79

17 INTERPERSONAL AND ORGANIZATIONAL COMMUNICATION AIE-84

PART 4 CASE AIE-88

Part 5 CONTROLLING

18 EFFECTIVE CONTROL AIE-91

19 FINANCIAL CONTROL METHODS AIE-95

20 PRODUCTIVITY AND OPERATIONAL CONTROL AIE-100

21 INFORMATION SYSTEMS AND CONTROL AIE-105

PART 5 CASE AIE-110

Part 6 EMERGING CONCEPTS IN MANAGEMENT

22 ENTREPRENEURSHIP AIE-111

23 ORGANIZATIONAL CAREERS AND INDIVIDUAL DEVELOPMENT AIE-116

24 INTERNATIONAL MANAGEMENT AIE-122

PART 6 CASE AIE-126

Preface to the AIE

Of all the supplements in the package accompanying *Management*, the *Annotated Instructor's Edition (AIE)* is perhaps the most innovative and the one that will be of the most help in teaching your course. Basically, the *AIE* combines two kinds of support materials. First, the *Instructor's Manual (IM)* is bound into the front of the *AIE*. The second component of the *AIE* includes the text itself supplemented with various kinds of marginal teaching notes or tips.

The concept of the *AIE*, then, puts into actual practice what professors have done for years—making brief notes in the margins of their lecture notes; clipping bits and pieces of relevant information or anecdotes from magazine or newspaper articles; jotting down thoughts on slips of paper and filing them away to enhance the teaching of a particular topic or chapter. An *AIE* pulls all of these common practices together into a convenient format and then combines with the *Instructor's Manual* to provide not only general help in teaching the course but also answers to text questions and analyses of cases included in the text.

The Fourth Edition of *Management* is the first principles of management text to offer an *Annotated Instructor's Edition*. Following is a more complete description of its features.

The Instructor's Resource Manual

The *Instructor's Manual* was written by Jack Hill of the University of Nebraska and includes as a major feature instructions written by Gary Yunker of Jacksonville University for using *Acumen: Educational Version with Management, Fourth Edition*.

In the introduction to the *Instructor's Manual*, Professor Hill provides an overview of the general philosophy, ideas, and structure of the text, suggestions for developing the course, examples of course-grading policies, suggestions for oral and written assignments (including term papers and alternatives to them), four alternate course outlines, and a complete description of all of the supplements available for both the professor and the student.

Following the introductory material in the *IM* is the instructor material for using *Acumen: Educational Version with Management*. It provides background information on the Acumen program and shows how students can link their profiles to topics and issues discussed in the text chapters.

Then, for each text chapter, the *Instructor's Manual* contains a chapter outline, list of key terms, chapter overview, analysis of the Illustrative Case Study, answers to end-of-chapter review questions, analysis of chapter-ending cases, suggested term paper topics and suggestions for guest speakers. Finally, the *IM* provides an analysis of the comprehensive integrative cases that conclude each major section or unit of chapters.

Chapter Annotations

Specific types of annotations in every chapter of the textbook include the following:

CLASS COMMENTS

These annotations provide anecdotes or factual data that you might want to emphasize for students as you lecture.

HERE'S AN EXAMPLE

Numerous and varied examples of management practices are provided. Each is tied to a certain concept presented in the chapter. In most chapters, several examples are presented, providing you with ample opportunities to pick and choose those that you want to use as you teach.

THOUGHT-PROVOKERS

These questions are designed to get students to think! Naturally, there may be no easily available answers to every question, but at least the students will begin to appreciate the complexity and dynamics of the management process.

DISCUSSION QUESTIONS

These questions are meant to prompt open discussion during class. Pose them to the students as you lecture, get their feedback, and use the discussion practice to make your points.

TEACHING TIPS

Throughout most of the chapters, we have provided you with some suggestions for making the class more exciting and manageable. Some professors may not need to use these, but others may find them useful as they teach.

QUOTATIONS FROM MANAGERS/ OTHERS

These quotations are usually short enough to be copied on the board or reproduced on a transparency. Instructors have found that students usually have some type of reaction to what the manager is saying and that lively class discussions often ensue.

COORDINATED RESOURCE

When applicable, we have attempted to provide you with some practical resources that can be used in conjunction with a given chapter. Some of these are videotapes, some are films, some are books, and some are other types of periodicals. As you know, resources that carefully complement the textbook can often add much to the learning experience.

BACKGROUND ON . . .

In some of the chapters, we thought it would be helpful to those teaching the course to have some background information on the topics and/or the people discussed in the text. Much of this background information is not only inherently interesting, but will also give students a concrete ''handle'' on topics that are otherwise being analyzed in new terms and new contexts.

A HUMOROUS NOTE

Managers and organizations sometimes do ''funny'' things. When we found something that we thought would pique student interest because it was amusing, we included it as a laugher! Hopefully, by helping your students to see the humor in these pieces, you'll be able to emphasize the point that, although management is serious business, managers are human!

EXTRA EXERCISES

These exercises supplement cases and questions included at the end of the chapters. They are designed to enhance and illustrate certain chapter concepts.

We hope you'll find this teaching tool to be state-of-the-art, interesting, exciting, and useful. We honestly believe that it will enhance and enrich your basic management course.

Mary Coulter
Jack A. Hill
Gary W. Yunker

Introduction to the Instructor's Manual

The Instructor's Manual (IM) portion of this annotated edition follows the format of the text based on the well-established *processes of management* point of view. The IM is written to provide a balance of ideas about teaching management and presenting the text to students; it offers an integrated approach to teaching the course through the use of the package of supplements.

This manual includes an overview of the text—its philosophy and structure; ideas about developing the course, especially developing student interest; examples of course policies; guidelines for written assignments, including cases and term papers; selected sources for assistance in writing research papers; ideas for writing better papers; oral reports; sample course outlines; and a brief discussion of the teaching supplement package.

Objectives of the Instructor's Manual

The sole purpose of the IM is to conserve your time in preparation for teaching this basic course in management. This manual should assist you in identifying and selecting teaching aids and topics from an extensive menu of material available through the comprehensive set of supplements.

The IM first undertakes a series of discussions on selected topics pertaining to teaching this dynamic course in management. Included are suggestions of ways to increase student interest in the study of management, for workable course policies and approaches to using written assignments, including term papers, alternatives to term papers such as book reports, and abstracts. A brief listing of library sources is provided for research purposes. The first section concludes with suggestions to help students improve the quality of their written work. With very little editing, parts of the IM could readily become handouts for student use. For instructors who desire to have students present oral reports, a few recommendations are included for improving the quality of such reports.

To cover teaching terms of varying lengths, four course outlines are presented. These outlines do not include course policies since individual preferences are too numerous to contemplate.

This Instructor's Manual is organized to provide:

- Chapter outline (1st, 2nd & 3rd level heads as applicable)
- List of key terms
- Chapter overview/synopsis
- Analysis of the "Illustrated Case Study:
  Introduction"
  Continuing"
  Concluding"
- Answers to end-of-chapter review questions
- Analysis of end-of-chapter cases with answers to case questions
- Suggested term paper topics
- Suggested guest speakers
- Analysis of comprehensive cases that conclude each part of the text

You will find the annotations in the margins and the teaching tips to be useful aids in teaching the comprehensive subject of the process of management. These annotations provide the kind of information instructors often write in book margins to remind themselves about points to stress or questions to ask to stimulate class discussion.

General Philosophy, Ideas, and Structure of the Text

The authors approach management from both a comprehensive and an integrative viewpoint in that management is presented as a *process* rather than as a series of unrelated steps. Thus, when management is said to be "the art of getting things done through people," the attainment of "getting things done" occurs as a result of the blending of many functions. The blending is seen to vary according to the purposes to be realized as a result of human endeavor. Every manager needs a system that works to get things done—in this text, the system is a process. The process requires not only goal setting but planning to ensure that things happen that otherwise would not occur. It takes resources to achieve goals, and managers have two types: human resources and material resources. Resources, however, do not apply themselves—*leading* becomes the means to directing people to use the resources necessary to reach a goal. Finally, the authors emphasize that a means of reviewing organizational efforts is necessary. Therefore, controlling becomes an essential part of a manager's process since both the effort made to attain a result and the result itself are measured against a predetermined standard.

The overall approach to the book appears vast because so much is involved in understanding and applying what has been identified in the previous paragraphs. The authors, however, approach the subject in a way that permits the components of the managerial process to be studied separately. Second, they provide comprehensive cases and other illustrative means to help students see the integrated whole of the processes of management.

The organization of this Instructor's Manual section follows the format of the text. This format will simplify making cross-references between matching parts of the manual and the text.

OVERALL STRUCTURE OF THE BOOK AND CHAPTER FORMAT

The text is presented in six parts: Introduction, Planning and Decision Making, Organizing for Stability and Change, Leading, Controlling, and Emerging Concepts in Management. Each major section concludes with a comprehensive case. The chapters of each section are organized in the following manner:

- Chapter outlines by 1st-level headings
- Learning objectives
- An illustrated case study (referred to throughout the chapter)
- A chapter introduction
- Chapter boxes (Ethics in Management, International Management, and Applications)
- Key terms as applicable
- Summary
- Chapter review and discussion questions
- Two chapter-ending cases with questions

Developing the Course

Principles courses are presented in a variety of ways, including large group lectures, small group discussions, and seminars. No one instructional method works to the exclusion of others, but the situational approach is commonly adopted by most professors—a variety of factors must be considered. Quite often, the "right electricity" between students and instructor makes the difference. In addition, each faculty member has a preferred style of teaching and an idea of what constitutes an optimum class size. Some of us feel comfortable in a large lecture hall, while others believe the best teaching occurs in a small group seated in a circle. Instruction, therefore, is highly individualized, and it would be presumptuous to prescribe a "best" method. On the other hand, this guide will review key items in the text and its supplements to assist instructors in the development and teaching of a basic course in management.

INCREASING STUDENT INTEREST IN THE STUDY OF MANAGEMENT

Students and, for that matter, many of us see the results of what managers do but give little consideration to what goes on behind the scenes to bring things and ideas to people in useful and wanted forms. Managerial plans do not execute themselves, choices made among alternatives are not automatic, and leadership is more than a series of slogans. Nor is control a self-starting process within organizations. Managers do much of their work through a series of interconnected processes. One of an instructor's goals early in a course is to heighten student interest in the subject.

Being a Student Is Not a Spectator Sport. Students regularly carry note-taking paraphernalia and expect to take notes to help prepare for examinations. In the so-called real world referred to earlier, employees do not come to a job, take notes, and sit for scheduled examinations. Employees are expected to be *part* of their organizations rather than *apart* from their organizations. Therefore, to the extent class size and personal philosophy toward teaching permit, students should be encouraged to involve themselves in the course through active participation. At times the educational process gives students the impression they are safest when they remain quiet—and, it is true, some teachers do not like students to ask questions. One way of encouraging class participation is to make such activity a graded part of the course.

Grading student participation may seem to be a near impossibility, but it is little different than grading written materials. The judgments, however, need to be made more quickly. One essential for grading participation is to know each student by sight. If participation is to be evaluated as part of the course, students need regular feedback. This information can be handed out separately or be shown on the cover of papers being returned. If participation is evaluated, its weight needs to be told to students. About 50 percent of what would be the value of an examination seems acceptable to most students.

Good Management Is More than Applied Common Sense. Regardless of teaching method, experienced faculty members find it worthwhile to invest time to build student interest in the subject. This is especially true with management since students often feel knowledgeable about business administration. They are in contact with business on a daily basis; they see movies and television programs, read books, and in other ways develop a feeling that management is "common sense." Such a student belief may be an excellent point of departure. Why not discuss the meaning of "common sense"? What is it? Where does it come from? Does it have anything to do with one's personal values?

Some persons believe common sense to be reason applied to experience. If this belief is reasonable it would follow that to exhibit common sense a person would (a) have had experiences, and (b) have learned something from the experiences. The ideal situation requires persons to be in a state of readiness to learn. A common impediment to learning is the belief that "I already display common sense." The lack of learning readiness needs to be confronted early in the course.

One way to confront this unwillingness to learn is to pose several "commonsense" sayings and beliefs to the students and ask which statements make good sense:

> "Do unto others, as you would have them do unto you."

After obtaining general agreement about the Golden Rule, ask if the following makes "common sense" as well:

> "God helps those who help themselves."

Here are a few more contradictory statements:

> "Absence makes the heart grow fonder" and "Out of sight, out of mind."
>
> "No person should receive things which have not been earned" and "You can't let people starve."
>
> "Education is a fine thing for everyone" and "It is practical people who get things done."

The above set of seeming contradictions should help put students in a state of learning readiness. There is much more to management than a series of sayings or quotations from popular books about management. In fact, more than one person has used the letters "MBBS," Management by Best Seller.

Examples of Course Policies (Classes of 30 to 40 students)

(Several approaches are given, to be modified as necessary)

GRADING (STRUCTURED)

3 Exams @ 100 points	300
1 Final @ 100 points	100
1 Paper @ 100 points	100
TOTAL	500

GRADING (HOLISTIC AND SUBJECTIVE)

The participative nature of this course means students should expect subjectivity in the grading of their written submissions and on their class participation. A 50-point base is used to record judgment (any point base will work). Under this system, grades will be recorded as follows: A+ = 50 points, A = 48 points, A− = 46 points, etc. Percentages are *not* part of this point grading system. Participation will be reviewed every few weeks, and students will be notified regarding the point level achieved. The participation grade is cumulative, which means a "good" grade early in the course can become a "poor" grade later if the level and quality of participation are not maintained. Conversely, a "poor" grade early in the course can be improved through high-level and -quality participation for the remainder of the course.

Class Attendance. (A somewhat permissive model.) Attendance is expected and will be a contributing factor when course grades are borderline. Keep in mind that examinations include text as well as materials from class sessions.

Class Attendance. (A restrictive model based on a semester of three meetings per week of 50 minutes each.) Attendance is expected in the same manner as employees are expected to be on-the-job. Each of the first three absences will cost three points, with the penalty doubled for the fourth absence and beyond.

Written Assignments: Term Papers and Their Alternatives

Employers frequently criticize today's college students for their inability to prepare useful letters, memorandums, and reports. Faculty members generally share this feeling even though possibly contributing to the problem by overreliance on objective methods of evaluating student progress. Writing cannot be learned through responses to objective questions. The Stoner and Freeman text has a variety of discussion questions and exercises that may be used to help students express themselves in writing. Many of the supplements also present a series of topics and assignments suitable for written responses. Students sometimes feel the usual writers' manuals stress thesis preparation rather than writing needed on the job. Students can be directed to texts on business communication and report writing for assistance in writing for a business audience.

The purposes of written work are (a) to help students develop research skills using secondary sources, (b) to further enhance their writing skills, and (c) to expand their knowledge regarding the literature in the field of management.

TERM PAPERS

Library research is a proven method of helping students learn about a variety of subjects. Research-based writing provides a degree of evidence that students both understand subject matter and are able to convey their understanding to others.

The finished draft of the paper should be carefully proofread for both content and mechanical errors. The submitted theme should be free of grammatical and typographical faults. Grading is holistic and includes a consideration of both content and mechanical factors. This approach is consistent with what occurs in the world of work where both content and the "package" are evaluated. All persons have a list of things they find difficult to tolerate—even in written papers. Careful attention to detail prevents the instructor from focusing on intolerable actions and downgrading the paper as a result. To the student, the lowered grade might appear to be out of proportion to the fault cited. Yet this is a common occurrence in life: people lose out because of such things as mismatched accessories, slovenly appearance, scuffed shoes, and term papers submitted on "tissue paper" (less than 20# stock), misspelled words, redundancies, overworked words, and phrases that merely take up space without contributing to the discussion.

Suggested Guidelines for the Term Paper. The paper should be planned to cover the subject matter in a range of 10–15 pages. The paper must be typewritten, double-spaced, and submitted on 20# paper. The format should follow the *Publication Manual* of the American Psychological Association (APA). Students need experience in writing to specification. In addition, a variety of writer's manuals exist that provide students with opportunities to follow other kinds of research formats in their formal writing.

The bibliography must contain at least five references. Other than papers dealing with management history, at least half the sources must have been issued since 1983. No more than two textbooks may be used for bibliographical reference.

At least two levels of headings are to be used to display the explicit organization of the paper. The first level should be capitalized at the left margin; the second level should be upper- and lower-case underlined at the left margin. Headings help contain the topic within a framework. The absence of headings allows a rambling format similar to what occurs in speech when a person adds interjections within ideas. While listeners tend to tolerate such speech patterns, writing that deviates from the express purpose is not as readily endured.

While the content portion of the paper will be subject-matter specific, the introduction will contain at least the following:

- Purpose of the paper
- Statement of limitations (a paper cannot cover an entire subject, and this statement, together with the defense of what is being omitted, is critical to a research-based paper).
- Definition of terms. (This will save later misunderstandings on the part of the reader. While we commonly think of words as having dictionary meanings, words also have human meanings. Where ambiguities might occur, provide the needed definitions.)
- Review of the literature to be cited in the paper. (In an abbreviated form, this review covers many of the points called for in the section dealing with book reviews.)

SELECTED LIBRARY REFERENCES FOR BETTER TERM PAPERS

- *Encyclopedia of Management*—Definition of terms, a few biographies.
- *Directory of Corporate Affiliations* (annual)—Lists ownership of subsidiaries, affiliates, and divisions.
- *Golden Book of Management*—Biographies of 70 early leaders in management and their major publications.
- *Business Periodicals Index*—Comprehensive index for business subjects in major business periodicals.
- *Business Reference Sources* by Lorna Daniells—Considered to be the *bible* of business information sources.
- *Encyclopedia of Business Information Sources*—Comprehensive coverage of business subjects.
- *History of Management*—Brief history about management from the time of Moses. Includes considerable biographical information.
- *Evolution of Management Thought* by Daniel A. Wren—Outstanding! Includes some biographical information.

ALTERNATIVES TO TERM PAPERS

Two term paper alternatives might be considered to assist students to learn more about the field of management through library sources. Book or journal reports, while shorter than term papers, contribute to student research and writing capabilities. Abstracts of books or journal articles are another means of helping students become knowledgeable about management.

Book or Journal Reports. Students do a better job of reviewing books and journal articles when they adhere to a format designed to emphasize the major points of interest and the findings of the study being reported. Here is a suggested format to help ensure that students reviewing books and articles do more than sketchy writing:

1. What was the special competence of the author for undertaking the writing of this book (article)? How well did he/she succeed? (Students need to seek other writings by the author, reviews of writing, biographical sketches, speeches and papers given, etc.)
2. What, if declared or revealed, was the author's purpose(s) in undertaking this book (article)? How well was the goal achieved? (Part of this is in the introduction to the book or article, but the student must also set forth a thesis about this point and present supporting arguments for the viewpoint taken. A response to this question also reveals how well the student studied the material for relevance.)
3. What special contribution do you think this book (article) made to its field? Was it worth the effort? (While opinion is called for, students will need to make an attempt to document their reasoning through citations in the material being reviewed.)
4. What did the book (article) do for you? In other words, what was new to you? Was the material interestingly presented? (Even though opinion is called for, students need to build a case for their viewpoints rather than simply assert them.)
5. Did the book (article) stimulate your interest in its area or field? Along what lines did it interest you in pursuing further reading, investigation, or inquiries? (As before, students need to develop writing skills to document positions taken.)
6. What were the shortcomings of the book (article)? What material was omitted or developed to too small a degree? What suggestions would you have for the author to consider when and if it is revised? (Specific references to content and comparisons to other writings will help support responses to this question. The suggestions for improvement may be personal, but to the extent possible, comparisons with other writers help.)
7. Would you care to re-read the book (article) later? If yes, was this because the material was not too clearly presented? Or was the richness of the material such that one would have difficulty in absorbing it all at first reading? If no, was the book too "thin" to warrant further attention? Or was the presentation done with such clarity and simplicity that its content could be understood at first reading? (Documentation to support one's ideas always helps.)
8. Any other comments you feel relevant and beneficial?

Abstracts of Books and Articles. The viewpoint to be conveyed to students who prepare a series of abstracts about a topic is that the instructor will read the abstracts with the "mind's eye" and try to visualize a finished term paper on the basis of the abstracts. This approach helps students expand the horizons of their search for material to abstract and also emphasizes the idea that students are ''writing'' a term paper without actually writing the paper.

Abstracts may be written on 4″ × 6″ cards, or it may be suitable to have no more than two on a regular typewritten page. The dictionary concept of an abstract suggests that an abstract concentrates in itself the essential qualities of a larger thing. Here are key points for students to cover in their abstracts, but the topics covered in each abstract will need to be adjusted to fit the peculiar requirements of the book being reviewed:

- Name and source of book. (Full bibliographical description)
- What are the author's qualifications? (This may require outside research)
- What are the main points of the text? (Write a series of declarative sentences)
  What problems or issues are presented?
  What drawbacks exist with the author's analysis?
  What would be the ''payoff'' with respect to the author's ideas?
- What additional information is provided?
- In what way is the book a contribution to its field?

IMPROVING THE QUALITY OF WRITTEN PAPERS

Student complaints and questions about grades on their written work can often be traced to a lack of understanding of what instructors appraise when assigning a grade. Written papers are assigned to enhance a student's educational experience. Since written assignments, by definition, are not voluntary efforts by students, students need to know the evaluative means to be applied to their reports. The actual detail of grading needs to be developed by the instructor; however, the following represents a few items to consider when explaining subjective grading to students.

Papers assigned high grades (distinction quality) are specific in nature. The writing takes the reader to the core of the issue(s) being presented and relies on a minimum of generalized, abstract, or ''textbook'' type of thinking. This high-quality work involves the writer in appraising situations from various viewpoints used by the authorities in the field being cited in the references. The writer's main responsibility is that of combining facts and authoritative viewpoints into a logical order that leads persuasively to specific conclusions.

Papers assigned good grades are mostly specific with few lapses into generalized, abstract, or ''textbook broad brush'' type of writing. Good quality is differentiated from distinction quality by a degree of ''glossing over'' points in the conclusion or conclusions not supported by the analysis.

Average-quality work is punctuated with mentioned specifics without offering a penetrating analysis. How factors influence other factors will often be omitted, or covered so superficially as to be tantamount to being omitted. Information is presented in random order without a logical pattern. Average work is differentiated from poor-quality work by at least some indication that factor analysis has been attempted.

The mark of poor-quality writing is the attention to symptoms of problems while ignoring specifics of the situation. There will be little if any appraisal of facts or the viewpoints of other writers. Little attempt will be made to demonstrate an understanding of what is occurring within the subject being discussed. The student often writes from the position of being the authority in the field rather than making the effort to cite the authorities in the field. If recommendations are made, few, if any, reasons to support them will be demonstrated to show an awareness of cost/benefit analysis, or other points regarding the time frame required for implementation, nor the overall feasibility of implementing the recommendations with the available resources.

Failing work will be generously sprinkled with throw-away phrases of ''fix responsibility,'' ''establish job descriptions,'' ''appoint persons with better qualities of leadership,'' and similar vacuous phrases. When strategy is being discussed, opening clauses may read, ''On the whole. . . .'' Assumptions will lack factual foundations strengthened with analysis.

Oral Assignments

Several times during the semester, students may be requested to report to the class on outside assigned readings or researched topics. Oral reports serve the following objectives:

To bring to the class the viewpoint presented in the study undertaken.

To make available to class members information they might not be able to obtain currently because of the limited numbers of book copies in the library.

To give students practice in organizing information for oral presentation as well as to provide additional experience in speaking before a group for the purpose of conveying specific information.

Seasoned speakers follow proven procedures for successful presentations. Students should make note of the following aspects of effective talks:

- The facts of the report should be arranged to present only those parts of the material that have a bearing on the central thesis of the assignment. The article or book may contain other information that is interesting but with little or no relevance to the subject for discussion. Such detail should be omitted.
- In arranging the materials, the student should bear in mind the time needed for an effective presentation. Within a class, time for oral presentation will be in the ten-minute range.
- Review the report notes prior to the presentation to prevent constant referral to such notes. While making this review, keep in mind the question: "What do I expect my fellow students to learn from my presentation?"
- The report should be sufficiently outlined so that a copy can be given to the instructor. In addition, it would be helpful to provide class colleagues copies of this outline. Appropriate visual aids may be substituted for distributed copies of the outline.
- The content of the outline and the "packaging" of the presentation will be evaluated. Verbosity and inconsequential details should be avoided.
- Lists should be avoided in oral reports. If lists or statistical data are needed, they are best provided through visual aids that include transparencies, charts and graphs fastened to an appropriate surface, slides, and computer attachments that permit computer monitor images to be displayed on a regular visual aid screen.

Sample Course Outlines

The following outlines include most time configurations of quarter and semester systems:

SCHEDULE A (10-week quarter; 2 meetings a week for 75 minutes each)

Week	Meeting	Topic	Chapter
1	1	Introduction to Course	
		Managing and Managers	1
	2	The Evolution of Management Theory	2
2	1	The External Environment of Organizations	3
		Social Responsibility and Ethics	4
	2	Effective Planning	5
3	1	Problem Solving and Decision Making	6
	2	Stragetic Planning and Management	7
		Strategy Implementation	8
4	1	Division of Work, Organizational Structure, and Coordination	9
	2	Authority, Delegation, and Decentralization	10
5	1	Human Resource Management	11
	2	Managing Organizational Change and Development	12
		Managing Organizational Conflict and Creativity	13
6	1	Motivation, Performance, and Satisfaction	14
	2	Leadership	15
7	1	Groups and Committees	16
		Interpersonal and Organizational Communication	17
	2	Effective Control	18
8	1	Financial Control Methods	19
	2	Productivity and Operational Control	20
9	1	Information Systems and Control	21
	2	Entrepreneurship	22
10	1	Organizational Careers and Individual Development	23
	2	International Management	24

Examinations need to be scheduled to meet the instructor's teaching philosophy. In addition to a schedule built upon text chapters, teaching selections of ancillary assignments might be made. The Lecture Extras Supplement and visual materials should be considered.

SCHEDULE B (15-week semester; 3 meetings a week for 50 minutes each)

Week	Meeting	Topic	Chapter
1	1	Introduction to Course	
	2	Managing and Managers	1
	3	The Evolution of Management Theory	2
2	1	The Evolution of Management Theory	2
	2	The External Environment of Organizations	3
	3	The External Environment of Organizations	3
		Social Responsibility and Ethics	4
3	1	Social Responsibility and Ethics	4
	2	Effective Planning	5
	3	Effective Planning	5
4	1	Problem Solving and Decision Making	6
	2	Problem Solving and Decision Making	6
	3	Strategic Planning and Management	7
5	1	Strategic Planning and Management	7
	2	Strategy Implementation	8
	3	Strategy Implementation	8
6	1	Examination covering Chapters 1–8	
	2	Division of Work, Organizational Structure, and Coordination	9
	3	Division of Work, Organizational Structure, and Coordination	9
7	1	Authority, Delegation, and Decentralization	10
	2	Authority, Delegation, and Decentralization	10
	3	Human Resource Management	11
8	1	Human Resource Management	11
	2	Managing Organizational Change and Development	12
	3	Managing Organizational Change and Development	12
9	1	Managing Organizational Conflict and Creativity	13
	2	Managing Organizational Conflict and Creativity	13
	3	Motivation, Performance, and Satisfaction	14
10	1	Motivation, Performance, and Satisfaction	14
	2	Leadership	15
	3	Leadership	15
11	1	Groups and Committees	16
	2	Groups and Committees	16
	3	Interpersonal and Organizational Communication	17
12	1	Interpersonal and Organizational Communication	17
	2	Examination covering Chapter 9–17	
	3	Effective Control	18
13	1	Effective Control	18
	2	Financial Control Methods	19
	3	Financial Control Methods	19
14	1	Productivity and Operational Control	20
	2	Information Systems and Control	21
	3	Entrepreneurship	22
15	1	Entrepreneurship	22
	2	Organizational Careers and Individual Development	23
	3	International Management	24

Examinations need to be scheduled to meet the instructor's teaching philosophy. In addition to a schedule built upon text chapters, teaching selections of ancillary assignments might be made. The Lecture Extras Supplement and visual materials should be considered.

SCHEDULE C (15-week semester; 1 meeting a week for 150 minutes each)

Week	Meeting	Topic	Chapter
1	1	Introduction to Course	
		Managing and Managers	1
		The Evolution of Management Theory	2
2	1	The Evolution of Management Theory	2
		The External Environment of Organizations	3
		Social Responsibility and Ethics	4
3	1	Social Responsibility and Ethics	4
		Effective Planning	5
4	1	Problem Solving and Decision Making	6
		Strategic Planning and Management	7
5	1	Strategic Planning and Management	7
		Strategy Implementation	8
6	1	Examination covering Chapters 1–8	
		Division of Work, Organizational Structure, and Coordination	9
7	1	Authority, Delegation, and Decentralization	10
		Staffing and Human Resource Management	11
8	1	Human Resource Management	11
		Managing Organizational Change and Development	12
9	1	Managing Organizational Conflict and Creativity	13
		Motivation, Performance, and Satisfaction	14
10	1	Motivation, Performance, and Satisfaction	14
		Leadership	15
11	1	Groups and Committees	16
		Interpersonal and Organizational Communication	17
12	1	Interpersonal and Organizational Communication	17
	2	Examination covering Chapters 9–17	
13	1	Effective Control	18
		Financial Control Methods	19
14	1	Productivity and Operational Control	20
		Information Systems and Control	21
		Entrepreneurship	22
15	1	Entrepreneurship	22
		Organizational Careers and Individual Development	23
		International Management	24

Examinations need to be scheduled to meet the instructor's teaching philosophy. In addition to a schedule built upon text chapters, teaching selections of ancillary assignments might be made. The Lecture Extras Supplement and visual materials should be considered.

SCHEDULE D (15-week semester; 2 meetings a week for 75 minutes each)

Week	Meeting	Topic	Chapter
1	1	Introduction to Course	
	2	Managing and Managers	1
		The Evolution of Management Theory	2
2	1	The External Environment of Organizations	3
	2	Social Responsibility and Ethics	4
3	1	Social Responsibility and Ethics	4
	2	Effective Planning	5
4	1	Problem Solving and Decision Making	6
	2	Strategic Planning and Management	7

continued

SCHEDULE D CONTINUED

Week	Meeting	Topic	Chapter
5	1	Strategic Planning and Management	7
	2	Strategy Implementation	8
6	1	Examination covering Chapters 1–8	
	2	Division of Work, Organizational Structure, and Coordination	9
7	1	Authority, Delegation, and Decentralization	10
	2	Human Resource Management	11
8	1	Human Resource Management	11
	2	Managing Organizational Change and Development	12
9	1	Managing Organizational Conflict and Creativity	13
	2	Motivation, Performance, and Satisfaction	14
10	1	Motivation, Performance, and Satisfaction	14
	2	Leadership	15
11	1	Groups and Committees	16
	2	Interpersonal and Organizational Communication	17
12	1	Interpersonal and Organizational Communication	17
		Examination covering Chapters 9–17	
13	1	Effective Control	18
	2	Financial Control Methods	19
		Productivity and Operational Control	20
14	1	Information Systems and Control	21
	2	Entrepreneurship	22
15	1	Organizational Careers and Individual Development	23
	2	International Management	24

Examinations need to be scheduled to meet the instructor's teaching philosophy. In addition to a schedule built upon text chapters, teaching selections of ancillary assignments might be made. The Lecture Extras Supplement and visual materials should be considered.

Additional Supplementary Aids for the Instructor

INSTRUCTOR'S RESOURCE PACKAGE

The supplements have been assembled in an attractive slip case for ready accessibility of needed items.

SUPPLEMENTS GUIDE

The guide is arranged to parallel the text outline and contains suggestions for including material from each supplement as appropriate for specific sections of the text. More information is contained in the package of supplements than can be covered during a teaching term, but the instructor can readily adapt recommendations from the guide in ways suitable for his/her individual teaching style.

DIPLOMA—CLASSROOM MANAGEMENT SYSTEM

Diploma combines four microcomputer programs into one package: an examination generator, a grade management system, a study guide generator, and a convenient scheduling tool. Since all of DIPLOMA's programs operate in a similar manner, the time required to master the entire package is minimal.

Exam combines the editing features of a word-processor with the file-handling capabilities of a data base manager to expedite creation and editing of test question banks. EXAM accommodates an unlimited number of questions in each format: multiple choice, true/false, matching, and short answer/essay.

Once a test bank has been created, examinations may be built either manually or randomly in just a few minutes. The main header and each section subheader may be up to ten lines long, and space for figures or graphs will be allocated if specified. Questions referring to the same figure are automatically printed together.

Appearance of the printed examination may be customizéd via fourteen print options. Among other things, these options enable you to adjust all four margins, scramble questions and multiple-choice answers, optimize paper space, control numbering, and print answer sheets for student responses.

Gradebook is organized in the familiar grid pattern of manual grade books: Student information is displayed on the left side, and test information on the right. Students and grades may be sorted in four different ways, and desired grade distribution, maximum score, and weight can be set for each test. A test's bell curve is automatically displayed whenever a curve is entered or adjusted.

In addition to maintaining student averages, *Gradebook* enables you to keep a detailed record for every student, every test, and the entire class. Each of these records contains pertinent statistics, space for up to six lines of comments, and multiple-function graphs.

Student-report graphs chart each student's progress, telling you at a glance the student's grade on each test, performance in relation to the rest of the class, the class high and low score on each test, and the class average. Graphs for tests inform you of each test's effectiveness, and class graphs indicate the overall performance of entire classes.

Study Guide enables instructors to create study diskettes or test diskettes for their students. After specifying the learning objectives for each study session, instructors can draw from EXAM-generated files to create an unlimited number of customized study diskettes.

Students proceed at their own pace, answering as many questions as they can. Grading commences when the student is finished. Test results are graphically displayed, showing overall performance and performance in each of the topic areas specified by the instructor. Questions—showing both the correct answer and the student's response—may be reviewed again once grading is completed.

Calendar is designed to help you plan upcoming events and manage your schedule. When *Calendar* is invoked, the current month is automatically displayed and the current day's events and messages listed. Any day's events may be viewed by moving the cursor to the desired date, or *Calendar* can scan automatically, stopping at the first day containing events. Up to eleven events or messages may be scheduled for each day. Recurring activities may be transferred from one day to another and need not be entered repeatedly.

TEST ITEM FILE

A comprehensive **test item file** contains more than 2,000 questions. The questions are identified as "applied" or "factual." Question placement in the file follows the topical outline of the text. Also, questions are identified according to level of difficulty. Each question with its correct answer is referenced to a text page.

TELEPHONE TEST PREPARATION SERVICE

Prentice Hall's **Telephone Test Preparation Service,** free to adopters, provides a letter-quality printed examination prepared error-free on a sophisticated computer. To use this service, simply choose questions from the Test Item File; indicate your selections on the Computerized Testing Service Request Form, the number of questions you want, and the order in which they should appear. You may:

- Choose up to 200 questions per test from the Test Item File
- Order as many as 5 tests per semester/quarter
- Alter the sequence of the questions you choose to get multiple versions of the same test

Within 48 hours of receiving your request, Prentice Hall will mail the examination master to you. Correct answers will be keyed to the text.

You can make your request by mail or use the toll-free number: (800) 560-0485 (all states but New Jersey); (201) 592-3263 (New Jersey).

TRANSPARENCY MASTERS

A set of transparency masters includes all of the figures from the text, chapter outlines, and selected tables. If you use the recommended type of acetate film, these masters are suitable for processing on most infrared transparency makers or on electrostatic copying machines. Suggestions for using these transparencies are included in the **Supplements Guide** that is part of the Prentice Hall teaching package.

COLOR TRANSPARENCIES

A set of approximately 150 color transparencies is available to adopters of the text. The transparencies are a mix of art from the text and from other applicable sources. Suggestions for using these transparencies are included in the **Supplements Guide** that is part of the Prentice Hall teaching package.

LECTURE EXTRAS

The three-part Lecture Extras Supplement should be one of the most-used items in your teaching package. Each part of this supplement is briefly described below.

- Part I There will be three Lecture Extras per chapter. One will be concept-oriented; one will be a digest of anecdotal articles from such applied periodicals as *Business Week, Fortune,* and *Wall Street Journal;* one will be an application activity, experiential exercise, or case study.
- Part II The following special interest lectures should be welcome additions to the teaching of management because of the timeliness of the topics:
  - ''Women in Management''
  - ''Performance Appraisal''
  - ''Alternate Methods of Dispute Resolution''
  - ''Labor Relations''
  - ''Health Care Management''
- Part III A series of business profiles pertaining to selected corporations and business leaders will help instructors relate chapter materials to both corporations and the leaders of corporations. These profiles will feature businesses and business leaders in such industries as:
  - Banking and finance
  - Light and heavy manufacturing
  - Retailing
  - Service organizations (lodging, food, law, hospital, security, etc.
  - Communication
  - Entertainment

Each of the lecture extra items will provide suggestions for how and when to use the unit with the text material and how the text material will be enhanced as a result of using the lecture extra. The lectures will be followed by discussion questions. In the case of application exercises, special instructions will be provided. Where appropriate to the materials, test questions with answers will be furnished.

VIDEOS AND FILMS

A **Video Guide Supplement** lists and reviews selected videos, including the *Enterprise* series, *Harvard Business Review* series, and other visual subjects reinforcing the text.

This supplement will include the following kinds of information for each film or video:

- A synopsis
- A discussion showing how the film relates to the teaching/learning objectives of the chapter in the book
- Major points of the video and teaching suggestions
- Multiple-choice and discussion questions with answers
- Follow-up assignments
- Bibliography

Additional Supplements for the Student

A comprehensive set of learning aids has been developed for student use in both learning and applying the processes of management to a variety of circumstances. Each supplement has been designed to accomplish a specific objective or set of objectives to assist students in their learning about management and managing for results.

The **Study Guide for Review and Application** provides students with points of view about the subject along with commentary dealing with how to obtain the best results from using the study guide. The guide follows established principles of behavioral research findings that disclose how organized practice lessons assist one's learning. Student test scores ought to be improved through the use of the study guide, but the more important goal is to further student understanding of the processes of management.

The study guide is arranged chapter-by-chapter to include the following:

- Chapter pretest—to help identify student strengths and knowledge gaps.
- Chapter overview—to offer a condensation of the main topics of the chapter to help students study the chapter in a more organized manner, especially to identify weakness disclosed during the pretest.
- Learning objective—to reinforce the overview by pointing out key topics.
- Key terms—to help build a vocabulary about management.

- Fill-in-the-blanks regarding chapter content—to help test comprehension.
- Chapter posttest—to help students determine how well they understand the chapter's objectives.
- Answers to exercises and tests.
- Application exercises—to help separate rote learning from the ability to apply what has been learned to practical situations.

Management Applications: Exercises, Cases, and Readings by John T. Samaras provides a selection of cases representative of situations and conditions faced by practicing managers. The readings extend many of the key sections and issues in the text. The exercises help remove some of the possible passivity felt by students from listening to lectures. The exercises require involvement by students as they undertake to work through the requirements of an interesting assignment. An Instructor's Manual provides pertinent data to assist professors in working with students regarding the cases, readings, and application exercises.

Micromanaging: Transforming Business Leaders with Personal Computers by George T. Geis and Robert L. Kuhn—Prentice Hall will provide one free book to adopters plus a site license to copy the Micromanaging software for student use. The Micromanaging exercises have been designed to help students better understand and apply how microcomputers can assist them in (a) transforming the concept of information, (b) transforming the character of organizations, and (c) transforming the nature of managerial thinking.

Readings in Management by Philip B. DuBose furnishes further background regarding classical management, planning and decision making, organizing for excellence, the management of human resources, managing for results through controlling, and emerging concepts in global management.

Modern Business Decisions by Richard V. Cotter and David J. Fritzsche. Computer-simulated business experience has become an accepted means of assisting students to deal with the kinds of situations they will experience in the so-called real world. Managers in business also obtain valuable decision-making seasoning through simulation exercises. The microcomputer is used for this simulation rather than a mainframe in order to provide features generally unavailable on mainframes. Features such as screen-oriented decisions and data management utilities assist the students in this exercise. The capability to backup diskettes on a microcomputer also minimizes the risk of lost data when "things go wrong."

This supplement includes the following aids:

- Player's Manual
- Instructor's Manual
- Program Disk
- Decision Disk

Managing an Organization: A Workbook Simulation by Gary R. Oddou is a workbook simulation that provides students with experiences similar to those obtained with the computer simulation exercise. This simulation stresses *applications* of what students have been studying in their courses of management. A stated advantage of using the non-computer simulation is that students have no need to take time to learn the necessary attributes to make a computer simulation work. The Instructor's Manual contributes to the usefulness of this supplement.

Twin Applications for Management, Fourth Edition, is a spreadsheet to help students become more knowledgeable about working with information in a decision-making environment.

***Acumen*™, Educational Version,** a self-assessment program widely used in management development programs, will be made available to adopters to help students assess their management styles and to learn how to improve upon their capabilities to become more effective as managers. A comprehensive manual covering ACUMEN™ is part of the instructor's package of teaching supplements. *Acumen*™ is available to students in a specially priced shrink-wrapped package. Instructors should contact their Prentice Hall representative for more information about making *Management, Fourth Edition—Acumen™ Special Edition* available for students.

Using *Acumen: Educational Version*

Introduction

The Fourth Edition of *Management* by Stoner and Freeman is accompanied by an IBM-compatible, self-assessment program called *Acumen*. The educational version of *Acumen* consists of 120 questions that measure the self-concept of the examinee. The results of this self-assessment generate a profile based upon 12 basic management traits. The instructor may wish to use *Acumen* and its assessment as part of the management course.

This overview will provide a description of *Acumen* and how it relates to the text. Specifically the following points will be addressed:

- What is *Acumen*?
- How *Acumen* measures self-concept
- How self-concept relates to management style
- Interpretation of the graphic profile
- Suggested uses of *Acumen* results in relation to the text

What Is Acumen?

Acumen is a managerial assessment and development program. The Educational Version of *Acumen* consists of three parts: instructions, a self-assessment, and an assessment report. *Acumen* requires about 20 to 30 minutes to digest the instructions, answer the questions, and review the results. The results are displayed in graphic form, and each individual score is interpreted.

Acumen presents the student with 120 questions composed of descriptive words and phrases such as "cynical," "dependent on others," "goes to the heart of the matter," and "critical of others." The student must choose among three frequency options for each question:

1 = Essentially unlike you
2 = Like you quite often
3 = Like you most of the time

The program allows two self-assessments.

Acumen's assessment report is based upon comparison of the student's self-assessment with "a cross-section of seasoned, professional managers." Previous research has indicated that effective managers (using dependent variables such as co-worker evaluations, number of promotions, and salary increases) obtain a very different profile than less effective colleagues. Specifically, effective managers consistently score high on the Humanistic-Helpful, Affiliation, Achievement, and Self-Actualization scales and low or average on the other eight scales. The report gives specific guidance concerning how students can work to change their attitudes and behavior to approximate more closely effective managers in the norm group used by *Acumen*.

Acumen was originally developed by Human Synergistics and is based upon ten years of applied research involving a sample of 250,000 managers at 6,000 companies. It is currently used as a managerial assessment tool in many well-known organizations, including Apple Computer, Chase Manhattan Bank, Equitable Life Assurance, E. I. du Pont Nemours, General Motors, Marriott, Miles Laboratories, Southland Corporation, Touche-Ross, the U.S. Navy, and the United Parcel Service.

Research results indicate a longer version of the instrument has acceptable levels of internal reliability and validity. For additional information, see R. Cooke and D. Rousseau, "Relationship of Life Events and Personal Orientation to Symptoms of Strain," *Journal of Applied Psychology* 68 (1983): 446–458; R. Cooke and D. Rousseau, "The Factor Structure of Level I: Life Styles Inventory," *Educational and Psychological Measurement* 43 (1983): 449–457; R. Cooke, D. Rousseau, and J. Lafferty, "Thinking and Behavioral Styles: Consistency between Self-Descriptions and Descriptions by Others," *Educational and Psychological Measurement* 47 (1987): 815–823; and M. Ware, G. Leak, and N. Perry, "Life Styles Inventory: Evidence for Its Factorial Validity," *Psychological Reports* 56 (1985): 963–968. Briefly, these studies agree that three factors are measured by the 12 *Acumen* (Life

Styles Inventory I) scales: People/Security Orientation (Approval, Conventional, Dependence, and Apprehension), Satisfaction Orientation (Humanistic-Helpful, Affiliative, Achievement, and Self-Actualizing), and Task/Security Orientation (Oppositional, Power, Competition, and Perfectionism).

How Acumen Measures Self-Concept

The way we behave towards other people often reflects the way we think about ourselves. These thoughts may be largely positive or negative and influence our motives, affect, and information processing as well as relationships with others. Whether we have a positive or negative view of ourselves is determined by our values, needs, attitudes, and behaviors. All these factors contribute to the self-image we hold or what is called our self-concept.

Self-concept is the way we see ourselves not only physically, but also emotionally, intellectually, socially, and psychologically. Our self-concepts are based mainly on our total life experiences. For example, a manager might feel unskilled at giving presentations. This manager feels insecure about his or her public speaking ability whenever confronted with the task of speaking in front of others. He or she is convinced that his or her skill level is low in this area. Whether an outside observer would agree with this manager's viewpoint is irrelevant. What is important is that since the manager has a negative view of his or her public speaking ability, he or she is going to behave in ways that validate this view. Our self-concept plays a significant role in how we respond to situations or to other people.

Although our self-concepts are influenced by our life experiences, this does not mean that they are static and constant for the remainder of our lives. Self-concepts are dynamic and adjust in response to feedback, challenges, and new experiences. Therefore, it is quite possible to develop a more positive self-concept. The first step in any personal change program is to understand what you are like now and what causes you to be that way. *Acumen* used as a self-assessment tool can help you take this initial step.

The words we use to describe ourselves reveal how we think of ourselves (our self-concept). If you have a positive self-concept you are likely to use words that reflect confidence, self-respect, and enthusiasm. If you have a more negative self-concept, you may use words such as "shy" or "afraid to make a mistake." When people use many of the same types of words to describe themselves, they build a pattern that reflects their self-image. The descriptive words in *Acumen*'s assessment section are selected in such a way as to reveal certain thinking styles. How you respond to these words or phrases reflects how you view yourself, which in turn reveals your motivational and behavioral styles.

How Self-Concept Relates to Management Style

Your self-concept affects the way you behave, whether on the job or in your personal life. For example, if you think of yourself as honest, you will probably see other people as basically honest, and you will treat them with respect and trust. If you are less trusting of others, establishing good working relationships will be difficult. These negative interactions eventually take their toll—not only can they cause the loss of career opportunities, but they can also lead to increased stress, with its related health problems.

Acumen is based on the belief that there is an optimal way for managers to carry out their responsibilities. Research conducted on thousands of managers over the last ten years shows significant associations between a healthy self-concept and several desirable factors. For example, certain thinking styles are associated with advancing in the organization, with lowered stress levels, and with increased salaries. In addition, managers with these thinking styles are seen as better candidates for promotion, as appreciating life experiences more, and as having more self-confidence.

There is no single method for managers to become more effective. For one manager, attaining a more effective management style may mean being less aggressive and more social; for another manager, it may require being more results-oriented and focusing less on gaining others' approval. *Acumen* is designed to help you understand your personal developmental needs. It then helps you formulate specific action plans to achieve your own optimal management style.

Interpretation of the Graphic Profile

When you complete the self-assessment, *Acumen* analyzes your responses and generates scores on 12 major scales. Each scale represents a particular attitude, or thinking style. The way you think (your thinking style) affects:

- What you strive to achieve (your goals)
- Your effectiveness as a leader
- How you relate to and communicate with other people
- Whether you view change as positive or negative
- How you respond to crises and stress

The major aim of *Acumen* is to help you develop a fuller understanding and appreciation of how your own thinking styles and personal dispositions play a role in your productivity and management effectiveness. *Acumen*'s analysis of your assessment responses, presented in graphic or textual form, provides this information.

When you request a graphic display of your assessment results, *Acumen* displays your score on each of twelve thinking styles, arranging the information on a circular profile (as in Figure 1) if you have a color display, and on a bar graph (as in Figure 2) if you have a monochrome display.

Notice that the circular profile in Figure 1 is numbered from 1 through 12, as on a clock face. The bar graph in Figure 2 is also numbered from 1 through 12, but the numbers are arranged on the *y*-axis (the vertical line). Each number represents one of the following twelve thinking styles:

1. *Humanistic-Helpful*. Measures the inclination to see the best in others, to encourage their growth and development, and to be patient and supportive. This style characterizes people who like to teach and assist others and provide them with positive rewards and support.
2. *Affiliation*. Measures the degree of friendliness, sociability, and outgoing tendencies you are likely to exhibit. This style is based on needs for a wide circle of friends and friendly relationships. Persons with high scores on this scale consider people to be more important than things, are generally cooperative, sincere, and at ease in social situations.
3. *Approval*. Measures the need to seek others' approval and support in order to feel secure and worthwhile. Approval seeking individuals tend to be agreeable and

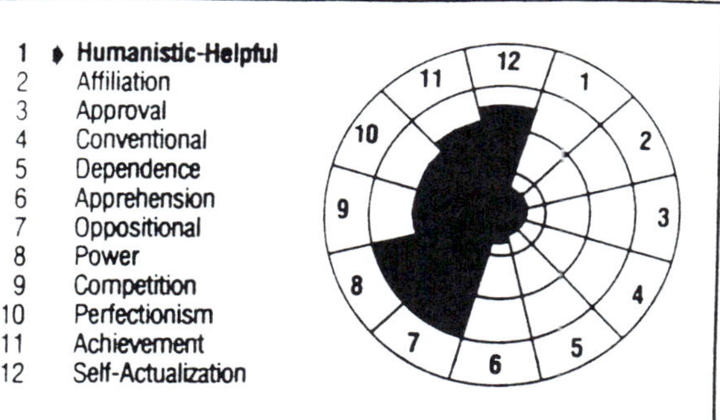

FIGURE 1

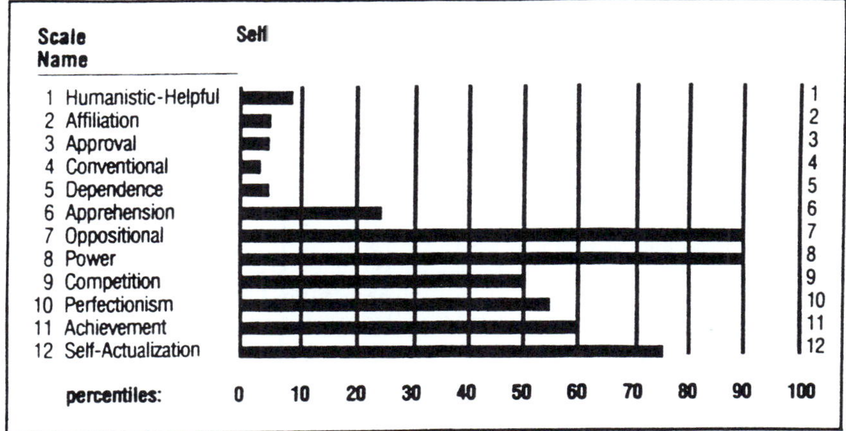

FIGURE 2

generous in their efforts to be liked and accepted by others. These people also generally set low, easily met performance standards and get along by doing what is expected of them by the organization.

4. *Conventional*. Measures the need to conform, follow the rules, and meet the expectations of those in authority. Conventional people wish to appear normal, avoid conflict, and follow standard policies, rules and regulations, and procedures.
5. *Dependence*. Measures the tendency to be compliant, passive, and dependent on others. Dependent people are good followers in that they look to others for direction and do what they are told. They also seek frequent advice and counsel from others before making a decision. Dependent individuals tend to worry about their situation and are cautious and meek in interpersonal relationships.
6. *Apprehension*. Measures the tendency to experience anxiety, self-blame, and low self-esteem. Apprehensive people are nervous and worried. They tend to be hesitant decision makers, avoid responsibilities, and lack self-confidence.
7. *Oppositional*. Measures the tendency to take a critical, questioning, and somewhat cynical attitude. Individuals with a high score in this area are often dogmatic, rigid, and mistrustful of others. They tend to be more concerned with personal recognition rather than effective cooperation with colleagues.
8. *Power*. Measures the tendency to be authoritarian and controlling. Individuals with a high score on this scale tend to be forceful and aggressive and are concerned with gaining prestige and authority. However, they may not show much concern for the feelings of colleagues and subordinates in their pursuit of these objectives.
9. *Competition*. Measures the need to be seen as the best and, to some extent, to maintain a self-centered attitude. Competitive people need to win and are driven by a need to be better than others. They tend to see life's activities measured on a big scorecard of wins and losses. They may lose their focus on the pursuit of excellence and achievement because of this overemphasis on winning.
10. *Perfectionism*. Measures the need to seek perfection and the tendency to base self-worth on personal performance. Perfectionists set very demanding performance standards that are often higher than those of their colleagues. Achievement of these high standards is used to demonstrate competence. These individuals often are obsessed with the elimination of even the tiniest mistakes and with doing things even better in the future.
11. *Achievement*. Measures the need to achieve and have an impact on things. High achievers are interested in attaining high-quality results. They enjoy challenges and encourage others to set realistic, challenging goals. Often they have effective planning, goal-setting, and problem-solving skills.
12. *Self-Actualization*. Measures the level of self-esteem, interest in self-development, and general drive to learn about and experience life to the fullest extent. Self-actualizers are usually confident and articulate. They tend to have a wide range of interests and knowledge. In addition, self-actualizers are generally healthy, vital, energetic, and open to new experiences.

These thinking styles have been arranged like the numbers on a clock for a specific reason. The behavior represented by one style is similar to, or works with, those styles represented on either side of it. For instance, 4 o'clock (Conventional) behavior frequently occurs with the 3 and 5 o'clock styles of Approval and Dependence. Styles on opposite sides of the clock, or a six-hour difference, often work in opposition, and may lead to conflict for the individual. For example, a person showing tendencies in both the 2 o'clock and 8 o'clock styles is likely to feel frustrated—it is difficult to be effective in your attempts to maintain good relations when you also have a tendency to push people around.

When you view a graphic profile display, you will notice that each scale's extension is of varying length. On the circular graph, some scales extend a long way from the center of the circle while other segments are relatively short. Similarly, scales on the bar graph will vary in length. The longer extensions indicate styles that are more prominent in your profile. By comparing the extensions, you will be able to find the thinking styles that have the most impact on your own behavior.

If you have a color display, you will notice four concentric circles when the graphic appears. These represent the 25th, 50th, 75th, and 100th percentile points for the graphic displays of the 12 scales. Percentiles indicate what percentage of respondents obtained the same, higher, or lower score on a given assessment scale. The smallest, innermost circle corresponds to the 25th percentile, while the largest circle represents the 100th percentile, or highest score, for each of the scales. (See Fig. 1.) On a monochrome display, the circular graphs are automatically replaced by bar graphs, and the four concentric circles are replaced by ten vertical lines representing the 10th through 100th percentiles. (See Fig. 2.)

The length of a scale's extension, relative to the percentile circles, indicates the percentage of sampled managers who scored higher or lower than you on any particular scale. For example, if one of your scale extensions falls exactly on the innermost grid, you know that 25 percent of managers scored lower than you, and 74 percent scored higher than you on that particular scale.

Acumen derives your percentile score by comparing your responses to those of a representative, standardized sample of managers, supervisors, and other professionals. This means that, as with other standardized rating instruments, your score compares to that of any other manager who might use the instrument within a narrow margin of statistical error.

By using standardized scores expressed in percentiles, *Acumen:*

- Allows you to see where you stand in comparison to other managers on a given scale.
- Lets you directly compare your score on any two scales by looking at the difference in the length of their extensions as reflecting a difference in percentage points.
- Corrects for the general tendency to choose socially desirable words and qualities, such as "open and generous," over less socially desirable ones, such as "rude and offensive."

Suggested Uses of Acumen Results in Relation to the Text

Acumen is a feedback tool. Standardized on practicing managers, it gives students insights into what their strengths and weaknesses *as managers* might be. While students may not yet be managers, they can benefit from being exposed to profiles of effective managers and assessing the kinds of changes they may need to make in order to become successful executives. Of course, this premise is based on the assumption that "effective" managerial thinking styles are relatively time-independent, i.e., that the successful profile based upon samples of managers assessed in the past will continue to indicate successful thinking styles in the future. This cautionary note, plus the fact that students may by virtue of being students score higher on scales 4 and 5 (Conventional and Dependence) than effective managers would, should guide the instructor away from any tendency to inflate the significance of the results.

It is recommended that students take *Acumen* at the beginning of the course before they have been exposed to the material and again at the end of the course. *Acumen: Educational Version* allows two self-assessments. Profile differences could be indicative of a changed self-concept.

The instructor can have students link their profiles to topics and issues discussed in Stoner and Freeman, *Management, Fourth Edition*. Students who score high on scales 4 and 7, for example, have a strong tendency to resist change and hesitate to try new and creative methods. Change and creative methods; change and creativity are discussed in Chapters 13 and 14, respectively. Following are *some* suggested relationships between profile scores and topics discussed in the text. Overall, using *Acumen: Educational Version* should help make selected management concepts become more real, alive, and relevant.

Key: H-H = Humanistic-Helpful, AFF = Affiliation, APR = Approval, CON = Conventional, DEP = Dependence, APH = Apprehension, OPP = Oppositional, POW = Power, COM = Competition, PER = Perfectionism, ACH = Achievement, S-A = Self-Actualization, (H) = High, and (L) = Low

CHAPTER 1: MANAGING AND MANAGERS

General Subject	Specific Issue(s)	Relevant *Acumen* Scale(s)
Case study	Alison questioned agenda of weekly staff meeting	CON (L)
	Handling of performance review	H-H (H)
	Luncheon with new manager	AFF (H)
	Planning and discussing budget with her boss	ACH (H)
	Unplanned meeting with key customer	AFF (H)
	United Way task force meeting	H-H (H)
	Sense of security with boss	APR, DEP (H)
	Efforts to stop smoking as an example	PER, S-A (H)
Four typical managerial activities	Planning and Organizing activities	ACH (H)
	Leading	H-H (H)
	Controlling	POW (H)
	All four activities	DEP, APH, CON (L)

General Subject	Specific Issue(s)	Relevant *Acumen* Scale(s)
What managers do	Managers work with and through other people	All 12 scales give insight into style of interacting
	Managers are responsible and accountable	S-A (H)
	Managers balance competing goals and set priorities	APH (L), ACH (H)
	Managers are mediators and politicians	H-H, AFF (H)
	Managers make difficult decisions	APH (L)
Managerial and organizational performance	Efficiency Effectiveness	POW, COM (H)S-A (H)
Management levels and skills	Katz's Human Skill	H-H, AFF (H)
Managerial roles	Mintzberg's Interpersonal Roles	H-H, AFF (H)
	Mintzberg's Decision Making Roles	CON, DEP, APH (L); COM, PER (H)
Management as anticipation	Livingstone's three qualities of successful managers: Need to manage	POW, ACH (H)
	Need for power	POW, (H)
	Capacity for empathy	H-H, AFF (H)

CHAPTER 2: THE EVOLUTION OF MANAGEMENT THEORY

General Subject	Specific Issue(s)	Relevant *Acumen* Scale(s)
Forerunners of scientific management	Robert Owen's management practices	H-H, AFF, ACH, S-A (H)
Taylor's four basic principles	First three principles	POW, COM, PER, (H)
	Last principle	H-H, AFF (H)
Lillian Gilbreth	Management must help workers reach their full potential	S-A (H)
Gilbreth's three-position plan of promotion	Workers train their successors	H-H (H)
Contributions and limitations of scientific management	Emphasized efficiency but slighted the human factor (social needs)	POW, COM (H); AFF (L)
Fayol's five functions	Specifically Planning, Commanding, and Controlling	H-H, POW, ACH (H)
Transitional theories	Follett and Barnard	H-H, AFF, S-A (H)
Limitations of human relations	Overemphasized "social man"	H-H, AFF (H)
Behavioral science approach	"Self-actualizing man"	S-A (H)
Contributions of the behavioral science school	*Acumen* is a product created by behavioral scientists	All 12 scales
Management application	Neo-human relations	H-H, AFF, ACH, S-A (H)

CHAPTER 3: THE EXTERNAL ENVIRONMENT OF ORGANIZATIONS

General Subject	Specific Issue(s)	Relevant *Acumen* Scale(s)
External stakeholders	Coping with governmental intervention	COM, ACH, S-A (H)
Internal stakeholders	Special role of managers in balancing conflicting claims	ACH, S-A (H)
Elements of the indirect-action environment	Changing attitudes in the United States and Japan	H-H, AFF (H)

General Subject	Specific Issue(s)	Relevant *Acumen* Scale(s)
Case study	Eastman Kodak's problems and needed managerial orientation for change	COM, ACH, S-A (H); CON, APH (L)
The problem of competitiveness	Public and private sector emphasis on competitiveness	COM (H)
Monitoring the indirect-action environment	Sources of information	H-H, AFF (H)

CHAPTER 4: SOCIAL RESPONSIBILITY AND ETHICS

General Subject	Specific Issue(s)	Relevant *Acumen* Scale(s)
Friedman's argument	Business should maxim ze profits	COM (H)
CSR-1	Paternalistic bases	APR, POW (H)
The spirit of "The Credo" at Johnson and Johnson	"Our credo" statements	H-H, AFF, APR, COM, PER, ACH, S-A (H); APH, OPP, POW (L)
Cultural relativism	Problems concerning personality type required	APR, CON, DEP, APH (H)
A kernel of truth	Relativism requires tolerance of diversity	OPP, POW (L)

CHAPTER 5: EFFECTIVE PLANNING

General Subject	Specific Issue(s)	Relevant *Acumen* Scale(s)
Case study of Chrysler	Iacocca's decisions	COM, ACH, S-A (H); CON, DEP, APH (L)
The four basic steps in planning	Establish a goal or set of goals	CON, APH (L)
	Define the present situation	H-H, AFF, COM, ACH (H)
	Identify the aids and barriers	OPP (L)
	Develop a course of action	CON, APH (L); COM, ACH, S-A (H)
Reluctance to set goals	Unwillingness to give up alternative goals	PER (H)
	Fear of failure	APH (H)
	Lack of organizational knowledge	AFF (L); CON, DEP (H)
	Lack of knowledge of the environment	AFF (L)
	Lack of confidence	DEP, APH (H); S-A (L)
Operational plans	Serve as vehicles for communication	H-H, AFF (H)
Standing plans	May cause inflexibility	CON, DEP, APH (H)
Helping individuals establish goals	Development of informal contacts	H-H, AFF (H)
Overcoming resistance to change	Participation, communication and humanitarian treatment	H-H, AFF, S-A (H); POW (L)

CHAPTER 6: PROBLEM SOLVING AND DECISION MAKING

General Subject	Specific Issue(s)	Relevant *Acumen* Scale(s)
Stage 3: Evaluate alternatives and select the best one	Determine willingness of subordinates to execute decision	H-H, AFF (H)

General Subject	Specific Issue(s)	Relevant *Acumen* Scale(s)
Stage 4: Implement and monitor the decision	Analysis of potential adverse consequences	OPP (H)
The problem-finding process	Informal and intuitive nature of the process	H-H, AFF, ACH, S-A (H); APR, CON, DEP, APH, OPP (L)
Opportunity finding	The dialectical inquiry method Exploitation of opportunities	OPP (H) AFF, COM, ACH, S-A (H)
Deciding to decide	Is this my decision to make?	H-H, AFF (H); DEP, APH, POW, PER (L)
Programmed and nonprogrammed decisions	Ability to decide when to use each type	ACH (H); CON, DEP, APH (L)
Simon's bounded rationality model	Satisficing	POW, PER (L)
Biases in decision making	Overuse of heuristics	CON, DEP, APH (H)
The game of "prisoner's dilemma"	Individuals fare better by cooperating	H-H, AFF, S-A (H); POW (L)
Barriers to individual problem solving	Relaxed and defensive avoidance and panic Relaxed change	APH (H) CON (H)
Deciding who decides	Involving others: quality and acceptance	H-H, AFF (H); POW (L)

CHAPTER 7: STRATEGIC PLANNING AND MANAGEMENT

General Subject	Specific Issue(s)	Relevant *Acumen* Scale(s)
Case study	Federal Express's competitive reputation as a trendsetter and the ZapMail venture	COM, PER, ACH, S-A (H); CON, DEP, APH (L)
The strategic management approach	Hofer and Schendel's 6 basic tasks	OPP (L); POW (H)
Ethics in management	"What's your business?"	S-A (H)
Porter's framework for industry analysis	Critique of Porter's framework	POW (H)
The formal strategic planning process: The example of SBU	Nine steps in SBU planning	H-H, AFF, COM, PER, ACH, S-A (H); CON, DEP, APH (L)

CHAPTER 8: STRATEGY IMPLEMENTATION

General Subject	Specific Issue(s)	Relevant *Acumen* Scale(s)
Case study: Merck & Co.	Chairman Roy Vagelos's innovative style	H-H, AFF, ACH, S-A (H)
The Seven-S model	Style Staff Superordinate goals	H-H (H) H-H, AFF, ACH, S-A (H) ACH, S-A (H)

General Subject	Specific Issue(s)	Relevant *Acumen* Scale(s)
Case study, continued	Vagelos's effort to shorten the regulatory approval cycle	CON, DEP, APH (L); COM, ACH (H)
Ethics in management: whistleblowing	Managerial challenge to build in processes for constructive disagreement and dissent	H-H, AFF, S-A (H); CON, DEP, APH, OPP, POW (L)
Setting annual objectives	Clarify managers' tasks and promote understanding of strategy	ACH (H)
Management by Objectives (MBO)	Cooperative goal setting and appraisal	H-H, AFF, ACH, S-A (H); DEP, APH, OPP, POW, (L)
Reward systems	Shape individual and group behavior	H-H, POW (H)
The role of the CEO	Example: Roy Vagelos does not allow unfounded claims nor criticizing of competitors' products	S-A (H)
Internal constraints	Inflexibility	H-H, AFF (L); CON, APH (H)
	Parochialism	APR, DEP (H)
	Values, styles, traditions	APR, CON, DEP (H)
	Power	POW (L)

CHAPTER 9: DIVISION OF WORK, ORGANIZATIONAL STRUCTURE, AND COORDINATION

General Subject	Specific Issue(s)	Relevant *Acumen* Scale(s)
Case study: Hewlett-Packard	Reorganization	CON, APH (L), COM (H)
Ethics in management: Hertz	Alan Blicker's activities	APR, DEP, CON, APH (H)
Matrix organization	Requires flexibility and cooperation	H-H, AFF (H); CON, DEP, APH, OPP, POW (L)
The informal organization	More organizations are relying on informal organizational structures	H-H, AFF (H)
Problems in achieving effective coordination	Constructive conflict	APR, DEP, APH (L); OPP (H)
Approaches to achieving effective coordination	Boundary-spanning and integrating roles	H-H, AFF (H)
The neo-classical approach to organizational design	The ideas of McGregor, Argyris, and Likert	H-H, AFF, ACH, S-A (H); POW (L)

CHAPTER 10: AUTHORITY, DELEGATION, AND DECENTRALIZATION

General Subject	Specific Issue(s)	Relevant *Acumen* Scale(s)
Case study	IBM's traditional approaches	APR, CON, DEP, APH (H)
	Restructuring effort	DEP, POW (L); H-H, AFF (H)
	No layoffs	S-A (H)

General Subject	Specific Issue(s)	Relevant *Acumen* Scale(s)
The basis of formal authority: Two views	The classical view	DEP, APH (H)
	The acceptance view	DEP, APH (L); S-A (H)
The sources of power	Reward, coercive, and legitimate power	POW (H)
	Expert power	PER (H)
	Referent power	H-H, AFF, ACH, S-A (H)
Ethics in management	Obedient individuals	APR, CON, DEP, APH, POW (H)
Power in organizations	McClelland's negative face of power	APR, DEP (L); POW (H)
	McClelland's positive face of power	H-H, AFF, POW, ACH, S-A (H)
Line and staff authority	Line authority	POW (H)
	Staff authority	H-H, AFF, PER (H)
Effective delegation	Reluctance to delegate	CON, OPP, POW (H); H-H, AFF, DEP, APH (L)
Approaches to job design	Motivational job design	H-H, AFF, POW, ACH, S-A (H); CON, DEP, APH, OPP (L)
	Job rotation	ACH (H)
	Job enrichment	POW, ACH, S-A (H)
	Empowerment	H-H, AFF, POW (H)
Decentralization	Advantages	H-H, S-A (H); APH, OPP, POW (L)

CHAPTER 11: HUMAN RESOURCE MANAGEMENT

General Subject	Specific Issue(s)	Relevant *Acumen* Scale(s)
Case study	Akio Morita's ideas about Sony	H-H, AFF, ACH, S-A (H)
The law	Use of Employee Assistance Programs (EAPs)	H-H, AFF (H)
Ethics in management	Corporate day care and the company's best interest	H-H, AFF, ACH (H)
Orientation and socialization	Effective socialization programs	H-H, AFF (H)
Management development programs	Manager-centered development	H-H, ACH (H)
On-the-job methods	Coaching	H-H, AFF, S-A (H); OPP, POW (L)
	Planned work activities	H-H, AFF (H)
Performance appraisal	Informal performance appraisal and formal systematic appraisal	H-H, AFF (H); APH (L)
Problems of appraisal	Joint goal setting and evaluation in participatory appraisal	H-H, AFF (H); APH, OPP, POW (L)
International management	Plant closure disclosure	H-H, AFF, S-A (H)
The 4 C's for human resources	High commitment	H-H, AFF (H)
	High competence	CON, DEP, APH (L); ACH, S-A (H)
	Higher congruence	H-H, AFF (H)

General Subject	Specific Issue(s)	Relevant *Acumen* Scale(s)
	CHAPTER 12: MANAGING ORGANIZATIONAL CHANGE AND DEVELOPMENT	
Case study	James E. Olson's ideas for AT&T	CON, DEP, APH (L); ACH (H)
Managerial responses to pressures for change	A program of planned change	H-H, AFF, ACH, S-A (H); CON, DEP, APH, OPP, POW (L)
The process of change	Changing Refreezing	H-H, ACH (H) H-H (H)
Sources of resistance to change	The three general sources of resistance	CON, DEP, APH, OPP (H)
Overcoming resistance to change	GM's joint union-management committees and flexible production schedules	H-H, ACH (H); CON, DEP, APH, OPP, POW (L)
Structural approaches	Decentralization	H-H, ACH (H)
Combining technological and structural approaches	Sociotechnical approaches	H-H, AFF, ACH (H)
Organizational development	Collaborative management	H-H (H); POW (L)
Ethics in management: OD assumptions and values	On the personal level On the group level On the organizational level Equalization of power	H-H, ACH, S-A (H)AFF (H) OPP, COM (L) POW (L/H)
OD techniques in closeup	Team building	H-H, AFF, ACH (H); POW, COM (L)
Organizational culture	A smart manager must stop perpetuating an unresponsive culture	CON, DEP, APH (L)
	CHAPTER 13: MANAGING ORGANIZATIONAL CONFLICT AND CREATIVITY	
Changing views of conflict	The traditional view The interactionist view	H-H, AFF (H); APH, OPP (L) CON, DEP, APH (L); ACH (H)
Sources of organizational conflict	Differences in values or perceptions Individual styles and organizational ambiguities	OPP (H) POW, COM (H)
Conflict stimulation methods	Exxon CEO Lawrence Rawl's style	APR, CON, DEP, APH (L); OPP, POW, COM, PER, ACH, S-A (H)
Suggestions for stimulating conflict	Bringing in outsiders, going against the book, restructuring the organization Encouraging competition	CON, DEP, APH, POW (L) H-H, COM (H)
Dominance and suppression	Forcing Smoothing Avoidance	POW (H) AFF, APR (H) APH (H)
Compromise	Compromise	H-H, CON (H)

General Subject	Specific Issue(s)	Relevant *Acumen* Scale(s)
Integrative problem solving	Consensus, confrontation, superordinate goals	H-H, AFF, ACH (H); POW (L)
Minimizing negotiation conflict	Guidelines for conducting negotiations	H-H, AFF, ACH, S-A (H); APH, OPP, POW (L)
Managing organization creativity and innovation	Individual creativity	CON, DEP, APH (L); PER, S-A (H)
Establishing a climate for organizational creativity	Kanter's "ten rules for stifling innovation"	H-H, AFF (L); OPP, POW, PER (H)
Some prescriptions for fostering organizational creativity	Develop an acceptance of change; permit more interaction	H-H, AFF (H)
	Encourage new ideas	CON (L)
	Tolerate failure	OPP, PER (L)
	Provide clear objectives and freedom to achieve them	ACH (H)
	Offer recognition	H-H (H

CHAPTER 14: MOTIVATION, PERFORMANCE, AND SATISFACTION

General Subject	Specific Issue(s)	Relevant *Acumen* Scale(s)
Case study	Monaghan's traits	H-H, AFF, ACH, S-A (H)
The importance of motivation	People are responsive to praise and encouragement	H-H (H)
The traditional model	Perspective on worker motives	POW (H)
The human relations model	Manipulation of workers	POW (H)
The human resources model	Facilitate worker self-motivation	H-H, S-A (H)
Maslow's hierarchy of needs theory	Security	DEP, CON (H)
	Belongingness and Love	H-H, AFF, APR (H)
	Esteem	H-H, AFF, ACH (H); APH (L)
	Self-actualization	ACH, S-A (H)
Alderfer's ERG theory	Relatedness	H-H, AFF, APR (H)
	Growth	ACH, S-A (H)
McClelland's needs	Need for Achievement	COM, PER, ACH, S-A (H)
	Need for Affiliation	H-H, AFF (H)
	Need for Power	POW (H)
Herzberg's two-factor approach	Satisfiers	ACH, S-A (H)
Management application	Chaparral Steel's human resources approach	POW (L); H-H, S-A (H)
Hammer's rules for using behavior modification	Rule 1	APR, APH (L)
	Rules 3 and 4	H-H, AFF (H)
	Rule 5	H-H (H)
	Rule 6	S-A (H)
Expectancy model: Nadler and Lawler's six implications	Implication 1	AFF (H)
	Implication 2	APH (L)
	Implication 3	PER (L)
	Implications 4 and 6	H-H (H)
The button experiments	Give people control over their work	POW (L)

General Subject	Specific Issue(s)	Relevant *Acumen* Scale(s)
Guidelines for effective motivation	Premium on understand ng subordinates	H-H, AFF (H)

CHAPTER 15: LEADERSHIP

General Subject	Specific Issue(s)	Relevant *Acumen* Scale(s)
Case study: Jack Welch	Delegated authority to lower levels	POW (L)
	Rewarded streamliners, changers, and risktakers	CON, DEP, APH (L)
	Competitor	COM (H)
Theories of leadership	Five bases of power	POW (H)
Two leadership styles:	Task-oriented, initiating structure, production-centered, style 9, 1, low LPC, and AI and AII styles	POW, COM (H)
	Employee-oriented, consideration, employee-centered, style 1, 9, high LPC, and GII style	H-H, AFF, APR (H)
Ethics in management	Ethical leadership	S-A (H)
Influences on choice of leadership	Choosing a style	APH (L)
	Subordinate characteristics	H-H, AFF
	Influence of organization's hierarchy	CON (H)
The managerial grid	Style 9,9	H-H, AFF, ACH, S-A (H)
Case study continued	Welch's confrontative and intense style	COM, PER, ACH, S-A (H); APR, CON, APH (L)
Hersey and Blanchard's situational model	Knowing the "maturity" of subordinates	H-H, AFF (H)
Path-Goal approach to leadership	Influence gained through rewards and clarification of "paths"	H-H, ACH (H); DEP, APH, OPP (L)
Deciding when to involve subordinates: The Vroom-Yetton and Vroom-Jago Models	Potential flexibility	CON, APH (L)
The future of leadership theory	Transformational or charismatic leadership	POW, ACH, S-A (H); DEP, APH (L)

CHAPTER 16: GROUPS AND COMMITTEES

General Subject	Specific Issue(s)	Relevant *Acumen* Scale(s)
Case study: Team Taurus at Ford	Parallel processing	H-H, AFF, ACH, S-A (H); CON, DEP, APH, OPP, POW (L)
Informal groups	Social satisfaction to members	AFF (H)
Informal leadership	Task role	POW, COM (H)
	Group building and maintenance role	H-H, AFF, APR, (H)
Group norms and conformity	Pressure to meet expectations	APR, CON, DEP, APH (H)
Ethics in management	"Authority of violence"	APR, CON, DEP, APH (H)
Cohesiveness and performance	Managers should give each group a "charter"	H-H (H); POW (L)

General Subject	Specific Issue(s)	Relevant *Acumen* Scale(s)
Advantages and disadvantages of committees and task forces	"Groupthink"	APR, CON, DEP, APH (H)
Guidelines for leaders	Detecting inappropriate work and avoiding it Manage discussions	APH (L) POW (H)

CHAPTER 17: INTERPERSONAL AND ORGANIZATIONAL COMMUNICATION

General Subject	Specific Issue(s)	Relevant *Acumen* Scale(s)
Role of communication in Mintzberg's three managerial roles	Interpersonal and informational roles Decisional roles	H-H, AFF (H) APH (L)
One- and two-way communication	One-way communication Two-way communication	POW (H) H-H, AFF (H)
Overcoming barriers to interpersonal communication	Overcoming differing perceptions Overcoming emotionality Overcoming distrust	H-H, AFF (H) AFF (H) AFF, S-A (H)
Problems of vertical communication	Filtering, modification, alteration, etc.	H-H, AFF (L)

CHAPTER 18: EFFECTIVE CONTROL

General Subject	Specific Issue(s)	Relevant *Acumen* Scale(s)
Case study	Characteristics of Kaizen at GenCorp	H-H, AFF, ACH, S-A (H)
Steps in the control process	Establish standards and methods for measuring performance Take corrective action	AFF, ACH (H) APH (L); POW (H)
Finding the right degree of control	Find the proper balance between control and individual freedom	H-H, AFF, S-A (H); POW (L)
Ethics in management	Ethical policy as a control device at Mead Corp.	ACH, S-A (H)
Establish standards for predictors and results	Set standards that are well understood and accepted	H-H, AFF (H); POW (L)
Evaluate information and take corrective action	Deciding what action (if any) to take	APH (L)
Key considerations in establishing a control system	Flexibility of standards Direction of feedback	CON (L) H-H (H)
Problems in establishing effective control systems	All three problems	CON, DEP, APH, POW (H)

CHAPTER 19: FINANCIAL CONTROL METHODS

General Subject	Specific Issue(s)	Relevant *Acumen* Scale(s)
How budgets are drawn up and approved	Top-down budgeting Bottom-up budgeting	POW (H) H-H, AFF (H); POW (L)
Some problems in budget development	Tosi's four important reactions to budget anxieties	OPP, POW, COM (H)
Zero-base budgeting	The normal budgeting process	CON (H)

General Subject	Specific Issue(s)	Relevant *Acumen* Scale(s)
Potentially functional aspects of budgets	1. Positive impact on motivation and morale	AFF (H)
	2. Coordinate work	ACH (H)
	3. Warning device for corrective action	APH (L)
	4. Helps experiential learning	COM, PER (H)
	5. Improve resource allocation	ACH (H)
	6. Improve communication	H-H, AFF (H)
	7. Imparts knowledge of fit in the organization	H-H (H)
	8. Imparts knowledge of organizational direction	H-H (H)
	9. Means of evaluation	ACH (H)
	CHAPTER 20: PRODUCTIVITY AND OPERATIONAL CONTROL	
Case study	Ford's emphasis on quality	H-H, AFF, ACH, S-A (H); POW (L)
Productivity through people	Management's failure to reward hard work and high performance	H-H (L)
	Peters and Waterman's separate ideas on excellence	H-H, AFF, ACH, S-A (H); CON, DEP, APH, POW (L)
Designing production/ operations systems	What, how many, how, where, and who decisions	APH (L); ACH (H)
Operations planning and control	"What if," trade-off calculations	CON, APH, OPP (L)
	CHAPTER 21: INFORMATION SYSTEMS AND CONTROL	
Management information systems	Managers should maintain effective informal communication channels	H-H, AFF (H)
Guidelines for effective design	Include users on the design team	H-H, AFF (H); POW (L)
	Provide adequate training and documentation	H-H (H)
Problems in implementing a computer-based MIS	Operating management's loss of control as a source of anxiety	POW (H)
Overcoming the implementation problems	User orientation	H-H, AFF (H)
	Participation	POW (L)
	Communication	H-H, AFF (H)
	Redefinition of performance measurements	CON, DEP, APH, OPP (L)
	New challenges	COM, ACH, S-A (H)
	CHAPTER 22: ENTREPRENEURSHIP	
Productivity	Improving production techniques	COM, PER, ACH, S-A (H)
Psychological and sociological factors	Need achievement	COM, PER, ACH, S-A (H); CON, DEP, APH, OPP (L)
	Evans' managing entrepreneurs	DEP (H)
	Evans' innovating entrepreneurs	CON, DEP, APH (L); ACH (H)

General Subject	Specific Issue(s)	Relevant *Acumen* Scale(s)
	Evans' controlling entrepreneurs	POW (H)
	Begley and Boyd's "locus of control"	S-A (H)
	Begley and Boyd's willingness to take risks	CON, DEP, APH (L)
	Begley and Boyd's tolerance for ambiguity	CON, DEP, APH (L)
	"Type A" behavior	COM (H)
Planning and strategy	Drucker's "fustest with the mostest" and "entrepreneurial judo"	CON, DEP, APH, OPP (L); COM (H)
Management application	3M's respect for people and their natural urge to create	H-H, AFF (H); CON, DEP, APH, OPP (L)
The dark side of entrepreneurship	Need for control	POW (H)

CHAPTER 23: ORGANIZATIONAL CAREERS AND INDIVIDUAL DEVELOPMENT

General Subject	Specific Issue(s)	Relevant *Acumen* Scale(s)
Hall's six factors in "reality shock syndrome"	3. Lack of performance appraisal	H-H, AFF (L)
	6. Threats to superiors	S-A (L)
Actions of the first supervisor	Attributes required of first supervisors	H-H, AFF, ACH, S-A (H); DEP, POW, PER (L)
Political insensitivity and passivity	Forming political alliances	AFF, POW (H)
Loyalty dilemmas	"Obey me"	POW (H)
	"Protect me and don't make me look bad"	CON (H)
	"Work hard"	COM, PER (H)
	"Be successful"	COM (H)
	"Tell me the truth"	AFF (L)
Personal anxiety: Schein's three individual responses	Conformity	APR, CON, DEP, APH (H)
	Rebellion	OPP (H)
	Creative individualism	S-A (H)
Effects of stress	Maddi and Kobasa's concept of "hardiness'	DEP, APH (L); POW, COM, ACH, S-A (H)
Reducing stress throughout the organization	Decentralizing authority, allowing participation, and enriching jobs	POW (L)
	Adjusting reward systems	H-H (H)
	Improving communication	H-H, AFF (H)
	Enlarging jobs	CON (L)
Driver's career concepts	Linear concept	POW, COM, ACH (H)
	Steady state career concept	DEP (H); COM (L)
	Spiral career concept	ACH, S-A (H)
	Transitory career concept	COM (L)
Schein's five factors in career motivation	Technical/functional competence	ACH, S-A (H)
	Managerial competence	H-H, AFF, POW (H); APH (L)
	Security	DEP (H)
	Creativity	CON, APH (L); COM, PER (H)
	Autonomy	S-A (H)
Four career roles and relationships	Apprentices	DEP (H)
	Colleague	AFF (H)
	Mentors	H-H (H)
	Sponsors	H-H, POW (H)
Individual career planning	Realistic career strategies	AFF, ACH, S-A (H); APH (L)

General Subject	Specific Issue(s)	Relevant *Acumen* Scale(s)
Managing the work situation	Do excellent work	COM, PER, ACH (H)
	Develop good working relationships and help your boss succeed	H-H, AFF (H)
	Be mobile	APH (L)
	Find a sponsor	AFF (H)
	Become visible	COM (H)
	Present the right image	CON (H); OPP (L)
Mentors and mentoring relationships	Career functions	H-H (H)
	Psychosocial functions	AFF (H)

CHAPTER 24: INTERNATIONAL MANAGEMENT

General Subject	Specific Issue(s)	Relevant *Acumen* Scale(s)
Managerial attitudes toward internationalization	Ethnocentric managers	CON, POW (H)
	Polycentric managers	APH (H)
	Geocentric managers	CON, APH (L); COM, S-A (H)
Becoming an international business	Japanese reliance on long-term relationships and personal trust	H-H, AFF (H)
Managing in a multinational environment	Managers must know and adapt to the nature of a foreign country	H-H, AFF (H); CON, APH, OPP (L)
Two prevailing control models used by MNEs	Bureaucratic control	CON, POW (H)
	Culture control	H-H, POW (H)
Applying Japanese approaches abroad and synthesizing differing approaches	Japanese managers encourage subordinates to participate	H-H, AFF (H); POW (L)

ANNOTATED INSTRUCTOR'S EDITION

MANAGEMENT

CHAPTER 1
Managing and Managers

Chapter Outline

DEFINING MANAGEMENT

WHY ORGANIZATIONS AND EFFECTIVE MANAGERS ARE NEEDED

- Organizations Serve Society
- Organizations Accomplish Objectives
- Organizations Preserve Knowledge
- Organizations Provide Careers

THE KEY ATTRIBUTES OF MANAGERIAL RESPONSIBILITY

MANAGERIAL AND ORGANIZATIONAL PERFORMANCE

TYPES OF MANAGERS

- Management Levels
  - First-Line Managers
  - Middle Managers
  - Top Managers
- Functional and General Managers
  - Functional Managers
  - General Managers

THE MANAGEMENT PROCESS

- Planning
- Organizing
- Leading
- Controlling

MANAGEMENT LEVEL AND SKILLS

MANAGERIAL ROLES

- Interpersonal Roles
- Informational Roles
- Decision-Making Roles

EXCELLENCE IN MANAGEMENT

ETHICS IN MANAGEMENT

EDUCATING MANAGERS

- Management Education Criticized
  - Management as Social Practice
  - Management as Anticipation
- Management Learning: Books and Experience

THE PURPOSE OF THIS BOOK

SUMMARY

Key Terms

- **management** The process of planning, organizing, leading, and controlling the work of organization members and of using all available organizational resources to reach stated organizational goals.
- **ethics** The study of who is—and should be—benefited or harmed by any action.
- **managerial performance** The measure of how efficient and effective a manager is: how well he or she determines and achieves appropriate objectives.
- **first-line managers** Managers who are responsible for the work of operating employees only and do not supervise other managers. They are the "first" or lowest level of managers in the organizational hierarchy.
- **middle managers** Managers in the midrange of the organizational hierarchy: they are responsible for other managers and sometimes for some operating employees.
- **top management** Managers responsible for the overall management of the organization. They establish operating policies and guide the organization's interactions with its environment.
- **functional manager** A manager responsible for just one organizational activity, such as finance or human resource management.
- **general manager** The individual responsible for all activities, such as production, sales, marketing, and finance, for an organization like a company or subsidiary.

Chapter Overview/Synopsis

Management is introduced as a concept of getting things done through people by employing the interrelated processes of planning, organizing, leading, and controlling. Through organizations people are better able to accomplish desired objectives. Further, the hierarchical arrangement of duties permits career paths. In effect, organizations serve a useful purpose in society. To meet such a wide variety of expectations, successful managers tend to possess attributes of working through other people, accepting responsibility, setting priorities, thinking analytically, resolving issues, and being diplomatic. Above all, they serve as symbols in society.

While the term *manager* may be used in a generic sense to mean anyone responsible for subordinates and the use of other organizational resources, the authors identify and discuss types of managers. First-line managers are those who do not supervise other persons; middle managers generally direct the work of other managers as well as rank-and-file employees; top managers are the persons responsible for the overall management of the organization since their responsibility includes that of setting policies. Functional managers have responsibility for only once activity, such as purchasing or plant maintenance.

The decision-making aspects of managers are discussed within a framework of business ethics. When managers operate in an ethical framework, decisions are influenced by answers to such questions as who benefits and who is harmed by their actions. This approach to ethics is further reinforced through a discussion of the need for managers to be accountable—accountable for their own actions as well as for the actions of others under their jurisdiction.

Although several types of managers exist and operate on different organizational levels, each is shown to require three basic skills: technical, human, and conceptual. The balance required of these necessary skills varies at each level; that is, a first-level manager needs more technical than conceptual skill. The discussion of skill levels is expanded through a review of the Henry Mintzberg analysis of ten managerial roles. These roles range from symbolic, where the manager is essentially a figurehead, to one of representing the organization to its internal and external publics through negotiation.

Management is presented as an interrelated set of processes: planning, organizing, leading, and controlling. Management is considered an applied discipline where practice preempts theory. Thus the practice of management exists in much the way law and medicine are practiced—there is an art to being successful. Several problems regarding management education are reviewed, especially the way educators approach management as a science rather than an art.

Analysis of Illustrative Case Study

INTRODUCTION—A TYPICAL DAY IN THE LIFE OF ALISON REEVES

To an outsider, Alison's typical day appears to be chaotic, but to her, such days have become normal. For such a day to be *normal* Alison has been able to accommodate herself to the idea that today's managers can work in a climate of uncertainty and ambiguity. Managers plan to cause events to happen that otherwise would not occur; this replaces uncertainty with certainty. Managers exercise control (measuring anything capable of being measured) against a predetermined standard; this reduces the level of ambiguity. Alison does not have full control over her destiny because outside situations often alter her plans. In general, however, she can leave the job at the end of the day with resolve to return another day.

Alison operates with an "open door policy" in that she appears to be accessible at any time. This availability to others helps them maintain their productivity, but it might also be preventing Alison from reaching a fuller potential of effectiveness. Thus, she has to determine if her approach to management is helping the organization reach its objectives better than if she isolated herself from her people from time to time. Her perception appears to be that top management is pleased with the way she handles her responsibilities.

Alison is partially meeting the need to plan, organize, lead and control. The case reveals she is leading and exercising elements of control during the meeting she has with her associates. Even so, she tends to operate more in a reactive than a proactive mode. While the present seems reasonably secure, her lack of future planning, with no inventory of resource needs, could cause future difficulties. On the other hand, since she appears to have top management's support, she may be acquiring the needed "quiet" time for planning when she is away from the job, such as when she rides the commuter train.

CONTINUED—A TYPICAL DAY IN THE LIFE OF ALISON REEVES

Alison's day reveals abilities to adjust to a variety of demands on her time. Adjusting means the capacity to change from one activity—sometimes right in the middle—to mount an assault on something more important. Her approach to being a manager is that of serving her people. By helping them to be effective, her worth to the organization increases.

WRAP-UP—A TYPICAL DAY IN THE LIFE OF ALISON REEVES

The Henry Mintzberg model of managerial roles (interpersonal, informational, and decision-making) is exemplified in the typical day of Alison Reeves. She spent much of her day dealing with people, even working with a person whose goals appeared to be at variance with those of the organization, she provided information to group members, and made a variety of decisions. A typical day for Alison is also typical for the unnamed Alisons and Alberts in the world of management.

Answers to End-of-Chapter Review Questions

1. How would you define the term *management?*

Management is both an art and a science of achieving organizational goals through people as a result of the judicious application of available resources.

2. Describe management in terms of the functions of managers. Describe management in terms of what managers do.

Managers attempt to meet their responsibilities by performing a series of interrelated functions (in a process format): they plan (provide for the future), they organize (assemble organizational resources), they lead (provide direction to subordinates), and they control (measure whatever they want to measure against predetermined standards).

3. How does the concept of ethics relate to the study of managerial roles?

Managers occupy a variety of roles in carrying out their responsibilities. Some of the roles require the balancing of priorities that may be in conflict with one another. Managers represent stockholders who desire a continuation of quarterly profits. The same managers may also need to plan for a capital expansion program that will reduce quarterly profits. Thus managers face the ethical dilemma posed in the chapter of being concerned about who is—and should be—benefited or harmed by any action.

4. What levels of management are discussed in this chapter?

First-line managers direct operating employees only; they do not supervise other managers. They are sometimes called foreman or supervisor.

Middle managers direct the work of other managers and sometimes the work of operating employees. Their main role is to help implement organization policies and serve in a liaison role between the level of management above them and managers in subordinate positions.

Top managers carry responsibility for the overall success of an organization. A main obligation is to set policies, strategies and objectives for the organization. Top managers often take the leadership in the organization's interactions with its many publics that include employees, stockholders, suppliers, customers, bureaucrats, and self-appointed stakeholders who feel affected by the activities of the organization.

Functional managers direct a single organizational activity such as production, sales, human resources department, and public relations. The important point is an organizational unit engaged in common activities.

5. How would you distinguish between efficient management and effective management?

Efficiency is the ability to get things done correctly, which includes economically in terms of organizational resources. Effectiveness is getting things done, but meeting the needs of efficiency may not result. Overall, being effective is the most critical attribute of a manager since it means the ability to size up situations and conditions and make the right decisions. Efficiencies can come later with people trained as efficiency experts. ''The pertinent question is not how to do things right, but how to find the right things to do, and to concentrate resources on them'' (Drucker).

6. According to Robert L. Katz, what three basic skills do managers need? Discuss each of these skills in terms of management level.

All managers need technical, interpersonal, and conceptual skills. The level of management, however, influences the relative importance of each skill in terms of the overall responsibility involved. Interpersonal skills tend to be about the same for all levels of management since the need to get along and work with others is not differentiated by job level. On the other hand, first-line managers have great need for technical skills since people under their jurisdiction look to them for guidance in doing their jobs. Top managers have greatest need for conceptual skills since they are looking to the future of the organization.

7. According to Mintzberg, what are the three different roles that a manager may assume in an organization? Briefly discuss each.

   Mintzberg reduced his ten managerial roles to three broad categories: interpersonal roles, informational roles, and decision-making roles.

   Working with people is one of the most important roles a manager can occupy since without people, an organization's purposes do not get accomplished. The interpersonal role has several parts. The manager might be *figurehead* in representing the organization to its publics; the manager might be a *leader* since people have to be selected, trained, and motivated; and managers sometimes have to work between groups in a *liaison* capacity as part of smoothing the communication process.

   Without information and effective information processing, managers are unable to make effective decisions. Thus the informational role is one of the most critical for all managers. Not only is information gathered, but it is also *monitored* in terms of what it means to the organization. Nevertheless, knowing what information means does little to enhance the state of the organization until knowledge is *disseminated* to others in terms they understand and accept.

   Decision making is the result of processing information and selecting a course of action from among alternatives. Mintzberg feels that decision making occurs within such frameworks as entrepreneurship, disturbance handling, and negotiating.

Answers to End-of-Chapter Case Questions

CASE 1: THE VICE-PRESIDENT, THE PRODUCT MANAGER, AND THE MISUNDERSTANDING

1. What do you think was the effect on Brewster and the other managers of Smith's outburst at the meeting?

   Brewster was obviously crushed by the attack on his inability to answer questions about his area of responsibility. His boss, Reynolds, noted the criticism was unfair but did not feel able to take corrective action during the meeting. Since Smith recognized he had made an error in dealing with Brewster, the group more than likely knew that while Smith might be impetuous in dealing with people, he was equally quick to make amends if he was wrong.

2. Was Smith right to apologize to Brewster, or should he have left well enough alone?

   Smith took the correct course of action in apologizing to Brewster. The apology, however, was in private. Smith needs to take some type of public action to demonstrate to others involved that conditions have been rectified. This implies the need for a public display of confidence more than it does a need for a public apology. This could be accomplished by having Brewster make a report at future meeting where Smith could respond publicly about an outstanding job. Smith could not leave well enough alone because it was not "well enough." There was damage that had to be corrected.

3. What do you think the apology meant to Brewster?

   It probably redirected his thinking about needing to find another job to resolving to be an effective member of the management team. While a person might refuse an apology on the grounds the situation should never have occurred, Brewster gave no such indication.

4. What would it be like to have Nick Smith as a superior? As a subordinate?

   A person working for Nick Smith would recognize him to be curt with unprepared persons and would never make that mistake again. A subordinate would also know that Smith was basically decent and if he was wrong about something, he would attempt to make amends.

   A person like Nick Smith could be counted on to get things done. Smith has achieved considerable rank and status in the organization which means that before a new boss begins to remove a person like Smith, time should be taken to see what kind of results Smith gets from people in his part of the organization. In short, a person cannot expect everyone to "walk on water." Given the choice of having a person who scores high on a socialization scale but is non-productive against a rough-hewn individual who gets results, the decision to go with the effective manager is inescapable.

5. How does Smith define Brewster's responsibilities as an assistant product manager? How does he define his own role as a top manager?

   The supervision of Brewster lies more with Reynolds than Smith. Nick Smith made no attempt to override the direct supervision of Reynolds when he made the remark to Brewster that "your job is to make sure that people like myself don't make stupid decisions." That says quite a bit about management's expectations of doing a good job, and keeping the boss fully informed about things that might prove embarrassing in the light of incomplete information.

   Smith's description of his own job was to ask questions so that he would be able to make intelligent decisions. He could only do his job if people in subordinate positions did theirs.

6. What is the most important aspect of the relations between management levels in this company?

   The organization, with respect to that part headed by Nick Smith, appears to have a culture of tension. That is, Smith expects to ask tough questions and to get complete answers. He does not expect to take time for pleasantries in meetings he conducts. When Smith is edgy, his subordinates are edgy. However, his management group has worked with him over time, and it appears the job is being done even though Smith's bias toward action appears somewhat severe to outsiders.

Suggested Term Paper Topics

1. The contributions to management thought by Mary Parker Follett
2. The nature of planning
3. Foundations for making ethical decisions in the face of uncertainty
4. Social responsibility and representing stockholder interests
5. A book review of Peters and Waterman, *In Search of Excellence*
6. Technical skills needed by top managers contrasted with technical skills needed by first-line managers
7. Management education for the 1990s
8. A book review of Peter Drucker's *The Practice of Management*
9. Can management theory be practical?

Suggested Guest Speakers

1. A top manager or someone from at least the upper echelons of middle management to discuss what goes on in a "typical day." In short, students ought to have a chance to compare the Alison Reeves case with what a practicing manager has to say.
2. The chapter provides an illustration of ethics in management by presenting a discussion of social responsibility. Bring in a speaker who represents a local big business that includes a social agenda in its annual budget. What considerations are made before declaring an organization to be "worthy" and to receive funding from the corporation?
3. Invite a management consultant to discuss the Peters and Waterman concept of what characteristics constitute excellence in management. Quite likely the instructor can obtain such a speaker through his contacts; if not, most of the Big Eight accounting firms have major divisions that emphasize management development.

CHAPTER 2
The Evolution of Management Theory

Chapter Outline

THE CLASSICAL MANAGEMENT THEORISTS

Forerunners of Scientific Management Theory
Scientific Management: Frederick W. Taylor
Other Contributors to Scientific Management
- Henry L. Gantt (1861–1919)
- The Gilbreths

Contributions and Limitations of Scientific Management Theory
- Contributions
- Limitations

Classical Organization Theory
- Henry Fayol
- Max Weber

Contributions and Limitations of Classical Organization Theory
- Contributions
- Limitations

Transitional Theories: Becoming More People-Oriented
- Mary Parker Follett
- Chester I. Barnard

THE BEHAVIORAL SCHOOL: THE ORGANIZATION IS PEOPLE

The Human Relations Movement
- The Hawthorne Experiments

Contributions and Limitations of the Human Relations Approach
- Contribution
- Limitations

From Human Relations to the Behavioral Science Approach
Contributions and Limitations of the Behavioral Science School

THE QUANTITATIVE SCHOOL: OPERATIONS RESEARCH AND MANAGEMENT SCIENCE

Contributions and Limitations of the Management Science Approach

THE EVOLUTION OF MANAGEMENT THEORY

The Systems Approach
- Some Key Concepts

The Contingency Approach

SUMMARY

Key Terms

- **scientific management** A management approach, formulated by Frederick W. Taylor and others between 1890 and 1930, that sought to determine scientifically the best methods for performing any task, and for selecting, training, and motivating workers.
- **theory** Principle or set of principles designed to explain the relationship between two or more observable facts.
- **differential rate system** Frederick W. Taylor's compensation system involving the payment of higher wages to more efficient workers.
- **classical organization theory** An early attempt, pioneered by Henri Fayol, to identify principles and skills that underlie effective management.
- **behavioral school** A group of management scholars trained in sociology, psychology, and related fields, who use their diverse knowledge to understand and improve the way organizations are managed.
- **Hawthorne effect** The possibility that workers who receive special attention will perform better simply because they received that attention: one interpretation of Elton Mayo and his colleagues' studies.
- **management science** (MS) Mathematical techniques for modeling, analysis, and solution of management problems. Also called operations research.
- **system approach** View of the organization as a unified, directed system of interrelated parts.
- **subsystems** Those parts comprising the whole system.

- **synergy** The situation in which the whole is greater than its parts. In organizational terms, the fact that departments that interact cooperatively can be more productive than if they operate in isolation.
- **open system** A system that interacts with its environment.
- **closed system** A system that does not interact with its environment.
- **system boundary** The boundary that separates each system from its environment. It is rigid in a closed system, flexible in an open system.
- **flows** Components such as information, material, and energy that enter and leave a system.
- **feedback (job-based)** The part of system control in which the results of actions are returned to the individual, allowing work procedures to be analyzed and corrected.
- **contingency approach** The view that the management technique that best contributes to the attainment of organizational goals might vary in different types of situations or circumstances.

Chapter Overview/Synopsis

This chapter focuses on three established schools of management thought: classical, behavioral, and management science. In addition, the systems approach and contingency approach to management are discussed to integrate the best components of the three major schools of thought.

Classical organization theory attempted to improve managerial effectiveness through adherence to the functions of planning, organizing, commanding, coordinating, and controlling. Management theory became more people-oriented through the contributions of Mary Parker Follett and Chester I. Barnard, both of whom focused extensively on the social framework of employment situations. Elton Mayo's Hawthorne experiments added substance to the human relations concept.

Systems theory follows a more eclectic view of organizations and considers each part as an essential component to be recognized and understood. Work must be performed effectively and economically (classical management) by motivated persons (behavioral management) in a manner that brings together all components of the objective to be reached in a timely manner (operations research).

Many of today's managers no longer attempt to subscribe to one school of management thought. Instead, they follow the contingency view that permits a leader to assess the situation, select, and apply the designated tools of management deemed appropriate for the situation.

Analysis of Illustrative Case Study

INTRODUCTION—THE APOSTLE OF MASS PRODUCTION

Henry Ford focused on producing an automobile the masses could afford. His management philosophy reflected the kind of thinking about specialization of labor advocated by Adam Smith centuries before and further developed by Frederick W. Taylor in his quest to find the "one best way" to perform work.

Ford's improvement to his plants through capital additions led to improved productivity. He believed the worker's increased productivity resulted from his capital investments; therefore, he felt justified in pushing his workers to do more. While Ford's production genius is often extolled, he is remembered also for having gained much of his success at the expense of his workers.

CONTINUED—THE APOSTLE OF MASS PRODUCTION

Henry Ford reflected the management thought prevalent in the 19th century—workers are born saddled, bridled, and ready to be ridden, while managers are born wearing boots with spurs to do the riding. Ford reflected the scientific management style of Frederick W. Taylor. The consequence was combativeness with the employees.

Ford demonstrated the entrepreneurial spirit of taking risks, but ignored the freedom of choice by consumers, who shifted loyalties to other producers when better value and choice were offered. In effect, Ford's magic lost much of its shine. The company had a poor labor relations record, which was reflected in the public's lack of support of the product.

WRAP-UP—THE APOSTLE OF MASS PRODUCTION

Ford's success were shared with the public through extensive philanthropy. To this extent, he was socially responsible, but it was easy for critics to charge that his success was built on a crumbling foundation of unenlightened management with respect to labor relations.

The case illustrates many attributes of classical management, especially the parts developed by Frederick W. Taylor and Frank W. Gilbreth. Taylor sought the one best way, and the assembly line was a "best way." Gilbreth worked to obtain economy of motion. The way Ford cars were assembled demonstrated adherence to many elements of motion analysis.

Answers to End-of-Chapter Review Questions

1. Why is it important for you to understand the various management theories that have developed?

First, good theory produces practical results. Classical management with its emphasis on functions of management continues today in many concepts of the processes of management. Yet there is an important distinction between functions and processes: functions may be performed in isolation, whereas processes flow together to achieve a result.

2. What environmental factors enhanced the growth and development of each of the three major schools of thought?

The Taylor theory was built on a closed environment where the enterprise was the center of the universe. The social environment concept, however, led to an increased awareness that workers were people with feelings, aspirations, and expectations. Quantitative analysis has added another dimension to the environment of management. To compensate for some of the inherent human relations problems created by these approaches to management, systems theory attempts to weave the best parts of management doctrine into a more workable set of assumptions.

3. What were some of the work methods and tools that Taylor introduced to productivity?

Time study was utilized to determine how long a task required. Taylor applied concepts of selection and placement in hiring first-rate persons. He conducted studies of fatigue in order to develop a way of increasing production by determining when workers should rest and when they should work. The differential piece rate pay plan was an attempt at behavior modification since he believed workers to be rational and would pursue their self-interests in seeking rewards.

4. Was Taylor's assumption that management and labor had a common cause valid? Why or why not?

The assumption was valid initially since Taylor lived when the factory system was in its infancy. It was common for workers and owners to work side-by-side with a resulting natural blending of interests.

5. Why did Follett believe that individual freedom and self-control should come through the activities of the group?

In a literary sense, Follett felt that "no man is an island." People had to live within a group to be whole. She maintained, like Taylor, that workers and owners had a commonality of interest, *provided* they remained in a group where the necessary steps of control arose.

6. Which of Fayol's principles and functions of management do you believe still apply today?

Division of labor, authority, discipline, unity of command, unity of direction, subordination of individual interest, remuneration, centralization, hierarchy, order, equity, stability of staff, and initiative.

7. What was Mayo's principal contribution to management knowledge? What is the Hawthorne effect?

Mayo helped bring about the realization that workers were more than hired hands. They brought all of themselves to the job—especially the social part of themselves.

The Hawthorne experiment revealed an inference that employees would work harder if they believed management was concerned about their welfare and supervisors paid special attention to them.

8. Distinguish between the "rational" and "social" models in human relations.

When people follow predictable patterns of behavior based on known stimuli, they are said to be rational. When people succumb to group pressures more than external sources, they are socially motivated.

9. What is OR (Operations Research), and how does it work?

OR is a problem-solving approach to managing drawn from the expertise of a mixed team of specialists from relevant disciplines established to analyze a problem and propose a course of action to management. The team relies extensively on building a mathematical model of the problem so that the variables can be manipulated in a series of "what if" statements to see the effect of each.

10. Why is the systems approach more appropriate today than it would have been in Fayol's time?

In Fayol's day, the environment of a business was more closed and the need to interact with a variety of constituents was less important. Today's businesses are more complex. Systems management relies on feedback to help the system operate in a self-correcting manner, and a continuous flow of information is essential.

11. What is the major task of the manager, according to the contingency approach?

The primary task is to determine which technique should be applied to a particular situation in a particular fashion. Contingency theory holds that for any given situation, a best or preferred set of actions should be implemented.

12. Which approach or school of management thought makes the most sense to you? Why?

    It is appropriate to consider the backgrounds of the responding students. For example, John T. Malloy, a popular "dress-for-success writer," often points out that people dress in a way that reflects their socio-economic background. Thus some students probably harbor a suspicion of management's motives. They would reply to this question in a manner reflecting a prescribed approach to being socially responsible. Other students might take the approach of Milton Friedman, a conservative economist, that the most socially responsible action for management is to make a profit. Society, through taxation, can take a share of the profits to support social programs.

Answers to End-of-Chapter Case Questions

CASE: THEORY AND POLICY ENCOUNTER POWER AND MOTIVATION AT CONSOLIDATED AUTOMOBILE

1. What is the real problem in this case?

   Two employees violated a union contract and undertook their own version of collective bargaining. The problem is worsened by the union steward supporting an illegal action and the plant manager's failure to have security personnel remove the workers and charge them with interfering with the safe operation of the plant.

2. How would each of the approaches to management in this chapter analyze the case?

   Frederick W. Taylor would follow the union contract and have the employees face disciplinary action.

   Henri Fayol might look into failures by managers to adhere to his principles, but would also look to the legal document negotiated by the union and the management for guidance.

   Elton Mayo would be fascinated by the social forces at work and how the disgruntled employees were supported by the idled workers whose pay was continuing during the stoppage. Mayo would probably ignore the collective bargaining concept and attempt to deal with the situation by seeking an acceptable group norm.

3. How should the plant manager restore production on the assembly line?

   Plant security needs to remove the wildcat striking workers from the unauthorized area; the workers are to be placed on disciplinary layoff pending a review based on the collective bargaining agreement. Plant maintenance employees are to restore power to the equipment, repair any broken locks, and secure the power distribution area according to pertinent safety standards. While this is occurring the idled workers have a choice: return to work, or face individual disciplinary action for failure to follow lawful management instructions. At the same time, the company's legal counsel is to be asked to file a legal action against the union and seek compensatory damages resulting from the wildcat strike.

4. What policy, if any, should be developed to prevent future production interruptions?

   Prevention is a goal, but the reality is that workers sometimes fail to accept the slowness of collective bargaining bureaucracy. The preventive approach should be one of speeding the process by which employee complaints are dealt with before they become grievances.

5. If there is an underlying struggle for power in this situation, precisely where does it lie? Which theoretical approach to management policy is best suited to answer this question?

   The union workers, supported by their steward, wanted to exercise prerogatives in determining company policies even if such actions compromised the effective and efficient management of plant facilities. The root of the difficulty most likely can be traced to past weakness by management in capitulating to union work-rule demands.

   The most suitable theoretical approach to management policy here is the kind advocated by Edward Deming. He would open the company's books to the employees to let them know what kinds of problems must be resolved for the plant to be competitive. Small groups will be organized to discuss what each can do to bring about a better operation.

   In the final analysis, the problem will be met through an eclectic approach of taking the best from several of the theories. Classical management offers a context for cooperation, behavioral theories provide ideas for practical application, and the mathematical school brings measurement to the actions agreed upon.

Suggested Term Paper Topics

1. In what ways can theory and practice be compatible?
2. An analysis of present practices of management rooted in classical theory
3. Contributions and limitations of behavioral theories of management
4. Contributions and limitations of operations research management
5. The contributions of the Hawthorne studies to the practice of management
6. The studies of Frank B. Gilbreth applied to modern work methods
7. Principles of management contrasted with the processes of management

8. Contrasting the social setting of work and management perceived need to institute control systems
9. The influence of Douglas McGregor on modern theories of management

Suggested Guest Speakers

1. The labor relations issues of the Consolidated Automobile case can be expanded by inviting a union leader and a management representative to discuss the issues from their respective points of view.
2. Invite a business historian, possibly from the Department of History, to discuss the early years of mass production as it influenced labor relations between workers and managers.
3. Invite a production manager to discuss how decision theory is applied in the planning and scheduling of work under conditions of job lot production and continuous production.

CHAPTER 3
The External Environment of Organizations

Chapter Outline

CHANGE AND THE ENVIRONMENT

COMPONENTS OF THE EXTERNAL ENVIRONMENT

ELEMENTS OF THE DIRECT-ACTION ENVIRONMENT

Environmental Evolution
Organizational Stakeholders
External Stakeholders
Internal Stakeholders
Multiple Stakeholder Environments

ELEMENTS OF THE INDIRECT-ACTION ENVIRONMENT

Environmental Variables
Social Variables
Economic Variables
Political Variables
Technological Variables

THE INTERNATIONAL ENVIRONMENT OF ORGANIZATIONS

New Technology
The Emergence of International Competitors
The Problem of Competitiveness
The Blurring of Public and Private Spheres of Influence
The Opening of China and the Eastern Bloc

CHARACTERISTICS OF TOTAL ORGANIZATION ENVIRONMENTS

The Theory of Uncertainty and Dependence
Other Theories of Environments
Natural Selection
Resource Dependence

MANAGING THE TOTAL ENVIRONMENT

Influencing the Direct-Action Environment
Monitoring the Indirect-Action Environment
Adjusting to the Environment

SUMMARY

Key Terms

- **collective bargaining** The process of negotiating and administering agreements between labor and management concerning wages, working conditions, and other aspects of the work environment.
- **stakeholders** Those groups or individuals who are directly or indirectly affected by an organization's pursuit of its goals.
- **inputs** Resources from the environment, such as raw materials and labor, that may enter any organizational system.
- **outputs** Transformed inputs that are returned to the external environment as products or services.
- **direct-action elements** Elements of the environment that directly influence an organization's activities.
- **indirect-action elements** Elements of the external environment that affect the climate in which an organization's activities take place, including economic and political situations, but that do not affect the organization directly.
- **external stakeholders** Groups or individuals who affect an organization's activities from its external environment.
- **internal stakeholders** Groups or individuals, such as employees, who are not strictly part of an organization's environment but for whom an individual manager remains responsible.
- **social variables** Factors, such as demographics and social values, that may influence an organization from its external environment.
- **economic variables** General economic conditions and trends that may be factors in an organization's activities.
- **political variables** Factors that may influence an organization's activities as a result of the political process or climates.

- **technological variables** New developments in products or processes, as well as advances in science, which may affect an organization's activities.
- **uncertainty** According to Hannan and Freeman, the theoretical problem posed to an organization by lack of information.
- **dependence** According to Hannan and Freeman, the theoretical problem faced by an organization because of its need for vital resources from outside sources.
- **forecasting** The attempt, using specific techniques, to predict outcomes and project future trends.

Chapter Overview/Synopsis

Chapter 2 noted the extensive influence social and environmental pressures have had on management thought. Managers of the classical school concentrated on direct control of such elements as conditions of employment, relations with customers, and dealings with suppliers. They failed to note the shift of public perception of business, but external forces had become a power that could not be ignored. Chapter 3 focuses on the significant environmental forces influencing the managing of organizations.

Effective managers identify those external forces relevant to the continued operations of their respective businesses. In all instances, organizations exchange resources with the environment. Inputs such as labor, materials, energy, and money come from without, and become outputs through various transformation processes before being returned to the environment.

Stakeholders have no common identity; they may be customers, competitors, suppliers, employees, self-styled watchdog groups, or governmental agencies. This lack of common identity combined with a lack of common purpose adds to the complexity facing managers as they attempt to anticipate and satisfy the demands of such groups.

The external environment of American businesses now includes global competition. Cultural and national values of other nations compound the complexity that managers must deal with. Technological change is another variable of the external environment. Many American citizens have little loyalty to "buy American" when they feel greater value and quality exists from foreign producers.

American managers will probably do the most for their businesses by taking steps to monitor their external environment continually in a way that helps them forecast pressures that could jeopardize the survival of their organization. From this careful set of observations, strategic planning can be done to help maintain the business in a proactive, rather than reactive, mode of operation.

Analysis of Illustrative Case Study

INTRODUCTION—IMAGE AND IMAGING PROBLEMS AT EASTMAN KODAK

Kodak's sure grip on the U.S. camera and camera film market slipped as a result of Kodak's inability to read the signs of change regarding photography. For most Americans, camera film came in yellow boxes, and family-style pictures were taken with a Brownie. True, other brands of film such as Agfa existed, and cameras such as Argus had a limited market. Kodak was a solid name that garnered respect from both the general public and those who trusted their future to the company—the employees. With such a firm position in the market, Kodak management failed to keep abreast of the changes in technology being pioneered by other producers.

While Kodak's share of the U.S. camera film market has remained substantial, Fuji from Japan is making inroads with its higher-speed film that can be used in the popular 35mm cameras. Also, Fuji's television sponsorship of the 1984 summer Olympics provided extensive brand name exposure to the public. Polaroid's unique picture-making capability has also captured a significant share of the market.

The overall consequence of Kodak not keeping up has resulted in employment reductions—about 12,000 throughout the world. Management's realization that the company was lagging behind its competition meant that drastic action had to be taken to position the company for renewal.

CONTINUED—IMAGE AND IMAGING PROBLEMS AT EASTMAN KODAK

During the time Kodak was contemplating its future, other producers of camera film, magnetic tape and disks, and cameras were moving into existing markets and developing new ones. The videocassette recorder (VCR) in particular had found a niche in the public's fancy.

Kodak's strategy for corporate rejuvenation has resulted in new products, notably office copying machines. It has also developed a computer program, Datashow®, that permits slide-type presentations on large-sized screens. Regardless of Kodak's movement toward corporate revitalization, the public recognizes that other producers are willing to serve them. Kodak is no longer the only name in photography.

WRAP-UP—IMAGE AND IMAGING PROBLEMS AT EASTMAN KODAK

The turn-around strategy of Kodak has begun to achieve results. The monolithic managerial style has been replaced by decentralization where managers have the freedom to fail (two failures of the same kind are unacceptable). Decentralization has resulted in Kodak expanding its product base. Kodak is involved in pharmaceuticals, electrostatic copiers, computer software, medical technology, and other areas where it feels able to compete. Part of this change has occurred because Kodak is willing to enter ventures with other companies since it no longer has to be so strongly centralized. A variety of problems face Kodak in its quest for resurgence. For example, it has to pay damages to Polaroid because of a patent infringement lawsuit. Also, its solid base of employee support may have been eroded as a result of layoffs of almost 13,000 employees.

Answer to End-of-Chapter Review Questions

1. Distinguish between the direct-action and indirect-action components of the environment and give examples of each.

The direct-action environment has a known composition that enables managers to use established means to know with whom they are interacting. The indirect-action environment is composed primarily of unlimited informational resources that may be used to monitor company progress.

2. Who are the stakeholders of an organization, and how have their stakes changed in recent years?

Stakeholders are self-identified individuals or groups who claim to be affected by actions of an organization; they may be either internal or external. Having a "stake" in the outcome of organizational actions is the basis for the claim. Probably the most significant change in and of stakeholders is their vigorous pursuit of new goals as they expand their level of expectations from businesses.

3. What are stakeholder networks and coalitions? How can managers use them to influence stakeholders?

Stakeholder networks are coalitions of diverse groups who have combined forces because of a common interest or set of interests. An organization may enlist the aid of stakeholder groups to gain support for its agenda when the interests of both groups are parallel. For example, competitively disadvantaged businesses may become linked to labor unions to obtain protective trade legislation.

4. Discuss the four factors that make up the indirect-action environment of organizations.

The indirect-action environment is composed of social, economic, political, and technological factors. Social values affect how people view politics, economics, and technology. Subsumed are demographics, lifestyles, and value systems. Economic variables influence the degree to which an individual's values retain their practicality. A person who feels the unemployed are lazy might have a different belief a year following a corporate blood-letting where his/her job was eliminated. The political value system changes rapidly under some conditions, but seems set in concrete when people seeking change are frustrated by political inaction. One of the main factors affecting the political value system held by people is access to persons possessing political power. Technological variables include scientific as well as method research. Skill in management can be a type of technology.

5. Describe some recent changes in U.S. demographics, lifestyles, and social values. How do they affect organizations?

The nation is getting older with the result that such disparate things as health care, employment in fast-food outlets, and recreational activities have been affected. An increased number of elderly persons need more of a nation's resources. Demographics also includes the different composition of ethnic, racial, and sex groups. Hispanic persons comprise one of the fastest growing groups in America. Black persons are growing in political and economic influence. An increasing number of women now occupy the professions as evidenced by more women physicians, lawyers, architects, and accountants, to identify but a few.

The single-parent family is commonplace—this has influenced the demand for affordable day care centers. More women are working and also raising families.

The recent downsizing and pay-cutting actions taken by many organizations to become more competitive has caused extensive shifts in social values. The fervent loyalty many employees once showed their employers has given way to an increase in willingness to place the employer's interests in a secondary position.

6. What is the difference between structural and cyclical economic change? What are their implications for organizations?

Structural changes are major shifts between different sectors of the economy. Cyclical economic changes occur periodically as determined by changes in the economy. Levels of employment vary according to demand; fresh food prices change according to the season and weather-related growth factors. One of management's challenges is to determine whether a shift is cyclical or periodic.

7. How does technological development proceed? At which stages in its life cycle is technology critical to competition?

   Technological development begins with basic research, when a scientist discovers some new phenomenon or advances some new theory. Technological change can be linear or non-linear. In the first instance research proceeds from step to step. One problem must be solved before the next one can be undertaken. On a non-linear basis, research may proceed on many fronts since each success can stand alone, even though better results might be obtained if more successes could be combined to form a larger solution. Base technology is knowledge held by all competitors and provides no competitive edge. Key technology gives a firm a competitive edge because the knowledge is neither widely known nor well protected by patents.

8. What are the management challenges and opportunities posed by growing international trade?

   The growth of international business has brought about a shift from some nations being a primary source of supply to being just another source of supply. The initial reaction to competition from abroad is to push for trade restrictions. Pressures for protectionist measures mount when American businesses know that foreign suppliers are heavily subsidized by their own nations. The best opportunity for today's managers appears to be to focus on long-term strategies based on stockholder support.

9. Define uncertainty and dependence and describe the environmental characteristics that affect them.

   Uncertainty occurs when information is lacking. Such lack may occur when the environment is differentiated and changing, and the interconnections between its elements are numerous. Dependence exists when organizations must rely on an external environment for the resources necessary to carry out their goals.

10. Contrast the natural selection, resource-dependence, and industrial-organizational models.

    The natural selection model "is based on biological theories of population ecology" and emphasizes the competition for scarce resources as the means of survival. Survival in this mode might depend as much on knowing how to get along with the environmental constraints as in overcoming them. The resource-dependent model assumes that organizations rely on other segments of the environment to supply the necessary resources. The industrial-organizational model assumes a selective approach to dealing with its environments. Where dependence cannot be changed to independence, it works with its external environments but does not abandon its quest for independence.

11. What techniques can managers use to influence the direct-action environment? To adjust to the indirect-action environment?

    The most likely approach to dealing with the direct-action environment is through the processes of monitoring, forecasting, and planning. Managers monitor the indirect-action environment to detect signs of impending forces that will eventually affect the survivability of the firm.

Answers to End-of-Chapter Case Questions

CASE: TRI-STATE TELEPHONE

1. Who are the stakeholders in this case?

   Tri-State Telephone Company, its customers, employees, suppliers, regulators, various media, and interested observers.

2. Which stakeholders are most important?

   Importance is relative. The elderly stakeholders might be most significant because they are newsworthy with the capability to present an emotional case to the public that Tri-State is out to deprive them of their "life line to the world." Other stakeholders who could assume positions of importance are business customers, computer enthusiasts, bankers, and other companies in the telecommunications business.

3. What are the critical trends in Tri-State's environment?

   People have not yet settled down to the deregulated telephone business. While long-distance rates declined, the general public experienced an escalation of local telephone rates. The result has been disillusionment with the telephone industry and a tendency to view rate proposals with distrust. The environment is a mix of indirect-action and direct-action coupled with a mounting force of technological change. The term *voice-communication* no longer describes the industry because, in addition to the traditional telephone call, telephone lines now carry pictures and digital information and have been tied to household appliances to provide additional services. Tri-state feels its pay-for-service idea will provide equity to a situation that has become inequitable.

4. Why are the customers of Tri-State upset, in your opinion?

   Threat of change is unsettling. People do not necessarily resist change, but they resist being changed. The proposed telephone rate structure is perceived as requiring telephone users to measure every minute of local conversation in much the way a taxi meter measures mileage. Telephone users are accustomed to timed long distance calls, but local service measurement appears as a threat to an entitlement. Another reason the customers are upset is that the rate structure did not provide alternatives. That is, flat rates should have been continued as an option. Those who wanted to pay for measured service could make the choice.

5. What should Mr. Godwin do?

   He should first identify leaders of the opposition and meet with them. This meeting should be for discussion, and he should make clear that he made a mistake in not researching his plan further. He should then point out the problem faced by the company as people use its services for different purposes and that he would appreciate their help in developing a plan that not only is fair but appears to be fair.

Suggested Term Paper Topics

1. An analysis of how organizations utilize public relations firms or the public relations firms function to work with special interest groups.
2. Public relations problems associated with shifting from being a regulated company to one free from economic regulation.
3. An identification and analysis of leading bellwethers used by firms to forecast changes in their operating environment.
4. Conditions that foster the emergence of stakeholder groups.
5. Characteristics of direct-action and indirect-action environments.
6. Role of strategy and strategic management in dealing with the international dimension of stakeholders.
7. Ways of measuring benefits accruing to stakeholder groups from organizational endeavors.
8. Technology and internal relationship of organizations.
9. Managing organizational change in the face of hostile stakeholder opposition.

Suggested Guest Speakers

1. Invite a manager of a formerly regulated company to discuss the changes faced by the organization as it became part of a non-regulated environment.
2. Invite a person from the local Chamber of Commerce or other individual with a direct interest in extending the international dimension of business. Ask to have the subject of protectionism discussed.
3. Politicians tend to identify "dragons that need slaying" as part of their electioneering. Invite an incumbent politician and ask him/her to describe how the selection is made to identify the "dragon" that will be mostly likely to draw votes for their candidacy.

CHAPTER 4 Social Responsibility and Ethics

Chapter Outline

THE CHANGING CONCEPT OF RESPONSIBILITY

The Public View of Business

CORPORATE SOCIAL RESPONSIBILITY

Milton Friedman's Argument
A History of Corporate Social Responsibility
Corporate Social Responsiveness
- Ackerman's Model
- Preston and Post's Model
- Carroll's Model
- The Limitations of Corporate Social Responsiveness Models

THE SHIFT TO ETHICS

What Is Ethics?
Four Levels of Ethical Questions in Business

THE TOOLS OF ETHICS

Ethical Language
- Values
- Rights and Duties
- Moral Rules

Common Morality
- Promise-Keeping
- Nonmalevolence
- Mutual Aid
- Respect for Persons
- Respect for Property

Applying Ethics
Institutionalizing Ethics

THE CHALLENGE OF RELATIVISM

Naive Relativism
Cultural Relativism
A Kernel of Truth

SUMMARY

Key Terms

- **stewardship principle** Biblical doctrine that requires businesses and wealthy individuals to see themselves as stewards, or caretakers, holding their property in trust for the benefit of society as a whole.
- **charity principle** Doctrine requiring the more fortunate members of society to voluntarily assist the less fortunate members, either directly or indirectly.
- **corporate social responsiveness** The second theory of corporate social responsibility, a more pragmatic, action-oriented view than the philosophical concepts of the charity or stewardship principles.
- **primary relations** Interaction between a business and market-oriented groups, such as customers, employees, shareholders, and creditors.
- **secondary relations** Interaction between a business and non-market-oriented groups, such as customers, employees, shareholders, and creditors.
- **corporate social performance** A single theory of corporate social action encompassing social principles, processes, and policies.
- **naive relativism** The idea that all human beings are themselves the standard by which their actions should be judged.
- **cultural relativism** The idea that morality is relative to a particular culture, society, or community.
- **values** Relatively permanent desires that seem to be good in themselves.
- **rights** Claims that entitle a person to take a particular action.
- **duties** Obligations to take specific steps or obey the law.
- **moral rules** Rules for behavior that often become internalized as moral values.
- **common morality** The body of rules covering ordinary ethical problems.

Chapter Overview/Synopsis

Society questions both the means businesses use to obtain profits and how those profits affect society's well-being. New social stipulations demand that businesses be conducted in a responsive and responsible manner. Those demands are not necessarily raised as one voice, and businesses are pulled and pushed by opposing forces. This chapter approaches the many issues of social responsibility by considering questions such as: Where does business responsibility to society begin and end? What rules of conduct should govern business and its managers? Is it proper for business to consider stockholder needs ahead of society's needs? What kinds of regulations are needed to balance society's concerns with the needs of business to be conducted in a manner that improves its likelihood of continued operation?

Neither answers nor analysis regarding the above questions exist that satisfy all the interest groups in society. The beginning point of gaining an understanding of the issues is the recognition that public opinion polls generally reveal the public's low esteem of business. Newspaper headlines draw attention to insider trading, bribery of officials, and products that cause harm to the public. Political populists promise to punish greedy businesses. Before reviewing the populism concept further, we consider several arguments regarding business ethics, including those of Milton Friedman, a Nobel Prize-winning economist who maintains that the most socially responsible function of business is to make a profit. This is followed by several arguments advocating different approaches to businesses being socially responsive.

The authors define ethics as the "study of how our decisions affect other people." Included in their analysis are people's rights and duties along with the rules people apply in making their decisions. Within this setting, ethics has both a *descriptive* and a *normative* perspective. There is also the relative circumstance surrounding the decision being reviewed. The question of relativism refers to a contingency approach of determining what is right or wrong, depending on a manager's values coupled with the situation.

People often feel the need for guidance in conducting themselves ethically and morally in a way that generates approval from others. The legal system provides much of this base, but there is a gray area where laws do not exist. Organizations may attempt to institutionalize ethical and moral behavior through codes of conduct. The decisions of managers *always* affect people.

Analysis of Illustrative Case Study

INTRODUCTION—AN ETHICAL AND SOCIAL DILEMMA AT CHEMICAL BANK

Matthew McPartland, a divisional manager for the retail division of New York's Chemical Bank, faces a decision regarding the future of two money-losing branches of the bank. The problem is compounded because the two branches are located in an economically depressed neighborhood. The likelihood of short-run economic conditions improving for the community are bleak. If the branches are closed, a 40-block area would be without a Chemical branch office. The people of the affected area feel the tensions of being without bank services and have voiced their feelings to local politicians. Chemical Bank's policies have been to be a good citizen wherever it conducts its business.

The case extends beyond the simpler and abstract issues of personal values and ethics. The bank's strategy clearly stresses the need to improve profitability, and McPartland accepts his paycheck from Chemical Bank. Accepting pay from an employer indicates a requirement to demonstrate loyalty to support ethical and lawful decisions. McPartland is not without help, however, since he can obtain guidance from bank officials.

CONTINUED—AN ETHICAL AND SOCIAL DILEMMA AT CHEMICAL BANK

Decision-making does not occur in a vacuum. McPartland will have difficulty tying his decision to philosophical reasoning about ethics, values, and corporate responsibility. If he follows the Friedman analysis and decides to improve profitability by closing down, a press conference staged by various stakeholder groups would picture Chemical Bank as a scourge on society, especially its poorer members. McPartland is in that uncomfortable spot "between a rock and a hard place."

WRAP-UP—AN ETHICAL AND SOCIAL DILEMMA AT CHEMICAL BANK

McPartland needs to consider the following questions that deal with the ethics of the situation:

1. Who will be affected by the decision? This is not just a matter of identifying who will be affected, but must also include the severity of the effect.
2. Who has rights? Rights exist only to the extent an enforcement agency exists; therefore, a claim of having a right is virtually meaningless. In this instance, however, the "rights" could come into existence through moral suasion created through the embarrassment of public protests.

3. What decision rule should be used? The sought-after decision is one in which all parties win. Mary Parker Follett noted three approaches to resolving conflict: domination, compromise, and integration of interest. The first two are almost the same since winners and losers exist, and even with compromise, concessions are made only because strength is lacking to exact a concession from the opposing party. This leaves integration of interest as the desired basis for making the decision.

   McPartland, community merchants, politicians, and officials from the Small Business Administration need to investigate ways to improve the business climate. Politicians need to consider looking into state and federal grants for redevelopment. These types of activities need to be the first course of action so that if the branches have to be closed in the future, the decision, while not popular, will most likely be viewed as an inevitability.

Answers to End-of-Chapter Review Questions

1. What is the "ethics crisis"?

   The public view about the role business should play in the economic and social scheme of things is rapidly changing. Critics charge that much of what is wrong can be traced to the greed and dishonesty of business. They point to such factors as high profits (without defining "high"), dangerous products or practices, shabby treatment of employees, and a general disdain for the well-being of society.

2. Why does Milton Friedman believe that the only responsibility of business is to maximize the profits of the shareholders?

   Friedman believes in specialization of endeavor. People should concentrate on doing what they understand and do best. Business managers understand how to process resources into profitable outputs, while such persons as social workers, educators, and penologists know how to carry out social programs using the resources supplied through tax monies.

3. In what ways was the idea of corporate responsibility paternalistic? Why did the critics of unrestricted free enterprise attack it?

   Advocates of corporate responsibility advocated both charity and stewardship. Charity meant for those possessing wealth to assist the less fortunate members of society. Such assistance could be direct or indirect. Yet the fortunate persons also made the decisions regarding who was unfortunate and how much assistance to render. Making decisions for others in the name of "in their best interests" epitomizes paternalism.

   Stewardship requires businesses and wealthy people to view themselves as stewards in which they return to society that which is entrusted to them. This creates somewhat of a contradiction since a steward or caretaker preserves and returns that which is given in trust. Business managers prefer to take wealth and put it to work so that money makes more money. Critics argue that businesses able to create wealth from wealth can do so only at the cost of impoverishing many members of the public.

4. Describe the objections to the concept of corporate responsiveness.

   Corporate responsiveness leaves the meaning of social responsiveness to the business to decide. As stated, it means what the business community intends it to mean. The objectors feel this leaves too much latitude in the hands of business managers.

5. What are the two major categories of relativism? What are the arguments against them? What is their kernel of truth?

   Naive relativism is based on the concept that human beings are themselves the standard by which their actions should be judged. Naive relativism considers moral decisions as deeply personal and individuals as ultimately responsible for their own actions. Naive relativism is built on a basis of tolerance for the beliefs of others.

   Cultural relativism claims that "morality is relative to particular cultures, societies, or communities." Thus moral behavior can best be understood when viewed in a cultural context. Behavior directed toward discriminating against women by a Saudi Arabian business person might appear strange, if not immoral, to a person from the United States. Cultural relativism creates problems for Americans who work for internationally-oriented businesses. They know the dictum about "when in Rome" but feel it would be improper to live by some of the rules of a host nation.

   The "kernel of truth" notes that "ours is a very big and complex world in which we must be tolerant of diversity. . . . tolerance is a real virtue, but taken to extremes it can be an alibi for just about any refusal to make judgments that must ultimately be made."

6. What is common morality? What are its basic principles?

   "Common morality is the body of rules covering ordinary ethical problems. These are the rules we live by most of the time." Thus, common morality is doing the *decent* thing. Here are several basic principles:

   —Keep promises—People need to feel that a person's word is a bond.
   —Show malice toward none—there is an expectation that people can deal openly with others.
   —Mutual aid—come to the aid of others without being asked.
   —Respect for persons—deal with others as you would want to be treated.
   —Respect for property—obtain consent before using the property of others.

7. What basic questions must we answer to apply moral rules?

   Exhibit 4-1 presents a *Harvard Business Review* list of twelve questions for examining moral rules. Key items in the list include defining the problem properly, seeking the cause, identifying stakeholder interests to determine points of view to be considered, identifying the objective to be gained in resolving the problem, and resolving whether the solution can be reversed and at what point and under what conditions.

8. How have companies attempted to institutionalize ethics?

   Ethics are institutionalized to provide predictability to how people in the organization will deal with the same type of situation. Ways of assuring this anticipation include corporate codes of ethics, ethics committees, ombudsman offices, judicial boards, ethics training programs, and social audits.

Answers to End-of-Chapter Case Questions

CASE: ALEXANDER GAVIN'S DILEMMA: CULTURAL RELATIVISM AND BUSINESS AS USUAL

1. What rights are at stake in this case?

   While the term *right* has a generally accepted meaning in the United States, a right has significance only in the context where enforceability exists. Thus, the "rights" identified below may not include the essential of enforceability.

   —The right of a buyer of services to obtain an honest contract.
   —The right of Alexander Gavin to be safe from physical harm.
   —The right of the employer to expect honest dealings from employees who occupy positions of trust. (The company can enforce this right if it has knowledge of the situation.)
   —The right of Gavin to quit his job. (Gavin probably can do this since his boss would still be able to kite the contract with a more willing subordinate, and Gavin would not have to suffer physical harm).
   —Gavin could withdraw the bid.
   —Gavin could seek outside assistance such as England's Scotland Yard.

2. What decision rule should Mr. Gavin use?

   Within the parameters of Gavin's situation, cultural relativism provides a decision basis. But two cultures are involved—the U.S. and Kuwait's. He is working for a Kuwait company in a nation of cultural ethos rather than for an American company with its institutionalized rules of conduct. He acknowledges the common practice of bribery in Middle Eastern nations, but this is his first experience in a morally compromising circumstance.

   One special point for Gavin to consider is that even though bribery is common in Islamic nations, the nations involved have severe penalties for persons caught accepting bribes. Justice in Middle Eastern nations lacks "American due process." To avoid being caught and punished, Gavin's boss is forcing Gavin to become a party to an illegal act. The decision rule for Gavin to use at this point is *role relativism* because his employer expects to be dealt with fairly. Gavin has no obligation to his boss nor to adapt to *cultural relativism* since the activity is occurring within a limited sphere of the culture—a business with an excellent reputation. He has no right to jeopardize his company nor to violate its trust in him. Therefore, Gavin needs to undertake an action that will both protect his physical well-being and the reputation of his employer. A British-based company, Ajax, Ltd., is involved.

   To accomplish his dual goals, Gavin needs to contract Scotland Yard, expose the scheme, and offer assistance. At this point he can take direction from experts in thwarting such acts of dishonesty. The main thing is that he remove himself from being a party to a dishonest act.

3. Will this rule work in different cultures?

   Ethics and morals tend to be quite personal. The culture of the Middle East includes bribe offering and accepting *(baksheesh)*. Therefore, the decision point would remain to determine which set of ethical values to follow: the ones in use in the United States or the ones of the host nation. The decison based on protecting the interests of the employer, obeying the concepts of moral relativism, and of not compromising one's own moral and ethical standards can apply in any culture as long as it is not a culture of thieves.

Suggested Term Paper Topics

1. A review of what businesses do that meet tests of social responsibility.
2. A review of business activities that violate the sense of public trust.
3. An analysis of allegations by activist groups against business situations or products that prove to lack merit.
4. An analysis of allegations by activist groups against business situations that result in society instituting corrective actions.
5. A collection and analysis of ethical codes of selected businesses and trade associations.
6. The ethics involved in a firm's decision to reduce its costs through permanent reductions in force.
7. The ethics involved in being a "good person in business" or a "good business person."

8. A review of selected business practices acceptable and unacceptable in Japan, Saudi Arabia, and the United States.
9. Educational backgrounds of business executives convicted of such crimes as insider trading, bribing public officials, or engaging in anti-trust activities.

Suggested Guest Speakers

1. Invite the director of the local Better Business Bureau to discuss businesses practices in the geographic area of that agency's jurisdiction.
2. Invite a member of the clergy to discuss whether obeying religious principles interferes with the profit-seeking objectives of business.
3. Invite a business executive whose responsibilities include international business to discuss doing business overseas. He should be asked to include such things as what prompted the firm to seek an overseas market, the issues of communication, meeting the documentation (paper work) requirements of the nations involved, what kinds of "cultural shock" arose, and receiving payment for services.

Part 1 Case Studies

SEAFOOD AMERICA: CORPORATE RESPONSE TO THE COSTS OF AIDS

1. Who are the stakeholders of Seafood America?

   Not arranged by priority, major stakeholders include:

   —Corporate owners
   —Employees
   —Public health services
   —Customers
   —Special interest activist groups
   —News media
   —Employees of suppliers
   —Garbage disposal employees

   The stakeholder group includes persons who ordinarily would be unconcerned about an employee's illness if it were a cold or the flu, but AIDS carries a special stigma in the public mind along with a fear of infection from casual contact. This fear remains relatively true despite repeated statements from the Surgeon General of the United States, along with ones from other respected public health bodies, that AIDS is not communicable through ordinary casual contact.

2. What is the indirect environment like? What political, technological, and economic trends will affect Mathews' decision?

   The indirect environment is composed of demographics, lifestyles, and social values. Demographics affect such factors as the restaurant's customer base, location decisions, and labor supply. The locations of the restaurants suggest lifestyles and social values of the geographic areas to be conservative. The political factors also tend to be ones supported by legislation, that persons with AIDS are to be accorded the same considerations as disabled persons. Technologically, major research continues to seek a cure for AIDS as well as treatments to ameliorate its affects on afflicted individuals. Because a customer spoke openly about an employee having AIDS, there is likelihood the restaurants will suffer an economic decline if a fearful public withholds patronage.

3. What is Mathews' responsibility to his employees? To his customers? To his employee with AIDS? To the employee accused of having AIDS?

   Regardless of AIDS, Mathews continues to be responsible to provide his employees and customers with environmental conditions that comply with all applicable regulations. Despite many public fears, Mathews must deal with the employees in a normal manner—that is, he may not discriminate. He could offer them transfers to company divisions where contact with the general public is minimal; however, neither their earnings nor other employment opportunities can be affected adversely by such a transfer.

4. What would you do if you were Mathews?

   For this question, ask students to research AIDS and base their answers accordingly.

PRECISION MACHINE TOOL: MANAGEMENT IN A CHANGING ENVIRONMENT

1. Describe the environment of Precision Machine Tools—the stakeholders and the trends.

   The environment is one of worn-out equipment beyond economic repair, supported by some modern equipment. Customers threaten to locate other sources if Precision cannot provide products that meet their quality needs. Stakeholders include employees, suppliers, the community, transportation companies, customers, and stockholders. The sales trend is downward. Customers have alternate sources of supply, and regardless of "Buy American" beliefs, they operate businesses that must have machine tools reliably capable of producing products to precise tolerances.

2. How has the emergence of foreign competition affected the company.

   The company had allowed quality to slip during a time period when outside competition was not considered to pose a threat. Thus, while Precision Tool slept, outsiders were gearing up to enter a market deficient in quality products because companies like Precision Tool were complacent.

3. Should the fact that the proposal is from a Japanese firm matter to Garner? Why or why not?

The text points out that decision-making cannot exist outside of a manager's personal value systems. Therefore, Garner's strong bias toward the concept of "Buy American" must have an inescapable affect on his decision-making. Such a bias need not mean he will not sell to a Japanese firm, however, only that it will take more time for him to rationalize the decision.

4. What would you do if you were Garner? Why? Could you defend your answer to your employees? Your community leaders? Your Congressperson?

Five choices appear to face Garner: (1) continue as at present, (2) take on heavy debt to modernize the plant, (3) become a dealer in foreign-made machine tools, (4) sell out to a willing buyer, (5) cease doing business.

Logic suggests choice 4 to be the appropriate alternative. A new owner would provide the likelihood that employment would continue. However, the number of jobs involved would most likely be fewer because foreign owners would not accept the work rule practices in American plants that tend to create more jobs than actually needed. The community should be willing to welcome a new owner who will increase investment in the plant and add to the overall tax base in the community. As in the other choices, the member of Congress could be told that protecting American jobs for Americans would have prevented this sale.

5. Role play the telephone call to Mr. Wang.

Two role-playing situations should be done. The first needs to accept Mr. Wang's offer and should include the conversation about protecting the jobs of all employees and continuing the overall culture of the company. Mr. Wang's conversation should counter many of these arguments.

The second role-play needs to inform Mr. Wang that his offer is refused. A refusal need not contain any justification. Mr. Wang's side of the conversation might contain some counterproposals designed to get negotiations reopened.

CHAPTER 5
Effective Planning

Chapter Outline

PLANNING AND THE MANAGEMENT PROCESS

Plans and Decision Making
The Four Basic Steps in Planning
- Establish a Goal or Set of Goals
- Define the Present Situation
- Identify Aids and Barriers
- Develop a Course of Action

The Link Between Planning and Controlling
- Controlling
- Budgeting

OPERATIONAL PLANS

Single-Use Plans
Standing Plans
- Policies
- Standard Procedures
- Rules

TOOLS AND TECHNIQUES FOR PLANNING

Forecasting
- Forecasting for Economic and Sales Information
- Forecasting Technological Change

Planning Complex Projects
- The Gantt Chart
- Milestone Scheduling
- Network-Based Scheduling

SUMMARY

Key Terms

- **planning** The process of establishing objectives and suitable courses of action before taking action.
- **effectiveness** The ability to determine appropriate objectives: "doing the right things."
- **efficiency** The ability to minimize the use of resources in achieving organizational objectives: "doing things right."
- **decision making** The process of identifying and selecting a course of action to solve a specific problem.
- **single-use plans** Detailed courses of action used once or only occasionally to solve problems that do not occur repeatedly.
- **program** A single-use plan that covers a relatively large set of organizational activities and specifies major steps, their order and timing, and unit responsible for each step.
- **project** The smaller and separate portions of the programs.
- **budgeting** Process for providing formal quantitative statements of the resources allocated to specific programs or projects for a given period.
- **standing plans** An established set of decisions used by managers to deal with recurring or organizational activities; major types are policies, procedures, and rules.
- **policy** A standing plan that establishes general guidelines for decision-making.
- **procedure** A standing plan of detailed guidelines for handling organizational actions that occur regularly.
- **rules** Standing plans that detail specific actions to be taken in a given situation.
- **controlling** The process of monitoring actual organizational activities to see that they conform to planned activities and correcting flaws or deviations.
- **forecasting** The attempt, using specific techniques, to predict outcomes and project future trends.
- **premises** The basic assumptions upon which planning and decision-making are based.
- **qualitative forecasting** A judgment-based forecasting technique used when hard data are scarce or difficult to use.
- **quantitative forecasting** Forecasting techniques used when enough hard data exist to specify relationships between variables.
- **Gantt chart** A graphic method of planning and control that allows a manager to view the starting and ending dates for various tasks.
- **milestone scheduling** A technique that adds detail and precision to the Gantt chart by marking particular dates by which the various phases of the entire project are to be completed.
- **network analysis** A technique used for scheduling complex projects that contain interrelationships between activities or events.
- **program evaluation and review technique (PERT)** A network analysis technique, using esti-

mates of the time required to complete tasks, that is used to schedule and control projects for which task completion times cannot be predicted with any precision.

- **critical path method (CPM)** A network analysis technique used to schedule and control work on projects for which the time required to complete tasks is known fairly precisely.

Chapter Overview/Synopsis

Plans exist to provide purpose and direction to organized endeavor so that events that otherwise would not occur, do occur. Plans provide managers with the knowledge necessary to assemble the human and material resources to achieve a desired result. Plans can be for short-, middle-, and long-range objectives. Planning consists of at least four significant phases:

1. Establish a goal or set of goals
2. Define the present situation
3. Identify the aids and barriers to the goals
4. Develop a plan or set of actions for reaching the goal(s)

Operational plans may be single-use or standing plans. Single-use plans are essential to the completion of one-time projects. Examples include erecting a new building, renovating existing facilities, or moving to a new location. Standing plans permit persons further down in an organization's hierarchy to compare situations to guidelines and take action accordingly.

Policies serve as guides to action. Guidance occurs because a policy establishes the degree of acceptable latitude to the person making a decision. As long as decisions remain within the guidelines, no questions need be raised regarding the decision-maker's rationale.

Forecasting exists to predict outcomes and trends for use in planning. Forecasts may be qualitative or quantitative. While qualitative forecasts suggest a person's opinion is involved, a manager's analytical ability and past experience lead to judgments that frequently can be reinforced by quantitative study.

Several approaches exist to assist management in completing projects. A widely used method dating back almost 100 years is the Gantt Chart. This is a graphic means of identifying time and expected completion dates of projects. Gantt Charts provide a "running report" of progress being made. Additional detail may be added to the Gantt Chart though a technique known as "milestone scheduling" that identifies when critical parts of a project are to begin or to be completed. Today's quantitative techniques permit use of other approaches to scheduling, such as network-based scheduling.

The two major scheduling network techniques are PERT, which stands for Program Evaluation and Review Technique, and CPM, Critical Path Method. PERT is widely used for non-repetitive undertakings such as construction projects. CPM is well suited for repetitive processes in which tasks are of fixed duration and the completion time is known. The primary use of PERT and CPM is to determine and control the time needed to complete a project. These approaches save time, and there is truth to the maxim that time is money. Although few managers would deny the necessity of forecasting and planning, there are impediments to overcome.

Analysis of Illustrative Case Study

INTRODUCTION—REVERSING THE FLOW AT CHRYSLER CORPORATION

By 1978, it was apparent Chrysler had made a series of forecast errors in predicting the sizes of cars its customers would buy. The error was compounded by the oil shortage of the late 1970s. Even though Chrysler attempted to adjust to the market by changing the size of its product, customers were unwilling to wait. New management was brought in, with Lee J. Iacocca named both board chairman and CEO.

Mr. Iacocca's analysis of Chrysler was that managers had been rotated from position to position so frequently that they no longer had the requisite expertise in any specialized area. Accordingly, Iacocca undertook the following:

—Replaced almost all senior managers

—Initiated meetings between sales managers and dealers

—Sold excess inventory to generate cash

—Became a public figure when he assumed the primary role in the advertising campaign of the "new" Chrysler Corporation.

Chrysler's problems were beyond the scope of the company to solve through internal means. Iacocca turned to the federal government for financial assistance. The government imposed a variety of stringent requirements as a condition for granting help. A good-faith effort by Chrysler resulted in a federal loan guarantee of $1.5 billion. By 1983, Chrysler's rebuilding allowed the company to repay all of its loans.

This case reveals the need for management to maintain an ongoing planning process. Chrysler's former managements relied too heavily on past experience as the means of forecasting the future. They failed to investigate the external environment sufficiently to identify threats to the organization. Complacency by management courts disaster.

CONTINUED—REVERSING THE FLOW AT CHRYSLER CORPORATION

Some persons involved in management development insist that managing is universal. That is, the skills and abilities of managing are more important than knowing about what is being managed. In effect, a manager of a hotel could manage a steel-producing company. Chrysler's rotation of managers through a variety of positions attempted to demonstrate the universality approach, but actually created a team of managers-in-training. One of Iacocca's first steps was to identify managers and what they were best suited to manage and reassign them accordingly.

The most important part of Iacocca's work lay in helping managers to believe in themselves and in Chrysler. They had to feel the company's problems could be solved. The main thing was to develop a plan and to work the plan.

WRAP-UP—REVERSING THE FLOW AT CHRYSLER CORPORATION

Chrysler's financial comeback had, by 1987, permitted it to acquire American Motors, Lamborghini, and a share of Maserati. Iacocca, however, still exhibits fear of failure, as discussed in the chapter, since he continues to lobby the federal government to undertake protectionist measures to insulate his firm from some of the rigors of foreign competition. He feels that with protection his firm could give Japanese manufacturers more competition. Lee Iacocca is attempting to identify and remove external threats to the company.

Answers to End-of-Chapter Review Questions

1. Why is flexibility a characteristic of a good plan? Why might flexibility impede planning?

The danger to existing organizations is that they will become inflexible through too much reliance on rules, systems, and procedures. Thus managers need to identify ahead of time the kinds of conditions that will cause the formation of alternate plans—flexibility.

Flexibility can be an impediment to planning if plans change too often, since this kind of change can lead to doubts about whether planning actually exists. Plans need to have a time frame built in and have sufficient organizational commitment through resources to help ensure completion as intended. Changes in planning are best justified when the present plan is not bringing about the goals and expectations of management.

2. Describe the basic steps in the planning process. Why is each step important?

a. Establish a goal or set of goals. Planning begins with decisions about what the organization or subunit wants or ought to be. Such goals help identify priorities of what the organization needs to accomplish with its available resources.

b. Define the present situation. The planning gap is identified by determining where the organization is, compared to where it ought to be, within the framework of its timetable for growth.

c. Identify the aids and barriers to the goals. Some experts refer to this as a SWOT (strength, weaknesses, opportunities, and threats) analysis. This helps identify what kinds of events might result in threats to the survival of the organization.

d. Develop a plan or set of actions for reaching the goal(s). More than one path should be available to accomplish a given plan. While one approach may be preferred for the sake of effectiveness and efficiency, a fixation with one plan can bring about inaction.

3. How are planning and controlling linked? Why is it important for you as a manager to keep these two management functions formally separated?

Planning is the process of establishing both objectives and courses of action, and controlling is the process of monitoring activities to determine how well they are achieving the intended goals. Separation of the two functions helps ensure that each is recognized as being important. Also, separation places quality control apart from the influence of those performing the activities.

4. What are the main types of operation plans? Under what conditions is each type of plan appropriate?

The two types are single-use and standing plans. Plans for one-time situations exist for non-repeatable occurrences such as entering a newly defined market, building a new plant, remodeling an existing facility, and similar cases.

Standing plans cover repeatable situations. Managers can delegate decision-making further down in the organization where standing plans exist to cover the circumstance. Approvals for such things as bank loans, installment purchases, returns of merchandise, and promoting employees need to follow guidelines readily identified with standing plans.

5. Justify the use of standing plans.

   Standing plans free managers from making decisions over routine matters. There is no need to have a decision-making manager review situations that have already been decided.

6. Why do you think forecasts do not have to be completely accurate to be meaningful?

   The authors point out: "forecasts do not have to be right in order to be useful—they simply have to predict future events closely enough to guide present actions in a valid and purposeful way." Time is an important element of forecasting. Managers want to know trends far enough in advance to make meaningful plans. Forecasting is a continuing activity so that early trends either become more fixed as additional information is acquired, or become insignificant because of other influences.

7. Why is forecasting an important part of the planning or decision-making process? What are the two types of forecasts that serve as planning premises?

   "The most important use of forecasts is as premises for planning." Two broad types of forecasts are involved: "First, forecasts of events that will be influenced, at least in part, by the organization's behavior." In addition, there are many economic and social variables not affected by things the organization does. In the latter instance, management is looking for bellwethers to serve as indicators of future events.

8. Describe and give examples of quantitative and qualitative forecasting.

   Quantitative forecasting uses statistical techniques to identify relationships between data. Computers are often utilized to manipulate additional variables in an attempt to find multiple relationships. Examples include obtaining relationships between pricing and sales volume, and domestic water use as related to the time television commercials are shown.

   Qualitative forecasting is judgment-based and is used when hard data are scarce or difficult to obtain and use. Even so, managers experienced in a given field often have a feel for information they receive and from which they make judgments. Such a feel exists in the fashion industry.

9. Briefly describe the principal characteristics of Gantt Charts, milestone scheduling, and network analysis, including PERT and CPM.

   Gantt Chart. Tasks are separated, each having both an estimate of both time required for completion and the progress to date. The chart identifies the starting as well as the completion date.

   Milestone scheduling. Time for specific parts of a project are added to a Gantt Chart to provide additional information. Milestones can also be specified to identify when special reports or reviews are to be made.

   Network Analysis. This term describes both PERT and CPM techniques for scheduling. PERT (program evaluation and review technique) is an advanced method of estimating and controlling scheduling needs.

Answers to End-of-Chapter Case Questions

Case: The Dashman Company

1. How would you evaluate the goal(s) of the new purchasing program?

   The goals are appropriate. The company is attempting to take steps to assure itself of a continued supply of necessary raw materials and components. One of the means for achieving this goal was to introduce a communication component into the process so that overlapping and perhaps wasteful actions would be monitored. An important goal such as this requires top management's "blessing," which was done by appointing an expert in the field and by informing the respective plant managements of the company's intention.

2. How would you evaluate the control process that Mr. Post has established?

   Having the support of top management does not assure support by affected persons. A common method for subordinates to deal with dictatorial bosses is to agree with the demands but continue "business as usual." While Post's control process had a predetermined standard, it had no means of follow-through. Post did not say what his central office would do with the information. Consequently, the local managers did not see advantages to the new system.

3. Might the problems, if any, with the purchasing procedures be symptomatic of a larger problem in the company?

   The problem identified was one of assuring a continued supply of materials. The company's solution was to bring in a purchasing expert who proceeded to take charge by instituting a centralized procedure. Centralization is one way to bring about control in a loose-knit operation. The problem, rather than appearing to be company-wide, arises from Mr. Post's failure to undertake the steps necessary to bring about a change in the organization.

4. What would you have done if you were Mr. Post?

   Student responses ought to target the speed with which the change was forced. There is a saying that "If there is not enough time to do a job right, there is always time to do it over."

5. What would you have done if you were Mr. Larson?

   Larson was named to be the assistant to Mr. Post and let himself be too easily brushed aside. A person who is in an assistant position needs to be willing to restate the case more than once. Since Larson's advice was turned down, the next step would be to write a short memorandum to Mr. Post in which the advice is restated together with predictions of unwanted results from undertaking so major a change without investing the time to sell the affected people on the need for the change.

6. Mr. Manson, president of the Dashman Company, has hired you as an outside consultant to advise him about the purchasing policy. What planning model would you use in determining your recommendations?

   A change such as this falls in the category of a single-use plan. The first step would be a study of present purchasing procedures. Included in this first step would be a series of meetings with personnel from the decentralized plants to let them know what was taking place and the reasons. Their help would be requested.

   Information from the local managers would form the basis for a set of recommendations to Mr. Manson. Thus if I do the consulting job right, the recommendations would most likely have been suggested by the local managers; therefore, they would be supportive of the changes.

Suggested Term Paper Topics

1. Ways of achieving more accurate information in the forecasting process.
2. Decision making in the face of uncertainty.
3. An analysis of Peter Drucker's statement that effectiveness is doing the right things, and efficiency is doing things right.
4. The process of determining that alternative courses of action remain alternatives rather than main courses of action.
5. Reducing the costs of control while maintaining control.
6. A case study of a selected process involving PERT.
7. Ways of improving judgmental decision making.
8. The history, development, and current uses of Gantt charts.
9. Implementing plans while minimizing barriers resulting from resistance to change.

Suggested Guest Speakers

1. Invite a top manager of a company that has undergone extensive ''downsizing'' by reducing the number of personnel. Ask the speaker to discuss what kinds of information led to a forecast resulting in a plan to reduce the number of personnel. This speaker should also include the kinds of situations that arose that were unexpected. If such a decision had to be implemented again, what changes in the planning would be made?
2. Ask an industrial engineer of a local manufacturing company to discuss the kinds of quantitative approaches they use in production scheduling. Ask the speaker to pay special attention to any steps they use with respect to PERT and CPM.
3. Invite a union leader to discuss ways union members are being consulted (or ignored) in company production planning.

CHAPTER 6
Problem Solving and Decision Making

Chapter Outline

THE RATIONAL PROBLEM-SOLVING PROCESS

Stage 1: Investigate the Situations
- Define the Problem
- Identify the Decision Objectives
- Diagnose the Causes

Stage 2: Develop Alternatives
Stage 3: Evaluate Alternatives and Select the Best One
Stage 4: Implement and Monitor the Decision

PROBLEM AND OPPORTUNITY FINDING

The Problem-Finding Process
Opportunity Finding
Deciding to Decide

THE NATURE OF MANAGERIAL DECISION MAKING

Programmed and Nonprogrammed Decisions
- Programmed Decisions
- Nonprogrammed Decisions

Certainty, Risk, and Uncertainty
Rational Decision Making
Bounded Rationality: A Challenge to the Rational Model

HEURISTICS AND BIASES IN DECISION MAKING

Three Heuristics
- Availability
- Representativeness
- Anchoring and Adjustment

Biases in Decision-Making
- Easy Recall
- Easy Search
- Insensitivity to Prior Probability
- Insensitivity to Sample Size
- Misconceptions of Chance
- Insufficient Adjustment
- Overconfidence
- The Confirmation Trap
- Hindsight

Some Conclusions

IMPROVING THE EFFECTIVENESS OF PROBLEM SOLVING AND DECISION MAKING

Improving Individual Problem Solving
- Barriers to Individual Problem Solving
- Overcoming Barriers to Individual Problem Solving

Deciding Who Decides
- Involving Others: Quality and Acceptance

SUMMARY

Key Terms

- **decision making** The process of identifying and selecting a course of action to solve a specific problem.
- **planning** The process of establishing objectives and suitable courses of action before taking action.
- **programmed decisions** Solutions to routine problems determined by rule, procedure, and habit.
- **nonprogrammed decisions** Specific solutions created through an unstructured process to deal with nonroutine problems.
- **bounded rationality** The concept that managers make the most logical decisions they can within the constraints of limited information and ability.
- **dialectical inquiry method** A method of analysis in which a decision-maker determines and negates his or her assumptions, and then creates "counter solutions" based on the negative assumptions.
- **heuristic principles** A method of decision making that proceeds along empirical lines, using rules of thumb, to find solutions or answers.
- **incremental adjustment** A method of managerial problem solving in which each successive action represents only a small change from activities.

Chapter Overview/Synopsis

Managers as well as non-managers make decisions. Decision making is a fact of life for everyone. This chapter concentrates on decision making at the managerial level, commencing with the planning process.

Decision making occurs under conditions of certainty, risk, and uncertainty. Under certainty, outcomes are known; under uncertainty, probabilities of outcome are assessed; and under risk, neither the probabilities nor outcomes are predictable. Managers attempt to add information where risk is encountered as a means of reducing risk. On the other hand, without elements of risk, there would be few elements of gain. Managers, therefore, seek problem-solving methods to bring more certainty into their decision-making.

Several approaches are used to solve problems on a rational basis. Tradition is common since similarity of situations is assumed. Judgment of others may be valued. A priori reasoning, based on what makes good sense may be used. None of the above is best, but managerial opinions are an important part of decision making: part of managerial pay is for the value of opinions. Rational decision making follows a process.

The first part of a rational problem-solving technique is to investigate the situation, which includes defining the problem, formulating the objectives to be attained, and identifying causes of the problem. Second, managers try to increase their "degrees of freedom" by developing alternative courses of action. If no alternatives exist, the decision is already made. Third, alternatives are evaluated against a set of criteria stemming from the objectives. This stage also includes selecting the alternative course of action. The fourth part of the process is the control aspect of following up on the decision to be certain its implementation achieves the desired result.

Managers lack full freedom to make decisions since they must operate within a "bounded" environment. Such things as laws, customs, values, policies, and mental capacities influence the kinds of decisions made. Rather than trying to improve or enlarge the boundaries within which decisions must be made, managers, according to Herman Simon, *satisfice* themselves by making a decision that best suits their purposes. They see no need to go further.

While individuals are criticized at times because they "go looking for trouble," the text emphasizes that for managers "a critically important skill . . . is the ability to select the right problem or opportunity." Managers rely on various skills and abilities to uncover things to do that will improve the organization's capacity to survive.

Decision-making cannot be divorced from a manager's values and the organizational environment. Therefore, part of the decision process involves understanding heuristics and biases. It is considered common for people to place great value on their opinions. Out of opinions come such things as "rules of thumb" and stereotypes. While heuristic decision-making often produces excellent results, managers must prudently take extra steps to understand and temper the sources of their value systems.

An important element of making decisions is determining who should make the decision. A part of a manager's job is to delegate. Delegation means giving other persons freedom to take actions bounded by the scope of the delegation. "The extent to which managers and subordinates should jointly make decisions depends on the type of problem and conditions under which the decision is being made."

Analysis of Illustrative Case Study

INTRODUCTION—DIPLOMACY AND DETERMINATION IN HIGH-LEVEL DECISION MAKING

The chapter emphasizes the need for managers to identify the kinds of problems to attack as a means of improving the organization's capability to survive. Texaco had the problem of depleting its oil reserves more rapidly than it was locating new ones, and its competitiveness in the industry was lagging.

Question: How should Mr. McKinley go about making his decision, and what barriers might he encounter?

Hindsight suggests that Mr. McKinley should have adhered to the Texaco policy of non-involvement in "hostile" takeovers. But some parts of the decision process should have been avoided, especially the heuristic part where judgments become colored by a feeling of intellectual superiority. Managers have high levels of ego, and the approach to follow here would have been that of following the route of the "devil's advocate," where everything that could go wrong would be targeted for analysis. The dialectical inquiry method might have highlighted the legal exposure of Texaco if it proceeded to be part of the takeover. The most likely approach would be to undertake the rational problem-solving approach, but it places too much weight on a priori reasoning.

CONTINUED—DIPLOMACY AND DETERMINATION IN HIGH-LEVEL DECISION MAKING

Texaco's decision to become a "player" resulted in Pennzoil filing suit and obtaining a multimillion dollar judgment against Texaco. At this point, Texaco is faced by a new set of problems: how to survive in the face of its bankruptcy. The important thing for Texaco's management is to look forward rather than to dwell on the past. While the past is useful for teaching lessons, Texaco's salvation will come from how well it makes decisions for its future survival.

WRAP-UP—DIPLOMACY AND DETERMINATION IN HIGH-LEVEL DECISION MAKING

The Texaco case reveals that companies are not democracies where time and coalitions work to slow decision making. A company can move quickly—even though in error. Once Texaco undertook the bankruptcy route to put its financial affairs in order, including the court-ordered payment to Pennzoil, it was able to make new decisions, and it is now in a position to pay dividends to its stockholders. Texaco accomplished this by liquidating all or part of its interests in Canada, West Germany, and Saudi Arabia. This generated $6 billion, of which $3 billion was needed for debt, and of the remaining, $1.7 billion is slated for shareholder participation. (See *Business Week,* August 15, 1988, pg. 52.)

Answers to End-of-Chapter Review Questions

1. Describe the four basic stages in the rational problem-solving process.

Stage 1: Investigate the Situation. Foremost is determining whether a "situation" exists. As the text points out later, it is an important part of a manager's job to identify problems and opportunities.

Stage 2: Develop Alternatives. Even though no alternatives seem to appear, managers are expected to look deeper and find alternatives. This is sometimes done by breaking a problem into components so that the solving of a problem can be done through a series of integrated steps. Alternatives need to be developed thoroughly so the evaluation is not cut off because of prejudices. This approach is borrowed from the concept known as *brainstorming,* in which ideas are placed on the table without their applicability being questioned at the time. This technique helps avoid a "chill" in the air that hampers the thinking of other persons participating in the search for alternatives.

Stage 3: Evaluate Alternatives and Select the Best One. The key to selecting the best alternative is that of determining which will be the most effective under the circumstances that must constrain the decision. The most likely constraints are time, goals, and available organizational resources.

Stage 4: Implement the Decision and Follow Up on It. A decision is but a message until action occurs. Important to implementation are the visible support of appropriate levels of management, the allocation of resources, and a procedure to monitor the execution of the decision by the persons involved. This stage is the significant part of the control process of decision making and implementation.

2. What is the principal difference between problem finding and opportunity finding?

According to Guth and Tagiuri, both problems and opportunities exist in the eye of the beholder. That is, human values and attitudes affect how managers view their world. Even so, a problem poses a dilemma to a manager and requires resolution before the manager's view of things has returned to equilibrium. Problems arise from such eventualities as deviations from past experience, a plan that is not proceeding "according to plan," minutiae to be dealt with, and competitor actions that cause the organization's goals to be more difficult to attain.

3. Contrast programmed and nonprogrammed decisions.

Programmed decisions are made according to policies, rules, procedures, or systems, while nonprogrammed decisions deal with the unusual or exceptional situations. Situations calling for nonprogrammed decisions can border on triviality compared to those that can affect an organization's survival. Clerical persons generally deal with programmed decisions, while managers work with the exceptional or nonprogrammed situations.

4. What are the differences between decisions made under conditions of uncertainty, certainty, and risk? Why do managers try to assess probabilities before reaching a decision?

Managers have very little knowledge about conditions when decisions are made under circumstances of uncertainty. Such decisions tend to arise when the manager is going into what qualifies as "uncharted waters." Under conditions of certainty, a manager knows the outcome before announcing the decision. Decision making under conditions of risk indicates that outcomes are sufficiently unknown and that ordinary approaches to probability analysis are not involved. Managers rely heavily on judgments based on experience and intuition. When probabilities are assessed prior to making a decision, the costs or the decision "going wrong" are better known.

5. What three questions should managers ask when they are presented with a problem?

   Is the problem easy to deal with? Might the problem resolve itself? Is this my decision to make?

6. What three heuristic principles do decision makers routinely employ? How can they help or hinder the decision-making process?

   (a) Making decisions against information already *available* in one's memory. (b) Viewing the conditions in terms of their representativeness to the larger set of experiences the person has had. (c) Making anchors of experiences that reinforce the belief.

   Heuristics tend to be reasonable and generally produce the correct results, but heuristics also produce biases in judgment. Therefore, managers need to exercise caution to recognize and eliminate biases that interfere with sound judgment.

7. What does Norman R. R. Maier suggest for improving the effectiveness of managerial problem solving and decision making?

   Maier feels two criteria have been isolated that affect the potential effectiveness of a decision: *objective quality* of the decision and its *acceptance* by those who must do the implementation. Even though a decision has been developed through the best means available, its results may be undesirable as a consequence of unforeseen circumstances. On the other hand a poor decision can achieve excellent results because of a fortunate turn of events.

Answers to End-of-Chapter Case Questions

CASE: BUSINESS AND POLITICAL ACTION—TO PAC OR NOT TO PAC?

1. What recommendations should Jessica Smythe make to the board of directors?

   First, Jessica should review the company's commitment to maintain stores in urban locations and the problems associated with that commitment. Following this review, Jessica should recommend that they, as individuals, provide financial support to candidates more willing to support urban renewal in areas where their stores are located. This recommendation should also include an appeal to a wider public to support their efforts. Her recommendation should go no further because the situation is a personal matter with her to maintain loyalty to stores in neighborhoods suffering economic deterioration.

2. Should a PAC be formed? If not, what other alternatives should be considered, and on what criteria should decisions be made to accept or reject them?

   A PAC should not be formed because of the obligations the corporation must undertake to keep it operational. The alternatives include Jessica and members of the board who share her feeling becoming personally involved in supporting candidates of their choice. They can work with neighborhood groups to bring public exposure to a congressional candidate who believes in "urban decay." With press conferences and help from local TV news teams, the plight of the neighborhoods can be made better known. The criteria should remain that of ensuring the company's financial survival despite the personal views of Jessica and some board members.

3. If a PAC is formed, what criteria should be used in making the following decisions: the selection of candidates to be supported? The solicitation of funds from various individuals and groups? The expansion of the PAC to an organizational level beyond the firm?

   Since a PAC tends to be a single-issue interest group, the criteria to support candidates need to include their sensitivity to the need to maintain the existence of established neighborhoods. Funds can be solicited from persons and groups with interests compatible with those of the PAC. In addition, since the goal is to halt the decline of the neighborhood, it is essential that broad-based support for the PAC be sought. While large donations are helpful, this PAC will do better by organizing neighborhood groups to solicit funds from as many individuals as possible. The number of supporters of this PAC could be almost as important as the dollars it obtains.

   The PAC should keep its identity and not allow a loss of identity to result from alliances.

4. Beyond a wealth of practical political decisions, which of Smythe's decisions have ethical ramifications for the activities of her organization and its responsibilities to its stakeholders?

   A stakeholder group that cannot be ignored is the stockholder group. Owners expect managers to look after their interests. Yet the firms must be socially responsible. Jessica had to balance stockholder interests with her inclination to allow company resources to support the needs of stores located in areas of economic decline.

   On a broader basis are those stakeholders who are employed in the stores in question as well as persons who live in those areas who need local sources of supply for many of their fix-up projects. A decision is needed to cover the size and scope of stores to remain open in the neighborhoods of economic decline. She has to decide whether to be one of the first to leave or become one of the last should other businesses vacate the locality.

Suggested Term Paper Topics

1. Pitfalls and strengths of systematic management for decision making.
2. A discussion of selected topics included in management development programs that help managers improve their ability to make nonprogrammed decisions
3. "Freedom to fail" as a component of delegated decision making.
4. A situational analysis of how managers turn problems into opportunities and how opportunities turn into problems.
5. What kinds of factors need to be analyzed to make one alternative stand out from the others?
6. An analysis of Herbert Simon's concept of "bounded rationality."
7. An examination of the dialectical inquiry method of decision making.
8. Creative decision making in a bureaucratic organization.
9. Heuristic decision making in a regulated business.

Suggested Guest Speakers

1. If there is a nuclear power plant in the area, invite a top manager to discuss how decision making is done to reduce the opportunities for unwanted consequences. An alternative would be to invite an official from a branch office of the Nuclear Regulatory Commission to speak on the same topic.
2. Invite a director of an Equal Opportunity Commission to discuss pitfalls of heuristic decision making in the field of personnel.
3. Ask a director of marketing for a manufacturing company to provide a case history of a promotional campaign that succeeded or failed.

CHAPTER 7
Strategic Planning and Management

Chapter Outline

THE CONCEPT OF STRATEGY

What Is Strategy?
Why Strategic Planning Is Important
Evidence for the Effectiveness of Strategic Planning

THE EVOLUTION OF THE CONCEPT OF STRATEGY

Strategy as the Grand Plan
Strategic Planning and Strategic Management
The Policy-Formulation Approach
The Initial Strategy Approach
The Strategic Management Approach
A Practical Point of View

LEVELS OF STRATEGY: SOME KEY DISTINCTIONS

The Three Levels of Strategy
Corporate-Level Strategy
Business-Unit Strategy
Functional-Level Strategy
Strategic versus Operational Planning

FRAMEWORKS FOR STRATEGY

The Portfolio Approach to Strategic Formulation: the BCG Matrix
Critiques of the BCG Matrix
Porter's Framework for Industry Analysis
Critique of Porter's Framework

THE FORMAL STRATEGIC PLANNING PROCESS: THE EXAMPLE OF BUSINESS-UNIT STRATEGY

Step 1: Goal Formulation
Step 2: Identification of Current Objectives and Strategy
Step 3: Environmental Analysis
Step 4: Resource Analysis
Step 5: Identification of Strategic Opportunities and Threats
Step 6: Determination of Extent of Required Strategic Change
Step 7: Strategic Decision Making
Identification of Strategic Alternatives
Evaluation of Strategic Alternatives
Selection of Strategic Alternatives
Step 8: Strategy Implementation
Step 9: Measurement and Control of Progress

SUMMARY

Key Terms

- **strategy** The broad program for defining and achieving an organization's objectives; the organization's response to its environment over time.
- **policy-formulation approach** The concept of implementing day-to-day rules that puts boundaries around what a functional area can and cannot do.
- **initial strategy approach** According to Alfred D. Chandler, "The determination of the basic long-term goals and objectives of an enterprise, and the adoption of courses of action and the allocation of resources necessary for carrying out these goals."
- **strategic management approach** A pattern based on the principle that the overall design of the organization can be described only if the attainment of objectives is added to policy and strategy as one of the key factors in management's operation of the organization's activities.
- **strategy-formulation task** A model of strategy formulation that must take into account the organization's goals and its strategy.
- **strategy implementation** The fifth task in the strategy management process that is a basically administrative task.
- **administration** Setting aside individual goals in favor of larger organizational goals.
- **strategic control** The process of checking strategy implementation progress against the strategic plan at periodic or critical intervals to determine if the corporation is moving toward its strategic objectives.
- **the portfolio framework** An approach to corporate-level strategy advocated by the Boston Consulting Group.
- **strategic business unit (SBU) planning** Grouping business activities within a multibusiness corporation because they generate closely related products or services.

- **performance gaps** The difference between the objectives established in the goal formation process and the results likely to be achieved if the existing strategy is continued.

Chapter Overview Synopsis

Strategy deals with what an organization proposes to do as well as what it ultimately does with its available resources. Strategies, therefore, tend to be broader statements of goals and objectives than are plans.

Strategic management, while usually associated with determining what to do and how to go about doing it, also includes identifying things not to do. This broader approach to strategy has evolved from earlier models of planning that were useful for businesses with a narrower focus. Today, however, an increasing number of businesses are global, or of the conglomerate type where resources are managed in much the way investors look after their portfolios.

Strategic planning would not consume the time and talents of managers if it were not important. It serves such purposes as improving the functioning of an organization since broad planning helps arrange the parts of an organization into an improved synergistic whole. The improved functioning also includes providing direction regarding how the organization can and will be responsive to its internal and external environments. Strategic management, as is true of other functions, has costs to be compared to its benefits. Analytical studies reveal ample evidence that firms engaging in strategic planning outperform ones that rely on informal planning.

Several models for strategic planning have been developed and advocated by various scholars and consultants. Two have had good acceptance by the business community as well as by scholars in the field: the Boston Consulting Group model better known as the BCG Matrix, and Porter's Approach to Strategy Formulation. The BCG Matrix labels organizations, products, divisions, or whatever is being assessed with investment-type names: cash cows, dogs, stars, and question marks.

The BCG Matrix is not without critics. The names used to describe market share and rate of growth do not have an academic ring; some people criticize the matrix because the labels are ''clever and colorful.'' Further, the names seem to imply a managerial action to be taken without further analysis. For instance, a cash cow needs to be ''milked,'' a ''star'' needs to be given the consideration of a prima donna, and a ''dog'' is to be dispatched from the organization with due haste.

Porter's Approach to Strategy Formulation lacks an easy-to-remember title or set of boxes forming a quadrant, as is true of the BCG Matrix. Instead, Porter ''focuses on the factors influencing success in a particular business or industry, and his approach is more appropriate to business unit-level strategy.'' From Porter's perspective, ''growth (and perhaps even survival) depends upon strategy formulation that protects the company from ill-advised head-on competition and monitors its shifting fortunes as it deals with buyers, suppliers, and substitute goals.''

Strategic planning at the business-unit level is a straightforward set of steps to be followed. While the steps can be enumerated, skill at performing managerial duties establishes the acid test for effective strategic planning. In the final analysis, managers seek to determine an organization's strengths, weaknesses, opportunities, and threats to survival.

Analysis of Illustrative Case Study

INTRODUCTION—PLANNING FOR THE FUTURE AT FEDERAL EXPRESS

Federal Express had grown from a small overnight delivery service to a major player in the industry. Businesses need timely and reliable deliveries of documents, small packages, and what are called large boxes. Federal Express had concentrated primarily on the delivery of document-filled envelopes. The pioneering work of Federal Express encourage other carriers to enter this lucrative market. Federal Express management is at the point of rethinking their master strategy. From their perspective, the company had moved beyond being an overnight delivery service of small packages to one of delivering ''information.''

The case illustrates the ongoing need of organizations to have an information-gathering and -analyzing function as a part of prudent management. While the information is given toward the end of this chapter, the conclusion by Michael Porter regarding strategic management is appropriate: ''growth (and perhaps even survival) depends upon strategy formulation that protects the company from ill-advised head-on competition and monitors its shifting fortunes as it deals with buyers, suppliers, and substitute goals.''

CONTINUED—PLANNING FOR THE FUTURE AT FEDERAL EXPRESS

Electronic transfer of information, as an additional part of Federal Express, proved irresistible to management. The company's name for its electronic transfer of documents had the catchy name "ZapMail." The system worked well but attracted too few customers for Federal Express to continue its operation. Federal Express researched the technology regarding electronic transfer of information, but did too little study of how business would view such a service. Businesses could install a FAX system of their own and bypass Federal Express. The company overlooked basic elements in its research of ZapMail—it appears to have concentrated on the best-case scenario and did not utilize the worst-case scenario that would have been considered with a devil's advocate method of studying ZapMail. Federal Express looked at too small a segment of the business and did insufficient study of the larger picture of competition from such organizations as United Parcel, United States Postal Service, and other organizations offering similar time-saving deliveries of packages.

WRAP-UP—PLANNING FOR THE FUTURE AT FEDERAL EXPRESS

Federal Express has shown leadership in its visionary planning to retain its superiority in a highly competitive market stressing overnight delivery of documents. The case illustrates that a firm, such as Federal Express, having an adequate business plan can compete head-to-head with larger organizations.

Answers to End-of-Chapter Review Questions

1. Why do you think it would be important for you as a junior manager to understand strategic planning?

   Studies of business failure emphasize that causes stem more from poor management than from inadequate financing. Poor management usually translates as managers failing to develop a business plan. The result is managers reacting to situations and being unable to position their respective businesses to take leadership roles.

2. Why has strategic planning become even more important to managers and their organizations?

   "Organizations function better as a result [of strategic planning] and become more responsive to a changing environment." Functioning better means determining what areas of the business to emphasize or add emphasis, and which ones to deemphasize or to cause stress. Strategic planning enables managers to prepare for and deal with a rapidly changing environment, especially the external environment.

3. What are the two most important factors in the evolution of contemporary management theory?

   (a) The rate of change in the environment has accelerated. There is less time to retrace steps if incorrect planning is done. The caliber and number of competitors have increased. This increased competition indicates a shorter life cycle for many new ideas and products. An organization has to move ahead to stay ahead. (b) Business size and complexity have quickened. More businesses have become multiunit in nature. International business has become customary, and with internationalism, organizations now operate on a multicultural basis.

4. How is strategic planning different from operational planning?

   Operational planning tends to be short-term and constitutes the *implementation* stage of strategic planning. Strategic planning is the long-term approach to viewing an organization's future—essentially that of defining its mission. Thus, strategic plans deal with such questions as "What business are we in, and what business ought we to be in?" and "Which of the alternative courses of action will be most consistent with our strategy?"

5. What are the key differences between the policy-formulation and strategy frameworks?

   Alfred D. Chandler proposed that strategy be defined as "the determination of the basic long-term goals and objectives of an enterprise, and the adoption of courses of action and the allocation of resources necessary for carrying out these goals." The Policy-Formulation Approach is the concept of implementing day-to-day rules that put boundaries around what a functional area can and cannot do.

6. What are the three levels of strategy? How do they differ from one another? How do they complement one another?

   The corporate level of strategy is formulated by top management to help it oversee the interests and operations of the organization, especially those comprised of more than one line of business. Two major questions are posed in determining the corporate level of strategy: What kind of businesses should we engage in? How should resources be apportioned among those businesses?

   Business-unit strategy is directed toward the managing of a particular line of business. Strategies are developed by seeking answers regarding: How will the business compete within its market? What products and services should it offer? Which customers should be served? How will the functional units of the operation be coordinated to meet the organization's market goals? How will resources be distributed within the business?

Function-level strategy creates the operational framework for the management of the operational functions of areas like production, sales, finance, research and development, and so on.

7. Why might managers perform corporate portfolio analysis? How is this done? According to Porter, what are the five "forces" influencing an organization's venture into a new market?

Portfolio analysis helps managers compare strategic variables, such as market share, against business growth rate. One of the most common portfolio techniques is known as the Boston Consulting Group Matrix, which places things to be compared in one of four quadrants. Products and/or units that generate large cash flows fit the cash cow quadrant; products and/or units that generate profits and have growth potential fit the star quadrant; products or business units that are not fully self-sustaining and need close monitoring are assigned to the question mark quadrant; and noncontributing products that are candidates for elimination are consigned to the dog quadrant.

Porter has identified the following five forces that influence an organization's decision to enter a new market:

1. *Threat of entry*. Management may reconsider a decision to enter a new market when other competitors can enter the market and, in effect, piggy-back on the firm's marketing strategy.
2. *The bargaining power of customers*. When a firm "is the only game in town," it has a different freedom to control supply and price than when competitors exist to provide customers more options in selecting a supplier.
3. *The bargaining power of suppliers*. If a producer must buy components or supplies from one or just a few suppliers, the suppliers have inordinate control over the customer.
4. *The threat of substitute products*. It is virtually a truism that at some price customers will turn to another source for supply or to an alternate product as a substitute.
5. *Jockeying for position*. Some persons refer to heavy advertising outlays and other approaches to product promotion as "the power to lose money." This is often a situation where similar products are differentiated in the minds of consumers through intensive advertising.

8. What are the nine steps in the formal planning approach?

(1) Goal formulation; (2) Identification of current objectives and strategy; (3) Environmental analysis; (4) Resource analysis; (5) Identification of Strategic Opportunities and Threats; (6) Determination of Extent of Strategic Change Required; (7) Strategic Decision Making; (8) Strategy Implementation; and (9) Measurement and Control of Progress.

Answers to End-of-Chapter Case Questions

CASE: PLANNING FOR DIVERSIFIED ACTIVITIES IN A CHANGING ENVIRONMENT

1. Use the BCG approach to help John Sullivan think about the strategy for DCI. Are there obvious products that are stars, cash cows, question marks, and dogs?

The Boston Consulting Group Matrix "focuses on three aspects of a particular business unit: its sales, the growth of its market, and whether it absorbs or produces cash in its operations." The four quadrants are composed of stars, question marks, cash cows, and dogs.

While the baby beds division is in a growing market with a good share of that market, DCI finds the buying power of mass retailers such that profitability is not particularly high. Selling to mass retailers also means the beds can and must be produced in volume. Volume production requires that costs be kept under control. Under the conditions of high volume of sales and low unit costs of production, profitability can be sufficient to justify the continued production of baby beds. The BCG category of baby beds is in the question mark area but bordering on the star category. The fear about "sleep carrousels" may be moot since consumer activists charge that these sleep units with their soft bottoms surrounded by high padding can cause crib deaths by reducing the supply of oxygen to a baby whose face is nestled against both the soft mattress and the padded side.

2. How would Porter's model analyze George Russell's situation?

Porter identifies five topic areas for analysis: (a) threat of entry, (b) bargaining power of customers, (c) bargaining power of suppliers, (d) threat of substitute products, and (e) jockeying for position. Of these five issues, threat of entry and bargaining power of both suppliers and customers are the critical ones. The Taiwanese supplier has the capability to enter the market. This is a real concern since baby beds tend to be a generic type of item and buyers are not particularly brand-conscious. Instead they look for appearance and safety features. The Taiwanese supplier also has power through the partial control of components. The oligopsonist power of K-Mart, Wal-Mart, and Sears is considerable, and they have freedom to seek other sources of supply.

3. To what extent can methods of strategic planning give the managers at DCI a method to talk to each other about their common problems? What are some disadvantages?

Strategic management helps reduce elements for comparison to a common denominator of identifying objectives. DCI, as a conglomerate, looks upon its acquisitions as parts of an investment portfolio and can be dispassionate in its decision making. On the other hand, the units of DCI are products that need employees to produce them. While the products can be viewed as part of a portfolio, if a product is dropped, the factory has unused capacity since it cannot be immediately turned off when a product line is discarded.

The disadvantages tend to arise because of human failings rather than from the process of planning. First, a bureaucracy of corporate planners could be formed at DCI, and it would not take bureaucrats long to create a maze of systems and procedures. Second, since strategic management planning identifies objectives as well as a means of assessing how well the objectives are attained, the danger exists that mangers will seek to carve out risk-free objectives for themselves.

Suggested Term Paper Topics

1. A critique of strength, weaknesses, opportunities, and threats analysis.
2. Types of forecasting most useful in strategic management planning.
3. An analysis of how structure follows strategy.
4. An analysis of selected strategic mistakes of major companies together with the identification of the gaps that existed in their forecasting mode.
5. A critical analysis of the Boston Consulting Group portfolio matrix.
6. "Number-crunching" strategic management goal setting compared to the human side of determining management strategies.
7. Determining what should be measured and the costs of measuring the attainment of goals identified in strategic management.
8. What kinds of differences, if any, apply to strategic management planning in the international arena as compared with those applicable to domestic companies in the United States.
9. An analysis of the human relations implications of portfolio analysis.

Suggested Guest Speakers

1. Invite a representative from a local public utility company to discuss strategic planning from that company's standpoint.
2. Invite the director of a local charitable organization to discuss the extent his/her organization can do long-range planning and its degree of effectiveness.
3. Invite the planning officer from a major corporation, if it has major offices in your city, to discuss the kinds of techniques or methods employed in his/her company's strategic planning operation.

CHAPTER 8
Strategy Implementation

Chapter Outline

STRATEGY IMPLEMENTATION

STRATEGY AND STRUCTURE

- Chandler's Thesis
- Further Research
  - Overseas Experience
  - Multinational Firms
- The Seven-S Model
  - Structure
  - Strategy
  - Systems
  - Style
  - Staff
  - Skills
  - Superordinate Goals

OPERATIONALIZING STRATEGY

- Developing Functional Strategy
  - Marketing
  - Finance
  - Production/Operations
  - Research and Development
  - Human Resource/Personnel
- Setting Annual Objectives
- Management by Objectives
  - Elements of the MBO System
  - Evaluation of MBO
- Reward Systems
- Matching Managers and Strategies

INSTITUTIONALIZING STRATEGY

- The Role of the CEO
- The Role of Key Managers
- Culture and Strategy

BARRIERS TO EFFECTIVE STRATEGY IMPLEMENTATION

- Environmental Constraints
  - Scarcity
  - Politics
  - Attitudes
  - Power Shifts
  - Technology
- Internal Constraints
  - Inflexibility
  - Executive Obsolescence
  - Parochialism
  - Values, Styles, Traditions
  - Power

SUMMARY

Key Terms

- **vertical integration** Broadening the scope of an organization's operations while retaining the original single product.
- **functional organization** A form of departmentalization in which everyone engaged in one functional activity, such as marketing or finance, is grouped into one unit.
- **multidivisional firm** An organization that has expanded into different industries and diversified its products.
- **management by objectives (MBO)** A formal set of procedures that establishes and reviews progress toward common goals for managers and subordinates.
- **organizational culture** The set of important understandings, such as norms, values, attitudes, and beliefs, shared by organizational members.
- **operational strategy** Organizational strategy spelling out facility locations and including marketing and financial strategies.
- **functional strategy** Implementation strategy providing the details necessary to put organizational strategy into action.
- **turnover situation** Strategy situation in which poor performance entails major changes that can be handled by insiders.
- **selective blend situation** Strategy situation entailing major changes in organizational strategy that blend both outsider and insiders to perform corrective measures.
- **stability situation** Strategy situation in which good past performance and the minor nature of needed changes make insiders the best choice for implementing.
- **reorientation situation** Strategy situation in which poor performance despite sound strategy calls for change to be implemented by outsiders.
- **Seven-S Model** According to Waterman and others, framework for change identifying seven key factors that can adversely affect successful change in an organization.

Chapter Overview/Synopsis

Without implementation, a business strategy remains but a future dream. Since strategy is multifaceted, its implementation must occur throughout an organization. Some areas of strategic management have little effect on parts of an organization other than where the strategy is applied, while other aspects of strategy can ripple throughout an organization. A manager needs to consider these parts of strategy as part of the implementation process. Some managers approach this point by saying, "the first thing to do is stop the bleeding." Further corrections can be taken when time is not so critical. Yet people in the organization must also feel the sense of urgency.

The implementation of strategy proceeds on a more successful course when the structure of the organization is compatible with the strategy. The significance of this point arises when one considers the Chandler thesis that organizations progress though three stages. The first stage is the unit where entrepreneurial leadership is sufficient to resolve the kinds of issues that confront the organization. The next logical step in growth is vertical integration, in which steps are undertaken to gain more control of raw materials needed and of distribution channels to assure an outlet for the company's products. Last, the successful organization becomes multidivisional, which tends to make it resemble many smaller units operating in a unified way.

The need for managers to be involved in both the developing and the implementation of strategy signifies the need for an organized way to initiate and monitor the process. While several techniques exit, a commonly used process is called Management by Objectives (MBO). The MBO system provides for the active involvement of managers at all organizational levels. Regardless of the claimed merits of MBO, the system is not without its critics. Since a desire for personal competence is seen as an attribute of contingency theory, participants in MBO may tend to focus their objectives on improving past performance to help guarantee their success. Other critics point to the number of variables involved in MBO, and it is difficult to identify accurately why a given plan works and another one does not.

No matter the support given for organizations to develop and implement strategy, barriers exist. There may be conflict of goals among and between organizational units. The goals identified may be inappropriate for the circumstances. Goal setting and implementation require resources that may be already stretched. The goals may lack the needed flexibility to meet the challenges of rapidly changing circumstances. In addition, problems can occur when managers feel the goals are not their own and refuse to accept them.

Analysis of Illustrative Case Study

INTRODUCTION—MAINTAINING THE COMPETITIVE EDGE AT MERCK & CO.

The time lag between the discovery of a drug and its market entry can be quite long—about ten years. This time factor makes it difficult for scientists at Merck to be evaluated on the basis of their products penetrating the consumer market. Scientists at Merck need other kinds of incentives to be recruited, recognized, and retained. The chairman of Merck, Roy Vagelos, takes nothing for granted with the company's personnel policies. He seeks to improve the productivity of his scientists. The working atmosphere is considered crucial to improving productivity.

Merck can do very little about the external environment of control that requires years of experimentation before a drug can be released to the consumer market. The company can lobby legislators to change the regulatory climate, but the probabilities of success in this quest are apparently limited because the public, especially those who claim to be consumer activists, point to the thalidomide tragedy to maintain stringent testing procedures.

CONTINUED—MAINTAINING THE COMPETITIVE EDGE AT MERCK & CO.

The CEO's desire to reduce the testing time for new drugs, while up against the resistance of consumer activists, may have an ally in a new illness—AIDS. Many protracted illnesses remove the urgency of shortening the research and development time of drugs, but with AIDS, the time factor from the time of laboratory confirmation of the disease and death of the victim is only three years. Persons suffering from AIDS constitute a formidable pressure group to press the government to relax its rules requiring extended drug testing before introduction to the public.

WRAP-UP—MAINTAINING THE COMPETITIVE EDGE AT MERCK & CO.

The Merck case appears to embody the principles of effective strategy setting and implementation as discussed in this chapter. The proof of this conclusion surfaces in the literature, where the company is considered to be one of the best managed in the United States. This level of management does not exist on its own: someone has to work toward its attainment.

Answers to End-of-Chapter Review Questions

1. What are the differences between evolutionary, managerial, sequential, and complex interventions?

   Evolutionary interventions occur when an organization's problems are small. There is little pressure to take such action, however, since the symptoms appear to be relatively unimportant and the ones that are manifested tend to be the kind that fall within regular managerial routines. Sequential intervention occurs when problems can be divided into issues that can be addressed in an orderly manner. It is important when undertaking such changes that interrelationships among units be maintained. Complex intervention occurs when the diversity of parties involved in implementing the decision need to work on the problem in a coordinated manner.

2. Describe the three stages in the growth and development of an organization's strategy and structure that were set out by Arthur Chandler.

   Stage 1. The organization is small, usually operating in a single location with a single product, and managed by a single owner. At this level of operation, the organization can, through growth, outstrip the capability of managers to manage effectively. *Stage 2*. The broadened scope of a single-product-type firm requires further efforts to rationalize its management. One of the most common approaches is vertical integration, in which the company may seek to have better control over the supply of raw materials or components used in the production of its product. *Stage 3*. The logical extension of a firm with vertical integration is to move horizontally by adding unrelated units so the firm becomes one of many individual businesses operating under a central management.

3. What are the seven factors of the Seven-S model?

   (1) Structure to link the vertical and horizontal parts of the organizations; (2) Strategy, while important, of less significance than its implementation; (3) Systems that bring predictable uniformity to the way the organization functions; (4) Style that communicates the substantive and symbolic actions of top managers; (5) Staff development, considered essential to successful organization; (6) Skills, the things organizations do best; and (7) Superordinate goals that serve as guiding concepts that help unite an organization toward a common purpose.

4. What are the weaknesses of traditional incentive plans? How can organizations improve them?

   Critics identify four problems of conventional incentive plans: (a) The incentive may be inappropriately correlated with the size of the firm instead of the rate of return. (b) Short-term performance may be emphasized to the exclusion of the attainment of long-term strategic objectives. (c) Incentives may be coupled to accounting factors such as earnings per share and return on investment rather than to the creation of economic value for the owners. (d) Accounting measures ignore the portfolio concept of corporate strategy that holds managers to the same standards of performance regardless of the rate of growth of their respective divisions.

   In response to the criticism directed toward rewarding short-term gains, organizations are focusing on such time periods as three- to five-year stretches. Deferred stock option plans help managers do more long-range planning. Companies are also developing more meaningful ways to determine returns on assets and other ways to connect managerial effort to results achieved.

5. What are functional strategies? How can they reduce their natural conflicts between functional areas of an organization?

   All functional areas of a business need functional strategies. Example of functions that need specialized strategies include production, sales, and finance. Functional strategies provide operating managers with what they need to know to implement the strategy.

   Natural conflicts are reduced through coordination that arises from centralized decision-making and control steps. It also helps for each functional area to have different responsibilities and, therefore, different priorities.

6. Give some examples of well- and poorly designed annual objectives.

   Well-designed objectives are linked to an organization's long-term goals, and they are measurable against a predetermined value. Here are examples from Table 8–2 of measurable objectives:

   > To reduce turnover (absenteeism, number of rejects, etc.) among sales managers by 10 percent by January 1, 1988; to increase the number of individuals capable of performing *X* operation in manufacturing by 20 percent by July 15, 1988.

   Deficient objectives lack specificity and are not readily measurable against verifiable values. Here are examples from Table 8–2 of deficient objectives:

To improve morale in the divisions (plan, department, etc.); to enhance or improve the training effort.

7. What is management by objectives? What are its strengths and weaknesses?

   Management by Objectives (MBO) refers to a formal or moderately formal set of procedures that begins with goal setting and continues through performance review. MBO tends to increase the likelihood that organization members will be successful in the implementation of organizational objectives. This occurs because MBO helps focus managerial attention, and this brings abut a more common set of goals.

   MBO is also said to be difficult and time-consuming to initiate and to operate. The process of setting up MBO also changes duties and responsibilities of people, and this can necessitate retraining time along with complicating something that did not need "fixing."

8. How can a CEO help implement an organization's strategy?

   "The chief executive officer (CEO) has a unique relationship with an organization's strategy because they spend the majority of their time developing and guiding strategy. Their personal goals and values inevitably shape organizational strategy, and they become closely identified with it." A CEO is able to help implement strategy in the following ways: (a) Interpret strategy for the organization to operating managers who may be in disagreement; (b) Enact through words and actions the seriousness of the organization's commitment to the selected strategy; (c) Motivate by setting a personal example.

9. What are the advantages and disadvantages to assigning an existing member of an organization to a key management position? To hiring someone from outside the organization?

   Advantages and disadvantages tend to exist according to a set of conditions. In a stable situation where people understand what is wanted, an insider may well be the best choice to guide the organization in the implementation stage of its strategies. On the other hand, in a turnover type of situation, an outsider has greater leverage in bringing about the changes necessary to cause the strategies to be implemented.

10. List some factors that can prevent effective strategy implementation. How can an organization overcome these obstacles?

   The text identifies a list developed by Kjell Ringbakk as being significant obstacles in implementing strategies; six appear below:

   —Formal planning is not accepted by all managers.
   —Some aspects of formal planning are not understood by some planners.
   —Managers at some levels are not included in pertinent planning activities.
   —Primary responsibility for planning is surrendered by top management to lower staff.
   —Long-range plans solidify and are considered unchangeable.
   —An overly elaborate or overly expensive planning system is chosen.

   Ways to overcome the barriers to effective planning include using persons familiar with the business and the industry of which it is a part, identifying steps of the planning process that have proven effective for similar firms, and being certain that people in line management positions are both involved in the process and committed to implementing the strategic plans.

Answers to End-of-Chapter Case Questions

CASE 1: "SACRED TRUSTEES" AND WHISTLEBLOWING AT BEECH-NUT

1. What should Mr. LiCari do?

   Given the circumstance that management refused to listen, the choice for Mr. LiCari was simple—to take his concerns to the consumer division of the attorney general's office of the state where the product was being packaged.

2. What measures could LiCari have taken, within the confines of his own position at the company, to make his case to upper-level management more compelling?

   The memorandums could have been accompanied by news clippings showing the kinds of penalties that have been applied to firms and managers for involvement in adulterating products. Further, he should have built a base of colleague allies to share his concerns.

   A single voice is more readily ignored than that of a chorus.

3. If it is discovered that Beech-Nut's synthetic juice did cause harm, how should product management be reprimanded for suppressing the advice of lower-level management.

   Three levels of direct action are possible: (a) The parent company could fire the managers, (b) criminal penalties could be levied from an appropriate court, and (c) civil damages could be assessed as a result of a class-action suit. Nestlé cannot limit its actions to ones of an internal nature since public confidence needs to be restored.

CASE 2: THE COMPETITION CHIPS AWAY AT CRAY RESEARCH

Cray Research is a leading producer of supercomputers. Recently a key computer designer, Steven Chen, resigned to start his own computer company. He was reputed to have received $10 million from IBM as seed money. The departure of Chen has left Cray's CEO, John Rollwagen, with a major problem because Chen's contribution's to Cray's success has no parallel

1. What kind of strategy-implementation problems can arise at Cray now that Chen has left?

   The CEO does not have freedom for *managerial intervention* since the problem created by Chen's departure is major. Therefore, in addition to the complex intervention described, sequential intervention is necessitated by the need to identify a series of things to be done to restore Cray to its former capability.

2. What kind of problems can arise when a research lab like the one in Chippewa Falls, is isolated from the main part of the organization?

   At this point in the discussion, reference is made to the Illustrative Case Study of Merck & Co. Merck's approach to dealing with scientists was to create an atmosphere of support and to remove distracting concerns from them. Cray, by having its scientific work done away from the corporate office, may also be creating a climate where scientists are free to work without staff bureaucrats from a home office demanding progress reports.

3. What should Rollwagen do to be sure that each function at Cray integrates its strategy with the others?

   Structure is said to follow strategy. One part of the structure can be a top management advisory team to work with Rollwagen. Each member of the team would represent a major area of Cray. Thus when strategies are agreed upon, the division manager is committed to supporting the implementation of the strategy to his/her people.

4. What, if anything, should Rollwagen do now that Chen has left the Company?

   Rollwagen's main path is to look forward with his new team and not look to the past with any feelings of "what might have been." Studies mentioned in the chapter show the critical importance of leadership and the need for leaders to set a positive tone for a company. This is what Rollwagen needs to continue. The text states that "CEOs *motivate*, [by] providing extra sources of motivation in addition to the tangible rewards offered by the organization's incentive plan; they can mobilize support for the strategy by appealing to the values, beliefs, and loyalty of organization members."

Suggested Term Paper Topics

1. An analysis of Chandler's thesis regarding the relationships between organizational structure and organizational strategy.
2. Multinational strategy setting: introducing strategies across cultural borders.
3. Theory X and Theory Y revisited: What remains applicable today?
4. Symptoms and cures of short-run strategy setting in organizations.
5. Dealing with managers whose competence has not kept pace with the needs of a growing and dynamic organization.
6. Ways of determining when one's loyalty to an employer is replaced by loyalty to one's set of principles.
7. Avoiding "risk-free" objective setting in a Management by Objectives organization.
8. In an MBO situation, measuring intangible goals such as morale, public relations, and loyalty.
9. Blending culture and strategy following a merger.

Suggested Guest Speakers

1. Invite a key manager of a firm that has recently undergone "downsizing" to discuss how the strategy was implemented. Especially, who were the key players, and what occurred to obtain their commitment to the action?
2. Ask the owner of a medium-sized business to discuss his/her business plan. What does that person expect the company to be like in one year? Three years? Five years?
3. Ask a management consultant (perhaps a professor) to discuss working with companies to help them determine and implement their strategic plans.

Part 2 Case Study

THE ADAMS CORPORATION

1. What are the key strengths of the company?
   - —Reputation for product in the industry and among consumers
   - —Corporate climate that breeds loyalty among employees
   - —Overall high ethical standards
   - —Efficiency of manufacturing
   - —Widespread channels of both domestic and international distribution
   - —New leadership
2. What are the weaknesses of Adams Corp.?
   - —Low profitability with high sales volume
   - —Loss of experienced management, with block retirements predicated on advanced age of executive team
   - —Lack of flexibility based on centralized decision-making
   - —Non-current status of operating reports
   - —Cost accounting system based on "guesstimate"

—Unattractive compensation package that discourages bright young people from applying for positions
—Out-of-date product packaging
—Pressure to increase sales "no matter what," which creates a situation of low profitability

3. Develop a plan of action for Millman.

In the manner of Lee Iacocca when he assumed command of Chrysler, Mr. Millman should take stock of the management team. Because of the conservative nature of the company, Millman will probably find several key managers who are "semi-retired on-the-job." The company's reputation for fair dealing suggests that employees and managers no longer needed will be granted an attractive severance package. In short, Millman's first task is to put an executive team in place. This implies a new chain-of-command along with a review of what should be centralized and what should be decentralized.

Part of developing a new executive team requires the development of an improved compensation plan. Because of the company's size, an experienced personnel director should be hired rather than retaining the services of a management consulting firm to set up a compensation plan. The personnel needs of the company extend beyond improving compensation.

To help executives focus on the same set of goals, Millman should institute Management by Objectives. This will ensure the involvement of managers, which will also signify their commitment to goal attainment. Periodic review of progress will help managers avoid posturing themselves in "risk averse" situations. Thus, managers who make progress will be rewarded.

A new financial expert is needed to revise all phases of financial reporting. This might involve a reconstruction of the accounting system and probably necessitates the services of a CPA firm

4. What are some important factors and potential barriers to implementing your plan?

—Managers set in their comfortable ways
—Suspicion of a new leader unacquainted with the firm's traditions
—Managers who protect themselves through a long chain of approvals before decisions are made
—Protective managers who can divert attention through "games playing." Therefore, priorities need to be set, information gathering must be timely and accurate, and biases must be replaced by objectivity.
—The tendency for managers to be "satisficed"

CHAPTER 9

Division of Work, Organizational Structure, and Coordination

Chapter Outline

DIVISION OF WORK

- Job Specialization
- Span of Management

ORGANIZING AND ORGANIZATIONAL STRUCTURE

- The Organization Chart
- The Formal Organizational Structure
- Functional Organization
- Product/Market Organization
  - Pros and Cons of Product/Market Organization
- Matrix Organization
  - Advantages and Disadvantages of Matrix Organizations
- The Informal Organization

COORDINATION

- Problems in Achieving Effective Coordination
- Approaches to Achieving Effective Coordination
  - Basic Management Techniques
  - Increasing Coordination Potential
  - Reducing the Need for Coordination
- Selecting the Appropriate Coordination Mechanisms

ORGANIZATIONAL DESIGN: STRUCTURING FOR SPECIALIZATION AND COORDINATION

- Early Approaches to Organizational Design
- The Classical Approach to Organizational Design
  - Criticisms of the Classical Approach
- The Neoclassical Approach to Organizational Design
  - Douglas McGregor
  - Chris Argyris
  - Rensis Likert
  - Criticisms of the Neoclassical Approach
- Modern Approaches to Organizational Design
- External Environment and Structure
  - The Stable Environment
  - The Changing Environment
  - The Turbulent Environment
  - Matching the Structure to the Environment
- Task-Technology and Structure

SUMMARY

Key Terms

- **division of work** The breakdown of a complex task into components so that individuals are responsible for a limited set of activities instead of for the task as a whole.
- **departmentalization** The grouping into departments of work activities that are similar and logically connected.
- **coordination** The integration of the activities of the separate parts of an organization to accomplish organizational goals.
- **organizational design** The determination of the organizational structure that is most appropriate for the strategy, people, technology, and tasks of the organization.
- **job specialization** The division of work into standardized, simplified tasks.
- **organizing** The process of arranging an organization's structure and coordinating its managerial practices and use of resources to achieve its goals.
- **organizational structure** The arrangement and interrelationships of the various component parts and position of a company.
- **organization charts** A diagram of an organization's structure, showing the functions, departments, or positions of the organization and how they are related.
- **functional organization** A form of departmentalization in which everyone engaged in one functional activity, such as marketing or finance, is grouped into one unit.
- **product or market organizational structure** The organization of a company by divisions that brings together all those involved with a certain type of product or customer.
- **matrix organization** An organizational structure in which each employee reports to both a functional or division manager and to a project or group manager.

- **traditional pyramid** The most common type of organizational structure in which command is unified at the top level.
- **temporary overlay** A short-term structure in which project teams are created only for special needs.
- **permanent overlay** Organizational structure in which project teams are continued for ongoing purposes.
- **mature matrix** Organization in which both dimensions of structure are permanent and balanced, with power held equally by both a functional and a project manager.
- **informal organization** The undocumented and officially unrecognized relationships between members of an organization that inevitably emerge out of the personal and group needs of employees.
- **integration** The degree to which employees of various departments work together in a unified way.
- **vertical information system** Means through which data are transmitted up and down the managerial hierarchy.
- **lateral relationship** A relationship that cuts across the chain of command, allowing direct contact between members of different departments. Examples include committees, liaison roles, and integrating roles.
- **direct contact** The simplest form of lateral relationship, communication between individuals who must deal with the same situation or problem.
- **boundary-spanning roles** Jobs in which individuals act as liaisons between departments or organizations that are in frequent contact.
- **integrating roles** Roles that are established when a specific product, service, or project spans several departments and requires coordination and attention from a single individual not in the departments in question.
- **managerial linking role** A role that may be required if an integrating position does not coordinate a particular task effectively.
- **span of management** The number of subordinates reporting directly to a given manager.
- **bureaucracy** Organization with a legalized formal and hierarchical structure.
- **System 1** Traditional organizational structure where power and authority are distributed according to the manager-subordinate relationship.
- **Systems 2 and 3** Intermediate stages between traditional structure and ideal structure.
- **System 4** Ideal organizational structure where there is extensive group participation in supervision and decision making.

Chapter Overview/Synopsis

Organization is done to assemble the human and material resources necessary to fulfill planned goals. Major functions are divided into individual jobs arrayed into departments or units for supervisory purposes. The number of persons under one person's supervision signifies what is called the span of supervisory control. The divided functions most generally are identified in an organization chart that distinguishes units from one another and also shows the formal channels of communication. Organizations may be functional, product/market, or matrix in nature. The need for personal communication, as opposed to formal communication, arises through the informal organization.

Managers strive to obtain optimal results from the various units of an organization through coordination of effort. Much of the work of coordination exists as information processing through the formal hierarchy, eliminating the need for managerial coordination through the establishment of independent units. Coordination may be accomplished in traditional pyramidal structures, or in ones in which people achieve more independence and power through participation. The complexities of some businesses require matrix organizations where people have both a functional manager in the hierarchical organization and a project manager at the operational level.

Analysis of Illustrative Case Study

INTRODUCTION-COORDINATION AND INTEGRATION AT HEWLETT-PACKARD

Hewlett-Packard had operated with emphasis on human freedom in order to obtain better creativity. Its market leadership in many products provided evidence of the success of this approach. Even so, individuality without coordination of effort allowed Hewlett-Packard to become more engineering-oriented than market-oriented. The consequence was a loss of market position. To retain the best of individuality and also achieve coordination of effort, Hewlett-Packard was reorganized to emphasize markets to be served rather than products to be developed and produced.

CONTINUED-COORDINATION AND INTEGRATION AT HEWLETT-PACKARD

When one part of a structure is changed, other parts are also affected. This occurred at Hewlett-Packard when the two divisions of sales were combined without also instituting procedures to achieve coordination at the production level. The shift of the company to being market-driven, therefore, created the need to coordinate production to take care of the special needs of customers rather than Hewlett-Packard's design engineers.

WRAP-UP-COORDINATION AND INTEGRATION AT HEWLETT-PACKARD

Earlier chapter of this text noted the need for an organization to exhibit flexibility when conditions warrant. Hewlett-Packard's capability to shift from production-orientation to market-orientation displayed managerial perception.

Answers to End-of-Chapter Review Questions

1. What is the difference between division of work and departmentalization?

   Division of work is the breaking-down of complex tasks into components that individuals can perform, while departmentalization is the grouping of similar division-of-work activities into an integrated unit called a department.

2. What are the advantages of job specialization? Why did it emerge?

   The main advantage is increased productivity: each part of a job can be broken into components that can be efficiently and economically performed by one worker. Job specialization emerged when, as tasks increased in complexity, it became difficult for workers to perform all the complex tasks effectively, as well as to master all the skills necessary to perform the entire operation.

3. What does an organization chart illustrate? What are its advantages and disadvantages? How do you think you might be affected by seeing your name or position on one?

   An organization chart illustrates the organization's hierarchical structure—its chain of communication. A claimed advantage is that persons can see how an organization is structured since a chart highlights the responsibility level of managers and subordinates. The primary disadvantage is that charts do not disclose the hidden relationships. Also, charts may give a person a sense of superiority or inferiority according to how he or she is placed on the chart. In general, a student should feel good about seeing his/her name on an organizational chart, since names tend to be attached to positions of importance, such as "Director of Human Resources Jennifer Ryan."

4. What are the different ways a product/market unit can be organized? What are the advantages and disadvantages of this form of organization?

   (a) Division by product, where each department is responsible for a product or related family of products; (b) division by geography, which allows departmental activities to be grouped according to the region where its business is conducted; and (c) division by customer, usually a class.

   Organization by division permits the necessary focusing of managerial expertise to produce and market products. Such a divisional structure permits managers to be evaluated in terms of profitability. A primary disadvantage is that divisional managers may stress the importance of their respective divisions to the detriment of the needs of the larger organization. Since more than one division would exist, there will also be a duplication of areas of specialization.

5. Under what conditions would a matrix structure be most suitable? What are its advantages and disadvantages?

   The primary condition to support a matrix structure is the need to resolve a complex problem that relies on the coordination of a network of job skills. This condition also serves as an advantage to matrix structures. Other advantages include organizational flexibility, interdisciplinary cooperation, and the development of employee resourcefulness. Disadvantages include the encouragement of power struggles, the realignment of people that may lower morale, divided control that may lead to more discussion than action, and effort that may be duplicated between teams working on similar projects.

6. What is coordination? What kinds of differences in attitude and work style can develop in the departments of an organization? How do such differences make coordination more difficult? How do they help organizations?

   Coordination is the process of integrating the objectives and activities of organizational units to focus on attaining organizational goals. Since coordination requires the managing of information, it follows that people in key positions do not stifle the flow of necessary information. Problems associated with coordination include differences in orientation toward individual goals, difference in time orientation so that what seems important to one person may be delayed by another individual, differences in interpersonal orientation, and differences in the formality of the organization's structure.

   Coordination occurs more readily in organizations where there is a known managerial hierarchy, where there are rules and procedures, and where plans and goals of the organization are known, understood, and accepted. Important to the effectiveness of coordination is the determination of how much information is needed to accomplish given goals. For instance, more information may be needed than is available—this stymies coordination. Organizations my find it cost effective to purchase an information system that reduces bottlenecks in the flow of critical information.

7. What are the advantages and disadvantages of the classical bureaucratic model of organizational design?

   Claimed advantages include seeking the "one best way" for performing work, separating planning from doing though a hierarchy, specialization of tasks, appointment by merit, and a rational, impersonal organization. Disadvantages include neglect of the psychological and sociological needs of workers, lack of flexibility in a rapidly changing environment, assumption of acceptance and respect of position of authority, and the possibility that organizational members will protect themselves through risk-averse decisions.

8. What are the differences between a System 1 and System 4 organization, as described by Likert?

   System 1 is a traditional organization structure where power and authority are distributed according to the manager-subordinate relationship, where the chain of command is considered all important. System 4 requires organizations to accept that managers and work activities should enhance members' sense of worth; group decision making is encouraged, and high performance goals are important.

9. What form of organization is best suited to a simple and static environment? A simple and dynamic environment? A complex but simple environment? A complex and dynamic environment?

   For a simple and static environment, the classical design with its hierarchy would be adequate but would ignore the human needs of employees. In a simple and dynamic environment, trends would be apparent regardless of the rate of change; therefore, an organic organization with roles relatively loosely defined would permit adjustments to technological changes. A complex but simple environment would need an organization that permits a rapid flow of information, and this also requires the use of a functional type of organization. A complex and dynamic environment requires a flow of information with appropriate analysis; therefore, more levels of management are needed, with bureaucratic safeguards to ensure that all factors receive due appraisal.

Answers to End-of-Chapter Case Questions

CASE 1: ORGANIZING THE STRUCTURE OF CLUB MED

1. In what ways would functional organization be an appealing option for structuring Club Med? Product/market organization?

   Functional organization occurs to bring together those engaged in one activity or several related activities. Club Méditerranée operates a series of resorts that cater to "yuppies" as well as to families, with increasing emphasis on providing activities for children as a means of attracting parents. In this sense, Club Med is a functional organization. Its product is recreation, and its market is people who desire a relaxing atmosphere devoid of many anxieties associated with the rest of the world.

2. How would you describe the current structure of Club Med according to the model of matrix organization?

   A matrix structure requires a boss in the traditional hierarchy of the pyramid as well as another boss on a horizontal plane in charge of a specific project. The project part requires highly specialized leadership or skill unavailable in the conventional organization. To the extent that regional cultures can affect operations, a matrix-type manager to provide local direction would add effectiveness to Club Med. The club, however, operates more as a divisionalized organization that achieves the uniformity of centralization by having the managers fly to Paris monthly to review the club's operations.

3. Which factors in Club Med's situation should be given the most weight in determining formal arrangement for a new organizational design?

   Club Med is built on obtaining and retaining clients. The market factor must be the overriding elements to dictate the organization structure. Customers expect first-class treatment and that the resort they visit be operated in a non-stressful manner. The formal operating structure reflects this attention to market factors.

4. What are the peculiar or unique factors in the environment of Club Med that may affect its decisions about further organizational design?

   It operates in many parts of the world and needs geographic divisions as well as able persons to deal with governmental offices. Club Med is in an expanding market; therefore, it needs a strong financial office to help carry out its expansion plans. Each club depends on obtaining and retaining employees, whose demeanor contributes to the enjoyment of guests. Therefore, considerable attention needs to be directed to the development of a human resource division to oversee the recruiting and training. Because most visits originate through contact with a travel or tour agent, a further key division should serve in a liaison capacity with travel agents and tour operators.

CASE 2: OPTIONS FOR CHANGES AT IMPERIAL CHEMICAL INDUSTRIES

1. What factors are most important in deciding the structure of the board of directors?

   The survival of ICI is the overriding factor. Related to its survival are such elements as setting up a mechanism to coordinate the work of the board and the organization and establishing a system to monitor the effectiveness of the decisions of the board as carried out by organizational members. Other factors depend on the decision whether to become a holding company or to remain in the present format.

2. Who should make the final decision about the shape of the board of directors?

This is a function of the board of directors, nevertheless, the board should give a full hearing to any proposal from the newly named chairman of the board. Providing this full hearing is logical since it was a board decision to name a new chairman.

3. What should the shape be?

The "final option" is having the board responsible for the overall direction and performance of the entire company. The present structure pits one member against another, with the result that decisions resemble the give-and-take of political trade-offs rather than ones of objective decision making.

Suggested Term Paper Topics

1. Ethical and legal obligations of members of boards of directors.
2. Problems in shifting from functional to product organization structure.
3. Human factors contributing to boundary-maintaining rather then boundary-spanning activities.
4. Ways of determining effective spans of management.
5. Responding to problems associated with achieving coordination in matrix organizations.
6. Ways the formal organization contributes to or inhibits the formation of informal organizational structures.
7. Job specialization and workers having higher educational attainments.
8. Basic management techniques contrasted with System 4 with respect to achieving coordination.
9. Max Weber's contributions to rationalizing organization design.

Suggested Guest Speakers

1. A member of a board of directors to talk about how boards can contribute to the effectiveness or organizations.
2. Identify a company, such as a major construction company, whose manager is asked to review how matrix management is viewed in that company.
3. A labor leader to discuss the extent to which members of the unions are involved in decision making in their respective companies. Without necessarily using the term "System 4," ask to have the elements of participative management included in the presentation.

CHAPTER 10
Authority, Delegation, and Decentralization

Chapter Outline

AUTHORITY, POWER, AND INFLUENCE

The Basis of Formal Authority: Two Views
- The Classical View
- The Acceptance View

The Sources of Power
Power in Organizations

DIVISION OF AUTHORITY

Line Authority
Staff Authority
Functional Authority

DELEGATION

Delegation, Authority, Accountability, and Responsibility
Classical Guidelines of Effective Delegation
- Accountability, Authority, and Responsibility
- The Scalar Principle
- Unity of Command

Limitation of the Classical Guidelines
Effective Delegation

JOB DESIGN

Approaches to Job Design
- Mechanistic Job Design
- Motivational Job Design
- Biological Job Design
- Perceptual/Motor Job Design

Job Design and Job Satisfaction

DECENTRALIZATION

Factors Influencing Decentralization
- Strategy and the Organization's Environment
- Size and Rate of Growth
- Characteristics of the Organization

Trends in Decentralization

SUMMARY

Key Terms

- **influence** Any actions or examples of behavior that cause a change in attitude or behavior of another person or group.
- **power** The ability to exert influence; that is, the ability to change the attitudes or behavior of individuals or groups.
- **formal authority** Power rooted in the general understanding that specific individuals or groups have the right to exert influence within certain limits by virtue of their position within the organization. Also called legitimate power.
- **reward power** Power derived from the fact that one person, known as an influencer, has the ability to reward another person, known as an influencee, for carrying out orders, which may be expressed or implied.
- **coercive power** The negative side of reward power, based on the influencer's ability to punish the influencee.
- **legitimate power** Power that exists when a subordinate or influencee acknowledges that the influencer has a "right" or is lawfully entitled to exert influence—within certain bounds. Also called formal authority.
- **expert power** Power based on the belief or understanding that the influencer has specific knowledge or relevant expertise which the influencee does not.
- **referent power** Power based on the desire of the influencee to be like or identify with the influencer.
- **delegation** The act of assigning formal authority and responsibility for completion of specific activities to a subordinate.
- **empowerment** The act of delegating power and authority to a subordinate so that the goals of the manager can be accomplished.
- **scalar principle** The concept that a clear line of authority through the organization must exist if delegation is to work successfully.
- **decentralization** The delegation of power and authority from higher to lower levels of the organization, often accomplished by the creation of small, self-contained organizational units.
- **centralization** The extent to which authority is concentrated at the top of the organization.
- **"zone of indifference"** or **"area of acceptance"** According to Barnard and Simon, respectively, inclinations conditioning individuals to accept orders that fall within a familiar range of responsibility or activity.

- **job design** The division of an organization's work among its employees.
- **job enlargement** The combination of various operations at a similar level into one job to provide more variety for workers and thus increase motivation and satisfaction. An increase in job scope.
- **job enrichment** The combining of several activities from a vertical cross section of the organization into one job to provide the worker with more autonomy and responsibility. An increase in job depth.
- **flextime** A system that permits employees to arrange their work hours to suit their personal needs.
- **line authority** The authority of those managers directly responsible, through the organization's chain of command, for achieving organizational goals.
- **staff authority** The authority of those groups of individuals who provide line managers with advice and services.
- **functional authority** The authority of staff department members to control the activities of other departments that are related to specific staff responsibilities.
- **unity of command principle** A guideline for delegation that states that each individual in an organization should report to only one superior.
- **divisionalization** Organizational structure whereby autonomous, decentralized units can make decisions on their own level.

Chapter Overview/Synopsis

The hierarchical grouping of jobs within organizations places power, authority, and influence into a perspective used to achieve coordination of resources. Authority can be traced from its classical origins rooted in the private property concept to the more modern approach that authority is effective only to the extent persons having authority are accepted by subordinates as being legitimate users of that authority. Power—the use of influence—has five sources: reward, coercive, legitimate, expert, and referent. The use of authority, power, and influence occurs within all parts of a structure—the line and the staff. Line positions have direct responsibility for achieving the organization's goals, while staff positions exist to provide expert advice and service to the line.

Authority moves downward in an organization through a process called delegation. Delegation is accepted as being accountable to the person having the ultimate responsibility—the one doing the delegating. Managers delegate in order to provide themselves with time to do things not delegable at the time. Jobs tend to be structured to achieve efficiency in achieving the organization's goals. Today's managers may help a person grow on a job by enlarging that job, or to have more autonomy and influence through having the job enriched. Bringing about the human willingness to perform assigned tasks generally requires the use of motivational techniques that range from the coercive use of power to the voluntarism that arises from people wanting to be part of a successful undertaking. All of this occurs within organizations that may be centralized where information is closely held and parceled out as needed from the top, or decentralized where people who need information have freedom to obtain the necessary details in order to take initiative in using that knowledge.

Analysis of Illustrative Case Study

INTRODUCTION—RESPONSIVENESS AND RESTRUCTURING AT IBM

IBM's management was moving too slowly to keep abreast of the market, but was unaware of the problem because of the market momentum carrying the company. But when Digital Equipment Company garnered a slice of "their" market and competitors' products were outperforming theirs, management was forced to take notice. The result was a major restructuring where payroll was reduced by more than 16,000 (mostly early retirements), and many staff persons were transferred to sales where they could generate revenues. The decentralization approach freed operating units from the centralized review of decision making by a multitude of staff reviews.

CONTINUED—RESPONSIVENESS AND RESTRUCTURING AT IBM

The decision to abandon the six-person executive committee to obtain decentralization of decision making provided the impetus for the concept of "entrepreneurship" to take hold where managers of a large organization could make decisions as though they were entrepreneurs. They, of course, had to produce results for IBM. One result was shortening the time needed to take an idea from inception to the market. Some observers feel this time factor has been reduced by more than 50 percent.

WRAP-UP—RESPONSIVENESS AND RESTRUCTURING AT IBM

While critics of IBM sometimes contend its best days are past, they may be forgetting that the momentum of a company as large as a battleship takes energy to slow and alter direction. Before selling IBM short, critics need to keep in mind that IBM is more than an organization; it is a culture. Many people believe in that company and will give more than a fair day's work to move it along the route toward improved success.

Answers to End-of-Chapter Review Questions

1. What are the two major views of authority? How do you think each view would affect a manager's attitude and behavior toward subordinates?

   In the classical view of authority, authority is legalistic or, as in the United States, stems from the Constitution that permits the ownership of private property. It follows that a person who owns property can employ others to use that property for lawful purposes while retaining enforcement powers to use, if needed, to obtain compliance. A second view of authority is acceptance, in which the only truly effective authority arises when subordinates accept the superior's "right" to exercise the authority. In the first instance, a manager's attitude would reflect the idea of telling rather than selling, while under acceptance the manager would do selling rather than telling.

2. What is the "zone of indifference"?

   According to Barnard and Simon, this zone is the inclination that conditions individuals to accept orders falling within a familiar range of responsibility or activity. Thus, if a person's job were to repair washing machines, it would make little difference which machine among several was to be repaired first.

3. What are the five bases of power described by French and Raven? Give one example of a manager's exercise of each type of power.

   —*Reward power:* A manager has the capability to assign jobs that may be looked upon as being rewarding or punishing, such as making salads or carrying out the garbage.

   —*Coercive power:* The manager gives a command making it quite clear that something deemed a punishment will occur if the job is not completed as specified. People who fail are assigned to work in "Outer Siberia."

   —*Legitimate power:* The subordinate acknowledges the "legitimate right" of the superior to give commands. A secretary transcribes a letter dictated by an executive.

   —*Expert power:* Is based on the belief that the person being asked a question has the expertise to provide a correct answer. A student asks a professor of English the correct punctuation for a complex sentence.

   —*Referent power:* Is based on the subordinate's desire to identify with the superior by acting in an acceptable manner, such as wearing the same type of apparel.

4. What are the two "faces of power" described by David McClelland?

   There is a positive as well as a negative face. The negative face is one of dominance in that if "I win, you lose"; the positive face is "win-win."

5. What are the characteristics of successful power users?

   Kotter noted six characteristics of successful users of power: the users (a) are sensitive to the source of their power, (b) recognize costs and benefits of using power, (c) appreciate that each power base has conditions for use, (d) possess career goals that allow for the development and use of power, (e) exercise self-control through mature behavior, and (f) understand that power has a legitimate use in reaching objectives.

6. What is the difference between line positions and staff positions? Is the difference always clear in organizations?

   Line positions exist in an organization for the purpose of having direct responsibility for the achievement of organizational goals. Staff positions exist to provide services and advice to line positions. An organization chart does not necessarily make clear a line from a staff position, but job descriptions indicate the key responsibilities. Line persons may seem to perform staff functions at times, and vice versa.

7. What does the phrase "functional staff authority" mean?

   Functional staff authority is a delegated right for staff offices to obtain compliance for specified actions from others in the organization regardless of whether they are in line or staff positions. For example, a university registrar (staff) sets deadlines for faculty (line) to submit course grades.

8. What are the advantages of delegation? Describe the classical guidelines of effective delegation. What are the limitations of these guidelines?

   Delegation provides more time for the superior to address other responsibilities. Delegation helps subordinates grow in the organization and accept accountabilities. Delegation is a legitimate means of transferring power in an organization.

   The classical guidelines are based on established principles of accountability, authority, and responsibility; the scalar principle; and unity of command. Accountability relates to the fact that the subordinate is answerable to the superior for the proper exercise of the authority. Authority, by definition, is a right to command, but the right may arise through legalistic means or through acknowledgment by subordinates.

Responsibility relates to the assignment to be carried out through the exercise of authority. The scalar principle provides that the full amount of authority vested at the top of the organization can be divided and subdivided downward in an organization to the lowest point where competence to exercise it exists. Unity of command means a person can have but one boss for a given set of responsibilities.

Several limitations exist. Foremost is that of the subordinates not necessarily recognizing the legitimacy of the order-giver. Another problem arises from the complexity of modern organizations where the idea of unity of command may be difficult to achieve because so many experts are needed to provide information necessary to carry out a given function. Another problem is that of human fallibility: a boss may be unable to define a task so that the subordinate has the same degree of understanding as does his boss.

9. What are the advantages of job specialization? Why did it emerge?

Advantages include less training time, higher levels of production, less chance of mental overload, and a larger labor pool. Specialization arose for a variety of reasons. During the early parts of the classical era, the majority of workers were thought to be lazy so that it was necessary for others to do the thinking. Today, however, the sheer complexity of many jobs necessitates specialization, such as in personnel departments where some persons specialize in wages and benefits, others specialize in affirmative action, and still others deal with labor relations.

10. What is the purpose of job enlargement and job enrichment?

The goal of job enlargement is to combine various operations of a similar skill level into one job to increase variety for workers and to add to their satisfaction with a further increase in their motivation. Job enrichment provides workers with more autonomy and responsibility by combining several activities from a vertical cross section of the organization in order to obtain greater job depth for workers.

11. How are decentralization and delegation related?

Delegation is the process of assigning authority from one level of management to another. Decentralization refers to a philosophy or concept of management regarding the extent to which it is considered appropriate to have decision making occur without obtaining prior review from a superior. Decentralization may be accompanied by the creation of relatively small autonomous units.

12. What factors influence the extent to which an organization is decentralized?

Pressure from competition often necessitates quick decision making—centralization impedes this process. This slowing of the decision process often occurs because of the number of bureaucratic levels associated with centralization. An increase in size of a business generally provides reason to decentralize. Other influences include the organizational culture, the abilities of managers to assume greater responsibilities, the costs and risks associated with the decision, and the preference of key managers.

13. Do you believe there will be a trend toward centralization or decentralization over the next several years? Why?

Many firms are restructuring and eliminating layers of management. This fact alone sets a strong trend for further decentralization. One result of this business downsizing is the reduction of the need for middle managers to occupy decision-screening staff positions.

CASE: THE USE AND ABUSE OF JOYCE ROBERTS

1. What are the sources and uses of power in this case?

The sources of power include reward, legitimate, expert, and referent. Reward, since Roberts could be rewarded or punished. As it turned out, she may have been punished by her boss once Peach was transferred. Legitimate power, because without it, the other kinds of power would not exist in a formal organization. Expert power, since Roberts had expertise to carry out her assignment. Referent power, as indicated by Roberts thinking of herself being associated with a possible future CEO.

2. What problems does Joyce Roberts have now?

She has to make peace with her boss. He has an apparent grudge because Peach had the capability to get Roberts reassigned and to keep Roberts' boss out of the picture. Roberts' boss now has the power to seek some type of punishment by questioning Roberts' performance. But Roberts could not have accomplished her task without involving other people of influence. Since her ideas were accepted at the top level, it would appear peculiar if her performance were now brought into question. Actually, Roberts' boss may have more of a problem by questioning Roberts' performance.

3. What advice would you give Roberts?

Let ordinary conversation with her associates bring into the open the difficulty she is having with her boss. Roberts can certainly ask her boss for an interview to explore the problem, since the work she had just completed had received acceptance from top management. The question to be asked: "In what way have I failed to perform properly in the light of the acceptance of my plans?"

Suggested Term Paper Topics

1. Ways of achieving a successful implementation of decentralization following a long period of centralization.

2. Job enrichment and ways of "working smarter, not harder."
3. An analysis of how conflict arises between line and staff departments.
4. Reconciling differences between line and staff departments.
5. An analytical book report of Chester I. Barnard's *The Functions of the Executive*.
6. Referent power as a tool of motivation.
7. The flow of authority, responsibility, and accountability.
8. An analysis of the kinds of authority that cannot be delegated.
9. Job design as an element of job enrichment.

Suggested Guest Speakers

1. Someone from a military-type organization (police, fire, or armed forces) to discuss the extent to which participation can exist in such an organization.
2. A manager of a large group of clerical workers, such as might work in a large insurance company, to discuss how authority is used and how jobs are kept interesting.
3. A politician to discuss how power is exercised to attain results.

CHAPTER 11
Human Resource Management

Chapter Outline

THE HRM PROCESS: A TRADITIONAL VIEW

HUMAN RESOURCE PLANNING

Planning Procedures
Forecasting and the Human Resource Audit
Forecasting
Human Resource Audit

RECRUITMENT

Job and Position Descriptions
Sources for Recruitment
Outside Recruitment for Managers and Professionals
Recruitment from Within
Equal Employment Opportunity and Affirmative Action
The Law
Implications for Managers

SELECTION

Steps in the Selection Process
Interviewing
Manager Selection
Selecting Experienced Managers
Selecting Potential Managers
Assessment Centers

ORIENTATION AND SOCIALIZATION

TRAINING AND DEVELOPMENT

Training Programs
Management Development Programs
On-the-Job Methods
Off-the-Job Methods
Conditions for Effective Management Development Programs

PERFORMANCE APPRAISAL

Informal and Formal Appraisal
Formal Appraisal Approaches
Problems of Appraisal

PROMOTIONS, TRANSFERS, DEMOTIONS, AND SEPARATIONS

Promotions
Transfers
Discipline, Demotions, and Separations

HRM AND STRATEGY

HRM and Environmental Pressures
The Four C's Model for Human Resources

SUMMARY

Key Terms

- **human resource management (HRM)** The management function that deals with recruitment, placement, training, and development of organization members.
- **human resource planning** Planning for the future personnel needs of an organization, taking into account both internal activities and factors in the external environment.
- **recruitment** The development of a pool of job candidates in accordance with a human resource plan.
- **orientation or socialization** A program designed to help employees fit smoothly into an organization.
- **forecasting** The attempt, using specific techniques, to predict outcomes and project future trends.
- **human resource audit** The analysis and appraisal of the organization's current human resources.
- **replacement chart** A chart that diagrams an organization's positions, showing the incumbents, likely future candidates, and readiness of candidates to enter those positions.
- **realistic job preview** (RJP) A description provided by the organization to applicants and new employees that gives both the positive and negative aspects of a job.
- **computer-assisted instruction (CAI)** A training technique in which computers are used to shorten training time with instructors and to provide additional help to individual trainees.
- **comparable worth** The principle that jobs requiring comparable skills and knowledge merit equal compensation even if the nature of the work activity is different.

- **training program** A process designed to maintain or improve current job performance.
- **development program** A process designed to develop skills necessary for future work activities.
- **selection** The mutual process whereby the organization decides whether to make a job offer and the candidate decides on the acceptability of the offer.
- **informal performance appraisal** The process of continuously feeding back to subordinates information regarding their work performance.
- **formal or systematic appraisal** A formalized appraisal process for rating current subordinate performance, identifying subordinates deserving raises or promotions, and identifying subordinates in need of further training.

Chapter Overview/Synopsis

Human Resources Management (HRM) involves those activities necessary to obtain and maintain an adequate working force: (a) human resource planning; (b) recruitment; (c) selection; (d) socialization; (e) training and development; (f) performance appraisal; (g) transfer, promotion, and demotion; and (h) separation. HRM planning is based on the organization's strategic management and endeavors to have the necessary people available for work according to the forecast. Bringing people into the organization requires an energetic program of recruitment and selection based on an analysis of the work to be done and identification of persons considered to be the most able to perform the needed work. One of the best sources for workers exists within the organization since they have already satisfied the entry requirements of the organization.

Crucial to the recruitment and selection process is adherence to a variety of laws and regulations relating to equal employment opportunity for all persons. Within legal guidelines the selection process consists of seven steps: (a) satisfactory completion of the application, (b) passing the screening interview, (c) testing, (d) background search, (e) in-depth interview, (f) physical examination, and (g) job offer. Assessment centers are often used to help select persons who will occupy higher-level or sensitive positions. Following selection, employees undergo a socialization process to help them better accommodate themselves to each other and the organization's culture.

Training and development is an ongoing process to help ensure that employees remain capable. Determination of capability depends on performance appraisal. While part of a formal process, it also has an informal aspect of review as needed rather than waiting for the elapse of a time period. Performance review, in addition to evaluating current job performance helps identify persons for transfers and/or promotions. Such change of work, however, must also adhere to legal guidelines established to assure impartiality in dealing with employees. A four C's model exists to help HRM executives assess the extent to which this function contributes to the organization's strategic objectives.

Analysis of Illustrative Case Study

INTRODUCTION—HUMAN RELATIONS AT SONY CORPORATION

Many managers claim their people are the most important resource in their respective organizations. The Sony Corporation's approach to managing reveals that the employer also has an obligation to help people be and remain a company's most valuable resource. Sony attempts to deal with people more as helpers and colleagues rather than as employees or hired hands. This case identifies many elements of HRM discussed in the chapter.

CONTINUED—HUMAN RELATIONS AT SONY CORPORATION

The idea that HRM deals with obtaining and maintaining an adequate work force appears to be exemplified at Sony. Workers receive training to do their jobs, and receive retraining as their present jobs are eliminated through change. Workers are seen as "rough stones" to be shaped and polished by managers to make them even more valuable to the company. Sony has also led other Japanese firms in providing workers a shorter work week while maintaining quality production.

WRAP-UP—HUMAN RELATIONS AT SONY CORPORATION

HRM exists to further an organization's efforts to attain its strategic goals. Sony understands that its workers are assets more than costs. Its approach to understanding and developing employees contributes significantly to its high level of success among world companies.

Answers to End-of-Chapter Review Questions

1. What are the steps in the HRM process? Are managers likely to be engaged in more than one step at a time? Why or why not?

The traditional HRM process consists of (a) human resource planning, (b) recruitment, (c) selection, (d) socialization, (e) training and development, and (f) performance appraisal. The process is considered ongoing, thus managers will most likely be engaged in a series of concurrent steps.

2. Why is human resource planning necessary? Name the four steps in human resource planning. What factors must managers of a human resource planning program consider?

HRM planning stems from forecasts of future personnel needs. The planning is done to help the organization meet its forecasted needs for people. This HRM planning consists of planning for future needs, planning for future balance, planning for recruiting and selecting or for laying off, and planning for development. To accomplish this planning process, managers must first consider the organization's strategic plan; second, managers need to be aware of internal and external influences that will change the company's need for people; and third, managers must observe the legal and ethical boundaries for the practice of effective management for human resources.

3. What methods of recruitment can managers use? What are the advantages and disadvantages of recruitment from within?

Methods are limited only by human imagination. Common methods include personal contacts, employment agencies, advertising, external and internal recruiting, obtaining recommendations from friends, and responding to applications from candidates. Advantages for recruiting from within include worker familiarity with the organization, loyalty fostered by internal recruiting, and a less expensive process. Disadvantages of the internal source of employees: (a) good candidates from without are overlooked, (b) company inbreeding can thrive, and (c) employee complacency can exist based on the belief their seniority and company policy will take care of them.

4. What changes have occurred in EEO and affirmative action in recent years? What are the implications for managers?

Where the basic law was designed to provide for equal opportunity, interpretations, together with additional legislation and regulation, have extended civil rights protection to almost any identifiable group able to show itself as disadvantaged without such protection. The implications for managers are still evolving through legislation, regulations, and court decisions. The primary implication is to adhere to both the letter and the spirit of applicable rules of law. A further implication is to avoid taking actions that increase an organization's legal exposure. For example, if an employer provides day care and a child suffers injury or illness while in the facility, is the company liable? To avoid this type of legal liability, managers may favor a grant or subsidy for employees to use as they see fit.

5. What is the standard, seven-step hiring sequence? Is this sequence the same under all conditions? Why or why not?

(1) Completed job application, (2) initial screening interviews, (3) testing, (4) background investigation, (5) in-depth selection interview, (6) physical examination, and (7) job offer. The sequence varies according to company conditions and the kinds of jobs in question. Relatively unskilled jobs will have a different hiring process than skilled or professional jobs. In general, companies place first the elements of the process that eliminate the greatest number of candidates. This approach saves on costs for all involved.

6. What are the defects of in-depth interviews? How can these defects be minimized?

(1) An unbalanced situation: the interviewee is at a relative disadvantage with the interviewer, who is perceived as having power to hire or not to hire. (2) The interviewee may be playing the role understood to be necessary to obtain a favorable interview reaction. (3) Interviewers may ask questions that have no useful purpose in deciding the candidate's qualifications. (4) The interviewer, in his zeal to hire a desirable person, may oversell the company. Companies may reduce the defects of interviews through the publication of a realistic job preview statement.

7. What information is socialization designed to provide?

The socialization process includes (a) general information about the company and the daily work routine, (b) a review of the organization's history, purpose, operations, products, and how the employee's job contributes to the company's needs, and (c) a detailed presentation, or even a brochure, of the organization's policies, work rules, and employee benefits.

8. What is the difference between training and development?

Training is directed toward the development, maintenance, and improvement of current job performance. Development, on the other hand, seeks to develop skills for future jobs.

9. What development approaches and methods can managers use? Which method is most effective?

Development involves technical skills as well as those needed for conceptual reasoning. The level of the employee's work determines, to a large extent, emphasis to be received during the development program. The most common approaches to training and development include on-the-job, off-the-job, internships, and apprenticeships. The acid test of developmental programs occurs on the job when the employee has an opportunity to apply what he has learned.

10. What are the basic differences between systematic and informal appraisal? What are the four basic appraisal approaches? How may formal appraisals be made more effective in leading to improved performance? What appraisal pitfalls do managers need to avoid?

Systematic appraisal is formal and occurs on a regular basis, such as semi-annually. Informal appraisal is conducted as needed, often spontaneously, as conditions are deemed appropriate.

The four basic appraisal approaches are (a) superiors rate their subordinates, (b) a group of superiors rate subordinates, (c) a group of peers rate a colleague, and (d) subordinates rate their respective bosses.

Formal appraisal, where the superior and subordinate jointly set performance goals and the means of determining their attainment; has the best likelihood of leading to improved performance. Participatory appraisal minimizes the possibility of the superior acting in the role of a judge and the employee being a defendant.

Common pitfalls to avoid: (a) shifting standards, (b) rater biases, (c) different rater patterns, and (d) negative and positive halo effects.

11. What are the problems associated with promotions? How may these problems be overcome?

Bypassed persons may feel resentful, and discrimination may prevent qualified persons from being promoted. Organizations can avoid these major problems through a systematic appraisal system that requires documentation, joint review of appraisals so that employees have an opportunity to respond to their appraisals, and close monitoring of the promotion process by an affirmative action officer.

12. When are transfers used in organizations?

A variety of purposes is served through transfers, chief of which are (a) employees obtain broader job experience, (b) promotable people are identified, and (c) employees who have become inadequate may be shifted to positions they can perform rather than being fired.

13. Explain how the four C's criteria may be used to evaluate the effectiveness of a human resource management policy.

The four C's consist of commitment, competence, congruence, and cost-effectiveness. High commitment improves communication between employees and managers and engenders mutual trust. High competence is revealed through the existence of versatile employees who can undertake new jobs as conditions demand. Cost-effectiveness relates to personnel programs that keep costs such as wages, benefits, and work stoppages equal to or less than those of competitors. Higher congruence means that employees and managers share a common bond in seeking success for themselves and their company.

Answers to End-of-Chapter Case Questions

CASE: THE GANNETT COMPANY—A LEADER IN MINORITY EMPLOYMENT

1. Why do newspapers have a substantially lower representation of minority employees?

The case points out that newspapers need a large number of technical and professional employees. Colleges enroll few minority persons as English or journalism majors; labor unions have been slow to open to minority persons their apprenticeship programs for skilled jobs. The Gannett Company obtains a significant number of its minority employees on the basis of quotas that managers must attain. The case noted the lowered morale of non-minority employees who feel that qualified persons are being passed over to obtain full quotas. Other newspapers could apply the same hiring standard and also obtain the same kind of result.

2. Why has the program at Gannett been successful in attracting minority employees?

Individuals like to go where they feel welcome. Gannett's policy of seeking minority persons makes the company attractive. This helps draw more applicants for the available positions, especially when it is known that jobs will remain open until a minority person applies.

3. What are some possible problems with this program, now and in the future?

The case indicates that minority persons, regardless of qualification, are being placed in jobs with the result that non-minority persons feel resentment. In addition to possible reverse discrimination legal actions, non-minority persons could keep their résumés up-to-date and take opportunities to change jobs. While this could sound as though Gannett will be left with unqualified persons to run the business, the reverse is more likely to be the case as a result of training and development. Gannett's main goal is to hire people with the capability to be trained and developed. More and more businesses have discovered that the majority of its new employees—minority and non-minority—lack many basic skills that should have been acquired in high school. To compensate, businesses are providing their own in-house educational opportunities for employees. Thus, the winners in the case can be the minority employees, who receive the training, as well as the company, which increases its supply of qualified employees. The short-range problem is for Gannett to work with its non-minority employees to enlist their cooperation in upgrading all employees.

4. What advice would you give Mr. Neuharth as he ponders the future of the program?

Maintain the program for the reasons offered in the previous question.

Suggested Term Paper Topics

1. Human resource management as a career choice.
2. Recruiting, selecting, and placing non-traditional persons.
3. Factors that add to or detract from the effectiveness of management development programs.
4. To what extent can interviews be replaced by other selection devices?
5. Costs and benefits of assessment centers in selecting managers.
6. Advantages and disadvantages of main kinds of on-the-job training.
7. Comparable worth contrasted with the economics of wage setting.
8. Minimizing morale problems during performance appraisal interviews.
9. Using the employee discharge as part of human resources management.

Suggested Guest Speakers

1. A personnel director from a service-type company to discuss how the company recruits people for positions that lack a career path.
2. An affirmative action director, such as a government official, to discuss the successes and problems in getting more effective use of affirmative action.
3. A recent graduate to discuss his/her experiences in obtaining the job he/she now holds.

CHAPTER 12

Managing Organizational Change and Development

Chapter Outline

FORCES FOR CHANGE

External Forces
Internal Forces

MANAGERIAL RESPONSES TO PRESSURES FOR CHANGE

The Role of the Change Agent

MODELS OF THE CHANGE PROCESS

Forces for Stability
The Process of Change

RESISTANCE TO CHANGE

Sources of Resistance to Change
Overcoming Resistance to Change

APPROACHES TO PLANNED CHANGE

Interdependence of the Three Approaches
Structural Approaches
Technological Approaches
Combining Technological and Structural Approaches
People Approaches

ORGANIZATIONAL DEVELOPMENT

Types of OD Activities
OD Techniques in Closeup
Survey Feedback
Team Building
Evaluating OD

ORGANIZATIONAL CULTURE

SUMMARY

Key Terms

- **change agent** The individual leading or guiding the process of a change in an organizational situation.
- **client system** The individual, group, or organization that is the target of a planned change.
- **unfreezing** Making the need for change so obvious that the individual, group, or organization can readily see and accept that change must occur.
- **refreezing** Transforming a new behavioral pattern into the norm through reinforcement and supporting mechanisms.
- **organizational development (OD)** A long-range effort supported by top management to increase an organization's problem-solving and renewal processes through effective management of organizational culture.
- **collaborative management** Management through power sharing and subordinate participation; the opposite of hierarchical imposition of authority.
- **organizational culture** The set of important understandings, such as norms, values, attitudes, and beliefs, shared by organizational members.
- **action research** The method through which organizational development change agents learn what improvements are needed and how the organization can best be aided in making improvements.
- **sensitivity training** An early personal growth technique, at one time fairly widespread in organizational development efforts, that emphasizes increased sensitivity in interpersonal relationships.
- **transaction analysis** An approach to improving interpersonal effectiveness, sometimes used in organizational development efforts, that concentrates on the styles and content of communication.
- **process consultation** A technique by which consultants help organization members understand and change the ways they work together.
- **team building** A method of improving organizational effectiveness at the team level by diagnosing barriers to team performance and improving interteam relationships and task accomplishment.

Chapter Overview/Synopsis

Organizations change as a result of both internal and external forces. The rate of change can be adjusted to some extent by managerial intervention since managers are considered to be change agents. Some change occurs as part of daily operation, while other change is long-range in nature with its success dependent on how well the human factor is committed to the change. People tend to resist being changed because of an unwillingness to undertake a new set of behaviors. Kurt Lewin's three-position model is significant in obtaining change: (a) unfreeze people's behavior, (b) change the behavior, and (c) freeze the new behavior.

Organizations can change structurally, technologically, and in human terms. Structure can include the management philosophy, as well as the flow of work; and technology can change through new equipment and job design. Human factor change includes such things as values, attitudes, technical and social skills, and conceptual understanding. This type of change occurs through a process referred to as organizational development (OD).

The interworkings of all aspects of an organization become known as its culture. An organization cannot be culture-free because it has almost predictable ways to reacting to given situations, and its people reflect such a set of behaviors.

Analysis of Illustrative Case Study

INTRODUCTION—ORGANIZATIONAL TRAUMA AND TRIUMPH AT AT&T

The changes at AT&T stemmed from a long-standing policy of resisting the forces of change. The company insisted on customers leasing their telephones, not making attachments to AT&T equipment, and that anything new had to be compatible with anything old. A court decision gave producers of telephone equipment the opportunity to provide more modern devices at lower costs. This change, coupled with the consent decree in 1983, set the basis for revolutionary change. The main change was a shift from being a telephone company to a telecommunications company with a marketing emphasis. This marketing emphasis created trauma for many employees who had been trained to provide service regardless of costs. Bringing costs into line necessitated severe reductions of the labor force together with changes in work rules. In effect, a new culture had to be forged.

CONTINUED—ORGANIZATIONAL TRAUMA AND TRIUMPH AT AT&T

The business and legal environment forced change on AT&T. The result was management seeking ways to implement new strategies. Management had to deal with such employee concerns as uncertainty, fear, and doubts whether the changes were really needed. Reassurances about employment would remove uncertainty, but massive layoffs added to employee apprehension. Renegotiated contracts with the union settled some misgivings about the continuation of benefits. The implementation of structural changes, while not eliminating doubts about the wisdom for making changes, fostered a realization among employees that changes were coming, ready or not. Company-sponsored programs to involve employee participation in the restructuring did much to help ensure the company's survival and repositioning for renewed growth.

WRAP-UP—ORGANIZATIONAL TRAUMA AND TRIUMPH AT AT&T

While organizational culture changed, certain constants remained at AT&T to provide a degree of stability for the employees. Employees had no reason to doubt what they perceived to be the "basic decency" of top management, that most of the beliefs, values, expectations, and norms of the company would be a part of a restructured business. Top management at AT&T appears to have been successful in communicating these relative constants to their stakeholders as part of the process of transforming the company to its new position in the economy.

Answers to End-of-Chapter Review Questions

1. What are some external and internal sources of change in organizations?

External sources include technological advances, competitive pressures, legislation, social expectations, and political responses. Internal sources include revised strategic goals, technology, collective bargaining, and employment development programs.

2. What are some nonconstructive responses to change pressures? Can you think of some examples of these nonconstructive responses in any of our society's political, business, or not-for-profit organizations?

The most common nonconstructive response is denying that the pressure for change really exists. Even after admitting the existence of the forces of change, the response may be to do as little as possible, often with the result that the force increases. A classic political example of a nonconstructive response was President Nixon's reaction to the Watergate situation, which led to his resignation from office. Firestone's refusal to recognize a problem with a series of tires resulted in a court decree to refund money to buyers of that particular tire. More than one charity has suffered as a consequence of failing to control its costs of soliciting donations.

3. What two major approaches do managers use to deal with change? When is each approach likely to be used?

First, managers attempt to make small, day-to-day adjustments that are part of a manager's duty. Such adjustments may forestall the need for more dramatic changes later. The second approach is a program of planned change—in effect a series of major structural shifts in operation. These major shifts often include management philosophy, organizational strategy, and even product alignment.

4. What major obstacles to change were noted by Lewin? According to the model developed by Lewin and elaborated by Schein, what are the two mechanisms through which individuals learn new attitudes?

First, persons prefer to hold to their past beliefs, values, and behaviors. Second, without some type of reinforcement to maintain the change, persons will revert to their former behaviors. New attitudes have the best chance of success if the person does not see the new behavior as a threat. Thus, a manager trying to bring about change will attempt to reduce the intensity of the restraining forces that would engender resistance to change.

5. What are the three categories of resistance to change? Which type of resistance should be encouraged? How may resistance to change be overcome?

(a) Uncertainty about the causes and effect of the intended change, (b) unwillingness to give up existing benefits, and (c) awareness of weaknesses in the proposed changes. Awareness of weaknesses may be considered a desirable form of conflict since it causes change agents to reexamine the changes thought to be desirable.

Six approaches to overcome resistance to change have been identified: (a) education and communication, (b) participation and involvement, (c) facilitation and support, (d) negotiation and agreement, (e) manipulation and co-optation, and (f) explicit and implicit coercion.

6. What are the three structural approaches to change?

(a) Rearranging an organization's managerial systems, such as lines of communication work flow and managerial hierarchy; (b) changing an organization's technology, such as altering its equipment, engineering processes, research methods, or production patterns; and (c) changing an organization's people through modifying such factors as selection, training, socialization, attitudes, or roles of employees.

7. What do technostructural approaches to change attempt to do? Why were these approaches to change developed? What are some approaches to technostructural change?

The goal is to improve performance by altering selected aspects of both an organization's structure and its technology. Technical change or structural change, when taken alone, often led to decreased morale and lowered productivity; the combination of technical and structural change retained job features that enhanced morale while also introducing the needed changes. Common technostructural changes include job enlargement and job enrichment programs.

8. How does the assumption underlying the people approach to change differ from the assumption underlying the structural and technical approaches?

While technostructural change attempts to improve organizational performance by changing the work situation, the people approach attempts to change behavior. Behavioral change is sought through such actions as teaching new skills and developing worker abilities to perceive and analyze their expectations.

9. What is a good working definition of OD?

Organizational Development (OD) has been inconsistently defined, but French and Bell provide the following working definition: "a top-management-supported, long-range effort to improve an organization's problem-solving and renewal processes, particularly through a more effective and collaborative diagnosis and management of organization culture—with special emphasis on formal work team, temporary team, and intergroup culture—with the assistance of a consultant-facilitator and the use of the theory and technology of applied behavioral science, including action research."

10. What assumptions about people do most OD practitioners make? Do you also hold these assumptions?

(a) Individuals have a natural desire for personal development and growth, (b) people want to be accepted by their work group, (c) groups do better when they can interact, and (d) the long-term health of an organization depends on the equalization of power between hierarchical levels. Answers to part (b) will be based on the value systems of individual students. Most likely, each assumption will receive at least some qualified disagreement from students.

11. What are the values upon which OD is based? Which of these values do you share?

OD practitioners value helping people achieve their aspirations; they also appreciate that people should be free to enjoy the open expression of their feelings; and they believe that situations should be of the win-win variety so that one group or individual does not excel at the expense of another. Answers to part (b) will depend on the value systems of individual students. Most likely each OD value will be subjected to some element of questioning—especially the value that one person should not be able to "win" over another.

12. What are three widely used OD techniques?

    For individual development, sensitivity training has been useful. For two or three people, transaction analysis has proven useful for helping people improve their level of interpersonal communication. For teams and groups, process consultation has been effective in helping people better understand group dynamics. For overall assessment of an organization's health, intergroup relations where confrontational meetings have been used have helped managers explore common problems. Survey feedback has been useful in identifying the kinds of issues requiring further study.

13. According to French and Bell, what conditions are required for a successful OD program?

    (1) Recognition by top management that the organization has problems; (2) use of an outside behavioral scientist; (3) top management support; (4) involvement of work group leaders; (5) early initial success; (6) education of organization members about OD; (7) acknowledgment of managers' strengths; (8) involvement with managers of human resource departments; (9) development of internal OD resources; (10) effective management of the OD program; (11) measurement of results.

14. What is organizational culture? How does it affect an organization's ability to change?

    An organization's culture is the shared understandings comprising norms, values, attitudes, and beliefs. The culture holds the key to how well change can occur. Change can be part of an organization's culture, or a stable organization may find itself culture-ridden with resistance to change.

15. How can the Seven-S model be used to understand cultural change?

    The Seven-S model focuses on an organization's superordinate goals:—skills, staff, and style—and helps managers take a broad view of how well an organization is meeting its objectives. Further, these superordinate goals further a review of each remaining S.

Answers to End-of-Chapter Case Questions

CASE: UNDERGOING CHANGE AT THE DIGITAL EQUIPMENT CORPORATION

1. Describe the culture at DEC. To what extent does the proliferation of networks and open network technology influence employee behavior?

   Culture is a set of important understandings that members of a community (DEC) share in common. The members appear to share these understandings: that customer problems are more important than just obtaining sales; that they listen to what customers have to say; a belief that the company is unique in its approach to letting computers of different makes "talk" to one another; knowledge that employees can deal directly with the president if considered important; and an ongoing willingness to reexamine its values with the idea of changing them if necessary.

   The open network permits information to flow freely, and employees take advantage of that openness to perform their jobs more effectively. This, in effect, gives employees an entrepreneurial spirit even though they are members of a large company.

2. What are the central issues of change at DEC?

   The main theme, the driving force, is to become a leader in the field. DEC has built its hardware so that software designed for other computers can be utilized through its network systems. Another key force of change is the organization's desire to maintain open channels of communication for its employees. An ongoing issue of change is to retain its interest in being of service to customers. DEC is also interested in obtaining the best talent in the field of electronics—it has no hesitancy in recruiting top-flight persons from IBM.

3. What advice would you give to Mr. Olsen?

   Maintain the rate of development at DEC to improve the quality of decision making and further company interest in being a leader in the computer field. The company has already scored many successes with its line of VAX computers, and rival IBM has received criticism because its machines are not capable of the open communication links available with DEC computers. Therefore, keep expanding the market niche for DEC.

Suggested Term Paper Topics

1. An update of "Organizational Trauma and Triumph at AT&T."
2. OD for persons whose culture stems from "Inshallah": if I were supposed to be a better manager, Allah would have made me a better manager.
3. A longitudinal study of change in a selected organization as it goes through the change from a regulated to an unregulated company.
4. Performance appraisal interview techniques where the goal is to shift an employee's unsatisfactory behavior to meritorious achievement.
5. An analysis of Kurt Kewin's "force field" theory.
6. Overcoming a labor union's resistance to change with respect to eliminating work rules that have more persons on the job than necessary.
7. Strengths and weaknesses of sensitivity training in organizational development.
8. An analysis of transaction analysis as it affects interpersonal communication.
9. Costs and benefits of team-building programs in OD.

Suggested Guest Speakers

1. From the Yellow Pages, or some other source, find a management consultant to discuss the implementation of an OD program.
2. The director of a Human Resource Department that has been involved with an OD program conducted by an outside consultant, to share his/her experiences regarding the program.
3. A panel of three classmates to identify and discuss what they perceive to be the culture of the college or university. Include in the discussion any changes that have occurred over the past five years.

CHAPTER 13
Managing Organizational Conflict and Creativity

Chapter Outline

CONFLICT, COMPETITION, AND COOPERATION

CHANGING VIEWS OF CONFLICT
- The Traditional View
- The Interactionist View

Functional and Dysfunctional Conflict
- Types of Conflict

Sources of Organizational Conflict
- Shared Resources
- Differences in Goals
- Interdependence of Work Activities
- Differences in Values or Perceptions
- Individual Styles and Organizational Ambiguities

DYNAMICS AND CONSEQUENCES OF ORGANIZATIONAL CONFLICT

Three Factors in Organizational Conflict
- The Level of Conflict
- Organizational Structure and Culture

METHODS FOR MANAGING CONFLICT

Conflict-Stimulation Methods
- Suggestions for Stimulating Conflict

Conflict-Reduction Methods

Conflict-Resolution Methods
- Dominance and Suppression
- Compromise
- Integrative Problem Solving

LINE AND STAFF CONFLICT

MANAGEMENT-LABOR CONFLICT

Workers and Unions

Minimizing Negotiation Conflict

MANAGING ORGANIZATIONAL CREATIVITY AND INNOVATION

Creativity and Innovation

Individual Creativity

Stimulating Individual and Group Creativity
- Brainstorming
- Nominal Group Process
- Synectics (The Gordon Technique)
- Creative Group Decision Making

Organizational Creativity and Innovation
- Generation of Ideas
- Idea Development
- Implementation

Establishing a Climate for Organizational Creativity

SUMMARY

Key Terms

- **organizational conflict** Disagreement between individuals or groups within the organization stemming from the need to share scarce resources or engage in interdependent work activities, or from differences in status, goals, or cultures. See also dysfunctional and functional conflict.
- **competition** A situation in which two or more parties are striving toward mutually incompatible goals but cannot interfere with each other.
- **cooperation** The process of working together to attain mutual objectives.
- **functional conflict** Any conflict that has positive, constructive, and nondivisive results.
- **dysfunctional conflict** Any conflict that results in decreased efficiency and greater factionalism within the organization.
- **arbitration** A form of compromise in which opposing parties agree to submit to the decision of a third party.
- **consensus** A method of conflict resolution in which the parties attempt to find the best solution rather than to achieve a victory over each other.
- **superordinate goals** Higher-level goals that acknowledge lower-level goals, both encompassing the guiding principles that an organization impresses upon its members and contributing toward cohesive goal-oriented activity among groups whose objectives may not coincide.

Chapter Overview/Synopsis

The notion that conflict is always destructive and to be avoided has changed through time. Conflict, today, is viewed as being both inevitable as well as a necessity to an organization's survival. Conflict exists among and between individuals as well as groups. Causes stem from, for example, shared resources, the need to work together, differences in values, and difficulties in communication. Whether conflict is functional or dysfunctional, conflict tends to bring about an increase in group cohesion, identification of leaders, and the development of personal perceptions regarding both events and personalities. The extent to which conflict is beneficial for an organization depends to a large degree on how well conflict is managed.

Positive conflict management includes stimulation, reduction, resolution, and integration. Integration as a means of problem solving permits benefits to accrue to all involved parties. Negative conflict management includes suppression, compromise, and neglect.

Conflicts arise between organizational and interorganizational units. Conflict between organizational units includes conflicts between line and staff. Conflict between interorganizational units most often arises through competition.

A management responsibility is to release the creative forces that exist within individuals. Creativity can be stimulated through a variety of techniques that include brainstorming, nominal group process, synectics, and group decision making.

Analysis of Illustrative Case Study

INTRODUCTION—CONFLICT AND COMPROMISE AT THE ADOLPH COORS COMPANY

Coors Beer, a product with a mystique, became a product to be avoided as a result of a boycott by organized labor and sympathetic activists. The problem arose from (a) the conservative management of the company openly supporting ideas and political candidates deemed unacceptable to the liberals of organized labor, and (b) posturing the company to avoid unionization. A key element of a union is being recognized by an employer, which Coors refused to do. If one employer can avoid providing recognition, so can others. Therefore, the union enlisted support of other unions to undertake a boycott action as a means of crippling Coors in the marketplace. Following a decade of the boycott, Coors Brewing Company's management shifted to younger members of the Coors family, who were more willing to reach an accord with the union.

CONTINUED—CONFLICT AND COMPROMISE AT THE ADOLPH COORS COMPANY

The boycott illustrated a classic example of dysfunctional conflict since neither the company nor the union benefited during the boycott. The union lost members, and Coors lost sales. Since the union's survival was more important to it than the loss of members, it needed to continue the boycott. The union could also receive support from allied unions, while Coors had to stand its losses alone. To resolve a conflict where both parties are "dug in" requires something on the order of a "superordinate goal," something that disputants agree is more important than the original items of the dispute. Lacking this, one of the parties has to "blink."

WRAP-UP—CONFLICT AND COMPROMISE AT THE ADOLPH COORS COMPANY

One way of ending bitter conflict is through integration of interest where third-party intervention gets negotiations underway. In this instance, the National Education Association helped bring the parties together. The leadership at Coors had changed, and so had that of the unions. This made it possible for the negotiators to place a little personal distance between themselves and the original dispute. The result was that Coors agreed to remain neutral during union efforts to organize the workers.

Answers to End-of-Chapter Review Questions

1. What is the difference between conflict and competition?

Conflict is viewed as a disagreement arising from the fact that organizational members or groups need to share an interdependent activity or resource while not sharing the same values or perceptions. Competition exists as a result of organizational members or groups seeking an incompatible goal, while being unable to interfere directly with the activities of one another.

2. What are the traditional and interactionist views of conflict? With which view do you agree? Why?

   Traditionalists view conflict as harmful and best avoided. The presence of conflict indicated something was wrong in the organization, and sound management practices were needed to restore the organization to equilibrium. Interactionists, on the other hand, consider conflict both inevitable and necessary to the health of a dynamic organization. Students most likely will accept the interactionist view because conflict is a means for people to become involved in the decision-making process of their respective organizations.

3. What are the six types of conflict possible in organizations? Under what conditions will each type of conflict arise?

   —Conflict within the individual. Arises from one's uncertainty about what is expected or wanted, or from a sense of inadequacy.
   —Conflict among individuals. Stems most likely from personality differences or different perceptions about role expectations.
   —Conflict among individuals and groups. Most often arises from the way individuals react to pressures for conformity imposed by the group.
   —Conflict among groups in the same organization. This conflict often stems from disputes over authority such as line and staff feuds.
   —Conflict among organizations. This kind of dispute is usually considered to be competition and appropriate.
   —Conflict among individuals in different organizations. Usually stems from what might be perceived as inappropriate treatment, such as a purchasing agent of one company informing the sales manager of another company that an order should have been shipped "yesterday."

4. Why does differentiation of organization groups often lead to conflict?

   An organization's resources are viewed as being finite, with the result that groups and members of the organization feel a responsibility to take actions deemed appropriate to get their "fair" share. Under such a condition, it is often perceived that growth or enhancement of other divisions occurs "at our expense."

5. What are the effects of organizational conflict on group attitudes and behavior? What factors determine whether these effects will be functional or dysfunctional?

   When the conflict is dysfunctional, it tends to grow—almost feeding on itself as each party feels that he/she must get in the last word. Under such conditions, there are winners who solidify their position, and there are losers who seek solace in finding sympathetic listeners. Moderate levels of conflict are seen as having the best chance of being functional, while unresolved conflict escalates to the point where it becomes dysfunctional.

6. What are the consequences of a very low level of organizational conflict? What methods of conflict stimulation can managers use?

   A very low level of organizational conflict suggests a "punishing" organization in which persons who question the status quo learn to keep quiet. The consequence of a setting of low conflict is that individual creativity and ideas remain with individuals, and the organization is the loser. With a change in organizational culture, new managers might find any of the following methods helpful in stimulating constructive conflict: (a) bring in outsiders to get a new viewpoint, (b) do something contrary to the established custom, (c) restructure the organization to shift the power base, (d) encourage competition, and (e) select additional managers who see the positive attributes of useful conflict.

7. In the Sherifs' conflict-reduction experiment, what two methods proved effective? Why might these methods be effective in organizations?

   In the first instance it was found that antagonisms could be reduced by diverting attention from the disagreement and replacing the source of the conflict with shared experiences in the form of superordinate goals that would lead to successful cooperation. In the second instance, a situation needed to be created where the disputants had to work together to respond to a common problem. Both methods are realistic for organizations: an interventionist manager can redirect the attention of the disputants toward a superordinate goal that will benefit both parties.

8. What are three types of conflict-resolution methods? In what ways can these methods be manifested? Which method is usually best? Why?

   Conflicts may be resolved through domination, compromise, or integration. Domination simply suppresses the conflict until one of the parties feels in a better position to dominate. Domination can be manifested through force, smoothing, or majority rule through a voting bloc. Compromise is little different from domination, since giving in on a point arises from insufficient power to dominate. Integration of interest is viewed as the most beneficial conflict resolution model because each party to the conflict comes away as a winner. Instead of one person's solution being favored over another, a new solution is found that is acceptable to all parties.

9. How do line and staff members view each other and their role in the organization? How can line and staff conflict be reduced?

   Line persons view themselves as "profit centers" whose activities lead to the company's survival, and they consider staff persons as "cost centers" supported by efforts from the line. This provides a foundation for dispute. Staff persons see themselves with superior knowledge and expertise, whose ideas are either resisted or ignored. This type of sibling rivalry can be minimized in organizations by establishing the following kinds of guidelines: (a) make responsibilities explicit for both the line and the staff, (b) integrate line and staff activities through a process of consultation, (c) educate line persons on how to get the most benefit from staff expertise, and (d) hold staff accountable for results stemming from their suggestions.

10. Why do you think creativity is important in organizational life?

Creativity is the watershed for ideas that lead to an organization's continued existence in the face of intensive competition. Creativity has become increasingly important as a result of new technologies, products, and methods of doing work.

11. What is the difference between creativity and innovation?

Creativity is the generation of new ideas, while innovation is the translation of such ideas into new products, services, or methods of operation.

12. What techniques can be used to stimulate individual or group creativity?

Brainstorming is a method that encourages the free flow of ideas and does not inhibit responses or judgments. Brainstorming seeks ideas in quantity rather than quality, since the development of ideas is another step of the process. Research, however, shows that individuals working alone do a better job of thinking through a problem and arriving at a solution. An extension of brainstorming is the nominal group process where individuals work together in the same room but write their ideas to avoid the influence of tone of voice. The listed ideas are later shared and discussed. Synectics, called the Gordon technique, is radically different from brainstorming because it focuses attention on a related area of inquiry rather than on the actual problem. Since only the group leader knows the actual problem, the group members are unable to offer simplistic solutions. Only when ideas from the group center on the problem is the full issue explored. The goal of synectics is to solve a problem, while the two brainstorming methods avoid identifying solutions.

13. What are the three steps in the organizational creativity process? How can each step be facilitated or inhibited?

(a) Generating ideas that result from an uninhibited flow of information within the organization, (b) developing the ideas through the established processes within the organization, and (c) implementing the ideas through an integrative process in which each applicable unit of the organization contributes its talent and resources to the successful achievement of a goal.

14. How can managers establish an organizational climate that encourages creativity?

Six attitudes foster a climate for creativity: (a) developing an acceptance of change as desirable, (b) encouraging new ideas, (c) advocating interaction among and between organizational units and members, (d) tolerating failure, (e) providing clear objectives and the freedom to achieve them, and (f) offering recognition to creative persons.

Answers to End-of-Chapter Case Questions

CASE: IS THERE CREATIVE LIFE AFTER POST-IT NOTES?

1. Why was Post-it Notes successful?

The product served a useful purpose.

2. Can creativity be managed at all?

To manage means causing something to happen. In the ordinary concept of management where authority, accountability, and responsibility exist, a person cannot be ordered to produce creativity. On the other hand, persons can be encouraged to bring forth their ideas for ways of improving the effectiveness of the organization.

3. Why is Art Fry worried, and what can he do about it?

Worry is natural since his success is known and he feels compelled to produce another good idea. In this form of internal conflict, he experiences self-doubt regarding his ability to develop another profitable product. This self-doubt can become dysfunctional if he worries about the future. He can review his situation and recognize that new ideas do not pour forth from a cornucopia of ingenuity.

4. Suppose Art Fry reported to you. As his manager, what advice would you give him?

Art's job is not connected with product development. He developed his Post-it Notes because someone needed bookmarks that would stay put while pages were being turned. Therefore, Art should concentrate on doing his regular job. If additional needs arise where he might find a solution, he should ask for time and resources to develop the idea. After all, the company thrives on change and encourages its people to be agents for change.

Suggested Term Paper Topics

1. Ways participative-type managers can encourage managers of the classical school to encourage constructive conflict in their areas of responsibility
2. Developing methods of obtaining constructive contributions from dysfunctional individuals
3. Labor union management of picket lines
4. A history of the development of staff activities in organizations
5. An analysis of brainstorming with case histories
6. Ways to restructure organizations to encourage functional conflict

7. A review of Mary Parker Follett's writings pertaining to resolution of organizational conflict
8. Developing organizations that foster creativity in individuals while also attending to the routines of daily operation
9. An analysis of finding problem solutions through synectics

Suggested Guest Speakers

1. A hospital administrator to discuss the macro aspects of managing a hospital in an environment composed of micro-type situations.
2. A labor leader to discuss collective bargaining in a world where competitive pressures in business are being used to demand union concessions with respect to wages and work rules.
3. A local manager from the Better Business Bureau to discuss ways they resolve conflicts between customers and businesses.

Part 3 Case Studies

CHRIS CUNNINGHAM

1. What are the problems and issues in this case?
   - **a.** Four different companies with different organizational cultures have become one company trying to accommodate separate heritages. The process of adaptation is not complete, which leaves organizational areas of overlapping responsibility, especially with respect to sales territories. Salespersons can retain customers in old territories even though they now have new sales areas.
   - **b.** The sales director, a carryover from the old Stover Company, is a complacent subordinate who provides little leadership for the sales force. This lack of leadership permitted a problem with a new salesperson to become a disrupting influence within the sales as well as the production departments of the company. The new salesperson is Chris Cunningham, a college classmate of Elizabeth Stover, the company president. He is a super salesman but gains much of his personal success by bypassing organizational lines of communication.
   - **c.** Organizational disruption occurs when Chris Cunningham pushes the production department to give his orders special treatment. In some way, Cunningham is able to intimidate others to do his bidding.
   - **d.** Elizabeth Stover recognizes the difficulty with Cunningham but feels his independence is much like her own, and she hesitates to muzzle someone who brings in a high sales volume. Yet his personal sales production contributes to customer dissatisfaction with the inability of other salespersons to deliver sales as promised.
2. What factors in successful organizational behavior are suggested in this case? What possible weaknesses?

   The president has been able to weld several independent companies into a larger one, which ought to cause some element of efficiency. The president was able to release many persons while improving on sales. This reduction of personnel lowered wage costs.

   The company has separate divisions to provide a degree of specialization among its various functions. Each unit has its own head, which preserves the concept of unity of command.

   The primary weakness is in leadership. The sales manager is used to working in a smaller company where complexity was only a word in a dictionary. He fails to understand the need to provide leadership and make the painful decision to take hold of Chris Cunningham. Elizabeth Stover, while concerned about Cunningham, should not have to be involved in his supervision.
3. Where should the line be drawn between organizational control over personal initiative and the contribution of personal initiative to organizational effectiveness?

   While the line may have fuzzy edges, it should be at that point where an individual's personal needs are interfering with the attainment of overall organizational objectives. In this case, Cunningham's creativity could be redirected to help other members of the sales force push themselves harder. The sales manager, Bill Johnson, may need to be replaced with someone capable of providing leadership for Cunningham and the others. In this instance, Cunningham needs referent leadership to give him a point of identity and a vision of his future in the company.
4. What should Stover do to deal with each of the variety of problems raised by this case?

   With respect to Bill Johnson's lack of leadership, she should sit down with him in a MBO style of communication and work out a plan for him to take charge, identify what must be done, and set a time for accomplishment. His progress should be monitored. If Johnson is successful, most of Stover's problems with Cunningham will be resolved. In the event Johnson cannot act in a forceful manner, he needs to be replaced.

   Elizabeth Stover needs to work with her production director to help him/her understand that persons in sales can make requests but that the production plan is to be followed. If there are difficulties in getting the job done, the line of communication needs to be followed to get the matter resolved.

   Elizabeth Stover needs to look at the broader picture of managing a larger company. While she has combined several companies, her management style remains entrepreneurial "hands on," and she is not building a leadership team. She probably needs to attend some seminars designed for managers of growing businesses.

THE CONSOLIDATED LIFE CASE: CAUGHT BETWEEN CORPORATE CULTURES

1. How has the culture at Consolidated Life changed during Mike's absence?

The culture shifted from one of openness and a willingness to cooperate to one of oppression by a new divisional vice president, Jack Greely. People now wait to be told what to do, and initiative is looked upon by Greely as a challenge to his managerial authority.

2. Was sending the memo a good idea? What effects did it have? Why were some of them unforeseen?

Hindsight indicates that sending the memorandum was not a good idea. Mike, however, was operating on the assumption that the company still welcomed ideas designed to improve its effectiveness. The company probably has not changed in that respect, but Jack Greely has interposed himself between the company and the people in his division. Rick Belkner should have given Mike a clue, but Rick was known to reflect the strongest person around him. He therefore would have sensed a personal threat if he had talked to Mike about the "new" culture in the division. The memorandum, in addition to disturbing Greely, brought about the demoralization of the group who now saw no opportunity to restore morale and productivity to the department. The mistakes in the memorandum, however, were slow to emerge since Jack Greely waited for a mistake to occur that could be blamed on Mike. In this way, the error was the target rather than the memorandum. Thus Jack Greely could maintain his base of power without letting the issue with the group be drawn to the attention of persons higher in the organization.

3. Why is Mike now regarded as a thorn in the side rather than a "superstar"? What, if anything, can he do to change that perception?

Jack Greely has the division under his control. The return of Mike injected a free spirit that imbued the others with courage to try to restore the unit to its former state. Thus, Mike was seen as a threat—a thorn in the side. Mike can do little to change Jack's perception, since once a person is considered to be on the "outs" it is very difficult to be an "in" person again. He should arrange a meeting with Greely to find out if he has a future in the company or the division. He is young enough to make a fresh start, but should certainly learn if the company has a future for him.

4. What advice do you have for Mike?

Mike needs to polish his résumé. This should be done prior to arranging a meeting with Jack Greely. Mike needs to base his interview from a position of strength. If he has any future with the company, it would most likely come from the exit interview when he would be able to expose the oppressive leadership problem in a division where he formerly was an outstanding success.

CHAPTER 14
Motivation, Performance, and Satisfaction

Chapter Outline

THE IMPORTANCE OF MOTIVATION

EARLY VIEWS OF MOTIVATION IN ORGANIZATIONS

The Traditional Model
The Human Relations Model
The Human Resources Model

THREE TYPES OF MOTIVATION THEORIES

Content Theories
Process Theories
Reinforcement Theories

A SYSTEMS VIEW OF MOTIVATION IN ORGANIZATIONS

Characteristics of the Individual
The Hierarchy of Human Needs
ERG Theory
The Urge to Achieve and Entrepreneurial Behavior
Characteristics of the Job Task
A Two-Factor Approach to Work Motivation
Characteristics of the Work Situation
Organizational Policies, Reward Systems, and Culture
The Immediate Work Environment
Change in Work-Situation Variables

THE IMPACT OF PAST CONSEQUENCES ON BEHAVIOR

Behavior Modification

INTEGRATIVE APPROACHES TO MOTIVATION

The Expectancy Approach
Expectations, Outcomes, and Work Behavior
Implications for Managers
Implications for Organizations
The Equity or Inequity Approach
Goal-Setting Theory

GUIDELINES FOR EFFECTIVE MOTIVATION

SUMMARY

Key Terms

- **motivation** The factors that cause, channel, and sustain an individual's behavior.
- **role perception** The individual's understanding of the behaviors needed to accomplish a task or perform a job.
- **behavior modification** An approach to motivation based on the "law of effect": behavior that leads to rewarding consequences tends to be repeated, and behavior with negative consequences tends not to be repeated. Thus, managers can change behavior by changing the consequences of that behavior.
- **expectancy approach** A model of motivation specifying that the effort to achieve high performance is a function of the perceived likelihood that high performance can be achieved and will be rewarded if achieved, and that the reward will be worth the effort expended.
- **valence** The value of motivating strength of a reward to the individual.
- **equity theory** A theory of job motivation emphasizing the role played by an individual's belief in the equity or fairness of rewards and punishments in determining his or her performance and satisfaction. Also called inequity theory.
- **goal-setting theory** A cognitive approach to the theory of work motivation which holds that workers are conscious (cognitive) creatures who strive toward goals.

Chapter Overview/Synopsis

Motivation is what causes people to accomplish objectives. Motivation can be implicit, residing within the individual, or explicit, applied from without the individual. Effective managers channel human motivation toward the attainment of the organization's goals. People have both "can-do" and "will-do" capabilities. What a person can do is based on such factors as genes, acquired skills, and education; what a person will do stems from motivational factors. For instance, to carry out a command requires (a) that the command be capable of execution—the person has both the skill and organizational resources necessary, and (b) that the command be both understood and accepted. A person can understood what is wanted, but for a number of reasons he fails to perform (does not accept the order).

A variety of motivation theories exist. These theories may be content-, process-, or reinforcement-oriented. Content stresses the relevance of satisfying human needs as a means of achieving motivation, process emphasizes the kinds of goals and rewards that motivate people, and reinforcement theories deal with rewards and punishments so that people tend to repeat actions that result in rewards and avoid ones that cause punishment. The contributions of such individuals as McGregor, Maslow, and Herzberg are examined to further illustrate the subject of motivation.

The work situation and managerial actions bear on the degree to which employees feel motivated to achieve organizational goals. In many ways, managers seek to modify employee behavior to undertake an assignment and follow it through to its successful completion. The behavior modification approaches include the expectancy theory and the equity theory. Much work remains to be done to help managers obtain optimal results from applying the appropriate theory of motivation.

Analysis of Illustrative Case Study

INTRODUCTION—CREATING A COMMITTED WORK FORCE AT DOMINO'S PIZZA

A person who feels trusted tries to avoid behaviors that would betray such trust. Domino's display of confidence toward its employees is backed with a reward system the employees appreciate. The human relations approach couple with a business strategy of a limited menu, guaranteed delivery within 30 minutes, and a tasty product became a recipe for success for Domino's Pizza. While success has been punctuated by ups and downs of the business, maintaining the key philosophy regarding the product and the employee treatment paid off. While Domino's extrinsic reward system contributes to employee motivation, the company strives to hire persons intrinsically motivated.

CONTINUED—CREATING A COMMITTED WORK FORCE AT DOMINO'S PIZZA

Domino's operates on a theory of rewarding employees for desirable results—a modification of Alderfer's model of work motivation. The reward system is designed to contribute to the material wealth of employees; in addition, trips to the Indy 500 provide extra rewards that strengthen the motivational methods of the company. A reward system needs to have a degree of consistency. Domino's approach to its human resources helps employees develop a sense of belonging—to feel they are important parts of a company environment and culture. This feeling of "family" yields a sense of continuity that binds employees to the company and the company to them.

WRAP-UP—CREATING A COMMITTED WORK FORCE AT DOMINO'S PIZZA

Regardless of worker motivation, customers are key to Domino's continued success. In addition to perceiving a good product, customers want to feel that Domino's employees portray a sense of pride in the product. Such a sense carries over to customers. Therefore, in the final analysis the attention the company renders to motivating its employees is critical. Another major factor contributing to Domino's success is growth of the company. To this end, employees who wish to become managers are accorded that opportunity.

Answers to End-of-Chapter Review Questions

1. What is motivation, and why is it important? What other factors influence a person's performance?

   By definition, motivation consists of the factors that cause, channel and sustain an individual's behavior. Motivation alone does not bring high performance; also necessary are ability, understanding, and acceptance of what is wanted.

2. How have views of motivation in organizations evolved? How might each view affect the ways in which managers behave toward subordinates?

   Views regarding motivation have paralleled organizational theory. Under autocratic management, workers were considered "hired hands" to do what they were told. Motivation could be translated to "do it my way or hit the highway." The extrinsic reward was money. Under the human relations model, managers made efforts to understand workers as human beings with values and attitudes. Group norms were considered important since people like to be part of a group. Some critics of the human relations model contended it was only a fancier way than the traditional management theories to manipulate employees. Thus, the human resources model was suggested as a way to explain that motivation resulted from a combination of many factors. The end result was an advocacy of participative management.

3. What are Theory X and Theory Y? How might each theory be more applicable in different circumstances?

Theory X holds workers to be lazy and to consider work as only being necessary for survival. Theory X workers prefer to be directed and to avoid shouldering responsibility for goal accomplishment. Theory Y, on the other hand, considers that people consider work as normal as relaxation and play. People seek responsibility and strive to be part of activities that draw upon their ingenuity and imagination. Theory X has application under conditions where time for job performance is critical and employees are relatively unskilled. Theory X is best used in the short-run because of long-term destructiveness of the human sense of worth. It also requires that a supervisor be present. Theory Y has long-run benefits because it builds people and does not depend on continuous presence of a supervisor. Under Theory Y people tend to be "self-starters."

4. According to content theories, what motivates people? What theorists advocated this approach? Why are content theories difficult to apply?

People are motivated to fill their needs. These needs are in an ascending scale so that as one is fulfilled, another takes its place. Even at the zenith of needs, self-actualization, people find there are higher orders to be sought. The content theory is difficult to apply for a number of reasons. (a) A need for one person is not the same need for another, (b) ways of satisfying needs vary among people, (c) the need that motivates a person one time may not be as attractive under another condition, and (d) people react differently to how a need is presented to them.

5. What aspects of motivation do process theories emphasize? How do process theories relate the concepts of expectancy and valence to motivation?

Process theories view needs as only one element of motivation. Other aspects include the way people perceive their needs and the kinds of rewards they might receive for certain behaviors. The expectancy model comprises a person's expectation that a given reward will be received for a given behavior, and a valence (preference) for that outcome. Thus if a person has low valence but a high expectation, motivation is low because the person has no desire to receive the outcome.

6. How do reinforcement theories explain behavior? To what extent does the process of learning play a part in reinforcement theories?

Reinforcement theory, also called behavior modification, depends on rewarding desirable behaviors and not offering reinforcement of unwanted behaviors. People learn to avoid behaviors that do not result in pleasant outcomes.

7. In the systems perspective, what three variables affect motivation in the workplace?

(a) Each individual's characteristics such as interests, attitudes, and needs; (b) job characteristics such as tasks, responsibility, variety, and elements that bring satisfaction, and (c) work situation characteristics such as recognition from peers, a sense of belonging, and a culture that fosters concern for members of the organization.

8. How is Maslow's hierarchy of needs related to motivation in organizations?

Maslow feels people are motivated to fulfill whatever need is the most powerful at the time. It is said, "a fish discovers water last." Thus a worker with a strong sense of job security would not be particularly concerned about behavior directed at job security; but under conditions where employees face loss of jobs, behaviors would most likely be directed toward maintaining employment.

9. According to Atkinson, what determines the strength of an individual's motivation drive? How did McClelland relate Atkinson's work to management? What are the implications of his findings for managers?

Motivation stems from (a) the intensity of the basic need involved, (b) the person's expectation of succeeding, and (c) the incentive value the person attaches to the goal. McClelland related Atkinson's ideas to business drive or the need for achievement found in successful managers. From the standpoint of management, it is important that people be matched to their jobs for the mix of motivational drives to do their work. Managers can also arrange the work environment to foster a measure of independence, as well as increasing responsibility and autonomy, and making the tasks more challenging. Feedback on performance, coupled with praise and reward, also contribute to employee motivation.

10. What is Herzberg's two-factor approach to job satisfaction and dissatisfaction? Why has the approach been criticized?

Herzberg identified factors that lead to satisfaction (motivational factors) and ones that lead to dissatisfaction (hygiene factors). Satisfiers included achievement, recognition, responsibility, and advancement and stem from job content coupled with reward. Dissatisfiers included salary, working condition, company policy, and the relationship of the employee to the work environment.

The following represent criticisms of Herzberg's theory: People credit themselves for success and blame others for their failures. People tend to rate components of their jobs on a sliding scale, but Herzberg's model is limited to either satisfaction or dissatisfaction. The two-factor model does not allow for variables that change with people and job conditions. Herzberg did not include productivity as an element.

11. How may an organization's culture and its personnel and reward policies affect motivation?

Organizational culture, the system of shared norms, values, and beliefs, can enhance or diminish a person's job performance. A major element in whether culture heightens or lessens accomplishment depends on how well an employee's personality meshes with that of the organization. Thus an imaginative and free spirited individual would most likely be dissatisfied working in a conservative organization.

12. Why is behavior modification controversial? What do you think of behavior modification techniques?

Behavior modification is based on the belief that the consequence of an individual's behavior in one situation can influence that individual's behavior pattern in similar future situation. Thus behavior is learned, and people tend to repeat behaviors they find rewarding and avoid ones that bring forth unwanted consequences. Behavior modification is expressed as follows:

Stimulus → Response → Consequences → Future Response

Student response regarding their opinion should include at least the idea that rewards and punishments exist in the eye of the beholder. The result is that what managers perceive to be a reward might be considered by others as something to avoid. In effect, there are rewarding punishments as well as punishments viewed as rewards. Consider the child who is sent to the principal's office for misbehaving in the classroom who considers it rewarding to be sent from the "punishment" of being in the room with the teacher.

13. Upon what assumptions is the expectancy approach based?

a. Behavior is determined by a combination of forces in the individual and environment.
b. Individuals make conscious decisions about their own behavior in organizations.
c. Individuals have different needs, desires, and goals.
d. Individuals decide among alternative behaviors based on their expectation that a given behavior will lead to a desired outcome.

14. Define performance-outcome expectancy, valence, and effort-performance expectancy. How do they affect a worker's level of performance?

(a) Individuals expect (anticipate) a certain outcome from engaging in a given activity. (b) Valence (preference or desire for the outcome) controls the intensity of a person's effort to achieve a given outcome. (c) The combination of expectancy and valence determines a person's motivation: $M = E \cdot V$. A person with both a high preference for an outcome and an expectation that "it can happen to me" would be considered a motivated individual.

15. What does equity theory suggest about the motivation, performance, and satisfaction of individuals in the organization?

Equity theory arises from a belief that a major factor in job motivation, performance, and satisfaction arises from the individual's sense of fairness or equity regarding rewards and punishments received. A major element in this theory is the subjectivity of the employee. The implication for managers, therefore, is that not only should a reward or punishment be fair but that it must appear to be fair.

Answers to End-of Chapter Case Questions

CASE: IDEALISM, MOTIVATION, AND COMMUNITY SERVICE AT THE CENTER CITY YWCA

1. What are the major problems facing Harriet Bowen?

—The organization's community image needs to be assessed.
—The YWCA programs need to be compared to the community assessment.
—An apparent lack of community involvement in the operation of the organization would be supplied by an advisory group.
—The staff does not appear to be participating in developing the operational structure of the organization.
—Bowen faces a problem in enlisting support from key staff persons who feel the recruiting policies are unfair.
—There is a perspective problem of developing an organizational culture that can be adopted by the employees so that the YWCA becomes a dynamic place offering a variety of challenges to its staff.

2. If you were Herzberg, how would you advise Harriet Bowen to manage the YWCA?

Concentrate on identifying the satisfiers, those elements of the job such as achievement, recognition, responsibility, involvement, and advancement. Help the staff associate their individual interests with job satisfiers. Further assist the staff in seeing the content of their respective jobs as simply a means to bring satisfaction to the clients of the YWCA. Seek commitment from the staff in examining the operational policies of the YW for the purpose of improving the way the organization functions.

3. What would Nadler and Lawler tell Harriet Bowen to assist her in leading her staff?

   The staff's motivation depends on their subjective assessment of what kinds of rewards they expect from their behaviors and their desire or preference to receive such rewards. That is, be certain that what is offered as rewards is perceived as rewards by the staff. Since money is short and wages are frozen, the rewards will have to be intrinsic.

4. How might reinforcement theory apply to this case?

   Reinforcement theory can begin at the time Harriet Bowen calls her staff together and discusses the organization. She can enlist their participation and indicate approval for the positive comments. She should avoid indicating disapproval of ideas she does not like since negative reinforcement is to be avoided. Thus, she needs to concentrate on having the staff react to behaviors they want to repeat.

Suggested Term Paper Topics

1. A cross-cultural analysis of motivational theories
2. Motivational methods for use with volunteer workers
3. Motivating non-career person in minimum wage jobs
4. A review of the expectancy model as contrasted with behavior modification
5. Motivational theory applied to workers on assembly lines
6. Human inconsistency and motivational theories
7. Job design factors and motivation
8. Problems associated with motivating workers, such as civil servants or professors with tenure, who have a high level of job security
9. Situational factors of motivational theories

Suggested Guest Speakers

1. A manager of a fast-food business to discuss ways used to motivate employees. (Keep in mind the Domino's Pizza case that was part of this chapter).
2. The director of human resources from a major employer in the area to discuss ways and means used in the company to develop managers to improve their motivational skills.
3. A panel made up of several students from the class to compare their job experiences regarding the kinds of motivational efforts they find positive and ones that achieve negative results.

CHAPTER 15
Leadership

Chapter Outline

DEFINING LEADERSHIP

THEORIES OF LEADERSHIP

The Trait Approach to Leadership
The Behavioral Approach to Leadership
Leadership Functions and Styles
Influences on Choice of Leadership Style
The Ohio State and University of Michigan Studies
The Managerial Grid
Contingency Approaches to Leadership
Situational Factors in Leadership Effectiveness
Theoretical Perspectives on the Contingency Approach to Leadership
Hersey and Blanchard's Situational Model
Leadership Style and the Work Situation: The Fiedler Model
A Path-Goal Approach to Leadership
Deciding When to Involve Subordinates: The Vroom-Yetton and Vroom-Jago Models

THE FUTURE OF LEADERSHIP THEORY

Transformational or Charismatic Leadership
Is Leadership Really Necessary?
Self-Managed Groups and Self-Leadership

SUMMARY

Key Terms

- **leadership** The process of directing and inspiring workers to perform task-related activities of the group.
- **power** The ability to exert influence; that is, the ability to change the attitudes or behavior of individuals or groups.
- **influence** Any actions or examples of behavior that cause a change in attitude or behavior of another person or group.
- **reward power** The perceived ability to provide people with the things they would like to have.
- **coercive power** The negative side of reward power, based on the influencer's ability to punish the influencee.
- **legitimate power** Power rooted in the general understanding that specified individuals or groups have the right to exert influence within certain limits by virtue of their position within the organization.
- **referent power** Power based on the desire of the influencee to be like or to identify with the influencer.
- **expert power** Power based on the belief or understanding that the influencer has specific knowledge or relevant expertise that the influencee does not.
- **leadership functions** The group-maintenance and task-related activities that must be performed by the leader, or someone else, for a group to perform effectively.
- **leadership styles** The various patterns of behavior favored by leaders during the process of directing and influencing workers.
- **contingency approach** The view that the management technique that best contributes to the attainment of organizational goals might vary in different types of situations or circumstances.
- **situational leadership theory** An approach to leadership developed by Paul Hersey and Kenneth H. Blanchard that describes how leaders should adjust their leadership style in response to their subordinates' evolving desire for achievement, experience, ability, and willingness to accept responsibility.
- **leader-member relations** The quality of the interaction between a leader and his or her subordinates; according to Fred Fiedler, the most important influence on the manager's power.
- **task structure** A work situation variable that, according to Fred Fiedler, helps determine a manager's power. In structured tasks, managers automatically have high power; in unstructured tasks, the manager's power is diminished.
- **position power** The power, according to Fred Fiedler, that is inherent in the formal position the leader holds. This power may be great or small, depending upon the specific position.
- **path-goal model** A leadership theory emphasizing the leader's role in clarifying for subordinates how they can achieve high performance and its associated rewards.
- **charismatic or transformational leaders** Leaders who, through their personal vision and energy, inspire followers and have a major impact on their organizations.
- **transactional leaders** Leaders who determine what subordinates need to do to achieve objectives, who classify those requirements, and who help subordinates become confident that they can reach their objectives.
- **self-managed work groups** Work teams organized around a particular task and composed of members who possess both the skill necessary to accomplish the task and the power to determine such factors as method operation, assignment of responsibilities, and creation of work schedules.

- **self-leadership** The ability of workers to motivate themselves to perform both tasks that are naturally rewarding and those that are necessary but not appealing.

Chapter Overview/Synopsis

Leadership is a process of influencing and directing group members to accomplish task-related activities. Three approaches to leadership are considered: trait, behavior, and contingency. The trait approach, while not particularly useful because it yields inconsistent results, concentrates on such human traits as honesty, enthusiasm, loyalty, and perseverance. Behavioral leadership focuses on leadership functions and styles. Leadership styles have been further categorized into work-centered styles that include autocratic and bureaucratic styles, and people-centered styles that include initiative and democratic styles. Some students of leadership note the importance of the situation since the style needed for a given circumstance depends on the situation.

Considerable emphasis has been given to the study of situational leadership since research identifies the following as being important determinants of effective leadership: the leaders' personality and past experience; the expectations and behavior of superiors; the characteristics, expectations, and behavior of subordinates; job demands; the organization's culture; and the expectations and behavior of peers.

Attempts to identify the best explanation of leadership have surfaced in such theories as the contingency approach, the path-goal approach, and a variety of circumstances that require different kinds of leadership. Contingency leadership attempts to identify the situational factors that provide the most consistent results. The path-goal model focuses on the abilities of managers to dispense rewards and the perceptions employees have of what they must do to earn a reward. Still other research in leadership undertakes the analysis of permitting workers to manage themselves.

Analysis of Illustrative Case Study

INTRODUCTION—NEW LEADERSHIP POLICIES AT GE

Jack Welch assumed the position of CEO at General Electric at a time when most of American industry was feeling the stress from external competition. Managements generally felt the cure had to be increased productivity from fewer resources. Welch approached his job by focusing on the internal management structure composed of many layers of bureaucrats, and upon the work force constrained by work rules. His immediate goal was to eliminate the unnecessary layers of management and to trim the number of employees.

Leadership most generally is considered as positive guidence that inspires and directs employees to accomplish tasks. Welch identified one of his tasks as restructuring the company—his managers had difficulty being inspired to preside over a series of "funerals" involving their associates. Yet his managers had no alternative but to help install a new competitive culture at General Electric. Whether employees and unions of GE like Jack Welch is not the real issue. The main question is the kind of organization that will emerge as a result of his leadership. Some use an analogy of trimming trees to make them stronger. The branches initially removed appear to leave unsightly gaps, but the new growth provides vigorous strength.

CONTINUED—NEW LEADERSHIP POLICIES AT GE

Organizational change that cuts deep into the levels of management and the number of employees faces considerable criticism within and without the organization. Jack Welch steeled himself to this because his vision of the emerging General Electric Company had yet to be grasped by many of his critics. Yet he cannot bring about the needed changes himself. Thus his leadership style, of necessity, must obtain support within the organization. While Welch has adopted the Blake and Mouton model dealing with the way managers demonstrate their concern for tasks and demonstrate their concern for people, his critics contend that his focus remains on tasks and not on people. The implementation of the Blake and Mouton model will require employee perception that people are a significant part of the future of General Electric.

WRAP-UP—NEW LEADERSHIP POLICIES AT GE

The shift from a bureaucratic style of conservatism to one of undertaking risks unsettled many managers at General Electric. Jack Welch approached the task of CEO with enthusiasm and undertook many of his changes almost concurrently. The acid test of leadership at General Electric will be productivity. Many managers and workers approve of the changes being made since they perceive the reward system as tailored to benefit persons who produce results.

Answers to End-of-Chapter Review Questions

1. How is leadership defined in this chapter? Discuss three implications of this definition.

   Leadership is the process of directing and inspiring workers to perform the task-related activities of the group. First, leadership involves people—those who lead and those who follow. Second, leadership can occur only when there is an uneven distribution of power between superiors and subordinates. Third, the act of leadership also influences subordinates in a variety of psychological and sociological ways since they must react to the kind of leadership provided.

2. Why was the trait approach a logical attempt to understand leadership? What two approaches did the trait researchers take? What did the leadership trait studies reveal?

   A strong belief persisted that leaders were born, not made. Therefore, it was logical to seek to identify traits possessed by born leaders. The first approach to studying traits as evidence of leadership compared traits of persons acknowledged to be leaders with traits of persons not considered to be leaders. The second approach compared traits of persons in leadership roles who were considered to be successful with leaders considered unsuccessful. Such studies have failed to identify a common set of leadership traits.

3. Describe the two basic leadership functions needed for effective group performance. Must the leader perform both these functions?

   The first function is task-related or problem solving. The second function is group-maintenance or social. Studies indicate that the most effective groups have shared leadership where one person performs the task function while another member of the group performs the social functions. Research also indicates that a person able to perform both roles has a better likelihood of being a successful leader.

4. Outline the basic idea of the Tannenbaum and Schmidt model. What factors should influence a manager's style, according to Tannenbaum and Schmidt? What practical considerations do they suggest managers take into account in selecting a style?

   Tannenbaum and Schmidt felt a variety of factors influenced leadership style. Three forces had to be considered: those in the manager, those in the subordinate, and those of the situation. The factors that influence a manager's style include the style favored by the organization's upper management. The work group also affects the choice of style. Further, the characteristics of subordinates influence the choice of management style. These include the desire for independence, the desire to make decisions, the need to identify with the organization, the extent of job knowledge, and the experiences with previous managers.

5. What are the two basic leadership styles identified by the Ohio State and University of Michigan studies? Which style was thought to be more effective?

   The studies indicated two basic styles: production-oriented, and people-oriented. The Michigan studies noted that employee-centered managers consistently achieved higher production. Also, employee turnover and grievances were lower. The Ohio State studies indicated the work situation to be significant. Thus employees of a military-type organization expected direct leadership and felt employee-centered leadership an interference with taking action. Overall, however, employees work best in a participative type of environment where their opinions count.

6. What is the "situational leadership theory"? How should the manager's style vary in each of the four phases?

   Situational leadership describes how leaders should adjust their leadership styles in response to their subordinates' desires for achievement, experience, ability, and willingness to accept responsibility. Hersey and Blanchard believed the relationship between a manager and subordinates moved through a four-phase life cycle: high task orientation during an employee's early days on the job, a second phase in which an employee is trusted to make some decisions without prior approval, a third phase when the subordinates' ability and achievement permit the assignment of greater responsibilities, and a final phase when subordinates can be placed on their own.

7. Outline the basic theory of the Managerial Grid. Which leadership style in the grid do Blake and Mouton feel is most effective?

   The Managerial Grid combines two factors to identify leadership style: the way a manager evidences concern for getting work done, and the way a manager evidences concern for people. These concerns are placed in a matrix numbered from 1 through 9 for each ascending level of concern, with the first concern identified with that of work. Thus a 9,1 manager has a high concern for work and a low concern for people needs; a 1,9 manager has low concern for the job but a high concern for people; a 1,1 manager has a low level of concern for both job and employees; and a 9,9 manager has a high concern for getting work done and satisfying the needs of the people. Blake and Mouton feel the 9,9 style to be the most effective.

8. What basic assumptions underlie the Fiedler model? What is the LPC scale? What basic elements in the

work situation determine which leadership style will be most effective? In what situations is a high-LPC leader effective? In what situations is a low-LPC leader effective?

Fiedler assumes that most managers are fairly set in their ways and that attempting to train them to another management style is not especially productive. Fiedler advocates selecting managers best fitted to manage a given type of situation. Thus, authoritarian managers are placed in roles where that leadership is expected. Leaders of other persuasions would also be placed in situations that would correspond best to their respective styles. Managers are identified in terms of the coworker they would work with least well (LPC). A high-LPC works best in situations where warm-hearted leadership is expected. A low-LPC manager works best in situations where direct action is needed and a warm, close relationship with workers is not considered essential.

9. Describe the path-goal model. On what theory of motivation is the model based? According to this model, how do managers with different leadership styles differ in their ability to influence or reward subordinates? What variables, according to this theory, help determine the most effective leadership style? Why?

The path-goal model is a leadership theory emphasizing the leader's role in clarifying for subordinates how they can achieve high performance and its associated rewards. The path-goal approach is based on the expectancy model, which states that an individual's motivation depends on the expectation for a reward to happen, and a preference for it "to happen to me." A manager's individual style of leadership determines, to a large extent, how the path-goal will be described. An authoritarian manager, for instance, will provide a narrow concept of the path and make it clear that instructions are to be followed. Subordinates tend to gravitate to the leadership style they feel will most likely provide desired rewards.

10. What are the five styles of managerial decision-making suggested by Vroom and Yetton? What are the most important modifications made by Vroom and Jago in the Vroom-Yetton model of leadership?

Vroom and Yetton isolated five styles of leadership to represent a continuum from authoritiarian (AI, AII) to consultative (CI, CII) to a fully participative one (GII). Under AI, managers solve the problems and make decisions themselves. Under AII, managers obtain necessary information from subordinates and decide on the solution themselves. Under CI, managers share the problem with subordinates individually. Under GII managers share the problem with subordinates as a group, involve the subordinates in creating the alternatives for solution, and attempt to reach a consensus on the solution. Vroom and Jago extended the theory to include questioning both the quality and commitment to making decisions. To do this they ask managers to question if they have sufficient information or skill to solve a problem as well as what ways to follow in seeking group participation. They are also concerned whether the problem is structured and to what extent group acceptance of the solution is critical for success.

Answers to End-of-Chapter Case Questions

CASE: THREE MANAGERIAL DECISIONS

1. After reading the three situations and before analyzing them, decide which of the decision-making style alternatives (AI, AII, CI, CII, GII) you would personally prefer to use in making each decision. Then answer the remaining questions.

A stimulating way to address this question of choosing a managerial style would be to refer students to the Acumen™ Educational Version supplement. Students should then discuss the meaning of rule-centered management and people-centered management.

2. Which is more important in the situation, quality or acceptance of the decision?

Electronics plant: Every indication in the case points to the people not wanting to make the robots effective. The quality of the decision cannot be negated, but worker involvement in solving the production problem is essential. *Slurry pipeline:* Quality of the decision is most important. Acceptance of the decision is not a major factor since the decision involves setting times to receive materials at the next site. *Overseas assignment:* Acceptance is more critical than quality since each engineer is said to be qualified to handle the assignment.

3. How critical is time in making a decision?

Electronics plant: Time is money. The undesirable costs are revealed in not obtaining the expected increase in production, in lowered morale as it affects plant operations, and in increased labor turnover. *Slurry pipeline:* Materials must be at the next construction site, thus time is critical. *Overseas assignment:* Time can be subordinated to obtaining employee acceptance of the assignment—up to a point. An engineer is needed overseas, and a week's delay might not be overly critical.

4. Does the manager have the information necessary to make the decision?

Electronics plant: No, the supervisor needs to talk with people in the shop to learn their feelings and how they would react to various possible solutions to obtain the desired production. *Slurry pipeline:* Yes, a supervisor would have information about the variables and should have no difficulty providing the needed information.

Overseas assignments: No, following an announcement of the need, a series of individual discussions should be made to help find a ''volunteer.''

5. Is the decision-making situation highly structured?

   Electronics plant: The plant supervisor left the decision process up to the supervisor, asking only to be informed within a week what steps were planned. *Slurry pipeline:* Yes, the decision process is quantitative and leaves little room for the heuristic trial-and-error approach. *Overseas assignment:* No, the supervisor is free to follow any course of action as long as a decision about assigning a person to the overseas location is made within a reasonable time period.

6. Choose the best decision-making style (AI, AII, CI, CII, GII) and give the reason for your choice.

   Electronics plant: The approaches of CI, CII, and GII have possibilities depending on the value system of the students involved. It appears, however, that whatever decision is made, a follow-up must be possible to ensure that control exists. The need for control rules out the democratic approach (GII) of adopting a group's preferred solution. This leaves CI and CII as the remaining choices. Either can be argued effectively. Since there is a morale problem, the AI and AII approaches have elements of secretiveness that will only worsen the morale problem. *Slurry pipeline:* CII has a good possiblity since it keeps the group informed of what is happening and still permits the decision to be made in a timely fashion. Approaches AI and AII can be used, but in a small group situation a one-alone, decision-making stance can place communication distance between people who ought to be working together. *Overseas assignments:* GII has to be eliminated since it permits the group's preferred solution to prevail. If the location is undesirable, the group's preference will be to ''stay put.'' The other alternatives of AI, AII, CI, or CII could be placed into a supervisor's value system. To the extent that CI and CII can be combined, this offers possibilities since the group can meet together to discuss the situation, followed by individual meetings. Following this an assignment can be made, quite probably to the person who really would like a taste of adventure.

7. Did your choice of the ''best'' style in question 6 differ from the style you would personally have chosen in question 1? If so, why do you think they differed?

   Each student's style of managing should be fairly explicit by now. The main thing to examine is consistency in reasoning.

Suggested Term Paper Topics

1. Forms of leadership theories contrasted with forms of authority theories
2. Self-managed work groups
3. An analysis of why the possession traits generally considered to be desirable does not assure success as a leader
4. The nature of leadership in turbulent organizations contrasted with leadership in stable organizations.
5. The Managerial Grid as an instrument for management development
6. Immediate and long-term effects of production-centered managers
7. A review of the Fiedler model of leadership
8. Leadership strategies to attain goal congruence when group consensus does not exist
9. Fitting a ''Theory X'' leader into a ''Theory Y'' organization

Suggested Guest Speakers

1. A theologian to discuss ''leadership, ethics, and morality.''
2. A director of human resources from a major corporation to discuss how his/her firm conducts management development programs.
3. A labor leader to discuss what workers expect in the way of leadership from their immediate supervisors.

CHAPTER 16
Groups and Committees

Chapter Outline

TYPES OF GROUPS

Formal Groups
Informal Groups

CHARACTERISTICS OF GROUPS IN ORGANIZATIONS

Informal Leadership
Group Norms and Conformity
Group Cohesiveness

PROBLEM SOLVING IN GROUPS

Advantages and Disadvantages of Group Problem Solving
Key Factors in Group Decision Making: Assets or Liabilities

TASK FORCES AND COMMITTEES

Types of Formal Working Groups
- Task Forces
- Standing Committees
- Boards and Commissions

Key Differences between Task Forces and Committees
Advantages and Disadvantages of Committees and Task Forces

MAKING FORMAL GROUPS EFFECTIVE

Committee Problem Solving
- Formal Procedures
- Guidelines for Leaders
- Guidelines for Members

Special Procedures for Task Forces
Conflict within Groups

SUMMARY

Key Terms

- **reference group** A group with whom individuals identify and compare themselves.
- **command group** A group composed of a manager and his or her subordinates who interact with each other toward a common objective.
- **permanent formal group** A long-term command group or permanent committee, such as a planning committee.
- **temporary formal group** A group formed for a specific purpose, such as a task force or project group, that is disbanded when its purpose is accomplished.
- **task role** The specific role within a group performed by the leader, whether formal or informal.
- **group building and maintenance role** The group leader's specific function to fulfill the group's social needs by encouraging solidarity feelings.
- **cohesiveness** The degree of solidarity and positive feelings held by individuals toward their group.
- **task interdependence** The extent to which a group's work requires its members to interact with each other.
- **sense of potency** Collective belief of a group that it can be effective.
- **outcome interdependence** The degree to which the work of a group has consequences felt by all its members.
- **task force** or **project team** A temporary group formed to address a specific problem.
- **committee** A formal organizational group, usually relatively long-lived, created to carry out specific organizational tasks.
- **board** A group made up of individuals appointed or elected to manage a public or private organization.
- **commission** A group whose members are usually appointed by government officials, charged with administrative, regulatory, or legislative tasks.
- **synergism** "A condition in which the whole is greater than the sum of its parts."

Chapter Overview/Synopsis

Groups, both formal and informal, exist in organizations. Formal groups are established by managerial action to accomplish a given purpose or set of ongoing purposes. Informal groups arise to fill communication gaps perceived by people with an organization. Membership in groups of all kinds satisfies human needs for such goals as recognition, status, power, and belonging. Group members are subjected to group norms regarding their respective behaviors.

Formal groups include ones with a variety of names: command groups, task forces, and committees. A command group, such as a board, most often serves in a policy-making capacity; a task force is established to carry out a single purpose and dissolves at the completion of its objectives; and a committee is established to fulfill an ongoing responsibility.

Groups are often used in problem-solving capacities since a variety of experience and perception can be directed at a problem. While the rate of deliberation is slower than that of a single individuals, group decisions are less likely to contain mistakes, and recommendations tend to have wider acceptance since groups most often represent a variety of constituencies in the organization. On the other hand, groups can be dominated and reach premature decisions when individuals abdicate their personal responsibility for exercising judgment.

An important management responsibility is to work with groups to achieve organizational objectives. Effective group management includes setting up regular meetings, forming guidelines to evaluate effectiveness, and using formal procedures to conduct the business of a group. While conflicts can emerge in groups, conflict can be a creative part of effective management.

Analysis of Illustrative Case Study

INTRODUCTION—THE TEAM TAURUS APPROACH TO MANAGEMENT AT FORD

Project management has been shown to contribute positive results when complex tasks are being undertaken. Some organizations use the term ''skunk works'' to denote the group working on the project since interdependence and high morale seem to go hand-in-hand. The group focuses on the entire product rather than on just pieces of it, even though the pieces have to be built and assembled one at a time. The Taurus approach is a recognition that people can accomplish more working together than they can working alone and in ignorance of what others are doing. Team management appears to have won an accepted place in the management of the Ford Motor Company.

CONTINUED—THE TEAM TAURUS APPROACH TO MANAGEMENT AT FORD

The Taurus project leader, Lew Veraldi, was able to build a coalition of managers and workers in the classical style of leadership: a group under no coercion that shared a common interest, following a leader in the quest of a goal determined by the leader. In this instance the goal was an automobile under the slogan ''being better than the best.'' The group accepted the challenge, and with the cooperation of a labor union were able to attain success for Ford and personal satisfaction for themselves.

WRAP-UP—THE TEAM TAURUS APPROACH TO MANAGEMENT AT FORD

A major shift in managing is not without problems. One occurred when many Taurus cars required major repairs. Whether the repairs were a design fault or were traced to production remains to be disclosed. In a group it is difficult to assign accountability for results since many people are involved in the process. A present danger is ''groupthink'' where each member gets ''sold'' on the idea and fails to exercise responsibility to ask questions that lead to enlightenment by the group. Nevertheless, participative approaches to management appear to have an established place at Ford.

Answers to End-of-Chapter Review Questions

1. What are the three basic groups in organizations? Which type of group do you think is most important? Why?

   The three basic groups are command (for management purposes), committees (to carry on recurrent activities), and informal (groups without formal ties to the organization's structure). The command group sets overall direction for an organization; without the command group the other groups could not exist.

2. What are reference groups? Why is it important for managers to be aware of them? Can you identify your own reference groups?

   Reference groups are ones to which individuals identify and compare themselves. Reference groups influence individual attitudes and behavior since people tend to model their performance to conform to what they perceive to be acceptable behavior of the reference group. Student identification of a reference group can be most revealing since students who aspire to be outstanding affiliates with other outstanding students, while ones who desire to "just get by" will find a group comprised of students having a similar mindset.

3. Why do you think informal groups emerge in organizations? What organizational needs do they serve? What member needs do they serve?

Informal groups bridge the information gap that exists between what the formal organization releases to its members and what the organizational members wish to know. Informal groups provide a place for the exchange of information and a place where a person feels secure. Informal groups help to maintain and to strengthen the norms and values held by their members, they provide members with social satisfaction, they provide a channel of communication for their members, and they provide an outlet for problem solving.

4. How do informal leaders emerge in informal and formal work groups?

Whereas a formal leader achieves that position through an established organizational mechanism and the identification can be immediate, informal leaders emerge gradually as groups work together. Such leaders may volunteer the best information or undertake the tasks shunned by other members. By whatever means, group acknowledgment of an informal leader occurs. The informal leader can, under various circumstances, become the group's challenge to a formal leader.

5. What are the two leadership roles of formal and informal group leaders?

Both formal and informal leaders play a task role in that the leader directs the group toward the completion of activities seen to be important to the group. In addition, group leaders also serve in the role of group building and maintenance. In this role they attempt to fulfill the group's social needs by encouraging feelings of solidarity.

6. How do group members try to enforce conformity?

Through time, groups tend to have a culture of their own where expectations of group members become known. Group behavior tends to follow the lines of conformity. When a member deviates from a norm or set of norms, pressures are directed toward the nonconformist to move toward the equilibrium point of the group. Pressure may include private discussions, reasoning, criticism, sarcasm, ridicule, and exclusion from group activities.

7. What is the relationship between group cohesiveness and group performance? How can group cohesiveness be increased?

The stronger the members' belief in the group's objectives, the more likely are they to work to help the group achieve its objectives. Witness the behavior of pickets as they attempt to keep "non-believers" from crossing the picket line and "taking our jobs." Group effectiveness through cohesiveness can be increased through (a) task interdependence which strives to get group members to interact with one another, (b) an increase in the sense of potency to enhance the collective belief that the group can be effective, and (c) outcome interdependence that helps group members believe that the outcome of the group effort will be felt by each and every one.

8. On what bases would a manager decide whether to use individual or group problem solving?

Two critical factors are time and knowledge. The amount of time available can determine whether a problem can be handled by a group. Also, the amount of expertise each person involved can bring to the problem has a bearing. Beyond these factors are such considerations as the culture of the organization, the expectations of the group, and other kinds of internal and external forces.

9. What are the possible advantages and disadvantages of group decision making and problem solving?

There are four basic advantages and disadvantages to groups being used in decision making and problem solving. Advantages include (a) groups can suggest more approaches to resolving an issue, (b) groups bring more skill and knowledge to an issue than an individual could, (c) the existence of a group enhances the acceptability of the solution, and (d) people who help make a decision have a better understanding of the decision and can relay that understanding to persons not part of the group. Disadvantages include (a) groups may make premature decisions by adopting the first reasonable-sounding suggestion, (b) groups tend to be dominated by assertive individuals regardless of whether they are part of the informal or formal structure, (c) members may choose sides and become committed to a course of action, and (d) a person may be committed to some other course of action than the one selected.

10. According to Shea and Guzzo, how can astute managers create effective groups?

(a) By task interdependence, which strives to get group numbers to interact with one another; (b) by increasing the sense of potency to enhance the collective belief that the group can be effective, and (c) by outcome interdependence that helps group members believe that the outcome of the group effort will be felt by each and every one.

11. What is a task force? What are the different types of committees and their functions?

A task force is formed to deal with a specific problem or task—it is a form of committee. Two other committee forms are standing committees, and boards and commissions. A standing committee is formed to monitor recurrent activities, such as one that reviews personnel recommendations. Boards and commissions are comprised of individuals with the responsibility to set policies for public or private organizations.

12. What are the advantages and disadvantages of task forces and committees?

Task forces generally include representatives from key units that will be affected by a recommendation. Task forces have a built-in life span since they cease to exist at the completion of their mission. One of their most important advantages is that group decisions have a better likelihood of successful implementation. Committees have specific advantages. One is improved coordination; another is that committees serve the function of giving ideas time to incubate; and a third is that committees help organizations avoid unwanted concentrations of power.

Committees, including task forces, have pitfalls. These may include domination by aggressive people; members with other agendas, resulting in divided attention and incomplete support to the committee's work; and politically based compromise decisions just to keep peace in the organization. There is also the danger of "groupthink" when individuals succumb to the tendency to yield uncritically to group judgments.

13. What formal procedures help make committees effective? How can committee leaders and members help make it effective?

—The committee's goals should be clearly defined, preferably in writing.
—The committee's authority should be specified.
—The optimum size of the committee should be determined.
—Ability should be the criteria for selecting a chairperson.
—Agendas should be distributed in advance of each meeting.
—Meetings should have starting and ending times.

14. What are the "paradoxes" of group life as seen by Smith and Berg? Why do they feel that intragroup conflict is inevitable and basically good?

A paradox is said to exist because rather than seeing conflicts as something to be resolved, Smith and Berg view conflict as an essential component of group life. The paradox is seen in the form of a question: How can conflict be viewed as an essential of life?

Smith and Berg note seven aspects of the paradox: identity, disclosure, trust, individuality, authority, regression, and creativity. In identity, people cluster with individuals of different skills in order to maintain their identity. The paradox of disclosure is that people will disclose as little of themselves as possible even though full disclosure would better ensure group success. The paradox of trust is that only through mutual trust can the group succeed. The paradox of individuality means that a group derives its strength from the collective vitality of its individual members. The paradox of regression stems from the idea that while individuals join groups to "become more," the group asks them to be less so that the group can be more. The paradox of creativity stems from the idea that while a group must change in order to be successful, change also means the destruction of existing ideas and norms.

Answers to End-of-Chapter Case Questions

CASE: THE NEW-PRODUCTS GROUP

1. Why is Karen's group having problems?

The group appears to be dysfunctional since it was established by a person on about the same organizational level as its members, which set the stage for a continuing power struggle. It would have been helpful to have the initial meeting called by a company officer who would have presided until the group named a chairperson. An alternative would be for the officer to call the meeting and introduce the chairperson—this gesture would have placed management's support on the selected person. Other factors contributing to the problem are that group norms are being dictated by an aggressive member who is advocating his personal value system. The end result is the group lacks cohesiveness. Even though a common goal has been established, the group has not been able to focus attention on what the organization needs, only on what will serve the personal egos of group members.

2. Can you use the Shea-Guzzo model to give Karen a better idea of why the group is dysfunctional?

The Shea-Guzzo model is built on a triad of task interdependence, the group's sense of potency, and outcome interdependence. This group is not interacting with one another—several members are pursuing individual agendas. Karen has not yet given the kind of direction to the group to focus member attention toward a common goal. So far the group seems to feel a greater sense of potency to control Karen than to make a difference for the organization. At the moment, group members appear to have no conception that there may be a price to pay for their lack of cooperation. Karen has not brought forth these kinds of leadership ideas by placing them on the agenda for the group's discussion.

3. What should Karen do now?

Time has run out for Karen to have the group develop a series of recommendations for tomorrow's finished report. What she needs to do is develop the report as she sees it and present it to the group for review. She should explain to the group that their time has been squandered in personal disagreements. A report is due, and unless they see some substantive problems with the recommendations, she needs their approval. A report must be provided tomorrow, and if not this one, what report do they want submitted? This approach will be drastic and certainly will get attention. At least this action will force the group to focus on a finished report despite any recriminations about her.

Suggested Term Paper Topics

1. Ways of setting meeting agendas that bring forth positive results
2. Techniques useful to committee chairpersons in redirecting group attention to the agenda when digressions occur
3. An analysis of decisions made under conditions when unanimity is required as opposed to decisions made under majority rule
4. Quality of work circles as a form of committee in the work place
5. The "care and feeding of informal committees" by formal management
6. An analysis of brainstorming and group problem solving
7. Approaches to shortening the time needed by committees to reach decisions
8. Ways of conducting committee audits to determine when and if a committee has outlived its usefulness
9. Ways of managing group conflict when group members "choose sides"

Suggested Guest Speakers

1. The person on the campus who often is the one selected to chair major committees to discuss how he/she achieves the goal established for the committee.
2. A person who is or has served as chairman of a board of directors to discuss how such a body conducts its business.
3. A person who frequently disagrees with the majority to discuss the importance of "minority reports." Most likely this person will be a member of a legislative or judicial body.

CHAPTER 17
Interpersonal and Organizational Communication

Chapter Outline

THE IMPORTANCE OF COMMUNICATION

INTERPERSONAL COMMUNICATION

The Communication Process
- Sender (Source)
- Encoding
- Message
- Channel
- Receiver
- Decoding
- Noise
- Feedback

One-Way and Two-Way Communication

BARRIERS TO EFFECTIVE COMMUNICATION
- Differing Perceptions
- Language Differences
- Noise
- Emotionality
- Inconsistent Verbal and Nonverbal Communication
- Distrust

Overcoming Barriers to Interpersonal Communication
- Overcoming Differing Perceptions
- Overcoming Differences in Language
- Overcoming Noise
- Overcoming Emotionality
- Overcoming Inconsistent Verbal and Nonverbal Communication
- Overcoming Distrust
- Redundancy

COMMUNICATION IN ORGANIZATIONS

Factors Influencing Organizational Communication
- Formal Channels of Communication
- Authority Structure
- Job Specialization
- Information Ownership

Communication Networks within the Organization

Vertical Communication
- Problems of Vertical Communication

Overcoming Organizational Barriers to Communication

Communication and Advanced Information Technology

Openness: A Double-Edged Sword

SUMMARY

Key Terms

- **communication** The process by which people attempt to share meaning via the transmission of symbolic messages.
- **sender** The initiator of communication.
- **encoding** The translation of information into a series of symbols for communication.
- **message** The encoded information sent by the sender to the receiver.
- **channel** The medium of communication between a sender and a receiver.
- **receiver** The individual whose senses perceive the sender's message.
- **decoding** The interpretation and translation of a message into meaningful information.
- **noise** Anything that confuses, disturbs, diminishes, or interferes with communication.
- **feedback (interpersonal)** The reversal of the communication process that occurs when the receiver expresses his or her reaction to the sender's message.
- **one-way communication** Any communication from the sender without feedback from the receiver.
- **two-way communication** Communication that occurs when the receiver provides feedback to the sender.
- **redundancy** Repeating or restating a message to ensure its reception or to reinforce its impact.
- **job specialization** The division of work into standardized, simplified tasks.
- **information ownership** The possession by certain individuals of unique information and knowledge concerning their work.
- **communication network** A set of channels through which communication travels within an organization or group.
- **vertical communication** Any communication that moves up or down the chain of command.

- **lateral communication** Communication between departments of an organization that generally follows the work flow, thus providing a direct channel for coordination and problem solving.
- **grapevine chain** The various paths through which informal communication is passed through an organization; includes the "single-strand," "gossip," "probability," and "cluster" chains.
- **electronic mail** Data and text circulated through interlinked computers.
- **video conferencing** Meetings held via telecommunications, usually by satellite television transmission, rather than by face-to-face contact.
- **telecommuting** The use of computers to enable individuals to work at home and send only the work (via telephone or data worksheet) to the work place.

Chapter Overview/Synopsis

Few tasks of managers can be completed without communication between individuals through some form of mutually understood symbolism. Such symbolism includes speech, writing, and visual images. The communications model consists of the sender, encoding, message, channel, receiver, decoding, noise, and feedback. Each part of the model affects the success of the communication process. Encoding, for example, places a message into a form perceived as being appropriate for the receiver. A message, however, often competes with noise that interferes with reception. Noise includes such things as distractions, other messages, and environmental noise.

Communication may be one-way, two-way, or free flowing, such as during a group discussion. Two-way communication offers the best possibility for success since feedback permits the participants to let each other know the extent to which the message is being received, understood, and accepted. Various barriers exist to interfere with communication. Barriers include differing perceptions, language difficulties, noise, evaluating listening, and attitudes. The use of feedback helps the sender to determine how well the message is getting through and, if needed, to employ other means to reinforce the message to ensure its receipt, understanding, and acceptance.

The formal structure of an organization dictates channels for some communication, while interpersonal relationships govern the selection of other channels of communication. Messages within organizations may flow downward, up and down, or laterally. Ongoing research in organizational communication reveals strong beliefs by many persons that more-open communication would generate better communication since there would be fewer "games" between senders and receivers. But openness can interfere with organizational effectiveness: many matters are sensitive in terms of the people involved, and some subjects, if freely discussed, would compromise the competitive edge of a company.

Analysis of Illustrative Case Study

INTRODUCTION—COMMUNICATIONS FAILURES AT BHOPAL

The Bhopal tragedy dramatizes the need for effective communication where questions of safety exist. The case illustrates the difficult communications in cross-cultural situations where language barriers are compounded by factors such as attitudes toward work, job assignments, "tea time," and the product itself. A mixture of these factors set the stage for plant safety devices to be under repair or shut off, and workers to misread gauges or make faulty assumptions about what was happening. Thousands of people died, and many more suffer varying degrees of disability. Faulty communication contributed to this disaster, and better communications will help to avoid such catastrophes in the future.

CONTINUED—COMMUNICATIONS FAILURES AT BHOPAL

The problem of securing effective communication regarding the Bhopal tragedy is compounded by the litigious influences of the situation. The Indian government is charging Union Carbide with a variety of criminal acts, Union Carbide is responding in a variety of ways, and lawyers are signing up clients. Against this environment Union Carbide must work with its communication process to ensure that other plants making the same product are operated safely. This is difficult when "noise" of many varieties is interfering with communication, coupled with emotional barriers that impede both the forming and the receiving of messages.

WRAP-UP—COMMUNICATIONS FAILURES AT BHOPAL

The Bhopal catastrophe reveals that messages have meanings in terms of people rather than the symbols used. The word "danger," for example, may not elicit the idea of *immediate danger* from a receiver. In the Bhopal case workers were able to rationalize that they had time to take a break before tending to a situation they felt only portended danger. Managers, therefore, have much to learn about the communication process to ensure that the processes of planning, organizing, leading, and controlling achieve their intended purposes.

Answers to End-of-Chapter Review Questions

1. Why is effective communication important to the manager?

Two reasons stand out: communication is the process by which managers accomplish their purposes, and managers expend considerable time and energy in the communication process.

2. List the eight elements in the expanded communication model.

Sender (source), encoding, message, channel, receiver, decoding, noise, and feedback.

3. What are some of the considerations involved in choosing the correct channel for one's message?

The needs and requirements of the receiver, the suitability of the message for a given channel, the need for and speed of feedback, and the costs measured against the value of the message.

4. What is "noise" in a communication system?

Noise is anything that interferes with communication. The noise may arise from internal or external sources. Internal noise might result from a person's inattention; environmental disturbances can be the cause of external noise.

5. Describe the common barriers to effective interpersonal communication. How may these barriers be overcome?

A communication barrier is anything that impedes the exchange of information between a sender and a receiver. While barriers may be almost unlimited in number, they tend to fall into categories that may be environmental, physiological, or psychological. Environmental barriers may arise from an inappropriate physical facility, such as using a boiler factory as a setting for a personal conversation. Physiological barriers can arise from, for example, impaired hearing or vision. Psychological barriers generally stem from attitudes, values, and even perceptions about the meaning of words.

Overcoming barriers is a two-step process. The sender needs to recognize the existence of a potential barrier and to initiate action appropriate to either overcome or minimize the effectiveness of the barrier.

6. What four factors influence the effectiveness of organizational communication? How do they exert this influence?

Raymond V. Lesikar identifies four factors that influence organizational communication: (a) the formal channels of communication, (b) the organization's authority structure, (c) job specialization, and (d) "information ownership." The *formal channels* affect communication in two ways: formal channels become longer as an organization grows, and the levels in the formal channels inhibit the flow of information. The *authority structure,* in ways similar to the formal channels, also serves to impede the flow of information because of differences in the hierarchical level of individuals. *Job specialization,* while probably contributing to communication within the specialty, may interfere when the communication is interdisciplinary because of jargon. *Information ownership* affects communication since a person in possession of information has the power to share or to withhold it.

7. What are the functions of vertical communication? What hinders accurate and complete vertical communication?

The primary plan of downward communication is to inform, advise, direct, instruct, and evaluate persons on subordinate levels in the organization. The goals of upward communication are to supply information as required by superiors. Subordinates, depending on their perception of the organization's culture, initiate communications to persons in superior positions.

A variety of problems exist to hamper the accuracy of vertical communication. These range from blocking a message filtering its content, or even modifying its content.

8. What is the function of the grapevine? Why do managers sometimes use the grapevine to convey information? What are some possible grapevine chains according to Keith Davis? Which chain is most likely to be used in organizations?

The grapevine serves social and informal communications functions together with one work-related function. A grapevine may be used to convey information, which moves more quickly than the ordinary flow of communication through established channels. The grapevine can also be used to "test" an idea to determine its acceptability. If unacceptable, the planted information can be denied.

Keith Davis has identified four possible types of grapevine chains: (a) the single strand where information flows from one person to another, (b) the gossip chain where idle information is passed along to anyone with time and inclination to listen, (c) the probability chain where senders are indifferent about whom they tell, and (d) the cluster where one person tells a few selected persons who, in turn, pass along the information to others in new clusters. Some clusters overlap, and this provides checks and balances regarding the accuracy of the information. Davis believes the cluster to be the dominant form.

9. How may the barriers to organizational communication be overcome?

Managers, first, need to recognize that communication is a complex process and that simplistic solutions lack effectiveness. One of the most important ways of overcoming barriers is for managers to put themselves in the position of the receiver and search for and eliminate or reduce problems that may interfere with the message being received, understood, and accepted.

10. What are some of the consequences of the use of computer communications technology in the work place?

One consequence is that form, content, size, and frequency of messages has changed. Computer-literate employees may gain access to information not destined for them. Another consequence is that persons who work with computers may be isolated from the rest of the organization and valuable interpersonal relations may be lost. In addition, some persons are becoming "telecommuters" where they remain at home with a computer terminal. How they are supervised and how they interact with other employees become vital questions for the future.

11. Why is complete openness on the job not always possible? Why isn't it always desirable?

Eisenberg and Witten suggest that openness has three meanings: a willingness to reveal personal information, a willingness to reveal impersonal information, and the possibility that the accuracy of the information disclosed may be questionable. Researchers continue to press for open communication in organizations but insist that a belief in openness does not require that all information be freely accessible to individuals. Many reasons for suppressing information exist: an individual's feeling of personal worth may be jeopardized, premature disclosure can interfere with goal attainment, and the disclosure of some proprietary information could cause financial havoc for a company.

Answers to End-of-Chapter Case Questions

CASE: THE CORPORATE POLICY SEMINAR

1. What are some of the benefits that Redbird might enjoy from another round of seminars?

Organizational communications exist for a variety of purposes. One benefit already obtained that can be enhanced is cross-cultural exchanges of information. This alone will help weld the company into a more cohesive unit. Knowing people throughout the company will alleviate suspicions that develop through ignorance of what is going on—for in the absence of information, people will manufacture what they need to know. This can be one of the negative aspects of the informal organization. If the seminars are continued, the participants will begin to identify persons with skill and leadership potential. Organizational barriers to communication should lessen as individuals get to know one another better.

2. How would you structure these seminars to maximize the benefit of better communication?

The seminars need a mix of functional and cross-functional groups. Where the purpose is to improve functional knowledge, the seminars should be restricted to persons having specified job responsibilities. For purposes of broadening the base of management, the seminars can continue to be cross-cultural. Much of what is presented appears to be "nuts and bolts information," which videotapes could present to larger groups or telecommunications lectures could present to save costs. The actual seminars should be confined to discussions that place people and their discussion leaders at the virtuoso level. This higher order of discussion would deal with conceptual reasoning—the kind that managers need to carry out their main functions. A major component of this master-level of discussion would be to obtain group interactions, as opposed to a one-to-many type of communication that occurs with lectures.

3. What would bill McGee tell the Executive Committee? How should he address the inevitable question of costs and benefits?

He would recommend that the seminars be continued because the company is so vast. Only through communication interchanges can the company obtain the synergy necessary to secure results greater than the sum of its human resources. With respect to costs, the costs of training will be borne by the company—one way or another. If the company undertakes the direct costs, it has control over the content and a reasonable likelihood of achieving positive results. If the company avoids the direct costs, other costs will arise through miscommunication, people withholding needed information as a means of building a power base, or other kinds of interpersonal difficulties.

Suggested Term Paper Topics

1. Ways to use redundancy without insulting the intelligence of the receiver

2. An analysis of non-verbal communication in formal communication

3. Significant ways of reducing barriers in vertical communication

4. Ways grapevines can be nurtured without killing them
5. An identification of words, terminology, and phrases that serve inflammatory purposes and ones that do not provoke anger or hostility
6. Difficulties encountered in multicultural communication and ways of minimizing or avoiding them
7. Learning how to listen as part of improving the communications process
8. How organizations can undertake a communications audit to identify potential problems of securing effective communication
9. A comparison of formal and informal communication systems

Suggested Guest Speakers

1. The manager of an organization's secretarial pool to share observations regarding problems with written communications.
2. A person in the community who is an acknowledged authority on non-verbal communication. Invite this person to discuss this field of communication.
3. Most communities have a Toastmaster's club. Invite an officer of that group to discuss how the club contributes to the communications effectiveness of its members.

Part 4 Case Study

COOKIE WARS

1. What are the main differences in leadership style between David Liederman and Debbi Fields?

   While leadership is the process of directing and inspiring workers to perform task-related activities, leaders do not perform their functions uniformly. Liederman's leadership style is task-structure–oriented. The leadership of Debbi Fields is charismatic or transformational. Liederman's task-structure takes form in centralized management that also minimizes the number of human factors that can influence the product. Liederman determines the work to be done—most of it automatically—and he essentially needs no more than "machine tenders" in his stores. Fields sets a personal example for all employees. Employees are encouraged to "have fun" while they work. Employees have freedom to, for example, judge baking times and determine ways to improve customer relations.

2. What is the relationship between leadership style and organizational structure in the two companies.

   The structure follows the leadership philosophy of the managers. David Liederman has a centralized structure with policies and procedures determined at the top. Mrs. Field's operation, while having elements of centralization, is mostly decentralized. The centralized segment of the company deals with store ownership and quality control over raw materials, since contracts are set with suppliers to furnish the stores with ingredients meeting Mrs. Field's standards. In some ways centralization exists with respect to finished goods, since Debbi Fields has been known to discard slightly overage cookies, or even close down a store is its product is below her standards. A major element of success, however, is in the decentralized part of the organization where store managers have freedom to manage. Mrs. Fields allows considerable latitude in how the respective managers carry out their "feel good" functions.

3. How are employees motivated in Liederman's company? In Field's?

   Liederman related a tale that reflects his method of managing. A friend told him the secret of managing this type of business was to keep employees stealing as little as possible. This approach necessitates considerable internal control with checks and balances for each step of the operation. Motivation arises in Liederman's businesses by following instructions. Understandably, his employees do not object to jobs where the planning is done by others. Errors, if any, are the responsibility of a manager rather than an employee.

   Employees at Mrs. Fields are encouraged to "have fun." The cookies are baked in regular ovens, and employees in charge of the baking determine when to remove cookies from the ovens. There are some rules, such as how long cookies can remain unsold before being discarded. It may be stretching the point, but in many respects the Field's stores have many aspects of self-management. Roles perception is important since each employee understands and accepts the behaviors necessary to accomplish their respective tasks. It would appear that equity theory works in this company since employees believe they are treated fairly. This feeling stems, in large part, from the high degree of trust that Mrs. Fields places in the employees.

4. How are interpersonal and organizational communications handled in each company?

   At David Liederman's the flow of instructions is downward, and the flow of operating results is upward. Interpersonal relationships between Liederman and his managers appear to be one-sided; however, it is obvious that managers must be able to respond to Liederman with more than monosyllabic words of "yes, sir." The general culture at Liedermans is not one to promote two-way communication where messages can be initiated down the line.

   Communications flows in many directions at Mrs. Fields. It is clear, however, that the commands from headquarters are not ignored. On the other hand, Debbi Fields is not a punishing manager whom people in the company fear to keep informed. Much of the openness in communications is exemplified in a statement from Debbi Fields: "We're a people company."

5. Is Debbi Fields really the leader of her company? Does Liederman face threats to this business that Fields does not? Why?

From an employee standpoint, Debbi Fields is the leader because she is a frequent point of contact for all employees. The operations manager is Debbi's husband, but his part of financial management is not visible to rank-and-file workers. Debbi visits the many stores and works with managers and employees alike to help them develop what she calls selling customers a "feeling-good feeling."

Liederman may face a threat from a lack of employees willing to work in a "no brain" atmosphere. Liederman has no desire to offer jobs with career track opportunities. His franchise owners are the ones he works with—he wants them to have the "urge to kill for the business." In short, he wants hard-driving managers who focus attention on making money for themselves and who also watch over their employees to accomplish such objectives. The employment pool for both Liederman and Mrs. Fields consists primarily of persons willing to work on a part-time basis. Word gets around regarding which company is the "best" employer. Wages would not be particularly important in determining a "best" employer since pay most likely approximates the minimum wage. If Liederman has difficulty obtaining and retaining people, he can be in for trouble. Even though Liederman brags that "a chimpanzee could take cookies out of a bag," there must still be something that attracts and holds people to their jobs.

6. In you opinion, which company will utlimately be more successful?

Students will most likely focus attention on the fact that customer taste preferences will make this determination. Certainly the way the customer is treated by a sales clerk will affect the customer's perception of the business, but no franchise holder is going to tolerate a clerk whose attitude drives customers away.

CHAPTER 18
Effective Control

Chapter Outline

THE MEANING OF CONTROL

The Link between Planning and Controlling
Steps in the Control Process
Establish Standards and Methods for Measuring Performance
Measure the Performance
Determine Whether Performance Matches the Standard
Take Corrective Action

THE IMPORTANCE OF CONTROL

Organizational Factors Creating the Need for Control
Change
Complexity
Mistakes
Delegation
Finding the Right Degree of Control

TYPES OF CONTROL METHODS

Pre-Action Controls
Steering Controls
Yes/No or Screening Controls
Post-Action Controls
The Importance of Steering Controls

DESIGN OF THE CONTROL PROCESS

The Control Process
Define Desired Results
Establish Predictors of Results
Establish Standards for Predictors and Results
Establish the Information and Feedback Network
Evaluate Information and Take Corrective Action
Key Considerations in Establishing a Control System
Types of Measurement
The Number of Measurements
Authority for Setting Measures and Standards
Flexibility of Standards
Frequency of Measurement
Direction of Feedback
Key Performance Areas and Strategic-Control Points
Strategic-Control Points
Key-Performance Areas

CHARACTERISTICS OF EFFECTIVE CONTROL SYSTEMS

Problems in Establishing Effective Control Systems

SUMMARY

Key Terms

- **control** The process of assuring that actual activities conform to planned activities.
- **pre-action controls** (or **precontrols**) Control methods ensuring that human, material, and financial resources have been budgeted.
- **steering controls** (or **cybernetic** or **feedforward controls**) Control methods designed to detect deviations from some standard goal and to permit corrective measures.
- **yes/no controls** (or **go/no-go controls**) Control methods for screening procedures that must be followed or conditions that must be met before operations continue.
- **post-action controls** Methods of control for measuring the results of a completed activity.
- **control system** Multistep procedure applied to various types of control activities.
- **management by exception** The principle that the controlling manager be informed about operation progress only when there is a significant deviation from a plan or standard.
- **external standard** Type of measurement derived from other organizations or other units of the same organization.
- **predetermined standard** Type of measurement based on careful analysis of the organizational unit's internal and external environments.
- **engineered standard** Type of measurement concerned with machine capacities.
- **assembly-line productivity standard** Type of measurement to evaluate effects on efficiency and employee response to new plans.
- **subjective standard** Type of measurement based mainly on a manager's discretion.
- **key-performance** or **key-result areas** Those aspects of the organization or unit that must function effectively if the whole organization or unit is to succeed in its plans.
- **strategic control points** Critical points in a system at which monitoring or collecting information should occur.

Chapter Overview/Synopsis

The purpose of planning is to improve upon a forecasted result, while control is a process to help assure management that events conform to plans. The control process, therefore, is multifaceted since it requires, among other things, predetermined standards, the determination of the measuring method, when measurements should be taken, taking the measurement, and determining the conditions under which corrective actions should be taken.

Time constraints and the increased complexity of the business environment add to the importance of the control process. Further, many companies have accelerated their change to decentralized operations, and this requires a better information-monitoring system. Then, too the human factor cannot be discounted—people make mistakes. The control process helps detect mistakes when they occur, but more important, a well-designed control process identifies the kinds of occurrences that lead to mistakes. In effect, controls can do much to reduce the costs of human errors.

Four methods of control have been identified: pre-action control, steering controls, yes/no screening controls, and post-action control. All methods are important, but steering controls carry extra significance since they permit corrective actions to occur during the attainment of planned objectives. The following are essential aspects of the control process: controls need to be accurate, they need to be timely, objective, and focused on strategic points where information is most useful. Controls must be economical in that their cost does not exceed the intended benefits.

Analysis of Illustrative Case Study

INTRODUCTION—AN EXPERIMENT IN INTEGRATIVE CONTROL AT GENCORP

The management of GenCorp reflects the need perceived by managers of other corporations to improve the productivity of their businesses to better cope with the competitive pressures of a global economy. A major shift in GenCorp's approach to control involved every level of the organization as it replaced its traditional model of control rooted in a managerial hierarchy. GenCorp now practices a brand of participating management that includes everyone from top management to production workers.

CONTINUED—AN EXPERIMENT IN INTEGRATIVE CONTROL AT GENCORP

Since GenCorp is shifting from traditional management to a participative managerial style, executives recognize the need to have the company staffed by persons supportive of participative management. Each person hired must be comfortable with an egalitarian approach to working together and not seek to use the organization's hierarchical structure as a shield. To accomplish this, the hiring process has been geared to recruiting, selecting, and placing people who will be comfortable working in a participative organization.

WRAP-UP—AN EXPERIMENT IN INTEGRATIVE CONTROL AT GENCORP

GenCorp's experiment in bringing about an organization where everyone carries a share of the responsibility to achieve productivity may serve as a model for other U.S. corporations. Employees at GenCorp have been selected and trained to work in an environment of commitment to working together with respect to managing the company and achieving control over its costs and quality standards.

Answers to End-of-Chapter Review Questions

1. What is the importance of the control function?
Control occupies a pivotal spot in determining how well managers achieve effectiveness from the application of scarce resources assigned to them for accountability.

2. How are planning and controlling linked?
The working definition of control relates to "the process through which managers assure that actual activities conform to planned activities." The link, therefore, is multifaceted: (a) determine what must be done, (b) establish a mechanism to assess progress toward or completion of the goal, (c) apply the means of measurement, and (d) take necessary corrective action.

3. List the four basic steps in the control process. What are the key elements in each of these steps?
1. *Establish standards and methods for measuring performance.*
—Standards must be in meaningful terms
—Methods of measurement should be accepted as being accurate
—The standards should include targets

2. *Measure the performance.*
   —Determine frequency of measurements to be taken
3. *Determine whether performance matches the standard*
4. *Take corrective action as appropriate*
   —Determine what activities need to be changed
   —Determine if standards should be reevaluated.

4. What organizational factors create the need for control?

A variety of circumstances determine the need for control. A change within the organization's environment may be brought about by external factors such as lost sales due to poor quality, or the imposition of a governmental regulation. The process of a manager delegating authority also includes a need for control regarding the quality of decision making by the deputy. The need for controls, therefore, arises from such factors as change, complexity, human efforts, and the delegation process.

5. What are the four main types of control? How is each type used? Which is most important? Why?

Pre-action controls ensure that before an action is undertaken the necessary human, material, and financial resources have been budgeted. *Steering controls* are designed to detect deviations from a predetermined standard and allow corrections to occur during the time a process is being completed. Such controls rely on timely and accurate information being supplied to management. *Yes/no controls* serve to screen activities to determine whether a given step meets standards before another step commences. *Post-action controls* measure the results of a completed action. In addition, through the process of feedback, information from post-action control can affect pre-action control to prevent or minimize problems.

6. According to William Newman, what are the five steps in designing a control system? How do managers go about carrying out these steps?

Newman's five-step control system: (1) define desired results, (2) establish predictors of results, (3) establish standards for predictors and results, (4) establish the information and feedback network, and (5) evaluate the information and take corrective action.

Newman suggests that desired results should be linked to a responsible person. In this way credit can be given to individuals who are successful, and corrective measures instituted with persons who need assistance. With respect to other steps of the process, Newman identified several "early warning" indicators. These include input measurements that identify needed changes in time to avoid later costs, detection of symptoms of situations that can become problems, and changes in assumptions used to establish standards for measurement.

7. With what six issues do Jerome Schnee and Thomas Ference suggest managers must be concerned in designing a control system? How might managers resolve these issues?

—*Types of measurement*. Measurements, by definition, are made against a standard. The standard may be historical, may be determined by engineering specifications or legislation, or may be subjective.
—*The number of measurements*. Each measurement adds to overall costs; therefore, the number of measurements needs to be restricted to the minimum necessary to assure attainment of the standard.
—*Authority for setting measures and standards*. Performance standards can be set with or without participation by persons whose performance is being monitored. When people are not involved, however, the danger exists that they may feel the standards are unreasonable.
—*Flexibility of standards*. Standards need not be uniform, but the conditions that determine changed standards for similar circumstances need to be known. For example, one sales territory may not be equal to another sales territory, and different standards are needed to determine the effectiveness of sales efforts.
—*Frequency of measurement*. Frequency and time of measurements depends on the nature of the function being controlled. Each measurement requires the expenditure of organizational resources, so the determination of frequency affects overall efficiency of the organization.
—*Direction of feedback*. A well-designed control system has a means of using control information to bring about changes in the control system itself. For example, the use of more reliable equipment in the production process can reduce the frequency of measurements.

8. What are key performance areas?

Controls need to be applied at those strategic points (*key points* or key performance areas) that most effectively determine how well a function is progressing toward its intended goal.

9. What is the "management by exception" principle?

This principle holds that the controlling manager be informed about operation progress only when there is a deviation from a plan or standard. A shorthand statement regarding the exception principle is that "no news is good news."

10. What are strategic-control points? How may managers locate them?

A strategic control point is one critical to the monitoring of information to be collected. There should be fewer strategic control points than key performance areas. To identify a strategic control point, managers need to focus on the most significant elements in a given operation. Often these significant elements constitute but a small portion of the overall operation being conducted.

11. What are the characteristics of effective control systems? Which of these characteristics is most important?

Ten characteristics of effective control systems have been identified. Control systems are:

1. accurate. Information obtained causes one of three outcomes: (a) corrects a problem, (b) reports everything is going according to plan, (c) creates a problem because of inaccurate data.
2. timely. Information, like many things, can lose value through time.
3. objective and comprehensible. People need to understand the information and feel it was gathered and used objectively.
4. focused on strategic-control points. Control works most effectively when applied to points where effect on final outcome is greatest.
5. economically realistic. Costs of control should not exceed the expected benefits.
6. organizationally realistic. The control system needs to be compatible with organizational resources. People should not be directed to control things that are beyond their control.
7. coordinated with the organization's work flow.
8. flexible. Few organizations operate in a stable environment; therefore, control systems need built-in flexibility.
9. prescriptive and operational. The control should also indicate the kind of corrective action to be taken.
10. accepted by organization members. People respond to control systems best when the system is perceived as being meaningful.

While all the characteristics are important, acceptance by organizational members is of utmost relevance since without the willingness of people to work with the control system, the other features cease to be useful in an organization.

Answers to End-of-Chapter Case Questions

CASE 1: PLANNING AND CONTROLLING AT 3M

1. What pressures for organization-wide controls has 3M imposed on itself with its program to grow by taking advantage of changes in its complex environment?

Heading the list are pressures from global competition, changes in health care delivery systems, and internal needs for greater efficiency through cost containment and organizational restructuring. The goals include more than a 10 percent growth rate in earnings per share; more than a quarter of the company's annual sales are to come from products less than five years old; and a 35 percent reduction in the costs of manufacturing, direct labor, and quality-control.

2. Given its optimistic statement about its organizational structure, what would you expect to be 3M's advantages in imposing controls on its plans for growth?

The company should achieve its objectives. The reduction of layers of management will leave in charge people committed to the attainment of goals. An important element in any control system is the acceptance of the people—in this instance, acceptance by the people imposing the controls. While the ones being controlled are in less of a position to provide acceptance, there is little reason to doubt employees will not support efforts to contain costs identified with producing, selling, and distributing the company's products.

3. Which method of control is most likely to be of the greatest value in implementing 3M's strategies for growth?

The most important method will be pre-action controls since these set the objectives of the control system. Of no less importance will be steering controls for use in monitoring the progress of the control systems in place, and post-action controls to ascertain how well the control systems worked to help the company achieve its goals. The post-action controls serve as part of the feedback system to adjust the control system where appropriate.

4. In which areas of its plan is 3M best prepared to implement financial controls? What steps has 3M already taken to ensure flexibility in managing its control strategy?

It is in the best position to implement financial controls in those areas where it has direct capability, such as in costs of production, labor, marketing, and administration. It is less able to control the costs of raw materials, energy, and factors beyond its internal environment. A major step in flexibility occurred when it shifted its approach to marketing products from its medical division. It has already consolidated several operating groups—tapes, adhesives, and decorative products. The company has also obtained more cooperation between its line and staff units. In effect, 3M is willing to review every aspect of its operation. This is flexibility since it demonstrates a commitment from 3M's management.

CASE 2: TRW, INC.—ELECTRONIC MONITORING IN THE TRUCKING INDUSTRY

1. Why has the trucking industry found it profitable to install computerized controls in its vehicles?

Computerized controls reduce operating costs, comprising fuel, wages, and other truck expenditures. For example, one trucking firm estimates savings of $85,000 per year for each tenth of a mile increase in mileage resulting from better fuel consumption. Computers also determine how long a truck sits idle, which adds to wage costs along with imputed interest charges from a vehicle not in use. Further, computers provide an overall monitoring of driver efficiency by showing, for example, whether engine rpms are within specified limits for each gear speed.

2. Describe the monitoring and controlling systems in terms of the four basic categories of control methods.

   Pre-action—engine rpms, truck highway speeds, and waiting times are set by the employer. *Steering control*—the driver knows the standards and needs to stay within accepted limits. In addition, the employer can initiate a discussion with any driver whose computer printout shows deviations from standards. *Yes-no control*—the equipment monitors the vehicle and the driver, but is not capable of determining that one action has occurred before permitting the next one to take place. *Post-action*—all the printouts, added to other information available for each vehicle, permit the employer to review standards and adjust them, as deemed appropriate, for new conditions.

3. If you were a truck driver, how would you feel about such devices? Would they make the job more or less attractive?

   To respond to this query, students need to consider how much freedom of action they desire in the conduct of their lives and to what extent they prefer to be responsible for their actions.

4. Do you think organizations should rely on self-monitoring by employees in situations like this one? In other types of situations? Why?

   If the driver buys his/her own fuel, leases the vehicle, and covers most other expenses, self-monitoring appears acceptable. On the other hand, an employer bearing all financial costs has a right to set controls to protect his investment.

5. As the manager of a trucking firm, how would you explain to your drivers why installation of devices to improve driver safety and comfort is lagging behind the use of devices to improve driver productivity?

   The productive use of capital equipment generates the revenues needed to pay for everything else. Therefore, the first special equipment to be installed on the trucks must produce savings; future acquisitions of devices to improve safety and comfort can be made from such savings. But you also need to consider the trade-offs involved since an item of equipment that provides greater comfort may be at the expense of some other wanted benefit. Therefore, before driver-comfort equipment is purchased, you should review the options available at that time.

Suggested Term Paper Topics

1. Human factors involved in obtaining control of employee behavior.
2. A review of management control systems designed to improve managerial effectiveness.
3. Internal control from an accountant's perspective.
4. A comparison of strategic controls and operational controls.
5. The total systems concept of achieving control.
6. An analysis of the control cycle.
7. Human issues to be reconciled when installing a new system of control.
8. An analysis of the characteristics of effective control systems.
9. A review of ways to determine when the right degree of control has been achieved.

Suggested Guest Speakers

1. A financial accountant to discuss internal control methods and what is done to prevent or detect deviations from such controls.
2. An office manager of a company employing hundreds of employees at computer keyboards to discuss how control over such workers is achieved.
3. A quality-control engineer to discuss the means used to determine the desired level of quality and to achieve it.

CHAPTER 19
Financial Control Methods

Chapter Outline

FINANCIAL CONTROLS

Financial Statements
- Balance Sheet
- Income Statement
- Cash Flow: Sources and Uses-of-Funds Statements

Ratio Analysis

Break-Even Analysis
- Limitations of Break-Even Analysis

BUDGETARY CONTROL METHODS

Budgetary Control

Responsibility Centers
- Revenue Centers
- Expense Centers
- Profit Centers
- Investment Centers

THE BUDGETING PROCESS

How Budgets Are Drawn Up and Approved

The Role of Budget Personnel

How Budgets Are Revised

Some Problems in Budget Development

TYPES OF BUDGETS

Operating Budgets
- Expense Budgets
- Revenue Budgets
- Profit Budgets

Financial Budgets
- Capital-Expenditure Budgets
- Cash Budgets
- Financing Budgets
- Balance-Sheet Budgets

Variable versus Fixed Budgets
- Fixed Costs
- Variable Costs
- Semivariable Costs

Zero-Base Budgeting

Functional and Dysfunctional Aspects of Budget Systems
- Potentially Functional Aspects of Budgets
- Potentially Dysfunctional Aspects of Budgets

AUDITING

External Auditing

Internal Auditing

SUMMARY

Key Terms

- **financial statement** Monetary analysis of the flow of goods and services to, within, and from the organization.
- **balance sheet** Description of the organizaton in terms of its assets, liabilities, and net worth.
- **income statement** Summary of the organization's financial performance over a given interval of time.
- **ratio analysis** Reporting of key figures from the organization's financial records as percentages or fractions.
- **break-even analysis** (or **cost-volume-profit analysis**) Financial statement enabling managers to analyze the relationships among costs, sales volume, and profits.
- **budget** Formal quantitative statement of resources allocated for planned activities over stipulated periods of time.
- **responsibility center** Any organizational function or unit whose manager is responsible for all its activities.
- **revenue center** Organizational unit in which outputs measured in monetary terms are not directly compared to input costs.
- **expense center** Commonly, administrative, service, and research departments where inputs are measured in monetary terms, although outputs are not.
- **profit center** Organizational unit where performance is measured by numerical differences between revenues and expenditures.
- **investment center** Organizational unit that not only measures the monetary value of inputs and outputs but also compares outputs with assets used in producing them.
- **operating budget** Budget indicating the goods and services the organization expects to consume in a budget period.
- **financial budget** Budget detailing the money expected to be spent during the budget period and indicating its sources.
- **engineered cost budget** Budget describing material and labor costs of each item produced, including estimated overhead costs.

- **discretionary cost budget** Budget used for departments in which output cannot be accurately measured.
- **revenue budget** Budget measuring marketing and sales effectiveness by multiplying the unit price of each product by the predicted sales quantity.
- **profit budget** (or **master budget)** Budget combining cost and revenue budgets in one unit.
- **capital-expenditure budget** Budget indicating future investments to be made in buildings, equipment, and other physical assets of the organization.
- **cash budget** Budget combining estimates for revenues, expenses, and new capital expenditures.
- **financing budget** Budget that assures the organization of available funds to meet shortfalls of revenues when compared to expenses and that schedules potential borrowing needs.
- **balance-sheet budget** (or **pro forma balance sheet)** Budget combining all other budgets to project the balance sheet at the end of the budgeting period.
- **fixed costs** Those unaffected by the amount of work accumulated in the responsibility center.
- **variable costs** Expenses varying directly with the amount of work being performed.
- **semivariable costs** Those, like short-term labor costs, varying with the amount of work performed but not in a proportional way.
- **zero-base budgeting (SBB)** A budgeting approach in which all the organization's activities, existing and proposed, are considered on an equal footing in resource-allocation decisions, rather than using the previous year's budget as a starting point.
- **external audit** Verification process involving the independent appraisals of financial accounts and statements.
- **internal audit** Audit performed by the organization to ensure that its assets are properly safeguarded and its financial records reliably kept.

Chapter Overview/Synopsis

An organization resembles a major investment expected to yield profitable returns to its owners. Managers charged with overseeing this investment use a variety of financial tools to plan, organize, and control the productive use of assets. Some of the major financial controls include budgets, ratio analysis, break-even analysis, and a variety of other financial statements.

Budgets serve a most useful purpose in planning and controlling a firm's financial activities. The budgeting process begins when top management sets goals and strategies for the organization. Each level of the organization is expected to contribute information to be used in constructing the necessary budgets. Depending on use, budgets may be functional or dysfunctional. Positive results include improved coordination, communication, morale, and motivation. Dysfunctional results include different priorities by organizational members, and unnecessary and harmful pressures on organization members as a consequence of unattainable goals set within the budget.

Auditing is done to verify the accuracy and authenticity of financial information, to prevent fraud, and to uncover deception. Auditing, internal and external, is a safeguarding activity that serves an oversight function.

Analysis of Illustrative Case Study

INTRODUCTION—FINANCIAL RESOURCEFULNESS AT JOHN DEERE AND COMPANY

John Deere, a century-old manufacturer of farm equipment and allied products for home and garden care, depends primarily on the agricultural community for its profitability. The farm economy's ongoing depression is reflected in an earnings decline of John Deere. Despite the turbulence of the agricultural economy, the company remains committed to serving the needs of agriculture and controls about 40 percent of that market. To maintain this leadership, the company must devise a system of financial controls to improve its management of resources.

CONTINUED—FINANCIAL RESOURCEFULNESS AT JOHN DEERE AND COMPANY

It has been said that it takes money to make money. John Deere embarked on a capital expansion program to add more efficient production facilities that increased capacity while lowering its labor costs. This investment program also increased fixed costs as well as raising the break-even point. Deere's management targeted the reduction of fixed costs as the best way to lower the break-even point since each dollar of fixed-cost reduction also lowers the break-even point by a like amount. Other efforts at cost reduction included reorganization of production divisions, restructuring of product lines, and concentrating sales efforts where the best profits resulted.

WRAP-UP—FINANCIAL RESOURCEFULNESS AT JOHN DEERE AND COMPANY

Regardless of production efficiencies, John Deere cannot attain its goals without sales revenues. Since farmers are scattered throughout the nation, the dealership network is crucial to John Deere's success. A depressed farm economy has taken a toll of dealers; however, servicing existing farm equipment has helped many dealers to survive. Their survival has also been helped by John Deere's offering significant concessions on interest owed for past inventory purchases. The company's desire to maintain its dealership network should provide the basis for future sales growth based on an expected annual sales increase of about 3 percent.

Answers to End-of-Chapter Review Questions

1. Financial statements are used to control what three major conditions of an organization?

Liquidity—the ability of a firm to convert assets into cash; *general financial condition*—the long-term balance between debt and equity; and *profitability*—the ability to earn profits steadily through time.

2. What are the major types of financial statements? What information does each type provide?

Balance sheet—a description of a company's assets, liabilities, and net worth at the end of a given time period. *Income statement*—a summary of how well the company's resources are used over a period of time. *Cash flow: sources and uses-of-funds statements*—a report showing how cash funds are used.

3. What is ratio analysis? How may comparisons of ratios be made? What are the major types of ratios used by organizations? What information is each type expected to provide?

Ratios compare one number to another (ex.: sales revenues compared with costs of production). Comparisons may be made in one of two ways: over a time period, or with similar organizations or with ones within the industry. The major ratios express profitability, liquidity (capability to turn an asset into cash), asset or liability activity (frequency of transactions), leverage (capability to obtain results greater than inputs, such as paying 12 percent interest on a loan to generate 18 percent profits), return on investment (shows profit generated from use of assets), inventory turnover (number of times the dollar value of inventory turns over in a given time period), current ratio (the ability of the firm to repay its present short-term debt), and debt ratios (a firm's capability to repay its long-term financial commitments). A much wider variety of ratios also exist dealing with anything capable of being measured.

4. What is the purpose of break-even analysis? What are the steps involved in creating a profitgraph? What is the break-even point? What are the advantages and disadvantages of break-even analysis?

The purpose of break-even analysis is to enable managers to better assess relationships between costs, revenues, and profit. A profitgraph is best displayed on a square grid where revenues are shown as a 45° line, fixed costs are drawn horizontally, and variable expenses are added to fixed expenses to become total expenses. The point where total expenses cross the revenue line is called the break-even point. Thus a break-even point occurs when revenues equal the sum of variable and nonvariable costs. The limitations of break-even analysis include (1) an assumption that variable costs per unit are constant, (2) that fixed costs are constant, (3) that prices are constant, and (4) that the costs can be accurately classified as fixed or variable.

5. Why are budgets so widely used in organizations?

Budgets are widely used because they are stated in monetary terms. Dollar amounts are readily used as a common denominator with respect to most activities of an organization.

6. What are four major types of responsibility centers? What organizational units are commonly considered as belonging to each type of center? How is the performance of each center measured?

Any functional unit headed by a manager responsible for its activities is called a responsibility center. The four types of centers consist of revenue centers, expense centers, profit centers, and investment centers. Performance is measured by assessing how effectively each manager uses inputs to obtain outputs.

7. How are budgets prepared, approved, and revised? What are the advantages of lower-level participation in the budgeting process?

In a top-down budget-building process, budgeting begins when managers receive top management's economic forecasts along with sales and profit objectives for the budget period. Budgets are most often prepared by persons responsible for their implementation. In bottom-down budgeting, department heads and others with an intimate knowledge of conditions provide management with information for approval or revision. The lower-level participation has several key advantages: fewer factors are likely to be overlooked, and support will be greater since lower-level persons contributed to the budgeting process.

8. What four reactions has Henry Tosi described concerning the anxieties of budget development?

Political behavior as managers try to influence resource allocation through a variety of means to "get more than their share''; *dysfunctional reactions* from supervisors who are unhappy with their share of the resources and vent their hostility on their subordinates; *overstatement of needs* resulting from managers who feel their requests will be reduced in the budgeting process; and *covert information systems* that arise when managers hold back budget information from their subordinates.

9. What types of budgets are used for three of the responsibility centers described in the chapter? Describe each budget. What is the purpose of each budget?

The three responsibility centers deal with expense, revenue, and profit. Expense budgets are of two types: engineered cost budgets and discretionary cost budgets. Revenue budgets are sales quantity multiplied by the expected unit selling price of each product. Profit budgets combine cost and revenue budgets in one statement for use by managers with responsibilities for both expenses and revenues.

10. What are cash, expenditure, and balance sheet budgets? Why are they used?

A cash budget combines the organization's budgeted estimates for revenues, expenses, and new capital expenditures. This budget reveals information about the level of funds flowing through the organization to assist with planning future expenditures. Expenditure budgets are developed to assure the organization of the availability of funds to meet possible shortfalls of revenues relative to anticipated expenses. Balance-sheet budgets assemble the other budgets to project how the balance sheet will appear if actual results conform to planned results.

11. What are variable budgets? What types of costs must managers consider when devising variable budgets? Why? How may variable costs be determined?

Variable budgets are cost schedules that indicate how each cost should vary as the level of activity or output varies. Three kinds of costs must be considered when developing flexible budgets: fixed, variable, and semivariable. Fixed costs are unaffected by the amount of work undertaken in the responsibility center. Variable costs vary directly with the quantity of work being performed in the responsibility center. Semivariable costs fluctuate with the volume of work performed in the responsibility center, but not in a proportional manner. Variable costs are fixed per unit of output, and the total is computed by multiplying the direct costs by the quantity produced and sold.

12. What are the basic steps in zero-base budgeting? What are some benefits and problems in this approach?

(1) Break down each activity into a decision package that includes all information about an activity needed by managers to evaluate that activity, and compare its costs and benefits to other activities. (2) Evaluate and rank the various activities in order of decreasing benefit. (3) Allocate resources based on the rankings determined in step two. Zero-base budgeting benefits include the quantification of alternatives, the fact that low-priority programs can be cut or eliminated, and that alternative programs can be considered with greater clarity. Problems include the reluctance of managers to submit their programs as though they could be eliminated; managers may tend to inflate the importance of their programs.

13. What are the potentially functional and dysfunctional aspects of budgets?

Functional aspects. (1) Budgets can improve motivation and morale. (2) Budgets make it possible to coordinate the work of an entire organization. (3) Budgets can be used as a warning device to indicate corrective action. (4) The budget system helps people learn from experience. (5) Budgets improve resource allocation. (6) Budgets improve communication. (7) Budgets help lower-level managers see where they fit into the organization. (8) Budgets let new people see where the organization is going. (9) Budgets serve as a means of evaluation.

Dysfunctional aspects. (1) Differing perceptions of budgets by organization members; (2) mechanical considerations; (3) communication and budgets pertaining to developing and installing the budget system; (4) impairment of motivation; (5) goal difficulty and goal achievement that may appear to be set too high to achieve employee acceptance.

14. What are the two basic types of audits? What is the purpose of each type?

External and internal audits. External audits are largely a verification process involving an independent appraisal of the organization's financial condition. Internal audits are carried out by members of the organization. Their purpose parallels that of external audits; they also evaluate the organization's control system to determine that unit members are working toward organizational objectives.

15. How has computerization affected financial control?

Computers permit real-time information so that managers have up-to-the-minute knowledge of selected operations. Computers also link many parts of an organization so that managers can make better decisions regarding diverse parts of a company. Computers can also be programmed to make management by exception much more effective.

Answers to End-of-Chapter Case Questions

CASE: THE AUDIT REPORT

1. Who is at fault here?

Jay O'Malley is at fault since he is an accounting professional who is expected to follow standard accounting practices. Since he was ordered to deviate from such practices, he owed the internal audit committee a letter that outlined the nature of the improper order he had received.

2. Do you think the audit and resulting letters will achieve their purpose?

   They should, since the firm no doubt has a contract with an independent auditing firm. Without a statement from an external auditor that the company's accounting conforms to standard accounting practices, the company will be seriously impaired in securing working capital.

3. How would you have handled this situation if you had been the mine's controller?

   See response to question 1.

4. How would you have handled this situation if you were the vice-president for mining operations?

   Notify headquarters of the unexpected increase in compensation claims and that the anticipated profit would be a loss for the accounting period, but that steps were being taken to improve the forecasting model to prevent or detect such problems. Ask Jay O'Malley for a set of recommendations pertaining to better forecasting for compensation claims.

Suggested Term Paper Topics

1. An analysis of standards or norms used in performing ratio analyses.
2. A review and analysis of external sources for comparative ratio analyses.
3. A comparative analysis of fixed cash budgets and flexible cash budgets.
4. A review of cash management systems.
5. An appraisal of selected means of conducting break-even analyses.
6. A review of appropriations, flexible, and zero-base budgeting.
7. Motivational techniques based on financial budgeting.
8. A review of professional ethics of accountants and business problems.
9. Removing or reducing dysfunctional behavior associated with budgeting.

Suggested Guest Speakers

1. A corporate controller to discuss his/her company's budgeting process.
2. A partner of a CPA firm to discuss problems associated with obtaining full financial information from clients.
3. An officer of a regulatory agency (insurance, SEC, bank commissioner) to discuss public confidence and auditing practices.

CHAPTER 20
Productivity and Operational Control

Chapter Outline

CHANGING VIEWS OF PRODUCTION AND OPERATIONS

PRODUCTIVITY

What Is Productivity?
Improving Productivity in Organizations
Productivity through People
Factors Influencing Productivity
- Work Force
- Energy Costs
- Condition of Facilities and Investment in New Plants and Equipment
- Level of Research and Development Spending
- Growth of the Less-Productive Service Sector
- Changes in Family Structure
- Increased Use of Alcohol and Drugs
- A Shift in Workers' Attitudes and Motivation
- Cost to Industry of Government Regulation
- Financial Pressures
- Tax Policies

Productivity Management

COMPETITIVE PRIORITIES FOR BUSINESS

- Pricing
- Quality Level
- Quality Reliability
- Flexibility

CHARACTERISTICS OF PRODUCTION/ OPERATIONS SYSTEMS

The Operations System: A Model
- Operations Management and Strategic Planning
- Continuous and Assembly-Line Production and Job-Shop Production

DESIGNING PRODUCTION/ OPERATIONS SYSTEMS

Product/Service Planning and Design
- CAD

Capacity Planning
Process Selection
- Major Technological Choice
- Minor Technological Choice
- Specific-Component Choice
- Process-Flow Choice

Facility-Location Planning
Layout Planning
Job Design

OPERATIONAL PLANNING AND CONTROL DECISIONS

Operations Planning and Control
- Production Plans
- Detailed Scheduling
- Materials-Requirements Planning

Inventory Planning and Control System
- Just-in-Time Inventory
- Quality Control

SUMMARY

Key Terms

- **operations** The production activities of an organization.
- **operations management** Complex management activity that includes planning production, organizing resources, directing operations and personnel, and monitoring system performance.
- **productivity** Measure of how well an operations system functions and an indicator of the efficiency and competitiveness of a single firm or department.
- **competitive priorities** Four major criteria, including pricing, quality levels, quality reliability, and flexibility, on which products are evaluated.
- **operations system** Production/operations system denoting both manufacturing and service systems.
- **continuous and assembly-line system** System producing standardized output of its own design, usually in large volume.
- **job-shop system** System for making small amounts of custom-tailored products, usually to fulfill a contract.
- **computer-aided design (CAD)** Design and drafting performed interactively on a computer.
- **capacity planning** Operations decision concerned with the quantity of goods or services to be produced.
- **computer-aided manufacturing (CAM)** Use of machines to perform and control required work.
- **work-flow layout** Layout planning concerned with product layouts (for the sequential steps in produc-

tion), process layouts (for arranging production according to task), and fixed-position layouts (for handling large or heavy products such as ships).

- **function layout** Layout planning concerned with storage layouts (for minimizing inventory and storage costs), marketing layouts (for maximizing product exposure and sales), and project layouts (for building one-of-a-kind products such as a dam).
- **materials-requirements planning** Operational planning system whereby end products are analyzed to determine the materials needed to produce them.
- **just-in-time inventory system** Inventory system in which production quantities are ideally equal to delivery quantities, with materials purchased and finished goods delivered "just in time."
- **quality control** Strategy for managing each stage of production so that early corrections can be made instead of reworking the product after end-of-line inspection.
- **acceptance-sampling procedure** Quality-control procedure to determine if the finished product conforms to design specifications.
- **process-control procedure** Quality-control procedure for monitoring quality during production of the product rendering of the service.
- **computer-integrated manufacturing** The use of machines to link computer-aided design and computer-aided manufacturing systems so that new product designs can be manufactured automatically in the factory.

Chapter Overview/Synopsis

Organizations exist to produce something, a good or a service. Operations management is the descriptive term for managing the production of goods and services. Production management, the former name of operations management, was essentially a top-down engineering function. Today's operations management, while having strong components of engineering, involves all levels of modern organizations. Research has shown that greater worker involvement has brought improvements to process design and the achievement of both higher quality and productivity.

Operations systems take a set of inputs (money, materials, manpower, minutes, methods, machinery, etc.) and transform them into outputs. Design of an operations system includes deciding upon the thing to be produced, the quantity, the process, where to produce it, the layout for efficient production, and how jobs will be structured and assigned. Undergirding the process are various types of planning and control techniques dealing with production scheduling, routing, and quality control. The overall measurement is in terms of productivity obtained from the use of the inputs. Computer technology has enhanced the effectiveness of operations management.

Analysis of Illustrative Case Study

INTRODUCTION—AT FORD, QUALITY IS JOB ONE

Ford Motor Company instituted its rebirth in 1980 under the leadership of Philip Caldwell as Chairman of the Board and Donald Petersen as Chief Executive Officer. Between 1980 and 1987, Ford's market share climbed 3 points while GM's market share shrank 9 points. This rebirth was based on two major factors: cost cutting and improvement in product quality. Employees were informed of the new culture at Ford and were given no choice but to offer their cooperation. Reducing the labor force was a major part of reducing costs. Obtaining employee participation and pride in quality opened new vistas of self-esteem for production-line personnel who now had a say in whether a product met quality standards.

CONTINUED—AT FORD, QUALITY IS JOB ONE

Achieving lower costs and higher quality did not occur without effort. Old work and managing habits persisted, which resulted in a large number of substandard cars being reworked at the factory or by dealers. The company's outmoded sales forecasting resulted in large inventories. Ford's corrective approach was to institute a program of preventive quality control—to obtain parts from reliable suppliers and to inspect and pass on purchases before installation on the production line. Constant monitoring of quality control reduced the number of problems with the finished cars. Improved consumer forecasts helped Ford better determine production and shipping schedules. Computers permitted the many parts of operations management to be interconnected.

WRAP-UP—AT FORD, QUALITY IS JOB ONE

The car-buying public's increased recognition of Ford's quality has been reflected in expanded sales. Ford management recognized that people will buy quality, a lesson learned when Americans purchased higher-quality foreign-built automobiles. Ford's management is not fully certain of its ability to compete with foreign competition and is urging the U.S. government to tighten the quotas of foreign-built cars for the U.S. market. Overall, Ford has taken a long step on the comeback trail, and Petersen has reasserted his commitment to restoring the company to a former position of eminence.

Answers to End-of-Chapter Review Questions

1. What do the terms *production management* and *operations management* mean?

Production management is a more traditional term for manufacturing management, but because production of services has achieved greater emphasis, a broader term—operations management—has become the accepted name. Operations management employs all the standard processes of management: planning the production/operations system, assembling the necessary capital and human resources, directing the system and the personnel, and control through a monitoring process.

2. How do the authors define the operations subsystem within the organization?

A set of components whose function is to transfer a set of inputs into some desired output.

3. What are the five elements of a system as the authors define them?

Planning production, organizing resources, directing operations and personnel, and monitoring system performance.

4. The authors further define operations systems as continuous and assembly-line systems or job-shop systems. Discuss the characteristics and give an example of each.

Assembly-line characteristics include the continuous production of a standardized product with standardized components using standardized methods for assembly (example: a television set). *Job-shop* characteristics include general purpose equipment used to produce custom-tailored products (example: a custom-made cover for a boat).

5. Discuss the basic steps in the product/service design process.

1. *Research*. Generate the product/service ideas and test them for implementation.
2. *Selection*. From among the research-generated ideas, choose the ones meeting the tests of technological and financial feasibility, marketability, and fitting into the organization's overall objectives.
3. *Design*. Develop design specification for the product or service that meets the standards for quality based on intended use.

6. What is meant by capacity planning?

Operations decision concerned with the quantity of goods or services to be produced.

7. The third major decision in design is process selection, or how the product or service will be produced. Chase and Aquilano suggest that this is a four-part decision. What are those parts?

(1) Major technological choice to ensure the technology exists to produce the product in the desired quantity with the desired quality. (2) Minor technological choice to select the production processes to be employed together with alternatives available. (3) Specific-component choice to identify and select the equipment to be used, such as single-purpose or multiple-purpose. (4) Process-flow choice to determine how the product or service should flow through the operations system.

8. Distinguish between facility location planning and layout planning.

Facility location is a geographic decision but includes such considerations as economical distance to transportation, suppliers, customers, employees, and the governmental infrastructure. Layout planning is concerned with such factors as work stations, materials-handling equipment, storage areas, and maintenance, and support facilities such as offices, restrooms, reception areas, food service, and parking.

9. The final decision in designing an operations system is the structure of individual jobs, or job design. Specifically what is meant by the term *job design?*

Job design is concerned with two questions: *how* will the work be done, and *who* will do the work? Job design consists of three activities: (1) specifying individual work operations, (2) specifying the method of doing each function, and (3) combining related work tasks into jobs for assignment to individuals.

10. What are the objectives of operations planning control, and how are they related?

The objectives of operations planning and control are to maximize customer service, minimize inventory investment, and maximize system operating efficiency. The relationships may or may not be compatible, since there may be times that customer service may require a large inventory to reduce customer waiting times. The goal, therefore, is to plan a series of what-if decisions to obtain an optimal balance between the different objectives.

11. What do the acronyms MRP and BOM mean?

MRP = materials-requirements planning; BOM = bill of materials.

12. Inventories are an integral or important part of many production systems. What are the major opposing costs associated with inventories?

    In addition to the direct cost of the inventory, the following are associated costs: storage, imputed interest, breakage, theft, handling, and other kinds of carrying costs.

13. What is a productivity ratio, and what does it measure?

    John Kendrick defined productivity as "the relationship between output of goods and services (O) and the inputs (I) of resources . . . used in the production process." Thus, the ratio is O/I, and the higher the ratio, the higher the productivity index.

14. Describe the just-in-time concept of inventory control.

    This is an ideal state said to exist when production quantities are equal to delivery quantities. Thus, carrying costs are minimized by eliminating inactive inventory kept on hand for reserve purposes.

15. What is the difference between a "big bang" approach and an incremental approach to improving productivity?

    Adherents of the big bang method strive to increase productivity by large one-time investments in capital equipment, while advocates of the incremental method try to obtain productivity increases through small changes in equipment, worker training, and operational procedures.

16. What changes have recently occurred in the way managers view quality control?

    Quality control is a strategy for managing each stage of production so that early corrections can be made instead of reworking the product after end-of-the line inspection. An increasing number of managers no longer see quality control as an inspection task; they now consider quality control at every stage of a company's operations.

17. What benefits does computerization offer to the manager of a retail store?

    Here is a sampling of benefits that computerization offers retail store managers. Cash registers can be tied to the warehouse to improve purchasing decisions. Pricing and recording sales can be done through laborsaving bar-code readers and optical scanners Price changes can be made in the computer rather than on the merchandise—especially beneficial in grocery stores. Internal records for payroll, taxes, auditing, and management decision making can be readily completed.

18. Discuss how companies can compete on different product characteristics, or competitive priorities.

    Marketing experts advocate product differentiation through such means as advertising to cause customers to choose one product over another with less concern over price. Public relations also helps when companies make technological advances that are newsworthy. New models are often announced through press releases. Companies can also segment markets to enable the best-selling items to appear in markets where sales are most likely to occur. Firms can also be selective in direct mail advertising by using zip codes and mailing lists to target potential customers.

Answers to End-of-Chapter Case Questions

CASE: GE TURNS OLD INTO NEW IN KENTUCKY

1. Why did GE revamp its dishwasher plant?

   The company decided to remain in the appliance business rather than abandon it, as was done by Westinghouse. Based on this decision, the company wanted the GE symbol to be perceived positively by the public. The decision appears to be a mix of competition and company pride.

2. What changes were made, and how did they increase productivity?

   (1) The labor force was taken into management's confidence; the workers' support of the decision was instrumental in achieving increased productivity. (2) The assembly process was reengineered to standardize production of most models, saving individual treatment until the end of the line. (3) Technological innovations permitted better production methods, such as occurred through use of a GE-developed weight-bearing plastic. (4) The plant was extensively "robotized," and optical scanners were used for inventory and production control as well as for assembly operations. While the rate of production was increased by these additions, productivity was further enhanced by fewer rejects of components and finished goods. Inventory levels were reduced considerably (from $9.5 million to $3.9 million).

3. How has Japanese competition influenced GE's operations strategy in household appliances?

   Although Japanese producers do not offer dishwashers, GE management was convinced Japanese firms would soon compete in other appliances, namely refrigerators. GE would gain considerable experience at its Louisville facility and would be ready to market other appliances capable of equaling or exceeding ones from Japan. Japanese-style quality has become the benchmark in the world; therefore, GE felt it had to have this level of quality for its appliances. This is especially true for refrigerators, which serve a global need.

4. In your opinion, are foreign-made goods of higher quality than American-made goods? Support you opinion with specific examples.

Students might set up a few debate teams to work on this question. In this way, more involvement would occur and students would also have time to research their responses.

Suggested Term Paper Topics

1. Operations management applied to labor-intensive jobs—custodial.
2. The politics of unionism and national goals to achieve productivity.
3. Import quotas by the United States and their influence on plant modernization.
4. Incentive programs to increase productivity without impairing quality.
5. Quality circles and ways they affect plant productivity.
6. The economics of the *maquiladora* movement for plants to have production facilities in Mexico.
7. Productivity goals in the health care industry.
8. Ways of measuring productivity or value-added in education.
9. Management practices and problems of automated warehouses.

Suggested Guest Speakers

1. A leader of an industrial union (CIO) to discuss robotics.
2. The director of a vocational rehabilitation center to discuss the extent to which clients are finding increased job opportunities as a result of robotics and automation.
3. A factory plant manager to discuss the ''old'' and the ''new'' of his plant with respect to the way production is achieved.

CHAPTER 21 Information Systems and Control

Chapter Outline

INFORMATION AND CONTROL

The Computer Revolution
The Value of Cost of Information

MANAGEMENT INFORMATION SYSTEMS

The Evolution of MIS
- EDP
- MIS
- DSS
- Artificial Intelligence

Differing Information for Different Management Levels
- Operational Control
- Middle Management
- Top Management

DESIGNING A COMPUTER-BASED MIS

Guidelines for Effective Design

IMPLEMENTING A COMPUTER-BASED MIS

Problems in Implementing a Computer-Based MIS
- Organizational Resistance
- Security

Overcoming Implementation Problems

END-USER COMPUTING

Decision-Support Systems
- Differences between DSS and MIS
- Using DSS
- DSS versus EDP/MIS

Expert Systems and Artificial Intelligence
- Use of Expert Systems
- Design and Implementation of Expert Systems
- Natural-Language Processing
- The Future of Expert Systems

Managing End-User Computing

THE IMPACT OF COMPUTERS AND MIS ON MANAGERS AND ORGANIZATIONS

The Continuing Computer Revolution

SUMMARY

Key Terms

- **management information system (MIS)** Computer-based information system for more effective planning, decision making, and control.
- **information** Technically, processed data that supplies information about a specific situation or process.
- **management information** Information representing relevant and important features about a situation so that a manager can take specific action.
- **electronic data processing (EDP)** Computerized data processing and information management, including report standardization for operating managers.
- **computer-based information system (CBIS)** (or **computer-based MIS)** Information system that goes beyond the mere standardization of data to aid in the planning process.
- **end-user computing** The creative use of computers by those who are not experts in data processing.
- **decision-support system (DSS)** Computer system accessible to nonspecialists to assist in planning and decision making.
- **artificial intelligence (AI)** Development of computational approaches to simulate intelligent human thought or behavior.
- **Expert system** Application of artificial intelligence denoting the technology entailed by the development of computational approaches to human functioning.
- **natural-language processing** Use of everyday language instead of special codes or instructions to communicate with a computer system.

Chapter Overview/Synopsis

The processes of planning, organizing, leading, and controlling stem from effective use of appropriate information. The formal information in modern organizations tends to be computer-based, such as management information systems (MIS), decision-support systems (DSS), and expert systems that focus on specific problems. Each level of management has different needs for information that is timely, accurate, and supported by employees.

Computer-based information systems can cause problems in situations where established routines are disrupted. In such a circumstance, the human element can cause various forms of resistance, such as aggressive behavior, avoidance, and interference. Overall, however, computer technology has had more acceptance than rejection by managers and other involved employees even though many human relationships have changed as a result. Computer systems have enabled organizations to eliminate, reduce, or at least process paperwork with greater speed and accuracy.

Artificial intelligence has become a goal for many computer users so that computers can diagnose and explain problems and recommend solutions. Within this objective is that of communicating with computers through the use of natural language to eliminate extensive training of end-users.

Analysis of Illustrative Case Study

INTRODUCTION—USING TECHNOLOGY AT SEARS FOR STRATEGIC ADVANTAGE

Computers have moved from being used primarily for data processing, payroll, and accounting to almost every facet of a business. Sears made this transition and now ties its cash registers to central computes to maintain a timely review of inventories as well as to verify charge accounts for sales clerks who call a store's credit office.

CONTINUED—USING TECHNOLOGY AT SEARS FOR STRATEGIC ADVANTAGE

Only a few years after a cashier had to verify a customer's credit with a telephone call to a credit office, it became possible for electronics to do the same job—faster and better. A cashier now has to only place the charge card in the cash register card-reading slot and punch in a few numbers. The credit is checked, the purchase is recorded, and the customer is presented with a receipt for signature. Electronics at the point of sale has done much to revolutionize the way retailers conduct business.

WRAP-UP—USING TECHNOLOGY AT SEARS FOR STRATEGIC ADVANTAGE

With a computer system in place to speed charge account purchases, Sears turned its attention to further improving decision making by merchandise managers. These are the persons whose responsibility is to determine what to buy for the future: correct decisions mean profits. These managers are impatient and wish to have an expert system installed to take care of their specialized needs. They are cautioned by top management that an incorrectly designed system can spell disaster. Therefore, they need to continue using the computer assistance in place and to be confident that Sears is working to develop an expert system.

Answers to End-of-Chapter Review Questions

1. Why is an effective information system a key part of effective managerial planning, decision making, and control?

   Prior to computers, a manager simply had too much information to invest to make the most effective decisions. Today's managers have a wide array of electronic aids at their disposal to provide accurate and timely information for decision making. The information provided by computer systems helps managers compare standards with actual results, detect deviations, and institute timely corrective actions.

2. On what four factors does the value of information depend? How do managers weight these factors against the cost of a management information system (MIS)?

   The value of data depends on information quality, timeliness, quantity, and relevance. Managers need to transform data (raw facts) into information (analyzed raw data) into a coordinated stream of findings to be used in determining what to do about a given situation. This latter aspect is a management information system. Before managers can install such a system, they need to determine the economic costs of doing without timely, accurate, and relevant information.

3. How might MIS be defined?

   "MIS [is] a formal method of making available to management the accurate and timely information necessary to facilitate the decision-making process and enable the organization's planning, control, and operational functions to be carried out effectively."

4. What are the differences between data, information, and management information? Which is most desirable for managers? Why?

   Data are raw unanalyzed facts, figures, and events. *Information* results from the analysis of data. *Management information* is knowledge that has action implications because it is accurate, timely, and relevant. MIS is most desirable but can exist only because data have been analyzed to become information for use in a comprehensive management information system.

5. What are the differing information needs at different management levels? How may an MIS be designed to meet these different needs?

   Differing information is needed for managers with three levels of responsibilities: operational control, management control, and strategic planning. The MIS system needs to be designed to collect information for operational control from data within the organization, while information sources for strategic planning tend to arise outside the organization.

6. What are the four major stages in developing a MIS? How may these stages be carried out effectively?

   The design of a MIS follows four broad steps: (1) a preliminary survey and problem definition stage, (2) a conceptual design stage, (3) a detailed design stage, and (4) an implementation stage. In stage one, a task force is created to design the system based on a thorough assessment of the organization's needs. In stage two, alternative designs are developed, each attempting to minimize unwanted consequences based on different standards. In stage three, the MIS is flowcharted; its components and other specifications are set From this a model of the system is developed, tested, and refined until it meets the specified level of performance. In stage four, the organization's data bases are entered into the system and it is given a series of verification checks prior to actual implementation.

7. According to Dickson and Simmons, what five factors determine whether and to what extent the implementation of a new MIS will be resisted?

   (1) Disruption of established departmental boundaries; (2) disruption of the informal system; (3) specific individual characteristics that might occur when a person feels the system interferes with his/her ability to get things done; (4) the organizational culture and (5) how the change is implemented. Resistance to MIS tends to follow hierarchical levels in that top management can simply avoid the system, operating managers may display aggression or avoidance, clerical personnel may practice projection by predicting dire consequences in the future, and nonclerical persons may be aggressive.

8. What are the major security concerns associated with computer-based information systems? How may they be solved?

   Security issues should be addressed during the design stages rather than added as afterthoughts. Security problems fall into four broad categories: physical, software, data, and consequential loss. Physical security is attained by precautions such as controlled access, fire protection, protection from the elements, and detection systems. Software security can be addressed by controlling computer access to monitor persons with freedom to download software. Programs written in-house provide more accessibility to authorized individuals, but as before, access to areas where programs are developed can be monitored. Data security presents the risk of data erasure or unauthorized data addition. Control is attempted by screening alteration access, by limiting access to a computer only to the extent necessary to carry out a responsibility; for example, many persons might have ''read only'' clearance. Higher-level security can be achieved through such means as encryption, passwords, and separation of data sources and points of access.

9. In what three ways may individuals show the frustrations associated with the implementation of a computer-based MIS?

   Dickson and Simmons have identified three major types of frustrations: (1) aggression, where individuals hit back at the object (or person) frustrating them, (2) projection, a psychological means of blaming difficulties on someone or something else—such as a computer, and (3) avoidance, where individuals withdraw from the frustrating situation, often by continuing their own way of doing things.

10. What is a decision support system (DSS)? How does it differ from an MIS?

    DSS is an interactive computer system that may be operated by noncomputer persons to carry out their respective responsibilities. MIS emphasizes standard, periodical reports, and cannot respond well to nonroutine, or *ad hoc,* situations. DSS helps managers make nonroutine decisions in a relatively unstructured, decision-making environment.

11. How can a DSS be used?

    ''The ideal DSS solicits input data needed from the user and then prompts the user to consider all key decision points.'' Thus DSS has a built-in program to make the calculations necessary to figures keyed in by the user. Most spreadsheet applications offer some form of DSS, and off-the-shelf programs are readily available for most routine needs.

12. What is artificial intelligence? How is it applied in problem solving?

    ''Artificial intelligence refers to the use of the computer to simulate characteristics of human thought'' where variables are concurrently analyzed. At present, however, computer intelligence follows an iterative technique where successive trials are performed until the best solution is reached.

13. What is an expert system? How does it differ from an MIS and a DSS?

    An expert system is the ''application of artificial intelligence denoting the technology entailed by the development of computational approaches to human functioning.'' MIS is a computer-based information system for more effective planning, decision making, and control. DSS is a ''computer system accessible to nonspecialists to assist [them] in planning and decision making.''

14. To what kinds of tasks can expert systems be applied?

Four categories of tasks have been identified: (1) resource allocation such as would occur in managing an investment portfolio, making capital budgeting decisions, and even doing personal income tax; (2) problem diagnosis so that review may be made of such things as financial statements, accounts receivable and other numerical data; (3) scheduling and assignments to facilitate managerial decision making for allocating personnel to work assignments; and (4) information management that works on models so computer users can feed information to the system to see a variety of ''what if'' outcomes for use in making a decision from among the alternatives considered.

15. What are the building blocks of an expert system?

(1) Dialogue structure to enable the computer to ask questions in a sequence that provides for an efficient analysis, which reduces the training time for users. (2) Inference engine so that the program can perform its work using a set of realistic assumptions. The inference engine can work from facts to a conclusion (data-driven reasoning) or from a conclusion to the facts (goal-driven reasoning).

16. What are the opportunities and risks associated with end-user computing?

The important point is for management to develop a strategy for end-user computing so that managers know how end-user computing will contribute to productivity. ''The risks associated with end-user computing include increased exposure of both data and software, leading to threats of data security and integrity.'' Another risk is a human one: end-users who do not make effective use of the resources available to them and fail to document their activities.

17. How will future developments in computer technology have an impact on managers, organizations, and their use of information?

The most probable effect will be the capability of organizations to produce and process more information with greater accuracy, speed, and timeliness. Another possible effect is more computer-generated paperwork. From a human resource standpoint there is increasing evidence that the restructuring of businesses has reduced the number of middle managers, and many of those who remain have been relegated to being functionaries responding to computer information. Since information resides within the computer system, there is increasing likelihood that subordinates will have access to information that might formerly have been screened from their purview by zealous managers exercising their prerogatives to control the flow of information.

Answers to End-of-Chapter Case Questions

CASE 1: THE HUMAN EDGE IN SOFTWARE: ELECTRONIC ADVISERS

1. How is Gary Chapman using *The Management Edge* to make decisions?

He is relying on the computer's advice with respect to dealing with people. He first completes an interactive portion of the program to obtain a profile of himself. Then when faced with a situation where he must make a decision regarding another person, he enters data about the person into the computer. Based on a comparative analysis of Gary's human characteristics and those of the other person, the computer makes a recommendation for action. Gary generally follows the advice.

2. What are the limitations of the program? What are the advantages?

The program can be no better than the way it analyzes variables. Further, the majority of a manager's problems are unstructured, and a manager may have insufficient time to use the program as it was intended. Managers may have problem-solving styles unlike the one used in the interactive software, such as working in groups rather than alone. A limitation beyond the program is that new conditions can enter a situation between the time the computer analysis is made and the decision is implemented. The advantage is that the program may cause an individual to give more thought to a situation simply by being forced to obtain information for analysis.

3. Do you agree with Murray Weiner that *The Management Edge* and other such programs are no more than ''games''?

The goal of expert systems is to emulate the abilities and judgments of human experts so that non-experts can make the same level of high-quality decisions. This is not a game. Interactive programs are widely used with respect to financial matters; and while human problems have more variables, the opinions of experts regarding a wide variety of human situations can be focused through computer programs to enable non-experts to at least sharpen their human relations skills.

4. In your opinion, will most managers be using an information system like *The Management Edge* in the future? Explain. Would you be comfortable with such a system? Discuss why or why not.

No. The ego of an individual will continue to foster self-reliance when making many decisions. An expert system, such as the one in this case, will most likely be used in management development programs to help managers learn how to think through problems.

Whether a person would be comfortable with such a system requires a decision of values. Some persons have no difficulty adapting themselves to working in a mechanistic organization where little freedom of action is permitted, while other persons prefer organic structure that requires quick adaptation to new conditions. Students should at least discuss the concepts of *mechanistic* and *organic* as they contemplate discussing this question.

CASE 2: USING DECISION-SUPPORT SYSTEMS AT GENERAL MOTORS

1. Why would shipping large loads infrequently over a specified route reduce transportation costs? Why would inventory costs be increased using the large load approach?

Transportation companies typically charge less for truckloads than they do for less-than-truckloads. In addition to this savings, the receiving company (in this instance the same as the shipping company) has but one order to process. Other cost savings include fewer claims for damages to packages and improved delivery service, which should reduce the imputed costs associated with the goods in transit. Inventory costs will increase because the shipper has to assemble more goods to make up a single shipment; the receiver needs storage space to hold a supply of goods in excess of current needs.

2. Why has General Motors waited until now to develop a decision-support system to evaluate transportation and inventory costs?

An idea needs someone to serve as its champion—to see it through to implementation by overcoming whatever bureaucratic impediments are raised to kill the proposal. Without such a person to shepherd an idea to fruition, little progress is made.

3. To determine the minimum cost solution, what input data are needed for analyzing transportation and inventory cost trade-offs?

The system is built on trade-offs between variables. To do this, the following kinds of data are needed in the computer program: transportation costs, distances involved, inventory costs per item, available routes for each shipment, shipment size, interest rates, sensitivity weights for key variables, and freight tariffs.

4. Why would TRANSPART be useful in assessing just-in-time management strategies?

The concept of just-in-time inventory systems is one in which production quantities are ideally equal to delivery quantities, with materials purchased and finished goods delivered "just in time." This definition identifies what must be done to determine whether it would be better to pay storage costs for reserve inventory, or to avoid such charges and have goods produced, shipped, and delivered just in time.

5. What other manufacturing functions lend themselves to decision-support systems such as the one developed by General Motors?

Any aspect of logistical management since things that move need managerial oversight. Logistics management is part of a system that deals with fixed locations of factories, storage areas, and terminals involved with movement of goods. Thus logistics deals with the physical movement of things and the flow of information dealing with such movement.

6. How useful is a decision support system such as TRANSPART in decision-making activities of small business? Can these tools be used by a manager who has little or no computer experience?

Small businesses can be quite small, or be medium-sized but called small by definition of the Small Business Administration. The very small firms most likely rely on package services such as United Parcel Service, the Post Office, and freight forwarders who consolidate small shipments into large shipments. Thus, the smaller businesses have fewer decision-making options. Yet their managers still need to be aware that goods can be shipped in a variety of ways. The medium-sized businesses can use the same kind of sophistication used by General Motors. Such firms can buy software programs that permit the manager to enter variables and determine the optimum size of shipment and other factors to reduce costs and thereby increase productivity. Therefore, an expert computer system has the expertise in the software and the user of the system needs relatively little knowledge of how computers work.

Suggested Term Paper Topics

1. Avoiding misinformation from a MIS.
2. Techniques to induce managers who avoid computers to use computers.
3. A review and analysis of selected expert software programs.
4. Human rights of privacy in a world of computerized data bases.
5. The vulnerability of middle management as a result of the computer revolution.
6. Methods of minimizing problems of GIGO (garbage in, garbage out) with respect to the analysis of data.
7. The role of telecommunications in a computerized environment.
8. The robotized factory.
9. Maintaining computer security without irritating employees.

Suggested Guest Speakers

1. A manager of data processing from a major corporation to discuss the past, present, and future of the field.
2. A leader of the American Civil Liberties Union to discuss individual liberties and computer data bases.

3. A top manager known for his/her reliance on computer-based information to discuss how he/she became involved with the medium and what the measurable results have been.

Part 5 Case

OSBORNE COMPUTER: TRYING FOR RAPID GROWTH WITHOUT CONTROLS

1. What factors accounted for the surge of competition in the portable computer field? Would these have been anticipated by a prudent executive?

   Key factors include wider acceptance by business users, along with increased interest by sophisticated individuals, rapid technological advances, software-driven computers rather than owners doing all of the programming, price-sensitive demand curve for computers, availability of mass distribution networks, increased respectability for the product as evidenced by IBM's entry, and availability of venture capital.

   The period of rapid expansion, except for firms such as IBM and Tandy, was led by entrepreneurs. Entrepreneurs, by definition, are optimistic risk takers, and being prudent is not characteristic of an entrepreneur. Prudence implies conservatism, caution, and circumspection. the existence of a market and the vision that a niche remained to be filled was a primary motivating force for Osborne.

2. In what ways does this case reveal the importance of the linkage between planning and control?

   The bankruptcy of Osborne Computing provides ample evidence that many kinds of business controls were either not applied or not working as planned. Osborne's production was based on plant capacity rather than on rates of market absorption; this alone caused mounting supplies of finished goods. The company failed to plan for the introduction of its new computer with the result that sales for early models lagged when an inflow of cash was needed. The sales lag occurred because the buying public was waiting for the improved model. A lack of on-going knowledge about what the competition was doing caused another gap in the control process, because Osborne's products were virtually obsolete at the time when competitors were offering improved products. Another major gap between planning and control occurred in the financial arena as cash outflow was more rapid than cash inflow.

3. What kind of controls would you have advised Osborne to set up to prevent its debacle?

   The first control is difficult to apply, but Osborne needed to have ongoing advice to determine when to let an administrator provide guidance rather than to continue as an entrepreneur-administrator. Beyond this key philosophical concept, a series of pre-action controls were needed to ensure that appropriate data was on hand to analize as decision-making information. Pre-action controls force management to write out a strategic plan, the paths to follow to achieve the plan, and an applicable timetable. Steering controls were needed to maintain vigilance that each goal was being pursued according to the overall business plan. Finally, post-action controls were needed to review everything that had occurred and determine what changes were appropriate in the planning process.

4. Did Osborne Computer have any unique strengths that could have enabled it to survive in this hotly competitive industry?

   The strengths probably came into existence too late. The main strength was the administrative talent of several employed persons to take over the operation of the company. The company did have a good name, and had the development of new computers been based on the MS-DOS standard of IBM, Osborne Computer might have survived.

5. If you had been called in as a consultant to Osborne Computer in March 1983, what advice would you have given Jaunich?

   The operating loss in March exceeded $600,000, and this followed February when profits of more than $300,000 had been projected. Such a calamitous reversal in the flow of income should be a red flag. Accordingly, Jaunich should call for an immediate reporting of all resources of the company—especially the financial ones. Losses as described here tend to be the kind that flow from unsold finished goods piling up in a warehouse. Therefore, Jaunich should make an immediate price adjustment to get an inflow of cash to the company to carry it during the time needed to reassess the product, its market, and what changes were needed in both the product and the administrative organization.

CHAPTER 22
Entrepreneurship

Chapter Outline

THE MEANING OF ENTREPRENEURSHIP

Entrepreneurial Roles
Factors Affecting Entrepreneurship
Economic Factors
Noneconomic Factors

THE IMPORTANCE OF ENTREPRENEURSHIP

Economic Growth
Productivity
New Technologies, Products, and Services

THE ENTREPRENEUR

Psychological and Sociological Factors
The Theory of Need-Achievement
Psychosocial Theories
Competence

THE ENTREPRENEURIAL PROCESS

Steps in the Entrepreneurial Process
Choosing a Business

ENTREPRENEURIAL ORGANIZATIONS

Planning and Strategy
Organizing
Leading
Controlling the Entrepreneurial Culture

BARRIERS AND PROBLEMS

The Dark Side of Entrepreneurship

SUMMARY

Key Terms

- **entrepreneur** Either the originator of a new business venture or a manager who tries to improve an organizational unit by initiating productive changes.
- **entrepreneurship** As opposed to management, the seemingly discontinuous process of combining resources to produce changes in production.
- **start-up** Business founded by individuals intending to change the environment of a given industry by the introduction of a new product or production process.
- **research and development (R&D)** Entrepreneurial function devoting organizational assets to the design, testing, and production of new products.
- **macroeconomic policy** Decisions considering such factors as taxation, development costs, regulatory control, and other external factors that might affect the development of a new product.
- **need-achievement** According to McClelland, a social motive to excel that tends to characterize successful entrepreneurs, especially when reinforced by cultural factors.
- **distinctive competence** Entrepreneurial desire to start a business coupled with the ability or experience to compete effectively once the enterprise is initiated.
- **franchising** Entrepreneurial system whereby an individual runs a business based on the right granted by a manufacturer or other organization to market a good or service.
- **intrapreneuring** Corporate entrepreneurship whereby an organization seeks to expand by exploring new opportunities through new combinations of its existing resources.
- **entrepreneurial culture** According to Stevenson and Gumbert, corporate culture focusing on the emergence of new opportunities, the means of capitalizing on them, and the creation of the structure appropriate for pursuing them.
- **administrative culture** According to Stevenson and Gumpert, corporate culture focusing on existing opportunities, organizational structure, and control procedures.

Chapter Overview/Synopsis

Entrepreneurs are growing in both their economic and their political influence. A large number of the nation's new jobs are being created by entrepreneurs. Entrepreneurs also influence the nation's noneconomic sphere through their cultural values. Members of Congress now recognize the political clout of many thousands of small business owners who combine their self-interest to oppose or support legislation.

Studies indicate that it takes a special breed of individual to become an entrepreneur. David McClelland found that persons following the entrepreneurial route have high interest in personal achievement. Other researchers have concluded that entrepreneurs are comfortable with taking risks and have a tolerance for ambiguity and uncertainty.

Major corporations have discovered that the entrepreneurial spirit is not limited to small businesses: the entrepreneurial spirit can exist anywhere. Thus, larger businesses now strive to imbue their managers with a willingness to accept risk, uncertainty, and ambiguity. But a small business is not big business. Researchers, therefore, suggest that managers of big business should not try to combine the entrepreneurial spirit with administrative necessities of the corporation since they are different cultures. Yet such cultures can coexist in big businesses so that administrators can continue working toward the economies of scale, while the entrepreneurial managers can probe new frontiers to seek better ways to turn ideas into profits.

Analysis of Illustrative Case Study

INTRODUCTION—START-UP PAINS AT NOVA PHARMACEUTICAL CORPORATION

The entrepreneurial spirit moved Donald J. Stark to resign as president of Sterling Drug's Pharmaceutical Group to become president of a fledgling pharmaceutical company, Nova. Nova had been started by a three-man group who felt the ethical drug industry held promise of excellent rewards for persons willing to take leadership in the discovery and development of new products for the industry. Each person connected with Nova is assuming risk, because during the early stages of a company such as this one, speculation appears more prominent than security. Yet entrepreneurs see challenges in risk, uncertainty, and ambiguity. This is the early stage of Nova.

CONTINUED—START-UP PAINS AT NOVA PHARMACEUTICAL CORPORATION

Along with the problems associated with attempting to discover a new and effective drug, Nova needs sufficient financing to carry it through the time necessary to develop and obtain governmental approval of new drugs. Thus, in addition to the entrepreneurial spirit, a company such as Nova needs capital resources to sustain it. So far, Nova has been able to obtain sufficient infusions of money to maintain a place in the industry.

WRAP-UP—START-UP PAINS AT NOVA PHARMACEUTICAL CORPORATION

A significant component of larger businesses is the administrative resource that helps bring about the needed coordination of organizational resources to move the company toward its objectives. Smaller firms such as Nova lack the financial resources for a separate administrative section staffed with specialists; instead, the entrepreneurial organization needs its innovative people to also assume the regular duties of planning, organizing, staffing, directing, and controlling. Nova has been able to merge the needs of operation with administration, but more time will be needed to determine whether the company can become a stable part of a major industry.

Answers to End-of-Chapter Questions

1. What function do entrepreneurs play in the productive process? How does this role sometimes overlap with others?

Entrepreneurs have the vision to see how a need can be satisfied through their creativity in establishing and operating an organization of their own design. An entrepreneur, however, cannot remain aloof from the routine aspects of managing resources. In this sense, the role of being an innovator must also be combined with duties of being a capitalist and a manager.

2. How do societies sometimes differ in the extent to which they encourage entrepreneurship?

Entrepreneurship exists best in societies where individuals have governmental support to display personal initiative. In this environment they may undertake risk and reap the rewards of success or suffer a loss of personal resources if the enterprise does not succeed. Thus, capitalist nations have more publicly acknowledged entrepreneurial endeavors than socialistic ones.

3. How have scholarly attitudes toward entrepreneurship changed since 1960?

Scholars shifted their emphasis from the management of the supply of goods through manipulating interest and taxation rates to that of improving the supply of goods and services. This supply-side type of economic is the domain of the entrepreneur.

4. How does entrepreneurship contribute to economic growth, productivity, and change?

Studies indicate that small businesses are the engines for employment since they create more new jobs than do larger businesses. David Birch, a researcher, has concluded that "four-fifth of all new employment openings come from small businesses." With respect to productivity—the capability to produce more output with less input of resources—small businesses must be efficient in order to survive. Thus, they have been leaders in obtaining growth of productivity. Entrepreneurs, almost by definition, are agents of change since they find unfilled needs and establish ventures designed to fill the demand.

5. How can one entrepreneurial innovation give rise to many others?

Innovation often needs others to provide the means for widespread application. Thus, the invention of the semiconductor meant little without computers and computer-type products based on semiconductors. Similarly, the cotton gin of the 19th century spawned an entire industry—textiles.

6. How does David McClelland's theory of need-achievement account for the emergence of individual entrepreneurs? How have McClelland's ideas evolved over the years? What are other psychosocial theories of entrepreneurship?

Entrepreneurs are people who like the challenge of risk, along with the satisfaction that comes from beating the odds. McClelland was interested in both the psychological and sociological factors that caused people to become entrepreneurs. He concluded that entrepreneurship was the link between need-achievement and economic growth. Studies by Begley and Boyd built on McClelland's. These two researchers determined that a high need achievement existed in people who felt they controlled their own lives. Other studies of psychological behavior encapsulated many ideas about entrepreneurs into a behavioral type called Type A behavior—"a chronic, incessant struggle to achieve more and more in less and less time, and if required to do so, against the opposing efforts of other things or other persons."

7. What decisions must entrepreneurs make about the organizational form their ventures should have? How do they make these decisions?

Entrepreneurs consider such things as the intended size of the business, scope, growth vector, degree of risk to undertake, similar businesses, and personal preference. The primary legal forms of organization are the proprietorship, general partnership, limited partnership, and the corporation. Small businesses frequently organize as an S corporation. The S corporation operates under a special provision of the tax code that permits its owners to elect to be taxed the same as proprietorships or corporations. The number of stockholders is limited to thirty-five. The amount of capital needed may influence the organization choice since it is assumed a corporation can raise capital more readily than can a proprietorship or a partnership. Personal preference cannot be ignored since entrepreneurs have a high need achievement profile—therefore, the desire to be one's own boss may be a critical dimension in choosing the organizational form.

8. What are Druker's entrepreneurial strategies and the advantages and disadvantages of each?

Peter Drucker has identified a series of strategies used by successful entrepreneurs: (1) "Fustest with the mostest." The momentum of an early start carries a major advantage for a firm that judges the market correctly. Of course, being first in the market can also leave a firm all alone in a market that shifts in another direction. (2) "Creative imitation." While a firm may not be the first to develop a product or service, the one able to identify a potential beyond that envisioned by its creator may be the marketplace winner. As before, a firm can make an incorrect decision with respect to placing its faith in copying and improving on what other firms are doing. (3) "Entrepreneurial judo." A firm leaps over competitors by employing a process or technique that renders those of the competitor obsolete. The danger here, according to Drucker, is a firm becoming arrogant with its place in the market or lead in production processes. This arrogance arises because management believes their firm to be on the "cutting edge" and that competition is not a major factor. (4) "Maximizing rather than optimizing." Companies that charge a premium price may take the cream off the top of the market, but they may fail to recognize when the market depth holds far more promise of profitability.

9. Why does Drucker, unlike Burgleman, think that entrepreneurial ventures must always be kept separate from a company's conventional units?

Drucker states: "The entrepreneurial, the new, has to be organized separately from the old and existing. Whenever we have tried to make an existing unit the carrier of the entrepreneurial project, we have failed." Burgleman feels that "operational linkages should be strong, to take advantage of the existing capabilities and skills and to facilitate transferring back newly developed ones."

10. How do the "entrepreneurial" and the "administrative" corporate cultures differ?

Howard H. Stevenson and David E. Gumpert determined that there are significant differences between the culture of the entrepreneur and the administrator. They ask separate questions. While the administrator asks "What resources do I control?" the entrepreneur asks "Where is the opportunity? How do I capitalize on it? What resources do I need? How do I gain control over them? What structure is best?"

11. What internal and external problems do entrepreneurs face?

Psychologists recognize that one problem of the entrepreneur may be himself since the road to success is not smooth. Consequently, the entrepreneur can be faced with such problems as self-doubt, wondering whether the rewards are worth the risks, and that some other endeavor would have been better. External problems include obtaining adequate financing, retaining competent employees, marketing difficulties, and governmental regulations designed for large businesses applying to a small business.

Answers to End-of-Chapter Case Questions

CASE 1: SPACE SAVING AND COST CUTTING AT ASSOCIATED VIDEO HUT, INC.

1. What are the risks to Associated Video Hut, Inc.?

   A major risk stems from the assumption that people are willing to pay a premium price at a drive-up location rather than a lower price at a competing outlet, such as a chain grocery store, that also restricts its stock to the latest hits. Experts agree that the most critical factor in retailing is *location*. Video Hut will have less risk with location since its kiosks can be moved to other locations. Nevertheless, the risk remains regarding how long a person will wait behind another car whose driver is mulling over a selection. At least two decisions are involved in renting a movie: to rent the movie and to select the movie. While the first decision is made prior to arriving at a kiosk, the second decision may or may not be made before learning what is available and weighing one choice against another. Of course, all the standard risks associated with starting a business apply to Associated Video Hut.

2. How would Peter Drucker characterize the company's entrepreneurial strategy?

   The primary strategy could be ''creative imitation'' since the owners are seeking a niche within a crowded field. They hope a market exists for a highly specialized approach that limits product selection to ones desired by most customers.

3. How does Associated Video Hut, Inc., create value for customers? Suppliers? Employees? Communities where stores are located? The owners?

   Each rental, by definition, creates value for a customer. Otherwise, the person would have rented a movie. An economic utility is satisfied since a want is fulfilled. In a similar fashion, suppliers satisfy Associated Video Hut's desire to carry current video films in stock. Persons without employment of desiring to change occupations also satisfy a want through employment. Communities may benefit in several ways such as through property and occupation taxes, money remaining in the community for further spending, and persons being employed who might otherwise be on welfare. The owners have satisfied a need with a result of receiving a profit. But in this case the owners are seeking to maximize rather than to optimize—a problem Peter Drucker says may lead to difficulty because they are satisfying too few people to sustain the business.

CASE 2: PRO-LINE CORPORATION PUTS A NEW FACE ON AN OLD INDUSTRY

1. How would you characterize Pro-Line's strategy?

   Pro-Line is following the creative imitation strategy identified by Peter Drucker. While hair care products already existed and were supplied by other companies, Pro-Line set out to target an ethnic market by marketing variations of such products. This strategy also includes the marketing approach of appealing to ethnic pride.

2. What have been the key factors in its success so far?

   The product filled a need that existed in the target market. The company expanded its product line to meet additional needs of its customers. Beyond the product are the leadership factors of Comer Cottrell and his belief in his ability to operate the business, which starts small and then becomes a larger business needing administrative talents as well.

3. What are some potential problems? Do you think there is a worldwide market for Pro-Line's products?

   A key problem area arises from competition since Pro-Line does not ''own'' its market. Johnson Products is well known, and Revlon, while not black-owned, has considerable marketing expertise in selling to ethnic markets. Pro-Line needs to reflect the hair needs of its markets since Pro-Line's customers have changing tastes regarding their hair styles. Yet hair care and cosmetics have assumed increased importance to black women who have professional-type jobs. The world market already exists: Johnson Products generates considerable sales volume from African nations. Pro-Line will need to have contacts with a distributor that can help the company penetrate foreign markets.

4. What are the key factors of a five-year plan?

   Cottrell's main strategy in a five-year plan is steady growth. In order to obtain this steady growth, the strategy needs to include the development of an administrative organization to mange the resources and guide the company through its growth evolution from medium-sized to a larger business. All of this requires the development of an administrative hierarchy to oversee each stage of the growth without being bogged down with the bloat of an unimaginative bureaucracy.

Suggested Term Paper Topics

1. An analysis of jobs created by entrepreneurs and those by big business.
2. Ways of interesting college students to consider entrepreneurship.
3. An analysis of the growth of a business that began as an entrepreneurship.
4. Entrepreneurial freedoms emerging in the Soviet Union.
5. Entrepreneurial success in political lobbying activities.
6. A review of major trade associations that cater to small businesses, such as the National Restaurant Association, and the National Federation of Independent Business.
7. Unionization successes and problems in organizing employees of small businesses.
8. Contribution to the Gross National Product by small business.
9. A study of entrepreneurial activities by persons whose jobs had been eliminated through downsizing of major corporations.

Suggested Guest Speakers

1. The owner of an emerging business to provide a ''case history'' of the trials and tribulations of a person embarking on a new business.
2. A representative of the Small Business Administration to discuss that agency's work in assisting entrepreneurs.
3. Many communities have a venture capital group. The Small Business Administration should be able to identify the president of such a group who could address the class about how its members assess requests for capital.

CHAPTER 23
Organizational Careers and Individual Development

Chapter Outline

EARLY ORGANIZATIONAL CAREER EXPERIENCES

The Formation of Expectations
- The Reality Shock Syndrome
- The Realistic Job Preview

Early Job Experiences
- Initial Job Assignment
- Actions of the First Supervisor
- How Individuals Fit in the Organizational Culture

EARLY CAREER DILEMMAS

Political Insensitivity and Passivity
Loyalty Dilemmas
Personal Anxiety
Role Conflict
Stress
- Causes of Stress
- Effects of Stress
- Managing Stress

CAREERS OVER TIME

Careers and the Life Cycle
- The Erikson Model
- The Levinson Model

Career Patterns and Themes
- Driver's Career Concepts
- Schein's Career Anchors

Careers within Organizations
- Schein's Conical Model
- Four Career Roles and Relationships

The Career Plateau
- Management Career States
- Options at the Career Plateau

INDIVIDUAL CAREER MANAGEMENT

Individual Career Planning
- Realistic Career Strategies
- Managing the Work Situation

Handling Specific Career Issues
- Dual-Career Couples
- Mentors and Mentoring Relationships
- Women's Careers in Management

SUMMARY

Key Terms

- **syndrome of unused potential** or **reality shock syndrome** According to Hall, an individual's reaction to the difference between high job expectations and the frustrating day-to-day realities of the workplace.
- **realistic job preview (RJP)** Description provided by an organization to applicants and new employees that summarizes both the positive and negative aspects of the job.
- **role conflict** According to Katz and Kahn, a situation in which an individual is confronted by two or more incompatible demands.
- **stress** The tension and pressure that result when an individual views a situation as presenting a demand that threatens to exceed his or her capabilities or resources.
- **stressor** Source of pressure and tension that creates stress.
- **quantitative overloading** Situation that occurs when an individual is given more tasks than he or she can accomplish in a given time.
- **qualitative overloading** Situation occurring when an individual lacks the abilities or resources necessary for the satisfactory completion of a task.
- **underloading** Stress, resulting in boredom and monotony, produced when an individual has insufficient work to do.
- **burnout** State of emotional, mental, and physical exhaustion that results from continued exposure to high stress.
- **transformational coping** According to Maddi and Kobasa, the process whereby commitment to work values, a sense of control over work variables, and the view of problems as challenges can turn stressful situations in less stressful directions.
- **coping skills training** Programs teaching people to recognize and cope with situations in which they feel helpless.
- **relaxation training** Popular methods, including mediation and biofeedback, by which individuals learn to control muscle tension and ease the experience of stress.

- **career concepts** According to Driver, four basic career patterns—linear, steady state, spiral, and transitory—by which people perceive their careers.
- **linear career concept** According to Driver, career concept by which an individual chooses a field, develops a plan for advancement, and executes it.
- **steady-state career concept** According to Driver, career concept by which an individual chooses a field but, even through improving professionally and financially, does not seek to move up the organizational hierarchy.
- **spiral career concept** According to Driver, career concept by which individuals motivated by personal growth perform well enough to advance in status and rank.
- **transitory career concept** According to Driver, career concept by which an individual moves from one job to another with no apparent pattern or progress.
- **career anchor** According to Schein, an occupational self-concept—an individual's sense of the kind of work he or she seeks to pursue and what that work implies about the individual.
- **vertical movement** According to Schein, hierarchical change in one's formal rank or management level.
- **radial movement** According to Schein, movement either toward or away from an organization's central "core" of power.
- **circumferential movement** According to Schein, transfer from one division, function, or department to another.
- **apprentice** Starting worker who usually does routine work under a supervisor or mentor.
- **colleague** Worker who, while still subordinate, makes independent contributions to organizational activities.
- **mentor** Employee who develops ideas, supervises others, and assumes responsibility for the work of subordinates.
- **sponsor** Upper-level manager involved in the major decision-making activities of the organization.
- **career plateau** Career stage in which the likelihood of additional hierarchical promotion is very low
- **psychosocial funciton** According to Krain, the aspect of a professional relationship that improves one's sense of competence, identity, and effectiveness.

CHAPTER OVERVIEW/SYNOPSIS

First jobs may not meet a person's expectations. Some persons think to themselves, "If only I had known . . . . " Individuals often have inflated desires to be achieved in a job and learn that the wanted progress is either not materializing or appears too far in the future. Thus, one aspect of a person's career growth is often called the reality shock syndrome. Employers can prevent much of this syndrome by offering a realistic job preview to prospective employees, and certainly the job applicant can ask questions to bring out the key elements of a job.

New employees prefer stimulating challenges from their work as a means of identifying with the employer to increase prospects for a brighter future. Lacking such challenge and a realistic job preview, employees may experience stress. Inner stress drives a person to greater achievement, but external stress can be dysfunctional when it arises from the organizational environment.

The starting point for persons desiring to embark on a career is to understand one's desires and wants from work, a career, or life itself. Most investigators advocate early career planning to enable a person to follow a series of planned steps to the desired level of success.

Other aspects of career-choice problems involve dual-career couples who have to balance personal demands with those of employment. Women, even though many job barriers have been surmounted, continue to face problems with respect to such things as attitudes of co-workers, organizational politic, policies, and procedures.

Analysis of Illustrative Case Study

INTRODUCTION—SELINA PROCTOR: PARENT AND PROFESSIONAL

Selina faces a problem common to mothers, whether working for wages or working as a homemaker: balancing the demands for personal attention. In this instance, Selina feels the following demands: (1) Her daughter has an apparent ear infection and needs medical attention, (2) Selina has an early job-related appointment that was difficult to arrange, (3) her husband is perceived as not carrying a share of child care responsibilities, and (4) all the other pressures of being a mother, wife, housekeeper, and wage earner. Selina is lying awake in bed trying to sort out these kinds of demands.

CONTINUED—SELINA PROCTOR: PARENT AND PROFESSIONAL

The pressures from work and home have created a stressful situation for Selina. Too many strains have converged at once with respect to working out today's dilemma of balancing her need to attend an important meeting, to secure medical treatment for Elizabeth, and to reconcile her attitudes toward her husband. While there are no textbook answers for Selina, she will have to make a decision within the next few hours.

WRAP-UP—SELINA PROCTOR: PARENT AND PROFESSIONAL

Even though Selina will get through the day one way or another, she still has the stress of considering whether she can continue working while carrying out her perceived responsibilities as a parent, employee, wife, and homemaker. Selina can continue to work part-time and take care of her child because day care centers work with children who need special help. There are also organizations that supply practical nurses for occasions when the mother cannot take care of the need of her child. Thus in addition to making a career choice, Selina needs to obtain information regarding what kind of support is available for a working parent.

Answers to End-of-Chapter Review Questions

1. Why do you think individuals develop unrealistic expectations about their first jobs? Why is this tendency especially severe among business school graduates?

The recruiting process may contribute to unrealistic expectations. Also, as an applicant, a person might overstate job qualifications, which leads to unrealized expectations when job performance is not up to the employer's expectations. MBAs learn about business from a top management perspective and see themselves in such roles. The clash between the graduate's job expectations and the realities of the job often leads to job turnover.

2. What is reality shock? What factors contribute to it?

Reality shock is the disparity between initial job expectations and the realities of the job. Reality shock can stem from learning that employees have to conform to many job requirements such as starting and stopping times, work rules, dress codes, learning the culture, and other ways of working within a fairly rigid structure.

3. What three factors in an individual's early job experiences have an especially strong influence on subsequent job success? Why are these factors so influential?

The three factors are initial job assignment, actions of the first supervisor, and how the individual fits in with the organization's culture. Berlew and Hall suggest the individual job assignment is critical since early success with challenging assignments leads to internalizing the performance standards of the company. The first supervisor imparts values and attitudes about the company to the new employees. The supervisor also imparts work expectations of the new personnel. Each organization has a culture, and while a perfect fit is not necessary, employees and organizations need to be compatible.

4. Why are young business school graduates often insensitive to the political dimension of organizational life. What is the proper function of political alliances in an organization?

Business school graduates may tend to feel their background should earn them an inside track to the top. The realities of organizational life, however, suggest that people "have to pay their dues" as part of making their way through the organization. Rather than learn how to work within the political structure of an organization, some employees may withdraw and become passive and just take what comes. Therefore, Webber's research finding is that people "who learn to accept organizational realities as they are can adapt more quickly to the organization."

5. Webber describes five common ways by which loyalty may be defined by a superior. What are these five ways? What ethical and other conflicts arise sometimes for subordinates in applying these directives?

(1) "Obey me." Managers expect legitimate directives to be accepted. (2) "Protect me and don't make me look bad." The boss is ultimately responsible and expects subordinates to contribute to that success. The ethical dimension is one of avoiding a situation where a mistake is covered up to protect a boss. (3) "Work hard." This is part of the work ethic held by many managers. The ethical dilemma is one of working so hard that quality standards suffer. (4) "Be successful." People say, "think success, act success, and be successful." Therefore, get the job done is what managers want. A worker has to distinguish between competition and contention for the spoils of an unfair advantage. (5) "Tell me the truth." Bosses are willing to defend their employees but they object to be placed in a position of having to explain them. The ethical problem is one of avoiding punishment for a mistake while still keeping the boss informed.

6. In what three ways can people respond to the organization's efforts to enforce compliance with its expectations? Which way do you think is best? Why?

Conformity, rebellion, and creative individualism. To determine which way seems best depends on whether the organization is mechanistic (structure) or organic (unstructured). In the mechanistic organization, employees are expected to conform or find another type of employment. In an organic organization, an employee is expected to make decisions and question directives when a better way appears to be possible.

7. What are the six types of role conflict identified by Katz and Kahn?

(1) *Intrasender conflict* arises when a supervisor gives a subordinate a set of incompatible orders or expectations. (2) *Intersender conflict* arises when orders or expectations from an executive through a supervisor cause the work group to let their immediate supervisor know that too much is being asked. (3) *Person-role conflict* exists when a person's job is incompatible with his/her expectations. (4) *In role overload conflict* too many sources are providing an individual with the feeling that too much is being asked. (5) *Role ambiguity* exists when a person is unclear about his assigned responsibilities. (6) *Inter-role conflict* arises when different roles undertaken by one person give rise to conflicting demands on how each role should be carried out.

8. What are the most common causes of stress? How can stress affect health? Describe the various procedures that can be used to reduce stress and help people deal with it.

The most common causes: responsibility for others, lack of participation in decisions, undergoing a performance evaluation, and feeling that a change in the organization will have personal repercussions. The belief among many doctors is that 50 to 70 percent of all physical illnesses are related to stress. There is a known link between stress and heart disease. Stress management includes changing one's life style, seeking social supports, and being committed to one's work rather than being alienated by it. Managers can help by decentralizing authority, being certain that procedures are not only fair but appear to be fair, and using forms of job enlargement and enrichment.

9. What are the ten stages in Levinson's model of adult development?

—Age 40–45: Mid-life transition with respect to son must successfully break away from family ties.
—Age 22–28: Entering the adult world following the completion of one's education and making commitments for future accomplishments.
—Age 28–33: A transition period where a person reviews progress to date and makes appropriate adjustments to goals if needed.
—Age 33–40: The individual settles down and focuses on career advancement.
—Age 40–45: Mid-life transition with respect to career goals. If goals are not being met, a mid-life crisis may ensue.
—Age 45–50: The person enters middle adulthood and reassesses the mid-life transition. There may be a sense of fulfillment also.
—Age 50–55: Another transition period where a crisis may develop.
—Age 55–60: Culmination of middle adulthood—a stable period.
—Age 60–65: Late adult transition where a person may reflect on life's accomplishment or even retire from the activities of employment.
—Age 65 and older: Late adulthood where a person takes time to sum up life and even undertake activities that had been neglected earlier.

10. Compare Driver's career concepts notion with Schein's idea of career anchors.

Driver's concepts: (1) The linear concept where life progresses step-by-step. (2) The steady-state concept where a person starts a job and stays with it as a career. (3) The spiral career concept that permits a person to "spiral" upward by changing fields from time to time. (4) The transitory career concept that exists for people who drift through a series of jobs without ever evidencing commitment. Schein, on the other hand, traces a person's work life through categories such as (1) technical/functional/managerial competence, (2) a need for security, (3) a need for creativity, and (5) a need for autonomy.

11. Identify individuals you know who work for organizations and try to fit them into the career stages or states of the various models presented in the chapter. Can they be accurately placed?

Other than testing each person for fitting the category, no other help can be offered.

12. According to Schein, what three types of movement are possible within organizations? What three types of organizational boundaries exist? How does the organization attempt to influence the individual who is making a position change? What can the individual do to most effectively influence the organization?

Schein proposed a conical model for depicting an individual's movement within an organization: (1) Vertical movement: this is the traditional hierarchical change in one's rank, and the boundaries are the entry point of each rank. (2) Radial movement: this is movement either toward or away from the organization's center of power. The boundaries are points where a person is either a part of a power group or not. (3) Circumferential movement: a transfer from one organizational unit to another with the boundary being the acceptance by members of the group to be joined. Organizational attempts to influence the individual depends on the type of movement being made. In a vertical or radial movement, members of the new unit attempt to socialize the new member to "do things their way." With respect to circumferential movement, members of the new unit will emphasize training. Each of these kinds of influence help the new member become both accepted and successful in the new assignment. The ability of a new member to influence members of the new unit depends a great deal on position, experience, and age. Thus a relatively new and young employee will have less success in attempting to influence the new unit with ideas than will a more experienced employee with a record of success.

13. List the nine steps in Schoonmaker's career strategy. How reasonable do they sound to you?

1. Accept the fact that there are some inescapable and irreconcilable conflicts between you and your organization.
2. Accept the fact that your superiors are essentially indifferent to your career ambitions.
3. Analyze your own goals.
4. Analyze your assets and liabilities.
5. Analyze your opportunities.
6. Learn the rules for company politics.
7. Plan your career.
8. Carry out your plan.
9. Chart your progress.

Students will most likely agree the steps are reasonable.

14. What are three most important steps one can take in the work situation to further one's career?

(a) Do excellent work; (b) develop good working relationships with one's boss; (c) help your boss to succeed. It also helps to be mobile, to find a sponsor, to be visible, and to present a positive image.

15. What are the special issues that must be confronted by dual-career couples? Discuss the four general styles of managing two careers.

There is a need to plan both careers cooperatively. Each person needs to be flexible and to be willing to compromise to achieve balance between competing desires. Francine and Douglas Hall identified four general styles of effectively managing two careers: (1) Accommodaters—couples resemble the traditional family where one person is looked upon in a focal role. (2) Adversaries—the members are deeply involved in each of their respective careers, and neither is willing to make career sacrifices. (3) Allies—"the two spouses are both highly involved in either their career or home roles and place little emphasis on the other area." (4) Acrobats—couples are highly involved in their respective roles and may take over roles for both the family and the career rather than ask the other partner to assume any responsibility.

16. According to Kram, what are the two categories of functions served by mentors? Should one assume that it is imperative to find an individual to serve as one's mentor? Why or why not?

The two categories are career functions and psychosocial functions. Kram feels it is better for a person to develop a network of mutually supporting relationships to serve the mentoring function than to restrict mentoring to one person. Which is best depends on the mentoring relationship. The problem to avoid, according to Kram, is misdirected efforts to identify a mentor.

17. What are some of the special problems faced by women in management?

Women deal with the same issues as men but with additional obstacles. There may be stereotyped images of a woman's role to overcome—both by colleagues and the woman herself. A married woman often faces conflicting demands of a job and a home. There may also be company policies and procedures built on a male-dominated structure that serve as barriers to full membership in the management fraternity.

Answers to End-of-Chapter Case Questions

CASE: ANDREW KRIEGER'S CAREER DECISION AT SOROS FUND

1. In what stage of his career is Mr. Krieger?

Mr. Krieger faces a career choice of becoming his own boss with the accompanying risks or satisfactions, or of becoming part of a team operation with an established business. On Driver's scale, Krieger is following a transitory career concept where he moves from one job to another with no apparent progress. According to the Levinson model, Krieger is in the transition stage where progress is not what he wants and he is thinking of a radical change in his career.

2. What are the factors that are causing stress in Mr. Krieger's life?

Much of his success stems from being a star, but he knows that some of his "winning" comes at the expense of colleagues who are unable to do their jobs because of his monopolizing needed resources. Stemming from this is pressure placed on him by his superiors, who question whether he is working toward organizational goals or personal attainments. Having one's performance appraised is a known source of stress. His lack of support from colleagues contributes to his stress. He is also experiencing some stress from home since family members are questioning how his work contributes to the good of society.

3. What can he do to manage this stress?

Some stress is part of living. Mr. Krieger's stress level appears too high because of personal demands conflicting with those of the job as well as pressures at home regarding how his work benefits other people. Since most of his stress exists because of his personal decisions rather than those of his employer, the main approach to stress management resides with Krieger. Mostly, he needs to decide whether to continue employment with a major organization or branch out on his own. If he remains with a major employer, he will need to reconcile himself to being a team player—something he has not yet demonstrated. Therefore, it appears he needs to embark on a career choice where he is the main player. This, too, will have stress, but its source will not be that of an employer and his colleagues. He cannot delegate much of what he does because he makes decisions that involve personal judgments that would not accompany a grant of delegated authority.

Suggested Term Paper Topics

1. Employer approaches to minimizing employee "burn-out."
2. An analysis of successful job searches by persons in mid-life.
3. An analysis of job failures by young employees.
4. Ways of using stress as an element of personal motivation.
5. A review of techniques for the relief of stressful job situations.
6. An analysis of factors that influence the selection of a career path.
7. All "deadwood" was once alive: a review of factors that cause people to become organizational "deadwood."
8. A review of adjustments made by successful dual-career couples.
9. A series of profiles of successful women top managers.

Suggested Guest Speakers

1. The director of career placement of a college or university to speak about the service available to students through that center.
2. An expert on mental health to discuss how factors on and off the job affect a person's stress level and what kinds of activities the person can engage in to reduce stress or what agencies offer necessary assistance.
3. An organization's affirmative action director to discuss the activities of that office in helping protected classes of persons find employment that is considered nontraditional.

CHAPTER 24 International Management

Chapter Outline

THE INCREASING INTERNATIONALIZATION OF THE WORLD ECONOMY

A Brief History
Why Companies Go International
How Companies Go International
Managerial Attitudes Toward Internationalization

THE MULTINATIONAL ENTERPRISE

The Rise and Spread of Multinational Enterprises
The Impact of MNE Operations
The Impact of MNEs on Host Countries
The Impact of MNEs on Home Countries

THE CHALLENGES OF MULTINATIONAL MANAGEMENT

Managing in a Multinational Environment
Handling the Differences
Adjusting the Management Process
Planning
Organizing
Staffing
Leading
Controlling

SELECTING A MANAGERIAL APPROACH

Applying U.S. Approaches Abroad
Applying Japanese Approaches Abroad and Synthesizing Differing Approaches

SUMMARY

Key Terms

- **Multinational companies** Those which operate in more than one country, including investing in foreign manufacturing facilities.
- **product-cycle theory** According to Vernon, the process whereby products originally developed for home markets earn enough foreign demand to justify direct foreign investment in their production.
- **ethnocentric management** Attitude that the home country's management practices are superior to those of other countries and can be exported along with the organization's goods and services.
- **polycentric management** Attitude that since a foreign country's management policies are best understood by its own management personnel, the home organization should rely on foreign offices.
- **geocentric management** Attitude that accepts both similarities and differences between domestic and foreign management policies and so attempts to strike a balance between those that are most effective.
- **multinational enterprise (MNE)** Large corporation with operations and divisions spread over several countries but controlled by a central headquarters.
- **political risk** Possibility that political changes, either in the short or long run, can affect the activities of an organization doing business in foreign countries.
- **global strategic partnership** An alliance formed by an organization with one or more foreign countries, generally with an eye toward exploiting the other countries' opportunities and toward assuming leadership in either supply or production.
- **bureaucratic control** A method of control that employs strict regulations to ensure desired behavior by organizational units; often used by multinational enterprises to control subsidiaries.
- **culture control** The method of control, often associated with large Japanese companies, that emphasizes implicit and informal direction based on a broad company culture.

Chapter Overview/Synopsis

The economic interdependence of nations fosters the growth of multinational firms that conduct business on a global scale where markets are more important than political boundaries. Some critics argue that multinational businesses are primarily oligopolistic since a relative few dominate world markets. Managers may also view ownership of foreign businesses as a prudent way to diversify the company's ''portfolio'' of production and marketing facilities.

Following World War II, multinationalism grew rapidly with the emphasis on open markets, partly as a result of increased prosperity with its concomitant purchasing power. Multinational enterprises (MNEs) appear to have a positive effect on their host nation through, for example, infusion of capital, transfer of both technical and managerial technology, and improvement in the nation's balance of payments.

Managers operating in an international environment deal with a variety of unique challenges growing out of such factors as politics, economics, and cultures. The size of MNEs indicates the existence of a high degree of bureaucracy, which emphasizes uniformity—this creates special problems for managers involved in cross-cultural situations. Probably no single method of managing works for all cultures; however, many arguments have asserted that the success of Japanese firms indicates the existence of a successful approach to managing that is effective between cultures.

Analysis of Illustrative Case Study

INTRODUCTION—SUMITOMO: THE THRUST TOWARD INTERNATIONAL BANKING

Advancements in technology and an increased need for political and economic interdependence have fostered an environment where global businesses can flourish. Japan's Sumitomo Bank represents a business that now has worldwide banking and investment activities. To capitalize on favorable conditions, a business must be ready. Sumitomo Bank began preparing itself to take advantage of business opportunities in the 1960s when it first committed itself to state-of-the art electronic banking. This was followed by other technological refinements such as electronic cash dispensers. Thus Sumitomo has been able to position itself in other countries to achieve greater profitability in its overall operations.

In 1984, Sumitomo bought 52.7 percent of Luxemburg Bank—this permitted a Japanese bank to gain a foothold in another nation. Two years later the bank acquired 12.5 percent of Goldman-Sachs & Company, one of the largest investment banks in the United States. While U.S. laws currently prevent Sumitomo's full involvement in the management of Goldman-Sachs, Sumitomo is looking ahead to the future when present laws may be modified or even repealed.

Sumitomo has adopted several techniques to promote efficiency in its operations. It streamlined its internal operations, and it has also diversified into fee-generating services not subject to typical economic regulation by political entities. Clearly, Sumitomo has a long-range goal of becoming the CitiBank of Japan.

CONTINUED—SUMITOMO: THE THRUST TOWARD INTERNATIONAL BANKING

Sumitomo's operations reveal the wisdom of its Banca del Gottardo acquisition because of leverage possible with direct investment. Its ownership interest in Goldman-Sachs indicates how indirect foreign investment can enhance a foreign company's involvement in global business. Sumitomo is moving toward attaining its global goals; yet each expansion into a new market further stretches the bank's managerial capability to meet the challenges of dealing with different conditions, people, and diverse cultures.

WRAP-UP—SUMITOMO: THE THRUST TOWARD INTERNATIONAL BANKING

One reason for Sumitomo's venture into the United States is the environment of deregulation. The deregulation of many aspects of banking permits a climate conductive to more competition. The bank is taking a position that further deregulation of U.S. banking will occur. Watchers of global businesses predict that Sumitomo has the managerial skills to succeed among businesses in an increasingly competitive global market.

Answers to End-of-Chapter Review Questions

1. Why do companies become internationalized?

No one set of explanations answers the question since most decisions are business-specific rather than generalized. Academic theories vary depending on one's point of view. One theory maintains that capital moves from where returns on capital are lower to where returns are higher. This "commonsense" answer was questioned by Steven Hymer, who noted that firms may have different reasons to operate in foreign markets, such as to avoid tariffs or import quotas levied within the market nation. Raymond Vernon noted the existence of a product-cycle. As a domestic market becomes saturated, a logical move is to take the product to a new market where the product-cycle can begin anew. Thus no single theory explains a company's expansion into a foreign market, but for any expansion there will be a theory to explain the decision.

2. Describe the four degrees of corporate internationalization identified by Christopher Korth.

	First-Degree Internationalization	Second-Degree Internationalization	Third-Degree Internationalization	Fourth-Degree Internationalization
Nature of contact	Indirect, passive	Direct, active	Direct, active	Direct, active
Locus of operations	Domestic	Domestic	Domestic and international	Domestic and international
Orientation	Domestic	Domestic	Primarily domestic	Multinational
Type of activity	Foreign trade of goods and services	Foreign trade of goods and services	Foreign trade, foreign assistance contract, foreign direct investment	Foreign trade, foreign assistance contracts, foreign direct investment
Organizational structure	Traditional hierarchical	International department	International division	Global structure

3. In what international activities might a company engage?

While an unending list probably exits, each activity will fit into the category of a good or a service.

4. List the three attitudes toward internationalization that managers may adopt.

Ethnocentric: where domestic managers view foreign countries and their people as being inferior. *Polycentric:* where managers see each country as being different and hard to understand, and leave foreign operations up to people in the field who are closest to the concerns. *Geocentric:* where managers recognize that nations have both similarities and differences and situational management is practiced to obtain the best results from various kinds of circumstances.

5. Define a multinational enterprise (MNE).

"Large corporation with operations and divisions spread over several countries but controlled by a central headquarters."

6. What are the possible impacts of MNEs on their host countries? On their home countries?

Effects on the host country: Infusions of capital, technology, entrepreneurship, improved balance of payments, creation of jobs, more local competition, and availability of products for host nation consumers.

Effects on home country: Availability of and steadier supply of raw materials, acquisition of technology from competing firms, exports of components and finished goods for assembly elsewhere, inflow of income from overseas profits, and job and increased career opportunities.

7. What aspects of the international environment must managers by aware of?

While the areas of requisite knowledge vary with the job requirements of the managers, each person assigned overseas needs the following: a sensitivity to and acceptance of cultural differences; a knowledge of local politics; language skills beyond those needed for trading in local bazaars; an interest in living within the local economy rather than in a compound known as a "little America," knowledge of currency and financial arrangements; and how the host nation generally receives foreigners living and working among its citizens.

8. How can familiarity with and responsiveness to foreign sociocultural characteristics aid international managers?

Most important, a manager's familiarity and responsiveness to foreign sociocultural characteristics hastens acceptance of the manager and the company he represents. It helps to know local customs and avoid making comparative statements designed to prove American ways are better or make more sense. A knowledge of how things are done will tend to keep persons in the host country from taking advantage of the "foreigner's" ignorance. The way the first managers behave sets both the tone and the degree of acceptance for those who follow.

9. How should managers adjust management practices when planning for the international environment?

The managements of MNEs need to consider such issues as the extent to which reward systems can cross national borders, how to factor time into planning based upon how different cultures value time, and whether a global strategy will be better than a series of microstrategies geared to local conditions. Within the latter issue is one dealing with how the MNE goes about allocating and structuring its resources toward the attainment of objectives. Management also needs to determine whether it is better to join forces with a host nation company or to operate on its own. Compensation is a yardstick by which many companies measure the contributions of managers; MNEs have to consider compensation plans in terms of the local living conditions. The problem may be exacerbated when managers are transferred from country to country.

10. What special problems do the managers of MNEs face when organizing international operations?

The focus of organization is to assemble and allocate resources—human and nonhuman. Two conflicting demands have to be balanced: the need to determine the optimum way to set up the needed strategic business units, such as departments or divisions, and the need to coordinate the work of each unit to attain the MNE's overall objectives.

11. According to Rosalie Tung, how can the managers of American MNEs learn from the human resource management practices of Japanese MNEs?

Rosalie Tung noted that Japanese MNEs have more success with managers that have been carefully selected and trained for overseas assignments. American firms need to sponsor training programs for managers and families that accept overseas assignments. Managers should be willing to develop long-term commitments to foreign assignments, and their support from the home office is readily apparent.

12. Discuss Hofstede's findings on variations in national character. How might these be relevant to managers?

Geert Hofstede studied the national character of 40 nations and concluded that people vary a lot [and the] variations seriously challenge the rules of effective managerial practice based on Western theories and peoples.'' He noted four dimensions of national character: (1) individualism versus collectivism, (2) how inequality among people is handled, (3) uncertainty avoidance (a nation with a strong uncertainty avoidance establishes institutions to reduce future uncertainty) and (4) masculinity versus femininity (a nation with strong division between sexual roles is termed masculine).

Hofstede's studies indicate that western-style management stressing individual accomplishment will not be effective in cultures where collectivism is stressed. Hofstede ranks the United States in the middle of the scale and concludes that ''organizational practices favored by U.S. managers may be reasonably acceptable to people from cultures at other ends of the scale.''

13. How does Japanese management style differ from U.S. management style?

William G. Ouchi conducted comparative studies of management style between Japanese and American companies. Below is a list of these comparisons:

JAPANESE ORGANIZATIONS	AMERICAN ORGANIZATIONS
Lifetime employment	Short-term employment
Slow evaluation and promotion	Rapid evaluation and promotion
Nonspecialized career paths	Specialized career paths
Implicit control mechanisms	Explicit control mechanisms
Collective decision making	Individual decision making
Collective responsibility	Individual responsibility
Holistic concern	Segmented concern

Answers to End-of-Chapter Case Questions

CASE 1: LUCKY-GOLDSTAR: MANAGEMENT, KOREAN STYLE

1. Describe the Korean method of management. What advantages and disadvantages does it have over U.S. methods? How has it borrowed from U.S. methods?

Lucky-Goldstar's management appears to be a cross of the findings from the Hawthorne Experiment, McGregor's Theory ''Y,'' Blake and Mouton's 9,9, and Likert's System 4. The important point for Lucky-Goldstar is that it practices the management that American research has shown to be effective. The stereotype of American management is that managers are from the Scientific Management school where managers plan and employees work. Advantages for the Korean style at Lucky-Goldstar include reduced absenteeism, employee loyalty toward the company, lower costs of production, employees who look to the company for leadership rather than to a union, and high product quality.

2. Why are Korean manufacturers setting up manufacturing operations in the United States?

American managers and union leaders believe that foreign imports are produced with unfair subsidies so that American jobs and company profits are affected. Their solution has been to pressure Congress to enact protectionist legislation and to put pressure on the president to use his powers to set quotas and other limits on foreign imports. Korea and other foreign producers have established factories in the United States to counter the effects of protectionist measures.

3. In your opinion, will the entry of foreign electronics manufactures have a positive or negative impact on the domestic electronics industry? Explain.

All opinion answers should be supported by a review of information available from the U.S. Department of Commerce and other sources. Also, students should define what is meant by domestic industry.

4. Can the recent success of Japanese and Korean MNEs be explained best by political, economic, or cultural factors?

These three factors are interrelated. The political system of the United States has fostered open-trade policies for many years, even though many unions and American managers are now pushing for protectionist strategies. Since the American political process can be fragile in that laws can be enacted or changed as a result of intense pressure, foreign firms can insulate themselves from some of this pressure by opening factories in the United States. Foreign managers would not seek to do business in the United States if expectations for profits were not favorable. Cultural factors appear to be somewhat neutral. People from Asian nations are not particularly welcomed, nor are they led to believe they are unwelcome. This is the cultural heritage of the United States—a nation built on immigrants and the contributions they have made.

CASE 2: THE COLONEL GOES TO JAPAN

1. How did Kentucky Fried Chicken overcome the so-called trade barriers to American companies doing business in Japan?

   Accommodation is the key term. Kentucky Fried Chicken (KCF) joined forces with Mitsubishi and was fortunate in hiring a dynamic Japanese man to serve in an executive capacity. Whenever cultures clashed, KFC moved to accommodate the Japanese style. Examples include changing the menu from mashed potatoes to French fries, altering the degree of sweetness in the cole slaw, and in store design. A major accommodation occurred when KFC adopted the employment-for-life concept and placed emphasis on the selection and training of persons who would look upon KFC as a career employer.

2. Describe planning, organizing, leading, and controlling at KFC–Japan.

   Strategic plans were to accomplish what has been identified in the above response. Leading was based on the Japanese style of consultation and involvement. Leading also included intensive training to help each employee be a successful addition to the company. Controlling followed traditional methods that do not have cultural bias. Inventory is controlled, sizes of servings are monitored, cash flow and capital needs are scrutinized, and reviews are made to determine that plans are being achieved.

3. What barriers might exist to the continued success of KFC in Japan?

   A primary barrier is the cultural insularity of the Japanese people, who tend to be xenophobic. The consequence is to feel superior to persons from other cultures and that Japanese products are superior to foreign ones. Nevertheless, KFC, along with many other American franchises, has been in Japan for several years, and there is a Japanese predisposition for things and ideas from the West. The main barrier would most likely arise from an indirect source such as a breakdown of American and Japanese trade negotiations and Japan retaliation.

4. What lessons can be learned from other organizations doing business in Japan? In other cultures?

   Regardless of the culture involved, managers need to be geocentric and recognize similarities as well as differences among countries, and draw upon the most effective techniques and practices that work in a given culture.

Suggested Term Paper Topics

1. Pitfalls of exporting U.S. ethics to foreign nations.
2. The growth of a domestic company to that of being a multinational.
3. Key differences involved in doing business with Islamic nations.
4. An analysis of international currency exchanges between businesses.
5. A review of conditions that bring calls for protectionist legislation.
6. An analysis of non-tariff trade barriers between nations.
7. A review of an American firm's experience in opening a sales office in a foreign nation.
8. A study of employee relations in a U.S.–based, Japanese-owned factory.
9. A review of the Japanese concept of lifetime employment and the employment of women in Japanese businesses.

Suggested Guest Speakers

1. The foreign business expert from a local Chamber of Commerce to speak of his/her efforts to either attract foreign business or to export the goods and services of local businesses.
2. The leader of an industrial union to speak about union attempts to unionize American factory workers employed by Japanese or Korean businesses.
3. If a foreign-owned or managed factory or office is in your area, ask the manager to talk about experiences in doing business in the United States.

Part 6 Case

CAREER AND ETHICS: ACTIVE OR PASSIVE MANAGEMENT?

1. What would you advise Rick Montrose to say in the rest of his report? Be as specific and practical as possible—put yourself in his shoes.

   The second part of the report covers personnel matters: the flow of communication, morale, and a personal assessment of the company and how Rick would fit the overall operation.

   The main thrust of personnel matters should address the counterproductive flow of information since Mr. Larton often got involved in day-to-day activities and by-passed regular department heads. This section should also indicate that Robin has assumed responsibilities of an executive vice president and has been issuing line-type orders in the absence of Mr. Larton. This part would conclude with the need for Mr. Larton to make clear the lines of communication in the business so that all affected employees would know the boundaries of their jobs and, more important for some, the boundaries of other jobs.

2. Write any additions to Rick Montrose's report that you feel are appropriate (try limiting yourself to less than 200 words). Be prepared to defend your position and the decision you are going to give Mr. Larton.

The first section of this report identified the kinds of strategic policies needed to help guide PlasTech for the next five years. A five-year plan has been included to identify each major step and the time table to be followed in implementing this plan for growth. Plans are not self-implementing, however, nor are goals self-achieving. To this end, the next few sections will deal with some personnel issues that cannot be ignored if this company's growth is to occur as planned.

It will be difficult for an entrepreneur such as yourself to "let go" and give your managers an opportunity to manage. However, PlasTech has grown to the point where it needs administrative direction. You have qualified managers in place—let them manage. Allow your entrepreneurial initiatives to continue in the growth stages of PlasTech rather than in those sections that are now well established. This will be a major departure from your regular style of managing, but you must not ignore the need for this vital change in management.

Part of this "letting go" must include having your secretary, Robin, also "let go" of attempting issue directives—in your name—to your operating managements. While it is true that Robin has considerable first-hand knowledge of operations, her official job is secretary. Whether her role is to be that of secretary or as an administrator, you need to clarify her function—for her benefit as well as that of the organization.

You have made not secret of the relationship between you and Robin. While you are comfortable with this, a large number of your employees are not comfortable because they feel Robin is using this relationship to exert power over their behavior. Therefore, in addition to making clarification of formal positions and authority, you need to have a personal discussion with Robin regarding her official duties and those she regards as a personal relationship with you.

I feel sufficiently committed to the recommendations about the need to clarify your secretary's role that my acceptance of your job offer must be made contingent on this point. I say this knowing that Robin and I have also have had a close relationship in the past. However, I am confident that I have separated my past affection for Robin from these recommendations. I like this job and its potential. I ask you to talk with me about these recommendations before reaching your final decision.

4. How has Rick managed his career so far? What are his strong points and successes? What are his shortcomings and mistakes? What should he concentrate on in the future?

Rick has followed a fast track toward the top and may have left a few gaps in his maturing process. Nevertheless, he has made several changes that have caused his career to prosper. He takes jobs that serve his career needs. While he was willing to share Robin's apartment with her during a visit to the city, once he had a job, he moved out with a resolve not to let personal involvements interfere with his success.

Shortcomings and mistakes appear to be minor ones since Mr. Larton is pleased with his work and the employees of PlasTech have taken him into their trust. He feels strongly that he should take no actions that would betray that confidence.

Rick's career could be side-tracked if he does not remain in one place long enough to establish himself. He has moved rather quickly, but at some point he will have a reputation of seeking only quick satisfactions for himself rather than building long-term benefits for his employer. Therefore, the job at PlasTech is one that he should accept and continue with for at least five years. However, he needs a commitment from Mr. Larton that Robin's influence will be kept within bounds.

Notes

Notes

Notes

Notes

Notes

Notes

Notes

MANAGEMENT

MANAGEMENT

Fourth Edition

James A. F. Stoner
Fordham University

R. Edward Freeman
University of Virginia

Prentice Hall
Englewood Cliffs, New Jersey 07632

Library of Congress Cataloging-in-Publication Data

Stoner, James Arthur Finch.
Management/James A. F. Stoner, R. Edward Freeman.—4th ed.
p. cm.
Includes bibliographies and indexes.
ISBN 0-13-548421-9
1. Management. I. Freeman, R. Edward. II. Title.
HD31.S6963 1989 88-30350
658—dc19 CIP

To W. Edwards Deming, whose example of constancy of purpose might be a benchmark for any of us, and to Marta Mooney, who saw what needed to be done long before I even suspected the possibilities.

J.A.F.S.

R. Edward Freeman would like to dedicate this edition to Benjamin Wellen Freeman.

Development editor: Ronald S. Librach
Editorial/production supervision: Eleanor Perz
Interior/cover design: Jayne Conte
Cover photo: The Metropolitan Museum of Art/George A. Hearn Fund, 1968
Photo research: Kay Dellosa
Interior art: Network Graphics
Manufacturing buyer: Ed O'Dougherty

Printed in the United States of America.

10 9 8 7 6 5 4 3 2 1

ISBN 0-13-548421-9

Prentice-Hall International (UK) Limited, *London*
Prentice-Hall of Australia Pty. Limited, *Sydney*
Prentice-Hall Canada Inc., *Toronto*
Prentice-Hall Hispanoamericana, S.A., *Mexico*
Prentice-Hall of India Private Limited, *New Delhi*
Prentice-Hall of Japan, Inc., *Tokyo*
Simon & Schuster Asia Pte. Ltd., *Singapore*
Editora Prentice-Hall do Brasil, Ltda., *Rio de Janeiro*

BRIEF CONTENTS

Part One **Introduction to Management**

1 MANAGING AND MANAGERS
2 THE EVOLUTION OF MANAGEMENT THEORY
3 THE EXTERNAL ENVIRONMENT OF ORGANIZATIONS
4 SOCIAL RESPONSIBILITY AND ETHICS

Part Two **Planning and Decision Making**

5 EFFECTIVE PLANNING
6 PROBLEM SOLVING AND DECISION MAKING
7 STRATEGIC PLANNING AND MANAGEMENT
8 STRATEGY IMPLEMENTATION

Part Three **Organizing for Stability and Change**

9 DIVISION OF WORK, ORGANIZATIONAL STRUCTURE, AND COORDINATION
10 AUTHORITY, DELEGATION, AND DECENTRALIZATION
11 HUMAN RESOURCE MANAGEMENT
12 MANAGING ORGANIZATIONAL CHANGE AND DEVELOPMENT
13 MANAGING ORGANIZATIONAL CONFLICT AND CREATIVITY

Part Four **Leading**

14 MOTIVATION, PERFORMANCE, AND SATISFACTION
15 LEADERSHIP
16 GROUPS AND COMMITTEES
17 INTERPERSONAL AND ORGANIZATIONAL COMMUNICATION

Part Five **Controlling**

18 EFFECTIVE CONTROL
19 FINANCIAL CONTROL METHODS
20 PRODUCTIVITY AND OPERATIONAL CONTROL
21 INFORMATION SYSTEMS AND CONTROL

Part Six **Emerging Concepts in Management**

22 ENTREPRENEURSHIP
23 ORGANIZATIONAL CAREERS AND INDIVIDUAL DEVELOPMENT
24 INTERNATIONAL MANAGEMENT

CONTENTS

PREFACE xxi

PART ONE Introduction to Management

1

MANAGING AND MANAGERS 1

Illustrative Case Study: A Typical Day in the Life of Alison Reeves 2
Defining Management 3
Why Organizations and Effective Managers Are Needed 5
Organizations Serve Society 5 Organizations Accomplish Objectives 5
Organizations Preserve Knowledge 6 Organizations Provide Careers 6
The Key Attributes of Managerial Responsibility 6
Managerial and Organizational Performance 8
Management Application: From the Land of Opportunity to the Land of the Rising Sun 9
Types of Managers 10
Management Levels 10 Functional and General Managers 11
The Management Process 11
Planning 12 Organizing 13 Leading 13 Controlling 13
Management Level and Skills 14
Managerial Roles 15
Interpersonal Roles 17 Informational Roles 17 Decision-Making Roles 18
Excellence in Management 18
Ethics in Management 20
Ethics in Management: Footing the Bill and Having a Heart 20
Educating Managers 21
Management Education Criticized 21 Management Learning: Books and Experience 24
The Purpose of This Book 25
Summary 26
Review Questions 27
Case Study: The Vice-President, the Product Manager, and the Misunderstanding 27

2

THE EVOLUTION OF MANAGEMENT THEORY 31

Illustrative Case Study: Henry Ford—The Apostle of Mass Production 32
The Classical Management Theorists 34
Forerunners of Scientific Management Theory 35
Scientific Management: Frederick W. Taylor 35
Other Contributors to Scientific Management Theory 37
Contributions and Limitations of Scientific Management Theory 38
Classical Organization Theory 41
Contributions and Limitations of Classical Organizations Theory 43
Ethics in Management: Muckrakers, Monopolies, Meat Packers, and Medicines 44
Transitional Theories: Becoming More People-Oriented 46
The Behavioral School: The Organization Is People 48
The Human Relations Movement 48
Contributions and Limitations of the Human Relations Approach 49
From Human Relations to the Behavioral Science Approach 51
Contributions and Limitations of the Behavioral Science School 52
International Management: Some Renaissance and Ancient Roots of Management Theory 52
The Quantitative School: Operations Research and Management Science 53
Contributions and Limitations of the Management Science Approach 54
The Evolution of Management Theory 55
The Systems Approach 56 The Contingency Approach 57
Management Application: The Neo-Human Relations Approach (or, The Social Animal in the Humanist's Maze) 60
Summary 62
Review Questions 62
Case Study: Theory and Policy Encounter Power and Motivation at Consolidated Automobile 64

3

THE EXTERNAL ENVIRONMENT OF ORGANIZATIONS 67

Illustrative Case Study: Image and Imaging Problems at Eastman Kodak 68
Change and the Environment 69
Components of the External Environment 70
Ethics in Management: Ethics and Ethnicity in Global Merchandising 70
Elements of the Direct-Action Environment 71
Environmental Evolution 71 Organizational Stakeholders 73
Elements of the Indirect-Action Environment 83
Environmental Variables 83

The International Environment of Organizations 90
New Technology 90 The Emergence of International Competitors 90
International Management: Biotechnology—The Race to Build a Better Pig 92
The Problem of Competitiveness 94
The Blurring of Public and Private Spheres of Influence 94
The Opening of China and the Eastern Bloc 95
Characteristics of Total Organization Environments 95
The Theory of Uncertainty and Dependence 95
Other Theories of Environments 96
Managing the Total Environment 96
Influencing the Direct-Action Environment 98
Monitoring the Indirect-Action Environment 98
Adjusting to the Environment 99
Summary 100
Review Questions 100
Case Study: Tri-State Telephone 102

4

SOCIAL RESPONSIBILITY AND ETHICS 105

Illustrative Case Study: An Ethical and Social Dilemma at Chemical Bank 106
The Changing Concept of Responsibility 107
The Public View of Business 108
Corporate Social Responsibility 108
Milton Friedman's Argument 109
A History of Corporate Social Responsibility 110
Corporate Social Responsiveness 112
The Shift to Ethics 116
What Is Ethics? 116 Four Levels of Ethical Questions in Business 116
The Tools of Ethics 117
Ethical Language 117
Management Application: A Code of Conduct at J. C. Penney 118
Common Morality 119 Applying Ethics 120 Institutionalizing Ethics 121
Ethics in Management: The Spirit of "The Credo" at Johnson & Johnson 122
The Challenge of Relativism 123
Naive Relativism 124 Cultural Relativism 125 A Kernel of Truth 126
International Management: The Sullivan Principles in South Africa 127
Summary 128
Review Questions 129
Case Study: Alexander Gavin's Dilemma—Cultural Relativism and Business as Usual 129
PART CASES: Seafood America—Corporate Response to the Cost of AIDS 132 / Precision Machine Tool—Management in a Changing Environment 133

PART TWO Planning and Decision Making

5

EFFECTIVE PLANNING 137

Illustrative Case Study: Reversing the Flow at Chrysler Corporation 138
Planning and the Management Process 139
Plans and Decision Making 140 The Four Basic Steps in Planning 141
International Management: Planning in the USSR—Gorbachev as CEO 143
The Link Between Planning and Controlling 144
Operational Plans 145
Single-Use Plans 146 Standing Plans 147
Tools and Techniques for Planning 148
Forecasting 149
Ethics in Management: When Planning Goes Awry, Who Pays the Price? 150
Planning Complex Projects 152
Summary 158
Review Questions 159
Case Study: The Dashman Company 160

6

PROBLEM SOLVING AND DECISION MAKING 163

Illustrative Case Study: Texaco—Penzoil—Getty Oil 164
The Rational Problem-Solving Process 165
Stage 1: Investigate the Situation 166
Stage 2: Develop Alternatives 167
Stage 3: Evaluate Alternatives and Select the Best One 167
Stage 4: Implement and Monitor the Decision 168
Problem and Opportunity Finding 169
The Problem-Finding Process 170 Opportunity Finding 171 Deciding to Decide 172
The Nature of Managerial Decision Making 174
Programmed and Nonprogrammed Decisions 174 Certainty, Risk, and Uncertainty 175
Rational Decision Making 176
Bounded Rationality: A Challenge to the Rational Model 176
Heuristics and Biases in Decision Making 177
Three Heuristics 177
Management Application: How Biased Are You? 178
Biases in Decision Making 179 Some Conclusions 181
Improving the Effectiveness of Problem Solving and Decision Making 182
Improving Individual Problem Solving 182
Ethics in Management: The Game of "Prisoner's Dilemma" 184
Deciding Who Decides 185
Summary 186
Review Questions 187
Case Study: Business and Political Actions—To PAC or Not to PAC? 187

7

STRATEGIC PLANNING AND MANAGEMENT 191

Illustrative Case Study: Planning for the Future at Federal Express 192

The Concept of Strategy 193

What Is Strategy? 193 Why Strategic Planning Is Important 193

The Evolution of the Concept of Strategy 196

Strategy as the Grand Plan 196 Strategic Planning and Strategic Management 197

A Practical Point of View 200

Levels of Strategy: Some Key Distinctions 202

The Three Levels of Strategy 202

Ethics in Management: What Do You *Stand* for? 204

Strategic versus Operational Planning 205

Frameworks for Strategy 206

The Portfolio Framework for Strategic Formulation: The BCG Matrix 206

Porter's Framework for Industry Analysis 208

The Formal Strategic-Planning Process: The Example of Business-Unit Strategy 211

Step 1: Goal Formulation 212

International Management: Strategic Partnerships Are In 213

Step 2: Identification of Current Objectives and Strategy 214

Step 3: Environmental Analysis 215 Step 4: Resource Analysis 215

Step 5: Identification of Strategic Opportunities and Threats 216

Step 6: Determination of Extent of Required Strategic Change 216

Step 7: Strategic Decision Making 217 Step 8: Strategy Implementation 218

Step 9: Measurement and Control of Progress 218

Summary 218

Review Questions 219

Case Study: Planning for Diversified Activities in a Changing Environment 219

8

STRATEGY IMPLEMENTATION 223

Illustrative Case Study: Maintaining the Competitive Edge at Merck & Co. 224

Strategy Implementation 225

Strategy and Structure 226

Chandler's Thesis 227 Further Research 228 The Seven-S Model 230

Operationalizing Strategy 233

Developing Functional Strategy 233

Ethics in Management: Whistleblowing 236

Setting Annual Objectives 237 Management by Objectives 238 Reward Systems 242

Matching Managers and Strategies 243

Institutionalizing Strategy 244

The Role of the CEO 244 The Role of Key Managers 244

Management Application: Death in the Executive Suite 245

Culture and Strategy 247

Barriers to Effective Strategy Implementation 248
Environmental Constraints 248 Internal Constraints 249
Summary 250
Review Questions 251
Case 1: "Sacred Trustees" and Whistleblowing at Beech-Nut 251
Case 2: The Competition Chips Away at Cray Research 253
PART CASE: The Adams Corporation 256

PART THREE Organizing for Stability and Change

9

DIVISION OF WORK, ORGANIZATIONAL STRUCTURE, AND COORDINATION 259

Illustrative Case Study: Coordination and Integration at Hewlett-Packard 260
Division of Work 262
Job Specialization 262 Span of Management 263
Organizing and Organizational Structure 264
The Organization Chart 265
Ethics in Management: When Is Top Management Responsible? 266
The Formal Organizational Structure 267 Functional Organization 267 Product/Market Organization 268 Matrix Organization 271 The Informal Organization 274
Coordination 275
Problems in Achieving Effective Coordination 276
Approaches to Achieving Effective Coordination 277
Selecting the Appropriate Coordination Mechanisms 280
Organizational Design: Structuring for Specialization and Coordination 280
Early Approaches to Organizational Design 281
The Classical Approach to Organizational Design 281 The Neoclassical Approach to Organizational Design 283
Management Application: Downsizing the American Management Lifestyle 284
Modern Approaches to Organizational Design 285
External Environment and Structure 285
Task-Technology and Structure 287
Summary 292
Review Questions 293
Case 1: Organizing the Structure of Club Med 293
Case 2: Options for Change at Imperial Chemical Industries 294

10

AUTHORITY, DELEGATION, AND DECENTRALIZATION 297

Illustrative Case Study: Responsiveness and Restructuring at IBM 298
Authority, Power, and Influence 299
The Basis of Formal Authority: Two Views 300 The Sources of Power 302 Power in Organizations 303

Ethics in Management: Obedience and Conscience 304
Line and Staff Authority 307
Line Authority 307 Staff Authority 308 Functional Authority 309
Delegation 310
Delegation, Authority, Accountability, and Responsibility 310
Classical Guidelines for Effective Delegation 311
Limitations of the Classical Guidelines 312 Effective Delegation 313
Job Design 315
Approaches to Job Design 316
Management Application: Quality at Huffy Corporation 318
Job Design and Job Satisfaction 319
Decentralization 321
Factors Influencing Decentralization 322 Trends in Decentralization 323
Summary 324
Review Questions 324
Case Study: The Use and Abuse of Joyce Roberts 325

11

HUMAN RESOURCE MANAGEMENT 327

Illustrative Case Study: Human Relations at Sony Corporation 328
The HRM Process: A Traditional View 329
Human Resource Planning 330
Planning Procedures 331 Forecasting and the Human Resource Audit 332
Recruitment 332
Job and Position Descriptions 334 Sources for Recruitment 334
Equal Employment Opportunity and Affirmative Action 335
Selection 339
Ethics in Management: The Issue of Corporate Day Care 340
Steps in the Selection Process 341 Manager Selection 342 Assessment Centers 343
Orientation and Socialization 344
Training and Development 345
Training Programs 345 Management Development Programs 346
Performance Appraisal 348
Informal and Formal Appraisal 349 Problems of Appraisal 350
Promotions, Transfers, Demotions, and Separations 351
Promotions 352 Transfers 352 Discipline, Demotions, and Separations 352
International Management: The Case for the Disclosure of Plant Closure 353
HRM and Strategy 354
HRM and Environmental Issues 354 The Four C's Model for Human Resources 355
Summary 357
Review Questions 358
Case Study: The Gannett Company: A Leader in Minority Employment 359

12

MANAGING ORGANIZATIONAL CHANGE AND DEVELOPMENT 361

Illustrative Case Study: Organizational Trauma and Triumph at AT&T 362
Forces for Change 363

External Forces 363 Internal Forces 363
International Management: "The Devil's Night" in Bhopal 364
Managerial Responses to Pressures for Change 365
The Role of the Change Agent 366
Models of the Change Process 366
Forces for Stability 367 The Process of Change 368
Resistance to Change 368
Sources of Resistance to Change 368 Overcoming Resistance to Change 369
Approaches to Planned Change 370
Interdependence of the Three Approaches 371 Structural Approaches 372
Technological Approaches 373 People Approaches 373
Organizational Development 375
Types of OD Activities 376
Ethics in Management: OD Assumptions and Values 377
OD Techniques in Closeup 378
Management Application: Change at Southwestern Bell and Honeywell 380
Evaluating OD 380
Organizational Culture 382
Summary 385
Review Questions 385
Case Study: Undergoing Change at the Digital Equipment Corporation 386

13

MANAGING ORGANIZATIONAL CONFLICT AND CREATIVITY 389

Illustrative Case Study: Conflict and Compromise at the Adolph Coors Company 390
Conflict, Competition, and Cooperation 391
Changing Views of Conflict 391
Functional and Dysfunctional Conflict 392 Sources of Organizational Conflict 394
Dynamics and Consequences of Organizational Conflict 395
Three Factors in Organizational Conflict 396
Management Application: Intergroup Conflict at Robber's Cave 396
Methods for Managing Conflict 398
Conflict-Stimulation Methods 398
Conflict-Reduction Methods 400 Conflict-Resolution Methods 401
Line and Staff Conflict 403
Management-Labor Conflict 404
Workers and Unions 405 Minimizing Negotiation Conflict 406
Ethics in Management: New Approaches to Union Activism 406
Managing Organizational Creativity and Innovation 408
Creativity and Innovation 408 Individual Creativity 408
Stimulating Individual and Group Creativity 409
Organizational Creativity and Innovation 411
Establishing a Climate for Organizational Creativity 413
Summary 415
Review Questions 416

Case Study: Is There Creative Life after Post-It Notes? 417
PART CASES: Chris Cunningham 418 / The Consolidated Life Case—Caught Between Corporate Cultures 419

PART FOUR Leading

14

MOTIVATION, PERFORMANCE, AND SATISFACTION 423

Illustrative Case Study: Creating a Committed Work Force at Domino's Pizza 424
The Importance of Motivation 425
Early Views of Motivation in Organizations 426
The Traditional Model 426 The Human Relations Model 426
The Human Resources Model 427
Ways of Looking at Motivation 428
Content Theories 429 Process Theories 430 Reinforcement Theories 430
A Systems View of Motivation in Organizations 431
Characteristics of the Individual 432
International Management: Questioning the Applicability of Universal Theories of Motivation 434
Characteristics of the Job Task 437 Characteristics of the Work Situation 439
Management Application: Succeeding through Technology and Human Resources at Chaparral Steel 442
The Impact of Past Consequences on Behavior 443
Behavior Modification 444
Integrative Approaches to Work Behavior 444
The Expectancy Approach 444 The Equity or Inequity Approach 448
Ethics in Management: The Button Experiments 449
Guidelines for Effective Motivation 451
Summary 452
Review Questions 453
Case Study: Idealism, Motivation, and Community Service at the Center City YWCA 454

15

LEADERSHIP 457

Illustrative Case Study: New Leadership Policies at GE 458
Defining Leadership 458
Theories of Leadership 460
Ethics in Management: Is Moral Leadership Different? 460
The Trait Approach to Leadership 461 The Behavioral Approach to Leadership 462
International Management: Questioning the Applicability of American Theories of Leadership 465
Contingency Approaches to Leadership 467
Theoretical Perspectives on the Contingency Approach to Leadership 470

The Future of Leadership Theory 479
Transformational or Charismatic Leadership 480 Is Leadership Really Necessary? 482
Management Application: Innovative Leadership at W. L. Gore and Associates 486
Summary 487
Review Questions 487
Case Study: Three Managerial Decisions 488

16

GROUPS AND COMMITTEES 491

Illustrative Case Study: The Team Taurus Approach to Management at Ford 492
Types of Groups 493
Formal Groups 494 Informal Groups 494
Characteristics of Groups in Organizations 496
Informal Leadership 496 Group Norms and Conformity 496
Ethics in Management: The "Authority of Violence" 498
Group Cohesiveness 500
Problem Solving in Groups 502
Advantages and Disadvantages of Group Problem Solving 503
Key Factors in Group Decision Making: Assets or Liabilities 504
Task Forces and Committees 505
Types of Formal Working Groups 505
Management Application: Winter Survival—A Test 506
Some Differences between Task Forces and Committees 508
Advantages and Disadvantages of Committees and Task Forces 509
Making Formal Groups Effective 510
Committee Problem Solving 510 Special Procedures for Task Forces 512
Conflict within Groups 514
Summary 515
Review Questions 516
Case Study: The New-Products Group 517

17

INTERPERSONAL AND ORGANIZATIONAL COMMUNICATION 519

Illustrative Case Study: Communications Failures at Bhopal 520
The Importance of Communication 521
Interpersonal Communication 523
The Communication Process 523 One-Way and Two-Way Communication 527
Barriers to Effective Communication 528
Management Application: Corporate Jargon 530
Overcoming Barriers to Interpersonal Communication 531
Communication in Organizations 533
Factors Influencing Organizational Communication 534
Ethics in Management: One Memo Too Many 535
Communication Networks within the Organization 536 Vertical Communication 538
Lateral and Informal Communication 539

Overcoming Organizational Barriers to Communication 540
Communication and Advanced Information Technology 541
International Management: Communication in an Increasingly Global Economy 542
Openness: A Double-edged Sword 544
Summary 545
Review Questions 546
Case Study: The Corporate Policy Seminar 547
PART CASE: Cookie Wars 548

PART FIVE Controlling

18

EFFECTIVE CONTROL 554

Illustrative Case Study: An Experiment in Integrative Control at GenCorp 554
The Meaning of Control 556
The Link between Planning and Controlling 556 Steps in the Control Process 556
The Importance of Control 559
Organizational Factors Creating the Need for Control 559
Ethics in Management: Ethical Policy at Mead Corp. 561
Finding the Right Degree of Control 560
Types of Control Methods 562
Pre-Action Controls 562 Steering Controls 563 Yes/No or Screening Controls 563
Post-Action Controls 563 The Importance of Steering Controls 564
Design of the Control Process 564
The Control Process 564 Key Considerations in Establishing a Control System 567
Key-Performance Areas and Strategic-Control Points 570
Management Application: The High-Tech Cookie 571
Characteristics of Effective Control Systems 572
Summary 574
Review Questions 575
Case 1: TRW, Inc: Electronic Monitoring in the Trucking Industry 576
Case 2: Planning and Controlling Growth at 3M 578

19

FINANCIAL CONTROL METHODS 581

Illustrative Case Study: Financial Resourcefulness at John Deere and Company 582
Financial Controls 583
Financial Statements 583 Ratio Analysis 586 Break-Even Analysis 587
Management Application: Where to Find Financial Ratios 589
Budgetary Control Methods 589
Budgetary Control 590 Responsibility Centers 590
The Budgeting Process 592
How Budgets Are Drawn Up and Approved 592 The Role of Budget Personnel 593
How Budgets Are Revised 594 Some Problems in Budget Development 595

Types of Budgets 595
Operating Budgets 596 Financial Budgets 597 Variable versus Fixed Budgets 599
Zero-Base Budgeting 601
Ethics in Management: The Jimmy Carter Years 602
Functional and Dysfunctional Aspects of Budget Systems 603
Auditing 606
External Auditing 606 Internal Auditing 606
Summary 608
Review Questions 608
Case Study: The Audit Report 610

20

PRODUCTIVITY AND OPERATIONAL CONTROL 613

Illustrative Case Study: At Ford, Quality Is Job One 614
Changing Views of Production and Operations 615
Productivity 617
What Is Productivity? 617 Improving Productivity in Organizations 618
Productivity through People 619 Factors Influencing Productivity 621
Productivity Management 623
International Management: The *Maquila* Industry—The U.S. Searches for Improved Productivity in Mexico 624
Competitive Priorities for Business 625
Characteristics of Production/Operations Systems 628
The Operations System: A Model 628
Designing Production/Operations Systems 632
Product/Service Planning and Design 632 Capacity Planning 632 Process Selection 633
Facility-Location Planning 636 Layout Planning 637 Job Design 637
Operational Planning and Control Decisions 639
Ethics in Management: The Traveling Circus Show 640
Operations Planning and Control 640 Inventory Planning and Control System 642
Summary 646
Review Questions 647
Case Study: GE Turns Old into New in Kentucky 648

21

INFORMATION SYSTEMS AND CONTROL 651

Illustrative Case Study: Using Technology at Sears for Strategic Advantage 652
Information and Control 653
The Computer Revolution 654 The Value and Cost of Information 654
Management Application: Information Power—How Companies Are Using New Technologies to Gain a Competitive Edge 656
Management Information Systems 656
The Evolution of MIS 657 Differing Information for Different Management Levels 658
Designing a Computer-Based MIS 660
Guidelines for Effective Design 661

Implementing A Computer-Based MIS 665
Problems in Implementing a Computer-Based MIS 666
Overcoming Implementation Problems 658
Ethics in Management: Security Issues and the Computer 670
End-User Computing 672
Decision-Support Systems 672
Expert Systems and Artificial Intelligence 674
International Management: Information-System Strategies 676
Managing End-User Computing 679
The Impact of Computers and MIS on Managers and Organizations 680
The Continuing Computer Revolution 681
Summary 683
Review Questions 683
Case 1: The Human Edge in Software: Electronic Advisors 684
Case 2: Using Decision-Support Systems at General Motors 686
PART CASE: Osborne Computer—Trying for Rapid Growth Without Controls 688

PART SIX Emerging Concepts in Management

22

ENTREPRENEURSHIP 695

Illustrative Case Study: Start-Up Pains at Nova Pharmaceutical Corporation 696
The Meaning of Entrepreneurship 697
Entrepreneurial Roles 698 Factors Affecting Entrepreneurship 699
The Importance of Entrepreneurship 700
Economic Growth 700 Productivity 700
New Technologies, Products, and Services 701
Ethics in Management: "Competing with the Biggies" 702
The Entrepreneur 703
Psychological and Sociological Factors 703 Competence 709
International Management: Economic Experiments in the People's Republic of China 706
The Entrepreneurial Process 711
Stages in the Entrepreneurial Process 711 Choosing a Business 712
Entrepreneurial Organizations 712
Planning and Strategy 712 Organizing 715 Leading 715
Management Application: The Care and Flourishing of Entrepreneurs at 3M 717
Controlling and Entrepreneurial Culture 717
Barriers and Problems 718
The Dark Side of Entrepreneurship 718
Summary 721
Review Questions 722
Case 1: Space Saving and Cost Cutting at Associated Video Hut, Inc. 722
Case 2: Pro-Line Corporation Puts a New Face on an Old Industry 724

23

ORGANIZATIONAL CAREERS AND INDIVIDUAL DEVELOPMENT 727

Illustrative Case Study: Selina Proctor—Parent and Professional 728
Early Organizational Career Experiences 729
The Formation of Expectations 729 Early Job Experiences 732
Ethics in Management: The Art of Writing a Résumé 733
Early Career Dilemmas 734
Political Insensitivity and Passivity 734 Loyalty Dilemmas 735 Personal Anxiety 736
Role Conflict 737 Stress 738
Careers Over Time 740
Careers and the Life Cycle 741 Career Patterns and Themes 745
Careers within Organizations 748 The Career Plateau 750
Individual Career Management 754
Individual Career Planning 754 Handling Specific Career Issues 756
Summary 761
Review Questions 762
Case Study: Andrew Krieger's Career Decision at Soros Fund 763

24

INTERNATIONAL MANAGEMENT 765

Illustrative Case Study: Sumitomo—The Thrust toward International Banking 766
The Increasing Internationalization of the World Economy 767
A Brief History 767 Why Companies Go International 768
How Companies Go International 769
Ethics in Management: Japanese Manufacturers in America 770
Managerial Attitudes toward Internationalization 771
The Multinational Enterprise 771
The Rise and Spread of Multinational Enterprises 772 The Impact of MNE Operations 772
The Challenges of Multinational Management 775
Managing in a Multinational Environment 776
International Management: Becoming an International Business 777
Handling the Differences 778 Adjusting the Management Process 780
Selecting a Managerial Approach 785
Applying U.S. Approaches Abroad 785
Applying Japanese Approaches Abroad and Synthesizing Differing Approaches 786
Summary 789
Review Questions 789
Case 1: Lucky-Goldstar—Management, Korean Style 790
Case 2: The Colonel Goes to Japan 792
PART CASE: Career and Ethics—Active or Passive Management? 794

GLOSSARY 797
COMPANY INDEX 803
NAME INDEX 805
SUBJECT INDEX 809

PREFACE

This Fourth Edition introduces R. Edward Freeman as a co-author and carries *Management* into the 1990s with what we've worked hard to make a state-of-the-art revision.

Management was published in its first edition in 1978. Since then, the book has gained tenure as the most widely used and all-time best-seller in the Principles of Management field. The book has succeeded not only in the United States but around the world, not only in its English edition but in its Portuguese, Spanish, Indonesian, and Bahasa Malayan translations.

While the Fourth Edition carefully revises and completely updates the content to bring the text abreast of recent developments and to point the way toward the future, it continues to build on the solid foundation that has made the first three editions highly regarded teaching and learning tools.

As always, this book is about the job of the manager. It describes how men and women go about managing the people and activities of their organizations so that the goals of those organizations, as well as their personal goals, can be achieved.

We have attempted in this book to convey the very positive view we have of the manager's job. We believe the job of a manager is among the most exciting, challenging, and rewarding careers a person can have. Individuals can, of course, make great contributions to society on their own. But it is also possible to realize major achievements in managed organizations—not only businesses, but also universities, hospitals, research centers, government agencies, and other organizations. Such organizations bring together the talent and resources that such achievements require. A manager working within an organization has a better chance to be involved in significant and far-reaching activities than would an individual working alone.

We also believe that in addition to being exhilarating and rewarding, a managerial career is critically important. The problems our society faces today—and, most likely, the problems it will face in the foreseeable future—require both large- and small-scale solutions that only businesses, governments, and other organizations can provide. The extent to which we learn to manage such problems as pollution, nuclear proliferation, overpopulation, and poverty may help determine whether we survive as nations, cultures, or even as a species. The extent to which we take advantage of such new opportunities as semiconductor and superconductor technology, the exploration of space, and the development of human potential may determine whether or not our cultures, having survived, will continue to flourish. The skill of organization managers will be a vital factor in our ability to meet a vast array of cultural tasks and challenges. The information in this text is designed to help you, the reader, develop these vital managerial skills.

In this text, we have chosen to address the reader as a potential manager. At times, in fact, we even adopt a tone that suggests the reader already *is* a manager. This is done intentionally: We want to encourage the reader to start thinking like a manager as soon as possible. Obviously, the earlier one learns to think like a manager, the sooner one can develop managerial effectiveness. But there is another, more basic reason. All managers—but especially young managers just beginning their careers—are evaluated in large part on how effective they are as subordinates. The more successful an individual is as a subordinate, the more likely that his or her career will be successful. And one of the best ways of learning how to be an excellent subordinate is to learn how to think like a manager. Thus, addressing the reader as a manager (or at least a prospective manager) is meant to be a helpful way of improving the reader's chances for future managerial and career success.

ORGANIZATION

This book is organized around the classical or functional approach to Management: planning, organizing, leading, and controlling.

The four chapters in **Part One** introduce the **field of management** and the issues involved in both the practice and study of management. Chapters 3 and 4 are new to this edition and engage topics of increasingly crucial importance to prospective managers and students of management practice. Chapter 3 focuses on the effects of an often turbulent *external environment* on organizations past and present. Chapter 4 addresses the critical issues of the *ethical and social responsibilities* of contemporary managers.

Part Two is devoted to the topics of **planning and decision making.** Chapters 7 and 8 incorporate a great deal of material new to this edition. Chapter 7 focuses in detail on *strategic planning* and outlines the key methods by which organizations analyze and formulate practical strategies. Chapter 8, which is entirely new, is designed to reflect the growing concern for the critical concept of *implementation* among managers and management theorists.

We turn in **Part Three** to the subject of the **organizing function.** Throughout this section of the book, we have tried not only to analyze the *division and coordination of work,* but to examine the influence of these processes on *organizational structure*. We have attempted to apply this approach to a closely related set of topics that includes not only such broad subjects as *human resources* and *organizational conflict* but such specific areas as *task delegation, job design,* and the encouragement of *individual creativity*.

In **Part Four,** we analyze the fundamental psychological principles that underlie the concept of the **manager as leader.** We look not only at *leadership* itself but the related practical phenomena of *motivation, communication,* and *group interaction*.

Part Five examines the important area of **control.** In addition to discussing *control systems* and the specifics of *financial means of control,* we emphasize the importance of the relationship between *operational control and productivity*. Toward this end, we have placed the chapter dealing with these subjects as the conceptual summary of Part Five, revising Chapter 8 of the Third Edition and making it Chapter 20 of the Fourth. We conclude with an updated overview of *management information systems*—the incredibly fast-paced evolution of the technology producing the tools with which managers can apply the concepts detailed in the first three chapters of the part.

In **Part Six,** we look at some of the **emerging issues in management theory and practice.** We examine the ways in which individual *careers* are affected by the influences on and changes in organizations, and we devote full chapters to the topics of *entrepreneurship* and *international management*.

We have organized the book this way because (1) we believe managers themselves still find the classical approach quite useful; (2) students find it to be a good "handle" on the management field; and (3) it provides an excellent organizing framework for a broad spectrum of management approaches. While it is impossible to describe the work of every theorist and writer in a field that has grown so rich, we have always tried to be balanced in our coverage. Thus, we describe the classical, behavioral, and quantitative approaches, as well as the increasingly important systems and contingency approaches, in Chapter 2, and we continue in other chapters to refer to major contributors from each of these schools as appropriate. Frequently, we give not only the viewpoint of certain schools but some discussion of the advantages and limitations of those perspectives as well.

CHANGES TO THE FOURTH EDITION

The External Environment, Ethics, and Social Responsibility

We have in the Fourth Edition decided to emphasize what we believe to be some critically important areas in management. First, we have taken Chapter 3 of the Third Edition on External Environment, Social Responsibility, and Ethics and revised and expanded it into two chapters: Chapter 3 on The External Environment of Management and Chapter 4 on Ethics and Social Responsibility.

In addition, every chapter in the text highlights ethical issues with an insert entitled "Ethics in Management." Believing that ethical issues pervade management practice at all levels, we have tried to address the subjects of ethics and social responsibility as routine matters of course rather than as afterthoughts. These inserts are designed to demonstrate that each topic covered in the book—and each problem encountered in the world of management practice—evokes ethical issues with which the beginning student of management should become acquainted.

International Management

International aspects of management continue to become increasingly important. While we have expanded our coverage of this topic in each successive edition, we have in the Fourth Edition focused attention on the topic throughout the book. In addition to the final chapter on international management, which was heavily revised, we have whenever appropriate added a highlighted section in individual chapters. Some of the Chapter and Part Cases also concern international issues or companies. As with the "Ethics in Management" sections, these "International Management" sections reflect the fact that management has become a genuinely global activity that encompasses a vast range of cross-cultural encounters, activities, and problems.

Relevance

Perhaps one of the most pervasive goals that has guided our revision was to bring relevance to the forefront of the text and the student's learning experience. In some ways, this has been one of our goals since the First Edition, as we have always tried to include chapters with a practical orientation, such as Careers and Individual Development, in the text. Over the editions, we have added chapters such as Information Systems Management, and, as we have seen, a chapter on International Management. In this edition, the new chapters on Entrepreneurship and Ethics and Social Responsibility continue this commitment to address and emphasize some of the more concrete or applied facets of management.

In the Fourth Edition, however, we have gone well beyond adding a few chapters with a more practical flavor. Even the most casual glance at the text provides considerable insight into how our goal of relevance governed every aspect of the revision. The

"Ethics in Management" and "International Management" boxes are in themselves examples of how we've shown how concepts in the text are applied in day-to-day business activities. "Management Application" boxes present opportunities for the student to use or experience knowledge from the text, as in Bazerman's exercise entitled "How Biased Are You?" and a guide on "How to Find Financial Ratios."

Perhaps the most obvious way we've increased relevance is through the cases in the text. Overall, we have more than doubled the number of cases from the Third Edition. Every chapter now opens with a case. Both this feature and the cases we've used for them are new to this edition. Every chapter ends with a separate case and every part ends with an integrative case. As a special feature, whenever possible we've provided two chapter-ending or part-ending cases.

However, the most important aspect of the cases is not their number, but the fact that they are good vehicles for applied learning. The cases that open each chapter are Illustrative Case Studies and focus on the efforts of such well-known organizations as Federal Express, Sony, Adolph Coors, Domino's Pizza, Chrysler, and Texaco to grapple with the issues being discussed in that particular chapter. At strategic points within the chapter, we return to the Illustrative Case Study in order to complement the ongoing discussion with a review of its application to the world of management practice as it has been and is being experienced by organizations and individuals in the everyday reality of business activity. Finally, we wrap up the case and its relation to the concepts in the chapter just before the chapter summary. As much as possible, the chapter-ending and part-ending cases, as with the boxes and in-text examples, are also based on real, identified companies. A dual goal, equally important, is to give the student tools with which they can increase their problem-solving and decision-making skills.

STRATEGY FOR ACHIEVING OUR GOALS

These, then, have been our goals. How have we gone about the business of achieving them? As the subsequent *Acknowledgments* section of this Preface makes clear, the development of the Fourth Edition of *Management* involved not only our efforts but those of a large and talented team at Prentice Hall—an acquisitions editor, a market-research specialist, a book designer, a production editor, a supplements editor, a supplements coordinator, a development editor, and many, many more people. This team was formed early during the development process and saw the project through to final publication. The Fourth Edition of *Management* is thus the culmination of years of careful market research, intensive editorial development, in-depth reviewing, and our own commitment to effective teaching.

We began preparing the Fourth Edition of *Management* in the spring of 1987, when Prentice Hall developed a detailed market-research questionnaire and mailed it to approximately 1600 management professors. The results gave us information on current trends in content, pedagogy, and supplements. From this, we developed an initial revision plan and a questionnaire specifically tailored to get feedback from users of the Third Edition. When we had collected and collated all of this information, we finalized our revision goals and plans, developed a comprehensive outline (which was also tested with reviewers), and began more focused work on individual chapters.

First, every chapter in the Third Edition was reviewed by at least one specialist in that particular area. While these reviewers may or may not have taught principles of management, they were able to give us both evaluations on whether the chapter covered the important ideas in the field and expert advice on what sources to use to update the material in terms of content, examples, and applications. To complement their input with the needs of those who regularly teach courses in principles of management, we used not only the feedback from the market-research and user-survey reviews described above but reviews on the entire text by professors who teach principles of management.

We continued to use a similar process on the first and second drafts of the manuscript. In the first draft, a panel of professors who teach principles of management reviewed every chapter as we developed it, and specialists again reviewed each major section of every chapter. A separate team of principles of management professors offered comments and suggestions on each chapter in the second draft. Finally, we prepared a third draft that is the culmination of all of these efforts.

As each draft of each chapter was written, a skilled development editor worked with us in analyzing the reviews and the manuscript. Part of the development editor's role was to adopt the students' perspective in reading the material and then combine it with his experience in developing a variety of college textbooks. Sentence by sentence and paragraph by paragraph, the development editor worked to ensure that we had succeeded in laying out for the student reader—interestingly and unambiguously—the fundamental topics in management theory and practice. This editorial procedure was applied to each of the drafts that finally became the Fourth Edition of *Management*.

The Fourth Edition of *Management* thus benefits not only from our years of teaching and writing experience but from many years of combined publishing experience. We feel strongly that the intensive process of development and manifold resources of our publisher have enabled us to prepare a state-of-the-art revision that continues the book's tradition of being the standard by which other texts are judged.

SUPPLEMENTS PACKAGE

The supplements packages for Principles of Management have become so large and complex as to be almost unwieldy. Rather than offering a supplements package guided by the rule that more is better, we decided to have a very complete and innovative package where the various pieces also work well together. To help us achieve that goal, we asked Jack Hill of the University of Nebraska, who had worked with Prentice Hall on several previous supplements, to be the Supplements Coordinator for the book. Jack's role was first to help plan the package by looking at each item individually and then as part of the whole. He then helped evaluate and offer suggestions on samples from various supplement author candidates. Aside from working with various supplements authors as they developed their own materials, Jack also wrote the Instructor's Manual for the text and a Supplements Guide which, on a chapter-by-chapter basis, shows how all the supplements can be used with the text. Finally, Jack acted as a quality-assurance partner with Prentice Hall and the other supplements authors, especially regarding the Test Item File.

We want to thank Jack for helping plan, organize, and coordinate the Test Item File and its conversion to the Diploma Computerized Test Generator, the Study Guide for Review and Application and its conversion to a computerized program called Proctor (which, along with Calendar and Gradebook, form part of the Diploma package), the Lecture Extras book, the Video Guide, the Supplements Guide, the Transparency Masters, the Color Transparencies, *Management Applications* by John Samaras, *Modern Business Decisions* by Richard Cotter and David Fritzsche, *Micromanaging* by George Geis and Robert Kuhn, *Readings in Management* by Phil DuBose, *Managing an Organization: A Workbook Simulation* by Gary Oddou, *Twin Applications for Management, Fourth Edition,* by Dennis Pitta, the videos, the Instructor's Manual, which includes instructions written by Gary Yunker of Jacksonville University for using *Acumen: Educational Version* with the text, and the Annotated Instructor's Edition of the text.

Most of these supplements are contained in an Instructor's Resource Package (a convenient slipcase) and all of them are fully described in the Annotated Instructor's Edition. We want to say a few words here about the Annotated Instructor's Edition (AIE) itself. Of all the supplements, this is the one which is most innovative (although, as with most innovations, this idea is gleaned from past input and professional evaluation). The AIE is designed to make teaching both easier and richer. It contains basically two kinds of support materials. First, the Instructor's Manual to the text is actually bound into the front of the AIE. It contains general guidelines for teaching the course, chapter outlines, a list of the key terms with their definitions, an annotated chapter outline, answers to review and discussion questions in the text, and analyses of the text cases. The second part of the AIE, written by Dr. Mary Coulter of Southwest Missouri State University, complements the text with a variety of teaching aids, such as extra examples, thought-provokers, discussion questions, teaching tips, quotes from managers, coordinated resources, background and humorous notes, and extra exercises in the margins of the text chapter. The concept of the AIE, then, puts into practice what professors have done for years—making brief notes in the margins of lecture notes, clipping bits and pieces of relevant information from articles and newspapers and jotting down thoughts on slips of paper that then go into files. Putting all of this together in one convenient location both benefits the professor and enhances the educational process.

ACKNOWLEDGMENTS

One of the most pleasant parts of writing a book is the opportunity to thank those who have contributed to it. Unfortunately, the list of expressions of thanks—no matter how extensive—is always incomplete and inadequate. These acknowledgments are no exception.

Our first thanks must go to the editor of the First Edition of this book, Sheldon Czapnik. Sheldon's unflagging patience, constant good humor, and astounding capacity for creative work and long hours made the First Edition both possible and successful. Others who contributed greatly to earlier editions include Stuart Whalen, Robert DeFillippi, Peter Pfister, Samuel and Della Dekay, Arthur Mitchell, and Jim McDonald.

The following people also helped immensely with their reviews of the material for this edition: Gib Akin, University of Virginia; John R. Anstey, University of Nebraska at Omaha; J. Scott Armstrong, The Wharton School of the University of Pennsylvania; Aline Arnold, Wayland Baptist University; Larry G. Bailey, San Antonio College; Don Baynham, Eastfield College; Don R. Beeman, University of Toledo; Allen Bluedorn, University of Missouri-Columbia; Jean Boddewyn, Baruch College-CUNY; Nakiye Boyacigiller, San Jose State University; Rogene A. Buchholz, The University of Texas at Dallas; Allen L. Bures, Radford University; John F. Burgess, Concordia College; Richard J. Butler, Empire State College of SUNY; John F. Byrnes, Bentley College; Herschel N. Chait, Indiana State University; Paul J. Champagne, Old Dominion University; Norman Coates, University of Rhode Island-Kingston; John W. Collis, Iowa Wesleyan College; Edward J. Conlon, University of Iowa; Anne C. Cowden, California State University-Sacramento; James A. Craft, University of Pittsburgh; Robert P. Crowner, Eastern Michigan University; Richard Cuba, University of Baltimore; W. Michael Donovan, Westbrook College; Ernie Englander, George Washington University; Bob Fisher, Henderson State University; Taggart F. Frost, University of Northern Iowa; Jerry L. Geisler, Sangamon State University; Thomas R. Gulledge, Jr., George Mason University; Richard H. Hall, University at Albany-SUNY; Stephen C. Harper, University of North Carolina-Wilmington; Frank Harrison, San Francisco

State University; Roger P. Hill, University of North Carolina-Wilmington; Bernard L. Hinton, California State University-Chico; Marie R. Hodge, Bowling Green State University; W. Michael Hoffman, Center for Business Ethics, Bentley College; Phyllis G. Holland, Valdosta State College; Steven E. Huntley, Florida Community College at Jacksonville; Dewey E. Johnson, California State University-Fresno; Douglas E. Jones, Jacksonville University; William Keller, Framingham State College; Robert H. Kessner, University of Hawaii; Jerry Kinard, Western Kentucky University; James W. Klingler, Villanova University; John L. Kmetz, University of Delaware; Michael H. Korzeniowski, La Salle University; Gerald H. Kramer, University of Wisconsin-Platteville; Charles Kuehl, University of Missouri-St. Louis; John W. Lloyd, Monroe Community College; John P. Loveland, New Mexico State University; Ronald W. Maestas, New Mexico Highlands University; Harry J. Martin, Cleveland State University; W. A. Meinhart, Oklahoma State University; Fekri Meziou, Augsburg College; Joseph F. Michlitsch, Southern Illinois University at Edwardsville; Benita H. Moore, Clayton State College; David R. Moorehouse, Franklin Pierce College; Edward J. Morrison, University of Colorado; Eugene J. Muscat, University of San Francisco; Donald G. Muston, Elizabethtown College; Robert V. Nally, Villanova University; Reed Nelson, Louisiana Tech University; Michael A. Novak, University of Massachusetts, Boston; Winston Oberg, Michigan State University; William D. Patzig, James Madison University; Gerald Perselay, Winthrop College; Milo C. Pierce, Corpus Christi State University; Gary N. Powell, University of Connecticut-Storrs; John M. Purcell, State University Agricultural & Technical College; Samuel Rabinowitz, Rutgers University-Camden; Phyllis K. Rettew, Vanderbilt University; Stephen J. Rosen, Edward Williams College of Fairleigh Dickinson University; Robert Sands, SUNY-Alfred State College; Gary C. Sanger, Louisiana State University; Milan Savan, Walsh College; Borge O. Saxberg, University of Washington-Seattle; Lloyd Seaton, Tusculum College; Michael Shapiro, Dowling College; Brad Shrader, Iowa State University; Robert L. Smoot, Northern Virginia Community College-Annandale Campus; Dixon G. Stevens, College of Saint Rose; Barbara A. Sylvia, Salve Regina College; Larry R. Taube, University of North Carolina-Greensboro; Ernest M. Teagarden, Dakota State College; Kenneth R. Thompson, De Paul University; Roger Volkema, George Mason University; William F. Webster, University of Florida-Gainesville; James K. Weeks, The University of North Carolina-Greensboro; Michael A. Weininger, The University of Wisconsin-Milwaukee; Alan G. Weinstein, Canisius College; Gary L. Whaley, Norfolk State University; Paul L. Wilkens, Florida State University; Gary E. Willard, Purdue University; David G. Williams, West Virginia University; Beth Wilson, College of Great Falls; and Lawrence E. Zeff, University of Detroit.

Many people at Prentice Hall have contributed to the development of this revision: Dennis Hogan, Publisher, Business and Vocational Books; Senior Managing Editor Alison Reeves and her assistant, Frances Falk; Art Director Florence Silverman and Interior Designer Jayne Conte; Director of Photo Archives Lorinda Morris-Nantz and Photo Researchers Page Poore and Kay Dellosa; Director of Scheduling Debra Kesar; Buyer Ed O'Dougherty; Production Manager Jeanne Hoeting; Lisa Garboski, Managing Editor for Supplements, and Supplemental Books Editor Ellen B. Greenberg; Director of Book Development Ray Mullaney and his assistant, Asha Rohra.

The production of the Fourth Edition was supervised by Eleanor Perz, whose professionalism and dedication to this project have been in evidence since the First Edition. The work of the following people in contributing to the content of this book has been invaluable: Professors Robert Behling (Bryant College), Hrach Bedrosian (New York University), Anne C. Cowden (California State University, Sacramento), Giusseppi A. Forgione (University of Maryland at Baltimore), and Larry Taube (University of North Carolina at Greensboro). We are also indebted to Roger Draper, Adrienne Kols, and Elizabeth Mastalski for their writing skills and assistance in the preparation of the manuscript.

Without the untiring efforts of Development Editor Ron Librach, this edition simply would not exist. Rebecca Villa, Patricia Bennett, Anurag Sharma, and Craig Wynett cheerfully prepared a number of cases and boxed inserts under the pressures of impossible deadlines. Karen Dickinson gave her usual superb support to everyone involved. The Sponsors of the Darden School and the Olsson Center for Applied Ethics provided resources and a wonderful environment in which to work. Maureen Wellen was again both critic and confidant.

MANAGEMENT

Josef Albers, *Homage to the Square—Impact*. 1965. 60.5 x 60.5 cm. Oil on Masonite. Josef Albers Museum, Bottrop. "Good design—proportion of effort to effect," Josef Albers. "Without effectiveness, there is no 'performance,' no matter how much intelligence and knowledge goes into the work, no matter how many hours it takes," Peter Drucker, *The Effective Executive*. "Do less in order to do more," Josef Albers. "The less an organization has to do to produce results, the better it does its job," Peter Drucker, *Ibid*.

1

MANAGING AND MANAGERS

Upon completing this chapter you should be able to:

1. Explain the concept of management and why managers are needed.
2. Describe the key attributes of managerial responsibility.
3. Define the difference between "efficiency" and "effectiveness" as aspects of managerial performance.
4. Identify what is meant by top, middle, and first-line managers, and functional and general managers, and explain the differences in their work activities.
5. List and explain the four basic functions of managers according to the common model of the management process.
6. Describe Mintzberg's additional roles and responsibilities of managers.
7. Explain what Peters and Waterman mean by "excellence" in management, including the role played by ethical considerations in managerial decision making.
8. Describe what management education can and cannot do for you and explain why you must be involved in continually learning to become an effective manager.

Chapter Outline

Introduction
Defining Management
Why Organizations and Effective Managers Are Needed
The Key Attributes of Managerial Responsibility
Managerial and Organizational Performance
Types of Managers
The Management Process
Management Level and Skills
Managerial Roles
Excellence in Management
Ethics in Management
Educating Managers
The Purpose of This Book

ILLUSTRATIVE CASE STUDY Introduction

A Typical Day in the Life of Alison Reeves

Alison Reeves is a middle-level manager at Gulf + Western, a large conglomerate headquartered in New York. As she boards the train to go home to New Jersey, she reflects on a hectic day—the kind that had become more normal for her.

She had arrived in the office at 7:45 to find a market-research report on her desk. One of her subordinates, Bob Jones, had spent most of the night finishing the final product to be reviewed by Alison before it could be presented to her vice-president. She spent 20 minutes or so talking to Bob, drinking coffee, and planning the logistics for preparing final copy of the report. Word processing and graphics had demanded a 48-hour notice of schedule changes.

By the time Alison got back to her office, she had already received three phone messages. She placed return calls to two of the callers but only reached one of them and scheduled a future meeting. She was now late for an 8:30 departmental staff meeting, which was finally over at 10:30. By the time she got back to her office, she had five new phone messages, including one of the people whom she failed to reach earlier and who had returned her call in the meantime.

Budget projections for next year were also due tomorrow, as were suggested revisions to the division-objectives statement. Meanwhile, Alison had a meeting scheduled with her boss at 2:00 in order to explain why her department was over-budget in the current year. Alison considered working through lunch but decided that she shouldn't cancel a planned luncheon with a new manager in a department that often competed with hers for the time and attention of her boss. Alison returned from lunch at 1:30, determined to plan her budget for next year so that she could offer a more feasible explanation as to why she was currently spending over budget.

Her 2:00 meeting went well. Alison's boss was pleased that she was ahead of the game on next year's budget and gained a better appreciation of her plans for her department. They spent 15 minutes on their planned agenda and 45 minutes discussing a variety of people in the division, Alison's boss telling her that he had considered reorganizing the division in an effort to diminish some duplication of effort in certain areas. At the end of the meeting, Alison mentioned the report that she and Bob had prepared and commented on what a good job Bob had done.

At 3:00, Alison went for coffee and ran into one of the division's top salespeople, who was giving a tour to a key customer. Alison mentioned the just-completed marketing-research report, particularly since it concerned a product that this customer had bought. They talked for 20 minutes, and Alison conceived some important illustrations for the report that was in progress.

At 3:30, Alison attended a meeting of an interdivisional task force established to coordinate the company's United Way campaign. By the time she returned to her office at 5:30, her desk was papered in pink telephone messages. She counted eight and began returning those from time zones where callers were still at work.

By 7:00, Alison left the office feeling tired but good. She had made some important progress on a number of issues. Her boss had taken her into his confidence for the first time and she felt a comfortable sense of security. Bob's report looked like a real winner, and the customer information incidentally accumulated that afternoon was going to help. As she boarded the train, she reached for a cigarette and headed for the smoking car, only to remember that she had stopped smoking in response to a request that company managers set better health examples for employees. Oh well, she thought, maybe her health club would still be open by the time she reached home.

TEACHING TIP

Try to build some enthusiasm in your students for the study of management. Let them know that management is fun, dynamic, challenging, and exciting.

TEACHING TIP

Point out that the study and practice of management is applicable to all *types* (retail, government, church, factory, profit, nonprofit, service), *sizes* (small to large), *levels* (upper to lower), and *functional* areas (finance, marketing, production, etc.) of organizations.

CLASS COMMENT

Managers must have people to manage. Managers must manage within a hierarchical organizational setting. Relate to the students that hierarchy refers to the vertical arrangement of jobs within the organization.

Alison is a "manager" in a large organization. What is *management,* and what do thousands of people like Alison really do every day for such long hours? For most of our lives, we are members of one *organization* or another—a college, a sports team, a musical or theatrical group, a religious or civic association, a branch of the armed forces, or a business. The organizations we belong to will obviously differ from one another in many ways. Some, like the army or a large corporation, may be organized very formally. Others, like a neighborhood basketball team, may be more casually structured. But regardless of how they differ, all the organizations we belong to have several basic elements in common.

Perhaps the most obvious common element our organizations will have is a *goal* or purpose. The goals will vary—to win a league championship, to entertain an audience, to sell a product—but without a goal no organization would have any reason to exist. Our organizations will also have some program or method for achieving their goals—to practice playing skills in order to win games, to rehearse a certain number of times before each performance, to manufacture and advertise a product. Without some *plan* for what it must do, no organization is likely to be very effective. Our organizations must acquire and allocate the resources necessary to achieve their goals—a playing field or rehearsal hall must be available; money must be budgeted for wages. Our organizations are not self-contained; they are comprised of people and they always exist in an environment with other organizations that they depend on for the resources they need—a team cannot play without the required equipment; most manufacturers must maintain contracts with many different suppliers. Finally, our organizations will all have leaders or *managers* responsible for helping the organizations achieve their goals. Who the leaders actually are probably will be more obvious in some organizations than in others. But without some manager—a coach, a conductor, a sales executive—the organization is likely to flounder.

This book is about how organizations are managed—or, more specifically, how managers can best help their organizations set and achieve their goals. Our emphasis will be on the so-called *formal* organizations—such as businesses, religious organizations, government agencies, or hospitals—that provide goods or services to their customers or clients and offer career opportunities to their members. It is easier to discuss the management of these organizations, because in such organizations people will usually have various well-defined responsibilities and because the role of the manager will be clear-cut and visible. But regardless of how formal their role is, all managers in all organizations have the same basic responsibility: to help other members of the organization and the organization itself set and reach a series of goals and objectives. Helping you to understand how managers accomplish this task is the subject of this book.

DEFINING MANAGEMENT

management The process of planning, organizing, leading, and controlling the work of organization members and of using all available organizational resources to reach stated organizational goals.

Management has been called "the art of getting things done through people." This definition, by Mary Parker Follett, calls attention to the fact that managers achieve organizational goals by arranging for *others* to perform whatever tasks may be necessary—not by performing the tasks *themselves*.

Management is that, and more—so much more, in fact, that no one simple definition has been universally accepted. Moreover, existing definitions change as the environments of organizations continue to change. Our discussion will start with a fairly complex definition, so that we may call attention to additional important aspects of managing:

TEACHING TIP

Stress to students that core issue of management is: accomplishing work (organizational goals) through combined efforts of all types of resources.

> Management is the process of planning, organizing, leading, and controlling the efforts of organization members and of using all other organizational resources to achieve stated organizational goals.[1]

A *process* is a systematic way of doing things. We define management as a process because all managers, regardless of their particular aptitudes or skills, engage in certain interrelated activities in order to achieve their desired goals. Exhibit 1-1 categorizes and describes the four basic activities in which managers are typically involved. You will also notice that our definition indicates that managers use *all* the resources of the organization—its finances, equipment, and information as well as its people—to attain their goals. People are the most basic resource of any organization, but managers would be limiting their achievements if they did not also rely on the other available organizational resources. For example, a manager who wishes to increase sales might try not only to motivate the sales force but also to increase the advertising budget, thus using both human and financial resources to attain the goal.

Finally, our definition stresses that management involves achieving the organization's "stated goals." This means that managers of any organization—a university, the Internal Revenue Service, the Washington Redskins—try to attain specific ends. These ends are, of course, unique to each organization. The stated goal of a university might be to give students a well-rounded education in an academic community. If, however, it succeeds only in processing students through its programs, it is functioning *efficiently* but, as regards its stated goals, not *effectively*. Whatever the stated goals of a particular organization, management is the process by which the attainment of those goals is enhanced.

EXHIBIT 1-1 FOUR TYPICAL MANAGERIAL ACTIVITIES

1. *Planning* implies that managers think through their goals and actions in advance. Their actions are usually based on some method, plan, or logic, rather than on a hunch.
2. *Organizing* means that managers coordinate the human and material resources of the organization. The effectiveness of an organization depends on its ability to marshal its resources to attain its goals. Obviously, the more integrated and coordinated the work of an organization, the more effective it will be. Achieving this coordination is part of the manager's job.
3. *Leading* describes how managers direct and influence subordinates, getting others to perform essential tasks. By establishing the proper atmosphere, they help their subordinates do their best.
4. *Controlling* means that managers attempt to assure that the organization is moving toward its goals. If some part of their organization is on the wrong track—if it's not working toward stated goals or is not doing so effectively—managers try to find out why and set things right.

BACKGROUND ON MANAGEMENT FUNCTIONS

Henri Fayol first noted the functions common to all managers: planning, organizing, commanding, coordinating, and controlling. His contributions will be further explored in Chapter 2.

[1]Michael H. Mescon, Michael Albert, and Franklin Khedouri, *Management: Individual and Organizational Effectiveness*, 2nd ed. (New York: Harper & Row, 1985), stress that "resources" should be defined to include not just general economic categories like labor and capital, but information and technology as well.

WHY ORGANIZATIONS AND EFFECTIVE MANAGERS ARE NEEDED

FOR DISCUSSION

Why are reports of organizational management/mismanagement considered so newsworthy? (Consider the size, pervasiveness, importance of, and impact of these organizations. For example, General Motors alone has some 100,000 managers. The Communications Workers of America union represents some 148,000 AT&T employees.)

FOR DISCUSSION

In what ways do business organizations influence your daily life? (Shampoo and soap used in quick shower made by Procter & Gamble, leading *consumer products* company; fast-food breakfast at McDonald's, a *restaurant* well known for its tasty morsels; jump in car, an older *Camaro* that is not much to look at but still runs; hit traffic lights in wrong sequence in morning dash across *town*—why can't they do something about sequencing those lights; just make it to management class and pull out felt tip pen made by Parker Brothers, a leading *manufacturer* and listen intently to professor; etc.)

TEACHING TIP

Relate the importance of organized activity to society by describing what role organizations play.

Almost every day, it seems, headlines like these greet us from the front pages of our daily newspapers:

- "Dollar Plunges After News of Record Trade Deficit"
- "Auto Imports Gain Market Share"
- "Federal Budget Deficit Figures Revised Upward"
- "Dow-Jones Falls for Third Straight Day"
- "Manville Files for Chapter 11"
- "EPA Levies Fines for Illegal Toxic Dumping"
- "SEC Investigates Allegations of Insider Trading on Wall Street"

The stories behind these headlines make us wonder whether our social organizations have failed. Some Americans feel that government, business, and labor organizations have become too large to keep in touch with people's needs and that their leaders lack high ethical standards. Criticizing organizations is, of course, a time-honored American custom but organizations are a necessary element of civilized life for several reasons: They enable us to accomplish things that we could not do as well—or at all—as individuals; they serve society; they help provide a continuity of knowledge; they serve as an important source of careers.

Organizations Serve Society

First of all, organizations are important because they are social institutions and must be managed within the confines of certain culturally accepted values and needs. They allow us to live together in a civilized way and to accomplish things as a society. Many organizations—and the people who manage them—have been responsible for achievements ranging from the conquest of outer space to the invention of computers because their managers have been responsive to the social needs served by these achievements. From local police departments to large multinational corporations, organizations serve society by making the world a better, safer, cheaper, and more pleasant place to live. Without them, we would be little more than animals with unusually large brains. Naturally, this is the ideal scenario that is not always necessarily played out. For instance, acid rain from the United States is not making life "better" for a lot of Canadians.

Organizations Accomplish Objectives

Let us consider for a moment how many organizations were involved in bringing us the paper on which this book is printed: loggers, a sawmill, manufacturers of various types of equipment and supplies, truckers, a paper mill, distributors, telephone and electric power companies, fuel producers, the postal service, banks and other financial institutions, and more. Even if an individual acting alone could do all the things that those organizations did to produce a ream of paper (which is doubtful) he or she could never do them as well or as quickly.

It is clear, then, that organizations and the people who manage them perform this essential function: *By coordinating the efforts of different individuals, they enable us to reach goals that would otherwise be much more difficult or even impossible to achieve.*

Organizations Preserve Knowledge

We know from history that when recorded knowledge is destroyed on a large scale (as when the museum and library at Alexandria were burned in the third century A.D.), much of it is never regained. We depend on records of past accomplishments because they provide a foundation of knowledge on which we can build to acquire more learning and achieve greater results. Without such records, science and other fields of knowledge would stand still.

Organizations (such as universities, museums, and corporations) are essential because they store and protect most of the important knowledge that our civilization has gathered and recorded. In this way, they help to make that knowledge a continuous bridge between past, present, and future generations. In addition, organizations themselves add to our knowledge by developing new and more efficient ways of doing things.

Organizations Provide Careers

THOUGHT-PROVOKER

Would you want to accept a job with a large, well-known national organization or with a small but growing firm? What are the advantages and disadvantages of each? Tie in to Chapter 23 on Careers.

Finally, organizations are also important because they provide their employees with a source of livelihood, depending on the style and effectiveness of their managers, and perhaps even personal satisfaction and self-fulfillment. Many of us tend to associate career opportunities with business corporations, but in fact a variety of other organizations, such as churches, government agencies, schools, and hospitals, also offer managerial guidance toward rewarding careers.

As we learn more about management and organizations, two basic questions will concern us: First, how can we make large and small organizations more effective in meeting social needs? Second, which of society's aims can be accomplished by which organizations?

THE KEY ATTRIBUTES OF MANAGERIAL RESPONSIBILITY

QUOTATION FROM A MANAGER

"Management's job is to see the company not as it is . . . but as it can become."—John W. Teets, Chairman of Greyhound Corporation

TEACHING TIP

Emphasize what managers *do* and how this relates to what managers *are* by examining functions, roles, and skills.

Our working definition describes *managers* as organizational planners, organizers, leaders, and controllers. Actually, every manager—from the program director of a college club to the chief executive of a multinational corporation—takes on a much wider range of roles to move the organization toward its stated objectives. In this discussion of the more detailed aspect of what managers *do,* we will also specify more completely what managers *are*.

Managers work with and through other people. The term *people* includes not only subordinates and supervisors but also other managers in the organization. "People" also includes individuals outside the organization—customers, clients, suppliers, union representatives, and so on. These people and others provide goods and services or use the product or service of the organization. Managers, then, work with anyone at any level within or outside their organizations who can help achieve unit or organizational goals. In addition, in working toward organizational goals, managers work to achieve personal goals.

Finally, managers in any organization should work with each other to establish the organization's long-range goals and to plan how to achieve them. They also work together to provide one another with the accurate information needed to perform tasks. Thus, *managers act as channels of communication within the organization*.

Managers are responsible and accountable. Managers are in charge of seeing that specific tasks are done successfully. They are usually evaluated on how well they arrange for these tasks to be accomplished. Managers are responsible also for the actions of their subordinates. The success or failure of subordinates is a direct reflection of managers' success or failure. Naturally, all members of an organization, including those who are not managers, are accountable for their particular tasks. Managers, however, are held responsible, or accountable, not only for their own work but also for the work of others.

Because managers have subordinates and other resources for getting a job done, they are able to accomplish more than nonmanagers, who have only their own resources to rely on. This, of course, means that managers are also *expected* to accomplish more than other members of the organization; that is, they are held responsible for greater achievement and for the allocation of the organization's resource during the pursuit of that achievement.

Managers balance competing goals and set priorities. At any given time, every manager faces a number of organizational goals, problems, and needs—all of which compete for the manager's time and resources (both human and material). Because such resources are always limited, each manager must strike a balance between various goals and needs. Many managers, for example, arrange each day's tasks in order of priority—the most important things are done right away, while the less important tasks are looked at later. In this way managerial time is used more effectively.

Managers must think analytically and conceptually. To be an *analytical* thinker, a manager must be able to break a problem down into its components, analyze those components, and then come up with a feasible solution. But even more importantly, a manager must be a *conceptual* thinker, able to view the entire task in the abstract and relate it to other tasks. Thinking about a particular task in relation to its larger implications is no simple matter but it is essential if the manager is to work toward the goals of the organization as a whole as well as toward the goals of an individual unit.

A HUMOROUS NOTE

Jeno F. Paulucci, founder of Chun King Corp. and Jeno's, Inc., is a manager with sheer spunk. Threatened with losing one of his biggest accounts, he personally flew to the location to conduct a quality test with the chief buyer. He opened a can of chop suey, saw a huge grasshopper staring up at him, and promptly ate it before the buyer noticed! (*Business Week*, 2/29/88, p. 81)

Managers are mediators. Organizations are made up of people, and people within the same organization will often disagree about goals and the most effective way of attaining them. Disputes within a unit or organization can lower morale and productivity, and they may become so unpleasant or disruptive that competent employees decide to leave the organization. Such occurrences hinder work toward the goals of the unit or organization; therefore, managers must at times take on the role of mediator and resolve disputes as they occur. Settling quarrels requires skill and tact; managers who are careless in their handling of disputes may be dismayed to find that they have only made matters worse.

Managers are politicians. Managers must build relationships and use persuasion and compromise to promote organizational goals, just as politicians do to move their programs forward. Managers should also develop other political skills. All effective managers ''play politics'' by developing networks of mutual obligations with other managers in the organization. They may also have to build or join alliances and coalitions. Managers draw upon these relationships to win support for proposals or decisions or to gain cooperation in carrying out various activities.[2]

HERE'S AN EXAMPLE

The newly appointed Chairman and CEO of AT&T, Robert E. Allen, brings a different style of management to AT&T's executive offices. He is low-key, quiet, and undemonstrative. However, he isn't afraid to tell a joke on himself. When asked to name his weaknesses, he grinned and said he couldn't confess his weaknesses because one of the people who hired him, a corporate director, was waiting in the back of the room!

Managers are diplomats. They may serve as official representatives of their work units at organizational meetings. They may represent the entire organization as well as a particular unit in dealing with clients, customers, contractors, government officials, and personnel of other organizations.

Managers are symbols. They personify, both for organizational members and for outside observers, an organization's successes and failures. Here, too, managers may

---

[2]Politics in business is *per se* neither good nor bad. The importance of political skills in management is becoming increasingly apparent. See Rosabeth Moss Kanter, ''Power Failure in Management Circuits,'' *Harvard Business Review* 57, no. 4 (July–August 1979):65–75; and Graham Astley and Paramjit S. Sachdeva, ''Structural Sources of Intraorganizational Power: A Theoretical Synthesis,'' *Academy of Management Review* 9, no. 1 (January 1984):104–113.

be held responsible for things over which they have little or no control, and it may be useful for the organization to hold them so responsible. The frequent dismissals of professional sports managers, for example, often have symbolic importance.[3]

FOR DISCUSSION

Being a manager is becoming more demanding. Agree or disagree and why. (New tools and techniques are making it easier but the rapidity and complexity of environmental changes are making it more difficult.)

Managers make difficult decisions. No organization runs smoothly all the time. There is almost no limit to the number and types of problems that may occur: financial difficulties, problems with employees, differences of opinion concerning organization policy, to name just a few. Managers are the people who are expected to come up with solutions to difficult problems and to follow through on their decisions even when doing so may be unpopular.

The brief descriptions of these managerial roles show that managers must "change hats" frequently and be alert to the particular role needed at a given time: As a rule, a manager is a peer, a superior, *and* a subordinate at one and the same time. The ability to recognize the appropriate role to be played and to change roles readily is one mark of an effective manager.

ILLUSTRATIVE CASE STUDY Continued

A Typical Day in the Life of Alison Reeves

Our initial example of Alison Reeves at Gulf + Western illustrates most of these managerial roles. She must plan, organize, lead, and control, but in order to perform these functions, she needs a variety of means at her disposal. As this case illustrates, management is not a methodical activity constituting a discrete and predictable series of steps. Rather, it is usually a miscellaneous accumulation of details and procedures. Alison has to keep half a dozen balls in the air at the same time and accomplish tasks through others, her boss, as well as her subordinates and peers. Some writers have even described Alison's world as one of "chaos."* Alison has to be simultaneously analytical in setting her budget and people-oriented in order to motivate Bob and to manage her boss. Perhaps symbolically, Alison gave up smoking, and for what were perhaps political reasons, she had lunch with a rival. All of these activities are entailed in her managerial responsibilities.

*Thomas J. Peters, *Thriving on Chaos: A Handbook For Management Revolution* (New York: Alfred A. Knopf, 1988).

MANAGERIAL AND ORGANIZATIONAL PERFORMANCE

How successfully an organization achieves its objectives, satifies social responsibilities, or both, depends upon how well the organization's managers do their jobs. If managers do not do their jobs well, the organization will fail to achieve its goals. Just as managers function within the organization, organizations function within the larger society. The performance of its organizations is a key factor in the performance of a society or a nation.

managerial performance The measure of how efficient and effective a manager is—how well he or she determines and achieves appropriate objectives.

How well managers do their jobs—**managerial performance**—is the subject of much debate, analysis, and confusion in the United States and many other countries.[4] How well the organizations of a society do *their* "jobs"—organizational performance—gives rise to an equally lively debate.[5] The chapters that follow discuss a number of

[3]On the symbolic role of managers, see Jeffrey Pfeffer and Gerald R. Salancik, *The External Control of Organizations: A Resource Dependence Perspective* (New York: Harper & Row, 1978), pp. 16–18, 264–265.

[4]For a popular critique of American management practice, see Steve Lohr, "Overhauling America's Business Management," *New York Times Magazine,* January 4, 1981, pp. 15ff.

[5]For a popular analysis of some of the apparent successes and possible failures of Japanese organizations, see Peter F. Drucker, "Behind Japan's Success," *Harvard Business Review* 59, no. 1 (January–February 1981):83–90.

MANAGEMENT APPLICATION

FROM THE LAND OF OPPORTUNITY TO THE LAND OF THE RISING SUN

Once upon a very long time ago, Japanese-manufactured goods were proverbial for their shoddiness. It's true—ask your teachers or parents. When the Japanese realized that they had a problem, they did not try to improve their "image," as a lot of U.S. companies might have done. Instead, they strove to improve their manufacturing techniques. Today, we know only too well that they succeeded.

What most of us don't know is that just as so many of the products that the Japanese now sell successfully were invented in America, the man who helped them achieve their reputation for quality was also an American. Here, in his own country, he is largely unknown—almost a prophet without honor. Yet in Japan, he is a national celebrity.

The man's name is W. Edwards Deming, and in books and articles he has preached the "quality crusade" to anyone who would listen. Japan discovered him in 1950, when he went there to give a lecture on his ideas about quality control. A year later, Japan set up a nationwide quality-improvement contest whose winner was to receive what is now called the Deming Prize. It is one of the country's greatest honors.

Deming has set forth 14 points for top managers who want to promote quality:

1. Plan for the long-term future, not for the next month or year.
2. Never be complacent concerning the quality of your product.
3. Establish statistical control over your production processes and require your suppliers to do so as well.
4. Deal with the fewest number of suppliers—the best ones, of course.
5. Find out whether your problems are confined to particular parts of the production process or stem from the overall process itself.
6. Train workers for the job that you are asking them to perform.
7. Raise the quality of your line supervisors (see Chapter 10).
8. "Drive out fear."
9. Encourage departments to work closely together rather than to concentrate on departmental or divisional distinction.
10. Do not be sucked into adopting strictly numerical goals, including the widely popular formula of "zero defect" (see Chapter 19).
11. Require your workers to do quality work, not just to be at their stations from 9 to 5.
12. Train your employees to understand statistical methods.
13. Train your employees in new skills as the need arises.
14. Make top managers responsible for implementing these principles (see Chapter 8).

Some of these points make common sense; others will become clearer as you acquaint yourself with the material discussed throughout this book.

Source: W. Edwards Deming, "Improvement of Quality and Productivity through Action by Management," *National Productivity Review* 1 (Winter, 1981–1982):12–22.

HERE'S AN EXAMPLE

The co-owner of a conspicously growing restaurant chain, Mazzio's Pizza, in Springfield, Missouri, attributes their success to *corporate management*. The management team has stated their foremost goal of customer satisfaction through quality, and this quality emphasis is carried through to the product, customer service, and the physical plant.

CLASS COMMENT

The cost of poor management is great. The choice is: good management or poor management. How can poor management be prevented and good management be implemented? The study of management we are undertaking this semester will help us answer these questions.

criteria and concepts for evaluating managers and organizations.[6] Underlying many of these are two concepts suggested by Peter Drucker, one of the most respected writers on management.[7] Drucker has argued that a manager's performance can be measured in terms of two concepts: efficiency and effectiveness. As he puts it, *efficiency* means "doing things right," and *effectiveness* means "doing the right thing."

Efficiency—that is, the ability to get things done correctly—is an "input-output" concept. An efficient manager is one who achieves outputs, or results, that measure up to the inputs (labor, materials, and time) used to achieve them. Managers who are able to minimize the cost of the resources they use to attain their goals are acting efficiently.

Effectiveness, in contrast, is the ability to choose appropriate objectives: An effective manager is one who selects the right things to get done. A manager who selects an inappropriate objective—the production only of large cars when demand for small cars is soaring—is an ineffective manager. Such a manager would be ineffective even if the large cars were produced with maximum efficiency. No amount of efficiency can compensate for lack of effectiveness.

A manager's responsibilities require performance that is both efficient and effective, but although efficiency is important, effectiveness is critical. For Drucker, effectiveness is the key to the success of an organization. The manager's need to make the most of opportunities, says Drucker, implies that effectiveness rather than efficiency is essential to business. The pertinent question is not how to do things right, but how to find the right things to do, and to concentrate resources and efforts on them.[8]

TYPES OF MANAGERS

FOR DISCUSSION

As the level of management changes, so do the different competencies demanded. What does this imply? (Think in terms of what functions/activities are performed; what training or background is required; what performance evaluations might be used; etc.)

We have been using the term *manager* to mean anyone who is responsible for subordinates and other organizational resources. There are many different types of managers, with diverse tasks and responsibilities. Managers can be classified in two ways: by their *level* in the organization—so-called first-line, middle, and top managers—and by the *range* of organizational activities for which they are responsible—so-called functional and general managers.

Management Levels

first-line (or **first-level**) **managers** Managers who are responsible for the work of operating employees only and do not supervise other managers; they are the "first" or lowest level of managers in the organizational hierarchy.

First-Line Managers. The lowest level in an organization at which individuals are responsible for the work of others is called **first-line** or **first-level management.** First-line managers direct operating employees only; they do not supervise other managers. Examples of first-line managers are the "foreman" or production supervisor in a manufacturing plant, the technical supervisor in a research department, and the clerical supervisor in a large office. First-level managers are often called "supervisors."

---

[6]For a discussion of the complexity of evaluating organizational performance, see Terry Connolly, Edward J. Conlon, and Stuart Jay Deutsch, "Organizational Effectiveness: A Multiple-Constituency Approach," *Academy of Management Review* 5, no. 2 (April 1980):211–217.

[7]Peter F. Drucker, *The Effective Executive* (New York: Harper & Row, 1967).

[8]Peter F. Drucker, *Managing for Results* (New York: Harper & Row, 1964), p. 5. The pressures to focus on efficiency versus effectiveness are great in all organizations. Drucker also observed, in a seminar for federal executives during the Eisenhower administration, that "the greatest temptation is to work on doing better and better what should not be done at all."

middle managers Managers in the midrange of the organizational hierarchy; they are responsible for other managers and sometimes for some operating employees.

Middle Managers. The term **middle management** can include to more than one level in an organization. Middle managers direct the activities of lower-level managers and sometimes also those of operating employees. Middle managers' principal responsibilities are to direct the activities that implement their organizations' policies and to balance the demands of their superiors with the capacities of their subordinates.

top management Managers responsible for the overall management of the organization. They establish operating policies and guide the organization's interactions with its environment.

Top Managers. Composed of a comparatively small group of executives, **top management** is responsible for the overall management of the organization. It establishes operating policies and guides the organization's interactions with its environment. Typical titles of top managers are "chief executive officer," "president," and "senior vice-president." Actual titles vary from one organization to another and are not always a reliable guide to membership in the highest management classification.

Functional and General Managers

The other major classification of managers depends on the scope of the activities they manage.

functional manager A manager responsible for just one organizational activity, such as finance or human resource management.

Functional Managers. The **functional manager** is responsible for only *one* organizational activity, such as production, marketing, sales, *or* finance. The people and activities headed by a functional manager are engaged in a common set of activities.

general manager The individual responsible for all activities, such as production, sales, marketing, and finance, for an organization like a company or subsidiary.

General Managers. The **general manager,** on the other hand, oversees a complex unit, such as a company, a subsidiary, or an independent operating division. He or she is responsible for *all* the activities of that unit, such as its production, marketing, sales, *and* finance.[9]

A small company may have only one general manager—its president or executive vice-president—but a large organization may have several, each at the head of a relatively independent division. In a large food company, for example, there might be a grocery-products division, a refrigerated-products division, and a frozen-food-products division, with a different general manager responsible for each. Like the chief executive of a small company, each of these divisional heads would be responsible for all the activities of the unit.

THE MANAGEMENT PROCESS

It is easier to understand something as complex as management when it is described as a series of separate parts, or *functions,* that make up a whole process. Descriptions of this kind, known as *models,* have been used by students and practitioners of management for decades. A model is a simplification of the real world used to convey complex relationships in easy-to-understand terms. In fact, we used a model—without identifying it as such—when we said earlier that the major management activities were planning, organizing, leading, and controlling. This model of management was developed

[9]Because of their responsibilities for many diverse functions, it is increasingly important for top managers to have broad corporate experience. See W. Walker Lewis, "The CEO and Corporate Strategy in the Eighties: Back to Basics," *Interfaces* 14, no. 1 (January–February 1984):3–9.

"I've supervised. I've managed. I've directed. I've presided. I've chaired. What else is there?"

at the end of the nineteenth century and is still in use today.[10] Our knowledge about each of these aspects has increased dramatically, and our contemporary model is thus quite complex.

We have already described briefly these four main management activities. Now that we have acquired some insights into the manager's many roles and responsibilities, we will examine these activities or functions in greater detail.

Planning

Plans give the organization its objectives and set up the best procedure for reaching them. In addition, plans become the guides by which (1) the organization obtains and commits the resources required to reach its objectives, (2) members of the organization carry on activities consistent with the chosen objectives and procedures, and (3) progress toward the objectives is monitored and measured, so that corrective action can be taken if progress is unsatisfactory.

CLASS COMMENT

"I'm going with my gut feeling" could be the management wave of the future. In a survey conducted by Learning International of the USA's 1200 largest industrial and service companies, they discovered that 32 percent of the 300 respondents wanted their management styles to be more intuitive in the future.

The first step in planning is the selection of goals for the organization. Then objectives are established for the *subunits* of the organization—its divisions, departments, and so on. Once the objectives are determined, programs are established for achieving them in a systematic manner. Of course, in selecting objectives and developing programs, the manager considers their feasibility and whether they will be acceptable to the organization's managers and employees.

Plans made by top management for the organization as a whole may cover periods as long as five or ten years. In a large organization, such as a multinational energy corporation, those plans may involve commitments of billions of dollars. Planning at the lower levels, by middle or first-line managers, covers much shorter periods. Such plans may be for the next day's work, for example, or for a two-hour meeting to take place in a week.

---

[10]See also Stephen J. Carroll and Dennis J. Gillen, "The Classical Management Functions: Are They Really Outdated?" *Proceedings of the Forty-Fourth Annual Meeting of the American Academy of Management* (August 1984):132–136.

Organizing

Once managers have established objectives and developed plans or programs to reach them, they must design and staff an organization able to carry out those programs successfully. Different objectives will require different kinds of organizations. For example, an organization that aims to develop computer software will have to be far different from one that wants to manufacture blue jeans: Producing a standardized product like blue jeans requires efficient assembly-line techniques, whereas writing computer programs requires teams of professionals—systems analysts, software engineers, and operators. Although they must interact effectively, such people cannot be organized on an assembly-line basis. It is clear, then, that managers must have the ability to determine what type of organization will be needed to accomplish a given set of objectives. And they must have the ability to develop (and later to lead) that type of organization.

Leading

After plans have been made, the structure of the organization has been determined, and the staff has been recruited and trained, the next step is to arrange for movement toward the organization's defined objectives. This function can be called by various names: *leading, directing, motivating, actuating,* and others. But whatever the name used to identify it, this function involves getting the members of the organization to perform in ways that will help it achieve its established objectives.

Whereas planning and organizing deal with the more abstract aspects of the management process, the activity of leading is very concrete; it involves working directly with people.

Controlling

Finally, the manager must ensure that the actions of the organization's members do in fact move the organization toward its stated goals. This is the controlling function of management, and it involves four main elements:

1. Establishing standards of performance.
2. Measuring current performance and comparing it against the established standards.
3. Detecting deviations from standard goals in order to make corrections before a sequence of activities is completed.
4. Taking action to correct performance that does not meet those standards.

Through the controlling function, the manager can keep the organization on its chosen track, keeping it from straying from its specified goals.

THOUGHT-PROVOKER

What's it like to be a manager? How would management differ between a new, small business and an established, growing business?

We have presented here a model of the management process. But the relationships described above are interrelated more than our model implies. For example, we saw that standards and benchmarks are used as a means of controlling employees' actions, but, obviously, establishing such standards is also an inherent part of the planning process and an integral factor in motivating and leading subordinates. And taking corrective action, which we also introduced as a control activity, often involves an adjustment in plans. In practice, the management process does not involve four separate or loosely related sets of activities but a group of *interactive* functions. We should also point out that the four functions do not necessarily occur in the sequence presented. In fact, various combinations of these activities are going on simultaneously in every organization.

QUOTATION FROM A MANAGER

John Rollwagen, head man at Cray Research, the organization that makes supercomputers, says, "The CEO used to be the boss. He's not anymore. He's had to relinquish day-to-day control. The job of the CEO is to let people be creative."

In addition, the existence of these distinct management functions does not imply that any manager has complete freedom to perform them whenever he or she wishes. Managers are generally faced with various limitations on their activities, depending on their role in the organization, their designated position in its hierarchy, and the kind of organization they work for. Some managers, for example, may find that limits are set on their dealings with subordinates—on what they can do to direct, guide, or motivate them—because their leadership style conflicts with the style that prevails in their organization. And a manager may not be able to hire new staff to pursue a new set of objectives because the organization cannot carry the added expense of their salaries.

In spite of their limitations, models provide a useful approach to understanding—as long as we remember their shortcomings and that they are not meant to be exact descriptions of the real world. By analyzing the management process—that is, by separating it into distinct pieces that we call "management functions"—this model can improve our understanding of what managers do. And that, after all, is the purpose of this book.

MANAGEMENT LEVEL AND SKILLS

Managers at every level plan, organize, lead, and control. But they differ in the amount of time devoted to each of these activities. Some of these differences depend on the kind of organization in which the manager works, some on the type of job the manager holds.

Managers of small private clinics, for example, spend their time quite differently from the way the heads of large research hospitals spend theirs: Managers of clinics spend comparatively more time practicing medicine, and less time actually managing, than do directors of large hospitals. The technical supervisor of research physicists at AT&T Bell Labs will have a job that in some respects is quite different from that of a production supervisor on a General Motors assembly line. Yet both are first-line managers. And yet there will also be important similarities in the jobs of all these managers.

Other differences in the ways managers spend their time depend upon their levels in the organizational hierarchy. In the sections below, we shall consider how management skills and activities differ at these various levels and look at the various roles that managers perform.

Robert L. Katz, a teacher and business executive, has identified three basic kinds of skills: technical, human, and conceptual. Every manager needs all three. *Technical skill* is the ability to use the procedures, techniques, and knowledge of a specialized field. Surgeons, engineers, musicians, and accountants all have technical skills in their respective fields. *Human skill* is the ability to work with, understand, and motivate other people, as individuals or in groups. *Conceptual skill* is the ability to coordinate and integrate all of an organization's interests and activities. It involves the manager's ability to see the organization as a whole, to understand how its parts depend on one another, and to anticipate how a change in any of its parts will affect the whole.

FOR DISCUSSION

Why is it important to recognize that managerial skills vary by level? (All three skills are essential but the relative importance of each is determined by organizational level. At each level, the mix of skills needed is dictated by the demands of the manager's job.)

Katz suggests that although all three of these skills are essential to a manager, their relative importance depends mainly on the manager's rank in the organization. (See Fig. 1-1.) Technical skill is most important in the lower levels. Human skill, by contrast, is important for managers at every level: Because they must get their work done primarily through others, their ability to tap the technical skills of their subordinates is more important than their own technical skills. Finally, the importance of

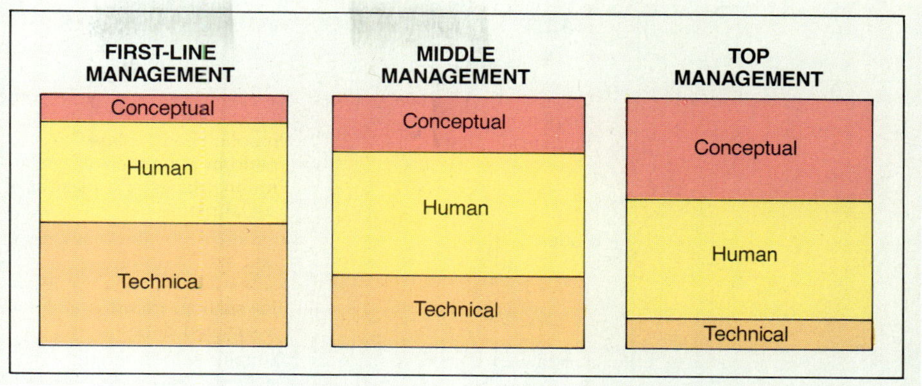

FIGURE 1-1 RELATIVE SKILLS NEEDED FOR EFFECTIVE PERFORMANCE AT DIFFERENT LEVELS OF MANAGEMENT

conceptual skill increases as one rises through the ranks of a management system based on hierarchical principles of authority and responsibility.

MANAGERIAL ROLES

As we have seen, a functional manager is someone responsible for *one* organizational activity or *one* unit within the organization. In a broad sense, a "role" consists of the behavior patterns expected of an individual within a social unit. For the purposes of managerial thinking, a *role* is thus the behavioral pattern expected of someone within a functional unit. Roles are thus inherent in functions.

Henry Mintzberg made an extensive survey of existing research on the subject of managerial roles and integrated his findings with the results of a study of five chief executive officers.[11] In an effort to catalog and analyze the various roles of managers, the combined review covered all kinds and levels of managers—from street-gang leaders to CEOs. Table 1-1 shows that, according to Mintzberg, managers perform basically ten roles that can be grouped according to three main functions.

Mintzberg concluded that, to a considerable extent, the jobs of many managers are quite similar. All managers, he argued, have formal authority over their own organizational units and derive status from that authority. This status causes all managers to be involved in interpersonal relationships with subordinates, peers, and superiors, who in turn provide managers with the information they need to make decisions. All managers thus play a series of interpersonal, informational, and decision-making roles that Mintzberg defined as "organized sets of behaviors." (See Fig. 1-2.) Here, we will summarize Mintzberg's findings and theories about managerial roles.

---

[11]Henry Mintzberg, "The Manager's Job: Folklore and Fact," *Harvard Business Review* 52, no. 4 (July–August 1975):49–61, and *The Nature of Managerial Work* (Englewood Cliffs, N.J.: Prentice Hall, 1973). Important precursors of Mintzberg's work include Sue Carlson, *Executive Behavior: A Study in the Work Load and Working Methods of Managing Directors* (Stockholm, Sweden: Stromberg Aktiebolag, 1951); Peter F. Drucker, *The Practice of Management* (New York: Harper & Row, 1954); and Rosemary Stewart, *Managers and Their Jobs: A Study of the Similarities and Differences in the Ways Managers Spend Their Time* (London: Macmillan, 1967). More recent studies of the manager's job include Colin P. Hales, "What Do Managers Do? A Critical Review of the Evidence," *Journal of Management Studies* 23 (January 1986):88–115; and two articles by Hugh C. Willmott, "Images and Ideals of Managerial Work: A Critical Examination of Conceptual and Empirical Accounts," *Journal of Management Studies* 21 (1984):349–368 and "Studying Managerial Work: A Critique and a Proposal," *Journal of Management Studies* 24 (May 1987):249–270.

TABLE 1-1 MINTZBERG'S MANAGERIAL ROLES

ROLE	DESCRIPTION	IDENTIFIABLE ACTIVITIES
Interpersonal		
Figurehead	Symbolic head; obliged to perform a number of routine duties of a legal or social nature	Ceremony, status requests, solicitations
Leader	Responsible for the motivation and activation of subordinates; responsible for staffing, training, and associated duties	Virtually all managerial activities involving subordinates
Liaison	Maintains self-developed network of outside contacts and informers who provide favors and information	Acknowledgements of mail; external board work; other activities involving outsiders
Informational		
Monitor	Seeks and receives wide variety of special information (much of it current) to develop thorough understanding of organization and environment; emerges as nerve center of internal and external information of the organization	Handling all mail and contacts categorized as concerned primarily with receiving information (e.g., periodical news, observational tours)
Disseminator	Transmits information received from outsiders or from other subordinates to members of the organization; some information factual, some involving interpretation and integration of diverse value positions of organizational influencers	Forwarding mail into organization for informational purposes, verbal contacts involving information flow to subordinates (e.g., review sessions, instant communication flows)
Spokesperson	Transmits information to outsiders on organization's plans, policies, actions, results, etc.; serves as expert on organization's industry	Board meetings; handling mail and contacts involving transmission of information to outsiders
Decision Making		
Entrepreneur	Searches organization and its environment for opportunities and initiates "improvement projects" to bring about change; supervises design of certain projects as well	Strategy and review sessions involving initiation or design of improvement projects.
Disturbance handler	Responsible for corrective action when organization faces important, unexpected disturbances	Strategy and review sessions involving disturbances and crises
Resource allocator	Responsible for the allocation of organizational resources of all kinds—in effect the making or approval of all significant organizational decisions	Scheduling; requests for authorization; any activity involving budgeting and the programming of subordinates' work
Negotiator	Responsible for representing the organization at major negotiations	Negotiation

Source: From *The Nature of Managerial Work* by Henry Mintzberg. Copyright © 1973 by Henry Mintzberg. Reprinted by permission of Harper & Row, Publishers, Inc.

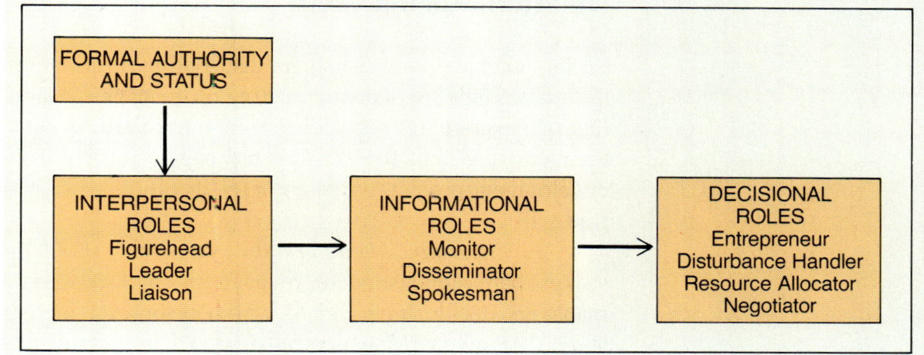

FIGURE 1-2 THE MANAGER'S ROLES

Source: Reprinted by permission of the *Harvard Business Review*. An exhibit from "The Manager's Job: Folklore and Fact" by Henry Mintzberg (July–August 1975). Copyright © 1975 by the President and Fellows of Harvard College; all rights reserved.

Interpersonal Roles

Three sometimes routine interpersonal roles help managers keep their organizations running smoothly. The first is that of the *figurehead* who performs ceremonial duties as head of the unit: greeting visitors, attending subordinates' weddings, taking customers to lunch. Second, there is the role of *leader:* hiring, training, motivating, and encouraging. First-line managers, in particular, stress effectiveness in this role. Finally, managers must play the interpersonal role of *liaison* in dealing with people other than subordinates or superiors: peers within the organization, as well as suppliers or clients outside it.

Informational Roles

Receiving and communicating information, Mintzberg suggests, are the most important aspects of a manager's job.[12] Managers need information to make intelligent decisions, and other people in their units or organizations depend on information received or transmitted through them.

Managers gather and disseminate information in three informational roles. The first is *monitoring,* whereby managers constantly look for useful information. They question subordinates and collect unsolicited information, usually through networks of contacts. The role of monitor usually makes managers the best informed members of their groups.

In the role of *disseminator,* managers distribute to subordinates important information they would not otherwise know. Last, in the role of *spokesperson,* managers transmit information to people outside their own groups. Keeping superiors well-informed is one important aspect of this role. Another is communicating with the world outside the organization.

[12]This suggestion has been supported by the work of John P. Kotter. See *The General Manager* (New York: Free Press, 1982) and "What Effective Managers Really Do," *Harvard Business Review* 60, no. 6 (November–December 1982):156–167.

Decision-Making Roles

So far, we have seen managers distributing information to others. Information is also the "basic input to decision-making for managers," according to Mintzberg, who says that managers play four decision-making roles. As *entrepreneurs,* they try to improve their units. When, for example, managers receive a good idea, they might launch a development project to make it a reality. In this role, they initiate change of their own free will.

As *disturbance handlers,* they respond to problems beyond their control, such as strikes, bankrupt customers, breaches of contract, and the like. As *resource allocators,* managers decide how and to whom resources, including the managers' own time, should be given. Managers also screen important decisions made by subordinates.

The fourth and last decision-making role is that of *negotiator*. A company president might, for example, deal with a consulting firm; a production head might draw up a contract with a supplier. Managers spend a lot of their time as negotiators because only they have the knowledge and authority this role demands.

HERE'S AN EXAMPLE

Seventy-seven percent of the people at the helms of 200 of America's largest corporations say their job is harder than their predecessor's was. Reasons given are the many external and unforeseen factors bombarding CEOs.

Mintzberg's work is particularly interesting because it calls attention to the uncertain, turbulent environment faced by managers in the real world. Reality is predictable and controllable only in part. For Mintzberg, managers should have neither the time nor the desire to be deep thinkers. They are, above all, *doers,* coping with life's dynamic parade of challenges and surprises.

EXCELLENCE IN MANAGEMENT

In 1982, a study by management consultants Thomas J. Peters and Robert H. Waterman examined the qualities of 43 "excellently managed" U.S. companies, including IBM, Eastman Kodak, 3M, Boeing, Bechtel, Procter & Gamble, and McDonald's.[13] Not only were these firms consistently profitable over a 20-year period, but they were also unusually successful in responding to customer needs, providing a challenging and rewarding working environment for their employees, and being good corporate citizens by meeting their social and environmental obligations effectively. Peters and Waterman concluded that these companies were "brilliant on the basics." Rather than having some secret strategy or unique market situation, they simply did the most fundamental organizational tasks very well.

CLASS COMMENT

Although attributes of excellence are widely quoted and recognized, it is important to understand where and how these attributes fell short. For example, Peters and Waterman were criticized for relying too heavily on unsupported generalizations and not taking into account environmental considerations, among other things.

Peters and Waterman emphasize the critical role played by management at all levels, especially at the top, in creating the values and practices that encourage excellence. In stressing the importance of organizational culture, Peters and Waterman cite such strongly held managerial values as IBM's "respect for the individual" and Frito-Lay's commitment to a "99.5 percent" level of satisfactory service as keys to each company's success.

However, a danger in labeling any firm "excellently run" is that internal and external conditions may change, so that a company which embodies excellence in one year may founder the next. In fact one of Peters' later books, *Thriving on Chaos,* goes so far as to argue that, in this sense, "There are no excellent companies." Why? Because "No company is safe. IBM is declared dead in 1979, the best of the best in 1982, and dead again in 1986."[14] Other companies also suffer such frequent ups and

[13]Thomas J. Peters and Robert H. Waterman, Jr., *In Search of Excellence* (New York: Harper & Row, 1982). The themes from this book are discussed further in Thomas J. Peters and Nancy Austin, *A Passion for Excellence* (New York: Random House, 1985); in Thomas J. Peters, *Thriving on Chaos: Handbook for a Management Revolution* (New York: Alfred A. Knopf, 1987); and in Robert H. Waterman, Jr., *The Renewal Factor: How the Best Get and Keep the Competitive Edge* (New York: Bantam Books, 1987).

[14]Peters, *Thriving on Chaos,* p. 3.

FOR DISCUSSION

Why would managers even want someone to tell them how to succeed? Are universal prescriptions for success even possible? Why or why not?

downs. In fact, the "champ to chump cycle," as Peters calls it, seems to be growing shorter and shorter.

For example, Levi Strauss and Company, one of the companies that Peters and Waterman described as excellent, later fell on hard times because it lost close contact with its customers: the retailers who carried its products and the consumers who wore them. When styles changed and the jeans market became glutted with suppliers, Levi's was slow to sense the changes and lost much of its retailers' loyalty. Recently, however, Levi's has made a comeback by deliberately trying to be a more responsive vendor.

In their subsequent research, Peters and Waterman (working separately) have stressed two principles. The first, as Peters says, is "a set of new basics: world-class quality and service, enhanced responsiveness through greatly increased flexibility, and continuous, short-cycle innovation and improvement" of all a company's products.[15] Companies must pursue what Waterman calls "informed opportunism"; in other words, they must respond to opportunities and challenges quickly, as they arise.

The second principle, as Waterman puts it, is to recognize that people are "the main engine" of any company, not just "interchangeable parts of the corporate machine."[16] Only a company's people can make it succeed and then help it defend its turf. These people have to be given more authority to make decisions and must be treated as individuals. Their loyalty must be won through a new sort of social contract. As Peters says:

> For managers this path means continuously retraining employees for more complex tasks, automating in ways that cut routine tasks and enhance worker flexibility and creativity, diffusing responsibility for innovation, taking seriously labor's concern for job security, and giving workers a stake in improved productivity via profit-linked bonuses and stock plans. For workers this . . . path means accepting flexible job classifications and work rules, agreeing to wage rates linked to profits and productivity improvements, and generally taking greater responsibility for the soundness and efficiency of the enterprise.[17]

Waterman is in essential agreement. Exhibit 1-2 lists and discusses his eight prescriptions for the renewal of corporate success.

EXHIBIT 1-2 WATERMAN'S LESSONS IN CORPORATE RENEWAL

- **INFORMED OPPORTUNISM**
  Information is their main strategic advantage, and flexibility is their main strategic weapon. They assume opportunity will keep knocking, but it will knock softly and in unpredictable ways.
- **DIRECTION AND EMPOWERMENT**
  Managers at renewing companies define the boundaries, and their subordinates figure out the best way to do the job within them. Managers give up some control to gain results.
- **FRIENDLY FACTS, CONGENIAL CONTROLS**
  Renewing companies love information that provides context and removes decision-making from the realm of mere opinions. Their people regard financial controls as the benign checks and balances that allow them to be creative and free.
- **A DIFFERENT MIRROR**
  Leaders are open and inquisitive. They get ideas from almost anyone in and out of the hierarchy—customers, competitors, even next-door neighbors.

(continued)

[15]Ibid., pp. 3–4.

[16]Robert J. Waterman, "The Renewal Factor," *Business Week*, September 14, 1987, p. 104.

[17]Peters, *Thriving on Chaos*, p. 22.

EXHIBIT 1-2 (CONTINUED)

- **TEAMWORK, TRUST, POLITICS, AND POWER**
Renewers stress the value of teamwork and trust their employees to do the job. While relentless at fighting office politics, they acknowledge politics are inevitable in the workplace.
- **STABILITY IN MOTION**
Renewing companies undergo constant change against a base of underlying stability. They understand the need for consistency and norms. But they also realize that the only way to respond to change is to deliberately break the rules.
- **ATTITUDES AND ATTENTION**
Visible management attention, rather than exhortation, gets things done. Action may start with the words, but it has to be backed by symbolic behavior that makes those words come alive.
- **CAUSES AND COMMITMENT**
Commitment results from management's ability to turn grand causes into small actions so that everyone can contribute to the central purpose.

Source: Robert H. Waterman, Jr., *The Renewal Factor: How the Best Get and Keep the Competitive Edge* (New York: Bantam Books, 1987).

ETHICS IN MANAGEMENT

Since managers play more than one role, they must also pursue multiple objectives and sets of priorities. Thus, they have to juggle goals and priorities, sometimes having to chose among them.

Because of this obligation, managers affect the ability of employees, customers, stockholders, and everyone else to get what they want (naturally, their own self-interest is usually at stake as well). Often, managers must decide who has a right to what, and when. Because the actions of managers affect other people, those managers allocate benefits and detriments no matter what they do—or fail to do.

ethics The concept and the study of the concept of who is—and should be—benefited or harmed by any action.

As applied to the study of management, **ethics** refers to the concept of interactive responsibility: of who is—and should be—benefited or harmed by any action. It is also the study of who does—and who should—have rights of any kind. Once you start to look for them (and often even if you don't), ethical questions materialize everywhere, at all levels of business.

On the surface, it is relatively simple to judge a business practice as ethically

ETHICS IN MANAGEMENT

FOOTING THE BILL AND HAVING A HEART

Ostensibly, the primary function of Reebok International is to outfit active young people in athletic shoes for jogging, playing tennis, and attending casual get-togethers in fashionable sportswear. But Reebok has not lost sight of more socially conscious roles that can be played by an organization with its resources. Recently, Reebok assumed an ethical obligation to an unlikely stakeholder—namely, an organization in the forefront of the human-rights movement.

Reebok plans to underwrite—to the tune of $10 million—a five-continent tour sponsored by Amnesty International featuring such popular artists as Sting and Peter Gabriel. "Their objective dovetailed with our corporate philosophy about the right to live your life the way you want," explains company president Joseph LaBonte. Reebok will encourage retailers to participate, establish a yearly $10,000 prize to reward the expression of the right to freedom, and merchandize such correct or incorrect. The hard part—especially when conventional rules don't seem to help—is understanding *the concepts and techniques of ethical decision making,* so that you can reach better decisions and so that your moral judgments amount to more than mere personal eccentricities. (See the Ethics in Management box entitled ''Footing the Bill and Having a Heart,'' which illustrates the relationship between organizational ethics and social responsibility.)

EDUCATING MANAGERS

FOR DISCUSSION

Why do I have to take a course to learn how to be a manager? What's the advantage of formal management training?

Management, as you can see, is thus an *applied* discipline—not primarily a theoretical one. Many theories and models are useful for managers, but the test is always the test of practice, of reality. Ideas that work well only in theory may be very good in theoretical physics—but not in management, because managers have to manage real human beings and everyday situations, not theoretical ones. In this respect, it resembles other arts that are concerned with good practice, such as the law and medicine.

Management education must reflect these facts. Like medical and legal education, it must include ''clinical'' practice, not just lecture-hall erudition. That world is also becoming increasingly international—and increasingly competitive. (See Management Application.) Working effectively in such an environment means working smarter, and working smarter means learning from one's mistakes.

Management Education Criticized

TEACHING TIP

Point out the usefulness of looking at management as: a *science*—organized body of knowledge; and as an *art*—application of knowledge. Use the *science* of management to master the *art* of management.

Thomas Mulligan argues that, currently, management education is ''almost entirely science based.''[18] Mulligan's point that management education tends to focus on management *science* and to ignore the *art* of management—especially the ethical issues it involves—suggests one criticism of the way we educate managers. Yet even some aspects of management science may also be neglected in our business schools.

As Robert H. Hayes and William Abernathy write, ''Success in most industries requires an organizational commitment to compete in the marketplace on technical

[18] Thomas M. Mulligan, ''The Two Cultures in Business Education,'' *Academy of Management Review* 12, no. 4 (1987): 593.

auxiliary items as T-shirts and jackets to promote the tour, all proceeds going to Amnesty International.

Last year, the pharmaceutical company G. D. Searle gave away $10,000 worth of a costly hypertension drug to needy patients and plans to continue a similar program this year, when it will donate an unlimited supply of seven different medications manufactured for the treatment of heart diseases.† A patient unable to reimburse a physician or clinic will be issued a certificate that Searle will then redeem. If one of the attributes of an excellent company is "a bias for action"—a preference for doing *something, anything,* in the interest of its customer community—Searle intends to continue pursuing that policy. Says chairman Sheldon Kilgore: "We view it as the cost of doing business, making drugs available to the needy. We plan to make available every new drug that we introduce on the same basis."

Sources: "Reebok Foots the Bill for Human Rights," *Business Week,* April 25, 1988; "Free Heart Drugs for Needy," *USA Today,* April 6, 1988.

grounds—that is . . . by offering superior products.'' But until recently, management education tended to promote

> (1) analytic detachment rather than the insight that comes from ''hands on'' experience and (2) short-term cost reduction rather than long-term development of technological competitiveness. It is this managerial gospel, we feel, that has played a major role in undermining the vigor of American industry.[19]

Robert G. Harris, an economist who accepts this critique, adds that ''the value assumptions of mainstream economics are at least partly responsible for these deficiencies.''[20] Why? Because those values tend to belittle the importance of leadership and to exalt income and wealth. On the individual level, this tends to promote an abstract careerism that has little to do with the role played by specific work satisfactions in overall life fulfillment. On the social and global level, it leads companies to seek short-term gains at the expense not only of the future but of the present: In particular, the environment is already beginning to feel (and express) the impact of shortsighted managers trained in our universities. The solution, according to Harris: ''Educating managers to understand changing values, philosophies, and lifestyles . . . and to appreciate the roles of other institutions in our society.''[21]

Management as Social Practice. Tom Burns, working often with G. M. Stalker, has tried for over twenty years to analyze the problems that occur because values and lifestyles continue to change. He has suggested two categories of decision-making factors in management that mirror those that virtually everyone uses in his or her daily decision making. In making decisions, we (1) acknowledge the diverse, unpredictable factors that affect our lives every day and (2) accept that diversity as leading to moments of ''social ambiguity'' in which decisions concerning others are not necessarily clear-cut. When we acknowledge and accept these factors, we enter structured, organizational, or even institutional social units and become part of a ''work organization'' practicing collective social interaction.[22] In short, we work together to fend off fragmentation, reduce dilemmas, and coordinate resources—we institute ''social practice.''

Those who agree with Burns argue that management decision making reflects the same problems of ''social practice.'' For example, if a manager wonders how the problems and needs of Division A can be made compatible with those of Divisions B and C rather than trying to figure out how the goals of all three divisions can be subordinated to some grand overall organizational design or formal statement of purpose, he or she is integrating the procedures of social practice.[23] More importantly, he or she is acknowledging managerial problems which institutionally reflect much more pervasive social processes, which are often ''messier'' than policy analysts would like

---

[19]Robert Hayes and William J. Abernathy, ''Managing Our Way to Economic Decline,'' *Harvard Business Review* 58 (July–August 1980):68. See also Robert B. Reich, *The New American Frontier* (New York: Times Books, 1983)

[20]Robert G. Harris, ''The Values of Economic Theory in Management Education,'' *American Economic Review* 74 (May 1984):123.

[21]Ibid., p. 126.

[22]Tom Burns, *The B.B.C.: Public Institution and Private World* (London: Macmillan, 1977); Burns, *A Comparative Study of Administrative Structure and Organizational Processes in Selected Areas of the National Health Service* (London: Social Science Research Council, 1982); Burns and G. M. Stalker, *The Management of Innovation* (London: Tavistock, 1961). See also M. I. Reed, ''Management as a Social Practice,'' *Journal of Management Studies* 21, no. 3 (1984):273–285.

[23]J. Tomlinson, *Unequal Struggle: British Socialism and the Capitalist Enterprise* (London: Methuen, (1982).

to believe, and which tend to be obscured by the belief that the organization's formal structure can handle, if not eliminate, them.

According to Burns and Stalker, management is an "organic" or systematically interrelated *process* of fighting off fragmentation, coordinating diverse mechanism of productive progress, and integrating means of finding solutions that satisfy broad social needs and values. Such an approach, they argue, is superior to the view of the organization as a structured hierarchy or formal unit committed to nothing more than a particularized socioeconomic system. Burns and Stalker write: "The growth and accretion of institutionalized values, beliefs, and conduct, in the form of *commitments,* ideology and manners, around an image of the concern in its industrial and commercial setting make good the loss of formal structure."[24]

Management as Anticipation. J. Sterling Livingstone agrees with the position of Mulligan, Burns, and Stalker, and adds that most management training programs also neglect to teach people what they must do in order to become fully effective managers.[25] These programs, Livingstone maintains, emphasize only problem solving and decision making. Thus, they help to develop analytical ability but do little to improve other, more important capacities a manager will need.

What managers really should be taught, Livingstone says, is problem *finding* and *opportunity* finding: that is, finding problems that inhibit growth and expansion and opportunities that enhance growth and expansion. Analytical skills are important, but a manager's success will ultimately depend on his or her ability to anticipate problems long before they arise. Even more important to the manager is the ability to find and take advantage of opportunities. After all, it is not problem solving but making the most of opportunities that helps organizations succeed.[26]

While Livingstone suggests that these abilities can and should be taught, he also maintains that certain characteristics of effective managers are almost impossible to teach—personal qualities that people develop long before they enter management training programs. According to Livingstone, three such qualities are associated with successful managers:

1. *The need to manage.* Only those people who want to affect the performance of others and who derive satisfaction when they do so are likely to become effective managers.
2. *The need for power.* Good managers have a need to influence others. To do this, they do not rely on the authority of their positions but on their superior knowledge and skill.
3. *The capacity for empathy.* The effective manager also needs the ability to understand and cope with the often unexpressed emotional reactions of others in the organization in order to win their cooperation.

With this discussion of the limitations of management education, Livingstone joins Katz and Mintzberg in calling attention to the wide variety of skills and abilities possessed by successful managers. Many of these skills can be and are being taught. But many are qualities of character and style that are difficult to develop in a classroom.[27] Prospective managers will have to look inside themselves to discover whether they have the personal qualities and abilities required of effective managers. If they are

---

[24]Burns and Stalker, *The Management of Innovation,* p. 122.

[25]See *Harvard Business Review* 49, no. 1 (January–February 1971):79–89.

[26]For a good discussion of problem finding, see William F. Pounds, "The Process of Problem Finding," *Industrial Management Review* 11, no. 1 (Fall 1969):1–19.

[27]Donald H. Bush and Betty Jo Licata, "The Impact of Skill Learnability on the Effectiveness of Managerial Training and Development," *Journal of Management* 9, no. 1 (Fall 1983):27–39.

truly motivated toward management, they will take the initiative in pursuing the self-development they will eventually need.[28]

Management Learning: Books and Experience

FOR DISCUSSION

What role does education play in management training? What role does experience play in management training?

Let's consider the following scenario. You are a middle manager in an organization that has decided to change its formal organizational structure (see Chapter 12). As part of its plan, the organization has instructed you to promote one of your subordinate managers by transferring him to a position in an organizational division located in another city. However, the man declines the promotion because he does not want to relocate—perhaps he does not want to remove his children from their school or perhaps his wife has established a successful business in the community. You may have to inform him that he thus faces an "up-or-out" situation—his position is such that promotion is possible within the organization only if he accepts the transfer. However, the *individual* decision is firm—the man has decided that, for various reasons, he does not have to accept the company's proposal and does not intend to. The *organizational* decision is also essentially firm: it has decided to reorganize in order to solve a problem or in order to seize an opportunity. *Managerial* decisions, however, remain to be made. Should the lower-level manager be terminated? Is it possible to move him horizontally—to some other position in the local headquarters (with or without promotion)? In either case, your original responsibility still has to be fulfilled: The position that one person has declined must still be filled if the organization's goals are to be carried out. How can you best fill that position?

Of course, no textbook by itself can teach you to become an effective manager and prescribe solutions to problems like this one. Learning how to be an effective manager requires not only knowledge and personal ability but also considerable practice in using the various management skills.

However, a major function of a textbook is to present relevant information in an orderly, systematic way. We say "relevant" because the knowledge in this textbook is based on the experience of managers and on studies by management researchers. Obviously, you will not be ready to assume all the responsibilities of a manager when you finish this book, but you will know many of the tools you will be using as a manager, and you will be more aware of the kinds of opportunities and problems you will be facing.

In order to help you develop your managerial abilities, this book includes numerous case studies that require you to describe and anticipate problems and decide what to do about them and that will provide you with an opportunity to develop your judgment and skill. To the extent that you will work with others in analyzing the cases, you will also be able to practice the human skills Katz described.

Students who have had some working experience, either before returning to management studies or concurrently with them, have the opportunity to observe managers in action. Community service and part-time employment provide a chance to watch managers and organizations at close range. Observe the interactions between levels of management, the characteristics of effective supervisors and leaders, and the qualities that seem to hinder communication and accomplishment. As your study of management progresses, try to find examples in *your* experience that illustrate the points you will be reading about and discussing.

---

[28]The importance of the motivation to manage has been studied extensively by John B. Miner; see "The Real Crunch in Managerial Manpower," *Harvard Business Review* 51, no. 6 (November–December 1973):146–158 and *Motivation to Manage* (Atlanta: Organizational Measurement Systems Press, 1977). This topic is also addressed by David McClelland and David H. Burnham in "Power Is the Great Motivator," *Harvard Business Review* 54, no. 2 (March–April 1976):100–110.

Furthermore, try putting your own management skills to work by assuming leadership roles in extracurricular activities. You might also work in and lead some of the group projects that many colleges offer in connection with formal course work. In addition, you can take advantage of whatever skills-oriented courses are available. These courses help develop specific abilities through the use of experiential exercises, unstructured groups, role playing, and other techniques.

The best way to learn to be an effective manager is by working with and observing good managers. Analyze what they do, how they do it, and how things turn out. It is difficult to learn from ineffective managers—but not impossible. You can notice and analyze what they are doing wrong and you can develop hypotheses about what you might do instead. In this way, you may learn some things *not* to do.[29] Knowing what not to do is important, but it is far more important to learn what *to do*. For this reason, good managers are easier to learn from—and they are much more enjoyable to work with. Finally, it is always good practice to try out new concepts for oneself—and to modify them in order to make them one's own.

In every career, it is inevitable that one will work with both effective and ineffective managers; however, keep in mind that a good manager to work under is one of the most important things to look for in a prospective job.

THE PURPOSE OF THIS BOOK

Most readers of this book will spend a good part of their lives working in organizations, either as employees or managers, or both. The chief purpose of this book is to prepare them for both of these roles. It will help them understand how organizations are managed—that is, what tasks managers must perform to keep their organizations running smoothly and effectively. They will also learn how managers accomplish those tasks, what managers need to know in order to manage effectively, and how they apply their skills and knowledge in order to meet organizational goals (as well as their own).

Usually, when people become employees, their first task is learning to be successful subordinates—a task that should not be underestimated. One of the best ways to be an effective subordinate is to understand the job of the employer. This means understanding the demands placed upon the employer by the needs of the organization. Effective subordinates should also be able to view their own roles in relation to others in the department or subdivision, the role of the subdivision in relation to the organization, the responsibilities of the subdivision manager, the goals of the organization as a whole, and perhaps its whole environment.[30]

The person who has acquired a basic understanding of how organizations are managed will be able to put this understanding to good use when he or she becomes a member of an organization. For example, by watching various managers in action, an alert, knowledgeable employee can identify the kinds of managerial behavior that seems to be successful (or unsuccessful) in moving the organization toward its goals. The employee can use this learning experience to improve his or her chances of becoming not only a manager but an *effective* manager—that is, one who attains organizational goals.

Last but not least, an understanding of management should prove helpful to the reader in many situations and activities outside the formal organization. Organizations are a necessary and useful fact of life. All of us have to live with a variety of organizations and managers during the course of our daily lives.

---

[29]And see Manfred F. R. Kets de Vries, "Managers Can Drive Their Subordinates Mad," *Harvard Business Review* 57, no. 4 (July–August 1979):125–134.

[30]A discussion of subordinate/supervisor relations can be found in John J. Gabarro and John P. Kotter, "Managing Your Boss," *Harvard Business Review* 58, no. 1 (January–February 1980):92–100.

ILLUSTRATIVE CASE STUDY Wrap-Up

A Typical Day in the Life of Alison Reeves

The case of Alison Reeves illustrates each of the main managerial activities with which this book is concerned. She has to plan her budget for the next year, and she has to understand why she is currently spending more than she had been budgeted—she has to *control.* Alison talked with her boss about reorganizing her department, and her decision to give up smoking derived from a desire to set a better example of *leadership.*

Each of these activities is also more subtle than at first appears. *Planning* isn't just figuring out the budget for the coming year: Alison is also planning when she decides what phone calls to return and whether or not to keep her lunch appointment. She has to decide what objectives were important, and she must do this almost routinely. Similarly, giving feedback to subordinates is a way of controlling—for example, telling Bob that he is doing a good job or simply spending a few minutes casually talking to him. Talking with her boss is an obvious case of *organizing,* but equally important was Alison's lunch, where she *coordinated* the efforts of two departments, and her task force meeting, at which the company's United Way campaign was organized. Finally, leadership is more than symbolic behavior. When Alison spent time with the customer whom she had met, she got important information that she could transmit both to Bob for his report and to her boss. Matching tasks and people, *motivating* and *communicating,* are also important parts of the leadership function.

Management is a dynamic process. Sometimes it does not have a beginning, middle, and end, and if Alison is not in the proper frame of mind, her day can seem an endless series of frustrating interruptions or disconnected activities. If she understands management as Mintzberg and others want us to—and if she understands it as an important kind of social practice—she will continue to be successful. Alison has not run a marathon on this particular day, but she may well feel as if she has—both tired and satisfied. ■

SUMMARY

Organizations are needed in our society because they accomplish things that individuals cannot do, help provide continuity of knowledge, are a source of careers, and serve society. The management of organizations involves planning, organizing, leading, and controlling the work of organization members in order to achieve stated goals.

In moving organizations toward their goals, managers adopt a wide range of interpersonal, informational, and decisional roles. Because the actions of managers affect other people, there is an ethical dimension to their jobs: Judgments should be fair decisions and not the result of preference or eccentricity.

Recent attempts have been made to isolate and describe the qualities of managerial excellence in organizations. The effort to identify and learn from organizations that are doing many things right is a positive stimulus to managers seeking to create the conditions of excellence in their own companies. Recent theorists have cautioned that the term "excellence" needs monitoring, because some companies respond better than others to changing environments; they also emphasize that "excellence" is largely a function of managing human resources—people.

There are two ways that managers can be classified: by level and by organizational activity. Management levels include first-line, middle, and top managers. Functional managers are responsible for only one organizational activity, such as sales. General managers are responsible for all the varied activities in a complex organizational unit.

Managers at different levels of the organization require and use different types of skills. Lower-level managers require and use a greater degree of technical skill than higher-level managers, whereas higher-level managers require and use a greater degree of conceptual skill. Human skill is important at all managerial levels.

Managers work with and through other people; they are responsible and accountable; they must balance competing goals and set priorities; they must be able to think analytically and conceptually; they are mediators, politicians, diplomats, symbols, and decision makers. Above all, managers must be alert to the need to change roles as the occasion arises. Managerial roles can be divided into three basic categories; interpersonal, informational, and decision-making roles.

REVIEW QUESTIONS

1. How would you define the term *management*?
2. Describe management in terms of the functions of managers. Describe management in terms of what managers do.
3. How does the concept of ethics relate to the study of managerial roles?
4. What are the levels of management discussed in this chapter?
5. How would you distinguish between efficient management and effective management?
6. According to Robert L. Katz, what three basic skills do managers need? Discuss each of these skills in terms of management levels.
7. According to Mintzberg, what are the three different roles that a manager may assume in an organization? Briefly discuss each.

CASE STUDY

The Vice-President, the Product Manager, and the Misunderstanding

Tom Brewster, one of the field sales managers of Major Tool Works, Inc., had been promoted to his first headquarters assignment as an assistant product manager for a group of products with which he was relatively unfamiliar. Shortly after he undertook this new assignment, one of the company's vice-presidents, Nick Smith, called a meeting of product managers and other staff to plan marketing strategies. Brewster's immediate superior, the product manager, was unable to attend, so the director of marketing, Jeff Reynolds, invited Brewster to the meeting to help orient him to his new job.

Because of the large number of people attending, Reynolds was rather brief in introducing Brewster to Smith, who, as vice-president, was presiding over the meeting. After the meeting began, Smith—a crusty veteran with a reputation for bluntness—began asking a series of probing questions that most of the product managers were able to answer in detail. Suddenly, he turned to Brewster and began to question him quite closely about his group of products. Somewhat confused, Brewster confessed that he really did not know the answers.

It was immediately apparent to Reynolds that Smith had forgotten or had failed to understand that Brewster was new to his job and was attending the meeting more for his own orientation than to contribute to it. He was about to offer a discreet explanation when Smith, visibly annoyed with what he took to be Brewster's lack of preparation announced, "Gentlemen, you have just seen an example of sloppy staff work, and there is no excuse for it!"

Reynolds had to make a quick decision. He could interrupt Smith and point out that he had judged Brewster unfairly; but that course of action might embarrass both his superior and his subordinate. Alternatively, he could wait until after the meeting and offer an explanation in private. Inasmuch as Smith quickly became engrossed in another conversation, Reynolds followed the second approach. Glancing at Brewster, Reynolds noted that his expression was one of mixed anger and dismay. After catching Brewster's eye, Reynolds winked at him as a discreet reassurance that he understood and that the damage could be repaired.

After an hour, Smith, evidently dissatisfied with what he termed the "inadequate planning" of the marketing department in general, abruptly declared the meeting over. As he did so, he turned to Reynolds and asked him to remain behind for a moment. To Reynold's surprise, Smith himself immediately raised the question of Brewster. In fact, it turned out to have been his main reason for asking Reynolds to remain behind. "Look," he said, "I want you to tell me frankly, do you think I was too rough with that kid?" Relieved, Reynolds said, "Yes, you were. I was going to speak to you about it."

Smith explained that the fact that Brewster was new to his job had not registered adequately when they had been introduced and that it was only some time after his own outburst that the nagging thought began to occur to him that what he had done was inappropriate and unfair. "How well do you know him?" he asked. "Do you think I hurt him?"

For a moment, Reynolds took the measure of his superior. Then he replied evenly, "I don't know him very well yet. But, yes, I think you hurt him."

"Damn, that's unforgivable," said Smith. He then telephoned his secretary to call Brewster and ask him to report to his office immediately. A few moments later, Brewster returned, looking perplexed and uneasy. As he entered, Smith came out from behind his desk and met him in the middle of the office. Standing face to face with Brewster, who was 20 years and four organization levels his junior, he said,

"Look, I've done something stupid and I want to apologize. I had no right to treat you like that. I should have remembered that you were new to your job, but I didn't. I'm sorry."

Brewster was somewhat flustered but muttered his thanks for the apology.

"As long as you are here, young man," Smith continued, "I want to make a few things clear to you in the presence of your boss's boss. Your job is to make sure that people like myself don't make stupid decisions. Obviously we think you are qualified for your job or we would not have brought you in here. But it takes time to learn any job. Three months from now I will expect you to know the answers to any questions about your products. Until then," he said, thrusting out his hand for the younger man to shake, "you have my complete confidence. And thank you for letting me correct a really dumb mistake."

Source: From *Cases and Problems for Decisions in Management,* by Saul Gellerman. Copyright © 1984 by Random House, Inc. Reprinted by permission of the publisher.

Case Questions

1. What do you think was the effect on Brewster and the other managers of Smith's outburst at the meeting?
2. Was Smith right to apologize to Brewster, or should he have left well enough alone?
3. What do you think the apology meant to Brewster?
4. What would it be like to have Nick Smith as a superior? As a subordinate?
5. How does Smith define Brewster's responsibilities as an assistant product manager? How does he define his own role as a top manager?
6. What is the most important aspect of the relations between management levels in this company? ■

Paul Klee (1879–1940), *Monuments by G.* Gypsum and watercolor on canvas. H.69 cm. W.50 cm. The Metropolitan Museum of Art, The Berggruen Klee Collection, 1984. The pyramids were built by at least a hundred thousand people over a 20-year period. Although it's only within the last 100 years that Management has become a discipline, the pyramids are evidence that people have practiced managerial concepts of planning, organizing, leading, and controlling for thousands of years.

2

THE EVOLUTION OF MANAGEMENT THEORY

Upon completing this chapter you should be able to:

1. Describe the three major schools of management thought and how they evolved.
2. Discuss how each of these schools can contribute to a balanced understanding of and approach to your job as a manager.
3. Identify the models of human behavior that underlie each of these schools.
4. Discuss the contributions and limitations of each school.
5. Describe two recently developed approaches to management that attempt to integrate the various schools.

Chapter Outline

Introduction
The Classical Management Theorists
The Behavioral School: The Organization Is People
The Quantitative School: Operations Research and Management Science
The Evolution of Management Theory

ILLUSTRATIVE CASE STUDY
Introduction

The Apostle of Mass Production

Henry Ford and the Model T have long been symbols of the modern industrial age. Even the subsequent growth and success of Ford's rival, General Motors, was due in large part to GM's need to find an innovative response to the Model T. In large measure, the managerial approach of Henry Ford, as well as his preferences in managerial theory, is a paradigm of much that was constructive—and much that was imperfect—in early approaches to management.

The son of a poor Irish immigrant, Henry Ford, born in 1863, grew up on a farm in rural Michigan. He was fascinated by machinery and was quite skilled in repairing and improving almost any machine. In 1903, he started the Ford Motor Company, and by 1908 the first Model T was built.

In the early part of the century when automobiles were first introduced, they were a symbol of status and wealth, almost the exclusive province of the rich. More than anything, Ford wanted to change that: The Model T was to be a car for the masses—one that virtually anyone could afford. He also understood that the only way to make such a car was to produce it at a high enough volume and low enough cost. In short, he had to invent the assembly line. Ford focused his factory efforts on efficiency, mechanizing wherever possible and breaking down tasks into their smallest components. One worker would perform the same task over until he had produced not a finished part, but one of the operations necessary for the production of the whole; the incomplete part would then be passed on to another worker, who would contribute a successive operation. Ford was able to achieve remarkable efficiencies: Although the first Model T took over 12 ½ hours to produce, by 1920, only 12 years later, Ford was producing one Model T every minute. By 1925, at the peak of their popularity, Model T's rolled off Ford's assembly lines once every 5 seconds.

However, the increasing mechanization of the plant had other effects. The faster Ford pushed his workers, the more disgruntled they became. In 1913, turnover was 380 percent, and Ford had to hire 10 times more workers than he needed just to keep the line moving. In an action that, at the time was unprecedented, Ford simply decided to double wages in order to get the best people and motivate them to work even harder. In the days following the announcement of doubling the wage, thousands and thousands of men came to the Ford plant in search of work. Police had to be called in to control the crowds.

Ford's management style was perhaps the darker side of this innovative personality, and it led to chaos in the management ranks. Ford did not take criticism well, especially of the Model T. Changes suggested by his top engineers were ignored, and some were fired as a result of suggesting that the Model T needed change. As a result, competitors like Chevrolet were able to make a great deal of headway in the automobile market. Additionally, Ford liked to play his subordinates against each other, to the point of assigning two of them the same title and seeing which one (the weaker one, according to Ford) would back down first. Competent managers abandoned the firm, which remained overly dependent on the irrascible Ford himself.

When he died in 1945, Ford was worth over $600 million. He left an indelible mark on both American industry and society. His name is synonymous with mass production, and the development of modern management theory has its roots in Ford Motor Company.

Source: Adaptation compiled from *The Reckoning* by David Halberstam. Copyright © 1986 by David Halberstam. By permission of William Morrow and Company, Inc.

Henry Ford made cars by managing a factory that manufactured them efficiently, and his place in the history of American business and culture is secured as much by his concern for efficient, calculated management as it is by the famous image of the Model T. Henry Ford, as the head of an organization who worked to develop the *ideas* according to which that organizaton developed and functioned, was a management *theorist;* moreover, despite a highly paternalistic attitude toward his own hierarchy of managers, Ford was not reluctant to call upon the advice of other theorists—especially those with whom he was theoretically compatible. For example, Frederick Winslow Taylor began much of his work on scientific industrial management at Ford's Model T plant. What is the story of the development of management theory? How did managers like Henry Ford and the theorists to whom he so often turned conceive the ideas that are so commonplace in the management practice of today's organizations? How did those ideas *evolve*? The purpose of this chapter is to examine questions such as these.

TEACHING TIP

Stress the importance of looking at history: to see how management thought has evolved, to see the mistakes and the achievements, and to contribute to your ultimate understanding of the field of management.

Beyond the fact that many theorists are practicing researchers whose work frequently produces practical results, just what does *theory* contribute to the *practice* of management? The theory of relativity, for example, helps physicists control the atom; through the laws of aerodynamics, engineers can predict the effects of a proposed change in airplane design. Similarly, the theories and principles of management make it easier for us to understand underlying processes and, on that basis, decide what we must do to function most effectively as managers. Without theories, all we have are intuition, hunches, and hope—all of which are of limited use in today's increasingly complex organizations.

theory Principle or set of principles designed to explain the relationship between two or more observable facts.

Our approach in this text will include the contributions of all schools and approaches—all *theories*. First, however, we should explain the concept of theory as it applies to the purpose of this text. In essence, a **theory** is a principle or set of principles that explains or accounts for the relationship between two or more observable facts or events. Let's use a simple example involving some observable facts about a current problem that has concerned a number of researchers in the fields of psychology and sociology. Observable fact one: the incidence of the eating disorder known as anorexia nervosa has increased dramatically in this country over the past several years. Observable fact two: about 90 percent of all anorexics are upper-middle- and upper-class young women. What accounts for this correspondence? Some research points to cultural factors—the media tend to promote the relationship between attractiveness and a pencil-thin physique. Other research points to such psychological factors as adolescent emotional disturbances resulting from the onset of sexual maturity. Yet other students of the problem focus on basically sociological factors, pointing out that the socioeconomic group at high risk is highly represented in certain environments—say, the socially and academically competitive environment of a college campus.

Obviously, there is a certain amount of validity in each of these explanations. Moreover, each of these explanations has research-supported ramifications far more complex that our quick survey of them imples. As our example suggests, then, a theory is much more than a ''rule of thumb'' that provides a hard-and-fast explanation for the relationship between facts as they are observed or events as they occur. Ideally, a theory should be testable, and its validity and durabiltiy should rest on research-based findings.

In addition, it should be clear that a number of theoretical approaches can be applied to any given issue. Many of us find ourselves naturally inclined to be more comfortable with one general theory than another, and we tend to resort to that theory when confronted by new facts or events. It is important to remember, however, that, in the study of management as in most social sciences, no general theory has emerged to unify or dominate the field. At present, the eclectic approach—the practice of borrowing principles from different theories as they best suit one's needs—appears to be the state of the art in management theory and practice. The future promises new perspectives that will not only help us to do our jobs better, but will also help us to re-evaluate ideas from the past.[1]

As managers, we will have at our disposal many ways of looking at organizations and at the activities, performance, and satisfaction of people in organizations. Each of these ways may be more useful in dealing with some problems than with others. For example, a management theory that emphasizes the importance of a good work environment may be more helpful in dealing with a high employee turnover rate than with production delays. Because there is no single, universally accepted management theory, we must be familiar with each of the major theories that currently coexist.

In this chapter we will focus on three well-established schools of management thought:[2] the *classical school* (which has two branches—*scientific management* and *classical organization theory*), the *behavioral school,* and the *management science school*. Although these schools developed in historical sequence, later ideas have not *replaced* earlier ones. Instead, each new school has tended to complement or coexist with the previous ones. At the same time, each has continued to develop. Some merging has also occurred, as later theorists have attempted to integrate accumulated knowledge.[3] Thus, we will also discuss two recent approaches to management that attempt to integrate the various theories—the *systems approach* and the *contingency approach*.

THE CLASSICAL MANAGEMENT THEORISTS

FOR DISCUSSION

Has there always been a need for managers? Explain. How do managers of today differ from those of years ago? How can an understanding of the history of management help the practice of management today?

People have been managed in groups and organizations since prehistoric times. Even the simplest of hunting and gathering bands generally recognized and obeyed a leader or a group of decision makers responsible for the welfare of the band. As societies grew larger and more complex, the need for organizations and managers became increasingly apparent. A town government could not, for example, be run by a few individuals. Administrators and bureaucrats were needed to manage the operations of a state or nation.

Attempts to develop *theories* and *principles* of management, however, are relatively recent. In particular, the industrial revolution of the 18th and 19th centuries gave rise to the need for a systematic approach to management. The development of new technologies concentrated great quantities of raw materials and large numbers of workers in factories; goods were produced in quantity and had to be distributed widely. That all these elements had to be coordinated called attention to the problems of management.

---

[1] For an excellent treatment of the process of change in theories, see Thomas S. Kuhn, *The Structure of Scientific Revolutions,* 2nd ed., enlarged (Chicago: University of Chicago Press, 1970). See also Richard G. Brandenberg, "The Usefulness of Management Thought for Management," in Joseph W. McGuire, ed., *Contemporary Management: Issues and Viewpoints* (Englewood Cliffs, N.J.: Prentice Hall, 1974), pp. 99–112.

[2] Much of the discussion in this chapter on the evolution of management theory is based on Claude S. George, Jr., *The History of Management Thought,* 2nd ed. (Englewood Cliffs, N.J.: Prentice Hall, 1972), and Daniel A. Wren, *The Evolution of Management Thought,* 2nd ed. (New York: Wiley, 1979).

[3] An excellent discussion of this evolutionary process appears in Harold J. Leavitt, "Structure, People, and Information Technology: Some Key Ideas and Where They Come From," *Managerial Psychology,* 4th ed. (Chicago: University of Chicago Press, 1978).

Forerunners of Scientific Management Theory

Imagine that you live in an English town in the early 1800s. The new factory system has been spreading, and a local entrepreneur has put you in charge of a new plant. What do you think would be foremost in your mind—profits, efficiency, craft? The forerunners of scientific management confronted questions very much like this one and had no previous experience to guide them. Robert Owen was a manager of several cotton mills at New Lanark, Scotland, during the early 1800s. At that time, working and living conditions for employees were very poor, and Owen conceived of the manager's role as one of *reform*. He built better housing for his workers and operated a company store where goods could be purchased cheaply. He reduced the standard working day to 10½ hours and refused to hire children under the age of 10.

Owen argued that improving the condition of employees would inevitably lead to increased production and profits. Where other managers concentrated their investments in technical improvements, Owen stressed the fact that a manager's best investment was in the workers, or "vital machines," as he called them.

Aside from making general improvements in working conditions at his mills, Owen openly rated an employee's work on a daily basis. Owen believed that these open ratings not only let the manager know what the problem areas were but also instilled pride and spurred competition. In our organizations today, the practice of posting and publicizing sales and production figures is based on the same psychological principle of *feedback*—of letting workers know how they are performing.

At about the same time, a British professor of mathematics, Charles Babbage became convinced that the application of scientific principles to work processes would both increase productivity and lower expenses.

Babbage was an early advocate of division of labor, believing that each factory operation should be analyzed so that the various skills involved in the operation could be isolated. Expensive training time could be reduced, and the constant repetition of each operation would improve the skills and efficiency of workers. Our modern assembly line, in which each worker is responsible for a different repetitive task, is based on many of Babbage's ideas.

Scientific Management: Frederick W. Taylor

scientific management A management approach, formulated by Frederick W. Taylor and others between 1890 and 1930, that sought to determine scientifically the best methods for performing any task, and for selecting, training, and motivating workers.

Scientific management arose in part from the need to increase productivity. In the United States especially, skilled labor was in short supply at the beginning of the 20th century, and to expand productivity, ways had to be found to increase the efficiency of workers. In an effort to address these problems, Frederick W. Taylor (1856–1915) built the body of principles that now constitute the essence of *scientific management*.

Taylor based his managerial system on production-line time studies. Instead of relying on traditional work methods, Taylor analyzed and timed steel workers' movements on a series of jobs. With time study as his base, Taylor broke each job down into its components and designed the quickest and best methods of operation for each part of the job. He thereby established how much workers should be able to do with the equipment and materials at hand. Taylor also encouraged employers to pay more productive workers at a higher rate than others. The increased rate was carefully calculated and based on the greater profit that would result from increased production. Thus, workers were encouraged to surpass their previous performance standards and earn more pay. Taylor called his plan the **differential rate system.** He believed that workers who met the higher standards need not fear layoffs because their companies benefited from the increase in productivity. The higher payments would continue because they were "scientifically correct" rates set at a level that was best for the company and

differential rate system Frederick W. Taylor's compensation system involving the payment of higher wages to more efficient workers.

for the worker. At the same time, no one would be hurt by the differential system. Workers who fell below the standard in productivity would find other work "in a day or two," as he put it, because of the existing labor shortage.

THOUGHT-PROVOKER

What were the economic, cultural, and political forces like at this time? How would these have contributed to the development of this scientific management approach?

By 1893, Taylor decided he could best put his ideas into effect as a private consulting management engineer. He was soon able to report impressive improvements in productivity, quality, worker morale, and wages while working with one client, Simonds Rolling Machine Company. In one operation, Simonds employed 120 women to inspect bicycle ball bearings. The work was tedious, the hours were long, and there seemed little reason to believe improvements could be made. Taylor proved otherwise. First, he studied and timed the movements of the best workers. Then he trained the rest in the methods of their more effective co-workers and transferred or laid off the poorest performers. He also introduced rest periods during the workday, along with his differential pay rate system and other improvements. The results were impressive: Expenses went down while productivity, quality, earnings, and worker morale went up. (See Exhibit 2-1.)

EXHIBIT 2-1 IMPROVEMENTS IN PRODUCTIVITY AT THE SIMONDS ROLLING MACHINE COMPANY.

Task:	Inspection of the balls used in bicycle ball bearings. An established operation employing 120 workers who were "old hands" and skilled at their jobs.
Major Changes Made:	Additional training based on study of higher-performing workers. Selection on the basis of appropriate skills, laying off or transferring lower performers. Workday shortened from 10½ to 8½ hours. Rest periods introduced. Efficiency of control system increased (but with no change in inspection standards).
Results Reported:	Thirty-five inspectors did work formerly done by 120. Accuracy improved by two-thirds. Wages received rose by 80 to 100 percent. Apparent improvements in worker morale.

CLASS COMMENT

Taylor, in his early years, carefully analyzed the game of croquet, the best method with the least fatigue of taking a cross-country walk, and developed other ingenious devices to help find the "one best way." (Daniel A. Wren, *The Evolution of Management Thought,* Ronald Press)

Although a number of researchers are skeptical about its faithfulness to the facts, a popular story has long been circulated about Taylor and Bethlehem Steel. In 1898 (or so the story goes), Bethlehem Steel Company engaged Taylor as a consultant. Taylor set out to make the work of the company yard gang more efficient. The members of the yard gang unloaded raw materials from incoming railcars and loaded the finished product on outgoing cars. Each worker earned $1.15 a day for loading an average of 12½ tons. Taylor was told that the workers were habitually slow and unwilling to work faster.

After he and a co-worker studied and timed the operations involved in unloading and loading the cars, Taylor concluded that with frequent rest periods, each man could handle about 48 tons a day. Setting 47½ tons as the standard, Taylor worked out a piece rate that would net $1.85 a day to those who met that standard. Thus, the workers were encouraged to adopt Taylor's work methods. Even though this story may well be false, it illustrates the high expectations that were set for scientific management and set the stage for subsequent theoretical conflict.

Although Taylor's methods led to dramatic increases in productivity and to higher pay in a number of instances, workers and unions began to oppose his approach. Like the workers at Midvale, they feared that working harder or faster would exhaust whatever work was available and bring about layoffs. The fact that workers had been laid off at Simonds and in other organizations using Taylor's methods encouraged this fear. As Taylor's ideas spread, opposition to them continued to grow. Increasing numbers of workers became convinced that they would lose their jobs if Taylor's methods were adopted.

By 1912, resistance to Taylorism had caused a strike at the Watertown Arsenal in Massachusetts, and hostile members of Congress called on Taylor to explain his ideas and techniques. Both in his testimony and in his two books, *Shop Management* and *The Principles of Scientific Management,* Taylor outlined his philosophy.[4] It rested, he said, on four basic principles:

QUOTATION FROM MANAGEMENT THEORIST

"And I want to make it perfectly clear, because I do not think it is clear, that my interest, and I think the interest of any man who is in any way engaged in scientific management, in the introduction of the principles of scientific management must be first the welfare of the working man."—Frederick W. Taylor, testimony before Industrial Relations Commission, 1914

1. *The development of a true science of management,* so that the best method for performing each task could be determined.
2. *The scientific selection of the workers,* so that each worker would be given responsibility for the task for which he or she was best suited.
3. *The scientific education and development of the worker.*
4. *Intimate, friendly cooperation between management and labor.*

Taylor also contended that in order for these principles to succeed, "a complete mental revolution" on the part of management and labor was required. Rather than quarrel over whatever profits there were, they should both try to increase production; by so doing, profits would be increased to such an extent that labor and management would no longer have to compete for them. In short, Taylor believed that management and labor had a common interest in increasing productivity.

Other Contributors to Scientific Management Theory

Henry L. Gantt. Henry L. Gantt (1861–1919) had worked with Taylor on several projects, including Simonds and Bethlehem Steel. But after he began to work on his own as a consulting industrial engineer, Gantt reconsidered Taylor's incentive system.

Abandoning the differential rate system as having too little motivational impact, Gantt came up with a new idea. Every worker who finished a day's assigned work load would win a 50¢ bonus for that day. Then he added a second motivation. The *supervisor* would earn a bonus for each worker who reached the daily standard, plus an extra bonus if all the workers reached it. This, Gantt reasoned, would spur a supervisor to train workers to do a better job.

Gantt also built upon Owen's idea of rating an employee's work publicly. Every worker's progress was recorded on individual bar charts—in black on days he or she made the standard, in red when he or she fell below. Going beyond this, Gantt originated a charting system for production scheduling; the "Gantt chart," is still in use today. In Chapter 5, an illustration of a Gantt chart is presented to show how its principles can be adapted to the process of formally reviewing costs, progress, and the need for replanning or rescheduling.

The Gilbreths. Frank B. and Lillian M. Gilbreth (1868–1924 and 1878–1972) made their contribution to the scientific management movement as a husband and wife team.

[4]Both books, in addition to Taylor's testimony before the Special House Committee, appear in Frederick W. Taylor, *Scientific Management* (New York: Harper & Brothers, 1947). For an assessment of Taylor's impact on contemporary management, see Edwin A. Locke, "The Ideas of Frederick W. Taylor: An Evaluation," *Academy of Management Review* 7, no. 11 (January 1982):14–24. See also Allen C. Bluedorn, Thomas L. Keon, and Nancy M. Carter, "Management History Research: Is Anyone Out There Listening?" in Richard B. Robinson and John A. Pearch, II, eds., *Proceedings of the Academy of Management* (Boston, 1985), pp. 130–133.

Lillian's doctoral thesis, which later appeared in book form as *The Psychology of Management,* was first published in the magazine *Industrial Engineering* in 1912.[5] Although she and Frank collaborated on fatigue and motion studies, Lillian also focused her attention on ways of promoting the welfare of the individual worker. To her, scientific management had one ultimate aim: to help workers reach their full potential as human beings.

CLASS COMMENT

Through Frank Gilbreth's study of a brick layer's motions, he was able to reduce the number of motions necessary to lay the brick from 18 to 4½ on exterior bricks and from 18 to 2 on interior bricks.

Frank Gilbreth began work as an apprentice bricklayer and worked his way up the managerial ladder. Bricklayers, he noticed, used three different sets of motions: one for teaching apprentices, another for working fast, and a third for deliberately holding down the pace of their work. After careful study of the different motions involved, Frank was able to develop a technique that tripled the amount of work a bricklayer could do in a day. His success led him to make motion and fatigue study his lifework.

BACKGROUND ON GILBRETHS

The Gilbreths refined hand motions into 17 basic or fundamental motions that they termed *therbligs* (Gilbreth spelled backwards with the *th* transposed).

In Frank Gilbreth's conception, motion and fatigue were intertwined—every motion that was eliminated also reduced fatigue. Using motion picture cameras, he tried to find the most economical motions for each task, thus upgrading performance and reducing fatigue. Both Gilbreths argued that motion study would raise worker morale because of its obvious physical benefits and because it demonstrated management's concern for the worker.

The Gilbreths developed a *three-position plan* of promotion that was intended to serve as an employee-development program as well as a morale booster. (See Fig. 2-1.) According to this plan, a worker would do his or her present job, prepare for the next highest one, and train his or her successor, all at the same time. Thus, every worker would always be a doer, a learner, and a teacher and would continually look forward to new opportunities.

Contributions and Limitations of Scientific Management Theory

TEACHING TIP

A good way to compare and contrast the various perspectives is to list on the board or prepared transparency the relative merits of each of the approaches to management. Emphasize to students that each approach contributes something of value to our knowledge of management.

Contributions. A team of people working together, each tending expertly to one or a few tasks, can outproduce the same number of people each performing all of the tasks. The prime example of this fact is the vastly increased productivity of the modern assembly line, in which conveyor belts bring to each employee the parts needed to do one specific job and then carry the completed work to the next employee on the line. Today's assembly lines pour out their finished products faster than Taylor could ever have imagined. This American production ''miracle'' is the legacy of scientific management.

The methods of scientific management can be applied to a variety of organizational activities, besides those of industrial organizations. The *efficiency techniques* of scientific management, such as time and motion studies, have made us aware that the

[5] Lillian M. Gilbreth, *The Psychology of Management* (New York: Sturgis and Walton, 1914).

FIGURE 2-1 THE GILBRETHS' THREE-POSITION PLAN

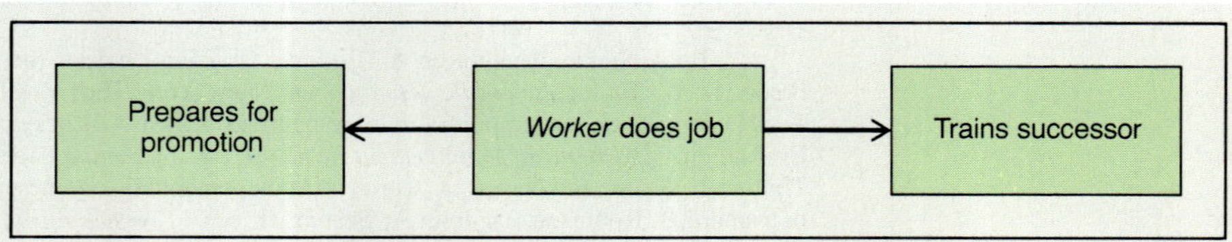

tools and physical movements involved in a task can be made more efficient and rational. The stress it placed on *scientific selection and development* of workers has made us recognize the importance of both ability and training in increasing worker effectiveness. The importance that scientific management gave to *work design* also encouraged managers to seek the "one best way" of getting a job done. Thus, scientific management not only developed a rational approach to solving organizational problems but also pointed the way to the professionalization of management.[6]

Finally, one of the most recent contributions of scientific managment theory and its emphasis on efficiency techniques has been the advent of automation and the use of robots to do a variety of jobs ranging from welding machine pistons to dusting crops.[7] (The effects and applications of automation and technology are discussed at length in Chapter 20.)

Limitations. Unfortunately, little if any of the "mental revolution" called for by Taylor came about in practice. While the new *technology* was readily adopted by management, the *philosophy* that Taylor espoused was not. Too often, increases in productivity led to layoffs or changes in piece rates that left workers producing more output for the same income. The higher wages and better working conditions enjoyed by today's workers did not result from the voluntary redistribution of increased profits by management; instead, the tremendous growth of unionism after the depression and the labor shortage in the years following World War II produced many of labor's gains. Today, labor and management frequently are at odds.

Proponents of scientific management were hampered by the notions of human behavior prevalent in Taylor's time. The then-popular economic model of human behavior was that people were "rational" and thus motivated primarily by a desire for material gain; it was assumed that they would therefore act in a manner best suited to satisfy their *economic* and *physical* needs. Thus, Taylor and his followers overlooked the *social* needs of workers as members of a group and never considered the tensions created when these needs were frustrated. They assumed that if one simply told people exactly what to do to increase their earnings, they would go right ahead and do it, as rational people should.[8] But, as many managers have since discovered, people need to feel important and want a say in the things that matter to them. Financial gain, while significant, is not the only thing that matters to workers.[9]

The proponents of scientific management also overlooked the human desire for job satisfaction. Paradoxically, as the principles of scientific management were successfully applied and affluence spread, there was a growing tendency on the part of workers to question traditional management practices. Thus, workers became more willing to go out on strike over job conditions rather than salary demands and to leave a job if they were unhappy in it. The result was that the scientific management model of a purely rational worker, interested *only* in higher wages, became increasingly inappropriate.

---

[6]Another important contributor to scientific management was Harrington Emerson. See his book *The Twelve Principles of Efficiency,* published in 1913.

[7]See *The Annals of the American Academy of Political and Social Science,* November 1983, the whole of which is devoted to the subject of robots and work.

[8]For a rich discussion of "rational, economic, social, self-actualizing, and complex man," see Edgar H. Schein, *Organizational Psychology,* 3rd ed. (Englewood Cliffs, N.J.: Prentice Hall, 1980), pp. 52–72 and 93–101.

[9]One observer, reporting on an automobile plant, wrote: "Some assembly-line workers are so turned off, managers report in astonishment, that they just walk away in midshift and don't even come back to get their pay for the time they have worked." See Judson Gooding, "Blue Collar Blues on the Assembly Line," *Fortune,* July 1970, pp. 69–70.

ILLUSTRATIVE CASE STUDY Continued

The Apostle of Mass Production

According to contemporary writers of a politically "liberal" point of view, Henry Ford's managerial practices and cultural attitudes entitled him to the epithet "robber baron," a status enjoyed by such other business luminaries as John D. Rockefeller, Andrew Carnegie, and Andrew Mellon. Roughly during the era (1902–1912) dominated by Theodore Roosevelt and the so-called "Progressive Republicans," many journalists began analyzing and assaulting the nature of American industrial practices and, as we have seen, soon earned the label "muckrakers"—exposers of political and commercial corruption among people and corporations who were threatening to perfect industrial managerial theory to an extent that these writers considered dangerous. Why was Henry Ford included on the muckrakers' list?

[Taking the advice of efficiency expert Walter Flanders in 1908,] Ford bought grounds in Highland Park, where he intended to employ the most modern ideas about production, particularly those of Frederick Winslow Taylor. These would bring, as Taylor had prophesied, an absolute rationality to the industrial process. The idea was to break each function down into much smaller units so that each could be mechanized and speeded up and eventually flow into a straight-line production of little pieces becoming steadily larger—continuity above all. What he wanted, and what he soon got, in the words of Keith Sward, was a mechanized process that was "like a river and its tributaries," with the subassembly tributaries merging to produce an ever more assembled car. The process began to change in the spring of 1913. The first piece on the modern assembly line was the magneto coil assembly. In the past, a worker—and he had to be a skilled worker—had made a flywheel magneto from start to finish. A good employee could make 35 or 40 a day. Now, however, there was an assembly line for magnetos, divided into 29 different operations performed by 29 different men. In the old system it took 20 minutes to make a magneto; now it took 13.

Ford and his men soon moved to bring the same rationality to the rest of the factory. Quickly, they imposed a comparable system for the assembly of motors and transmissions. Then, in the summer of 1913, they took on the final assembly, which, as the rest of the process had speeded up, had become the great bottleneck. The workers [were now maneuvered] as quickly as they could around a stationary metal object, the car they were putting together. If the men could remain stationary as the semifinished car moved up the line through them, less of the workers' time—Ford's time—would be wasted.

Charles Sorensen, who had become one of Ford's top production people, [initiated the assembly line by pulling] a Model T chassis slowly by a windlass across 250 feet of factory floor, timing the process all the while. Behind him walked six workers, picking up parts from carefully spaced piles on the floor and fitting them to the chassis. . . . [Soon,] the breakthroughs came even more rapidly. . . . [By installing an automatic conveyor belt,] Ford could eventually assemble a car in an hour and a half. . . . Just a few years before, in the days of stationary chassis assembly, the best record for putting a car together had been 728 hours of one man's work; with the new moving line it required only 93 minutes. Ford's top executives celebrated their victory with a dinner at Detroit's Pontchartrain Hotel. Fittingly, they rigged a simple conveyor belt to a five-horsepower engine with a bicycle chain and used the conveyor to serve the food around the table. It typified the spirit, camaraderie, and confidence of the early days.

Nineteen years and more than fifteen million cars later, when Ford reluctantly came to the conclusion that he had to stop making the T, the company balance was $673 million. And this was not merely a company's success; it was the beginning of a social revolution. Ford himself [believed] he had achieved a breakthrough for the common man [—at least a breakthrough for the common man as consumer.] "Mass production," he wrote later, "precedes mass consumption, and makes it possible by reducing costs and thus permitting both greater use-convenience and price-convenience."

[Not surprisingly,] price of the Model T continued to come down, from $780 in the fiscal year 1910–11 to $690 the following year, then to $600, to $550, and, on the eve of World War I, to $360. At that price, Ford sold 730,041 cars, outproducing everyone in the world. In 1914, the Ford Motor Company, with 13,000 employees, produced 267,720 cars; the other 299 American auto companies, with a total of 66,350 employees, produced only 286,770. Cutting his price as his production soared, Ford saw his share of the market surge—9.4 percent in 1908, 20.3 in 1911, 39.6 in 1913, and with the full benefits of his mechanization, 48 percent in 1914. By 1915, the company was making $100 million in annual sales; by 1920 the average monthly earning after taxes was $6 million. . . .

Henry Ford, immigrant's son and one-time machinist's apprentice, had indeed become a very rich man. Obviously, he had become so by being a venturesome and successful theorist of industrial management. But both his practices and his personality drew fire from those who were critical of his implicit attitude toward those "masses" for whom he had originally perfected and priced the Model T. For example, his widely publicized doubling of wages for employees in 1914 was seen by some as a trailblazing maneuver in management-labor relations, by others as a scheme to solidify Ford's paternalistic power over those who depended upon him for a living. In addition, Ford stubbornly resisted the unionization of his employees long after his major competitors had made agreements with union organizations. Repression on the part of company police against union "agitators" was common on the company's grounds until, finally, having lost an election conducted by the National Labor Relations Board, [a government agency established in 1935 to affirm labor's right to bargain collectively] Ford contracted with the United Auto Workers in 1941.

Classical Organization Theory

classical organization theory An early attempt, pioneered by Henri Fayol, to identify principles and skills that underlie effective management.

CLASS COMMENT

Management theory and research originated in the lower operative levels of the organization and subsequently were applied to the upper administrative levels.

Scientific management was concerned with increasing the productivity of the shop and the individual worker. The other branch of classical management—**classical organization theory**—grew out of the need to find guidelines for managing such complex organizations as factories.

Henri Fayol. Students of management theory generally acknowledge Henri Fayol (1841–1925) as the founder of the classical management school—not because he was the first to investigate managerial behavior but because he was the first to systematize it. Fayol believed that sound managerial practice falls into certain patterns that can be identified and analyzed. From this basic insight, he drew up the blueprint for a cohesive doctrine of management—one that retains much of its force to this day. Fayol was a contemporary of Taylor, and it is important to note that, while Taylor was basically concerned with organizational *functions,* Fayol was interested in the *total* organization.

Fayol believed that "with scientific forecasting and proper methods of management, satisfactory results were inevitable." His insistence that management was not a personal talent but a skill like any other was a major contribution to management thought. It had generally been believed that "managers were born, not made"—that practice and experience would be helpful only to those who already had the innate qualities of a manager. Fayol, however, believed that management could be taught—once its underlying principles were understood and a general theory of management was formulated. To this day, many of the managerial concepts we take for granted today were first articulated by Fayol.

In setting out to develop a science of management, Fayol began by dividing business operations into six activities, all of which were closely dependent on one another. These activities were (1) technical—producing and manufacturing products; (2) commercial—buying raw materials and selling products; (3) financial—acquiring and using capital; (4) security—protecting employees and property; (5) accounting—recording and taking stock of costs, profits, and liabilities, keeping balance sheets, and compiling statistics; and (6) managerial.

Fayol's primary focus, of course, was on this last activity, because he felt managerial skills had been the most neglected aspect of business operations. He defined managing in terms of five functions: planning, organizing, commanding, coordinating, and controlling. In this definition, *planning* means devising a course of action that will enable the organization to meet its goals; *organizing* means mobilizing the material and human resources of the organization to put the plans into effect; *commanding* means providing direction for employees and getting them to do their work; *coordinating* means making sure that the resources and activities of the organization are working harmoniously to achieve the desired goals; *controlling* means monitoring the plans to ensure that they are being carried out properly. (See Fig. 2-2.)

Finally, note that Fayol carefully chose the term *principles* of management rather than *rules* or *laws* (see Exhibit 2-2):

> I prefer the word principles in order to avoid any idea of rigidity, as there is nothing rigid or absolute in administrative matters; everything is a question of degree. The same principle is hardly ever applied twice in exactly the same way, because we have to allow for different and changing circumstances, for human beings who are equally different and changeable, and for many other variable elements. The principles, too, are flexible, and can be adapted to meet every need; it is just a question of knowing how to use them.[10] Fayol listed the 14 principles of management he ''most frequently had to apply.''

Max Weber. Reasoning that any goal-oriented organization consisting of thousands of individuals would require the carefully controlled regulation of its activities, the German sociologist Max Weber (1864–1920) developed a theory of bureaucratic management that stressed the need for a strictly defined hierarchy governed by clearly defined regulations and lines of authority.[11] For Weber, the ideal organization was a *bureaucracy* whose activities and objectives were rationally thought out and its divisions of labor explicitly spelled out. Weber also believed that technical competence should be empahsized and that performance evaluations should be made entirely on the basis of merit.

---

[10]Henri Fayol, *Industrial and General Administration,* trans. J. A. Coubrough (Geneva: International Management Institute, 1930). Fayol used the word *administration* for what we call *management.*

[11]Max Weber, *The Theory of Social and Economic Organizations,* ed. Talcott Parsons, trans. A. M. Henderson and Parsons (New Yc-k: Free Press, 1947).

FIGURE 2-2 FAYOL'S DIVISION OF BUSINESS OPERATIONS AND MANAGERIAL FUNCTIONS

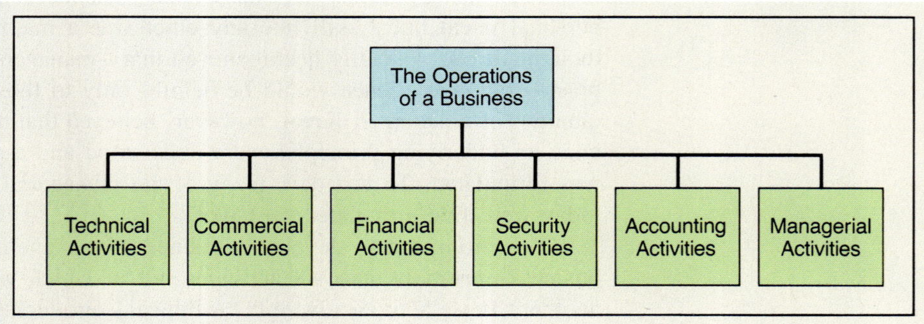

Source: Henri Fayol, *Industrial and General Administration,* J. A. Coubrough, trans. (Geneva: International Management Institute, 1930).

TEACHING TIP

Make a point to go over Fayol's 14 principles and describe them. To keep this from becoming overly boring, engage students in discussion of examples of each of these in student organizations to which they belong.

EXHIBIT 2-2 FAYOL'S 14 PRINCIPLES OF MANAGEMENT

1. *Division of Labor.* The more people specialize, the more efficiently they can perform their work. This principle is epitomized by the modern assembly line.
2. *Authority.* Managers must give orders so that they can get things done. While their *formal* authority gives them the right to command, managers will not always compel obedience unless they have *personal* authority (such as relevant expertise) as well.
3. *Discipline.* Members in an organization need to respect the rules and agreements that govern the organization. To Fayol, discipline will result from good leadership at all levels of the organization, fair agreements (such as provisions for rewarding superior performance), and judiciously enforced penalties for infractions.
4. *Unity of Command.* Each employee must receive instructions about a particular operation from only one person. Fayol believed that when an employee reported to more than one superior, conflicts in instructions and confusion of authority would result.
5. *Unity of Direction.* Those operations within the organization that have the same objective should be directed by only one manager using one plan. For example, the personnel department in a company should not have two directors, each with a different hiring policy.
6. *Subordination of Individual Interest to the Common Good.* In any undertaking, the interests of employees should not take precedence over the interests of the organization as a whole.
7. *Remuneration.* Compensation for work done should be fair to both employees and employers.
8. *Centralization.* Decreasing the role of subordinates in decision making is centralization; increasing their role is decentralization. Fayol believed that managers should retain final responsibility but also need to give their subordinates enough authority to do their jobs properly. The problem is to find the best amount of centralization in each case.
9. *The Hierarchy.* The line of authority in an organization—often represented today by the neat boxes and lines of the organization chart—runs in order of rank from top management to the lowest level of the enterprise.
10. *Order.* Materials and people should be in the right place at the right time. People in particular should be in the jobs or positions most suited for them.
11. *Equity.* Managers should be both friendly and fair to their subordinates.
12. *Stability of Staff.* A high employee turnover rate is not good for the efficient functioning of an organization.
13. *Initiative.* Subordinates should be given the freedom to conceive and carry out their plans, even though some mistakes may result.
14. *Esprit de Corps.* Promoting team spirit will give the organization a sense of unity. To Fayol, even small factors could help to develop this spirit. He suggested, for example, the use of verbal communication instead of formal, written communication whenever possible.

Source: Henri Fayol, *Industrial and General Administration,* J. A. Coubrough, trans. (Geneva: International Management Institute, 1930).

We should be careful, however, not to apply automatically overly negative connotations to the word *bureaucracy* as Weber used it. We often think of "bureaucracies" as vast, inflexible organizations that prefer impersonal efficiency to human values and needs. But much like scientific management theorists, Weber sought basically to improve the performance of socially important organizations by making their operations models of predictable productivity. In addition, although we now tend to value innovation and flexibility as much as efficiency and predictability, it is also clear that Weber's model of bureaucratic management has contributed to the type of organizational thinking that has made possible such large corporate organizations as Coca-Cola, Exxon, and many, many others. (Weber's contributions to the theory of organizational design are discussed further in Chapter 9.)

Contributions and Limitations of Classical Organization Theory

Contributions. Like all theorists, the classical organization theorists were limited by the knowledge that was available to them and the conditions that existed in their time. Nevertheless, much in classical organization theory has endured. For example, the concepts that management skills apply to all types of group activity have, if anything, increased in importance today—in our schools, government, and other organizations.

ETHICS IN MANAGEMENT

MUCKRAKERS, MONOPOLIES, MEAT PACKERS, AND MEDICINES

The press, particularly the journalists who wrote for popular magazines, played an important role in bringing to public consciousness the injustices and tragedies wrought by industrialization and the social changes that accompanied it. . . . A great deal of [so-called "muckraking"] literature detailed the corruption and inequities inherent in big business, trusts and monopolies being the special objects of public wrath, however much [their practices seemingly contributed to the national economic well-being]. Oddly, however, the muckrakers who uncovered frauds and adulterations in the food and drug industries recognized free-market competition—the relative absence of trusts and monopolies—as the prime stimulus to such practices. If an intensely competitive industry produced immoralities of one sort, and if monopolistic enterprise produced other kinds of immoralities, then perhaps the federal government was duty-bound to intervene in the marketplace to protect the voiceless and to ensure that the free market could operate without excess.

Ida Tarbell's classic *History of Standard Oil,* [detailing the monopolistic practices of the rapidly growing conglomerate, was published in 1904. Among other things, Tarbell discovered Standard Oil's purchase of illicit information about competitors and routine practice of receiving rebates and kickbacks from smaller companies dependent upon it. During the course of her four-year investigation, Tarbell uncovered John D. Rockefeller's premeditated subversion of Pennsylvania state banking laws, encountered mysteriously missing archival documents, and was physically threatened.]*

In 1905, an investigation of the New York insurance and gas industries, led by Charles Evans Hughes (a politician, not a journalist) uncovered appalling corporate practices, "among them bribes, payoffs, and large campaign contributions."† David Graham Phillips . . . detailed corruption in Washington in his series "The Treason of the Senate," published serially in *Cosmopolitan* magazine between March and November, 1906, and Upton Sinclair's infamous novel *The Jungle,* [an unsavory exposé of common practices in the meat-packing industry,] also appeared in 1906.

If corporate financial chicanery was seen as so appalling, what could be said of Sinclair's book . . .? Sinclair intended his book to be a powerful plea for socialist revolution; as he himself remarked, the book "aimed for the hearts of the American

*Ida Tarbell, *History of Standard Oil Co.,* 2 vols. (Rpt. Lexington, Mass.: Peter Smith, 1904).

†Lewis J. Gould, *Reform and Regulations: American Politics, 1900–1916* (New York: Wiley, 1978).

The concept that certain identifiable principles underlie effective managerial behavior and that these principles can be taught also continues to be valid. (For one thing, it is the justification for this book.)

Although classical organization theory has been criticized by members of other schools of management thought, its perspectives have for some time been well received by *practicing* managers. This may be because classical organization theory helped to isolate major areas of practical concern to the working manager. More than anything else, then, the classical organization school raised issues that remain important to managers; it has made them aware of basic kinds of problems that they would face in any organization.

Limitations. However, classical organization theory has been criticized on the ground that it was more appropriate for the past than for the present. When organizations were in a relatively stable and predictable environment, the classical principles people and hit them instead in their stomachs." The following passage provides a sample of the language that horrified the American nation and its President:

> There was never the least attention paid to what was cut up for sausage; there would come all the way back from Europe old sausages that had been rejected, and that was mouldy and white—it would be doused with borax and glycerine, and dumped into the hoppers, and made over again for home consumption. There would be meat that had tumbled out on the floor, in the dirt and sawdust, where the workers had tramped and spit uncounted billions of [tuberculosis] germs. There would be meat stored in great piles in rooms: and the water from leaky roofs would drip over it, and thousands of rats would race about on it. It was too dark in these storage places to see well, but a man could run his hand over these piles of meat and sweep off handfuls of the dried dung of rats. These rats were nuisances, and the packers would put poisoned bread out for them: they would die, and then rats, bread, and meat would go into the hoppers together.[‡]

President [Theodore] Roosevelt appointed an investigatory commission to verify Sinclair's tale of filth and fraud in the making of processed meats. Although only a few pages of the book actually relate such practices as the use of tubercular animals . . . to make "canned hams" [and recount such stories as that] of the laborer who slipped . . . to a lower level of the plant and was thereafter shipped out to an unsuspecting public bearing the label "Durham's Pure Beef Lard," the commission indeed reported to the President that Sinclair's story was essentially accurate; the Meat Inspection Act of 1906 was promptly enacted by Congress.

Popular commentary on adulterated and misbranded foods was [furthered more] by state agricultural and food-inspection officials, chemists, members of Congress, and representatives of various groups such as the General Federation of Women's Clubs than by "muckrakers" per se. [In particular, the subject of patent medicines became relatively popular:] There were two series of popular magazine articles decrying the immorality of patent-medicine vendors—one by Samuel Hopkins Adams in *Collier's Weekly,* the other by Edward Bok and Mark Sullivan in *The Ladies Home Journal.* These series seem to have been quite influential in spurring the passage of the 1906 Pure Food Act and in ensuring that the act contained provisions to regulate the content and labeling of medicines.

[‡]Upton Sinclair, *The Jungle* (1906; rpt. Cambridge, Mass.: Bentley, 1971).

Source: Adapted from Donna J. Wood, *Strategic Uses of Public Policy: Business and Government in the Progressive Era.* Copyright © 1986 by Donna J. Wood. Reprinted by permission of Ballinger Publishing Company.

seemed valid. Today, with organizational environments becoming more turbulent, the classical organization guidelines seem less appropriate. For example, it was important to classical theorists that managers maintain their formal authority. Today's better-educated employees, however, are less accepting of formal authority, especially when it is applied arbitrarily. They are also more likely than workers of the past to leave an organization if they are dissatisfied in it.

The principles of classical organization theorists have also been criticized as being too general for today's complex organizations. For example, in modern companies specialization has increased to the point where the lines of authority are sometimes blurred. The maintenance engineer, for instance, may take orders from the plant manager *and* the chief engineer. Here we have a conflict between the classical principles of division of labor and unity of command. Yet classical theory provides little or no guidance for deciding which principle should take precedence over the other.

The idea that management principles and practices could and should be studied, both academically and in the workplace, was firmly established by the dawn of the 20th century. As a discipline of study, the primary subject matter of management theory was *productivity*—and by extension, of course, *profitability*. As we have seen, theorists such as Frederick Taylor and Henry Gantt were active as consultants to organizations like the Ford Motor Co. and Bethlehem Steel, neither of which was in business as a nonprofit organizaton. By the first decade of the century, then, management theory and practice were key factors in the activities of organizations that were pursuing and realizing profits on an unparalled scale. The history of this era in American cultural and business life is replete with stories of fabulous fortunes and daring entrepreneurial ventures in a climate of fierce competition, vast productivity, and the availability of immense sums of capital profit. It is also replete with chronicles of abuse and social irresponsiblility on the part of many businesses in pursuit of more than their fair share of the nation's wealth. As the Ethics in Management box illustrates, such practices did not go unnoticed either by social critics or by the government.

Transitional Theories: Becoming More People-Oriented

Among others, Mary Parker Follett and Chester Barnard built on the basic framework of the classical school. However, they introduced many new elements, especially in the area of human relations and organizational structure. In this, they anticipated trends that would be further developed by the emerging behavioral and management science approaches.

QUOTATION FROM MANAGEMENT THEORIST

''Different situations require different kinds of knowledge, and the man possessing the knowledge demanded by a certain situation tends to be in the best-managed businesses, and other things being equal, to become the leader of the moment.'' (Mary Parker Follett, ''Some Discrepancies in Leadership Theory and Practice,'' 1928)

Mary Parker Follett. Follett (1868–1933) was convinced that no one could become a whole person except as a member of a group (see box). Thus, she took for granted Taylor's assertion that labor and management shared a common purpose as members of the same organization. She believed, however, that the artificial distinction between managers and subordinates—order givers and order takers—obscured this natural partnership.[12] The result was a behavioral model of organizational control (see Fig. 2-3),

[12]See Mary P. Follett, *The New State* (Gloucester, Mass.: Peter Smith, 1918); Henry C. Metcalf and Lyndall Urwick, eds., *Dynamic Administration* (New York: Harper & Brothers, 1941); and L. D. Parker, ''Control in Organizational Life: The Contribution of Mary Parker Follett,'' *Academy of Management Review* 9, no. 4 (October 1984):736–745.

FIGURE 2-3 THE FOLLETT BEHAVIORAL MODEL OF CONTROL

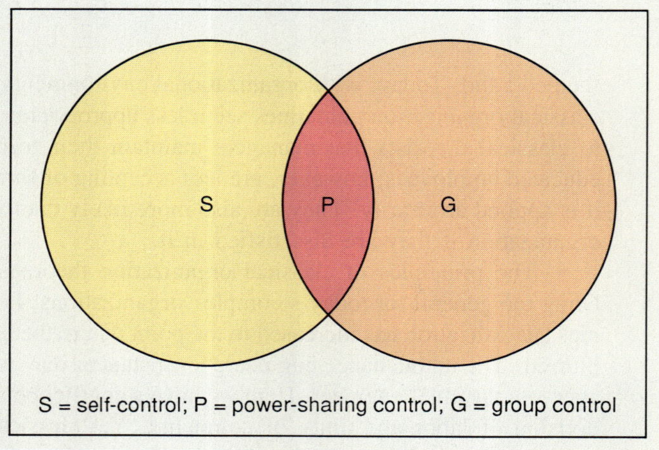

Source: L. D. Parker, ''Control in Organizational Life: The Contribution of Mary Parker Follett,'' *Academy of Management Review* (1984): 742.

in which control was sponsored by and oriented toward the group; self-control (*S*) was exercised by both individuals and groups (*G*) with the result being shared control or power (*P*). Moreover, Follett took into account such factors as politics, economics, and biology (designated as *E* for environment in Fig. 2-4), which influenced the interactive or integrative nature of self-control groups (*I*). Because she saw this system as an integrated whole, Follett characterized it as a ''holistic'' model of control.

BACKGROUND ON CHESTER I. BARNARD

Chester Barnard personified the Horatio Alger ideal of a farm boy who made good. Although he never received his degree from Harvard because he lacked a laboratory science course, he has earned a place in history as an eminent management scholar.

Chester I. Barnard. Barnard (1886–1961) became president of New Jersey Bell in 1927. He used his work experiences and his extensive readings in sociology and philosophy to formulate his theories on organizational life. According to Barnard, people come together in formal organizations to achieve things they could not achieve working alone. But as they pursue the organization's goals, they must also satisfy their individual needs. And so Barnard arrived at his central thesis: An enterprise can operate efficiently and survive only when both the organization's goals and the aims and needs of the individuals working for it are kept in balance.

For example, to meet their personal goals within the confines of the formal organization, people come together in informal groups, such as cliques. To ensure its survival, the firm must utilize these informal groups effectively, even if they sometimes work at cross-purposes to management's objectives. Barnard's recognition of the importance and universality of the ''informal organization'' was a major contribution to management thought.

Barnard believed that individual and organizational purposes could be kept in balance if managers understood a subordinate's ''zone of indifference'' or ''zone of acceptance''—that is, what the subordinate would do without questioning the manager's authority. Obviously, the more activities that fell within an employee's zone of

FIGURE 2-4 THE FOLLETT HOLISTIC MODEL OF CONTROL

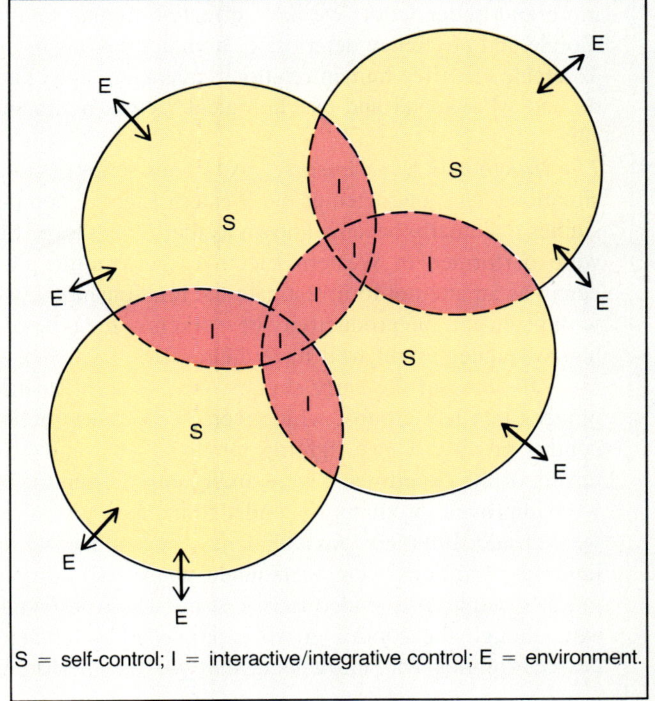

Source: L. D. Parker, ''Control in Organizational Life: The Contribution of Mary Parker Follett,'' *Academy of Management Review* (1984): 743.

acceptance, the smoother and more cooperative an organization would be. Barnard also believed that the executives of an organization had a duty to instill a sense of moral purpose in their employees. Executives were required to think beyond their narrow self-interest and to make an ethical commitment to society. Although Barnard placed much of his emphasis on the work of *executive* managers, he also focused considerable attention on the role of the individual worker as "the basic strategic factor in organization." When he went further to emphasize the organization as the cooperative enterprise of individuals working as *groups,* he actually departed from the mainstream of classical management theory and set the stage for the development of a great deal of current managmement thinking.[13]

THE BEHAVIORAL SCHOOL: THE ORGANIZATION IS PEOPLE

behavioral school A group of management scholars trained in sociology, psychology, and related fields, who use their diverse knowledge to understand and improve the way organizations are managed.

The **behavioral school** emerged in part because managers found that the classical approach did not achieve sufficient production efficiency and workplace harmony. Managers still encountered difficulties and frustrations because people did not always follow predicted or expected patterns of behavior. Thus, there was increased interest in helping managers deal more effectively with the "people side" of their organizations. Several individuals tried to strengthen classical organization theory with the insights of sociology and psychology. As we shall see in Chapter 14, many of these insights contributed to further thinking about the issue of employee motivation in the workplace.

The Human Relations Movement

"Human relations" is frequently used as a general term to describe the ways in which managers interact with their subordinates. When "employee management" stimulates more and better work, we have effective human relations in the organization; when morale and efficiency deteriorate, human relations in the organization are ineffective. To create effective human relations, managers must know why employees act as they do and what social and psychological factors motivate them.

The Hawthorne Experiments. A famous series of studies of human behavior in work situations was conducted at the Western Electric company from 1924 to 1933. These studies eventually became known as the "Hawthorne Studies" because many of them were performed at Western Electric's Hawthorne plant near Chicago. The studies began as an attempt to investigate the relationship between the level of lighting in the workplace and the productivity of workers—the type of question Frederick Taylor and his colleagues might well have addressed.

In some of the early studies, the Western Electric researchers divided the employees into test groups, which were subjected to deliberate changes in lighting, and control groups, whose lighting remained constant throughout the experiments. The results of the experiments were ambiguous. When the test group's lighting conditions were improved, productivity tended to increase just as expected, although the increases were erratic. But there was a tendency for productivity to continue to increase when the lighting conditions were then made worse. To compound the mystery, the control group's output also tended to rise as the test group's lighting conditions were altered, even though the control group experienced no changes in illumination. Something besides lighting was influencing the workers' performance.

---

[13] See Chester I. Barnard, *The Functions of the Executive* (Cambridge, Mass.: Harvard University Press, 1938).

In a new set of experiments, a small group of workers was placed in a separate room and a number of variables were altered: Wages were increased; rest periods of varying lengths were introduced; the workday and workweek were shortened. The researchers, who now acted as supervisors, also allowed the groups to choose their own rest periods and to have a say in other suggested changes. Again the results were ambiguous. Performance tended to increase over time, but it also rose and fell erratically. Part way through this set of experiments, Elton Mayo (1880–1949) and some associates from Harvard, including Fritz J. Roethlisberger and William J. Dickson, became involved.

QUOTATION FROM MANAGEMENT THEORIST

". . . if our technical skills are to make sudden and radical changes in methods of working, we must develop social skills that can balance these moves . . . ." (George Elton Mayo, *The Social Problems of an Industrial Civilization*, 1945)

Hawthorne effect The possibility that workers who receive special attention will perform better simply because they received that attention: one interpretation of Elton Mayo and his colleagues' studies.

COORDINATED RESOURCES

An excellent and engaging description of the Hawthorne Experiments can be found in *The Evolution of Management Thought* by Daniel A. Wren, published by Ronald Press.

In these and subsequent experiments, Mayo and his associates decided that financial incentives, when these were offered, were not causing the productivity improvements. They believed that a complex chain of attitudes had touched off the productivity increases. Because they had been singled out for special attention, the test and the control groups developed a group pride that motivated them to improve their work performance. Sympathetic supervision had further reinforced their increased motivation. The researchers concluded that employees would work harder if they believed management was concerned about their welfare and supervisors paid special attention to them. This phenomenon was subsequently labeled the **Hawthorne effect,** which has remained a quite controversial idea to this day. Since a control group that received no special supervisory treatment or enhancement of working conditions also improved in performance, some people, including Mayo himself, have speculated that the workers' increased productivity resulted from the special attention not of the company's management, but that of the researchers themselves.

The researchers also concluded that informal work groups—the social environment of employees—have a positive influence on productivity. Many of the employees found their work dull and meaningless, but their associations and friendships with co-workers, sometimes influenced by a shared antagonism toward the "bosses," imparted some meaning to their working lives and provided a partial means of protection from management. For these reasons, group pressure, rather than management demands, frequently had the strongest influence on how productive workers would be.

To Mayo, then, the concept of "social man"—motivated by social needs, wanting rewarding on-the-job relationships, and responding more to work-group pressures than to management control—was necessary to complement the old concept of "rational man" motivated by personal economic needs.[14]

Contributions and Limitations of the Human Relations Approach

Contributions. By stressing social needs, the human relations movement improved on the classical approach, which treated productivity almost exclusively as an engineering problem. In a sense, Mayo had rediscovered Robert Owen's century-old dictum that a true concern for workers, those "vital machines," paid dividends.

In addition, these researchers spotlighted the importance of a manager's style and

[14]For extensive discussions of Mayo's work, see Elton Mayo, *The Human Problems of an Industrial Civilization* (New York: Macmillan, 1953), and F. J. Roethlisberger and W. J. Dickson, *Management and the Worker* (Cambridge, Mass.: Harvard University Press, 1939). Also see Roethlisberger's autobiography, *The Elusive Phenomena,* ed. by George F. F. Lombard (Boston: Division of Research, Graduate School of Business Administration, Harvard University, 1977). Analysis, criticism, and defense of the Hawthorne studies can be found in George C. Homans, *The Human Group* (New York: Harcourt, Brace, and Co., 1950), pp. 48–155; Alex Carey, "The Hawthorne Studies: A Radical Criticism," *American Sociological Review* 32, no. 3 (June 1967); Henry A. Landsberger, *Hawthorne Revisited* (Ithaca, N.Y.: Cornell University Press, 1958); Jon M. Shepard, "On Carey's Radical Criticism of the Hawthorne Studies," *Academy of Management Journal* 14, no. 1 (March 1971):23–32; and Dana Bramel and Ronald Friend, "Hawthorne, the Myth of the Docile Worker, and Class Bias in Psychology," *American Psychologist* 36, no. 8 (August 1981):867–878.

thereby revolutionized management training. More and more attention was focused on teaching people-management skills, as opposed to technical skills. Finally, their work led to a new interest in the dynamics of groups. Managers began thinking in terms of group processes and group rewards to supplement their former concentration on the individual worker.

Limitations. Although the Hawthorne experiments profoundly influenced the way managers approached their jobs and the ways research on management was subsequently conducted, the research had many weaknesses of design, analysis, and interpretation. Whether Mayo and his colleagues' conclusions are consistent with their data is still the subject of lively debate and considerable confusion.[15]

The concept of "social man" was an important counterweight to the one-sided "rational-economic man" model. But it, too, failed to describe completely individuals in the workplace. Many managers and management writers assumed that satisfied workers would be more productive workers. However, attempts to increase output during the 1950s by improving working conditions and employee satisfaction did not result in the dramatic productivity increases that had been expected.

Apparently, the social environment in the workplace is only one of several interacting factors that influence productivity. Salary levels, regardless of the interest levels of given tasks, organizational structure and culture, and labor-management relations also play a part. Thus, the entire matter of productivity and worker satisfaction has turned out to be more complex than was originally thought.

For example, a more recent and rigorous study concluded by social psychologists P. Mirvis and E. E. Lawler in 1977 also proved inconclusive in its findings on the relationship between job satisfaction and performance.[16] Mirvis and Lawler attempted to measure the performance of bank tellers in terms of cash shortages and proposed two arguments: (1) satisfied tellers were less likely to show shortages through either carelessness or dishonesty; (2) satisfied workers were less likely to leave their jobs and so saved their employers considerable expense in the recruitment and training of replacements. However, subsequent analysis of this study tends to support the contention that when the quantity of a worker's output is used as a measure of the relationship between satisfaction and performance, the correspondence is generally lower than one would expect. Such analysis also raises a crucial question: Does a worker perform well because he or she is satisfied, or does the worker's perception that he or she is performing well lead to satisfaction?

It does seem to be true that satisfaction lowers absenteeism and job turnovers, but analysis of the Mirvis-Lawler data shows that even this correspondence is lower than expected. Finally, even the correlation between dissatisfied workers and those who quit is smaller than one might assume (even if the observation that dissatisfied workers are more likely to quit than satisfied workers were worth making).[17]

In conclusion, there seem to be at least two reasons why it is difficult to study the relationship between job satisfaction and performance or productivity. First, job satis-

---

[15]Personal communications with Gary Yunker and a paper by him were particularly helpful in clarifying some of the confusions associated with these experiments. See Gary Yunker, "The Hawthorne Studies: Facts and Myths," *Faculty Working Papers,* Department of Psychology, Jacksonville State University, Summer 1985. One example of the confusions associated with the research focuses on the fact that the Hawthorne effect suffers from many different definitions. Some researchers doubt that it exists at all, and many others feel its power to improve performance is greatly exaggerated. See Berkeley Rice, "The Hawthorne Defect: Persistence of a Flawed Theory," *Psychology Today,* February 1982, pp. 70, 72–74; and John G. Adair, "The Hawthorne Effect: A Reconsideration of the Methodological Artifact," *Journal of Applied Psychology* 69, no. 2 (1984):334–345.

[16]P. Mirvis and E. E. Lawler, "Measuring the Financial Impact of Employee Attitudes," *Journal of Applied Psychology* 62 (1977):1–8.

[17]P. M. Muchinsky, *Psychology Applied to Work* (Homewood, Ill.: Dorsey Press, 1983).

"Now available for the first time: 'A Treasury of Management Opinions'—a complete collection of management opinions for the past ten years on your choice of L.P. recordings or eight-track tapes. Here's how to order."
Drawing by W. Miller; © 1979 The New Yorker Magazine, Inc.

faction is largely an emotional response to one's work, and emotional factors, in addition to involving numerous variables, are hard to *measure* in any terms sufficiently precise to satisfy the requirements of social-scientific study. Second, as we shall see in Chapter 14, it is difficult to separate the issue of job *satisfaction* from the equally complex issue of job *motivation*.

From Human Relations to the Behavioral Science Approach

FOR DISCUSSION

What do "behavioral scientists" do differently from "human relations theorists"? (Note their training, emphasis in organizational studies, and explanations for behavior as some suggestions for discussing this question.)

Mayo and his colleagues pioneered the use of the scientific method in their studies of people in the work environment. Later researchers were more rigorously trained in the social sciences (psychology, sociology, and anthropology) and used more sophisticated research methods. Thus, these later researchers became known as "behavioral scientists" rather than "human relations theorists."

Mayo and the human relations theorists introduced a "social man" motivated by a desire to form relationships with others. Some behavioral scientists, such as Argyris, Maslow, and McGregor, believed that the concept of "self-actualizing man" would more accurately explain human motivations.[18] (MacGregor's contributions will be discussed more fully in Chapter 14, Argyris's work in Chapter 9.)

According to Maslow, the needs that people are motivated to satisfy fall into a hierarchy. At the bottom of the hierarchy are physical and safety needs. At the top are ego needs (the need for respect, for example) and self-actualizing needs (such as the need for meaning and personal growth). In general, lower-level needs must be satisfied before higher-level needs can be met. Since many of our lower-level needs have been satisfied in our society, most of us are motivated, at least in part, by the higher-level

[18]Abraham H. Maslow, *Motivation and Personality* (New York: Harper & Row, 1964).

INTERNATIONAL MANAGEMENT

SOME RENAISSANCE AND ANCIENT ROOTS OF MANAGEMENT THEORY

There are two classic works that have many useful ideas to modern managers. The first is Niccolò Machiavelli's *The Discourses,* in which he writes about how to manage a republic. (It may be only mildly ironic that Machiavelli is known for his book *The Prince,* from which we get the perjorative adjective *Machiavellian* meaning *manipulative, insidious, cunning, opportunistic,* and a host of other less–than–admirable character traits; in fact, Machiavelli was a great believer in the virtues of a republic.) Machiavelli wrote the book in 1531 while living in the early Italian republic of Florence. Paraphrasing some of his principles to apply to organizations rather than governments, we might conclude that Machiavelli advises us that:

1. An organization is more stable if members have the right to express their differences and solve their conflicts within it.
2. While one person can begin an organization, "it is lasting when it is left in the care of many and when many desire to maintain it" (201).
3. A weak manager can follow a strong one, but not another weak one, and maintain authority.
4. A manager seeking to change an established organization "should retain at least a shadow of the ancient customs" (231).

ego and self-actualizing needs. Being aware of these different needs enables a manager to use different ways to motivate subordinates. (The hierarchy of needs is discussed in greater detail in Chapter 14.)

Some later behavioral scientists feel that even this model is inadequate to explain fully all the factors that can motivate people in the workplace. They argue that not everyone goes predictably from one need level to the next. For some people, work is only a way to meet their lower-level needs; others are satisfied with nothing less than the fulfillment of their highest-level needs and may even choose to work in jobs that threaten their safety to attain uniquely personal goals. To these behavioral scientists, the more realistic model of human motivation is ''complex man.'' The effective manager is aware that no two people are exactly alike and tailors his or her attempts to influence people according to their individual needs.

Contributions and Limitations of the Behavioral Science School

Behavioral scientists have made enormous contributions to our understanding of individual motivation, group behavior, interpersonal relationships at work, and the importance of work to human beings. Their findings have enabled managers to become much more sensitive and sophisticated in dealing effectively with subordinates. They continue to offer new insights in such important areas as leadership, conflict resolution, the acquisition and use of power, organizational change, and communication.

In spite of the impressive contributions of the behavioral sciences to management, many management writers—including behavioral scientists—believe that the potential of this field has not been fully realized. Managers themselves may resist behavioral scientists' suggestions, because they do not like to admit that they need help in dealing with people. The models and theories proposed by behavioral scientists are seen by many managers as too complicated or abstract to be useful or relevant to their specific problems. The tendency of behavioral scientists to use jargon rather than

While Machiavelli did not have a systematic view of management or organizations, it does seem obvious that he did have some important insights that are still relevant to us today.

A second ancient figure is the Chinese philosopher Sun Tzu, who wrote *The Art of War* more than 2000 years ago. While there is some controversy about the historical accuracy of the book, here too are some important lessons for management, as modified somewhat by one of Sun Tzu's followers, Mao Tse-tung:

1. When the enemy advances, we retreat!
2. When the enemy halts, we harass!
3. When the enemy seeks to avoid battle, we attack!
4. When the enemy retreats, we pursue!

While metaphors coined by men devoted to professional polity and professional hostility may or may not be of much value in thinking about management and organizations, it can be useful in thinking about overall strategy. The modern concern with competition, with avoiding head-on competition (see the discussion of Porter's view of strategy in Chapter 7), and with the signals that competitors send to each other, was well understood in both Renaissance Italy and ancient China.

Sources: The Portable Machiavelli, Peter Bondanella and Mark Musa, ed. and trans. (New York: Penguin, 1979); Sun Tzu, *The Art of War,* Samuel B. Griffith, trans. (London: Oxford University Press, 1963).

everyday language in communicating their findings has also inhibited understanding and acceptance of their ideas. Finally, because human behavior is so complex, behavioral scientists often differ in their recommendations for a particular problem, making it difficult for managers to decide whose advice to follow.[19]

THE QUANTITATIVE SCHOOL: OPERATIONS RESEARCH AND MANAGEMENT SCIENCE

At the beginning of World War II, Great Britain was faced with a number of new, complex problems in warfare that it needed desperately to solve. (For example, new tactics in antisubmarine warfare had to be developed.) With their survival at stake, the British formed the first operational research (OR) teams—groups of mathematicians, physicists, and other scientists who were brought together to solve such problems. By pooling the expertise of various specialists in these OR teams, the British were able to achieve significant technological and tactical breakthroughs. When the Americans entered the war, they formed what they called *operations research* teams, based on the successful British model, to solve similar problems.

When the war was over, the applicability of OR to problems in industry gradually became apparent. New industrial technologies were being put into use; transportation and communication had become more complicated. These developments brought with them a host of problems that could not be solved easily by conventional means.

[19]See Edgar H. Schein, ''Behavioral Sciences for Management,'' and Edwin B. Flippo, ''The Underutilization of Behavioral Science by Management,'' in Joseph W. McGuire, ed., *Contemporary Management: Issues and Viewpoints* (Englewood Cliffs, N.J.: Prentice Hall, 1974), pp. 15–32 and pp. 36–41. See also James A. Lee, ''Behavioral Theory vs. Reality,'' *Harvard Business Review* 49, no. 2 (March–April 1971):20–28 passim; and Jay W. Lorsch, ''Making Behavioral Science More Useful,'' *Harvard Business Review* 57, no. 2 (March–April 1979):171–180.

OR specialists were called on increasingly to help managers come up with new answers to these new problems. With the development of the electronic computer, OR procedures were formalized into what is now called the "management science school."[20]

management science (MS) Mathematical techniques for modeling, analysis, and solution of management problems. Also called operations research.

Today, the **management science** approach to solving a problem begins when a mixed team of specialists from relevant disciplines is called in to analyze the problem and propose a course of action to management. The team constructs a mathematical model to simulate the problem. The model shows, in symbolic terms, all the relevant factors that bear on the problem and how they are interrelated. By changing the values of the variables in the model (such as increasing the cost of raw materials) and analyzing the different equations of the model with a computer, the team can determine what the effects of each change would be. Eventually, the management science team presents management with an objective basis for making a decision.[21]

EXTRA EXERCISE

Have students identify some organizational problems that could be solved by the management science approach. (Examples: reducing waiting time in a grocery store express lane checkout, reducing the number of rejects for unacceptable product quality, opening a new building on a college campus, etc.)

Contributions and Limitations of the Management Science Approach

The techniques of management science are a well-established part of the problem-solving armory of most large organizations, including the civilian and the military branches of government. Management science techniques are used in such activities as capital budgeting and cash flow management, production scheduling, development of product strategies, planning for human resource development programs, maintenance of optimal inventory levels, and aircraft scheduling.

In spite of widespread use for many problems, however, management science has not yet reached the stage where it can effectively deal with the behavioral side of an enterprise. Its contributions to management have been greatest in planning and control activities, and more progress has been made in the areas of organizing, staffing, and leading the organization. Some managers have complained that the concepts and language of management science are too complicated for ready understanding and implementation. Others feel they are not enough involved with management scientists in developing decision-making techniques, with the result that the later, ongoing implementation of these techniques is often unsuccessful because it fails to address the psychological and behavioral components of workplace activities.[22] Management scientists, for their part, sometimes feel that they have not achieved their full potential for solving management problems because of their remoteness from and lack of awareness of the problems and constraints actually faced by managers.[23]

---

[20]Larry M. Austin and James R. Burns, *Management Science* (New York: Macmillan, 1985); Robert J. Thierauf, *Management Science: A Model Formulation Approach with Computer Applications* (Columbus, Ohio: Merrill, 1985); and Kenneth R. Baker and Dean H. Kroop, *Management Science: An Introduction to Decision Models* (New York: Wiley, 1985).

[21]The management science approach has been applied to other uses besides industrial problem solving. Jay Forrester and his colleagues, for example, have pioneered attempts to simulate the operations of whole enterprises. He and others have also simulated economic activities of Third World nations and even of the world system as a whole. See Jay W. Forrester, *Industrial Dynamics* (Cambridge, Mass.: MIT Press, 1961) and *World Dynamics,* 2nd ed. (Cambridge, Mass.: MIT Press, 1979); Dennis H. Meadows et al., *The Limits to Growth* (New York: Universe Books, 1972); Dennis H. Meadows, ed., *Alternatives to Growth—* Vol. 1, *A Search for Sustainable Futures* (Cambridge, Mass.: Ballinger, 1977); and Mihajlo Mesarovic and Eduard Pestel, *Mankind at the Turning Point* (New York: Dutton, 1975).

[22]See James R. Miller and Howard Feldman, "Management Science—Theory, Relevance, and Practice in the 1980s," *Interfaces* 13, no. 5 (October 1983):56–60; and Leonard Adelman, "Involving Users in the Development of Decision-Analytic Aids: The Principal Factor in Successful Implementation," *Journal of the Operational Research Society* 33, no. 4 (1982):333–342.

[23]For a discussion of how management science should reorient itself to compete with other approaches, see A. M. Geoffrion, "Can MS/OR Evolve Fast Enough?" *Interfaces* 13, no. 1 (February 1983):10–25.

THE EVOLUTION OF MANAGEMENT THEORY

THOUGHT-PROVOKER

If you had the opportunity to sit down and talk with any one of the management theorists discussed, who would it be? What questions would you want to ask this person?

FOR DISCUSSION

Can the various approaches to management be more appropriate in some organizations or industries than in others? How? (For example, people-intensive organizations might find behavioral approaches more appropriate. Machine-intensive organizations might find scientific or classical approaches more useful.)

We have described the three major schools of management thought in terms of their chronological emergence. All continue to maintain their importance today. The behavioral science and the management science schools both represent vital and energetic approaches to researching, analyzing, and solving management problems. The classical school, too, continues to evolve. It has incorporated much of the research produced by the behavioral sciences, along with the new perspectives of both the behavioral science and the management science schools, and even the newer systems and contingency approaches.

Classical theory remains important because it has been able to integrate newer developments into the basic framework of the traditional issues identified by the classical writers. These issues—division of labor, authority and responsibility, initiative—remain important, although in many cases the particular focus has shifted. For example, concern with division of labor has led to speculation about the point at which specialization may become excessive in terms of the values and expectations of today's employees.

As the classical school has evolved, much of its emphasis and many of its perspectives can still be traced back to the early classical writers. In fact, while the special focus of each remains, the other two major schools also tend to borrow insights and concepts. Indeed, it often seems that the boundaries between the various schools are becoming progressively less distinct.[24]

But the growing similarities should not be exaggerated. Just as there are many individuals who integrate the perspectives of all the schools, so are there many whose training and background are firmly in a single school and who have little or no awareness of other approaches. One benefit of studying the history and perspectives of the three schools is to understand the perspectives of your future colleagues in management and thus be prepared to work effectively with them.

Moreover, current management theory continues not only to draw on the past, but to generate exciting concepts of its own. (Exhibit 2-3 presents at least five possible directions for the evolution of management theory.) It is impossible to predict what future generations will be studying, but at this point we can identify at least three additional perspectives on management theory that will become important in this book: the systems approach, the contingency approach, and a neo-human relations approach.

EXHIBIT 2-3 FIVE POSSIBLE DIRECTIONS FOR THE EVOLUTION OF MANAGEMENT THEORY

1. *Dominance.* One of the major schools could emerge as the most useful. Incorporating some ideas from other schools, the dominant approach would drive the others from the field. This has not been happening. Currently, each approach is recognized as contributing powerful insights, perspectives, and tools to the growing body of management theory.
2. *Divergence.* The major schools could each go off on their own paths, with decreasing cross-fertilization as they show little interest in each other's perspectives. Clearly, this, too, is not happening.
3. *Convergence.* The schools could become more similar, with the boundaries between them tending to blur. This indeed seems to be happening. The convergence is uneven, though. For example, the special tools and mathematically sophisticated models of management science have not been widely accepted by less technically oriented thinkers.* In fact, some view the current tendency toward convergence as promising eventual domination by one school over the others.†

(continued)

[24]For an example of interaction among the various management theories, see Sang M. Lee, Fred Luthans, and David L. Olson, "A Management Science Approach to Contingency Models of Organizational Structure," *Academy of Management Journal* 25, no. 3 (September 1982):553–566.

EXHIBIT 2-3 (CONTINUED)

4. *Synthesis*. Other theorists, however, see the apparent convergence now taking place leading to an integration of the perspectives of the existing schools. This would not be the "layered" buildup of the schools we described earlier. Rather, the integration would be a fresh conceptual approach to the field of management. Two candidates for the honor of integration already exist: the systems approach and the contingency approach, to be discussed below.
5. *Proliferation*. As a final possibility, more schools or perspectives may still appear. Again, to some extent this may already be happening. In 1961, in a famous article, "The Management Theory Jungle," Harold Koontz discerned six major schools of management theory.‡ Nearly 20 years later he found 11—almost twice as many—flourishing.§ However, many of the new approaches seem less to be new schools than specific focuses on a relatively limited set of issues.

*For an excellent approach to the field of management from the management science perspective, see Martin S. Starr, *Management: A Modern Approach* (New York: Harcourt Brace Jovanovich, 1971).
†William T. Greenwood ("Future Management Theory: A 'Comparative' Evolution to a General Theory," *Academy of Management Journal* 17, no. 3 [September 1974]:503–511) and Harold Koontz ("The Management Theory Jungle Revisited," *Academy of Management Review* 5, no. 2 [April 1980]:175–187) have also suggested that convergence is occurring around the operational management process school as other schools adopt and expand its basic concept.
‡Harold Koontz, "The Management Theory Jungle," *Journal of the Academy of Management* 4, no. 3 (December 1961):174–188.
§Koontz, "The Management Theory Jungle Revisited."

The Systems Approach

systems approach View of the organization as a unified, directed system of interrelated parts.

The **systems approach** to management attempts to view the organization as a unified, purposeful system composed of interrelated parts. Rather than dealing separately with the various segments of an organization, the systems approach gives managers a way of looking at an organization as a whole and as a part of the larger, external environment. (See Chapter 3.) In so doing, systems theory tells us that the activity of any segment of an organization in varying degrees affects the activity of every other segment.[25]

CLASS COMMENT

General Systems Theory (GST), upon which the systems approach to management is based, assumes that everything is part of a larger, interdependent arrangement. Ludwig von Bertalanffy, a biologist and founder of GST says, "In order to understand an organized whole we must know both the parts and the relations between them." (Ludwig von Bertalanffy, "The History and Status of General Systems Theory," *Academy of Management Journal*, December 1972, p. 411)

As production managers in a manufacturing plant, for example, we would like to have long uninterrupted production runs of standardized products in order to maintain maximum efficiency and low costs. Marketing managers, on the other hand, would like to offer quick delivery of a wide range of products and therefore may want a flexible manufacturing schedule that can fill special orders on short notice. As systems-oriented production managers, we would make scheduling decisions only after we have identified their impact on other departments and the entire organization. This means that managers cannot function wholly within the confines of the traditional organization chart. To mesh their department with the whole enterprise, managers must communicate with other employees and departments, and frequently with representatives of other organizations as well.[26]

Some Key Concepts. Many of the concepts of general systems theory are finding their way into the language of management. As managers, we should be familiar with the systems vocabulary, so that we can keep pace with current developments.

subsystems Those parts comprising the whole system.

Subsystems. The parts that make up the whole of a system are called **subsystems.** And each system in turn may be a subsystem of a still larger whole. Thus, a department is a subsystem of a plant, which may be a subsystem of a company, which may be a

[25]See Ludwig von Bertalanffy, Carl G. Hempel, Robert E. Bass, and Hans Jonas, "General System Theory: A New Approach to Unity of Science," I–VI, *Human Biology* 23, no. 4 (December 1951):302–361; and Kenneth E. Boulding, "General Systems Theory—The Skeleton of Science," *Management Science* 2, no. 3 (April 1956):197–208.

[26]See Seymour Tilles, "The Manager's Job—A Systems Approach," *Harvard Business Review* 41, no. 1 (January–February 1963):73–81.

subsystem of a conglomerate or industry, which is a subsystem of the national economy as a whole, which is a subsystem of the world system.

synergy The situation in which the whole is greater than its parts. In organizational terms, the fact that departments that interact cooperatively can be more productive than if they operate in isolation.

open system A system that interacts with its environment.

closed system A system that does not interact with its environment.

system boundary The boundary that separates each system from its environment. It is rigid in a closed system, flexible in an open system.

flows Components such as information, material, and energy that enter and leave a system.

feedback (job-based) The part of system control in which the results of actions are returned to the individual, allowing work procedures to be analyzed and corrected.

FOR DISCUSSION

How can an organization be viewed as a system? (Illustrate on the board or with prepared transparencies various examples of organizations as systems.)

Synergy. Synergy means that the whole is greater than the sum of its parts. In organizational terms, **synergy** means that as separate departments within an organization cooperate and interact, they become more productive than if each had acted in isolation. For example, it is more efficient for each department in a small firm to deal with one financing department than for each department to have a separate financing department of its own.

Open and Closed Systems. A system is considered an **open system** if it interacts with its environment; it is considered a **closed system** if it does not. All organizations interact with their environment, but the extent to which they do so varies. An automobile plant, for example, is a far more open system than a monastery or a prison.

System Boundary. Each system has a boundary that separates it from its environment. In a closed system, the **system boundary** is rigid; in an open system, the boundary is more flexible. The system boundaries of many organizations have become increasingly flexible in recent years. For example, oil companies wishing to engage in offshore drilling have increasingly had to consider public reaction to the potential environmental harm.

Flow. A system has **flows** of information, materials, and energy (including human energy). These enter the system from the environment as *inputs* (raw materials, for example), undergo transformation processes within the system (operations that alter them), and exit the system as *outputs* (goods and services).

Feedback. **Feedback** is the key to system controls. As operations of the system proceed, information is fed back to the appropriate people or perhaps to a computer so that the work can be assessed and, if necessary, corrected.[27]

Systems theory calls attention to the dynamic and interrelated nature of organizations and the management task. Thus, systems theory provides a framework within which we can plan actions and anticipate both immediate and far-reaching consequences; at the same time, it allows us to understand unanticipated consequences as they may develop. With a systems perspective, general managers can more easily maintain a balance between the needs of the various parts of the enterprise and the needs and goals of the firm as a whole.

Although systems theory advocates believe that it will absorb concepts of the other management schools until it becomes dominant or that it may eventually develop into a well-defined school by itself, at present it seems most likely to emerge as a perspective incorporated into the thinking of all the major schools. The systems approach has already permeated management thinking and the concepts just described are an integral part of the thought processes and research designs of both on-the-job managers and academic theorists of all three major schools. Although partisans of this approach hail it as the eventual and long-sought integrating development, only time will tell if the systems approach to management will continue to evolve to the point at which it does absorb, synthesize, and integrate all other approaches.

The Contingency Approach

The well-known international economist Charles Kindleberger was fond of telling his students at MIT that the answer to any really engrossing question in economics is: "It depends." The task of the economist, Kindleberger would continue, is to specify *upon what* it depends, and *in what ways*.

[27]Fremont E. Kast and James E. Rosenzweig, "General Systems Theory: Applications for Organization and Management," *Academy of Management Journal* 15, no. 4 (December 1972):447–465. See also Arkalgud Ramaprasad, "On the Definition of Feedback," *Behavioral Science* 28, no. 1 (January 1983):4–13.

"It depends" is an appropriate response to the important questions in management as well. Management theory attempts to determine the predictable relationships between situations, actions, and outcomes. It is therefore not surprising that a recent approach seeking to integrate the various schools of management thought focuses essentially on the interdependence of the various factors involved in the managerial situation.

contingency approach The view that the management technique that best contributes to the attainment of organizational goals might vary in different types of situations or circumstances.

The **contingency approach** (sometimes called the *situational approach*) was developed by managers, consultants, and researchers who tried to apply the concepts of the major schools to real-life situations. Often finding that methods highly effective in one situation would not work in other situations, they sought an explanation for these experiences. Why, for example, did an organizational development program work brilliantly in one situation and fail miserably in another? Advocates of the contingency approach had a single and logical answer to such questions: Results differ because situations differ; a technique that works in one case will not necessarily work in all cases.

QUOTATION FROM MANAGEMENT THEORIST

". . . Allowance must be made for different and changing circumstances . . . ." (Henri Fayol, "Administration: Industrielle et generale," 1916)

According to the contingency approach, then, the task of managers is to identify which technique will, *in a particular situation, under particular circumstances, and at a particular time,* best contribute to the attainment of management goals. Where workers need to be encouraged to increase productivity, for example, the classical theorist may prescribe a new work-simplification scheme. The behavioral scientist may seek to create a psychologically motivating climate and recommend some approach like *job enrichment*—the combination of tasks that are different in scope and responsibility and allow the worker greater autonomy in making decisions. (The relationship between such approaches and job satisfaction and motivation is discussed in more detail in Chapter 14.) But the manager trained in the contingency approach will ask, "Which method will *work best here*?" If the workers are unskilled and training opportunities and resources are limited, work simplification might be the best solution. With skilled workers, driven by pride in their abilities, a job enrichment program might be more effective.

As we have seen, while the systems approach emphasizes the interrelationships between parts of an organization, the contingency approach builds upon this perspective by focusing in detail on the nature of relationships existing between these parts, seeking to define those factors that are crucial to a specific task or issue and to clarify the functional interactions between related factors. For this reason, advocates of the contingency approach see it as the leading branch of management thought today.[28]

The primacy of the contingency approach is challenged, however, by several other theorists.[29] They argue, for one thing, that the contingency approach does not incorporate all aspects of systems theory, and they hold that it has not yet developed to the point at which it can be considered a true theory. Critics also argue that there is really not much that is new about the contingency approach. For example, they point out that even classical theorists such as Fayol cautioned that management principles must be flexibly applied.

---

[28]See Fred Luthans, "The Contingency Theory of Management: A Path Out of the Jungle," *Business Horizons* 16, no. 3 (June 1973):62–72; Fred Luthans and Todd I. Stewart, "A General Contingency Theory of Management," *Academy of Management Review* 2, no. 2 (April 1977):181–195; Jon M. Shepard and James G. Hougland, Jr., "Contingency Theory: 'Complex Man' or 'Complex Organization'?" *Academy of Management Review* 3, no. 3 (July 1978):413–427; Fred Luthans and Todd I. Stewart, "The Reality or Illusion of a General Contingency Theory of Management: A Response to the Longenecker and Pringle Critique," *Academy of Management Review* 3, no. 3 (July 1978):683–687; and Jay W. Lorsch, "Making Behavioral Science More Useful," *Harvard Business Review* 52, no. 2 (April 1979):171–180. A recent assessment of contingency theory can be found in Henry L. Tosi, Jr., and John W. Slocum, Jr., "Contingency Theory: Some Suggested Directions," *Journal of Management* 10, no. 1 (1984):9–26.

[29]Among the more outspoken critics of contingency theory are Harold Koontz ("The Management Theory Jungle Revisited") and Justin G. Longenecker and Charles D. Pringle ("The Illusion of Contingency Theory as a General Theory," *Academy of Management Review* 3, no. 3 [July 1978]:679–682).

EXTRA EXERCISE

Assign individual students or groups of students the roles of Taylor, Fayol, Barnard, Follett, Maslow, Kast and Rosenzweig (systems), and Luthans (contingency). How would each of these scholars interpret and manage the following situations: the introduction of robots into the workplace, actual sales inconsistent with sales projections, employee dissatisfaction, product quality decline? Other examples could be developed.

To these critics, contingency approach supporters point out that many classical and management process theorists forgot the pragmatic cautions of Fayol and others. Instead, they tried to come up with "universal principles" that could be applied without the "it depends" dimension. Encouraged by the elimination of contingencies—of unpredictable factors—many working managers applied the absolute principles advocated by these theorists—and re-encountered reality, complete with all its shades and complications.

As managers who have studied the contingency approach, then, we would not be satisfied with simply analyzing a particular problem: We would be equally concerned with how well a particular solution fits in with the structure, resources, and goals of our entire organization. Should we try to increase productivity through work simplification or through a job-enrichment program? We must take into account more than the needs of the workers. If top management is opposed to increasing specialization of work for policy reasons, then a work-simplification program will not gain support. Environmental factors must be considered also. In a depressed economy, for example, job-enrichment programs might be too expensive or too uncertain in their outcome. The contingency approach asks us to be aware of the complexity in every situation and to take an active role in trying to determine what would work best in each case.

The *neo-human relations* approach detailed in the Management Application is indicative of a movement toward an *integrative* approach to management theory that began in the 1950s and gained momentum in the 1960s, when organizational-research studies started to report on the relationship between changes in organizational environment and organizational commitment to technology. In England, for example, Joan Woodward and a team of researchers conducted studies into the nature of organizational "task-technology"—the relationship between an organization's technological orientation and the performance of its employees.[30] At least two themes emerged from the Woodward studies: (1) in certain circumstances (although not in all), a *flexible* management system—one that could respond to necessary adjustments in the relationship between technological and human resources—is more effective than a system based essentially on cut-and-dried classical management principles; (2) the impact of technological orientation on employee motivation and productivity must be regarded as a key factor in organizational management.

The first of these conclusions confirmed the earlier contention of Tom Burns and G. M. Stalker that "the beginning of administrative wisdom is the awareness that there is no optimum type of management system."[31] As we have seen, such "wisdom" underlies the contingency approach to management, and as this proposition relates to organizational structure, we shall discuss it further in Chapter 9. At this point, however, let us focus on the second of the two Woodward themes—the effect of an organization's technological commitment upon its *human* resources. As Jay W. Lorsch and Paul R. Lawrence point out, *contingency* theory refers to the fact that organizational processes are "contingent upon external requirements *and* member needs."[32]

For example, machines work 24 hours a day without complaint, but *humans* find themselves in *situations* that change—that may or may not satisfy their "needs" as "members" of an organization. Thus the focus on "member needs" is playing a major role in the efforts of contemporary management theorists to develop an integrative approach to the practice of management: At present, it appears that any such approach will be successful only if it can integrate scientific management techniques with emerging concepts about human relations within organizations.

[30]Joan Woodward, *Industrial Organization* (London: Oxford University Press, 1965)..

[31]Tom Burns and G. M. Stalker, *The Management of Innovation* (London: Tavistock, 1961), p. 125.

[32]Jay W. Lorsch and Paul R. Lawrence, eds., *Studies in Organization Design* (Homewood, Ill.: Richard D. Irwin/Dorsey, 1970), p. 1.

MANAGEMENT APPLICATION

THE NEO-HUMAN RELATIONS APPROACH (OR, THE SOCIAL ANIMAL IN THE HUMANIST'S MAZE)

The hallmark of the human relations approach to management is *people* management, and the behavioral school tried to make this concept more specific by studying "people" more scientifically. The result, as we have seen, is generally known as the contingency approach but in recent years some management thinkers have combined these approaches in a way that goes beyond contingency theory. The neo-human relations approach is explicitly normative. Edwards Deming, Tom Peters, and others have articulated principles that combine a view of "human nature" with the scientific study of the contexts within which human interactions actually occur, focusing on the concept of "quality" in work and on the individual worker's relationships with others. They believe that this concept can be used to build a comprehensive and practical set of principles of management, much in the way that Fayol did in the early part of the century. While there may be situational aspects—unpredictable factors, unforeseen events—to management, each of these thinkers propose to tell us how management should act in *most* circumstances to be successful. Because this view is based on both scientific studies and clinical experience, a mix of principles and case histories are used to illustrate them.

EXTRA EXERCISE

Read a corporate case study in a business periodical (*Business Week, Fortune,* or others). What management approaches can be identified? (The professor can either assign a specific reading or leave the assignment open-ended.)

COORDINATED RESOURCE

The videotape, "In Search of Excellence: The Film," could be shown as an upbeat and fun ending to this chapter since it illustrates several examples of companies that have different approaches in their bids to be excellent. (Available from AMA Film/Video, 85 Main Street, Watertown, MA 02172, or call 800-225-3215.)

Morever, any such approach must implicitly reject many of the tenets of traditional management theory. For example, Peter Drucker, writing in 1985, attributed "the astonishing job growth of the American economy" over the preceding 20 years to the emergence of "growth enterprises" founded and nourished by entrepreneurs who had broken free of conventional ways of organizational thinking. He envisions an "entrepreneurial society" in which "individuals will increasingly have to take responsibility for their own continuous learning and relearning, for their own self-development and for their careers. . . . Tradition, convention, and 'corporate policy' will be a hindrance rather than a help."[33] Tom Peters contends that this emphasis on the specifically human resource in the development of new ways of organizational thinking requires "flexibility by empowering people." More specifically, he argues that "this power can most effectively be tapped when people are gathered in human-scale groupings—that is, teams, or more precisely, self-managing teams."[34]

If writers like Drucker, Peters, and others[35] are accurate in their analyses, then it seems clear that the emphasis on the human resource—and thus on human-relations management—foresees an important step in the evolution of organizational structures themselves. At this point, then, an integrative approach to management theory will have to analyze the role of human-relations management within the context of this evolutionary prospect. One such effort has been made by William Ouchi, an American familiar with Japanese organizational practices.[36] Ouchi first observed that many of the most successful American companies displayed organizational behavior quite similar

[33]Peter F. Drucker, *Innovation and Entrepreneurship: Practice and Principles* (New York: Harper & Row, 1985), pp. 11, 264.

[34]Tom Peters, *Thriving on Chaos: Handbook for a Management Revolution* (New York: Alfred A. Knopf, 1988), pp. 281–282.

[35]See Rosabeth M. Kanter, "The Middle Manager as Innovator," *Harvard Business Review,* July–August 1982, pp. 95–105; "Shaping Corporate Change," *Productivity Brief,* no. 35 (April 1984):2–8; *The Change Masters* (New York: Simon & Schuster, 1983).

In Chapter 1, we briefly looked at Deming's 14 principles, but it is important to note here an underlying view of human nature—namely, that fear is not essential to management strategy and that people can do quality work if they are given the knowledge to do so and the proper conditions under which to do it.

In a little-read chapter of their *In Search of Excellence,* Peters and Waterman describe the scientific research on which their claims about successful organizations are based. This research, some of which will be discussed in the remainder of this book, is explicitly about human nature and the ways that people interact in organizational settings. Building on the work of Herbert Simon (discussed in Chapter 6), organization theorist Karl Weick, social psychologist Stanley Milgram (discussed in Chapter 10), and others, Peters and Waterman deduce some general rules for treating others with dignity and respect and proper expectations about their work capabilities. This general approach is carried out in their later work, and the theme has been picked up by other scholars. Peters' latest book, *Thriving on Chaos,* elaborates these principles in the explicitly normative language of "promises".

Whether or not the neo-human relations approach becomes a major contribution to management theory—or just another conceptual and academic fad—is too early to tell, at this time, but it is safe to say that this approach is having a tremendous impact on management thinking in both universities and in organizations.

to practices common in Japanese organizations. For example, Japanese organizations place more emphasis on collective decision making and group responsibilities; quality control is often handled during periodic meetings or by on-site personnel; most Japanese expect their relationship with the organizaiton to be a lifetime commitment, and the organization often develops its relationship with an employee outside the work environment.

At the same time, much of the Japanese managerial style was borrowed from Western models based primarily on scientific management principles, and Ouchi has proposed a management model that *integrates* the successful practices of both culturally different approaches. Ouchi recommends that certain tenets of classical theory—for example, scientific work methods—be incorporated into an integrative approach to management theory, but he also advises the adoption of principles that are much more common in Japanese practice than in typical American practice. In particular, he endorses greater emphasis on human-relations management as a complement to the techniques of scientific management. He proposes that the organization devote more energy to satisfying the needs of its human resources, both as individuals and as groups, and he suggests that such goals can be attained if the organization focuses on changes in two crucial areas: *decision making* should become a participatory activity for a greater number of employees, and *responsibility* should be considered a collaborative function, preferably the product of group or team processes.

Since their publication in 1981, Ouchi's proposals have met with enthusiastic response among practicing managers. Whether they prove to point in the direction of a valid integrative theory depends upon both their inherent feasibility and the evolution of organizational culture.

[36]William Ouchi, *Theory Z—How American Business Can Meet the Japanese Challenge* (Reading, Mass.: Addison-Wesley, 1981).

ILLUSTRATIVE CASE STUDY Wrap-Up

The Apostle of Mass Production

We have discovered at least two things in this chapter and its Illustrative Case Study: (1) managerial theory, like theories in all fields, must *evolve* in order to meet practical needs and everyday realities; (2) theorists, whatever their fields of endeavor, tend to be people and products of their times.

Henry Ford was certainly an apostle of the so-called *charity principle*—the contemporary notion that it was the responsibility of society's financial fortunates to tend to the needs of its unfortunates (see Chapter 4). He was a philanthropist of the first order: He donated $5 million to establish a museum in Dearborn, Michigan, and $7.5 million to build the Henry Ford Hospital in Detroit. As we shall also see in Chapter 4, Ford could legitimately be characterized as a practitioner of the *stewardship principle,* another contemporary theory that proposed that wealthy individuals were essentially "caretakers" of property that would occasionally have to be turned over and devoted to larger public interests: Although he staunchly advocated an isolationist policy when World War II broke out in Europe, Ford immediately converted his plants to produce war material when the U.S. entered the war in 1941.

And yet, many of Ford's managerial practices were conservative or unresponsive to changing times, and his hold on the automotive market was eventually wrested from him by companies more farsighted in their managerial theories and practices. Hostile to the banking community, for example, Ford refused outside investments in his company throughout his lifetime, borrowing capital only when absolutely necessary and preferring to finance corporate activities solely through the company's own income. He was also inclined to ignore the dynamics of the industry that he had largely founded. Although he opened up Ford Motor Co. to include branch factories to cater to a growing European market, he long failed to follow managerial advice to retool for both the hydraulic brake and the six- or eight-cylinder engine; he also resisted management counsel regarding advances in gearshift and transmission technology and even put off introducing color variety into his product line (Ford preferred his cars to be black). His disinterest in increasing consumer demands for comfort and style ultimately cost him his industry's leadership to General Motors, a conglomerate assembled from over 20 diverse firms by founder William Durant and a second generation of American industrial organizers. ■

SUMMARY

Three well-established schools of management thought—classical, behavioral, and quantitative—have contributed to managers' understanding of organizations and to their ability to manage them. Each offers a different perspective for defining management problems and opportunities and for developing ways to deal with them. In their current state of evolution, however, each approach also overlooks or deals inadequately with important aspects of organizational life. The newer systems approach, based on general systems theory, and the contingency approach have already been developed to the point where they offer valuable insights for the practicing manager. Eventually, these most recently evolved perspectives may lead to the integration of the classical, behavioral, and quantitative schools; on the other hand, some new approach not yet perceived on the horizon may accomplish this end.

It is also possible that the theoretical breakthrough may never occur. Managers will then have to continue on their own to select the perspective or perspectives appropriate to a given situation, and so it is likely that managers will find such a multiplicity of theories useful.

REVIEW QUESTIONS

1. Why is it important for you to understand the various management theories that have developed?
2. What environmental factors enhanced the growth and development of each of the three major schools of thought?

3. What were some of the work methods and tools that Taylor introduced to increase productivity?
4. Was Taylor's assumption that management and labor had a common cause valid? Why or why not?
5. Why did Follett believe that individual freedom and self-control should come through the activities of the group?
6. Which of Fayol's principles and functions of management do you believe still apply today?
7. What was Mayo's principal contribution to management knowledge? What is the Hawthorne effect?
8. Distinguish between the "rational" and "social" models in human relations.
9. What is OR and how does it work?
10. Why is the systems approach more appropriate today than it would have been in Fayol's time?
11. What is the major task of the manager according to the contingency approach?
12. Which approach or school of management thought makes the most sense to you? Why?

CASE STUDY

Theory and Policy Encounter Power and Motivation at Consolidated Automobile

On Tuesday morning at 6 A.M., two young automobile assembly-line workers, disgruntled over failing to get their supervisor transferred, shut off the electric power supply to an auto-assembly line and closed it down at Consolidated Automobile Manufacturers, Inc.

The electric power supply area, containing transformers, switches, and other high-voltage electrical equipment, was positioned near the center of the plant in a 6 × 7 foot area. Enclosing this area was a 10-foot high chain-link fence with a locked gate of equal height in order to form a protective cage around the facility and provide a measure of security.

The two assembly-line workers, William Strong and Larry Kane, gained access to the electric power supply area simply by scaling the fence. Once inside, they halted the assembly line by opening the switches and cutting off the electrical power.

Strong and Kane, who worked as spot welders, had taken matters into their hands when the union's grievance procedure had not worked fast enough to satisfy them. Co-workers, idled by the dramatic protest and the motionless assembly line, grouped themselves around the fenced area, shouting encouragement to the two men inside. In response, Strong and Kane were chanting, "When you cut the power you've got the power." They were in the process of becoming folk heroes among their co-workers.

Sam Winfare, who supervised Strong and Kane and who was the target of their protest, had been supervisor for only a short time. In explaining the events that led to the protest, Winfare said that production on the assembly line had been chronically below quota before he took charge. At the time Winfare was made supervisor, the plant manager had plainly told him that his job was to improve the production rate, and production had improved markedly in the short time that he had been supervisor.

Winfare advised the plant manager that his transfer would only set a serious, long-term precedent. "The company's action to remove me would create a situation where the operations of the plant would be subject to the whims of any employee with a grudge," he argued. His contention was confirmed by the comment of a union steward who said there were other conditions in the plant that needed improving—such as the cafeteria food and relief from the more than 100-degree heat in the metal shop. Moreover, the steward said, there was at least one other supervisor who should be removed. He implied that, if successful, the power cage protest would facilitate attaining both these ends—namely, employees' prerogatives to dictate the company's problem–solving agenda and to ensure that their own agenda compromised the company's decision–making priorities. The union steward's final comment was that two men on an unauthorized, wildcat strike might accomplish the same thing as a full-blown strike.

Each passing minute was costing the company a production loss of one automotive unit valued at $6,000; the cost of each lost production hour, therefore, was $360,000.

As he began a staff meeting to resolve his dilemma, the plant manager felt pressure to accomplish two objectives: (1) to restore production on the profitless assembly line (a solution about which he was uncertain), and (2) to develop policies for preventing future production interruptions by assembly-line workers.

Source: Adapted from John M. Champion and John H. James, *Critical Incidents in Management: Decisions and Policy Issues,* 5th ed. (Homewood, Ill.: Richard D. Irwin, 1985), pp. 36–37. Copyright 1985 by Richard D. Irwin, Inc.

CASE QUESTIONS

1. What is the real problem in this case?
2. How would each of the approaches to management in this chapter analyze the case?
3. How should the plant manager restore production on the assembly line?
4. What policy, if any, should be developed to prevent future production interruptions?
5. If there is an underlying struggle for power in this situation, precisely where does it lie? Which theoretical approach to management policy is best suited to answer this question? ■

The Hennepin County Center, Minneapolis. John Warnecke and Associates. Photo courtesy of the Hennepin County Public Affairs Dept.

3

THE EXTERNAL ENVIRONMENT OF ORGANIZATIONS

Upon completing this chapter you should be able to:

1. Identify the direct-action and indirect-action environments of organizations and explain why managers must be concerned about them.
2. Describe the stakeholders of an organization and how their stakes have changed in recent years.
3. Describe the four factors that make up the indirect-action environment and explain how they may affect an organization.
4. Discuss the recent changes in the international environment.
5. Define uncertainty and dependence and explain how they vary from one type of environment to another.
6. Describe the ways in which a manager can keep abreast of changes in the environment.

Chapter Outline

Introduction
Change and the Environment
Components of the External Environment
Elements of the Direct-Action Environment
Elements of the Indirect-Action Environment
The International Environment of Organizations
Characteristics of Total Organization Environments
Managing the Total Environment

ILLUSTRATIVE CASE STUDY
Introduction

Image and Imaging Problems at Eastman Kodak

Until the mid-1970s, the name *Kodak* was synonymous with the yellow boxes in which it marketed its products—boxes symbolizing quality film, technically excellent cameras for amateur photographers, and continued profits for investors. The company was known for its determined self-reliance, even maintaining a herd of cattle to provide gelatin for its film process. As an employer, Kodak was a lifetime safe bet for recent high-school and college graduates, and company loyalty among its employees was of the sort more commonly associated today with Japanese companies. There were no strikes in the U.S. plants, and the family-like corporate culture—generous, hierarchical, conservative, fiscally sound—pervaded the company and spun off benefits for the entire Rochester, New York, community. But then the world changed very quickly for Kodak.

Kodak had been slow to respond to new markets opening in its business. Customer tastes had shifted from the cheap but dependable standard product, like the familiar Brownie or Instamatic camera, to the sophisticated VCRs and feature-loaded instant cameras. The electronics revolution made many more options available to amateur photographers and radically altered the technology of the industry. The decline in the use of silver halide film and subsequent increases in electronic image processes made Kodak aware of the success of the instant camera. But when Kodak ventured into the instant camera market, it found itself involved in an embarrassing legal battle with Polaroid over patents; on January 9, 1986, Kodak lost the court battle, and a week later laid off 500 employees.

In addition, there was foreign competition in both cameras and film. While Kodak still has the lion's share of the U.S. color film market, one Japanese firm, Fuji, is moving up fast in quality and market share. In addition, high-end sophisticated equipment manufacturers like Nikon and Minolta developed "point and shoot" cameras for the amateur market as soon as electronics advances made these developments possible.

In light of these troubles, Kodak has reorganized and trimmed its work force—by some 12,000 people worldwide. It may have to close down facilities worth $230 million. Its managers have begun to pay more attention to the external environment and the changes in it. They have begun to speed up their product-development process and have made some acquisitions of innovative companies. In addition, they have begun to rely on others for partnerships in some businesses and have started ventures into biotechnology and electronic publishing.

Sources: Subrata N. Chakravarty and Ruth Simon, "Has the World Passed Kodak By?" *Forbes,* November 5, 1984, pp. 184–192; Barbara Buell, "Kodak Is Trying to Break Out of Its Shell," *Business Week,* June 10, 1985, pp. 92–95; William B. Glaberson, Marilyn A. Harris, and James R. Norman, "Polaroid vs. Kodak: The Decisive Round," *Business Week,* January 13, 1986, p. 37; Alex Taylor III, "Kodak Scrambles to Refocus," *Fortune,* March 3, 1986, pp. 34–39; Leslie Helm and James Hurlock, "Kicking the Single-Product Habit at Kodak," *Business Week,* December 1, 1986, pp. 36–37.

TEACHING TIP

Most students have a hard time seeing the changes taking place in our dynamic environment. However, this chapter provides prime opportunities for bringing in outside materials to illustrate the external environment.

The changes that affected Kodak are not unique to its industry: The external environment of most organizations has changed radically over the last 25 years. In addition to the internal forces to which organizations have always responded, today's organizations must respond to a variety of important external pressures. The purpose of this chapter is to analyze these changes and provide a framework for understanding them. Once we have explained that framework, most of the rest of this book will be devoted to discussing its relationship to management concepts and procedures.

CHANGE AND THE ENVIRONMENT

TEACHING TIP

Have students close their eyes. Tell them you want them to take today's class notes with their eyes closed. After they stop hooting and hollering, explain that a manager who doesn't know anything about his environment is just as ''blind'' as a student trying to take notes with his eyes closed.

FOR DISCUSSION

Why is so much emphasis placed today on examining the external environment? Hasn't the external environment always been important? (Of course it has always been important, but up until about the 1960s the environment was fairly static. We emphasize the external environment because as managers we must recognize that our organizations do not operate in a vacuum. We must be alert to changes happening in the environment that might potentially impact upon our organization.)

The classical, behavioral, and quantitative schools of management focused on aspects of the organization that managers could influence directly, advising managers on how many subordinates they should have, why working conditions should be improved, and how new technology could be used in decision making. But in their concern with the *internal environment* of organizations, they tended to underestimate the importance of the *external environment,* worrying little about the political climate or outside opinion of the organization's business practices. This predisposition was not necessarily bad. When an organization operates in a stable and predictable external environment, its managers need to pay only moderate attention to external conditions.

Today, however, the external environment continuously undergoes rapid changes having far-reaching effects on organizations and their management strategies. For example, Asian and European firms have emerged as strong competitors in a global marketplace; rapid and widespread technological change has become the norm; new information-processing technologies have made it possible to eliminate thousands of middle-management jobs. In addition, the roles of the private and public sectors have become less sharply delineated; even in the United States, a stronghold of capitalism, the government intervened to save Chrysler and exempted a joint research and development consortium of computer manufacturers from antitrust laws. Customer lifestyles, employee demographics, and government regulations are also in flux. Managers are under increasing pressure to think globally and to anticipate and respond to this host of external forces.

At the same time, the standards by which managers are judged have changed. Once it was enough for organizations to maximize profits; managers were judged according to whether they furthered the financial interests of the *stockholders.* Now, organizations must consider the effects of their actions on the quality of life, holding themselves responsible not only to their stockholders but also to the larger and more disparate community of **stakeholders**—those groups or individuals who are affected directly or indirectly by the organization's pursuit of its goals.[1]

stakeholders Those groups or individuals who are directly or indirectly affected by an organization's pursuit of its goals.

As the Ethics in Management box on ''Ethics and Ethnicity in Global Merchandising'' points out, Colgate-Palmolive, at least to some critics, sustained a long-standing policy of racial stereotyping and ethnic condescension in marketing a toothpaste called ''Darkie.'' Colgate's critics argue that such a policy should be unacceptable to the company's average stakeholder and that, to all intents and purposes, the company

[1]For a more complete exposition of the stakeholder approach to management, see R. Edward Freeman, *Strategic Management: A Stakeholder Approach* (Boston: Pitman, 1984).

violated its social responsibility to significant groups of both stakeholders and shareholders. External stakeholders may include unions, suppliers, competitors, customers, special-interest groups, and government agencies. Internal stakeholders consist of employees, shareholders, and the board of directors.

COMPONENTS OF THE EXTERNAL ENVIRONMENT

inputs Resources from the environment, such as raw materials and labor, that may enter any organizational system.

outputs Transformed inputs that are returned to the external environment as products or services.

direct-action elements Elements of the environment that directly influence an organization's activities.

indirect-action elements Elements of the external environment which affect the climate in which an organization's activities take place, including economic and political situations, but which do not affect the organization directly.

The external environment consists of elements outside an organization that are relevant to its operations. Organizations are neither self-sufficient nor self-contained. They exchange resources with the environment and depend on it for their survival. Organizations take **inputs** (raw materials, money, labor, and energy) from the external environment, transform them into products or services, and then send them back as **outputs** to the external environment.

The external environment has both **direct-action** and **indirect-action elements.**[2] Stakeholders directly influence an organization and so are elements of the direct-action environment. Indirect-action elements, such as the technology, economy, or politics of a society, affect the climate in which an organization operates and have the potential to become direct-action elements. This happened in the United States, for example, when changes in public expectations concerning corporate behavior led to the creation of new governmental regulatory agencies. Direct-action elements may also disappear, as in the late 1970s and early 1980s, when budget pressures and public disappointment with regulatory efforts led to the closing or shrinking of some government agencies.

[2]See Alvar O. Elbing, ''On the Applicability of Environmental Models,'' in Joseph W. McGuire, ed., *Contemporary Management: Issues and Viewpoints* (Englewood Cliffs, N.J.: Prentice Hall, 1974), pp. 283–89.

ETHICS IN MANAGEMENT

ETHICS AND ETHNICITY IN GLOBAL MERCHANDISING

After nearly 18 months of research and testing, Colgate-Palmolive Co. is still trying to mollify critics of its Darkie toothpaste brand amid renewed charges that it's moving too slowly to jettison the "racist stereotype" of the Asian-marketed product.

Colgate has tried to find a way to shush American critics of the product—whose logo is a grinning, top-hatted blackface minstrel—while sustaining the 60-year-old brand's appeal to Asians. But members of the Interfaith Center for Corporate Responsibility, a nonprofit New York organization of more than 240 church groups, remain dissatisfied with the pace of Colgate's efforts.

"Most people cannot believe that in the late 1980s this racist stereotype is still in existence anywhere," says Dara Demmings, an Interfaith Center executive, who says the company is dragging its feet.

Stung by such criticism, Colgate began market research on new versions of Darkie, in which it acquired its interest when it bought a 50 percent stake in Darkie's maker, Hawley & Hazel Chemical Co., in 1985. . . . "We've done an enormous amount of work on the logo, but it continues to be a problem," says Gavin Anderson, director of executive services for Colgate. "We thought the solution would be a lot easier," he adds. "Darkie is so ingrained in the culture, particularly in Taiwan. . . .

Meanwhile, critics say they're particularly disturbed that Colgate's Far Eastern partner this month is launching a new toothpaste in Japan, where Darkie has

Figure 3-1 outlines Kodak's environmental picture and shows the influence of both direct- and indirect-action stakeholders. The role of each is discussed in the next section.

TEACHING TIP

Stress Input, Transformation, Output cycle by showing environmental exchanges of organizations. Organizations input resources, transform them, and output goods and services, waste materials, etc.

The practical impact of each element of the environment determines whether it is a stakeholder in an organization and part of its direct-action environment. The same element may have different relationships with different organizations. For example, labor unions may have only a small, indirect impact on a nonunionized industry, such as book publishing, but a major and direct impact on a heavily unionized industry, such as automobile manufacturing. Labor unions would thus be stakeholders of an automaker but not of a book publisher.

ELEMENTS OF THE DIRECT-ACTION ENVIRONMENT

The purpose of this section of the book is to categorize and analyze the roles played by stakeholders in the activities of organizations. In so doing, however, we must first emphasize one major point: Not only do these roles *change,* but they do so in part because organizational environments *evolve*. They develop according to patterns of change that both management theorists and practicing managers must consider as they attempt to trace the various influences on an organization's behavior and to recommend appropriate responses to the fluctuation of those influences.

Environmental Evolution

For example, Emery and Trist have described four idealized environments, or ''causal textures'' which illustrate the natural progress of all environments towards increasing

never had a presence. The tube, labeled "Mouth Jazz," also bears a logo of a smiling, top-hatted blackface.

[This flap began when an American in Thailand sent a Darkie sample to] the Interfaith Center, which has targeted other companies in the past for advertising or product packages its members considered racist or sexist. In Colgate's case, the Interfaith Center; the School Sisters of St. Francis, an order of nuns; and other religious shareholders recently renewed their complaints. . . .

Darkie is sold in Hong Kong, Taiwan, Malaysia, Thailand, and Singapore. Mr. Anderson says Hawley's Chinese founder chose the name after he traveled to the U.S. in the 1920s "and literally fell in love with Al Jolson." Darkie became a big seller and, eventually, an archrival of Colgate. . . . By acquiring its interest, Colgate ended the fight and gained a new market in Taiwan.

Though the Interfaith Center is frustrated with Colgate's pace, Ms. Demmings and the center's director, Timothy Smith, praise Colgate Chairman Reuben Mark and other Colgate executives for their "moral sensitivity to the issue."

The protest has challenged New York-based Colgate, which has been forced to ask Hawley to change a product Asians apparently didn't find offensive in order to satisfy foreign concerns. Colgate says the issue was further complicated when its research showed that Asian consumers associated the logo with nothing more derogatory than clean white teeth. "We were concerned about the image all along, but after research we saw no racial connotations at all for those who buy it," says Mr. Anderson.

Source: Based on Ann Hagedorn, "Colgate Still Seeking to Placate Critics of Its Darkie Brand," *The Wall Street Journal,* April 18, 1988, pp. 36–37.

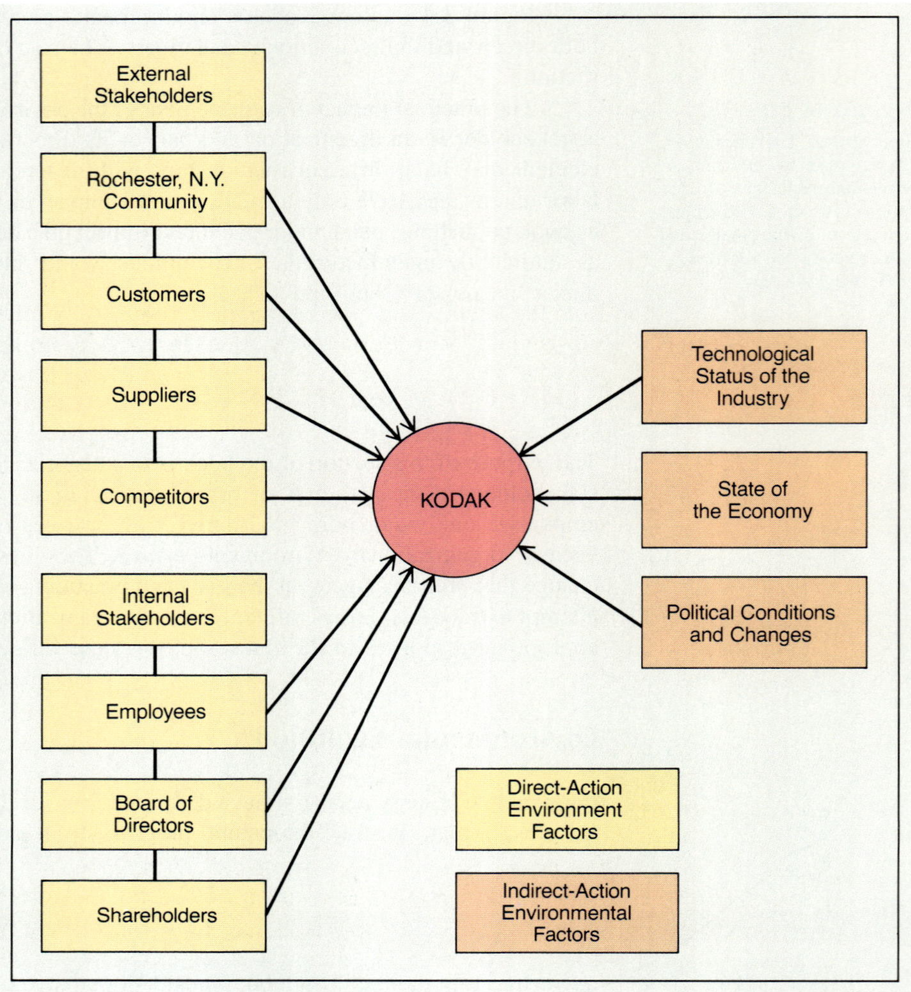

FIGURE 3-1 CHART OF KODAK'S DIRECT-ACTION AND INDIRECT-ACTION ENVIRONMENT

complexity and uncertainty.[3] The placid, randomized environment is stable and unchanging, with resources distributed almost randomly; in this type of environment there is no distinction between strategy and tactics, and managers must learn by trial and error. The placid, clustered environment is also stable, but resources are concentrated in certain locations that become the focus of the manager's job. The disturbed-reactive environment is unstable, with concentrated resources and multiple competing organizations; location is less important than the ability to meet competitive challenges. Change is even more rapid in the turbulent environment. The number of organizations and the linkages between them are growing, as are the connections among the social, political, economic, and technological spheres of society; competition depends increasingly on research and development.

Environments tend to become more turbulent over time, although turbulence grows more quickly in some industries than in others. Ansoff has described the organi-

[3] F. Emery and E. Trist, "The Causal Texture of Organizational Environments," *Human Relations* 18 (August 1965):124–51.

zational predicament as turbulence increases.[4] Events are less predictable, changes are more frequent, and past experience is less relevant to current decision making. Organizations need more time and greater knowledge of the environments in order to respond successfully, and they must devote more of their resources to monitoring the environment, applying increasingly complex forecasting technologies, and developing strategies.

Organizational Stakeholders

Both the internal and external stakeholder groups of most organizations have changed substantially over the past few years. In this section, beginning with **external stakeholders,** we will outline the stake of each group and how it has changed.

external stakeholders Groups or individuals that affect an organization's activities from its external environment.

BACKGROUND ON BABY BOOMERS

Consumers aged 35 to 44 will soon be the nation's biggest spenders. This group's purchasing power will grow an incredible $195 billion to $939 billion by 1997 (less than 10 years from now). A sizable market awaits those companies astute enough to have the right goods and services for this group. (*Fortune*, 2/1/88, pp. 68–77)

External Stakeholders. *Customers* exchange resources, usually in the form of money, for an organization's products and services. Selling tactics vary according to customer and market situations. Usually, a marketing manager analyzes the potential customers and market conditions and directs a marketing campaign based on that analysis. A customer may be an institution, such as a school, hospital, or government agency; it may be another firm, such as a contractor, distributor, or manufacturer; or it may be the individual consumer.

Naturally, the customer market may be highly competitive, with large numbers of potential buyers and sellers seeking the most congenial arrangements. In such markets, managers must be especially concerned about price, quality, service, and product availability if they want to keep old customers and attract new ones.

In recent years, as foreign firms have challenged the dominance of American business by offering customers more choices and setting new standards of quality, competition has begun to change customer relationships. For example, when Japanese television manufacturers found it difficult to set up service networks for their products in the United States, they responded by making televisions that simply were less likely to malfunction. Whereas the old customer relationship with a television manufacturer was once cemented by the availability of the local dealer and repair shop, customers were soon able to buy televisions at large discount retailers. A similar pattern has emerged in the U.S. auto industry.

New technology, by making communications and transportation inexpensive and accessible, has also led to some homogenization of markets throughout the world. People around the globe are now exposed to the latest and best products, and as a result, customers in different countries have become potential customers for the same goods.[5] Manufacturers can now think in terms of a world car, for example, or a worldwide computer networking system.

CLASS COMMENT

A one-page advertisement in the *Wall Street Journal,* in May 1988, listing several companies was Ford Motor Company's way of saying "Thanks for the Quality" to its suppliers. Ford's Q1 Preferred Quality Award is a special tribute to those suppliers helping the car company produce the highest quality American cars and trucks. Ford made clear by this advertisement that they recognized the role suppliers take in helping them achieve their goal of Quality Job 1.

Suppliers. Every organization appropriates raw materials, services, energy, equipment, and labor from the environment and uses them to produce its output. What the organization brings in from the environment—and what it *does* with what it brings in—will determine both the quality and the price of its final product, and every organization is therefore dependent upon the suppliers of materials and labor.

Organizations usually deal with suppliers of materials, services, and energy through a purchasing manager or an agent. The purchasing manager has relationships with several competing suppliers, and he or she may choose on occasion to pay a higher unit price in order to keep the organization from becoming overly dependent on

[4] I. Ansoff, *Strategic Management* (New York: Halsted Press, 1981).

[5] Theodore Levitt, *The Marketing Imagination,* (New York: Free Press, 1983), pp. 20–49.

a single supplier. The purchasing agent takes advantage of competition among suppliers to obtain lower prices, better quality work, and faster deliveries.

Today, as organizations look overseas for more and more of their raw materials, their relationships with suppliers have changed, sometimes dramatically. For example political considerations can be as important as those of price and quality. Witness the strategy used by the OPEC nations to quadruple the price of oil in 1973–74 and then double it in 1979–80.[6] In this instance, the supplier organization has become less effective in recent years, since the rise in the price of oil led to energy conservation and made both oil-extraction in marginal areas and alternative energy sources more cost-effective. From a manager's standpoint, however, the power in the relationship has shifted irrevocably away from the oil refiners to the petroleum-exporting nations—that is, to the suppliers. In this instance, we also have a good example of the environmental complexity facing today's manager: Managers not only have to know which organizations affect them *directly,* but which organizations affect the organizations affecting them!

Advances in inventory control and information processing have also changed supplier relationships. Under the conventional system, the manufacturer was usually responsible for all of the inventory necessary for production capability. Today, however, some companies keep zero inventory, relying on several "just in time" deliveries each day. Suppliers such as American Hospital Supply have used new information technology to put computer terminals on the customer's premises so that the customer can directly order a product whenever it is needed. Regular customers of Emery Air Freight receive personal computer systems that not only weigh packages, calculate charges, and generate air bills, but also consolidate shipments, give them a direct link to Emery's computer tracking system, and generate management reports about their shipping activity. Changes in the supplier relationship continue.

Finally, we should note the increasingly important role played by a particular group of suppliers called *vendors.* Vendors supply materials and services necessary to an organization's specific production activities (for example, parts, either finished or ready for assembly) or general operations. A company that produces airplanes will contract with a vendor that specializes in the design and production of guidance systems and another that specializes in flying-control systems. Automobile manufacturers rely on vendors for such items as windshields and tires. Purchasing managers must develop firm relationships with vendors and maintain constant, careful control over those relationships. Shortages, untimely deliveries, and fluctuating prices are only a few of the variables that can develop in an organization's relationship with its vendors.

COORDINATED RESOURCES

Three videotapes from the Enterprise series that would clearly illustrate the economic impacts of deregulation are: "Dogfight over New York" (about upstart New York Air's drive to become a competitor in the lucrative northeast corridor long dominated by Eastern Airline's Shuttle); "Gulliver's New Travels" (a critical look at AT&T's future as its telephone monopoly ends); and "Tailspin" (an in-depth look at the airline industry's first combatant to declare bankruptcy, Braniff). These videotapes are available from LCA, 108 Wilmont Road, Deerfield, IL 60015-9990, or call 800-621-2131.

Governments. From World War I through the early 1980s, the government has been regarded as increasingly involved with the private sector in its role as "watchdog." It regulates organizations in the public interest and enforces strict antitrust laws to ensure adherence to market principles. Regulatory agencies, such as the Federal Communications Commission (FCC) and the Occupational Safety and Health Administration (OSHA), establish and enforce ground rules within which an industry must operate. In addition, Congress and the courts have always played a major role, at least indirectly, in shaping the strategies and policies of the modern organization. Anyone who would like to know just how careful an eye the U.S. government keeps on our organizational activities may consult Exhibit 3-1. Our list is drawn from a recent source. However, its contents reflect much about the evolution of American history and the role that government has attempted to play in it: Even this abbreviated list runs the gamut from the Railroad Retirement Board to the National Aeronautics and Space Administration. Needless to say, the names and numbers of the players change with some frequency.

[6] "Beware Cheap Oil," *The Economist,* March 12, 1988, pp. 12–13.

EXHIBIT 3-1 U.S. GOVERNMENT INDEPENDENT AGENCIES

Appalachian Regional Commission—Winifred A. Pizzano, federal co-chmn.; Gov. Arch A. Moore Jr. of West Virginia, states' co-chmn. (1666 Connecticut Ave. NW, 20235).

Board for International Broadcasting—Malcolm S. Forbes Jr., chmn. (1201 Connecticut Ave., 20036).

Central Intelligence Agency—Robert M. Gates, act. dir. (Wash., DC 20505).

Commodity Futures Trading Commission—Susan M. Phillips, chmn. (2033 K St. NW, 20581).

Consumer Product Safety Commission—Terrence Scanlon, chmn. (5401 Westbard Ave., Bethesda, MD 20207).

Environmental Protection Agency—Lee M. Thomas, adm. (401 M St., SW, 20460).

Equal Employment Opportunity Commission—Clarence Thomas, chmn. (2401 E St., NW, 20507).

Farm Credit Administration—Frank W. Naylor Jr. chmn., Federal Farm Credit Board (1501 Farm Credit Drive, McLean, VA 22102).

Federal Communications Commission—Dennis R. Patrick, chmn. (1919 M St. NW, 20554).

Federal Deposit Insurance Corporation—L. William Seidman, chmn. (550 17th St. NW, 20429).

Federal Labor Relations Authority—Jerry L. Calhoun, chmn. (500 C St. SW, 20424).

Federal Reserve System—Chairman, board of governors: Alan Greenspan. (20th St. & Constitution Ave. NW, 20551).

Federal Trade Commission—Daniel Oliver, chmn. (Pennsylvania Ave. at 6th St. NW, 20580).

General Accounting Office—Comptroller General of the U.S.: Charles A. Bowsher (441 G St. NW, 20548).

General Services Administration—Terence C. Golden, adm. (18th & F Sts. NW, 20405).

Interstate Commerce Commission—Heather J. Gradison, chmn. (12th St. and Constitution Ave. NW, 20423).

Library of Congress—James H. Billington, librarian (101 Independence Ave. SE, 20540).

National Aeronautics and Space Administration—James C. Fletcher, adm. (600 Independence Ave., SW 20546).

National Labor Relations Board—Donald L. Dotson, chmn. (1717 Pennsylvania Ave. NW, 20570).

National Transportation Safety Board—James E. Burnett, chmn. (800 Independence Ave. SW, 20594).

Nuclear Regulatory Commission—Lando W. Zech Jr., chmn. (1717 H St. NW, 20555).

Occupational Safety and Health Review Commission—E. Ross Buckley, chmn. (1825 K St. NW, 20006).

Postal Rate Commission—Janet D. Steiger, chmn. (1333 H. St. NW, 20268-0001).

Railroad Retirement Board—Robert A. Gielow, chmn. (1333 H St. NW, 20268-0001). Main Office (844 Rush St. Chicago, IL 60611).

Securities and Exchange Commission—David S. Ruder, chmn. (450 5th St. NW, 20549).

Selective Service System—Wilfred Ebel, act. dir. (National Headquarters, 20435).

Small Business Administration—James Abdnor, adm. (1441 L St. NW, 20416).

United States Arms Control & Disarmament Agency—Kenneth L. Adelman, dir. (320 21st St. NW 20451).

United States International Trade Commission—Susan Wittenberg-Liebeler, chairwoman (701 E St. NW, 20436).

United States Postal Service—Preston R. Tisch, postmaster general (475 L'Enfant Plaza West SW, 20260).

Veterans Administration—Thomas K. Turnage, adm. (810 Vermont Ave. NW, 20420).

Note: Address—Washington, D.C. Location and ZIP codes of agencies are in parentheses.

Source: National Archives Records Administration.

The scope of government intervention in the economy has expanded since World War II. Gone are the days when an organization could rely on trade and lobbying groups such as the U.S. Chamber of Commerce to manage its relationship with government. And as government intervention has grown, it has also become increasingly controversial. On the one hand, it promises genuine social benefits, such as cleaner air and water, safer automobiles, and a general increase in the standard of living; it can also be argued that regulation benefits and protects the regulated industries themselves. On the other hand, regulation is costly and may inhibit free enterprise.

This debate became even more heated when the Reagan administration began its attempts to reform regulatory law in 1981, claiming that deregulation would result in savings of $150 billion by 1990.[7] While supporters argued that regulation did not always achieve its goals and that free enterprise could do the job more cost-effectively,[8] opponents claimed that deregulation was a return to the law of the jungle.[9]

Whatever the merits of regulation as a specific governmental prerogative, managers must deal with a complex web of local, state, federal, foreign, and international governments, each with the potential to affect an organization through legislative initiatives, judicial action, and executive regulation. (See Fig. 3-2.) For example, they must cope with contradictory regulations by different federal agencies. They have to understand the workings of foreign governments, which may be deliberately placing obstacles in their path in an effort to protect domestic organizations. They must deal with conflicting state laws, such as the tax and packaging requirements for beer. They have to fight product-liability, equal-opportunity, and antitrust suits in court. They must weigh state incentive plans in their decisions about plant locations and plant closings. They even have to cope with citizen initiatives such as bottle deposit laws. Obviously, the cumulative effect of all this governmental consideration is enormous.

However, even though managers must respond to government activity, effective managers can also help shape the direction of public policy. In 1984, for example, corporations successfully blocked government efforts to tighten controls on the export of high-technology products in the interest of national security. They advocated self-regulation instead. If the concept of corporate social responsibility continues to gain ground, agreements and compromises between corporations and stakeholders may reduce the pressure for government intervention.

CLASS COMMENT

Fast-food outlets are opening in, of all places, hospitals across the United States. Hospital spokespeople are supporting the practice by saying the restaurants supplement a hospital's regular food services and are targeted at staff and visitors, not patients. Medical advocacy groups are opposing the move. Howard Lewis, spokesman for the American Heart Association says, "We feel hospitals should provide leadership in health care." (*Springfield News-Leader*, 7/15/88, p. 5)

Special Interest Groups. Consumer and environmental advocates are examples of a more general trend towards "special interest groups" (SIGs) that use the political process to further a position on some particular issue such as gun control, abortion, or prayer in the schools. Managers can never be sure that an ad hoc group will not form to oppose the company on any particular issue—selling nonstandard infant formula in the Third World, for example, or investing in South Africa.

While special interest politics is hardly a new phenomenon, modern communications technology and election financing have allowed SIGs to flourish.[10] The media provide such groups with national attention, while Political Action Committees (PACs) use campaign contributions to influence legislators.[11] Managers must take both present and future special interest groups into account when setting organizational strategy. Among the most important special interest groups are *consumer advocates* and *environmentalists*.

The modern consumer movement dates from the early 1960s, with President Kennedy's announcement of a "Consumer Bill of Rights" and Ralph Nader's crusade against the General Motors Corvair. While government agencies became less responsive in the Reagan era, consumer advocates still exist.

Hirschmann's model of exit, voice, and loyalty provides a framework for understanding the consumer movement.[12] Dissatisfied customers can choose either to *exit*—that is, to take their business elsewhere—or to *voice* their complaints; the customers' *loyalty* to the organization will determine the option. Exit can of course cripple an

---

[7]Henry Eason, "Deregulation: Dream Deferred," *Nation's Business*, February 1984, pp. 24–26.

[8]See Robert A. Leone, "Examining Deregulation," *Harvard Business Review* 62, no. 4 (July–August 1984):56–58.

[9]Susan J. Tolchin and Martin Tolchin, *Dismantling America: The Rush to Deregulate* (Boston: Houghton-Mifflin, 1983).

[10]G. Wilson, *Interest Groups in the United States* (New York: Oxford University Press, 1981).

[11]E. Epstein, "Business Political Activity: Research Approaches and Analytical Issues," in L. Preston, ed., *Research in Corporate Responsibility and Social Policy, Volume 2* (Greenwich: JAI Press, 1980).

[12]A. Hirschmann, *Exit, Voice and Loyalty* (Cambridge: Harvard University Press, 1970).

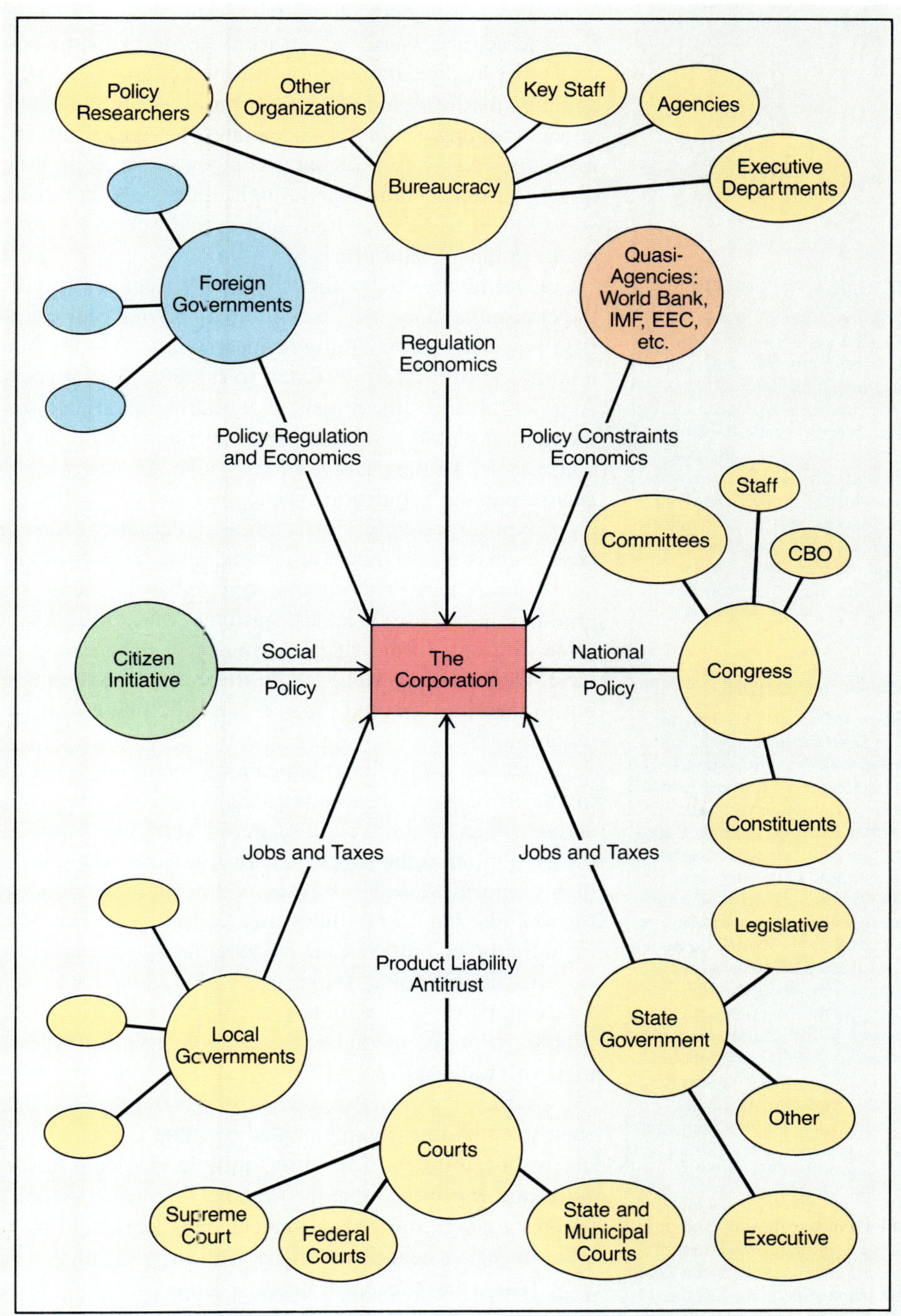

Source: R. Edward Freeman, *Strategic Management: A Stakeholder Approach* (Boston: Pitman, 1984), p. 15. Copyright 1984 by R. Edward Freeman.

FIGURE 3-2 BUSINESS–GOVERNMENT RELATIONSHIPS IN THE UNITED STATES

organization because it removes the customer base without giving managers time to make changes; in contrast, voice is a political strategy designed to signal the need for change and to seek redress for grievance. Filing lawsuits requesting regulatory intervention of a regulatory agency and lobbying a law-making body are examples of the exercise of voice.

From this perspective, the consumer movement and its use of voice is constructive and not necessarily adversarial. Recognizing the costs of government intervention, consumer leaders are often open to voluntarism and negotiation, and it is in fact management that is all too often adversarial despite the fact that managers should welcome voice as an opportunity to understand customer needs and to learn about changes in the marketplace. Many successful companies, such as Procter & Gamble, do make handling consumer complaints a high priority. AT&T has even formed Consumer Advisory Panels (CAPs) to help understand consumer reactions to proposed changes in rates, products, and services.

HERE'S AN EXAMPLE

DuPont Company has announced plans to phase out production of environmentally harmful chlorfluorocarbons, which have been scientifically linked to the ozone depletion problem. However, the phase-out and substitution of environmentally safer products could take several years and would require global cooperation. (See Lecture Extras Supplement for an additional lecture on this topic.) (*Wall Street Journal*, 3/25/88, p. 2)

During the 1960s, the public also became aware of the threat sometimes posed to the environment by new technology. The first national debate over the costs and benefits of a particular technology concerned the building of the supersonic transport (SST), a commercial aircraft designed to fly routinely at speeds greater than that of sound. Activists attacked the project as wasteful and argued that the sonic boom generated by the aircraft would harm the ozone layer and the oceans. These and other environmental concerns led to the passage of the Clean Air and Water Acts and to the creation of the Environmental Protection Agency.

Not surprisingly, environmental regulations have imposed extra burdens on business. Emissions standards, for example, required the development of the catalytic converter as part of the automotive exhaust system, reduced engine performance by eliminating the use of leaded gasoline, and, of course, added to the overall purchase price of a car. In the chemical industry, the cleanup costs for generations of neglect have become staggering. While there are no easy answers, managers have no choice but to take into account today's current climate of broad and genuine concern for the environment.

CLASS COMMENT

Firms are setting up plans to help deal with corporate crises. When a Boston area supermarket received a phone call from a man claiming to have poisoned several cans of Campbell Tomato juice with strychnine, Campbell Soup Company's new crisis-planning and management team was ready to act. Within six hours, Campbell employees had removed the tomato juice stock from all 84 stores in the supermarket chain. Robert A. Smith, Director of Corporate Safety and Services for Dow Chemical Company, states, "We have to be prepared in case the unimaginable ever happens." (*Wall Street Journal*, 12/7/87)

Media. Mass communications technology has revolutionized the role of the media in business. Large organizations today live in a fishbowl, with virtually all activity open to some form of public scrutiny. As investigative reporters have turned their attention to the private sector, managers have had to face "unfair" stories about their companies, their products, and even their characters in the press or on television. Movies like *Wall Street* have made corporate maneuvering a subject fit for big-screen melodrama, and in 1984, dramatic same-day newsreel footage made the Union Carbide catastrophe in Bhopal, India, much more than a mere news story about one company's safety policies in a remote part of the world. (See the Illustrative Case Study for Chapter 17.) The media, pervasive and provocative, provides yet another challenge to modern managers.

collective bargaining The process of negotiating and administering agreements between labor and management concerning wages, working conditions, and other aspects of the work environment.

Labor Unions. Personnel specialists generally deal with an organization's labor supply, sometimes supplemented by other managers with specific hiring and negotiating responsibilities. They use multiple channels to locate workers with the varying skills and experience that the organization needs. When an organization employs labor union members, union and management normally engage in some form of **collective bargaining** to negotiate wages, working conditions, hours, and so on.

There have been dramatic changes in labor relations in recent decades. Both personnel and union management have been professionalized. Also, employers generally accept the collective bargaining process and, in cooperation with the unions, have increased worker responsibility and participation. The sit-down strikes and violence that so often characterized the unions' early days are for the most part gone. Instead, unions urge stock-ownership, profit-sharing, and gain-sharing programs that give the workers a stake in the organization, and quality-of-worklife programs that give workers more control over what they do and how they do it.[13]

[13]See David H. Rosenbloom and Jay M. Shafritz, *Essentials of Labor Relations* (Reston, Va.: Reston Publishing, 1985), and Arthur A. Sloane and Fred Witney, *Labor Relations*, 6th ed. (Englewood Cliffs, N.J.: Prentice Hall, 1988).

Financial Institutions. Organizations depend on a variety of financial institutions, including commercial banks, investment banks, and insurance companies, to maintain and expand their activities. Both new and well-established organizations may rely on short-term loans to finance current operations or long-term loans to build new facilities or acquire new equipment. Because effective working relationships with financial institutions are so vitally important, establishing and maintaining such relationships is normally the joint responsibility of both the chief financial officer and the chief operating officer of the organization—a responsibility that has been made considerably more difficult by the many enormous changes taking place in the financial industry.

One change is that large full-service investment houses are replacing older partnership arrangements. For example, in order to broaden the financial services that it could offer, American Express acquired international and investment banks, insurance companies, and mutual funds in the 1980s. Another recent development is insider-trading charges against investment bankers that have caused turmoil in the industry, as has the 1987 stock market crash—which has been linked in part to sophisticated computer trading programs. Similarly, arbitrage departments have fueled the takeover and merger trend, and there are growing linkages among world stock and money markets. Moreover, deregulation of the banking industry is increasing competition at the same time that many banks have been weakened by the failure of loans to domestic energy companies and developing countries.

HERE'S AN EXAMPLE

Sun Microsystems, a fast-growing computer maker, is taking aim at the computer industry's long-time reliance on competing on proprietary technology. Company executives have outlined a bold strategy to lead a revolution in the computer industry by offering industrywide standards for hardware and software. Sun's president and CEO, Scott McNealy, is being bombarded with a lot of criticism, but stoically replies, "I guess that's what happens when you're trying to change the whole industry." (*Wall Street Journal,* 3/18/88, p. 1)

Competitors. In order to increase its share of the market, a firm must take advantage of one of two opportunities: (1) it must gain additional customers, either by garnering a greater market share or by finding ways of increasing the size of the market itself; or (2) it must beat its competitors in entering and exploiting an expanding market. In either case, it must therefore analyze the competition and establish a clearly defined marketing strategy in order to provide superior customer satisfaction.[14]

Airline firms such as Eastern, American, Piedmont, TWA, and their foreign counterparts are clearly competitors in the American air-carrier market. But competition can also come from organizations that provide substitute products or services. In the northeast corridor, for example, Amtrak metroliners compete with airlines for intercity shuttle service. The world petroleum crisis that started in the 1970s drew attention to the competitive interrelationships in the energy industry; thus, while Texaco, Mobil, and Exxon compete against one another in the sale of petroleum, they share the common problem of competition from the coal, nuclear, solar, and geothermal industries, all of which provide energy-producing substitutes.

Sometimes, competition is limited. In an oligopolistic market, for example, relatively few sellers confront large numbers of buyers; the sellers may then informally divide the market up among themselves and set prices. In a monopoly, every customer must buy from one available source, such as an electric utility. Sometimes a firm enjoys a temporary monopoly, as was the case with Xerox when it first introduced the electrostatic copier. Monopolies are frequently subject to government regulation.

In recent years, the competition for U.S. organizations has broadened to include foreign firms. In the 1950s "Made in Japan" meant "junk" or "cheap"; in the 1980s, however, it became a hallmark of quality because the success of Japanese products ranging from cars to cameras has been enormous. Many products, such as televisions and video cassette recorders, are often not made in the United States today. There is competition from abroad in almost every "U.S. dominant" industry.

Foreign competition poses a special problem. As long as all significant competition is domestic, everyone must play by the same rules. Each competitor bears the burdens and shares the benefits of the same government, the same fickle consumer population, and the same special interest groups. Firms within an industry can implic-

---

[14]See Lyn S. Wilson, "Managing in the Competitive Environment," *Long Range Planning* 17, no. 1 (February 1983):59–64.

itly or explicitly coordinate their responses to various issues, and theoretically no one is at a competitive disadvantage. Not only does foreign competition upset this balance, but it is much more difficult to analyze the competition when that entails learning about another culture.

Other Stakeholder Groups. Each individual organization will have a host of different stakeholders. For instance, a hospital will have to consider the American Hospital Association, groups of doctors, nurses, and other caregivers, and of course, patients. Any organization will have a fairly unique stakeholder map that will in essence be a picture of the direct action component of its external environment. Figure 3-3 is just one example of how one organization, a hypothetical "major oil company," may experience changes in its stakeholder map over a 30-year period.

internal stakeholders Groups or individuals, such as employees, which are not strictly part of an organization's environment but for whom an individual manager remains responsible.

CLASS COMMENT

A 1986 poll, conducted by *Business Week* and Louis Harris and Associates, of middle managers at 600 corporations from the Business Week 1000 showed that employee loyalty toward corporations has dropped dramatically. A large majority (65 percent) of the respondents felt that salaried employees were less loyal to their companies compared with 10 years ago.

BACKGROUND ON CORPORATE BOARDS

The legal principle that directors and managers must be responsible to shareholders is beginning to be honored by companies. Through proxy fights and lawsuits, aggressive shareholders are winning more control of the companies they own. Directors are being forced to shape up and do their jobs. What will occur ultimately is a change in the way companies are managed. (*Fortune,* 7/18/88, pp. 58–67)

Internal Stakeholders. Even though, strictly speaking, **internal stakeholders** are not part of the organization's environment, they are a part of the environment for which an individual manager is responsible. While we shall return to these stakeholders in other chapters, it is worth spending a few minutes here to complete the stakeholder picture.

Employees. The nature of the work force is changing in most organizations, in part because of demographic factors. The so-called baby-boom generation is getting older, and the declining birth rate means that the United States will soon face a labor shortage. At the same time, the skills needed by employees are changing. As more companies find it necessary to experiment with quality programs, team approaches, and self-managed work groups, employees must be better educated and more flexible.

Employee involvement paid off at an AMAX coal mine, for example, when the miners, not the engineers, thought of a way to keep open the main operating face of the mine at moderate expense; it was also the miners who were able to reclaim old, cast-off equipment until it was among the best in the company's inventory.[15]

Shareholders and Boards of Directors. The governing structure of large public corporations gives shareholders the opportunity to influence a company by exercising voting rights. Traditionally, however, shareholders have been interested primarily in the return on their investment and have left the actual operation of the organization to its managers.

In recent years, however, certain groups of social activists have begun purchasing small quantities of stock for the purpose of forcing votes on controversial issues at annual corporate meetings.[16] Ralph Nader pioneered the technique in 1969, when he launched "Campaign GM," whereby an ad hoc group bought two shares of General Motors stock with the intention of waging a proxy fight on social and business issues, including the need for public transportation, the rights of women and minorities, product design for safety, and emissions control.[17] A Securities and Exchange Commission ruling of 1983 made it more difficult to carry out this particular tactic,[18] but the tactic of share ownership to seize control of entire companies continues to be common business policy. Mergers and hostile takeovers, often spurred by the legitimate need to reorganize American manufacturing methods, nevertheless have to justify large expenditures of capital by cutting back operations and liquidating assets, and many managers are thus on the defensive, sometimes ignoring the long-term health of their

---

[15]Tom Peters, *Thriving on Chaos* (New York: Alfred A. Knopf, 1988), p. 289.

[16]David Vogel, "Trends in Shareholder Activism: 1970–1982," *California Management Review* 25, no. 3 (Spring 1983):68–87.

[17]Ralph Nader, *Unsafe at Any Speed* (New York: Grossman Publishers, 1972).

[18]Richard L. Hudson, "SEC Tightens Annual Meeting Proposal Rules," *Wall Street Journal,* August 17, 1983, p. 4.

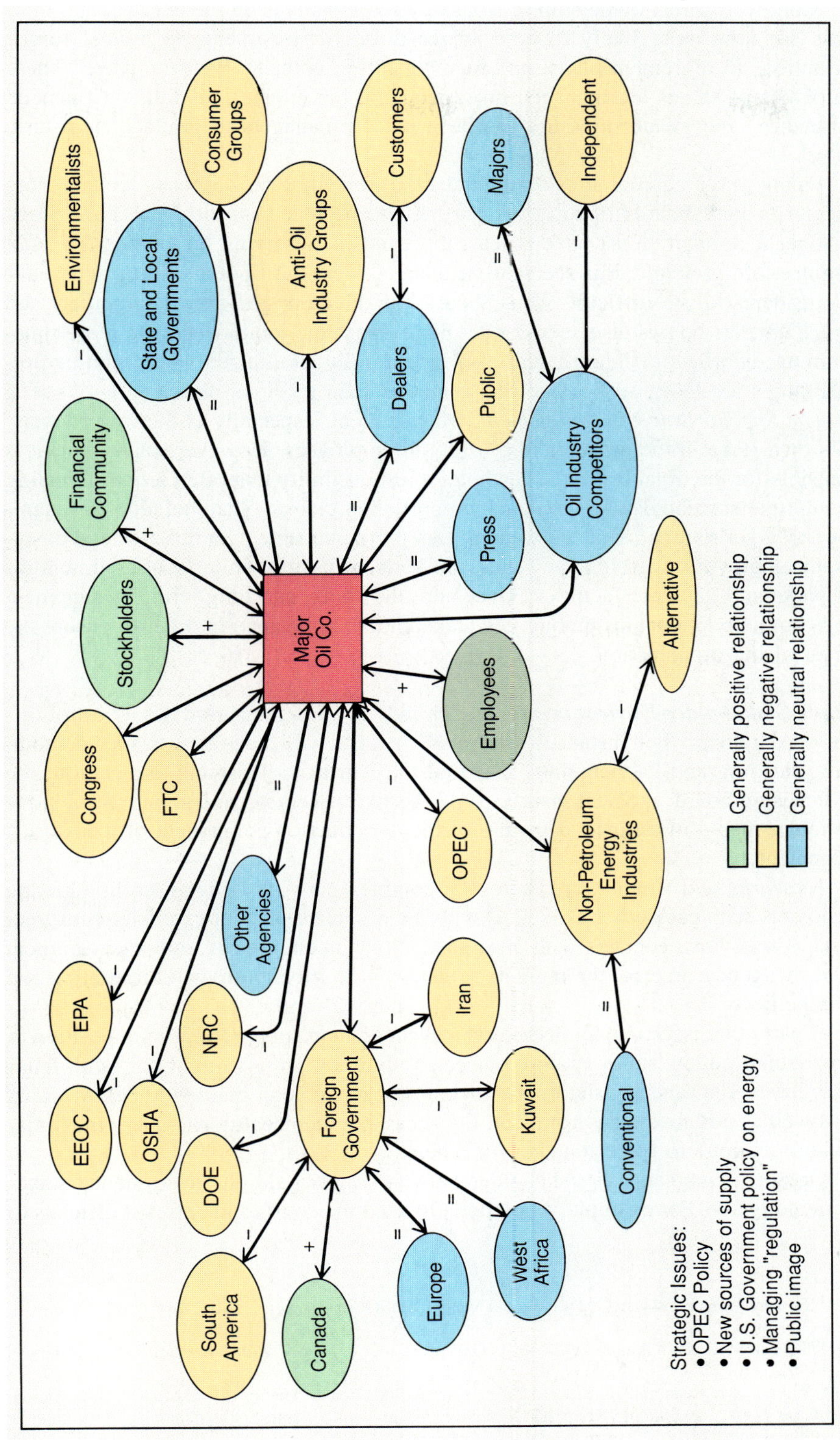

FIGURE 3-3 STAKEHOLDER MAP OF MAJOR OIL CO. IN 1980s

organizations in their efforts to keep current profits and stock prices up so as to discourage takeover attempts.[19]

Moreover, direct ownership of stocks by individuals is on the decline, and individuals are now more likely to hold shares through investments in mutual funds, contributions to retirement plans, and membership in company pension plans. These large blocks of shares are managed professionally; the emphasis is thus on financial performance, and greater pressure has been put on managers to produce short-term results.

Finally, political pressures during the 1970s forced organizations to include more outsiders on their boards of directors. In fact, to be listed on the New York Stock Exchange, a company must have at least three outsiders serving on the board's audit committees. In principle, this seems to be a sound idea, but finding willing and qualified outsiders can be difficult. Thus, boards of directors are growing smaller, and although smaller boards also seem to get more done, the job has become more time-consuming; conflicts of interest will also be carefully scrutinized and committee responsibilities are likely to become greater rather than lesser in number.[20]

TEACHING TIP

Emphasize the *balance* among key stakeholders and how this ensures organizational survival. Use a company example (such as McDonald's or DuPont Chemical or Chrysler) to illustrate how overemphasis on or ignorance of key stakeholders could harm the organization. What if Chrysler ignored consumer advocates? What if McDonald's listened only to its suppliers? etc.

The Special Role of Management. Management, especially at the lower levels, has its own stake in the organization, as do all employees. However, management is responsible for the organization as a whole, a responsibility that often requires dealing with multiple stakeholders and balancing conflicting claims. Shareholders, for example, want larger returns, while customers want more investment on research and development; employees want higher wages and better benefits, while local communities want parks and day-care facilities. Over both the short- and long-term, management must keep the relationships among key stakeholders in balance in order to ensure the survival of the organization.[21]

EXTRA EXERCISE

Have students develop unique stakeholder maps for some companies (Wal-Mart, American Ballet Theatre, Coca-Cola, a small business in your town, etc.). It might be interesting and revealing to put these examples side-by-side for comparison and contrast purposes.

Multiple Stakeholder Environments. Each individual organization has a host of different stakeholders. For instance, a hospital manager will have to consider doctors, nurses, cleaning and kitchen staff, patients, the American Hospital Association, the state licensing board, medical insurers, and the like. Every organization has a unique stakeholder map—in essence, a picture of the direct-action component of its external environment.

Networks and Coalitions. There is a complex network of relationships linking stakeholders with each other as well as with the organization. For example, consumer advocates may have contacts with an organization, its employees, and a government regulatory agency; in turn, the regulatory agency will affect both the organization and its competitors.

A particular issue may unite several stakeholders in support of or in opposition to organizational policy.[22] For example, special advocacy groups might join with labor unions, the media, and legislators to block a new technology that could cost workers jobs as well as pollute the environment. On occasion, such coalitions outlive the initial issue and continue to work together on others.

Organizations can use stakeholder networks and coalitions to influence stakeholders indirectly. For example, Marathon Oil used the courts and antitrust officials to

---

[19]Edward L. Hennessy Jr., "The Raiders Make It Harder to Compete," *New York Times,* March 13, 1988, p. F3.

[20]George Melloan, "A Good Director Is Getting Harder to Find," *Wall Street Journal,* February 9, 1988, p. 39.

[21]William M. Evan and R. Edward Freeman, "A Stakeholder Theory of the Modern Corporation: Kantian Capitalism," in *Ethical Theory and Business,* 3rd ed., ed. by Tom L. Beauchamp and Norman E. Bowie (Englewood Cliffs, N.J.: Prentice Hall, 1988), pp. 102–103.

[22]W. Graham Astley, "Toward an Appreciation of Collective Strategy," *Academy of Management Review* 9 (1984):526–35; W. Graham Astley and Charles J. Fombrun, "Collective Strategy: Social Ecology of Organizational Environments," *Academy of Management Review* 8 (1983):576–87.

delay a takeover bid from Mobil and give it time to search for another company to come to its rescue; other companies have even enlisted employees and stockholders in letter-writing campaigns. Such strategies have been known to work but, at present, little has been done to formulate their details.

Multiple Roles. A single individual or group may have multiple relationships with an organization.[23] A toy company employee, for example, may also be a parent who purchases the company's products, a shareholder with an investment in the company, a member of a consumer advocate group lobbying for stricter safety codes for children's products, and a member of a political party with pronounced ideas about free trade and protectionism. Thus, stakeholders may have to balance conflicting roles in determining what action they want the organization to take.

ELEMENTS OF THE INDIRECT-ACTION ENVIRONMENT

FOR DISCUSSION
Cite some instances in which an indirect-action element could become a stakeholder in a firm's direct-action environment. (Example: Hairdressers and beauticians testifying before Congressional committees could force changes in labeling and packaging; changing societal attitudes towards AIDS could bring about changes in employee hiring and firing; etc.)

The indirect-action component of the external environment affects organizations in two ways. First, forces may dictate the formation of a group that eventually becomes a stakeholder. Second, indirect-action elements create a climate—rapidly changing technology, economic growth or decline, changes in attitudes toward work—in which the organization exists and to which it may ultimately have to respond. For example, today's computer technology makes possible the acquisition, storage, coordination, and transfer of large amounts of information about individuals. Banks and other business firms use this technology to maintain, store, process, and exchange information about the credit status of potential borrowers. Individuals concerned about the misuse of such data might thus form a special-interest pressure group to seek voluntary changes in bank business practices. If this group were to organize a successful boycott of a particular bank, it would become a stakeholder of that bank and enter its direct-action environment.

Environmental Variables

Fahey and Narayanan have grouped these complex interactions into four broad factors that influence the organization and must be considered by its managers: social, economic, political, and technological.[24] Figure 3-4 illustrates the interrelationships of the indirect-action and the direct-action environments and the organization.

Social Variables. Values are the foundation of our lives and our world. They drive all the other social, political, technological, and economic changes, and they determine all the choices we make in life.

social variables Factors, such as demographics and social values, that may influence an organization from its external environment.

Fahey and Narayanan divide **social variables** into three categories: demographics, lifestyle, and social values. Demographic and lifestyle changes affect the composition, the location, and the expectations of an organization's labor supply and customers. Values underlie all other social, political, technological, and economic changes and determine all the choices that people make in life. Social values also set the guidelines that determine how most organizations and managers will operate. Sometimes the guidelines will be relatively narrow, such as the restrictions on black workers

[23]R. Edward Freeman and Daniel R. Gilbert, Jr., "Managing Stakeholder Relationships," in *Business and Society: Dimensions of Conflict and Cooperation,* ed. by S. Prakash Sethi and Cecilia M. Falbe (Lexington, Mass.: Lexington Books, 1987).

[24]Our discussion of the indirect-action variables in the following sections is largely drawn from Liam Fahey and V. K. Narayanan, *Macroenvironmental Analysis for Strategic Management* (St. Paul: West Publishing, 1986).

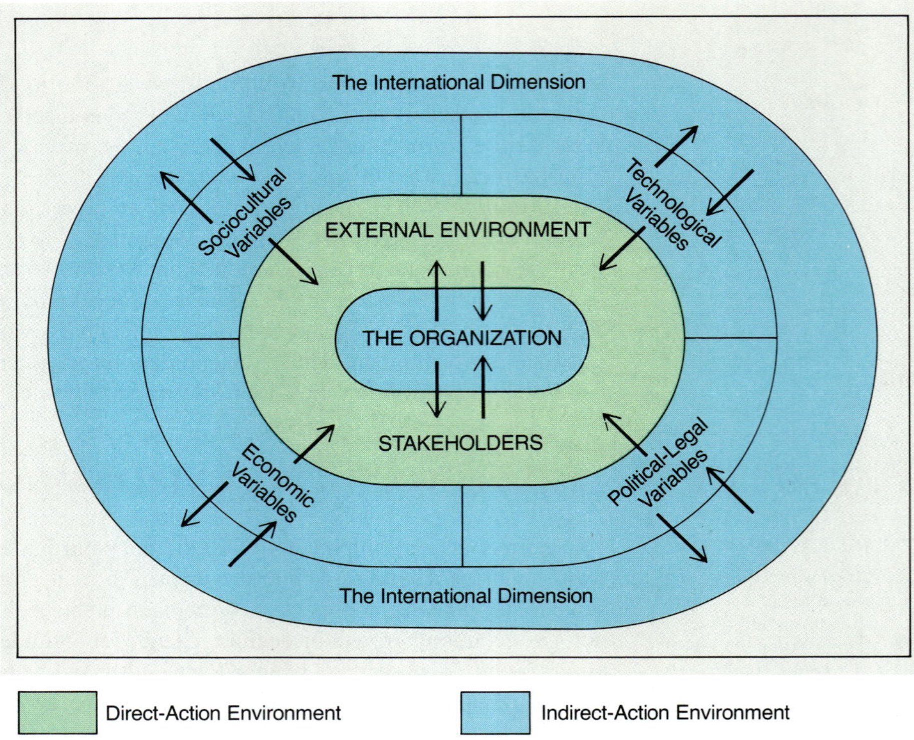

FIGURE 3-4 THE DIRECT-ACTION AND INDIRECT-ACTION ENVIRONMENTS OF AN ORGANIZATION

in South Africa, who are denied both by law and by custom the right to managerial positions where they might have to supervise whites. In other areas the guidelines may be quite broad. Acceptable boss-subordinate relationships, for example, run the gamut from informal camaraderie with little outward evidence of rank to deferential formality toward superiors.

BACKGROUND ON BABY BOOMERS

Baby Boomers, that bulge of 77 million individuals born from WWII to about 1964, are parenting a new wave of kids. This group has also made early middle age the fastest growing segment of society. That aging, along with the rapidly growing numbers of the elderly, is contributing to an older national population. Experts predict that society's focus may change to reflect the aging population. (*Springfield News-Leader*, 1/28/88, p. 5B)

Demographics. There have been major demographic changes in the United States since World War II. The population as a whole is growing only slowly, increasing just 6.9 percent from 1980 to 1987. However, some segments of the population, such as Hispanics and blacks, are growing much faster than others.

Table 3-1 highlights the aging of the American population in terms of the number

TABLE 3-1 THE AGING OF THE POPULATION: PERCENTAGE OF THE POPULATION 65 YEARS AND OVER.

YEAR	TOTAL
1950	8.1%
1960	9.2
1970	9.8
1980	11.3
Projected	
1990	12.3
2000	12.2
2010	12.7
2020	15.6
2030	18.3

Source: Historical figures from the *Statistical Abstract of the United States,* 1981; projected figures from Allan & Brotman, 1981.

TABLE 3-2 THE INCREASE IN THE AVERAGE LIFE EXPECTANCY IN THE UNITED STATES

	LIFE EXPECTANCY	
Year	Male	Female
1920	53.6	54.6
1930	58.1	61.6
1940	60.8	65.2
1950	65.6	71.1
1960	66.6	73.1
1970	67.1	74.8
1980	70.0	77.4
1986	71.3	78.3

Source: Statistical Abstract of the United States, 1988.

of people 65 years or older. Table 3-2 demonstrates the increase in American life expectancy over a recent 60-year period. There have also been dramatic shifts in age structure, that is, the relative sizes of different age groups. Babies born from 1946 to 1964 account for more than one-third of the country's population, and as this cohort has grown up, the society in which it plays a dominant role has naturally begun to reflect its interests and demands. Moreover, despite an increase in fertility since the baby boomers themselves have started to become parents, the median age of the population continues to rise. By 1986, it had grown to 32.7, compared with a post-war low of 28 in 1970. Fast-food restaurants and other traditional employers of teenagers are beginning to turn to housewives and retirees to fill their part-time jobs.

Geographically, as Figure 3-5 demonstrates, the West and South have been growing more quickly than other parts of the country. Nonmetropolitan areas within

FIGURE 3-5 REGIONAL POPULATION OF THE UNITED STATES, 1940–1984

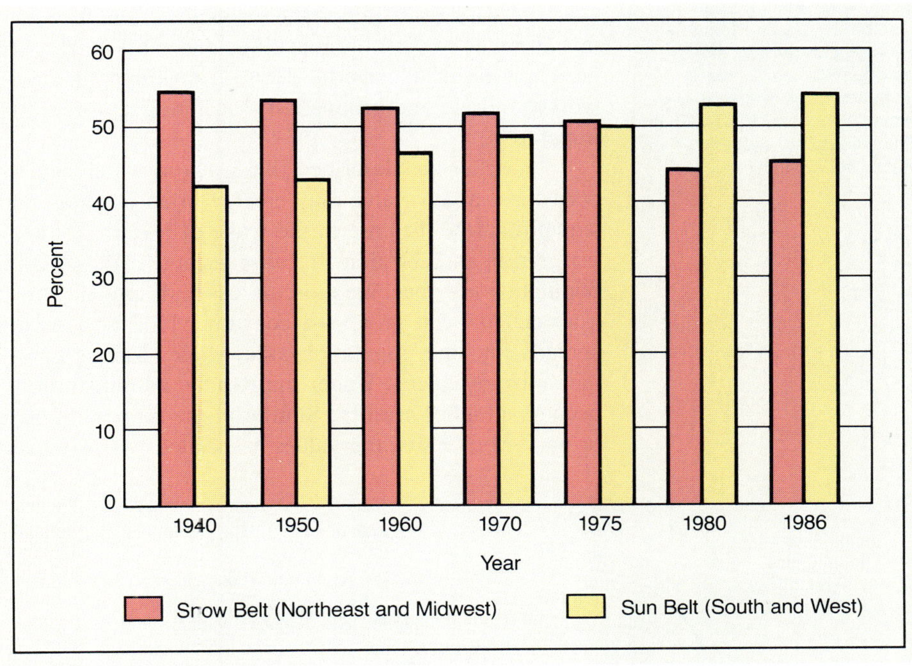

Source: U.S. Bureau of the Census.

commuting distances of cities have also been growing more quickly than metropolitan areas. This has reversed a long-time trend, but it still leaves 73 percent of the nation's population in metropolitan areas. Economically, low growth and changes in the composition of families led to a three percent decline in median family income in real terms during the 1970s; by the mid-1980s, real family income had begun to rise once more.

BACKGROUND ON SOCIO-CULTURAL CHANGES

Couch potatoes. Cocooning. These terms refer to the socio-cultural phenomenon of staying at home. No longer do Yuppies bop till they drop. Makers and marketers of consumer electronics, apparel, gardening equipment, and swimming pools are enjoying increasing sales while discos and clubs are crying in their drinks. As one analyst stated, "Saturday-night studs turned sofa spuds now leave the house only to shop for products that keep them indoors." (*Fortune*, 5/23/88, p. 9)

Lifestyles. According to Fahey and Narayanan, lifestyles are the "outward manifestations of people's attitudes and values."[25] In recent decades, change rather than stability has become the norm for lifestyle in this country. For example, families account for a shrinking proportion of U.S. households, and fewer and fewer of these families include married couples; households consisting of single adults and one-parent families are become more numerous.

With respect to work, the most striking trend is the increasing participation of women in the labor force. More than half of all adult women now work. In most countries, social barriers are raised against women who seek managerial careers, so reaching the top may mean considerable personal sacrifice for women.[26] In the United States, however, women are penetrating this male stronghold in increasing numbers: the number of women managers doubled from 1972 to 1980. (This is not to say that women are reaching "the top" at the same significant rate. In the United States as elsewhere, becoming a manager is not the same thing as reaching the top. Reaching the top ranks of management is generally a slow process for everyone.)

Other lifestyle changes include a trend toward better education: More people now complete high school and go on to college. Smaller cars, condominiums, diet soft drinks, and paid household help are only a few examples of new consumption patterns. Physical fitness has experienced a recent surge in popularity, and other home-centered activities—notably cable TV and video recorders—are becoming more prevalent as Americans distribute their leisure time.

CLASS COMMENT

"A Nutrition Minded McDonald's" is the title of a pamphlet available at the chain's outlets. The pamphlet describes McDonald's efforts to enhance the healthfulness of their food products. Many outlets also prominently display bulletin boards and posters emphasizing McDonald's concern about nutrition. (This pamphlet should be available at any McDonald's outlet.)

Social Values. Changing social values have in recent years weakened our commitment to equality of opportunity and the regulation of industry, altered our assessments of the costs and benefits of new technology such as life-support systems for the seriously ill, and increased the social and economic expectations of consumers, women, and minorities.

Perhaps most important for managers is the way in which values have affected our attitudes toward organizations and work itself. For example, whereas employee participation in managerial decision making was once seen as a means of improving worker morale and productivity, it is now regarded by some observers as an ethical imperative.[27]

Rescher has described five ways in which social values may change.[28] On rare occasions, a new value may emerge or an existing value may totally disappear. Such was ultimately the case in the wake of historic Supreme Court decisions about racial integration and abortion. In other instances, the distribution of a value throughout the population may become more or less widespread. This occurs when the values held by a special interest group—a consumer bloc or a political movement, for example—spreads into the population as a whole. Values may also move up or down in our hierarchy of values. Under the Reagan administration, for instance, national defense became a higher priority. Similarly, the scope of a particular value may be broadened or narrowed. Thus, the values associated with civil rights were expanded to apply to

---

[25]Fahey and Narayanan, p. 73. The remainder of this section is based on Fahey and Narayanan, pp. 74–78.

[26]Frank Taylor, "Women Grab Management Power," *International Management* 39, no. 2 (February 1984):24, 25ff.

[27]Marshall Sashkin, "Participative Management is an Ethical Imperative," *Organizational Dynamics* 12, no. 4 (Spring 1984):5–22.

[28]N. Rescher, "What Is a Value Change? A Framework for Research," in *Values and the Future*, ed. by K. Baier and N. Rescher (New York: Free Press, 1969).

employment and education as well as to voting and religion. Finally, the standard by which a value is measured may change, as is constantly happening to our assessment of a minimum standard of living.

Naturally, social values vary from one country to another. In Japan, for example, where employees may work for the same company all their lives, lower-level workers participate in policy and decision making more freely than American workers do. French organizations, which operate in a society where relationships are somewhat formal, tend to be more rigidly structured than their American and Japanese counterparts.

Economic Variables. Obviously, general economic conditions and trends are critical to the success of an organization. Wages, prices charged by suppliers and competitors, and government fiscal policies affect both the costs of producing products or offering services and the market conditions under which they are sold. Each is an **economic variable.** For example, the 1984 devaluation of the peso and imposition of currency controls by the Mexican government benefited American-owned assembly plants on the Mexican side of the border while devastating wholesalers and retailers in the United States who catered to visiting Mexicans.

economic variables General economic conditions and trends that may be factors in an organization's activities.

HERE'S AN EXAMPLE

A recent study by the Public Policy Center, SRI International, and the American Association of State Colleges and Universities, illustrated the implications for universities of the change from a traditional economy to a new economy. For example, under the new economic focus on global markets, universities will have to provide knowledge of new cultures and languages; rapidly changing skill requirements will imply lifelong learning and education extension programs; etc. (*The Higher Education-Economic Development Connection: Emerging Roles for Public Colleges and Universities in a Changing Economy*, p. 5)

THOUGHT-PROVOKER

Economic experts are predicting that our nation is on the brink of economic changes that could be as far-reaching as those of the Industrial Revolution. Carl Shepherd, policy analyst for the Commerce Department's Division of Productivity, Technology, and Innovation says, "We're talking about a revolutionary change that's happening very fast." Changes will include: investing in research on products and management/labor mix attitudes; identifying what business the company is in, not just what products it produces; engaging in long-term thinking; and retraining employees to change their mind-set of doing only one job for their entire work life. (*Springfield News-Leader*, 9/8/87, p. 6B)

Common economic indicators measure national income and product, savings, investment, prices, wages, productivity, employment, government activities, and international transactions. (See Exhibit 3-2.) All these factors vary over time, and managers devote much of their organizations' time and resources to forecasting the economy and anticipating changes. Since economic change is now the norm rather than the exception, this task has become more complicated in recent decades.

There are two types of economic change. First, *structural* changes in the economy are major alterations, whether permanent or temporary, in the relationships between different sectors of the economy and key economic variables; such changes challenge our basic assumptions about how the economy works. The shift from an industrial to a service economy and the rise in energy costs relative to the cost of other raw materials are examples of structural changes.

In contrast, *cyclical* economic changes are periodic swings in the general level of economic activity. Some examples are the rise and fall of interest rates, inflation, and

EXHIBIT 3-2 COMMON ECONOMIC INDICATORS

- National Income and Product
  - Gross national product
  - Personal income
  - Disposable personal income
  - Personal consumption expenditures
  - Retail sales
- Savings
  - Personal savings
  - Business savings
- Investment
  - Industry investment
  - Investment expenditures
  - New equipment orders
  - Inventory investment
  - Housing starts
- Prices, Wages, and Productivity
  - Inflation rate
  - Consumer price (index) changes
  - Producer price (index) changes
  - Raw material price (index) changes
  - Average hourly earnings
  - Output per hour per business sector
- Labor Force and Employment
  - Numbers employed by age/sex/class of work
  - Unemployment rate
- Government Activities
  - Federal surplus/deficit
  - Expenditures by type
  - Government purchases of goods and services
  - State and local expenditures
  - Defense expenditures
  - Money supply changes
- International Transactions
  - Currency exchange rates
  - Exports by type
  - Imports by type
  - Balance of trade
    - Merchandise
    - Goods and services
  - Investment abroad

Source: Reprinted by permission from *Macroenvironmental Analysis for Strategic Management* by Liam Fahey and V. K. Narayanan.

housing starts. Cyclical changes have far different implications for organizational strategies than structural changes, because they are a function of normal economic volatility. The real problem lies in *distinguishing* cyclical and structural changes from one another.

political variables Factors that may influence an organization's activities as a result of the political process or climate.

Political Variables. Will a government agency adopt a rigorous or a lenient stance in its relations with the management of a company with which it is dealing? Will antitrust laws be rigidly enforced or ignored? Will government policy inhibit or encourage management's freedom to act? These questions concern **political variables,** and the answers to such questions depend in large part on the nature of the political process and on the political climate of a given time. The political process involves the competition between different interest groups, each seeking the power to advance its own values and goals. Some of these interest groups are direct stakeholders in an organization, others are not. Since they all interact with one another, even the non-stakeholders may influence the organization.

In the United States, the political climate has ranged from strong support of corporate autonomy—epitomized in President Coolidge's dictum that "the business of America is business"—to the deep suspicion and distrust of business and government that began in the 1960s and has continued ever since. Both the number and activities of interest groups have increased, as has the diversity of the issues that they bring into the courts and legislatures for consideration. Government responsibilities have expanded to include, for example, the protection of consumers, the preservation of the environment, and the ending of employment discrimination.

As interest groups, particularly special interest groups, become more committed to their goals, political conflicts can grow more intense and last longer. Not surprisingly, the issues to which such groups become committed often bring them into conflict with other groups, including business organizations. These conflicts often enter the legal system at one end and come out the other quite complex in their ramifications. For instance, the issue of the rights of businesses to free speech, involving ethical as well as legal questions, has been raised more than once in the last 15 years and has not been resolved despite several court rulings. Is it ethical for a business to take a stand on a public issue that is not necessarily related directly to its particular type of business activity? Is it legal? In 1980, in the case of *Consolidated Edison Company of New York v. Public Service Commission of New York,* the Supreme Court held that the Public Services Commission could not prohibit Consolidated Edison from including pro-nuclear energy brochures in its monthly statements. In such cases, as interest groups prepare to do battle with large businesses, ethical issues still tend to remain even after legal ones have theoretically been decided. In the *Consolidated Edison* case, for example, the Court took into consideration the argument that businesses have so much power and so much financial means at their disposal that their influence on both legislators and certain segments of society is inherently "unfair." Proponents of this position also argue that this fact is especially important when the positions of businesses differ from what the interest group interprets as being in the best "public interest."

At the same time, the nature of the contemporary media is such that interest groups (in this case, public rather than private) can compete more effectively with well-financed organizations for national attention and resources. Thus the potential for interest groups to influence the political process is greater than ever before.

technological variables New developments in products or processes, as well as advances in science, which may affect an organization's activities.

Technological Variables. **Technological variables** include advances in basic sciences such as physics, as well as new developments in products, processes, and materials. The level of technology in a society or a particular industry determines to a large extent what products and services will be produced, what equipment will be used, and how operations will be managed.

BACKGROUND ON TECHNOLOGY ADVANCES

Much like their human counterparts, robots are moving into services. They are especially useful in jobs people find dangerous or boring, such as cleaning up nuclear plants, picking oranges, or guarding commercial buildings. (*Fortune*, 9/14/87, pp. 81–88)

The Course of Development. Technological development begins with basic research, when a scientist discovers some new phenomenon or advances some new theory; other researchers then examine the breakthrough for its potential utility. If further development leads to a workable prototype and engineering refinements make commercial exploitation practical, then the technology is finally put to use and may be widely adopted.[29] Government institutions such as NASA, independent research establishments such as Bell Labs, universities, and large corporations all carry out basic research. Independent entrepreneurs, business firms, and some government agencies carry the developments out of the laboratory and into the marketplace.

Technological change takes place in many directions at once—that is, it is *multifinal*. Bar codes, for example, are used to track items not only in grocery stores, but also in warehouses, assembly lines, shipping docks, libraries, even in the Department of Defense. Technological change is also *nonlinear:* developments take place irregularly. There are many dead ends, and each highly visible advance may depend on a host of small developments (including failures). Thus, the production of 100 percent solid-state televisions came only after five frustrating years of unsuccessful attempts.

Life Cycles. As development proceeds and a specific technology moves through its life cycle, its functional performance characteristics improve. This change in performance characteristics often follows an S–shaped curve. Figure 3-6, for example, indicates quite clearly the increase in speed due to the performance characteristics of transportation technology over the past two centuries.

Any single product or process will also contain many specific technologies in different phases of their life cycles. *Base* technologies are fully mature; their performance has peaked, and they are shared by all competitors. Although base technologies may pose an entry barrier to the industry, they are not the focus of competition. *Key* technologies, in contrast, are growing and changing rapidly; improvements in this area

FIGURE 3-6 TECHNOLOGICAL DEVELOPMENT AND THE GROWTH OF SPEED

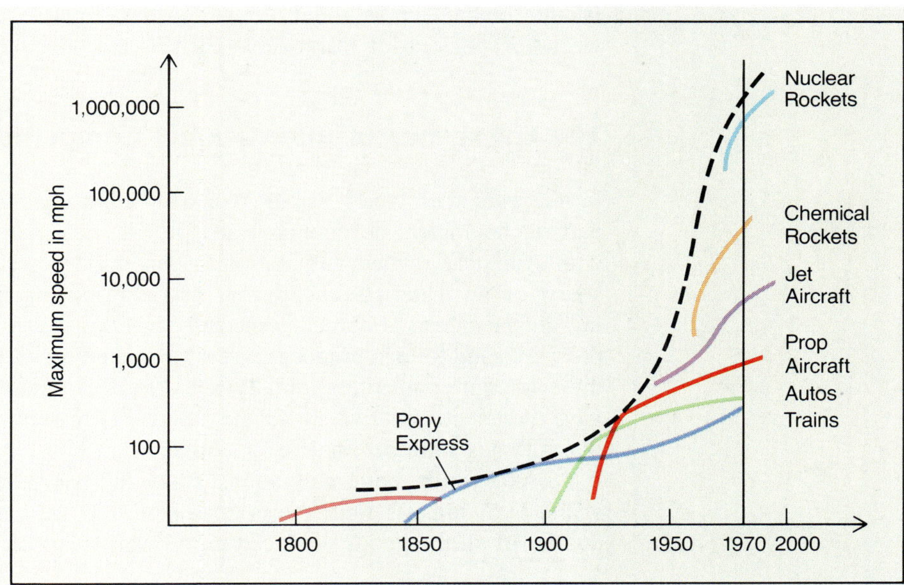

Source: S. C. Wheelwright and S. Makridakis, *Forecasting Methods for Management*, Third Edition. Copyright © 1980 by Ronald Press. Reprinted by permission of John Wiley & Sons, Inc.

[29] J. B. Quinn and J. A. Mueller, "Transferring Research Results to Operations," *Harvard Business Review* 41 (January–February 1963).

give firms competitive edges. *Pacing* technologies are those which may eventually replace key technologies but whose potential use has not yet been proven. *Peripheral* technologies, which are not by their design intended to add much to a product's features, do not play a major role in competition.[30]

THE INTERNATIONAL ENVIRONMENT OF ORGANIZATIONS

HERE'S AN EXAMPLE

Two large corporations, one USA-based and the other Canadian-based, have formed a joint organization called Corporate Networks Operation that will develop and market automated office equipment. Northern Telecom, Ltd. makes telecommunication equipment and Hewlett-Packard Company makes computers and scientific instruments. The joint alliance is viewed as a defense against giant IBM (and its Rolm Corporation subsidiary) and AT&T (with its investments in Ing. C. Olivetti & Co., S.p.A. and Sun Microsystems, Inc.). (*Wall Street Journal*, 5/12/88, p. 13)

The globalization of business is one of the most important changes in the external environment of most organizations. A growing number of companies operate production facilities outside the United States and market their products abroad; even companies with only ostensibly domestic operations face international competition and rely on foreign suppliers. The daily press is filled with reports of trade deficits, calls for protectionism or for free trade, and the latest-breaking news on China, the Soviet Union, and other countries that are experimenting with alternative market mechanisms. Managers can no longer afford to concentrate solely on a domestic point of view. In this section, we will briefly survey a few selected aspects of the international situation that must be classified as aspects of an organization's *environment*. Chapter 24 will be devoted to a full-scale discussion of the nature and nuances of global culture and competition.

New Technology

Technological advances have radically reduced the costs of communication and transportation. Radio and television bring the news simultaneously to people around the world. Even people in deserted corners of the globe share in the craving for Western clothing, movies, cigarettes, and Coca-Cola. In 1979, for example, American television broadcast the day-to-day details of uprising in Iran, as young men fought for Islamic fundamentalism and a return to the principles of the past, wielding modern weapons and wearing fashionable French-cut pants and open-body shirts.[31]

The Emergence of International Competitors

In the years after World War II, American companies expanded abroad. For the most part, technological development and product design remained in the United States, with American-owned multinationals generally viewing the rest of the world as a source of raw materials, cheap labor, and supplemental markets. However, as purchasing power increased abroad, especially in Europe and Japan, indigenous production prospered and foreign producers grew beyond their own national boundaries. Although these foreign competitors initially relied on U.S. technology, lower costs eventually gave them a competitive advantage, and today they have taken a technological initiative that has furthered their competitiveness.[32]

As a result, both international trade and competition have intensified in recent years. U.S. imports and exports more than doubled between 1970 and 1981.[33] One-quarter of all the goods produced in the world now cross national boundaries, while

---

[30] Arthur D. Little and Co., "Strategic Management of Technology," Paper presented at the European Forum, 1981.

[31] Levitt, *Marketing Imagination*, p. 22.

[32] Russell E. Palmer, "Trends in International Management: Toward Federations of Equals," *Business Quarterly* 152, no. 1 (Summer 1987):116–20.

[33] *Economic Report of the President*, 1984, p. 221.

ILLUSTRATIVE CASE STUDY Continued

Image and Imaging Problems at Eastman Kodak

By 1986, it had become increasingly evident that Kodak had spent at least one decade (other estimates place it at closer to five) perfecting the art of foot-dragging. Between 1975 and 1985, for example, Kodak had been unaccountably slow in entering such markets as 35mm cameras and VCRs—markets that would seem to be natural extensions of a company that depends on photography-related business for about 80 percent of its over $10 billion in sales. When, in January of 1986, Kodak re-entered the 35mm camera field after an inexplicable absence of 17 years, it was obliged to manufacture its cameras not in its own once-vaunted facilities but in Japan.

Besides waking to discover vigorous competition from such formidable American rivals as RCA and GE (in consumer electronics), IBM and Xerox (in copiers and office-publishing equipment), and Memorex and 3M (in floppy disks), Kodak found that it also *shared* a problem with its American counterparts: In the fields of film, VCRs, and video cameras, Japanese concerns like Fuji, Konica, Nikon, Canon, Minolta, Sony, and Toshiba had made ominous inroads into both American technology and profits. Says Columbia University management professor E. Kirby Warren, who served as a consultant at Kodak for seven years: "Psychologically, I don't know whether some of those people in Rochester can get it into their heads that they got whooped by the Japanese, and they have to fight harder, tougher, and meaner."

For example, Japanese manufacturers are now making a frontal assault on one of Kodak's long-standing market bastions, amateur photography. When Fuji introduced a 400 ASA-speed film in 1977, Kodak matched it in six months; in 1983, however, Fuji introduced a new 1600-speed film that Kodak is still trying to duplicate. In addition, Kodak permitted Fuji to waltz off with sponsorship of the 1984 Los Angeles Olympics. Kodak "was *so* arrogant," recalls Olympic organizing president Peter Ueberroth. "They wanted to give us $1 million and a bunch of film. They thought they had a lock on it, that nobody else could afford it." Fuji saw the matter differently, bidding $7 million: "The Olympics," explains Carl Chapman, vice president of Fuji Photo Film U. S. A., "is the greatest vehicle you can have for a promotional tie-in. We've increased our position in the marketplace, and we're not going to sit back and relax."

As a result, although Fuji currently commands less than 10 percent of the U.S. market for film, its volume has increased at the rate of over 20 percent per year since it purchased the Olympic sponsorship in 1981—despite a market which, on the whole, has grown much more slowly. Now, according to Ueberroth, Kodak is "spending *ten* times [its original offer] to get in on the fringes."

nearly three-quarters of the goods produced in the United States face foreign competition.[34] As Lester Thurow notes, we now live in a world where transportation costs are so unimportant that everything that can be traded soon will be.[35] In this world market, organizations must fight to capture overseas markets while defending their home markets from foreign competition, subjects that we will discuss in greater detail in Chapter 24.

The United States has been slow to recognize and respond to this rise in international competition, with Japan having become our most visible competitor. For example, although home video technology was originally developed and patented in the United States, not one video cassette recorder has ever been manufactured in this country. Japan's estimated 1984 production was 20 million machines. The Japanese have also taken over a large portion of the semiconductor market, once an American

[34]John A. Young, "Global Competition: The New Reality," *California Management Review* 37, no. 3 (Spring 1985):12.

[35]Lester Thurow, "Revitalizing American Industry: Managing in a Competitive World Economy," *California Management Review* 27, no. 1 (Fall 1984):10.

INTERNATIONAL MANAGEMENT

BIOTECHNOLOGY: THE RACE TO BUILD A BETTER PIG

Following up on its success in attracting American consumers to everything from robots to optical fibers, Japanese industry, in conjunction with its universities and its government, is now preparing to challenge American superiority in the domain of biotechnology. Still an infant scientific and commercial field, "biotech" is nevertheless a potentially multibillion-dollar industry that promises to employ genetic engineering to develop products ranging from cancer treatments to brand-new types of pigs.

Professor Hajime Nashimura of Tokyo University admits that the U.S. maintains a large lead "and the gap isn't closing." However, one strong indication of Japan's determination to close that gap is the attention given to biotech by the country's Ministry of International Trade and Industry (MITI). Already, MITI has seeded funds for research on gene-splicing, an important technique for creating one chemical out of another; MITI has also initiated a 10-year program to encourage work in the field known as bioelectronics, which envisions computers that will function more like human brains. Moreover, Japanese companies have bankrolled bioscience laboratories at such institutions as Harvard University, hoping to expedite the catch-up process by participating in the development of American breakthroughs.

The problem for American competitors is the twofold issue of cash flow and delayed gratification. Many American firms are wary of joint ventures with Japanese partners: "We terminated one possible joint venture," explains an official of Genetics Institute of Cambridge, Massachusetts, because "we didn't feel very comfortable giving away proprietary information and scientific know-how." However, many American biotech companies are small start-up firms who see few options other than exchanging scientific secrets for capital offered by immensely large Japanese corporations that are cash-rich from a huge variety of other operations. Moreover, American companies are sensitive to investor demands and cannot normally allocate the large sums of money entailed by the long-term planning, research, and resources typical of biotechnology. For example, the Philadelphia company of Rohm and Haas abandoned plans for developing a new strain of rice precisely because of such pressures. "We [still] believe there will be a potential," laments R & H president Ruben Salazar, "but the time it will take is so long, and the investment is so big." By contrast, Japanese corporations frequently issue shares to other friendly Japanese firms that buy and hold rather than demand dividends or hefty quarterly profits; other Japanese firms depend on financing from banks that also tend to abide a long-term view.

Table 3-3 summarizes the current status of three key areas of American, Japanese, and European biotech competition.

Source: Based on Bernard Wysocki, Jr., "Gene Squad: Japanese Now Target Another Field the U.S. Leads: Biotechnology," *Wall Street Journal,* December 17, 1987.

monopoly, and they have even taken the lead in the development of new drugs.[36] The Japanese are not our only competitors, however. European products, such as the Airbus, are also taking market shares away from American organizations,[37] while other Asian countries are becoming strong competitors. Korean exports, for example, ranked thirteenth in the world in 1985 and are growing over 30 percent annually.[38]

[36]Ibid., pp. 10–12.

[37]Ibid., p. 12.

[38]Sangjin Yoo and Sang M. Lee, ''Management Style and Practice of Korean Chaebols,'' *California Management Review* 29, no. 4 (Summer 1987):95–110.

TABLE 3-3 BIOTECH'S GLOBAL COMPETITION AND COOPERATION

LEAD COMPANY	PARTNER	U.S. STATUS*	JAPANESE STATUS*
Tissue Plasminogen Activator (heart attacks)			
Genentech (U.S.)	Mitsubishi (Japan), Boehringer (Germany)	Approved	Phase 2
Genetics Institute (U.S.)	Wellcome PLC (Britain), Sumitomo (Japan)	Phase 3	Phase 2
Integrated Genetics (U.S.)	None		
	Toyobo (Japan)	—	Phase 2
Asahi Chemical and Kowa (Japan)	None	—	Phase 3
Meiji Milk (Japan)	Meiji Seika (Japan)	—	Phase 1
Biogen (U.S.)	SmithKline Beckman (U.S.)	—	—
Chiron (U.S.)	Hoechst (Germany)	Preclinical	—
Damon (U.S.)	SmithKline Beckman (U.S.), Yamanouchi (Japan)	Preclinical	Preclinical
Bio-Response (U.S.)	None	Preclinical	—
Green Cross (Japan)	None	—	NDA
Monsanto (Searle) (U.S.)	None	Preclinical	—
Lilly (U.S.)	None	Preclinical	—
Gamma Interferon (cancer, rheumatoid arthritis)			
Biogen	Baxter Travenol (U.S.), Shionogi (Japan)	Approved	Approved
Amgen (U.S.)	Johnson & Johnson (U.S.)	Phase 2,3	—
Genentech	Toray/Daiichi (Japan)	Phase 3	Phase 2
Interferon Sciences (U.S.)	None	Phase 1	—
Kyowa (Japan)	None	—	Preclinical
Daiichi/Toray (Japan)	None	—	Preclinical
Human Growth Hormone			
Genentech	None	Approved	Approved
Lilly	Shionogi (Japan)	Approved	Approved
Biotech. General (U.S.)	Du Pont (U.S.)	Phase 3	—
Cell Technology	Serono Labs (U.S.)	Phase 3	NDA
Sumitomo Chemical (Japan)	None	—	Approved
Yamanouchi	Nordisk (Demark)	Phase 2	NDA
Kabivitrum (Sweden)	Sumitomo	—	Approved

*NOTES ON STATUS:
Preclinical: Animal or lab tests
Phase 1: Human tests to determine safety
Phase 2: Human tests to determine dosage range
Phase 3: Large-scale human tests of effectiveness
NDA: New drug submitted for approval

Source: Prudential-Bache Securities. Reprinted and updated from *The Wall Street Journal,* December 17, 1987.

The automobile market is a good example of the changes in international competition over the past three decades. American automakers initially had a stranglehold on the domestic market, but German and Japanese manufacturers eventually flooded the country with less expensive, well-built cars, forcing American automakers on the defensive. Only government intervention kept Chrysler afloat. Today, there is a world auto market, with firms from all countries locked into ever-closer competition—and cooperation. Volkswagen, Honda, and Nissan have assembly plants in the United States; other foreign manufacturers are following their lead, and General Motors and Toyota actually alternate production in a California factory. Some ''Chrysler'' cars and

"Why should I be worried about fish contaminated with dioxin? . . ."
Reprinted by permission of Tribune Media Services.

trucks are designed and made by Mitsubishi, while the inexpensive end of the American market is increasingly being left to Korean and Yugoslavian manufacturers.

The Problem of Competitiveness

COORDINATED RESOURCES

Some sources for more information on this timely topic: "How the Best Get Better," *Business Week,* 9/14/87, pp. 98–120; "America's Leanest and Meanest," *Business Week,* 10/5/87, pp. 78–84; "It's Time for America to Wake Up," *Business Week,* 11/16/87, p. 158–177; "Look Out World, Here We Come," *Fortune,* 6/20/88, pp. 54–55. For an anecdotal digest of these articles, see the Lecture Extras Supplement.

John A. Young, Chairman of the President's Commission on Industrial Competitiveness, has reported that the ability of the United States to compete in the world economy has declined for the past two decades.[39] Productivity is growing more slowly in the United States than among its major trading partners. Real hourly wages have been stalled for more than a decade, and the return on manufacturing assets has dropped since the mid-1960s to a point where investments in financial assets have higher returns; trade deficits are at all-time highs, and high-technology industries are losing world market share.

The commission concluded that both the public and private sectors need to place a higher priority on international competitiveness and made some specific recommendations. According to the commission, the responsibility for formulating international trade policy and encouraging exports, which is currently fragmented among multiple government agencies, should be unified. The government also needs to cut the deficit, encourage savings, and stabilize its monetary policy in order to bring down the cost of capital. Civilian research and development, including university training and research programs, need more funding. The successful implementation of such policies, plus a renewed interest in manufacturing, may help overcome our disappointing track record in developing manufacturing applications. Finally, the private sector must use stock purchase and profit-sharing plans to motivate its employees.

The Blurring of Public and Private Spheres of Influence

As mentioned earlier, government has played an increasingly active role in the marketplace in the post-World War II environment, because international competition has increased the pressure on governments to intervene to protect their own industries. In the United States, this role crystallized when the federal government bailed out the Chrysler Corporation in 1980 by guaranteeing its loans. Shortly thereafter, the government exempted a number of computer manufacturers from antitrust laws in order to allow them to perform joint research and development and to increase their ability to compete with the Japanese.

Under President Reagan, the first tax-reform bill led to an enormous influx of venture capital into the economy. The Reagan administration also actively promoted

[39] Young, "Global Competition," pp. 11–25.

American business over international competitors in defense contracting. For example, a low foreign bid to install a glass cable between New York and Washington was rejected in favor of AT&T on the grounds that the cable had "national defense" implications. Thus, the American ideal of "laissez-faire" is today a fiction.

This blurring of public policy and private enterprise is not limited to the United States. In Japan, the Ministry of International Trade and Industry actively assists some industries rather than others, and government takes an active role. The Group of Five (the United States, West Germany, Japan, France, and the United Kingdom) routinely meet to plan their monetary policy in concert. And, in the wake of the October 19, 1987, stock market crash, there have been suggestions to coordinate the stock markets in these nations.

Changes in government policy can help or hurt an industry or an organization overnight. Many organizations are therefore spending more time and resources in an attempt to influence policy among governments around the world.

The Opening of China and the Eastern Bloc

Chinese leadership announced a new policy of "economic readjustment" in 1978, since which time free market forces have begun to supplement China's planned economy. The greatest changes have so far taken place in the countryside, where the "economic responsibility" system stops just short of giving individual families title to their land. In addition, there are now some private companies in China as well as a growing number of foreign ones (Volkswagen has opened a $200 million assembly plant, and American companies have invested about $5 billion in Chinese industrial development). The state plan no longer sets strict production quotas for state-owned firms or assigns their entire output to buyers. Managers are being induced to take the initiative in choosing suppliers, deciding what to produce, and finding customers.[40] Bonus plans have emerged, and managers are now being promoted on the basis of productivity.

FOR DISCUSSION

What implications do these new reforms have for U.S. companies? (P.S. Don't just think about the increased sales, although that is a big part of it!)

In 1988, Soviet leader Mikhail Gorbachev announced plans for similar reforms in the economy of the U.S.S.R. Called "Peristroika." These reforms call for a gradual end to central economic coordination. Market mechanisms will be allowed to influence production quotas, wages, salaries, and even whether or not certain factories remain open. In both China and the U.S.S.R., economic reform has been imposed by leaders at the top but has encountered fierce political resistance that has slowed the pace of reform and made its long-term prospects uncertain. Thus while it is too early to tell whether these changes will be successful, they have already begun to be felt among such Soviet allies as Hungary, Rumania, and Czechoslovakia.

CHARACTERISTICS OF TOTAL ORGANIZATION ENVIRONMENTS

The Theory of Uncertainty and Dependence

The environment as a whole may be viewed both as a source of information and as a stock of resources.[41] Depending on its approach to its environment, an organization therefore faces one of two theoretical problems: **uncertainty,** caused by a lack of information, and **dependence** on others for vital resources. M. T. Hannan and J. H. Freeman have described six environmental factors that affect an organization's level of uncertainty and dependence. (See Exhibit 3-3.) Petroleum refiners, for example, be-

uncertainty According to Hannan and Freeman, the theoretical problem posed to an organization by lack of information.

dependence According to Hannan and Freeman, the theoretical problem faced by an organization because of its need for vital resources from outside sources.

[40] Richard H. Holton, "Marketing and the Modernization of China," *California Management Review* 27, no. 4 (Summer 1985):33–45.

[41] H. E. Aldrich and S. Mindlin, "Uncertainty and Dependence: Two Perspectives on Environment," in *Organization and Environment,* ed. by L. Kerpit (Beverly Hills, Calif.: Sage, 1978), pp. 149–70.

EXHIBIT 3-3 HANNAN AND FREEMAN'S FACTORS AFFECTING AN ORGANIZATION'S UNCERTAINTY AND DEPENDENCE.

The environment is more uncertain and less easy to understand when:

- it is more differentiated,
- it is changing, and
- there are numerous interconnections among its various elements.

A manufacturing organization in an uncertain environment, for example, might have to contend with many different types of customers, the rapid introduction of new products, and connections with a large number of suppliers. Organizations are more dependent in an environment where:

- required resources are not widely available,
- those resources are not evenly distributed, and
- increasing connectedness disturbs elements of the environment and the linkages among them.

Source: M. T. Hannan and J. H. Freeman, "The Population Ecology of Organizations," *American Journal of Sociology* 82 (1977):929–64.

THOUGHT-PROVOKER

Why would environments tend to become more turbulent over time?

came more dependent in the 1970s when crude oil supplies were less readily available and when they were concentrated in the Middle East. By the 1980s, the Iran-Iraq War, which had embroiled the Persian Gulf, had rendered the supply of oil even less dependable, as had the web of entangling of uncertain alliances in the region.

Other Theories of Environments

Other theorists have developed strategic models of the environment in an effort to explain the relationships between organizations and the environment.

Natural Selection. This model is based on biological theories of population ecology and shares their emphasis on competition for resources.[42] In the variation stage, organizations make different responses to environmental pressures; error and chance are as important as problem-solving abilities in determining which organizations acquire information and resources more efficiently. In the selection stage, those organizations survive which best fit the constraints imposed by the environment. In the retention stage, the selected organizations persist until the environment changes or different organizations arise.

Resource Dependence. This model assumes that organizations are dependent on the environment for resources, such as suppliers, customers, competitors, and regulators.[43] The organization may take action on its own to acquire and maintain those resources—for example, negotiating long-term contracts or adopting a technological innovation. It may also act collectively with other organizations—participating in trade associations that lobby government agencies and set informal industry norms. The organization's strategy will vary according to the relative importance of each of its dependencies.

MANAGING THE TOTAL ENVIRONMENT

The external environment is more or less important to managers depending on the types and purposes of their organizations, their positions and functions, and their places in the organizational hierarchy. Thus, managers at Exxon may be more influenced by

[42]Aldrich, *Organizations and Environments;* M. T. Hannan and J. H. Freeman, "The Population Ecology of Organizations," *American Journal of Sociology* 82 (1977):929–64.

[43]M. E. Porter, *Competitive Strategy* (New York: Free Press, 1980).

ILLUSTRATIVE CASE STUDY Continued

Image and Imaging Problems at Eastman Kodak

When 60-year-old Colby H. Chandler, an engineer in Kodak's ponderous bureaucracy for over 30 years, became Chairman and CEO of the company in 1983, he was the most recent of only 12 presidents who had headed the company since its origins in the 1880s. Chandler was quite familiar with the outmoded managerial establishment that had originated in 1880, when founder George Eastman determined that his company would become a centralized, self-sufficient decision-making, producing, and marketing entity. Eventually, the company organized itself along quite strictly functional lines (see Chapter 10), with its manufacturing and marketing divisions operating virtually autonomously. If an idea from one functional area affected another, it would have to percolate to the top of the organizational hierarchy and then dribble back down again to the appropriate level. The decision-making process was obviously sluggish and often faulty. In the 1940s, for example, Kodak rejected an instant-photography system offered it by Edwin Land, who then turned to Polaroid; 20 years and $94 million later, when Kodak had finally succeeded in duplicating the product, Polaroid superseded it with an SX-70 camera that produced litter-free color prints and sent Kodak scampering forth to avoid a $6.5 billion loss by introducing a competitive system. The astonishing success of the VCR has been no secret since at least 1982, but Kodak still does not manufacture a model of its own.

"Historically this company has been risk-adverse," understates new Executive Vice President J. Phillip Samper, but Samper is part of a new managerial organization that is currently looking at Kodak's business environment quite differently. "Today," he explains, "we're saying, 'Making a mistake isn't bad. Just don't make it twice.'" Chandler agrees—"It's essential that we take more risks," he demands—and in 1985 reorganized Kodak's core Photographic Division into 17 operational units. Each unit is responsible for its own profitability and is managed by an executive who oversees every aspect of the division from design to production. In a paternalistic corporation that once promoted top-level managers primarily on the basis of seniority and loyalty to the company, Chandler passed over senior managers in selecting the heads of 15 of the company's 17 new units. In an effort to promote innovation, clarify profit goals, and expedite decision making, Chandler forced decision-making responsibilities downward from the executive staff to the unit-manager level. Now decisions can be made in a few days (Charles L. Trowbridge, Vice-President for Copy Products, has been known to okay a new district office in half an hour).

Decentralization has also helped Kodak kick its "one-product habit." For example, the new Life Sciences Division has made use of the company's expertise in imaging and chemicals to apply film-coating techniques to the production of blood analyzers that have become invaluable in the diagnosis of anemia and diabetes. Moreover, Kodak's new entrepreneurial system has both encouraged and facilitated new acquisitions policies, especially in markets traditionally related to its own. When it purchased Fox Photo Inc. in 1986, Kodak not only became the nation's largest wholesale photo finisher but secured a huge customer for its own photographic paper and chemical products. Exhibit 3-4 sketches out some of Kodak's "extracurricular" activities over a two-year period.

Perhaps most importantly, as its conventional silver-based film technology inevitably gives way to electronics, Kodak has ventured into new technologies with uncharacteristic zeal, especially into the field of *electronic imaging*—systems that manipulate photos and graphics the same way that computers manipulate texts. Unveiled in 1985, Kodak's Ektaprint Electronic Publishing System underscores not only its commitment to new technology but a willingness to merchandize products made by other manufacturers: Sun Microsystems will build the computer, Interleaf Inc. will provide the software, and Canon will supply the printer. Here, too, acquisitions play a major role in Kodak's $300 million game plan. In 1985, Kodak completed seven acquisitions, including Eikonix Corp., a maker of digital image-processing equipment, and Garlic Technology, which develops digital magnetic recording heads for disk drives.

Kodak has also purchased sponsorship rights for the 1988 Olympic Games for $10 million.

EXHIBIT 3-4 WHERE KODAK IS FOCUSING OUTSIDE PHOTOGRAPHY

	1984
June	Invests $8.4 million in ICN Pharmaceuticals and its Viratek subsidiary for drug research
September	Announces deal to market Canon's mid-volume copiers under Kodak name
October	Invests $20 million in Sun Microsystems, maker of graphics work stations
	Invests more than $2.5 million in Interleaf, a software developer and vendor of electronic publishing systems
November	Forms Life Sciences Division for push into medical technology
	1985
January	Forms Videk unit to make factory machine vision systems
March	Says it will buy floppy-disk maker Verbatim for $175 million
	Announces acquisition of Eikonix, maker of digital scanning and color image processing systems, for $56 million
April	Invests $45 million to develop anti-viral and anti-aging drugs
May	Introduces electronic publishing and microfilm management systems

Data: Company Reports.

Source: Reprinted from June 10, 1985 issue of *Business Week* by special permission. Copyright © 1985 by McGraw-Hill, Inc.

A HUMOROUS (BUT SERIOUS!) NOTE

First Children's Bank, opened in the F.A.O. Schwarz store in New York City in May 1988, was inspired by the 5-year-old daughter of the President of First Women's Bank when she asked why only grownups could get money from cash machines. First Children's Bank joins the ranks of Young American's Bank, which opened in Denver during the summer of 1987. (*Fortune*, 4/11/88, p. 14)

TEACHING TIP

Be sure to emphasize the role of the manager in *influencing* the direct-action environment and *monitoring* the indirect-action environment. Do this by describing how different managers might perform each of these.

CLASS COMMENT

A manager's actions, which will be explained and described in the remainder of the book, are in response to changes in the external environment.

factors in the external environment than managers at A&P, pollution control engineers more than sales-division managers, and executives more than clerical workers.

Because of their greater power and broader perspectives, managers at the higher levels bear greater responsibilities for managing relations with the external environment than do lower-level managers. Top managers play key roles in balancing the interests of the various stakeholders in the organization and in forecasting and adjusting to trends in the indirect-action environment.

Influencing the Direct-Action Environment

The direct-action environment is a known quantity with which the organization has regular and established patterns of interaction. For the most part, managers use such standard and reliable techniques as advertising, lobbying, and collective bargaining to influence an organization's stakeholders. The real challenge for managers is to decide the relative importance of each stakeholder and to balance managerial decisions accordingly.

Monitoring the Indirect-Action Environment

Managers monitor the indirect-action environment for early-warning signs of changes that will later effect their organization's activities. For example, rather than waiting for specific sales to fall, a savvy manager could reduce production of luxury items when he or she first spots a downward trend in general consumer spending.

Information about the indirect-action environment comes from many sources: an industry's grapevine, managers in other organizations, the data generated by an organization's own activities, government reports and statistics, trade journals, general financial and business publications, on-line computer data-bank services, and others. Hints, predictions, statistics, gossip—any of these may alert a manager to a trend that should be monitored. The manager can then order further research in order to clarify potentially important developments. By using *forecasting* techniques, managers can anticipate change in social, economic, political, and technological variables and so prepare alternative courses of action and concrete plans for the future.

Adjusting to the Environment

Managers generally adjust to the external environment through the planning process. They develop and implement strategic plans in order to guide the organization's attempts to influence the behavior of stakeholders and its adaptations to the indirect external environment.[44]

Another type of adjustment to the environment involves changes in the organization's formal structure—its work flows, authority patterns, reporting relationships among managers, and the like. This kind of "organizational design" implies a conscious structuring of the organization so that it will best meet the demands of the environment at a given time. Although few organizations operate according to such an ideal design, many are regularly reorganized and restructured in accord with environmental dictates (we will describe this process in Part Three of this book). In both cases, adjustment demands that the manager deal with a critical paradox: With the environment changing ever more rapidly and areas of "relevant uncertainty" increasing, strategic planning, fundamentally a process for *stabilizing* an organization's activities, must now be more *flexible* than ever before.

[44] A useful discussion of how managers respond to the challenges of the environment is found in Rosemary Stewart, "Managerial Agendas—Reactive or Proactive?" *Organizational Dynamics* 8, no. 2 (Autumn 1979):34–47. According to Stewart, *reactive* managers respond to events after they have taken place, while *proactive* managers provide for future eventualities in their plans and programs.

ILLUSTRATIVE CASE STUDY Wrap-Up

Image and Imaging Problems at Eastman Kodak

With $10.8 billion in assets, Kodak's products, in their familiar yellow boxes and bold black imprint, are not likely to disappear from store shelves across the country regardless of the success or failure of CEO Chandler's organizational revamping. Yet, the company faces a twofold problem: (1) How many *different,* if related, products will Kodak be able to put on those shelves? (2) How *rapidly* will those products be consumed from store shelves, especially in comparison to the sales rates of competitors both domestic and foreign? And an even larger question looms behind the Kodak story chronicled in our Case Study: In an industry in which *innovation* has always clearly been the touchstone of success, how could Kodak have so seriously lost sight of that criterion? As we have seen, one result of that shortsightedness is the loss, in 1986, of a monumental lawsuit filed by Polaroid (the settlement is expected to be over $130 million). What might be the ramifications of alienating 16.5 million external stakeholders—that is, the owners of now-obsolete cameras that accounted for only 3 percent of Kodak's annual revenues in the first place? What should Kodak do? Agree to accept the return of cameras for which it can no longer manufacture film, some of which retailed for as much as $78, in exchange for disk cameras worth $50? Accept them in return for stock that is now worth about $47.50 per share (minus a brokerage fee that can run as high as $25)? Buy out Polaroid, whose current market value is only about $1.5 billion?

The company's stakeholders are involved in other issues facing the company. Because of the Polaroid suit and Chandler's reorganizational plan, Kodak was forced to cut its payroll by almost 13,000 by 1986—at a cost of $300 million in 1986 but a savings of $500 million in 1987. How is such a decision likely to affect Kodak's relations with such internal stakeholders as employees (interestingly, Kodak is one of the few big American corporations with no domestic unions) and such external stakeholders as the Rochester, N.Y., community? Wage increases were also delayed, although Chandler and President Kay Whitmore accepted raises of 12 and 18.5 percent, respectively.

What sort of managerial problems remain to be encountered because of Kodak's new entrepreneurial stance? For example, in 1981 Kodak paid $79 million in stock to acquire Atex, a producer of newspaper and magazine publishing systems. Kodak's operational pace had not yet gained the momentum intended by Chandler, customers complained about delays, key managers defected (including the company's founders), and technological advantages were squandered. Why has this trend at Atex started to reverse because Kodak's new management has decided to keep such acquisitions at greater arm's length from its central headquarters in Rochester?

Finally, a question that you may be able to address only at the conclusion of this course: What does the story of Eastman Kodak tell us about the evolution of American business culture between the 1880s and the 1980s? ■

■ SUMMARY

The many rapid changes taking place in the external environment of organizations require increasing attention from managers. The direct-action component of the environment consists of the organization's stakeholders—that is, the groups with direct impact on the organization's activities. External stakeholders include customers, suppliers, governments, consumer and environmental advocates, special interest groups, labor unions, financial institutions, the media, and competitors. Internal stakeholders include employees, shareholders, and the board of directors.

Managers must balance the interests of the various stakeholders for the good of the organization as a whole. They may be able to use the network of relationships among the stakeholders and the organization to influence stakeholders individually. For their part, stakeholders may unite in coalitions to exert influence over the organization. Individual stakeholders may also hold conflicting stakes in an organization.

The indirect-action component of the environment consists of their factors that influence the organization indirectly. Not only do these factors create a climate to which the organization must adjust, but they have the potential to move into the direct-action environment. Demographic and lifestyle variables mold an organization's labor supply and customer base, and changes in values are at the heart of every other social, economic, political, and technological change. Managers must distinguish between and adjust to structural and cyclical changes in the economy. In addition, they must contend with the growing influence of special interest groups in politics, and technological developments also fuel the competition between organizations.

Technological advances in communications and transportation have made the international environment increasingly important. Greater international competition has made the U.S. lag in competitiveness critical, and has also blurred the distinction between the private and public sectors.

The environment determines the extent to which organizations face uncertainty and to which they are dependent on others for vital resources. In turbulent environments, organizations must devote more of their resources to monitoring the environment. The natural-selection, resource-dependence, and industrial-organization models provide alternative views of the relationship between organizations and the environment.

Managers—especially at higher levels—must monitor the external environment and try to forecast changes that will affect the organization. They may use strategic planning and organizational design to adjust to the environment.

■ REVIEW QUESTIONS

1. Distinguish between the direct-action and indirect-action components of the environment, giving examples of each.
2. Who are the stakeholders of an organization, and how have their stakes changed in recent years? What *new* categories of stakeholders are now developing?

3. What are stakeholder networks and coalitions? How can managers use them to influence stakeholders?
4. Discuss the four factors that make up the indirect-action environment of organizations.
5. Describe some recent changes in U.S. demographics, lifestyles, and social values. How do they affect organizations?
6. What is the difference between structural and cyclical economic change? What are their implications for organizations?
7. How does technological development proceed? At which stages in its life cycle is a technology critical to competition?
8. What are the management challenges and opportunities posed by growing international trade?
9. Define uncertainty and dependence, and describe the environmental characteristics that affect them.
10. Contrast the natural selection, resource-dependence, and industrial-organizational models.
11. What techniques can managers use to influence the direct-action environment? To adjust to the indirect-action environment?

CASE STUDY Tri-State Telephone

John Godwin, Chief Executive of Tri-State Telephone, leaned back in his chair and looked at the ceiling. How was he ever going to get out of this mess? At last night's public hearing, 150 angry customers had marched in to protest Tri-State's latest rate request. After the rancorous shouting was over and the acrimonious signs put away, the protesters had presented state regulations with some sophisticated economic analyses in support of their case. Additionally, there were a number of emotional appeals from elderly customers who regarded phone service their lifeline to the outside world.

Tri-State Telephone operated in three states and had sales of over $3 billion. During the last five years, the company had experienced a tremendous amount of change. In 1984, the AT&T divestiture sent shock waves throughout the industry, and Tri-State Telephone had felt the effects, as pricing for long-distance telephone service changed dramatically. The Federal Communications Commission instituted a charge to the effect that customers should have "access" to long-distance companies whether or not they were in the habit of making long-distance calls. Consumer groups, including the Consumer Federation of America and the Congress of Consumer Organizations, had joined the protest, increasing their attention on the industry and intervening in regulatory proceedings wherever possible. The FCC was considering deregulating as much of the industry as possible, and Congress was looking over the Commissioner's shoulder. Meanwhile, the Department of Justice and Judge Harold Greene (both of whom were responsible for the AT&T divestiture) continued to argue about what businesses companies like Tri-State should be engaged in.

In addition, technology was changing rapidly. Cellular telephones, primarily used in cars, were now hand-held and could be substituted for standard phones. Digital technology was increasing, leading to lower costs and requiring companies like Tri-State to invest to keep up with the state of the art. Meanwhile, rate increases negotiated during an inflationary period during the 1970s were keeping earnings higher than regulators would authorize. New "intelligent" terminals and software developments gave rise to new uses for the phone network (such as using the phone for an alarm system), but as long as customers paid one flat fee, the phone company did not benefit from these new services.

Godwin's company had recently proposed a new pricing system, whereby users of local telephone services would simply pay for what they used rather than a monthly flat fee. All of the senior managers were convinced that the plan was fairer, even though some groups who used the phone with notable frequency like real estate agents, would pay more. Now the company would have an incentive to bring new services to their customers, and customers could choose which ones to buy. No one anticipated the hue and cry from the customers who would actually save money, as Godwin's studies showed that the elderly were among very light users of local service and could save as much as 20 percent under the new plan.

After the debacle at the hearing the previous night, Godwin was unsure how to proceed. If he backed off the new pricing plan, he would have to find a different way to meet the challenges of the future—maybe even different businesses to augment company income. Alternatively, the company could not stand the negative press from a protracted battle, even though Godwin thought that the regulators were favorably disposed towards his plan. In fact, Godwin himself believed the company should help its customers rather than fight with them.

Source: This case was written by R. Edward Freeman, Olsson Professor of Business Administration, the Darden School, University of Virginia.

Case Questions

1. Who are the stakeholders in this case?
2. Which stakeholders are most important?
3. What are the critical trends in Tri-State's environment?
4. Why are the customers of Tri-State upset, in your opinion?
5. What should Mr. Godwin do? ■

Lewis Hine, *Carolina Cotton Mill*. 1900–1909. Photo courtesy of the Library of Congress. Like ethical insights, compelling artistic images frequently refuse to remain confined to the realm of the abstract or aesthetic: Some of Hine's photographic images were so powerful that they helped prompt laws prohibiting child labor.

4

SOCIAL RESPONSIBILITY AND ETHICS

Upon completing this chapter you should be able to:

1. Describe public attitudes toward business.
2. Explain Milton Friedman's attitude toward the social responsibilities of business.
3. Outline the two basic principles of the first theory of corporate social responsibility.
4. Sketch the two models of the second theory of corporate social responsiveness.
5. Define the descriptive and normative meanings of the word "ethical."
6. Describe two kinds of moral relativism, the arguments against each, and the kernels of truth that each contains.
7. Understand the basic tools of ethics.
8. Indicate how companies attempt to institutionalize ethics.

Chapter Outline

Introduction
The Changing Concept of Responsibility
Corporate Social Responsibility
The Shift to Ethics
The Tools of Ethics
The Challenge of Relativism

ILLUSTRATIVE CASE STUDY Introduction

An Ethical and Social Dilemma at Chemical Bank

In mid-1983, Matthew McPartland, a divisional manager for Chemical Bank's retail operations in certain parts of New York City, had to consider the pros and cons of shutting down two branches in a poor neighborhood. Together, they were losing about $100,000 a year at a time when the bank as a whole was trying to cut expenses. Chemical, however, had a tradition of involvement in the affairs of the communities where it did business. McPartland fully supported this policy and had consistently acted upon it. By doing so, he had given the bank an even larger share of the market in a part of his district than competitors who had more branches there.

Unfortunately, the commerce and housing of the area immediately around the two branches were deteriorating, and no improvement was likely in the short term. One solution would be to vacate the neighborhood entirely, but this would leave Chemical with no branch in a 40-block area. Another alternative would be to consolidate the two branches. However, the expense of setting up a combined branch would have made it also unprofitable for some time to come, although less so than maintaining two separate branches. In addition, the proposed location of the new branch would have been much closer to one of the old branches than to the other. It seemed likely that if the bank moved, it would lose deposits in the latter area.

Moreover, the residents of the area protested to local politicians, with whom the bank had formerly had good relations because it had faithfully complied with the terms of the Community Reinvestment Act of 1977. The Act encourages banks to respond to the credit needs of local neighborhoods, especially poor ones. Under the regulation, federal supervisory agencies have the right to limit or delay the expansion of banks that fail to serve the neighborhoods where they operate. As McPartland noted, the bank had maintained many unprofitable branches in poor neighborhoods and so had never had a CRA problem. Closing or consolidating the two branches might create one.

Moreover, McPartland believed that the bank's community policy attracted new business, contributing to the core of stable retail accounts that constituted the bank's safety net in hard times. If the branches were closed, he worried, neighborhood business conditions might further deteriorate and thus damage more deeply the bank's viability in the area. He also feared for Chemical's thriving business, cultivated through its community program, with area nonprofit organizations.

With Chemical's increasing emphasis on profitability, McPartland knew that he would have to decide quickly. Although he could cut expenses by consolidating the two branches, the only clearly *profitable* choice was to leave the area entirely—an option that McPartland found particularly unappealing because he and his branch managers had spent a good deal of time there. Closing down altogether seemed to negate everything that they and Chemical Bank had stood for. If Chemical "deserted" the area, McPartland feared, the bank would undermine its own reputation in the community. But he also feared that not closing the two branches would be contrary to the bank's current policy of stressing corporate profits.

Source: This case was prepared by Susan E. Woodward, Research Assistant, under the supervision of Lynda Sharp Paine, Visiting Assistant Professor, and Henry W. Tulloch, Executive Director, the Olsson Center for Applied Ethics.

TEACHING TIP

Start this chapter off by asking students to write down what a "socially responsible organization" would be like. Get some answers and write them down on the board. Compare and contrast the responses.

Ask them to write down what an "ethical manager" would be like. Again use the responses as a basis for comparing and contrasting.

Mr. McPartland's dilemma involves many forces and pressures from the environment in which his business functioned—factors such as we discussed in Chapter 3. However, that dilemma has also arisen because of the changing nature of corporate responsibility. McPartland must determine Chemical Bank's responsibility to the community and how that responsibility can be reconciled with its responsibility to the bank's stockholders. In short, McPartland faces a dilemma of social responsibility and *ethics*. The purpose of this chapter is to explain these concepts and to show how they relate to our understanding of the processes and practice of management.

THE CHANGING CONCEPT OF RESPONSIBILITY

THOUGHT-PROVOKER

Ask your students if their attitudes toward work are any different from their parents' attitudes. How? Ask them if their lifestyles are any different from their parents' lifestyles. How? How do these changes affect the changing concept of responsibilities?

During our century, there has been much change in what society expects of its institutions and in what managers regard as their proper role in organizations. In different ways, the Depression of the 1930s, stimulating President Franklin D. Roosevelt's New Deal and bringing active government involvement in the nation's economy through job creation and the passage of such legislation as social security and labor-relations laws, stimulated mounting criticism of business behavior. So, too, did the activist movements of the 1960s and 1970s, including the civil rights and consumer movements, which encouraged legislation that directly affected the management of corporations and stimulated continuing debate—often critical—of corporate management. This criticism was directed against the view that a commercial enterprise should pursue profit singlemindedly, with little or no consideration of the society and community in which the corporation resides. Increased attention has been focused on the ethics of corporate ventures, the social role to be played by corporations, and the level of responsibility that corporations have to a society.

In the 1980s, it became quite clear that the far-reaching changes of this century were, for the most part, necessary. As a new contract between business and society evolved, we have seen the traditional ethic of *caveat emptor* ("let the buyer beware") gradually erode into a new concept of corporate social responsibility. Meanwhile, many individuals, including many managers, believe that, besides their responsibility to the organizations they serve, they have a personal responsibility to society. Managers within organizations are increasingly held accountable for the social effects of their actions. Warren Anderson, President of Union Carbide, has been indicted by the government of India for events surrounding the Bhopal disaster. Two executives from Beech-Nut were recently sentenced to prison terms for consumer fraud. Managers in the defense industry have been accused of kickbacks and bribes, while whistleblowers have lost their jobs.

Where does that responsibility begin? Where does it end? What rules of conduct should govern the exercise of executive authority? Should a company place stakeholders' interests before those of society or of the environment? Should a company be responsible for the social consequences of its operations? When is regulation necessary, and when is it excessive? What, if anything, does the corporation owe to its employees? To what extent should corporations be held accountable for their products? These are the kinds of questions we must answer.[1]

The Public View of Business

THOUGHT-PROVOKER
''If it's legal, it's ethical.'' Debate pro and con.

This changing concept of responsibility is manifested in what some call the ''ethics crisis.'' We see headlines that touch upon it almost daily. Wedtech and other companies have been accused of exerting improper influence upon the federal government's awarding of contracts; Wall Street's already low reputation plunged still lower with the insider-trading scandal. Not surprisingly, pollster Louis Harris has found that 70 percent of the public answers no to the question, ''Does business see to it that its executives behave legally and ethically?''[2]

Gallup, another polling organization, reported similar findings from a poll in 1983. According to this poll, almost 50 percent of all Americans think that business ethics had declined during the previous ten years.[3] More than 60 percent believe that corporate executives file dishonest tax returns; upwards of 70 percent believe that corporate expense accounts are also calculated dishonestly. The dominant opinion is that business executives are significantly less ethical than doctors and even lawyers—though slightly more ethical than members of Congress. (The poll had nothing to say about the relative morality of Congressional investigators and various witnesses testifying before their committees.) Executives themselves are less than sanguine in regarding the current climate of business practices: Close to 40 percent say ''superiors have at some point asked them to do something they considered unethical.''[4]

Although public opinion polls, especially different ones taken at different points in time, cannot be taken as definitive reflections of business conditions, they do all point in the same direction. Public confidence in business ethics has declined. This fact is all the more striking because it came at a time when business had a friendly government in Washington—a government that has largely devoted itself to ''getting off the back of business.'' Indeed, President Reagan came to power in part because public opinion during the 1970s had become somewhat more pro-business than it had been previously.

These possibilities and realities call for a closer examination of the role that business plays in society at large and of the role of ethical thinking in business.

CORPORATE SOCIAL RESPONSIBILITY

At least some people believe that the only social responsibility of business is the maximization of profits. In espousing this view, Milton Friedman has become the leading opponent of the idea that business has a social responsibility other than being profitable.

---

[1]This chapter as a whole is based on William C. Frederick, ''Corporate Social Responsibility and Business Ethics,'' in S. Prakash Sethi and Cecilia M. Falbe, *Business and Society* (Lexington, Mass.: Lexington Books, 1987), pp. 142–161; and R. Edward Freeman and Daniel Gilbert, Jr. *Corporate Strategy and the Search for Ethics* (Englewood Cliffs, N.J.: Prentice Hall, 1988).

[2]Louis Harris, *Inside America* (New York: Vintage Books, 1986), p. 236.

[3]Roger Ricklefs, ''Executives and General Public Say Ethical Behavior Is Declining in U.S.,'' *Wall Street Journal,* October 31, 1983, p. 33.

[4]Roger Ricklefs, ''Public Gives Executives Low Marks for Honesty and Ethical Standards,'' *Wall Street Journal,* November 2, 1983, p. 33.

Milton Friedman's Argument

According to Friedman, "There is one and only one social responsibility of business: to use its resources and energy in activities designed to increase its profits so long as it stays within the rules of the game . . . [and] engages in open and free competition, without deception and fraud. . . ." Friedman contends that corporate officials are in no position to determine the relative urgency of social problems or the amount of organizational resources that should be committed to a given problem.[5] He also insists that managers who devote corporate resources to pursue personal, and perhaps misguided, notions of the social good unfairly tax their own shareholders, employees, and customers. In short, businesses should produce goods and services efficiently and leave the solution of social problems to concerned individuals and government agencies.

More recently, Friedman has also argued that government intervention is often undesirable;[6] he charges that bureaucratic officials responsible for implementing programs actually have little incentive to solve the problems that their organizations were created to deal with.

Friedman favors eliminating many Social Security and government benefits and adopting instead a limited set of government policies to influence national income. Citing growing productivity problems, he believes that our present system discourages work, and he wants to give individuals greater freedom to make their own economic decisions, without government controls. He believes, not without opposition, that this freedom would lead to less waste and greater productivity.

CLASS COMMENT

An advisory panel to the Food and Drug Administration recommended that extraordinarily strict restrictions be put on the use of a popular acne drug, Accutane, which has been shown to cause severe birth defects when taken by pregnant women. It also recommended that the drug's availability to doctors be restricted and that the FDA implement a number of Hoffmann-LaRoche's proposals to intensify product warnings (Hoffman-LaRoche makes Accutane). If the FDA accepts these recommendations to tighten the drug's availability, it would be one of the first times such restrictive measures had been placed on a drug already sold in the marketplace. (*Wall Street Journal*, 4/27/88, p. 3)

Friedman's views are generally considered to represent one extreme on a continuum that recognizes some division of social responsibility among the various segments of society, including government and the business community. Most managers and other people believe that both the government and the business community do have some responsibility to act in the interest of society. As the two most powerful institutions in the country, the sheer size of business and government obliges them to address problems of public concern. Both corporations and government depend upon acceptance by the society to which they belong. For them to ignore social problems might in the long run be destructive. In any case, if business does not amend its public image voluntarily, it will almost inevitably be subject to increased government regulation.

Keith Davis has said that there is "an iron law of responsibility which states that in the long run those who do not use power in a manner that society considers responsible will tend to lose it."[7] Procter & Gamble's quick action in voluntarily removing from the market a tampon that may have been responsible for toxic-shock syndrome is a recent example of one company's awareness of this "law."[8] In a January 1988 survey by *Fortune*, Procter & Gamble was ranked third behind Johnson & Johnson and Eastman Kodak as corporations most admired for their community and environmental responsibility.

The recent case of Beech-Nut knowingly selling bogus apple juice for babies illustrates what can happen if corporations ignore the "iron law" of responsibility: as much as $25 million in fines, legal fees, settlement of a class-action suit, two top executives sentenced to jail, and a tarnished reputation causing a loss in its market share to rivals Gerber and Heinz.

---

[5]Milton Friedman, *Capitalism and Freedom* (Chicago: University of Chicago Press, 1963), p. 133.

[6]Milton Friedman and Rose Friedman, *Free to Choose* (New York: Harcourt Brace Jovanovich, 1980).

[7]Keith Davis, "The Meaning and Scope of Social Responsibility," in Joseph W. McGuire, ed., *Contemporary Management* (Englewood Cliffs, N.J.: Prentice Hall, 1974), p. 631.

[8]Susan B. Foote, "Corporate Responsibility in a Changing Legal Environment," *California Management Review* 26, no. 3 (Spring 1984):217–228.

In the following sections, we will first address the idea that business has a social responsibility and examine a few proposals for how to understand this social role. Then we will address the more general and more current concept of the ''ethics'' of business and demonstrate some of the tools and techniques of ethics as they affect managerial decision making. Finally, we will address one challenge—the position known as *relativism*—which claims that ethics and social responsibility can be reduced to matters of opinion.

A History of Corporate Social Responsibility

In 1901, the conglomerate U.S. Steel Corporation was created, primarily out of the assets of the former Carnegie Steel Company. A few years earlier, Andrew Carnegie, the founder of U.S. Steel, had published a book called *The Gospel of Wealth* (1889), in which he argued that the rich hold their money ''in trust'' for the rest of society. Carnegie himself had practiced what he preached by giving away millions of dollars for charitable and civic purposes.

Nevertheless, the immense size of U.S. Steel inspired fears that it, and other big corporations like it, might threaten both free enterprise and democracy. Yet U.S. Steel, like Carnegie before it, embarked upon an active program of philanthropy. Admittedly, U.S. Steel, acting on Carnegie's ideas about capitalism and philanthropy, was the exception rather than the rule, and between the Civil War and the Great Depression, most management commitments to social welfare were encouraged either by law or labor-movement pressure.[9]

Not until the Great Depression of the 1930s did large numbers of executives take an independent interest in the social impact of business. In 1936, for example, Robert Wood (the CEO of Sears, Roebuck) pointed proudly to his ''stewardship'' of ''those general broad social responsibilities which cannot be presented mathematically and yet are of prime importance.''[10] Such views were the starting point for a new vision of the social responsibilities of business.

It was Andrew Carnegie (1835–1919), an American industrialist and philanthropist, who set forth the classic statement of *corporate social responsibility*. Carnegie's view was based upon two basic ideas: the charity principle and the stewardship principle. Both were frankly paternalistic.[11]

charity principle Doctrine of social responsibility requiring more fortunate individuals to assist less fortunate members of society.

The **charity principle** required the more fortunate members of society to assist its less fortunate members, including the unemployed, the handicapped, the sick, and the elderly. These unfortunates could be assisted either directly or indirectly, through such institutions as churches, settlement houses, and (from the 1920s onward) the Community Chest movement. Of course, well-to-do people themselves decided how much to contribute, and charity was an obligation of wealthy individuals, not of business itself. By the 1920s, however, ''community needs outgrew the wealth of even the most generous wealthy individuals.''[12] Business was now expected to contribute its resources to charities aiding the unfortunate.

stewardship principle Biblical doctrine that requires businesses and wealthy individuals to see themselves as stewards, or caretakers, holding their property in trust for the benefit of society as a whole.

The **stewardship principle** came from the Bible. It required businesses and wealthy individuals to see themselves as the stewards, or caretakers, of their property.

---

[9] Lee E. Preston, *Social Issues and Public Policy in Business and Management: Retrospect and Prospect* (College Park: University of Maryland College of Business and Management, 1986), pp. 3–4.

[10] J. C. Worthy, *Shaping an American Institution: Robert E. Wood and Sears, Roebuck* (Urbana: University of Illinois Press, 1984), quoted in Preston, *Social Issues and Public Policy.*

[11] This discussion is based upon William C. Frederick, ''Corporate Social Responsibility and Business Ethics,'' in Sethi and Falbe, *Business and Society,* pp. 142–161.

[12] Ibid., p. 143.

Holding it in trust for society as a whole, they could use it for any purpose that society deemed legitimate. However, it is also a function of business to multiply society's wealth by increasing its own through prudent investments of the resources that it is caretaking.[13]

By the 1950s and 1960s, these two principles had become widely accepted in American business, as more and more companies began to recognize that "power begets responsibility." Many companies that rejected the principle nonetheless realized that if business did not accept social responsibilities of its own free will, they would be forced upon it by the government. Many others thought that accepting these responsibilities was a matter of "enlightened self-interest." Dayton Hudson in Minneapolis has been a leader in applying principles of corporate social responsibility to the area of corporate philanthropy and the support of a group of companies called "the 5% club," which give 5 percent of their pre-tax earnings to charity. After a number of years of giving to the community, Dayton Hudson was in a position to get an anti-takeover law passed by the Minnesota legislature.

FOR DISCUSSION

Are organizations more socially responsible today than they were in past years? Why or why not?

Even at the high point of concern for corporate social responsibility, in the 1950s and 1960s, doubts began to undermine it. In 1953, H.R. Bowen insisted that business managers are morally bound to "pursue those policies, to make those decisions, or to follow those lines of action which are desirable in terms of the objectives and values of our society."[14] This rather different concept of the social responsibilities of business—one which saw business both as a reflection of social "objectives and values" and as an agency for promoting them—inspired much new thinking on the subject.

The charity and stewardship principles appealed chiefly to those who maintained a vested interest in the preservation of the free enterprise system and its freedom from other forms of social pressure. It thus attracted "an odd coalition of critics" that included just about anyone who was skeptical about corporate commitment to balancing social needs with economic needs:

> Included among the opponents were leftist critics ("It's a capitalist smokescreen hiding profits and greed"); free-market advocates ("It reduces market efficiency"); liberal critics ("Its impact is marginal"); and a large but unknown number of hard-nosed business executives ("It's impractical, too costly, and unworkable").[15]

One problem with the idea had to do with the meaning of the term "social responsibility." Some critics suggested that the concept of "social responsibility" did not indicate the appropriate magnitude of corporate concern, nor did it suggest how a company should actually weigh its social responsibilities against its other responsibilities. For example, when Ford was developing the model that it called the Pinto, the company discovered that the gas tank was unusually prone to catching fire in crashes. The company undertook a cost-benefit analysis to see if fixing the problem would be worthwhile. The analysis showed that the company could have made the car much safer by installing an $11 shield for the gas tank. Ford decided not to do so: In effect, it decided that the human lives disrupted and destroyed by the faulty gas tanks were worth less than $11 per Pinto.[16]

Finally, some critics charged that the notion of "social responsibility" permitted wealthy individuals and business executives to chose their social obligations according

---

[13]Ibid., p. 143.

[14]H. R. Bowen, *Social Responsibilities of the Businessman* (New York: Harper & Row, 1953), p. 6, quoted in Steven L. Wartick and Philip L. Cochran, "The Evolution of the Corporate Social Performance Model," *Academy of Management Review* 10 (1985): pp. 758–759.

[15]Frederick, "Corporate Social Responsibility and Business Ethics," pp. 145–146.

[16]These issues were litigated in *Grimshaw v. Ford Motor Company,* 119 Cal. App. 3d 757 Cal. Rptr 348 (1981).

to their own lights. In this sense, the notion of corporate responsibility became a smokescreen for the personal values of those individuals. As a result, the moral justification "for corporate decisions could be as varied as the lives and values of the executives making the decisions."

TEACHING TIP

Stress to students the distinctions between *responsiveness* and *responsibility*.

Eventually, many managers and theorists began to talk about corporate social *responsiveness* rather than *responsibility*. *Corporate social responsiveness* developed as a concept that was more pragmatic and concerned with the kinds of concrete results in which business managers are normally interested.

Corporate Social Responsiveness

corporate social responsiveness The second theory of corporate social responsibility, a more pragmatic, action-oriented view than the philosophical concepts of the charity or stewardship principles.

There are two basic approaches to the concept of **corporate social responsiveness.** Some theorists, focusing on the "micro" level of analysis, try to show individual companies how they can be more socially responsive. Other researchers concern themselves with the "macro" level of analysis, assuming that the government, not individual companies, should establish our country's social goals.

Ackerman's Model. Micro-level theorist Robert Ackerman was among the earliest people to suggest that responsiveness, not responsibility, should be the goal of corporate social endeavor. Ackerman described three phases through which companies commonly tend to pass in developing a response to social issues (see Table 4-1).[17]

[17]Robert W. Ackerman, "How Companies Respond to Social Demands," *Harvard Business Review* 51, no. 4 (July–August 1973):88–98. See also Sandra L. Holmes, "Adapting Corporate Structure for Social Responsiveness," *California Management Review* 21, no. 1 (Fall 1978):45–54.

TABLE 4-1 ACKERMAN'S THREE STAGES OF SOCIAL RESPONSIBILITY

ORGANIZATIONAL LEVEL	PHASES OF ORGANIZATIONAL INVOLVEMENT		
	Phase 1	Phase 2	Phase 3
Chief Executive	Issue: Corporate obligation Action: Write and communicate policy Outcome: Enriched purpose, increased awareness	Obtain knowledge Add staff specialists	Obtain organizational commitment Change performance expectations
Staff Specialists		Issue: Technical problem Action: Design data system and interpret environment Outcome: Technical and informational groundwork	Provoke response from operating units Apply data system to performance measurement
Division Management			Issue: Management problem Action: Commit resources and modify procedures Outcome: Increased responsiveness

Source: Reprinted by permission of the *Harvard Business Review*. An exhibit from "How Companies Respond to Social Demands" by Robert W. Ackerman (July–August 1973).

EXTRA EXERCISE

Have students find examples of socially responsible actions taken by organizations and bring them to class. Use current business periodicals.

In phase 1, a corporation's top managers learn of an existing social problem. At this stage, no one asks the company to deal with it. The chief executive officer merely acknowledges the problem by making a written or oral statement of the company's policy toward it.

In phase 2, the company hires staff specialists or engages outside consultants to study the problem and to suggest ways of dealing with it. Up to this point, the company has limited itself to declaring its intentions and formulating its plans.

Phase 3 is implementation. The company now integrates the policy into its ongoing operations. Unfortunately, implementation often comes slowly—and often not until the government or public opinion forces the company to act. By that time, the company has lost the initiative. Ackerman thus advises that managers should ''act early in the life cycle of any social issue in order to enjoy the largest amount of managerial discretion over the outcome.''[18]

For example, it has recently been suggested that women who spend a great deal of time working at video display terminals, such as word processors or computer operators, stand a higher than average chance of having problem pregnancies. The research is preliminary, tentative, and disputed by some investigators. Ackerman's point is that as this issue unfolds, as more actors and competing interests become involved in efforts to resolve it, managers could conceivably lose control over their ability to handle the issue at their own discretion. We can easily imagine several studies confirming these early indications and the resulting drama of Congressional hearings, work stoppages, lawsuits, and bureaucratic regulation. Ackerman's model suggests developing options early in the life cycle of an issue. In this case, ''enlightened'' companies could make the best information available to their employees, encourage them to ask questions, and even seek transfers or retraining if they believe it is warranted. Being responsive may well be the only responsible course of action.

Preston and Post's Model. Yet, as Ackerman himself knew, companies react slowly to just about any social problem. Even the most responsive of them take up to eight years to reach the third and highest stage of response. No wonder that by the late 1960s, many social activists had concluded that business would act decisively on social problems only if prodded by the government.[19]

It was Lee Preston and James Post[20] who put forward one of the first definitive statement of the macro approach to the concept of corporate responsiveness. In this model, Preston and Post suggested that business and society interact in two distinct ways. The **primary relations** of business—its relations with customers, employees, shareholders, and creditors—are market-oriented. When these relations create social problems, **secondary** (or nonmarket) **relations,** such as law and morality, come into play.

primary relations Interaction between a business and market-oriented groups, such as customers, employees, shareholders and creditors.

secondary relations Interaction between a business and non-market-oriented segments of society, such as the law and moral forces.

Government and public opinion, say the two researchers, fix the limits both of market and nonmarket relations. For when managers face a social problem, they do not merely examine their own consciences in deciding what to do about it. They also have to think about the law—federal, state, and local. They have to think about rulings by courts and regulatory agencies on all three levels. And they have to think about public opinion.

For example, a company may consider whether to institute an affirmative-action program to broaden the base of its employees, and it may decide to give special treatment to women and minorities. But even noble sentiments cannot be enacted as

[18]Frederick, ''Corporate Social Responsibility and Business Ethics,'' p. 150.

[19]Edwin M. Epstein, *The Corporation in American Politics* (Englewood, N.J.: Prentice Hall, 1969).

[20]Lee E. Preston and James E. Post, *Private Management and Public Policy: The Principle of Public Responsibility* (Englewood Cliffs, N.J.: Prentice Hall, 1975).

policy without a clear knowledge of the law. When Proctor and Gamble took the Rely Tampon off the market, it did so by studying the regulatory climate and was quite aware of the effects of continuing to market Rely if there were liability suits from victims of Toxic Shock Syndrome.

Carroll's Model. We have already seen that the idea of corporate social responsibility deals mainly with the philosophical basis of social action and that it deals mainly with the institutional basis (business and government) and its consequences for social policy. We are thus concerned here with three dimensions of social action: social principles, social processes, and social policies. In 1979, Archie Carroll attempted to combine these three dimensions—principle, process, and policy—into a single theory of corporate social action: **corporate social performance.**[21]

corporate social performance A single theory of corporate social action encompassing social principles, processes and policies.

Carroll suggested that principles, processes, and policies are three phases of one phenomenon. On the micro level, "corporate social performance" refers to the relationship between the firm and its environment; on the macro level, it "continued to use social responsibility"—that is, the philosophical principles that underlie social action—"as the starting point for corporate social involvement."[22]

The principles that give business its philosophical bearings are economic (the free market), legal, and ethical. They create a "social contract" between business and society, permitting companies to act as moral agents. In attempting to implement these principles, business carries out decision-making processes. Some are reactive, occurring only after a challenge has been made. Some processes are defensive, providing an excuse for a course of action. Other processes are accommodative, since they bring the company's position into line with the views of external organizations, especially the government. Finally, certain processes are proactive—the company anticipates demands that have not yet been made.

HERE'S AN EXAMPLE

International health officials have praised Merck and Co.'s multimillion dollar giveaway of a drug to fight "river blindness," the world's leading cause of blindness. The disease, caused by a fly-borne parasitic worm is a serious problem in mostly poor tropical areas of Africa, the Middle East, and Latin America. Dr. Bruce Greene, an infectious disease expert says, "If all companies were expected to make magnanimous gestures like Merck, it could cut off what little research exists." Merck officials are still worried about industry response to their decision because the company doesn't want to discourage research by setting a precedent whereby poor countries will regularly expect profitable companies to donate new drugs. (*Wall Street Journal*, 10/22/87, p. 42)

Four years later, in 1983, R. Strand extended Carroll's ideas by defining the connections among social principles (responsibilities), social processes (responsiveness), and social policies (responses).[23] Strand argued that society as a whole decides which social principles are binding upon business. Each company has three duties: "(a) to identify and analyze society's changing expectations . . . (b) to determine an overall approach for being responsive to society's changing demands, and (c) to implement appropriate responses to social issues."[24] These three interrelated duties correspond to principles, processes, and policies.[25]

The Limitations of Corporate Social Responsiveness Models. For several reasons, the shift from concern for "responsibility" to "responsiveness" and "performance" was an advance. It gave business executives a more realistic framework for making

HERE'S AN EXAMPLE

Wal-Mart Stores, Inc., the discount retail chain, announced it would donate 10,000 box fans during July 1988 to residents in heat-damaged areas in its 25-state trade territory. David D. Glass, president of Wal-Mart said, "This fan distribution is a way for Wal-Mart Associates to help our neighbors in need, especially those most affected by the heat—our young children, the elderly and infirm." (*Springfield News-Leader*, 7/15/88, p. 5B)

---

[21] Archie B. Carroll, "A Three-Dimensional Conceptual Model of Corporate Social Performance," *Academy of Management Review* 4 (1979):497–506; see also Carroll, *Social Responsibility of Management* (Chicago: Science Research Associates, 1984); and Kenneth E. Aupperle, Archie B. Carroll, and John D. Hatfield, "An Empirical Examination of the Relationship between Corporate Social Responsibility and Profitability," *Academy of Management Journal* 28 (1985):446–463.

[22] This account of corporate social performance is based chiefly on Wartick and Cochran, "The Evolution of the Corporate Social Performance Model, pp. 758–759.

[23] R. Strand, "A Systems Paradigm of Organizational Adjustment to the Social Environment," *Academy of Management Review* 8 (1983):90–96.

[24] Wartick and Cochran, "Evolution of the Corporate Social Performance Model," p. 763.

[25] Yet another attempt to unify the insights of CSR–1 and CSR–2 came from Edwin M. Epstein, who proposed what he called the *corporate social-policy-process model*. Like anyone who speculates about business ethics, Epstein stressed "value-based *moral reflection* and *choice* concerning individual and organizational behavior." Like those who tried to promote corporate social responsibility, Epstein wished to institutionalize awareness of the social consequences of corporate activity. And like the champions of corporate social responsiveness, he focused on "the individual and organizational *processes* through which value-based, issue-oriented reflection occurs." See Edwin M. Epstein, "The Corporate Social Policy Process: Beyond Business Ethics, Corporate Social Responsibility, and Corporate Social Responsiveness," *California Management Review* 29, no. 3 (Spring 1987):99–114.

FOR DISCUSSION

Who should be expected to bear the costs of corporate social activities? (Responses will generally be: the consumer, the company, maybe employees, etc.)

decisions about social policy. Meanwhile, the ideas put forward by champions of the micro and macro approaches shifted the focus of the debate over the socially oriented activities of business from abstract speculation to concrete operational decisions.[26] Most business executives would rather implement programs inspired by the concrete demands of external forces than speculate abstractly about the nature of their social responsibilities, as required by the concept of corporate social responsiveness.

But a practical and basic problem remains to be solved: Precisely which values social responsiveness should try to encourage. For example, which social demands should business be responsive to—all of them, or only some? If the latter, which ones? Should companies change social priorities when the government changes them—as happened, for example, when the moderately liberal Carter Administration gave way to President Reagan's militantly conservative one? Or should it hold fast to one set of priorities, no matter what government does?

FOR DISCUSSION

Is a company behaving in a socially responsible manner if it refuses to make necessary changes that will keep it in business? (This question will stir up some interesting discussion!)

The meaning of social "responsiveness" depends upon both the issue at hand and a given company's shifting attitude toward it. It seems to mean simply what the business community intends it to mean at a given time and in a given case.[27] When restaurants in racist towns refused to serve blacks, were they not being "responsive" to community sentiment? By contrast, when a company like Control Data tries to make a business out of inner-city redevelopment and train the hard-core unemployed, it is being technically "unresponsive" because they are striking out in a new direction. Similar ambiguities and questions apply to companies that bolster regimes in other countries. Who defines community or national interest in countries such as South Africa? Is apartheid, maintained by a white minority, in the interests of the total community, both black and white? While many U.S. corporations have left South Africa because of its political situation, those that remain must struggle with such dilemmas.

The real difficulty with all of the models in this section is that they have no way of effectively managing a conflict in *values*. They give little advice about *how* to solve disputes that represent fundamentally different visions of our world. Hence, they need to have a more direct concern with ethics.

[26]Frederick, "Corporate Social Responsibility and Business Ethics," p. 153.

[27]Ibid., p. 154.

ILLUSTRATIVE CASE STUDY Continued

An Ethical and Social Dilemma at Chemical Bank

Now that we are armed with an arsenal of theories about social responsibility, let's return to the case of our Mr. McPartland and ask if any of these theories of corporate social responsibility help him in deciding whether or not to close his two unprofitable branches.

Milton Friedman would tell him to do whatever he thinks will maximize the bank's profits. If that means closing the two branches, so be it. The theory of corporate social responsibility suggests that before McPartland acts, he should determine his responsibilities to the neighborhoods where his bank does business. By these lights, too, he should decide who has a stake in his decision and what the company owes each of those stakeholders.

To be responsive, McPartland must try to assign priorities to those key stakeholders. He probably can't satisfy all of them, but he must try to get a better idea of the real consequences—economic, social, and political—of closing the branches in question. Unfortunately, McPartland is forced to make a critical decision very late in the life cycle of the issue at hand. A better approach would have been to generate more options for revitalizing the branches when the company had received early warning signs that they were in trouble. There is no rulebook for making decisions as difficult as this one.

THE SHIFT TO ETHICS

Not surprisingly, modes of corporate social responsibility, responsiveness, and performance have become even more complex. The external environment of most organizations contains a host of conflicting stakeholder demands (see Chapter 3), and, organizations have responded by introducing changes in their management systems ranging from internal restructuring to basic compliance with the law of the land. Many theorists and managers, however, continue to call for a broader examination of business in terms of ethics. Although assessing an organization's social responsibility covers its relationships with the external world, ethics is a more general umbrella covering both internal and external relationships. Much of the current research on corporate social responsibility has thus been brought together under the broad phrase "business ethics."

EXTRA EXERCISE

Have students identify business situations they might face where questions of ethics might arise. (For example: padding expense accounts like everyone else in my department; sending my secretary on my personal errand; knowing about a safety hazard in my work area; etc.)

Business ethics is a topical subject. There are daily stories in *The Wall Street Journal* and in the popular press. Television news carries the latest scandal and eagerly depicts major corporate figures headed for court or prison. But business and ethics—that is to say, organizations and ethics—are connected in more significant ways than the news media and some pundits would have us believe. Almost every business decision has an ethical component, and effective managers must add the methods, tools, concepts, models, and ideas of ethics to their managerial tool kits.

What Is Ethics?

To begin with, some writers distinguish between "ethics" on the one hand and "morals" on the other. But this distinction leads only to confusion. Here we will define *ethics* broadly and simply as the study of how our decisions affect other people. It is also the study of people's rights and duties and of the rules that people apply in making decisions.[28]

Four Levels of Ethical Questions in Business

We cannot avoid ethical issues in business any more than we can avoid them in the other areas of our lives. In business, most of these questions fall into one of four levels, which are not mutually exclusive.

The first level we might call "societal." At this level, we ask questions about the basic institutions in a society. The problem of apartheid in South Africa is a societal-level question: Is it ethically correct to have a social system in which a group of people—indeed, the majority—is systematically denied basic rights?

Another societal-level moral question is the debate over the merits of capitalism. Is capitalism a just system for allocating resources? What role should the government play in regulating the marketplace? Should we tolerate gross inequalities of wealth, status, and power? Such societal-level questions usually represent an ongoing debate among major competing institutions. As managers and individuals, each of us can try to shape that debate. The early theorists of corporate social responsibility such as Andrew Carnegie worked at this level by arguing that the proper role of a business such as his own U.S. Steel was to apply the principles of charity to assist the poor and unfortunate groups in society.

The second level might be called that of stakeholders—employees, suppliers, customers, shareholders, bondholders, and the rest. Here we ask questions about how a

[28] Our discussion of this issue is based on R. Edward Freeman, Alexander Horniman, and John W. Rosenblum, "A Note on Ethics in Business" (Charlottesville: The Sponsors of the Darden School, 1988).

company should deal with the external groups affected by its decisions, and also about how the stakeholders should deal with the company.

There are many such issues. Insider trading is one, as is the limitation on a company's obligation to inform its customers about the potential dangers of its products. What obligations does a company have to its suppliers? To the communities where it operates? To its stockholders? How should we attempt to decide such matters? Notice that at this level, the questions deal with business policy. Stakeholder questions are about a company's relations with its key resources. Managers make such decisions each and every day.

The third level of moral discourse might be called ''internal policy.'' At this level, we ask questions about the nature of the relations between a company and its employees, both managers and others. What kind of contract is fair? What are the mutual obligations of managers and other workers? What rights do employees have? Is there a right to due process in matters of employment? To free speech in the workplace? To meaningful work? To participate in the management of companies that employ us? These questions, too, pervade the workday of a manager. Layoffs, perks, work rules, motivation, and leadership are all ethical categories in the descriptive sense. It is on this level that companies have a chance to be socially responsive to stakeholders. In Chapter 1, for example, we saw how companies as diverse as Merck and Reebok were using their products and financial resources to be responsive to the values of key groups in their environments.

Finally, we come to the ''personal'' level of moral issues. Here we ask questions about how people should treat one another within a corporation. Should we be honest with one another, whatever the consequences? What obligations do we have—both as human beings and as workers who fill specific work roles—to our bosses, our subordinates, and our peers? These questions deal with the day-to-day issues of life in any organization. Behind them lie two broader issues: Do we have the right to treat other people as means to our ends? Can we avoid doing so?

Ethical questions are everywhere, at all levels of business activity. Business ethics concern the ground rules of individual, company, and societal behavior. As such philosophers as Mark Pastin have argued, our behavior—on individual, company, and societal levels—implies ground rules that are already in place.[29] ''Doing ethics'' is the hard part because it requires that we be critical of our own ground rules and that we improve them.

THE TOOLS OF ETHICS

COORDINATED RESOURCE

A recently completed landmark study on business ethics entitled, ''Corporate Ethics: A Prime Business Asset'' is available from The Business Roundtable, 200 Park Avenue, New York, NY 10166, or call (212) 682-6370. An excerpt from this document on Johnson & Johnson's Credo is found in the box on Ethics in Management. In addition, see the Lecture Extras Supplement for an anecdotal digest of the contents of the report.

We engage in some kind of ethical reasoning every day of our lives, but in order to improve it, we must analyze it explicitly as well as practice it casually. Business will not overcome the moral uncertainties that now plague it until it addresses ethical issues in ethical terms.

Ethical Language

Some companies, such as IBM, have an open-door policy to encourage employees to speak about problems. Others, such as J. C. Penney, have spelled out policies about conflict of interest. (See the Management Application box entitled ''A Code of Conduct at J. C. Penney.'')

[29]Mark Pastin, 'Ethics as an Integrating Force in Management,'' *Journal of Business Ethics* 3 (November 1984):293–304; and ''Business Ethics, by the Book,'' *Business Horizons* 28 (1986):2–6.

MANAGEMENT APPLICATION

A CODE OF CONDUCT AT J. C. PENNEY

J. C. Penney is one of many companies that have corporate codes of ethical conduct. Called "Conflicts of Interest," this code was meant to ensure that Penney's employees (whom it calls "Associates") do nothing that "could impair, or appear to impair, an Associate's ability to perform his or her Company duties or to exercise his or her judgment in a fair and unbiased manner."

The statement covers gifts, loans, and entertainments offered to Penney employees by people who do business with them. Penney recognizes in the statement that employees have a "right to conduct their personal affairs without interference." Nonetheless, the statement also points out that the company must also know if its employees have behaved in ways that are opposed to its own interests.

First, it must do so because some of the things that its employees could do—take bribes, for instance—are illegal. But what is a bribe? Let's suppose that a company doing business with Penney invites one of its employees to a lavish and expensive lunch. Does this constitute a "bribe"?

Not in principle, says the Penney statement, since attendance at "business-related functions, including the acceptance of lunches or other meals . . . is a normal and permissible business practice." Penney merely advises its employees to make sure that "their value and frequency are not excessive." Dinners, theater tickets, hunting trips, and other kinds of business entertainment "may be accepted only if it is practicable for the Associate to reciprocate." If employees cannot do so, they should take the problem to their supervisors.

The statement provides several such cases and the proper resolution of each. Suppose, for example, that another company were to invite a Penney employee to attend a two-day seminar at a fashionable resort. The seminar is the most important commercial event of the year in the employee's specialty, but he or she cannot reciprocate in any practical way. She therefore takes the problem to her supervisor, who should rule in favor of attendance, since it is "necessary or desirable at times in order that Associates remain current in their areas of responsibility for the Company."

Source: Ronald Berenbeim, *Corporate Ethics* (New York: The Conference Board, 1987), pp. 26–27.

Ethics uses a language that has been curiously absent from a lot of management theory. The key terms of the ethical language are *values, rights, duties,* and *rules.* Let's consider each in its turn.

values Relatively permanent desires that seem to be good in themselves.

Values. When you value something, you want it or you want it to happen. **Values** are relatively permanent desires that seem to be good in themselves, like peace or goodwill.

Values are the answers to the "why" questions. Why, for example, are you reading this book? You might reply that you want to learn about management. Why is that important? To be a better manager? Why do you want that? To be promoted and make more money sooner? Why do you need more money? To spend it on a VCR? Such questions go on and on. You reach a point when you no longer want something for the sake of something else. At this point, you have arrived at a value. Corporations have values. For some, it is power in size or profitability or making a quality product. Obviously, individuals also have values.

rights Claims that entitle a person to take a particular action.

Rights and Duties. A **right** is a claim that entitles a person the "room" in which to take action. In more formal terms, one might call this room a person's "sphere of autonomy" or, more simply, his or her freedom. Rights are rarely absolute; most people would agree that the scope of individual rights is limited by the rights of others. Ordinarily, for example, you have a right to speak your mind freely. But suppose that in doing so you would take away another person's right to compete on equal terms for a job. You would do this if, for example, you were to make slanderous statements about that person.

duties Obligations to take specific steps or obey the law.

Moreover, rights are correlated with duties. Whenever someone has a right, someone else has a duty to respect it. A **duty** is an obligation to take specific steps—to pay taxes, for example, and to obey the law in other respects.

moral rules Rules for behavior that often become internalized as moral values.

Moral Rules. It is **moral rules** that guide us through situations where competing interests collide. You might think of moral rules as "tie breakers"—guidelines that can resolve disagreements. Moral rules, which are rules for behavior, often become internalized as moral values.

Common Morality

common morality The body of rules covering ordinary ethical problems.

Common morality is the body of rules covering ordinary ethical problems. These are the rules we live by most of the time. Let's briefly examine some basic principles of common morality to see how they work.

Promise Keeping. Most of us want to have some assurance that other people will do what they say. Without the simple convention of promise keeping, social interaction would grind to a halt; business would be impossible. Every moral theory thus asserts, at the very least, that human beings should keep most of their promises most of the time. Insider-trading became such a scandal in part because those who were caught had promised not to engage in such activities.

Nonmalevolence. Among other things, rights and duties are a way of preventing violent conflict. If we constantly had to worry about our basic physical safety, we would be much less willing to trust other people and have more complex dealings with them in which disputes may arise and require resolution. Most moral theories thus require that most people, most of the time, refrain from harming other human beings.

There are, of course, exceptions—we allow the police to use force to subdue criminals; we accept wars that we regard as just; we let people defend themselves when they are attacked without cause. But morality, by its very nature, requires us to avoid violence in settling disputes.

Mutual Aid. Morality and moral codes regulate the behavior of human communities that include individuals who pursue both the group's common interests and their own separate interests. Much as we have a negative desire that these individuals should refrain from harming us, we also have a positive desire that they should help us. From this desire, we derive the principle that individuals should help one another if the cost of doing so is not great.

Respect for Persons. By and large, common morality also requires us to regard other people as ends in themselves, not as mere means to our own ends. Treating people as ends involves taking them seriously, accepting their interests as legitimate, and regarding their desires as important.

Respect for Property. The preceding principle, unlike those before it, is controversial. Even more controversial is the principle that most people, most of the time, should get the consent of others before using their property. If you think of people as owning their own bodies, respect for property is a corollary of respect for persons.

Applying Ethics

CLASS COMMENT

"If greed is the main motivator in the surge of white-collar crime, pressure to perform also plays a part." (*Time*, 5/25/87, p. 23)

As in any other institution or organization, and perhaps even more so, modern corporations enlist certain rules that may conflict with the rules of common morality. For example, invoking the principle of mutual aid to assist a person who needs help might draw sneers from corporate managers if the distressed party was a competitor. We must know *how* to apply the principles of common morality and the language of ethics to business situations.

Let's consider one of the most important business events of recent history. On January 1, 1984, what had until then been the largest corporation in the world ceased to exist. The American Telephone and Telegraph Company, AT&T, was broken up into eight separate multimillion-dollar telephone-operating companies.

Why? Two years earlier, AT&T and the U.S. Justice Department had signed a consent decree in which the government agreed to drop its antitrust suit against the company and to permit AT&T to compete in the relatively unregulated computer business. In return, AT&T agreed to divest its large distribution network and local-telephone business, the eight wholly owned Bell System operating companies.

The future of AT&T was up for grabs. Billions of dollars were at stake. But there were even more important issues. More than one million people worked for AT&T. Local communities throughout the United States depended on it for much of their employment base. Many smaller companies depended on sales to it. Tens of millions of people, in the United States and abroad, were customers. There were more than three million shareholders. Many people had come to expect that AT&T would provide everything from low-cost phone service to lifetime employment.

The AT&T divestiture was a matter of ethics because it distributed harms and benefits to various groups with a stake in the decision. Let us suppose that Charles Brown, the CEO of AT&T, decided to use the language of ethics in making this decision. To keep things simple, let us also suppose that Mr. Brown had only two choices: to go on fighting the Justice Department or to accept the divestiture. Mr. Brown will now have to answer four questions. (Of course, these are not the only questions that might be asked. For another set of questions, see Exhibit 4-1.)

First, Mr. Brown must find out whom his decision will affect—for instance, stockholders, employees, customers, the government, suppliers, local communities,

EXHIBIT 4-1 TWELVE QUESTIONS FOR EXAMINING THE ETHICS OF A BUSINESS DECISION

1. Have you defined the problem accurately?
2. How would you define the problem if you stood on the other side of the fence?
3. How did this situation occur in the first place?
4. To whom and to what do you give your loyalty as a person and as a member of the corporation?
5. What is your intention in making this decision?
6. How does this intention compare with the probable results?
7. Whom could your decision or action injure?
8. Can you discuss the problem with the affected parties before you make your decision?
9. Are you confident that your decision will be as valid over a long period of time as it seems now?
10. Could you disclose without qualm your decision or action to your boss, your CEO, the board of directors, your family, society as a whole?
11. What is the symbolic potential of your action if understood? If misunderstood?
12. Under what conditions would you allow exceptions to your stand?

Source: Laura L. Nash, "Ethics Without the Sermon," *Harvard Business Review* 59 (November–December 1981):78–90.

and competitors. He will also have to make an effort to see these groups as embodiments of real flesh-and-blood people, not as a mere mass of faceless individuals.

Next, Mr. Brown must know how his decision will affect the people in each group. The two strategic alternatives may yield different results. If AT&T continues to fight the Justice Department, the outcome would be far from clear. Should AT&T prevail, its stockholders, its employees, its customers, its suppliers, its competitors, the government, and the local communities where it does business will all experience "business as usual." If the Justice Department prevails, the existing allocation of harms and benefits will change, and it will change differently for different groups.

Now Mr. Brown needs to know the interests and desires of each group. He also wants to identify each group's rights. The stockholders have rights because they have risked their capital and are thus entitled to a return; the company's employees have what they regarded as a virtual right to lifetime employment by AT&T, and that expectation was encouraged by the company itself; customers feel they have a right to the good low-priced service that the company had provided in the past.

Finally, Mr. Brown has to decide which rules to use in making his decision. He might begin by examining the rules accepted by each stakeholding group. Traditionally, management has claimed to believe that it should maximize the wealth of the stockholders. He could also view the decision from the standpoint of other stakeholders, and he must be prepared for the likelihood that these various standpoints will conflict. Whatever rules Mr. Brown decides to use, he will be allocating harms and benefits among the various stakeholders.

Institutionalizing Ethics

Mr. Brown and other CEOs do not have to confront these questions all alone. Instead, they can institutionalize the process of ethical decision making by ensuring that each moral decision builds upon decisions that preceded it. There are several ways of institutionalizing ethical policy, including corporate codes of conduct, ethics committees, ombudsman offices, judicial boards, ethics-training programs, and **social audits** (reports describing the company's activities in such areas of social interest as community involvement, environmental protection, equal opportunity, product quality, and workplace safety).

CLASS COMMENT

Is there an ethics crisis in American management? Companies are scrambling to adopt codes of ethics. Business schools are re-emphasizing ethics in their basic courses and even adding courses in business ethics. Hundreds of consultants are helping companies put "integrity" into corporate cultures. ". . . Ethics seems to be moving up the corporate priority list." (*Business Week*, 2/15/88, pp. 56–57)

One survey found that more than 90 percent of the companies that have tried to institutionalize ethics have created codes of ethics requiring and prohibiting specific practices. Although no more than 11 percent of these companies actually display their codes in offices and factories, most of them will dismiss, demote, or reprimand employees who intentionally violate those codes.[30] For one code that has become a model—especially given the company's trauma over the Tylenol-tampering disaster—see the box on "The Credo" at Johnson & Johnson.

Even though another survey reports that "codes have a limited effect in deterring the misbehavior of intentional wrong-doers," many companies feel that these codes assure employees that business decisions should take account not only of economic and social considerations but of ethical ones as well. "More importantly," the study concludes, codes of conduct remind employees "that the company is fully committed to stating its standards and is asking its workforce to incorporate them into their daily activities."[31] Figure 4-1 indicates the groups to whom corporate ethics codes apply.

---

[30]The foregoing statistics about ethics codes come from the Center for Business Ethics, Bentley College, "Are Corporations Institutionalizing Ethics?" *Journal of Business Ethics* 5 (1986):86.

[31]Ronald Berenbeim, *Corporate Ethics* (New York: The Conference Board, 1987), p. 13.

ETHICS IN MANAGEMENT

THE SPIRIT OF "THE CREDO" AT JOHNSON & JOHNSON

In its beginnings, when it specialized in baby powder and bandage products, Johnson and Johnson was a highly centralized organization. Now, it is both highly diversified, operating over 160 businesses in over 50 countries, and highly decentralized. Under a program begun by General Robert Wood Johnson, a son of one of the company's three founders who took it over in 1932, the process of decentralization was started, and today each company has a president or managing director who reports to a Company Group Chairperson but who generally manages his or her particular company with a fair amount of independence. Because Johnson and Johnson's decentralized structure depends so heavily on individual autonomy and decision making, the company established a "Credo" in 1945, not only to insure its essential dedication to product quality, but to encourage personal commitment to the goals of a loosely structured organization. "The Credo," says Chairman James Burke, "is our common denominator."

Our Credo

—We believe our first responsibility is to the doctors, nurses and patients, to mothers and all others who use our products and services.
—In meeting their needs everything we do must be of high quality.
—We must constantly strive to reduce our costs in order to maintain reasonable prices.
—Customers' orders must be serviced promptly and accurately.
—Our suppliers and distributors must have an opportunity to make a fair profit.
—We are responsible to our employees, the men and women who work with us throughout the world.
—Everyone must be considered as an individual.
—We must respect their dignity and recognize their merit.
—They must have a sense of security in their jobs.
—Compensation must be fair and adequate, and working conditions clean, orderly and safe.
—Employees must feel free to make suggestions and complaints.
—There must be equal opportunity for employment, development and advancement for those qualified.
—We must provide competent management, and their actions must be just and ethical.
—We are responsible to the communities in which we live and work and to the world community as well.
—We must be good citizens—support good works and charities and bear our fair share of taxes.
—We must encourage civic improvements and better health and education.
—We must maintain in good order the property we are privileged to use, protecting the environment and natural resources.
—Our final responsibility is to our stockholders.
—Business must make a sound profit.
—We must experiment with new ideas.
—Research must be carried on, innovative programs developed and mistakes paid for.
—New equipment must be purchased, new facilities provided and new products launched.
—Reserves must be created to provide for adverse times.
—When we operate according to these principles the stockholders should realize a fair return.

Source: Laura L. Nash, Nash Associates, Cambridge, Massachusetts, "Johnson & Johnson's Credo," in James Keogh, ed., *Corporate Ethics: A Prime Business Asset* (New York: The Business Roundtable, 1988), pp. 77–104.

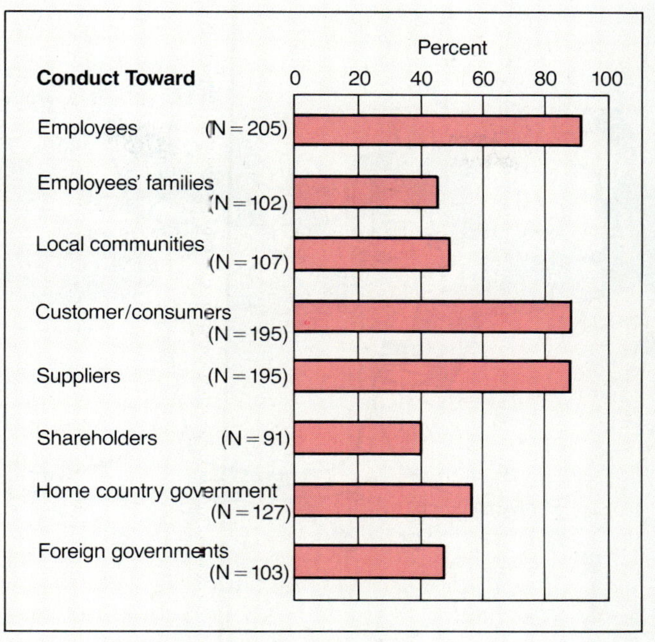

Source: Ronald Berenbeim, *Corporate Ethics* (New York: The Conference Board, 1987), p. 15.

FIGURE 4-1 GROUPS TO WHOM CORPORATE ETHICS CODES APPLY (SURVEY OF 225 CORPORATIONS)

QUOTATION FROM A MANAGER

Frank A. Olson, chairman of Hertz Corporation, the car rental company that admitted overcharging motorists and insurers $13 million for repairs, vows, "If I catch one guy billing at something other than cost, I'll throw him out the window myself." (*Business Week*, 2/15/88, p. 57)

Many companies trying to institutionalize ethical policy have created specific organizations to enforce that policy. Of these companies, more than 40 percent have also set up programs to teach their employees how to confront moral problems in business. Some 18 percent have set up ethics committees; 3 percent have appointed an ombudsman (an officer to investigate decisions from an ethical point of view); and 3 percent have judicial boards that rule on ethical questions.[32] Ethics training programs very often include discussion programs and workshops in which employees thrash out hypothetical moral problems. Participating companies report that "the give-and-take of these programs helps to sensitize employees to ethical issues, broaden and deepen employee awareness of code directives, and underscore the commitment of the company to its ethical principles."[33]

THE CHALLENGE OF RELATIVISM

Finally, we must confront the challenge of relativism to moral theory in general. There are many versions of moral relativism, but all of them hold that we cannot decide matters of right and wrong, good and evil, in any rational way.

Moral relativism seems to imply that since right and wrong are relative to whomever makes the decision, there are no answers—except individual answers—to any

[32]Center for Business Ethics, "Are Corporations Institutionalizing Ethics?" p. 87.
[33]Berenbeim, *Corporate Ethics*, p. 17.

"Miss Johnson will now pass out the moral blinders."
Drawing by Richter; © 1988 The New Yorker Magazine, Inc.

moral question. It also suggests that constructive moral argument is impossible, for each person will do what is right for himself or herself. Each of us may agonize over every moral problem, but there is no way of deciding that one decision is morally better than another.

Naive Relativism

naive relativism The idea that all human beings are themselves the standard by which their actions should be judged.

QUOTATION FROM CONVICTED CORPORATE CROOK

Albert Miano, a former $35,000/year middle manager at *Reader's Digest* who embezzled $1 million from 1982 to 1987: "Greed was the biggest motivator" he confesses. Philosophizing from prison, he states, "For a nickel or for $5 million it doesn't pay. You enjoy the money for a while, but you lose your pride and self-respect. It ends up hurting your family, and no money can ever change that." (*Fortune*, 4/25/88, p. 194)

Perhaps the most widespread form of relativism might be called **naive relativism**—the idea that all human beings are themselves the standard by which their actions should be judged. The naive relativist believes that because ethical decisions are personal, important, and complex, only the decision maker's opinion is relevant.

However, it does not follow from the personal and serious nature of morality that we can't reason about it—quite the contrary. Because morality is so vital to our lives, we must do our very best thinking in precisely this area. If other areas of our lives are anything to judge by, we need the help of everyone who is engaged in the process of moral reasoning. If no one's moral beliefs have to stand up to scrutiny and criticism, how will anyone get better at making moral choices? If there are no standards for deciding if one moral decision is better or worse than any other—if any decision will do—how can we believe that morality is important?

Tolerance for others is necessary and good, but naive relativism can take tolerance beyond the limits of basic reflection upon our selves and our lives. People often disagree about moral questions, much as they disagree about everything else, but we should not conclude that there can never be any reason for anything we do, or that one course of action is always just as good as another. Instead, we must try to sort things out; if we don't, we have admitted defeat in coming to terms with our own lives. Besides, the naive relativist's tolerance for all points of view is a contradiction, for it is itself an absolute point of view: ''We must always be tolerant.''

There is an even more compelling argument against naive relativism. From that point of view, the moral test for any action is whether or not the agent believed it to be correct. Therefore, we need not check on the *content* of a particular action; we must only find out if the agent acted in accord with his or her beliefs. Such realities as abortion, infanticide, civil liberties, capital punishment, and so forth are undoubtedly the content of many an ethical discussion, but any judgment about an action taken regarding such issues—say, protesting pro or con—is necessarily suspended.

Ultimately, the real failing of naive realism is its laziness: It is not a belief but rather an excuse for not having beliefs. Admittedly, it is hard to marshal facts and construct theories, and the naive realist just doesn't want to bother, despite the price that must be paid—giving up any hope of living in a better world or becoming a better human being.

Cultural Relativism

cultural relativism The idea that morality is relative to a particular culture, society, or community.

A second form of relativism, **cultural relativism,** claims that morality is relative to particular cultures, societies, or communities. It further asserts that no standards can help us *judge* the morality of a particular culture, and that the best anyone can do is to *understand* the particular moral codes and customs of a given society.

Cultural relativism tells us to understand, for example, South African morality or Russian morality, but not to judge them. If norms and customs are shared by the members of any society, what right does someone outside it have to criticize from some external standpoint? Why should South Africans or Russians have any obligation to accept our ideas of morality?

The implications of cultural relativism are vast as, today, more and more corporations operate in a global marketplace. Employees maintain allegiances to different nations, races, and creeds; managers may have to do business in such dissimilar places as Japan, Korea, Saudi Arabia, France, Mexico, China, and Brazil. They confront a diversity of cultural norms, from different table manners to different religions and moral principles. Cultural relativism is a critical ethical issue for businesses and managers operating in a global environment.

If the proponents of cultural relativism are right, managers must obey only the local moral code in countries where they operate. Must American managers in Saudi Arabia treat women as the Saudis treat them? Must American managers in South Africa treat blacks as white South Africans treat them?

Like it or not, we must do business in countries whose cultures and laws differ from ours. Take the People's Republic of China. A corporation operating there must accept the denial of basic political freedoms. Sometimes, moreover, companies find themselves torn between the requirements of two different governments and legal systems. For instance, the government of France once instructed the French subsidiary of Dresser Industries to sell the Soviet Union materials for a gas pipeline linking it to Western Europe. Meanwhile, our government forbade Dresser or any of its subsidiaries to sell such materials to the Soviets.[34]

---

[34]For an interesting view of the Dresser case, see B. Crawford and S. Lenway, ''Decision Modes and International Regime Changes: Western Collaboration on East–West Trade,'' *World Politics* 37, no. 3 (1985):375–402.

If the cultural relativists are right, the search for morals, at least in the business arena, is over. We must merely obey local customs, codes, and laws. But are they right? The Dresser case suggests one problem: the fact that companies find themselves caught between conflicting moral and legal demands from more than one culture. Dresser had to act. The only advice a cultural relativist could give would be: "Do whatever you like, because you will violate legal stricture whatever you do." So, far from helping us out of this difficult situation, cultural relativism can only confirm the realization that we cannot possibly escape it.

The second problem with cultural relativism is that most cultures are fairly diverse. In South Africa, for instance, whose moral norms should be obeyed—those of the white minority or those of the black majority? It is all too easy to accept as norms what are merely the beliefs of a society's elite—beliefs that may be nothing more than a way for the strong to oppress the weak.

A Kernel of Truth

THOUGHT-PROVOKER

A new survey by Ward Howell International, a New York recruiting firm, found that only 55 percent of human resource executives say they would *always* provide accurate references to a prospective employer. (*Fortune*, 4/25/88, p. 198)

Relativism represents an admission that human reason cannot solve the most important of all questions: How shall we live as human beings? It tells us, on the contrary, that we *should* live in any way that we actually *do* live. In business, where ethical decisions are often regarded as separate from business decisions, relativism would prevent us from trying to find consistent moral principles to help us solve our business problems. It would also make it impossible for us to resolve conflicting moral demands in any satisfactory way. This is a very high price to pay for a theory.

Relativism warns us that ours is a very big and complex world in which we must be tolerant of diversity. To be sure, a proper level of tolerance is a real virtue, but taken to extremes it can be an alibi for just about any refusal to make judgments that must ultimately be made. Should we be tolerant of the white-majority regime in South Africa? Should we be tolerant of the Sandinista regime in Nicaragua? Should we be equally tolerant of both? Strictly speaking, relativism requires that we answer yes in all cases—but it has also asked us to forgo the exercise of any reasoned judgment.

In order to behave morally, we must believe that we are acting correctly, but that belief is not a sufficient condition for morality. We must also take into account the community of individuals whose lives could be changed by our actions. Here, in the interplay between individuals and the community, is the kernel of truth in relativism.

The notion of a broad human community is an important one, for in fact it gives us not only the institutions that make relativism attractive but also the intuitions that defeat it as a theory. Human communities give rise to communication and to language. Without a community, language itself would be impossible. In fact, we must all communicate through some language, and to communicate we must literally speak the same language. To speak the same language is to share the same kinds of experience, to live together with a sense of solidarity. We must know the accepted and proper use of words or we cannot communicate. If we share the same kinds of experience—for example, the experience of learning a language, of enjoying family ties, and meaningful work—we have a common base from which to look for principles. If we have no basis for communication, we have no reason for morality and moral principles except as a way of codifying our beliefs about our obligations to "persons" or "things" with which we have no communication.

Suppose we encountered an alien society and that all attempts to communicate with it failed. If we could nevertheless infer that the aliens were living creatures, we would probably continue our efforts to communicate. But if we could make no such

INTERNATIONAL MANAGEMENT

THE SULLIVAN PRINCIPLES IN SOUTH AFRICA

In an effort to change business practices in South Africa, a black minister from Philadelphia, Reverend Leon Sullivan, put forward a set of principles to guide U.S. firms who did business in South Africa. Sullivan, a member of the Board of Directors of General Motors, then lobbied corporations to sign the principles and to report on their progress in implementing them. Most of the major companies in the U.S. signed a statement by which they promised to abide by the principles. Sullivan's six principles are:

Principle 1 Nonsegregation of the Races in All Eating, Comfort, Locker Rooms, and Work Facilities

Principle 2 Equal and Fair Employment Practices for All Employees

Principle 3 Equal Pay for All Employees Doing Equal or Comparable Work for the Same Period of Time

Principle 4 Initiation and Development of Training Programs that Will Prepare Blacks, Coloreds and Asians in Substantial Numbers for Supervisory, Administrative, Clerical and Technical Jobs

Principle 5 Increasing the Number of Blacks, Coloreds and Asians in Management and Supervisory Positions

Principle 6 Improving the Quality of Employees' Lives Outside the Work Environment in Such Areas as Housing, Transportation, Schooling, Recreation and Health Facilities

However, these principles, as innocuous as they may seem to us, are controversial. On the one hand, they require companies to disobey South African Law. On the other, critics such as Bishop Desmond Tutu have argued that the principles do not go far enough. Tutu has proposed principles requiring companies to ignore the so-called "Passbook laws," which can have the effect of splitting up family members, as men sometimes go to areas to work where they are not allowed to live with their families.

Recently, Reverend Sullivan has repudiated his principles as the controversy around divestment in South Africa has become a more viable issue. He has admitted that although the principles may have made life better for some blacks in South Africa, they have not produced change at a fast enough pace.

Source: R. Edward Freeman, Olsson Professor of Business Administration, The Olsson Center for Applied Ethics, Colgate Darden Graduate School of Business Administration, University of Virginia, Charlottesville, Virginia.

inference, we would have very little, if anything, in common with the aliens, and there would be no basis for communication. We would see the aliens much as we see rocks and trees; morality would be irrelevant.

Theories of relativism should remind us that although two sets of consistent and coherent cultural norms and legal systems can sometimes be equally justified, further investigation may clarify some of the key questions in dispute and may find important similarities where only differences were once perceived. What, for example, generally happens when two scientists or two conflicting schools of thought propose competing hypotheses? The fact that two hypotheses can be simultaneously conflicting and sensible suggests the need for further research to resolve the conflict. Moral theory should work in the same way. Like other theories, it is incomplete and fallible, and we often get it wrong. Therefore, we often find ourselves in need of new theories, and such a need is an argument for further work, not for giving up.

ILLUSTRATIVE CASE STUDY Wrap-Up

An Ethical and Social Dilemma at Chemical Bank

How should Mr. McPartland of Chemical Bank approach his decision from the standpoint of ethics? First, he might answer any or all of four questions: "Who will be affected by the decision?" "How will each be affected?" "Who has rights?" and "What decision rule should be used?" Along the way, he would uncover an analysis of the harms and benefits of his alternatives. Clearly, whatever rule he uses must work in other circumstances, so McPartland must put his rules to the test of a variety of cases.

Ethical theories are rather like road maps: They are useful, even indispensable, but they are guidelines that must be used critically, with constant attention paid to the textures of the landscape. McPartland has a difficult decision. He must understand the ground rules at work at Chemical Bank—Chemical Bank's answer to the question "What do you stand for?"—and then he must make a decision either to proceed in accord with those rules or to challenge them. ■

SUMMARY

In 1983, the Gallup organization reported that almost 50 percent of all Americans thought that business ethics had declined during the previous decade.

Such thinkers as Milton Friedman believe that the only social role business should play is the maximization of profits. A company's contribution to the general welfare should be the efficient production of goods and services. Social problems should be left to concerned individuals and government agencies.

Friedman's views are generally considered extreme. More commonly, people accept the proposition that both the government and the business community have some responsibility to act in the interest of society. The idea of corporate social responsibility, the first attempt to make sense of the relations between business and society, was based upon two frankly paternalistic ideas: the charity principle (whereby society's more fortunate members are obligated to help those less fortunate) and the stewardship principle (whereby the wealthy should see themselves as caretakers of public property).

This theory was thus based largely on abstract speculation about the nature of their social responsibilities. By the 1950s and 1960s, critics had begun to address the shortcomings of this concept, placing more emphasis on the concept of concrete corporate social responsiveness instead of the abstract concept of corporate responsibility. On the "micro" level of analysis, this meant trying to show individual companies how they could be more socially responsive. The "macro" approach to the idea of corporate social responsiveness assumes that government regulation and public opinion affect business decisions, which should thus be made with these considerations in mind.

Efforts have been made to overcome the shortcomings of each model and to synthesize the virtues of both.

It is important to distinguish between two aspects of the word "ethical": the descriptive and the normative. A norm is held to be binding on individuals. Moral relativists argue that there can be no such norms. There are several versions of moral relativism, but all of them hold that we cannot decide matters of right and wrong, good and evil, in any rational way.

To behave morally, we must believe that we are acting correctly, but that belief is not a sufficient condition for morality. We must also take into account the community of individuals whose lives could be changed by our actions. In business, most ethical questions fall into one of four levels, which are not mutually exclusive: the societal, the stakeholder, the internal-policy, and the personal levels. The key terms of the ethical language are *values, rights, duties,* and *rules*.

Companies institutionalize the process of ethical decision making, so that each decision builds upon decisions that preceded it. There are several ways of doing so, including corporate codes of conduct; ethics committees, ombudsmen, or judicial boards; ethics training; and social audits.

REVIEW QUESTIONS

1. What is the "ethics crisis"?
2. Why does Milton Friedman believe that the only responsibility of business is to maximize the profits of the shareholders?
3. In what ways was the idea of corporate responsibility paternalistic? Why did the critics of unrestricted free enterprise attack it?
4. Describe the objections to the concept of corporate responsiveness.
5. What are the two major categories of relativism? What are the arguments against them? What is their kernel of truth?
6. What is common morality? What are its basic principles?
7. What basic questions must we answer to apply moral rules?
8. How have companies attempted to institutionalize ethics?

CASE STUDY Alexander Gavin's Dilemma: Cultural Relativism and Business as Usual

April 10, 1983

Dear Professor Hennessey:

I have not talked with you since my participation in The Executive Program at Tuck School in the summer of 1978. Many times I've hoped I might come back to visit but my life has been one surprise after the other, and I have been too busy to take any vacations in recent years.

I want to tell you about a situation that happened to me recently. I know you will be interested in it, and if you have time I'd like you to tell me what you would have done had you been in my position.

As I think you know, I am Senior Project Manager for the El Sahd Construction Company in Kuwait. The company is a prosperous one, with an excellent reputation for producing in a timely and cost-effective way on major construction projects in the Middle East. The Chairman and Chief Executive Officer is a well-known Kuwaiti and my direct boss is another American expatriate who is Senior Vice President for urban construction projects.

Two months ago, we put in a bid to be the principal subcontractor on a project in Iran. Our bid was $30 million, and we expected to bargain with Ajax, Ltd., the British-based company asking for the bids. We had built a heavy profit into the $30 million.

I was asked to go to Tehran on March 3rd to talk with the Ajax manager of the major project. That manager told me that we were going to get the job. I was delighted. The job meant a lot to us. We had put a great deal of planning into it, and it was exactly the kind of work that we do best.

Then came the surprise. I was told our bid had to be $33 million. My response was that we can always raise our price but that I would like to know why we were being asked to do so. The reply was, "Our way of doing business requires that because $1 million will go directly to the Managing Director of our Company in London. I will get $1 million and you, Alexander, will get $1 million in a numbered Swiss account." "Why me?," I asked. "Because we need to have you on the hook as insurance that you will never talk about this with anybody else."

I went back to Kuwait to ponder the matter. I was particularly disturbed because I had heard of cases like this in which, should the bidder fail to cooperate, the next message was that physical harm might be part of the exchange. I had been involved in "pay-offs" before. They are a common part of doing business in the Middle East, but I had never been in a situation where I was being coerced into taking a "cut" myself. I didn't like that. It went against my ethics.

At that point, I really didn't know what to do. I thought, among other things, how helpful it would have been to put my dilemma before a Tuck class and listen to the discussion.

Sincerely,
Alexander Gavin

Source: This case has been prepared for instructional purposes only. Most names have been disguised.

Case Questions

1. What rights are at stake in this case?
2. What decision rule should Mr. Gavin use?
3. Will this rule work in different cultures? ■

CASES ON INTRODUCTION TO MANAGEMENT

Seafood America: Corporate Response to the Cost of AIDS

Jack Mathews, CEO of Seafood America, returned the phone to its cradle and slowly shook his head. He had to give an answer to his restaurant managers in Cheyenne and St. Louis. Nothing that he had learned in business school or 25 years of industry experience had prepared him to deal with the issue facing him: AIDS.

Jack Mathews was Chief Executive Officer of a national chain of restaurants that catered to the 18- to 35-year-old upwardly mobile consumer and provided both a "meeting place" and "good but not gourmet" food that was moderately priced. Entrees were priced at $7.95 on average and were almost exclusively fresh seafood. Roughly 35 percent of the revenue came from the bar business, as typical customers spent some time in the bar before being seated, or just came to Seafood America to graze on appetizers, drink, and meet friends. In 1985, sales had grown 24 percent, to $100 million. Net profits increased 13 percent to $8 million. The prospects for growth were excellent, as the eating habits of Americans continued to change to "whiter and lighter" food.

Seafood America had been founded in 1975 by John Andrews of Cheyenne, Wyoming. The fourth son of a rancher, Andrews was vice president of a regional meat distributor. On several business trips to the East and West Coasts, Andrews had become convinced that the excellent seafood that he always ordered in restaurants would sell in Cheyenne. So, he quit his job, sold his house to raise capital, and started Seafood America. At first, he struggled because he knew little about the restaurant business. However, at the end of the third year the initial restaurants opened in Cheyenne, Albuquerque, and Phoenix had turned the corner, and he prepared to grow quickly. By 1983, he had opened 25 restaurants in 22 cities in the western part of the country. By providing fresh seafood at reasonable prices in a pleasant and sociable atmosphere, Seafood America had become enormously successful.

By the end of 1983, Andrews decided to sell the business to Amalgamated Foods, a distinguished food-processing company that was increasing its presence in the restaurant business. From 1983 to 1985, Amalgamated doubled the number of restaurants and planned to add 10 new "properties" every year for the next four years.

Employees at Seafood America fit the profile of the restaurant industry. Most were young and looking forward to the days when they would be doing something else. Few saw long-term careers as waiters, waitresses, bartenders, or buspersons. However, since Andrews tried to treat his employees "like family," Seafood America experienced significantly lower turnover than the industry average. Each Seafood America restaurant employed an average of 40 people. In most large cities, at least half of Seafood America's employees were members of minorities or low-income groups, and the majority of employees were single and male.

Jack Mathews had spent his entire business career of 15 years with Amalgamated Foods. For the last eight years, he had been involved in Amalgamated's move into the restaurant business. Initially, he was a corporate planner responsible for designing the "restaurant strategy," and his request to help actualize the plans was granted. Starting as manager of a small chain of fast-food restaurants, Jack had learned the business from the inside. He had spent the past year presiding over the incredible growth of Seafood America.

The AIDS Problem. Acquired Immune Deficiency Syndrome (AIDS) is now a household word.* As most of us know, the virus works by destroying the body's immune systems, making it vulnerable to a host of diseases, and incapacitates a special type of white blood cell—a cell that coordinates the activities of other immune cells. Without this "helper" cell, the body cannot respond effectively to many external challenges.

It is estimated that between one and two million Americans have already been infected with the virus. It is not known whether all these people will eventually

*This section is based primarily on the Institute of Medicine and National Academy of Sciences report *Mobilizing Against AIDS* (Cambridge, Mass.: Harvard University Press, 1986).

develop AIDS, but it is believed by scientists that anyone who carries the virus can infect others. Since there is a long time between initial infection and the appearance of AIDS—up to five or more years—it is extremely difficult to predict the overall impact of the disease on the population. However, it is estimated that by 1991, there will be over 270,000 cases of AIDS in the United States.

Transmission is thought to be primarily through sexual contact, as the virus is present in blood, semen, and vaginal secretions, or through the practice of using unsterile needles passed from AIDS victims to others. Most blood transfusions are now routinely screened for the AIDS virus. AIDS has given rise to great public fear about its transmission, primarily because it is such a deadly disease and because so little is known about it. Demonstrations have taken place to keep infected children away from schools. AIDS victims have lost their jobs, been ostracized, and had to cope with virtual isolation in addition to the knowledge of impending death. Rarely does a victim live longer than three years after onset of the disease.

The Institute of Medicine and National Academy of Sciences has tried to allay the fears that AIDS can be transmitted by casual contact:

> It must be emphasized at the outset that there is no evidence that AIDS can be transmitted by "casual" contact. . . . Thus, the disease cannot be transmitted by a handshake, by a cough or sneeze, or by the consumption of food prepared by someone with AIDS.

Subsequent studies have shown . . . that the virus is very rare in secretions such as tears and saliva, and even when it is present, the levels are probably too low to play a role in infection.

The economic impact of AIDS is difficult to calculate. One study estimates that economic loss from the first 10,000 victims is over $4 billion. The medical costs of AIDS victims is estimated to be between $42,000 and $147,000 for hospital care alone. Public health officials estimate the cost of caring for AIDS patients in the United States to be $16 billion by 1991. According to *Fortune,* most of this burden will fall on corporations, as 70 percent of the population is covered by health insurance with their employers.

While there is hope of a vaccine to prevent AIDS, the scientific and public issues are complex. It is far from certain that the AIDS virus will lend itself to the development of vaccines, since it seems to mutate into other forms rather quickly. There are a number of drugs that scientists have used or developed to alleviate the disease and, it is hoped, prolong life, but for now there is no cure and no cure in sight.

The first case of AIDS at Seafood America was brought to the attention of the Cheyenne restaurant manager by the employee himself. The second case was more difficult to deal with. In St. Louis, a regular customer who happened to be a nurse came up to the restaurant manager and said, "You should know that your waiter, John, is being treated for AIDS at my clinic."

In keeping with the family tradition established by Mr. Andrews, the normal policy for Seafood America was to give a certain amount of sick leave and to pay the full cost of medical care for its employees.

Given the prognosis for continued growth of the AIDS epidemic, especially among high-risk groups, Mathews knew that he needed a formal policy to help restaurant managers decide what to do in these tragic cases.

Source: This case was adapted from R. Edward Freeman, Visiting Associate Professor, the Olsson Center for the Study of Applied Ethics. Copyright © 1986 by the Colgate Darden Graduate Business School Sponsors, University of Virginia, Charlottesville, Virginia. Note: Although this case is based on a factual situation, such particulars as industry, city, and proper names have, of course, been changed.

Case Questions

1. Who are the stakeholders of Seafood America?
2. Describe the indirect environment. What political, technological, and economic trends will affect Mathews's decision?
3. What is Mathews's responsibility to his employees? To his customers? To his employee with AIDS? To the employee accused of having AIDS?
4. What would you do if you were Mathews? ■

Precision Machine Tool: Management in a Changing Environment

John Garner, president of Precision Machine Tool, watched the elegantly tailored Mr. Wang leave the office after making his disturbing proposition. Of course, John had known that his own production people were working with Suzuki Machines on developing specifications for a machining center that would help solve Precision's nagging quality problems. Negotiations were winding down, and the Japanese firm's price quotation was expected. Ako Wang's name on today's appointment calendar, therefore, was no surprise. From past dealings with Asian firms, Garner had expected the traditional old-world formalities that precede the closing of a sale for a major piece of capital equipment. In fact, he had braced himself for the usual rich combination of urbane courtesy and sharp technology. The U.S. machine tool industry has a strong bias to "buy American," and Precision was no exception.

This morning, Wang had performed as expected, but this time Suzuki was not intent on making a sale. True, the proposal on Garner's desk contained a purchase document, but it was not a quotation for a $250,000 heavy-duty machining center. Instead, it was a formal invitation to discuss the purchase of Precision Machine Tool by Suzuki Machines.

"Lorraine," Garner said into the intercom on his desk, "see if you can find Tom and ask him to come up."

While waiting for his partner, Garner stood by the window that overlooked a big machining bay on the floor below. Even through the heavy insulated glass he could hear the ceaseless clamor of the big machines that were making high-precision parts for the lathes that Precision produced and sold to the automobile industry. He watched as an operator checked the control panel of a new cobalt-blue lathe that stood among the aging machines on the shop floor. The hulking lathe was state-of-the-art machine technology, precise and sophisticated—with a manufacturer's nameplate that read "Suzuki/Made in Japan."

The machine tool industry is unique in that it uses its own products to make its own products, and much of Precision's old equipment was becoming dulled by decades of use. In a desperate move to stem customer complaints about quality, it had bought the computer-controlled Japanese lathe to use for making parts for the machines it produced. To buy foreign-made machinery went against the grain, but many domestic toolmakers were buying imported machines because they were more efficient to operate, gave a higher quality of output, and were cheaper than American-made equipment. For some toolmakers, it was the alternative to joining the 20 percent of the nation's machine tool companies that had gone out of business in the first years of the 1980s.

Garner turned away from the window and took a sales printout from a desk drawer. His company was in better shape than many medium-sized toolmakers, but that was not saying a lot. Sales were down 30 percent from the bellwether year of 1979. Booked orders were weak, and quality rejects due to the aging and long-used equipment ate into profits. Precision was a victim of the 1980–1981 recession in the automobile industry. Like many other machine toolmakers, it had never fully recovered. Garner looked up as his partner entered the office.

Tom Avery flung himself into the chair that had been occupied by Ako Wang. Precision's works manager was a big man, blunt and outspoken, and a first-class tool-design engineer. He ran the manufacturing and materials management end of the business and, with John Garner, had founded Precision Machine Tool in 1966. His reaction to John's news about Wang's proposition was expressed in a single word that was short, direct, and explosively negative.

Despite excess capacity in American plants, Japan's share of the American machine tool market was increasing and was hotly resented by the domestic industry. The fire was currently being fueled by Japan's determination to increase exports of cars to the United States now that the voluntary quota system had expired. There was no corresponding assurance that there would be any increase in the trickle of American goods allowed to enter Japan. As a result, the decrease in American market share could be significant in an industry linked so closely with automobiles and steel. Employment would be hard hit as well, and Precision's 312 employees were down 22 percent from 1979.

"That was my first reaction, too, Tom. But I think we should think this through." John held up his hand to silence his partner as Tom leaned forward, scowling. "Let me go on for a minute. Our industry is in its worst crisis since the Depression. Sure, Precision's done better than some, but our sales are down to $16 million and you know what the reject rate is doing to costs. Orders have softened steadily, Tom, and that's what worries me most. We've had a reputation for top-quality machine tools from the time we opened our shop.

"Precision Machine Tool has always been synonymous with precision quality. We're losing that, Tom." John went over to the bay window. "Sixty percent of our equipment is old, some of it more than 20 years. Accuracy of these machines is unreliable, they're expensive to operate and not worth any more rebuilding. We're in a spiral, Tom: Without profits, we can't afford to modernize the plant, and with obsolete machines, we can't compete with foreign imports, not in price and not in quality."

The late 1970s had been the apex of the domestic machine tool industry. There was a record backlog in orders that could not be filled because of inadequate production capacity. Industrial customers waited two years for machine tool orders they needed today. The domestic industry was too busy to notice that several years before, Japan had identified machine tools as a growth industry and started subsidizing modern factories. Now was the time to cash in. American manufacturers were turning overseas for fast delivery of high-quality, inexpensive machines and machine tools to use in their production processes. During the 1980–1981 recession in the automobile industry, American tool firms had little capital for investment. When the economy recovered, they were left behind in the marketplace. Lately, subsidiaries of big Japanese toolmakers had begun to appear in the United States, along with an occasional Japanese acquisition of a domestic firm.

"What are you telling me, John? That you want to sell out?" Tom's voice was tight. "This is the most exciting industry around right now. We've got the wonders of automation to sell these days, the futuristic manufacturing systems. You want them all to be Japanese, John? Or West German, or Korean, or everything but American? You want to get out of the race just when we've survived the cash crunch from buying the new equipment we do have? That Japanese lathe, for starters."

It had taken Tom a long time to accept the idea of using an imported machine in Precision's production process, but the harshness in his voice was gone as he said, "Listen, John. You're a financial expert, but I know that yesterday's production gives us yesterday's dollars. Why not get rid of this patch-and-mend philosophy and shop for some real capital to modernize the plant? The U.S. capabilities for producing the computer software that meshes the tools together is superior to anybody's. We've got access to that, John, and all Precision needs is modern machines to get the edge we need to stay in the race." Tom waited. He knew that John was a financial conservative, dedicated to financing capital improvements from profits.

John turned from the window and sat down in the chair across from his partner. Tom knew as well as he did that it was not a matter of catching up with the competition; it would be necessary to leapfrog over a moving target. A big capital investment meant a big debt, and interest rates would tend to be high for a firm in the troubled machine tool industry. Precision would become highly leveraged and could risk ruin. There were too many "ifs." What if there was a downturn in the economy . . . or if too many customers were irrevocably lost during the transition . . . or if foreign toolmakers slashed prices to protect their market share . . . or if software companies outside the machine tool industry won important orders in the area of software expertise where American toolmakers had the edge? It was ironic, but John knew that Tom would infinitely prefer bankruptcy to selling out to foreign competition.

"All right, Tom." John took a deep breath. "Look at *this* scenario, and think about it for a minute. If we wanted to go the retrenchment route, maybe it makes sense to sell a line of imports to help us finance some new equipment. I don't like the idea any better than you do, but it would be temporary, Tom, and it's profitable. They wouldn't have to be Asian. The dollar's strong, and we might be able to buy West German machine tools at a price that would give us a good markup." John stopped, expecting Tom's outburst to be as vehement as his response to the Wang proposition.

Both men, especially Tom, had always been critical of the strategy of some of the hard-up domestic toolmakers who acted as distributors of imported machines and machine tools, or who bought imported products and customized them for special-order customers. John had to agree with the tone of derision and contempt in Tom's words. Selling imported machine tools in direct competition with your own industry was quite different from using a couple of pieces of imported equipment to beef up your own production process in a crisis.

Not only could the practice spell doom for the domestic industry, but the knife cut a lot deeper. One of the oportunity costs of selling foreign goods is that while a manufacturer is doing it, he tends not to improve his own technology and capabilities. The machine tool industry is at the core of modern manufacturing, and the country that controls state-of-the-art machines and machine tools has the advantage of being able to make better cars and aircraft and drilling equipment—and ballistic missles.

It was inconsistent that an industry that had spent so much time and resources trying to get the federal government to provide protection from foreign competition by limiting imports was itself buying those same imports. Buying foreign was repugnant; John knew that, but it was a trade-off. Was it worth it?

"What are our options, Tom?" John's voice was quiet. "Is it better to commit ourselves to a debt that could wipe us out? Is it better to fold? Whatever we do, we've both got to buy into it, right? We always have." Tom smiled, and John knew that they were both remembering the early days of Precision Machine Tool, when they operated on a shoestring and sat down together every Thursday to decide what bills they could afford to pay.

Things seemed more complex now, and even more uncertain. During the life of Precision, its industry had experienced a revolutionary change in products, and the past ten years had been either feast or famine for domestic machine tools. Now the race to build the factories of the future would be won by the nation that had the most efficient computerized operations to produce the cheapest, most reliable products. For the owners of Precision Machine Tool, the price paid for falling behind was high, and the risks in trying to stay in the race were great.

. . . Lorraine sent out for sandwiches and coffee, and as the afternoon passed the two men examined the future of their industry and their place in it. When they parted late that night, their decision had been made—and they agreed to meet in John's office the next morning at ten for his telephone call to Ako Wang.

Source: This case was prepared by Janet Barnard, College of Business, Rochester Institute of Technology. See *Journal of Management Case Studies* 2 (1986):94–97. Copyright © 1986 by Elsevier Science Publishing Co., Inc. Reprinted by permission.

Case Questions

1. Describe the environment of Precision Machine Tools—the stakeholders and the trends.
2. How has the emergence of foreign competition affected the company?
3. Should the fact that the proposal is from a Japanese firm matter to Garner? Why or why not?
4. What would you do if you were Garner? Why? Could you defend your answer to your employees? Your community leaders? Your Congressperson?
5. Role play the telephone call to Mr. Wang. ■

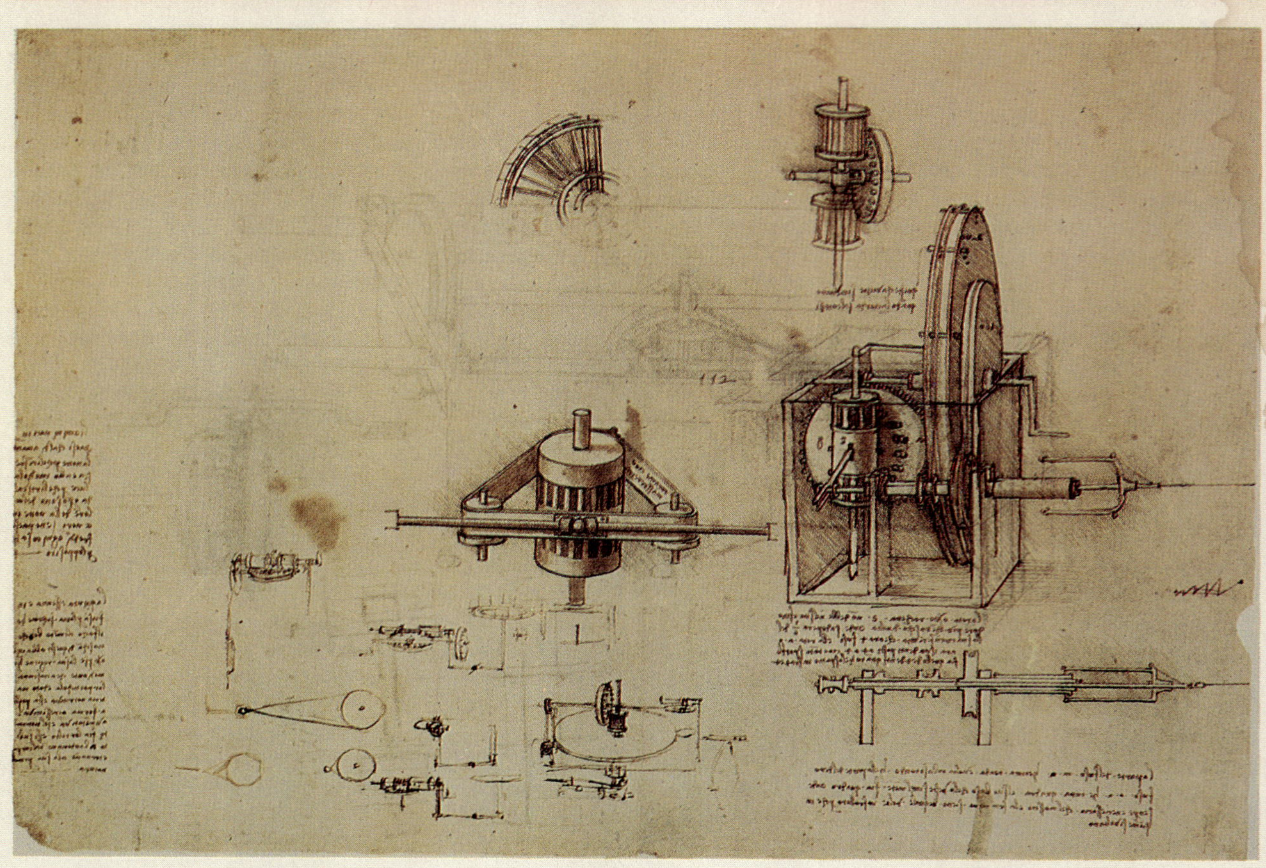

Leonardo de Vinci, Plans for a Spinning Wheel. © 1490. Bibliotica Ambrosiana, Milan.

5

EFFECTIVE PLANNING

Upon completing this chapter you should be able to:

1. Describe the basic steps in the planning process.
2. Explain how the functions of planning and controlling are linked.
3. Identify and describe the different types of plans.
4. Identify and describe management science techniques that can make planning effective.

Chapter Outline

Introduction
Planning and the Management Process
Operational Plans
Tools and Techniques for Planning

ILLUSTRATIVE CASE STUDY Introduction

Reversing the Flow at Chrysler Corporation

On November 2, 1978, Chrysler made two announcements: The company had suffered a record loss of $158.5 million in the third quarter, and Lee J. Iacocca would become Chrysler's new chairman and CEO. The first of these announcements was due to a series of forecasting and planning errors:

1. In 1971, Chrysler instituted a new strategy to sell primarily full-size family cars. They became available in 1973, just in time for the OPEC oil embargo.
2. New compact-size cars were introduced in 1975, but sales were slow because of a temporary decline in demand for small cars.
3. In 1978, Chrysler heavily promoted its new, smaller luxury models. Manufacturing problems prevented their delivery until late November. By then, customers had bought other cars.

Mr. Iacocca's initial impression of Chrysler was that people were doing the wrong jobs. Years of shuffling meant that no one was doing what he or she had been trained to do. He moved on several fronts to assert control:

1. He replaced virtually all senior managers.
2. He ordered monthly meetings between sales managers and dealers.
3. He took losses in order to sell off the huge inventory.
4. He became the company's advertising spokesman.

The company's most serious problem was its lack of cash. Iacocca petitioned Congress to approve loan quarantees covering $1.5 billion of Chrysler's loans, maintaining that the only alternative to federal help was bankruptcy. Congress agreed, insisting that Chrysler, through its own initiatives, win about $2 billion in concessions from unions, suppliers, and others, whittling itself down to a leaner and more viable core.

Iacocca then initiated a strategy of severe retrenchment and divestiture aimed at reducing operating expenses and improving productivity, profit margins, and cash flow. Salary expenses dropped when half the work force was laid off; through concession bargaining with unions, Iaccoca was able to achieve wage cuts of 13 percent and major reductions in fringe benefits. Fixed plant costs fell as the company closed a third of its plants, sold extensive foreign operations, and terminated about a quarter of its domestic dealerships. With the introduction of robot welding and computerized quality control, the remaining 40 plants were modernized to make them more productive and cost-efficient. Savings in inventory came from reducing the number of different parts required throughout the manufacturing system.

From 1978 to 1981, the company lost a staggering $3.5 billion. In 1982, a modest profit resulted from the sale of the company's tank division, and as the national economy moved out of the 1981–82 recession, Chrysler's profitability rose steadily. By 1984, earnings had reached $2.38 billion. Cash flow also improved.

In 1983, Iacocca announced that Chrysler had repaid all outstanding loans—seven years ahead of the 1990 deadline. In addition to its value as a public relations move, retiring the debt saved the company $350 million in interest payments.

Sources: James K. Glassman, "The Iacocca Mystique," *New Republic,* July 16–23, 1984, pp. 20–23; Lee Iacocca with William Novak, *Iacocca* (New York: Bantam Books, 1984); Iacocca, "The Rescue and Resuscitation of Chrysler," *Journal of Business Strategy* 4, no. 1 (Summer 1983): 67–69; Iacocca with Sonny Kleinfield, *Straight Talking* (Toronto: Bantam Books, 1988); Alexander L. Taylor, III, "Iacocca's Tightrope Act," *Time,* March 21, 1983, pp. 50–61; Michael Schwartz and Glenn Yago, "What's Good for Chrysler Is Bad for Us," *Nation,* September 12, 1981, pp. 200–203; Janice Castro, "Iacocca II, the Sequel," *Time,* June 13, 1988, p. 48.

TEACHING TIP

The Chrysler Corporation case study is an excellent example of a corporate turnaround and illustrates the crucial role that planning played. Don't overlook or underemphasize it!

Chrysler's revival under Lee Iacocca's leadership was obviously not the result of some predictable mechanics of business momentum—like the swinging of some great economic pendulum from one extreme to another. It was partially the result of *planning*—the successful establishment and attainment of goals coordinated with the successful modification of the organization's structure. In this chapter, we shall see how the idea of planning has evolved into a complex set of conceptual and practical principles of enabling organizations to set and meet goals.

planning The process of establishing objectives and suitable courses of action before taking action.

Individuals and organizations both need to plan. Whether we plan for a party, a vacation, the next step in a career, or a new sales program, **planning** is the basic process we use to select our goals and determine how to achieve them.

In the overview of management in Part One of this text, the function of planning was noted several times. We have seen that a major task for managers is to plan the efforts of organization members and the use of other resources to achieve stated organizational goals. We have also described the activities of managers in ways that implied the central importance of planning. For example, Peter Drucker's distinction between **effectiveness**—doing the right things—and **efficiency**—doing things right—is paralleled in the steps of selecting goals and then determining how to achieve them.

effectiveness The ability to determine appropriate objectives: "doing the right things."

efficiency The ability to minimize the use of resources in achieving organizational objectives: "doing things right."

TEACHING TIP

This would be a good time to do a little wrap-up and review with the students. Stress the important building blocks covered in Chapters 1–4 and how these are laying the foundation for our in-depth study of management functions.

In Part Two of this book, we will focus on the specific elements of the planning process and the closely related processes of decision making and the development and implementation of strategy. This chapter introduces the concept of planning and suggests ways to make planning effective. Chapter 6 examines managerial decision making under routine and non-routine circumstances. Chapter 7 focuses on strategic planning and presents processes for developing strategies. Chapter 8 describes the ways in which strategies are implemented and identifies techniques that are particularly useful in the implementation process. In this chapter, we will first examine the basic steps in the planning process, briefly discussing the linkage between planning and control. Next, we will explain the various types of plans and their purposes. Finally, we will discuss some tools and techniques to assist managers with the four basic stages in planning.

PLANNING AND THE MANAGEMENT PROCESS

Planning is every manager's job: Before managers can organize, lead, or control, they must make the plans that give purpose and direction to the organization—deciding what needs to be done, when and how it needs to be done, and who is to do it.

Plant managers must plan how their facilities are going to be used, how many of what products to make, and when to make them. Marketing managers must plan how to introduce products, what distribution channels to use, and how to price the products. Even financial managers must plan how to structure the debt and equity of the firm and how to budget and spend resources.

CLASS COMMENT

Why plan? (1) Protective purpose (minimize risk), (2) affirmative purpose (increase success), (3) coordinative purpose (increase coordination efforts).

The need for planning exists at all levels and actually increases at higher levels, where it has the greatest potential impact on the organization's success. Upper-level managers generally devote most of their planning time to the distant future and the strategies of the entire organization; managers at lower levels plan mainly for their own subunits and for the shorter term. Variations in planning responsibilities depend also on the organization's size and purpose and on the manager's specific function or activity.

Thus a multinational company would be more concerned with planning for the distant future than would a local retailer since its operations around the world may well be more complex. Some organizations—say, mining companies, airlines, the Department of Defense—must make long-range commitments because of their particular purposes and objectives. On the other hand, a bookstore might concentrate on seasonal or annual goals. Still other types of organizations must strike a balance between short- and long-term planning responsibilities. For example, because of frequently changing styles, dress manufacturers might make only short-range plans in design and purchasing while retaining long-term plans for personnel selection and improvement of production techniques and capacity. It is important, therefore, for managers to understand the roles of both long-range and short-term planning in the overall planning scheme.

HERE'S AN EXAMPLE

The Ozark Empire Fair based in Springfield, Missouri, knew it had to take drastic steps to insure its survival. After several years of operating in the red and not having sufficient cash flow to maintain its physical properties, several changes were implemented. Establishing an organizational plan was instrumental in helping to turn the situation around. The fair now operates in the black and has had enough cash surplus to make some much-needed improvements in its facilities.

Plans and Decision Making

Managers who develop plans but do not commit themselves to action are simply wasting time: Ideas that are not accompanied by definite ways to utilize them have no practical effect. Planning is a process that does not end when a plan is agreed upon; plans must be implemented. Moreover, at any time during the implementation and control process, plans may require modification to avoid becoming useless or even damaging. "Replanning" can sometimes be the key factor leading to ultimate success.

An important aspect of planning is **decision making**—the process of developing and selecting a course of action to solve a specific problem. Decisions must be made at many points in the planning process. Managers must decide which predictions in such areas as the economy and the actions of competitors are likely to be most accurate. They must analyze organizational resources and decide how to allocate them to achieve goals most effectively. Because decision making is such an important part of planning, it will be discussed at length in Chapter 6.

decision making The process of identifying and selecting a course of action to solve a specific problem.

Organizations that have operated for a long time in stable environments tend to lose flexibility and thus find change difficult or impossible. In Chapter 3, we looked at numerous examples of organizations get into trouble by ignoring change. Steel factories, automobile manufacturers, banks, telecommunications companies have all witnessed changes in their respective industrial environments over the last 25 years. Consequently, in order to avoid chaos and decline, they have had to plan in more flexible ways.[1] Even socialist planners in countries such as China and the Soviet Union have begun to recognize the need for more flexibility in their plans (See the International Management box entitled "Planning in the USSR".)

TEACHING TIP

Emphasize that the decision is not whether or not to plan but how to plan *most effectively*.

Managers must frequently monitor relevant environmental factors so that the organization can adapt to new situations as quickly as possible; they should manage surprises before they occur.[2] To do this, managers must establish ongoing processes to collect data on the organization's internal functioning, in order to maintain fresh information on its efficiency and the attitudes of its personnel. Whatever information comes from data-collecting processes must be regularly compared with previously established standards or benchmarks of performance. Serious divergences from these benchmarks should sound an alarm so that corrective action can be taken.

---

[1]Of course, Tom Peters has argued that "chaos" is the wave of the future for managers, and that they must understand the current environment as one of continual change. Even so, managers must plan for this continual change. See Thomas Peters, *Thriving on Chaos* (New York: Knopf, 1988).

[2]See David W. Fischer, "Strategies Toward Political Pressures: A Typology of Firm Responses," *Academy of Management Review* 8, no. 1 (January 1983):71–78.

EXTRA EXERCISE

Have students formulate a post-graduation plan. Have them follow the four steps in planning: identify goals, define the present situation, identify aids and barriers, and develop set of actions for reaching goals.

The Four Basic Steps in Planning

Planning is a fundamental process and can be condensed into four basic steps that can be adapted to all planning activities at all organizational levels. (See Fig. 5-1.)

Establish a Goal or Set of Goals. Planning begins with decisions about what the organization or subunit wants or needs. Without a clear definition of goals, organizations spread their resources too broadly. Identifying priorities and being specific about aims enable organizations to focus their resources effectively. (Goals for individuals in organizations are discussed more fully in Chapter 14.)

When Jack Welch became CEO of General Electric, he immediately set a goal for each of GE's businesses to be number one or number two in their industries. Welch reasoned that global competitiveness would increase and only the top two firms in each industry would be winners. Setting this clear goal gave every manager a focus—namely, how to become number one or number two.

Goal setting is equally important on a smaller scale. You need to establish goals for each class that you take in school, for finding a job, and for preparing your career. Goals are an indispensable part of planning.

Because goal setting is the essential first step in planning, managers who are unable to set meaningful goals will be unable to make effective plans. There are a number of reasons why some managers hesitate—or fail entirely—to set goals for their organizations or subunits.[3]

- *Unwillingness to give up alternative goals.* The decision to establish new goals and commit resources to their achievement requires that other choices be forgone. At times, each of us finds it difficult to accept the fact that we cannot achieve all of the things that are important to us; as a result, we may be reluctant to make a firm commitment to one goal because it is too painful to give up desirable alternatives.
- *Fear of failure.* A person who sets a definite, clear-cut goal takes the risk of failing to achieve it. Managers are as likely as anyone else to see failure as a threat to their self-esteem, to the respect others have for them, and even to their job security; thus, the fear of failure keeps some managers from taking necessary risks and establishing specific goals.
- *Lack of organizational knowledge.* Managers cannot establish meaningful objectives for their subunits without having a good working relationship with the organization as a whole. Part of each manager's job is keeping his or her own subunits' plans consistent with those of top management. A new or uninformed manager may well hesitate to set objectives if he or she senses that they may conflict with those already set at higher levels. Similarly, in order to avoid conflict or duplication, the manager must be aware of other subunits' objectives. A manager whose information network is undeveloped or faulty may try to avoid making new plans altogether and instead fall back on already established goals.

---

[3]See David A. Kolb, Irwin M. Rubin, and James M. McIntyre, *Organizational Psychology: An Experiential Approach to Organizational Behavior,* 4th ed., Englewood Cliffs, N.J.: Prentice Hall, 1984), p. 102. The authors discuss why individuals are reluctant to set personal goals regarding their careers, but their reasons are also applicable to the reluctance of managers to commit themselves to setting organizational goals. Similarly, the solutions that the authors offer can be applied to improving a manager's effectiveness in goal setting.

FIGURE 5-1 THE FOUR BASIC STEPS IN PLANNING

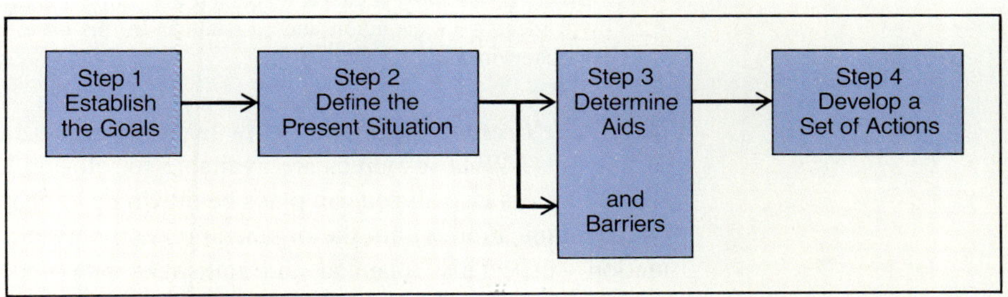

- *Lack of knowledge of the environment.* In addition to understanding the organization's internal environment, the manager needs to understand its external environment— the competition, clients or customers, suppliers, government agencies, and the general public; without knowledge of the external environment, managers are apt to become confused about which direction to take and are reluctant to set definite goals.
- *Lack of confidence.* To commit themselves to goals, managers must feel that both they and the subunit or organization have the ability to achieve those goals; obviously, if managers lack confidence in themselves or the organization, they will hesitate to establish challenging goals.

What can be done to help an individual overcome the impediments to effective goal-setting? Some of the answers are implied by the problems themselves. Managers who lack knowledge of the organization or its external environment need assistance in developing a viable information system that can be provided in a variety of ways. For example, one of the most important benefits of in-company management development programs is that they help participants establish informal contacts with people from different departments, divisions, and locations. These contacts help managers find things out and get things done. This, in turn, raises their confidence both in others and in themselves.

The barriers due to fear of failure and unwillingness to give up attractive alternative goals are reduced in companies that have effective and well-communicated systems for planning. Where planning is a well-understood process, it is easier for each individual to develop his or her own goals—and to obtain help in developing plans to achieve those goals. Where effective decision-making techniques are widely used, it is easier to determine which are the more attractive alternatives and to recognize the necessity of forgoing some alternatives in order to achieve others.

Fear of failure and lack of confidence are also reduced by setting realistic goals and achieving them. The individual's immediate superior plays a key role in creating a climate in which difficult to attainable goals will be set. Providing training and guidance in ways to achieve such goals is one important step. Recognition and reward for successful goal achievement is a second step; providing constructive and supportive responses when targets are occasionally missed constitutes a vital third step that is too often overlooked.

Planning implies change, and implementing and managing change are important parts of a manager's job. There are a number of ways for managers to reduce or eliminate resistance to planned changes:

- Involve employees and other concerned groups, including stakeholders, in the planning process.
- Provide more information to employees about plans and their probable consequences so that they will understand the need for change, the expected benefits, and what is required for effective implementation.
- Develop a pattern of effective planning and effective implementation. A successful track record encourages confidence in the planners and acceptance of new plans.
- Be aware of the impact of proposed changes on organization members and minimize unnecessary disruptions. If introduction of a new manufacturing process led to sizable layoffs in the past, it can be expected that implementation of a new process in the future will meet with suspicion and resistance. In this case, employment guarantees would be one step in allaying suspicion.

Define the Present Situation. How far is the organization or the subunit falling short of its goals? What resources are available for closing the gap? Only after the current state of affairs is analyzed can plans be drawn up to change future progress. Open lines of communication within the organization and between its subunits provide the information—especially financial and statistical data—necessary for this second stage.

INTERNATIONAL MANAGEMENT

PLANNING IN THE USSR: GORBACHEV AS CEO

Imagine a country whose economic plan has been controlled through a closed command economy for 50 years. A command economy is one in which the state owns property resources and controls centralized economic planning. Production is set by the state, the state plans what is to be produced and by whom, time lines are planned in increments that do not always bear a relationship to what needs to be produced, quality is not regarded as a key element in production, and profit is not a part of the planning process.

In such economies, planning generally means "centralized planning." One bureau must decide how to structure the output of entire sectors of the economy, such as agriculture. Central planners decide how much steel to produce and set appropriate goals—not just for one factory but for all steel-producing factories. So, if too much steel is produced, there are costly inventory overruns, and if too little steel is produced, a shortage occurs. Because production decisions are centralized, if a shortage occurs and is accompanied by a rise in prices, increased production of that particular item does not necessarily follow. Small wonder that, in times of shortages resulting from poor centralized planning, there are thriving "black markets" to compensate for shortages in most command economies.

Command economies, then, are virtually synonomous with "planned economies," and when such economies become troubled, planning is almost certainly a key factor. So imagine now how you would change a troubled command economy into an economically viable, quality-oriented, mixed economy with state enterprise still a central part of the economy but with some room made available for a market economy, profit in firms, wages based on performance, joint ventures with other countries, and a spirit of entrepreneurism.

Soviet leader Mikhail Gorbachev is trying to change his country's 50-year-old socialist economy into a new and vital economy, to lead his country into this part of the twentieth century, with its advancing technology and innovation, and to prepare the USSR for the next century. Gorbachev is creating reforms, referred to as *perestroika,* or "restructuring," which are far-reaching in a country accustomed to closed bureacratic planning. The new approach, called *glasnost,* or "more openness," appears to allow much greater participation on the part of the Soviet people in the workplace and in the economy as a whole. As Gorbachev moves toward a combination of socialist thinking and the freedoms inherent in the mechanisms of a market economy, he is seeking changes that will inevitably entail less planning by central planners and more planning by individual entrepeneurs and factory managers. Along with economic reforms, there are plans for such political reforms as elections and a greater openness in political as well as economic systems.

Sources: Marshall Goldman, "Gorbachev, Turnaround CEO," *Harvard Business Review,* 66, no. 3 (1988):107–113; "Reforming the Soviet Economy," *Business Week,* December 7, 1987, pp. 76–80; and "Can Gorbachev Control the Nationalism Glasnost Unleashed?" *Business Week,* March 28, 1988, p. 43.

Donald Peterson, Chairman of Ford, had a clear goal in the early 1980s—namely, to return Ford to profitability. To do so, he had to conduct an in-depth analysis of Ford's strategies and operations to determine just how far away from that goal the company really was.

Identify Aids and Barriers. What factors in the internal and external environments can help the organization reach its goals? What factors might create problems? It is comparatively easy to see what is taking place now, but the future is never clear.

Although difficult to do, anticipating future situations, problems, and opportunities is an essential part of planning.

In the fall of 1987, Wall Street firms were riding high after a long bull market. Many of them foresaw a market downturn, but none predicted the disastrous drop of October 19, 1987. As a result, many plans had to be abandoned and many new goals established.

Develop a Course of Action. The final step in the planning process involves developing various alternative courses of action, evaluating these alternatives, and choosing the most suitable (or at least the most satisfactory) alternative. This is the step in which decisions about future actions are made and during which the guidelines for effective decision making are most relevant.

As Presidential candidates, Michael Dukakis and George Bush had to develop detailed plans for winning votes in each state of the Union. They had to allocate time, people, and money in ways that helped in the achievement of their mutual objective—winning the Presidency. The development of such plans established guidelines for many day-to-day campaign decisions.

The fourth step is not necessary if, after examining current trends, the manager predicts that the plan already in effect will carry the organization or subunit to its desired goal. In such a case, the manager usually monitors progress under the old plan closely and reacts quickly if it deviates from expectations. Most of the time, however, we engage in planning because present conditions are not meeting goals and expectations; in such cases a new plan has to be developed.

The Link Between Planning and Controlling

We have described planning as an analytic and decision-making process that ends when a specific plan is developed. Plans are implemented through detailed actions aimed at realizing specified objectives. It is at this action-taking stage that planning moves into another function—controlling.

controlling The process of monitoring actual organizational activities to see that they conform to planned activities and correcting flaws or deviations.

budgeting Process for providing formal quantitative statements of the resources allocated to specific programs or projects for a given period.

Controlling. **Controlling** can be defined simply as the process of ensuring that actions conform to plans. Controlling cannot take place unless a plan exists, and a plan has little chance of success unless some efforts are made to monitor its progress.[4]

Budgeting. **Budgeting** is the most common link between planning and controlling. A budget is almost always a key part of the planning process because it guides decisions about allocating resources toward the attainment of goals. A well-planned budget harmonizes an organization's strategy and structure, its management and personnel, and the tasks it needs to accomplish.[5] Overrunning a budget is frequently an early signal that activities are not proceeding as planned. Excessive expenditures may be due to inadequate planning, to changed conditions, or to other unforeseen events. When budget overruns become too large, the entire plan may need to be revised.

In some organizations, planning and controlling are also linked by the process of employee participation in planning. When employees participate in establishing goals, they are more likely to control their own activities in order to make sure the goals are met. For example, in order to develop the Ford Taurus, a team of engineers, stylists and manufacturing personnel worked together with assembly line workers, and even customers, to plan the best possible car. General Foods has found apparent success by

---

[4]See Neil C. Churchill, "Budget Choice: Planning vs. Control," *Harvard Business Review* 62, no. 4 (July–August 1984):150–164.

[5]See Peter Lorange and Declan Murphy, "Considerations in Implementing Strategic Control," *Journal of Business Strategy* 4, no. 4 (Spring 1984):27–35.

organizing its work force into interfunctional, multidisciplinary work teams which focus on and are fully dedicated to a specific business, groups of businesses, or a fairly long-term project.

Although planning and controlling are linked, there are advantages in keeping the two functions formally separated. Separation emphasizes the importance of each; it encourages employees to take control seriously and to ensure that relevant activities are not neglected or performed haphazardly. Such separation may on occasion lead to disputes between planners and controllers over how well the control system is functioning, but a strong controller will play a key role in maintaining the integrity of the system.[6]

ILLUSTRATIVE CASE STUDY Continued

Reversing the Flow at Chrysler Corporation

Iacocca first had to determine a set of goals for Chrysler. The starting point in this process was easy enough to determine, since Chrysler was in danger of becoming extinct: The goal was simply for Chrysler to *survive* in some form. Next, he had to determine how bad the present situation really was. Again, the answer was readily available: Chrysler was on the brink of bankruptcy. The cause of the crisis was equally evident in terms of high costs of production and poor design, coupled with increasing competition from more sophisticated and farsighted organizations, both foreign and domestic. The barriers to Chrysler's goals were substantial: The government had a large stake, as did suppliers who were owed money, unions who stood to lose jobs, and other businesses who did not want the government to "bail out" Chrysler. Finally, Iacocca had to formulate a set of action plans to overcome the barriers.

Even after accomplishing these four steps in *planning,* Chrysler was far from out of the woods, as these plans had to be translated into concrete plans throughout the organization.

OPERATIONAL PLANS

Plans have many functions in an organization: they provide the objectives to be met by plans at the lower level; they provide the means for achieving the objectives set in the plans of the next higher level; and serve as vehicles for communication among organizational members.

There are two main types of plans. Strategic plans are designed to meet the broad objectives of the organization—to implement the mission that provides the unique reason for the organization's existence. Operational plans provide details as to how the strategic plans will be accomplished. We will discuss strategic plans in more depth in Chapter 7. The remainder of this section will be concerned with operational plans.

In turn, there are two main types of operational plans. Single-use plans are developed to achieve specific purposes and to be dissolved when these have been accomplished; standing plans are standardized approaches for handling recurrent and predictable situations (see Fig. 5-2). We will discuss strategic plans in detail in Chapter 7, but at this point we will focus our attention on the single-use and standing plans that translate the broad objectives of strategic plans into day-to-day decisions and actions of organization members.[7]

---

[6] See Vijay Sathe, "The Controller's Role in Management," *Organizational Dynamics* 11, no. 3 (Winter 1983):31–48.

[7] Our discussion draws upon the classification and description of plans in William H. Newman, *Administrative Action: The Techniques of Organization and Management,* 2nd ed. (Englewood Cliffs, N.J.: Prentice Hall, 1963), pp. 13–54. The types of plans we include in the classification and our specific interpretation of their use differ somewhat from Newman's version.

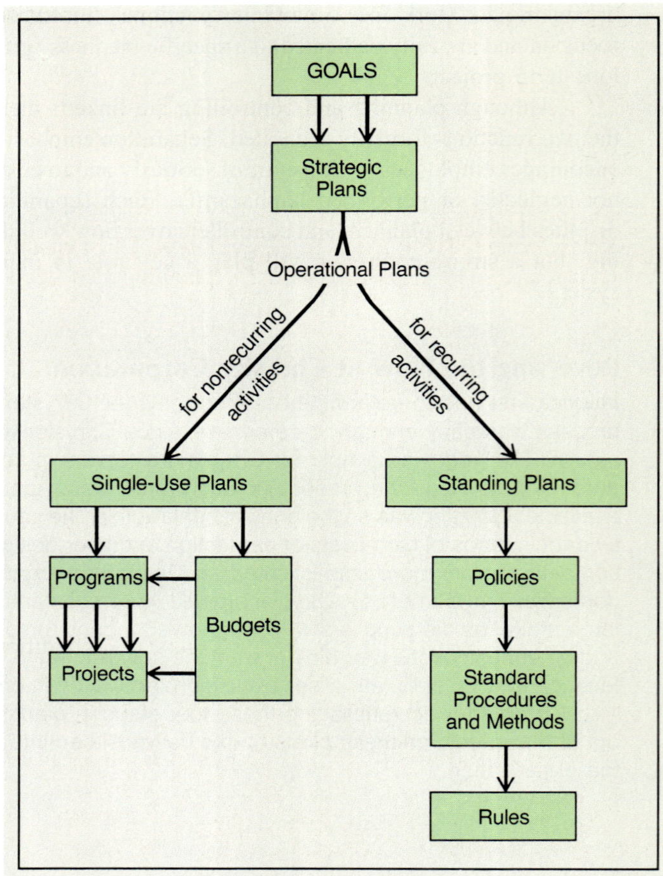

FIGURE 5-2 THE HIERARCHY OF ORGANIZATIONAL PLANS

Single-Use Plans

single-use plans Detailed courses of action used once or only occasionally to solve problems that do not occur repeatedly.

program A single-use plan that covers a relatively large set of organizational activities and specifies major steps, their order and timing, and unit responsible for each step.

project The smaller and separate portions of the programs.

budgets Formal quantitative statements of the resources allocated to specific programs or projects for a given period.

Single-use plans are detailed courses of action that probably will not be repeated in the same form in the future. For example, a rapidly expanding firm, planning to set up a new warehouse, will need a specific single-use plan for that project even though it has established a number of other warehouses in the past. It will not be able to use an existing warehouse plan, because the projected warehouse presents unique requirements of location, construction costs, labor availability, zoning restrictions, and so forth. The major type of single-use plans include programs, projects and budgets. For example, in 1982 when AT&T agreed to split itself into eight separate companies, it created a single-use plan called "The Plan for Divestiture." Many person-years of work went into the creation of this document, which served as a blueprint for the unique events that were to occur.

A **program** covers a relatively large set of activities. The program shows (1) the major steps required to reach an objective, (2) the organization unit or member responsible for each step, and (3) the order and timing of each step. **Projects** are smaller, separate portions of programs of limited scope and distinct directives concerning assignments and time. If the program is to transfer inventory from one warehouse to another, one related project might be to evaluate floor space at the proposed installation. **Budgets** are statements of financial resources set aside for specific activities in a given period of time; they are primarily devices to control an organization's activities and are thus important components of programs and projects.

Standing Plans

standing plans An established set of decisions used by managers to deal with recurring or organizational activities; major types are policies, procedures, and rules.

Whenever organizational activities occur repeatedly, a single decision or set of decisions can effectively guide those activities. Once established, **standing plans** allow managers to conserve time used for planning and decision making because similar situations are handled in a predetermined, consistent manner. For example, bank managers can more easily approve or reject loan requests if criteria are established in advance to evaluate credit ratings, collateral assets, and related applicant information.

In some cases, however, standing plans can be disadvantageous because they commit managers to past decisions which, although venerable, may no longer be appropriate. For this reason, it is particularly important that standing plans be continuously reinterpreted and analyzed for their potential flexibility. For example, for many years, the standard workday began at 9:00 A.M. and ended at 5:00 P.M. Yet in recent years, companies have both officially and unofficially implemented the concept of "flextime," whereby employees might determine their own starting and ending times. This practice has been adopted in response to such factors as greater employee responsibility in the home, increasingly crowded traffic conditions on the nation's highways, and additional stress on an aging mass-transit system. It represents the ability of corporate management to adjust standing plans in response to changing conditions.

The major types of standing plans are policies, procedures, and rules.

policy A standing plan that establishes general guidelines for decision making.

TEACHING TIP

Covering this section on policies, standard procedures, and rules, provides a prime opportunity to relate these types of standing plans to your school. For example, identify *policies* (admissions, grading, prerequisite requirements, etc.); *standard procedures* (registering for classes, registering your car, cashing a check, getting a transcript, etc.); and *rules* (no smoking in classrooms, books checked out for a maximum two-week period, etc.) that are in force at your institution. Then, ask your students why these are necessary. (Some of them will probably think they aren't!)

Policies. A **policy** is a general guideline for decision making. It sets up boundaries around decisions, including those that can be made and eliminating those that cannot. In this way, it channels the thinking of organization members so that it is consistent with organizational objectives. Some policies deal with very important matters, such as those requiring strict sanitary conditions where food or drugs are produced or packaged. Others may be concerned with relatively minor issues, such as the way employees dress; IBM, for example, has a strict dress code requiring dark business dress, while informal dress is the rule rather than the exception at Apple and Tandem Computers.

Policies are usually established formally and deliberately by top managers who may set policy because (1) they feel it will improve the effectiveness of the organization; (2) they want some aspect of the organization to reflect their personal values (for example, dress codes); or (3) they need to redress some conflict or confusion that has occurred at a lower level in the organization.

Policies may also emerge informally and at lower levels as the result of a seemingly consistent set of decisions on the same subject made over a period of time. For example, if office space is repeatedly assigned on the basis of seniority, the practice may become organization policy. In recent years, policy has also been set by factors in the external environment—for example, the issuance of governmental guidelines for an organization's activities (such as requiring certain safety procedures).

Many organizations have recently developed policies in South Africa. Some companies, including General Motors and IBM, have policies not to do business in South Africa, while other companies have established a policy to abide by the Sullivan Principles (see Chapter 4). Other organizations, such as universities and institutional investors, have developed policies for investment in the stocks of companies with holdings in South Africa. In most cases, these policies are the result of protracted debate and careful planning.

procedure A standing plan of detailed guidelines for handling organizational actions that occur regularly.

Standard Procedures. Policies are carried out by means of more detailed guidelines called "standard procedures" or "standard methods." A **procedure** provides a detailed set of instructions for performing a sequence of actions that occurs often or regularly. For example, the refund department of a large discount store may have a policy of "refunds made, with a smile, on all merchandise returned within seven days of purchase." The procedure for all clerks who handle such merchandise might then be (1) smile at customer, (2) check receipt for purchase date; (3) check condition of merchandise . . . and so on. Such detailed instructions guide the employees who perform these tasks and help insure a consistent approach to a specific situation.

At The Limited, a specialty clothing store, standard procedure ensures that customers get an offer of assistance within the first few seconds of entering the store. At Wal-Mart, a discount merchandiser, store procedure requires that one person greet all customers and smile at them. At the Red Cross, the advent of AIDS has meant numerous changes in the standard procedure for accepting blood donations and handling blood products.

rules Standing plans that detail specific actions to be taken in a given situation.

Rules. **Rules** are statements that a specific action must or must not be taken in a given situation. They are the most explicit of standing plans and are not guides to thinking or decision making, rather, they are substitutes for them. The only choice a rule leaves is whether or not to apply it to a particular set of circumstances. For example, in an office where the rule requires all employees to work until five o'clock, the manager may decide to suspend the rule in order to dismiss the staff earlier on a hot day if the air-conditioning system breaks down. The proliferation of rules can often adversely affect employee morale.[8] This is especially true when employees have been accustomed to working without many rules, as was the case with Apple Computer under its innovative founders Steven Jobs and Stephen Wozniak. When they hired professional manager John Sculley, he instituted a more traditional set of rules, from tough product-development deadlines to formal reporting procedures. Given the once informal nature of these activities, the changes created quite a morale problem, particularly for those accustomed to the less formal approach.

While some organizations have many policies, procedures, and rules, others have few. Even though each particular instance of a policy, procedure, or rule may be well-intentioned, some organizations, such as the Dana Corporation, have found that, overall, there are just too many policies, procedures, and rules. They have taken steps to eliminate those that are unnecessary and to give people more autonomy in the exercise of their judgment.

In particular, the neo-human relations school, mentioned in Chapter 2, has argued that the existence of such rules constrains creativity and makes organizations unresponsive to change. If such is the case, then it is all the more ironic because most rules, policies, and procedures are supposed to *adapt* the organization to a particular change.

TOOLS AND TECHNIQUES FOR PLANNING

We have examined the components of the planning process and described various kinds of plans; we have also noted the link between planning and controlling. The creation of effective plans, their successful implementation, and the imposition of effective controls upon them are all vital to an organization's achievement. In this section, we will examine some tools and techniques for making planning more effective.

---

[8] See Lloyd L. Byars, *Concepts of Strategic Management: Planning and Implementation* (New York: Harper & Row, 1984), p. 212.

The first step in the planning process is goal setting. Second, in order to set realistic and achievable goals, managers must try to understand what the future holds for them. In turn, the third step in the planning process, identifying aids and barriers to an established goal, depends crucially on an understanding of future events.

forecasting The attempt, using specific techniques, to predict outcomes and project future trends.

Forecasting is the attempt to predict outcomes and future trends that can serve as the basis for these planning steps. We will define and describe two techniques for forecasting economic and sales trends and present some considerations for forecasting technological change.

Complex projects, such as designing and building the Boeing 747 or the space shuttle, require that planning be pursued continuously. Goals continually have to be updated. Managers must constantly recognize and describe any discrepancy between the present situation and future goals. There are constant barriers that arise, and plans must be made for overcoming them. The shuttle is a good example. Although forecasts were useful tools for predicting the future, once the *Challenger* disaster took place, NASA needed a whole new set of plans and schedules.

COORDINATED RESOURCE

If your school has a planning official (most have someone acting in that capacity), ask that person to come in and speak to the class about effective planning and forecasting in institutions of higher education. Or you might want to invite a planner from your city or any businesses in your locale who can share their thoughts with the class.

We will examine some of the comprehensive tools and techniques that managers can use to plan large and complex projects. We will trace the development of those techniques from the early use of Gantt charts, to the concept of milestone scheduling, and finally to descriptions of PERT and CPM, two closely related strategies that enable management to monitor the progress of more intricate projects and to analyze the interrelationship between the activities within those projects. The four basic steps in planning are continuous in projects as large as these.

Forecasting

An observation popular with many forecasters is that "the only certain thing about a forecast is that it will be wrong." Beyond its irony, this observation touches on an important point: Forecasts do not have to be right in order to be useful—they simply have to predict future events closely enough to guide present actions in a valid and purposeful way. The fact that many forecasts made by meteorologists, economists, politicians, and managers prove inaccurate may make us forget how widespread and important forecasts really are. Most daily actions are based on some type of forecast, and forecasts are necessary; without them, individuals as well as organizations are at the mercy not only of the future but of its uncertainty. Sometimes, of course, forecasts are wrong, and there is a price to be paid (See the Ethics box entitled "When Planning Goes Awry . . .").

The most important use of forecasts is as premises for planning. When managers assess the alternatives, they try to forecast how events both within and outside the organization will affect each alternative and what the outcome of each will be. These forecasts are the **premises,** or basic assumptions, upon which planning and decision making are based.[9]

premises The basic assumptions upon which planning and decision making are based.

Two broad types of forecasts are used as planning premises. First are forecasts of events that will be influenced, at least in part, by the organization's behavior. Second are certain basic economic and social variables that are unaffected by any one organization's behavior. Thus, managers need not take their organization's possible actions into account when making predictions about such variables. Instead, they will look to leading broad-based indicators—such as Department of Commerce statistics—in finding the information they need. For example, if administrators want to decide whether to expand their college's facilities, federal statistics can give them some idea of long-term college enrollment trends.

[9]See George A. Steiner, *Strategic Planning: What Every Manager Must Know* (New York: Free Press, 1979), pp. 18–20 and 122–148.

ETHICS IN MANAGEMENT

WHEN PLANNING GOES AWRY, WHO PAYS THE PRICE?

Planning is one of the central tasks of management, and all organizations, large and small, engage in some form of planning. The real world, however, does not always cooperate. Practical work activities do not always proceed according to the best-laid plans; sometimes, the plans were based on faulty information or just bad logic, and sometimes unexpected events render even well-conceived plans irrelevant. An ethical dilemma is posed when the following question must finally be asked: Who should pay the price when things go wrong?

In the late 1960s, for example, oil companies didn't take OPEC very seriously. They planned on "business as usual," building production facilities and retail outlets as if there would always be a cheap source of oil and gasoline from the dependable region of the world known to a few as the Mid East, whose need for American and European revenues routinely figured into oil company planning. In 1970, however, Libya nationalized Occidental Petroleum, capping a decade-long struggle for control of the country's oilfields. Finally in 1973 OPEC organized the now famous boycott. Geopolitical reality exposed the oil companies' plans as short-sighted and perhaps even arrogant, and yet it was consumers who paid dearly through higher prices and shorter supply.

Similarly, when big steel in the U.S. underwent severe competitive pressures from Japan, their suppliers were also hurt. Utilities such as Duquesne Light Company in Pittsburgh lost a major portion of their business as steel mill after steel mill shut down. Managers at large steel companies had underestimated the Japanese threat or underinvested in new plant and equipment, but employees, suppliers, and communities paid a large part of the price.

As we saw in Chapter 4, ethical questions like "Who should pay the price?" are inevitably easier to ask than they are to answer. For that matter, as we saw in Chapter 3, the increasing complexity of the external environments in which organizations must operate ensures that, in incidents like those detailed above, the problem of providing reasonably practical answers to ethical questions becomes even more difficult. If we take the idea of *price* literally, there are a few easy answers: Consumers pay the "price" in terms of higher living costs, and numerous conglomerate organizations pay the "price" in terms of decreased profitability and less latitude in planning options. But if the deceivingly simple issue of *price* is translated into the thornier issue of *responsibility,* both questions and answers become more difficult. *Who* is "responsible" for effective long-term planning that can potentially affect millions of people? If the "responsible" parties can be isolated, how can "responsibility" be enforced?

As you can see, most ethical questions are usually single questions in a chain of questions, and as the chain gets longer, each and every answer reveals itself as more and more simplistic, leading to more complex questions and raising more complex issues.

Forecasts that are affected by an organization's behavior are more difficult to make, because they require assumptions about the organization's actions as well as assumptions about events outside the organization's control. A sales forecast, for example, may become a company objective. In the forecasting process, managers' analyses of anticipated company actions and probable competitor responses—together with their projections of the economic environment—may indicate that the sales objective will not be realized if existing programs and policies are left unchanged. In such a case, a "planning gap" is said to exist. Accordingly, the managers must rework previously adopted plans until the forecast indicates that the planning gap has been closed—that is, until forecasted sales under the new program and the sales objectives are the same.

Forecasting for Economic and Sales Information. Because of the importance of predicting future economic and sales trends, our discussion of forecasting techniques will focus on these areas. The same techniques can, of course, be used for forecasting other variables (such as the anticipated number of job applicants in a town where the company may open a plant or the number of votes a political candidate will receive).

qualitative forecasting A judgment-based forecasting technique used when hard data are scarce or difficult to use.

Qualitative forecasting is appropriate when hard data are scarce or difficult to use. For instance, when a new product or technology is introduced, past experience is not a reliable guide for estimating what the near-term effects will be. Qualitative forecasting thus involves the use of subjective judgments and rating schemes to transform qualitative information into quantitative estimates. Examples of qualitative forecasting include the jury of executive opinion, sales-force composite, and the survey of expert opinion.

quantitative forecasting Forecasting techniques used when enough hard data exist to specify relationships between variables.

Quantitative forecasting extrapolates from the past or is used when there is sufficient "hard" or statistical data to specify relationships between key variables. Extrapolation forecasting, such as time-series analysis, uses past or current trends to project future events. Sales records of the past several years, for example, could be used to extend the sales pattern into the coming year. Causal models are used where good data exist for a number of related variables and where the relationships between variables can be clearly expressed. The computer is invaluable for handling the complex mathematical formulas and the values assigned to variables in quantitative forecasting.[10]

Qualitative forecasting does not demand numerical or statistical data in the same way that quantitative forecasting does. (Quantitative forecasting can be used if information exists about the past, if this information can be specified numerically, and if it can be assumed that the pattern of the past will continue.) Inputs to qualitative forecasts are mainly the results of intuitive thinking, judgment, and accumulated knowledge. Specialists from a variety of fields are sometimes called upon to provide such input. Qualitative techniques may be used alone or in combination with quantitative methods. Most (although not all) studies comparing the two forecasting techniques, however, find that quantitative methods are generally more accurate than qualitative ones.[11] Table 5-1 outlines several subcategories of qualitative and quantitative forecasting and lists the main drawback of each.[12]

HERE'S AN EXAMPLE

Matsushita Electric Industrial Company, after getting to the top in consumer electronics, now is taking aim on the industrial electronics market. Akio Tanii, Matsushita's president, says about the difficulties of developing the industrial side of the product line, "It's been harder than we expected, but we don't take a short-term view."

Forecasting Technological Change. The rapid pace of technological change has led many firms, hospitals, government agencies, and other institutions to recognize the importance of predicting future technological developments. Discoveries in such areas as lasers, jet aircraft, energy, data communications, biotechnology, and advanced plastics have drastically affected many organizations.[13] As managers, we may often have to ascertain what technological developments are likely to occur in order to prepare our organization for change.

A HUMOROUS NOTE

Sometimes organizations have to make plans to phase out products. Vermont Castings Inc. of Randolph, Vermont, is phasing out production of its 375-lb. cast-iron Defiant wood-burning stove in favor of a new emissions-control model. The company threw a "Heavy Metal Party" in honor of the phase-out over the July 4th, 1988 weekend and celebrated with 20,000 of their best customers, the governor of Vermont, and the media! (*Business Week*, 7/11/88, p. 36.)

---

[10] M. J. Lawrence, "An Exploration of Some Practical Issues in the Use of Quantitative Forecasting Models," Journal of *Forecasting* 2, No. 2 (April–June 1983):169–179.

[11] See Essam Mahmoud, "Accuracy in Forecasting: A Survey," *Journal of Forecasting 3,* no. 2 (1984):139–159; and Joseph P. Martino, *Technological Forecasting for Decision Making,* 2nd ed. (New York: North Holland, 1983).

[12] Our discussion of forecasting techniques is heavily indebted to J. Scott Armstrong, *Long-Range Forecasting: From Crystal Ball to Computer* (New York: Wiley, 1985). See also Spyros Makridakis and Steven C. Wheelwright, eds., *The Handbook of Forecasting* (New York: Wiley, 1982).

[13] See Daniel D. Roman, "Technological Forecasting in the Decision Process," *Academy of Management Journal* 13, no. 2 (June 1970):127–138.

TABLE 5-1 TYPES OF FORECASTS

QUALITATIVE	QUANTITATIVE
Judgmental Methods	**Extrapolation Methods**
Use intentions and opinions as data 1. Intentions studies—how people say they will act 2. Surveys of opinions —jury of executive opinion —sales force composite —Delphi technique (queries to panel of experts; each reviews others' opinions and works toward consensus) Caution: Allows bias to creep in, e.g., in selecting judges and posing questions	Project past and/or current trends in future; "naive" method (looks at only one key variable) 1. Time series analysis—used to detect seasonal or annual trends and patterns Caution: Often changes in trend are key
Projective Methods (Technological Forecasting)	**Causal Models**
Start with informed ideas and build on them 1. Brainstorming —groups focus intensively on given problem —generates many new ideas/alternatives rapidly —no evaluation until idea generation is completed 2. Scenario construction —builds logical, hypothetical sequences of events (stories) —answers question "if ... then ..." Caution: Little research on efficacy	Deal with relationships between several variables (dependent and independent) 1. Econometric methods —use statistical regression techniques to measure economic data —equations express known relationships among key variables 2. Segmentation methods —equations work with groupings or classes or related variables that do not respond identically in all respects Caution: Often expensive
Bootstrapping Methods	
Develop an explicit model from the judgmental forecast of an individual to attain more consistent performance. Caution: Difficult to wean people away from strictly judgmental methods	

Source: Adapted from discussion in J. Scott Armstrong, *Long-Range Forecasting: From Crystal Ball to Computer.* 2nd ed. (New York: Wiley-Interscience, 1985). Copyright 1985 by John Wiley & Sons.

The forecasting techniques described on the preceding pages imply that the future often will be similar to the past, but where technological change is concerned, we can anticipate that the future often will be quite different from what has gone before. The consequences of new developments may be either subtle or massive. Often even the most knowledgeable observers have under- or overestimated the effects of a key development. For nearly 30 years, for example, the computer industry has outstripped predictions of its impact on society and the individual; computing power has grown faster and its costs have declined more rapidly than nearly anyone imagined. On the other hand, although early predictions of the impact of atomic energy indicated that energy would be so inexpensive it would virtually be given away, no such inexhaustible, cheap, safe energy supply has materialized.

Planning Complex Projects

EXTRA EXERCISE

How would you use planning tools to help you in: writing a term paper, taking a weekend skiing trip, throwing a birthday party for your roommate, etc.?

We have seen how forecasting can help management identify not only proper goals, but aids and barriers to them, and we have seen how managers may develop programs based upon those factors. Once such programs are determined, it is critical that management have access to the tools that are instrumental in planning, controlling, and evaluating the projects that comprise those programs.

In this section, we will discuss several widely used project-management approaches. We begin with the Gantt chart, an early graphic project management technique, and move on to milestone scheduling, which extends the utility of the Gantt chart by incorporating completion dates for project phases; finally, we will focus on

PERT and CPM, two network-based scheduling methods that can incorporate data about the interrelationships between project elements and thereby facilitate the management of larger, more complex projects.

Gantt chart A graphic method of planning and control that allows a manager to view the starting and ending dates for various tasks.

CLASS COMMENT

Keep in mind that planning is not just a managerial function in the for-profit sector. Many nonprofit organizations (such as governmental agencies, community organizations, arts groups, etc.) are engaging in planning. (See Lecture Extras Supplement for a descriptive lecture on one arts organization's foray into planning.)

The Gantt Chart. One of the earliest and best-known approaches to project management was developed by Henry L. Gantt (see Chapter 2). A **Gantt chart** (Fig. 5-3) is a graphic planning and control method. A project is broken down into separate tasks, for each of which estimates are made regarding the amount of time required and the termination date necessary to meet the specified completion date for the project. This information is shown as a pair of brackets, one of which indicates the starting date and the other the end date, for each task. The Gantt chart enables a manager to make commitments based on the planned completion times, to acquire extra resources to shorten some of the times, and so on. In addition, filling in the brackets (''accomplishment'' in Fig. 5-3) enables the manager to see immediately what tasks are behind (or ahead of) schedule and how far. (In Fig. 5-3, shipping of product B is slightly behind schedule.) Extra effort can be applied to problematical parts of an operation before the overall completion date is threatened.

milestone scheduling A technique that adds detail and precision to the Gantt chart by marking particular dates by which the various phases of the entire project are to be completed.

Milestone Scheduling. If you select a date when a certain accomplishment, decision, or event is to take place and indicate that date on the horizontal bar of a chart, you have created a milestone.[14] The milestone may be the date when a decision is to be made concerning outside financing, when announcement of the project to the trade press is planned, or when a thorough project progress review is scheduled. **Milestone scheduling** indicates selected dates by which the various phases of the entire project are to be completed. Milestones thus add detail to the Gantt chart. They serve as formal review

[14]See James L. Riggs and Charles O. Heath, *Guide to Cost Reduction through Critical Path Scheduling* (Englewood Cliffs, N.J.: Prentice Hall, 1966).

FIGURE 5-3 GANTT CHART FOR MANUFACTURING DEPARTMENT

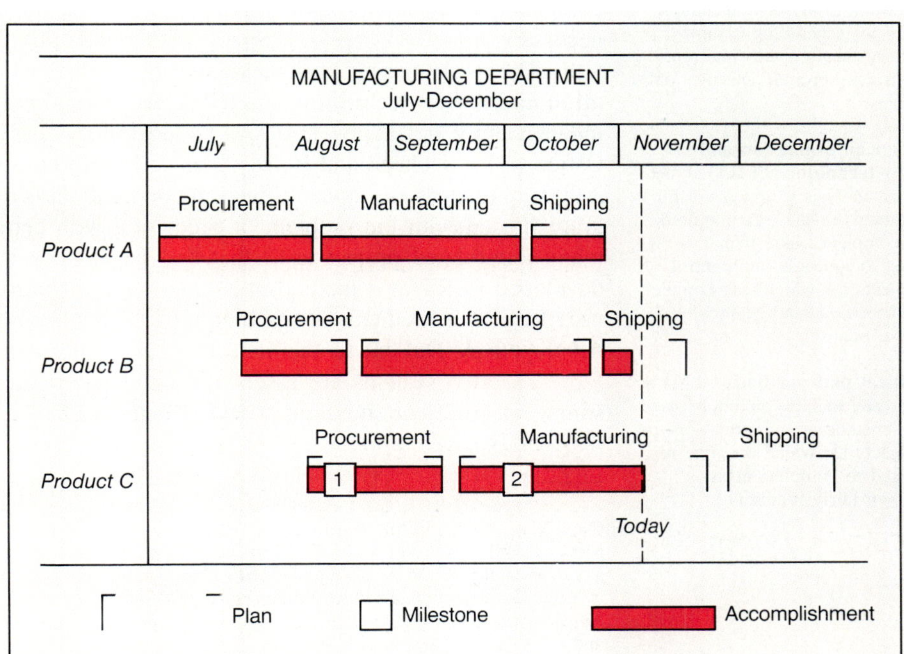

Drawing by M. Stevens; © 1983 The New Yorker Magazine, Inc.

points at which costs, progress, and the need for replanning or schedule modification can be reviewed. In Figure 5-3, milestones appear on the bars for product C to indicate (1) mailing of final purchase orders and (2) completion of the first quality inspection. Gantt charts show the relationship between milestones within the same task but not among different tasks. Modifying a Gantt chart to overcome this limitation leads to the formation of a network.[15]

Network-Based Scheduling. Gantt charts are appropriate for scheduling series of unrelated activities, such as separate production runs in job-shop operations. Milestone scheduling can be used to divide a major project into subactivities so that managers can achieve greater control over the project. Neither approach, however, can adequately deal with the interrelationships between activities or events that characterize more complex projects and programs. In such situations, some form of **network analysis** is necessary.

network analysis A technique used for scheduling complex projects that contain interrelationships between activities or events.

program evaluation and review technique (PERT) A network analysis technique, using estimates of the time required to complete tasks, which is used to schedule and control projects for which task completion times cannot be predicted fairly precisely.

critical path method (CPM) A network analysis technique used to schedule and control work on projects for which the time required to complete tasks is known fairly precisely.

The two major network techniques are **PERT,** which stands for **program evaluation and review technique,** and **CPM,** the **critical path method.** Both systems were independently developed in 1957–58, PERT by the U.S. Navy's Special Projects Office with Lockheed and Booz, Allen & Hamilton to help coordinate the more than 3,000 contractors and agencies working on the Polaris missile–nuclear submarine program. Faced with the problem of predicting with certainty the completion time for many interrelated project tasks that had never been attempted before, the planners developed PERT as a method of estimating and controlling scheduling needs.[16] The use of PERT is credited with trimming two years from the Polaris program. CPM was developed by DuPont to facilitate its control of large, complex industrial projects.

The two systems are essentially similar but can be used to best advantage in somewhat different situations: CPM is better suited to repetitive processes in which

[15] See Robert J. Thierauf and Richard A. Grosse, *Decision Making through Operations Research* (New York: Wiley, 1970); and Robert W. Miller, *Schedule, Cost, and Profit Control with PERT* (New York: McGraw-Hill, 1963); see James B. Dilworth, *Production and Operations Management: Manufacturing and Nonmanufacturing,* 3d ed. (New York: Random House, 1986).

[16] See Harold E. Fearon, William A. Ruch, Vincent G. Reuter, C. David Wieters, and Ross R. Reck, *Fundamentals of Production/Operations Management,* 3rd ed. (St. Paul, Minn.: West, 1986; W. J. Erickson and O. P. Hall, *Computer Models for Management Science* (Reading, Mass.: Addison-Wesley, 1986).

tasks are of fixed duration and the completion time is known, while PERT can best handle nonrepetitive processes in which the duration and completion time of tasks can be only roughly estimated.

The use of PERT and CPM is widespread and has significant impact on the planning and control of projects and programs. Formerly, establishing a PERT or CPM system was generally too time-consuming and expensive for all but the most complex, time-critical projects, such as highway construction, shipbuilding, or the installation of a large-scale data-processing system.[17] Now, however, network analysis software for microcomputers has made PERT and CPM accessible to managers who did not previously have the technical background or the resources. Such software makes these methods available to managers of much smaller projects, who can now quickly develop and frequently update schedules and rapidly check the effects of such "what-if" factors as a supplier's possible delay in shipping a crucial component.[18] There are a number of PERT and CPM techniques with different names and slight variations of methods. All, however, are essentially systems for network analysis—systems for planning projects and implementing plans. Their approach is to divide the project into separate operations and then chart the order in which the operations should be carried out, when each should be started and completed, and when the entire project should be completed. Since PERT and CPM are basically similar in technique, we will discuss them together, pointing out the differences between them whenever appropriate.

There are four requirements for translating a program into a PERT or CPM network.[19]

1. The activity must be broken down into individual tasks that will then be put into the network in the form of events and activities. Events are usually indicated in circles on the chart; they represent those parts of the tasks to be accomplished at specific points in time. Activities represent the time or the resources required to progress from one event to another and are usually indicated by arrows. For example, the official start of a design project would represent the chart's first event; the five weeks necessary to prepare preliminary blueprints would represent the chart's first activity.
2. Events and activities are placed in the chart in a logical, sequential, and integrated way. For example, each activity is preceded and followed by the appropriate events; no activity may start until its preceding event has been completed.
3. The length of time required for each activity is estimated and written in on the network. In CPM, a single time estimate is established for each activity. In PERT, however, each activity may be assigned four time estimates: an "optimistic" estimate for the length of time the activity would require under ideal conditions; a "most probable" estimate of the normal time that such an activity should take; a "pessimistic" estimate taking into account the possibility that just about everything will go wrong; and an "expected" time estimate based on a probability analysis of the other three estimates.
   The times are shown on the network diagram as:
   $$\frac{\text{optimistic, most probable, pessimistic}}{\text{expected}}$$
4. A critical path through the network must be determined. This requirement will be discussed in the next section.

---

[17]See Riggs and Heath, *Guide to Cost Reduction through Critical Path Scheduling*, pp. 16–20; and Richard J. Schonberger, "Custom Tailored PERT/CPM Systems," *Business Horizons* 15, no. 6 (December 1972):64–66; and Everett Adam and Ronald Ebert, *Production and Operations Management*, 3rd ed. (Englewood Cliffs, N.J.: Prentice Hall, 1986.).

[18]For an overview of recent project management software, see Andres Pollack, "Software Aids Small Projects," *New York Times*, October 25, 1984, p. D2. Typical microcomputer project management programs are Pro-Ject 6 (Clearwater, Fla.: SoftCorp, 1984); Project Scheduler 5000 (Sunnyvale, Calif.: Scitor Corp., 1985); and Pertmaster (Palo Alto, Calif.: Westminster Software, 1985).

[19]Robert W. Miller, "How to Plan and Control with PERT," *Harvard Business Review* 40, no. 2 (March–April 1962):93–104. See also Miller, "Schedule, Cost, and Profit Control with PERT," pp. 32–38.

We can illustrate the construction of a network, using as an example the development of a new cordless vacuum cleaner.[20] The major activities in this job and their immediate predecessors are listed in Table 5-2. For example, preliminary product testing, activity G, cannot begin until activity D, construction of a prototype model, is completed. Also included in the table are a range of estimates for the duration (in weeks) of each activity: optimistic time, most probable time, pessimistic time, and the expected time of completion. In this case, since it is not possible to make accurate time estimates, the PERT system will be used; if accurate estimates based on ample prior experience were available, the CPM system would be more applicable.

From the information in the table, we can construct the network shown in Figure 5-4. This network illustrates which activities can be performed simultaneously and which must wait for predecessors to be completed. For example, once the cordless vacuum cleaner has been designed, construction and testing of the prototype, routing (manufacturing engineering), and cost estimation can go on at the same time. But the market survey cannot be started until the market research plan and the marketing brochure have been completed.

The longest route through the network in terms of time is called the critical path and is determined by totaling the amount of time required for each sequence of tasks (as opposed to tasks that are performed simultaneously). The task chain with the longest time is the critical path. In Figure 5-4, the critical path is marked with the thicker arrows. For example, once the path reaches 2, there are three possible routes to 8. Because we are looking for the longest route, the critical path will follow 2, 3, 6, 7, 8, since that will add the most weeks (9) to the total.

The significance of the critical path is that it determines the total length of time, or completion date, of the entire project. If an event on the critical path is delayed, the entire project will be delayed.

[20]This example is taken from David R. Anderson, Dennis J. Sweeney, and Thomas A. Williams, *Quantitative Methods for Business* (New York: West Publishing, 1983).

TABLE 5-2 ACTIVITY LIST AND TIME ESTIMATES FOR CORDLESS VACUUM CLEANER PROJECT, IN WEEKS

ACTIVITY	DESCRIPTION	IMMEDIATE PREDECESSORS	OPTIMISTIC TIME ESTIMATE	MOST PROBABLE TIME ESTIMATE	PESSIMISTIC TIME ESTIMATE	EXPECTED TIME
A	R & D product design	—	4	5	12	6
B	Plan market research	—	1	1.5	5	2
C	Routing (manufacturing engineering)	A	2	3	4	3
D	Build prototype model	A	3	4	11	5
E	Prepare marketing brochure	A	2	3	4	3
F	Cost estimates (industrial engineering)	C	1.5	2	2.5	2
G	Preliminary product testing	D	1.5	3	4.5	3
H	Market survey	B, E	2.5	3.5	7.5	4
I	Pricing and forecast report	H	1.5	2	2.5	2
J	Final report	F, G, I	1	2	3	2
						Total 32

Source: Reprinted by permission from *Quantitative Methods for Business*. Second Edition, by Anderson et al.

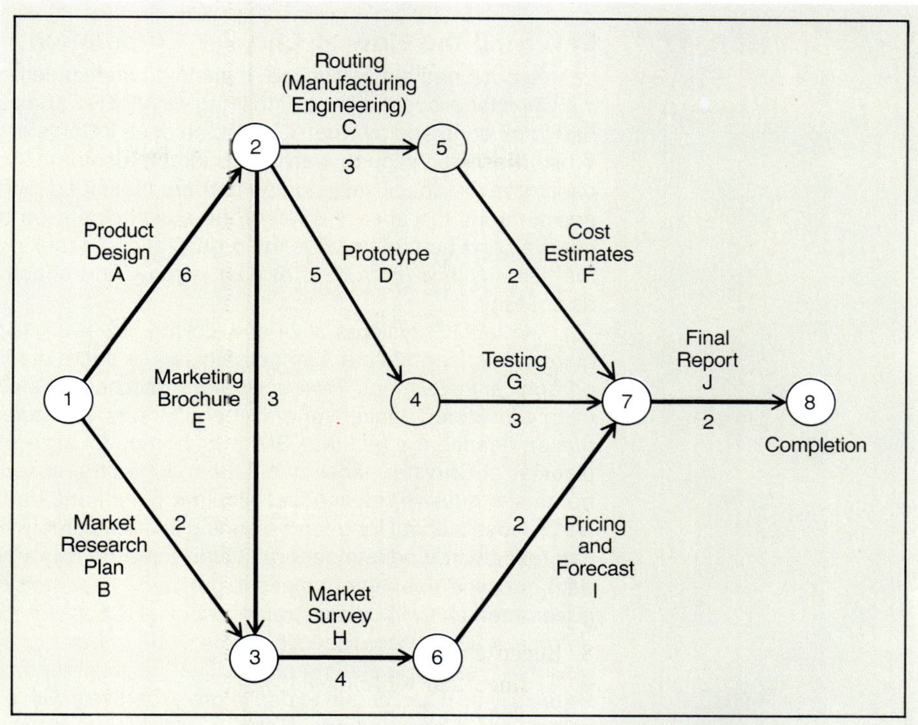

FIGURE 5-4 PERT CHART FOR CORDLESS VACUUM CLEANER PROJECT WITH EXPECTED ACTIVITY TIMES (IN WEEKS)

Source: Reprinted by permission from *Quantitative Methods for Business,* Second Edition, by Anderson et al. Copyright © 1973 by West Publishing Company. All rights reserved.

Paths other than the critical path are called subcritical. These contain some slack since the total time for their completion is less than that of the critical path. Both PERT and CPM can reduce project completion time by indicating resources that can be transferred from activities on subcritical paths to activities on the critical path. For example, transferring staff from F, cost estimates, to I, pricing and forecast report, might increase the time for F on the subcritical path by a week, but the time required for I might be reduced by a week. Since I is on the critical path, this would reduce completion time for the whole project by a week.

The main function of PERT and CPM is to determine and control the time required to complete a project; the main benefit is time saved through the scheduling of tasks, both initially and as the project progresses. Since time and cost are closely related, saving time usually leads to savings in costs. In addition, both PERT and CPM have been adapted and applied explicitly to costs. They can, for example, be used to develop an optimum cost-efficiency schedule that can help managers determine the savings and costs involved in achieving a shorter production schedule. Using extra labor to reduce the duration of an activity, for instance, may cost more than the bonus for early completion. Other extensions of PERT and CPM, such as pinpointing problem areas, improving communication, and comparing alternative actions, also enhance their usefulness.[21]

---

[21] See Riggs and Heath, "Guide to Cost Reduction through Critical Path Scheduling"; and T. M. McCann and H. W. Lanford, "Effective Planning and Control of Large Projects—Using Work Breakdown Structure," *Long Range Planning* 16, no. 2 (April 1983):38–50.

ILLUSTRATIVE CASE STUDY Wrap-Up

Reversing the Flow at Chrysler Corporation

Lee Iacocca had a massive job of planning and implementation on his hands in turning Chrysler around. It is easy to imagine a PERT analysis or a GANTT chart of what had to be done and by when it had to be done if Chrysler were to stave off bankruptcy. While these techniques were undoubtably useful to Chrysler, Iacocca also had to overcome the specifically human barriers that stood in the way of the turnaround. He had to focus the energy of all of the stakeholders on achieving the difficult goal of survival, and he had to focus the organization on making decisions differently than in the past. With a great deal of pain, agony, and effective management, Chrysler is alive today.

In fact, Chrysler is alive and kicking. By 1987, Iacocca's organization had acquired American Motors, Lamborghini, and a share of Maserati. In his second autobiographical installment, *Talking Straight,* Iacocca revealed in 1988 that Chrysler had even considered a takeover of General Motors, now another troubled American automaker, despite the fact that GM is four times the size of Chrysler. Having staved off disaster at Chrysler, Iacocca has abandoned the essentially defensive (although by no means passive) stance first required of him and has become more aggressive in his proposals about long-term planning in the automotive industry in particular and the external environment in general. Often rejecting the suggestion that he run for President, Iacocca has nevertheless expressed himself on numerous issues concerning governmental and business relationships. He has, for example, called on the U.S. to enforce a 20 percent reduction in its trade imbalance with Japan, and his proposal obviously reflects a lifetime of effective, flexible planning in the automotive industry, especially as it has begun to deal more assertively with newly emergent complications in its external environment. "Take my word for it," he says in his new book, as tough-talking as his first, "the Japanese like to work toward objectives. It's time we gave them one."

By 1988, however, critics were noting that while Iacocca was becoming a corporate superstar, Chrysler was suffering. In fact, after four years of improved car sales, Chrysler's sales fell 22.8 percent in 1987—a bigger decline than rival GM's drop of 21.6 percent.

Refocusing his efforts at Chrysler, Iacocca is again restructuring the corporation, reshuffling top management, focusing on engineering and development capacity, and entertaining thoughts of a joint partnership with such companies as Nissan or Volkswagen. Only time will tell if Iacocca's excellent management skills, his charismatic leadership abilities, and a less hostile competitive environment will enable him to launch a second major comeback for Chrysler. ■

SUMMARY

FOR DISCUSSION

Managers often complain of being "too busy to plan." What advice could you give them?

Planning is the first step in managing an organization and can be seen as the manager's most fundamental responsibility at all levels. Planning involves four basic steps: (1) establishing goals, (2) defining the present situation, (3) determining aids and barriers to goal achievement, and (4) developing courses of action.

Single-use plans are established for unique situations; standing plans provide standardized responses to recurring situations. Single-use plans include programs, projects, and budgets. Standing plans include policies, procedures, and rules.

Planning and controlling are closely linked; without planning there can be no controlling. To ensure that performance conforms to plans, progress must be monitored and corrective action taken when necessary.

Forecasting techniques for economic and sales information include qualitative forecasting (such as a jury of executive opinion) and quantitative forecasting (such as time series analysis). The Gantt chart graphically indicates the tasks involved in each project and the time it will take to complete them. Milestones on a Gantt chart indicate important dates in a project—usually when a certain phase of the project is to be completed. PERT and CPM networks illustrate the tasks involved in a project, the time it will take to complete them, and the interrelationships between those tasks.

Models for planning and control include forecasting and various project management techniques such as Gantt charts, milestone scheduling, PERT, and CPM.

REVIEW QUESTIONS

1. Why is flexibility a characteristic of a good plan? Why might flexibility impede planning?
2. Describe the basic steps in the planning process. Why is each step important?
3. How are planning and controlling linked? Why is it important for you as a manager to keep these two management functions formally separated?
4. What are the main types of operation plans? Under what conditions is each type of plan appropriate?
5. Justify the use of standing plans.
6. Why do you think forecasts do not have to be completely accurate to be meaningful?
7. Why is forecasting an important part of the planning or decision-making process? What are the two types of forecasts that serve as planning premises?
8. Describe and give examples of quantitative and qualitative forecasting.
9. Briefly describe the principle characteristics of Gantt charts, milestone scheduling, and network analysis, including PERT and CPM.

CASE STUDY

The Dashman Company

The Dashman Company was a large concern making many types of equipment for the armed forces of the United States. It had over 20 plants, located in the central part of the country, whose purchasing procedures had never been completely coordinated. In fact, the head office of the company had encouraged each of the plant managers to operate with their staffs as independent units in most matters. When it began to appear that the company would face increasing difficulty in securing certain essential raw materials, Mr. Manson, the company's president, appointed an experienced purchasing executive, Mr. Post, as vice-president in charge of purchasing, a position especially created for him. Mr. Manson gave Mr. Post wide latitude in organizing his job, and he assigned Mr. Larson as Mr. Post's assistant. Mr. Larson had served the company in a variety of capacities for many years, and knew most of the plant executives personally. Mr. Post's appointment was announced through the formal channels usual in the company, including a notice in the house organ published by the company.

One of Mr. Post's first decisions was to begin immediately to centralize the company's purchasing procedures. As a first step, he decided that he would require each of the executives who handled purchasing in the individual plants to clear with the head office all purchase contracts made in excess of $10,000. He felt that if the head office was to do any coordinating in a way that would be helpful to each plant and to the company as a whole, he must be notified that the contracts were being prepared at least a week before they were to be signed. He talked his proposal over with Mr. Manson, who presented it to his board of directors. They approved the plan.

Although the company made purchases throughout the year, the beginning of its peak buying season was only three weeks away at the time this new plan was adopted. Mr. Post prepared the following letter to send to the 20 purchasing executives of the company:

Dear _____:

The board of directors of our company has recently authorized a change in our purchasing procedures. Hereafter, each of the purchasing executives in the several plants of the company will notify the vice-president in charge of purchasing of all contracts in excess of $10,000 that they are negotiating at least a week in advance of the date on which they are to be signed.

I am sure that you will understand that this step is necessary to coordinate the purchasing requirements of the company in these times when we are facing increasing difficulty in securing essential supplies. This procedure should give us in the central office the information we need to see that each plant secure the optimum supply of materials. In this way the interests of each plant and of the company as a whole will be best served.

Yours very truly,

Mr. Post showed the letter to Mr. Larson and invited his comments. Mr. Larson thought the letter an excellent one, but suggested that, since Mr. Post had not met more than a few of the purchasing executives, he might like to visit all of them and take the matter up with each of them personally. Mr. Post dismissed the idea at once because, as he said, he had so many things to do at the head office that he could not get away for a trip. Consequently he had the letters sent out over his signature.

During the following two weeks replies came in from all except a few plants. Although a few executives wrote at greater length, the following reply was typical:

Dear Mr. Post:

Your recent communication in regard to notifying the head office a week in advance of our intention to sign contracts has been received. This suggestion seems a most practical one. We want to assure you that you can count on our cooperation.

Yours very truly,

During the next six weeks the head office received no notices from any plant that contracts were being negotiated. Executives in other departments who made frequent trips to the plants reported that the plants were busy, and the usual routines for that time of year were being followed.

Source: This case was prepared by George F. F. Lombard as the basis for class discussion rather than to illustrate either effective or ineffective handling of an administrative situation. Reprinted by permission of the Harvard Business School.

Case Questions

1. How would you evaluate the goal(s) of the new purchasing program?
2. How would you evaluate the control process that Mr. Post has established?
3. Might the problems, if any, with the purchasing procedures be symptomatic of a larger problem in the company?
4. What would you have done if you were Mr. Post?
5. What would you have done if you were Mr. Larson?
6. Mr. Manson, president of the Dashman Company, has hired you as an outside consultant to advise him about the purchasing policy. What planning model would you use to aid you in determining your recommendations? ■

Guy Billout, *Solutions.* Courtesy of the Artist.

6

PROBLEM SOLVING AND DECISION MAKING

Upon completing this chapter you should be able to:

1. Describe the rational problem-solving process and explain why it is sometimes preferable to informal methods of problem solving.
2. Explain why an important part of a manager's job is to find the right problem to work on.
3. Explain why it is important for managers to be aware of their own values and backgrounds when they work on problems.
4. Identify the different types of decisions made by managers.
5. Describe the various conditions under which managers make decisions.
6. Explain why managers often settle for a satisfactory decision, rather than trying to make the ideal decision.
7. Explain some heuristics that managers use to make decisions and some biases that result.
8. Describe ways in which managers can improve their decisions and make them more acceptable to subordinates.

Chapter Outline

Introduction
The Rational Problem-Solving Process
Problem and Opportunity Finding
The Nature of Managerial Decision Making
Heuristics and Biases in Decision Making
Improving the Effectiveness of Decision Making and Problem Solving

ILLUSTRATIVE CASE STUDY Introduction

Diplomacy and Determination in High-Level Decision Making

Mr. John McKinley, CEO of Texaco, knew he was faced with a difficult issue, both for his career and for the future of his company. Did Texaco want to become an active bidder to acquire Getty Oil? Getty and Pennzoil had already reached an "agreement in principle" for a Pennzoil takeover, so any action taken by Texaco would have to be made immediately, before the Getty-Pennzoil deal was finalized.

The situation was very complicated. It had begun when Getty Oil began searching for a buyer. Getty was largely controlled by the Getty family trust, Getty trust shares, and the shares held by the Getty Museum, a total constituting 52 percent of the outstanding shares. The remaining 48 percent were publicly held. Mr. Gordon Getty had begun by seeking a partner to buy the publicly held shares, planning to combine the family shares with those held by the Museum and thus take control of the company. However, he needed to eliminate the board of directors, which represented the public, in order to gain his ultimate goal—total control. Pennzoil had agreed to purchase the outstanding public shares at a value of $112.50 per share.

Since the Getty Oil board of directors objected to this proposal on the grounds that the public was being cheated, they sought a company to make a counteroffer, buying the public and Museum shares and thereby thwarting Gordon Getty's bid for control of Getty Oil. It was this role of "white knight" that Texaco was being asked to fill. Texaco would have to pay approximately $125 per share—a price that would not only assure the public of receiving full value, but would also entice the Museum to sell rather than join with Mr. Getty in taking control. Additionally, the investment bankers advising Texaco thought this price would be high enough to lure Mr. Getty into selling, rather than buying, the family shares.

The purchase of Getty could solve a number of problems for Texaco, which was currently draining its reserves much faster than it was locating new sources of oil. Although refinery modernization guaranteed efficiency in turning crude oil into marketable products, Texaco was fast losing its competitive position within the industry, currently spending nearly double the industry standard to explore for new oil reserves and consistently coming up empty-handed. The purchase of Getty Oil would almost double its oil reserves—and at a quarter of the price Texaco was presently paying for exploration. In addition, the purchase of such a large company would greatly enhance Texaco's position in an industry in which it was a large but not key player.

However, McKinley was not entirely comfortable with the proposed deal. It had long been a Texaco policy not to engage in any hostile takeovers, and the situation with Getty was so unclear that he could not tell how welcome his offer might be. Certainly the Getty Oil board members who had approached him would welcome an offer. But how would Gordon Getty respond? If he was against Texaco, then McKinley did not want to pursue the possibility any further. Unfortunately, it was not as simple as merely asking Mr. Getty: Takeover negotiations are extremely delicate, and any such overt action on Texaco's part could irrevocably disturb the process as it was currently evolving. The lawyers and investment bankers were encouraging McKinley to move forward, but their advice was suspect, since their fees would be considerably higher if the deal were pursued further.

All of these considerations weighed heavily on McKinley. Any move would have to be made within the next 24 hours, and the sooner the better: Taking too long to consider all the options would be the same as deciding against pursuing the deal. Once any move was made, McKinley would be obligated to continue. Therefore, he had to be totally committed to pursuing the takeover of Getty Oil before making even preliminary moves, including the gathering of any more information.

Source: Steve Coll, *The Taking of Getty Oil,* (New York: Atheneum Books, 1987).

CLASS COMMENT

Decision making is often viewed as an integral managerial function, an important aspect of the manager's job.

decision making The process of identifying and selecting a course of action to solve a specific problem.

planning The process of establishing objectives and suitable courses of action before taking action.

People at all levels in an organization must constantly make decisions and solve problems. *Problems* arise when an actual state of affairs differs from a desired state of affairs. Sometimes, however, problems give rise to opportunities. For example, if an organization is faced with the problem of too many employees, the problem could also be seen as an opportunity to restructure, whereby twice as many jobs may ultimately be saved as lost. In this case, management would simultaneously be solving a problem and seizing an opportunity. Moreover, in solving a particular problem, many decisions may have to be made. Sometimes, the solution will require an entire chain of decisions. **Decision making**—that is, identifying and selecting a course of action to deal with a specific problem or take advantage of an opportunity—is a particularly important part of managers' jobs. How should profits be invested? Which employee should be assigned a particular task? Large problem or small, it is usually the manager who must confront it and decide what action to take. Managers' decisions provide the framework within which other organization members make their decisions and act.

Problem solving and decision making are thus key parts of a manager's activities. They play a particularly important role, however, when the manager is engaged in **planning.** Planning involves the most significant and far-reaching decisions a manager can make. In the planning process, managers decide such matters as what goals or opportunities their organization will pursue, what resources will be used, and who will perform each required task. The entire planning process involves managers in a continual series of decision-making situations. The quality of their decisions plays a large role in determining how effective their plans will be.

THE RATIONAL PROBLEM-SOLVING PROCESS

If a manager is faced with an unusually difficult problem or issue, if it is an important problem that will not resolve itself, and if the manager is the person who must decide what to do about it, then he or she is in a problem-solving situation.[1] Many managers rely on informal problem-solving methods. They may, for example, rely on tradition and make the same decisions that were made when similar problems or opportunities arose in the past. They may also appeal to authority and make a decision based on suggestions from an expert or a higher-level manager. Finally, they may use what philosophers called *a priori reasoning:* They assume that the most superficially logical or obvious solution to a problem is the correct one.[2]

These three methods may be useful in some cases. In others, however, they will lead the manager to make the wrong decision. For example, one company was plagued by a serious quality problem: Too many of the parts it was making were returned because of defects. The obvious management decision was to tighten up quality control procedures. However, this did not solve the problem. Further investigation revealed that the real culprit was excess worker fatigue caused by a faulty ventilation system. In this case, the most obvious solution to the problem was not the correct one.

[1] In this section we will use the terms *problem solving* and *decision making* more or less interchangeably because most of our discussion focuses on the decision-making portion of the total process.

[2] Francis J. Bridges, Kenneth W. Olm, and J. Allison Barnhill, *Management Decisions and Organizational Policy* (Boston: Allyn and Bacon, 1971).

TEACHING TIP

Emphasize to students the simplicity yet thoroughness of the problem-solving process.

No approach to decision making can guarantee that a manager will always make the right decision, but managers who use a rational, intelligent, and systematic approach are more likely than other managers to come up with high-quality solutions to the problems they face.

The basic process of rational decision making is similar to the process of planning discussed in Chapter 4. It involves diagnosing, defining, and determining the sources of the problem, gathering and analyzing the facts relevant to the problem, developing and evaluating alternative solutions to the problem, selecting the most satisfactory alternative, and converting this alternative into action. The model of this process that we shall use consists of four major stages. (See Fig. 6-1.)[3]

Stage 1: Investigate the Situation

The problem-solving process begins when the problem has been identified for action. The manager's first task is to search for all the factors that may have created the problem or that may be incorporated into the eventual solution. A thorough investigation has three aspects: problem definition, identification of objectives, and diagnosis.

Define the Problem. Confusion in problem definition arises in part because the events or issues that attract the manager's attention may be symptoms of another, more fundamental and pervasive difficulty. A manager may be concerned about an upsurge in employee resignations, but the increase in employee turnover is not a problem unless it interferes with the achievement of organizational objectives. If the individuals resigning are relatively low performers and more qualified people can be readily found to replace them, the resignations may represent an opportunity rather than a problem. Curing the turnover problem, then, may be the last thing the manager should do. Defining the problem in terms of the organizational objectives that are being blocked helps to avoid confusing symptoms and problems.

[3]The discussion that follows is based on John Dewey, *How We Think* (Boston: Heath, 1933), pp. 102–118; Drucker, *The Practice of Management* (New York: Harper & Row, 1954), pp. 354–365; Charles H. Kepner and Benjamin B. Tregoe, *The Rational Manager: A Systematic Approach to Problem Solving and Decision Making* (New York: McGraw-Hill, 1965); and Ernest R. Archer, "How to Make a Business Decision: An Analysis of Theory and Practice," *Management Review* 69, no. 2 (February 1980):43–47. We have adapted and modified Archer's approach for our basic model.

FIGURE 6-1 THE RATIONAL PROBLEM-SOLVING PROCESS

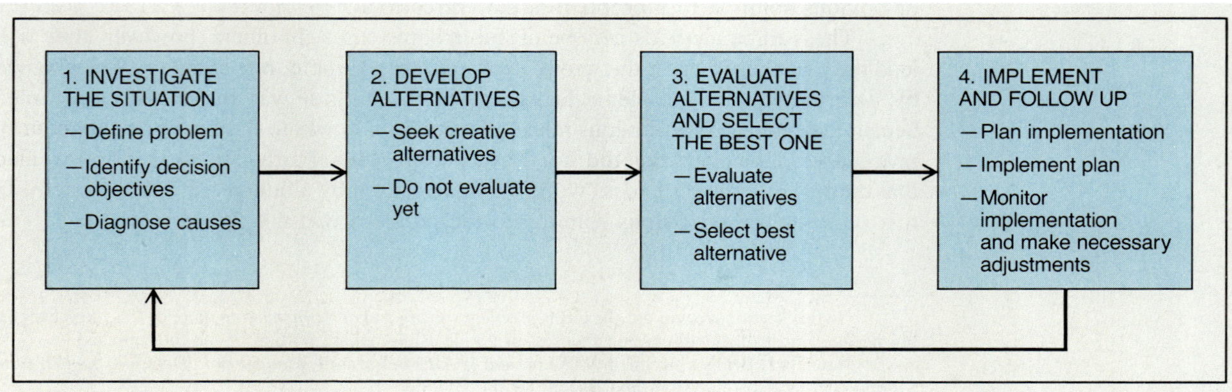

Identify the Decision Objectives. Once the problem has been defined, the next step is to decide what would constitute an effective solution. How will things be different when the problem has been solved? As part of this process, managers should begin to determine which parts of the problem they *must* solve and which they *should* try to solve. Most problems consist of several elements, and a manager is unlikely to find one solution that will work for all of them. Managers therefore need to distinguish between their ''musts'' and their ''shoulds'' so that they will have a basis for proposing and evaluating alternative solutions. For example, if a manager has a staffing problem, he or she *must* hire someone who can do a good job in a difficult position at a certain salary—someone who has had some experience and who will fit in well with others in the organization. Managers can eliminate all candidates who do not meet their ''musts'' criteria; they will evaluate all the other candidates by how well they meet their ''shoulds.''

If their solution enables them to achieve their organizational objectives, it is a successful one. More ambitious objectives, however, may be appropriate. The immediate problem may be an indicator of future difficulties that a manager can prevent by taking early action. Or the problem may offer the opportunity to improve, rather than merely restore, organizational performance.

Diagnose the Causes. When managers have found a satisfactory solution, they must determine the actions that will achieve it. But first, they must obtain a solid understanding of all the sources of the problem so they can formulate hypotheses about the causes. They should ask such questions as: What changes inside or outside the organization may have contributed to the problem? What people are most involved with the problem situation? Do they have insights or perspectives that may clarify the problem? Do their actions contribute to the problem?

Causes, unlike symptoms, are seldom apparent, and managers have to rely on intuition to ferret them out. Different individuals, whose views of the situation are inevitably colored by their own experiences and responsibilities, may perceive very different causes for the same problem. It is up to the manager to put all the pieces together and come up with as clear a picture as possible.

Stage 2: Develop Alternatives

CLASS COMMENT ON ALTERNATIVES IN DECISION MAKING

In Bartlesville, Oklahoma, duck-crossing warning signs were popular targets for taking by teenagers. Forced to protect their ducks and their signs, city administrators decided to sell the signs for $35 and so far have sold a dozen! (*Business Week,* 7/18/88, p. 82)

The temptation to accept the first feasible alternative too often prevents managers from achieving the best solutions to their problems. Developing a number of alternatives allows them to resist the temptation to solve their problems too quickly and makes reaching an effective decision more likely.

No major decision should be made until several alternatives have been developed. Problem solving at this stage frequently requires finding creative and imaginative alternatives. (Chapter 13 offers some techniques managers can use to uncover original and unusual alternative solutions for complex problems.)

Another temptation often interferes with the development of an adequate number of alternatives: the inclination to appraise alternatives as they are developed. This temptation, too, should be resisted. Evaluation at this stage is premature, preventing managers from generating other viable alternatives.

Stage 3: Evaluate Alternatives and Select the Best One

THOUGHT-PROVOKER

Why did you decide to come to class today? What were your alternatives and what consequences affected your decision?

Once managers have developed a set of alternatives, they must evaluate them to see how effective each would be. Effectiveness can be measured by two criteria: how realistic the alternative is in terms of the goals and resources of the organization, and how well the alternative will help solve the problem.

Each alternative must be judged in light of the goals and resources of the organization. An alternative may seem logical, but if it cannot be implemented, it is useless. For example, if sales are high but profits are declining, we may want to reduce overhead costs. But if costs have already been cut sharply, or if further cuts would reduce the quality of the product, this alternative may not be feasible.

In addition, each alternative must be judged as to its consequences for the organization. Will new problems arise when a particular course of action is followed? Managers must determine how willing their subordinates will be to carry out a decision and what might happen if the decision is not implemented wholeheartedly. Practical problems may be involved in implementing the decision, such as the need to obtain additional funding. Other departments in the organization that would be affected by the decision must be consulted.[4] Competitors may be affected by the decision, and their reactions will have to be taken into account.

Each alternative must also be evaluated in terms of how well it will achieve the "musts" and "shoulds" of the problem. In some cases, managers may be able to experiment with possible solutions by trying one or more of the alternatives in different parts of their organization to see which is most effective. In other cases, they may use simulation techniques to explore the possible outcomes of alternative solutions. But usually they will simply use their knowledge, judgment, and experience to decide which alternatives are most attractive.

The selected alternative will be based on the amount of information available to the managers and/or their imperfect judgment. More likely than not, the selected alternative will also represent a compromise among the various factors that have been considered. (Some modern tools to help managers evaluate and choose among alternatives are described in Chapter 8.)

Stage 4: Implement and Monitor the Decision

A HUMOROUS NOTE

Decisions are often made that, upon reflection, we wish could be changed. When the Beatles auditioned for Decca Recording Company in 1962, the company executives refused to sign the group because they didn't like their sound and said groups with guitars were on their way out. M&M Mars (the candy company) decided that they would gain nothing by allowing M&M's to be used in the movie *E.T.* So the little boy in the movie lured the lovable E.T. with Hershey's Reese's Pieces, causing a dramatic increase of 65 percent in Hershey's sales! (Taken from *The Mis-Fortune 500* by Bruce Nash and Allan Zullo, Pocket Books, 1988.)

Once the best available alternative has been selected, managers must make plans to cope with the requirements and problems that may be encountered in putting it into effect.[5]

Implementing a decision involves more than giving appropriate orders. Resources must be acquired and allocated as necessary. Managers set up budgets and schedules for the actions they have decided upon. This allows them to measure progress in specific terms. Next, they assign responsibility for the specific tasks involved. They also set up a procedure for progress reports and prepare to make corrections if new problems should arise.

Potential risks and uncertainties have been identified during the earlier evaluation-of-alternatives stage, and these must be kept in mind. There is a human tendency to forget possible risks and uncertainties once a decision is made. By taking extra time to reexamine their decision at this point and to develop detailed plans for dealing with these risks and uncertainties, managers can counteract this tendency.

After managers have taken whatever steps are possible to deal with adverse consequences if they arise, actual implementation can begin. Ultimately, a decision (or a solution) is no better than the actions taken to make it a reality. A frequent error of managers is to assume that once they make a decision, action on it will automatically

---

[4]A "corporate devil's advocate" who would specifically search for the flaws in solutions has been suggested by Theodore T. Herbert and Ralph W. Estes in "Improving Executive Decisions by Formalizing Dissent: The Corporate Devil's Advocate," *Academy of Management Review* 2, no. 4 (October 1977):662–667.

[5]Kepner and Tregoe, *The Rational Manager: A Systematic Approach to Problem Solving and Decision Making,* pp. 190–194. See also Morgan W. McCall, Jr., and Robert E. Kaplan, *Whatever It Takes: Decision Makers at Work* (Englewood Cliffs, N.J.: Prentice Hall, 1985).

follow. If the decision is a good one but subordinates are unwilling or unable to carry it out, then that decision will not be effective.

Actions taken to implement a decision must be monitored. Are things working according to plan? What is happening in the internal and external environments as a result of the decision? Are subordinates performing according to expectations? What is the competition doing in response? Decision making is a continual process for managers—and a continual challenge.

ILLUSTRATIVE CASE STUDY Continued

Diplomacy and Determination in High-Level Decision Making

The model suggested by the rational problem-solving process, sound as it may seem, nevertheless poses several difficulties for Mr. McKinley of Texaco. While he must investigate the situation, he is receiving conflicting information. The very fact that he is investigating and considering making an offer for Getty can affect the outcome of the decision. He must investigate and gather more information, but he cannot get all the information he needs.

Clearly, he needs to think through the alternatives. In a similar case, when Bendix made an approach to buy Martin Marietta, Bendix's William Agee and his advisors were taken completely by surprise when Martin Marietta launched the so-called "Pac Man Defense," countering with its own tender offer for Bendix. So McKinley must consider the possible results of proceeding with the decision to buy Getty.

Evaluation is easier for McKinley since he has a team of bright analytical minds on which to rely. However, it is important to get multiple points of view as to what may happen in the environment if a particular alternative is chosen. Of course, he has to be ready to implement his decision, and the implementation of such a takeover is far from trivial; it involves proxies, regulatory filings, and the eventual integration of Getty into Texaco.

It is interesting to note that what happened to Texaco *can* be partly explained by this model. Another creative solution to an increasingly complicated series of interactions—one which McKinley had not considered or had discounted—occurred to other parties involved. Pennzoil filed suit in a Texas court claiming that Texaco had interfered with its deal with Getty. A Texas court agreed with Pennzoil and awarded it multibillion-dollar damages. After several legal challenges, Texaco was forced to file for bankruptcy. When the company emerged from bankruptcy proceedings it found itself a prime takeover target. Late in 1988, it had begun a process of restructuring in order to avoid takeover. Thus, although the original decision to buy Getty would have solved Texaco's reserves problem, it also created several other problems that had driven the company to the brink of disaster.

PROBLEM AND OPPORTUNITY FINDING

The idea that managers are problem solvers may conjure up an image of managers sitting behind their desks, calmly deciding what to do about every problem that arises. In fact, effective managers do not try to solve every problem thrust upon them by subordinates, superiors, and peers; they conserve their time and energy for those problems that really require their decision-making ability. Minor problems are handled by quick judgments or assigned to a subordinate.

Some problems come to managers, while others must be found. Managers try to anticipate problems, deciding how to prevent them or what to do if they occur. In addition, managers actively seek opportunities, deciding first which opportunities to pursue and then what to do to make them a reality. Since organizations face a great number of problems and opportunities, a critically important skill for managers is the ability to select the right approach to a problem or to recognize worthwhile opportunities.

As Guth and Tagiuri have noted, the types of problems and opportunities managers choose to work on are influenced by their values and backgrounds.[6] If managers are motivated primarily by economic values, they usually want to make decisions on practical matters, such as those involving marketing, production, or profits. If they have a more theoretical orientation, they may be concerned with the long-term prospects of their organization. If their orientation is political, they may be more concerned with competing with other organizations or with their own personal advancement.

The backgrounds and expertise of managers will also influence what they see as problems and opportunities. A study of executives by De Witt C. Dearborn and Harbert A. Simon found that managers from different departments will define the same problem in different terms.[7] In this study, a group of executives were presented with a complex business case and asked to describe what they saw as the most important problem facing the company. Each executive tended to be sensitive to those parts of the case that related to his or her department, defining opportunities and problems from his or her particular perspective. For example, marketing managers want inventory to be high and view low inventory as a problem situation. Finance managers, on the other hand, view a high-inventory situation as a problem, preferring low inventory in most situations.[8]

Managers' particular sensitivities to certain types of problems and opportunities can sometimes be an advantage, as they may be aware of possibilities that others ignore. But it can also work to the organization's disadvantage, because experts in one area may not see problems and opportunities in other areas. Clarifying their own values and being conscious of the blinders imposed by past experiences, training, and successes can help managers guard against seeing only a few of the problems and opportunities facing their organizations.

The Problem-Finding Process

William Pounds has described four situations that alert managers to possible problems: when there is a deviation from past experience, when there is a deviation from a set plan, when other people present problems to the manager, and when competitors outperform the manager's organization.[9]

When there is a *deviation from past experience,* a previous pattern of performance in the organization is broken. This year's sales are falling behind last year's; expenses have suddenly increased; employee turnover has increased. Events such as these are signals to the manager that a problem has developed.

When there is a *deviation from the plan,* the manager's projections or expectations are not being met. Profit levels are lower than anticipated; a department is exceeding its budget; a project is off schedule. Such events tell the manager that something must be done to get the plan back on course.

Other people often bring problems to the manager. Customers complain about late deliveries; higher-level managers set new performance standards for the manager's department; subordinates resign. Many decisions that managers make daily involve problems presented by others.

---

[6]See William D. Guth and Renato Tagiuri, "Personal Values and Corporate Strategy," *Harvard Business Review* 37, no. 5 (September–October 1965):123–132.

[7]De Witt C. Dearborn and Herbert A. Simon, "Selective Perception: A Note on the Departmental Identification of Executives," *Sociometry* 21, no. 2 (June 1958):140–144.

[8]Robert J. Graham, "'Give the Kid a Number': An Essay on the Folly and Consequences of Trusting Your Data," *Interfaces* 12, no. 2 (June 1982):41.

[9]W. E. Pounds, "The Process of Problem Finding," *Industrial Management Review* (Fall 1969):1–19. See also Peter F. Drucker, *The Practice of Management* (New York: Harper & Brothers, 1954), pp. 351–354.

The *performance of competitors* can also create problem-solving situations for the manager. When other companies develop new processes or improvements in operating procedures, the manager may have to reevaluate processes or procedures in his or her own organization. Competitors within the same organization may also pose problems for the manager. If a company has many plants, for example, top management may compare the performance of each plant. The manager of a plant that is performing below average will have to decide what can be done to bring the plant's performance up to par.

Pounds suggests that management science techniques can also be used to help managers locate problems in addition to solving them. However, such techniques are difficult for many present managers to learn.[10] Pounds found that problem finding is informal and intuitive. Therefore, the four methods described are likely to be those most often used in the years ahead.

A study by Marjorie A. Lyles and Ian I. Mitroff supports Pounds's view that the problem-finding process is informal and intuitive. Lyles and Mitroff collected case histories from upper-level managers of major organizations. Eighty percent of these managers said they had become aware of the existence of a major problem before it showed up on financial statements or as a result of other formal indicators—and even before it was presented to them by superiors or subordinates. "Informal communication and intuition" were described as the sources of their information.[11]

Problem finding is not always straightforward. Sara Kiesler and Lee Sproull have identified some of the more common errors made by managers in sensing problems. Kiesler and Sproull describe three main categories of pitfalls that managers may encounter: false association of events, false expectation of events, and false self-perceptions and social image. For example, under the category of false expectations might be listed the belief among managers of mainframe computer manufacturing companies during the 1960s and early 1970s that a significant demand for personal computers did not and probably would not exist. The idea of a market for personal computers did not fit their expectations.[12]

Opportunity Finding

EXTRA EXERCISE

Have students look at making a job choice from a problem-finding and an opportunity-finding perspective.

It is not always clear whether a situation faced by a manager presents a problem or an opportunity. For example, missed opportunities create problems for organizations, and opportunities are often found while exploring problems.[13] David B. Gleicher, a management consultant, provides a useful distinction between the two terms. He defines a problem as something that endangers the organization's ability to *reach* its objectives, while an opportunity is something that offers the chance to *exceed* objectives.[14]

---

[10]A useful model of how problems are recognized and dealt with by organizations is provided by Thomas P. Ference, "Organizational Communications Systems and the Decision Process," *Management Science* 17, no. 2 (October 1970):B83–B96.

[11]Marjorie A. Lyles and Ian I. Mitroff, "Organizational Problem Formulation: An Empirical Study," *Administrative Science Quarterly* 25, no. 1 (March 1980):102–119. For a discussion of the use of intuition by managers, see Thomas S. Isaack, "Intuition: An Ignored Dimension of Management," *Academy of Management Review* 3, no. 4 (October 1978):917–922; W. H. Agor, "Tomorrow's Intuitive Leaders," *Futurist,* August 1983, pp. 49–53; and W. H. Agor, "The Logic of Intuition: How Top Executives Make Important Decisions," *Organizational Dynamics* 14 (Winter 1986), 5–18.

[12]Sara Kiesler and Lee Sproull, "Managerial Response to Changing Environments," *Administrative Science Quarterly* 27, no. 4 (December 1982):548–570.

[13]The author uses the phrase "the Pollyanna theory of management" to describe the belief that every problem has an opportunity embedded in it. Robert J. Graham uses the maxim that "problems are merely opportunities in disguise" in "Problem and Opportunity Identification in Management Science," *Interfaces* 6, no. 4 (August 1976):79–82.

[14]Personal communication.

Henry A. Mintzberg, Duru Raisingham, and André Théorêt distinguish between crises, problems, and opportunities. Their research indicates that crisis decisions are usually triggered by a sudden, single event (a fire or bankruptcy of a key supplier, for example) that requires immediate attention. Problems become apparent through a stream of ambiguous and frequently verbal data stimulated by the accumulation of multiple events. Opportunities, on the other hand, are often evoked by an idea or a single (noncrisis) event. When dealing with problems and opportunities, managers accumulate and process information until a certain threshold is reached. When the threshold is reached, the manager is ready to make a decision. The threshold varies among managers and with the nature of the decision to be made.[15]

dialectical inquiry method A method of analysis in which a decision maker determines and negates his or her assumptions, and then creates ''counter solutions'' based on the negative assumptions.

The **dialectical inquiry method** sometimes called ''The Devil's Advocate Method,'' is useful in problem solving and opportunity finding.[16] In this method, the decision maker determines possible solutions and the assumptions they are based on, considers the negation, or opposite, of all of his or her assumptions, and then develops countersolutions based on the negative assumptions. This process, in turn, may generate more useful alternative solutions as well as bringing to the forefront any hitherto unnoticed opportunity.

An enormous amount of research has been devoted to problem solving, whereas a very small amount concerns problem finding, and even less concerns opportunity finding. Yet, as Peter Drucker makes clear, opportunities rather than problems are the key to organizational and managerial success. Drucker observes that solving a problem merely restores normality, but results ''must come from the exploitation of opportunities.'' Drucker links exploitation of opportunities to finding ''the right things to do, and . . . [concentrating] resources and efforts on them.[17]

Deciding to Decide

As we have seen, while some problems come to managers, some they must locate for themselves. But no manager can possibly handle every problem that arises in the daily course of business. It is important to learn how to establish priorities for problems and how to delegate to subordinates responsibility for taking care of the minor ones.

Thus, when managers are presented with a problem, they should ask themselves the following questions:

1. *Is the problem easy to deal with?* Some problems are difficult and expensive to deal with, others are not. Questions such as whether to acquire a subsidiary obviously require extensive consideration. Most problems, however, require only a small amount of the manager's attention. Even if the decision turns out to be wrong, correcting it will be relatively speedy and inexpensive. To avoid getting bogged down in trivial details, effective and efficient managers reserve formal decision-making techniques for problems that require them. A manager who gives the same level of attention to every problem will get very little work done.
2. *Might the problem resolve itself?* The classic illustration of this principle concerns Napoleon, who was reputed to have let incoming mail pile up on his desk for three weeks or more. When he finally read the accumulated mail, he was pleased to find that most matters had been resolved in the interim. In like manner, managers find that an amazing

---

[15]Henry A. Mintzberg, Duru Raisingham, and André Théorêt, ''The Structure of 'Unstructured' Decision Processes,'' *Administrative Science Quarterly* 21, no. 2 (June 1976):246–275.

[16]For a discussion of dialectical inquiry, see Richard A. Cosier, ''Approaches to the Experimental Examination of the Dialectic,'' *Strategic Management Journal* 4, no. 1 (January–March 1983):79–84; Lyle Sussman and Richard Herden, ''Dialectical Problem Solving,'' *Business Horizons,* January–February 1982, pp. 66–71, and David M. Schweiger and Phyllis A. Finger, ''The Comparative Effectiveness of Dialectical Inquiry and Devil's Advocate: The Impact of Task Biases on Previous Research Findings,'' *Strategic Management Journal* 5 (1984):335–350.

[17]Peter F. Drucker, *Managing for Results* (New York: Harper & Row, 1964), p. 5. See also J. Sterling Livingston, ''Myth of the Well-Educated Manager,'' *Harvard Business Review* 49, no. 1 (January–February 1971):79–89.

number of time-wasting problems can be eliminated if they are simply ignored. Therefore, when establishing priorities for dealing with several problems, managers should rank them in order of importance. Those at the bottom of the list usually take care of themselves or can be dealt with by others. If one of these problems worsens, it moves to a higher priority level on the list.

3. *Is this my decision to make?* When confronted with an important problem requiring a decision, a manager must determine if he or she is responsible for making the decision. Here is a general rule that can be of help: The closer to the origin of the problem the decision is made, the better. This rule has two corollaries: (a) Pass as few decisions as possible to those higher up, and (b) pass as many as possible to those lower down. Usually, those who are closest to a problem are in the best position to decide what to do about it.

FOR DISCUSSION

"Not making a decision is a decision." Explain. (A course of action, nonaction actually, was chosen.

When managers refer an issue to someone higher up for a decision, they have to be sure they are not simply passing the buck instead of being properly cautious. (Referring a matter to a subordinate is not passing the buck because the manager still retains ultimate responsibility.) Managers are usually closer to the problem than their superiors, but they must pass along all decisions that would be better or more appropriately made by someone else. How can they decide when they should pass a problem on to a superior? If our basic rule and its corollaries do not supply the answer, managers can supplement them with a few other questions:

- Does the issue affect other departments?
- Will it have a major impact on the superior's area of responsibility?
- Does it require information available only from a higher level?
- Does it involve a serious breach of our departmental budget?
- Is this problem outside my area of responsibility or authority?

A "yes" answer to any of these questions is an indication that the issue should probably be referred to a superior. Perhaps the Reagan Administration would not have found itself embroiled in the Iran-*contra* affair had Oliver North, John Poindexter, and others asked themselves these questions.

"Then again, gentlemen, we're in complete agreement in the sense that nobody knows the answer to any of the questions that have been raised."

Drawing by Stan Hunt; © 1983 The New Yorker Magazine, Inc.

THE NATURE OF MANAGERIAL DECISION MAKING

As we have seen, decision making is an important part of the problem-solving process. Managers make different types of decisions under different circumstances. Deciding where to locate a new plant requires extensive investigation of the alternatives; deciding what salary to pay a new employee demands less intensive analysis; when to schedule the annual Christmas party requires even less.

Similarly, the amount of information available to the decision maker varies. A manager can be relatively confident that a supplier chosen on the basis of price and past performance will live up to expectations. However, when there is little past experience or information to serve as a guide, the outcome of a decision is much less certain. For example, a manager considering whether to enter a new market must take much more care in making the decision.

Programmed and Nonprogrammed Decisions

Managers have to vary their approach to decision making, depending on the particular situation. It is useful to distinguish between situations that call for programmed decisions and those that call for nonprogrammed decisions.[18]

programmed decisions Solutions to routine problems determined by rule, procedure, or habit.

COORDINATED RESOURCE

The Enterprise videotape "Chef's Special" would be an excellent companion to talking about programmed and nonprogrammed decisions. Ask the students to note places in the film where the owner/manager has to make decisions. Then at the end of the videotape, talk about whether these are programmed or nonprogrammed. (Available from Learning Corporation of America, 108 Wilmot Road, Deerfield, IL 60015-9990, or call 800-621-2131.)

Programmed Decisions. **Programmed decisions** are those made in accordance with some habit, rule, or procedure. Every organization has written or unwritten policies that simplify decision making in recurring situations by limiting or excluding alternatives. For example, we would not usually have to worry about what to pay a newly hired employee; organizations generally have an established salary scale for all positions. Routine procedures exist for dealing with routine problems.[19]

Routine problems are not necessarily simple ones; programmed decisions are used for dealing with complex as well as with uncomplicated issues. If a problem recurs, and if its component elements can be defined, predicted, and analyzed, then it may be a candidate for programmed decision making. For example, decisions about how much inventory to maintain on a given product can involve a great deal of fact-finding and forecasting; however, careful analysis of the separate elements in the problem may yield a series of routine, programmed decisions.

To some extent, of course, programmed decisions limit our freedom, because the organization rather than the individual decides what to do. However, programmed decisions are intended to be liberating. The policies, rules, or procedures by which we make programmed decisions free us of the time needed to work out new solutions to old problems, thus allowing us to devote attention to other, more important activities. For example, deciding how to handle customer complaints on an individual basis would be time-consuming and costly, but a policy stating "exchanges will be permitted on all purchases within 14 days" simplifies matters considerably.

We should note, however, that effective managers lean on policy to save time but remain alert for exceptional cases. For example, company policy may put a ceiling on the advertising budget for each product. A particular product, however, may need an extensive advertising campaign to counter the newly aggressive marketing strategy of a competitor, such as the one launched by Anheuser Busch to defend its market share

---

[18]These terms are from the computer field. A program provides the computer with a sequence of coded instructions for carrying out tasks. See Herbert A. Simon, *The Shape of Automation* (New York: Harper & Row, 1965), pp. 58–67. See also Simon, "Using Cognitive Science to Solve Human Problems." Paper presented at a Science and Public Policy Seminar, Washington, D.C. Sponsored by the Federation of Behavioral, Psychological, and Cognitive Sciences, 1985.

[19]See also Herbert A. Simon, *The New Science of Management Decision,* rev. ed. (Englewood Cliffs, N.J.: Prentice Hall, 1977), pp. 45–49.

when Miller introduced its new Miller Lite. A programmed decision—that is, a decision to advertise the product in accordance with budget guidelines—might be a mistake in this case. Ultimately, managers must use their own judgment in deciding whether a situation calls for a programmed decision.

nonprogrammed decisions Specific solutions created through an unstructured process to deal with non-routine problems.

Nonprogrammed Decisions. **Nonprogrammed decisions,** on the other hand, are those that deal with unusual or exceptional problems. If a problem has not come up often enough to be covered by a policy or is so important that it deserves special treatment, it must be handled by a nonprogrammed decision. Such problems as how to allocate an organization's resources, what to do about a failing product line, how community relations should be improved—in fact, most of the significant problems a manager will face—will usually require nonprogrammed decisions. As one moves up in the organizational hierarchy, the ability to make nonprogrammed decisions becomes more important because progressively more of the decisions are nonprogrammed.

For this reason, most management-development programs try to improve managers' abilities to make nonprogrammed decisions—usually by trying to teach them to analyze problems systematically and to make logical decisions. The decision-making process we describe in this chapter is used mainly for nonprogrammed decisions.

Certainty, Risk, and Uncertainty

FOR DISCUSSION
Why should it even matter knowing whether a decision must be made under certainty, risk, or uncertainty?

Managers make decisions in the present for actions that will be taken and goals that they hope to achieve in the future. All important decision-making situations contain some aspects that are unknowable and very difficult to predict: a specific competitor's reaction, interest rates in three years, the reliability of a new supplier using a promising but unproven technology. Although uncertainty exists in many situations, the amount of uncertainty varies greatly.

In analyzing a situation requiring a decision, managers frequently find it useful to categorize decisions on a continuum ranging from predictable situations to situations extremely difficult to predict. Three words to describe different positions on this continuum are: "certainty," "risk," and "uncertainty."[20]

There are two possible sources of uncertainty. First, there may be external conditions partially or entirely beyond a manager's control. Second and equally important is the manager's access to information about those conditions. The manager may not be aware of all the information available about a set of conditions, or the necessary information may simply not exist. In either case, the manager's ability to predict the future is impaired.

Under conditions of *certainty,* we know what will happen in the future. Under *risk,* we know what the probability of each possible outcome is. Under *uncertainty,* we do not know the probabilities—and maybe not even the possible outcomes.

Under conditions of certainty, there is accurate, measurable, reliable information available on which to base decisions. The future in this case is highly predictable. Diamond merchants, for example, can be so confident of their relationship with one another, even across international boundaries, that they customarily seal multimillion dollar transactions with a handshake. They can act in complete confidence that their agreements will be honored, informal though those agreements may be.[21]

Where predictability is lower, a condition of risk exists. Complete information is unavailable, but we have a good idea of the probability of particular outcomes. Oil

---

[20]See F. H. Knight, *Risk, Uncertainty, and Profit* (New York: Harper & Brothers, 1920); and Stephen A. Archer, "The Structure of Management Decision Theory," *Academy of Management Journal* 7, no. 4 (December 1964):269–287.

[21]Murray Schumach, *The Diamond People* (New York: Norton, 1981).

companies, for example, may not know if any particular well will produce oil; but in a drilling program involving a great many wells, good estimates can be made of the number of wells that will be successful.

Under conditions of uncertainty, however, very little is known. For example, managers engaged in international business may face for the first time cultural customs radically different from their own and for which they may have no preparation. In some parts of the world, a written contract does not carry the binding force we associate with it but merely signals the start of a new round of negotiations. Decisions made under these conditions lead to sleepless nights. At the same time, conditions of uncertainty. generally accompany our most crucial—and most interesting—decisions.

But managers do have tools at their disposal to make the unknown future a little more comfortable to anticipate and deal with. Although few management situations are likely to fit precisely the definitions of certainty and risk, it is frequently useful for managers to analyze some situations as though they did. Oil companies often assume situations of uncertainty about where to drill for oil and about resources to spend for information and then determine optimal levels of risk, drilling where they are most *likely* to find oil.

Rational Decision Making

The rational model of decision making parallels the rational problem-solving process. This model prescribes that managers define alternatives in terms of the potential outcomes of each. Next, the value of each outcome is calculated and weighted by the probability of its occurrence. If the decision is under conditions of certainty, then the probability of the given outcome is calculated at *one*. If there are conditions of *risk,* then each risk must be assessed through the same method. If there are conditions of uncertainty, then the decision maker might either assume each outcome to be equally likely or assume that the worst will happen. If the decision maker is rational, he or she will choose that course of action most likely to yield the greatest overall value.

The rational model tends to conjure up a picture of the decision maker as a kind of super calculating machine, but we know that, in reality, human beings simply do not make decisions in this manner. Among others, Herbert Simon has tried to describe the factors that affect real-life decisions and has proposed a theory of "bounded rationality."

Bounded Rationality: A Challenge to the Rational Model

bounded rationality The concept that managers make the most logical decisions they can within the constraints of limited information and ability.

Simon's theory of **bounded rationality** points out that real-life decision makers must cope with:

- Inadequate information about the nature of the problem and its possible solutions
- The lack of time or money to compile more complete information
- Distorted perceptions of the information available
- The inability of the human memory to retain large amounts of information
- The limits of their own intelligence to determine correctly which alternative is best

Instead of searching for the perfect or ideal decision, managers frequently settle for a decision that will adequately serve their purposes. In Simon's terms, they *satisfice,* or accept the first satisfactory decision they uncover, rather than *maximize,* or search until they find the optimal decision.[22] Oil companies, for example, simply do not enjoy the time or money to gather all of the information that could encourage or discourage a specific drilling project. Rather than spend all of their time (and capital) getting information, they choose to *satisfice*.

Managers simply lack the time to do all of the calculations required by the rational model, especially for routine decisions. It is important to try to follow the rational model when making major decisions—for example, whether or not to venture into a new line of business or to restructure an organization. But it would be foolish, and thus irrational, to go to the same degree of detail for every decision a manager makes. Simon points out that human psychology is more in line with bounded rationality. The so-called ''rational model'' of decision making is probably the exception, not the rule.

HEURISTICS AND BIASES IN DECISION MAKING

heuristic principles A method of decision making that proceeds along empirical lines, using rules of thumb, to find solutions or answers.

COORDINATED RESOURCE

The Enterprise videotape ''Room at the Top'' is another good resource for showing decision making. The videotape is about Westin Hotel's decision to enter the suddenly crowded Boston luxury hotel market. Have students try to identify some heuristics and biases the managers use as they make their various decisions. (Available from Learning Corporation of America, 108 Wilmot Road, Deerfield, IL 60015-9990, or call 800-621-2131.)

Research by Amos Tversky and Daniel Kahneman has extended Simon's ideas on bounded rationality. They have demonstrated that people rely on **heuristic principles,** or rules of thumb, to simplify the process of making decisions.[23] Loan officers, for example, may screen mortgage applicants by assuming they can afford to spend no more than 35 percent of their income on housing. Alternatively while heuristics are great time-savers and often produce good results, they can also lead to systematic biases in decision making. For one thing, people are often unaware of the heuristics upon which they rely; they are overconfident about the quality of their decisions because they do not appreciate the weakness of their assumptions or the extent of their ignorance. Good managers need to be conscious of heuristics and the biases they produce in order to make better decisions.

Three Heuristics

There are three heuristics that show up repeatedly in human decision making.[24] These are not specific rules, but general cognitive strategies that people apply to a wide variety of situations because they make intuitive sense.

Availability. People sometimes judge the likelihood of an event by testing it against the information stored in their memories. In principle, it is easier for people to recall frequently-occurring events. Thus events that are more readily ''available'' in memory are assumed to be more likely to occur in the future. This assumption is based on the experience of a lifetime, and it seems reasonable enough. However, the human memory is affected not just by the frequency of an event, but also by how *recently* it has occurred and how *vivid* the experience was. Thus, a risk manager recently caught in a flood is likely to overestimate the importance and frequency of flooding the next time he or she procures insurance.

---

[22] Herbert A. Simon, *Models of Man: Social and Rational* (New York: Wiley, 1957). See also James G. March and Herbert A. Simon, *Organizations* (New York: Wiley, 1958); Herbert A. Simon, *Administrative Behavior*, 3rd ed. (New York: Free Press, 1976); Herbert A. Simon, *Reason in Human Affairs* (Stanford, Calif.: Stanford University Press, 1983), pp. 12–23; Anna Grandori, ''A Prescriptive Contingency View of Organizational Decision Making,'' *Administrative Science Quarterly* 29, no. 2 (June 1984):192–209; and Neil M. Agnew and John L. Brown, ''Bounded Rationality: Fallible Decisions in Unbounded Decision Space,'' *Behavioral Science,* July 1986, pp. 148–161.

[23] A. Tversky and D. Kahneman, ''Judgment under Uncertainty: Heuristics and Biases,'' *Science* 18 (1974):1124–1131.

[24] Tversky and Kahneman, ''Availability: A Heuristic for Judging Frequency and Probability,'' *Cognitive Psychology* 5 (1973):207–232.

MANAGEMENT APPLICATION

HOW BIASED ARE YOU?

Judgment biases described in this chapter can be insidious. They so pervade the human thinking process that we are not even aware of them. Max Bazerman has put together the following test to illustrate some common flaws in our judgment. Try to develop logical answers to the following questions—without bias. You may be surprised by the traps you fall into.

Quiz Item 1: The following 10 corporations were ranked by *Fortune* magazine to be among the 500 largest U.S.-based firms according to sales volume for 1982:
Group A: American Motors, Wang Laboratories, Lever Brothers, Kellogg, Scott Paper
Group B: Coastal, Signal Companies, Dresser Industries, Agway, McDermott
Which group (A or B) had the largest total sales volume for the total of the five organizations listed?
Quiz Item 2: The best student in the author's introductory MBA class this past semester writes poetry, is rather shy, and is small in stature. What was the student's undergraduate major: (A) Chinese studies or (B) psychology?
Quiz Item 3: Are there more words in the English language (A) that start with an "r" or (B) for which "r" is the third letter?
Quiz Item 4: Assume that two research groups sampled consumers on the driving performance of a 1986 Dodge Omni versus a 1986 Plymouth Horizon in a blind road test (the consumers did not know when they were driving the Omni or the Horizon). As you may know, these cars are identical; only the marketing varies. One research group (A) samples 66 consumers each day for 60 days (a large number of days to control for such factors as weather); the other research group (B) samples 22 consumers each for 50 days. Which consumer group would observe more days in which 60 percent or more of the consumers tested would prefer the Dodge Omni?
Quiz Item 5: You are the sales forecaster for a department store chain with nine locations. The chain depends on you for quality projections of future sales in order to make decisions on staffing, advertising, information system developments, purchasing, renovation, and so on. All stores are similar in size and merchandise selection. The main difference in their sales occurs because of location and random fluctuations. Sales for 1985 were as follows:

Representativeness. People also tend to assess the likelihood of an occurrence by trying to match it with a pre-existing category. For example, employers may rely on stereotypes of sexual, racial, and ethnic groups to predict an individual job candidate's performance. In a similar way, product managers may predict the performance of a new product by comparing it to other products with proven track records. In fact, however, each individual or product is a new commodity, not just the representative of a group, and should be judged accordingly.

Anchoring and Adjustment. People do not pull decisions out of thin air. Usually, they start with some initial value—even if it is randomly chosen—and then make adjustments to that value in order to arrive at a final decision. Salary decisions, for example, are routinely calculated by assuming last year's salary to be an initial value to which an adjustment must be made. Unfortunately, depending heavily on the single

Store	85	87
1	$12,000,000	________
2	11,500,000	________
3	11,000,000	________
4	10,500,000	________
5	10,000,000	________
6	9,500,000	________
7	9,000,000	________
8	8,500,000	________
9	8,000,000	
TOTAL	90,000,000	99,000,000

Your economic forecasting service has convinced you that the best estimate of total sales increases between 1985 and 1987 is 10 percent (to 99,000,000). Your task is to predict 1987 sales for each store. Because your manager believes strongly in the economic forecasting service, it is imperative that your total sales are equal to $99,000,000.

Quiz Item 6: A newly-hired engineer for a computer firm in the Boston metropolitan area has four years experience and good all-around qualifications. When asked to estimate the starting salary for this employee, my secretary (knowing very little about the profession or the industry) guessed an annual salary of $17,000. What is your estimate?

Quiz Item 7: It is claimed that when a particular analyst predicts a rise in the market, the market always rises. You are to check this claim. Examine the information available about the following four events (cards):

Card 1	*Card 2*	*Card 3*	*Card 4*
Prediction: Favorable report	Prediction: Unfavorable report	Outcome: Rise in the market	Outcome: Fall in the market

You currently see the predictions (cards 1 and 2) *or* outcomes (cards 3 and 4) associated with four events. You are seeing one side of a card. On the other side of cards 1 and 2 is the actual outcome, whereas on the other side of cards 3 and 4 is the prediction that the analyst made. Evidence about the claim is potentially available by turning over card(s). Which cards would you turn over for the the *minimum* evidence that you need to check the analyst's claim? Circle the appropriate cards.

Source: Max H. Bazerman, *Judgment in Managerial Decision Making* (New York: John Wiley & Sons, 1986), pp. 15–17.

factor of initial value tends to obscure relevant criteria. In addition, different initial values lead to different decisions.

Biases in Decision Making

Each of these three heuristics leads to a number of biases that are so deeply imbedded in the human thinking process that it is difficult to recognize them as illogical. (See the application entitled "How Biased Are You?") Even scientific training does not prevent these biases from distorting people's judgment.[25] We will describe some of the most common biases here.[26]

[25]Tversky and Kahneman, "The Belief in the 'Law of Numbers,'" *Psychological Bulletin* 76 (1971):105–110.

[26]The following discussion and many of the examples cited are drawn from Chapter 2 of *Judgment in Managerial Decision Making* by Max H. Bazerman (New York, John Wiley & Sons: 1988).

Easy Recall. The more easily people can recall examples of an event, the more frequently they believe it occurs. However, both the recentness and the vividness of an event can bias this judgment. Thus, annual performance appraisals are consistently biased towards employee performance during the most recent three months, because that is what stands out in managers' memories. In another example, a purchasing agent selected a supplier because the firm's name was familiar; as it turned out, he remembered the name because the firm had recently been in the news for extorting funds from its clients!

Easy Search. Our search strategies are based on our assumptions about the way the world is organized. Thus, managers may seek advice about computers from the Management Information Systems (MIS) division of their company. If the expertise they need is elsewhere in the organization, they will not find it. Consumers work the same way. The Cadillac Cimarron, a compact car, was a marketing failure because potential small-car buyers did not associate compacts with the Cadillac name and price tag.

Insensitivity to Prior Probability. People tend to overrate the importance of representative information and underrate the importance of basic trends. Take, for example, an MBA student who is interested in the arts and once considered a career as a musician. Given a choice, most people would guess that he or she is more likely to take a job in the management of the arts than with a management consulting firm. Why? Because the student fits a stereotyped image of a person working in the arts better than an image of a management consultant. People may ignore the fact that he or she is an MBA student and that far more MBAs find jobs in management consulting than in the management of the arts. This basic trend is a better predictor than the personal description.

Insensitivity to Sample Size. Few people appreciate the role of sample size when they evaluate information. Statistically, the smaller the sample, the more likely it is to stray from the mean. Consumers are regularly misled by advertising claims such as "Four out of five dentists surveyed recommend sugarless gum for their patients who chew gum." The claim is worthless without knowing how many dentists were surveyed. A sample of five or ten dentists may not reflect the opinions of the entire profession.

Misconceptions of Chance. Most people do not understand the nature of random events.[27] They often assume that multiple random events are somehow connected. In a series of coin tosses, for example, the average person believes that the odds of tails coming up is greater after heads has come up ten times in a row. In fact, each toss of the coin is an independent event with fifty-fifty odds.

Insufficient Adjustment. People sometimes arrive at final decisions by adjusting some initial value to suit a specific situation. Their adjustments, however, are usually inadequate.[28] Salaries, for example, typically consist of last year's wages plus a raise. Even though last year's salary may not reflect an employee's true worth, it will bias this year's salary; thus someone who is initially overpaid or underpaid may never be equitably paid.

---

[27] D. Kahneman and A. Tversky, "Subjective Probability: A Judgment of Representativeness," *Cognitive Psychology* 3 (1972):430–454.

[28] P. Slovic and S. Lichtenstein, "Comparison of Bayesian and Regression Approaches in the Study of Information Processing in Judgment," *Organizational Behavior and Human Performance* 6 (1971):649–744.

Overconfidence. People tend to be overconfident when answering questions on subjects with which they are unfamiliar; overconfidence is much less likely in an individual's area of expertise. This is a problem when people do not adjust their level of confidence in their judgment so as to reflect their actual knowledge about a specific subject.[29] It is possible to reduce overconfidence by providing people with feedback on their judgments or by prodding them to think about why their answer might be wrong.[30]

The Confirmation Trap. Frequently, people do not actively try to discredit their tentative decisions; rather, they tend to look for evidence in their favor.[31] After employers make preliminary hiring decisions, for example, they usually follow up by trying to get more information about the candidate's skills and accomplishments. They usually do not search for evidence of the candidate's incompetence. According to the rules of logic, however, no proof is complete without some attempt to discredit a theory.

Hindsight. Once people know the outcome of a decision, they may start to believe that they could have predicted it ahead of time.[32] They do not remember how uncertain the situation originally looked and may remember the evidence as more clear-cut than it actually was. Unfortunately, this means that managers may be judged entirely on results even when the results are out of their control. Take, for example, a hiring decision that turns out poorly. Senior managers may claim, after the fact, that there was plenty of evidence to show that the new employee would not work out. Some leading researchers have suggested that a better system would reward managers for how they make their decisions, not how the decisions turn out.[33]

Some Conclusions

The use of heuristics to simplify the decision-making process has two strengths. First of all, heuristics have reasonable rationales and so generally produce the correct results. Secondly, they save enormous amounts of time for the decision maker. Often, but not always, the time-savings itself outweighs any loss in the quality of the decisions.

At the same time, however, the most commonly employed heuristics produce systematic biases in judgment—biases of which we are not always aware. Such heuristics are not obvious rules that we choose to employ, but rather the intuitive approaches of the human mind; in a very real sense, we use them involuntarily. If managers learn how to recognize and eliminate such biases, the quality of their decisions will improve.

[29]R. S. Nickerson and C. C. McGoldrick, "Confidence Ratings and Level of Performance on a Judgmental Task," *Perceptual and Motor Skills* 20 (1965):311–316; G. F. Pitz, "Subjective Probability Distributions for Imperfectly Known Quantities," in *Knowledge and Cognition,* L. W. Gregg, ed. (New York: Wiley, 1974), pp. 29–41.

[30]A. Koriat, S. Lichtenstein, and B. Fischoff, "Reasons for Confidence," *Journal of Experimental Psychology: Human Learning and Memory* 22 (1980):107–118; S. Lichtenstein, B. Fischoff, and L. D. Phillips, "Calibration of Probabilities: State of the Art to 1980," in *Judgment under Uncertainty: Heuristics and Biases,* D. Kahneman, P. Slovic, and A. Tversky, eds. (New York: Cambridge University Press, 1982).

[31]H. J. Einhorn and R. M. Hogarth, "Confidence in Judgment: Persistence in the Illusion of Validity," *Psychological Review* 85 (1978):395–416; P. C. Wason, "On the Failure to Eliminate Hypotheses in a Conceptual Task," *Quarterly Journal of Experimental Psychology* 12 (1960):129–140; P. C. Wason, "Reason about a Rule," *Quarterly Journal of Experimental Psychology* 20 (1968):273–283.

[32]B. Fischoff, "Hindsight ≠ Foresight: The Effect of Outcome Knowledge on Judgment under Uncertainty," *Journal of Experimental Psychology: Human Perception and Performance* 1 (1975):288–299.

[33]H. J. Einhorn and R. M. Hogarth, "Behavioral Decision Theory: Process of Judgment and Choice," *Annual Review of Psychology* 32 (1982):53–88; J. M. Feldman, "Beyond Attribution Theory: Cognitive Process in Performance Appraisal," *Journal of Applied Psychology* 66 (1981):127–148.

IMPROVING THE EFFECTIVENESS OF PROBLEM SOLVING AND DECISION MAKING

Norman Maier has isolated two criteria by which a decision's potential effectiveness can be appraised. The first is the *objective quality* of the decision, and the second is the *acceptance* by those who must execute it.[34]

QUOTATION FROM A MANAGER

CEO Scott G. McNealy of Sun Microsystems, Inc., the fast-growing computer maker, on decision making, "Consensus if possible, but participation for sure." (*Business Week*, 7/18/88, p. 115)

The objective quality of the decision is determined by how well the formal decision-making process is carried out. The manager has a choice of making decisions alone or with the help of others. For example, many companies, including corporations as large as General Foods and Burlington Industries, have initiated policies of using teams to assist management in decision making at several levels. However, there is little choice when it comes to implementation. A number of people are almost always involved in implementing decisions; gaining their acceptance and cooperation is essential.

Improving Individual Problem Solving

Most managers realize that an apparently excellent decision—that is, one based on information that has been gathered, analyzed, and evaluated effectively—may turn out poorly because of an unforeseeable event. Conversely, an unlikely and unpredictable event may turn a bad or illogical decision into a fortunate choice. Even if a decision works as well as predicted, a manager can never be completely sure another one would not have been equally effective or even better.

Most managers experience some tension in deciding how to go about solving a problem and then implementing the solution. They know they will frequently be evaluated according to the success or failure of their solution, and they know that almost all second-guessing will be aimed at their less successful decisions. It is not unusual for people in such situations to set up barriers to problem solving or to devote time and energy to developing justifications for avoiding difficult problems that confront them. To make effective decisions, managers must first overcome the barriers that discourage them from recognizing and attacking emerging problems in their organizations. Sometimes, however, matters are not quite so simple. Imagine the situation posed in the box on "The Prisoner's Dilemma."

Barriers to Individual Problem Solving. Irving L. Janis and Leon Mann have identified four defective problem-recognition and problem-solving approaches that can hinder people who must make important decisions in situations of conflict.[35] (See Fig. 6-2.)

1. *Relaxed avoidance:* The manager decides not to decide or act after noting that the consequences of inaction will not be very great. This might be the attitude of a manager who has been informed by a superior that a promotion will depend on improved performance. Learning through the grapevine that the superior may be dismissed, the manager does nothing. But if he or she did not know of the superior's shaky position, that same manager would eagerly work harder and put in longer hours.
2. *Relaxed change:* The manager decides to take some action, noting that the consequences of doing nothing will be serious. However, rather than analyzing the situation, the man-

[34] Norman R. F. Maier, *Problem-Solving Discussions and Conferences: Leadership Methods and Skills* (New York: McGraw-Hill, 1963).

[35] Irving L. Janis and Leon Mann, *Decision Making: A Psychological Analysis of Conflict, Choice, and Commitment* (New York: Free Press, 1977). We have used a somewhat different terminology for their four approaches.

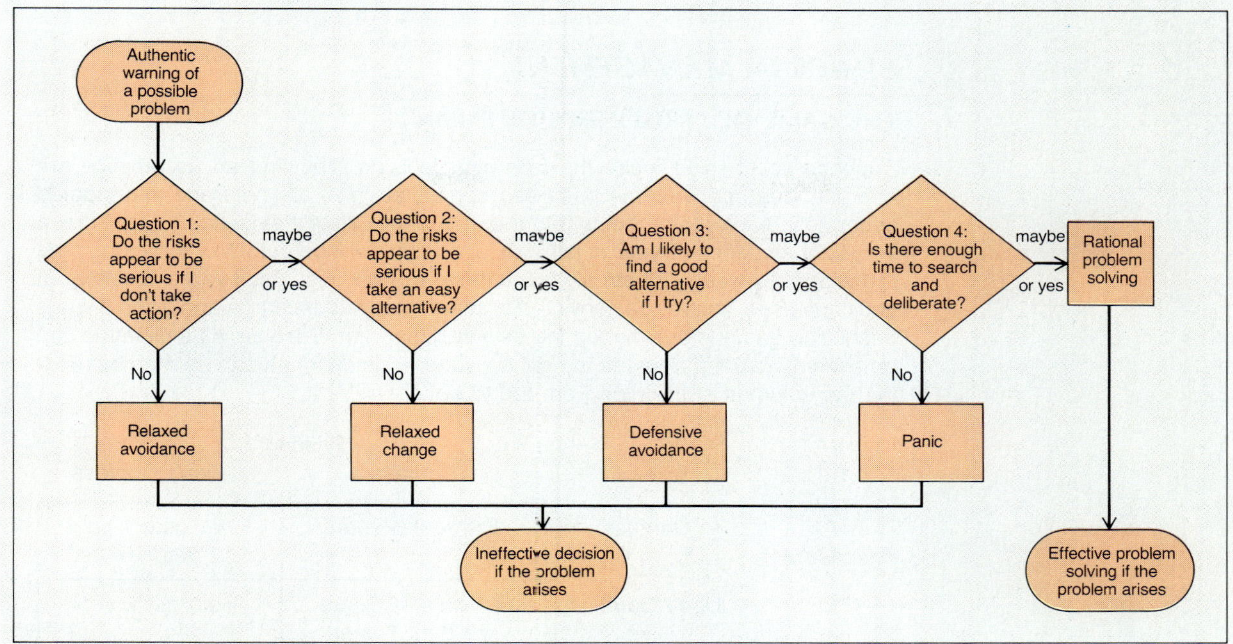

Source: Adapted by permission of the publisher, from "A New Look at Managerial Decision Making," by Victor H. Vroom, *Organizational Dynamics*, Summer 1973, p. 70. Copyright © 1973 by American Management Association, New York. All rights reserved.

FIGURE 6-2 EFFECTIVE AND INEFFECTIVE PROBLEM-SOLVING APPROACHES

This model shows the preferred management styles for various types of problems. The most "time-efficient" feasible alternative for each problem is circled. (See also the box on the opposite page.)

ager takes the first available alternative that appears, on the surface, to involve low risk. Careful analysis is avoided.

3. *Defensive avoidance:* Faced with a problem and unable to find a good solution based on past experience, this manager seeks a way out. He or she may put off considering the consequences or may try buck passing. He or she may let someone else make the decision (and suffer the consequences) or simply ignore the risks and choose the most obvious solution. This resigned posture may prevent consideration of more viable alternatives.
4. *Panic:* The manager feels pressured not only by the problem itself but by time. This produces a high level of stress that may manifest itself in sleeplessness, irritability, and other forms of agitation; in extreme form, physical illness may result. In the panic state, the individual may be so agitated that he or she is unable to appraise the situation realistically or accept help from subordinates. And given inappropriate handling, the situation is likely to deteriorate.

incremental adjustment A method of managerial problem solving in which each successive action represents only a small change from activities.

Managers who react to problems in the above ways often opt for a simplistic approach to decisions. A frequent method is **incremental adjustment**—choosing an alternative that represents only a minor change from existing policies.[36] In many instances, this is indeed the most sensible approach, because it avoids extensive investigation of the problem and thus saves time and money. It presents the manager with familiar, nonspeculative, and relatively stable and predictable data for analysis. But such an approach often results in inferior solutions because it is a substitute for gathering new information and for innovative thinking. When managers use incremental adjustment, it is highly unlikely that new ideas will be considered; and it is quite likely that long-run advantages will be sacrificed to short-term gains.

[36]Charles E. Lindblom, *The Intelligence of Democracy* (New York: Free Press, 1965), pp. 143–145.

ETHICS IN MANAGEMENT

THE GAME OF "PRISONER'S DILEMMA"

Suppose you had to make the following decision. You and an accomplice are apprehended after a crime has been committed. You are held and interrogated separately, each of you being told that if you turn state's evidence you will get a very light sentence (1 year in jail), while the other will be put away for a long time (10 years). However, if *both* of you confess, you will each get 8 years. If *neither* of you confesses, you will be convicted of some more minor charge and given 2 years each. The game is depicted in the following diagram. Prisoner #1's dilemma can be seen by reading from left to right; Prisoner #2's dilemma can be read by reading the columns at the right from top to bottom.

		Prisoner #2	
		Confess	Don't Confess
Prisoner #1	Confess	Both get 8 years	#1 gets 1 year #2 gets 10 years
	Don't Confess	#1 gets 10 years #2 gets 1 year	Both get 2 years

#1 reasons this way: "The best outcome for me is to confess while #2 does *not* confess. But #2 will realize this and confess and we'll *both* be worse off, so I won't confess. But if I choose this route, then #2 will realize I may do this and confess—which will be the best outcome for *him* and the worst for *me*." And so on.

This simple game is at the heart of many ethical dilemmas in decision making. When *each* fails to cooperate with the other in not confessing, *each* acting in accordance with *his own* self-interest, *both* the prisoners fare worse. In a pathbreaking book, Robert Axelrod showed that, over time, if the game is repeated an indefinite number of times, cooperation will begin to emerge as the dominant strategy adopted by each of the players. But the result is paradoxical: Sometimes when we try to be selfish we end up faring worse. Axelrod shows in "Prisoner's Dilemma" that in such situations, we can generally do better for *ourselves* by *cooperating.*

Sources: Robert Axelrod, *The Evolution of Cooperation* (New York: Basic Books, 1984); Anatol Rappoport and Albert Chammah, *Prisoner's Dilemma* (Ann Arbor: University of Michigan Press, 1965).

Overcoming Barriers to Individual Problem Solving. Familiarity with the rational problem-solving process described earlier gives managers confidence in their ability to understand and deal with difficult situations. This confidence is important for two reasons. First, it increases the likelihood that managers will actively try to locate problems—and opportunities—in their organizations. Second, it increases the likelihood that they will, in fact, find good solutions to the problems they confront.

In addition to using the rational problem-solving process, there are other specific ways individuals can manage their decision making more effectively.

1. *Set priorities*. Managers are faced with numerous problems and tasks every day. Sometimes, the sheer quantity of the workload is overwhelming. To avoid being snowed under by tasks and unfinished business, managers should review the priorities of their workload daily. After setting, or resetting, priorities, they should allocate time according to those

priorities. (Some effective managers review their priorities and replan their work a number of times a day.)[37]

2. *Acquire relevant information.* As they work on identifying and solving a problem, managers should collect the information that they will eventually need to make the final decision. This information consists of the potential alternatives and their consequences, any relevant events that may occur in the future (termed ''states of nature'' by the management scientist), and the criteria for evaluating the eventual decision and solution.[38]
3. *Proceed methodically and carefully.* There are many forms of the rational problem-solving model outlined above, but none of them works well if it is not used well. In following a rational problem-solving model, managers should keep in mind some common mistakes. For example, in stage 1 many people tend to define a problem in terms of only one possible solution, to focus on lower priority goals, or to diagnose the problem in terms of its symptoms but not its underlying causes. In stage 2, when alternatives are being developed, there is a tendency to evaluate them right away—a tendency that prevents creation of a sufficient number of alternatives. In stage 3, evaluating alternatives, people fail to use information systematically and tend to proceed in hit-or-miss fashion. Finally (in stage 4), mistakes crop up during implementation. Managers may not motivate staff members or give them clear instructions; they sometimes do not gain acceptance of the decision, allocate appropriate resources, or provide in advance the information needed to monitor the solution program.[39] By knowing these common pitfalls, we can avoid them as we make and follow through on decisions.
4. *Be aware of heuristics and biases.* As we have seen, these rules of thumb can be both good and bad. Managers need to understand how heuristics can lead to biases, to bad decisions, and to overconfidence. Once managers are aware of their faulty assumptions, they can make a deliberate effort to avoid relying on them and so to improve the quality of their decisions.

Deciding Who Decides

Managers make decisions as individuals, and managers involve other individuals in the decision-making process. The first decision that a manager must make is: Who will decide? In making this decision, Maier's concepts of objective quality and acceptance are useful guidelines.

As we noted earlier, the objective quality of the decision is determined by how well the manager carries out some form of the rational problem-solving process. In doing so, the manager may work alone or may be involved with many other individuals. If the problem is properly defined and diagnosed, the facts gathered and evaluated carefully, and the attractive alternatives developed and well evaluated, then the resulting decision should have high objective quality. Maier suggests that where the problem is largely a technical one, a quality decision may be enough to solve it.

If people are involved in the problem, however, then a quality decision may not be sufficient, according to Maier. The acceptance of the people involved may also be required to make it effective. A difficulty arises for managers if ''quality'' considerations conflict with ''acceptance'' considerations: The decision that objectively would work best may not be acceptable to the people affected. On the other hand, the decision most favored by subordinates may not be the best one for the organization.

---

[37]This process is known as time management, and it may be the single most important way for managers to improve their overall efficiency. Some useful books are Kenneth Blanchard and Spencer Johnson, *The One-Minute Manger* (New York: Morrow, 1982), which emphasizes a process for establishing and remaining focused on a limited set of priorities (''one-minute goal-setting''); and Peter Turla and Katherine Hawkins, *Time Management Made Easy* (New York: Dutton, 1984).

[38]George P. Huber, *Managerial Decision Making* (Glenview, Ill.: Scott, Foresman, 1980), pp. 30–40.

[39]Ibid., pp. 11–12.

HERE'S AN EXAMPLE

Procter & Gamble, the mammoth consumer products company, is undergoing some revolutionary organizational changes. One area in which change is evident is in the administrative committee, 40 members strong, the highest-ranking body within the organization that had ratified all significant promotions and spending plans. On July 1, 1988, the company took away the decision-making authority from this group and reorganized a 20-member executive panel to meet weekly to deal with only the most important issues. Other decisions now will be made by lower-level managers. (*Business Week*, 7/25/88, p. 76)

Involving Others: Quality and Acceptance. Traditionally, the final responsibility for making decisions belongs to managers, who may have to persuade or compel subordinates to obey. But this approach is not always appropriate. Sometimes, subordinates have excellent reasons for resisting a decision. Perhaps they are aware, for example, of alternatives or relevant factors that were not considered in the original analysis. In such cases, a managerial decision may fail because the manager is unable to convince subordinates to carry it out willingly. In other cases, subordinates may implement a decision loyally even though they disagree with it—the results being poor because the decision was poor.

When subordinates are given the responsibility for dealing with a problem, their self-esteem increases and they take pride in their demonstrated value to the organization. Of course, there are disadvantages as well as advantages to involving a number of individuals in the problem-solving process. Because individuals' time is valuable, we should involve them when the benefits—quality, acceptance, morale, development—are greater than the likely costs in time, money, or the frustration of employees who feel they should not be involved.

ILLUSTRATIVE CASE STUDY Wrap-Up

Diplomacy and Determination in High-Level Decision Making

As we mentioned earlier, the decision-making process at Texaco took a very difficult and unexpected turn for the company. Undoubtedly, some of the heuristics that Texaco's managers used did not work in this set of unusual circumstances. Perhaps "Easy Search" and "Easy Recall" were at work. After all, who would have thought that a David like Pennzoil could bring down a Goliath like Texaco? Since the Texas court set a precedent with this case, the heuristic of availability simply would not have worked. In thinking through the precedents, McKinley should have discovered that no court had ever done what the Texas court did in this case—after all, Texaco's offer was higher than Pennzoil's. In addition, it's likely that a number of the actors in this large-scale drama were simply overconfident in their roles as parties to a major corporate takeover—roles in which they had little expertise (no one does) with multiple-party deals in a world of "Pac Man defenses" and any number of other exotic defenses, attacks, and counterattacks in a company's arsenal. In short, what had begun as a fairly easy, nonprogrammed decision quickly generated a political morass of conflicting groups, laws, and situations. ■

■ SUMMARY

Managers must solve problems and make decisions. The types of problems and the conditions under which they must be solved vary. Decision-making approaches, therefore, must be tailor-made to fit particular circumstances.

Effective managers do not merely wait for problems to arise; they actively look for both problems and opportunities. One of the more significant responsibilities of managers is deciding which problems and opportunities should receive their full attention. Opportunity finding, problem finding, and problem solving are all important managerial activities. Although opportunity finding is the most important of these three processes, it is the least understood.

COORDINATED RESOURCE

More information on decision-making styles can be found in the Lecture Extras Supplement.

Programmed decisions are those made by habit or policy; nonprogrammed decisions are made under new or unusual conditions and require creative thinking and rational consideration. This chapter is concerned with nonprogrammed decision making.

Managers make decisions about conditions that are not always under their control and with varying amounts of information. Therefore, it is frequently useful for managers to approach decisions as though they were being made under conditions of certainty, risk, or uncertainty. Under conditions of certainty, managers assume they know precisely the results of each of the available alternatives. Under conditions of risk, they act as though they know the probabilities of the outcomes of each alternative. Under conditions of uncertainty, the outcome probabilities are assumed not to be known.

It is often useful for managers to follow formal and rational procedures for solving problems. One model of that process can be described in four stages: (1) define, diagnose, and find the sources of the problem; (2) develop alternatives; (3) evaluate the alternatives and select the best one; and (4) implement the selected alternative and follow up on the implementation. Rational decision making is limited, however, by the availability of information and by the manager's ability to utilize that information. Thus, managers may settle for a satisfactory rather than an ideal decision.

Managers should be aware that common heuristic principles can cause systematic biases in decisions. Managerial decisions may be distorted by (1) the way that memories absorb and deliver information, (2) a reliance on representative stereotypes, and (3) a need to derive final decisions from some initial, and often meaningless, value.

Although managers are presented with many problem situations in the course of their daily activities, not all of them require the formal problem-solving process. Ranking problems in the order of importance, or setting priorities and making daily schedules, helps managers decide which ones should receive their immediate and full attention.

REVIEW QUESTIONS

1. Describe the four basic stages in the rational problem-solving process.
2. What is the principal difference between problem finding and opportunity finding.
3. Contrast programmed and nonprogrammed decisions.
4. What are the differences between decisions made under conditions of uncertainty, certainty, and risk? Why do managers try to assess probabilities before reaching a decision?
5. What are three questions managers should ask when they are presented with a problem?
6. What three heuristic principles do decision makers routinely employ? How can they help or hinder the decision making process?
7. What does Norman R. F. Maier suggest for improving the effectiveness of managerial problem solving and decision making?

CASE STUDY

Business and Political Action: To PAC or Not to PAC?

Jessica Smythe, founder and chief executive officer of a chain of 17 hardware and hobby stores in a heavily populated midwestern state, had seen the firm grow in 15 years from a single store on a neighborhood shopping street to a corporation with assets of $9 million and annual sales of $22 million: 12 of the stores were located in large thriving suburban shopping malls, 2 were in urban neighborhoods undergoing a renaissance, and the remaining 3, including the original store, were in declining urban areas and undergoing a decrease in sales concurrent with a surge in operating expenses.

At its last meeting, the board of directors had voted to leave these last three stores in their present locations rather than move them to more profitable settings. This decision to become involved in efforts to rejuvenate the neighborhoods was motivated both by concern for the maintenance of urban neighborhoods and by the knowledge that renovation efforts in the two renaissance areas had produced heavy demand for hardware and other remodeling aids.

Each of the three declining areas had formed a neighborhood association, largely in response to the urging of the local merchants, and had sought public development funds with which to renovate the older buildings. Partly owing to financial entrenchment severely limiting the money available at all levels of government, and partly because of insensitivity to the needs of the communities on the part of their congressional representatives, available federal funds in the form of block grants were not forthcoming. It was apparent that the neighborhood associations had little political clout.

As Jessica Smythe pondered the insensitivity of locally elected officials to neighborhood interests, she was aware that the next congressional election was just six months away. Most likely, some form of political involvement was needed . . . perhaps in the form of campaign financing.

Smythe would like to see one congressman in particular defeated. Not only had he voted against the enabling legislation for neighborhood development funds, he also had refused to discuss the matter on her recent visit to his local office during the congressional recess.

The other two congressmen were neither antagonistic nor helpful, and Smythe felt that they would listen to reason once the political clout of one neighborhood group was established.

Smythe reviewed the strengths and weaknesses of the neighborhoods. All three were heavily populated with middle-aged and older adults with a common, foreign ethnic origin. They had remained in the neighborhood in which they had settled and raised their children, even though in many instances the children had moved away, leaving a customer base of individuals on fixed incomes. Other less affluent families had been attracted to the neighborhoods in recent years because of their close proximity to the urban center and because rental and home-sales prices were reasonable.

Each neighborhood association wished to maintain the identity of the neighborhood; both the older and the more recent residents agreed about this. Furthermore, the residents cooperated with each other in keeping the neighborhood clean and in a modest state of repair. Each could point out specific improvements that had resulted from community effort: One or more homes that had been repainted using volunteer labor and paint supplied by an elderly homeowner, or porch steps replaced in similar fashion. However, the age of the homes and the lack of financial resources clearly indicated that outside funding was needed even to retain the status quo.

Faced with the prospect of seeing the neighborhoods decline further, and of losing the equity the residents and merchants had in their properties (frequently a high percentage of their total worth), everyone involved believed that each neighborhood group would be cohesive and would actively support a group effort. Smythe felt certain of this.

It would be possible to calculate the financial cost to the city of lost property, business, and sales and personal income taxes if local merchants and residents were forced to move from the area. Moreover, there would be increased costs for protection services to avoid property damage, fires in empty buildings, and crime on dark streets. It also was doubtful that any new enterprises could be found to move into the neighborhoods to occupy empty store spaces and to create new jobs.

The best approach appeared to be immediate action directed at elected officials, such as Congressman X.

For a political action committee (PAC) to be formed, several things had to occur quickly. Jessica Smythe knew that her firm could provide administrative services for a PAC associated with it. However, she would need the support of the board of directors. Jessica Smythe owned 40 percent of the stock, but approval of the remaining stockholders would be critical.

Smythe knew of a firm of similar size that had raised $50,000 for a PAC, and she wondered how she might be able to accomplish such a goal. Funds could be solicited directly from stockholders and employees. Would employees from suburban areas and nearby cities where branch stores were located be willing to contribute funds? What type of internal network would be needed? Since PAC can solicit funds from individuals outside the parent organization twice a year, the Smythe PAC could approach merchants and residents within the area and appeal as well to civic-minded individuals from a wider geographic region.

If like-minded groups could be identified, such as party committees for candidates the PAC wished to support, the League of Women Voters, and perhaps groups interested in neighborhood preservation, the efforts of the Smythe PAC could be extended. Since the election was just six months away, the PAC might not be able to qualify as a multicandidate committee; therefore it would have to follow the dollar limitations established for individuals and other such groups acting in concert. Each candidate that was supported could receive $1,000 per election (primary, general, run-off); however, $5,000 could be given to any other committee in support of one or more candidates the PAC favored, and $20,000 could be given to a national party committee for use in congressional elections. Adding this together, the PAC could contribute $3,000 directly to the three congressional candidates it selected for the general election, as much as $20,000 to the party of the candidate opposing Congressman X, and $10,000 to two committees that loaned their support to the opposing candidate. Together, this meant that $33,000 could be allocated for contributions, and ;the remaining money used for the preparation of leaflets and for solicitation expenses.

There were additional considerations. To qualify eventually as a multicandidate PAC and be able to contribute $5,000 per candidate per election another time, it would be necessary to contribute to at least five federal candidates and to obtain funds from at least 50 individuals.

Would it be wise to plan for the long term and to qualify as a multicandidate PAC? Smythe knew that the 17 stores were scattered throughout 12 congressional election districts in the state and that some employees lived in still other districts. How would five candidates be selected for support? Should small amounts be given to a large number of candidates, with larger sums reserved for the three targeted districts? The uncle of one suburban store manager was running in a "safe" election. How much money should be diverted for his campaign? Would a wider dispersal of funds to include the suburbs hinder solicitation efforts from groups interested primarily in urban neighborhood preservation? There were five stores in urban areas, each in a different congressional district.

Of course, other types of PAC organization were possible. Each neighborhood association could form a PAC, but this would prevent the Smythe firm from providing administrative services. There was a national trade association of hardware dealers, but if support was sought from this group, other firms learning of these efforts might try to acquire a large share of the block grant money for areas they serve, even if they provided little support for the association PAC. On another level, the effort could boomerang through negative publicity or through retaliatory action on the part of developers interested in tearing down the buildings and creating large office or apartment buildings.

Source: This case was prepared by Carol J. Fritz. Copyright © 1982 by Pittman Press. Reprinted with permission.

Case Questions

1. What recommendations should Jessica Smythe make to the board of directors?
2. Should a PAC be formed? If not, what other alternatives should be considered, and on what criteria should decisions be made to accept or reject them?
3. If a PAC is formed what criteria should be used in making the following decisions: The selection of candidates to be supported? The solicitation of funds from various individuals and groups? The expansion of the PAC to an organizational level beyond the firm?
4. Beyond a wealth of practical political decisions, which of Smythe's decisions have ethical ramifications for the activities of her organization and its responsibilities to its stakeholders? ■

John Tenniel illustration colored by Fritz Kredel, *Alice and the Cheshire Cat.* Print courtesy of Historical Pictures Service, Chicago. Alice asked, "Cheshire-Puss . . . Would you tell me, please, which way I ought to go from here?" "That depends a good deal on where you want to get to," said the Cat.

7

STRATEGIC PLANNING AND MANAGEMENT

Upon completing this chapter you should be able to:

1. Explain what a strategy is and how it differs from normal planning.
2. Explain why strategic planning is important.
3. Discuss the trends in modern concepts of strategic planning, especially in terms of increasing environmental and organizational complexity.
4. Identify the three levels of strategy and describe the differences in strategy between these levels.
5. Understand the differences between strategic and operational planning.
6. Describe the current frameworks for strategy, including the portfolio approach and the theory based on competitive factors.
7. Describe how strategic planning takes place in large organizations.
8. Identify and describe the nine steps in the formal strategic-planning approach at the business-unit level.

Chapter Outline

Introduction
The Concept of Strategy
The Evolution of the Concept of Strategy
Levels of Strategy: Some Key Distinctions
Frameworks for Strategy
The Formal Strategic Planning Process: The Example of Business-Unit Strategy

ILLUSTRATIVE CASE STUDY Introduction

Planning for the Future at Federal Express

The managers of Federal Express were concerned. They had grown from a small package-delivery service into the major force in overnight delivery. However, they needed to decide on directions for the future: Competition was closing in from several sides, and Federal Express felt the need to move quickly if it was to continue to grow and thrive.

Federal Express did not consider itself simply a package "delivery service." It saw itself as part of a larger and more complex industry that should be more properly thought of as "information delivery." Thus, although they competed with such traditional rivals as other overnight carriers like United Parcel Service and the United States Postal Service, they also worried about other information carriers, such as MCI, AT&T and other telecommunication companies. Therefore, it was important for company managers to speculate on the future directions of all these companies.

Federal Express had a reputation for being at the forefront of a trend, and it wanted to keep both its position and its reputation. The company had started long before anyone thought that overnight-delivery service would be such an important part of doing business. Although it had taken over three years for the concept to catch on and make the company profitable, it was now the leader in the industry. The technology, as well as the company's overall attitude of innovation, that was needed to make the transition from handling 40 packages a night to 400,000 was still very much a part of the company's corporate thinking. These were also important assets, and the question that now arose was: How should these assets be used?

The postal service was obviously impinging on their overnight-delivery business, the "Express Mail" package being a direct and serious challenge. However, the Post Office was somewhat limited as to future directions. It could challenge in terms of price and service but would probably continue to specialize in the same type of product. United Parcel Service (UPS) was also a direct challenger—one that priced its service considerably under Federal and that was improving its service noticeably. Where would UPS go in the years to come?

Despite the obvious challenges of other package-delivery services, Federal Express was far more concerned about the competition from other methods of information transfer. MCI, for example, had recently introduced its MCI Mail System, which transferred documents from one computer to another in far fewer hours than Federal Express could promise. Was this what business in the information age wanted? More importantly, was this the way of the future? If it was, precisely how should Federal counter the threat?

Since 1978, the mechanics of doing business have changed drastically; the rapid development of technology has changed business attitudes and expectations forever. It is no longer acceptable that a business letter take a week to move from one coast to the other; important documents are always needed sooner, and businesses now think in terms of hours instead of days. The development of a truly global marketplace has also affected the document-delivery business: As international business becomes more common, information-transfer systems have to keep pace.

The people at Federal Express knew that they had to move forward in order to survive. Federal Express had to be ready to meet the needs of *tomorrow's* businesses as they developed, and in order to do this, they had to anticipate those needs today. But which needs were going to be the most important? What could they do to get ready now?

Sources: Larry Reibstein, "Turbulence Ahead: Federal Express Faces Challenges to Its Grip on Overnight Delivery," *Wall Street Journal,* January 8, 1988, pp. 1, 10; Arthur M. Lewis, "The Great Electronic Mail Shootout," *Fortune,* August 20, 1984, pp. 167–169; Joan M. Feldman, "Federal Express: Big, Bigger and Biggest," *Air Transport World,* November 1985, pp. 46–48; John J. Keller with John W. Wilson, "Why Zapmail Finally Got Zapped," *Business Week,* October 13, 1986, pp. 48–49; David H. Freedman, "Redefining an Industry through Integrated Automation," *Infosystems,* May 1985, pp. 26–27; Katie Hajner, "Fred Smith: The Entrepreneur Redux, *Inc.,* June 1984, pp. 38, 40; John Merwin, "Anticipating the Evolution," *Forbes,* November 4, 1985, pp. 163–164.

TEACHING TIP

This is a fascinating chapter to teach! There are so many current examples of company strategies. Remind your students to be alert to these and to bring examples in to share with the class. Also, you can find many examples to use just by picking up current issues of *Business Week, Fortune,* and the *Wall Street Journal.*

In the last two chapters, we discussed ways of planning and decision making effectively. We looked at the major types of plans, described some obstacles to effective planning, and outlined ways of overcoming them. In particular, we learned that *planning* is the basic process whereby an organization selects goals and decides *how* to achieve them. In this chapter, we discuss *strategic* planning, the process by which top management establishes an organization's goals and selects specific means for achieving them. At first glance, the two definitions seem quite similar, but as Robert H. Hayes and Steven C. Wheelwright show in Exhibit 7-1, there are at least five ways in which *strategy* can be distinguished from more general types of *planning*.

THE CONCEPT OF STRATEGY

What Is Strategy?

strategy The broad program for defining and achieving an organization's objectives; the organization's response to its environment over time.

Strategy can be defined from at least two different perspectives: from the perspective of what an organization *intends to do,* and also from the perspective of what an organization eventually *does,* whether or not its actions were originally intended.

From the first perspective, strategy is "the broad program for defining and achieving an organization's objectives and implementing its missions."[1] The word "program" in this definition implies an active, conscious, and rational role played by managers in formulating the organization's strategy.

From the second perspective, strategy is "the pattern of the organization's responses to its environment over time." In this definition, every organization has a strategy—although not necessarily an effective one—even if that strategy has never been explicitly formulated: That is, every organization has a relationship with its environment that can be examined and described. This view of strategy includes organizations whose managers' behavior is reactive—managers who respond and adjust to the environment as the need arises.[2]

CLASS COMMENT

Strategic management is much more than just strategic planning. Strategic management involves formulating, implementing, and evaluating the strategy.

Our discussion of strategy will use both definitions, but we will emphasize the active role. The active formulation of a strategy is known as *strategic planning* or, more recently, strategic management, and it takes a broad and usually long-range focus.

Why Strategic Planning Is Important

Most organizations now recognize the importance of strategic planning to their long-range growth and health. Managers have found that by specifically defining the mis-

[1]For a history of the concept of strategy, see Roger Evered, "So What *Is* Strategy?" *Long Range Planning* 16, no. 3 (June 1983):57–72. Recent research is contributing to our understanding of organizational strategy. See Ari Ginsberg, "Operationalizing Organizational Strategy: Toward an Integrative Framework," *Academy of Management Review* 9, no. 3 (July 1984):548–557; and James W. Fredrickson, "Strategic Process Research: Questions and Recommendations," *Academy of Management Review* 8, no. 4 (October 1983):565–575.

[2]Our discussion of strategy and strategic planning in this chapter draws upon Dan E. Schendel and Charles W. Hofer, eds., *Strategic Management: A New View of Business Policy and Planning* (Boston: Little, Brown, 1979). However, our classifications and interpretations differ somewhat from theirs.

TEACHING TIP

Be sure to emphasize these characteristics of strategy, as students will tend to confuse strategy with other general types of planning.

EXHIBIT 7-1 MAJOR CHARACTERISTICS DISTINGUISHING STRATEGY FROM GENERAL TYPES OF PLANNING

1. *Time horizon.* Generally, the word *strategy* is used to describe activities that involve an extended time horizon, with regard to both the time it takes to carry out such activities and the time it takes to observe their impact.
2. *Impact.* Although the consequences of pursuing a given strategy may not become apparent for a long time, their eventual impact will be significant.
3. *Concentration of effort.* An effective strategy usually requires concentrating one's activity, effort, or attention on a fairly narrow range of pursuits. Focusing on these chosen activities implicitly reduces the resources available for other activities.
4. *Pattern of decisions.* Although some companies need to make only a few major decisions in order to implement their chosen strategy, most strategies require that a series of certain types of decision be made over time. These decisions must be supportive of one another, in that they follow a consistent pattern.
5. *Pervasiveness.* A strategy embraces a wide spectrum of activities ranging from resource allocation processes to day-to-day operations. In addition, the need for consistency over time in these activities requires that all levels of an organization act, almost instinctively, in ways that reinforce the strategy.

These five characteristics clearly indicate that an organization's strategy is the central hub around which other major organizational activities revolve. Strategy is long-term and wide-ranging; it pervades and controls important organizational actions, and is an important determinant of an organization's success or failure over time.

Source: Robert H. Hayes and Steven C. Wheelwright, *Restoring Our Competitive Edge: Competing Through Manufacturing* (New York: Wiley, 1984), pp. 27–28.

QUOTATION FROM A MANAGER

Former President of Matsushita Electric Industrial Company, Toshihiko Yamashita: "Instant success would weaken the company, since strength is born of struggle." (*Business Week*, 2/1/88, p. 84D)

sion of their organizations they are better able to give them direction and focus their activities. Organizations function better as a result and become more responsive to a changing environment.

As an example of how the introduction of strategic planning can have positive results for an organization, consider the case of Servus Rubber, which had been operating at a loss for several years. Then entered two young entrepreneurs, Tommy Hewitt, 35, and Michael Cappy, 33, both former employees of GE. Servus Rubber had been a manufacturer of high-quality rubber boots worn by farmers, construction workers, electricians, military personnel, and industrial workers.

However, with the advent of South Korean products that were considerably cheaper in price and lower in quality, the managers of Servus decided on a new strategy: Rather than continuing in their niche as high-quality bootmaker, they would try to compete with the South Koreans on price. Servus changed its tactics, using cheaper materials and neglecting equipment—a strategy which created an atmosphere of declining morale at the company. The consequences of this strategy were that, by 1981, Servus was down by 50 percent in profits.

Hewitt and Cappy bought Servus and applied new strategies to save the company and bring it back to its former reputation. Their strategy was to differentiate Servus from its competition, offering products that represented the best value and a mix of price and quality. To implement their strategic plan, they developed new markets and new products, worked with the employees to improve morale, fired the prior management, and repositioned Servus into its former prosperity.

Hewitt and Cappy had a clearcut concept of the organization, making it possible to formulate plans and activities to bring the organization from the brink of disaster to renewed vigor.[3]

Strategic planning, then, helps to develop a clear-cut concept of an organization. This, in turn, makes it possible to formulate the plans and activities that will bring an organization closer to its goals.

---

[3]Joshua Hyatt, "Sole Survivors," *Inc.*, October 1987.

FOR DISCUSSION

The environment is so uncertain that strategic planning is a waste of time. Discuss. (Emphasize that although systematic strategic planning can help managers predict and forecast, there may be some instances where the environment is so complex and changing so rapidly that strategic planning might not be useful.)

Another reason strategic planning has become important for managers is that it enables them to prepare for and deal with the rapidly changing environment in which their organizations operate. When the pace of change was slower, managers could operate on the assumption that the future would be similar to the past. They could establish goals and plans simply by extrapolating from past experiences. Today, events move too rapidly for experience to be a reliable guide, and managers must develop new strategies suited to the unique problems and opportunities of the future.

As we saw in Chapter 3, the external environment of many organizations contains a host of stakeholder groups. One telephone company used a strategic planning process to reposition its basic service and in doing so was able to meet the concerns of over 700 separate stakeholder groups.

The major disadvantage of formal strategic planning is the danger of creating a large bureaucracy of planners that may lose contact with the business's products and customers. According to a *Business Week* study, in their efforts to develop effective strategic-planning systems some companies have invested heavily in consultants, planning staffs, and sophisticated models and planning programs. These planning staffs can usurp the initiative and power of operating managers. From their ivory towers, staff planners may make decisions based on abstract concepts rather than on close familiarity with the real needs of the business.[4]

The considerable investment in time, money, and people that a formal planning system requires may take years to pay off. Until the strategic planning process begins to function smoothly, the organization may move slowly and uncertainly on important decisions. This can result in lost opportunities. A further disadvantage is that strategic planning sometimes tends to restrict the organizations to the most rational and risk-free option. Managers learn to develop only those strategies and objectives that can survive the detailed analysis of the planning process, and may avoid attractive opportunities that involve high degrees of uncertainty or are difficult to analyze and communicate.[5]

HERE'S AN EXAMPLE

"What would you do if someone handed you $3 billion?" This was the amount Texaco, Inc. was scheduled to hand over to Pennzoil Company for legal damages from the Getty Oil takeover. And Pennzoil is going to take its time in spending it. They want to avoid making hasty acquisitions and, in fact, must first decide on its (Pennzoil's) identity, what type of company it wants to be. (*Business Week,* 4/11/88, p. 63)

Evidence for the Effectiveness of Strategic Planning. A number of research studies have compared organizations that use formal strategic planning with those that do not. J. Scott Armstrong reviewed these studies—some of which are summarized below—and concluded that formalized strategic planning pays off.[6] Although most studies have been limited to large companies, it is likely that this conclusion is valid for small organizations as well.

Most organizations do not face a choice between no planning and a complete, full-blown, finely tuned strategic planning system. Instead, the choice is often between no explicitly stated strategy and a conscientious attempt to develop one. In an organization already accustomed to sophisticated operational planning, the choice may be between a very rough, informal process of developing a strategy and a somewhat more formalized process. In other words, the practical option open to most organizations is to move toward more formality in strategy making.

An early study by Stanley S. Thune and Robert J. House found that firms with formal, long-range planning procedures consistently outperformed those that confined themselves to informal planning.[7] The advantage of formal strategic planning was

---

[4]The New Breed of Strategic Planner," *Business Week,* September 17, 1984, pp. 62–68.

[5]See Richard B. Robinson, Jr., and John A. Pearce II, "The Impact of Formalized Strategic Planning on Financial Performance in Small Organizations," *Strategic Management Journal* 4, no. 3 (July–September 1983):197–207. Some recent best-selling management books suggest that we should be wary of rational plans that suppress managers' entrepreneurial impulses. See Thomas H. Peters and Robert S. Waterman, *In Search of Excellence* (New York: Warner Books, 1982); Tom Peters and Nancy Austin, *A Passion for Excellence: The Leadership Difference* (New York: Random House, 1985); and Rosabeth M. Kanter, *The Changemasters* (New York: Simon & Schuster, 1983).

[6]J. Scott Armstrong, "The Value of Formal Planning for Strategic Decisions: Review of Empirical Research," *Strategic Management Journal* 3, no. 3 (July–September 1982):197–211.

[7]Stanley S. Thune and Robert J. House, "Where Long-Range Planning Pays Off," *Business Horizons* 13, no. 4 (August 1970):81–87.

most evident in industries in a rapidly changing environment (such as the drug or computer industries). Managers in such industries had to chart their course carefully to help their organizations survive and grow. A follow-up study supported this conclusion.[8]

A more recent analysis of 38 chemical/drug, electronics, and machinery firms found that on nine out of 13 financial measures (sales volume, earnings per share, net income, and so on) "formal, integrated long-range planners" far outperformed "informal planners."[9] A study of large U.S. banks[10] also confirmed the advantages of formal planning in a service industry.[11]

QUOTATION FROM A MANAGER

Richard Rainwater, the legendary Texas dealmaker, describing attempts to save Western Union from Chapter 11 of the Bankruptcy Act: "Guys tried, but there is no margin for error anymore for a second-rate company in a fast-changing business. Change is going to make a lot of businessmen look stupid. Most aren't. But one wrong turn and they'll be out of business anyway". (*Business Week,* 12/14/87, p. 114)

The research just cited focuses on the presence or lack of formal strategic planning systems. Other studies have related performance to the presence or lack of a formal strategy. Not surprisingly, the findings are similar. For example, of 100 firms drawn from four industries, those with clear, well-defined strategies generally outperformed companies that had informal, unclear stategies. The "winners" in this study identified their distinctive areas of competence and took advantage of them through planning. The "losers" more often simply reacted to the external environment. The only case in which this reactive approach seemed to work was in the air transport industry, which was heavily regulated and protected at the time of the study and subject to very little uncertainty.[12]

THE EVOLUTION OF THE CONCEPT OF STRATEGY

Strategy as the Grand Plan

CLASS COMMENT

As you can see, the concept of strategy has a long and colorful history. As noted in Chapter 2 on the evolution of management thought, the military has played a key role in the development of many management concepts.

The concept of strategy is ancient. The word "strategy" comes from the Greek *strategeia,* which means the art or science of being a general. The Greeks knew the importance of generalship in winning and losing battles. Effective generals needed to define the purpose of leading an army, winning, holding territory, protecting a city from invasion, wiping out the enemy, and so forth. Each kind of objective required a different deployment of resources—different programs. Likewise, an army's strategy could be defined as the actual pattern of *actions* that it took in response to the enemy.

Now, the Greeks also knew that strategy was more than just fighting battles. Effective generals had to determine the right lines of supply, decide when to fight and when not to fight, and manage the army's relationships with citizens, politicians, and diplomats. Effective generals not only had to plan but to *act* as well. Dating back to the Greeks, the concept of strategy thus was both *planning* components and decision-making or *action* components.[13] Taken together, these two concepts form the basis for the "grand" strategic plan.

---

[8]David M. Herold, "Long-Range Planning and Organizational Performance," *Academy of Management Journal* 15, no. 1 (March 1972):91–102.

[9]Zafar A. Malik and Delmar W. Karger, "Does Long-Range Planning Improve Company Performance?" *Management Review* 64, no. 9 (September 1975):27–31.

[10]D. Robley Wood, Jr., and R. Lawrence LaForge, "The Impact of Comprehensive Planning on Financial Performance," *Academy of Management Journal* 22, no. 3 (September 1979):516–526. Also see Lawrence C. Rhyne, "The Relationship of Strategic Planning to Financial Performance," *Strategic Management Journal* 7 (1986):423–436.

[11]In contrast, no positive relationship was found in the service sector by two other investigators: Robert M. Fulmer and Leslie W. Rue, "The Practice and Profitability of Long-Range Planning," *Managerial Planning* 22, no. 6 (May–June 1974):1–7. This may be because many of the service organizations studied had begun their planning activities too recently for the systems to begin to have an effect.

[12]Charles C. Snow and Lawrence G. Hrebiniak, "Strategy, Distinctive Competence, and Organizational Performance," *Administrative Science Quarterly* 25, no. 2 (June 1980):317–336. For a review of studies relating strategy, structure, and organizational performance, see Jay R. Galbraith and Daniel A. Nathanson, *Strategy Implementation: The Role of Structure and Process,* 2nd ed. (St. Paul, Minn.: West Publishing, 1986). The accuracy of some studies is questioned in Alfred Rappaport, "Corporate Performance Standards and Shareholder Value," *Journal of Business Strategy* 3, no. 4 (Spring 1983):4–8, 26.

[13]Daniel Gilbert, Edwin Hartman, John Mauriel, and Edward Freeman, *A Logic for Strategy* (Boston: Ballinger Press, 1988).

General Robert E. Wood, president of the giant mail-order house of Sears, Roebuck and Co., sounded a similar theme in the 1920s. Wood realized that the growing popularity of the automobile would allow increasing numbers of people access to urban areas. A population no longer confined to the countryside, he reasoned, would abandon the mail-order catalog in favor of the retail store. So Sears embarked on the long-range strategy of converting to a retail chain. According to Wood, the company "made every mistake in the book" at first, but its carefully laid plans spelled success in the end. "Business is like war in one respect," the general wrote. "If its grand strategy is correct, any number of tactical errors can be made and yet the enterprise proves successful."[14]

Strategic Planning and Strategic Management

HERE'S AN EXAMPLE

Michael R. Quinlan, CEO of McDonald's Corporation, is planning major growth despite some obstacles: generally flat sales in the fast-food industry, chronic shortage of minimum-wage workers, and creeping inflation in food prices. Here are some comments made by associates and observers about Quinlan: "He's like a shark"; "That's Quinlan's willingness to experiment with new ideas"; "Mike has made us more aggressive in the marketplace"; "He's got a keen competitive instinct."

In more modern terms, the methods for the development of such grand strategies have undergone a series of important changes, even though it has been only recently that students of management practice have recognized strategy as a key factor in organizational success. (Recall our discussion in Chapter 3.) The main reason for this recognition has been environmental change. Since World War II, significant changes have taken place in the environment in which businesses must operate, and they have found it necessary to keep pace with these changes by giving more elaborate thought to their own processes—including management strategies.

These changes were particularly significant in the early 1970s. The environment was beginning to change and become increasingly complex as technology developed rapidly, international competition was starting to have an impact, markets were maturing and energy was becoming a crisis issue. Assumptions that the future would continue to look just like the past, with increased growth and prosperity, gave way to new realities.[15] New approaches to management strategy were needed in the face of general changes in the business environment.

First, the *rate* of change in the environment has increased rapidly, partially because the greater interdependence of environmental factors has led not only to more complex demands on management operations but to a much more rapid birth-and-death cycle of innovative ideas. Second, there has been an obvious growth in the size and complexity of business organizations. For example, in 1949 the majority of *Fortune* 500 companies were single-product line or single-key idea organizations; by 1970, not only had a majority shifted to multi-industry organizations, but many had become multinational organizations as well.[16] Integrating the interests and needs of a diverse group of functional areas (and sometimes of different cultures) is a *strategic* enterprise. It can be distinguished as such because, among other problems, it takes time to accomplish such integration.

Dan Schendel and Charles Hofer have identified two approaches that have governed the strategic-management practices of businesses over several decades and proposed a third which, they predict, will develop into the approach of the future.[17]

The Policy-Formulation Approach. When an individual entrepreneur offered one class of product to a restricted range of customers, he or she could coordinate the activities of the firm quite informally. But when the product was modified or supple-

---

[14]Quoted in Alfred D. Chandler, Jr., *Strategy and Structure* (Cambridge, Mass.: MIT Press, 1962), p. 325.

[15]Larry J. Rosenberg and Charles D. Schewe, "Strategic Planning: Fulfilling the Promise," *Business Horizons*, July–August 1985, pp. 54–62.

[16]Richard Rumelt, *Strategy, Structure, and Economic Performance* (Boston: Graduate School of Business Administration, Harvard University, 1974).

[17]Schendel and Hofer, *Strategic Management*, pp. 7–18.

policy-formulation approach The concept of implementing day-to-day rules that puts boundaries around what a functional area can and cannot do.

mented or sales territories expanded, the number of the firm's functions increased. The task of integrating functions soon required more formal procedures so that the firm could coordinate activities both within and between functional areas. Thus the **policy-formulation approach** arose—that is, the concept of implementing day-to-day rules that put boundaries around what a functional area could and could not do.

The concept of "business policy" soon became part of the country's educational curriculum, but by the 1950s and early 1960s, the policy-formulation approach had begun to prove inadequate. Organizations were increasing in size and complexity, and the magnitude and unpredictability of their environments presented them with problems that the policy-formulation approach—even one based on the assumption that improved policy would be sufficient to face new challenges—could not solve.

The Initial Strategy Approach. In 1962, business historian Alfred D. Chandler proposed that "strategy" be defined as

> the determination of the basic long-term goals and objectives of an enterprise, and the adoption of courses of action and the allocation of resources necessary for carrying out these goals.[18]

initial strategy approach According to Alfred D. Chandler, "The determination of the basic long-term goals and objectives of an enterprise, and the adoption of courses of action and the allocation of resources necessary for carrying out these goals."

Chandler's formula, now recognized as the **initial strategy approach,** embraced at least four implications for a redefinition of "strategy" that may not be obvious at first glance. First, he was as interested in "courses of *action*" for attaining objectives as he was in the objectives themselves; second, he emphasized the process of *seeking* key ideas rather than the routine principle of implementing policy in the interest of a key idea that may or may not need re-examination; third, Chandler was similarly interested in *how* strategy was formulated and not just in *what* that strategy turned out to be; fourth, Chandler abandoned the conventional notion that the relationship between a business and its environment was more or less stable and predictable. Chandler developed his ideas using historical methods and by analyzing the growth and development of such classic American companies as DuPont, General Motors, Sears, Roebuck, and Standard Oil.

As Chandler thus defined the idea of "strategy," it was eventually refined by people interested in business education. Kenneth Andrews, H. Igor Ansoff, and others brought the idea of strategy as *process* instead of fixed formula (policy) into the classroom, and in the decade between 1965 and 1975, the term *strategy,* as opposed to *policy,* came into wide use in the nation's business schools.[19]

Two factors soon became evident: (1) *strategic planning* paid off in the world of real business activity, but (2) the role of the manager in the implementation of strategic planning had not yet been clarified. (See Chapter 8 for a more complete discussion of strategy implementation.) What could top management do to deal with the two major problems faced by modern organizations—namely, rapid changes in the organization-environment inter-relationship and the rapid growth in size and complexity of modern business organizations? In an effort to address this problem, the strategic management paradigm began to take shape.

The Strategic Management Approach. Many students of the subject of strategy have proposed different definitions and descriptions of it, and Charles Hofer and Dan Schendel have surveyed the resulting literature in order to arrive at a composite definition and

---

[18] Alfred D. Chandler, *Strategy and Structure: Chapters in the History of the American Industrial Enterprise* (Cambridge, Mass.: M.I.T. Press, 1962), p. 16.

[19] Kenneth Andrews, *The Concept of Corporate Strategy* (New York: Dow Jones/Irwin, 1965; H. Igor Ansoff, *Corporate Strategy: An Analytic Approach to Business Policy for Growth and Expansion* (New York: McGraw-Hill, 1965). See Edmund P. Learned, C. Roland Christensen, Kenneth R. Andrews, and William D. Guth, *Business Policy: Text and Cases* (Homewood, Ill.: Richard D. Irwin, 1965).

strategic management approach A pattern based on the principle that the overall design of the organization can be described only if the attainment of objectives is added to policy and strategy as one of the key factors in management's operation of the organization's activities.

a **strategic management approach.** They developed a definition that considers four components:

1. The need to match products or markets with geographic territories (known as *scope*).
2. The need to deploy a large quantity and variety of resources, both human and material.
3. The need to recognize and seize competitive advantages.
4. The need to convince a complex variety of functional divisions that departmental cooperation is better for overall organizational performance than isolated departmental activity (a principle known as *synergy;* see Chapter 2).[20]

BACKGROUND ON SYNERGY

Synergy, as we learned earlier, is a systems concept. Strategic synergy can be achieved by: market synergy (one product or service enhances the sales of others); cost synergy (shared costs of development, production, marketing, etc.); technological synergy (transferring technology from one application to another); and management synergy (transferring knowledge). (William R. King and David I. Cleland, *Strategic Planning and Policy,* Van Nostrand Reinhold, 1978.)

Although this composite does not mention goals and objectives as such, it is based on the principle that the overall design of the organization can be described only if the attainment of *objectives* is added to *policy* and *strategy* as one of the key factors in management's operation of the organization's activities—that is, in the strategic management process.

Hofer and Schendel went on to propose six basic tasks in the strategic management process. First, a set of organizational goals must be established. Ideally, goals should simply make common sense economically, but in practice *power* frequently plays a role in their designation: That is, not only the economic status of the organization but the personal goals and power of various stakeholders must be considered in the final determination of goals.[21] Second, if we consider the "environment" to consist of external elements that can influence an organization's operations (see Chapter 3), we must also remember that this environment can be influenced but not controlled. One aspect of strategic management, then, must be the *forecasting* of environmental conditions that the organization can expect to face in the future.[22]

strategy-formulation task A model of strategy formulation that must take into account the organization's goals and its strategy.

Third, there is the question of *how* to formulate strategy—what Hofer and Schendel call the **strategy-formulation task.** It raises controversial issues because it remains a highly theoretical topic. Hofer and Schendel point out that theoretical models of strategy formulation must take into account two factors: (1) the organization's *goals* (that is, *what* it wants to accomplish) and (2) its *strategy* (that is, *how* it will proceed toward its goals). Not surprisingly, there tend to be two theoretical models of the strategy-formulation task: those that combine the goal- and strategy-formulation tasks and those that separate them.[23] Numerous researchers have tried to reconcile the two camps, but differences persist.

Fourth, organizations need to evaluate past strategy and to estimate the success of future strategy. If existing strategy has failed, examination of it may help in determining the proper direction in which to turn. The second procedure, estimating future success, requires that the organization anticipate such factors as changes in the environment, resources, and objectives.

strategy implementation The fifth task in the strategy management process that is a basically administrative task.

administration Setting aside individual goals in favor of larger organizational goals.

The fifth task in the strategic management process, which Hofer and Schendel call **strategy implementation,** differs from the first four tasks in the sense that implementation is a basically *administrative* task, not a process of analysis, formulation, or evaluation. **Administration** means that individual goals must be set aside in favor of larger organizational goals, and a key question arises: Even if strategy formulation is

---

[20] Charles W. Hofer and Dan E. Schendel, *Strategy Formulation: Analytical Concepts* (St. Paul: West Publishing, 1978).

[21] See Henry Mintzberg, *Power In and Around Organizations* (Englewood Cliffs, N.J.: Prentice Hall, 1983); Mintzberg, "Power and Organizational Life Cycles," *Academy of Management Review* 9 (April 1984):207–224.

[22] See Harold E. Klein and Robert E. Linneman, "Strategic Environmental Assessment: An Emergent Typology of Corporate Planning Practice," *Contribution of Theory and Research to the Practice of Management* (Proceedings of the Southern Management Association, New Orleans, November 1982):4–9.

[23] On this debate, see Thomas J. McNichols, *Policy Making and Executive Action: Cases on Business Policy* (New York: McGraw-Hill, 1972); Frank T. Paine and William Naumes, *Strategy and Policy Formation: An Integrative Approach* (Philadelphia: Saunders, 1974); Hugo Uyterhoeven, Robert Ackerman, and John Rosenblum, *Strategy and Organization* (Homewood, Ill.: Richard D. Irwin, 1973).

the product of rational, analytical thinking, how can this be reconciled with the fact that administrative tasks, which cannot be performed independently of the organization, are often achieved through internal "political" processes? Moreover, some studies show that administrative structure, encompassing most of the organizational hierarchy, actually influences strategic decisions. Therefore, administrating strategy (essentially, "getting the job done") might seem to be the logical "last" (or next-to-last) step in the strategic management process, but if administrative considerations must be taken into account during earlier steps, then ordering the tasks of strategic management sequentially is basically a convenience. As Hofer and Schendel point out, "In practice, [these steps] are interactive, recycle and repeat themselves and do not move forward in sequence as neatly as described here."[24] (We discuss strategy implementation in more detail in Chapter 8.)

strategic control The process of checking strategy implementation progress against the strategic plan at periodic or critical intervals to determine if the corporation is moving toward its strategic objectives.

Consequently, even the "last" step in the strategic management process—what Hofer and Schendel label **strategic control**—need not necessarily be considered in strict sequential order. Once a strategy has been implemented, its progress must be monitored. Is the strategy being implemented and administered as it was supposed to be? Has it produced the intended results? In order to answer such questions, management may have to reconsider both the contingencies of the strategic plans and the practicality of the expected results. If the strategic management process has deviated from its intentions, then the "feedback" resulting from re-evaluation initiates a process of "recycling" strategic plans. An overview of this procedure is schematized in Figure 7-1.

HERE'S AN EXAMPLE

Martin Marietta Company, the large aerospace and data systems organization, is beginning to enjoy the successes in the defense industry it had systematically planned for. The company has garnered 50 percent of the contracts it targeted, surpassing industry averages. According to Mr. Norman Augustine, Vice-Chairman and CEO, the successes have been gained through a carefully planned four-stage strategy that is only half over. Indeed, the company's strategic management will have to guide them through the rough waters ahead for the defense industry. (*Wall Street Journal*, 2/18/88, p. 6)

A Practical Point of View

Peter Lorange has articulated a much less complex way of thinking about the concept of strategy. He says that any particular method of strategic management must answer four very simple questions that take into consideration both the *planning* and *action* components of the concept of strategy:

1. Where are we going?
2. How do we get there?
3. What's our blueprint for action?
4. How do we know if we are on track?[25]

EXTRA EXERCISE

Either interview company owners or do some library research (using company magazines, annual reports, or business periodicals, etc.) to find examples of mission statements.

In Lewis Carroll's novel *Alice in Wonderland,* the Cheshire Cat says to Alice, "If you don't know where you're going, then any road will take you there." The concept of strategy requires that we begin with some sense of which road we want to go down. The answer to this question goes by various names—"mission," "objective," "goal," "purpose." However, we don't see much to be gained by stipulating formal definitions of these terms, because each of them refers to the same general idea—namely, that strategy (and planning in general) make sense only if some endpoint, some desired outcome, is defined.

Even then, simply defining the endpoint does not complete the process. Oftentimes, there are many different ways to achieve a particular outcome, so strategic

[24]Hofer and Schendel, "Strategic Management," p. 14. For a discussion of some of the finer distinctions between the formulation and implementation of strategy, see also Arthur A. Thompson and A. J. Strickland, Jr., *Strategy Formulation and Implementation,* 3rd ed. (Dallas: Business Publications, 1986).

[25]Peter Lorange, *Corporate Planning: An Executive Viewpoint* (Englewood Cliffs, N.J.: Prentice Hall, 1980).

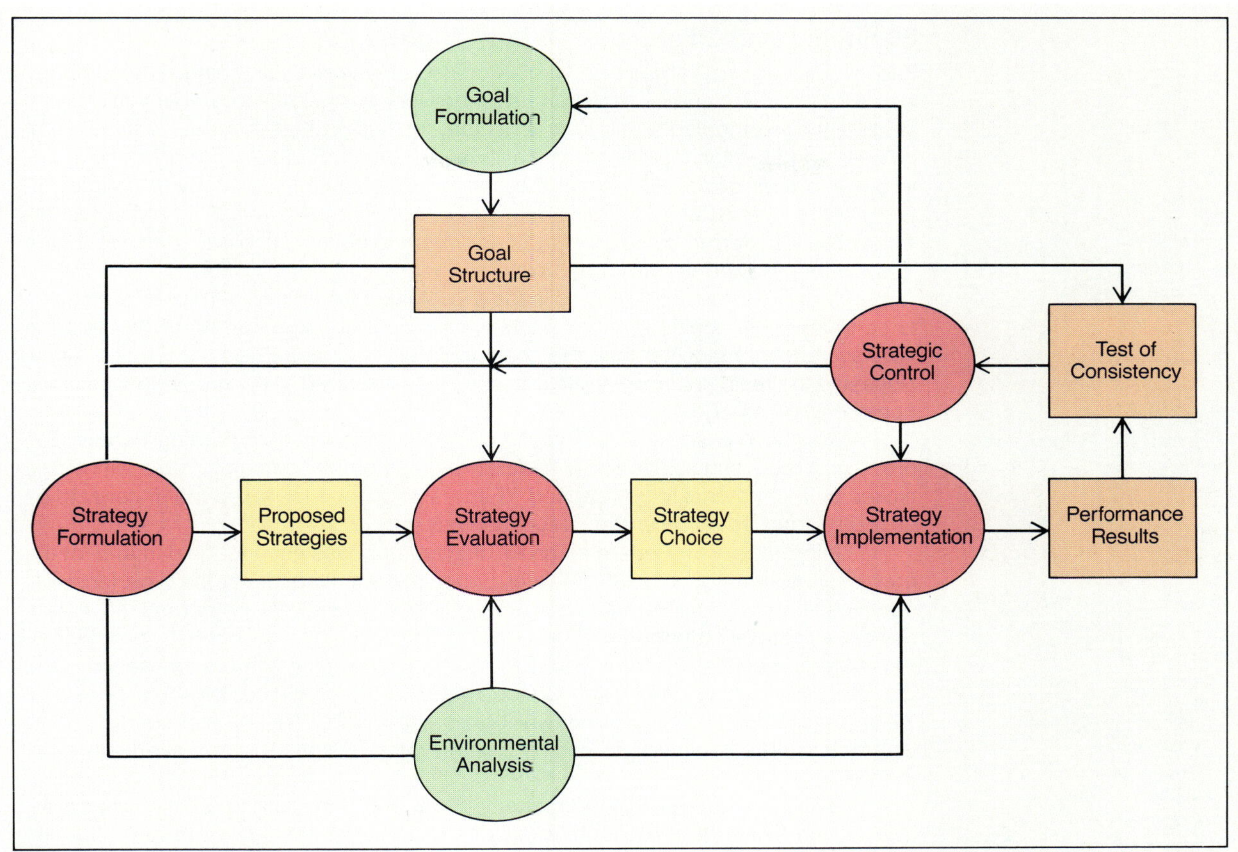

Source: Daniel E. Schendel and Charles W. Hofer, eds., *Strategic Management: A New View of Business Policy and Planning*. Copyright © 1979. By permission of the authors.

FIGURE 7-1 SCHENDEL AND HOFER'S OVERVIEW OF THE STRATEGIC MANAGEMENT PROCESS

management must also *specify* a set of programs that will lead to the desired outcome. If the first question is one of *ends,* then the second question is one of *means*. IBM's mission is to be the leading computer company in the world. Obviously, there are a lot of different ways to realize that mission. Recently, having experienced its worst profit slide ever, IBM has had to develop new strategies to realize its mission. With an increasingly competitive environment littered with now established, viable competitors such as Apple, DEC, and Compaq, IBM is developing new strategies, ranging from a decentralized management structure to new product-design approaches to improved relations with those outside "Big Blue" (IBM's nickname), particularly customers. (The case of IBM is discussed more fully as the Illustrative Case Study for Chapter 10.)[26]

A third question asks if we have concrete plans of actions with which to implement our programs, and we will deal with implementing strategy in Chapter 8. Finally, the fourth question asks us to pay attention to *control* in order to be sure that the strategy is on track. Control is a large subject and we will defer it until Chapters 18–21.

[26]Fred Guterel, "IBM's Very Tough Guy," *Business Month,* February 1988.

ILLUSTRATIVE CASE STUDY Continued

Planning for the Future at Federal Express

Federal Express had always had a clear sense of where it was going: The company wanted to be the leader in the information-delivery business. As company managers studied their competitors, they came to the conclusion that they had defined their business and the technology on which it was based too narrowly. Therefore, in order to achieve their desired direction, they began by planning a strategy to counter directly MCI's Mail System. Federal Express called their new service "ZapMail," a service which transferred documents from anywhere to anywhere in less than two hours. The system worked in one of two ways.

First, large businesses could lease a ZapMailer from Federal Express and use it to send facsimile copies to other ZapMailers around the country. If the recipient did not have such a machine, then the document was sent to the Federal Express office closest to the recipient. From there, the copy was delivered to the proper location by a Federal Express agent.

Alternatively, smaller businesses could use the service by calling Federal Express and requesting ZapMail. A Federal Express employee came to the office and picked up the material to be "zapped." Federal Express then faxed the material to be delivered from its office in the destination city.

Unfortunately for Federal Express, there simply was not enough demand for the new service. Finally, in 1986 Federal Express discontinued ZapMail; as facsimile machines began to proliferate in business offices all over the country (and the world), there was simply no need for it.

More recently, Federal Express has renewed its emphasis on service and begun to compete squarely with United Parcel in the so-called "big box" business, which deals in the delivery of heavier boxes and freight. This project comes just as United Parcel is beginning to compete with Federal Express in the overnight letter market.

As these examples of continuous thinking and rethinking in competitive corporate offices illustrate, the simple questions of strategic management and planning must be augmented with a more complete understanding not only of why strategic planning is important, but, perhaps more importantly, the competitive dynamics that influence a particular organization's strategy.

LEVELS OF STRATEGY: SOME KEY DISTINCTIONS

The Three Levels of Strategy

TEACHING TIP

These three levels of strategy are important to stress to students. Make sure they understand the levels. A good example to use is General Motors Company. You can discuss *corporate-level strategy,* from GM headquarters' point of view; then you can discuss *business-unit strategy,* from each of the separate car company's points of view—Chevrolet, Pontiac, Cadillac, etc; then *functional-level strategy* can be discussed within each of these separate car company's marketing, production, R&D plans, etc. Also important to stress is how all these levels of plans must be interrelated and support each other.

Arthur A. Thompson and A. J. Strickland detect the operation of these five principles on at least three levels of strategy—corporate, line-of-business or business unit, and functional area (see Fig. 7-2)—and describe each level as follows.[27]

Corporate-Level Strategy. Corporate strategy is formulated by top management to oversee the interests and operations of organizations that contain more than one line of business. The two major questions at this level are: What kind of businesses should the company be engaged in? And how should resources be allocated among those businesses? To answer these basic questions, corporate strategic planners, usually top management, must address a further series of questions, such as: What businesses should we get into, and which should we get out of? Which customers should the

---

[27]The discussions on levels of strategy and on corporate-level strategy are drawn largely from Arthur A. Thompson, Jr., and A. J. Strickland III, *Strategy Formulation and Implementation: Tasks of the General Manager,* 3rd ed. (Plano, Texas: Business Publications, 1986). Thompson and Strickland also note a fourth level of strategy—operating-level strategy, which regulates the day-to-day activities of departmental and supervisory managers. Also see Paul Miesing and Joseph Wolfe, "The Art and Science of Planning at the Business Unit Level," *Management Science* 31, no. 6 (June 1985):773–781.

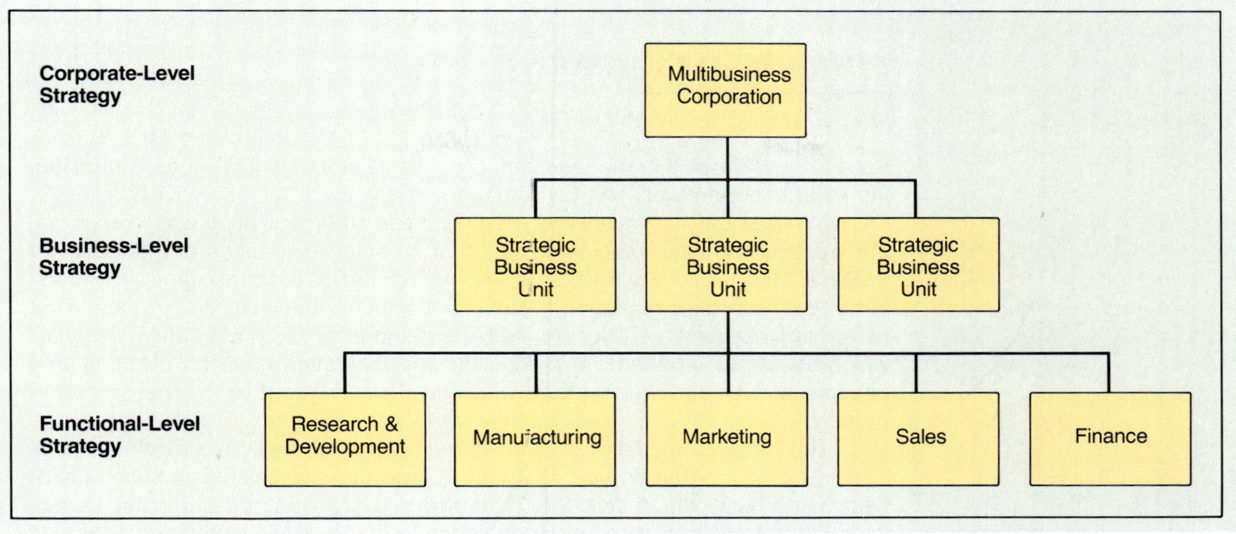

Source: Adapted from Robert H. Hayes and Steven C. Wheelwright, *Restoring Our Competitive Edge: Competing Through Manufacturing,* p. 28. Copyright 1984 by John Wiley & Sons, Inc.

FIGURE 7-2 THREE LEVELS OF STRATEGY

organization serve? What new technologies should it use? How do we manage the range of our activities, and how do we acquire and allocate resources for the activities we choose to pursue? Corporate level strategy addresses the actions the total organization is taking and should take, and attempts to determine the roles each business activity is playing and should play in the organization.

Business-Unit Strategy. Business-unit strategy is concerned with managing the interests and operations of a particular business. It deals with such questions as: How will the business compete within its market? What products/services should it offer? Which customers does it seek to serve? How will the various functions—manufacturing, marketing, finance, and so on—be managed in order to meet market goals? How will resources be distributed within the business? Business unit strategy attempts to determine what approach the business should take to its market and how the business should conduct itself, given its resources and the conditions of the market.

Many corporations have extensive interests in different businesses. Top managers of these companies have difficulty organizing their corporations' complex and varied activities. One approach to dealing with this problem is the creation of strategic business units. A *strategic business unit (SBU)* groups together all business activities within a multibusiness corporation that produce a particular type of product or service and treats them as a single business unit. The corporate level provides a set of guidelines for the SBUs, which then develop their own strategies on the business unit level. The corporate level then reviews the SBU plans and negotiates changes if necessary. Single-business corporations use business-unit-level strategy making unless they are contemplating expanding into other types of business. At that point, strategic planning on the corporate level becomes necessary.

Functional-Level Strategy. Functional-level strategy creates the framework for the management of functions—such as finance, research and development, and marketing—so that they conform to the business-unit-level strategy. For example, if the business unit strategy calls for the development of a new product, the R&D department will create plans on how it will develop that product.

ETHICS IN MANAGEMENT

WHAT DO YOU *STAND* FOR?

Peter Drucker and other management consultants and theorists used to argue that the most important question for managers to ask was: "What's your business?" The emphasis on clearly defining *what* business an organization was in captured the creative and intellectual imagination of an entire generation of management thinkers. The literature of the field is filled with stories about consultants who made fortunes by informing managers: "You aren't in the tin can business, you are in the packaging business." Theodore Leavitt's famous article, "Marketing Myopia," which sought to broaden the production and marketing horizons of managers, became a Bible for a generation who sought to define their businesses more broadly.

But there is another question at the heart of strategic management decisions—namely "What do you *stand* for?" This question calls for a statement of values and principles. It calls for an answer to critics who question company actions in terms of *why* a company did what it did. The critic who asks, "Why did AT&T agree to divest the Bell Operating Companies?" may want to know about the options available to the company when it decided to do so, but even more likely, the critic wants to know precisely what values and principles lay behind AT&T's decision. Drucker and others have now begun to call such a statement of values and principles "Enterprise Strategy" (or "E-Strategy" for short).

At least seven different "Enterprise Strategies" have been identified in the literature concerned with this issue:

1. Stockholder E-Strategy: The corporation should maximize the interests of stockholders.
2. Managerial Prerogative E-Strategy: The corporation should maximize the interests of management.
3. Restricted Stakeholder E-Strategy: The corporation should maximize the interests of a narrow set of stakeholders, such as customers, employees, and stockholders.
4. Unrestricted Stakeholder E-Strategy: The corporation should maximize the interest of all stakeholders.
5. Social Harmony E-Strategy: The corporation should maximize social harmony.
6. Rawlsian E-Strategy: The corporation should promote inequality among stakeholders only if inequality results in raising the level of the worst-off stakeholder.
7. Personal Projects E-Strategy: The corporation should maximize its ability to enable corporate members to carry out their personal projects.

Although these brief statements become immensely more complicated when a given organization attempts to put them into actual practice, this trend towards looking at the ethical foundations of strategy is likely to continue, especially given both the uncertain environment of today's organizations and the increasingly critical eye with which its decisions are being examined.

Source: R. Edward Freeman and Daniel J. Gilbert, Jr., *Corporate Strategy and the Search for Ethics* (Englewood Cliffs, N.J.: Prentice Hall, 1988).

As we move from corporate to business to functional-level strategies, the plans become more detailed and specific. Obviously, corporate-level strategy entails difficulties that must be met on the most fundamental level of managerial terms. In Exhibit 7-2, Steven C. Wheelwright describes two major approaches that managers can take in

EXHIBIT 7-2 WHEELWRIGHT'S TWO MAJOR APPROACHES TO DEVELOPING CORPORATE STRATEGY

1. *The values-based approach.* In this approach, the beliefs and convictions (values) of managers and workers about how the firm should conduct its business are the key to setting the organization's long-term direction. Values-based strategies develop gradually and incrementally and provide general guidance rather than a narrowly focused plan. Consensus by organizational members is important; often there is a "company way" of doing things that determines what strategies will be pursued. Major strategic decisions evolve over time and are confirmed by the entire organization. Firms such as S. C. Johnson and Hewlett Packard, as well as many Japanese companies, take this approach.
2. *The corporate portfolio approach.* In this approach, top management evaluates each of the corporation's various business units with respect to the marketplace and the corporation's internal makeup. When all business units have been evaluated, an appropriate strategic role is developed for each unit to improve the overall performance of the organization. The corporate portfolio approach is rational and analytical, is guided primarily by market opportunities, and tends to be initiated and controlled by top management only. Texas Instruments is one company that has used the corporate portfolio approach extensively.

Source: Steven C. Wheelwright, "Strategy, Management, and Strategic Planning Approaches," *Interfaces* 14, no. 1 (January–February 1984):19–33.

developing corporate strategy. While Wheelwright includes the *values-based approach,* we will focus on the corporate portfolio approach and BCG matrix and Michael Porter's competition-oriented approach.

Strategic versus Operational Planning

When organizations become complex and diversified—perhaps even multinational—*strategic planning* is the planning activity of an organization in which top management's role is most crucial because coordination of the organization's functional areas becomes crucial. Planning done at lower levels is called *operational planning,* as we saw in Chapter 5. To distinguish the two types of planning, remember that strategic

"These projected figures are a figment of our imagination. We hope you like them."
Drawing by Weber; © 1982 The New Yorker Magazine, Inc.

planning focuses on doing the *right things* (effectiveness), while operational planning focuses on *doing* those things right (efficiency).

Because strategic planning provides guidance and boundaries for operational management, the two types of planning overlap. Both are necessary. Effective management must have a strategy *and* must operate on the day-to-day level to achieve it. Remember, too, that operational strategy at every functional level should be considered in the formulation of overall organizational strategy.

FRAMEWORKS FOR STRATEGY

There are a number of ways to think about the concept of strategy, each useful in different circumstances. We are going to consider two main approaches that have developed over recent years.

The Portfolio Framework for Strategic Formulation: The BCG Matrix

portfolio framework An approach to corporate-level strategy advocated by the Boston Consulting Group.

TEACHING TIP

The BCG matrix, even with its limitations, is still a good vehicle to introduce students to the concept of portfolio strategy. Have the students try to think of examples for each of the cells.

The first is an approach to corporate-level strategy called the **portfolio framework** to corporate strategy. Its best known advocate is the Boston Consulting Group, which developed the now famous BCG Matrix.[28]

The BCG approach focuses on three aspects of a particular business unit: its sales, the growth of its market, and whether it absorbs or produces cash in its operations. The approach seeks to develop a balance among business units that use up cash and those that supply cash.

Figure 7-3 shows a four-square BCG matrix in which business units can be plotted according to the rate of growth of their market segment and their relative market share. Each cell in the matrix has its own significance. For instance, a business unit in the ''question mark'' category (a business with a relatively small market share in a rapidly growing market) can be an uncertain and expensive venture. The rapid growth of the market may force it to invest heavily simply to maintain its low share of the market, even though that low market share may yield low or even negative profits and cash flow. Increasing the question mark's market share relative to the market leader would require still larger investments. Yet the rapid growth of the market segment offers exciting opportunities if the proper business strategy—and the funds to implement it—can be found.

A business in the ''star'' category—high relative market share in a rapidly growing market—should be quite profitable. However, the need to keep investing in order to keep up with the market's rapid growth may consume more cash than is currently being earned. The *cash cow*—high relative market share in a slowly growing market—is both profitable and a source of excess cash from its operations: The slow growth of the market does not require large investments to maintain market position. Finally, the *dog*—low relative market share in a slowly growing or stagnant market—is seen as a moderate user or supplier of cash.

A ''success sequence'' in the BCG matrix involves investing excess cash from cash *cows* and the more successful *dogs* in selected question marks to enable them to become stars by increasing their relative market shares. When the rate of market

[28]See Allan Gerald, ''A Note on the Boston Consulting Group Concept of Competitive Analysis and Corporate Strategy,'' *Intercollegiate Case Clearing House* 9 (June 1976):175; Milton Leontiades, *Strategies for Diversification and Change* (Boston: Little, Brown, 1980), p. 63; Schendel and Hofer, eds., *Strategic Management: A New View of Business Policy and Planning* (Boston: Little, Brown, 1979), pp. 11–14.

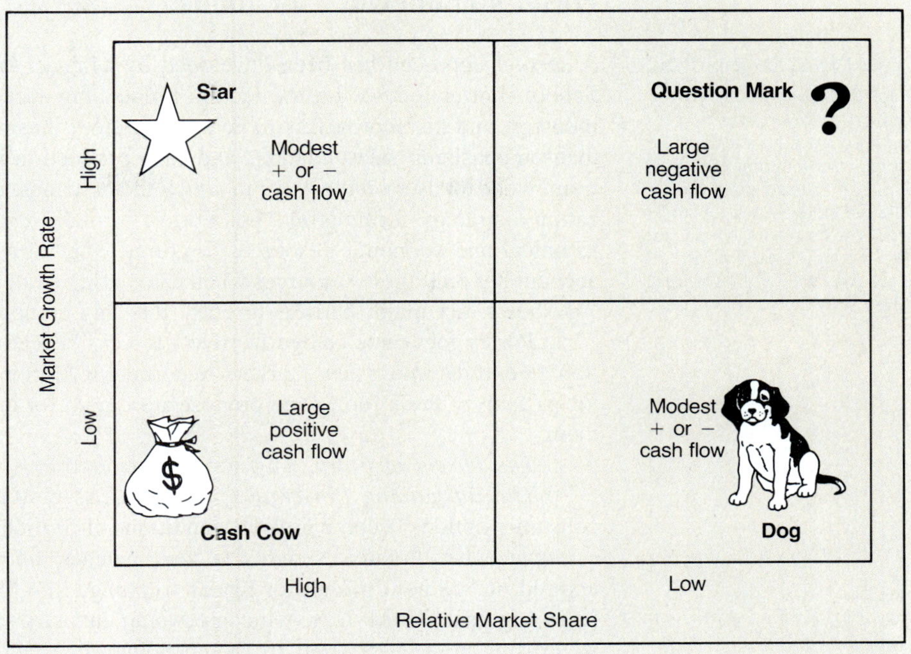

Source: Reprinted by permission of Arnoldo C. Hax and Nicolas S. Majluf, "The Use of the Growth-Share Matrix in Strategic Planning," *Interfaces* 13, no. 1 (February 1983). Copyright © 1983, The Institute of Management Sciences.

FIGURE 7-3 THE BCG MATRIX

growth slows, the stars will become cash cows, generating excess cash in their turn to invest in the next generation of promising question marks.

Critiques of the BCG Matrix. The BCG matrix approach has been the most widely used corporate portfolio approach in the 1970s and 1980s.[29] However, it has received its share of criticism[30]—not the least of which is associated with the clever and colorful names of the business units in the matrix's various cells. With the dividing line in Figure 7-3 between high and low market growth typically being chosen at 10 percent per year in physical units, and with only the single market share leader being classified as "high" in market share, about 60 to 70 percent of business units would be classified as "dogs." However misleading, that label encourages managers to look negatively on the prospects and opportunities that those businesses possess.[31] Similarly, the name and concept underlying "cash cow" encourage it to be "milked"—used to supply funds for other businesses—when it may actually be an excellent candidate for further investment. Obviously, skillful analysis can avoid dangers such as these, but like many potentially useful concepts, the BCG approach to simplicity and abstractness can encourage simplistic approaches to complex problems and situations.

---

[29] A survey of U.S. companies by Phillipe Haspeslagh (*Harvard Business Review* 60, no. 1 [January–February 1982]:58–73) concluded that by 1979, 36 percent of *Fortune* 1000 and 45 percent of *Fortune* 500 industrial companies had introduced this approach.

[30] For a further discussion of the BCG matrix, see Barry Hedley, "A Fundamental Approach to Strategy Development," *Long Range Planning* 9, no. 6 (December 1976):2–11. For a critique, see Thompson and Strickland, *Strategy Formulation and Implementation*.

[31] For example, "dogs" are frequently seen as providing only minimal cash flow, if any. However, recent research has concluded that the average dog has enough positive cash flow to finance one question mark. Donald C. Hambrick, Ian C. MacMillan, and Diane L. Day, "Strategic Attributes and Performance on the BCG Matrix—A PIMS-Based Analysis of Industrial Product Businesses." *Academy of Management Journal* 25, no. 3 (September 1982):510–531.

Porter's Framework for Industry Analysis

COORDINATED RESOURCE
Porter's books, *Competitive Strategy* and *Competitive Advantage,* are both excellent sources for additional information. If you have some outstanding students who would benefit from reading these, they can be a good learning experience. Available from The Free Press, New York, New York.

A second approach has been developed by Michael Porter of the Harvard Business School. Porter focuses on the factors influencing success in a particular business or industry, and his approach is more appropriate to business unit-level strategy. Rather than emphasizing sales, market, and cash production like the BCG Matrix, Porter's framework focuses on the ways in which the demands to *compete* influence an organization's strategy formulation. For Porter, virtually every organization possesses the technical and economic resources to compete in a given market and must take into account not only these resources when calculating strategy formulation, but, as Exhibit 7-3 shows, six major barriers to entry into any competitive market.[32]

Porter goes on to categorize five "forces," each of which threatens an organization's ventures into a new market. According to Porter, it is the corporate strategist's job to analyze these forces and propose a program for influencing or defending against them.

The Threat of Entry. This topic is covered extensively in Exhibit 7-3.

The Bargaining Power of Customers. As new companies enter the field and consumer options become greater, conditions of profitability can change radically. For example, when Polaroid's rights to basic patents and proprietary camera technology expired, it was not difficult for Kodak to plunge into the market. Conversely, when a large segment of the U.S.-wine producing industry stepped up diversification and advertising in the 1960s and 1970s, entry into the field became more difficult because consumers were being made aware of an already existing broad range in choice and price. Consumers also have power when products are particularly expensive or if advertising helps them to realize that a range of products is relatively undifferentiated.

The Bargaining Power of Suppliers. If an industry is not realistically able to raise prices to cover the cost of necessary goods and services (say, soft-drink producers facing competition from powdered mixes and concentrated beverages), then the power of the supplier of goods and services naturally increases. Among other things, the supplier is generally powerful if the industry is dominated by only a few competitors or if the purchasing industry is only of moderate importance to the supplier. By contrast, the buyer can exercise power if it purchases in large volume, if the low-profit performance of the product makes the buyer cost-conscious about its material or ingredients, or if the buyer can threaten to manufacture the seller's product itself (U.S. automakers, for example, have often used the threat of self-manufacture in their negotiations with suppliers).

The Threat of Substitute Products. If a product can be upgraded or differentiated in the interest of higher profitability, buyers can substitute products normally furnished by traditional suppliers. Strategic managers must pay special attention to products with an ongoing or current history of improved price performance because of substitute products. (The sugar industry has certainly learned its lesson in an era of American weight-consciousness and the availability of fructose corn syrup.)

Jockeying for Position. What Porter calls "advertising slugfests" have become a staple of everyday television programming, and when competitors are numerous and roughly equal in advertising energy (say, fast-food chains), competition can become intense, especially if competitors are fighting for market shares of slow-growth indus-

---

[32]Michael E. Porter, "How Competitive Forces Shape Strategy," *Harvard Business Review* 57, no. 2 (1979):137–145. See also Porter, *Competitive Strategy: Techniques for Analyzing Industries and Competitors* (New York: Free Press, 1980); Porter, *Competitive Advantage: Creating and Sustaining Superior Performance* (New York: Free Press, 1985). See also Gregory G. Dess and Peter S. Davis, "Porter's (1980) Generic Strategies and Performance: An Empirical Examination with American Data—Part I: Testing Porter," *Organization Studies,* No. 1 (1986):37–55; Dess and Davis, "Porter's (1980) Generic Strategies and Performance: An Empirical Examination with American Data—Part II: Performance Implications," *Organization Studies,* No. 3 (1986):255–261.

EXHIBIT 7-3 PORTER'S SIX BARRIERS TO MARKET ENTRY

1. *Economies of scale.* These economies deter entry by forcing the aspirant either to come in on a large scale or to accept a cost disadvantage. Scale economies in production, research, marketing, and service are probably the key barriers to entry in the mainframe computer industry, as Xerox and GE sadly discovered.
2. *Product differentiation.* Brand identification creates a barrier by forcing entrants to spend heavily to overcome customer loyalty. Advertising, customer service, being first in the industry, and product differences are among the factors fostering brand identification. For example, to create high fences around their businesses, brewers couple brand identification with economies of scale in production, distribution, and marketing.
3. *Capital requirements.* The need to invest large financial resources in order to compete creates a barrier to entry, particularly if the capital is required for unrecoverable expenditures in up-front advertising or R&D. Capital is necessary not only for fixed facilities but also for customer credit, inventories, and absorbing start-up losses. For example, an industry like mineral extraction is likely to entail immense initial capital requirements.
4. *Cost disadvantage independent of size.* Entrenched companies may have cost advantages not available to potential rivals, no matter what their size and attainable economies of scale. These advantages can stem from the effects of the learning curve (and of its first cousin, the experience curve), proprietary technology, access to the best raw material sources, assets purchased at preinflation prices, government subsidies, or favorable locations.
5. *Access to distribution channels.* The new boy on the block must, of course, secure distribution of his product or service. A new food product, for example, must displace others from the supermarket shelf via price breaks, promotions, intense selling efforts, or some other means
6. *Government policy.* The government can limit or even foreclose entry to industries with such controls as license requirements and limits on access to raw materials. Regulated industries like trucking, liquor retailing, and freight forwarding are noticeable examples; more subtle government restrictions operate in fields like ski-area development and coal mining.

Porter also advices that any organization desiring to compete in a new market analyze its incumbent competitors' likely reactions, especially if:

1. The incumbents possess substantial resources to fight back, including excess cash and unused borrowing power, productive capacity, or clout with distribution channels and customers.
2. The incumbents seem likely to cut prices because of a desire to keep market shares or because of industrywide excess capacity.
3. Industry growth is slow, affecting its ability to absorb the new arrival and probably causing the financial performance of all the parties involved to decline.

Source: Adapted from Michael E. Porter, "How Competitive Forces Shape Strategy." Reprinted by permission of the *Harvard Business Review* 57, no. 92 (March–April 1979).

tries, when competitive products are relatively undifferentiated (and thus subject to raiding), or when *exit barriers*—a variety of factors that may cause a company to persist in competing despite questionable profitability—prove costly or unflexible. Figure 7-4 represents a schematic view of Porter's concept of the forces influencing a company's competitive decisions.

What do Porter's hypotheses tell us about the larger issue of strategy formulation? For one thing, an analysis of these five factors can contribute to an evaluation of a company's strengths and weaknesses. More importantly, the strategist should be capable of providing his or her company with the best possible position in the competitive field—including its defenses against current or potential competitors.

This framework has implications for strategy formulation. Porter hypothesizes that the greater the forces in an industry, the lower the average returns. Therefore, in order to be successful in an industry with many new entrants, numerous substitute products, high bargaining power on the part of customers and suppliers, and a constant jockeying for position by competitors, a company must carefully craft a strategy that takes these forces into account.

Crown, Cork and Seal is a company that has grown from $200 million in the early 1960s to over $1 billion today by understanding the forces at work in the con-

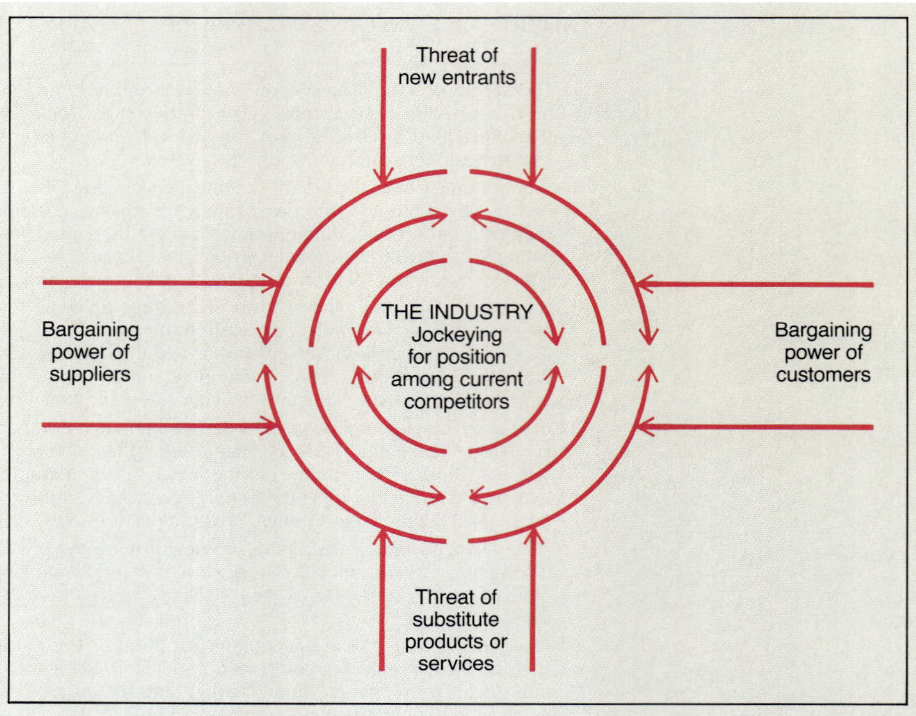

Source: Michael E. Porter, "How Competitive Forces Shape Strategy," *Harvard Business Review* 57, no. 2 (March–April 1979):141.

FIGURE 7-4 PORTER'S SUMMARY OF FORCES GOVERNING INDUSTRIAL COMPETITION

tainer industry. For the last 35 years, there have existed many large single customers for beverage and food cans and other can-industry products. These customers can affect prices and quality with a single order. In addition, the suppliers to can companies like Crown are large integrated steel and aluminum companies, and Crown has no effect on the price of its raw materials. New technologies, such as plastics, cardboard, and new metals, threatened Crown, while large customers began to integrate backwards into can-making activities. There was fierce competition among National Can, Continental Can, Crown, and others. It was only by understanding these forces and executing a focused strategy that Crown, Cork and Seal was able to survive and flourish, posting over 20 years of increased returns to shareholders.

Critique of Porter's Framework. Although Porter's framework has become widely used in the last ten years, it has been criticized from two perspectives. The first involves a famous case of the United States Football League in its struggle for survival against its entrenched rival, the National Football League. Critics charged that the NFL followed Porter's model, tried to erect entry barriers to the USFL, and in general endeavored to influence the five forces in a way that seemed to violate the anti-trust laws. Of course, this was a complex case involving unions, media, and other groups. However, it does seem that both legal and ethical analyses of the role of organizational power are missing from Porter's approach. A second criticism holds that Porter's approach ignores many of the external stakeholders that we discovered in Chapter 3.[33]

[33]R. E. Freeman, *Strategic Management: A Stakeholder Approach* (Boston: Pitman Publishing, 1984).

By focusing only on the five forces, it is possible to overlook many groups, such as consumer activists and environmentalists, that can have major effects on an organization. One possible response is that these groups are important only in so far as they can affect the competitive dynamics—the five forces—in an industry. But, from a managerial point of view, it is the stakeholder relationships which must be managed, not the five forces.

ILLUSTRATIVE CASE STUDY Continued

Planning for the Future at Federal Express

Like any other, Federal Express needs to understand its businesses in detail. ZapMail, for instance probably had a different competitive dynamic than did the overnight-parcel business. Surely, the freight business that Federal Express is trying to take away from United Parcel is different from both ZapMail and the overnight-delivery business. At the corporate level, Federal Express must understand how these businesses work together in an overall strategy of related business projects, and at the business-unit level, they must understand the critical factors for success in each different industry.

THE FORMAL STRATEGIC-PLANNING PROCESS: THE EXAMPLE OF BUSINESS-UNIT STRATEGY

strategic business-unit (SBU) planning Grouping business activities within a multibusiness corporation because they generate closely related products or services.

In this section, we will describe the formal approach to **strategic business-unit (SBU) planning** and explain how managers carry it out. Our description of the process (as shown in Fig. 7-5) combine the planning steps suggested by several writers.[34] Although generally applicable to any type of organization, our model best describes the planning process as it would be conducted in a medium-size, single-product-line business.

Figure 7-5 looks formidable, but it is surprisingly straightforward and easy to understand if we translate each step into a simple question or statement. Simply refer to Exhibit 7-4 for a list showing the various steps of Figure 7-5 as a series of basic questions or statements that could be used to develop a strategy for an organization (or to develop a personal career strategy).

EXHIBIT 7-4 THE NINE STEPS IN STRATEGIC BUSINESS-UNIT PLANNING

- What do we want? (Step 1)
- What are we now doing to get what we want? (Step 2)
- What's "out there" that needs doing? (Step 3)
- What are we able to do? (Step 4)
- What can we do that needs doing? (Step 5)
- Will continuing to do what we are now doing take us where we want to go? (Step 6)
- This is what we'll do to get what we want. (Step 7)
- Do it. (Step 8)
- Check frequently to make sure we're doing it right. (Step 9)

Now let's consider in more detail each of the nine steps specified in Exhibit 7-5:

[34]Figure 5-4 and our discussion are based mainly on Charles W. Hofer, *Strategy Formulation: Issues and Concepts*, 2nd ed. (St. Paul, Minn.: West Publishing, 1986); Dan E. Schendel and Charles W. Hofer, eds., *Strategic Management: A New View of Business Policy and Planning* (Boston: Little, Brown, 1978); Kenneth R. Andrews, *The Concept of Corporate Strategy* (Homewood, Ill.: Dow Jones-Irwin, 1971); and J. Kalman Cohen and Richard M. Cyert, "Strategy: Formulation, Implementation, and Monitoring," *Journal of Business* 46, no. 3 (July 1973):349–367. See also Max Richards, *Setting Strategic Goals and Objectives* (St. Paul, Minn.: West Publishing, 1986); and Glenn Boseman, Arvind Phatak, and Robert Schellenberger, *Strategic Management* (New York: Wiley, 1986).

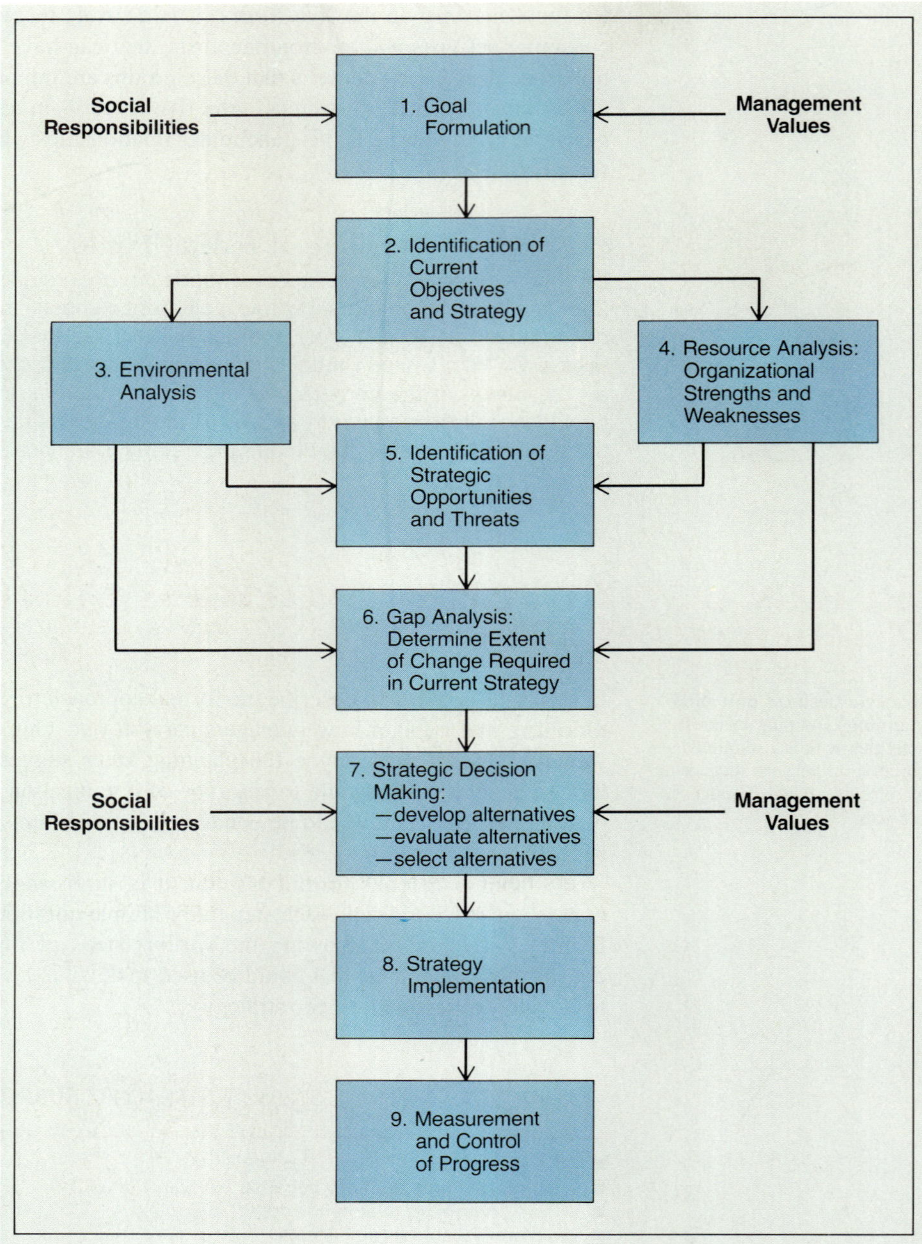

Source: This figure draws heavily upon the concepts of Andrews in *The Concept of Corporate Strategy* as interpreted by Hofer in *Strategy Formulation.* Hofer's model has been modified for this figure.

FIGURE 7-5 STEPS IN THE FORMULATION AND IMPLEMENTATION OF STRATEGY

Step 1: Goal Formulation

Setting the goals of the organization is the most essential step in the business-unit strategic planning process. Because the goals chosen will take up a large amount of the business's resources and govern many of its activities, goal formulation is a key responsibility of upper-level managers.

INTERNATIONAL MANAGEMENT

STRATEGIC PARTNERSHIPS ARE IN

Pick up *The Wall Street Journal* on any given day and you'll be sure to find at least one announcement of a partnership formed by companies from different countries. Strategic partnerships are the wave of the future, as companies try to cope with a complex and changing external environment. At one time, seemingly sound logic dictated that a company simply take the products developed for its home market and try to sell them around the world, possibly adapting them to local conditions whenever necessary. However, both products and markets have become more complex, and U.S. companies have responded by becoming more adept at negotiating "win-win" agreements with other companies all over the world.

For example, AT&T signed a joint-venture agreement with Philips, a Dutch telecommunications company, to bid together on the installation of large telephone systems in Europe, Asia, and the Middle East. AT&T had little international experience, but it did have an abundance of the high-quality products that Philips needed. AT&T also signed a joint-venture agreement with and bought a minority stake in Olivetti, an Italian computer company, both to supply it with personal computers for the U.S. market and to market some of AT&T's products in Europe. An Olivetti executive, Vittorio Cassoni, served as head of AT&T's computer subsidiary for several years.

Two newcomers to joint-venture partnerships are China and the USSR. Both socialist countries are attempting to move away from command economies through a series of economic reforms. One form that those changes has taken is that of joint partnerships. In China, with its over one billion potential consumers, Coca-Cola, Kentucky Fried Chicken, Bausch & Lomb, Johnson & Johnson, RJR Nabisco, Seagram, and Procter & Gamble have established joint partnerships with the Chinese. Occidental Petroleum, Combustion Engineering, PepsiCo, and others have entered into joint partnerships with USSR companies.

Obviously the course of true partnership does not always run so smoothly; such marriages are made not in heaven but in usually turbulent business environments. Many problems arise, ranging from differences in culture and language to differences in what each partner wants out of the partnership. Managing in these hybrid organizations also creates special difficulties, because business winds shift and the management of the partnership may quickly find itself in an "us" versus "them" climate. No contract, joint-venture, or partnership agreement can spell out all of the areas of conflict, whether potential or already evident, and at present, management theorists understand very little about how and why these new global partnerships really do or do not work.

As we defined goal formulation at the beginning of this chapter, it includes reviewing and understanding the organization's purpose, defining its mission, and establishing the objectives that translate the mission into concrete terms. The key step in goal formulation is defining the mission of the organization. Identifying the organization's mission can take managers a long way toward selecting objectives. For example, AT&T's visionary mission some 80 years ago was described by a former chairman in this way: "The dream of good, cheap, fast, worldwide telephone service . . . is not a speculation. It is a perfectly clear statement that you're going to do something."[35] Faced with its recent divestiture, AT&T has since altered its mission; the company now

[35]Quoted in Charles H. Granger, "The Hierarchy of Objectives," *Harvard Business Review* 42, no. 3 (May–June 1964):63–74.

aims to be "a major factor in the worldwide movement and management of information."[36] Most observers would probably agree that this mission statement does not have the clarity and potential for excitement that the earlier one possessed. Before deciding what their objectives are going to be, managers must know the purpose and mission of their organization.[37] This includes knowing which businesses to stay out of as well as which to pursue.

Figure 7-5 indicates that the values held by managers will affect the kinds of goals they select. As we noted in Chapter 3, these values may be social or ethical, or they may involve practical matters, such as the size that managers would like their organization to be, the kind of product or service they would like to produce, or simply the way they prefer to operate. Peters and Waterman, Pascale and Athos, and other researchers have concluded that many excellently managed companies are "value-driven"; that is, organizational values actually guide many managers' actions. An early leader of a value-driven organization, often the founder, is usually seen as playing a key role in creating these values.[38] The Walt Disney Company is an excellent example of this phenomenon.

HERE'S AN EXAMPLE

Walt Disney Company had to undergo some radical changes in order to transform itself from a prime candidate for takeover to the hottest all-around entertainment maker in America. Walt Disney's successors were terrified of tampering with a previously winning formula and tended to contemplate all new ideas with "What would Walt have done?" comments. Roy Disney (son of one of the co-founders of Disney), one of the largest individual shareholders of the company, knew that Disney could not function creatively and profitably without new leadership. Michael Eisner and Frank Wells were brought in as chairman and president, respectively, and have pulled off one of the most dazzling corporate turnarounds since Iacocca and Chrysler. (*Time*, 4/25/88, pp. 66–76)

Step 2: Identification of Current Objectives and Strategy

Once the organization's mission has been defined and translated into concrete objectives, managers are ready for the next stage in the process. Steps 2 through 6 provide the basis for determining what must be done differently to achieve those objectives. The first step in this series is to identify the organization's existing objectives and strategy. Sometimes, the newly defined mission and objectives will be quite similar to the mission and objectives on which the existing strategy is based. Sometimes, however, the goal formulation process yields a substantial change in mission and objectives; this is especially true if the organization has been failing to meet key objectives.[39]

The existing objectives and strategy may be well defined and clearly communicated throughout the organization. This optimal situation usually follows earlier formal strategic planning or informal but explicit strategy making by a strong organizational leader. All too often, however, Step 2 uncovers no explicit strategy; managers then face the task of inferring from its day-to-day actions what the organization's top leadership is attempting to accomplish. Managers in small businesses and not-for-profit organizations often face this situation because such organizations have rarely developed formal strategic plans.

Many managers determine their organization's current strategy by asking themselves such questions as: What is our business and what should it be? Who are our customers and who should they be? Where are we heading? What major competitive advantages do we enjoy? In what areas of competence do we excel?

---

[36]Jeremy Main, "Waking Up AT&T: There's Life After Culture Shock," *Fortune*, December 24, 1984, pp. 66–74.

[37]Our definition of organizational purpose (see p. 111) suggests that managers must understand the relationship of their organization to society. This perspective, while essentially accurate, does not emphasize the active debate concerning the proper societal roles (purposes) of business, government, and other types of organizations, and it minimizes both the ambiguity of their roles and the role changes that continue to take place today.

[38]Peters and Waterman, *In Search of Excellence;* and Richard Tanner Pascale and Anthony G. Athos, *The Art of Japanese Management: Applications for American Executives* (New York: Simon & Schuster, 1981).

[39]Our model of the formal strategic planning process starts with the goal formulation process, but other approaches are also used. For example, the process can start by focusing on current strategies and organizational strengths. The preexisting objectives are accepted with little or no further scrutiny. See Steven C. Wheelwright, "Strategic Planning in the Small Business," *Business Horizons* 14, no. 4 (August 1971):51–58; and Michael B. McCaskey, "A Contingency Approach to Planning: Planning with Goals and Planning without Goals," *Academy of Management Journal* 17, no. 2 (June 1974):281–291. Also see Peter Grinyer, Shawki Al-Bazzaz, and Masoud Yasai-Ardekani, "Towards a Contingency Theory of Corporate Planning," *Strategic Management Journal* 7 (1986):3–28.

THOUGHT-PROVOKER

What major issues face our school in the next decade? How are we going to prepare for these changes?

Step 3: Environmental Analysis

Knowledge of the organization's goals and existing strategy provide a framework for defining which aspects of the environment will have the greatest influence on the organization's ability to achieve its objectives. The purpose of environmental analysis is to identify the ways in which changes in an organization's economic, technological, sociocultural, and political/legal environment can indirectly influence the organization and the ways competitors, suppliers, customers, government agencies, and others can directly influence it (see Chapter 3).[40] For example, a manufacturer of steel shelving might find the usual market for its product reduced during a recession. Careful analysis, however, would show that while industrial users may purchase less shelving, individual consumers are likely to buy more, since steel shelving costs less than wood shelving. In response, the company might make its produce line more attractive for home use—and thus beat the recession.

It is important in this planning step to develop a list solely of those factors judged to be truly crucial. No list is likely to identify all potentially relevant factors; yet a serious effort to do so can aid in planning. Useful sources of information include customers and suppliers, trade publications and exhibitions, and technical meetings.

Forecasting and management science methods for analyzing the environment are discussed in Chapter 5. As James M. Utterback has noted, one key to successful environmental analysis for strategy formulation is the early detection of changes. Late identification of changes in the environment often increases an organization's vulnerability to competitors.[41] Although forecasts rarely predict with complete accuracy, environmental analysis helps the organization adjust to changes in the indirect-action environment and anticipate and influence activity in the direct-action environment.

Strategic anticipation of the reactions of stakeholders to the implementation of a strategy is becoming increasingly important. Strategic anticipation can be rather subtle. For example, Ian C. MacMillan has reported that one firm delayed launching a new product until the marketing manager of its main competitor had departed for an extended business trip and vacation. The company established a dominant position in the market while its competitor was paralyzed as the absent manager's stand-in slowly grappled with this new threat and eventually acted too late.[42] This illustrates the value of systematically gathering information on competitors—a technique that, according to a recent study, is too little used in American business.[43]

Step 4: Resource Analysis

The organization's goals and existing strategy also provide a framework for analyzing its resources. This analysis is necessary to identify the organization's competitive advantages and disadvantages. Competitive advantages and disadvantages are the strengths and weaknesses of the organization relative to its present and likely future competitors.

The question is not "What do we do well or poorly?" but rather, "What are we doing better or worse than anyone else?" If all the universities in an area provide excellent teaching, then University X does not gain a competitive advantage in attract-

---

[40]Hofer, *Strategy Formulation*.

[41]James M. Utterback, "Environmental Analysis and Forecasting," in Schendel and Hofer, eds., *Strategic Management*, p. 135. See also Utterback's article, pp. 134–144, and Harold E. Klein's commentary on it, pp. 144–151, for discussions on the use of environmental analysis in strategy formulation.

[42]Ian C. MacMillan, "Commentary," in Schendel and Hofer, eds., *Strategic Management*, p. 171.

[43]See William L. Sammon, Mark A. Kurland, and Robert Spitalnic, *Business Competitor Intelligence* (New York: Wiley, 1984); and Liam Fahey and V. K. Narayanah, *Environmental Analysis* (St. Paul, Minn.: West Publishing, 1986).

ing students because its faculty performed well in the classroom. By contrast, if University X offers only good, but not excellent, teaching while the other universities do a poor job, then it would have a competitive advantage in this dimension. Furthermore, relative strength also depends on what an organization is trying to do. A strong sales force will be of little or no use to a firm that plans to shift its operations to direct-mail selling.

As Exhibit 7-5 shows, all of these considerations are essentially matters of analyzing and, where possible, forecasting an organization's resources. Note that this author, Charles Hofer, combines our Steps 2 and 3, analysis of existing strategy and environment into a single step.

EXHIBIT 7-5 HOFER'S FOUR STEPS FOR ANALYZING RESOURCES

1. Develop a profile of the organization's principal resources and skills in three broad areas: financial; physical, organizational, and human; and technological.
2. Determine the key success requirement of the product/market segments in which the organization competes or might compete.
3. Compare the resource profile to the key success requirements to determine the major strengths on which an effective strategy can be based and the major weaknesses to be overcome.
4. Compare the organization's strengths and weaknesses with those of its major competitors to identify which of its resources and skills are sufficient to yield competitive advantages in the marketplace.*

*Strengths and weaknesses may also be related to the structure of organizations. See Ian C. MacMillan and Patricia E. Jones, "Designing Organizations to Compete, *Journal of Business Strategy* 4, no. 4 (Spring 1984):11–26.

Source: Charles W. Hofer, *Strategy Formulation: Issues and Concepts,* 2nd ed. (St. Paul, Minn.: West Publishing, 1986).

FOR DISCUSSION

How often do you think a SWOT (strengths, weaknesses, opportunities, threats) analysis should be done? Why?

Step 5: Identification of Strategic Opportunities and Threats

Identifying strategy, analyzing the environment, and analyzing the organization's resources (Steps 2, 3, and 4) come together in the fifth step: determining the opportunities available to the organization and the threats it faces. Opportunities and threats may arise from many factors: Land purchased for farming activities by a large agribusiness corporation may become so valuable that the company considers forming or acquiring a housing development division. In this instance, changed market conditions present a new opportunity.

In the 1960s, organizations owing their success to expertise in designing and manufacturing complex electromechanical products, such as cash registers, found that advances in electronic technology rapidly made both their skills and their plants and equipment obsolete. Here, technological changes were a clear threat. But firms that could move ahead rapidly with the new technology had the opportunity to do so. Thus, the same environment that posed a threat to some organizations offered opportunities to others.

Step 6: Determination of Extent of Required Strategic Change

performance gaps The difference between the objectives established in the goal formation process and the results likely to be achieved if the existing strategy is continued.

After resources and the environment have been analyzed, the results of the existing strategy can be forecast. The longer that strategy has been in place and the more stable the environment, the easier it will be to make this prediction. Then managers can decide whether or not to modify that strategy or its implementation. This decisions should be based on whether **performance gaps** can be identified. A performance gap is the difference between the objectives established in the goal formulation process and the results likely to be achieved if the existing strategy is continued. Performance gaps can result from choosing more difficult objectives or from the failure of past performance to meet expectations because of effective responses by competitors, changes in the environment, loss of resources—a failure by the firm to properly implement the strategy—or because the strategy itself had not been well thought out.

HERE'S AN EXAMPLE

Some directors at CBS, Inc. are unhappy with what's happening to their company. Says one disgruntled director, "We're not happy. Tisch [Laurence C. Tisch, CEO of CBS] has dismantled the company in a piecemeal fashion, and it's too late to stop him. We've asked for a plan or a strategy. But it's not in his nature to lay out a strategy." (*Business Week*, 7/25/88, p. 52)

Step 7: Strategic Decision Making

If a change in strategy appears necessary to close the performance gap, the next step involves identifying, evaluating, and selecting alternative strategic approaches. The process of decision making is discussed in detail in chapter 6; our discussion here highlights those aspects that concern strategic alternatives.

Identification of Strategic Alternatives. In a given instance, a variety of alternatives for closing the performance gap probably exist. New markets may be entered; key products may be redesigned to enhance quality or reduce cost; new investments may be undertaken or old ones terminated.

If only a minor change in the existing strategy is needed, the logical alternatives may be few. If, for example, a lag in new-product introduction has been identified as a major cause of dwindling sales, a program to improve the performance of the research and development department may be the obvious choice. But if a significant change in the strategic approach is required, more alternatives must be identified and greater care will be needed later to avoid attempting to blend incompatible options into a new strategic approach.

Evaluation of Strategic Alternatives. As Exhibit 7-6 indicates, Richard P. Rumelt has described four criteria for evaluating strategic alternatives.

EXHIBIT 7-6 RUMELT'S FOUR CRITERIA FOR EVALUATING STRATEGIC CRITERIA

1. The strategy and its component parts should have consistent goals, objectives, and policies.
2. It should focus resources and efforts on the critical issues identified in the strategy formulation process and separate them from unimportant issues.
3. It should deal with subproblems capable of solution, given the organization's resources and skills. [For example, he has noted that "A strategy for competing in the electric typewriter market . . . by creating a radically cheap yet durable machine defines a subproblem (inventing the machine) that is probably no more amenable to attack than the original strategic problem."]
4. Finally, the strategy should be capable of producing the intended results—that is, it should show promise of actually working.

Source: Richard P. Rumelt, "Evaluation of Strategy," in Schendel and Hofer, eds., *Strategic Management: A New View of Business Policy and Planning.*

In addition, in evaluating alternatives it is also important to focus on a particular product or service and on those competitors who are direct rivals in offering them. A strategy that does not create or exploit a particular advantage of the organization over its rivals should be rejected.

Selection of Strategic Alternatives. In choosing among the available possibilities, managers should select the alternatives that are best suited to the organization's capabilities. Successful strategic plans utilize the existing strengths of the organization. New capabilities can be acquired only through investment in human resources and/or equipment and cannot be built up quickly. Therefore, it is seldom advisable to embark on a strategic plan requiring resources or skills that are weak or nonexistent. Instead, recognized strengths should be fully exploited.

HERE'S AN EXAMPLE

Anheuser-Busch Company's dependence on Budweiser beer (Bud and Bud Light account for more than 75 percent of brewery volume and 56 percent of its sales) will need to be reduced sooner or later. After a major scandal over a distributor kickback scheme, in which several top officials were fired or resigned, the company seems energized. Admits August A. Busch III, A-B's chairman, the shakeup might have its benefits. "You learn from your mistakes, not your successes," he says. (*Business Week*, 5/2/88, p. 121)

Step 8: Strategy Implementation

Once the strategy has been determined, it must be incorporated into the daily operations of the organization. Even the most sophisticated and creative strategy will not benefit the organization unless it is carried out. Whether or not the strategy is recorded in a formal and detailed strategic plan, it must be translated into the appropriate tactical plans, programs, and budgets.

Let us assume our strategic plan calls for the introduction of a new line of products in five years. The personnel department might have to develop a short-term hiring program. The marketing department might have to make up a short-term budget for the first year of the plan, perhaps to cover preliminary market testing for new product concepts. The research and development department might set forth preliminary plans for the entire period of the new strategy. The production department may work up preliminary cost estimates during the early stage of the strategic plan, becoming more actively involved as the new products achieve final form in the research and development department.

Step 9: Measurement and Control of Progress

As implementation proceeds, manager must check progress against the strategic plan at periodic or critical stages to assess whether the organization is moving toward its strategic objectives. Company controllers often play an important role in designing systems of *strategic control* (as this process is generally known). The two main questions in strategic control are: (1) Is the strategy being implemented as planned? and (2) Is the strategy achieving the intended results?[44]

ILLUSTRATIVE CASE STUDY Wrap-Up

Planning for the Future at Federal Express

Federal Express is a prime example of how a company can have a vision—namely the business of getting important information from one place to another as fast as possible. Realizing this vision meant taking on the Postal Service and United Parcel Service—entrenched organizations with well-established ways of doing business. Federal Express's success, as well as such failures as ZapMail, is illustrative of the kind of strategic thinking that managers must practice if organizations are to survive in today's rapidly changing environment. ■

■ SUMMARY

Strategic planning has become increasingly important to managers in recent years. Defining fundamental goals and objectives in specific terms, and determining the means to achieve them, provides a basic, long-range framework into which other forms of planning can fit. Strategic planning can strongly influence the survival and growth of an organization, especially in a volatile environment.

---

[44] See David A. Aaker, "How to Select a Business Strategy," *California Management Review* 26, no. 3 (Spring 1984):167–175. Aaker has suggested that the accuracy of a strategy's evaluation can be increased by including factors beyond sales and profit forecasts, such as judgments of its flexibility, feasibility, consistency with the firm's mission, and responsiveness to the environment.

The concept of strategy has evolved significantly over the years, especially because of the increasing complexity of the environment and the rapid growth in organizational size. Policy-formulation stressed rules of boundaries governing a functional area's activities; later strategy paradigms emphasized courses of action and the *process* of seeking out key ideas; objectives must be considered as well as policy and strategy.

Strategy is defined at three levels: corporate, business-unit, and functional-area. On the corporate level, managers are concerned with developing a strategy for their organization's varied business interests. On the business-unit level, managers deal with the particular concerns of one line of business. On the functional level, managers administer corporate and business-level strategies in functional areas—manufacturing, marketing, and so on. Some organizations use corporate portfolio management. The BCG Matrix is one popular corporate portfolio model. Another framework, developed by Michael Porter, emphasizes the importance of competitive factors on business unit–level strategy.

To devise an appropriate strategy, managers must determine their organization's desired outcomes. What should the business of the organization be? Who are its customers, and who should they be? Where is the organization heading? By answering such fundamental questions, managers can determine the true capabilities of their organizations and devise the most effective strategies to utilize these capabilities.

In the formal strategic planning process, managers (1) formulate organizational goals; (2) assess their organization's current objectives and strategy; (3) analyze the environment; (4) analyze the organization's resources; (5) identify strategic opportunities and threats; (6) determine the extent of change required in the current strategy; (7) identify, evaluate, and select the best strategic alternatives; (8) implement the strategy; and (9) measure and control the process of implementation.

These basic steps in the formal planning approach are handled differently in various types of organizations. Large organizations are likely to use a specialized planning staff to formulate objectives and strategies and to coordinate the strategic planning process.

REVIEW QUESTIONS

1. Why do you think it would be important for you as a junior manager to understand strategic planning?
2. Why has strategic planning become even more important to managers and their organizations?
3. What are the two most important factors in the evolution of contemporary management theory?
4. How is strategic planning different from operational planning?
5. What are the key differences between the policy-formulation and strategy frameworks?
6. What are the three levels of strategy? How do they differ from one another? How do they complement one another?
7. Why might managers perform corporate portfolio analysis? How is this done? According to Porter, what are the five "forces" influencing an organization's venture into a new market?
8. What are the nine steps in the formal planning approach?

CASE STUDY Planning for Diversified Activities in a Changing Environment

John Sullivan is CEO of Diversified Conglomerate Incorporated (DCI), a leader in air compressors and basketball backboards, both low-growth industries, and coffee imports, a high-growth industry. In addition, DCI has a substantial presence in baby beds and inner-spring mattresses and has recently started ventures in biotechnology and retailing gourmet coffee; other ventures are planned. Also, there are 15 other businesses in which DCI engages to varying degrees. In short, DCI is a company with many diverse and unrelated businesses and with many diverse people with different projects.

John Sullivan has a problem that is solely a function of DCI's diversification. He needs to be able to allocate resources across a wide range of businesses that do not have much in common. He must compare baby beds with air compressors, and he needs a *"language"* of some kind to make such comparisons.

George Russell is the division manager at DCI responsible for baby beds. He finds the business in a difficult position. After years of flat sales, the market for baby beds has been growing for several years because baby-boom women are now starting families. However, an increasing share of DCI baby beds is going to K-Mart, Wal-Mart, and Sears—the large retailers. DCI manufactures the wooden parts of the beds and buys the brackets and other metal parts. Recently, one source of supply has gone out of business, leaving only one U.S. firm and one Taiwanese firm capable of supplying the quantity of parts that DCI needs. There are also several new companies in the industry that have more features than DCI's best bed and that command premium prices, and moreover, Russell suspects that the Taiwanese supplier is set to enter the U.S. market with two products that would compete directly with his low-end beds. To ice the cake, a recent study questioned the use of baby beds or cribs altogether, touting a new idea—the infant "sleep carousel" as producing a happier baby.

Both John Sullivan and George Russell have strategic problems that are of the utmost importance to DCI.

Source: Adapted from R. Edward Freeman and Daniel R. Gilbert, Jr., *Corporate Strategy and the Search for Ethics* (Englewood Cliffs, N.J.: Prentice Hall, 1988).

Case Questions

1. Use the BCG approach to help John Sullivan think about the strategy for DCI. Are there obvious products that are stars, cash cows, question marks, and dogs?
2. How would Porter's model analyse George Russell's situation?
3. To what extent can methods of strategic planning give the managers at DCI a method to talk to each other about their common problems? What are some disadvantages? ■

Jean Arp, Collage *According to the Laws of Chance*. (1916–1917). Torn and pasted paper, 19⅛ x 13⅝. Collection, The Museum of Modern Art, New York. Purchase.

8

STRATEGY IMPLEMENTATION

Upon completing this chapter you should be able to:

1. Discuss the relationship between organizational structure and strategy, and identify the three stages in the growth of an organization's structure.
2. Explain how functional strategies and annual objectives operationalize an organization's strategy.
3. Describe management by objectives (MBO) programs, including their role in the process of goal setting.
4. Explain how incentive plans and reward systems can motivate members of an organization to implement its strategy.
5. Describe the roles of the chief executive officer (CEO) and key managers in executing strategy.
6. Discuss the relationship between organizational culture and strategy.
7. Describe some barriers to effective strategy implementation and explain how they can be reduced or eliminated.

Chapter Outline

Introduction
Strategy Implementation
Strategy and Structure
Operationalizing Strategy
Institutionalizing Strategy
Barriers to Effective Strategy Implementation

ILLUSTRATIVE CASE STUDY Introduction

Maintaining the Competitive Edge at Merck & Co.

Primarily because drug patents last only a few years, a pharmaceutical company lives and dies by new drug discoveries. Once a patent expires, other companies can duplicate another company's formula, and consumers who want to save money purchase these duplications. For the consumer, this is a boon, but for the company that spent years to develop the original formula, it signals an end of the profit stream from that drug.

New drugs are incredibly expensive to develop. First, it often takes years of basic research before the idea for a drug is discovered. Then more years of research follow, as the idea is eventually turned into a prototype drug. Then animal studies are conducted. Nine out of ten prototypes fail during this stage because they cause too many side effects or are not as effective as anticipated. If the animal studies go well, then clinical, human, studies are initiated. After all these studies have been conducted, FDA approval is sought—a process that alone often takes one to two years. All told, it is often 10 years from the time an idea for a new drug was generated until it reaches the market.

This fact of life for the pharmaceutical company translates into an aggressive program for recruiting, and retaining the best scientists possible. Merck, a leading pharmaceutical company headquartered in Rahway, New Jersey, has long been successful at this process, and Merck has maintained its edge in large part because of its unwillingness to take anything for granted. In fact, Chairman Roy Vagelos is always searching for new ways to move forward, to improve the company primarily by improving the productivity of the people who comprised it.

One of his principal concerns is the atmosphere in which his scientists work and the policies that support and encourage them. What do the scientists want and need? What can he give them that will keep them working for Merck rather than for a competitor? What do they need to be as productive as possible? Merck already has a number of human resource policies that separate it from many of its competitors: Merck scientists are paid very well, and their contribution to the company, individually and as a group, are regularly recognized; liberal benefits include child care and continued education. So the usual answer of "more money" does not seem to apply when personnel problems threaten to arise.

The other principal concern Vagelos must ponder is the time frame under which new drugs are developed. Is there a way to shorten the procedure? Obviously, scientists cannot be forced to invent on a schedule. But can other parts of the process be speeded up? Can some action or policy of the company enable the scientist to work more quickly—to take ideas and turn them into realities faster?

Currently Merck's scientists are organized in several ways. The basic groups are organized around therapeutic classifications. For example, there might be a variety of scientific disciplines represented in a lab working on antibiotics. Particularly promising drug innovations are worked on by project teams—smaller subsets of the therapeutic group that work solely with the new drug. As a drug gets closer to becoming a possible market introduction, departments responsible for overseeing the testing, the approval process, and marketing become involved. The project team remains responsible for keeping the process organized and moving forward, keeping everyone involved enthusiastic about the progress being made.

The process works well, but Merck still faces many of the same difficulties as its competitors. How can Vagelos put all of these pieces together to sustain Merck's success and improve the implementation of developmental strategy?

Sources: John A. Byrne, "The Miracle Company," *Business Week,* October 19, 1987; Gordon Bock, "Merck's Medicine Man," *Time,* February 22, 1988, pp. 44–45.

QUOTATION FROM A MANAGER

"The best strategy isn't worth anything if it isn't implemented"—John H. Costello, Senior Vice-President, Pepsi-Cola USA. (Brochure on Management Books, Lexington Books, 1988)

No matter how well a plan is designed, it cannot succeed unless its ideas are *implemented*—are put into action. This chapter explains the major concepts and tools of the recently emerging subfield of "strategy implementation." Although the field is so new that there is as yet no consensus about its dimensions, scholars and managers alike agree on some central ideas that have emerged from its study.

First, successful strategy implementation depends in part on the organization's structure. We will examine *structure* in more detail in Chapter 9, but here we will review the classic work of Alfred Chandler and his followers in tracing the relationship between *strategy* and structure.

Second, before it can be implemented, a strategy must be *operationalized*—processed or systematized into specific actions and objectives that lower-level managers and employees can actually execute. Taken together, these objectives must be capable of achieving the desired organizational goal. We shall explain one commonly used method to do just this—namely, *management by objectives;* we shall also examine the role of reward systems.

Finally, strategy must be *institutionalized* in order to succeed: That is, it must become a routine part of the day-to-day life of the organization, pervading its culture, systems, and values. We will examine the Seven-S framework developed by McKinsey & Company as a way of thinking about institutionalization.

We end the chapter with an analysis of what can go wrong in the strategy process, describing some of the barriers to and pitfalls in successful strategic management.

STRATEGY IMPLEMENTATION

Lawrence Hrebeniak and William Joyce have described four different approaches to strategy implementation, each depending on the size of the problem facing an organization and on the time available to solve it. (See Fig. 8-1.)[1] Not surprisingly, the larger and more immediate the problem, the more difficult the manager's task.

Evolutionary interventions take place when an organization's problems are small and there is relatively little pressure to solve them. These interventions consist of managers' routine decisions, often concerning personnel, made in direct response to problems or in an attempt to improve a unit's performance. They do not involve a major shift in organizational strategy or basic operating procedures and are not usually perceived as strategic changes. The process may be inefficient, but it is generally tolerated since it involves only small changes.

HERE'S AN EXAMPLE

After losing a key defense contract, Grumman Corporation's future as a major manufacturer of military aircraft is uncertain. President John O'Brien will need " . . . the vision of a master strategist to maneuver Grumman through a time when, for defense companies, the competition is keener and the risks much higher." (*Business Week*, 2/1/88, pp. 54–55)

Minor problems that must be solved immediately call for *managerial interventions*. Since the situation is basically stable, the manager can afford to focus on the trouble spot and ignore the effects of decisions on other parts of the organization. These secondary effects are small and are thus absorbed by the organization without difficulty.

In contrast, serious problems demand planned interventions in more than one area of the organization: Managers must recognize and preserve the interrelationships among the different areas of the organization even during the course of making

[1]Lawrence G. Hrebeniak and William F. Joyce, *Implementing Strategy* (New York: Macmillan, 1984), pp. 19–22.

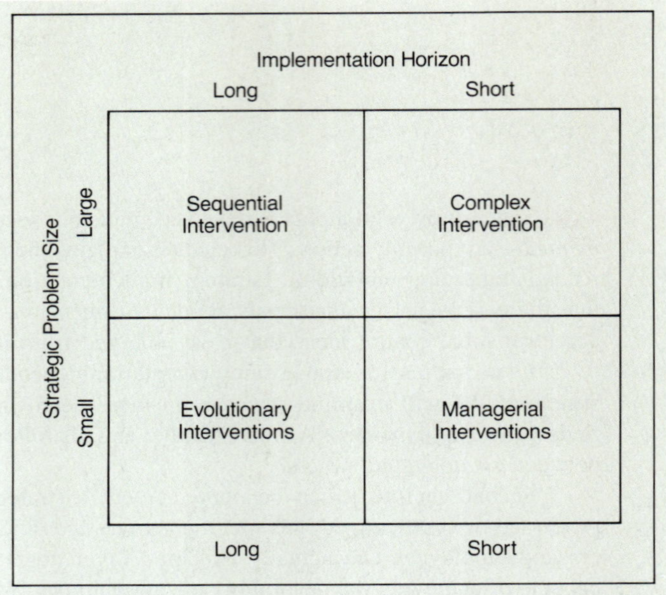

Source: Reprinted with permission of Macmillan Publishing Company from *Implementing Strategy* by Lawrence G. Hrebeniak and William F. Joyce. Copyright © 1984 by Macmillan Publishing Company, a Division of Macmillan, Inc.

FIGURE 8-1 A TYPOLOGY OF STRATEGY IMPLEMENTATIONS

changes. Given enough time, a manager can subdivide the problem and address each part in turn in a process called *sequential intervention*. Over a period of years, he or she can methodically carry out an entire series of changes.

When time is short, however, managers are forced to make those changes simultaneously and according to a process called *complex intervention*. Negotiating and coordinating this web of interdependent decisions generally demands a task force or some other mechanism to bring all interested parties together. A drastic shift in the environment most commonly calls for complex intervention (see Chapters 3 and 7). Moreover, as the environment grows more turbulent, complex interventions may be needed more frequently.[2] In their new books, Tom Peters' *Thriving on Chaos: Handbook for Management Revolution* and Robert H. Waterman's *The Renewal Factor: How the Best Companies Get and Keep the Competitive Edge,* both authors stress the turbulence of the enviromnent and the imperative that corporations adapt to the changing times or disappear from the scene. Both argue that change can effectively destroy an organization if it is not anticipated.[3]

QUOTATION FROM A MANAGER

''The best thing for me to do is to decide what's right for the business, get it approved, and get it implemented''—John M. Stafford, CEO, Pillsbury Company. (*Business Week,* 1/25/88, p. 58)

STRATEGY AND STRUCTURE

Successful implementation depends in part on how the organization's activities are divided, organized, and coordinated. In short, it depends on the structure of the organization. Not surprisingly, the chances that an organization's strategy will succeed are

[2]See L. J. Bourgeois, ''Strategic Goals, Perceived Uncertainty, and Economic Performance in Volatile Environments,'' *Academy of Management Journal,* September 1985, pp. 548–573.

[3]Tom Peters, *Thriving on Chaos: Handbook for a Management Revolution* (New York: Alfred A. Knopf, 1988); Robert H. Waterman, *The Renewal Factor: How the Best Get and Keep the Competitive Edge* (New York: Bantam Books, 1987.)

far greater when its structure matches its strategy. By the same token, as its basic strategy changes over time, so must its structure.[4]

Chandler's Thesis

In his ground-breaking study of the history of large corporations, Alfred Chandler examined the growth and development of 70 of the largest businesses in the United States, including Du Pont; General Motors; Sears, Roebuck; and Standard Oil.[5] He observed a common pattern in their development. Although the organizations changed their growth strategies to suit technological, economic, and demographic changes, new strategies created administrative problems and economic inefficiencies. Structural changes were needed to solve those problems and to maximize the organization's economic performance. Chandler thus concluded that organizational structure followed and reflected the growth strategy of the firm.

CLASS COMMENT
Structure follows strategy.

According to Chandler, organizations pass through three stages of development: moving from a unit, to a functional, and then to a multidivisional structure (see Fig. 8-2). At first, organizations are small: There is usually a single location, a single product, and a single entrepreneurial decision-maker. For example, when Bill Hewlett and Dave Packard founded a company to build an audio oscillator in 1939, they were personally responsible for its design, manufacture, testing, and marketing.[6] Eventu-

[4]Our discussion of structure and strategy draws heavily on Chapter 2 of *Strategy Implementation: Structure, Systems, and Process,* 2nd ed., by Jay R. Galbraith and Robert K. Kazanjian (St. Paul, Minn.: West Publishing, 1986).

[5]A. D. Chandler, *Strategy and Structure* (Cambridge, Mass.: MIT Press, 1962).

[6]This example is taken from Donald F. Harvey, *Strategic Management* (Columbus, Ohio: C. E. Merrill, 1982), pp. 269–270.

FIGURE 8-2 STRATEGIES AND STRUCTURE

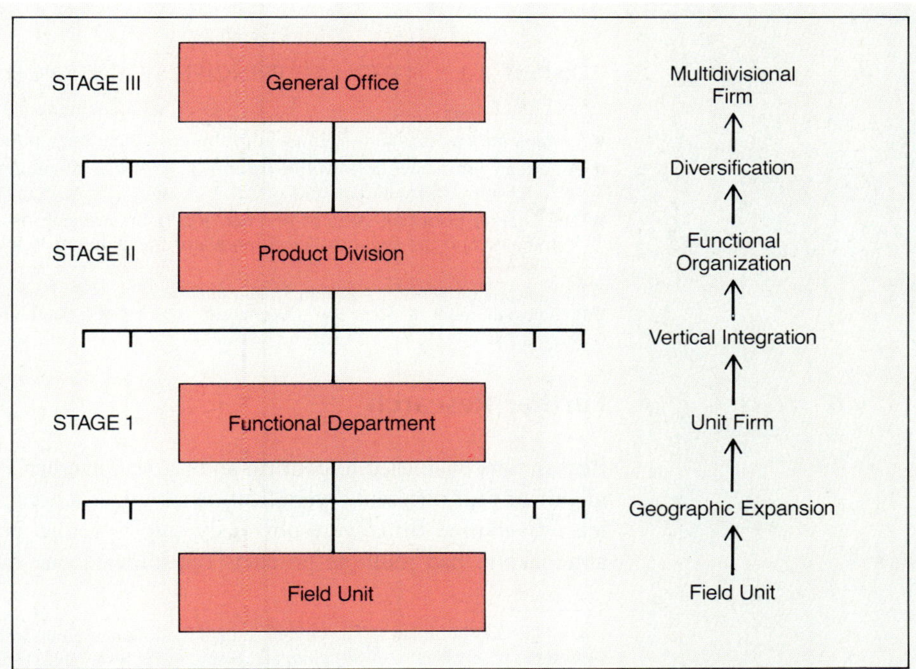

Source: Reprinted by permission from *Strategy Implementation: Structure, Systems, and Process,* by J. R. Galbraith and R. K. Kazanjian.

ally, increased volume and additional locations will create new problems. The organization will become a unit firm, with an administrative office to handle interunit coordination, specialization, and standardization.

vertical integration Broadening the scope of an organization's operations while retaining the original single product.

The next step is **vertical integration:** The organization broadens the scope of its operations while retaining the original single product. For example, the pioneers of vertical integration, the steel companies, eventually moved into mining. A manufacturer might naturally move into warehousing and wholesaling. However, vertical integration creates new problems in moving goods and materials through the organization's various functions. Therefore, the organization evolves into a **functional organization,** with finance, marketing, production, and other subdivisions and formalized budgeting and planning systems. Thus, as Hewlett-Packard's production of test equipment expanded, *functional* managers took over operating decisions.

functional organization A form of departmentalization in which everyone engaged in one functional activity, such as marketing or finance, is grouped into one unit.

In the third stage, an organization expands into different industries and diversifies its products. This phenomenon poses a significant new challenge: selecting products and industries in which to invest the organization's capital. The result is the **multidivisional firm,** which operates almost as a collection of smaller businesses. Semi-autonomous product divisions take responsibility for short-term operating decisions, with the central office remaining responsible for strategic decisions with a longer time horizon. Hewlett-Packard, for example, diversified into computers, calculators, and components. The company now has 42 divisions operating almost independently. The central office of Hewlett-Packard itself is primarily involved with strategic planning and fiscal controls. (We will examine some of Hewlett-Packard's current revenues in Chapter 9.)

multidivisional firm An organization that has expanded into different industries and diversified its products.

Chandler also observed that the transition from one structure to another was often both delayed and painful. He concluded that organizations do not readily change structure because the entrepreneurial founders of organizations who excel at strategy are generally neither interested in nor knowledgeable about organizational structure. Indeed, when the organization finally is restructured, the entrepreneur often leaves. This has happened frequently in recent years in rapidly growing, technology-oriented firms like Apple Computer.[7] Chandler's three main principles are summed up in Exhibit 8-1.

EXTRA EXERCISE

Have students select a large company to study. Trace its history to see if it follows Chandler's pattern: unit, functional, multidivisional. If it did follow this pattern, did it appear to succeed? If it didn't follow this pattern, what did it do and why?

EXHIBIT 8-1 CHANDLER'S PRINCIPLES OF STRUCTURAL TRANSITION

- Organizational structure follows from the growth strategy pursued by the firm.
- American firms have followed a pattern of stagewise development from unifunctional structure, to functional, to multidivisional.
- The change from one stage to another occurs only after provocation, because the strategy formulator and the organizational innovator are different types of people.

Source: Reprinted by permission from *Strategy Implementation: Structure, Systems, and Process,* Second Edition, by J. R. Galbraith and R. K. Kazanjian.

Further Research

Researchers have tried to confirm and refine Chandler's thesis. Wrigley, for example, identified four different diversification strategies among *Fortune* 500 companies.[8] The least diversified firms were obviously single-product businesses. Others, such as the automakers, had multiple products but allowed one business to dominate 70 to 95

[7] R. K. Kazanjian, "The Organizational Evolution of High Technology Venture: The Impact of Stage of Growth on the Nature of Structure and Planning Process," Ph.D. diss., The Wharton School, University of Pennsylvania, 1983.

[8] L. Wrigley, "Divisional Autonomy and Diversification," Ph.D. diss., Harvard Business School, 1970.

percent of their sales. Still other firms, while diversified, moved primarily into businesses which shared customers, distribution channels, or technology with their main business. The most diversified firms moved into completely unrelated businesses. Wrigley found that the more diversified the strategy, the more likely a firm had a multidivisional structure. The firms with a dominant business were sometimes hybrids, using a functional structure to manage the dominant business and a divisional structure for the rest.

In a similar study covering the years from 1949 to 1969, Rumelt found that the number of dominant-product and single-product business firms fell, while the proportion of the more diversified firms doubled from 30 to 60 percent.[9] Over the same time period, functional structures declined from 63 to 11 percent of the sample, while multidivisional structures grew from 20 to 76 percent. This pattern continued through 1974.[10] In addition, the greater a firm's diversity, the more likely it was to have a multidivisional structure.

FOR DISCUSSION

How do Miles and Snow's propositions fit in with contingency theory?

More recently, Raymond Miles and Charles Snow have done extensive studies analyzing the "fit" among an organization's strategy, structure, and management processes—that is, its balance between alignment with its environment and its maintenance of stable internal interrelationships. They argue that successful organizations achieve strategic fit with their market environments and support their strategies with appropriately designed structures and management processes, while less successful organizations typically exhibit poor fit externally and/or internally.

Miles and Snow developed a set of terms to describe the type of strategy used by organizations to survive in changing times. One industry they studied was tobacco. Few industries have come under the degree of negative pressure that has been and continues to be exerted on tobacco companies. Each of four major tobacco companies has reacted to this environment quite differently—and with different results. Philip Morris relied on a "prospector" strategy, engaging in a series of product and market innovations that propelled the company from last-place market share among the major firms in 1950 to first place today. R. J. Reynolds (now RJR Nabisco) used an "analyzer" strategy, pursuing a "second-in" goal by adopting the successful innovations of its competitors. This strategy has kept it a close second to Philip Morris. American Brands chose a "defender" strategy, trying to maintain a traditional approach despite changes in the environment—for example, moving away from nonfiltered to filtered cigarettes; it fell from first to fourth place in overall market share. Liggett and Meyers adopted a "reactor" strategy, holding on to its product-market strategy despite an unfavorable performance. By the late 1970s it was searching for a purchaser for its tobacco business.

HERE'S AN EXAMPLE

Pillsbury Company, whose performance has been lagging, has been described by one Wall Street analyst as "a conglomerate that's stagnating." However, company executives have chosen to stick with a strategy of competing in both packaged foods and restaurants. Remaining diversified goes against the trend among other food processors to strip down to core businesses. (*Business Week*, 1/25/88, pp. 56–58)

Thus, major environmental changes were analyzed well by two tobacco companies, poorly by one, and quite inadequately by a fourth.[11]

Overseas Experience. With mixed results, other researchers have tried to apply Chandler's thesis outside the United States.[12] They have found that, in itself, product

---

[9]R. P. Rumelt, *Strategy, Structure, and Economic Performance* (Boston: Division of Research, Harvard Business School, 1974).

[10]R. P. Rumelt, "Diversification Strategy and Profitability," *Strategic Management Journal* 3 (1982):359–369.

[11]Raymond E. Miles and Charles E. Snow, "Fit, Failure and the Hall of Fame," *California Management Review* 26, no. 3 (1984):10–28. See also Miles and Snow, *Organizational Strategy, Structure, and Process* (New York: McGraw-Hill, 1978); Miles and Snow, "Organizations: New Concepts for New Forms," *California Management Review* 28, no. 2 (1986):64–71; and Donald C. Hambrick, "Some Tests of the Effectiveness and Functional Attributes of Miles and Snow's Strategic Types," *Academy of Management Journal* 26 (1983):5–26.

[12]D. Channon, *The Strategy and Structure of British Enterprise* (London: Macmillan, 1973); G. Pooley-Dyas, "Strategy and Structure of French Enterprise," Ph.D. diss., Harvard Business School, 1972); B. R. Scott, "The Industrial State: Old Myths and New Realities," *Harvard Business Review* 51 (1973):133–148.

diversity is not enough to bring about a multidivisional structure: Competitive pressures are also required. For example, a study of leading Japanese firms found that the smaller domestic market caused businesses to diversify earlier while waiting much later to change to a multidivisional structure. (This delay is caused in part by the traditional clustering of companies around a major bank—a fact which effectively reduces competition.[13])

Multinational Firms. Chandler's thesis has also been confirmed by the experience of U.S. multinationals. As American firms expanded abroad during the 1960s, they first added an international division to their existing product divisions.[14] Ultimately, however, firms that internationalized entire or diversified product lines adopted worldwide product divisions. By contrast, firms that competed globally only in their dominant business tended to adopt geographic divisions dividing the world into regions.

European multinationals followed a different pattern, in part because prior agreements and cartels limited competition.[15] Initially, they combined a holding company for international operations with a functional structure for domestic business. By the early 1970s, however, many had shifted to a multidivisional structure.

Today, intensified global competition, greater demands by host governments, and growing participation in joint ventures are weakening the strategic control of the head offices of multinational organizations. For example, under the U.S.S.R.'s joint-venture law, the Soviet government must own 51 precent of the company and appoint the top manager. Structure itself has become less important to performance, and hybrid and matrix structures have become more common. Rather than reorganize, top management may upgrade personnel and implement new management systems in order to solve problems.[16]

Chandler's thesis remains a topic of active research. Some critics have argued that he reversed the relationship between strategy and structure. It may be that the structure of a company is so resistant to change that it constrains the kinds of strategies that are most feasible under given circumstances. For example, the structure of a large organization such as the old Bell System, organized functionally and geographically with over one million employees before divestiture in 1984, prevented the company from pursuing certain areas and attempting certain strategies.

Regardless of the final verdict on Chandler, it is impossible to understand an organization's strategy without examining its structure. Indeed, one framework for organizational effectiveness goes even further in its analysis of this relationship.

The Seven-S Model

Seven-S Model According to Waterman and others, framework for change identifying seven key factors than can adversely affect successful change in an organization.

Based on discussions with consultants, academics, and business leaders, the consulting firm of McKinsey & Company has proposed the **Seven-S Model** for organizational effectiveness.[17] McKinsey's consultants found that it is a slow and painful process for organizations to learn new ideas and make appropriate changes because there are seven key factors affecting an organization's ability to implement new strategies. Neglect of any one of these factors can adversely affect successful change.

---

[13] Y. Suzuki, "The Strategy and Structure of Top 100 Japanese Industrial Enterprises 1950–1970," *Strategic Management Journal* 1 (1980):265–291.

[14] J. Stopford and L. Wells, *Managing the Multinational Enterprise* (London: Longman, 1972).

[15] L. Franko, "The Move Toward a Multi-Divisional Structure in European Organizations," *Administrative Science Quarterly* 19 (1974):493–506; L. Franko, *The European Multinationals* (Greenwich, Conn.: Greylock Press, 1976).

[16] C. A. Bartlett, "MNCs: Get Off the Reorganization Merry-Go-Round," *Harvard Business Review* 62 (March–April 1983):138–147; C. K. Prahalad and Y. L. Doz, "An Approach to Strategic Control in MNCs," *Sloan Management Review* (Summer 1981):5–13.

[17] See Robert H. Waterman, Jr., Thomas J. Peters, and Julien R. Phillips, "Structure Is Not Organization," *Business Horizons* (June 1980).

TEACHING TIP

Emphasize these seven key factors and how they affect the organization's ability to implement new strategies successfully.

As Figure 8-3 illustrates, each of these factors is equally important and interacts with all the other factors; any number of circumstances may dictate which of the factors will be the driving force in the execution of any particular strategy.

Structure. We have already discussed the importance of organizational structure earlier in this chapter, but the Seven-S model adds a more contemporary perspective to the problem. The McKinsey consultants point out that in today's complex and ever-changing environment, successful organizations may make temporary structural changes to cope with specific strategic tasks without abandoning basic structural divisions throughout the organizations. Thus, the General Motors Corporation, while holding onto its traditional divisions, incorporated additional project centers during its major downsizing effort.

Strategy. Previous chapters have discussed strategy at length. In particular, the Seven-S model emphasizes that, in practice, the *development* of strategies poses less of a problem than their *execution*.

Systems. This category includes all the formal and informal procedures that allow the organization to function, including capital budgeting systems, training systems, and

FIGURE 8-3 THE SEVEN-S MODEL

Source: Robert H. Waterman, Jr., Thomas J. Peters, and Julien R. Phillips, "Structure Is Not Organization," *Business Horizons* (June 1980).

accounting systems. Systems can overpower expressed strategies. Thus, a consumer-goods manufacturer might find it impossible to implement a new portfolio strategy if its management information system does not adjust to produce the necessary cost data by segment. There was no way to compare the different segments of the business.

Style. "Style" does not refer to personality, but rather to the pattern of substantive and symbolic *actions* undertaken by top managers. It communicates priorities more clearly than *words* alone and may profoundly influence performance. For example, consultants have found that even oil- and mineral-exploration efforts, surely a matter of operational skills and luck, benefit from top management attention. Exploration is more successful in companies where top managers spend more of their own and the board's time participating in exploration activities, articulate better reasons for exploration, recruit more people with exploration experience, fund exploration more consistently, and assign exploration managers to report at higher organizational levels.

Staff. Successful organizations view people as resources to be managed aggressively—that is, to be nurtured, developed, guarded, and allocated. For example, top managers devote time and energy to planning the progress and participation of existing managers, while job assignment policies actively foster the development of new managers. Similarly, new hirees are given jobs in the mainstream of the organization, whether that be marketing or new product innovation. Talented individuals are assigned mentors, put into fast-track programs, exposed to top management, and rapidly moved into positions of real responsibility.

Skills. "Skills" refer to those activities which organizations do best and for which they are known. For example, DuPont is known for research, Procter & Gamble for product management, ITT for financial controls, and Hewlett-Packard for innovation and quality. Strategic changes may require organizations to add one or more new skills. Thus, the termination of their U.S. telephone monopoly forced the Bell System to add new marketing skills to its resources. Strategic initiatives that require the dismantling or revising of an old skill pose even more difficult implementation problems. Eastman Kodak, for example, has been forced to give up some of its traditional quality-control skills to accelerate product innovation.

Superordinate Goals. These are not formally stated organizational objectives, but rather guiding concepts, values, and aspirations that unite an organization in some common purpose. They are often expressed succinctly and often rather abstractly: "customer service" at IBM, for example, or "new products" at 3M. Superordinate goals have deep meaning within the organization. They provide a sense of purpose and a certain stability as other, more superficial characteristics of the organization change. Not every, or even most, organizations have superordinate goals—primarily those organizations that tend to perform most successfully. It is very often the drive to accomplish superordinate goals that separates superior performers from the crowd.

HERE'S AN EXAMPLE

Solarcare, Inc. out of Bethelem, Pennsylvania, founded by three young upstarts from an idea hatched in a business school class, is facing the common challenge of many start-ups—getting their product on already-jammed store shelves. Their solution: appealing to a niche in the market and putting their product in consumers' hands, for free, if necessary. (*Wall Street Journal*, 5/13/88, p. 27)

QUOTATION FROM A MANAGER

"We're trying to create an environment in which strange ideas don't get kicked out in a knee-jerk reaction"—Bob Groat, innovation manager at S.C. Johnson and Son, Inc. (makers of Johnson Wax and Raid bug sprays). (*Wall Street Journal*, 4/22/88, p. 35)

BACKGROUND ON FAST-GROWING COMPANIES

In general, the supergrowth champs began their rise by tapping into broad nationwide or worldwide trends. They followed these trends wherever they led. Then when industry shakeouts and intense competitive pressures hit, they found ways to survive. Who are some of these fast growers? Sun Microsystems, who saw sales of its computer workstations double after five years; Reebok International, athletic shoemaker in its eighth year, increased sales 50 percent; Compaq Computer, PC maker, saw 1987 sales soar 95 percent; and others. (*Fortune*, 5/23/88, pp. 28–40)

ILLUSTRATIVE CASE STUDY Continued

Maintaining the Competitive Edge at Merck & Co.

Because Merck is successful—some have selected it as the most admirably managed pharmaceutical company in the country—Vagelos cannot adopt a posture of complex intervention, as did Lee Iacocca at Chrysler (see Chapter 5). Rather, he must focus on how to sustain its success by means of incremental improvement. Vagelos is worried about the key implementation factors that will be necessary in any continued expansion, improvement, and success. What kinds of rewards do scientists want? Money? Fame? Does the team approach lead to greater or less time in developing new ideas? How much participation should scientists at various levels have in the overall strategy-making function of Merck?

For one thing, Vagelos wants to shorten the regulatory approval cycle that costs his company so much time and money in the development of its products; he must thus decide on the best approach to a major company (and, indeed, industrywide) program. He must decide whether his current public affairs and government relations staff is sufficient for taking on one of the most powerful decision-making forces in his company's external environment. Should Merck push for adjustments in present regulatory policy or should it seek revamped legislation? Vagelos must also decide how—and to what extent—to involve other key managers in these decisions. In other words, he must decide on the makeup and coordination of the *team* to implement the strategy of the project.

OPERATIONALIZING STRATEGY

In order to implement a strategy, we must go beyond such vague prescriptions as "harvest" or "grow" and lay out detailed blueprints for functional and individual actions. In the eight-step planning process for business units that we set out in the last chapter, we mentioned briefly how implementation involves making the plan a part of the daily life of the organization. In short, the strategy must be *operationalized*. In this section, we will consider some ways to do this: making explicit functional plans, setting annual objectives, initiating a process called management by objectives (MBO), and making reward systems consistent with strategy.

Developing Functional Strategy

operational strategy Organizational strategy spelling out facility locations and including marketing and financial strategies.

functional strategy Implementation strategy providing the details necessary to put organizational strategy into action.

FOR DISCUSSION

"Line managers should make strategy." Agree or disagree and why?

Production, marketing, finance, and all the other functional areas of an organization must each develop their own strategies in order to contribute to the greater organizational strategy. Take, for example, a chain of movie theaters. The **operational strategy** would spell out the type and location of its facilities, the marketing strategy would dictate what films are screened and what price to charge customers, and the financial strategy would determine whether the theaters are bought or leased.[18] A **functional strategy** provides operating managers with the details that they need to put the organizational strategy into action. Table 8-1 illustrates the way key functional strategies may vary depending on corporate strategy.

Functional strategies are more detailed than organizational strategies and also have shorter time horizons. Their purpose is to communicate short-term objectives and the actions needed on the part of operating managers to achieve them, as well as to create an environment which encourages their achievement. It is critical that lower-level managers participate in the development of functional strategies so that they better understand what needs to be done and are more committed to the plan.

Functional strategies must also be coordinated with each other to reduce the inevitable conflicts and to increase the likelihood that the organization's goals will be achieved. Each functional area has different responsibilities and, therefore, different priorities. Marketing, for example, is bound to want high inventories of finished goods so that customer orders can be filled quickly; finance naturally wants to keep inventories, and hence costs, down. It is the organization's strategy which should determine the successful settlement of such disputes.

[18] John A. Pearce II and Richard B. Robinson, Jr., *Formulation and Implementation of Competitive Strategy* (Homewood, Ill.: Richard D. Irwin, 1985), p. 300.

TABLE 8-1 KEY FUNCTIONAL STRATEGIES AS DETERMINED BY SELECTED CORPORATE STRATEGIES

CORPORATE STRATEGY		DESCRIPTION	MARKETING STRATEGY	PRODUCTION STRATEGY	FINANCE STRATEGY	TIMING
"Managed exit" from business (retrenchment)	Divest	Maximize cash flow and earnings Cut back R&D sales force technical service Sell proprietary technology and specialty business. Minimize EPA OSHA compliance	300MM lb. of current products (declining to 225MM with loss of productivity)	Patch up Newark and Houston plants to meet minimum EPA OSHA regulatory requirements	$2.0MM–2.5MM (nonmaintenance EPA OSHA expenditures)	Shut down both plants in 2½ years (by June 1979)
"Think lean" commodity producer (harvesting)	Harvest	Operate as "lean" as possible. Reduce R&D, technical service, and sales force to minimum Sell proprietary technology and specialty business. Contract 80+ percent of output Compete as a commodity rather than specialty producer	240MM lb. product A 190MM lb. product B 430MM lb.	Concentrate manufacturing at Houston plant Close Newark plant by end of 1979 Finish Houston expansion and open a second line for product B production	$14.0MM Houston expansion $ 5.0MM Product B line $ 3.25MM Refurbish 16th reactor from Newark $22.25MM	Houston expansion completed mid-1977 Product B capacity completed late 1977
"Think small" specialty producer (stable growth)	Selective investment	Complete only in those markets with a competitive advantage (e.g., products B and C)	220MM lb. product B 135MM lb. product C 355MM lb.	Convert product A expansion at Houston to product B Transfer 16th reactor at Newark to Houston on-line with five small reactors Locate specialty plant at either plant location	$14.0MM Houston expansion $ 3.25MM Refurbish 16th reactor $ 1.0MM Other $18.25MM	Product B capacity completed mid-1977 Product C capacity on-stream in late 1977
"Buy-time" approach (stable growth)	Selective investment	Consolidate current product lines at Houston Maintain current *potential* product mix Renew all productive capacity Operate small specialty business (25MM-30MM lb. at either Newark or Houston plants) Selectively trim and add to sales force, technical service, R&D, other overhead departments	210MM lb. product A 180MM lb. product B 310MM lb. product C 700MM lb.	Locate three product lines at Houston One-line: product A (two 18,000-gal. reactors) One-line: product B (16th reactor plus five old reactors) New-line 24,000-gal. reactor for product C Shut down Newark plant by December 1977	$14.0MM Houston expansion $ 5.0MM Product C line $ 1.25MM Refurbish 16th reactor $ 2.0MM Other $22.25MM	Houston product A capacity on-stream late 1978 Flexible plant (three lines) on-stream late 1979
"Consolidate position" build a flexible three-product plant (combination)	Selective investment	Load Houston plant with product A production Aggressively pursue specialty business at Newark plant If specialty program succeeds, expand Newark plant capacity for specialty products	*At Houston* 250MM lb. product A *At Newark* 180MM lb. product B 150MM lb. product C 330MM lb.	Houston expansion for product A production Begin Newark two-product expansion of specialty business in mid 1977 Product B line Products C and D line	$14.0MM Houston expansion $ 6.0MM –$7.0MM EPA OSHA $ 6.0MM Newark revitalization $26.0MM	250MM lb. product A capacity at Houston available 1978 130MM–150MM lb. expansion at Newark available 1981

Each functional area must also develop its own rules, procedures, and policies to guide its employees in the implementation of the functional strategy. An overabundance of rules, however, may dampen employee morale and initiative. (See the Ethics in Management box entitled ''Whistleblowing.'')

HERE'S AN EXAMPLE

Nordstrom, Inc., a Seattle-based apparel, shoe, and soft-goods retailer, is well known for its unbeatable customer service. Says a Nordstrom's clothing salesman, ''Nordstrom tells me to do whatever I need to do to make you happy. Period.'' Nordstrom is moving East, opening up stores, and competitors are already dreading their arrival. Says a Minneapolis-based service consultant, ''I think they will raise the level of service everywhere they go.'' (*Business Week*, 6/15/87, pp. 99–100)

Marketing. Marketing strategies match products and services with customer needs, decide where and when to sell and promote products, and set prices. The approach depends (1) on whether the company is addressing existing customers or is trying to attract new ones and (2) on whether the product is new or already established.[19]

Market penetration is an attempt to expand the organization's control of a market in which it already has a product or service. For example, the Hanes Corporation, already established in the market for men's hosiery, used innovative packaging and sales promotion, distribution through drugstores and supermarkets, discounts, and a massive ad campaign to win a larger share of the women's hosiery market with its L'eggs pantyhose offering.

Market development introduces an existing product or service to new customers. One example is the expansion of Coors Beer from the western part of the United States throughout the rest of the country. *Product development* does the reverse. It creates a new product or service for existing customers—for example, when a company specializing in frozen foods expands its product line.

Diversification marketing involves both a new product and new customers. For example, an entrepreneur might launch a new publication design and production service that relies on desktop publishing software and laser printers.

Finance. Finance strategies are concerned with the acquisition and allocation of capital and the management of working capital and dividends. Unlike other functional strategies, they must have long-term as well as short-term components. Some typical issues are record keeping, calculating financial needs, managing debt, and dealing with creditors.

HERE'S AN EXAMPLE

J. P. Morgan, the blue blood of the banking industry, is having its share of problems, too. As a Morgan executive concludes regarding company problems, ''Either we will freeze or move ahead.'' Changes are being implemented such as: scrutinizing employees for their contribution to the bottom line; increased aggressiveness for new markets; tightening up controls, etc. (*Wall Street Journal*, 3/22/88, p. 6)

Production/Operations. This functional area is concerned with the transformation of materials, labor, and capital inputs into products or services. Strategic decisions include plant size and location, the selection of equipment, inventory size and control, wages and supervision, and product design and engineering. In the mobile-home industry, for example, Winnebago has opted for a single, large production center located near critical raw materials as part of its strategy to automate and integrate production. One of its competitors, Fleetwood, has decided instead on multiple production facilities located near various markets. Fleetwood rarely replaces equipment and relies on labor-intensive production techniques.[20] For more on operations, see Chapter 20.

HERE'S AN EXAMPLE

AT&T, long the laughingstock of the computer industry, is executing a risky strategy aimed at controlling the next major computer standard. Their inability to succeed so far at selling computers at a profit illustrates the difficulties of blending the computer and telecommunications industries. (*Wall Street Journal*, 4/7/88, p. 6)

Research and Development. Organizations engage in research and development to ensure that their products, services, and production methods do not become obsolete. They may choose to carry out basic research to increase their technical knowledge, applied research to create a commercial application, or development research to develop a new or improved product or process. The research may be done in-house or contracted outside; it may be a long- or short-term program.

There are four possible research and development strategies, each depending on an organization's size, technical leadership, environment, and competitors.[21] Pharmaceutical companies espouse an *innovative strategy* primarily concerned with develop-

[19]Lloyd L. Byars, *Concepts of Strategic Management Planning and Implementation* (New York: Harper & Row, 1984), pp. 200–202.

[20]Pearce and Robinson, *Formulation and Implementation*, p. 310.

[21]Byars, *Concepts of Strategic Management*, pp. 206–207.

ETHICS IN MANAGEMENT

WHISTLEBLOWING

Strategic management is an area with ethical landmines strewn all about it. The very idea of dividing strategy into formulation and implementation poses a special ethical problem: If you think of formulating strategy as essentially a cognitive and analytical task, then implementation—getting employees to make a product that conforms to specifications—becomes in part a matter of persuasion. Many companies have found that the more lower-level employees participate in the strategy process, the easier is implementation. In any case, all companies want to avoid what happened to the space shuttle *Challenger* and one of its builders, Morton Thiokol.

At a lower level in the organization, engineers at Morton Thiokol suspected that something was wrong with the now-infamous "O-rings." Yet when they complained, wrote memos, and "blew whistles," nothing happened. (Whistleblowing can be defined as opposing decisions, policies, or practices within the organization that appear to be ill-advised, detrimental, or illegal; it can also include publicizing such behavior to the world outside the organization.) Their job was evidently seen by senior managers as implementing policy, not setting or questioning it. Of course, the space shuttle case had a particularly tragic ending—one that was highly public and highly publicized.

The challenge for managers in thinking about strategy implementation is to ensure that there are built-in processes for constructive disagreement and dissent—and that those who dissent have some due process and perhaps even protection under company "law." Obviously, such a process can be abused by employees who constantly cry wolf—management is nowhere foolproof and easy. IBM has an open-door policy, as do other companies; some have employed outside ombudsmen, while others rely on confidential surveys and questionnaires. All want to avoid the tragedy of the space shuttle and the public relations discomfiture suffered by Morton Thiokol, but many are not willing to pay the price of guaranteeing a basic right to disagree. The sound of a whistle blowing in the midst of the implementation process can be especially shrill if it is accurately sounded and entails replanning, redesign, and a reworking of the implementation strategy.

Sources: Judith H. Dobrzynski, "Morton Thiokol: Reflections on the Shuttle Disaster," *Business Week,* March 14, 1988, pp. 82–83, 86, 91; Judith Valente, "Thiokol Faces a New Shuttle Test Today," *Wall Street Journal,* April 20, 1988, p. 6.

ing new products. In contrast, a *protective strategy* tries to improve existing products in order to maintain the firm's current position in the industry. Firms facing foreign competition, such as American robotics and small-car manufacturers, may adopt a *catch-up strategy* in which they analyze a competitor's product and adopt its best features. A *combination strategy* combines any or all of the foregoing. IBM, for example, is committed both to innovating new products and protecting its existing products.

Human Resource/Personnel. Human resource management includes recruiting, training, and counseling employees; determining compensation; and maintaining contact with both unions and governments. Its objective is to attract, motivate, and retain those employees required by the organization. Depending on whether the organizational strategy calls for growth or retrenchment, the human resources strategy may be geared to increasing or reducing employee numbers. For more about human resource management, see Chapter 11.

"If we knew what conclusions the President wants our commission to come to, we would come to them, and that would be that."
Drawing by Handelsman; © 1971 The New Yorker Magazine, Inc.

Setting Annual Objectives

Annual objectives lie at the very heart of strategy implementation—especially when detailed functional strategies are being implemented. They identify precisely what must be accomplished each year in order to achieve an organization's strategic goals; in the process, they also provide managers with specific targets for the coming year's performance. For example, if strategy dictates an increase in market share, annual objectives for the coming year might include a 15 percent increase in sales, the opening of a regional distribution center in a specific area of the country, and the negotiation of a certain line of credit to pay for the increased production and distribution expenses.[22]

TEACHING TIP
Emphasize the role that objectives play in organizations.

Thus, annual objectives clarify managers' tasks and give them a better understanding of their role in the organization's strategy. Insofar as annual objectives challenge managers and give them a sense of purpose, they also increase motivation. At the same time, they furnish a quantitative basis for monitoring performance and make it easier to spot performance problems.

Well-designed annual objectives are clearly linked to the organization's long-term goals and they are measurable. It is important that they *quantify* performance in absolute terms, so there can be no dispute over a unit's results. Some areas, like production, naturally lend themselves to this kind of measurement. It is more difficult to create quantitative standards for personnel. The examples in Table 8-2 illustrate the difference between well- and poorly designed annual objectives.

Another important design issue is the way in which the annual objectives of different units interact with one another. Managers must *coordinate* the annual objectives of the organization, resolving their contradictions, setting priorities, and designing objectives to reinforce one other. Marketing, for example, often has a clearly defined annual objective for delivery time to customers, it is impossible for marketing to meet that objective unless manufacturing also has an annual objective regarding delivery time. Both sets of objectives must not only agree on the acceptable limits on

[22]Pearce and Robinson, *Formulation and Implementation*, p. 291.

TABLE 8-2 OPERATIONALIZING MEASURABLE ANNUAL OBJECTIVES

EXAMPLES OF DEFICIENT ANNUAL OBJECTIVES	EXAMPLES OF ANNUAL OBJECTIVES WITH MEASURABLE CRITERIA FOR PERFORMANCE
To improve morale in the divisions (plant, department, etc.).	To reduce turnover (absenteeism, number of rejects, etc.) among sales managers, by 10 percent by January 1, 1987. *Assumption:* Morale is related to measurable outcomes (i.e., high and low morale are associated with different results).
To improve support of the sales effort.	To reduce the time lapse between order date and delivery by 8 percent (two days) by June 1, 1987. To reduce the cost of goods produced by 6 percent to support a product price decrease of 2 percent by December 1, 1987. To increase the rate of before- or on-schedule delivery by 5 percent by June 1, 1987.
To develop a terminal version of the SAP computer program.	To develop a terminal version of SAP capable of processing X bits of information in time Y at cost not to exceed Z per 1,000 bits by December 1, 1987. *Assumption:* There virtually is an infinite number of "terminal" or operational versions. Greater detail or specificity defines the objective more precisely.
To enhance or improve the training effort.	To increase the number of individuals capable of performing X operation in manufacturing by 20 percent by April 15, 1987. To increase the number of functional heads capable of assuming general management responsibility at the division level by 10 percent by July 15, 1987. To provide sales training to X number of individuals, resulting in an average increase in sales of 4 percent within six months after the training session.
To improve the business's image.	To conduct a public opinion poll using random samples in the five largest U.S. metropolitan markets and determine average scores on 10 dimensions of corporate responsibility by May 15, 1987. To increase our score on those 10 items by an average of 7.5 percent by May 1, 1988.

Source: John A. Pearce II and Richard B. Robinson, Jr., *Formulation and Implementation of Competitive Strategy* (Homewood, Ill.: Richard D. Irwin, 1985). Copyright 1985 by Richard D. Irwin.

delivery time, but also spell out the changes in production and distribution that will accomplish the overall goal.

Managers should participate in the process of setting annual objectives to ensure that they are realistic and to screen out flaws in their design. Manager involvement has another potential benefit as well: The process may air political conflicts and provide a forum for their resolution before they begin interfering with strategy implementation.

Management by Objectives

management by objectives (MBO) A formal set of procedures that establishes and reviews progress toward common goals for managers and subordinates.

Management by objectives (MBO) is one method for operationalizing strategy. It goes beyond annual objectives for *organizational* units to performance goals for *individual* employees. The approach was first proposed by Peter Drucker in his 1954 book

The Practice of Management.[23] Since that time, MBO has spurred a great deal of discussion, evaluation, and research, and many similar programs have been developed.[24]

COORDINATED RESOURCE

For an extensive review of studies looking at the effectiveness of MBO, see: Jack N. Kondrasuk, "Studies in MBO Effectiveness," *Academy of Management Review,* July 1981, pp. 419–429.

MBO refers to a formal, or moderately formal, set of procedures that begins with goal setting and continues through performance review. Managers and their subordinates act together to set common goals. Each person's major areas of responsibility are clearly defined in terms of measurable expected results or "objectives" used by subordinates in planning their work and by both subordinates and superiors for monitoring progress. Performance appraisals are conducted jointly on a continuing basis, with provisions for regular periodic reviews.

The objectives, which are at the heart of MBO, spell out the individual actions needed to fulfill the unit's functional strategy and annual objectives. Thus, MBO provides a way to integrate and focus the efforts of all the members of an organization on the goals of higher management and overall organizational strategy.

Another key to MBO is its insistence on the active involvement of managers and staff members at every organizational level. Drucker, following the principles of Theory Y, insisted that managers and staff members set their own objectives or, at the very least, be actively involved in the objective-setting process; otherwise, people might refuse to cooperate or make only half-hearted efforts to implement "someone else's" objectives. Drucker also suggested that managers at every level help set objectives for levels higher than their own. This requirement gives them a better understanding of the broader strategy of the company and how their own specific objectives relate to the overall picture.

Elements of the MBO System. MBO programs can vary enormously. Some are designed for use in a subunit; others are used for the organization as a whole. Some emphasize corporate planning; others stress individual motivation. Managers, of course, may also choose to use different methods and approaches. Nevertheless, most effective MBO programs share the following six elements.[25]

1. *Commitment to the Program.* At every organizational level, managers' commitment to achieving personal and organizational objectives and to the MBO process is required for an effective program. Much time and energy are required to implement a successful MBO program. Managers must meet with subordinates, first to set objectives and then to review progress toward these objectives. There are no easy shortcuts. If objectives are set but not reviewed periodically, they are not likely to be achieved. If subordinates' progress is reviewed in an overly judgmental way, resentment and impaired functioning may result.
2. *Top-Level Goal Setting.* Effective MBO programs usually start with the top managers who determine the organization's strategy and set preliminary goals. These goals resemble annual objectives in their content and terms, for example, "a 5 percent increase in sales next quarter" or "no increase in overhead costs this year." This procedure gives both managers and subordinates a clearer idea of what top management hopes to accomplish and shows them how their own work directly relates to achievement of the organization's goals.
3. *Individual Goals.* In an effective MBO program, each manager and subordinate has clearly defined job responsibilities and objectives, for example: "The manager of Subunit

[23]Peter F. Drucker, *The Practice of Management* (New York: Harper & Brothers, 1954).

[24]See Dale D. McConkey, *How to Manage by Results,* 4th ed. (New York: American Management Association, 1983), p. 3. See also Stephen J. Carroll, Jr., and Henry L. Tosi, Jr., *Management by Objectives: Applications and Research* (New York: Macmillan, 1973), p. 3. For a comprehensive review of the literature on planning in general and goal setting in particular, see Scott Armstrong, "The Value of Formal Planning for Strategic Decisions: Review of the Empirical Research," *Strategic Management Journal* 3, no. 2 (1982):197–211.

[25]See W. J. Reddin, *Effective Management by Objectives: The 3-D Method of MBO* (New York: McGraw-Hill, 1971), pp. 13–19; and George S. Odiorne, *MBO II: A System of Managerial Leadership for the 80's* (Belmont, Calif.: Fearon Pitman, 1979), pp. 127–140, 161–165, and 320–321.

A will be responsible for increasing sales 15 percent over a 12-month period.'' The purpose of setting *objectives* in specific terms at every level is to help employees understand clearly just what they are expected to accomplish. This understanding—and insight into organizational strategy—helps each individual plan effectively to achieve his or her targeted goals.

Objectives for each individual should be set in consultation between that individual and his or her supervisor. Because they know best what they are capable of achieving, subordinates might well help managers develop realistic objectives; in turn managers might help subordinates ''raise their sights'' toward higher objectives by showing willingness to help them overcome obstacles and confidence in their abilities.

4. *Participation*. The degree of subordinate participation in setting objectives can vary enormously. At one extreme, subordinates may participate only by being present when objectives are dictated by management. At the other extreme, subordinates may be completely free to set their own objectives and methods for achieving them. Neither extreme is likely to be effective. Managers sometimes set objectives without full knowledge of the practical constraints under which their subordinates must operate; subordinates may possibly select objectives that are inconsistent with the organization's goals. As a general rule, the greater the participation of both managers and subordinates in the setting of goals, the more likely it is that the goals will be achieved.
5. *Autonomy in Implementation of Plans*. Once the objectives have been set and agreed upon, the individual enjoys a wide range of discretion in choosing the means for achieving the objectives. Within the normal constraints of organization policies, managers should be free to develop and implement programs to achieve their goals without being second-guessed by their immediate superiors—an aspect of MBO programs particularly appreciated by managers.
6. *Review of Performance*. Managers and subordinates periodically meet to review progress toward the objectives. During the review, they decide what problems, if any, exist and what they can each do to resolve them. If necessary, objectives may be modified for the next review period. To be fair and meaningful, review should be based on *measurable* performance results rather than on subjective criteria, such as attitude or ability. For example, rather than attempting to assess how energetic a salesperson has been in the field, a manager should emphasize actual sales figures and detailed knowledge of specific accounts.

Evaluation of MBO. Do MBO concepts really work? The lack of studies on MBO programs makes it difficult to answer this question. Although controlled field experiments would be the most informative kind of research in the question, such research requires active interference by experimenters with the management of the groups under study. Even if researchers found a manager willing to permit such experimentation, the results would not be clear-cut. For one thing, it would be too difficult to control numerous experimental variables and to exclude the influence of chance events for the length of time needed before improvements from MBO implementation would become visible.[26]

Some research conducted at General Electric, Purex, the University of Kentucky, and elsewhere has indicated generally that MBO can improve managerial planning and performance, but that successful implementation requires considerable time and effort. Moreover, the active support of managers and their continued attention to program requirements is also necessary to introduce MBO techniques effectively.

In their review of the literature on MBO research, Stephen J. Carroll and Henry L. Tosi focused on three key concepts—specific goal setting, feedback on performance, and participation—in order to determine if optimism about MBO was justified. They arrived at the following conclusions.[27]

---

[26]For a well-designed attempt to study an MBO program under ''experimental conditions,'' see Jan P. Muczyk, ''A Controlled Field Experiment Measuring the Impact of MBO on Performance Data,'' *Journal of Management Studies* 15, no. 3 (October 1978):318–329.

[27]Carroll and Tosi, *Management by Objectives,* pp. 1–19.

Goal Setting. The evidence clearly showed that, when it comes to goal setting, nothing succeeds like success. Individuals who determine their own goals tend to aim for an improvement on past performance. If they achieve this improvement, they again set themselves a higher goal; if they fail to reach their target, however, they tend to set more conservative levels of aspiration for the next period.

The research also suggests that when employees are given specific goals, they reach significantly higher performance levels than do those who are merely asked to do their best.[28] However, if employees feel that goals are impossible rather than challenging, it's not surprising that performance will decrease.

Although most of the research Carroll and Tosi reviewed was not performed in organizations with established MBO programs, it does indicate that MBO should improve performance if goals are realistic and accepted by the employees involved.[29] The actual *degree* of improvement, however, depends on many factors, such as the individual employee's past experience with success or failure in reaching goals and how difficult the actual goals are.[30]

Feedback on Performance. There was also clear evidence that providing feedback on employee performance generally led to better performance. In addition, the periodic review process was found to have positive effects on employees' attitudes, creating feelings of friendliness, confidence in management, and a more tolerant acceptance of criticism[31]

Several studies showed a relationship between the *quality* of the feedback and the degree of improvement: The more specific and timely the feedback, the more positive the effect. The manner in which the feedback is provided also affects performance. The feedback should be given in a tactful manner, particularly if it conveys a failure to meet objectives. Otherwise, hostility and reduced performance can result. (The effects of various management communication styles will be further examined in Chapter 17.)

Participation. Most research studies on participation indicate that subordinates who set or participate in setting their own goals are likely to show higher performance levels than those who have goals set for them. In one well-known study conducted at General Electric, subordinates who had more influence in setting objectives showed more favorable attitudes and higher levels of achievement. In contrast, subordinates who had little influence showed defensive behavior and, in some cases, lower levels of performance.[32]

Ultimately, then, the research suggests that there are at least two ways in which participating in setting goals can lead to higher performance. First, participation can lead to a greater likelihood that goals will be accepted, and *accepted* goals are more

---

[28]John M. Ivancevich, ''Different Goal-Setting Treatments and Their Effects on Performance and Satisfaction,'' *Academy of Management Journal* 20, no. 3 (September 1977):406–419. See also Gary P. Latham and Timothy P. Steele, ''The Motivational Effects of Participation versus Goal Setting on Performance,'' *Academy of Management Journal* 26, no. 3 (September 1983):406–417; and Mark E. Tubbs, ''Goal Setting: A Meta-Analytic Examination of the Empirical Evidence,'' *Journal of Applied Psychology*, August 1986, pp. 474–483.

[29]Gary P. Latham and Edwin A. Locke, ''Goal Setting—A Motivational Technique That Works,'' *Organizational Dynamics* 8, no. 2 (Autumn 1979):68–80. Latham and Locke reach the conclusion that goal setting increases performance whether goals are set unilaterally by the supervisor or with the participation of the employees—as long as the goals are *accepted* by the employees.

[30]A thorough review of the effects of goal setting on performance is provided in Gary P. Latham and Gary A. Yukl, ''A Review of Research on the Application of Goal Setting in Organizations,'' *Academy of Management Journal* 18, no. 4 (December 1975):824–845.

[31]See Jay S. Kim, ''Effect of Behavior plus Outcome Goal Setting and Feedback on Employee Satisfaction and Performance,'' *Academy of Management Journal* 27, no. 1 (March 1984):139–149.

[32]See Herbert H. Meyer, Emmanuel Kay, and John R. P. French, Jr., ''Split Roles in Performance Appraisal,'' *Harvard Business Review* 43, no. 1 (January–February 1965):123–129; and Miriam Erez, P. Christopher Earley, and Charles L. Hulin, ''The Impact of Participation on Goal Acceptance and Performance: A Two-Step Model,'' *Academy of Management Journal*, March 1985, pp. 50–66.

likely to be achieved. Second, participation can lead to the setting of higher goals, and *higher* goals lead to higher performance.[33]

Finally, Carroll and Tosi also concluded that, in addition to its impact on performance, the very process of participation leads to increased communication and understanding between managers and subordinates.[34]

Reward Systems

QUOTATION FROM A MANAGER

"Bad numbers will kill you every time"—John M. Stafford, CEO, Pillsbury Company. (*Business Week*, 1/25/88, p. 56)

Rewards and incentives contribute to strategy implementation by shaping individual and group behavior. Well-designed incentive plans are consistent with an organization's objectives and structure. They motivate employees to direct their performance toward the organization's goals.[35]

In setting up an incentive plan, the organization is faced with a series of choices: Should bonuses be in cash or stock? Current or deferred? How will performance be measured? How much discretion will managers have in awarding bonuses? How large will the bonuses be?[36] The object is to tailor the program to the organization's objectives. Incentive plans can encourage short-term or long-term decision making, greater or lesser risk taking, more or less cooperation with other managers, and the like. Table 8-3 reviews established practice in incentive plans for top management.

Critics have pointed out four problems faced by managers with conventional incentive plans. First, incentives may be inappropriately correlated with the absolute size of the firm instead of the rate of return.[37] Second, short-term performance may be emphasized at the expense of long-term strategic development.[38] Third, incentives may be tied to accounting measures, such as earnings per share and return on investment, which do not accurately reflect the creation of economic value for shareholders.[39] Finally, these accounting measures also ignore portfolio concepts of corporate strategy, holding managers to the same standards of performance regardless of the rate of growth of their division.[40]

In response to these criticisms, organizations have begun to make changes in their incentive plans.[41] They may use three- to five-year performance evaluation periods and deferred stock-option plans to encourage long-term planning. They may calculate a more meaningful return on assets for current operations by separating out expenses incurred by strategic projects. They may develop new performance measures that are more meaningful than simple accounting criteria. Finally, they may adjust the

---

[33]For a thorough discussion of the literature on participation, and the ambiguities in much of the research, see Edwin A. Locke and E. M. Schweiger, "Participation in Decision-Making: One More Look," in Barry M. Staw, ed., *Research in Organizational Behavior,* Vol. 1 (Greenwich, Conn.: JAI Press, 1979), pp. 265–339.

[34]For a discussion of how satisfaction is related to setting objectives, see Thomas I. Chacko, "An Examination of the Affective Consequences of Assigned and Self-Set Goals," *Human Relations* 35, no. 9 (September 1982):771–726.

[35]Hrebeniak and Joyce, *Implementing Strategy,* p. 15.

[36]M. Salter, "Tailor Incentive Compensation to Strategy," *Harvard Business Review* 51 (1973):94–102.

[37]A. Rappaport, "Corporate Performance Standards and Shareholder Value," *Journal of Business Strategy* 3 (Spring 1983):28–38.

[38]P. Lorange, *Corporate Planning: An Executive Viewpoint* (Englewood Cliffs, N.J.: Prentice Hall, 1980).

[39]A. Rappaport, "How to Design Value—Contributing Executive Incentives," *Journal of Business Strategy* 4 (Fall 1983):49–59.

[40]D. Norburn and P. Miller, "Strategy and Executive Reward: The Mis-Match in the Strategic Process," *Journal of General Management* 6 (Summer 1981):17–27.

[41]See Rappaport, "How to Design Value"; A. Rappaport, "Selecting Strategies That Create Shareholder Value," *Harvard Business Review* 60 (May–June 1981):139–149; P. J. Stonich, "Using Rewards in Implementing Strategy," *Strategic Management Journal* 2 (1981):345–352; and P. J. Stonich and C. E. Zaragoza, "Strategic Funds Programming: The Missing Link in Corporate Planning," *Managerial Planning* (September–October 1980):3–11.

TABLE 8-3 KEY ASPECTS OF INCENTIVE COMPENSATION

POLICY ISSUES	FINANCIAL INSTRUMENTS	PERFORMANCE MEASURES	DEGREE OF DISCRETION IN ALLOCATING BONUS AWARDS	SIZE AND FREQUENCY OF AWARDS
Short run vs. long run	Mix of current bonus awards and stock options should reflect the relevant time horizon for policy-level executives. Deferred instruments are weak reinforcers of short-term performance.	Mix of quantitative measures of performance and more qualitative measures should reflect the relevant time horizon for executives. Qualitative measures usually reflect long-run considerations more effectively than quantitative measures.	Nondiscretionary, formula-based bonuses tend to encourage a short-run point of view.	Frequent bonus awards encourage concentration on short-term performance.
Risk aversion vs. risk taking	Current bonus awards, in cash or stock, can reinforce risk-taking behavior.	Qualitative measures of performance can reinforce initiative by assuring executives that total performance will be evaluated for purposes of bonus awards.	Completely discretionary, highly personalized bonuses do not clarify the "rules of the game" and as a result can discourage risk-taking behavior.	The size of both salary and incentive awards should be commensurate with the business and personal risks involved.
Interdivisional relationships		Bonus pools can be based on divisional performance, total corporate performance, or some mix of the two. Each arrangement sends different signals in terms of interdivisional cooperation.	Nondiscretionary, formula-based bonuses for division managers are most practical in companies where little cooperation among divisions is required. Discretionary bonuses are practical when top management wants to encourage cooperation among divisions.	
Company-division relationships	Stock options can effectively link the interests of division personnel to the interests of the corporation.	Use of objective measures of performance for division managers is more meaningful where the primary role of headquarters is to allocate capital than it is in instances where the head office plays an important role in "managing the business" of the divisions.	Nondiscretionary, formula-based bonuses are most practical in companies where headquarters does not interfere in management of the profit centers. Discretionary bonuses are most useful when top management wants to exert a direct influence on decisions in the divisions.	

Source: Reprinted by permission from *Strategy Implementation: Structure, Systems, and Process,* Second Edition, by J. R. Galbraith and R. K. Kazanjian.

incentives for managers of high- and low-growth businesses within the same corporation, giving a different weight to market share, product quality, new-product development, and the like.

Matching Managers and Strategies

Different strategies call for different managerial skills, knowledge, and personality traits. In theory, of course, general managers should perform better if their skills, attitudes, and practices match the competitive setting and strategy of their organization.[42] Some corporations, including General Electric and Corning Glass Works, have tried to assess their managers and then place them in an appropriate setting, matching them with a particular stage of a product life cycle or a particular kind of business. However, no one has yet developed or rigorously tested specific rules for typing managers.

INSTITUTIONALIZING STRATEGY

A strategy cannot be implemented successfully unless it influences the *daily* decisions and actions of *every* member of the organization. It must *pervade* the organization's culture, systems, and values: In other words, strategy must be *institutionalized*.

HERE'S AN EXAMPLE

"Must Wins." This was the title of the list of 24 government contracts Martin-Marietta Corporation targeted as crucial. Twenty-two of these projects have been won, and Norman Augustine, Martin-Marietta's Vice-Chairman and CEO, attributes the successes to a carefully planned, four-stage strategy that is only half completed. The third and fourth stages of the strategy build upon forecasted industry changes and developments. (*Wall Street Journal*, 2/18/88, p. 6)

The Role of the CEO

Chief executive officers have unique relationships with organizations' strategies because they spend the majority of their time developing and guiding strategy. The personal goals and values of CEOs inevitably shape organizational strategy. For example, Merck's Roy Vagelos has communicated his own sales values to his 5,000 sales representatives. In the drug industry, exaggerated claims on a product's behalf are not unheard-of, but Vagelos will not allow his representatives to make claims that cannot be scientifically substantiated. Nor will he allow them to promote their products by criticizing the cheaper generic drugs of other companies. In addition, major changes in strategy can usually be associated with a change in CEO.

This fact gives CEOs a special role in strategy implementation. First, they *interpret* the strategy: They serve as final judges when managers disagree as to how strategy should be executed. Second, CEOs *enact*—in their words and actions—the seriousness of the organization's commitment to a strategy to doubtful managers, workers, and customers. Lee Iacocca, for example, helped Chrysler's new strategy to succeed by preaching its virtues on television and in the auto factories as well as in front of securities analysts. Third, CEOs *motivate,* providing extra sources of motivation in addition to the tangible rewards offered by the organization's incentive plan; they can mobilize support for the strategy by appealing to the values, beliefs, and loyalty of organization members. (See the Management Applications box entitled "Death in the Executive Suite.")

HERE'S AN EXAMPLE

What happens when the "hand-picked" successor to the top job doesn't perform? At Cullinet Software, Inc., the founder reassumes the top job, replacing the man he picked as successor. As industry analysts explained, "David [David Chapman, successor to John J. Cullinane, founder of Cullinet Software] was a strategist. At this point you need people who are ready to emphasize sales, support and customer service. . . . " Implementing the company's strategy will be Cullinane's task. (*Wall Street Journal*, 1/1/88)

The Role of Key Managers

Top managers believe that the most important factor in successful strategy implementation is placing the right people in key managerial positions. They look for individuals whose ability, education, experience, track record, and personality seem to fit the particular situation with which they are faced. They may, for instance, choose to assign or promote someone from within the organization, or they may opt to hire an outsider. Insiders have the advantage of knowing the organization and the important players, but these same ties may compromise their ability to make changes. Outsiders can bring in needed skills, experience, and enthusiasm, but they may be difficult to find and expensive to hire. (See Fig. 8-4.)

[42] A. Gupta, "Contingency Linkages Between Strategy and General Manager Characteristics," *Academy of Management Review* 27 (1984):25–41; N. M. Tichy, C. J. Fombrun, and M. A. Devanna, "Strategic Human Resource Management," *Sloan Management Review* (Winter 1982):47–61.

MANAGEMENT APPLICATION

DEATH IN THE EXECUTIVE SUITE

In this chapter, we have shown how the chief executive officer plays a vital role in strategy implementation. But CEOs are human. They die. What happens to a company and its strategy when it loses a CEO?

Some companies have *succession plans*—carefully worked out systems of who would replace who if a tragedy strikes or a better job opportunity costs them a key executive. Allied/Signal Corporation, for example, requires every senior manager to have succession plans for his or her organization. These plans are reviewed by the human resources department and ultimately the Board of Directors.

But many companies remain unprepared, especially for a sudden death. Sometimes, there is an heir apparent who is not yet ready to take the reins. This was the case at Dana Corporation, when President Stanley Gustafson died of a heart attack. It was necessary to divide his responsibilities among three executives and consolidate them later. Two weeks before his sudden death, AT&T Chairman James Olson told the board that Robert Allen should succeed him and the board agreed. Allen, a close friend of Olson, had to manage the awesome responsibility of running a large global firm at the same time as he grieved for the loss of his comrade. Even worse, Arrow Electronics lost 13 of its executives in a hotel fire; indeed, it is difficult to see how any company could have planned for a tragedy like the one that struck Arrow.

While no organization is totally dependent on one person, we have seen that the CEO's role in setting the tone for successful strategy implementation and in overseeing its reported progress is crucial to organization success. Sometimes it is easy to forget the very human element at the heart of organizations—and as a result, we sometimes gloss over the very difficult problems that all managers face.

Source: Based on Amanda Bennett, "Many Companies Aren't Prepared to Deal with Sudden Death of Chief Executive," *Wall Street Journal,* April 29, 1988, p. 25.

According to John Pearce and Richard Robinson, there are four different approaches that may be taken to such assignment decisions, each with its advantages and disadvantages. (See Fig. 8-5.) By and large, the relative advantages of insiders versus outsiders depends on how well the organization has already been performing and on the change and complications entailed by the prospective strategy.[43]

turnover situation Strategy situation in which poor performanace entails major changes that can be handled by insiders.

Outsiders are the better choice in a **turnover situation**—that is, when the organization has been performing poorly and the strategy calls for major changes. Outsiders have the experience to implement new strategies and are neither defensive about prior insufficiencies nor bound by prior commitments. In addition, employees are more likely to take the changes more seriously if new people are being brought in. Chrysler's near-bankruptcy is the classic example of a turnover situation. First, Lee Iacocca was brought in to serve as CEO. He, in turn, eventually filled over 80 percent of the company's top-management positions with outsiders. These decisions went a long way toward bringing Chrysler the skills and commitment that it needed to implement its new small-car strategy.

selective blend situation Strategy situation entailing major changes in organizational strategy that blend both outsiders and insiders to perform corrective measures.

The **selective blend situation** also requires major changes, but because of environmental fluctuations and not poor performance. Under these circumstances, the best solution seems to be to blend outsiders, who possess needed skills and experience, with insiders who can integrate the changes into the existing system. Take, for example, IBM's move into personal computers. Most positions were filled by existing IBM

[43]Pearce and Robinson, *Formulation and Implementation of Competitive Strategy,* pp. 336–341.

	Advantages	Disadvantages
Using existing executives to implement a new strategy	Already know key people, practices, and conditions. Personal qualities better known and understood by associates. Have established relationships with peers, subordinates, suppliers, buyers, etc. Symbolizes organizational commitment to individual careers.	Less adaptable to major strategic changes because of knowledge, attitudes, and values. Past commitments may hamper hard decisions required in executing a new strategy. Less ability to become inspired and credibly convey the need for change.
Bringing in outsiders to implement a new strategy	Outsider may already believe in and have "lived" the new strategy. Outsider is unencumbered by internal commitments to people. Outsider comes to the new assignment with heightened commitment and enthusiasm. Bringing in an outsider can send powerful signals throughout the organization that change is expected.	Often costly, both in terms of compensation and "learning-to-work-together" time. Candidates suitable in all respects (i.e., exact experience) may not be available, leading to compromise choices. Uncertainty in selecting the right person. The "morale" costs when an outsider takes a job several insiders wanted. "What to do with poor ol' Fred" problem.

Source: John A. Pearce II and Richard B. Robinson, Jr., *Formulation and Implementation of Competitive Strategy* (Homewood, Ill.: Richard D. Irwin, 1985), p. 339. Copyright © 1985 by Richard D. Irwin.

FIGURE 8-4 KEY CONSIDERATIONS IN MANAGERIAL ASSIGNMENTS TO IMPLEMENT STRATEGY

employees. The firm recruited only a limited number of outsiders, mostly those with experience in direct retail outlets—the one facet of the new strategy which was totally foreign to IBM.

stability situation Strategy situation in which good past performance and the minor nature of needed changes make insiders the best choice for implementing.

In a **stability situation,** past performance has been fine and few changes are needed. Insiders are clearly the best choice for implementing the strategy, since they are familiar with the firm, have a network of established relationships in the industry, and have a good track record. Thus, Wendy's used internal promotions to fill its management positions during the early 1980s, when its fast-food strategy required relatively few substantive changes in its operations.

reorientation situation Strategy situation in which poor performance despite sound strategy calls for change to be implemented by outsiders.

Sometimes, an organization's strategy appears to be sound even though its performance has been poor. If the organization's problems are due to bad management, such a **reorientation situation** calls for outsiders. Apple Computer found itself in this situation after IBM muscled into the personal computer market. Apple brought in a new CEO and key marketing and finance managers from outside the company in order to improve its competitive position. At the same time, the company transferred and clarified the role of younger product-development managers in an effort to reinvigorate its technical strengths.

Culture and Strategy

organizational culture The set of important understandings, such as norms, values, attitudes, and beliefs, shared by organizational members.

EXTRA EXERCISE

Find an example of a merger or acquisition that appears to have not worked and try to explain why. Scan any of the business periodicals from the last couple of years.

Organizational culture includes the shared values, beliefs, attitudes, and norms that shape the behavior and expectations of each member of the organization. "Culture," while less explicit than rules and procedures, may be an even more powerful influence on the way employees and managers approach problems, serve customers, and the like. Broadly speaking, organizational culture determines what behavior is appropriate for employees and which issues should take priority. (Organizational culture is discussed in more detail in Chapter 12.)

When an organization's culture is consistent with its strategy, the implementation of strategy is eased considerably. For example, the organizational cultures at Delta Airlines and IBM complement their strategic emphasis on service. Because of the nature of their services, members of those companies share people-oriented values: They are eager to help and go out of their way to solve individual customer problems.[44]

It is impossible to implement successfully a strategy that contradicts the organization's culture. Thus, AT&T's traditional belief in the importance of universal telephone service, which dates from the days of its monopoly, has been a major stumbling block in the implementation of its new market-oriented strategy that discriminates among customers needing different services.[45] Managers faced with this type of situation must somehow change the culture to fit the new strategy. In recent years, for example, managers at Eastman Kodak have implemented a new, entrepreneurial strategy designed to speed up the development of new products (recall the Illustrative Case in Chapter 3). This strategy has entailed replacing the old cautious, insular culture, which valued quality above all, with an aggressive, competitive culture that promotes risk taking.[46]

---

[44]Thomas J. Peters and Robert H. Waterman, Jr., *In Search of Excellence* (New York: Harper & Row, 1982), pp. xx–xxi.

[45]"The Corporate Culture Vultures," *Fortune*, October 17, 1983, p. 66.

[46]Claudia H. Deutsch, "Kodak Pays the Price for Change," *New York Times*, March 6, 1988, pp. F1, F7–F8.

FIGURE 8-5 FOUR MANAGERIAL ASSIGNMENT SITUATIONS

Changes required to implement the new strategy	Effective	Ineffective
Many	**"Selective blend"** *Current executives* via promotion and transfer where skills match new roles; otherwise, seek skills and experience via *outsiders*.	**"Turnover"** *Outsiders* should be a high priority to provide new skills, motivation, and enthusiasm.
Few	**"Stability"** *Current executives* and internal promotions should be a major emphasis in order to reward, retain, and develop managerial talent.	**"Reorientation"** *Outsiders* are important to replace weaknesses and "communication seriousness." *Current executives* should be a priority where possible via promotion, transfer, or role clarification.

Assessment of past organizational performance

Source: John A. Pearce II and Richard B. Robinson, Jr., *Formulation and Implementation of Competitive Strategy* (Homewood, Ill.: Richard D. Irwin, 1985), p. 339. Copyright © 1985 by Richard D. Irwin.

BARRIERS TO EFFECTIVE STRATEGY IMPLEMENTATION

There are many barriers to effective strategy implementation. While some result from changes in a complex environment, others stem from internal obstacles.

Environmental Constraints

Peter Lorange identifies five major trends in the environment that pose particular challenges to strategy implementation and argues that organizations must actively integrate these environmental concerns into their strategy planning.[47]

Scarcity. The first trend is the growing shortage of natural resources—energy, food, minerals—that causes the cost of raw materials to rise. In response, organizational strategies must (1) cultivate those businesses which use resources efficiently and whose profits are less vulnerable to the rising cost of raw materials and (2) forecast imminent shortages while seeking substitutes and alternative sources of supply.

HERE'S AN EXAMPLE

"You don't bite the hand that feeds you and you sure don't feed the hand that bites you." This is the way an industry source described the situation of an advertising agency that developed an ad campaign cheering the new no-smoking policy of Northwest Airlines but who also happened to hold the R. J. Reynolds Company account as one of its clients. RJR fired the ad agency. (*Wall Street Journal*, 4/6/88, p. 30)

Politics. Organizational fortunes often spin unpredictably as the globe turns according to changes in political stability, legal systems, and government attitudes toward business. Therefore, knowledge of an organization's external stakeholders (see Chapter 3) is increasingly important to its strategy, which must set out a consistent set of priorities to allow the organization to interact effectively with government, labor unions, consumer activists, and the like.

Attitudes. Like political realities, social values are in flux, and in particular two recent changes in social attitude may act to reduce organizational effectiveness. First is the change in attitude toward growth: The importance of growth has been devalued in the current social and economic climate, and organizational strategy must somehow counterbalance this attitude to ensure that the organization continues to recognize and pursue growth opportunities.

Second is the challenge to traditional expectations of strong commitment and performance on the part of organization members. Organizations must respond by encouraging managers to participate in the development and implementation of strategy: The better its managers understand the organization's strategic direction and the more they feel they are contributing to its success, the greater will be their sense of commitment.

Power Shifts. Interest groups and outside pressures on the organization are also constantly shifting. Organizations can monitor these trends and try to reduce their vulnerability to outside pressures by shifting their resources away from sensitive areas. Thus some pharmaceutical companies, fearing consumer lawsuits, have stopped producing pertussis vaccine, a controversial drug for certain infectious diseases in children, while many businesses have left South Africa in order to escape the attention of the anti-apartheid movement. By the same token, a flexible portfolio allows an organization to plan for more productive activities in which issues or geography are less volatile.

Technology. In the future, technical expertise may very well become the single most important strategic resource of all. Strategies will then have to manage technology in the same way that they currently manage money. Technical knowledge will be allo-

[47]Peter Lorange, "Where Do We Go from Here: Implementation Challenges for the 1980s," in *Implementation of Strategic Planning* (Englewood Cliffs, N.J.: Prentice Hall, 1982), pp. 209–226.

cated among the various parts of the organization and transferred between them as needed. In addition, methods of business departmentalization will be redefined as the transfer of knowledge will be facilitated, and as technology increases at greater rates, product life cycles will unquestionably be affected.

HERE'S AN EXAMPLE

IBM Corporation is ready for round two of the PC clone wars. In fact, many industry officials, dealers, and customers say clones of IBM's PS/2 (its year-old second line of PCs) will put far less pressure on IBM than did the first generation of clones. IBM models are likely to fare better in round two. (*Wall Street Journal*, 4/29/88, p. 25)

Internal Constraints

Lorange also observes that some of the greatest difficulties facing managers are created by the organization itself.[48] Strategy should, ideally, prevent such handicaps and free the organization from internal constraints; at the very least, it must learn to cope with them.

HERE'S AN EXAMPLE

Coca-Cola Company's diversification efforts have not had much success. A number of analysts and Coke watchers conclude that, " . . . away from the soda machine, the company is haunted by strategic confusion." Roberto Goizeuta, chairman of Coca-Cola Company, is wondering—what things really do go better with Coke? (*Forbes*, 3/21/88, pp. 34–35)

Inflexibility. All too often, functional divisions become rigidly independent fiefdoms which fail to communicate or cooperate with one other. Managers must thus become aware of the inherently *cross-functional* nature of the organization's major tasks. Lorange proposes a dual responsibility system that would assign managers to strategic cross-functional task forces in addition to their own functional operating responsibilities.

Executive Obsolescence. Members of an organization may become obsolete as environmental changes make their accumulated knowledge and experience irrelevant. Therefore, the strategic planning process should be a learning process for managers, keeping them up-to-date. In addition, strategy should view human competencies as transferable resources to be shifted from problem to problem rather than hired to cope with rigidly defined problems or problem areas and then fired when no longer needed.

Parochialism. Managers often feel loyalty to their particular business or country operation rather than to the organization as a whole. If the organizational strategy calls for a portfolio style (see Chapter 7), it must somehow develop values and attitudes that reinforce that point of view. Lorange recommends that feedback from the corporate executive office emphasize the role that each division plays within the organization, the organization's portfolio perspective being stressed, not the division's relative success or failure.

Values, Styles, Traditions. Organizational culture simplifies strategy implementation because it ensures that everyone involved approaches the issues from a similar point of view. But those same shared values, styles, and traditions can also act as vested interests, preventing managers from recognizing the significance of environmental changes and making them reluctant to modify their priorities or shift strategic resources. According to Lorange, central corporate planning must ensure that its style is responsive to strategic processes which, in turn, are receptive to goal modification, new-business developments, and environmental problems and opportunities.

Power. In many organizations, the CEO simply lacks the power to alter the firm's direction and reallocate strategic resources. This can happen when executive power is decentralized in favor of functional managers, when the CEO is a lame duck nearing retirement, when a poor track record has undermined all confidence in the CEO, or when there is no coalition of top executives to support or supplement the CEO's efforts. The best solution is to develop a group of managers at the top of the organization who are able and willing to work together to develop and execute strategy.

---

[48] Ibid., pp. 220–225.

ILLUSTRATIVE CASE STUDY Wrap-Up

Maintaining the Competitive Edge at Merck & Co.

Merck is a well-managed company in large part because it has successfully applied the lessons of strategy implementation. From recruiting and training, to teamwork and rewards, Merck has created an atmosphere in which a number of people can flourish at a variety of levels. The fact that Vagelos is concerned about the atmosphere of his company is a sign that, like any good contemporary CEO, he spends a great deal of his time fitting together the strategy and the culture of an organization which is built on a complexly integrated system of units that must be coordinated in the implementation of strategy for a vast variety of projects.

Successful implementation, however, is not simply a matter of establishing an internal harmony conducive to productivity. External factors also play an extremely important role in erecting barriers to successful strategy implementation. Among the external barriers faced by pharmaceutical manufacturers is the problem of securing the approval of the Food and Drug Administration (FDA) for the marketing of their products. In this respect, Merck, under Roy Vagelos' leadership, has been remarkably effectve in implementing long-term—and highly costly—strategies in its efforts to transform extremely expensive research-and-development commitments into profitable strategies.

A case in point is a product that the company markets as Mevacor, which can reduce cholesterol levels in the body by up to 40 percent. Merck had actually begun preliminary research on the product in 1956. Roy Vagelos joined the company in 1975 as senior vice-president for research and championed the project through a series of breakthroughs and setbacks in development until, by 1986, about 25 percent of the company's $530 million research and development were committed to the project.

In November of 1986, Merck presented the FDA with some 42,000 pages of documents supporting a request for a public review by an FDA advisory panel—a request that can wait as long as a year before it is granted. But Merck had begun implementing its campaign much earlier than 1986. Beginning in 1978, a special group for regulatory affairs had begun working with the FDA, advising the agency not only of progress but of problems. A team of over 100 people made sure that the FDA was continuously supplied with necessary information, and by February 19, 1987, the company had already met some 6,000 individual target deadlines. On that date—three months after filing its application—Merck won its hearing date. The next day, Mevacor received the panel's unanimous preliminary approval. Final approval was granted in August: Merck had accomplished in 9 months what normally takes about 30. The next step in implementation was marketing: Whereas Merck is an industry leader in spending $560 million in its laboratories each year, it also devotes $670 million per year to marketing and advertising as key functions in its implementation strategy.

Some industry analysts estimate that within five years, Mevacor (and its improved versions) will be the leading product in a $4.5 billion market composed of cholesterol-conscious consumers. ■

■ SUMMARY

Strategy implementation depends in part on organizational structure. In the United States, organizations typically pass through three stages of strategic and structural development. At first, they are single-product, unit firms with an administrative office to manage the business. The second stage is marked by vertical integration and a functional structure; operational decisions are now made by managers of such functional divisions as marketing, finance, and production. In the third stage, a multidivisional structure emerges to handle product diversification in a competitive environment. Product divisions operate semiautonomously, while a central office makes the long-term strategic decisions. Multidivisional structures may act as a substitute for market mechanisms in allocating resources among disparate businesses.

The Seven-S approach argues that successful strategy implementation depends on suitable adjustment among an organization's strategy, structure, operating systems, management style, staff development programs, organizational skills, and superordinate goals.

Suitably designed incentive plans can be used to motivate managers. They can reward risk taking, cooperation with other units, or a variety of behavior that best fits the organization's strategy. Another approach is to match a manager's personality and experience with the strategic needs of a particular division or product.

Marketing, production, finance, human resources, and other functional strategies translate the organizational strategy into action. They provide operating managers with detailed short-term goals as well as with a better understanding of their roles in the overall strategy. Annual objectives set absolute, numerical targets for managers for the coming year.

One popular method of operationalizing strategy down to the individual level is management by objectives (MBO). Managers and subordinates in MBO programs work together to establish for every member of the organization specific objectives that are derived from and support the organization's goals.

CEOs have both a symbolic and practical role to play in institutionalizing strategy. They interpret the strategy, demonstrate management's commitment to it, and motivate subordinates to implement it. Equally important are the managers holding certain key positions. Depending on the situation, it may be better on the one hand to select an executive already in the organization or, on the other, to bring in an outsider to fill these posts.

Organizational culture has the power to reinforce or to block strategy implementation. Other barriers to effective strategy include inappropriate responses to environmental changes and obstacles generated within the organization.

REVIEW QUESTIONS

1. What are the differences among evolutionary, managerial, sequential, and complex interventions?
2. Describe the three stages in the growth and development of an organization's strategy and structure that were set out by Arthur Chandler.
3. What are the seven factors of the Seven-S Model?
4. What are the weaknesses of traditional incentive plans? How can organizations improve them?
5. What are functional strategies? How can they reduce the natural conflicts between functional areas of an organization?
6. Give some examples of well and poorly designed annual objectives.
7. What is management by objectives? What are its strengths and weaknesses?
8. How can a CEO help implement an organization's strategy?
9. What are the advantages and disadvantages to assigning an existing member of an organization to a key management positions? To hiring someone from outside the organization?
10. List some factors that can prevent effective strategy implementation. How can an organization overcome these obstacles?

CASE STUDY "SACRED TRUSTEES" AND WHISTLEBLOWING AT BEECH-NUT

Mr. Jerome LiCari did not know what to do. He had tried everything he could think of to make his superiors aware of the fact that, in all probability, the apple juice that Beech-Nut was selling was not what the company said it was. So far, upper-level management had ignored his warnings that the juice appeared to be a blend of synthetic ingredients and not the "pure" juice the label claimed it to be. It appeared that upper-level managers had simply decided to ignore this fact. Mr. LiCari did not believe this attitude made much business, ethical, or public relations sense, but he was at a loss as to how to approach the problem.

In some ways, he could see why his managers had chosen to ignore his warnings. In 1981, Beech-Nut was not a very healthy company, having lost money for several years. The parent company, Nestlé, was getting impatient for profits, economizing wherever possible in an effort to increase Beech-Nut's small profit margins. The problems faced by Nestlé were compounded by the fact that Beech-Nut was the number-two brand—far behind Gerber, which controlled over 60 percent of the market for baby food products. Beech-Nut, as the smaller company, had to fight for every brand-share point.

In order to differentiate itself from Gerber, Beech-Nut emphasized its concern for the nutritional value of its baby food, promoting itself heavily as the only company that offered babies proper nutrition. As American mothers became more health-conscious, this strategy seemed even more appropriate, encouraging mothers to avoid the trouble of making their own baby food without sacrificing the extra nutrition of homemade food. However, to LiCari the company's apple juice seemed to be in direct conflict with this image.

Unfortunately, there was only circumstantial evidence that the juice was not pure. Beech-Nut purchased the concentrate from another supplier and then reconstituted, bottled, and distributed it from Beech-Nut plants. There was no test that would conclusively distinguish synthetic juice from the real thing, although there were tests that suggested the presence of synthetic ingredients. The suspicions of the research department were further aroused by the unusually low price that Beech-Nut was paying and by the fact that the supplier would not allow its facilities to be inspected.

Mr. LiCari had attempted to make upper management aware of his suspicions. He had written a memo documenting the suggestive test results and other circumstantial evidence. Management, however, refused to alter its purchasing patterns, claiming that the evidence was not sufficient to warrant the burdensome cost of changing suppliers. Its attitude seemed to be: "Everyone else does this too, so why shouldn't we save money the same way?" They also seemed to think that no one would actually be harmed if they continued their current practice.

LiCari was not convinced that this was the right attitude. After all, the company had staked its reputation on its commitment to "the sacred trust of feeding children." Surely it could be right to feed them something other than what deceptive packaging claimed.

Sources: Carol Hall, "A Juicy Bit of Bad News," *Marketing and Media,* January 1987, p. 8; Chris Welles, "What Led Beech-Nut Down the Road to Disgrace," *Business Week,* February 22, 1988, pp. 124–128.

Case Questions

1. Since it appears that top-level management knew about the problem, what could LiCari do to change the company's strategy in the face of a top-level "cover-up"?
2. What measures could LiCari have taken, within the confines of his own position at the company, to make his case to upper-level management more compelling?
3. If it is discovered that Beech-Nut's synthetic juice did cause harm, how should product management be reprimanded for suppressing the advice of lower-level management?
4. What are the barriers to implementing Nestlé's objective of increased profitibility for Beech-Nut?
5. What other ways do ethical and social concerns affect strategy implementation? ■

CASE STUDY

The Competition Chips Away at Cray Research

John Rollwagen, CEO of Cray Research, had a problem. One of his key supercomputer designers, Steven Chen, had just left the company. Cray had refused to fund a project proposed by Chen, and so Chen recruited a group of people from Cray and started his own firm. Moreover, IBM had reputedly offered $10 million in seed money to Chen's new company.

Cray Research was founded in 1972 by computer genius Seymour Cray, who had started out as a key designer at Control Data. Ever since Cray had introduced the world's first supercomputer, the Cray 1, in 1976, the firm had maintained a wide lead in the industry. Much of that success had been due to Cray and to Steve Chen, who had designed two of Cray's more successful products, the X-MP and the Y-MP, and who, by some accounts, was responsible for 90 percent of Cray's sales.

The world of "go-fast" computers is a complex one, and it seemed to be getting more difficult by the day. At one point, Cray had been the only game in town when it came to supercomputers, its machines used primarily not only by several large companies and universities but by the Defense Department. However, by 1986 there was a great deal of competition coming from Control Data's ETA Systems, Hitachi, NEC, Chopp Computer, Alliant, and Convex Corp. Several of these companies were in the process of designing machines that offered comparable performance at a lower cost. By customizing the performance capability to the needs of individual customers, many of Cray's competitors offered "minisupers" to the customer who did not need all the power available in a Cray or who could not afford one.

Since its founding in 1972, Cray had dedicated itself to bringing out a succession of the fastest machines on the market, all designed and built by a small group of talented engineers. After the Cray 1 appeared in 1976, it was followed by the X-MP in 1982, the Cray 2 in 1985, and, finally, the Y-MP in 1988. The Cray 3 was expected to reach the market in the mid-1990s.

Seymour Cray's formula for success had been to pursue his goal with single-mindedness, to isolate himself from the day-to-day chores of management, and to eschew gadgetry in favor of existing technology. He had set up a lab in rural Chippewa Falls, Wisconsin, away from the closest corporate offices in Minneapolis. His own contribution to the production of chips was the use of gallium arsenide instead of silicon, permitting faster transmission of information. By devoting 15 percent of its funds to research, Cray kept itself in the forefront of supercomputer design. Seymour Cray's ambition and drive pushed the company to the forefront, and Steven Chen's ability to deliver more of what the market wanted in the X-MP and Y-MP had been largely responsible for keeping the company successful.

In short—and for good reason—Rollwagen was uncertain what effects Chen's departure would have on Cray.

Sources: Tom Alexander, "Cray's Way of Staying Super-Duper," *Fortune,* March 18, 1985, pp. 66–68, 72, 76; Thomas J. Murray with Fred V. Guterl and Barbara Berkman, "Hot Tickets of High Tech," *Dun's Business Month,* June 1985, pp. 26–28; Steve Gross, "Breaking Out of the Shell," *Datamation,* January 1, 1987, pp. 112–113; Gross, "A Well-Kept Design Secret Drives Cray Research," *Electronic Business,* January 1, 1987, pp. 98–99; Mary J. Pitzer, "Now, Cray Is Only Way Ahead," *Business Week,* July 13, 1987, p. 109; Kenneth Labich, "The Shootout in Supercomputers," *Fortune,* February 29, 1988, pp. 67–70; Steve Gross, "Cray Designs Its Future without Designer Steve Chen," *Computer Business,* May 1, 1988, pp. 78–80.

Case Questions

1. What kind of strategy-implementation problems can arise at Cray now that Chen has left?
2. What kinds of problems can arise when research labs, like the one in Chippewa Falls, are isolated from the main part of the organization?
3. What should Rollwagen do to be sure that each function at Cray integrates its strategy with the others?
4. What, if anything, should Rollwagen do now that Chen has left the company? ■

CASE ON PLANNING AND DECISION MAKING
The Adams Corporation

In January 1972, the board of directors of the Adams Corporation simultaneously announced the highest sales in the company's history, the lowest after-tax profits (as a percentage of sales) of the post–World War II era, and the retirement (for personal reasons) of its long-tenured president and chief executive officer, Jerome Adams.

Founded in St. Louis in 1848, the Adams Brothers Company had long been identified as a family firm both in name and operating philosophy. Writing in a business history journal, a former family senior manager commented:

> My grandfather wanted to lead a business organization with ethical standards. He wanted to produce a quality product and a quality working climate for both employees and managers. He thought the Holy Bible and the concept of family stewardship provided him with all the guidelines needed to lead his company. A belief in the fundamental goodness of mankind, in the power of fair play, and in the importance of personal and corporate integrity were his trademarks. Those traditions exist today in the 1960s.

In the early 1950s, two significant corporate events occurred. First, the name of the firm was changed to the Adams Corporation. Second, somewhat over 50 percent of the corporation's shares were sold by various family groups to the wider public. In 1970, all branches of the family owned or influenced less than one-fifth of the outstanding shares of Adams.

The Adams Corporation was widely known and respected as a manufacturer and distributor of quality, brand-name consumer products for the American, Canadian, and European (export) markets. Adams products were processed in four regional plants located near raw material sources. (No single plant processed the full line of Adams products, but each plant processed the main items in the line.) The products were stored and distributed in a series of recently constructed or renovated distribution centers located in key cities throughout North America, and they were sold by a company sales force in thousands of retail outlets—primarily supermarkets.

In explaining the original, long-term financial success of the company, a former officer commented:

> Adams led the industry in the development of unique production processes that produced a quality product at a very low cost. The company has always been production-oriented and volume-oriented and it paid off for a long time. During those decades the Adams brand was all that was needed to sell our product; we didn't do anything but a little advertising. Competition was limited and our production efficiency and raw material sources enabled us to outpace the industry in sales and profit. Our strategy was to make a quality product, distribute it, and sell it cheap.
>
> But that has all changed in the past 20 years. Our three major competitors have outdistanced us in net profits and market aggressiveness. One of them—a first-class marketing group—has doubled sales and profits within the past five years. Our gross sales have increased to almost $250 million, but our net profits have dropped continuously during that same period. While a consumer action group just designated us as "best value," we have fallen behind in marketing techniques; for example, our packaging is just out of date.

Structurally, Adams was organized into eight major divisions. Seven of these were regional sales divisions with responsibility for distribution and sales of the company's consumer products to retail stores in their areas. Each regional sales division was further divided into organizational units at the state, county, and/or trading-area level. Each sales division was governed by a corporate price list in the selling of company products, but each had some leeway to meet the local competitive price developments. Each sales division was also assigned (by the home office) a quota of salespeople it could hire and was given the salary ranges within which these people could be employed. All salespeople were on straight salary with an expense-reimbursement salary plan—a policy which resulted in compensation under industry averages.

A small central accounting office accumulated sales and expense information for each of the several sales divisions on a quarterly basis, and it prepared the overall company financial statements. Each sales division received, without commentary, a quarterly statement showing the following information for the overall division: number of cases processed and sold, sales revenue per case, and local expenses per case.

Somewhat similar information was obtained from the manufacturing division. Manufacturing division accounting was complicated by variations in the cost of obtaining and processing the basic materials used in Adams's products. These variations—particularly in procurement—were largely beyond the control of the division. The accounting office, however, did have one rough external check on manufacturing-division effectiveness: a crude market price existed for case lot goods sold by smaller firms to some large national chains.

Once every quarter, the seven senior sales vice-presidents met with general management in St. Louis. Typically, management discussion focused on divisional sales results and expense control. The company's objective of being #1—the largest-selling line in its field—directed group attention to sales as compared to budget. All knew that last year's sales targets had to be exceeded, no matter what. The manufacturing division vice-president sat in on these meetings to explain the product-availability situation. Because of his St. Louis office location, he frequently talked with Jerome Adams about overall manufacturing operations and specifically about large procurement decisions.

The Adams Company, Price Millman knew, had a trade reputation for being very conservative with its compensation program. All officers were on a straight salary program. An officer might expect a modest salary increase every two or three years; these increases tended to be in the thousand-dollar range, regardless of divisional performance or company profit position. Salaries among the seven sales divisional vice-presidents ranged from $40,000 to $55,000 with the higher amounts going to more senior officers. Jerome Adams's salary of $75,000 was the highest in the company. There was no corporate bonus plan. A very limited stock-option program was in operation, but the depressed price of Adams stock meant that few officers exercised their options.

The corporate climate at Adams had been of considerable pride to Jerome Adams. "We take care of our family" was his oft-repeated phrase at company banquets honoring long-service employees. "We are a team and it is a team spirit that has built Adams into its leading position in this industry." No member of first-line, middle or senior management could be discharged (except in cases of moral crime or dishonesty) without a personal review of his case by Mr. Adams; as a matter of fact, executive turnover at Adams was very low. Executives at all levels viewed their jobs as lifetime careers There was no compulsory retirement plan, and some managers were still active in their mid-70s.

The operational extension of this organizational philosophy was quite evident to employees and managers. For over 75 years, a private family trust provided emergency assistance to all members of the Adams organization. Adams led its industry in the granting of educational scholarships, in medical insurance for employees and managers, and in the encouragement of its members to give corporate and personal time and effort to community problems and organizations.

Jerome noted two positive aspects of this organizational philosophy:

> We have a high percentage of long-term employees—Joe Girly, a guard at East St. Louis, completes 55 years with us this year and every one of his brothers and sisters has worked here. And it is not uncommon for a vice-president to retire with a blue pin—that means 40 years of service. We have led this industry in manufacturing-process innovation, quality control, and value for low price for decades. I am proud of our accomplishments and this pride is shown by everyone from janitors to directors.

Industry sources noted that there was no question that Adams was #1 in terms of manufacturing and logistic efficiency.

In December 1971, the annual Adams management conference gathered over 80 members of Adams's senior management in St. Louis. Most expected the usual formal routines—the announcement of 1971 results and 1972 budgets, the award of the "Gold Flag" to the top processing plant and sales division for exceeding targets, and the award of service pins to executives. All expected the usual social good times. It was an opportunity to meet and drink with "old buddies."

After a series of task force meetings, the managers gathered in a banquet room—good-naturedly referred to as the "Rib Room" since a local singer, Eve, was to provide entertainment. In the usual fashion, a dais with a long, elaborately decorated head table was at the front of the room. Sitting at the center of that table was Jerome Adams. Following tradition, Adams's vice-presidents, in order of seniority with the company, sat on his right. On his left sat major family shareholders, corporate staff, and a newcomer soon to be introduced.

After awarding service pins and the "Gold Flags" of achievement, Adams formally announced what had been corporate secrets for several months. First, a new investing group had assumed a control position on the board of Adams. Second, Price Millman would take over as president and CEO of Adams.

Introducing Millman, Adams pointed out the outstanding record of the firm's new president: "Price got his M.B.A. in 1958, spent four years in control and marketing, and then was named as the youngest divisional president in the history of the Tenny Corporation. In the past years, he has made his division the most profitable in Tenny and the industry leader in its field. We are fortunate to have him with us. Please give him your complete support."

In a later, informal meeting with the divisional vice-presidents, Millman spoke about his respect for Adams's past accomplishments and the pressing need to infuse Adams with "fighting spirit" and "competitiveness." He said: "My personal and organizational philosophy are the same—the name of the game is to fight and win. I almost drowned, but I won my first swimming race at 11 years of age! That philosophy of always winning is what enabled me to build the Ajax Division into Tenny's most profitable operation.We are going to do this at Adams."

In conclusion, Millman commented: "The new owner group wants results. They have advised me to take some time to think through a new format for Adams's operations—to get a corporate design that will improve our effectiveness. Once we get that new format, gentlemen, I have but one goal—each month must be better than the past."

Source: This case was written by Charles B. Weigle, research assistant, and Professor C. Roland Christensen. The names of the company and all of its executives, as well as the geographic location of offices, have been disguised.

Questions

1. What are the key strengths of the company?
2. What are the weaknesses of Adams Corp.?
3. Develop a plan of action for Millman.
4. What are some important factors and potential barriers to implementing your plan? ■

Paul Klee (1879–1940), *Clarification*. Oil on canvas. H. 29½ in. W. 37⅞ in. The Metropolitan Museum of Art, the Berggruen Klee Collection, 1984. As Robert Katz has said, conceptual skill "involves always thinking of patterns among elements," being able to see how separate elements—background and foreground, forest and trees—work together as one unified, coordinated whole.

9

DIVISION OF WORK, ORGANIZATIONAL STRUCTURE, AND COORDINATION

Upon completing this chapter you should be able to:

1. Describe the organizing process and explain why it is important for organizations.
2. Explain the division of work and span of management.
3. Understand the uses of organizational charts.
4. Define the formal structure of an organization and identify the various ways an organization can be structured.
5. Describe functional, product/market, and matrix structures, as well as identify the advantages and disadvantages of each.
6. Explain why the activities of an organization must be coordinated with its objectives.
7. Describe the three basic approaches to achieving effective coordination.
8. Identify the key variables in organizational design and explain how each of them can affect organizational structure.

Chapter Outline

Introduction
Division of Work
Organizing and Organizational Structure
Coordination
Organizational Design: Structuring for Specialization and Coordination

ILLUSTRATIVE CASE STUDY Introduction

Coordination and Integration at Hewlett-Packard

In July 1984, Hewlett-Packard Company (HP), a California-based manufacturer of computers and instruments, announced a major reorganization of its corporate structure. Company executives stated that the reorganization was undertaken to better coordinate HP's marketing efforts in the rapidly growing computer business. Declared president and CEO John Young: "We're determined to build a better awareness of the importance of marketing and give our people some tools to use."

HP had long been considered both an excellent place to work and an entrepreneurial, free-spirited company. In addition, HP's engineering talent and strong position in industrial and educational laboratories provided a solid base for the company's growing computer business. However, in the early 1980s HP was losing its market position because its customers began to demonstrate a preference for integrated, companywide computer systems instead of piecemeal, stand-alone computers of the sort that HP specialized in. HP's product lines were aging, new products were behind schedule, and competition from IBM, DEC, and a host of small, innovative start-up companies was increasing dramatically.

Many customers and industry analysts believed that HP's concentration on engineering excellence, radically decentralized operations, and orientation toward the quality of individual products read paradoxically, kept the company from capitalizing on such booming markets as engineering work stations and personal computers. Further, HP's two major divisions, computers and instruments, had their own separate sales forces, and little concern was given to coordination between them. As the market for computers and related instruments began to merge in factories, laboratories, and offices, HP's salespeople (each selling only the products of his or her specialized division) increasingly pursued the same customers in the same way—customers whose needs, however, were no longer the same.

HP's reorganization sought to correct these problems and to better position the company to compete. Under the new structure, marketing and sales functions were organized by markets rather than by products. One sales force now served business customers while the second served scientific and manufacturing customers. This new program successfully integrated once-independent groups from the computer side of the company with those from the instruments side.

In addition, CEO Young surprised HP watchers my moving executive vice-president Paul Ely, Jr., a long-time HP computer executive who was known as an aggressive, outspoken manager, who had built HP's position in computers, but who had retained his focus on the company's computer division, to a less visible, less influential assignment. Meanwhile, Dean Morton, previously Ely's equal as executive vice-president, was promoted to chief operating officer and given responsibilities for a new marketing structure charged with integrating the marketing of both computer and instruments sides of the company.

Sources: "Can Morton Calm Ruffled Feathers?" *Industry Week,* August 20, 1984, p. 64; "Hewlett-Packard: Continuing the Search for Excellence," *Business Marketing,* November 1985, pp. 74, 76; Kathleen K. Wiegner, "John Young's New Jogging Shoes," *Forbes,* November 4, 1985, pp. 42–44; John A. Young, "The Quality Focus at Hewlett-Packard," *The Journal of Business Strategy* 5 (Winter 1985):6–9; David Finn, "Growing up with the Founding Fathers," *Across the Board* 23 (March 1986):47–55; Wiegner, "Making the Short List Again," *Forbes,* June 15, 1987, pp. 124, 125–126; Jonathan B. Levine, "Mild-Mannered Hewlett-Packard Is Making Like Superman," *Business Week,* March 7, 1988, pp. 110–111, 114.

The word *organization* has two common meanings. The first meaning signifies an *institution* or functional group; for example, we refer to a business, a hospital, a government agency, or a basketball team as an organization. We discussed the importance of organizations in this sense in Chapter 1. The second meaning refers to the process of organizing—the way work is arranged and allocated among members of the organization so that the goals of the organization can be efficiently achieved. We will be dealing with various aspects of the organizing process in this section of the text (Chapters 9–13).

The organizing process involves balancing a company's needs for both stability and change. On the one hand, an organization's structure gives stability and reliability to the actions of its members. Stability and reliability are required for an organization to move coherently toward its goals. On the other hand, altering an organization's structure can be a means of adapting to and bringing about change, or it can be a source of resistance to change.

Chapters 9 and 10 in Part Three emphasize the stabilizing aspects of organizational structure. In them, we will see how managers create predictability of organizational behavior through the ways they structure the organization and define tasks, responsibilities, and relationships in the workplace. Then, in Chapter 11 we will consider the selection, training, and development of the organization's members. In the remaining two chapters of Part Three, our attention will turn to organizing in the face of change and to managing conflict and creativity within the organization.

Many organizations evolve haphazardly, making additions to and changes in their structure from time to time as tactical expedients to meet specific ends. A number of specific factors determine an organization's actual structure. Among those factors are the technology it uses, the environment in which it operates, and the values of its members. There is no "one best way" for all organizations to be designed. The most desirable structure is an individual matter that will vary from one organization to the next and within one organization over time.

division of work The breakdown of a complex task into components so that individuals are responsible for a limited set of activities instead of the task as a whole.

departmentalization The grouping into departments of work activities that are similar and logically connected.

coordination The integration of the activities of the separate parts of an organization to accomplish organizational goals.

organizational design The determination of the organizational structure that is most appropriate for the strategy, people, technology, and tasks of the organization.

As we saw in Part Two, the planning process results in a schedule of tasks for managers to accomplish. Strategic planning helps managers focus on the long-range goals of the organization. In Part Three, we will be examining how the managerial tasks defined in the planning stages can be divided and reintegrated to achieve the organization's objectives.

This chapter will focus on several aspects of organizational structure: division of work, departmentalization, coordination, and the design of organizations. **Division of work** is the breakdown of the work of an organization so that each person in it performs a limited set of activities, not its entire work. **Departmentalization** is the grouping of work functions so that similar and logically related activities occur together. **Coordination** means integrating the goals and tasks of an organization's separate units to achieve its goals efficiently. **Organizational design** is the process of choosing the best type of organization for any situation.

All these concepts engaged the attention of the earliest management writers and continue to interest writers and managers today. The subject of an individual's work tasks—how specialized or varied they should be—was one of the earliest concerns of management. It is still a major subject of debate and research. In Exhibit 9-1 Ernest Dale describes organizing as a multistep process.

EXHIBIT 9-1 THE MULTISTEP PROCESS OF ORGANIZING

1. *Detailing all the work that must be done to attain the organization's goals.* Every organization is created with a set of purposes—hospitals are created to care for the sick, basketball teams are created to win games, businesses are created to sell goods and services. Each of these purposes will obviously be accomplished in a different way. For the organization's goals to be achieved, therefore, the tasks of the organization as a whole must first be determined. For example, before the organizers of a hospital can help the sick, they will have to purchase equipment, hire physicians and other professional and nonprofessional personnel, set up various specialized medical departments, arrange for accreditation with professional organizations, coordinate with various agencies in the community, and so on.
2. *Dividing the total work load into activities that can logically and comfortably be performed by one person or by a group of individuals.* Organizations are created because the work they are meant to accomplish cannot be performed by one person alone. Thus, the work of the organization must be appropriately divided among its members. By "appropriate" we mean, first, that individuals will be assigned to tasks on the basis of their qualifications for those tasks and, second, that no individual will be charged with carrying too heavy or too light a work load.
3. *Combining the work of the organization's members in a logical and efficient manner.* As an organization expands in size and hires more people to perform various activities, it becomes necessary to group individuals whose assigned tasks are related. Sales, human resources, production, accounting, and marketing are some typical departments in manufacturing organizations. In a given department are workers with a number of different skills and levels of expertise, whose interactions with one another are governed by established procedures. This aggregation of work is generally referred to as departmentalization.
4. *Setting up a mechanism to coordinate the work of organization members into a unified, harmonious whole.* As individuals and departments carry out their specialized activities, the overall goals of the organization may become submerged or conflicts between organization members may develop. For example, marketing managers in a manufacturing company may press for larger advertising budgets to stimulate demand, even though the larger interests of the company may be best served by investment in more automated equipment to lower costs. In a university, various schools or departments may compete aggressively for limited funds. Coordinating mechanisms enable members of the organization to keep sight of the organization's goals and reduce inefficiency and harmful conflicts.
5. *Monitoring the effectiveness of the organization and making adjustments to maintain or increase effectiveness.* Because organizing is an ongoing process, periodic reassessment of the four preceding steps is necessary. As organizations grow and situations change, the organization's structure must be reevaluated to be sure it is consistent with effective and efficient operation to meet present needs.

Source: Ernest Dale, *Organization* (New York: American Management Association), p. 9. The five-step process detailed here elaborates on Dale's original three-step process.

DIVISION OF WORK

Many businesses as well as departments within companies start out small. A single entrepreneur or individual may be able to handle the entire operation. As the work load of the business or department grows, however, the entrepreneur or individual becomes a manager as assistants are added and work is divided among them. With further expansion it becomes necessary for the manager to group employees into departments.

Job Specialization

job specialization The division of work into standardized, simplified tasks.

The rise of civilization can be attributed to the division of labor. The greater productivity resulting from **job specialization** gave humanity the resources needed for art, science, and education.

Adam Smith's *Wealth of Nations* opens with a famous passage describing the minute specialization of labor in the manufacture of pins. Describing the work in a pin factory, Smith wrote: "One mans draws the wire, another straightens it, a third cuts it, a fourth points it, a fifth grinds it at the top for receiving the head." Ten men working in this fashion, he said, made 48,000 pins in one day. "But if they had all wrought separately and independently," each might at best have produced 20 pins a day. As

Smith observed, the great advantage of the division of labor was that in breaking down the total job into small, simple, and separate operations in which each worker could specialize, total productivity multiplied geometrically.[1]

TEACHING TIP

List the advantages and disadvantages of specialization side by side on the board or on a prepared transparency.

Why does division of work sometimes result in increases in productivity? (We use the more modern phrase "division of work" rather than the classic "division of labor" because the latter term implies that only routine tasks are specialized; in fact, specialization applies to all types of work activities, including those of managers and other professionals.) The answer is that no one person is physically able to perform all the operations in most complex tasks, nor can any one person acquire all the skills needed to perform the various tasks that make up a complex operation. Thus, to carry out tasks requiring a number of steps, it is necessary to parcel out the various parts of the tasks among a number of people. Such specialized division of work allows people to learn skills and become expert at their individual job functions. Simplified tasks can be learned in a relatively short time and be completed quickly. Also, the availability of a variety of jobs makes it possible for people to choose, or be assigned to, positions they will enjoy and for which they are well suited.

But job specialization also has its disadvantages. If tasks are divided into small, discrete steps, and if each worker is responsible for only one such step, then *alienation*—the absence of a sense of ownership—may easily develop. Karl Marx built his theory of socialist economics partly on the contention that division of work causes workers to take little pride in their work because they are responsible for only a small portion of the finished product. On the more practical, less theoretical level, boredom may set in—and absenteeism may rise—when a specialized task becomes repetitious and personally unsatisfying.[2] Many techniques of *job enlargement* and *job enrichment* (to be discussed in Chapter 12) are aimed at overcoming the problem of labor alienation. For example, General Motors and Toyota decided in their Fremont, California, joint venture to let work teams decide who performs what tasks and to train workers to perform multiple tasks.

Span of Management

span of management The number of subordinates reporting directly to a given manager.

Span of management (also called **span of control**) can be simply defined as the number of subordinates who report directly to a given manager. This aspect of organization has interested managers since ancient times. Both the Roman legions and the Chinese civil service, for example, had to address span of management questions (although neither explicitly recognized the concept as such).

The modern approach to the subject began with the Industrial Revolution. In the nineteenth and first half of the twentieth centuries, various writers attempted to determine the maximum number of subordinates one manager could supervise. Many concluded that the universal maximum was six. The ideal that a manager can control only a certain number of subordinates regardless of circumstances seems odd today, but the earlier writers must be given credit for recognizing that there is an optimal number of subordinates and also that there is a number beyond which supervision becomes less effective.[3]

---

[1]Adam Smith, *Wealth of Nations* (New York: Modern Library, 1937; originally published in 1776), pp. 3–4.

[2]Gareth R. Jones, "Task Visibility, Free Riding, and Shirking: Explaining the Effect of Structure and Technology on Employee Behavior," *Academy of Management Review*, October 1984, pp. 684–695.

[3]Some early writers did, however, consider situational factors. Early in this century, for instance, F. R. Mason referred to variables that affected the span of management in *Business Principles and Organization* (Chicago: Cree Publishing, 1909). Considerably later, Lyndall F. Urwick emphasized the interdependence of the work of subordinates, and Luther Gulick mentioned a variety of important factors, such as the type of work and the variety of tasks performed. See Lyndall F. Urwick, "The Manager's Span of Control," *Harvard Business Review* 34, no. 3 (May–June 1956):39–47; and Luther Gulick, "Notes on the Theory of Organization," in Luther Gulick and L. Urwick, eds., *Papers on the Science of Administration* (New York: Institute of Public Administration, Columbia University, 1937), pp. 1–46.

There are two major reasons why the choice of the appropriate span may be important: First, span of management may affect the efficient utilization of managers and the effective performance of their subordinates. Too wide a span may mean that managers are overextending themselves and that their subordinates are receiving too little guidance or control. Too narrow a span of management may mean that managers are underutilized.

CLASS COMMENT

Be sure to recognize the differences between "tall" and "flat" organizations.

Second, there is a relationship between span of management throughout the organization and organizational structure. Narrow spans of management result in "tall" organizational structures with many supervisory levels between top management and the lowest levels. Wide spans, for the same number of employees, mean fewer management levels between top and bottom. Either structure may influence the effectiveness of managers at any level.

If too wide or too narrow a span of management can influence productivity and costs, selecting the appropriate span may offer the opportunity to increase organizational performance. Rather than searching for the universally correct span, contemporary researchers have sought to determine the span of management most appropriate to a given situation.

The appropriate span of management cannot be calculated from any single formula or rule of thumb. There are, however, some guidelines that indicate whether a span should be relatively broad or relatively narrow. The guidelines include factors relating to the situation, subordinates, and the manager.

Some of these factors imply that the optimal span of management may not always be the same, even for the same manager and subordinates. For example, as a manager and subordinates improve in their work, the optimal span would increase. A change in the nature or quantity of work may require narrowing the span if closer supervision is required.

If the span of management appears to be inappropriate, either the span itself or the factors that influence it can be adjusted. For example, if "supervisors are harassed and subordinates are frustrated"—a symptom of too large a span—some subordinates and their work might be transferred to other supervisors. Alternatively, additional training for lower-level managers and subordinates, adding supervisory assistants, or arranging assistance with nonsupervisory tasks might be tried. By understanding the relationships between the variables, we can identify the most promising factors to adjust.[4]

ORGANIZING AND ORGANIZATIONAL STRUCTURE

organizing The process of arranging an organization's structure and coordinating its managerial practices and use of resources to achieve its goals.

organizational structure The arrangement and interrelationships of the various component parts and position of a company.

CLASS COMMENT

Organizational structure is a framework vital to the organization's well-being (much like the skeleton is to the human body).

Although we have been using the terms "organizing" and "organizational structure" throughout this chapter, we have not yet defined or discussed them in detail. In its broadest sense, **organizing** can be thought of as *the process of making the organization's structure fit with its objectives, its resources, its environment.* **Organizational structure** can be defined as *the arrangement and interrelationship of the component parts and positions of a company.* An organization's structure specifies its division of work activities and shows how different functions or activities are linked; to some extent it also shows the level of specialization of work activities. It also indicates the organization's hierarchy and authority structure, and shows its reporting relationships.[5] It provides the stability and continuity that allow the organization to survive the comings and goings of individuals and to coordinate its dealings with its environment.

---

[4]For subsequent research on span of management, see David Van Fleet and Arthur G. Bedeian, "A History of the Span of Management," *Academy of Management Review* 2, no. 3 (1977):356–372; and Van Fleet, "Empirically Testing Span of Management Hypotheses," *International Journal of Management* 2, no. 2 (1984):5–10.

[5]Robert H. Miles, *Macro Organizational Behavior* (Santa Monica, Calif.: Goodyear, 1980), p. 17.

The Organization Chart

The job functions of employees need to be divided among them and combined in logical ways. Workers with related functions usually share a common work area and constitute a work unit. Efficiency of work flow depends on the successful integration of various units within the organization. Division of work and logical combinations of tasks should lead to logical department and subunit structures.

As a company grows, the number of work units and subunits increases, and layers of supervision are added. Managers and subordinates alike become further removed from the eventual results of their actions. They need a clear understanding of how their activities fit into the larger picture of what the organization is and does. Most organizational structures are too complex to be conveyed verbally. To show the organization's structure, managers customarily draw up an **organization chart,** which diagrams the functions, departments, or positions of the organization and shows how they are related. The separate units of the organization usually appear in boxes, which are connected to each other by solid lines that indicate the *chain of command* and official channels of communication. (See Figs. 9-1 through 9-5 for examples of organization charts.)

organization chart A diagram of an organization's structure, showing the functions, departments, or positions of the organization and how they are related.

FOR DISCUSSION

What does an organization chart tell you about an organization? What does it not reveal? (See the information on this included in the text.)

Not every organization welcomes such charts. For example, Robert Townsend, the former president of Avis, suggested that organization charts are demoralizing, because they reinforce the idea that all authority and ability rest at the top of the organization.[6] Most organizations, however, do develop these charts and find them helpful in defining managerial authority, responsibility, and accountability. Exhibit 9-2 illustrates five major aspects of an organization's structure.

EXHIBIT 9-2 THE FIVE MAJOR ASPECTS OF ORGANIZATIONAL STRUCTURE

1. *The division of work.* Each box represents an individual or subunit responsible for a given part of the organization's work load.
2. *Managers and subordinates.* The solid lines indicate the chain of command (who reports to whom).
3. *The type of work being performed.* Labels or descriptions for the boxes indicate the organization's different work tasks or areas of responsibility.
4. *The grouping of work segments.* The entire chart indicates on what basis the organization's activities have been divided—on a functional or regional basis, for example.
5. *The levels of management.* A chart indicates not only individual managers and subordinates but also the entire management hierarchy. All people who report to the same individual are on the same management level, regardless of where they may appear on the chart.

EXTRA EXERCISE

Have your students obtain organization charts from local organizations and bring copies to class. (The fact that some organizations will not have one is also a good learning point! You can discuss the advantages and disadvantages of having and not having an organization chart.) Pass them around the room and see the variations. Talk about how the structure facilitates implementation of strategy. (This would be a good review of Chapter 8 on Implementation.)

The extent to which work in the organization is specialized can be estimated by reading the labels that indicate different work tasks and seeing how the tasks are grouped. The lines showing the chain of command indicate one of the key means of coordination in any organization. It may even be possible to judge the size of the organization from a chart of its structure. But while the organization chart contains some useful clues, it is possible to derive an inaccurate picture without additional information.[7]

The advantages and disadvantages of organization charts have long been a subject of debate among management writers.[8] One advantage is that employees and

[6]Robert Townsend, *Further Up the Organization* (New York: Alfred A. Knopf, 1984), p. 159.

[7]Harold Stieglitz, "What's Not on an Organization Chart," *Conference Board Record* 1, no. 11 (November 1964):7–10.

[8]See Dale, *Organization*, p. 238; Stieglitz, "What's Not on an Organization Chart," pp. 8–10; and Karol K. White, *Understanding the Company Organization Chart* (New York: American Management Associations, 1963), pp. 13–19.

ETHICS IN MANAGEMENT

WHEN IS TOP MANAGEMENT RESPONSIBLE?

A recent event surrounding Hertz rental cars illustrates the kind of ethical dilemma facing managers in today's world. It seems that one office of Hertz in Boston was creating phony damage-estimate reports from body shops that did not exist. As a result, insurers and customers were overcharged roughly $13 million. Moreover, Hertz was charging retail price for repairs even though its huge volume had normally entitled it to repairs at large discounts. Although top managers approved the practice on the advice of lawyers who assured them that others in the industry followed the same procedure, Hertz failed to notify its customers that they would pay retail for any repairs rather than the actual repair cost. It is also normal corporate practice at Hertz to have employees sign a compliance statement to the effect that their activities reflect the company's ethnics code.

Alan Blicker was head of the Boston outlet where the complaints originated. Frank Olson, chairman of Hertz, fired Blicker and 18 others, centralizing more control over operations and exercising more oversight on the activities and individual outlets. Blicker, however, claims that he is being made the scapegoat for practices the senior management approved. Now the catch—Blicker was five levels below Olson in the organization.

To what extent can a manager be held accountable for what his or her subordinates do, even when that manager may have little or no knowledge of the subordinates' activities?

Two recent presidents of the United States foundered on this very issue. Richard Nixon claimed that the famous Watergate break-in occurred without his knowledge or approval, yet it led to his resignation; Ronald Reagan claimed that the provision of arms to political groups in Nicaragua, financed by sales of arms to Iran, occurred without his knowledge. In fact, some witnesses at the Iran-Contra hearings said that they deliberately withheld information from the President so that he would have "plausible deniability."

One of the benefits of organization structure is that it specializes tasks, roles, and responsibilities: no given individual is responsible for each and every task. The effect, therefore, can be that certain information does not reach the levels at which corrective actions can be taken.

Nevertheless, many consumers and business analysts contend that top-level management should be held responsible for the activities of their subordinates—that is, for the activities of the organizations that they head. As in the case of Frank Olson, it is clear that organizational structure can either encourage or discourage corporate ethics, but the central question remains: Should top-level managers be held accountable in such cases? (In fact, there may be a simpler and more practical question at hand: As a rule, *are* they?)

Source: "Hertz Is Doing Body Work—On Itself," *Business Week,* February 15, 1988, p. 57.

others are given a picture of how the organization is structured. Managers, subordinates, and responsibilities are delineated. In addition, if someone is needed to handle a specific problem, the chart indicates where that person may be found. Finally, the process of making up the chart enables managers to pinpoint organizational defects—such as potential sources of conflict or areas where unnecessary duplication exists.

A major disadvantage of charts is that there are many things they obscure or do not show. They do not, for example, indicate who has the greater degree of responsibility and authority at each managerial level. Nor do they indicate the organization's informal relationships and channels of communication, without which the organization could not function efficiently. Also, people often read into charts things they are not intended to show. For example, employees may infer status and power on the basis of distance from the chief executive's box. These disadvantages can be minimized if charts are used only for their intended purpose—revealing the basic framework of the organization.

The Formal Organizational Structure

BACKGROUND ON ORGANIZATIONAL STRUCTURE

An interesting type of organization design—the hollow corporation—is appearing. A fascinating article on this topic that describes what a "hollow corporation" is and its good and bad points can be found in "The Hollow Corporation," *Business Week*, 3/3/86, pp. 57–85.

CLASS COMMENT

Organizational structure can have a significant impact on performance and can be modified or changed to help organizations meet their goals.

An organization's departments can be formally structured in three major ways: by function, by product/market, or in matrix form. While these three forms of structure are most frequently cited in discussing business organizations, they can be used in organizations of any type.

Organization by *function* brings together in one department all those engaged in one activity or several related activities. For example, the organization divided by function might have separate manufacturing, marketing, and sales departments. A sales manager in such an organization would be responsible for the sale of *all* products manufactured by the firm.

Product or *market* organization, often referred to as organization by division, brings together in one work unit all those involved in the production and marketing of a product or related group of products, all those in a certain geographic area, or all those dealing with a certain type of customer. For example, the organization might include separate chemical, detergent,and cosmetic divisions. Each division head would be responsible for the manufacturing, marketing, and sales activities of his or her entire unit. Currently, General Motors is a good example of this type of organizational structure.

In *matrix* organization, two types of design exist simultaneously. Permanent function departments have authority for the performance and professional standards of their units, while project teams are created as needed to carry out specific programs. Team members are drawn from various functional departments and report to a project manager, who is responsible for the outcome of the team's work. Many aerospace companies that rely on contract work use this matrix. On the whole, however, the matrix structure is found much less frequently in organizations than are the functional and product market structures.[9]

As we shall see, all three types of organization design have advantages and disadvantages. Few organizations rely on any one type exclusively.

Functional Organization

functional organization A form of departmentalization in which everyone engaged in one functional activity, such as marketing or finance, is grouped into one unit.

COORDINATED RESOURCE

If there is an organization in your community that uses assembly-line production, schedule a class visit. Note the groupings of functions, arrangement of work, etc.

Functional organization is perhaps the most logical and basic form of departmentalization. (See Fig. 9-1.) It is used mainly (but not only) by smaller firms that offer a limited line of products, because it makes efficient use of specialized resources. Another major advantage of a functional structure is that it makes supervision easier, since each manager must be expert in only a narrow range of skills. In addition, a functionalized structure makes it easier to mobilize specialized skills and bring them to bear where they are most needed. (See Exhibit 9-3.)

As an organization grows, either by expanding geographically or by broadening its product line, some of the disadvantages of the functional structure begin to become apparent. It becomes more difficult to get quick decisions or action on a problem because functional managers have to report to central headquarters and may have to

[9]Robert A. Pitts and John D. Daniels, "Aftermath of the Matrix Mania," *Columbia Journal of World Business* 19, no. 2 (Summer 1984):48–54; and John R. Adams and Nicki S. Kirchof, "The Practice of Matrix Management," in David I. Cleland, ed., *Matrix Management Systems Handbook* (New York: Van Nostrand Reinhold, 1984), pp. 13–30.

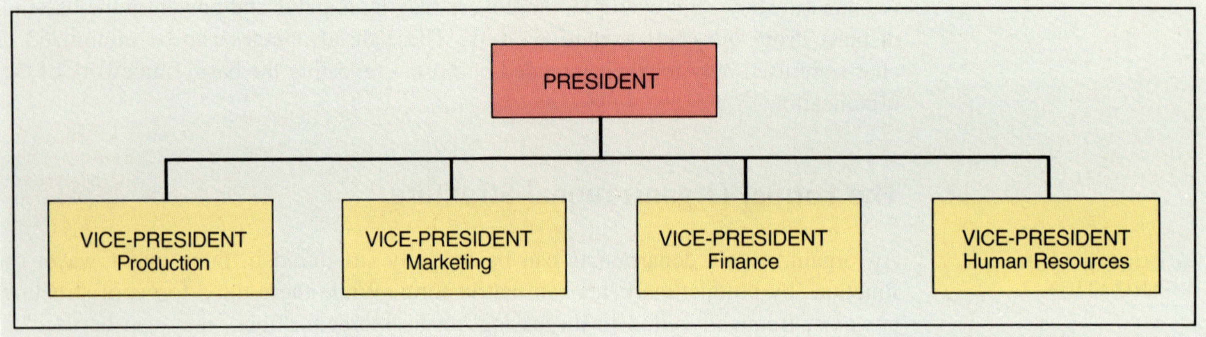

Note: Each vice-president is in charge of a major organizational function.

FIGURE 9-1 FUNCTIONAL ORGANIZATION CHART FOR A MANUFACTURING COMPANY

wait a long time before a request for help is acted on. In addition, it is often harder to determine accountability and judge performance in a functional structure. If a new product fails, who is to blame—research and development, production, or marketing? Finally, coordinating the functions of members of the entire organization may become a problem for top managers. Members of each department may feel isolated from (or superior to) those in other departments. It therefore becomes more difficult for employees to work in a unified manner to achieve the organization's goals. For example, the manufacturing department may concentrate on meeting cost standards and delivery dates and neglect quality control. As a result, the service department may become flooded with complaints.

EXHIBIT 9-3 CHARACTERISTICS OF FUNCTIONAL STRUCTURE

ADVANTAGES	DISADVANTAGES
1. Is suited to a stable environment.	1. Slows response time in large organizations.
2. Fosters development of expertise.	2. Causes bottlenecks due to sequential task performance.
3. Offers colleagues for specialists.	3. Does not encourage innovation; has narrow perspective.
4. Requires little internal coordination.	4. Fosters conflicts over product priorities.
5. Requires fewer interpersonal skills.	5. Does not foster development of general mangers.
	6. Obscures responsibility for the overall task.

Source: Arthur A. Thompson, Jr., and A.J. Strickland III, *Strategy Formulation and Implementation,* p. 324. Copyright © 1983 by Richard D. Irwin, Inc. Used with permission.

Top managers who wish to use a functional structure or add a functional department to an existing structure must weigh potential benefits against expected costs. The economic savings brought about by a functional structure may be outweighed by the additional managerial and staff salaries and other overhead costs that are required. Top managers also have to consider how often they expect to use the special skills of a functional department. In a small firm, for example, it may be more economical to retain outside legal services whenever necessary, rather than set up an in-house legal department.

Product/Market Organization

product or **market organizational structure** The organization of a company by divisions that brings together all those involved with a certain type of product or customer.

Most large, multiproduct companies, such as General Motors, are organized according to a **product** or **market organization** structure. At some point, sheer size and diversity of products make servicing by functional departments too unwieldy. When a com-

HERE'S AN EXAMPLE

Ross Johnson, CEO of RJR Nabisco, Inc., sees his constant reorganizations leading to a simplified management process. He believes that with fewer people and procedures to gum up the works, a company can make the most of its powerful brands. (*Fortune*, 7/18/88, pp. 32–46)

pany's departmentalization becomes too complex for the functional structure, top managers will generally create semiautonomous divisions, each of which designs, produces, and markets its own products. Exhibit 9-4 shows how a product or market organization can follow one of three major patterns.

EXHIBIT 9-4 THE THREE MAJOR PATTERNS OF PRODUCT OR MARKET ORGANIZATION

1. In *division by product,* each department is responsible for a product or related family of products. For example, General Foods has a different division for each of its major types of food products. Product divisionalization is the logical pattern to follow when a product type calls for manufacturing technology and marketing methods that differ greatly from those used in the rest of the organization. (See Fig. 9-2.)
2. *Division by geography* brings together in one department all activities performed in the region where the unit conducts its business. This arrangement follows logically when a plant must be located as close as possible to (a) its sources of raw materials, as with mining and oil-producing companies; (b) its major markets, as with a division selling most of its output overseas that must locate abroad; or (c) its major sources of specialized labor, as with diamond cutting operations in New York, Tel-Aviv, and Amsterdam. (See Fig. 9-3.) Service, financial, and other nonmanufacturing firms are generally organized on a geographic basis.
3. *Division by customer* occurs when a division sells most or all of its products to a particular class of customer. An electronics firm, for example, might have separate divisions for military, industrial, and consumer customers. As a general rule, manufacturing firms with a highly diversified line of products tend to be organized by customer or by product. (See Fig. 9-4.)

Unlike a functional department, a division resembles a separate business. The division head focuses primarily on the operations of his or her division, is accountable for profit or loss, and may even compete with other units of the same firm. But a division is unlike a separate business in one crucial aspect: It is not an independent entity; that is, the division manger cannot make decisions as freely as the owner of a truly separate enterprise, because he or she must still report to central headquarters. As a rule, a division head's authority will end at the point where his or her decisions have a significant effect on the workings of other divisions.

FIGURE 9-2 PRODUCT/MARKET ORGANIZATION CHART FOR A MANUFACTURING COMPANY: DIVISION BY PRODUCT

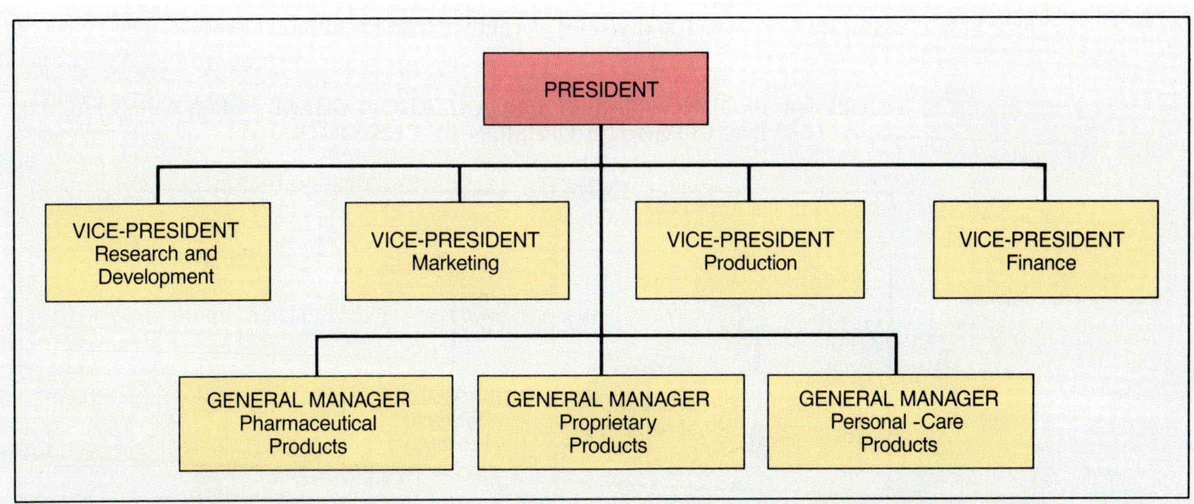

Note: Each general manager is in charge of a major category of products, and the vice-presidents of the functional areas provide supporting services to the general managers.

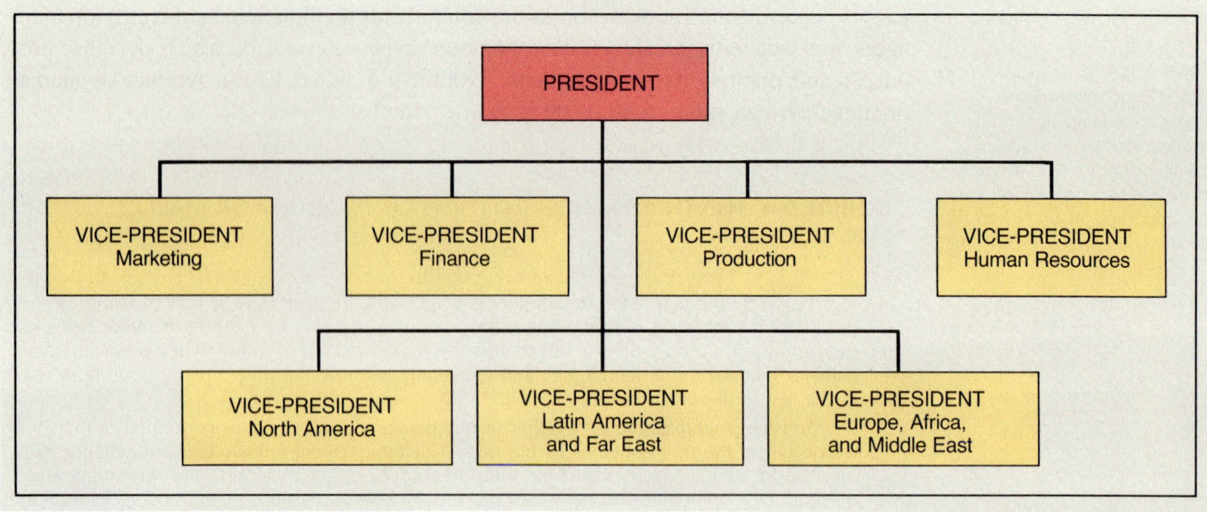

Note: Each area vice-president is in charge of the company's business in one geographic area. The functional vice-presidents provide supporting services and coordination assistance for their areas of responsibility.

FIGURE 9-3 PRODUCT/MARKET ORGANIZATION CHART FOR A MANUFACTURING COMPANY: DIVISION BY GEOGRAPHY

Pros and Cons of Product/Market Organization. Organization by division has several advantages. Because all the activities, skills, and expertise required to produce and market particular products are grouped in one place under a single head, a whole job can be more easily coordinated and high work performance maintained. In addition, both the quality and the speed of decision making are enhanced, because decisions made at the divisional level are closer to the scene of action. Conversely, the burden on central management is eased because divisional mangers have greater authority. Perhaps most important, accountability is clear. The performance of divisional management can be measured in terms of that division's profit or loss.

Recently, some organizations using the divisional organizational structure have come under increasing pressure to "restructure." Restructuring usually entails cutting not only labor but management personnel and often involves the sale of some of the company's divisions. In some cases, division managers will seek financing from banks and bondholders in order to buy the division themselves. Beatrice Foods, a very large company with over 100 divisions, recently experienced such a process. The divisional

FIGURE 9-4 PRODUCT/MARKET ORGANIZATION CHART FOR A MANUFACTURING COMPANY: DIVISION BY CUSTOMER

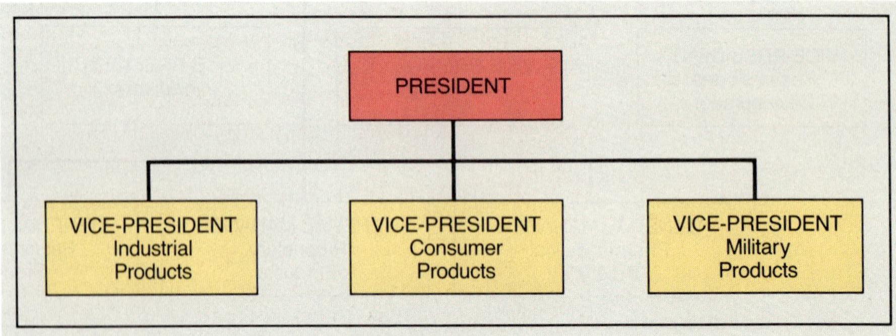

Note: Each vice-president is in charge of a set of products grouped according to the type of customer to whom they will be marketed.

organizational form makes it easy not only to treat each business autonomously but to isolate and calculate its contribution to the overall value of the organization. On the reverse side of the coin, some companies try to reduce their attractiveness as takeover targets by integrating divisions in such a way that it would be difficult for a hostile buyer to dissolve interdivisional ties and sell off certain divisions.

There are, however, some disadvantages to the divisional structure. The interests of the division may be placed ahead of the needs and goals of the total organization. For example, because they are vulnerable to profit and loss performance reviews, division heads may take short-term gains at the expense of long-range profitability. In addition, administrative expenses tend to increase. Each division, for example, has its own staff members and specialists, leading to costly duplication of skills. (See Exhibit 9-5.)

EXHIBIT 9-5 CHARACTERISTICS OF PRODUCT/MARKET STRUCTURE

ADVANTAGES	DISADVANTAGES
1. Is suited to fast change.	1. Fosters politics in resource allocation.
2. Allows for high product visibility.	2. Does not foster coordination of activities among divisions.
3. Allows full-time concentration on tasks.	3. Encourages neglect of long-term priorities.
4. Clearly defines responsibilities.	4. Permits in-depth competencies to decline.
5. Permits parallel processing of multiple tasks.	5. Creates conflicts between divisional tasks and corporate priorities.
6. Facilitates the training of general managers.	

Matrix Organization

Neither of the two types of structures we have discussed meets all the needs of every organization. In a functional structure, specialized skills may become increasingly sophisticated—but coordinated production of goods may be difficult to achieve. In a divisional structure, various products may flourish while the overall technological expertise of the organization remains undeveloped. The matrix structure attempts to combine the benefits of both types of designs while avoiding their drawbacks.[10]

matrix organization An organizational structure in which each employee reports to both a functional or division manager and to a project or group manager.

QUOTATION FROM A MANAGER

"One of the toughest things an executive has to do is say no. You can't say yes to everybody, then no one will need you. . . . "—Ross Johnson, CEO of RJR Nabisco, Inc. (*Fortune*, 7/18/88, p. 36)

In a **matrix organization,** employees have in effect two bosses—that is, they are under dual authority. One chain of command is functional or divisional, diagrammed vertically in the preceding charts. The second is shown horizontally in Figure 9-5, which depicts the multidimensional structure of Dow-Corning. This lateral chain depicts a project or a business team, led by a project or group manager who is expert in the team's assigned area of specialization. For this reason, matrix structure is often referred to as a "multiple command system." (In mathematics, a matrix is an array of vertical columns and horizontal rows; hence the name is applied to this two-directional organizational structure.)

Matrix organizations were first developed in the aerospace industry by firms such as TRW. The initial impetus was a government demand for a single contact manager for each program or project who would be responsible to the government for the project's progress and performance. To meet this need for a single coordination point, a project leader was established, sharing authority with the leaders of the preexisting technical or functional departments. This temporary arrangement then evolved into formal matrix organizations. Now matrix organization is used in the units of many major companies, in management consulting firms, and in advertising agencies,

[10]See John F. Mee, "Matrix Organizations," *Business Horizons* 7, no. 2 (Summary 1964):70–72; Jay R. Galbraith, "Matrix Organization Designs," *Business Horizons* 14, no. 1 (February 1971):29–40; Stanley M. Davis and Paul R. Lawrence, *Matrix* (Reading, Mass.: Addison-Wesley, 1977); and Harvey F. Kolodny, "Evolution to a Matrix Organization," *Academy of Management Review* 4, no. 4 (1979):543–553.

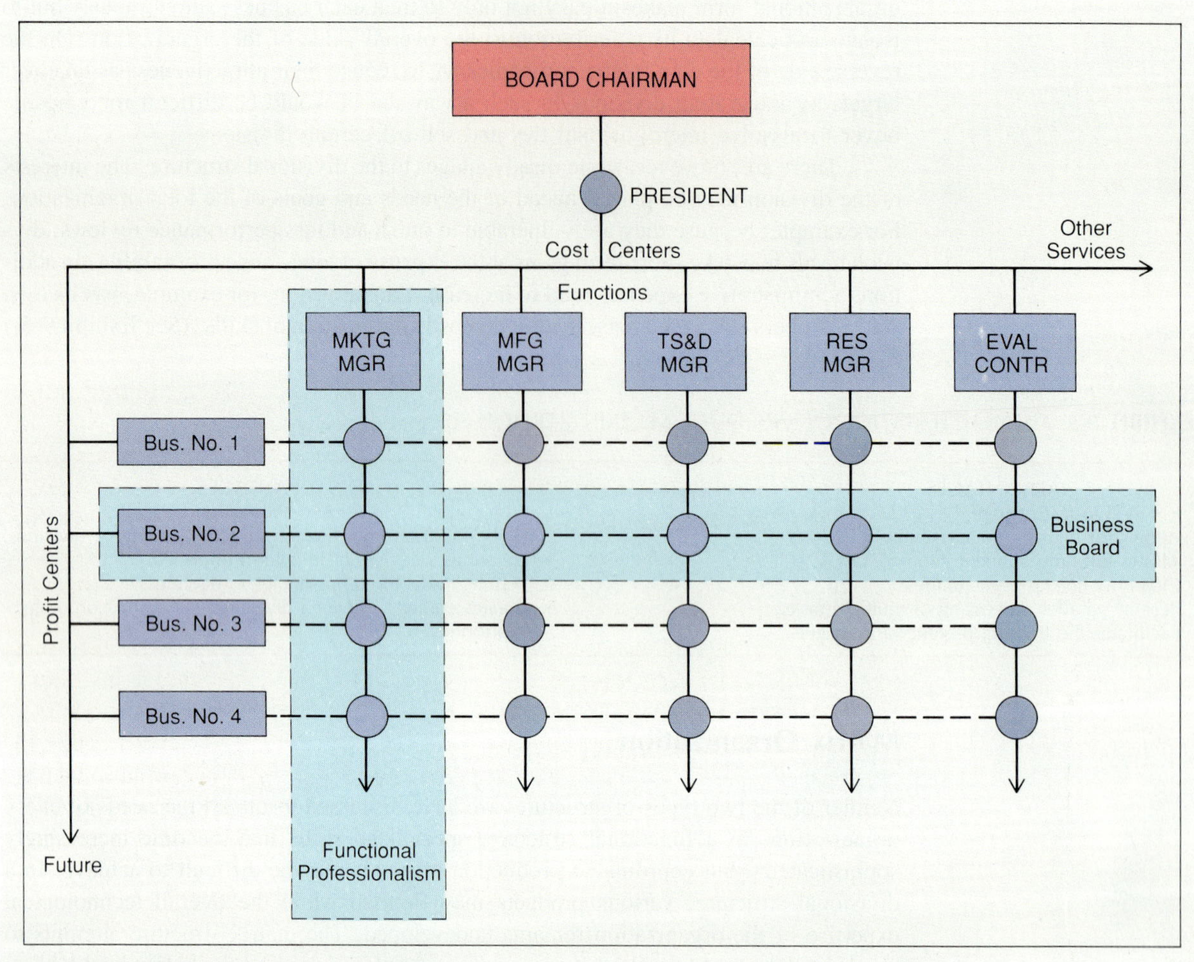

Source: William C. Goggins, "How the Multidimensional Structure Works at Dow Corning," *Harvard Business Review,* January–February 1974. Copyright © 1973 by the President and Fellows of Harvard College; all rights reserved.

FIGURE 9-5 THE DOW-CORNING MATRIX

among many other types of businesses. In some companies the matrix structure is found at all levels, while in others it is used only in certain departments.

As organizations have become more global, many use the matrix form in their international operations. There may be product or division managers, as in a divisionalized firm, and national managers for each country in which the company does business. Thus, a division employee would report to the divisional manager on product-related issues and to the national manager on political issues or those involving international relations.

Few organizations are able to make a sudden and effective transition from functional or divisional organization to a fully functioning matrix structure. When considering such a changeover, management must realize that much time and effort is required to make the matrix work.

Stanley M. Davis and Paul R. Lawrence outline four phases of matrix evolution: phase I, the **traditional pyramid,** in which command is unified at the top level; phase II, **temporary overlay,** in which project terms are created only for special and immediate needs; phase III, **permanent overlay,** in which project means are continued for ongoing purposes; and phase IV, a **mature matrix,** in which both dimensions of

traditional pyramid The most common type of organizational structure, in which command is unified at the top level.

temporary overlay A short-term structure in which project teams are created only for special needs.

permanent overlay Organizational structure in which project teams are continued for ongoing purposes.

mature matrix Organizational in which both dimensions of structure are permanent and balanced, with power held equally by both a functional and project manager.

structure are permanent and balanced, with power held equally by both a functional and a project manager.[11]

Not everyone adapts well to the matrix system. An effective matrix structure requires flexibility and cooperation from the people at all levels of the organization. The complexity of the structure requires open and direct lines of communication throughout both dimensions. Special training in new job skills or interpersonal relationships may be necessary for managers and subordinates when a matrix overlay is first introduced, or when a temporary overlay becomes permanent. To protect individuals who have functioned well in traditional structures but who have difficulty adjusting to a matrix structure, many companies make special efforts to retrain personnel before they are assigned to project teams, or select only volunteers for the teams.

EXTRA EXERCISE

Have students write a short paper on which type of organizational design they would work best in after they graduate.

Advantages and Disadvantages of Matrix Organizations. The matrix structure is often an efficient means for bringing together the diverse specialized skills required to solve a complex problem. (See Exhibit 9-6.) The problem of coordination—which plagues most functional designs—is minimized here, because the most important personnel for a project work together as a group. This in itself produces a side benefit—by working together, people come to understand the demands faced by those who have different areas of responsibility. A report from AT&T Bell Labs, for example, indicated that systems engineers and systems developers overcame their preconceptions about each other's jobs and acquired more realistic attitudes about each other after working together as a project team. (This was not, however, in a pure matrix structure.) Indeed, the exposure to workers in other areas was so effective that some systems developers decided to move into full-time systems engineering.[12] (See Chapter 13 for a related discussion on overcoming conflict between groups.) Another advantage of the matrix structure is that it gives the organization a great deal of cost-saving flexibility; each project is assigned only the number of people it needs, thus avoiding unnecessary duplication.

EXHIBIT 9-6 CHARACTERISTICS OF MATRIX STRUCTURE

ADVANTAGES	DISADVANTAGES
1. Gives flexibility to organization.	1. Risks creating a feeling of anarchy.
2. Stimulates interdisciplinary cooperation.	2. Encourages power struggles.
3. Involves and challenges people.	3. May lead to more discussion than action.
4. Develops employee skills.	4. Requires high interpersonal skills.
5. Frees top management for planning.	5. Is costly to implement.
6. Motivates people to identify with end product.	6. Risks duplication of effort by project teams.
7. Allows experts to be moved to crucial areas as needed.	7. Affects morale when personnel are rearranged.

Source: Some of the material in this box is from Harold Kerzner. "Matrix Implementation: Obstacles, Problems, Questions, and Answers," in David I. Cleland, ed., *Matrix Management Systems Handbook* (New York: Van Nostrand Reinhold, 1984), pp. 307–329; and William Jerkovsky. "Functional Management in Matrix Organizations," *IEEE Transactions on Engineering Management* 30, no. 2 (May 1983):89–97.

A disadvantage is that team members require more than the usual skill in interpersonal relations to deal intensively with other team members and to get the help they need from functional departments. In addition, morale can be adversely affected by personnel rearrangements when projects are completed and new ones are begun.[13]

[11]Davis and Lawrence, *Matrix*, pp. 39–45.

[12]R. F. Grantges, V. L. Fahrmann, T. A. Gibson, and L. M. Brown, "Central Office Equipment Reports for Stored Program Control Systems," *Bell System Technical Journal* 62, no. 7 (September 1983):2365–2395.

[13]See Harold Kerzner, "Matrix Implementation: Obstacles, Problems, Questions, and Answers," in Cleland, ed., *Matrix Management Systems Handbook*, pp. 307–329; and William Jerkovsky, "Functional Management in Matrix Organizations," *IEEE Transactions on Engineering Management* 30, no. 2 (May 1983):89–97.

Finally, if hierarchies of authority are not firmly established and effectively communicated, there is the danger, according to some analysts, that conflicting directives and ill-defined responsibilities may plunge certain managers into states of virtual chaos.[14]

Matrix structures will probably become more commonplace in the future. When organized and operating properly, they are an excellent mechanism for undertaking and accomplishing complex projects. For example, a major New York bank instituted matrix organization to enable it to expand the number of services it could offer. By creating project teams to handle special groups of accounts (such as physicians, lawyers, and professional athletes), the bank was able to supply a high level of expertise to the specific estate-planning, loan, an investment needs of these client groups.[15]

The Informal Organization

informal organization The undocumented and officially unrecognized relationships between members of an organization that inevitably emerge out of the personal and group needs of employees.

THOUGHT-PROVOKER

Why do organizations need structure? If everyone knows his or her job and does it, why do organizations need structure?

COORDINATED RESOURCE

An excellent reading on organizations and the "shocks" that can occur in them is *Rites of Passage* by Joanne Greenberg, Holt, Rinehart & Winston Publishers, 1972.

Relationships within an organization are certainly not restricted to those official ones outlined in formal organization charts. Managers have always realized that an **informal organization** exists side by side with the formal one. This informal organization grows inevitably out of the personal needs and group needs of company members. It has been described by Herbert A. Simon as "the interpersonal relationships in the organization that affect decisions within it but either are omitted from the formal scheme or are not consistent with it."[16]

Given the pace of change in today's business environment, more and more companies and enterprises of all sorts are relying on informal organizational structures. In this environment, a company's employees must be able to communicate and make decisions rapidly, and the traditional formal structures, with their elaborate hierarchies, are just too slow. Organizations such as Xerox accrued so many bureaucratic layers that new-product ideas were forced to follow such an ardurous path to actual product completion that Xerox, once "the name" in photo-copiers, allowed competitors like IBM and various Japanese firms to enter the competitive arena and severely reduce its market share. No wonder that many organizations are experimenting with relatively "flat" structures, with little if any hierarchy. (Management information systems, described in Chapter 19, can help them work especially well.) Yet even in organizations that have been slow to adapt to the new environment of business, informal structures are important.

Among the first to recognize the constructive possibilities of the informal organization was Chester Barnard, whom we discussed in Chapter 2. Barnard suggested that strict adherence to the formal structure—that is, always "going through channels"—could be detrimental. In emergencies, for example, an informal communication network makes faster decisions possible. Informal relationships also smooth the flow of personnel and materials across the lines of authority, and these relationships promote cooperation among departments that have only indirect points of contact on the organization chart. The informal relationships that develop in an organization not only help organization members satisfy their social needs but also assist them in getting things done.

---

[14]Ralph Katz and Thomas J. Allen, "Project Performance and the Locus of Influence in the R&D Matrix," *Academy of Management Journal*, March 1985, pp. 67–87.

[15]Martyn E. Gossen, "California Bank Personal Finance Group," case no. 9–478–055 (Cambridge, Mass.: Harvard Business Case Services, 1978). "California Bank" in a pseudonym for a well-known New York-based bank. For an example of successful use of a matrix structure in the public sector, see Mary E. Simon, "Matrix Management at the U.S. Consumer Product Safety Commission," *Public Administration Review* 43, no. 4 (July–August 1983):357–361.

[16]Herbert A. Simon, *Administrative Behavior*, 3rd ed. (New York: Macmillan, 1976). For other rich discussions of informal groups, see Chester I. Barnard, *The Functions of the Executive* (Cambridge, Mass.: Harvard University Press, 1938); F. J. Roethlisberger and William J. Dickson, *Management and the Worker* (Cambridge, Mass.: Harvard University Press, 1947); and Charles Perrow, *Complex Organizations*, 3rd ed. (New York: Random House, 1986).

Barnard, however, overlooked the fact that informal organization may also arise among employees as a protective device against management. In such cases, the aims of the informal organization may well run counter to the objectives of the enterprise. For instance, the informal group may set work norms well below the standards prescribed by management and enforce a slowdown in various ways, ranging from persuasion to violence.

COORDINATION

coordination The integration of the activities of the separate parts of an organization to accomplish organizational goals.

HERE'S AN EXAMPLE

W. L. Gore Associates, a high-technology company with over 5,000 employees, prides itself on the fact it has "no titles and no structure." The Gore Company appears to be doing well by ignoring organization theory.

Managers divide work into specialized functions or departments to increase productivity and efficiency. Once managers have done so, goals must be translated into appropriate objectives for each unit. Each unit must also be informed about the activities of other units, so that all of them work together smoothly.

Coordination is the process of integrating the objectives and activities of these separate units (departments or functional areas) in order to realize the organization's goals efficiently.[17] Without coordination, people and departments would lose sight of their roles within the organization. They would pursue their own special interests, often at the expense of organizational goals.

The activities of organizational units differ in the extent to which they need to be integrated with the activities of other units. The need for coordination depends on the nature and communication requirements of the tasks performed and the degree of interdependence of the various units performing them.[18] When these tasks require or can benefit from information flow between units, then a high degree of coordination is best. However, if there is no such requirement or benefit, the work might be better completed if less time were spent in interaction with members of other units. A high degree of coordination is likely to be beneficial for work that is nonroutine and unpredictable, for work in which factors in the environment are changing, and for work in which task interdependence is high (for example, if one unit cannot function without receiving information or a product component from another unit). A high level of coordination is also needed in organizations that set high performance objectives.[19]

ILLUSTRATIVE CASE STUDY Continued

Coordination and Integration at Hewlett-Packard

HP's reorganization was aimed at having all parts of the organization coordinate their tasks more effectively. By combining the sales forces of its two divisions, HP could more effectively serve customers. But now more coordination became imperative. Because each sales representative sold both instruments and computers, coordination was necessary between each of the two manufacturing units of the company. Changing an organization's structure can change the ways in which work is divided, and changes in the division of work can lead to changes in organizational structure.

Organizing by markets, rather than by products, served to give the company an added external focus. Under HP's new structure, employees had to pay attention to the special market needs of its customers and to the means by which their products could be adapted to fit those market needs. Their attention was no longer focused so narrowly on the otherwise commendable program of making the best possible product from a strictly engineering standpoint.

---

[17]James Mooney defines coordination as "the orderly arrangement of group effort, to provide unity of action in the pursuit of a common purpose." See *The Principles of Organization,* rev. ed. (New York: Harper & Brothers, 1947), p. 5.

[18]See Joseph L. C. Cheng, "Interdependence and Coordination in Organizations: A Role-System Analysis," *Academy of Management Journal* 26, no. 1 (March 1983):156–162.

[19]James D. Thompson, *Organizations in Action: Social Sciences Bases of Administrative Theory* New York: McGraw Hill, 1967), pp. 54–60.

Problems in Achieving Effective Coordination

HERE'S AN EXAMPLE

A reorganization at Chase Manhattan's investment banking operation led one person who stepped down from his job to say, "Chase has a good reputation but they can't constantly go through the shock effects of reorganization." (*Wall Street Journal*, 5/4/88, p. 26)

As the need for coordination increases, so does the difficulty of achieving it effectively. Similarly, increased specialization also increases the need for coordination. But the greater the degree of specialization, the more difficult it is for managers to coordinate the specialized activities of different units. Paul R. Lawrence and Jay W. Lorsch have pointed out that people in specialized units tend to develop their own sense of the organization's goals and how to pursue them.[20]

Lawrence and Lorsch have noted that division of work involves more than a difference in precise activities, such as tightening a bolt or writing advertising copy. It also influences how we perceive the organization, how we perceive our role in it, and how we relate to each other. These differences are desirable because they enable the organization to match individuals' talents, skills, and perspectives to the specialized needs of different tasks and activities.

As Exhibit 9-7 shows, the researchers also identified four types of differences in attitudes and working style that tend to arise among the various individuals and departments in organizations. These differences—which they call *differentiation*—complicate the task of effectively coordinating an organization's activities.

EXHIBIT 9-7 DIFFERENCES IN ATTITUDES AND WORKING STYLE

1. *Differences in orientation toward particular goals.* Members of different departments develop their own views about how best to advance the interests of the organization. To salespeople, product variety may take precedence over product quality. Accountants may see cost control as most important to the organization's success, while marketing managers may regard product design as most essential.
2. *Differences in time orientation.* Some members of an organization, such as production managers, will be more concerned with problems that have to be solved immediately. Others, like members of a research and development team, may be preoccupied with problems that will take years to solve.
3. *Differences in interpersonal orientation.* In some organizational activities, such as production, there may be relatively abrupt ways of communicating. Decisions may be made in a quick, "let's-get-on-with-it" manner in order to keep things moving. In other activities, such as R&D, the style of communication may be much more easygoing. Everyone may be encouraged to discuss their ideas with others.
4. *Differences in formality of structure.* Each type of unit in the organization may have different methods and standards for evaluating progress toward objectives and for rewarding employees. In a production department, for example, the standards may be quite explicitly defined in terms of cost, quality, and schedule, and a control system may exist for precise measurement of these criteria. In the personnel department, however, standards of performance may be quite broadly defined—such as "upgrading the quality of field personnel"; the control system for measuring progress against such standards will be correspondingly less precise.

integration The degree to which employees of various departments work together in a unified way.

In place of the term *coordination,* Lawrence and Lorsch use **integration** to designate the degree to which members of various departments worked together in a unified manner. Departments should cooperate and their tasks be integrated where necessary, without reducing the differences that contribute to task accomplishment. It may be useful for the sales department to give advice on advertisements to the graphic artists who will prepare them; however, if salespeople view themselves as adjuncts of the advertising department, then the functioning of both sales and advertising units will be impaired. Division of work and specialization help the organization use its resources most efficiently, even though they increase the coordination burden of managers.

[20]Paul R. Lawrence and Jay W. Lorsch, *Organization and Environment: Managing Differentiation and Integration* (Homewood, Ill.: Richard D. Irwin, 1967), p. 9.

Differentiation encourages conflict among individuals and organizational units. Various members of the organization present their viewpoints, argue them openly, and in general make certain that they get heard. In this way they force managers to consider the special needs and knowledge of individual departments when problems exist. Constructively resolved conflict is healthy for an organization's operations. A recent study of managers in eight nations and four national groupings found that most managers appeared to be rewarded more for noncooperativeness, *within reasonable limits,* than for cooperativeness. Exceptions included Japan and the Scandinavian countries, where cooperativeness was more rewarded.[21] Constructive conflict is seen as so important that modern management writers regard the absence of a reasonable level of conflict as a danger signal. (Creative uses of conflict will be dealt with more extensively in Chapter 13.)

QUOTATION FROM A MANAGER

"We had more problems to solve and decisions to make. We moved 20,000 people around. Nobody's ever done that. Nobody's every decentralized IBM to the degree we did last week. That's fun."—John F. Akers, CEO, IBM Corp. (*Business Week,* 2/15/88, p. 95)

Approaches to Achieving Effective Coordination

Communication is the key to effective coordination. Coordination is directly dependent upon the acquisition, transmission, and processing of information. The greater the uncertainty of the tasks to be coordinated, the greater the need for information. For this reason, it is useful to think of coordination as essentially an *information processing* task.[22]

In this section we will examine three approaches to achieving effective coordination: using basic management techniques, increasing the potential for coordination, and reducing the need for coordination. (See Fig. 9-6.)

[21] Eliezer Rosenstein, "Cooperativeness and Advancement of Managers: An International Perspective," *Human Relations* 38, no. 1 (January 1985):1–21.

[22] Our discussion of coordination is based to a large extent on Jay R. Galbraith, "Organization Design: An Information Processing View," *Interfaces* 4, no. 3 (May 1974):28–36; Jay R. Galbraith, *Organization Design* (Reading, Mass.: Addison-Wesley, 1977); and Michael L. Tushman and David A. Nadler, "Information Processing as an Integrating Concept in Organizational Design," *Academy of Management Review* 3, no. 3 (July 1978):613–624.

FIGURE 9-6 THREE APPROACHES TO EFFECTIVE COORDINATION METHODS FOR MANAGERS

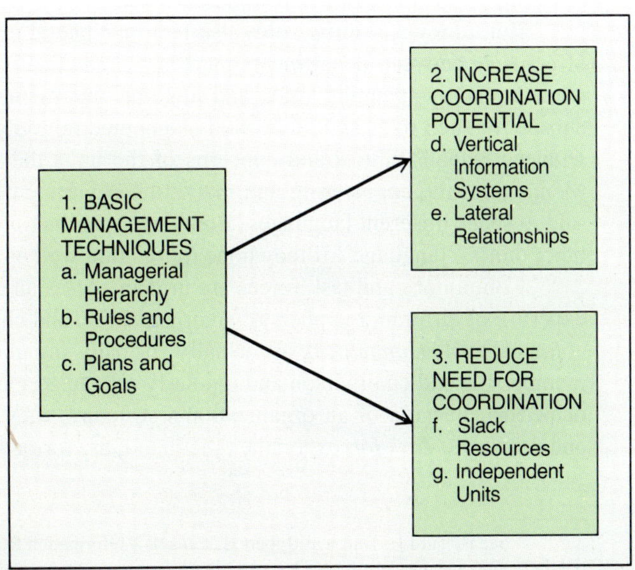

Source: Adapted from Jay R. Galbraith, "Organization Design: An Information Processing View," *Interfaces* 4, no. 3 (May 1974). Copyright © 1974 by The Institute of Management Sciences. Reprinted by permission.

Basic Management Techniques. The problems of organizations with relatively modest coordination requirements can often be resolved through the use of the basic managerial mechanisms for achieving control. These mechanisms are discussed at length in other chapters, so we will mention them only briefly here.

- *The managerial hierarchy.* The organization's chain of command specifies relationships among its members and the units they oversee, thereby facilitating the flow of information and work between units.
- *Rules and procedures.* An organization's rules and procedures are designed to handle routine events before they arise. If they are regularly followed, subordinates can take action quickly and independently, leaving more time for managers to devote to new or unique events.
- *Plans and goals.* Plans and goals achieve coordination by assuring that all units direct their efforts toward the same broad targets.

Increasing Coordination Potential. When an organization's various units become more interdependent or expand in size or function, more information is necessary for the organization to achieve its objectives, and thus its coordination potential must also be increased. When the basic management techniques just described are insufficient, additional mechanisms may be desirable. Coordination potential may be increased in two directions, vertically and laterally.

vertical information system Means through which data are transmitted up and down the managerial hierarchy.

Vertical Information Systems. A **vertical information system** is the means by which data are transmitted up and down the levels of the organization. The communication may occur within or outside of the chain of command. Management information systems have been developed in such activities as marketing, finance, production, and international operations to increase the information available for planning, coordination, and control.[23] (We will examine management information systems in detail in Chapter 21.)

lateral relationship A relationship that cuts across the chain of command, allowing direct contact between members of different departments. Examples include some committees, liaison roles, and integrating roles.

direct contact Simplest form of lateral relationship, communication between individuals who must deal with the same situation or problem.

boundary-spanning roles Jobs in which individuals act as liaisons between departments or organizations that are in frequent contact.

CLASS COMMENT

Managing an organization's suppliers (materials, parts, and services) requires creativity, *structured* efforts, discipline, and analytic support used to address any strategic issue. (*Wall Street Journal*, 4/18/88, p. 24)

Lateral Relationships. Cutting across the chain of command, **lateral relationships** permit information to be exchanged and decisions to be made at the level where the needed information actually exists. There are several kinds of lateral relationships; our discussion will begin with relatively simple ones and move toward more complex ones that require a greater investment of time and effort.

The simplest form of lateral relationship is **direct contact** between the individuals who must deal with the same situation or problem. This avoids the necessity for referring problems upward to division managers for resolution.

Boundary-spanning roles also facilitate lateral relationships. When the number of contacts between departments increases dramatically, it may be best to create explicit boundary-spanning roles and appoint unit members to them. The employees chosen for such roles should be well acquainted not only with their own units but also with the responsibilities and concerns of the units they are dealing with as liaisons. Members of the engineering and marketing departments, for example, can almost be said to speak different languages. Boundary-spanning individuals must be fluent in the other unit's "language" if they hope to function well as a channel for communication.

Committees and task forces are in many cases an effective means of pooling the expertise of different members of an organization and channeling their efforts toward a common goal. *Committees* are usually formally organized groups with a designated membership and chairperson and regularly scheduled meetings. Generally long-lasting or permanent parts of an organization's structure, they deal with recurring problems and decisions. *Task forces,* on the other hand, are formed as needed to deal with special

[23]See Richard L. Daft and Robert H. Lengel, "Information Richness: A New Approach to Managerial Behavior and Organization Design," in *Research in Organizational Behavior,* vol. 6 (Greenwich, Conn.: JAI Press, 1984), pp. 191–233.

problems. Each of the units concerned with the problem contributes one or more members. Once a solution is reached, the task force is dissolved. The distinctions between committees and task forces and their effective use are discussed more fully in Chapter 16.

integrating roles Roles that are established when a specific product, service, or project spans several departments and requires coordination and attention from a single individual not in the departments in question.

Integrating roles are roles established when a specific product, service, or project that spans several departments requires continuing coordination and attention from a single individual not in the departments in question. Integrators act like diplomats, speaking the languages of each department or group (for example, computer programmers and line supervisors). They can maintain neutrality when the groups to be integrated are excited and distrustful, and they can attempt to balance power differences between departments—restraining the more powerful ones and bolstering the less powerful.

managerial linking role A role that may be required if an integrating position does not coordinate a particular task effectively.

Managerial linking roles may be called for if the integrating position just described does not coordinate a particular task effectively. A linking manager has *formal authority* over all the units involved in a project. This authority often takes the form of control over the budgets of all units to assure that they work together toward the goals of the organization as a whole.

As we have already seen, a *matrix organization* has characteristics of both the managerial linking role and the task force. In a matrix structure, the managers of two areas supervise a group of employees responsible to them both, so the requirements of both areas are routinely taken into account. Like a task force, a particular matrix structure may be dissolved when a project has been completed.

Reducing the Need for Coordination. When basic management techniques are insufficient, coordination can be increased with the foregoing methods. When the need for coordination is so great that even these are ineffective, the best approach is to reduce the need for tight coordination. Jay Galbraith describes two ways to reduce the need for coordination: creating slack resources and creating independent units.[24]

[24]Galbraith, *Organization Design*, pp. 50–52. Galbraith also offers a third method: managing the organization's relationship with the environment so as to reduce uncertainty and the need for tight coordination. We do not discuss this as a separate method, preferring to consider it part of the basic task of relating the organization to the environment through its strategy-making and planning/control systems. However, Galbraith's discussion calls attention to the open nature of the organization as a system: It can reduce the need for internal capacity by altering the ways in which it deals with the external environment.

Drawing the Chas. Addams; © 1976 The New Yorker Magazine, Inc.

Creating Slack Resources. Providing slack (additional) resources gives units leeway in meeting each other's requirements.[25] Suppose, for example, that Mercedes-Benz anticipates that it will sell 10,000 cars in a given region of the United States over a three-month period beginning January 1. The manufacturer might establish a production quota of 12,000 cars, in case demand is larger than anticipated, and a production deadline of October 1 of the previous year to give itself a three-month safety margin should production or transportation difficulties arise.

Creating Independent Units. Another way to reduce the need for coordination is to create units that can perform all the necessary aspects of a task internally. A company that builds a variety of kitchen appliances, for example, could form an independent unit that designs, manufactures, and markets all of its food processors, thereby eliminating the need for continual consultations with centralized engineering, manufacturing, and marketing staffs. Apple Computer used this technique with Mackintosh, forming an entirely new unit to design and produce the machine. Similarly, GM created a new unit to produce the Saturn car. New labor agreements were negotiated, new advertising agencies hired, and completely new plants constructed.

Selecting the Appropriate Coordination Mechanisms

COORDINATED RESOURCE
See Lecture Extras for Chapter 9 for an interesting description of how top management personality affects organizational structure.

The key consideration in selecting the best approach to coordination is to match the organization's *capacity* for coordination with its *need* for coordination. How much information does the organization need to perform its operations? How much information is it capable of processing? If the need is greater than the ability, the organization must make a choice: It can either increase its coordination potential (by improving its performance of the basic management techniques, by introducing or expanding vertical information systems and lateral relationships, or both), *or* reduce the need (by appropriating slack resources or creating independent units). As information processing capacity increases, both complexity and cost increase as well.

In selecting appropriate coordinating mechanisms, managers in the 1980s need to recognize that organizational coordination capabilities are improving rapidly due to electronic information processing systems, which are simple, readily available, and increasingly inexpensive. It is practical and cost-effective for even small organizations to purchase information systems that reduce bottlenecks in information processing and that can grow and change with the organization and its needs.

ORGANIZATIONAL DESIGN: STRUCTURING FOR SPECIALIZATION AND COORDINATION

So far, we have been discussing specific aspects of organization—division of work, structure, and coordination—that help knit companies together and influence the efficiency of their operations. In this section we look at the topic of organizational design—choosing the best type of organizational structure for a given situation.

The process we describe here may sound neat, rational, and precise. In reality, it rarely is. Organizational design is, first of all, a continuing process because environments, organizations, and strategies inevitably change over time. Large changes in organizational structure may be required occasionally, and smaller changes may be needed often. Like many complex managerial issues, the problem of organizational design may never be permanently resolved in any particular organization. Second,

[25]See Kenneth E. Marino and David R. Lange, "Measuring Organizational Slack: A Note on the Convergence and Divergence of Alternative Operational Definitions," *Journal of Management* 9, no. 1 (Fall 1983):81–92.

changes in structure usually involve many trial-and-error attempts, accidents, and accommodations to political realities, rather than purely rational approaches.

It may seem logical to cut back a particular department, for example. But if its head has strong allies elsewhere in the organization, or perhaps even on the board of directors, plans for a cutback may go nowhere. It is not always possible to implement what may appear, at any one time, to be the best design.

FOR DISCUSSION

Why has "restructuring" become a new buzzword for U.S. industries? (Changing technology; new products; administrative changes such as cost-cutting, efficiency measures, quality emphasis; and human resource changes, among others.)

Even so, organizational design has long been an important consideration for managers in all types and sizes of organizations. For example, recent U.S. presidents, claiming that the federal bureaucracy is wasteful and inefficient, have attempted to restructure it to better meet its goals.

In the private sector, inappropriate structures can create high costs and even sink an entire organization. When the Pennsylvania Railroad merged with the New York Central Railroad to form Penn Central, for instance, the opportunities for a larger, more efficient organization seemed promising. The two companies did not, however, merge their organizations into one sound structure. The resulting rivalry and duplication of effort contributed to Penn Central's financial collapse in the early 1970s.[26] Following large losses by creditors and shareholders, Penn Central emerged from bankruptcy in 1980 with a very different organizational structure and strategy. In fact, it was no longer in the railroad business.

Early Approaches to Organizational Design

Early management writers attempted to find the "one best way" or the "universal" approach to designing organizations. They tried to establish a set of principles that would yield an organizational structure that was efficient and effective in all situations. Such an approach implied that organizational structure was affected by neither the organization's environment nor its strategy—that a sound structure would succeed regardless of external conditions and internal objectives.

Today, management writers have moved from a "one-best-way" approach to a contingency approach. They argue that an organization is highly interdependent with its environment and that different situations require different structures. Managers then, must identify the variables that affect their organization so that they can design it appropriately. Before discussing these key variables, we will briefly review the early management approaches to the organizing process. We will then look at more recent perspectives on how an organization should be designed.[27]

The Classical Approach to Organizational Design

The sociologist Max Weber[28] and management writers Frederick Taylor and Henri Fayol were major contributors to the so-called classical approach to organizational design. They believed that the most efficient and effective organizations had a hier-

---

[26]Joseph R. Daughen and Peter Binzen, *The Wreck of the Penn Central* (Boston: Little, Brown, 1971).

[27]For the overall perspective in this section, the authors are indebted to Kenneth N. Wexly and Gary A. Yukl, *Organizational Behavior and Personnel Psychology,* rev. ed. (Homewood, Ill.: Richard D. Irwin, 1984); Y. K. Shetty and Howard M. Carlisle, "A Contingency Model of Organizational Design," *California Management Review* 15, no. 1 (Fall 1972):38–45; and Jay R. Galbraith and Daniel A. Nathanson, "The Role of Organizational Structure and Process in Strategy Implementation," in Dan E. Schendel and Charles W. Hofer, *Strategic Management: A New View of Business Policy and Planning* (Boston: Little, Brown, 1979), pp. 249–283. See also Daniel Robey, *Designing Organizations,* 2nd ed. (Homewood, Ill.: Richard D. Irwin, 1986).

[28]Max Weber, *Economy and Society: An Outline of Interpretative Sociology* (New York: Bedminster Press, 1968; originally published in 1925), pp. 956–958.

bureaucracy Organization with a legalized formal and hierarchical structure.

archical structure based on a legalized formal authority. (Weber called an organization with such a structure a **bureaucracy**.) Members of the organization were guided in their actions by a sense of duty to the organization and by a set of rational rules and regulations. When fully developed, according to Weber, such organizations were characterized by specialization of tasks, appointment by merit, provision of career opportunities for members, routinization of activities, and a rational, impersonal organizational climate.

FOR DISCUSSION

How is our school like a bureaucracy? What is good about that? What is bad about that?

Today the word "bureaucracy" has many negative connotations. The early management writers, however, found much to commend in bureaucracy as an organizational design. Weber in particular praised its rationality, its establishment of rules for decision making, its clear chain of command, and its promotion of people on the basis of ability and experience rather than favoritism or whim. He also admired the clear specification of authority and responsibility, which he believed made it easier to evaluate and reward performance.

Criticisms of the Classical Approach. The classical approach has been criticized from two major perspectives. First, it has been criticized as a theory that may not have a basis in reality. Have organizations like those described by Weber and the others ever existed? And, if they existed, did they achieve the predicted results?[29]

Second, it has been criticized as a prescription for managers—one that claims organizations designed and managed according to bureaucratic principles will enjoy the predicted benefits. These critics argue that the world does not currently fit the assumptions in Weber's model (if it ever did), and so a bureaucracy is not likely to yield the results he describes.

In addition, because the word "bureaucracy" has come to imply large size, some criticisms of bureaucracies are more nearly criticisms of bigness per se rather than of a particular structure or of classical theory. Exhibit 9-8 indicates why this second group of criticisms of the bureaucratic model is of contemporary importance to managers.

[29]Weber addressed this criticism by defining a hypothetical "ideal" organization that incorporated every one of the characteristics of bureaucracy. He believed that the closer an actual institution approached this ideal one, the more fully it would enjoy the benefits of bureaucracy.

EXHIBIT 9-8 CRITICISMS OF THE BUREAUCRATIC MODEL

1. It neglects the human aspects of organization members, assuming they are motivated only by economic concerns. As educational levels, affluence, and work expectations have risen, this criticism has become more severe.
2. It does not suit rapidly changing and uncertain environments. Formalized bureaucratic organizations have difficulty in changing their established procedures.
3. It assumes that upper-level managers will be respected and obeyed by subordinates because of their superior knowledge and skills. Therefore, they can guide the work of subordinates effectively. But as the organization increases in size, top-level managers lose touch with lower levels. And in periods of rapid technological change, young newcomers frequently have relevant knowledge and skills not possessed by managers above them.
4. As organizational procedures become more formalized and individuals more specialized, means often become confused with ends. Specialists, for example, may concentrate on their own finely tuned goals and forget that their goals are a means for reaching the broader goals of the organization.
5. The bureaucratic structure has also been criticized for encouraging what Victor Thompson calls "bureaupathology."* Because managers compete for advancement, are held accountable for mistakes, and direct subordinates who may have superior technical knowledge, they may feel insecure. Thompson believes that bureaucratic structures permit counterproductive personal insecurities to flourish and that some managers try to protect their authority and position by aloof, ritualistic behavior. This is "pathological," according to Thompson, because it can prevent the organization from meeting its goals.

*Victor A. Thompson, *Modern Organization* (New York: Alfred A. Knopf, 1961), p. 152

The Neoclassical Approach to Organizational Design

Early human relations researchers and behavioral scientists attempted to deal with what they saw as the major inadequacy of the classical bureaucratic model: neglect of the human element within the organization. They argued that an industrial organization has two objectives: economic effectiveness *and* employee satisfaction.

As we saw in Chapter 2, the initial impetus for this point of view was provided by the Hawthorne studies, which were interpreted as implying that when management showed concern for employees, increased productivity resulted. Human relations researchers and behavioral scientists argued that the bureaucratic structure could be improved by making it less formal and by permitting more participation of subordinates in decision making. Because they did not reject the classical model, but only tried to improve it, these researchers are sometimes called neoclassicists. Among them are Douglas McGregor,[30] Chris Argyris,[31] and Rensis Likert,[32] whose work we describe in the paragraphs that follow.

CLASS COMMENT

This concept is often referred to as Theory X and Theory Y managers.

Douglas McGregor. McGregor believed that the vertical division of labor that characterized organizations under the bureaucratic system was based in part on a set of negative assumptions about workers. In vertical division of labor, activities are specialized by levels in the management hierarchy. Planning and decision making take place at upper levels of management, while implementation of the decisions is done by people at lower levels. Although this separation has always existed to some extent, it was increased by the application of scientific management techniques.

McGregor believed that many managers accept the assumption about lower-level employees that most people have little ambition, that they desire security above all, and that they avoid work unless coerced into it. In this view, a rigid, formal organizational hierarchy is necessary to maintain managers' authority over subordinates. McGregor claimed that organizations would better meet their members' needs and use their potential more effectively. By assuming that people can find satisfaction in work, that they desire achievement, and that they seek responsibility. Such organizations would permit employees more independence, a larger role in decision making, and greater openness in communication with their managers and with each other. McGregor's view will be discussed in more detail in Chapter 14.

CLASS COMMENT

This concept is called the *incongruency theory* and describes how organizational structures are incongruent with individual needs.

Chris Argyris. Argyris was also concerned that in a bureaucratic organization managers had nearly total responsibility for planning, controlling, and evaluating the work of their subordinates. Argyris argued that such domination of the workplace by managers can cause subordinates to become passive and dependent, as well as decrease their sense of responsibility and self-control.

To Argyris, such conditions were incompatible with the human needs for self-reliance, self-expression, and accomplishment. Members of the organization, particularly at lower levels, will become dissatisfied and frustrated in their work as these needs are blocked. The result, he suggested, it not only increased unhappiness among organization members but also increased problems in meeting organizational goals. For example, dissatisfied workers may change jobs frequently, increasing staffing costs, or do their work carelessly, increasing production costs. Employees may also insist on higher wages because their work is so psychologically unrewarding.

---

[30]Douglas McGregor, *The Human Side of Enterprise* (New York: McGraw-Hill, 1960), and *The Professional Manager* (New York: McGraw-Hill, 1967).

[31]Chris Argyris, *Personality and Organization* (New York: Harper & Brothers, 1957), and *Integrating the Individual and the Organization* (New York: John Wiley, 1964).

[32]Rensis Likert, *New Patterns of Management* (New York: McGraw-Hill, 1961), and *The Human Organization* (New York: McGraw-Hill, 1967); and Rensis Likert and Jane Gibson Likert, *New Ways of Managing Conflict* (New York: McGraw-Hill, 1976).

MANAGEMENT APPLICATION

DOWNSIZING THE AMERICAN MANAGEMENT LIFESTYLE

Many American companies adopted bureaucratic organizational structures when times where more stable, when they dominated their respective environments, and when assumptions about continued economic growth were regularly borne out in fact. Thus, such companies as Xerox, Exxon, IBM, and GM developed multilayered bureaucracies that eventually became overly complex and too cumbersome in making decisive responses to rapidly changing times.

The advent of increasingly complex national fiscal problems, an unprecedented wave of mergers, divestitures, and acquisitions, the deregulation of some industries, and an increasing number of new, entrepreneurial firms greatly accelerated both domestic and international competition. In addition, far-reaching technological advances further compelled complacent, highly bureaucratic companies to become less hierarchical and more adaptive to their environments. The important new concepts are efficiency and productivity, with organizations seeking to become leaner, more flexible structures that can respond more readily to the acceleration and maneuverability of market-driven economies. The term used to describe this complex process is *downsizing.*

While many people have been affected by the trend toward downsizing, middle managers have been particularly affected. Once seen as fairly impervious to termination, this group has been hard hit by downsizing. Between 1984 and 1988, over one million management and professional workers have been dismissed from their jobs. The trend continues as such corporations as CBS, AT&T, GE, IBM, Exxon, GM, and others continue to reorganize and restructure byzantine bureaucracies into more manageable configurations.

Once known for their almost paternalistic attitudes and operations, these large corporations have spawned great disillusionment for the many managers who have lost the lifetime job security that they once took for granted. Are there any ethical issues here for large scale corporations to be concerned with? Are middle managers less likely to be loyal to new firms than they once were? How is this alteration of the management contract likely to change the ethical contract between corporations and middle management?

Sources: Rod Willis, "What's Happening to America's Middle Managers?" *Management Review,* January 1987, pp. 24–33; "The Downside of Downsizing," *Fortune,* May 23, 1988, pp. 45–52.

As an alternative, Argyris argued for an organizational design that would better meet human needs and increase the satisfaction of organization members. Like McGregor, he favored allowing subordinates much more independence and decision-making power and creating a more informal organizational culture.

System 1 Traditional organizational structure where power and authority are distributed according to the manager-subordinate relationship.

Systems 2 and 3 Intermediate stages between traditional structure and ideal structure.

System 4 Ideal organizational structure where there is extensive group participation in supervision and decision making.

Rensis Likert. Likert shared the perspectives of McGregor and Argyris. In his research on effective group performance, he found that traditional authoritarian managers were less able to motivate their subordinates to high standards of achievement than managers who actively supported their subordinates' feelings of self-worth and importance. Based on these findings, Likert created a model to describe different organizational designs and their effectiveness.

In Likert's model, organizational structure can be based on one of four systems. In **System 1,** the traditional organizational structure, power and authority are distributed strictly according to the manager-subordinate relationship. Managers at one level tell members at lower levels what to do, and so on down the chain of command. **Systems 2** and **3** are intermediate stages. **System 4** organizations represent Likert's view of how an organization should ideally be designed and managed. At this stage, there is extensive group participation in supervision and decision making. The System 4 manager's primary task is to build a group that can make decisions and carry them out. To reach System 4, Likert says, organizations should (1) accept that managers and work activities should enhance individual members' personal sense of worth and importance, (2) use group decision making where appropriate, and (3) set high performance goals.

Criticisms of the Neoclassical Approach. The neoclassical approach to organizational design compensates for some limitations in the traditional classical model, but it, too, has been criticized.

1. The neoclassicists share the classical assumption that there is "one best way" to design an organization. They overlook environmental, technological, and other variables that might affect an organization's design.
2. The neoclassicists oversimplify human motivation. Not everyone is motivated by the nonmonetary aspects of work, nor can all work be made intrinsically challenging and rewarding.
3. The coordination of decentralized, fragmented groups to achieve organizational goals may be more difficult than the neoclassicists suggest, particularly when the objectives of lower-level employees are not consistent with the goals of upper-level managers.

Modern Approaches to Organizational Design

HERE'S AN EXAMPLE

Lawrence G. Rawl, CEO and Chairman of Exxon Corporation, is described as the "rebel shaking up Exxon." His tough, internally focused style seems to fit a more competitive world. (*Business Week*, 7/18/88, pp. 104–111)

We saw earlier that in today's fast-changing business environment, many companies have found that hierarchical organizational structures make it hard for employees to communicate with one another quickly. These structures therefore slow down decision making.

Hierarchical organizational structures are very centralized. Information flows, slowly, from the bottom to the top, and decisions flow, also slowly, from the top to the bottom. The decision makers at the top often lack the information they need to make intelligent choices. Subordinates at the bottom often don't know why any decision has been made. Little wonder that one expert[33] on corporate structure thinks "decentralization, that is, having more subordinates participate in the decision-making process, may generate the information needed" for sensible decisions. Is this possibility valid? Let's take a look at factors affecting modern approaches to organizational design.

More than anything else, the design of an organization's structure should reflect its business environment. Understanding that environment is the first and most important task of anyone who would design an organization's structure. Table 9-1 lists the internal (within the organization) and external (outside it) factors that define a business environment. Few, if any, organizations must deal with environments that include all factors, but all companies face some of them.

External Environment and Structure

In examining the effects of the environment on organizational design in greater detail, it is useful to distinguish between three types of environments: stable, changing, and turbulent.[34]

[33]This discussion of modern approaches to organizational design is based upon Robert Duncan, "What Is the Right Organizational Structure? Decision Tree Analysis Provides the Answer," *Organizational Dynamics* (Winter 1979):447–461.

[34]Ross A. Webber, Marilyn A. Morgan, and Paul C. Browne, *Management* (Homewood, Ill.: Richard D. Irwin, 1985), pp. 433–436; Fred E. Emery and E. L. Trist, "The Causal Texture of Organizational Environments," *Human Relations* 18, no. 1 (February 1965):21–31; Shirley Terreberry, "The Evolution of Organizational Environments," *Administrative Science Quarterly* 12, no. 4 (March 1968):590–613; Michael C. White, Michael D. Crino, and Ben L. Kedia, "Environmental Turbulence: A Reappraisal of Emery and Trist," *Administration and Society* 16, no. 1 (May 1984):97–116; and Gareth Morgan, "Rethinking Corporate Strategy: A Cybernetic Perspective," *Human Relations* 36, no. 4 (April 1983):345–360.

TABLE 9-1 ENVIRONMENTAL COMPONENTS OF AN ORGANIZATION

INTERNAL ENVIRONMENT	EXTERNAL ENVIRONMENT
Organizational personnel component Educational and technological background and skills Previous technological and managerial skill Individual member's involvement and commitment to attaining system's goals Interpersonal behavior styles Availability of work force for utilization within the system Organizational functional and staff units component Technological characteristics of organizational units Interdependence of organizational units in carrying out their objectives Intraunit conflict among organizational functional and staff units Intraunit conflict among organizational functional and staff units Organizational level component Organizational objectives and goals Integrative process integrating individuals and groups into contributing maximally to attaining organizational goals Nature of the organization's product service	Customer component Distributors of product or service Actual users of product or service Suppliers component New materials suppliers Equipment suppliers Product parts suppliers Labor supply Competitor component Competitors for suppliers Competitors for customers Sociopolitical component Government regulatory control over the industry Public political attitude toward industry and its particular product Relationship with trade unions with jurisdiction in the organization Technological component Meeting new technological requirements of own industry and related industries in production of product or service Improving and developing new products by implementing new technological advances in the industry

Source: Reprinted, by permission of American Management Association, from Robert Duncan, "What Is the Right Organizational Structure? Decision Tree Analysis Provides the Answer," *Organizational Dynamics* 7, no. 3 (Winter 1979):449.

The Stable Environment. A stable environment is one with little or no unexpected or sudden change. Product changes occur infrequently and modifications can be planned well in advance. Market demand has only minor and predictable fluctuations. Laws that affect the particular organization or product have remained the same for an extended period and are unlikely to change abruptly. New technological developments are unlikely to occur, so research budgets are either minimal or nonexistent.

Because of the increasing rate of technological change, stable organizational environments are hard to find. Still, they do exist. For example, E. E. Dickinson, the major distiller of witch hazel, a topical astringent, has been operating in essentially the same way since 1866. The product, the process, and the company's way of doing business have remained viable despite the passage of more than a century.[35]

The Changing Environment. Environmental changes can occur in any or all of the previously mentioned areas—product, market, law, or technology. Such changes however, are unlikely to take the top managers of the organization completely by surprise. Trends are likely to be apparent and predictable, and organizations are easily able to adjust. For example, a law firm like the Wall Street law firm of Willkie, Farr & Gallagher is in a changing environment because its lawyers must acquaint themselves with each new law. However, the basic body of law changes very gradually. Other organizations in changing environments include many in service, construction, appliance, computer, financial, transportation, and energy industries. The rate of change in the environment has accelerated in some industries—such as trucking, air carrying, natural gas, and savings and loans—because of the relatively recent institution of deregulation policies. A once-stable environment has become a very competitive one, causing the downfall of banks, airlines, and other organizations, both product manu-

[35]Peter Kerr, "Witch Hazel Still Made in Old-Fashioned Way," *New York Times*, May 11, 1985, pp. 27–28.

facturers and service providers. The advent of greatly increased international competition has also created a highly competitive, sometimes hostile environment for many firms.

EXTRA EXERCISE

Have students find examples of these types of environments by looking at current business periodicals. In fact, a good approach would be to assign each environment type to a different team of students and then have the teams do an oral class report on their findings.

The Turbulent Environment. When competitors launch new, unexpected products, when laws are passed without appreciable warning, and when technological breakthroughs suddenly revolutionize product design or production methods, the organization is in a turbulent environment.

Few organizations face a continuously turbulent environment. If a rapid and radical change does occur, organizations usually pass through only a temporary period of turbulence before making an adjustment. For example, hospitals had to adjust to a sudden increase in demand for their service when Medicaid legislation was passed. Similarly, new pollution-control laws and the energy crisis created a turbulent environment for some time. Some firms, however, experience almost constant turbulence—computer companies, for example, have been dealing with a rapid rate of technological and market change for three decades.

The recent rash of takeovers and leveraged buyouts, coupled with stock-market volatility, has added another dimension of turbulence to the environment in which today's organizations find themselves. The Pennzoil-Getty-Texaco episode recounted in Chapter 6 is the story of three companies sailing almost constantly turbulent industrial seas. Similarly, when Saul Steinberg, CEO of the acquisitive conglomerate Reliance Group Holdings, announced a hostile takeover attempt at Disney, shockwaves were felt throughout the company for some time.

International competition and the emergence of new and powerful domestic competitors have also been sources of increased environmental turbulence. Even the relatively stable U.S. automobile industry has experienced turbulence with the emergence of exerted competition from Toyota, Nissan, and Honda in Japan and Hyundai in Korea. Such external turbulence has resulted in virtually complete internal redesign at both Ford and Chrysler and a rethinking at General Motors of its overall organizational design.

Matching the Structure to the Environment. Tom Burns and G. M. Stalker have distinguished between two organizational systems: mechanistic and organic.[36] In a *mechanistic* system, the activities of the organization are broken down into separate, specialized tasks. Objectives and authority for each individual and unit are precisely defined by higher-level managers. Power in such organizations follows the classical bureaucratic chain of command described earlier.

In an *organic* system, individuals are more likely to work in a group setting than alone. There is less emphasis on taking orders from a superior or giving orders to subordinates. Instead, members communicate across all levels of the organization to obtain information and advice.

After studying a variety of companies, Burns and Stalker concluded that the mechanistic system was best suited to a stable environment, whereas organic systems were best suited to a turbulent one. Organizations in changing environments would probably use some combination of the two systems.

In a stable environment, organization members have little need for a flexible array of skills, since each is likely to continue performing the same task. Thus, skill specialization is appropriate. In turbulent environments, however, jobs must be constantly redefined to cope with the ever-changing needs of the organization. Organization members must be skilled at solving a variety of problems, not at repetitively performing a set of specialized activities. In addition, the creative problem solving and decision making required in turbulent environments are best carried out in groups in

[36]Tom Burns and G. M. Stalker, *The Management of Innovation* (London: Tavistock, 1961).

which members can communicate openly. Thus, for turbulent environments, an organic system is appropriate.

The findings of Burns and Stalker were supported and extended by the research of Paul Lawrence and Jay Lorsch discussed earlier in this chapter.[37] They examined 10 companies, measuring the degree of differentiation and integration these companies exhibited in relation to the type of external environment in which they operated.

Lawrence and Lorsch hypothesized that departments in organizations such as plastics manufacturing companies, which were operating in unstable environments, would be more differentiated than departments in organizations operating in stable environments, such as container manufacturing companies. They further reasoned that not all departments would be affected to the same extent by an unstable environment; therefore, different types of structures might be appropriate for different departments in the same organization. Last, they predicted that high-performing organizations in each type of environment would have a greater degree of integration than low-performing companies: Effective cooperation and coordination within an organization would make it more successful.

The results of their study confirmed their hypotheses. Of the companies studied, those operating in an unstable environment were the most highly differentiated, and those operating in a stable environment were least differentiated. In addition, high-performing organizations in both types of environments had a higher degree of integration than did the low-performing organizations. Those successful organizations with a high degree of differentiation integrated their operations effectively by using a variety of integrating mechanisms such as committees and task forces. The Lawrence and Lorsch study supports the importance of an organization's internal structure being appropriate for its environment.

TEACHING TIP

List the findings of Burns and Stalker, Lawrence and Lorsh, and Morse and Lorsh side by side for comparison and contrast. You also might want to add Woodward's findings (described in the next section).

John J. Morse and Jay W. Lorsch extended this line of research by comparing the *effectiveness* of departments that matched or failed to match their environments.[38] In their study, four departments of a large company were evaluated. Two of these departments, which manufactured containers, operated in a comparatively stable environment. Two other departments were in the unstable environment associated with communications research. In each pair, one department had been evaluated as highly effective and the other as less effective. They found that the most effective manufacturing department was structured in a mechanistic fashion, with clearly defined roles and duties, while the most effective research department was structured in an organic fashion, with roles and duties loosely defined. On the other hand, the less effective manufacturing department was structured in an organic way, while the less effective research department was mechanistically structured. In short, the structures of the most effective departments fit their environments, while the structures of the less effective departments did not.

Once an organization's business environment has been defined, it must be evaluated along two dimensions, simple-complex and static-dynamic. Simple business environments have relatively few factors; complex environments, more of them. Static environments change slowly; dynamic environments, quickly. Today's business environments are mostly complex and dynamic.

Let's begin by considering companies whose environment is simple and static. In the early 1970s, there were a number of such companies in the motor home/recreational vehicle industry. The market for its products was fairly homogeneous—that is,

---

[37]Lawrence and Lorsch, *Organization and Environment*.

[38]John J. Morse and Jay W. Lorsch, "Beyond Theory Y," *Harvard Business Review* 48, no. 3 (May–June 1970):61–68. See also Robert Duncan, "What Is the Right Organization Structure? Decision Tree Analysis Provides the Answer," *Organizational Dynamics* 7, no. 3 (Winter 1979):59–80. Duncan has classified environments in terms of their complexity and rate of change and offers guidelines for selecting between several forms of functional and divisional structures that vary according to the requirements of the environment.

simple. Demand for them remained high for a number of years—in other words, demand was static. Such companies should in most cases adopt the functional form of organization.

Yet an environment that is static today may become dynamic tomorrow. Managers must make an effort to recognize the signs of impending change. Change came to this industry after 1973, when the cost of oil began to soar.

Simple but dynamic environments—for example, that of the motor home/recreational vehicle industry after 1973—require a different kind of organization. They need a faster flow of information and greater closeness to markets than the pure functional form allows. A company may find that it makes sense to keep a basically functional form of organization but to modify it by providing for lateral relations among employees. Such organizations may, for example, create special task forces or committee to deal with specific problems or products.

When a business environment is complex, a new factor must be taken into account: whether the company's activities can be segmented along product, market, or geographical lines. Hospitals are typical of organizations whose activities are complex and static, but also unsegmentable by product or market. Here the correct form of organization will usually be functional—surgery, medicine, and so forth.

By contrast, many companies that market health-care products are complex and static, but segmentable. Such companies might segment their offerings into divisions responsible for, let's say, medical products, dental products, pharmaceuticals, and products for hospitals. Each of these divisions might have its own internal facilities for all functional areas, such as marketing, engineering, and production.

However, some companies that market health-care products must function in environments that are complex, and segmentable, and also dynamic. Suppose, for example, that the company's pharmaceuticals division has trouble introducing a new line of products. The line is directed at doctors, the province of the company's medical division, and likely to be used in hospitals, the province of the hospital division. In this case, the company might set up a task force with employees from all three divisions to study the problem.

Companies whose environments are complex, segmentable, and dynamic may, however, want to have the sophistication that a specialized functional department provides. A matrix organization, with both product and functional links, is usually the most appropriate choice.

Task-Technology and Structure

In addition to the environment-structure connection, it is also clear that there is an important relationship between an organization's technological commitments and the motivation and productivity of its employees—a relationship sometimes called the organization's "task-technology." Classical studies conducted in the mid-1960s by Joan Woodward and her colleagues also found that an organization's task-technology affected both its structure and its success.[39] Woodward's team divided about 100 British manufacturing firms into three groups according to their respective task-technologies: (1) unit and small-batch production, (2) large-batch and mass production, and (3) process production.

Unit production refers to the production of individual items tailored to a customer's specifications—custom-made clothes, for example. The technology used in unit

---

[39]Joan Woodward, *Industrial Organization* (London: Oxford University Press, 1965). See also Karl O. Magnusen, "A Comparative Analysis of Organizations," *Organizational Dynamics* 2, no. 1 (Summer 1973):16–31; James D. Thompson, *Organizations in Action* (New York: McGraw-Hill, 1967); Charles Perow, *Complex Organizations: A Critical Essay*, 2nd ed. (Glenview, Ill.: Scott, Foresman, 1979); and Paul D. Collins and Frank Hull, "Technology and Span of Control: Woodward Revisited," *Journal of Management Studies* 23 (1986):143–164.

production is the least complex of all groups because the items are produced largely by individual craftspeople. *Small-batch production* refers to products made in small quantities in separate stages, such as machine parts that are later assembled. *Large-batch* and *mass production* refer to the manufacture of large quantities of products, sometimes on an assembly line (such as automobiles). *Process production* refers to the production of materials that are sold by weight or volume, such as chemicals or drugs; these materials are usually produced with highly complex equipment that operates in a continuous flow.

As Exhibit 9-9 indicates, Woodward found a number of relationships between technological processes and organizational structure. The researchers discovered that the successful firms in each category had in fact similar structural characteristics—characteristics which tended to cluster around the median value for those characteristics at each technological level. For example, if the median span of management in process firms was five, the successful process firms would have spans near that number. Less successful firms, on the other hand, would have structural characteristics well above or below the median in each category.

EXHIBIT 9-9 WOODWARD'S FINDINGS ON THE RELATIONSHIP BETWEEN TECHNOLOGICAL PROCESSES AND ORGANIZATIONAL STRUCTURE

1. *The more complex the technology*—from unit to process production—*the greater is the number of managers and management levels.* In other words, complex technologies lead to tall organizational structures and require a greater degree of supervision and coordination. (See Fig. 9-7.)
2. *The span of management of first-line managers increases from unit to mass production and then decreases from mass to process production.* Lower-level employees in both unit and process production firms tend to do highly skilled work. As a result, they tend to form small work groups, making a narrow span inevitable. Assembly-line workers, on the other hand, usually perform similar types of unskilled tasks. Large numbers of such workers can be supervised by one manager.
3. *The greater the technological complexity of the firm, the larger are the clerical and administrative staffs.* The larger the number of managers in technologically complex firms require supportive services—to do the additional paperwork, for example, or to handle nonproduction-related work, such as human resource administration. In addition, complex equipment requires more attention in terms of maintenance and production scheduling to keep it in operation a high proportion of the time.

Source: Joan Woodward, *Industrial Organization* (London: Oxford University Press, 1965).

The significance of this finding is that *for each type of technology, there were specific aspects of organizational structure that were associated with more successful performance*. In other words, the successful firms were those with the appropriate structure for their level of technology. For mass-production firms, the appropriate structure conformed to the classical management principles. In the other two types of firms, however, the appropriate structure did *not* conform to classical guidelines.

Woodward's studies provided evidence of the influence of technology on organizational structure. Other research has suggested that the impact of technology on structure is strongest in small firms (which the firms studied by Woodward tended to be). For large firms, the impact of technology seems to be felt mainly at the lowest levels of the organization.[40]

There are several signs that a company's organizational design isn't working. Managers may consistently fail to predict changes in the business environment, or they

[40]See, for example, David J. Hickson, D. S. Pugh, and Diana C. Pheysey, "Operations Technology and Organizational Structure: A Critical Reappraisal," *Administrative Science Quarterly* 14, no. 3 (September 1969):378–397.

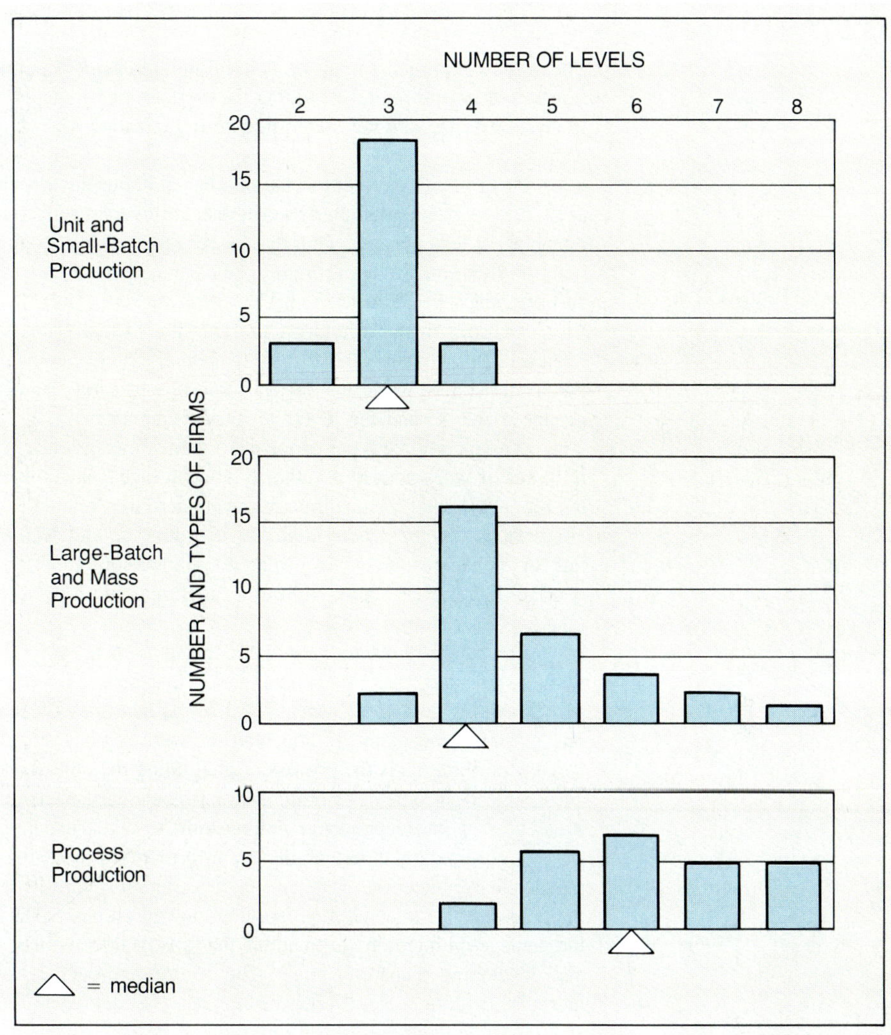

Source: Joan Woodward, *Industrial Organization.* Copyright 1965. By permission of Oxford University Press.

FIGURE 9-7 TECHNOLOGICAL COMPLEXITY AND MANAGEMENT LEVELS

may be unable to adapt to these changes. Perhaps, too, the right information often fails to get to the right people at the right time. When companies face such problems, it is time to rethink organizational design.

ILLUSTRATIVE CASE STUDY Wrap-Up

Coordination and Integration at Hewlett-Packard

Hewlett-Packard's approach to organizing is hardly unique. Yet HP has been able to sustain its success in part because of its flexibility: The company was willing to reorganize—a costly and sometimes painful process—even during times of relative strength. Too many organizations wait for severe trouble before undertaking major structural shifts. At such a point, there is the temptation to look upon reorganization as some kind of magic tonic to cure the company's sudden ills. By focusing on the coordination of marketing and customer needs, HP was better able to implement tasks across functional lines, and as we have seen throughout this chapter, reorganization is not generally an ad hoc or "stopgap" measure: It is the product of long-term planning and goal-oriented strategy. ■

SUMMARY

The organizing process involves determining the work that must be done to achieve an organization's goals, appropriately dividing the work among its employees, and setting up a mechanism to coordinate its activities. Dividing an organization's work among its employees is called job design.

Span of management is the number of subordinates who report directly to a given manager. Early writers attempted to establish a universal rule concerning how many subordinates a manager could supervise, but today we recognize that the optimal number of subordinates varies with the situation. An appropriate span of management may adversely affect productivity, costs, and efficiency.

Organizational structure represents the formal procedures through which a company is managed. A company can set forth its formal structure in an organizational chart, which identifies its division of work, its managers and subordinates, the types of work it performs, the way it groups its work, and the levels of its management.

There are three types of formal organization structure. A functional structure is organized by kinds of work activity. Authority is centralized, and specialized skills can be developed. In the product/market organization, different activities related to a single set of products or markets are grouped together; there is greater coordination and accountability, but also greater duplication of human resources. In a matrix organization, functional departments and project teams overlap. Employees report to both a functional and a project manager. Matrix organization is effective for complex projects.

Informal organization, which coexists with the formal one, comprises the interpersonal relationships and lines of communication that inevitably emerge when human beings work together. All of the various aspects of the organization—its strategy, people, technology, and so on—must be considered in choosing the right organizational structure.

Coordination is the process of integrating the objectives and activities of separate units of an organization to achieve organizational goals. The need for coordinating varies according to the degree of interdependence among units.

Coordination is essentially an information-processing task. Managers must attempt to match the organization's capacity for coordination with its need for coordination. The first of three approaches to achieving coordination call on basic management techniques, such as using the managerial hierarchy to facilitate the flow of information, establishing rules and procedures, and developing plans and goals. The second approach is to increase coordination vertically, laterally, or both. Lateral relationships can be established through mechanisms like boundary-spanning roles and the use of committees and task forces. The third approach is to reduce the need for coordination by creating slack resources and developing independent units. In practice, companies tend to combine different approaches. Designing an effective organizational structure is an ongoing process, because environments and strategies change.

Neoclassicists tried to improve the classical, relatively inflexible, model of organizational structure. McGregor suggested that organizational structures should increase the effectiveness and satisfaction of employees. Argyris argued for a more informal organizational design that gives members greater independence and power. Likert favored what he called a System 4 organizational structure, permitting greater participation in supervision and decision making. Although these approaches enrich the classical model, they overlook technological and environmental variables that can affect the organization, and they simplify the complexity of human motivation.

More than anything else, the design of an organization's structure should reflect its business environment. Once an organization's business environment has been defined, it must be evaluated along two dimensions: simple-complex and static-dynamic. An organization whose environment is simple and static should adopt the functional form of organization. Simple, dynamic environments require a faster flow of information and greater closeness to markets, so it makes sense for them to retain a functional organization but to modify it by providing for lateral relations.

Companies whose business environment is complex but static should if possible segment alone product/market lines. Companies whose environments are complex and dynamic have the greatest need for sharing information quickly. If possible, they too should segment their activities, but they may also want to have the sophistication that a specialized functional department provides. A matrix organization is often the right choice.

REVIEW QUESTIONS

1. What is the different between division of work and departmentalization?
2. What are the advantages of job specialization? Why did it emerge?
3. What does an organization chart illustrate? What are its advantages and disadvantages? How do you think you might be affected by seeing your name or position on one?
4. What are the different ways a product/market unit can be organized? What are the advantages and disadvantages of this form of organization?
5. Under what conditions would a matrix structure be most suitable? What are its advantages and disadvantages?
6. What is coordination? What kinds of differences in attitude and work style can develop in the departments of an organization? How do such differences make coordination more difficult? How do they help organizations?
7. What are the advantages and disadvantages of the classical bureaucratic model of organizational design?
8. What are the differences between a System 1 and a System 4 organization as described by Likert?
9. What factors did Lockheed's analysts select as significant in choosing a span of management? Which factors were confirmed by subsequent research? Which factor was found to have an opposite effect to that suggested by Lockheed's analysts?
10. What form of organization is best suited to a simple and static environment? A simple and dynamic environment? A complex but simple environment? A complex and dynamic environment?

CASE STUDY

Organizing the Structure of Club Med

For twenty years, Club Méditerranée's headquarters in Paris had much of the flavor of one of the club's free-wheeling holiday villages. The informal management structure, whereby executives in jeans dropped in and out of the office of the firm's chief executive, recently gave way to a more strait-laced corporate structure with four regional operational centers covering the globe.

According to chief executive Gilbert Trigano, the change in management style was dictated in part by the club's continuing spread around the world—a network of resorts that totals ninety installations in twenty-six countries. Another factor pushing the club to reorganize was the brief danger that Trigano might leave Club Med to assist French President, François Mitterrand, in determining whether Paris should be the site of the 1989 World's Fair. In the old structure, decisions seemed to be made on an ad hoc basis, reflecting Trigano's personal-management style. Centralization was the rule, to the point where such things as commercial policies to be pursued in the Japanese market or how to run a holiday village in Tahiti were dictated from Paris. An "animator" would fly from Paris to Agadir, Morocco, just to discuss evening entertainment at the company's Agadir resort.

The need for quick financial decisions in different parts of the globe, the need to adapt rapidly to changing market conditions and to maintain close links between marketing staff and operating personnel at the firm's resort villages all argued in favor of decentralization. Given the basic uniformity of the company's resort villages around the world, a geographic divisional structure made more sense than a product-based organizational structure. Under the current structure, the regional directors fly into Paris once a month to review world strategy and to discuss the financing of new villages and problems with tour operators, exchange controls, and the like.

Source: "Club Med Management Gives Up Some of Its Free-Wheeling Style," *International Management* Vol. 39 (May 1984), 27. Reprinted with special permission from *International Management,*

Case Questions

1. In what ways would functional organization be an appealing option for structuring Club Med? Product/market organization?
2. How would you describe the current structure of Club Med according to the model of matrix organization?
3. Which factors in Club Med's situation should be given the most weight in determining formal arrangements for a new organizational design?
4. What are the peculiar or unique factors in the environment of Club Med that may affect its decisions about further organizational design? ■

CASE STUDY

Options for Change at Imperial Chemical Industries

Mr. John Harvey-Jones sat at his desk and pondered the future. He had just taken over as chairman of board at Britain's Imperial Chemical Industries (ICI), and he knew he had some serious reorganization to do.

ICI is an international firm whose major business is commodity chemicals. It consists of 11 divisions doing business in the following areas: specialty chemicals, pharmaceuticals, agricultural chemicals and fertilizers, paints, explosives, oil, fibers, petrochemicals, and plastics. It is a British firm with a large market presence in the United States and Europe and smaller markets in almost all other countries.

The Current Situation. The 1980 world recession hit ICI hard. Earnings in 1979 had been $595 million, but in 1980 ICI lost $27 million; in 1982, the company earned only $196 million. This drastic decline in earnings was the result of several factors: a poor world economy, an inflated pound, the fall of commodity-chemical prices, and a rise in operating expenses all took their toll. However, an unfocused response to these outside factors also contributed to the problems. By 1982, some of these factors were reversing: The pound was weakening and the world economic picture was brightening. However, many of the underlying problems within ICI were still present and had to be addressed by ICI's new chairman.

The Alternatives. Harvey-Jones believed that the first step was to examine the current structure and functioning of the board of directors. In doing so, he recognized three basic alternatives for structuring the future management of ICI: maintain the status quo, become a holding company, or make the company more than the sum of its parts through a restructuring of responsibilities. Each alternative offered advantages and disadvantages, but one had to be chosen.

At the time, the company was structured so that each board member was responsible for a separate division. Thus, the board member planned the future of his division and tried to persuade other members to support it. Each member, then, had a vested interest in seeing his or her division receive capital expenditure funds, larger budgets, and the chance to pursue a goal that may or may not have been consistent with either the goals of another division or the company's overall goals. Each member mapped out a strategy for his or her own division, and no one oversaw the direction for the entire company. Not surprisingly, conflicting goals were likely, and self-interest was common.

One option for change was to become a holding company, whereby the board would give a minimum amount of guidance to each division. Each division would then be expected to contribute a certain amount of profit to the corporation; each would be independently responsible for meeting its profit goal. In large part, the holding-company option negated the necessity of an active board of directors.

The final option was to make the board responsible for the overall direction and performance of the entire company. Rather than overseeing one division per person, the entire board would set goals for every division, individually and corporately. Day-to-day responsibility would rest with the president of each division, but the process and decisions would be reviewed by the board.

Mr. Harvey-Jones knew he had some major decisions to make.

This case was prepared by Rebecca Villa.

Sources: Graham Turner, "ICI Becomes Proactive," *Long Range Planning* 17, no. 6 (December 1984):12–16; "ICI: Changing the Shape of a Giant," *Chemical Week,* July 25, 1984, pp. 28–32; Stephanie Cooke and John P. Tarpey, "Behind the Stunning Comeback at Britain's ICI," *Business Week,* June 3, 1985, pp. 62–63.

Case Questions

1. What factors are most important in deciding the structure of the board of directors?
2. Who should make the final decision about the shape of the board of directors?
3. What should that shape be?
4. How would any changes that were necessary be implemented? ■

Paul Klee, *Polyphony*. 1932. Emanuel Hoffman Foundation, Kunstmuseum, Basel. Color photo by Hans Hinz. Copyright © 1988 by COSMOPRESS, Geneva.

10

AUTHORITY, DELEGATION, AND DECENTRALIZATION

Upon completing this chapter you should be able to:

1. Define the relationship among authority, power, and influence and explain their importance in an organization's life.
2. Distinguish between the "classical" and the "acceptance" views of formal authority.
3. Identify and describe the sources of managerial power and informal power in organizations.
4. Distinguish between line and staff authority, and describe the various types of personal, specialized, and functional staffs.
5. Explain the importance of delegation in organizations, and describe how delegation can be made effective.
6. Explain the various ways that jobs can be designed.
7. Identify and describe the factors that influence the amount of centralization and decentralization in organizations.

Chapter Outline

Introduction
Authority, Power, and Influence
Line and Staff Authority
Delegation
Job Design
Decentralization

ILLUSTRATIVE CASE STUDY
Introduction

Responsiveness and Restructuring at IBM

IBM had always been the leader in many segments of the computer industry, but by 1987, it may have forgotten just exactly how it had gotten there. Over the years, IBM had become less responsive to consumer needs and was being perceived as a little arrogant. Consumers may have tolerated this attitude because they had little choice: After all, everyone assumed, IBM was really the only brand of computer equipment to buy. Naturally, any company contemplating a large capital expenditure for computers would naturally avoid the risk of purchasing an inferior product from an untested or less trustworthy source.

So, IBM prospered. As the computer age advanced, however, more and more competition entered the market. Suddenly, IBM was no longer unchallenged. Other companies began selling computers that people trusted, and frequently they outperformed IBM in the area of customer service. Some of IBM's new products did not succeed as well as had been expected, and older ones no longer met the more demanding needs of the consumer. For three years, IBM watched earnings decline, and investors became less enthusiastic about backing a company whose traditional approaches were no longer paying off so handsomely. Clearly, it was time to make changes before IBM was knocked from its traditional place at the head of the industry.

Ultimately, chairman John Akers decided it was time to decentralize a company that had grown over the years into a mammoth organization. IBM structured around a central management committee that made all major decisions. As the company grew, new layers of management were added, as were new policies and procedures. Akers wanted to remove many of these layers and allow decisions at much lower levels in the organization. For one thing, he moved thousands of employees into sales positions in order to increase the effectiveness of IBM's selling effort. But the biggest change—and the biggest challenge—was the program to decentralize the company's headquarters. Now, instead of a single management committee making all the decisions, there are six separate divisions organized according to product lines. The general manager of each division now functions more autonomously than any manager at IBM ever has. Since IBM is such a large organization, this restructuring displaced a great may people, but by offering early-retirement incentives and by taking advantage of natural attrition rates, Akers managed his changes without violating the company's history of declining to lay off employees.

Akers reasoned that the smaller groups within IBM would be better able to meet customer needs. The large bureaucracy that had long characterized IBM had made it difficult for IBM to move quickly enough to exploit market fluctuations and new market niches. Critics of IBM have claimed that it was this failure that allowed DEC to capture the mid-size market, and Apple to make such inroads into the personal-computer market. Smaller groups seem better able to spot opportunities and to move more quickly to take advantage of them. Since each manager at IBM now has fewer markets to consider, each division should be much better equipped to determine and respond to the needs of its particular consumers.

Sources: Paul B. Carroll and Michael W. Miller, "IBM to Realign Top Managers, Sources Say," *Wall Street Journal,* January 28, 1988, p. 3; Miller and Carroll, "IBM Unveils a Sweeping Restructuring in Bid to Decentralize Decision-Making," *Wall Street Journal,* January 29, 1988, p. 3; Larry Reibstein, "IBM's Plan to Decentralize May Set a Trend—but Imitation Has a Price," *Wall Street Journal,* February 19, 1988, Sec. 2, p. 21; Geoff Lewis with Anne R. Field, John J. Keller, and John W. Verity, "Big Changes at Big Blue," *Business Week,* February 15, 1988, pp. 92–98.

TEACHING TIP

The material in this chapter is critical to understanding the nature of the manager's task. (Recall from Chapter 1 that management is accomplishing work with and through others.) Authority, delegation, and decentralization are mechanisms to accomplish this. Try to keep the material from becoming routine and boring. Emphasize the examples, comments, and exercises annotated throughout the chapter. Also, encourage students to share any experiences they might have had with any of these topics.

Seventeenth-century European traders, soldiers, and missionaries were surprised by the unusual social organization of some Native American groups living near the Great Lakes. Several central Algonkian tribes there had no formal system of authority.[1] In fact, the Native Americans deeply resented any efforts to control their actions. Lifelong familiarity with the tasks of the community had taught them what was required of them. These tasks tended to be simple and repetitive, because the society changed slowly. Some groups, like the warriors, had acknowledged leaders, but no real authority was needed. Direct orders were considered insulting. Instead, members of the tribe would arouse others to action by persuasion, flattery, and example.

It would be difficult, if not impossible, to implement such a system in our own society. Most of us have grown up under one authority or another for as long as we can remember. Our parents, our teachers, our bosses, and our government all have the acknowledged right to tell us what to do in some circumstances. The concept of authority is so much a part of our culture that it is hard for us to imagine a workable society without some form of authority. What, for example, would happen to the federal government if the Internal Revenue Service lacked the authority to collect taxes? We would be neither comfortable nor competent in a system largely relying on flattery and persuasion.

Also, our society is too large and complex for the Algonkian system to be practical. There are simply too many tasks to be performed, often with strict limits on time and resources. Even projects as comparatively small as reorganizing an accounting department would result in chaos if clear lines of authority and accountability did not exist. A formal authority system is necessary if modern organizations are to achieve their objectives.

For an organization to function effectively, however, that system must be supplemented by informal bases of power and influence. Effective managers rarely have to resort to their official authority to obtain the cooperation of their subordinates. They rely instead on their knowledge, their experience, and their leadership ability. They may even use the Algonkian methods of persuasion, flattery, and example.

CLASS COMMENT

Note the emphasis again on goals. Also, be aware that managers will have personal, as well as organizational goals.

In this chapter, we first discuss the formal and informal methods of influence that managers use to achieve their personal and organizational goals. We then examine the line and staff structure through which authority is exercised. Next, the theory and practice of delegating authority effectively are reviewed before we conclude with a discussion of job design and decentralization.

AUTHORITY, POWER, AND INFLUENCE

formal authority Power rooted in the general understanding that specific individuals or groups have the right to exert influence within certain limits by virtue of their position within the organization. Also called legitimate power.

Writers on management have defined and used the terms *authority, power,* and *influence* in a variety of ways and have not always been in agreement.[2] **Formal authority** is one type of power. It is based on the recognition of the legitimacy or lawfulness of the attempt to exert influence. Individuals or groups attempting to exert influence are

[1] Walter B. Miller, "Two Concepts of Authority," in Harold J. Leavitt and Louis R. Pondy, eds., *Readings in Managerial Psychology* (Chicago: University of Chicago Press, 1964), pp. 557–576.

[2] See, for example, Dennis H. Wrong, "Some Problems in Defining Social Power," *American Journal of Sociology* 73, no. 6 (May 1968):673–681.

perceived as having the right to do so within recognized boundaries. This right arises from their formal position in an organization.

power The ability to exert influence; that is, the ability to change the attitudes or behavior of individuals or groups.

We define **power** as the ability to exert influence. To have power is to be able to change the behavior or attitudes of other individuals. In general, those persons who can exert influence over others in an organization are called stakeholders, as we mentioned in Chapter 3. For example, Jesse Jackson, recent candidate for the Democratic nomination for President, continued to exercise power as a politically important "stakeholder" in the party even after he lost the nomination to Michael Dukakis. Jackson had gained power through his charisma and his ability to attract and motivate a sizable coalition of groups that have traditionally wielded very little power in our society. Jackson's "Rainbow Coalition" of blacks, some whites, the poor, gays, Hispanics, and many other groups felt it had made great strides toward gaining power through Jackson's campaign; other Democrats, including Dukakis, consequently agreed to share party power with Jackson.

influence Any actions or examples of behavior that cause a change in attitude or behavior of another person or group.

Influence is defined here as actions or examples that, either directly or indirectly, cause a change in behavior or attitude of another person or group. For example, a hard-working person may, by setting an example, influence others to increase their productivity. This definition takes into account also those types of influence that do not lead to more tangible changes. For example, managers may use their influence to improve morale.

As Chrysler's CEO, for instance, Lee Iacocca used his influence to change traditional business strategies among management personnel, the United Auto Workers, government officials, and consumers. His influence enabled Chrysler to arrange a large federal bail-out loan, a new negotiated contract with cuts from the union, and a reduced management workforce which led to Chrysler's comeback as a major automobile maker. (Iacocca's tenure at Chrysler and the company's turnaround are discussed in detail as the Illustrative Case Study for Chapter 5.)

The Basis of Formal Authority: Two Views

"What gives you the right to tell me what to do?" This familiar question bluntly suggests that before we comply with an instruction, we must be satisfied that the person issuing it has the right to do so. It is unlikely that we would ask this question of a superior in our organization, since we assume that a superior does have the right to issue instructions to us. But why is this so? Where do managers get the right to direct subordinates' activities? There are two major views on the origin of formal authority in organizations: the classical view and the acceptance view.

The Classical View. The *classical view* supposes that authority originates at some very high level of society and then is lawfully passed down from level to level. At the top of this high level may be God, the bureaucracy (in the form of a king, a dictator, or an elected president), or the collective will of the people.[3]

In the classical view of formal authority in American organizations, management has a right to give lawful orders, and subordinates have an obligation to obey. This obligation is, in effect, self-imposed. Members of our society, in agreeing to abide by the Constitution, accept the rights of others to own private property and to own and control a business. By entering and remaining in an organization, subordinates in the United States accept the authority of owners or superiors and therefore have a duty to

[3]See Max Weber, "The Three Types of Managerial Rule," *Berkeley Journal of Sociology* 4 (1953):1–11 (orig. 1925); and Cyril O'Donnell, "The Source of Managerial Authority," *Political Science Quarterly* 67, no. 4 (December 1952):573–588.

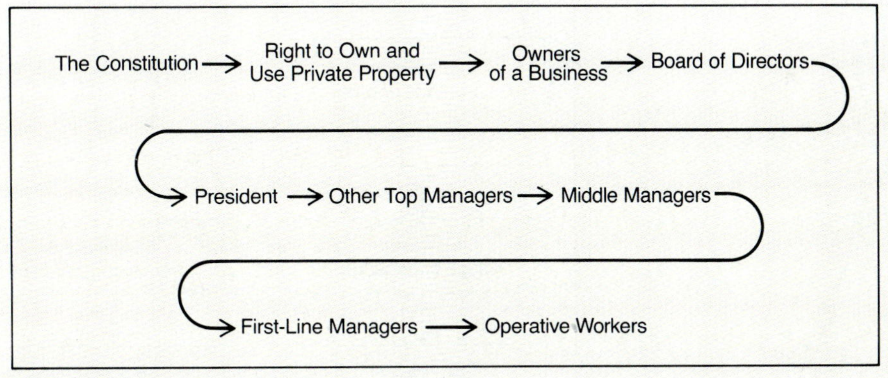

FIGURE 10-1 THE CLASSICAL VIEW OF THE FLOW OF AUTHORITY

obey lawful directives. Figure 10-1 presents a schematic view of formal authority in American life as envisioned by the classical view.

HERE'S AN EXAMPLE

Use yourself as an example to illustrate the differences between the classical and acceptance views of authority. Say your department head comes in and commands you to perform open-heart surgery on one of your students on the table in front of the class. Under the classical view of authority, you would obey the command. (Much to the disbelief of students!) Under the acceptance view of authority, however, you would go through the four conditions to determine whether or not to comply with the order. (This is really a crazy example, but it does get across the point to students that the acceptance view of authority is more realistic!)

The Acceptance View. The second perspective on the origin of formal authority, the *acceptance view,* finds the basis of authority in the *influencee* rather than in the *influencer*. This view starts with the observation that not all legitimate laws or commands are obeyed in all circumstances. Some are accepted by the subordinate or receiver of the order, and some are not. The key point is that it is the *receiver* who decides whether or not to comply. In the acceptance viewpoint, therefore, whether or not authority is present in any particular law or order is determined by the receiver, not the person issuing the order. For example, if a supervisor storms along an assembly line shouting at everyone to work harder, the subordinates may not question the supervisor's right to do so but, through anger or indifference, may choose not to comply with the order. The authority of the order will then be nullified.

This view should not suggest that insubordination and chaos are the norm in organizations; most formal authority is, in fact, accepted by the members of an organization. Chester I. Barnard, a strong proponent of the acceptance view, has defined the conditions under which a person will comply with higher authority:[4]

> A person can and will accept a communication as authoritative only when four conditions simultaneously obtain: (a) he can and does understand the communication; (b) *at the time of his decision* he believes that it is not inconsistent with the purpose of the organization; (c) *at the time of his decision* he believes it to be compatible with his personal interest as a whole; and (d) he is able mentally and physically to comply with it.

"zone of indifference" or **"area of acceptance"** According to Barnard and Simon, respectively, inclinations conditioning individuals to accept orders that fall within a familiar range of responsibility or activity.

In addition to these conditions, cooperation in accepting authority is fostered by what Barnard calls the **"zone of indifference"** and Herbert A. Simon refers to, perhaps more descriptively, as the **"area of acceptance."**[5] Both expressions refer to the inclination of individuals to accept most orders given to them by their superiors, provided the orders fall within a "normal" range. Most of us, for example, will accept the need for periodic progress reports on our work and will usually not stop to consider whether or not to comply with a request for such reports from our superiors. Figure 10-2 graphically contrasts the theoretical differences between the classical and acceptance views of authority.

---

[4]Chester I. Barnard, *The Functions of the Executive,* 30th anniversary ed. (Cambridge, Mass.: Harvard University Press, 1968), p. 165.

[5]Herbert A. Simon, *Administrative Behavior,* 3d ed. (New York: Macmillan, 1976), pp. 12, 18.

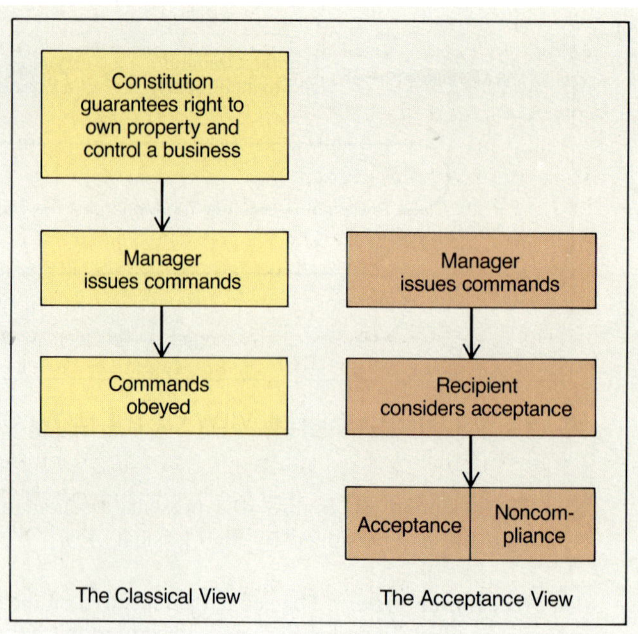

FIGURE 10-2 TWO VIEWS OF FORMAL AUTHORITY

The Sources of Power

reward power Power derived from the fact that one person, known as an influencer, has the ability to reward another person, known as an influencee, for carrying out orders, which may be expressed or implied.

coercive power The negative side of reward power, based on the influencer's ability to punish the influencee.

legitimate power Power that exists when a subordinate or influencee acknowledges that the influencer has a "right" or is lawfully entitled to exert influence—within certain bounds. Also called formal authority.

expert power Power based on the belief or understanding that the influencer has specific knowledge or relevant expertise which the influencee does not.

Power does not simply derive from an individual's level in the organizational hierarchy. John French and Bertram Raven have identified five sources or bases of power.[6] Each may occur at all levels.

Reward power is based on one person (the influencer) having the ability to reward another person (the influencee) for carrying out orders or meeting other requirements. One example is the power of a supervisor to assign work tasks to subordinates. The greater the attractiveness of a particular task in the eyes of the influencee, the greater the reward power of the influencer. However, rewards are best used to reinforce the desirable actions of subordinates and not as "bribes" to carry out tasks.[7]

Coercive power, based on the influencer's ability to punish the influencee for not meeting requirements, is the negative side of reward power. Punishment may range from loss of a minor privilege to loss of a job. Coercive power is usually used to maintain a minimum standard of performance or conformity among subordinates.

Legitimate power, which corresponds to our term *authority* (see above), exists when a subordinate or influencee acknowledges that the influencer has a "right" or is lawfully entitled to exert influence—within certain bounds. It is also implied that the influencee has an obligation to accept this power. The right of a manager to establish reasonable work schedules is an example of "downward" legitimate power. A plant guard may have the "upward" authority to require even the company president to present an identification card before being allowed onto the premises.

Expert power is based on the perception or belief that the influencer has some relevant expertise or special knowledge that the influencee does not. When we do what

---

[6]John R. P. French and Bertram Raven, "The Bases of Social Power," in Dorwin Cartwright, ed., *Studies in Social Power* (Ann Arbor: University of Michigan Press, 1959), pp. 150–167.

[7]Gary Yukl and Tom Taber, "The Effective Use of Managerial Power," *Personnel* 60, no. 2 (March–April 1983):37–44.

our doctors tell us, we are acknowledging their expert power. Expert power is usually applied to a specific, limited subject area. Although we may accept the advertising advice of our company's marketing specialists, we may discount their recommendations on how to lower production costs.

referent power Power based on the desire of the influencee to be like or identify with the influencer.

Referent power, which may be held by a person or a group, is based on the influencee's desire to identify with or imitate the influencer. For example, popular, conscientious managers will have referent power if subordinates are motivated to emulate their work habits. Referent power also functions at peer level—charismatic colleagues may sway us to their sides in department meetings. The strength of referent power is directly related to such factors as the amount of prestige and admiration the influencee confers upon the influencer.

These are potential sources of power only. They are the ways in which one person can influence another person. Possession of some or all of them does not guarantee the ability to influence particular individuals in specific ways. For example, we may have their respect and admiration as an expert in our field, but we still may be unable to influence them to be more creative on the job or even to get to work on time. Thus, the role of the influencee in accepting or rejecting the attempted influence remains the key one.

FOR DISCUSSION

Relate the sources of power to a contingency view of management. (A manager would use a particular source of power to influence others based upon characteristics of the situation. If, then . . . if this is the way my situation is, then this is the best way for me to influence.)

Normally, each of the five power bases is potentially inherent in a manager's position. A specific degree of legitimate power always accompanies a manager's job and is especially important because it shapes the hierarchical relationships within which the other forms of influence and power occur. Subordinates are assumed to accept a manager's formal authority and will generally obey him or her within reasonable limits. Managers usually have the power to reward subordinates with money, privileges, or promotions and to punish them by withholding or removing these rewards. Also, managers are assumed to possess some degree of expertise, at least until they prove otherwise. Since referent power so obviously depends on an individual's style and personality, it is least likely to be an expected part of a manager's position. Many examples of it, however, exist in organizations, for instance in the tendency of subordinates to model themselves after successful senior executives.

Power in Organizations

The concept of power is a difficult one for Americans to deal with objectively—perhaps because the United States was founded in opposition to an authoritarian regime and peopled by successive waves of immigrants who were seeking to avoid oppressive governments throughout the world. A distrust of excessive power is reflected in the United States Constitution, which, while establishing the powers of the federal government, clearly limits those powers as well, reserving a great deal of authority to the states. The Constitution's specific system of checks and balances was designed to give each of the three branches of government—legislative, executive, and judicial—the means of preventing the others from accumulating too much power. In addition, the Bill of Rights and subsequent amendments were enacted to protect the rights of individuals.

Some Americans, then, have ambivalent feelings about power, both admiring and resenting it in others. They may covet power but are reluctant to admit it openly because power has negative connotations in our culture. Power is seen as manipulation and the use of power as evil. This is only natural in a society which holds that "all persons are created equal." This uneasiness about power perhaps explains why management writers have neglected it in the past, even though the exercise of power is an obvious part of a manager's job. If we begin to think about power as influence, as is suggested here, then it can start to lose its negative meaning.

ETHICS IN MANAGEMENT

OBEDIENCE AND CONSCIENCE

In 1960, Stanley Milgram conducted the famous "Yale experiments" probing the conflict between personal conscience and obedience to an outside authority figure. He found that people ordered to act against their consciences entered an "agentic state." That is, they viewed themselves as merely instruments (agents) of the authority figure and felt no responsibility for their actions.

In the Yale experiment, Milgram asked a random sample of New Haven residents—excluding students—to help him test whether people learned best by negative or positive reinforcement. He asked the subjects to serve as "teachers" and told them that another subject would be the "learner." The teacher was to read a series of word pairs to the learner and then prompt the learner with the first word of one of the pairs.

If the learner responded correctly with the second word in the pair, the teacher would go on to another series. If, however, the learner answered incorrectly, the teacher was told to give the learner an electric shock. The strength of the shock increased with each wrong answer. A researcher, who served as an authority figure, stayed in the room with the teacher while the teacher read the word pairs and "punished" the learner.

In fact, no electric shocks were really being given. The learner was an actor who, as time went on, pretended to be in extreme pain and asked to withdraw from the experiment. Milgram wanted to know how many subjects would complete the experiment and administer up to 450 volts of "electricity" to a stranger. In the basic experiment, depending on the proximity of the teacher to the learner, 30 to 65 percent of the subjects obeyed the experimenter to the end of the test. Figure 10-3 dramatizes the nature of Milgram's experiment. (a) The shock generator used in the experiment. (b) With electrodes attached to his wrists, the "learner" provides answers by pressing switches that light up on an answer box. (c) The subject administers a shock to the "learner." (d) The subject breaks off the experiment. Milgram found out what he wanted to find out, but questions about the ethics of such experimentation still remain.

In variations on the experiment, Milgram tested to see how peer pressure, the sex of the subject, the clarity of the experimenter's commands, the affiliation of the experimenter to the university, the health condition of the learner, and the physical presence of the experimenter (the authority figure) would affect its outcome. The only factor that tended to cause the teacher to stop the experiment was the absence of the authority figure.

Milgram concluded that loyalty and discipline are so highly regarded in our society that disobedience produces no satisfaction. "The price of disobedience," he said, "is the growing sense that one has been faithless." And though a cooperative, hierarchical structure is necessary for a society's or a corporation's harmonious survival, he cautioned, "Accept nothing which contradicts our basic experience merely because it comes to us from tradition or convention or authority."

The response of other researchers to Milgram's experiment was occasionally one of outrage because he had misled his subjects about the nature of the experiment and manipulated them in a way that, at least from a psychological standpoint, was potentially dangerous. The American Psychological Association censured Milgram and instituted strict guidelines for the conduct of numerous types of experiments. In Milgram's defense, it must be said that he was in control of his procedure and had established a comprehensive debriefing and follow-up procedure to mitigate any potentially harmful consequences to his subjects.

Source: Stanley Milgram, *Obedience to Authority* (London: Tavistock Publications, 1975). © 1974 by Stanley Milgram.

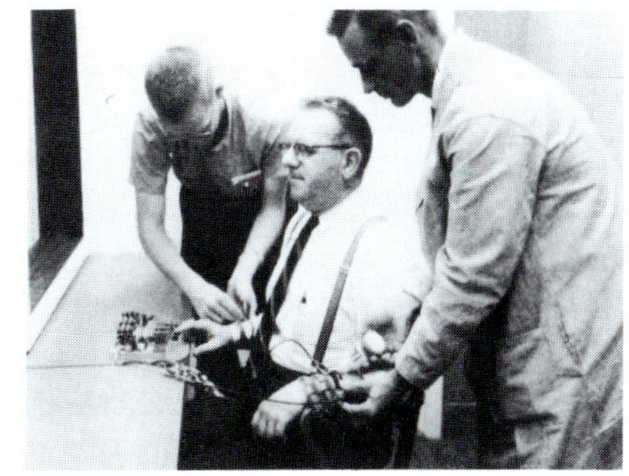

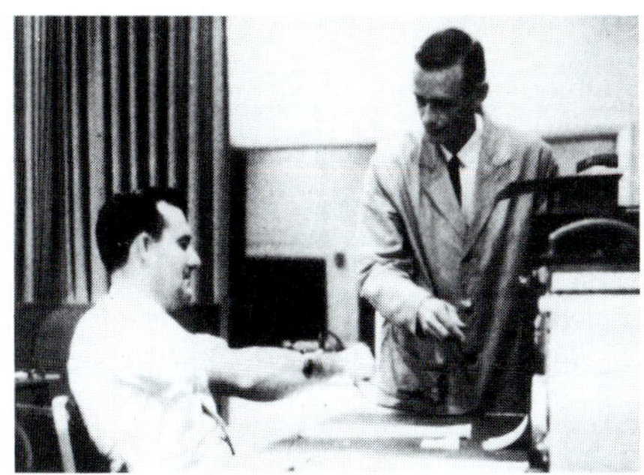

FIGURE 10-3 STANLEY MILGRAM'S OBEDIENCE EXPERIMENT

Note: See box entitled "Obedience and Conscience."

BACKGROUND ON OFFICE POLITICS

"Gamesmanship." "Office politics." Whatever you call it, students are often fascinated (or disgusted) by descriptions of these. See the Lecture Extras Supplement for more information on office politics.

In recent years, power and political processes in organizations have become major concerns of management writers.[8] Both our realistic understanding of the role of these factors and our understanding of how they can be used constructively have been increasing rapidly. For example, David McClelland has described "two faces of power"—a negative face and a positive one.[9] The negative face is usually expressed in terms of dominance-submission: If I win, you lose. To have power implies having power over another, who is less well off for it. Leadership based on the negative face of power regards people as little more than pawns to be used or sacrificed as the need arises. This is self-defeating, since people who feel they are pawns tend either to resist leadership or to become passive. In either case, their value to the manager is severely limited.

The positive face of power is best characterized by a concern for group goals—for helping to formulate and achieve such goals. It involves exerting influence on behalf of rather than over others. Managers who exercise their power positively encourage group members to develop the strength and competence they need to succeed as people and as members of the organization.

McClelland and David H. Burnham report that successful managers have a greater need to influence others for the benefit of the organization than for self-aggrandizement.[10] Managers who use their power with self-control will be more effec-

---

[8]Jeffrey Pfeffer has explored the basis for the unease about power and politics and has concluded that power processes are often ubiquitous and generally beneficial rather than harmful to organizations and the people who work in them. See Jeffrey Pfeffer, *Power in Organizations* (Marshfield, Mass.: Pitman, 1981); and Henry Mintzberg, *Power in and Around Organizations* (Englewood Cliffs, N.J.: Prentice Hall, 1983).

[9]David C. McClelland, "The Two Faces of Power," *Journal of International Affairs* 24, no. 1 (1970):29–47.

[10]David C. McClelland and David H. Burnham, "Power Is the Great Motivator," *Harvard Business Review* 54, no. 2 (March–April 1976):100–110.

tive than those who wield power to satisfy a need to dominate others or those who neglect to use their power out of a strong need to be liked. When a manager continually eases rules and changes procedures to accommodate subordinates, they will suspect that he or she is not flexible but weak and indecisive. McClelland concluded that good managers exercise power with restraint on behalf of others. Such managers encourage team spirit, support subordinates, and reward their achievements, thereby raising morale. Successful managers also employ certain proven techniques to channel their power productively. John P. Kotter has argued that the external environment of organizations has contributed to the growing need for power skills among managers. Some of his key characteristics of successful power skills are listed in Exhibit 10-1.

EXHIBIT 10-1 KOTTER'S KEY CHARACTERISTICS OF SUCCESSFULLY HANDLED POWER

Kotter maintains that managers who handle power successfully:

1. *Are sensitive to the source of their power.* They keep their actions consistent with people's expectations. For example, they do not try to apply expert power in one field to another field.
2. *Recognize the different costs, risks, and benefits of the five bases of power.* They draw on whichever power base is appropriate to a particular situation or person.
3. *Appreciate that each of the five power bases has merit.* They try to develop their skills and credibility so they can use whichever method is best.
4. *Possess career goals that allow him to develop and use power.* They seek jobs that will build their skills, make people feel dependent on them, and employ a type of power with which they are comfortable.
5. *Act maturely and exercise self-control.* They avoid impulsive or egotistical displays of their power, and they try not to be unnecessarily harsh on others around them.
6. *Understand that power is necessary to get things done.* They feel comfortable using power.

Sources: John P. Kotter, "Power, Dependence, and Effective Management," *Harvard Business Review* 54, no.2 (March–April 1976):100–110; *Power in Management* (New York: AMACOM, 1979); and *Power and Influence* (New York: Free Press, 1983).

Rosabeth Kanter has argued that power can easily become institutionalized. Those whom others believe to possess power seem to find it easier to influence other people around them—and thus to garner even more genuine power. By the same token, "powerlessness" is a difficult condition to overcome. Kanter claims, for example, that many of the real problems experienced by women and minorities can be traced through an analysis of power rather than through an examination focusing primarily on the disadvantages of race or sex.[11]

There are also a number of other arguments that can be raised to support French and Raven's typology of the five sources of power. For example, a changing business climate can make different functions within an organization more important than others at a crucial point in time. As the amount of uncertainty faced by an organization increases, the number of potential power bases also increases. Sometimes, formal authority is only the official ratification of power acquired through other means, and if that base of power is sanctioned by policies that may or may not be observed—may or may not be supported by actual influence—there remains room for other members of the organization to secure real influence and practical power.

Kanter proposes a number of ways for an organizational member to acquire power. Four of the most important means are categorized in Exhibit 10-2.

---

[11]Rosabeth Moss Kanter, *Men and Women of the Corporation* (New York: Basic Books, 1977), pp. 165–205. See also Kanter, "Men and Women of the Corporation Revisited," *Management Review*, March 1987, pp. 14–15; Kanter, *The Change Masters* (New York: Simon & Schuster, 1983), pp. 156–179; and Sharon Nelton, "Meet Your New Work Force," *Nation's Business* 76, no. 7 (1988):14–21.

EXHIBIT 10-2 KANTER'S KEY MEANS TO ORGANIZATIONAL POWER

1. *Extraordinary activities.* Making changes, being the first person to occupy a position, or being successful upon taking exceptional risks can lead to greater power.
2. *Visibility.* Being noticed, gaining "exposure" in the eyes of those in power, and even making certain activities appear to be riskier than they actually are can also increase power—a fact that has led Kanter to speculate that public appearance may be a more influential factor than genuine substance.
3. *Relevance.* Doing something that solves an authentic organizational problem can be a source of power and may well lend necessary credence to the factors of extraordinary activity and visibility.
4. *Sponsors.* Having a sponsor or mentor—someone who advises you on how to succeed in the organization—can be an informal sense of power, especially depending upon the power enjoyed by the sponsor; Kanter claims that sponsors are especially important for women who are inexperienced in organizational power politics.

Source: Rosabeth Moss Kanter, *Men and Women of the Corporation* (New York: Basic Books, 1977), pp. 165–205.

TEACHING TIP

Stress to students the concept that *informal* power may also be used to influence behavior. Try to have them come up with some examples of informal power from organizations to which they belong.

Power is not limited to managers. Lower-level members of an organization may have a great deal of informal power based on their knowledge, their skills, or the resources they control. Nurses, for example, gain influence over new doctors in a hospital when they "show them the ropes," and copy-machine attendants have the power to impede or improve a manager's work flow. Likewise, subordinate employees with computer skills can exercise increasing influence over an organization's day-to-day activities as organizations come to rely more and more on the use of computer technology. To an extent, knowledge, combined with hands-on input into daily activities, can be tantamount to power, and those members of an organization who possess in-demand skills are in positions to secure bases of practical power.

Power, then, is an important fact of organizational life. As managers we must not only accept and understand power as an integral part of our jobs, but we must learn how to use, and not abuse, it to further our own and our organization's goals.[12]

LINE AND STAFF AUTHORITY

CLASS COMMENT

Authority is the major device organizations use to integrate work.

Formal authority is the legitimate power associated with an organizational position. In this section we will use the word "authority" in a different way, in distinguishing between what are frequently called line authority and staff authority. Not all authors agree that this distinction is meaningful.[13] Line and staff authority are, however, such pervasive and confusing elements in organizations that they need to be examined and understood. Figure 10-4 elaborates on the various interactions possible in line- and staff-position systems.

Line Authority

line authority The authority of those managers directly responsible, throughout the organization's chain of command, for achieving organizational goals.

Every organization exists to achieve specific goals. Line managers may be defined as those in the organization directly responsible for achieving these goals. **Line authority** is represented by the standard chain of command, starting with the board of directors and extending down through the various levels in the hierarchy to the point where the basic activities of the organization are carried out.

[12]A key concern of current research is the integration of the various theories of power into a unified theory. See W. Graham Astley and Paramjit S. Sachdeva, "Structural Sources of Intraorganizational Power: A Theoretical Synthesis," *Academy of Management Review* 9, no. 1 (January 1984):104–113; and Anthony T. Cobb, "An Episodic Model of Power: Toward an Integration of Theory and Research," *Academy of Management Review* 9, no. 3 (July 1984):482–493.

[13]See, for example, Gerald G. Fisch, "Line-Staff Is Obsolete," *Harvard Business Review* 39, no. 5 (September–October 1961):67–79; and Vivian Nossiter, "A New Approach Toward Resolving the Line and Staff Dilemma," *Academy of Management Review* 4, no. 1 (January 1979):103–106.

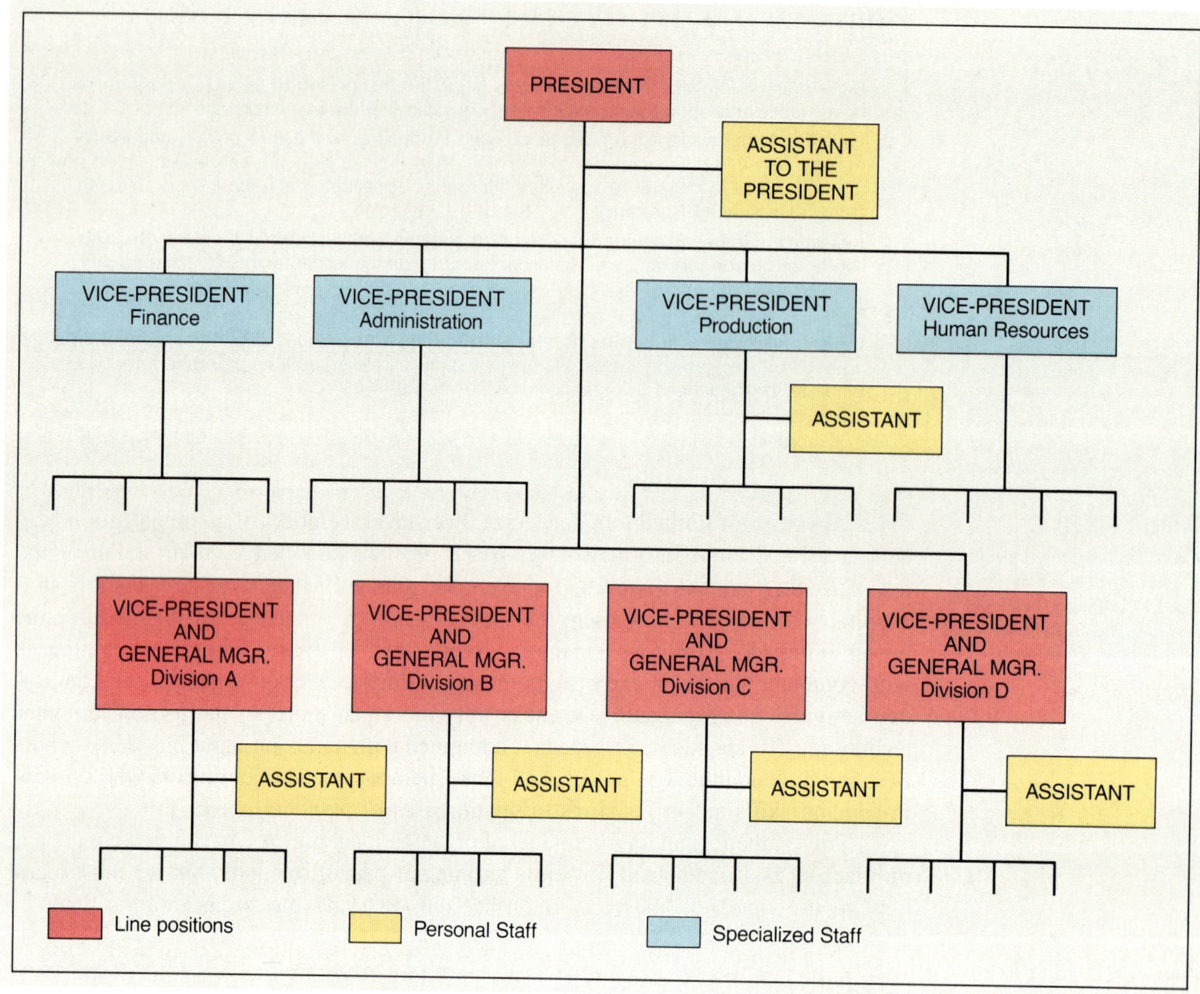

FIGURE 10-4 LINE AND STAFF POSITIONS

Since line activities are identified in terms of the company's goals, the activities classified as line will differ with each organization. For example, a manufacturing company may limit line functions to production and sales, while a department store, in which buying is a key element, will include the purchasing department as well as the sales department in its line activities.

When an organization is small, all positions may be line roles; staff roles are added as the organization grows and it becomes useful to hire specialists to assist the line members in doing their primary jobs.[14]

Staff Authority

staff authority The authority of those groups of individuals who provide line managers with advice and services.

Staff authority belongs to those individuals or groups in an organization who provide services and advice to line. The concept of staff includes all elements of the organization that are not classified as line. Advisory staffs have been used by decision makers from emperors and kings to parliamentary governments and dictatorships over the

[14]For a discussion of the various ways staff activities are integrated in the organizational structure, see Harold Stieglitz, "On Concepts of Corporate Structure: Economic Determinants of Organization," *Conference Board Review*, February 1974, pp. 148–150.

course of recorded history. The staffs of kings often included court jesters and fools.[15]

Staff provides managers with varied types of expert help and advice. Staff can offer line managers planning advice through research, analysis, and options development. Staff can also assist in policy implementation, monitoring, and control, in legal and financial matters, and in the design and operation of data-processing systems.[16]

It is sometimes difficult to distinguish between line and staff: Line managers seem to be performing staff functions, and staff members seem to have some line responsibilities. Staff personnel, however, will devote most of their time to providing services and advice to line members, while line managers will tend to focus their efforts directly on producing the organization's products or services.

Functional Authority

The role of staff members to provide advice and service to line members implies that staff lacks independent, formal authority. In reality, staff departments, especially those responsible for audit functions, may have formal authority over line members within the limits of their functions. The right to control activities of other departments as they relate to specific staff responsibilities is known as **functional authority.**

functional authority The authority of staff-department members to control the activities of other departments that are related to specific staff responsibilities.

In Figure 10-5, the finance manager of Division A reports through the chain of command to the general manager of Division A. The finance manager, however, is also responsible to the vice-president at the corporate level in a "dotted-line" relationship representing the functional authority between specialized staff and line managers.

The need for functional authority is very real. It arises from the need for a degree of uniformity and an unhindered application of expertise in carrying out many organizational activities. For this reason, functional authority is common in organizations.

EXTRA EXERCISE

Show students a copy of your school's organization chart. Try to determine line, staff, and functional authority positions from it.

[15]Alfred Kieser, "Advisory Staffs for Rulers: Can They Increase Rationality of Decisions?" Unpublished paper delivered at the seminar on "Improvement of Top-Level Decision-Making" at the Institute for Advanced Study, Berlin, February 1983.

[16]For an early discussion of ways in which staff members can support line managers, see Louis A. Allen, "The Line-Staff Relationship," *Management Record* 17, no. 9 (September 1955):346–349ff.

FIGURE 10-5 FUNCTIONAL AUTHORITY AND "DOTTED-LINE" RELATIONSHIPS

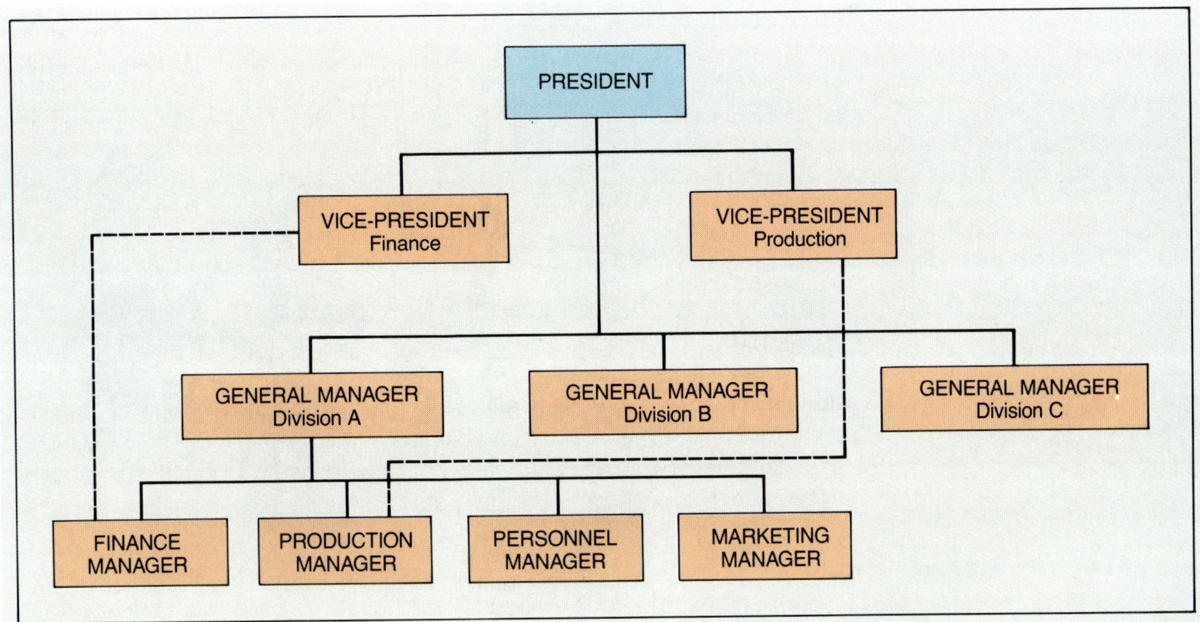

The skills required to manage functional authority relationships (and the problems arising from them) are similar to those required in the dual-boss relationships in matrix organizations.

DELEGATION

delegation The act of assigning formal authority and responsibility for completion of specific activities to a subordinate.

We may define **delegation** as the assignment to another person of formal authority and accountability for carrying out specific activities. The delegation of authority by superiors to subordinates is obviously necessary for the efficient functioning of any organization, since no superior can personally accomplish or completely supervise all the organization's tasks.

Delegation, Authority, Accountability, and Responsibility

Note that our definition designates precisely what can be delegated—*authority* and *accountability*. But note also that this definition implicitly raises two closely related questions: Can *authority* be delegated? Can *responsibility* be delegated? Our definition has already answered the first of these two questions: There is little debate concerning the delegation of *authority*—it can and should be delegated. For example, a manager might choose to delegate the authority to subordinates to make expenditures without approval—at least up to a stipulated amount. However, considerable debate often arises with regard to the delegation of *responsibility*. A close analysis of this debate often reveals that it is more the result of semantics—of the variables occurring in the use of language in different contexts—rather than a misunderstanding of the concepts involved.

Those contending that responsibility cannot be delegated support their position by stating that managers can never shed the responsibilities of their jobs by passing them on to subordinates. Those contending that responsibility can be delegated justify their position by pointing out that managers can certainly make subordinates responsible to them for certain actions.

"Miss Roth, send someone in here to roll up our sleeves."
Drawing by Leo Cullum; © 1982 The New Yorker Magazine, Inc.

However, delegation to subordinates does not make managers any less responsible to their superiors. Delegation of responsibility does not mean abdication of responsibility by the delegating manager. Responsibility is not like an object that can be passed from individual to individual. For example, suppose a loan manager for a bank decided to delegate to his or her loan officers the responsibility for insuring that all loans are processed within the 10-day limit stated by bank policy. The loan manager can certainly make the loan officers *accountable* regarding the matter. At the same time, the loan manager is no less *responsible* to his or her boss—that is, he or she is *responsible* for seeing that the activity is carried out, for explaining why it was not, and/or correcting any problems that are caused by the actions of his or her subordinates. In short, one does not delegate responsibility, because responsibility always remains with the delegating manager.

Perhaps we can get a better idea of what delegation *is* by looking at Exhibit 10-3, which specifies what delegation is *not*.

EXHIBIT 10-3 WHAT DELEGATION IS NOT

1. It is not abdication: It is not simply a matter of giving people jobs to do and telling them to get them done. When this approach is taken, the results the manager wants or expects are seldom achieved. The recipients of this type of delegation are put in the position of being second-guessed at the end of the job.
2. It is not abandonment of the manager's responsibility.
3. It does not mean that the manager loses control.
4. It does not mean that the manager avoids making decisions: The manager who delegates still makes decisions. The important point is that he or she can concentrate on those decisions and issues of most importance and allow subordinates to make those decisions which are best made at the point of direct contact.

Although delegation is the transfer of legitimate power, it relates to the other power bases as well. When formal authority is conferred, the power to reward and punish goes with it to some extent. Expert power can also be indirectly conveyed by delegation: The subordinate who now acts in place of the superior will acquire expert power to the extent that he or she develops the necessary skills to perform the task.

The extent to which managers delegate authority and accountability is influenced by such factors as the culture of the organization, the specific situation involved, and the relationships, personalities, and capabilities of the people in that situation.[17] While there are many contingency factors that managers will have to take into account in deciding what and how much to delegate, there are also some basic guidelines that apply to most situations.

Classical Guidelines for Effective Delegation

COORDINATED RESOURCE

The film *Delegating* describes the process of delegation and the basic steps managers should use to improve their overall managerial effectiveness. Available from CRM McGraw-Hill, P.O. Box 641, Del Mar, CA 92014.

Delegation was an important subject of the early management writers, and their basic considerations remain valid today. Many of the guidelines for effective delegation are therefore based on classical principles.[18]

Accountability, Authority, and Responsibility. Every position in an organization has, or should have, specified tasks and individuals or groups who are accountable for the success of those tasks. For the organization to make efficient use of its resources,

[17]See Gerald G. Fisch, "Toward Effective Delegation," *CPA Journal* 46, no. 7 (July 1976):66–67.

[18]Our discussion in this section is based on James D. Mooney and Alan C. Reiley, *The Principles of Organization* (New York: Harper & Brothers, 1939), pp. 14–19, 23–24; and S. Avery Raub, *Company Organization Charts* (New York: National Industrial Conference Board, 1964).

accountability for specified tasks is assigned to the lowest organizational level at which there exists sufficient ability and information to carry them out competently. For example, it would be a waste of a company president's time—which should be spent in directing achievement of the overall goals of the organization—to check personally the time cards of lower-level employees. Such a task can be performed most efficiently by lower-level supervisors.

A corollary of this rule is that *for individuals in the organization to perform their assigned tasks effectively, they must be delegated sufficient authority to do so*. For example, as sales managers, we would be accountable for a certain standard of performance in our sales department. But if we did not have the formal authority to assign territories, reward the most effective salespeople, and fire incompetents, we would not be able to fulfill our obligations.

A necessary part of the delegation of accountability and authority is *responsibility*—being held answerable for results. By accepting responsibility and authority, individuals in the organization also agree to accept credit or blame for the way in which they carry out their assignments. For managers, the concept of responsibility has an added dimension: Not only are managers held accountable for their own performance, but they are also held responsible for the performance of their subordinates. In fact, responsibility for the actions of subordinates is one of the defining characteristics of a managerial position.

scalar principle The concept that a clear line of authority through the organization must exist if delegation is to work successfully.

The Scalar Principle. For delegation to work effectively, members of the organization should know where they stand in the chain of command. Otherwise, they could neither accept nor assign responsibility with any confidence. The **scalar principle** suggests that there must be a clear line of authority running step by step from the highest to the lowest level of the organization. This clear line of authority will make it easier for organization members to understand (1) to whom they can delegate, (2) who can delegate to them, and (3) to whom they are accountable.

When establishing the line of authority, *completeness of delegation* is required; that is, all necessary tasks in the organization should be assigned. Unassigned tasks, called *gaps,* have to be avoided, because otherwise it is likely that the tasks will remain unperformed—or the people who voluntarily perform those tasks will resent their extra burden. For example, we should not assume that our purchasing manager will also take care of inventory control. Either we will clearly define the inventory tasks as his or her responsibility or we will delegate the task to someone else. Similarly, there should be no *overlaps* (responsibility for the same tasks assigned to more than one individual) and no *splits* (responsibility for the same task assigned to more than one organizational unit). Otherwise, confusion of authority and accountability will result.

unity of command principle A guideline for delegation that states that each individual in an organization should report to only one superior.

Unity of Command. The **unity of command principle** states that each person in the organization should report to only one superior. Reporting to more than one superior makes it difficult for an individual to know to whom he or she is accountable and whose instructions he or she must follow. For example, a computer graphics designer who must report to several managers will frequently receive conflicting orders about whose proposal or presentation has priority. The designer is then likely to feel confused and bullied. Reporting to more than one superior also encourages individuals to avoid responsibility, since they can easily blame poor performance on the fact that with several bosses they have too much to do.

Limitations of the Classical Guidelines

The guidelines we have been discussing are representative of the classical "top to bottom" view of authority in organizations. While they remain quite useful in many situations, they do have some limitations.

HERE'S AN EXAMPLE

W. L. Gore Associates (with over 5,000 employees in 1987) has always followed a strict policy of not having more than 200 employees at any one of its manufacturing facilities. The high-technology company prides itself on the fact that it has no titles and no structures. The Gore Company appears to be doing well even though it doesn't follow any of the traditional or new organizational theory.

One problem with the guidelines is that they overlook the fundamental point made earlier in this chapter—namely, that the acceptance of legitimacy of managers by subordinates determines whether those managers can exercise authority effectively. Managers may have the formal right to delegate tasks, but if subordinates do not accept that right, the delegation process breaks down. As we shall see, managers often must seek the support of subordinates in order to make delegation effective.

Experiments with participative management, have been implemented with varying degrees of success by General Foods, GE, GM, Ford, and many other companies, are attempts to secure the support of employees by including them in the management process. However, many such experiments have failed even after impressive initial results. For example, one study of 101 industrial companies found that those who had used participative management—quality circles, work teams, and the like—outscored others on 13 of 14 financial measures. Nevertheless, many of the same studies found that such strategies were ultimately subject to the law of diminishing returns. Although these efforts tended to produce results on the shoproom floor, they also tended to meet resistance at higher management levels. Fear of sharing power and of potential job loss in an era of downsizing are among the reasons cited for such resistance, especially among members of middle management.[19]

Another problem arises from the complexity of many modern organizational structures. The unity of command principle, for example, is explicitly violated in matrix organizations. The matrix structure exists because, in some situations, the advantages of the dual reporting system exceed the disadvantages, even though some of the disadvantages arise precisely from this violation.[20]

The utility of the classical guidelines also depends on the ability of a boss to define precisely the tasks to be done. In a dynamic organizational environment, task definition is an ongoing activity, with responsibility and authority frequently being reallocated. In such a situation, flexibility on the part of both subordinates and managers is essential.

Effective Delegation

When used properly, delegation has several important advantages. The first and most obvious is that the more tasks managers are able to delegate, the more opportunity they have to seek and accept increased responsibilities from higher-level managers. Thus, as managers we will try to delegate not only routine matters but also tasks requiring thought and initative, so that we can be free to function with maximum effectiveness for our organizations. In Exhibit 10-4, Harvey Sherman categorizes six typical degrees of delegation.

EXHIBIT 10-4 SHERMAN'S SIX DEGREES OF DELEGATION

1. Take action—no further contact with me is needed.
2. Take action—let me know what you did.
3. Look into this problem—let me know what you intend to do; do it unless I say not to.
4. Look into this problem—let me know what you intend to do; delay action until I give approval.
5. Look into this problem—let me know alternative actions available with pros and cons and recommend one for my approval.
6. Look into this problem—give me all the facts; I will decide what to do.

Source: Quoted from Harvey Sherman, *It All Depends: A Pragmatic Approach to Organizations* (University, Ala.: University of Alabama Press, 1966), pp. 83–84. © 1966 by the University of Alabama Press. Used by permission.

[19]Bill Saporito, "The Revolt Against 'Working Smarter,'" *Fortune*, July 21, 1986, pp. 58–65.

[20]John R. Adams and Nicki S. Kirchof, "The Practice of Matrix Management," in David I. Cleland, ed., *Matrix Management Systems Handbook* (New York: Van Nostrand Reinhold, 1984), pp. 13–30.

Another advantage of delegation is that it frequently leads to better decisions, since subordinates closest to the "firing line" are likely to have a clearer view of the facts. For example, the West Coast sales manager will be in a better position than the vice-president of sales to allocate the California sales territories.

Effective delegation also speeds up decision making. Valuable time is lost when subordinates must check with their superiors (who then may have to check with *their* superiors) before making a decision. This delay is eliminated when subordinates are authorized to make the necessary decision on the spot. In addition, delegation causes subordinates to accept accountability and exercise judgment. This not only helps train subordinates—an important advantage of delegation—but also improves their self-confidence and willingness to take initiative.

Finally, as Exhibit 10-5 shows, delegation can be most effective when its uses and effects are carefully considered and the process of delegation initiated through a series of planned steps.

EXHIBIT 10-5 STEPS IN DELEGATING

1. *Decide Which Tasks Can Be Delegated.* Many items can and should be delegated. Some of these are minor decisions, recurring chores, etc. However, unusually demanding and challenging assignments may often be delegated to your subordinates and will do much to develop them.
2. *Decide Who Should Get the Assignment.* Who has available time? Does the job require special competence? For whom would it be an appropirate and useful developmental experience? Ask yourself these questions when deciding which of your people should get the assignment.
3. *Delegate the Assignment.* Provide all relevant information on the task. As far as possible, delegate by results expected, not by methods to be used. Cultivate a climate of free and open communication between yourself and the person to whom you have delegated the task.
4. *Establish a Feedback System.* Provide for a system of checkpoints and/or feedback information so that you will remain advised of progress. Your feedback system ought to be selected carefully, however, since the tighter your controls the less the acutal delegation that takes place.

CLASS COMMENT

One of the hardest things for a young (or new) manager to do is to learn how to delegate. (The film on delegation described previously can illustrate this in an entertaining way!)

In spite of the advantages, many managers are reluctant to delegate authority and many subordinates are reluctant to accept it. There are a number of reasons that managers commonly offer to explain why they do not delegate: "I can do it better myself"; "My subordinates just aren't capable enough"; "It takes too much time to explain what I want done." These reasons are often excuses that managers use to hide the real reasons they avoid delegation.

An additional cause of reluctance to delegate is a manager's lack of ability. Some managers may simply be too disorganized or inflexible to plan ahead and decide which tasks should be delegated to whom or to set up a control system so that subordinates' actions can be monitored.

Insecurity may be a major cause of reluctance to delegate. Managers are accountable for the actions of subordinates, and this may make them reluctant to "take chances" and delegate tasks. Or the manager may fear a loss of power if the subordinate does too good a job.

Insecurity can also be a barrier to the acceptance of delegation. Some subordinates want to avoid responsibility and risks, and so would like their bosses to make all the decisions. Similarly, subordinates who fear criticism or dismissal for mistakes are frequently reluctant to accept delegation.

The most basic prerequisite to effective delegation is the willingness of managers to give their subordinates real freedom to accomplish delegated tasks. Managers have

HERE'S AN EXAMPLE

F. Ross Johnson, CEO of RJR Nabisco, Inc., certainly is dynamic, disarming, and unpredictable. Unlike his predecessor, Tylee Wilson, Johnson generally prefers to function as the sole strategist. He can be abrupt and snappish, but his executives remain loyal because he offers some of the highest compensation packages in the industry. (*Business Week*, 5/23/88, pp. 175–182)

to accept the fact that there are usually several ways to solve a problem and that subordinates may legitimately choose a path different from their own. And, subordinates will make errors in carrying out their tasks. But they must be allowed to develop their own solutions to problems and to learn from their mistakes. The solution to subordinates' mistakes is not for the manager to delegate less but to train or otherwise support subordinates more.

Improved communication between managers and subordinates will increase mutual understanding and thus help to make delegation more effective. Managers who know the abilities of their subordinates can more realistically decide which tasks can be delegated to whom. Subordinates who are encouraged to use their abilities and who feel their managers will back them up will in turn be more likely to accept responsibility.[21]

A useful method for overcoming barriers to delegation is to increase the complexity of delegated assignments and the degree of delegation over time. Thus, a manager can delegate successively more work and subordinates will accept more responsibility for particular tasks. If there is no progress within a planned period, then some problem in the superior-subordinate relationship is indicated (such as inadequate training, lack of mutual confidence, or poor communication).

ILLUSTRATIVE CASE STUDY Continued

Responsiveness and Restructuring at IBM

Although IBM had often reorganized during the course of its history, this most recent change may well be its most important in several decades. It represents a major attempt to delegate authority *down* in the organization. For years, most major decisions were made or reviewed by a six-person executive committee. Now, however, authority for a huge number of decisions has been delegated to the six divisional committees. Division heads are now authorized to act as if they were running their own businesses, without having constantly to seek and wait for permission to try new things that may modify or violate traditional IBM policy.

Paradoxically, Akers, *relinquished* some control and authority in order to *maintain* control and authority. This notion of giving up control to gain control is not peculiar to IBM, according to Robert Waterman, who argues that one of the hallmarks of companies that have successfully renewed themselves is their ability to delegate authority to all levels in the organization. For IBM, such an extensive program of decentralization represents a major change.

JOB DESIGN

job design The division of an organization's work among its employees.

The structure of authority in organizations is directly related to the ways in which jobs are designed: While some jobs are designed to afford employees wide latitude in decision making, others permit the exercise of very little authority. There is a growing body of research on the subject of **job design,** but before we explore some of the ideas that have resulted from these studies, let us recall a fateful day that affected the very idea of organizational behavior not only in the U.S. but throughout the world.

On a day in late March 1979, the core of a nuclear reactor on Three Mile Island, in Pennsylvania, almost melted down. The island happens to be near Harrisburg, the state capital. If a meltdown had actually occurred, many thousands of people might have died.

The problem was not in the reactor. The problem was that the jobs of the people who operated the reactor were "actually (though inadvertently) designed to be error-

[21] See Fisch, "Toward Effective Delegation," p. 67; and William Newman, "Overcoming Obstacles to Effective Delegation," *Management Review* 45, no. 1 (January 1956):36–41.

prone—that is, designed for disaster.''[22] For example, the hundreds of lights and gauges that told the operators what was happening inside the reactor were hard to see. Even when the workers could read the indicators, the equipment was hard to use, because the reactor's controls were often far removed from the lights and gauges that indicated what effect the controls were having.[23]

FOR DISCUSSION

What are the potential negative consequences of poorly designed jobs? (Think in terms of consequences for the individual, the organization, and society.)

These problems had nothing to do with the internal design of the reactor. Even if the reactor itself had been absolutely without flaw, its controls—the interface between the reactor and those who ran it—made a disaster quite likely. At bottom, that disaster was a failure of job design, not of equipment or people.

Approaches to Job Design

Experts have been thinking about job design for at least a century. We shall now take a look at the four basic ways of viewing the subject: the mechanistic, motivational, biological, and perceptual/motor approaches.

Mechanistic Job Design. Consider the jobs of factory workers on an assembly line. Those jobs are very limited, requiring each worker to do only one or two simple things, over and over again. Most of these jobs are fairly easy to learn and fairly easy to do. Such jobs are suited to the mechanistic approach to job design, inspired by the turn-of-the-century research of Frederick W. Taylor, the ''father of scientific management'' (see Chapter 2), who systematically attempted to make jobs simple and efficient.

Jobs designed in this way are usually rather boring. The workers who hold them tend to be dissatisfied and unmotivated and to have high rates of absenteeism and on-the-job injury. Jobs that require workers to be alert and to perform more than one function—for example, the jobs of the operators at Three Mile Island—are not suited to this approach.

CLASS COMMENT

Take time to go over these *core job dimensions* with students. Encourage them to provide examples from jobs that they have held.

Motivational Job Design. As the limits of the mechanistic approach became clear, researchers began to seek out ways of making jobs more varied and challenging. J. Richard Hackman and others[24] who wished to motivate workers to do their jobs have come up with five core jobs dimensions: skill variety, task identity, task significance, autonomy, and feedback. Table 10-1 describes these dimensions and gives examples of them.

Hackman argues that employees who have responsible jobs that they can understand are more motivated and satisfied with their positions.[25] People whose jobs involve high levels of skill variety, task identity, and task significance experience work as very meaningful. A high level of autonomy makes workers more responsible and accountable for their acts. Feedback gives workers a useful understanding of their specific roles and functions. The more a job has of all five characteristics, the more likely it is that the person who holds it will be highly motivated and satisfied.

---

[22] Michael A. Campion and Paul W. Thayer, ''Development and Field Evaluation of an Interdisciplinary Measure of Job Design,'' *Journal of Applied Psychology* 70, no. 1:29–43. The following discussion of the four approaches to job design is based this source.

[23] For a complete account of Three-Mile Island, see Charles Perrow, *Normal Accidents* (New York: The Free Press, 1985).

[24] J. Richard Hackman and Edward E. Lawler, ''Employee Reactions to Job Characteristics,'' *Journal of Applied Psychology, Monograph 55* (1971):269–286; J. Richard Hackman and Greg R. Oldham. ''Development of the Job Diagnostic Survey,'' *Journal of Applied Psychology* 60, no. 2 (April 1975):159–170; and J. Richard Hackman and J. Lloyd Suttle, eds., *Improving Life at Work* (Santa Monica, Calif.: Goodyear, 1977), pp. 130–131.

[25] J. Richard Hackman, ''Work Design,'' in Hackman and Suttle, eds., *Improving Life at Work,* pp. 128–130.

TABLE 10-1 TASK CHARACTERISTICS

CHARACTERISTIC	DESCRIPTION	HIGH DEGREE	LOW DEGREE
Skill variety—the extent to which a variety of skills and talents are required to accomplish the assigned tasks.	Perform different tasks that challenge the intellect and develop skills in coordination.	Dress designer	Messenger
Task identity—the extent to which the job involves completion of an identifiable unit, project, or other piece of work.	Handle an entire job function from start to finish and be able to show a tangible piece of work as the outcome.	Software designer	Assembly-line worker
Task significance—the extent to which the task affects the work or lives of others, inside or outside the organization.	Be involved in a job function that is important for the well-being, safety, and perhaps survival of others.	Air traffic controller	House painter
Autonomy—the extent of the individual's freedom on the job and discretion to schedule tasks and determine procedures for carrying them out.	Be responsible for the success or failure of a job function and be able to plan work schedule, control quality, etc.	Project manager	Cashier in a department store
Feedback—the extent to which the individual receives specific information (praise, blame, or other comment) about the effectiveness with which his or her tasks are performed.	Learn about the effectiveness of one's job performance through clear and direct evaluation from a supervisor or colleagues or the results of the work itself.	Professional athlete	Security guard

Much attention has been given to making routine jobs more rewarding. These attempts fall into three broad categories: job enlargement, job enrichment, and flexible work schedules.

job enlargement The combining of various operations at a similar level into one job to provide more variety for workers and thus increase motivation and satisfaction. An increase in job scope.

Job enlargement stems from the thinking of industrial engineers. The idea behind it is to break up the monotony of a limited routine and work cycle by increasing a job's scope. Work functions from a horizontal slice of an organizational unit are combined, thereby giving each employee more operations to perform. For example, the work from two or more positions may be combined, thereby restoring some sense of the wholeness of the job. Or workers may be shifted routinely from job to job within the same company and thus get a chance to develop a variety of skills. Job rotation of this sort motivates workers by challenging them.

job enrichment The combining of several activities from a vertical cross section of the organization into one job to provide the worker with more autonomy and responsibility. An increase in job depth.

Another basic strategy has been inspired by motivational theory. **Job enrichment** tries to deal with dissatisfied workers by increasing the depth of their jobs. Work activities from a vertical slice of the organizational unit are combined in one position, so that employees have more autonomy on the job. Some of them may develop a stronger sense of accountability by setting their own work pace, for correcting their own errors, or for deciding the best way to perform various tasks. They may also help make decisions that affect their own subunits. As work becomes more challenging and worker responsibility increases, motivation and enthusiasm increase as well.[26]

empowerment The act of delegating power and authority to a subordinate so that the goals of the manager can be accomplished.

CLASS COMMENT

Job enlargement is often described as *horizontal loading* of jobs. Discuss why.

CLASS COMMENT

Job enrichment is often described as *vertical loading* of jobs. Discuss why.

Because job enrichment involves the delegation of accountability, one way to think about this mode of delegation is through the concept of **empowerment.** The manager literally gives the subordinate the power to act and accomplish his or her goals. Empowerment means autonomy, and it rests on a relationship of trust between superior and subordinate. The obvious question becomes "Who is ultimately *responsible?*" According to the principle of empowerment, responsibility devolves upon the subordinates but can never be abdicated by the manager. The answer in this case, then, is both the subordinate and the manager. Consider the illustration provided in the Management Application box entitled "Quality at Huffy Corporation." At Huffy, the workers were urged to take responsibility for product quality. Authority was delegated to them and jobs were designed so that responsibility was jointly determined.

[26]A paper by Robert N. Ford, "Job Enrichment Lessons from AT&T," *Harvard Business Review* 51, no. 1 (January–February 1973):96–106, describes some of the techniques used by AT&T to redesign white- and blue-collar jobs in one of the most extensive job-enrichment programs in American industry.

MANAGEMENT APPLICATION

QUALITY AT HUFFY CORPORATION

Huffy Corporation, a bicycle manufacturer, was in a squeeze in 1982. Manufacturing costs had to be cut by at least 20 percent to meet the competition. Japanese imports had increased dramatically, and competition in the American market had never been so fierce. The usual way to cut costs was to increase plant automation and fire line workers, most of whom had been with Huffy all their lives. Early in 1983, however, Huffy had to close a brand-new plant in Oklahoma because the automated equipment simply could not do the job.

Huffy decided to take another approach. The company would enlist the support of its employees in a radical quality and productivity program. Management made the employees responsible for product quality, delegating to them both the authority to act and the responsibility for results. In short, they were "empowered." Now all workers and production teams routinely inspect their own work and fix any defects. Only perfect products count toward their quotas. They also act as a quality control on the people or machines just before them in the production process. In this way problems are noticed and corrected before the bikes are assembled.

Huffy's plant in Celina, Ohio, is now the most productive bicycle factory in the world. Workers there turn out bikes in a third to a quarter of the time it takes in Japan. At the same time, quality is up. Inspectors who randomly take apart finished bikes rarely find anything wrong these days. Huffy employees now collect a second check each month, worth about 5 to 8 percent of their basic wages, as part of a special gain-sharing program. The company calculates its cost savings each month by comparing the factory's output with the hours logged by employees. This money is split fifty-fifty with the employees.

Source: Ralph E. Winter, "Upgrading of Factories Replaces the Concept of Total Automation," *Wall Street Journal,* November 30, 1987, pp. 1, 8.

FOR DISCUSSION

What are the *individual* and *organizational* advantages of alternative work schedules?

Job enlargement and job enrichment are attempts to make work itself more meaningful. Alternative work schedules, by contrast, make work hours more convenient and may enhance the quality of nonwork time. Two kinds of alternative work schedules are today being incorporated into organizational structures: the compressed work week and flextime.

Employees whose schedules have been compressed usually exchange the traditional five-day week for a week of four or even three days. Instead of working eight hours a day for five days (5/40), they may work 10 hours a day for four days (4/40), or twelve hours a day for three (3/36), or any other combination that suits them and their employers. Such work schedules help employees share household responsibilities with their spouse, attend school, or pursue other activities of their own choosing.[27]

Compressed workweeks also reduce the costs of overtime, overhead, and personal-leave time. Small manufacturing or service operations are often well suited to such a schedule—especially where they demand little or no physical work, so there is no danger that tired workers will hurt themselves. Young or newly hired workers especially like the compressed work week because they can adapt their lifestyles to the extra leisure time it permits. By contrast, workers who are used to the standard Monday-to-Friday, 9-to-5 routine generally take longer to adjust to such changes. Sometimes these workers resist them altogether, because it is hard to change a lifestyle, especially when it is tied to the schedules of other family members.

[27]Riva Poor, *Four Days, Forty Hours* (Cambridge, Mass.: Bursk and Poor, 1970).

flextime A system that permits employees to arrange their work hours to suit their personal needs.

Flextime, which is more widespread in Europe than it is in the United States, permits employees to arrange their daily work hours to suit their personal needs and lifestyles. A very attractive aspect of flextime is the possibility of avoiding rush-hour travel. It is particularly suited to companies whose work loads fluctuate from hour to hour within a single day.

Flextime employees are responsible for coordinating their functions with other employees; in that way, they have more responsibility and autonomy than most workers do. Assembly-line operations, by contrast, are usually not suited to flexible time arrangements.[28] Flextime typically requires employees to be on the job during a core period—often about four hours in the middle of the day—but allows them to choose their own starting and ending times.

EXTRA EXERCISE

Have students interview the manager or a sales representative from a local office furniture store regarding furniture design. Or have the manager come speak to your class regarding office furniture design.

Biological Job Design. We have already seen that jobs involving little physical work are suited to compressed schedules, since there is less danger that tired workers will hurt themselves. Such considerations have given rise to a whole approach to job design. This biological approach, sometimes called "ergonomics," is a systematic attempt to make work as safe as possible.

The biological approach has been used extensively in heavy industry (such as steel, mining, and construction), both to make jobs safer and to help women do the kind of physically demanding work that used to be done only by men. In offices, ergonomic techniques can reduce the back- and eyestrain suffered by employees who spend their days sitting in chairs, looking at computer screens.

Perceptual/Motor Job Design. Experimental psychology has suggested yet another approach to job design. The biological approach, as we have seen, attempts to ensure that the physical demands of work do not exceed the physical capabilities of the people who do it. Likewise, the perceptual/motor approach seeks to ensure that the mental demands of their work do not exceed their mental capabilities. For example, the jobs of the people who operated the reactor at Three Mile Island had been poorly designed from the perceptual/motor point of view, since the operators had to respond to excessive amounts of information from the lights and gauges. The problem with the perceptual/motor approach, as with the mechanistic approach, is that jobs can be made so simple that they become boring.

Job Design and Job Satisfaction

As you can see in Table 10-2, each of these four ways of designing jobs has advantages and disadvantages. The mechanistic approach cuts training times and error rates, but also job motivation and satisfaction. The motivational approach promotes job motivation and satisfaction but involves more training time and a higher risk of error and stress. The biological approach can be expensive, although it cuts the effort and fatigue of many jobs. The perceptual/motor approach, like the mechanistic one, tends to make jobs less satisfying, although (like the biological approach) it also makes them safer.

In fact, these four approaches differ in degree rather than in kind. They can be described as a continuum. On one end of the continuum lie jobs designed with the motivational approach, to maximize the job satisfaction and motivation of individual workers, as well as to cut absenteeism. On the other end are jobs that have been designed with the mechanistic or perceptual/motor approaches, which tend to promote organizational (rather than individual) ends. By limiting the scope of any job, these approaches help companies use their equipment more efficiently, since each worker

[28] "Flextime in the Utilities Industry," *Personnel* 61, no. 2 (March–April 1984):42–44.

TABLE 10-2 SUMMARY OF OUTCOMES FROM THE JOB-DESIGN APPROACHES

JOB-DESIGN APPROACH	POSITIVE OUTCOMES	NEGATIVE OUTCOMES
Mechanistic	Decreased training time Higher utilization levels Lower likelihood of error Less chance of mental overload and stress	Lower job satisfaction Lower motivation Higher absenteeism
Motivational	Higher job satisfaction Higher motivation Greater job involvement Higher job performance Lower absenteeism	Increased training time Lower utilization levels Greater likelihood of error Greater chance of mental overload and stress
Biological	Less physical effort Less physical fatigue Fewer health complaints Fewer medical incidents Lower absenteeism Higher job satisfaction	Higher financial costs because of changes in equipment or job environment
Perceptual/Motor	Lower likelihood of error Lower likelihood of accidents Less chance of mental overload and stress Lower training time Higher utilization levels	Lower job satisfaction Lower motivation

Source: Reprinted, by permission of American Management Association, from Michael A. Campion and Paul W. Thayer, "Job Design: Approaches, Outcomes, and Trade-Offs," *Organizational Dynamics*, Autumn 1973, p. 76. © 1973 American Management Association, New York. All rights reserved.

will perform one repetitive task at one machine. Both approaches also make jobs easier to learn and perform, but easy, limited jobs tend to be boring.

The relationship between job design and job satisfaction is complex. Motivational theorists have argued that the more we use job-enrichment and job-enlargement techniques, the more satisfied individual employees will be. A study by Charles Hulin and Milton Blood concluded that employee satisfaction or dissatisfaction with specialized jobs depends to a great extent on the attitudes of the workers being studied.[29] Those who accept the "Protestant Work Ethic"—that is, who see work as important and meaningful and who strongly desire financial success—are likely to become dissatisfied in jobs that are too specialized.

Hulin and Blood suggest, however, that employees who feel alienated may prefer narrower, more restricted jobs because they are easier and require little attention or commitment. Hackman, who has drawn similar conclusions, refers to a "growth need," not to the Protestant work ethic. His studies indicate that people with high growth needs will be more satisfied in expanded and challenging jobs than individuals with low growth needs.[30]

One group of researchers reviewed 28 separate research studies of job satisfaction.[31] They found that the relationship between job satisfaction and the characteristics of jobs themselves is higher in those employees who have high growth needs. This conclusion supports Hackman's research. In those employees with lower needs for

[29]Charles L. Hulin and Milton R. Blood, "Job Enlargement, Individual Differences, and Worker Responses," *Psychological Bulletin* 69, no. 1 (1968):41–53.

[30]See Hackman, "Work Design," p. 118.

[31]Brian Lober, Raymond Noe, Nancy L. Moeller, and Michael Fitzgerald, "A Meta-Analysis of the Relation of Job Characteristics to Job Satisfaction," *Journal of Applied Psychology* 70, no. 2 (1985):280–289.

growth and development, situational characteristics—like work-group or management support for a job-enrichment program—may be more important.

Gerald Salancik and Jeffrey Pfeffer also argue that the social dimensions are important to job satisfaction. Social influences may affect not only the way people value their jobs but also the way they describe them. It has been shown, for example, that the extent to which a supervisor engaged in "small talk" and offers advice on how to do a job affects the extent to which employees feel independent.[32] In addition, a number of researchers have concluded that personality traits of workers have a great impact on job satisfaction.

CLASS COMMENT

Emphasize the importance of making sensible job design choices.

Job design is complex and often difficult. Managers must often make trade-offs between characteristics that are both good in themselves: between simplicity and motivation, for example. To make sensible choices, you must understand all four approaches, as well as the strengths and weaknesses of each.

DECENTRALIZATION

decentralization The delegation of power and authority from higher to lower levels of the organization, often accomplished by the creation of small, self-contained organizational units.

centralization The extent to which authority is concentrated at the top of the organization.

CLASS COMMENT

The concept of centralization-decentralization is not absolute but rather a relative one. It's a matter of how much, not a matter of are we or are we not.

HERE'S AN EXAMPLE

IBM Corporation announced during January of 1988 a major restructuring that would decentralize authority in the company. Five new, highly independent systems and technology businesses with significant worldwide responsibilities, and a new major organization, IBM United States, are being established. IBM will transfer day-to-day operational decisions from corporate headquarters to these six new operating entities. (*Business Week*, 2/15/88, pp. 92–98)

The delegation of authority by individual managers and the design of jobs in organizations are closely related to an organization's decentralization of authority. Delegation is the process of assigning authority or accountability from one level of management down to the next. Job design is based on the amount of authority and accountability delegated to an employee. The concepts of decentralization and centralization refer to the extent to which authority or accountability have been passed down to lower levels (**decentralization**) or have been retained at the top of the organization (**centralization**). This terminology derives from a perspective, held in many countries, of the organization as a series of concentric circles. The chief executive of the organization is situated in the very center and a "web" of authority radiates out from him or her. The greater the amount of authority delegated throughout the organization, the more decentralized the organization is. For example, to the extent that lower-level managers can expend significant sums for equipment or supplies without first checking with higher-level managers, the organization is more decentralized.

As we noted in Chapter 9, considerable confusion often arises between the terms *decentralization* and *divisionalization*. Part of the confusion is because of the tendency to refer to divisionalized firms as decentralized and to functionally structured firms as centralized. After all, the most obvious example of an increase in decentralization is an organization that moves from a centralized functional structure to a decentralized divisional structure. Furthermore, many of the advantages of divisionalization, as discussed in Chapter 9, also apply to decentralization. The two, however, are not the same and should not be regarded as such. Any divisionalized organization may be relatively centralized or decentralized in its operations.

The advantages of decentralization are similar to the advantages of delegation: unburdening of top managers; improved decision making because decisions are made closer to the scene of action; better training, morale, and initiative at lower levels; and more flexibility and faster decision making in rapidly changing environments. These advantages are so compelling it is tempting to think of decentralization as "good" and centralization as "bad."

But total decentralization, with no coordination and leadership from the top, would clearly be undesirable. The very purpose of organization—efficient integration of subunits for the good of the whole—would be defeated without some centralized control. For this reason, the question for managers is not whether an organization should be decentralized but to what extent it should be decentralized.

---

[32]Gerald Salancik and Jeffrey Pfeffer, "Determinants of Supervisory Behavior: A Role Set Analysis, *Human Relations* 28 (1975):139–154.

As we shall see, the appropriate amount of decentralization for an organization will vary with time and circumstances. It will also vary for the different subunits of the organization. For example, production and sales departments have gained a high degree of decentralization in many companies, whereas financial departments have tended to remain comparatively centralized.

Factors Influencing Decentralization

Decentralization has value only to the extent that it assists an organization to achieve its objectives. In determining the amount of decentralization appropriate for an organization, the following factors are usually considered.[33]

1. Influences from the business environment outside the organization, such as market characteristics, competitive pressures, and availability of materials.
2. Size and growth rate of the organization.
3. Characteristics of the organization, such as costliness of given decisions, top management preferences, the organization's culture, and abilities of lower-level managers.

The first two factors help to determine the logical degree of decentralization—that is, they suggest what top managers *should* do. The last factor suggests what managers are *likely* to do. For example, a particular supermarket chain might be better off if each store manager had some discretion in adapting purchasing and pricing policies to local conditions. An autocratic top management might be unwilling to delegate this authority. But it will have to either change its attitude or accept the fact that the organization will suffer losses in some areas at the hands of competitors.

BACKGROUND ON CHANDLER

Chandler's classic study, *Strategy and Structure: Chapters in the History of the American Industrial Enterprise,* also concluded that structure follows strategy. (Refer back to Chapter 8 for more information about this topic.)

Strategy and the Organization's Environment. The strategy of an organization will influence the types of markets, technological environment, and competition with which the organization must contend. These factors will, in turn, influence the degree of decentralization that the firm finds appropriate. Alfred Chandler, for example, found that firms such as Westinghouse and General Electric that developed new products through a strategy of research and development leading to product diversification chose a decentralized structure. Other companies, operating in industries in which markets were more predictable, production processes less dynamic technologically, and competitive relationships more stable, tended to remain or become more centralized. United States Steel, for example, became more, rather than less, centralized in the first half of this century.[34]

Size and Rate of Growth. It is virtually impossible to run a large organization efficiently while vesting all decision-making authority in one or a few top managers. This is almost certainly the strongest single force for delegation and, hence, for decentralization.

As an organization continues to grow in size and complexity, decentralization tends to increase. The faster the rate of growth, the more likely it is that upper management, bearing the weight of an ever-increasing work load, will be forced to accelerate

[33]See Ernest Dale, *Organization* (New York: American Management Associations, 1967), pp. 114–130.

[34]Alfred D. Chandler, Jr., *Strategy and Structure: Chapters in the History of the American Industrial Enterprise* (Cambridge, Mass.: MIT Press, 1962).

the delegation of authority to lower levels. When the growth rate slows, however, upper management may attempt to regain decision-making authority under the guise of "tightening things up" and protecting profits.

Characteristics of the Organization. The extent to which decision-making authority is centralized is also likely to be influenced by such internal characteristics of the company as:

1. *The cost and risk associated with the decision.* Managers may be wary of delegating authority for decisions that could have a heavy impact on the performance of their own subunits or of the organization as a whole. This caution is out of consideration not only for the company's welfare but for their own as well, since the responsibility for the results remains with the delegator.
2. *An individual manager's preference for a high degree of involvement in detail and confidence in subordinates.* Some managers pride themselves on their detailed knowledge of everything that happens within their area of responsibility. (This is known as "the good manager runs a tight ship" approach.) Others take equal pride in confidently delegating everything possible to their subordinates in order to avoid getting bogged down in petty details and to save their own expertise for the unit's major objectives.
3. *The organizational culture.* The shared norms, values, and understandings (culture) of members of some organizations support tight control at the top. The culture of other organizations support the opposite. The history of an organization helps to create its current culture. A firm that has had slow growth under a strong-willed leader may have a very centralized structure. In contrast, a firm that has grown rapidly through acquisitions will have learned to live with the greater independence of the acquired companies. (See Chapter 13 for a further discussion of corporate culture.)
4. *The abilities of lower-level managers.* This dimension is, in part, circular. If authority is not delegated because of lack of faith in the talent below, the talent will not have much opportunity to develop. In addition, the lack of internal training will make it more difficult to find and hold talented and ambitious people. This, in turn, will make it more difficult to decentralize.

HERE'S AN EXAMPLE

"For an organization to run smoothly, people need to know who's in charge." At Westinghouse Electric Company, CEO John C. Marous and President Paul E. Lego share an arrangement where Lego has already been designated as CEO after Marous retires in 1991. Both men are determined to make their partnership work. So far, whenever a final decision has had to be made, "We've never split over an issue," says Marous. (*Business Week*, 3/28/88, p. 52)

Trends in Decentralization

The period from the end of World War II to the early 1970s was a time of great economic growth. On balance, decentralization probably increased during this period. In the 1970s to mid-1980s, low rates of economic growth, pressure from foreign competition, and eventually the competitive disadvantages arising from the strength of the U.S. dollar encouraged centralization; many companies sought ways to increase productivity by eliminating costly duplication of functions.

The clear trend today is toward more decentralization. Many companies have "restructured," which often means simply eliminating staff jobs and pushing decision-making authority farther down the organization. GE, AT&T, and Eastman Kodak, to name but a few, have eliminated thousands of corporate staff jobs in an effort to decentralize. At the same time, advances in information technology have made centralized control systems much more sophisticated. At The Limited and other retailers, every sale feeds into an inventory system so that stores can be restocked automatically according to their own needs. Information systems allow some processes to be centrally controlled, while decentralizing decision-making to the managers closest to the customer. Indeed, the issue of decentralization promises to be one of the most hotly debated topics in the years to come.

ILLUSTRATIVE CASE STUDY Wrap-Up

Responsiveness and Restructuring at IBM

By delegating authority for a number of policy decisions to lower levels of management, IBM has tried to decentralize the authority in the company. IBM created essentially six new divisions to aid in this decentralization, but simple *divisionalization* and overall *decentralization* are not the same thing.

Obviously, IBM's environment had changed over the years. The advent of minicomputers and micros affected IBM's products, but it also affected the way that IBM could manage the business effectively. While many companies have sacrificed both jobs and morale by restructuring, removing layers of management, and downsizing, IBM, in keeping with its long and distinguished history, has been able to implement complex, long-term strategy without sacrifice of jobs or morals.

Nevertheless, the jury is still out on IBM. Every few years, pundits regularly declare IBM dead on late arrival, but once again the company has shown no reluctance to do what is necessary to adapt to an environment, both internal and external, that tends to change with virtually mind-boggling speed. ■

■ SUMMARY

Power, influence, and authority are necessary elements of organizational life. From a classical viewpoint, formal authority is a legitimate managerial right that subordinates are obligated to recognize. From an "acceptance" viewpoint, formal authority is legitimized by subordinates.

There are five sources or bases of power: reward, coercive, legitimate, expert, and referent. In exercising their power, managers may take a dominance-submission approach toward subordinates, or they may use a more positive style based on concern for group goals and the encouragement and support of subordinates. The latter approach seems to work better, and effective managers learn to temper their use of power with maturity and self-control.

Line positions can be defined as those directly responsible for achieving the organization's goals. *Staff positions* provide expert advice and service to the line.

Effective delegation helps an organization use its resources efficiently—it frees managers for important tasks, improves decision making, and encourages initiative. Classical guidelines for effective delegation include the need to give subordinates authority and accountability and the need to follow the scalar principle and the principle of unity of command. These guidelines, however, will not apply to all situations.

The structure of authority in organizations is directly related to the organization's policies for job design. The mechanistic approach to job design seeks to make all jobs as efficient and simple as possible. Jobs so designed tend to be dull. The motivational approach attempts to inspire workers by increasing the skill variety, task identity, task significance, autonomy, and feedback involved in their work. Job enrichment and job enlargement are ways to enhance such task characteristics and heighten work involvement. The biological approach attemtps to ensure that the physical demands of work do not exceed the physical capacities of those who do it. Likewise, the perceptual/motor approach seek to ensure that the mental demands of work do not exceed their mental capacities.

Delegation is closely related to decentralization in the sense that the greater the amount of delegation, the more decentralized the organization. The appropriate amount of decentralization for a particular organization will depend on external environmental forces, the organization's size and growth, and its culture. The current trend, fueled both by corporate restructuring and advances in information technology, is toward decentralization.

■ REVIEW QUESTIONS

1. What are the two major views of authority? How do you think each view would affect a manager's attitude and behavior toward subordinates?
2. What is the "zone of indifference"?
3. What are the five bases of power described by French and Raven? Give one example of a manager's exercise of each type of power.
4. What are the "two faces of power" described by David McClelland?

5. What are the characteristics of successful power users?
6. What is the difference between line positions and staff positions? Is the difference always clear in organizations?
7. What does the phrase "functional staff authority" mean?
8. What are the advantages of delegation? Describe the classical guidelines to effective delegation. What are the limitations of these guidelines?
9. What are the advantages of job specialization? Why did it emerge?
10. What is the purpose of job enlargement and job enrichment?
11. How are decentralization and delegation related?
12. What factors influence the extent to which an organization is decentralized?
13. Do you believe there will be a trend toward centralization or decentralization over the next several years? Why?

CASE STUDY The Use and Abuse of Joyce Roberts

Joyce Roberts, 29 years old, was a middle-level manager at Amalgamated Products Inc. (API). For the last nine months, she had been on special assignment to a key marketing-staff function at corporate headquarters, working directly with the Marketing Vice-President, Bernard Peach, even though there were two levels of management between them. Peach had come to Roberts' boss and told her not to give her any other assignments—that Roberts was to work directly for Peach. In order to communicate more closely, Peach had Roberts install a high-tech phone system in her office and gave Roberts access to an executive secretary.

API was a staid company, facing a number of changes in its external environment. It was highly centralized, and a number of key managers complained that the company was overly bureaucratic. Many older managers, like Roberts' boss (and her bosses' boss) were looked upon as "dead wood" incapable of operating in the new environment. Nevertheless, change was normally a slow process at API, and on a number of matters Roberts found herself in direct conflict with her boss even though she was acting on Peach's direct orders. She was unsure how much resentment was building up beneath the surface, but she found working directly with Peach, occasionally mentioned as a future CEO, exhilirating—even if she was frustrated by being caught in the middle of larger bureaucratic struggles.

Peach and Roberts worked together closely on a high-profile revamping of API's products, and by all measures the project promised to be quite successful. Two days before the presentation to API's Executive Committee, Peach dispatched Roberts to the resort where the meeting was to be held in order to double- and triple-check all of the arrangements. When Peach arrived, he called Roberts' room at 3 A.M. and together they checked the slide projector to be sure that the tops of the slides were straight when projected.

After the presentation, the committee adopted most of the recommendations, and two days later Bernard Peach was promoted to Group Vice-President—Asia. Joyce Roberts went into her office to find two memos on her desk. The first was the announcement that Bernard Peach had been promoted and had already left for his new job. The second was a handwritten note from her boss to talk about her performance problems over the last six months. Roberts wondered what she should do.

Source: This case was prepared by R. Edward Freeman, Olsson Professor of Business Administration, The Darden School, University of Virginia. It is based on an actual situation, but all names and some facts are disguised.

Case Questions

1. What are the sources and uses of power in this case?
2. What problems does Joyce Roberts now have?
3. What advice would you give Roberts? ■

Max Weber, *Rush Hour, New York*. 1915. Canvas 36½ x 30¼. National Gallery of Art, Washington D.C. Gift of the Avalon Foundation.

11

HUMAN RESOURCE MANAGEMENT

Upon completing this chapter you should be able to:

1. Explain why human resource management (HRM) is an essential management function.
2. Describe the HRM proccss.
3. State why human resource planning is important, what the aims of human resource planning are, and how the process of human resource planning is carried out.
4. Describe the process of recruitment both within and outside the organization.
5. Describe each step in the selection procedure.
6. Indicate how early job experiences have an effect on new employees' eventual success.
7. Describe the various types of training and management development programs.
8. Identify the four basic appraisal approaches and how appraisal can be managed so as to lead to improved employee performance.
9. Explain how HRM's connected to the organization's strategy.

Chapter Outline

Introduction
The HRM Process: A Traditional View
Human Resource Planning
Recruitment
Selection
Orientation and Socialization
Training and Development
Performance Appraisal
Promotions, Transfers, Demotions, and Separations
HRM and Strategy

ILLUSTRATIVE CASE STUDY Introduction

Human Relations at Sony Corporation

Akio Morita, founder of Sony Corporation, says that there is no "magic" in the success of Japanese companies in general and Sony in particular. The secret of their success is simply the way that they treat their employees. In his biography, *Made in Japan,* Mr. Morita says:

> The most important mission for a Japanese manager is to develop a healthy relationship with his employees, to create a familylike feeling within the corporation, a feeling that employees and managers share the same fate. Those companies that are most successful in Japan are those that have managed to create a shared sense of fate among all employees, what Americans call labor and management, and the shareholders.

While Morita was chairman of Sony, he made a personal point every year of addressing each class of college recruits, explaining his view of the differences between school and work. According to Morita, the world of work gave them an exam every day. Performance had to be continual, and mistakes resulted not in failed exams, but in costs to the company. Above all, Morita stresses that each employee had to seek happiness in his work and to decide personally whether he or she wanted to spend the rest of his or her working life at Sony.

At Sony there are few noticeable differences between management and labor (even though things are not as rosy as they are sometimes painted by writers extolling the virtues of Japanese management). One of the reasons for this fact can be isolated in the philosophy of managers like Morita. Sony has always endeavored to treat employees as colleagues and helpers rather than as mere means to profits. Morita believed that although investors are important, they established only a *temporary* relationship with Sony, a company that was not financed in the usual way—through large industrial groups. Rather, employees were more important because they really were a *permanent* part of the company, just as much as top management.

Morita also expected loyalty from his employees, but this expectation did not require that subordinates simply parrot Morita's opinion; in fact, he encouraged dissent and variety of opinion. Ironically, this attitude was partly inspired by Morita's experience with American managers and employees. In the early days of Sony, many employees were hired in the United States because Sony had to keep pace with the remarkable demand for its products, and one day Morita was stunned by an American colleague's advice about a problem employee. His American friend said "Fire him." Morita was equally surprised when an American employee walked into his office one day and announced that he was going to quit and take a job with a competitor who had offered to double his salary.

Under Morita, the whole process of recruitment, selection, socialization, training and development, performance appraisal, and rewards at Sony was built on the premise that employees were the most valuable part of the company. Granted, Sony was once a maverick in Japan, and Morita's policies may certainly seem out of keeping with policy in most American companies even today, but it is his approach to the human resource process which interests us here and which we will discuss in greater depth throughout this chapter. Note, however, that we should exercise caution in generalizing from this case: Morita has given us only his view of Sony, and sometimes the viewpoint of the CEO may well differ from that of other employees at all levels in the organization.

Source: Akio Morita, *Made in Japan* (New York: E. P. Dutton, 1986).

The most important resources of an organization are its human resources—the people who supply the organization with their work, talent, creativity, and drive. Thus, among the most critical tasks of a manager are the selection, training, and development of people who will best help the organization meet its goals. Without competent people at the managerial level—and indeed at all levels—organizations will either pursue inappropriate goals or find it difficult to achieve appropriate goals once they have been set.

human resource management (HRM) The management function that deals with recruitment, placement, training, and development of organization members.

TEACHING TIP

Emphasize the *recruitment, selection, placement, training,* and *development* of employees.

Human resource management (HRM) is the management function that deals with the recruitment, placement, training, and development of organization members. In this chapter, we will examine how organizations determine what human resources they need now and in the future, how managers recruit and select people with the best potential for each position, how managers train people so that they will perform effectively, and finally, what types of development programs will best assure a constant flow of managerial talent from lower to higher levels of the organization. More than ever, HRM is critical to an organization's success. Recall from Chapter 3 how the global environment puts more pressure on the HRM process. First, we will look at the traditional view of the HRM process, and then we will show how the environment of an organization demands that it coordinate HRM more closely with its strategy.

THE HRM PROCESS: A TRADITIONAL VIEW

The composition of an organization's work force changes over time. Managers in organizations do not stay in their positions permanently. Successful managers are usually promoted; many of those who are not promoted seek better jobs elsewhere; unsuccessful managers are, in many cases, transferred or replaced. The same is true of nonmanagerial staff. Thus, the organization and its managers must accommodate themselves to a constant change of personnel over time.

FOR DISCUSSION

Why is it so important to have the right people in the right positions at the right time?

The HRM process can be seen as a continuing procedure to keep the organization supplied with the right people in the right positions at the right time. The activities in this process include:

1. *Human Resource Planning*. Human resource planning is designed to ensure that the personnel needs of the organization will be constantly and appropriately met. Such planning is accomplished through analysis of (a) internal factors, such as current and expected skill needs, vacancies, and departmental expansions and reductions, and (b) factors in the external environment, such as the labor market. As a result of this analysis, plans are developed for executing the other steps in the HRM process. Human resource planning usually covers a period from six months to five years in the future. The use of computers to build and maintain information about all employees (HRIS) has enabled organizations to be much more efficient in their planning of human resources.
2. *Recruitment*. Recruitment is concerned with developing a pool of job candidates in line with the organization's human resource plan. The candidates are usually located through newspaper and professional journal advertisements, employment agencies, word of mouth, and visits to college and university campuses.
3. *Selection*. Selection involves evaluating and choosing among job candidates. Application forms, résumés, interviews, employment and skills tests, and reference checks are the most commonly used aids in the selection process.

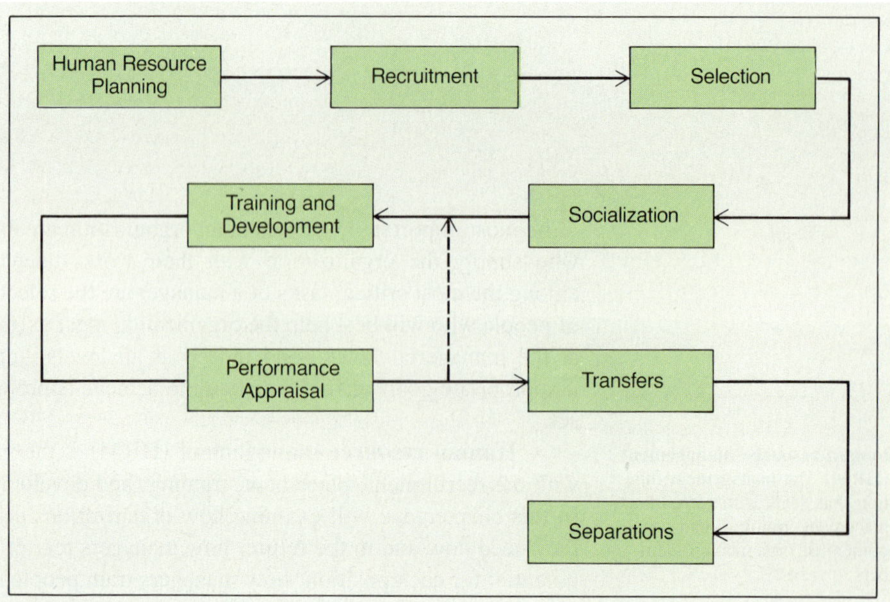

FIGURE 11-1 THE HRM PROCESS IN ORGANIZATIONS

4. *Socialization.* Socialization is designed to help the selected individuals fit smoothly into the organization. Newcomers are introduced to their colleagues, acquainted with their responsibilities, and informed about the organization's policies and goals. It is also the method whereby the organization presents its expectations regarding behavior to the individual.
5. *Training and Development.* The process of training and development aims at increasing the ability of individuals and groups to contribute to organizational effectiveness. *Training* is designed to improve skills in the present job; for example, employees might be instructed in new decision-making techniques or the capabilities of data processing systems. *Development* programs are designed to educate employees beyond the requirements of their present position so that they will be prepared for promotion and be able to take a broader view of their role in the organization.
6. *Performance Appraisal.* Performance appraisal compares an individual's job performance against standards or objectives developed for the individual's position. If performance is high, the individual is likely to be rewarded (by a bonus, for example, or by more challenging work assignments). If performance is low, some corrective action (such as additional training) might be arranged to bring the performance back in line with desired standards. (Figure 11-1 illustrates the HRM process.)

HUMAN RESOURCE PLANNING

human resource planning Planning for the future personnel needs of an organization, taking into account both internal activities and factors in the external environment.

The need for **human resource planning** may not be readily apparent. After all, one might ask, If an organization needs new people, why doesn't it simply hire them? In fact, an organization's human resource needs can hardly ever be met as quickly or as easily as this question implies. An organization that does not plan for its human resources will often find that it is not meeting either its personnel requirements or its overall goals effectively.

For example, a manufacturing company may hope to increase productivity with new automated equipment, but if the company has not started to hire and train people to operate the equipment before installation is begun, the equipment may remain idle for weeks or even months. Similarly, an all-male, all-white organization that does not plan to add women and minority group members to its staff is likely to become the defendant in a civil rights lawsuit. In rapidly changing times like those which have characterized the second half of the 20th century and which promise to proceed at an equally heady pace, planning for human resources will be a challenging task. With an increasingly competitive environment, projected labor shortages, changing demographics, and increased pressure on government to protect employee rights, organizations will need to be flexible and remain aware of the dynamics of their environments.[1]

Planning Procedures

There are four basic procedures in human resource planning.[2]

1. *Planning for future needs*. How many people with what abilities will the organization need to remain in operation for the foreseeable future?
2. *Planning for future balance*. How many people presently employed can be expected to stay with the organization? The difference between this number and the number the organization will need leads to the next step.
3. *Planning for recruiting and selecting or for laying off*. How can the organization locate and lure the number of people it will need?
4. *Planning for development*. How should the training and movement of individuals within the organization be managed so that the organization will be assured of a continuing supply of experienced and capable personnel?

To take these steps effectively, the managers of a human resource planning program must consider a number of factors. The primary factor is the organization's strategic plan. (See Chapter 7.) The organization's basic strategy and the detailed goals, objectives, and tactics for making that strategy a reality will define the personnel needs of the organization. For example, a strategy based on internal growth means that additional personnel will have to be hired. A strategy based on acquiring other companies suggests not only the need to hire managers who have had experience with the types of firms being acquired, but the need to plan for a reduction in the number of the organization's overall personnel. Many firms that have merged have identified redundancies among combined staffs and have had to discharge personnel whose activities overlapped with those of other members of the new organization.

BACKGROUND ON FUTURE JOBS

The "new job" market is facing a critical point—a growing mismatch between emerging jobs that call for increasingly higher levels of skills and the people available to fill them. The labor pool is shrinking, and the labor market is changing as U.S. companies cope with rapid technological change and an ever more-competitive global economy. (*Fortune*, 4/11/88, pp. 42–56)

Another factor to be considered by managers is potential change in the organization's external environment. As we saw in Chapter 3, this may mean a change in the market, in the availability of financing, or in the labor force. In a booming economy, for example, an organization might want to expand, and so its personnel needs will increase. At the same time, however, there may be fewer job candidates available because unemployment will be low. In a depressed economy, many organizations cut back on the number of employees; however, an organization that wishes to expand is likely to have an increased number of candidates available because of unemployment. As organizations expand internationally, they must find people conversant with the cultures of other countries. By agreeing to joint ventures with Philips and Olivetti, AT&T was able to take advantage of their partners' human resources; later, AT&T hired a number of European managers for its own operations in Europe.

In sum, the organization's internal environment (as exemplified by its strategic plan), as well as its external environment, will broadly define for managers the limits within which their human resource plan must operate. Once these broad limits have been established, managers can begin to compare their future personnel needs against

[1]See Allan Halcon, "Portfolio," *Personnel Journal* 67, no. 3 (1988): 12–13; and Sharon Nelton, "Meet Your New Work Force," *Nation's Business* 76, no. 7 (1988):14–21.

[2]See Edwin L. Miller, Elmer H. Burack, and Maryann H. Albrecht, *Management of Human Resources* (Englewood Cliffs, N.J.: Prentice Hall, 1980); and Burckhardt Wenzel, "Planning for Manpower Utilization," *Personnel Administrator* 15, no. 3 (May–June 1970):36–40.

the existing personnel situation in order to determine what recruitment, training, and development procedures they will need to follow.[3]

Forecasting and the Human Resource Audit

The two central elements in human resource planning are forecasting and the human resource audit. These two elements give managers the information they need to plan the other steps in the HRM process, such as recruiting and training.

forecasting The attempt, using specific techniques, to predict outcomes and project future trends.

Forecasting. Human resource **forecasting** attempts to determine what personnel the organization will need to maintain its growth and exploit future opportunities. Thus, forecasters try to predict the number, type, and quality of people needed in the future; specify the range of responsibilities that will have to be met; and establish what skills and knowledge organization members will need.[4]

Human Resource Audit. Once the forecasts are completed, the next step is to obtain information about the organization's present personnel. Two kinds of information are needed: Do organization members have the appropriate skills for their jobs? Are they performing effectively? The answers to these questions will enable planners to match the organization's personnel strengths and weaknesses against future requirements. Particular emphasis should be placed on locating existing skills and potential within the organization, since it is usually more economical to promote from within than to recruit, hire, and train people from outside—a practice that also fosters loyalty to the firm and acknowledges the possibility of career paths for personnel.

human resource audit The analysis and appraisal of the organization's current human resources.

In a **human resource audit,** the skills and performance of each individual in the organization are appraised. Within each department, individuals are ranked according to the quality of their work. The information thus obtained will give upper-level managers an idea of the effectiveness of staff in each department.

replacement chart A chart that diagrams an organization's positions, showing the incumbents, likely future candidates, and readiness of candidates to enter those positions.

For higher levels of management, the next step in the auditing process may be to develop a detailed succession plan or replacement chart. The **replacement chart** shows the positions in the organization, present incumbents in those positions, likely future candidates for those positions, and the readiness of those candidates to take over those positions. Replacement charts such as that in Figure 11-2 with this much detail are usually developed only for upper-level managers. However, the need to compare existing human resources with future requirements exists at all levels of the organization. GE uses a "slate system," whereby every senior manager at a certain level has a potential replacement. Both former chairman Reg Jones and current chairman Jack Welch have attested that managing the company's slate system is among their most important tasks and highest priorities.

RECRUITMENT

recruitment The development of a pool of job candidates in accordance with a human resource plan.

The purpose of **recruitment** is to provide a group of candidates large enough for the organization to select the qualified employees it needs. *General recruiting,* which is

[3]Jennifer McQueen, "Integrating Human Resource Planning with Strategic Planning," *Canadian Public Administration* 27, no. 1 (Spring 1984):1–13; Judy D. Olian and Sara L. Rynes, "Organizational Staffing: Integrating Practice with Strategy," *Industrial Relations* 23, no. 2 (Spring 1984):170–183; Randall S. Schuler and Ian C. MacMillan, "Gaining Competitive Advantage through Human Resource Management Practices," *Human Resource Management* 23, no. 3 (Fall 1984):241–255; Raymond E. Miles and Charles E. Snow, "Designing Strategic Human Resources Systems," *Organizational Dynamics* 13 (1984): 36–52; and Elmer H. Burack, "Corporate Business and Human Resource Planning Practices: Strategic Issues and Concerns," *Organizational Dynamics* 15 (1986):73–87.

[4]For a survey of recent advances in task analysis, see Kenneth N. Wexley, "Personnel Training," *Annual Review of Psychology* 35 (1984):522–525.

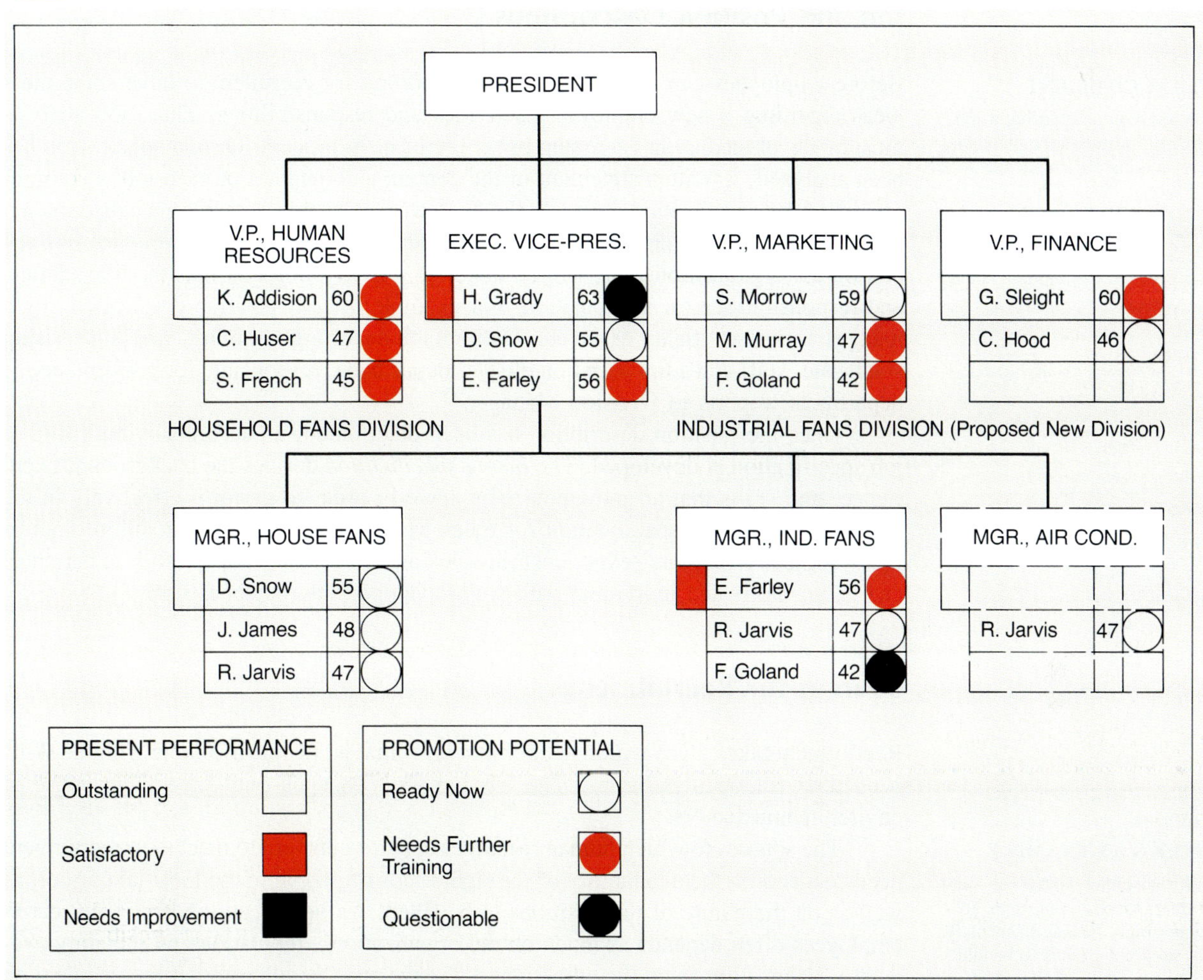

Source: Adapted from *Developing Managerial Competence* by Walter S. Wikstrom. Copyright © 1964 The Conference Board.

FIGURE 11-2 MANAGEMENT REPLACEMENT CHART

most appropriate for operative employees, takes place when the organization needs a group of workers of a certain kind—for example, typists or salespeople. It follows comparatively simple, standardized procedures. *Specialized recruiting,* which is used mainly for higher-level executives or specialists, occurs when the organization desires a particular type of individual. In specialized recruiting, candidates receive personalized attention over an extended period.[5]

The recruiting of college and MBA graduates falls somewhere between these two extremes. It resembles general recruiting in the sense that many candidates are screened for a given group of openings and many may be hired with only a vague idea about their initial jobs—especially if the first ''job'' is in a management training program. At some companies, the CEO and other top executives are directly involved in recruiting in order to symbolize its importance to company strategy.

[5]See John B. Miner and Mary G. Miner, *Personnel and Industrial Relations,* 3rd ed. (New York: Macmillan, 1977); Richard M. Coffina, ''Management Recruitment Is a Two-Way Street,'' *Personnel Journal* 58, no. 2 (February 1979):86–89; and John P. Wanous, *Organizational Entry: Recruitment, Selection, and Socialization of Newcomers* (Reading, Mass.: Addison-Wesley, 1980).

Job and Position Descriptions

CLASS COMMENT

Job analysis and writing a job description must take place *before* looking for employees to fill jobs.

Before employees can be recruited, it is important for recruiters to have some clear ideas regarding a new employee's activities and responsibilities. Thus, job analysis must be developed as an early step in the recruitment process. Once a specific job has been analyzed, a written statement of the content and location of each job is incorporated into the organization chart. At the operative level, this statement is called the *job description;* at the managerial level, the statement is called a *position description*. Each box on the organization chart will be linked to a description that lists the title, duties, and responsibilities for that position. For example, a brief position description might read as follows: "Sales Manager: Duties include hiring, training, and supervising small sales staff and administration of sales department; responsible for performance of department; reports to Division Manager."

Once the position description has been determined, an accompanying hiring or job specification is developed. The *hiring specification* defines the background, experience, and skills that an individual must have in order to perform effectively in the position. The hiring specification for Sales Manager might read: "Position requires BBA degree; five years' experience in sales and two years' supervisory experience; energetic, motivated individual with well-developed interpersonal skills."

Sources for Recruitment

Recruitment takes place within a *labor market*—that is, people available with the skills needed to fill open positions. The labor market changes over time in response to environmental factors.

HERE'S AN EXAMPLE

With unskilled workers in short supply, service companies are increasingly turning to mentally retarded individuals to handle mops and grills. The fast-food industry, where annual employee turnover rate approaches 200 percent, is glad for the loyalty exhibited by these individuals. Some companies that have hired mentally handicapped workers include McDonald's franchises in Long Island, New York; Kentucky Fried Chicken in company-owned restaurants in Virginia; and the Marriott Corporation. (*Fortune*, 9/26/88, pp. 10–11)

The sources to which human resources departments turn to meet their recruitment needs depend on the availability of the right kinds of people in the local labor pool, as well as on the nature of the positions to be filled. An organization's ability to recruit employees often depends as much on the organization's reputation and the attractiveness of its location as on the attractiveness of the specific job offer. If the people with the appropriate skills are not available in the organization itself or in the local labor pool, they may have to be recruited from competing organizations and/or from some distance away.

Some companies have enhanced the success of their recruitment policies by establishing good reputations as places to work. According to *Fortune's* 1988 list of "America's Most Admired Corporations," among those companies that attract, develop, and retain talented people are Philip Morris, J. P. Morgan, and Merck. Other firms have become known for providing particularly good opportunities for women: American Express, Hallmark, Honeywell, Pepsico, and Hewlett-Packard, among others.[6]

COORDINATED RESOURCE

This would be a good time to enlist a speaker from your school's job placement service to talk to students about job recruiting. This is a topic of high interest and importance to students. It also fits in well with the whole area of human resources management.

Outside Recruitment for Managers and Professionals. Large companies use various outside recruitment sources to fill vacancies at different levels of management. For many large companies, college and graduate school campuses are a major source of entry-level and new managerial help. Campus recruiting, however, has some disadvantages; the recruitment process can be quite expensive, and it is not uncommon for hired graduates to leave an organization after two or three years. When recruiting to fill middle-management and top-level positions, many large companies must resort to even costlier and more competitive hiring strategies than those used in campus recruiting. When top-quality ability is in short supply, middle-management recruitment often requires the services of placement agencies or the purchase of expensive ads in news-

[6]Ellen Schultz, "America's Most Admired Corporations," *Fortune*, January 18, 1988.

papers and national publications. And when recruiting is done to fill top-level positions, many corporate managements must turn to executive search firms for help in locating three or four carefully considered prospects who not only are highly qualified but who can be enticed from their present positions by the right offer. For example, in 1984 AT&T realized that its new environment would require more marketing expertise. Therefore, it immediately began enticing and eventually hiring a number of executives from a variety of companies in order to give the organization a better mix of talent in many areas. The difficulties inherent in recruiting outside the organization, especially for positions at senior levels, argue that organizations carefully weigh the costs and benefits involved in the process. Although the benefits often outweigh the costs, such is not always the case.

Recruitment from Within. Many firms, such as IBM, General Foods, and Procter & Gamble, have a policy of recruiting or promoting from within the organization except in very exceptional circumstances. There are three major advantages of this policy. First, individuals recruited from within will already be familiar with the organization; they are therefore likely to succeed because of their knowledge of the organization and its members. Second, a promotion-from-within policy helps to foster loyalty and inspire greater effort among organization members. Finally, it is usually less expensive to recruit or promote from within than to hire from outside the organization. The major disadvantages of this policy are the limitations that it places on available talent, it reduces the chance for a fresh viewpoint to enter the organization, and it may encourage complacency because employees may assume that seniority will assure promotion.

Equal Employment Opportunity and Affirmative Action

In the early 1960s, the growing civil rights and women's movements called national attention to the discriminatory effects of existing human resource practices. Responses to these efforts began with the Equal Pay Act of 1963 and the Civil Rights Act of 1964. These were expanded by the courts and most state legislatures and through various amendments and executive orders. The implications of such legislation for human

Drawing by Chas. Addams; © 1982 The New Yorker Magazine, Inc.

resource policies and practices are still evolving and being clarified by court decisions and administrative interpretations. The median annual earnings of women at work have increased significantly in the past quarter century, but the ratio of women's to men's wages, while increasing on the average, continues to vary widely from one occupation to another. Moreover, while the increase of women employed in some of the higher-status, higher-paid occupations is dramatic, the proportion of women in those occupations is still low (see Table 11-1). "For example," as Janet L. Norwood, U.S. Commissioner of Labor Statistics, noted, "the number of women lawyers increased more than fivefold over the last decade, but there are still less than 100,000 in the legal profession, and they make up only 15 percent of the total."[7]

The Law. The key legislation is Title VII of the Civil Rights Act of 1964 (amended in 1972 and establishing the Equal Employment Opportunity Commission [EEOC] to enforce the provisions of Title VII), which prohibits employment discrimination on the basis of race, sex, age, religion, color, or national origin. These requirements for nondiscriminatory treatment are called *equal employment opportunity* (*EEO*) requirements. They apply to virtually all private and public organizations. Executive Orders 11246 and 11375 of 1965 and 1968 (amended in 1977) required, in addition, that firms doing business with the federal government make special efforts to recruit, hire, and promote women and members of minority groups. These requirements are called *affirmative action* (*AA*).[8] The differences between equal employment opportunity and affirmative action are summarized in Table 11-2.

TEACHING TIP

Be sure to point out these differences, as the terms are often incorrectly used interchangeably.

The Equal Pay Act, originally introduced in 1946, prohibits discrimination by employers between employees on the basis of sex by paying men higher wages than women for jobs that are equal in skill, effort, responsibility, and working conditions. The Equal Pay Act established the foundation for another, related concern about pay—the concept known as **comparable worth.** Comparable worth refers to "comparable" skills, aptitudes, and knowledge applicable to a disparate variety of available positions; the Equal Pay Act itself requires like pay for like jobs. Critics thus point out that it is not only market forces which can establish salary levels; occupational segregation or the existence of an occupation dominated by one sex—such as nursing—create situa-

comparable worth The principle that jobs requiring comparable skills and knowledge merit equal compensation even if the nature of the work activity is different.

THOUGHT-PROVOKER

How can "comparable worth" issues ever be resolved?

[7]William Serrin, "Experts Say Job Bias Against Women Persists," *New York Times*, November 25, 1984, pp. A1, A32.

[8]See Ann Weaver Hart, "Intent vs. Effect: Title VII Case Law That Could Affect You (Part I)," *Personnel Journal* 63 (1984):31–47; and Hart, "Intent vs. Effect: Title VII Case Law That Could Affect You (Part II)," *Personnel Journal* 63 (1984):50–58.

TABLE 11-1 THE WAGE GAP BETWEEN THE SEXES

	WOMEN AS PERCENT OF ALL WORKERS		EARNINGS RATIO, FEMALE TO MALE	
	1979	1988	1979	1988
Accountants and auditors	34%	45%	0.60	0.79
Computer programmers	28	40	0.80	0.81
Computer systems analysts	20	30	0.79	0.82
Lawyers	10	15	0.55	0.63
Managers and administrators	22	29	0.51	0.67
Sales of business services	28	34	0.58	0.79
Teachers, elementary school	61	82	0.82	0.96

Note: Figures are for full-time workers in selected occupations.
Source: Census Bureau.

TABLE 11-2 SOME DIFFERENCES BETWEEN EEO (NONDISCRIMINATION) AND AA

	EEO	AFFIRMATIVE ACTION
Who is affected?	Virtuall everyone is covered by law	Legally applies only to certain organizations
What is required?	Employment neutrality Nondiscrimination	Systematic plan
What are the sanctions?	Legal charges can be filed Possible court action	Withdrawal of contracts or funds if noncompliant
What are some examples of compliance?	Not barring female, minorities, or disabled persons from employment Selecting, promoting, and paying people solely on the basis of bona fide job-related qualifications	Actively recruiting and hiring female, veteran, minority, or disabled persons Validating tests; rigorously examining company practices in selection, promotion, and benefits to eliminate non job-related qualifications that discriminate against protected persons

Source: The Management of Affirmative Action by Francine S. Hall and Maryann H. Albrecht. Copyright © 1979 by Scott, Foresman and Company. Reprinted by permission.

tions in which discrimation in pay can occur. 1988 statistics show women making only about 68 cents for every dollar earned by men; much of the difference is attributed to occupational segregation. Comparable worth takes into account the actual skills and knowledge which are needed for jobs and which define a candidate's suitability for a position or category of positions; it seeks to invalidate patterns of wage and job discrimination—such as those based on sex or occupational segregation—that have often established or influenced salary guidelines.[9]

Employment rights of persons 40 and older were protected in the Age Discrimination in Employment Act of 1967 (amended in 1986), while the Vocational Rehabilitation Act of 1973 (amended in 1974) added protection for the physically and mentally disabled or differently abled if they were qualified to perform job tasks with reasonable accommodation by the employer. The 1987 Supreme Court ruling[10] that those with contagious diseases are covered by this Act has potentially wide-ranging applications, because this decision offers hope, particularly given our current concern over AIDS, to employees dismissed from their jobs despite the fact that they do not pose a real health threat to other employees. The Vietnam-Era Veterans' Readjustment Act of 1974 requires those doing business with the federal government to extend affirmative action programs to veterans of that period and to disabled veterans in particular.

HERE'S AN EXAMPLE

A report entitled "AIDS: Corporate America Responds" says that only 5 percent of U.S. employers have developed an AIDS policy. One company, IBM, drafted its policy in 1985 and sent a letter to all its 240,000 employees, that stated, "IBM-ers affected by AIDS will be encouraged to work as long as they are able, and their privacy will be respected." (*Wall Street Journal*, 1/20/88, p. 31)

Sexual harassment (unwanted sexual requests or advances or the creation of a sexually harassing environment through sexual jokes and remarks) when related to hiring or promotion decisions or the work environment violates Title VII.[11] A 1978 amendment to Title VII, the Pregnancy Discrimination Act, prohibits dismissal of

[9]See George Ritzer and David Walczak, *Working: Conflict and Change*, 3rd ed. (Englewood Cliffs, N.J.: Prentice Hall, 1986), pp. 104–106; John B. Golper, "The Current Legal Status of 'Comparable Worth,' in the Federal Sector," *Labor Law Journal* 34 (1983): 563–580; Golper, *Pay Equity and Comparable Worth* (Washington, D.C.: Bureau of National Affairs, 1984), pp. 13–34; and Marsha Katz, Helen Lavan, and Maura Malloy, "Comparable Worth: Analysis of Cases and Implications for Human Resource Management," *Compensation and Benefits Review*, May–June 1986, pp. 26–38.

[10]*School Board of Nassau County v. Arline*, No. 85–1277 (1987).

[11]Our discussion of equal employment opportunity and affirmative action issues derives from Terry L. Leap, William H. Holley, Jr., and Hubert S. Field, "Equal Employment Opportunity and Its Implications for Personnel Practices in the 1980s," *Labor Law Journal* 31, no. 11 (November 1980):669–682; and Francine S. Hall and Maryann H. Albrecht, *The Management of Affirmative Action* (Santa Monica, Calif.: Goodyear, 1979), pp. 1–23. See also David P. Twomey, *A Concise Guide to Employment Law* (Cincinnati: South-Western, 1986).

women because of pregnancy alone and protects their job security during maternity leaves.[12] In various states, legislation extends these employment rights to employees of very small firms and to specific groups not yet mentioned in federal legislation, such as homosexuals and former prison inmates.[13]

This mass of legislation and subsequent legal decisions has attempted to deal with two kinds of discrimination of concern to managers. *Access discrimination* refers to hiring considerations and practices (different qualifying tests, lower starting salaries) that are not related in any way to an employee's present or future job performance but are based on the employee's membership in a particular population subgroup. *Treatment discrimination* involves practices unrelated to job performance (less favorable work assignments, slower promotion rates) that treat subgroup members differently from others once they are in the work force.[14]

Managers received practical assistance in implementing their responses to equal employment opportunity legislation in 1978, when the Uniform Guidelines on Employee Selection Procedures were issued. Under these guidelines, organization practices or policies that adversely affect employment opportunities for any race, sex, or ethnic group are prohibited unless the restriction is a justifiable job requirement. Thus, courts have found height and weight requirements illegal when they prevented employment of women and people of Hispanic or Asian origin and were not shown to be job-related. Called *bona fide occupation qualifications* (BFOQs), there are justifiable instances in which discriminatory hiring requirements are permitted—such as hiring only males to play male roles in theater productions. Race and color, however, have never been judged valid BFOQ criteria.

In a landmark decision on employment discrimination in 1982, the Supreme Court departed from the policy of the previous two decades and ruled that the fact that a seniority system at American Tobacco Company has a discriminatory impact is not in itself enough to make it illegal: Actual intent to discriminate must be proved.[15] Since 1981, the Justice Department has appeared to favor seniority systems over affirmative action programs.

BACKGROUND ON PRIVACY

Companies want to know more about employees' personal lives, and workers are fighting harder for the right to be left alone. The difficulty arises from trying to maintain a proper balance between the common good and personal freedom. The basic issues include: drug-testing, AIDS, lie detector tests, computer surveillance and genetic screening. (*Business Week*, 3/28/88, pp. 61–68)

In recent years, social problems have begun to affect the management of our corporations more and more. One of the most controversial and important policy matters is in the area of privacy. As concern focuses on such issues as drug testing, AIDS, lie detector tests, computer surveillance, and even genetic screening, many companies are delving further into employees' personal lives, and workers find themselves fighting harder for privacy rights.

One of the most controversial of these issues has been drug testing. Drug use costs U.S. industry about $50 billion a year in turnover and absenteeism. Countless dollars are lost in less reliable and productive workers. Lives have been lost due to accidents caused by employees under the influence of alcohol, drugs, or both. Such situations have caused companies such as Eastern Airlines to perform random drug testing of employees. However, whenever a company requires drug testing, the issue of employee civil rights is appropriately raised. While our country is still grappling

---

[12]Leap, Holley, and Field, "Equal Employment Opportunity," pp. 677–679. See also Bette Ann Stead, *Women in Management* (Englewood Cliffs, N.J.: Prentice Hall, 1978). Attitudes toward women in an organization might be assessed using the MATWES scale in Peter Dubno, John Costas, Hugh Cannon, Charles Wankel, and Hussein Emin, "An Empirically Keyed Scale for Measuring Managerial Attitudes Toward Women Executives," *Psychology of Women Quarterly* 3, no. 4 (Summer 1979):357–364.

[13]Leap, Holley, and Field, "Equal Employment Opportunity," p. 671. See also Richard A. Fear and James F. Ross, *Jobs, Dollars, and EEO* (New York: McGraw-Hill, 1983).

[14]Hall and Albrecht, *The Management of Affirmative Action*, pp. 9–10.

[15]The case was *American Tobacco* v. *Patterson*, cited in Karen Paul and George Sullivan, "Equal Employment Opportunity vs. Seniority Rights: The Emergence of a Changing Social Policy," *Business and Society* 23, no. 1 (Spring 1984):8–14. See also Philip Shenon, "U.S. Acts to Stop Quotas on Hiring It Once Supported," *New York Times*, April 30, 1985, pp. A1, A22.

QUOTATION FROM A MANAGER

Forced to take a drug test after five weeks of sick leave and never having used any kind of illegal drug, one employee said, "When I left the room I was angry, I was hurt, I was crying. I thought I'd lose my job." (*Business Week,* 3/28/88, p. 62)

with the drug problem on all levels within organizations, experts predict that except for a small number of occupations, such as operators of atom smashers and school buses, American workers will not be randomly tested. However, there are an increasing number of companies—IBM, American Airlines, Dupont, GE and Kodak among them—who are testing job applicants.

Some companies have addressed the reality of drug and alcohol problems on the job in a way that has been perceived by employees as more supportive—for example, by adding Employee Assistance Programs (EAPs) to employee benefits packages. Such programs offer confidentiality, appropriate referrals, and further support to employees whose job performance may be impaired due to chemical dependency or many other kinds of problems.[16]

Implications for Managers. In the recruitment process, the human resources department normally has prime responsibility for assuring compliance with equal employment opportunity and affirmative action provisions. Ultimately, however, all managers are affected, because these provisions determine the pool of applicants for available positions and influence the procedures that must be used in managing and developing the individuals who are recruited. The human resources department must instruct and educate other organization members in the implications of compliance for their respective departments. Even job titles can be sexist and reflect de facto discrimination. For example, the job titles *foreman* and *salesman* are now outmoded; they should be replaced by *supervisor* and *sales worker* or *salesperson,* respectively. Managers must realize that neither they as individuals nor the organization as a whole has completely free choice in the recruiting, hiring, training, and promotion of human resources. Individuals and organizations failing to comply may be reported to the Equal Employment Opportunities Commission (EEOC) for investigation or become defendants in class action or specific lawsuits. In one widely reported class action suit, several thousand female flight attendants won $52.5 million from Northwest Airlines when the company's employment practices were found to be discriminatory. Female employees elsewhere, including clerical workers who struck at Yale University in 1984, have demanded equal pay for jobs deemed by the employer to be of comparable worth. The Reagan administration, however, did not favor the idea of comparable worth as a means of correcting employment discrimination. There are many current developments on the issue of comparable worth, and it promises to be hotly debated in the coming years. Indeed, the whole area of how men, and women work together in today's organizations promises to be an exciting topic of discussion and study. (See the Ethics in Management box on corporate day care.)

HERE'S AN EXAMPLE

The number of employers offering child care has surged to approximately 3,500, up 40 percent since 1984. About 200 of these companies started their day-care programs in the past six months. (*Springfield News-Leader,* 10/1/88, p. 6B)

SELECTION

selection The mutual process whereby the organization decides whether or not to make a job offer and the candidate decides on the acceptability of the offer.

The **selection** process involves mutual decision making. The organization decides whether or not to make a job offer and how attractive the offer should be. The job candidate decides whether the organization and the job offer will fit his or her needs and goals. However, when the job market is extremely tight, the selection process will in practice be more one-sided. Several candidates will be applying for each position, and the organization will, on the basis of a series of screening devices, hire the candidate that it feels most suitable. The process is also one-sided when the candidate is a highly qualified executive or professional who is being courted by several organizations.

[16]See "Privacy," *Business Week,* March 28, 1988, pp. 61–68; and Craig Mellon, "The Dope on Drug Testing," *Human Resource Executive* 2, no. 4 (1988):34–37.

ETHICS IN MANAGEMENT

THE ISSUE OF CORPORATE DAY CARE

As the percentage of two-career households continues to rise, child care has become an increasing need among people engaged in the business world. Currently, over 50 percent of mothers with infants and toddlers hold jobs outside the home, and the children must be cared for during the working day. Naturally, as the number of children in need of care increases, it becomes continually harder to find resources for it. The number of day-care centers has not grown fast enough to meet the need, and fewer women—historically, the labor pool for this service industry—are available to care for children in the home. In some areas, the shortage is so acute that good day-care centers have waiting lists up to two years long—suggesting in some cases that a family enter its name on the list before the child is even conceived. These problems are even greater for employees who work hours other than conventional daytime hours. Finding child care from 9 A.M. to 5 P.M. is difficut enough—finding it from 6 P.M. to 2 A.M. is all but impossible.

Obviously, not every employee faces the problem of finding child care. Some people do not have children, and others solve the problem on their own (generally, with family help). But the issue clearly affects a significant number of people—and their employers. Studies have shown that parents at work devote a significant amount of energy to concern for their children, and a high percentage of absenteeism can be attributed to family conflicts resulting from child-care failures or sick children who could not attend their day-care centers.

There is a lively debate regarding the appropriate role of the company regarding child care. Should a company seek to provide some type of service to employees with children? What is the best way to meet the needs of this group?

Managers in some companies who believe that it is in their best interest to help employees find child care have gone about it in a variety of ways. A few companies have set up child-care centers for their employees, either on-site or near by. However, such centers are often filled to capacity and have long waiting lists as long as privately operated centers. Many larger companies sponsor information and referral centers where parents can go to get information and help in finding good child care in the community. Small companies which find these solutions out of their budget have instituted policies which make it a little easier for parents, including flexible hours and/or flexible leave policies for taking care of sick children.

However, many companies have done very little to assist employees in this area. There are a variety of reasons for this failure, most of them having to do with simple economics. Corporate day-care centers can be very expensive to set up and run; some companies fear the liability involved. Referral centers can be only as useful as the facilities available in the community. Other companies feel that day care is strictly the responsibility of the employee and that it would be inappropriate for the employer to get involved.

Should the company seek to provide child care or information about child care in the community? Should companies institute policies that make it easier for employers with children? The demographic data suggest that these questions are neither going to solve themselves nor cease to become more compelling issues in the coming years. In short, responsibility for child care is growing into an important issue in human resources management.

Sources: Cathy Trost, "Best Employers for Women and Parents," *Wall Street Journal,* November 30, 1987, p. 23; Trost, "Creative Child-Care Programs Aid Employees Who Work Odd Hours," *Wall Street Journal,* March 18, 1988, Sec. 2, p. 29; Albert R. Carr, "Child-Care Plans Provided by 11% of Surveyed Firms," *Wall Street Journal,* January 15, 1988, p. 12.

Steps in the Selection Process

COORDINATED RESOURCE

See the Lecture Extra from Chapter 10 for more information on "hiring smart."

The standard hiring sequence follows a seven-step procedure described in Table 11-3.[17] In practice, the actual selection process will vary with organizations and between levels in the same organization. For example, the selection interview for lower-level employees may be quite perfunctory; heavy emphasis may be placed instead on the initial screening interview or on tests. However, although written tests designed to define a candidate's interests, aptitudes, and intelligence have long been a staple of employment screening, their use has declined over the past 25 years: Many tests have proven to be discriminatory in their design and results, and it has been difficult to establish their job relatedness when they have been subjected to judicial review.

In selecting middle- or upper-level managers, on the other hand, the interviewing may be extensive—sometimes lasting eight hours or more—and there may be little or no formal testing. Instead of initially filling out an application, the candidate may submit a résumé. Completion of the formal application may be delayed until after the job offer has been accepted. Some organizations omit the physical examination (Step 6 in Table 11-3).

[17] Wendell L. French, *The Personnel Management Process*, 5th ed. Copyright © 1982 by Houghton Mifflin Company.

TABLE 11-3 STEPS IN THE SELECTION PROCESS

PROCEDURES	PURPOSES	ACTIONS AND TRENDS
1. Completed job application	Indicates applicant's desired position; provides information for interviews.	Requests only information that predicts success in the job.*
2. Initial screening interview	Provides a quick evaluation of applicant's suitability.	Asks questions on experience, salary expectation, willingness to relocate, etc.
3. Testing	Measures applicant's job skills and ability to learn on the job.	May include computer testing software, handwriting analysis, lie detector tests, and urinalysis.†
4. Background investigation	Checks truthfulness of applicant's résumé or application form.	Calls the applicant's previous supervisor (with permission) and confirms information from applicant.‡
5. In-depth selection interview	Finds out more about the applicant as an individual.	Conducted by the manager to whom the applicant will report.
6. Physical examination	Ensures effective performance by applicant; protects other employees against diseases; establishes health record on applicant; protects firm against unjust worker's compensation claims.	Often performed by company's medical doctor.
7. Job offer	Fills a job vacancy or position.	Offers a salary plus benefit package.

*See, for example, Robert Hershey, "The Application Form," *Personnel* 48, no. 1 (January–February 1971):38; and Irwin L. Goldstein, "The Application Blank: How Honest Are the Responses?" *Journal of Applied Psychology* 55, no. 5 (October 1971):491.

†David Tuller, "What's New in Employment Testing?" *New York Times*, February 25, 1985, p. F17.

‡Kirk Johnson, "Why References Aren't 'Available on Request,'" *New York Times*, June 9, 1985, pp. F8–F9.

Source: Wendell L. French, *The Personnel Management Process*, 5th ed. Copyright 1982 by Houghton Mifflin Co.

EXTRA EXERCISE

Interviewing provides an excellent opportunity for role-playing. Have students put on skits illustrating the good and bad points about interviewing.

Interviewing. For many positions, particularly in management, the in-depth interview is an important factor in the organization's decision to make a job offer and in the individual's decision to accept or decline the offer. The most effective interviews—that is, those that are best able to predict the eventual performance of applicants—are usually planned carefully and the same questions are usually asked of all candidates for the same position.[18] Most interviews, however, tend to be far less structured and deliberate.

Inadequate interviews can lead to poor employment decisions. Richard Nehrbass has identified three common defects in interviewing that may produce inaccurate information about job applicants.[19] The first defect is the imbalance of power in the interview situation. The interviewer is likely to be experienced and at ease. The interviewee, on the other hand, who is probably inexperienced in the interview situation and to whom the job may represent a livelihood, a career, and an important part of his or her self-image, is likely to feel ill at ease. The interviewee may therefore behave in an uncharacteristically tense manner.

The second defect of interviews is that they may cause the job candidate to adopt "phony" behavior. The applicant feels compelled to project an image that he or she thinks will be acceptable to the interviewer. Sometimes the "act" put on by a qualified applicant is obviously false or projects an image that is contrary to the organization's style. In such cases, a less qualified candidate who projects a realistic image may be offered the position.

BACKGROUND ON KEEPING EMPLOYEES

Here's some advice for keeping employees: be straight about job expectations up front; make sure the "fit" is right between applicant and organization; provide information on company requirements; make sure training programs have a readily apparent purpose; encourage mentoring; and give frequent performance appraisals. (*Fortune,* 6/6/88, pp. 271–274)

A third defect is the tendency of interviewers to ask questions that have no useful answers, such as "Tell me about yourself" or "What would you say is your greatest weakness?" Applicants are likely to sense the lack of skill and preparation of the interviewer who asks such open-ended questions. They may feel uneasy and give superficial answers, or they may try to second-guess the interviewer and go off on a lengthy tangent. As Nehrbass asserts, interviews that focus on the requirements of the job and the actual skills and abilities of candidates will provide interviewers with more useful information and be better predictors of performance.

The interview process may also prove unreliable because of the differing objectives of the interviewer and interviewee. The prospective employer wants to sell the organization as a good place to work and may exaggerate the organization's strengths; the prospective employee wants to be hired and may exaggerate his or her qualities. Some organizations have attempted to reduce this problem through the **realistic job preview (RJP),** in which candidates are exposed to the unattractive as well as the attractive aspects of the job, and by using structured, focused interviews to acquire a more accurate picture of each interviewer's likely job performance. (See Chapter 23.)[20]

realistic job preview (RJP) A description provided by the organization to applicants and new employees that gives both the positive and negative aspects of a job.

Manager Selection

The task of selecting managers is a difficult one because of the complexity of the manager's job. Because managers are required to utilize a wide variety of skills and abilities, their selection depends on accurate assessment of candidates' proven or potential skills and abilities.

[18]See Robert E. Carlson, Donald P. Schwab, and Herbert G. Heneman III, "Agreement among Selection Interview Styles," *Journal of Industrial Psychology* 5, no. 1 (March 1970):8–17.

[19]Richard G. Nehrbass, "Psychological Barriers to Effective Employment Interviewing," *Personnel Journal* 56, no. 2 (February 1977):60–64.

[20]See Wanous, *Organizational Entry;* and S. L. Premack and Wanous, "A Meta-Analysis of Realistic Job Preview Experiments," *Journal of Applied Psychology* 70 (1985):706–719.

Selecting Experienced Managers. Organizations may seek to hire experienced managers for a variety of reasons. A newly created post may require a manager with experience not available within the organization; an established post may exist and the talent to fill it is unavailable within the organization; a key position might suddenly open and there is no time to train a replacement; or a top performer in a competing organization is sought to improve the organization's own competitive position.

An experienced manager who is up for selection usually goes through several interviews before being hired by an organization. A candidate's interviewers are almost always higher-level managers who attempt to assess the candidate's suitability and past performance. Although past performance is generally expected to predict future performance, interviewers often find it difficult to obtain verifiable data on a manager's past performance. Therefore, they must frequently rely on other assessment tools during the interview process, such as paying close attention to the personal qualities of the candidate during the course of his or her interviews. The interviewers look for desirable qualities, such as emotional stability, self-confidence, and interpersonal skills, in the personality of the candidate. In short, interviewers try to determine how well the candidate seems to fit their idea of what a good manager should be; how compatible the candidate's personality, past experience, personal values, and style of operating are with the organization and its culture.

Selecting Potential Managers. Potential managers usually enter the organization after graduating from college. They will typically take entry-level positions—a research job or a staff job or a position in a training program. Their performance in these entry-level positions will have a strong influence on the type of managerial job they eventually will receive.

Assessing an individual's potential for managerial performance is difficult because the future manager must be judged on things he or she has not yet done. However, such an assessment is also extremely important, since potential managers may well determine the future success of the organization.

TEACHING TIP

Discuss with your students the implications of these statements.

Most assessments of prospective managers begin with a review of college grades. However, except for technical positions, college performance does not seem to be strongly associated with managerial performance. Other aspects of the college record, however, can provide some insights into nonacademic abilities, such as interpersonal skills, leadership qualities, and ability to assume responsibility. For this reason, many organizations look for evidence of extracurricular managerial interest or experience—working on a campus journal, for example, or directing part of a community project.[21] Finally, like experienced managers, prospective managers may be interviewed extensively to determine whether they have what the interviewers consider to be the appropriate personal styles for managers.

In general, the likelihood of making good candidate choices is improved when several managers interview each candidate. The multiplicity of viewpoints made available through this approach lessens the possibility that effective managers will be lost to the organization because of one interviewer's bias or point of view.

Assessment Centers

Another method that has proven effective in selecting qualified candidates is the assessment center. Assessment centers were originally used during World War II as a means of selecting OSS (Office of Strategic Services) agents. Assessment centers have

[21] See Frank Malinowski, "Job Selection Using Task Analysis," *Personnel Journal* 60, no. 4 (April 1981):288–291.

since been used with considerable success as devices for predicting the future management performance of both experienced and potential managers.[22] In the assessment center approach, candidates are asked to participate in a wide range of simulation exercises while trained observers note and assess their behavior. One common exercise is the *in-basket*. In this simulation, the candidate is informed that he or she has just been promoted to a newly vacant position and will have to leave town soon to attend an important meeting. The candidate is given one hour to deal with the memos, letters, reports, telephone messages, and other materials in the previous incumbent's in-basket. The candidate must handle each item in the most appropriate manner and in many cases will have an opportunity to explain or discuss his or her decisions in a follow-up interview.

In the activity known as the *leaderless group discussion* exercise, the participants are given a problem requiring a group decision. The way the candidates handle themselves in this situation helps to reveal their leadership qualities and interpersonal skills. Candidates may also participate in *management games* geared to the level of the job being filled, make oral presentations, and take any number of tests probing mental ability, general knowledge, and personality.

Assessment centers are not only excellent predictors of management potential but also can serve as part of a management development program. In fact, some graduate schools of business use some of the techniques to guide an individual's self-development program. However, the assessment center approach is so costly that it is restricted to a few relatively large, successful organizations. An assessment typically involves a number of assessors working with a small group of candidates over a period of several days.[23]

Assessment centers have also come under criticism on other grounds. Richard Klimoski, for example, has pointed out that the tests focus on maximum performance under certain conditions rather than *typical* performance. They prove that a person *can* perform well without evidence that he or she *will* perform well.[24]

ORIENTATION AND SOCIALIZATION

orientation or **socialization** A program designed to help employees fit smoothly into an organization.

QUOTATION FROM A MANAGER

''The first six months are absolutely critical, the most critical, in setting up an employee's work attitude.''—Daniel S. Fogel, Director Executive Education Center, Tulane University (*Fortune*, 6/6/88, p. 271)

Orientation or **socialization** is designed to provide a new employee with the information he or she needs in order to function comfortably and effectively in the organization. Typically, socialization will convey three types of information: (1) general information about the daily work routine; (2) a review of the organization's history, purpose, operations, and products or services, and how the employee's job contributes to the organization's needs; and (3) a detailed presentation, perhaps in a brochure, of the organization's policies, work rules, and employee benefits.

Many studies have shown that employees feel anxiety when they enter an organization. They worry about how well they will perform in the job; they feel inadequate compared to more experienced employees; and they are concerned about how well they will get along with their co-workers. For these reasons, effective socialization programs are deliberately aimed at reducing the anxiety of new employees. Information on

[22]See Larry D. Alexander, ''An Exploratory Study of the Utilization of Assessment Center Results,'' *Academy of Management Journal* 22, no. 1 (March 1979):152–157. An excellent description of the well-known AT&T assessment center can be found in Douglas W. Bray, Richard J. Campbell, and Donald Grant, *Formative Years in Business* (New York: John Wiley, 1974).

[23]For additional information on assessment centers, see Marilee S. Niehoff, ''Assessment Centers: Decision-Making Information from Non-Test-Based Methods,'' *Small Group Behavior* 14, no. 3 (August 1983):353–358; and Clive A. Fletchér and Victor Dulewicz, ''An Empirical Study of a U.K.-Based Assessment Centre,'' *Journal of Management Studies* 21, no. 1 (1984):83–97.

[24]Richard Klimoski, quoted in Barbara Lovenheim, ''A Test to Uncover Managerial Skills: Hopefuls Try Out, Watched by Assessors,'' *New York Times*, January 21, 1979, pp. D1, D4.

the job environment and on supervisors is provided, co-workers are introduced, and questions by new employees are encouraged.[25]

Early job experiences appear to play a critical role in the individual's career with the organization. It is during these experiences that the individual's expectations and the organization's expectations confront each other. If these are not compatible, dissatisfaction will result. As might be expected, employee turnover rates are almost always highest among the organization's new employees.[26]

TRAINING AND DEVELOPMENT

training program A process designed to maintain or improve current job performance.

development program A process designed to develop skills necessary for future work activities.

CLASS COMMENT

The burden of helping employees cope with uncertainties in the job market will increasingly fall on corporations, who will need to spend heavily on employee training programs.

HERE'S AN EXAMPLE

A revolutionary new work environment is being created by the crumbling employer-employee commitment in organizations. More and more companies are using temporary workers to complement their work force. Temps are no longer just the old standby—clerical workers—but include accountants, chemists, engineers, lawyers, and chief financial officers, to name a few. Managing these temps and creating a productive environment for them presents a human resource challenge. (*Fortune,* 2/15/88, pp. 110–116)

Training programs are directed toward maintaining and improving *current* job performance, while **development programs** seek to develop skills for *future* jobs. Both managers and nonmanagers may receive help from training and development programs, but the mix of experiences is likely to vary. Nonmanagers are much more likely to be trained in the technical skills required for their current jobs, while managers frequently receive assistance in developing the skills—particularly conceptual and human relations skills—required in future jobs. In our discussion of training and development, we will cover training briefly and then focus on management development.

Training Programs

The need to train new or recently promoted employees is self-evident: Such employees need to learn new skills, and since their motivation is likely to be high, they can be acquainted relatively easily with the skills and behavior expected in their new position. On the other hand, training experienced employees to make their performance more effective can be problematic. The training needs of such employees are not always easy to determine, and when they are determined, the individuals involved may resent being asked to change their established ways of doing their jobs.

There are four procedures that managers can use to determine the training needs of individuals in their organization or subunit:

1. *Performance appraisal*—each employee's work is measured against the performance standards or objectives established for his or her job.
2. *Analysis of job requirements*—the skills or knowledge specified in the appropriate job description are examined. Those employees without necessary skills or knowledge become candidates for a training program.
3. *Organizational analysis*—the effectiveness of the organization and its success in meeting its goals are analyzed to determine where differences exist. For example, members of a department with a high turnover rate or a low performance record might require additional training.
4. *Survey of human resources*—managers as well as nonmanagers are asked to describe what problems they are experiencing in their work and what actions they believe need to be taken to solve them.

Once the organization's training needs have been identified, the personnel department must initiate the appropriate training effort. There are a variety of training

[25]See, for example, Earl R. Gomersall and M. Scott Myers, "Breakthrough in On-the-Job Training," *Harvard Business Review* 44, no. 4 (July–August 1966):62–72. See also Gareth R. Jones, "Organizational Socialization as Information Processing Activity: A Life History Analysis," *Human Organization* 42, no. 4 (1983):314–320.

[26]For studies of the relationship between early job experience and subsequent job performance and career progress, see David E. Berlew and Douglas T. Hall, "The Socialization of Managers," *Administrative Science Quarterly* 11, no. 2 (September 1966):207–223; also James A. F. Stoner, John D. Aram, and Irwin M. Rubin, "Factors Associated with Effective Performance in Overseas Work Assignments," *Personnel Psychology* 25, no. 2 (Summer 1972):303–318.

approaches that managers can use. The most common of these are *on-the-job training* methods. These include *job rotation,* in which the employee, over a period of time, works on a series of jobs, thereby learning a broad variety of skills; *internship,* in which job training is combined with related classroom instruction; and *apprenticeship,* in which the employee is trained under the guidance of a highly skilled co-worker.

Off-the-job training takes place outside the actual workplace but attempts to simulate actual working conditions. This type of training includes *vestibule training,* in which employees work on the actual equipment and in a realistic job setting but in a room different from the one in which they will be working. The object is to avoid the on-the-job pressures that might interfere with the learning process. In *behaviorally experienced training,* some of the methods used in assessment centers—business games, in-basket simulation, problem-centered cases, and so on—are employed so that the trainee can learn the behavior appropriate for the job through *role playing.* Off-the-job training may focus on the *classroom,* with seminars, lectures, and films, or it may be undertaken by means of **computer-assisted instruction (CAI),** which can both reduce the time needed for training and provide more help for individual trainees.[27]

computer-assisted instruction (CAI) A training technique in which computers are used to lessen the time necessary for training by instructors and to provide additional help to individual trainees.

Management Development Programs

CLASS COMMENT

Some common topics for management development programs are: improving supervisory skills, developing good communication skills, time management and priority setting, becoming an effective listener, etc.

Management development, as we have already suggested, is designed to improve the overall effectiveness of managers in their present positions and to prepare them for greater responsibility when they are promoted. Management development programs have become more prevalent in recent years because of the increasingly complex demands being made of managers and because training managers through experience alone is a time-consuming and unreliable process. The investment of many companies in management development can be quite large. For example, for years a minimum of 40 hours of human resource management training has been required by IBM for all new managers,[28] and similar levels of training are continued after this initial involvement. Some companies, however, do not rely on costly formal training approaches. For example, Exxon prefers to nurture its new talent by providing it with practical job experience, dispatching executives at all levels to key positions around the world in order to broaden their outlook and hone their judgment.

Early management development activities were program-centered; that is, a program would be designed and administered to managers regardless of their individual differences. However, it is being increasingly recognized that managers differ in ability, experience, and personality. Thus, management development programs are becoming more *manager-centered*—tailored to fit the unique developmental requirements of the managers attending. Before a program is selected, a *needs analysis* is made to identify the particular needs and problems of the manager or group of managers. The appropriate training activities are then recommended.[29]

As in other training programs, there are a number of on-the-job and off-the-job management development approaches.[30]

---

[27]Dennis L. Dossett and Patti R. Hulvershorn, "Increasing Technical Training Efficiency: Peer Training via Computer-Assisted Instruction," *Journal of Applied Psychology* 68, no. 4 (November 1983):552–558; Stephen Schwade, "Is It Time to Consider Computer-Based Training?" *Personnel Administrator* 30, no. 2 (February 1985):25–28; and William C. Heck, "Computer-Based Training—The Choice Is Yours," *Personnel Administrator* 30, no. 2 (February 1985):39–48.

[28]Milkovich and Glueck, *Personnel,* pp. 72–73.

[29]On needs analysis, see F. L. Ulschak, *Human Resource Development: The Theory and Practice of Need Assessment* (Reston, Va.: Reston, 1983).

[30]Lynn S. Summers, "Out of the Ivory Tower: A Demand-Side Look at the Future of Management Development," *Training and Development Journal* 38, no. 1 (January 1984):97–101; and Jan Asplind, Håkan Behrendtz, and Frank Jernberg, "The Norwegian Savings Banks Case: Implementation and Consequences of a Broadly Scoped, Long-Term, System-Driven Program for Management Development," *Journal of Applied Behavioral Science* 19, no. 3 (1983):381–394.

On-the-Job Methods. On-the-job methods are usually preferred in management development programs. The training is far more likely than off-the-job training to be tailored to the individual, to be job-related, and to be conveniently located.

There are four major formal on-the-job development methods:

1. *Coaching*—the training of a subordinate by his or her immediate superior—is by far the most effective management development technique. Unfortunately, many managers are either unable or unwilling to coach their subordinates. To be meaningful, on-the-job coaching must be tempered by considerable restraint—subordinates cannot develop unless they are allowed to work out their problems in their own way. Managers too often feel compelled to tell their subordinates exactly what to do, thereby negating the effectiveness of coaching. In addition, some managers feel threatened by the idea of coaching their subordinates, for fear of creating a rival. In reality, it is the manager who has much to gain from coaching subordinates, since a manager frequently will not be promoted unless there is a successor available to take his or her place.

   Many firms, particularly those with MBO programs (see Chapter 7), make a point of training their managers in the fine art of coaching. Conscientious managers often keep a "development file" for each subordinate, indicating the training the subordinate is receiving, the skills the subordinate is acquiring, and how well the subordinate is performing. A record of *critical incidents*—situations in which a subordinate displayed desirable or undesirable behavior—may also be included. In discussing these incidents with the subordinate, managers can reinforce good habits ("You really handled that customer's complaint well"), gently point out bad habits ("Do you think you should be firmer with the suppler?"), and identify the areas in which the subordinate needs further development.
2. *Job rotation* involves shifting managers from position to position so that they may broaden their experience and familiarize themselves with various aspects of the firm's operations.
3. *Training positions* are a third method of developing managers. Trainees are given staff posts immediately under a manager, often with the title of "assistant to." Such assignments give trainees a chance to work with and model themselves after outstanding managers who might otherwise have little contact with them.
4. Finally, *planned work activities* involve giving trainees important work assignments to develop their experience and ability. Trainees may be asked to head a task force or participate in an important committee meeting. Such experiences help them gain insight into how organizations operate and also improve their human relations skills.

Off-the-Job Methods. Off-the-job development techniques remove individuals from the stresses and ongoing demands of the workplace, enabling them to focus fully on the learning experience. In addition, they provide opportunities for meeting people from other departments or organizations. Thus, they will be exposed to useful new ideas and experiences and will make contacts that may be useful to them when they return to their jobs. The most common off-the-job development methods include in-house classroom instruction and management development programs sponsored by universities and other organizations, such as the American Management Association.

FOR DISCUSSION

What are the advantages and disadvantages of having an in-house trainer instead of an outside consultant?

Almost every management development program includes some form of *classroom instruction*. Specialists from inside or outside the organization are asked to teach trainees a particular subject. To counteract possible passivity and boredom, classroom instruction may be supplemented with case studies, role playing, and business games or simulations. For example, managers may be asked to play roles on both sides in a simulated labor-management dispute.

Some organizations send selected employees to *university-sponsored management development programs*. Many major universities have such programs, which range in length from about a week to three months or more. Some universities (such as MIT and Stanford) also have one-year, full-time study programs for middle-level managers. These managers usually have been slated for promotion; their organizations send them to these university programs to broaden their perspectives and prepare them for movement into general (as opposed to functional) management. University programs will often combine classroom instruction with case studies, role playing, and simulation.

Large corporations are increasingly assuming many of the functions of universities with regard to advanced off-the-job training of employees. U.S. business now spends an estimated $60 billion each year on in-house education, a figure comparable with that spent by the nation's colleges and universities. By the 1990s, more than two dozen corporations and industry associations are expected to be offering advanced, accredited academic degrees. Xerox, RCA, Arthur Anderson, GE, and Holiday Inns have each acquired educational facilities that closely resemble university campuses, and IBM, Westinghouse, and Digital Equipment Company have established the National Technological University, a "satellite university" where high-level continuing education is transmitted via satellite to classrooms throughout the country and abroad.[31]

Conditions for Effective Management Development Programs. One of the greatest challenges to the development program takes place when the trainee returns to his or her job. If the on-the-job environment does not encourage or support the new managerial skills and knowledge, they will quickly disappear. This has been observed following human relations training, where individuals are taught to use more democratic, participative management styles. Those individuals whose supervisors do not favor such a style may become even more autocratic than they were before the training. For this reason, the support of top management and the trainees' supervisors is important in making a training program effective.

ILLUSTRATIVE CASE STUDY Continued

Human Relations at Sony Corporation

Sony has long been a leader in human resources management in Japan. The company has adopted such American concepts as the 5-day, 40-hour workweek even though Japanese law still provides for a maximum of 48 hours and the average in Japanese manufacturing remains 43 hours per week; in addition, Sony was one of the first Japanese firms to close its factories for one week every summer and thus allow all its employees to be off work at the same time.

In addition, the Japanese system enforces a different view of recruits. Morita urges managers to see recruits as rough stones and the managerial job as the task of building a strong and sturdy wall out of these rough stones. In the Japanese system, managerial recruits are, at least ideally, shaped and smoothed so that they fit together into the cohesive whole that reflects the cohesive structure of the company as a whole.

Japanese companies, at least the large ones, also have a different view of what happens in declining industries. Most companies offer retraining—which most workers eagerly accept. Even within companies like Sony, workers are retrained when their particular jobs are no longer needed.

PERFORMANCE APPRAISAL

TEACHING TIP

Have students relate experiences they have had with performance appraisals—both as appraiser and appraisee.

Although performance appraisal is one of the most important tasks any manager has, it is one that most managers freely admit they have difficulty in handling adequately. It is not always easy to judge a subordinate's performance accurately, and it is often even more difficult to convey that judgment to the subordinate in a constructive and painless manner.

[31]Edward B. Fiske, "Booming Corporate Education Efforts Rival College Programs, Study Says," *New York Times*, January 28, 1985, p. A10.

Informal and Formal Appraisal

informal performance appraisal The process of continuously feeding back to subordinate information regarding their work performance.

We will use the term **informal performance appraisal** to mean the continuous process of feeding back to subordinates information about how well they are doing their work for the organization. This process occurs both informally and systematically. *Informal appraisal* is conducted on a day-to-day basis. The manager spontaneously mentions that a particular piece of work was performed well or poorly, or the subordinate stops by the manager's office to find out how a particular piece of work was received. Because of the close connection between the behavior and the feedback on it, informal appraisal quickly encourages desirable performance and discourages undesirable performance before it becomes ingrained. An organization's employees must perceive informal appraisal not merely as a casual occurrence but as an important activity, an integral part of the organization's culture.[32]

formal or **systematic appraisal** A formalized appraisal process for rating current subordinate performance, identifying subordinates deserving raises or promotions, and identifying subordinates in need of further training.

Formal systematic appraisal occurs semiannually or annually on a formalized basis. Such appraisal has four major purposes: (1) It lets subordinates know formally how their current performance is being rated, (2) it identifies those subordinates who deserve merit raises, (3) it locates those subordinates who require additional training; and (4) it plays an important role in identifying those subordinates who are candidates for promotion.

It is important for managers to differentiate between the current performance and the promotability (potential performance) of subordinates. Managers in many organizations fail to make this distinction; they assume that a person with the skills and ability to perform well in one job will automatically perform well in a different or more responsible position. For this reason, people are often promoted to positions in which they cannot perform adequately.[33]

Formal Appraisal Approaches. Who is responsible for formal performance appraisals? In answer to this question, four basic appraisal approaches have evolved in organizations.

The first approach, *a superior's rating of subordinates,* is by far the most common. However, other approaches are becoming more popular and can be a valuable supplement to appraisal by a single superior.

A group of superiors rating subordinates is the second most frequently used appraisal approach. Subordinates are rated by a managerial committee or by a series of managers who fill out separate rating forms. This approach, because it relies on the view of a number of people, is often more effective than appraisal by a single superior. However, it is time-consuming and often dilutes subordinates' feelings of accountability to their immediate superior.

The third appraisal approach is *a group of peers rating a colleague*. The individual is rated separately and on paper by his or her co-workers on the same organizational level. This approach is uncommon in business organizations because of the difficulty of asking employees to make appraisals on which raise or promotion decisions can be based. It is used mainly in the military, particularly in military academies, to identify leadership potential.

The fourth approach, *subordinates' rating of bosses,* is the least common in business. In this approach, subordinates evaluate their superior's performance. This approach has a common analog in colleges, where students are often asked to evaluate their teacher on a number of performance measures. Although not widely used in

[32]Edward E. Lawler III, Allan M. Mohrman, Jr., and Susan M. Resnick, "Performance Appraisal Revisited," *Organizational Dynamics* 13, no. 1 (Summer 1984):20–35; and Roy Serpa, "Why Many Organizations—Despite Good Intentions—Often Fail to Give Employees Fair and Useful Performance Review," *Management Review* 73, no. 7 (July 1984):41–45.

[33]See Laurence J. Peter and Raymond Hull, *The Peter Principle* (New York: William Morrow, 1969).

business organizations, this approach is becoming a more common method of evaluating managers and helping them improve their performance.[34]

TEACHING TIP

It would be beneficial to have examples of the different types of appraisal forms to share with students. Check in any personnel management or human resources management textbook for examples.

Traditionally, appraisals have concentrated on such personal characteristics as intelligence, decisiveness, creativity, and ability to get along with others. Today, however, appraisals are increasingly based on the individual's performance—that is, on how well the subordinate is helping the organization achieve its goals. MBO (see Chapter 7) is an example of a performance-based appraisal approach that involves establishing specific objectives and comparing performance against those objectives. Exhibit 11-1 lists and defines the major current approaches to performance appraisal.

EXHIBIT 11-1 DEFINITIONS OF PERFORMANCE APPRAISAL APPROACHES

Graphic rating	Assessing performance by a graph or line representing the range of a personal trait or dimension of the job.
Behavioral rating	Assessing performance by specific descriptions of work behavior.
Work standards approach	Comparing actual performance against expected levels of performance.
Essay	Writing a commentary discussing an individual's strengths, weaknesses, and so forth.
Management by objectives (MBO) approach	Setting of future objectives and action plans jointly by subordinate and supervisor and then measuring outcome against goals.
Objectives-based approach	Setting of future objectives (without action plans) jointly by subordinate and supervisor and then measuring outcome against goals.
Forced distribution systems	Rating employees on scales with a set percentage of employees assigned for each scale point.

Source: Adapted by permission of the publisher, from "Strategic Issues in Performance Appraisal: Theory and Practice," by Charles J. Fombrun and Robert L. Laud, *Personnel,* November–December 1983, p. 25.

Problems of Appraisal

Probably the most influential study of performance appraisal was conducted at the General Electric Company in the early 1960s by Herbert Meyer and his associates.[35] They found that formal appraisals by managers are often ineffective in improving the performance of subordinates. Individuals who were formally criticized about their job performance once or twice a year tended to become defensive and resentful. Their performance after the appraisal interview tended to decline.

Meyer and his colleagues suggest that the goal of appraisal should be to improve the future performance of subordinates and that this goal is difficult to achieve if managers act in their traditional role of judge. Instead, Meyer and his colleagues argue, a manager and an individual subordinate should set performance goals together and then evaluate progress toward those goals. Participatory appraisal, they found, leads to both greater satisfaction and higher performance on the job. Meyer and his co-workers also suggest the appraisal process should be a continuous one; that is, it should become part of the day-to-day interaction between managers and subordinates rather than be imposed on subordinates once or twice a year.

[34]In a fifth approach, the training and development section of the human resources department appraises performance and assists line managers in implementing any of the four approaches already described. See R. Bruce McAfee, "Performance Appraisal: Whose Function?" *Personnel Journal* 60, no. 4 (April 1981):298–299.

[35]Herbert H. Meyer, Emanual Kay, and John R. P. French, "Split Roles in Performance Appraisal," *Harvard Business Review* 43, no. 1 (January–February 1965):123–129. See also Douglas M. McGregor, "An Uneasy Look at Performance Appraisal," *Harvard Business Review* 35, no. 3 (May–June 1957):89–94.

Aside from the tendency to judge subordinates, there are a number of other pitfalls managers must avoid in order to make their formal and informal appraisal programs effective:

1. *Shifting standards*. Some managers rate each subordinate by different standards and expectations. A low-performing but motivated employee, for example, might be rated higher than a top-performing but seemingly indifferent employee. To be effective, the appraisal method must be perceived by subordinates as based on uniform, fair standards.[36]
2. *Rater bias*. Some managers allow their personal biases to distort ratings. These biases may be gross prejudices regarding not only sex, color, race, or religion but also other personal characteristics, such as age, style of clothing, or political viewpoint. An increasing number of organizations try to deal with this problem by requiring documentation or explanations for rating reports.
3. *Different rater patterns*. Managers (like teachers) differ in their rating styles. Some managers rate harshly, others rate easily. The lack of uniform rating standards is unfair to employees, who can become confused about where they stand; it is also unfair to the organization, since it becomes difficult to decide which employees should be rewarded. Differences in rating patterns can be reduced through precise definitions of each item on the rating form.
4. *The halo effect*. There is a common tendency, known as the halo effect, to rate subordinates high or low on *all* performance measures based on *one* of their characteristics. For example, an employee who works late constantly might be rated high on productivity and quality of output as well as on motivation. Similarly, an attractive or popular employee might be given a high overall rating. Rating employees separately on each of a number of performance measures and encouraging raters to guard against the halo effect are two ways the halo effect can be reduced.

Approximately two decades after the original study by Meyer and his colleagues, a research team headed by Edward E. Lawler, Allan M. Mohrman, and Susan M. Resnick conducted a follow-up study at GE. Their study supported many of the original findings and led to the following additional recommendations:[37]

1. Top management should take care to integrate performance appraisal into the overall organizational culture and human resource strategy, to emphasize its importance, and to evaluate it continually.
2. The nature of an employee's job, as well as the performance expectations attached to it and the ways in which performance will be measured, should all be made clear at the outset of employment.
3. Discussions about the bases for pay increases and the relationship between pay and performance should be a natural and important part of appraisal process.
4. In a *separate* process, well integrated into the overall human resource management system, a manager should discuss an employee's career development opportunities and outline that employee's developmental needs to reach his or her potential.
5. The employee should be an equal and active partner with the manager throughout the appraisal process.

PROMOTIONS, TRANSFERS, DEMOTIONS, AND SEPARATIONS

The movement of personnel within an organization—their promotion, transfer, demotion, and separation—is a major aspect of human resource management. The actual

[36]See Ed Yager, "A Critique of Performance Appraisal Systems," *Personnel Journal* 60, no. 4 (February 1981):129–133.

[37]See Lawler, Mohrman, and Resnick, "Performance Appraisal Revisited," pp. 31–34. See also Charles J. Fombrun and Robert L. Laud, "Strategic Issues in Performance Appraisal: Theory and Practice," *Personnel* 60, no. 6 (November–December 1983):23–31; and Donald L. Kirkpatrick, "Two Ways to Evaluate Your Performance Appraisal System," *Training and Development Journal* 38, no. 8 (August 1984):38–40.

decisions about whom to promote and whom to fire can also be among the most difficult, and most important, a manager has to make.

Promotions

HERE'S AN EXAMPLE

A top GM official says that GM's bonus system should more closely link the fortunes of both managers and hourly workers to the performance of their units. (*Wall Street Journal,* 2/15/88, p. 4)

The possibility of advancement often serves as a major incentive for superior managerial performance, and promotions are the most significant way to recognize such superior performance. Therefore, it is extremely important that promotions be fair—that is, based on merit and untainted by favoritism. However, even when promotions are fair and appropriate, they can still create a number of problems. One major problem is that organization members bypassed for promotion frequently feel resentful, a fact which may affect their morale and productivity. Another major problem in promotions is discrimination. Most people accept the need, or at least the legal obligation, to avoid racial, sex, or age discrimination in the hiring process. However, less attention has been paid to discrimination against women, the aged, and minority groups in promotion decisions. Consequently, affirmative action programs, which seek to ensure that members of groups that have been discriminated against are groomed for advancement, have become more widespread. Such programs are one means of overcoming the effects of past discrimination.

Transfers

Transfers serve a number of purposes. They are used to give people broader job experiences as part of their development and to fill vacancies as they occur. Transfers are also used to keep promotion ladders open and to keep individuals interested in the work. For example, many middle managers reach a plateau simply because there is no room for all of them at the top. Such managers may be shifted to other positions to keep their job motivation and interest high. Finally, inadequately performing employees may be transferred to other jobs simply because a higher-level manager is reluctant to demote or separate them.

Discipline, Demotions, and Separations

BACKGROUND ON FIRING EMPLOYEES

The following are guidelines for firing employees: give poorly performing employees several warnings and a chance to improve before terminating them; make sure employees cannot claim age, gender, or race discrimination; be aware that oral agreements, initial-offer letters, and employee handbooks are implied contracts that are binding in some states; offer an outplacement service to senior executives; and avoid critical remarks if asked to give a reference for a terminated employee. (*Business Week,* 6/20/88, p. 168)

Discipline is generally administered when an employee violates company policy or falls short of work expectations and management must act to remedy the situation. Discipline usually progresses through a series of as many steps as are necessary to alleviate or eliminate the problem: warning, reprimand, suspension, disciplinary transfer, demotion, or, as a last resort, discharge.[38]

If a manager proves ineffective in a given position, that manager may be transferred, asked to go for retraining or further development, or be fired. The transfer may be a demotion, a shift to another same-level position, or even a "promotion" to a position with a more impressive title but with less responsibility.

Where demotion or other transfer is not feasible, it is usually better to separate than to let the poor performer stay on the job. A surprising number of times, a man or woman dismissed from one firm becomes a solid success in another. Thus, no matter how agonizing separation decisions may be, the logic of human resource planning and management development frequently requires that they be made. In recent times, a

[38]See Richard D. Arvey and Allen P. Jones, "The Use of Discipline in Organizational Settings," in L. L. Cummings and Barry M. Shaw, eds., *Research in Organizational Behavior,* Vol. 7 (Greenwich, Conn.: JAI Press, 1985)

INTERNATIONAL MANAGEMENT

THE CASE FOR THE DISCLOSURE OF PLANT CLOSURE

On May 24, 1988, President Reagan vetoed a trade bill that had been under Congressional and executive consideration for some time. The veto was aimed primarily at the bill's provision for plant-closing notification. The provision would have mandated that workers and local governments be informed 60 days in advance of a plant shutdown. However, the bill provided for several significant exceptions, including one for "unforeseeable circumstances." Those opposing the bill contended that notification of a plant closing can cause more harm than good, pointing out that such notification not only causes the company problems with its creditors and suppliers, but generates undue stress for its workers.

Some American companies already comply with the suggested provision. President Reagan supported the practice of voluntary disclosure but did not want it mandated by the government. He feared that such a policy would hamper American competitiveness at a time when the international trade picture was beginning to turn around. However, most of America's trading partners already had such legislation on their books. The bill in question would not thus have distinguished America from her trading partners, but rather would have aligned this country's policies more closely with theirs. Most European countries require notification from 2 to 12 weeks before a plant closes. Along with this requirement is the understanding that each case must be considered independently, with realistic notification schedules taking this principle into account. Japan requires "sufficient" warning so that workers can find other jobs and so that communities housing troubled firms will not be hurt by their actions. This principle reflects both the Japanese concern for the general welfare of the workers and the fact that most Japanese workers expect lifelong employment with the same company.

The requirement that a company notify those most closely affected by a plant closure did not appear to hamper business in other countries. Moreover, such laws need not be insensitive to the fact that each case is different, much as the U.S. law, given its number of exceptions provided for, would have been sensitive to the different variables of different circumstances. Such laws certainly do not appear to have hampered Japanese companies in their competition here.

After President Reagan's veto, legislative efforts were made to separate the trade bill issue from its plant-closing provisions. In July, 1988, the President accepted a new bill requiring 60-day notice of plant closings. In what ways might this new law cause problems for U.S. firms?

Sources: Monica Langley, "Conferees Clear Trade-Bill Provision for Advance Notice of Plant Closings," *Wall Street Journal,* March 30, 1988, p. 11; Walter S. Mossberg, "Plant-Closings Quarrel Distorts a Modest Idea," *Wall Street Journal,* April 25, 1988, p. 1; Richard B. McKenzie, "Fraud Law Could Shield Workers from Plant Closings," *Wall Street Journal,* April 27, 1988, p. 26.

turbulent environment, resulting in greater competition and a trend toward restructuring, has contributed to a growing rate of separations. (See the International Management box on "The Case for the Disclosure of Closure.") In order to assist separated employees, some companies provide *outplacement* services to help them find new and more suitable employment.

QUOTATION FROM A PROFESSOR

"Americans are coming to believe that the rights we attach to citizenship in our society—free expression, privacy, equality, and due process—ought to have their echo in the workplace."—Alan F. Westin, Columbia University professor who has studied individual rights in the corporation since 1950 (*Business Week,* 3/28/88, p. 62)

In addition, it has become increasingly important for companies to establish—and follow to the letter—a policy on termination. More and more companies are now finding themselves in court defending personnel decisions in what are called "wrongful termination" cases. For many years, it was accepted doctrine that managers could fire at their own discretion, but with the increasing number and complexity of rights won by employees through legislative and judicial action, jobs are increasingly being viewed as activities to which are attached rights roughly comparable to property rights.

Judgments against employers can be costly: The average settlement in California is currently about $450,000.

HRM AND STRATEGY

BACKGROUND ON EMPLOYEE BENEFITS

In 1986, Congress adopted a measure barring health plans from discriminating against lower-wage workers. The measure is giving corporate human resource managers headaches because of the processes involved in verification. (*Business Week,* 10/3/88, p. 35)

COORDINATED RESOURCE

Two well-written provocative articles on the crisis in education are: "How to Smarten Up the Schools," *Fortune,* 2/1/88, pp. 86–94, and "The Education Crisis: What Business Can Do," *Fortune,* 7/4/88, pp. 71–81.

HRM and Environmental Pressures

Given the number of changes constantly occurring in its environment, an organization should be certain that its human resource management function fits well with what the organization is trying to do. Many of today's environmental pressures are demanding much more of an organization's HRM policy. (See Table 11-4.)[39] If an organization wishes to retain its effectiveness, then it must formulate its HRM policy to incorporate long-term perspectives with regard to corporate performance, employee needs, and interpersonal well-being. In short, an organization must link its HRM policy to its business strategy.

Researchers at the Harvard Business School have proposed a broad way of understanding human resources management that takes HRM beyond the narrow connotation of just planning, selecting, training, and appraising. Figure 11-3 indicates how external stakeholder interests, such as union interests, and situational factors, such as the local labor market, can influence a variety of HRM policies. These policies naturally have consequences for the organization itself, which, in turn, reverberate in both the external and internal environments.

For example, for the 1990s many people are forecasting a labor shortage in the United States. If this is indeed true, then business strategies must take this fact into

[39]Michael Beer, Bert Spector, Paul R. Lawrence, D. Quinn Mills, and Richard E. Walton, *Human Resource Management,* (New York: Free Press, 1985), pp. 4–6.

TABLE 11-4 REACTIONS OF AN ORGANIZATION TO CHANGES IN ITS ENVIRONMENT

ACTIONS	REACTIONS
Situational/Stakeholder Pressures Influencing Effectiveness	Countervailing Measures by HRM to Retain Effectiveness
Increasing international competition	Improve human productivity Increase employee commitment Ensure long-term supply of competent people
Increasing complexity and size of organizations	Reduce levels of bureaucratization Improve HRM in diverse societies
Slower growth and declining markets	Reevaluate advancement opportunities to high potential employees Reevaluate employment security to long-service employees
Greater government involvement	Reexamine HRM policies and practices Develop new HRM policies and practices
Increasing education of the work force	Reexamine employee competency
Changing values of the work force	Reexamine employee autonomy
More concern with career and life satisfaction	Reexamine employee career paths, lifestyle needs, and work schedules
Changes in work force demography	Reexamine all policies, practices, and managerial values affecting minorities

Source: Adapted with permission of The Free Press, a Division of Macmillan, Inc., from *Human Resource Management* by Michael Beer, Bert A. Spector, Paul R. Lawrence, and Richard E. Walton, Copyright © 1985 by The Free Press.

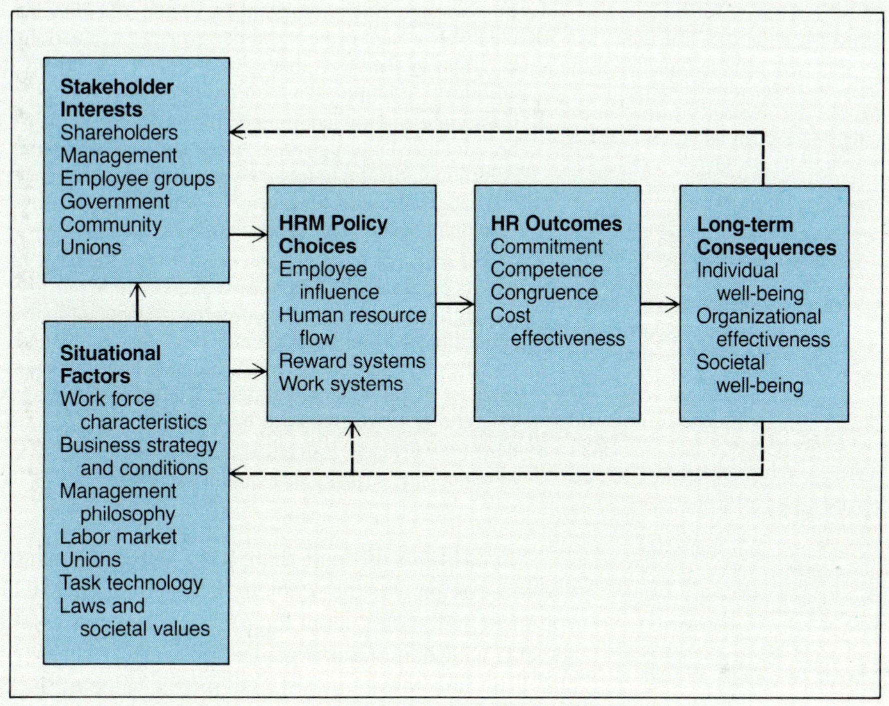

Source: Adapted with permission of The Free Press, a Division of Macmillan, Inc., from *Human Resource Management* by Michael Beer, Bert A. Spector, Paul R. Lawrence, and Richard E. Walton. Copyright © 1985 by The Free Press.

FIGURE 11-3 MAP OF THE HRM TERRITORY

account. Some labor-intensive activities may have to be transferred to other countries, or, alternatively, executives may have to lobby for a liberalization of immigration laws. Additionally, if there is a labor shortage, industries will be affected differentially. Companies may have to adopt a variety of new reward systems and even new ways of dividing and sharing work.

Such considerations as these strongly affirm that the HRM process cannot be divorced from the overall direction of the firm. The most important point to remember, however, is that unless HRM policies are influenced by all stakeholders, the organization will fail to meet the needs of the stakeholders in the long run and will fail as an organization.

The Four C's Model for Human Resources

In order to evaluate the efficacy of the HRM process within an organization, the Harvard researchers have proposed a four Cs model for human resources outcomes: commitment, competence, congruence, and cost-effectiveness. Managers are encouraged to consider the four Cs when evaluating their company's HRM process and policies. It is hoped that managers will develop creative solutions to human resource problems when questions related to the four Cs are addressed during the HRM evaluation. Examples of questions interrelated with the four Cs, as well as some methods used in measuring them, are as follows:[40]

[40]Ibid., p. 20–22.

HERE'S AN EXAMPLE

At the Goodyear Tire and Rubber Company plant in Mount Pleasant, Iowa, work is carried out by "self-directed" work groups—there are no bosses. Instead of having middle-level management positions, each work team chooses a "coordinator" who follows up on group ideas and complaints. The experiment here has been so successful that it is being used at other Goodyear plants, and at the Iowa plant, absenteeism and accidents have declined. (*Springfield News-Leader,* 9/11/88, p. 20E)

HERE'S AN EXAMPLE

Maytag Company's nonsupervisory employees turned in 6,346 suggestions during 1987 (an average of three per worker). More than 2,700 of the ideas were actually implemented.

1. *Competence.* How competent are employees in their work? Do they need additional training? Assessment centers and performance evaluations by managers can help a company in determining the talent that it has available. To what extent do HRM policies attract, keep, and develop employees with skills and knowledge needed now and in the future?
2. *Commitment.* How commited are employees to their work and organization? Surveys can be conducted through interviews and questionnaires to find answers to this question. Additional information can be gained from personnel records about voluntary separation, absenteeism, and grievances. To what extent do HRM policies enhance the commitment of employees to their work and organization?
3. *Congruence.* Is there congruence between the basic philosophy and goals of the company and its employees? Is there trust and common purpose between managers and employees? Incongruence can be detected in the frequency of strikes, conflicts between managers and subordinates, or an increase in grievances. A low level of congruence results in low levels of trust and common purpose—tension and stress between employees and managers may increase. What levels of congruence between management and employees do HRM policies and practices enhance or retain?
4. *Cost-effectiveness.* Are HRM policies cost-effective in terms of wages, benefits, turnover, absenteeism, strikes, and similar factors?

Even more difficult than addressing and measuring the extent of the four Cs within a company is the problem of assessing HRM *outcomes.* In other words, how do you make judgments about long-term consequences of HRM policies on employee and societal well-being and organizational effectiveness? How, for example, do you go about the formidable task of assigning a value to the commitment of employees or to the climate and culture of a firm that encourages motivation and growth its employees? Difficulties such as these are not easily overcome. In the final analysis, it is likely that if managers are to obtain the data needed to evaluate the impact of HRM practices and policies, the participation of a broad range of stakeholders (management, unions, governmental agencies) will be necessary.

By shaping HRM policies to enhance commitment, competence, congruence, and cost-effectiveness, an organization can increase its capacity to adapt to changes in its environment. High levels of the four Cs can contribute to employee and organizational adaptability in the following ways.[41]

- *High commitment* means better communication between employees and managers; mutual trust is enhanced, and all stakeholders are responsive to each other's needs and concerns whenever changes in environmental demands occur.
- *High competence* means that employees are versatile in their skills and can take on new roles and jobs as needed; they are better able to respond to changes in environmental demands.
- *Cost-effectiveness* means that human resource costs, such as wages, benefits, strikes, have been kept equal to or less than those of competitors; all stakeholders have undoubtedly faced the realities of the business.
- *Higher congruence* means that all stakeholders share a common purpose and collaborate in solving problems prompted by external changes in environmental demands.

Organizations that can adapt to changes in their environment are more effective organizations. Therefore, it is important that HRM be linked to strategy; by shaping its HRM policies to enhance the four Cs, an organization will be able to function more effectively in its ever-changing environment.

[41]Ibid., p. 37–39.

ILLUSTRATIVE CASE STUDY Wrap-Up

Human Relations at Sony Corporation

Clearly, Akio Morita's human resource policies accommodate the overall strategy of Sony. By focusing on the shared fate of management and employees, Sony develops among its workers a sense of commitment to the overall goals of the firm. In part because of employee commitment, Sony has been able to stay competitive in terms of wages and benefits and to motivate highly competent people to continue to innovate.

By focusing on people as resources rather than as costs, companies like Sony are writing the book on the future of management theory and practice. ■

SUMMARY

The HRM process includes (1) human resource planning; (2) recruitment; (3) selection; (4) socialization; (5) training and development; (6) performance appraisal; (7) transfer, promotion, and demotion; and (8) separation.

Human resource planning includes planning for the future personnel needs of the organization, planning what the future balance of the organization's personnel will be, planning a recruitment-selection or layoff program, and planning a development program. Human resource plans are based on forecasting, and the human resource audit, in which the skills and performance of organization members are appraised. To be meaningful, human resource plans have to take into consideration the strategic plan and the external environment of the organization.

General and specialized recruitment are designed to supply the organization with a sufficiently large pool of job candidates. Job recruits can be drawn from within or outside the organization. However, before recruitment can take place, a job analysis, consisting of the position description and job specification, must be made.

Successive federal and state legislation, executive orders, and legal decisions since the early 1960s have mandated equal employment opportunity (EEO) regardless of race, sex, age, color, religion, or ethnic group membership. EEO legislation also covers Vietnam era and disabled veterans and the physically and mentally handicapped. Nondiscriminatory procedures must provide equal access to jobs, training, and promotion and equal treatment in the work environment. Firms doing business with the federal government are subject to affirmative action (AA) programs to add and develop women and minority group members.

The selection process follows a seven-step procedure: completed job application, initial screening interview, testing, background investigation, in-depth selection interview, physical examination, and job offer. For managerial positions, the in-depth interview is probably the most important step. Ideally, it should be realistic and factually based. Assessment centers may also be used to select managers.

Socialization helps the new employee and the organization accommodate to each other. Giving new employees challenging assignments has been shown to correlate with future success.

Training programs seek to maintain and improve current job performance, while development programs are designed to impart skills needed in future jobs. The need for training may be determined through performance appraisal, job requirements, organizational analysis, and human resource surveys. Both training and development methods can be classified as on-the-job or off-the-job. Coaching is the most important formal on-the-job development method. Other development methods include job rotation and classroom teaching. Both training and development should be reinforced in the work situation.

Performance appraisal may be informal or systematic. To improve performance, appraisal should be based on goals jointly set by managers and subordinates. Problems of appraisal include shifting standards, rater bias, different rater patterns, and the halo effect.

To be useful as employee incentives, promotions must be fair. Discrimination in promotion, though illegal, has still not disappeared.

Transfers are used to broaden a manager's experience, to fill vacant positions, and to relocate employees whom the organization does not want to demote, promote, or fire. Demotions are an infrequently used option in dealing with ineffective managers. Separations, though painful, are more widely used and frequently prove beneficial to the individual as well as to the organization.

New trends call for linking HRM more closely with an organization's strategy. The Harvard researchers' four Cs model is useful in evaluating the effectiveness of an organization's human resource policy in supporting its business strategy.

REVIEW QUESTIONS

1. What are the steps in the HRM process? Are managers likely to be engaged in more than one step at a time? Why or why not?
2. Why is human resource planning necessary? Name the four steps in human resource planning. What factors must managers of a human resource planning program consider?
3. What methods of recruitment can managers use? What are the advantages and disadvantages of recruitment from within?
4. What changes have occurred in EEO and affirmative action in recent years? What are the implications for managers?
5. What is the standard, seven-step hiring sequence? Is this sequence the same under all conditions? Why or why not?
6. What are the defects of in-depth interviews? How can these defects be minimized?
7. What information is socialization designed to provide?
8. What is the difference between training and development?
9. What development approaches and methods can managers use? Which method is most effective?
10. What are the basic differences between systematic and informal appraisal? What are the four basic appraisal approaches? How may formal appraisals be made more effective in leading to improved performance? What appraisal pitfalls do managers need to avoid?
11. What are the problems associated with promotions? How may these problems be overcome?
12. When are transfers used in organizations?
13. Explain how the four Cs criteria may be used to evaluate the effectiveness of a human resource management policy.

CASE STUDY

The Gannett Company: A Leader in Minority Employment

In an industry not noted for minority employees, the Gannett Company, owner of 90 newspapers throughout the country, has placed minority employees in 20 percent of its jobs and boasts a professional, technical, managerial, and sales force consisting of 15 percent minority employees. The U.S. population is about 22 percent minorities, and the percentage of minorities in the journalism industry 7 percent, up from 4 percent in 1978, when the American Society of Newspaper Editors first took the count. Approximately half of the 1,600 daily newspapers in this country have no minority reporters.

Currently, only 2 of Gannett's 90 newspapers have no minority employees. Although praise has been lavished on the company for its achievements in hiring and promoting minorities, some of its white male employees have complained that *merit* is being given short shrift in staffing decisions. Company executives have denied these charges of reverse discrimination.

Some minorities are also critical of Gannett, saying that even more needs to be done and that management's concern is strictly with hiring quotas—whereby, paradoxically, minorities will always end up underrepresented since once a quota is met, other minority candidates may not be given a chance.

Gannett's hiring program is based on aggressive recruitment and promotion programs, where jobs may remain open until nonwhites apply for them. The company also sends recruiters to job fairs and publishes its job classifieds in magazines targeted to minorities. Managers at Gannett are trained in equal employment hiring goals, and they forward their figures in monthly or quarterly reports to keep track of their progress toward employment goals. Gannett also provides bonuses for managers who compile good records in hiring minorities. Although this reward must reflect a balanced consideration of both the hiring opportunities available to a manager and his or her hiring choices, the motivation to reach equal opportunity goals is made all the more clear by financial incentives.

Allan Neuharth, chairman of Gannett, is fully committed to the company's program. In 1979, he began a campaign called "Partners in Progress" that established an agenda for the hiring and promotion of minorities and women. Now, almost 10 years later, Neuharth wonders how he should evaluate the progress of the program.

Source: Adapted from Johnnie L. Roberts, "Gannett Surpasses Other Newspaper Firms in the Hiring and Promotion of Minorities," *Wall Street Journal,* May 11, 1988, p. 11.

Case Questions

1. Why do newspapers have a substantially lower representation of minority employees?
2. Why has the program at Gannett been successful at attracting minority employees?
3. What are some possible problems with this program, now and in the future?
4. What advice would you give Mr. Neuharth as he ponders the future of the program? ■

Herbert Bayer, Poster from the Great Ideas of Western Man Series. Courtesy of the Jefferson Smurfit Corporation, St. Louis.

12

MANAGING ORGANIZATIONAL CHANGE AND DEVELOPMENT

Upon completing this chapter you should be able to:

1. Identify two constructive responses to change pressures and suggest when each approach is appropriate.
2. Describe internal and external forces for organizational change.
3. Summarize Lewin's three-phase model of the organizational change process.
4. Understand the sources of resistance to change and the ways this resistance can be overcome.
5. Describe three approaches to planned change.
6. Describe a model of individual change.
7. Understand the organizational development approach to planned change and the assumptions and values upon which this approach is based.
8. Discuss the effect of organizational culture on change.

Chapter Outline

Introduction
Forces for Change
Managerial Responses to Pressures for Change
Models of the Change Process
Resistance to Change
Approaches to Planned Change
Organizational Development
Organizational Culture

ILLUSTRATIVE CASE STUDY Introduction

Organizational Trauma and Triumph at AT&T

In perhaps the most celebrated case in business history, AT&T agreed in 1983 to a consent decree with the Department of Justice to divest itself of three quarters of its $150 billion in assets. Until that time AT&T and the associated Bell Telephone Companies were widely and highly regarded as among the most consistently profitable and best managed companies in the world. The changes that resulted from divestiture were enormous. Each of the resulting multibillion-dollar companies had to establish new ways of planning and organizing, and AT&T itself was plunged fully into a brand-new competitive world.

In the early 1970s, AT&T recognized that its external environment was changing and that it was inevitably going to be more competitive. In an early effort at organizational development, AT&T took the unprecedented step of hiring Arch McGill, a fiery ex-IBM employee, to bolster its marketing expertise. Ten stormy years later, McGill left the company after having put an indelible mark on it. His style of confrontation and conflict, along with his marketing and customer orientation, began a process of change that is still ongoing.

Prior to 1983, AT&T was the largest private employer in the United States. It was well known for rewarding loyalty, perseverance, and hard work with responsibility and job security. The tradition of serving the public interest was deeply ingrained in AT&T employees. Under the stress of change, however, many of the company's traditions collapsed. As part of its cost-cutting efforts, AT&T eliminated 75,000 jobs, some via retirement but many more through layoffs. For a while, even top management seemed to be in shock, too paralyzed to prevent the disorganization and erosion of morale.

In the fall of 1986, a 22-year AT&T veteran killed himself when he discovered that he was probably going to be laid off—after three transfers and five jobs in two years. His suicide note wondered aloud how a company could do this to a loyal employee only a few years from retirement. According to James E. Olson, then AT&T's chairman, "Nobody's been through what this company's been through. We put our people through hell."

Olson began a move to unify the company and heal its wounds. He devised a broad new plan: to protect AT&T's core telecommunications business, drive its sagging computer business out of the red, and increase AT&T's overseas revenues. Part of his strategy was to do away with the multiple payroll procedures, phone systems, and ID badges that had characterized the old divisions of the company and to forge a single new corporate culture. In addition, he set more realistic goals for the computer division. Rather than challenge IBM directly in many markets, Olson focused the division on a few products and markets.

Olson began implementing this strategy during a special meeting of his 27 top executives. After five days of hard-fought battles over the new shape of AT&T, each of the executives had to stand individually and publicly affirm his commitment to the plan when asked: "Are you with me?"

Still troubled by the morale problem, Olson took to the road, toured seven cities, and spoke to over 40,000 AT&T workers in an effort to explain the company's problems and his proposed solutions. Unfortunately he died of cancer early in 1988. His successor, Mr. Robert Allen, faces a difficult job to continue the task of organizational change and development.

Sources: John J. Keller, Geoff Lewis, Todd Mason, Russell Mitchell, and Thane Peterson, "AT&T: the Making of a Comeback," *Business Week,* January 18, 1988, pp. 56–62; Steve Coll, *The Deal of the Century: The Break up of AT&T* (New York: Atheneum, 1986).

CLASS COMMENT

Anticipating change is *proactive* management as opposed to *reactive* management.

In Chapter 9, we saw how organizations can be designed to fit the environments in which they operate. Even if an organization's design is appropriate for its environment at a given time, the managers must anticipate changes in the environment that will require future adjustments in the organization's design. Anticipating such change effectively is not only a challenge but also a necessity for organizational survival.

This chapter will focus on systematic programs to bring about planned change in organizations or their subunits. The forces that create the need for organizational change, when to recognize that the time for change has come, and how to overcome resistance to change will be discussed in turn. Approaches to planned change, with an emphasis on the technique known as organizational development (OD), the assumptions and values on which it is based, and the role of organizational culture will complete our discussion.

FORCES FOR CHANGE

Organizations depend on and must interact with their external environment in order to survive. Any factor in the external environment that interferes with the organization's ability to attract the human and material resources it needs, or to produce and market its services or products, becomes a force for change.[1] Any factor in the internal environment that affects the way the organization carries out its activities is also a force for change. Given the great changes in the external environment of most organizations that we examined in Chapter 3, managing change has taken on increased importance.

External Forces

HERE'S AN EXAMPLE

Change has been slow in coming to UPS since the combination of employee ownership and tight operating controls has worked so well. However, UPS is now in the throes of major change, forced into the high-tech era by competitors. (*Fortune*, 1/18/88, pp. 56–64)

An enormous variety of external forces, from technological advances to competitive actions, can pressure organizations to modify their structure, goals, and methods of operation. Increasing costs and scarcity of natural resources, worker safety and antipollution regulations, consumer boycotts, higher levels of education in the labor market, volatile capital markets—the list of environmental factors that have changed our lives as workers and consumers in recent years are numerous. We all recall that a fatal leak of toxic chemicals from the Union Carbide plant in Bhopal, India, intensified worldwide public concern about safeguards and standards in the chemical industry (see the International Management box entitled "'The Devil's Night' in Bhopal"). More generally, the growing ability of Japanese, Korean, French, German, and other multinational companies to compete in the global marketplace (see Chapters 3 and 24) has led to pressure for the internal restructuring of many organizations.

Internal Forces

Pressures for change may also arise from a number of sources within the organization, particularly from new strategies, technologies, and employee attitudes and behavior. For example, a top manager's decision to seek a higher rate of long-term growth will

[1] Eliza Collins, "Taking Hold of Change," *Harvard Business Review*, May–June 1984, pp. 54–65.

HERE'S AN EXAMPLE

GM, the world's largest automaker, will shrink capacity in order to boost profits. However, GM needs union cooperation to increase efficiency by changing outmoded work rules. Says Donald Ephlin, head of the United Auto Workers' GM Department, "If they have a plan for going out of business, they don't want to talk to me about it. I don't want any part of it." (*Business Week*, 5/9/88, pp. 114–122)

affect the goals of many departments and may even lead to some reorganization. The introduction of automated equipment to perform tasks that previously required human labor may call for a complete change in work routines, training programs, and compensation arrangements. The entrance of more women and minorities into the work force may also force managers to consider the merits of flexible work schedules, innovative benefits like day care, and more substantial employee-training programs. Finally, worker dissatisfaction, as manifested in high turnover rates or strikes, may lead to changes in management policies and practices.

However, change, especially when it results in major reorganizational plans, can be traumatic, and changes in a company's actions may often beget reactions—even when the pressure for change issues from top-management levels. For example, at Alcoa (Aluminum Company of America), former CEO Charles Parry developed a strategy for company restructuring with 50 percent of its revenues coming from non-aluminum businesses and the company becoming a preeminent producer of new alloys and other space-age materials for the 21st century. However, because the board was unsure of Parry's strategy and Alcoa's customers and employees were confused about its direction, the board appointed a new CEO, Paul O'Neill, whose strategy returned the company to its focus on its core aluminum business after Parry took "early retirement."[2]

External and internal forces for change are often linked. The link is particularly strong when changes in values and attitudes are involved. Persons with new attitudes enter the organization and cause it to change from within. Many of the changes described in earlier chapters—such as job enrichment programs and the trend toward greater subordinate participation in decision making—represent in part a response to changes in people's attitudes toward authority and expectations of work satisfaction.

[2]"The Quiet Coup at Alcoa," *Business Week*, June 27, 1988, pp. 58–65.

INTERNATIONAL MANAGEMENT

"THE DEVIL'S NIGHT" IN BHOPAL

Although such companies as airlines maintain elaborate contingency plans for catastrophic crashes, companies in some industries do not foresee the possibility of catastrophic changes in their organizational futures. As a result, they may find themselves without planned responses to such changes, whether reactive responses to immediate problems or planned responses to long-term consequences.

Such was the case for Union Carbide on the morning on December 3, 1984, when its pesticide plant in Bhopal, India, leaked tons of lethal methylisocyanate gas into an overcrowded city of 700,000 people. By the time that death-toll reports reached the company's headquarters in Danbury, Connecticut, climbing first from 200 and 300 and ultimately to 2,000 with over 100,000 injured, Carbide's options for immediate reactive response had already been severely limited. There were only two telephone lines into the Bhopal area, and management in Connecticut had to rely on fragments of information funneled out of its Bombay subsidiary. The plant's supervisors had been placed under arrest, and when Carbide chairman Warren Anderson arrived to assess the situation and offer whatever resources were at the company's immediate disposal, he, too, was taken into custody. Freed on bail, Anderson was then informed that the Indian government expected Carbide to pay compensation damages that threatened to become astronomical—far beyond the resources of Carbide's reported $200 million in insurance.

MANAGERIAL RESPONSES TO PRESSURES FOR CHANGE

Managers can respond to pressures for change in ways that are ultimately destructive—for example, by denying that they exist, resisting them, or avoiding them. Companies that have lost millions of dollars in lawsuits because of flagrant violations of toxic waste disposal laws are paying the price for denying or resisting change in social values and government regulations. Companies forced to close down due to competition or to unwise financial maneuvers during the course of restructuring clearly had avoided responding in an adaptive or constructive way to changes in the environment.

QUOTATION FROM A MANAGER

"Management must guide the forces of change."—John W. Teets, Chairman, Greyhound Corporation (Greyhound Corporation advertisement)

To deal with change, managers use two major approaches. First, they *react* to the signs that changes are needed, making piecemeal modifications to deal with particular problems as they arise. Second, they develop a *program of planned change,* making significant investments of time and other resources to alter the ways their organizations operate. In the latter case, they deal not only with present difficulties but with anticipated problems not yet clearly observable.

The first response—which is simpler and less expensive than the second—is necessary for the small, day-to-day adjustments integral to the manager's job. Examples of such adjustments are easy to find: A sales form is modified because the old layout led to errors in specifying quantity and price; young managers are having difficulty with tasks involving financial analysis, so a two-week seminar on financial analysis is arranged; two managers, working together on a high-priority project, temporarily move into adjoining offices until the project is completed. These small changes require minimal planning because they can and should be handled in a quick and routine manner. We will not deal with this type of reactive response in this chapter, since we deal with it throughout the book in descriptions of the daily problems and decisions that managers confront.

Carbide immediately ceased its worldwide production of methylisocyanate gas, but its problems in taking quick reactive measures were far from being under the company's managerial control. In addition to having to stem the leakage of toxic fumes with an undertrained work force, Carbide found the city of Bhopal strewn with mass graves and hospitals reporting deaths at the rate of one every 60 seconds. The city's foliage had withered, and the dying, writhing in pain from the inhalation of a gas that swells lung tissue and drowns victims in internal fluids, scurried through shantytown streets littered with animal carcasses and teeming with flies.

The long-term outlook was no better. Carbide lost over $800 million in market value in a single week, and the company could look forward to lengthy and intensive scrutiny of its safety policies and procedures. Why, for example, had no computerized warning system been installed at the Bhopal plant? Moreover, the company could expect to find itself at the center of a long and volatile debate about the practices of U.S. firms engaged in risky ventures in underdeveloped nations—a fact that will no doubt hamper Carbide's efforts to defend both its ethical practices and its financial stability among present and potential investors for some time to come. Finally, every one of the company's problems is exacerbated by public-relations issues that will have to be addressed by intricate, long-term strategies for which it had not planned.

Sources: "India's Tragedy—A Warning Heard around the World," *U.S. News & World Report,* December 17, 1984, pp. 25–26; R. I. Kirkland, "Union Carbide: Coping with a Catastrophe," *Fortune,* January 7, 1985, pp. 50–53; R. W. King, "Early Steps to a Carbide Settlement: Carbide's Contractor in Bhopal," *Business Week,* January 28, 1985, p. 48; and Larry Everest, *Bhopal: The Anatomy of a Massacre* (New York: Banner Press, 1985).

HERE'S AN EXAMPLE

The employees of Weirton Steel are fully behind the employee buyout of their plant. They have no choice—Weirton is a one-industry town. But questions need to be raised about whether the effort is realistic as a business venture. (*Forbes*, 4/11/83, pp. 39–41)

UPDATE ON EXAMPLE

Weirton Steel still faces a bleak outlook but not as much so. Shipments in 1984 increased more than 17 percent as Weirton went after the smaller companies—a niche in the steel industry not touched by the big competitors. (*Forbes*, 3/25/85, p. 12)

The second response, a program of planned change, has been defined by John M. Thomas and Warren G. Bennis as "the deliberate design and implementation of a structural innovation, a new policy or goal, or a change in operating philosophy, climate, and style."[3] Such a response is appropriate when the entire organization, or a major portion of it, must prepare for or adapt to change.

Planned change is greater in scope and magnitude than reactive change. It is a means of dealing with those changes that may be crucial for survival. It involves a greater commitment of time and resources, requires more skills and knowledge for successful implementation, and can lead to more problems if implementation is unsuccessful. Because planned change has become so important to many organizations in today's world, it is the subject of the remainder of this chapter.

It is, however, difficult for planned change programs to accurately predict and respond to all the forces for change in today's complex environment. (See Chapter 3.) Therefore, some companies have turned to a different kind of planned change program that does not spell out specific innovations. Rather, management accepts change and the need to respond to it quickly as an important value for the organization. This kind of planned change program views change as a necessary and healthy part of life that fosters organizational and individual growth.

The Role of the Change Agent

change agent The individual leading or guiding the process of a change in an organizational situation.

client system The individual, group, or organization that is the target of a planned change.

In every situation in which a change is desired, some person or group must be designated as the catalyst for change. That person or group is called the **change agent.**

The change agent is the individual who is responsible for taking a leadership role in managing the process of change. The individual, group, or organization that is the target of the change attempt is called the **client system.** Change agents can be members of the organization or they can be consultants brought in from outside. For complex and lengthy change programs, it is often desirable that an outside change agent manage the process, since specialized expertise and skills may be required, freedom from distraction by day-to-day operating responsibilities may be essential, and the prestige of being an outsider can be helpful. Outsiders with no vested interests in the organization are often more likely to be confided in, listened to, and able to form objective judgments.[4]

MODELS OF THE CHANGE PROCESS

Although organizations are beset by many forces for change, it is important to recognize that other forces act to keep an organization in a state of equilibrium. Forces opposing change are also forces supporting stability or the status quo.

To understand how pressures for change and pressures for stability interact, we will present a model that describes how the level of behavior or performance in any organization is influenced by forces that push in opposing directions. Other models will show how an organization, department, or individual can be helped to change, and whether an organization is likely to mobilize the energies necessary for successful change.

---

[3]John M. Thomas and Warren G. Bennis, eds., *The Management of Change and Conflict* (Baltimore: Penguin, 1972), p. 209.

[4]For a review of the various types of change agents, see Richard N. Ottaway, "The Change Agent: A Taxonomy in Relation to the Change Process," *Human Relations* 36, no. 4 (April 1983):361–392. On the use of political skills by change agents, see Newton Margulies and Anthony P. Raia, "The Politics of Organization Development," *Training and Development Journal* 38, no. 8 (August 1984):20–23.

Forces for Stability

According to the "force-field" theory of Kurt Lewin, any behavior is the result of an equilibrium between *driving* and *restraining* forces.[5] The driving forces push one way, the restraining forces push the other. The performance that emerges is a reconciliation of the two sets of forces. An increase in the driving forces might increase performance, but it might also increase the restraining forces. For example, a manager may believe that he or she can get improved results by telling subordinates that there will be absolutely no time off until productivity increases. But the likely response of hostility, distrust, and greater resistance may cause additional declines in productivity, even though the formal prohibition against taking time off is observed.

The natural tendency for most of us, if we want change, is to push. However, the equally natural tendency of whomever or whatever is being pushed is to push back: Driving forces activate their own restraining forces. Decreasing the restraining forces, therefore, is normally a more effective way to encourage change than by increasing the driving forces. In the productivity example, the manager would be more likely to get results by identifying pointless bureaucratic bottlenecks and eliminating them.

Lewin's model (see Fig. 12-1) reminds us to look for multiple causes of behavior rather than a single cause. It is applicable to our purposes because it is generalized: The forces can be of many types, and the behavior or performance can be that of an individual, group, or entire organization. The equilibrium concept also suggests that organizations have forces that keep performance from falling too low, as well as forces that keep it from rising too high.

CLASS COMMENT
Remove or weaken *restraining forces*. Create or strengthen *driving* forces.

Programs of planned change are directed toward removing or weakening the restraining forces and toward creating or strengthening the driving forces that exist in organizations.

[5]Kurt Lewin, *Field Theory in Social Science: Selected Theoretical Papers* (New York: Harper & Brothers, 1951).

FIGURE 12-1 FORCE-FIELD DIAGRAM

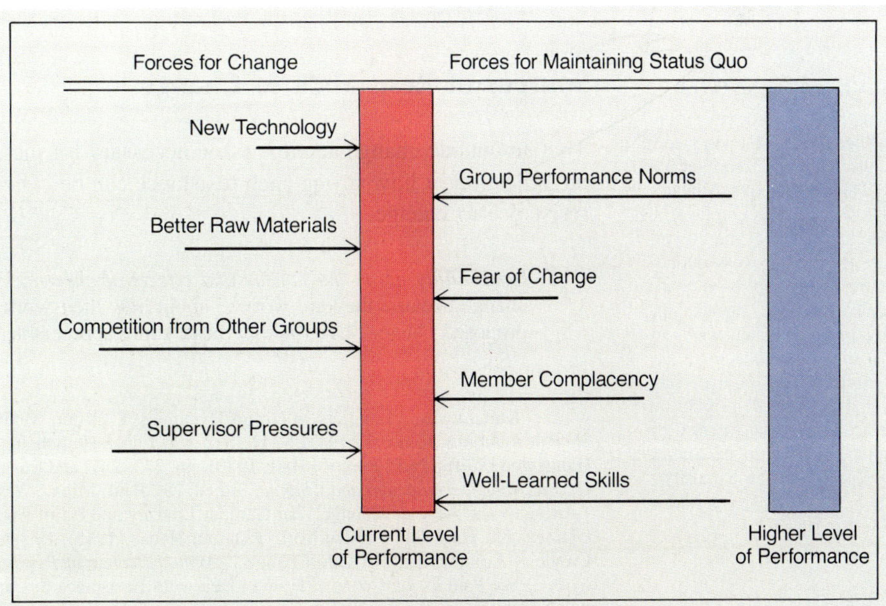

Note: Length of arrow is equal to amount of force.

Source: Adapted by permission from *Organization Development and Change,* 3rd ed. by Edgar F. Huse and Thomas G. Cummings, p. 73.

The Process of Change

Lewin also studied the process of bringing about effective change. He noted that individuals experience two major obstacles to change. First, they are unwilling (or unable) to alter long-established attitudes and behavior. A manager told that he or she needs to learn a new analytic technique may accept this information with little or no difficulty. But if that same manager is told that he or she is too aggressive and abrasive in dealing with others, he or she is much more likely to resent and reject the information. Suggesting the need to make a change in managerial style or attitude is perceived as a violation of one's self-image and an indication of inadequacy.

The second major obstacle noted by Lewin was that change frequently lasts only a short time. After a brief period of trying to do things differently, individuals often return to their traditional pattern of behavior.

To overcome obstacles of this sort, Lewin developed a three-step sequential model of the change process. The model, later elaborated by Edgar H. Schein and others, is equally applicable to individuals, groups, or entire organizations.[6] It involves "unfreezing" the present behavior pattern, "changing" or developing a new behavior pattern, and then "refreezing" or reinforcing the new behavior.

unfreezing Making the need for change so obvious that the individual, group, or organization can readily see and accept that change must occur.

refreezing Transforming a new behavioral pattern into the norm through reinforcement and supporting mechanisms.

1. **Unfreezing** involves making the need for change so obvious that the individual, group, or organization can readily see and accept it.
2. Changing requires a trained change agent to foster new values, attitudes, and behavior through the processes of *identification* and *internalization*. Organization members identify with the change agent's values, attitudes, and behavior, internalizing them once they perceive their effectiveness in performance.
3. **Refreezing** means locking the new behavior pattern into place by means of supporting or reinforcing mechanisms, so that it becomes the new norm.

RESISTANCE TO CHANGE

As we have already noted, a major obstacle to the implementation of new policies, goals, or methods of operation is the resistance of organization members to change.

HERE'S AN EXAMPLE

Bad efforts at reorganization can lead to more resistance of future legitimate reorganization. At Pacific Mutual's Atlanta claims office, an employee who complained about the 20 percent increase in work quotas implemented shortly after the company held a "leadership alignment" seminar was told that the new quotas were a "gravity issue" (a leadership alignment term describing uncontestable management decisions). The employee continued to object until the company fired her. (*Wall Street Journal*, 7/24/87, p. 19)

Sources of Resistance to Change

That an outside change agent is often necessary for the success of change programs is an indication of how strong such resistance can be. There are three general sources of resistance to change.[7]

1. *Uncertainty about the causes and effects of change*. Organization members may resist change because they are worried about how their work and lives will be affected by the proposed change. Even if they have some appreciable dissatisfaction with their present

---

[6]Kurt Lewin, "Frontiers in Group Dynamics: Concept, Method, and Reality in Social Science," *Human Relations* 1, no. 1 (1947):5–41. See also Edgar H. Schein, *Organizational Psychology*, 3rd ed. (Englewood Cliffs, N.J.: Prentice Hall, 1980), pp. 243–247; and Edgar F. Huse and Thomas G. Cummings, *Organization Development and Change*, 3rd ed. (St. Paul, Minn.: West, 1985), p. 20; William J. McGuire, "Attitudes and Attitude Change," in Gardner Lindzey and Elliot Aronson, eds., *Handbook of Social Psychology*, 3rd ed., Vol. 2 (New York: Random House, 1985), Chapter 6; and Joel Cooper and Robert T. Croyle, "Attitudes and Attitude Change," *Annual Review of Psychology* 35 (1984):395–426.

[7]See Paul R. Lawrence, "How to Deal with Resistance to Change," *Harvard Business Review* 47, no. 1 (January–February 1969); John P. Kotter and Leonard A. Schlesinger, "Choosing Strategies for Change," *Harvard Business Review* 57, no. 2 (March–April 1979):107–109; and Herbert Kaufman, *The Limits of Organizational Change* (Tuscaloosa: University of Alabama Press, 1971).

work, they may still worry that things will be worse when the proposed changes are implemented. When the change is initiated by someone else, they may feel manipulated and wonder what is the "real" intention behind the change.

2. *Unwillingness to give up existing benefits.* Appropriate change should benefit the organization as a whole, but for some individuals, the cost of change in terms of lost power, prestige, salary, quality of work, or other benefits will not be sufficiently offset by the rewards of change.
3. *Awareness of weaknesses in the changes proposed.* Organization members may resist change because they are aware of potential problems that have apparently been overlooked by the change initiators. Different assessments of the situation represent a type of desirable conflict (see Chapter 13) that managers should recognize and use to make their change proposals more effective.

BACKGROUND ON DOWNSIZING

Survivors of middle-management shakeouts are prone to distraction, disloyalty, and resentment. These problems can be minimized if companies will communicate clearly the need for new strategies; use technology to communicate information; use in-person pep-talks; treat the people let go with respect and kindness; let your stars know the company has a bright future and you want them to stick around; have a "grieving" process; etc. (*Fortune*, 5/23/88, pp. 42–52)

Overcoming Resistance to Change

Resistance to a change proposal is a signal to managers that something is wrong with the proposal or that mistakes have been made in its presentation. Managers, therefore, must determine the actual causes of resistance and then remain flexible enough to overcome them in an appropriate manner.[8]

In recent years, for example, American auto makers have experienced numerous forces pressing for relatively broad changes in long-standing policies and long-standing relationships with stakeholder groups that are resistant to those changes. In at least one instance—a top-level determination to downsize at General Motors—flexible, and even innovative, measures have both lessened resistance to change and increased the likelihood that all parties involved will ultimately benefit.

One of the enduring realities of the auto business in the U.S. is that management has long been dealing with unions over such issues as work rules, working conditions, and wages and benefits. As a rule, labor-management relations have been characterized by adversarial stances even when all appeared to be going well for both parties. However, as auto makers fell on tough times and were forced to seek changes in their commercial fortunes they have attempted to negotiate less traditional, more flexible relations with their union stakeholders. GM, which once made 52 percent of the new cars sold in the U.S., is now settling for less than 40 percent. Its current management is pledged to downsize the organization considerably by 1992—a policy which could mean at least 4 out of 26 plants closing and at least 100,000 jobs eliminated. This would be in addition to the almost 60,000 United Auto Workers members already on indefinite layoff.

To help create a changed relationship in which management and workers could work together and not at cross-purposes, each GM plant formed joint union/management committees to study ways to boost productivity. GM has also worked with the union to adopt more flexible production methods such as those used in Japanese-style team systems.

While there has been some progress, there is still some reluctance on the part of the union to change—reluctance based not just on changes in the ways work has traditionally been done, but also on the fear that as productivity increases, job security will decrease. Although GM has negotiated some job security, the 1987 contract stipulates that if sales continue to fall, GM can lay off more workers. With GM's plans to downsize coinciding with falling sales for its products, there would seem to be many barriers to success in changing both work patterns and the union-management relationship. And yet many people, both analysts and participants, are hopeful that new ap-

[8]See Paul C. Nutt, "Tactics of Implementation," *Academy of Management Journal* 29 (1986):230–261.

TABLE 12-1 METHODS FOR DEALING WITH RESISTANCE TO CHANGE

APPROACH	INVOLVES	COMMONLY USED WHEN . . .	ADVANTAGES	DISADVANTAGES
1. Education + communication	Explaining the need for and logic of change to individuals, groups, and even entire organizations.	There is a lack of information or inaccurate information and analysis.	Once persuaded, people will often help implement the change.	Can be very time-consuming if many people are involved.
2. Participation + involvement	Asking members of organization to help design the change.	The initiators do not have all the information they need to design the change, and others have considerable power to resist.	People who participate will be committed to implementing change, and any relevant information they have will be integrated into the change plan.	Can be very time-consuming if participators design an inappropriate change.
3. Facillitation + support	Offering retraining programs, time-off, emotional support and understanding to people affected by the change.	People are resisting because of adjustment problems.	No other approach works as well with adjustment problems.	Can be time-consuming, expensive, and still fail.
4. Negotiation + agreement	Negotiating with potential resisters; even soliciting written letters of understanding.	Some person or group with considerable power to resist will clearly lose out in a change.	Sometimes it is a relatively easy way to avoid major resistance.	Can be too expensive if it alerts others to negotiate for compliance.
5. Manipulation + co-optation	Giving key persons a desirable role in designing or implementing change process.	Other tactics will not work, or are too expensive.	It can be a relatively quick and inexpensive solution to resistance problems.	Can lead to future problems if people feel manipulated.
6. Explicit + implicit coercion	Threatening job loss or transfer, lack of promotion, etc.	Speed is essential, and the change initiators possess considerable power.	It is speedy and can overcome any kind of resistance.	Can be risky if it leaves people angry with the initiators.

Source: Reprinted by permission of the *Harvard Business Review.* An exhibit from "Choosing Strategies for Change" by John P. Kotter and Leonard A. Schlesinger (March–April 1979).

proaches and strategies will increase productivity and profits for GM—and thus bring greater job security for both management and union members.[9]

TEACHING TIP

Dealing with resistance to change is often difficult for managers. Be sure to go over these methods individually so students can absorb them.

John P. Kotter and Leonard A. Schlesinger have proposed six ways of overcoming resistance to change, including the two primary means adopted by GM and its union workers—namely, participation + involvement and negotiation + agreement. All six methods are summarized in Table 12-1. Each method has advantages and disadvantages, and no method is appropriate for all situations.

APPROACHES TO PLANNED CHANGE

In the previous sections, we described how the impetus for change develops in an organization and how the change process can be carried out. In this section, we will discuss the various elements of the organization to which the change process can be applied. Specifically, we will try to answer the question: What aspects of the organization can be changed?

---

[9] "GM Faces Reality," *Business Week,* May 9, 1988, pp. 114–122; "GM's New 'Teams' Aren't Hitting Any Homers," *Business Week,* August 8, 1988, pp. 46–47; and Stephen Kindel, "The Designated Hitter," *Financial World* 157, no. 14 (1988):20–21.

"We ought to consider taking Freedley off crisis management."

Harold J. Leavitt states that an organization can be changed by altering its structure, its technology, and/or its people.[10] Changing the organization's *structure* involves rearranging its internal systems, such as its lines of communication, work flow, or managerial hierarchy. Changing the organization's *technology* means altering its equipment, engineering processes, research techniques, or production methods. Changing the organization's *people* involves changing the selection, training, relationships, attitudes, or roles of organization members. Because we have already dealt with structure and technology to some extent in earlier chapters of this unit, we will deal with them only briefly here. Our main focus will be on change efforts aimed at the people in the organization; in particular, we will emphasize organizational development (OD) programs, which attempt to change the ways people work together to achieve the organization's and their own objectives.

Interdependence of the Three Approaches

Organizations are made up of interacting, interdependent elements under the influence of common forces; that is, organizations are systems. The three elements cited—structure, technology, and people—are therefore highly interdependent. A change in one is likely to affect the other elements as well.[11] (See Fig. 12-2.) Thus, an effective change program is likely to be one that acknowledges the interaction of these three elements and attempts to change all three, as necessary.

Normally, the greater the amount of change managers desire, the higher the likelihood that the change efforts will have to involve all three elements in order to be effective. For example, let us assume we are managers in a large company and wish

[10]Harold J. Leavitt, "Applied Organization Change in Industry: Structural, Technical, and Human Approaches," in W. W. Cooper, H. J. Leavitt, and M. W. Shelly II, eds., *New Perspectives in Organization Research* (New York: John Wiley, 1964), pp. 55–71. For an amplification of such a model, see David A. Nadler, "Managing Organizational Change: An Integrative Perspective," *Journal of Applied Behavioral Science* 17, no. 2 (April–May–June 1981):191–211.

[11]For a more detailed description of system element interdependence, see Wendell L. French and Cecil H. Bell, Jr., *Organization Development: Behavioral Science Interventions for Organization Improvement*, 3rd ed. (Englewood Cliffs, N.J.: Prentice Hall, 1984), pp. 54–62.

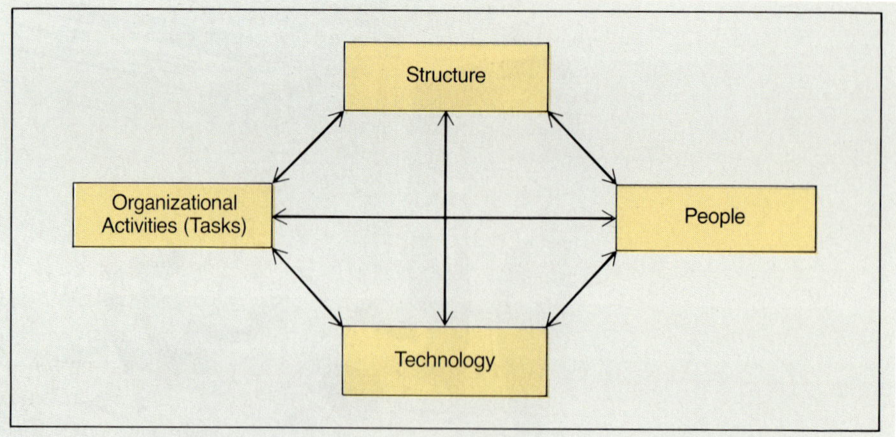

Source: Adapted from Harold J. Leavitt, "Applied Organization Change in Industry: Structural, Technical, and Human Approaches," in W. W. Cooper, H. J. Leavitt, and M. W. Shelly II, eds., *New Perspectives in Organization Research* (New York: John Wiley, 1964), p. 56. Used by permission.

FIGURE 12-2 INTERDEPENDENT ORGANIZATIONAL ELEMENTS

to increase sales in two product categories: proprietary drugs and personal care products. To achieve our goal, we might conclude that a major structural change will be required. The sales force will have to be divided into two separate units so that the efforts of salespeople are more focused on each product line and accountability is easier to determine. Such a structural change may well involve technological changes. For example, new computer programs may have to be used to transfer the old marketing and sales information into more appropriate formats, or new sales techniques and procedures may be developed to increase the professionalism of the sales force. In addition, people changes are also likely to be required. Some new sales personnel may have to be hired and trained, and previously hired personnel will have to be retrained or reassigned. IBM, for example, has instituted a no-layoff policy, but that policy has also forced the company to increase the number of its personnel transfers, either because facilities are closed or because positions are made available for personnel at other locations. Insiders at IBM often refer to the company as "I've Been Moved." At IBM as elsewhere, individuals unable to adjust to changing circumstances, whether in current locations or through transfer, may have to be replaced.

QUOTATION FROM A SURVIVOR OF DOWNSIZING

"Increases in stress, conflict, and ambiguity about each individual's role; decreases in job involvement; decreases in work satisfaction; dissatisfaction with leadership and co-workers; decreases in the quality of coordination within the organization—all of which had negative impacts on the overall performance of the organization"—William F. Joyce (*Fortune*, 7/22/88, p. 155)

Structural Approaches

Leavitt divides structural efforts to bring about organizational change into three areas. *Classical organizational design* seeks to improve organizational performance by carefully defining the job responsibilities of organization members and by creating appropriate divisions of labor and lines of authority. Managers can still improve the performance of their organizations by changing management spans, job descriptions, areas of responsibility, reporting relationships, and the like.

Decentralization creates smaller, self-contained organizational units that increase the motivation and performance of the members of those units and help them to focus their attention on the highest-priority activities. Decentralization also permits each unit to adapt its own structure and technology to the tasks it performs and to its external environment.

Modifying the *flow of work* in the organization and careful grouping of specialties may also lead directly to an improvement in productivity and to higher morale and work satisfaction.[12]

Technological Approaches

Frederick Taylor, through "scientific management" (see Chapter 2), attempted to analyze and refine the interactions between workers and machines to increase efficiency in the workplace. Through time and motion studies, setting piece rates, and other efforts to redesign work operations and reward systems, Taylor and later industrial engineers tried to improve organizational performance.

Technological changes are often difficult to implement successfully and may prove incompatible with an organization's structure. For example, Trist and Bamforth found that decreased satisfaction and performance followed the introduction of technological innovations in a mining operation.[13] The miners, who had performed a variety of tasks in small, closely knit work groups, were forced to work on more specialized tasks in a much larger, less cohesive group when the technical changes were implemented. The result was low productivity, more accidents, and a high turnover rate.

HERE'S AN EXAMPLE

Service industries are finding that computers don't always raise productivity. Some reasons why: some companies automate existing practices instead of changing them to exploit technology; companies are sometimes preoccupied with marketing maneuvers; data overload; precedence isn't necessarily given to computer projects that would be of greatest benefit to the whole company; etc. (*Wall Street Journal*, 4/19/88, p. 37)

HERE'S AN EXAMPLE

American manufacturing appears to be in a new stage of modernization. Some statistics reflecting this trend: an 8.9 percent rise in plant and equipment outlays by manufacturing industries is predicted, and output per worker in all manufacturing industry rose 30 percent from the end of 1982 to November 1987. (*Wall Street Journal*, 4/19/88, p. 35)

Combining Technological and Structural Approaches. *Technostructural* approaches to change, often called *sociotechnical* approaches, attempt to improve performance by changing some aspects of both an organization's structure and its technology. For example, in the mining operation mentioned, many of the original small work groups were eventually reintroduced in ways that would be compatible with the new mining machinery and led to dramatic improvements in morale and productivity.

Job enlargement and job enrichment programs are other examples of technostructural approaches to change. (See Chapter 10.) In these programs, the tasks that make up a job, the ways the tasks are performed, and employee relationships are altered to improve employee satisfaction and perhaps to increase productivity.[14] In *job enrichment*, some activities from a vertical slice of the organization are combined in one job to make it more challenging (thereby stimulating the jobholder's sense of responsibility). Under *job enlargement*, various tasks at the same level of the organization are combined to provide employees with greater variety on the job and increase their sense of work involvement.

QUOTATION FROM A MANAGER

"You're looking at bakeries that are going to be like oil refineries, they will have so few people. They will dump the flour in at night and out will come these things—bread, cookies or whatever—in the morning."—J. Tracy O'Rourke, President and CEO of Allen-Bradley (*Wall Street Journal*, 4/19/88, p. 35)

People Approaches

Both the technical and structural approaches attempt to improve organizational performance by changing the work situation— a factor which should cause employee behavior to become more productive. The people approaches, on the other hand, attempt to change the behavior of employees directly by focusing on their skills, attitudes, perceptions, and expectations. Improvements in these may lead to more effective job performance and to employee-initiated changes in the organization's structure and technology. Figure 12-3 summarizes the three major approaches to change.

QUOTATION FROM A PROFESSOR

Describing the change taking place at UPS, "People will make sure things work out because they want *their* company to succeed."—Jeffrey Sonnenfeld, Harvard University professor (*Fortune*, 1/18/88, p. 60)

---

[12]See, for example, Eliot D. Chapple and Leonard R. Sayles, *The Measure of Management* (New York: Macmillan, 1961).

[13]Eric L. Trist and K. W. Bamforth, "Some Social and Psychological Consequences of the Long-Wall Method of Coal-Getting," *Human Relations* 4, no. 1 (February 1951):3–38.

[14]See Dorothy Leonard-Barton and William A. Kraus, "Implementing New Technology," *Harvard Business Review*, November–December 1985, pp. 102–110.

Efforts to change people's behavior and attitudes can be directed at individuals, groups, or the organization as a whole. Many but not all such efforts are known as organizational development (OD) techniques. Non-OD approaches for changing people include management development (see Chapter 11), behavior modification (described in Chapter 15), and management by objectives (see Chapter 8).

ILLUSTRATIVE CASE STUDY Continued

Organizational Trauma and Triumph at AT&T

The managers at AT&T could no doubt identify with all of the concepts discussed in this chapter. Both internal and external forces for change clearly existed. Even before the divestiture, AT&T had undertaken programs designed to make changes, especially under the guidance of Arclu McGill; for example, the company had already negotiated a union agreement with the Communications Workers of America that included a new quality-of-work-life program to improve management-labor communications and cooperation.

Because AT&T was so large prior to its divestiture, overcoming the sheer inertia of over 1,000,000 employees and $150 billion in assets required constant vigilance. Once the layoffs started, resistance to change increased among some employees in proportion to the companys own uncertainty, but it lessened in others—those who were eager for something, almost anything, to happen.

Over the years, AT&T planned for and implemented each of the three approaches to planned change that we have discussed in this chapter. There have been numerous reorganizations, some mandated by regulatory changes, some undertaken to align AT&T more closely with customer needs and concerns. As technology has increased in the industry, AT&T has used a variety of technological approaches, ranging from time-and-motion studies of operators to the development of electronic monitoring devices that encourage some workers to spend less time on customer premises. Throughout these efforts, AT&T has sought to give its people the skills—especially marketing and technical skills—that they need to be more productive. Although all of these approaches have been at work, no one of them can be pointed out as the sole reason for AT&T's survival in managing its historic change.

FIGURE 12-3 THE THREE CHANGE APPROACHES

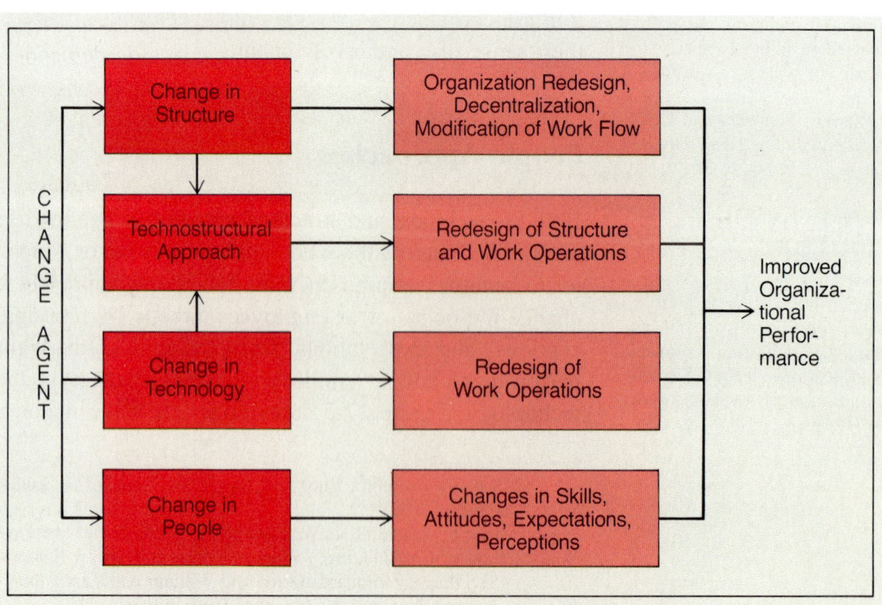

ORGANIZATIONAL DEVELOPMENT

organizational development (OD) A long-range effort supported by top management to increase an organization's problem-solving and renewal processes through effective management of organizational culture.

CLASS COMMENT

OD is more extensive and comprehensive than management development since it focuses on the entire organization.

QUOTATION FROM A PROFESSOR

"Corporations are so hard up for answers these days that I'd say there's a $3 billion or $4 billion market for transformational consulting out there."—Richard Beckhard, founding father of the OD field and a business professor at MIT (*Wall Street Journal*, 7/24/87)

The approaches to change just discussed are particularly appropriate for solving immediate and specific problems. **Organizational development (OD),** another approach to planned change, is a longer-term, more encompassing change approach meant to move the entire organization to a higher level of functioning while greatly improving the performance and satisfaction of organization members. Although OD frequently includes structural and technological changes, its primary focus is on changing people and the nature and quality of their working relationships. In addition, the OD approach differs from the three approaches discussed in the previous section in that it demands the expenditure of more time and is inherently more complex.

As a formal concept OD is relatively new, and "the term 'organizational development' itself remains inconsistently defined, being primarily a convenient label for a variety of activities."[15] We will use a definition that stresses certain aspects of and approaches to managing organizational change or development. However, no definition is sacred. Many activities quite different from the ones we describe are legitimately called OD by their practitioners and users. The field is also changing so rapidly, as we will see, that in a few years the label OD may well be applied to a somewhat different set of activities.

Organizational development has been defined by Wendell French and Cecil Bell as

> a top-management-supported, long-range effort to improve an organization's problem-solving and renewal processes, particularly through a more effective and collaborative diagnosis and management of organization culture—with special emphasis on formal work team, temporary team, and intergroup culture—with the assistance of a consultant-facilitator and the use of the theory and technology of applied behavioral science, including action research.[16]

In this definition, *problem-solving process* refers to the organization's methods of dealing with the threats and opportunities in its environment. For example, managers might choose to solve the organization's problems on their own, or they might participate with subordinates in problem solving and decision making.

Through a *renewal process,* the organization's mangers can adapt their problem-solving style and goals to suit the changing demands of the organization's environment. Thus, one aim of OD is to improve an organization's self-renewal process so that managers can more quickly adopt a management style that will be appropriate for the new problems they face.

collaborative management Management through power sharing and subordinate participation; the opposite of hierarchical imposition of authority.

organizational culture The set of important understandings, such as norms, values, attitudes, and beliefs, shared by organizational members.

Collaborative management means management through subordinate participation and power sharing rather than through the hierarchical imposition of authority.

The term **organizational culture** refers to prevalent patterns of activities, interactions, norms, values, attitudes, and feelings. Culture includes the informal aspects of organizational life as well as the formal—the "covert" attitudes that form the submerged part of the iceberg shown in Figure 12-4. Organizational culture will be discussed in greater detail at the end of this chapter.

[15]Robert L. Kahn, "Organizational Development: Some Problems and Proposals," *Journal of Applied Behavioral Science* 10, no. 4 (1974):485. See also Larry E. Greiner, "Red Flags in Organization Development," in J. R. Hackman, E. E. Lawler III, and L. W. Porter, eds., *Perspectives on Behavior in Organizations* (New York: McGraw-Hill, 1983), pp. 536–542; and Charles Kiefer and Peter Stroh, "A New Paradigm for Organization Development," *Training and Development Journal* 37 (1983):26–35.

[16]French and Bell, *Organization Development,* p. 17.

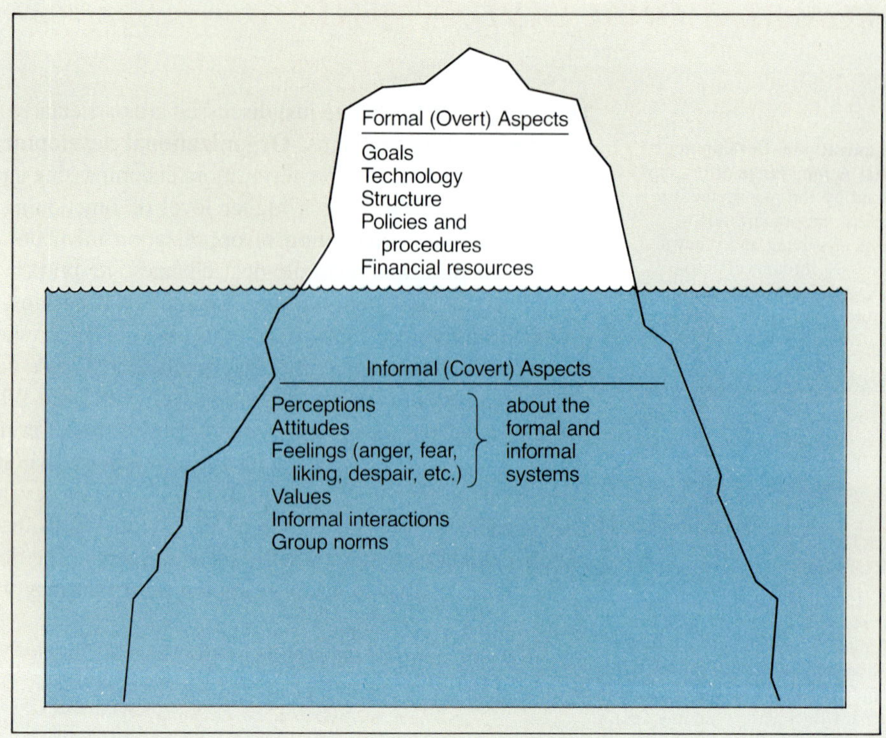

Source: Adapted from Stanley N. Herman, "TRW Systems Group," in Wendell L. French and Cecil H. Bell, Jr., *Organization Development: Behavioral Science Interventions for Organization Improvement,* 3rd ed., p. 19. © 1984. Used by permission of Prentice Hall, Englewood Cliffs, N.J.

FIGURE 12-4 THE ORGANIZATIONAL ICEBERG

action research The method through with organizational-development change agents learn what improvements are needed and how the organization can best be aided in making improvements.

Action research refers to the way OD change agents go about learning what aspects of the organization need to be improved and how the organization can be helped to make these improvements. Briefly, action research involves (1) a preliminary diagnosis of the problem by OD change agents, (2) data gathering to support (or disprove) the diagnosis, (3) feedback of the data to organization members, (4) exploration of the data by organization members, (5) planning of appropriate action, and (6) taking appropriate action.

Types of OD Activities

Change agents have many techniques and intervention approaches available to them, not all of which will be used in a given change program. One useful way of classifying these techniques is in terms of the target groups with which they might be employed. The techniques can be used to improve the effectiveness of individuals, the working relationship between two or three individuals, the functioning of groups, the relationship between groups, or the effectiveness of the total organization.[17] Some techniques described here are applicable to more than one target group.

---

[17]Ibid., p. 131. French and Bell also discuss other ways of classifying OD techniques and describe many of the techniques in detail.

ETHICS IN MANAGEMENT

OD ASSUMPTIONS AND VALUES

Organizational development is not value-neutral. There are a number of ethical assumptions and values which most OD practitioners share and which determine the kinds of changes they suggest.

On the personal level, OD change agents assume that individuals have a natural desire for personal development and growth and that most employees are willing and able to make a greater contribution to the organization. They also believe that satisfying human needs and aspirations is an important purpose of organizational life. Therefore, they are concerned with individual self-fulfillment and try to overcome organizational factors discouraging personal growth.

On the group level, OD practitioners assume that it is important for people to be accepted by their work group and that most groups do not encourage the open expression of feelings. However, OD practitioners believe that hiding feelings has a negative effect on group members' willingness and ability to solve problems constructively, on job satisfaction, and on job performance. Therefore, they encourage the awareness and development of feelings as an integral part of organizational life.

On the organizational level, OD practitioners assume that the links between work groups influence their effectiveness. For example, there will be more coordination and cooperation between work groups when all group members can interact, less when just the managers communicate. A second assumption is that the policies and methods of managers of large groups will affect the way smaller groups operate. Finally, OD practitioners assume that strategies based on one group or department winning at the expense of another will not be successful in the long run. Organizations should rely instead on approaches acceptable to all the groups involved.

OD change agents also value the equalization of power within an organization, arguing that it is necessary for the long-term health of the organization. In most cases, power equalization means increasing the influence of subordinates. In some organizations, however, such as universities, hospitals, and city administrations, lower-level people may possess too much power. The solution then is to enhance the power of the administrators at the top.

sensitivity training An early personal growth technique, at one time fairly widespread in organizational development efforts, that emphasizes increased sensitivity in interpersonal relationships.

transaction analysis An approach to improving interpersonal effectiveness, sometimes used in organizational development efforts, that concentrates on the styles and content of communication.

process consultation A technique by which consultants help organization members understand and change the ways they work together.

1. *OD for the individual.* **Sensitivity training** was an early and fairly widespread OD technique. In "T" ("training") groups, about 10 participants are guided by a trained leader to increase their sensitivity to and skills in handling interpersonal relationships. Sensitivity training is now less frequently used by organizations, and participant are usually screened to make certain that they can withstand the anxiety raised by a T group. Precautions are also taken to assure that attendance is truly voluntary.[18]
2. *OD for two or three people.* **Transaction analysis** (TA) concentrates on styles and content of communication (transactions or messages) between people. It teaches people to send messages that are clear and responsible and to give responses that are natural and reasonable. Transactional analysis attempts to reduce destructive communication habits or "games," in which the intent or full meaning of messages is obscured.[19]
3. *OD for teams or groups.* In **process consultation,** a consultant works with organization members to help them understand the dynamics of their working relationships in group or team situations. The consultant helps the group members to change the ways they work

[18]Morton. A. Lieberman, Irvin D. Yalom, and Matthew B. Miles, *Encounter Groups: First Facts* (New York: Basic Books, 1973).

[19]See Eric Berne, *Games People Play* (New York: Ballantine, 1978); and Abe Wagner, *The Transactional Manager: How to Solve People Problems with Transactional Analysis* (Englewood Cliffs, N.J.: Prentice Hall, 1981).

together and to develop the diagnostic and problem-solving skills they need for more effective problem solving.[20]

team building A method of improving organizational effectiveness at the team level by diagnosing barriers to team performance and improving interteam relationships and task accomplishment.

Team building, a related approach, analyzes the activities, resource allocations, and relationships of a group or team to improve its effectiveness. This technique can be used, for example, to develop a sense of unity among members of a new committee. Team building is described in more detail later in this chapter.[21]

4. *OD for intergroup relations.* To permit an organization to assess its own health and to set up plans of action for improving it, the *confrontation meeting* may be used. This is a one-day meeting of all of an organization's managers in which they discuss problems, analyze the underlying causes, and plan remedial actions. The confrontation meeting is typically used after a major organizational change, such as a merger or the introduction of a new technology.[22]
5. *OD for the total organization.* The *survey feedback* technique can be used to improve the total organization's operations. It involves conducting attitude and other surveys and systematically reporting the results to organization members. Members than determine what actions need to be taken to solve the problems and exploit the opportunities uncovered in the surveys.

OD Techniques in Closeup

We will take a more detailed look at two widely used OD techniques—survey feedback and team building—each for specific reasons. Survey feedback exemplifies the action research concept, and research suggests it is particularly effective. Team building is employed in many large-scale OD programs; it was chosen for a closer look because OD has historically had a group focus and has stressed the importance of the small group.

Survey Feedback. Survey feedback uses a familiar tool—the questionnaire—but does more than simply collect data. The collected data are returned to managers and subordinates so that the survey results can be employed as a basis for change. The survey feedback process (which is summarized and contrasted to traditional questionnaire use in Table 12-2) has been described by French and Bell as consisting of five steps:

- *Step 1:* Organization members at the top of the hierarchy are involved in the preliminary planning.
- *Step 2:* Data are collected from all organization members.
- *Step 3:* Data are fed back to the top executive team and then down through the hierarchy in functional teams . . .
- *Step 4:* Each superior presides at a meeting with his or her subordinates in which the data are discussed and in which (a) subordinates are asked to help interpret the data, (b) plans are made for making constructive changes, and (c) plans are made for the introduction of the data at the next lower level.
- *Step 5:* Most feedback meetings include a consultant who has helped prepare the superior for the meeting and how serves as a resource person.

---

[20]See Edgar H. Schein, *Process Consultation: Its Role in Organization Development* (Reading, Mass.: Addison-Wesley, 1969); and Larry Hirshhorn and James Krantz, "Unconscious Planning in a Natural Work Group: A Case Study in Process Consultation," *Human Relations* 33, no. 10 (October 1982):805–844.

[21]Examples of team-building efforts in a broadcast system and a university administration can be found in William G. Dyer, *Team Building; Issues and Alternatives* (Reading, Mass.: Addison-Wesley, 1977), pp. 64–67 and 82–83, respectively. An experiment in which this technique did not improve performance but did generate a perceptible increase in participation is reported in Richard W. Woodman and John J. Sherwood, "Effects of Team Development Intervention: A Field Experiement," *Journal of Applied Behavioral Science* 16, no. 1 (April–May–June 1980):211–227.

[22]See Richard Beckhard, "The Confrontation Meeting," *Harvard Business Review* 45, no. 2 (March–April 1967):149–155.

TABLE 12-2 SURVEY FEEDBACK VERSUS TRADITIONAL SURVEY APPROACH

	TRADITIONAL APPROACH	SURVEY FEEDBACK APPROACH
Data collected from:	Rank and file, and maybe manager	Everyone in the system or subsystem
Data reported to:	Top management, department heads, and perhaps to employees through newspaper	Everyone who participated
Implications of data are worked on by:	Top management (maybe)	Everyone in work teams, with workshops starting at the top (all superiors with their subordinates]
Third-party intervention strategy:	Design and administration of questionnaire, development of report	Obtaining concurrence on total strategy, design and administration of questionnaire, design of workshops, appropriate interventions in workshops
Acton planning done by:	Top management only	Teams at all levels
Probable extent of change and improvement:	Low	High

Source: Wendell L. French and Cecil H. Bell, Jr., *Organization Development: Behavioral Science Interventions for Organization Improvement,* 3rd ed., p. 182 © 1984. Reprinted by permission of Prentice Hall, Englewood Cliffs, N.J.

COORDINATED RESOURCE
An excellent film on team building is "Team Building: Making the Task the Boss," 1982 and 1983 versions. Available from CRM McGraw-Hill, P.O. Box 641, Del Mar, CA 92014.

Team Building. A fundamental unit of an organization, the team or working group, can be a logical focus for improving the effectiveness of the organization.[23] OD team-building activities can improve the performance of teams and the sense of participation among members. *Team building* can be directed at two different types of teams or working groups: first, an existing or permanent team made up of a manager and his or her subordinates, often called a *family group*, and second, a new group that may have been created through a merger or other structural change in the organization or formed to solve a specific problem, which we will call the *special group*.

For both kinds of groups, team-building activities aim at diagnosing barriers to effective team performance, improving task accomplishment, improving relationships between team members, and improving processes operative in the team, such as communication and task assignment. Table 12-3 summarizes these activities for both family and special groups.

Diagnostic meetings may involve the total group or several subgroups and require only a brief time—a day or less—to identify strengths and problem areas. Actual

[23]See French and Bell, *Organization Development,* pp. 138–154. For a discussion of the distinctions between the interactions of a *group* and the coordination of a *team,* see H. H. Emurian, J. V. Brady, R. L. Ray, J. L. Meyerhoff, and E. H. Mougey, "Experimental Analysis of Team Performance," *Naval Research Reviews* 36 (1984):3–19.

TABLE 12-3 TEAM-BUILDING ACTIVITIES

ACTIVITY	FAMILY GROUPS	SPECIAL GROUPS
Diagnosis	Diagnostic meetings: "How are we doing?"	Diagnostic meetings: "Where would we like to go?"
Task accomplishment	Problem solving, decision making, role clarification, goal setting, etc.	Special problems, role and goal clarification, resource utilization, etc.
Building and maintaining relationships	Focus on effective interpersonal relationships, including boss-subordinate and peer	Focus on interpersonal or interunit conflict and underutilization of other team members as resources
Management of group processes	Focus on understanding group processes and group culture	Focus on communication, decision making, and task allocations
Role analysis and role negotiation	Techniques used for role clarification and definition	Techniques used for role clarification and definition

Source: Adapted from Wendell L. French and Cecil H. Bell, Jr., *Organization Development: Behavioral Science Interventions for Organization Improvement,* p. 104. © 1984. Used by permission of Prentice Hall, Englewood Cliffs, N.J.

MANAGEMENT APPLICATION

CHANGE AT SOUTHWESTERN BELL AND HONEYWELL

In recent years, planned change programs have transformed Southwestern Bell and Honeywell Information Systems. Change was mandated at Southwestern Bell by the court-ordered breakup of the Bell System. The company was forced to become fully independent for the first time, taking over all the functions previously provided by AT&T. These ranged from purchasing to investor relations. Southwestern Bell, accustomed to the role of a protected utility, also had to learn how to compete in order to exploit the new opportunities created by divestiture. A new, entrepreneurial spirit was a top priority for the company.

In contrast, Honeywell's change program came in response to the sluggish growth, poor morale, and widespread infighting plaguing the organization. While a 1982 program of cutbacks temporarily restored profits, it did not provide a basis for long-term growth. Top management decided to use organizational development to renew the business. Outside consultants used survey feedback and process consultation techniques to infuse Honeywell with a new organizational culture that incorporated basic OD values about the importance of the individual.

While the impetus for change was different at the two companies, their change programs shared a people-oriented approach. Both companies, for example, implemented mandatory retraining programs for managers. At Southwestern Bell, all mid- and upper-level managers attended a week-long Corporate Policy Seminar which focused on stimulating intrapreneurship. The Honeywell Executive Leadership Program also consisted of week-long workshops, but the focus here was on the development of team spirit (the group struggled together with physical obstacles such as a 12-foot wall) and commitment to the change process.

team building requires a subsequent longer meeting, ideally held away from the workplace. The consultant interviews participants beforehand and organizes the meeting around common themes. The group proceeds to examine the issues, rank them in order of importance, study their underlying dynamics, and decide on a course of action to bring about those changes perceived as necessary. A follow-up meeting at a later time may then evaluate the success of the action steps.

Evaluating OD

BACKGROUND ON ORGANIZATIONAL CHANGE

See the Anecdotal Digest for Chapter 12 for an interesting description of managing organizational change.

Evaluation of OD programs is hard because of their complexity, scope, and long-term nature. Even limited activities, like a team development project, may be difficult to evaluate because of inability to prevent changes in membership and to control related organizational activities. In addition, a variety of approaches to team development may be used, so evaluation of one type of team development effort may not tell much about how a different approach will work. In response to different kinds of pressures, Honeywell Information Systems and Southwestern Bell have adopted different approaches to the problems of change and organizational development. As the Management Application box entitled "Change at Southwestern Bell and Honeywell" indicates, comparative evaluation of different approaches is difficult.

The existence of organizational politics can also make objective assessment difficult.[24] The individuals with the greatest commitment to the program may also have to play a leading role in the evaluation. And, as in any change in an organization, the results following an OD program may be due to other causes—for example, when changes in the economy lead to changes in the turnover rate. For these reasons, efforts

[24]Newton Margulies and Anthony P. Raia, "The Politics of Organization Development," *Training and Development Journal* 38 (1984):20–23.

Participative management is the new order of the day. Honeywell has systematically reeducated its managers and now encourages a participative management style by promoting those managers who employ it. Southwestern Bell rewards its managers with bonuses. The company also created a formal "Quality of Work Life" program to encourage employee contributions to the organization. A QWL team from Kansas City, for example, successfully developed a new plan for the efficient restoration of phone service after a storm.

Communication has also been a hallmark of both programs. The change team at Honeywell visited every company computer facility and produced a videotape for employees explaining their goals and the kinds of behavior they were trying to encourage. Southwestern Bell staged a satellite link-up of all 55,000 company employees and their spouses in 57 locations immediately after divestiture. This event allowed employees to vent their emotions about the change and gave management a chance to demonstrate their new leadership.

What else do the change programs at Southwestern Bell and Honeywell have in common? Both are success stories. At Southwestern Bell, intrapreneurship has caught hold: Individual employees have devised better ways to restore service to customers with defective lines, to monitor cellular systems, and to market the company's services. At Honeywell, the changes in information systems are now spreading throughout the rest of the corporation. Revenues and profits are up for both organizations.

Sources: Zane E. Barnes, "Change in the Bell System," *Academy of Management Executive* 1, no. 1 (February 1987): 43–46; James J. Renier, "Turnaround of Information Systems at Honeywell," *Academy of Management Executive* 1, no. 1 (February 1987):47–50.

to evaluate OD programs frequently yield ambiguous results.[25] As Exhibit 12-1 shows, French and Bell have identified a set of conditions that they feel necessary for a successful OD program. Although the evaluation of OD programs that have clearly failed has provided some insight into just what conditions are necessary for an OD program to succeed, it is important to remember that the conditions influencing *failure* may be qualitatively different from those conducive to *success*—that is, the conditions for success are by no means necessarily the *opposite* of the conditions for failure.

EXHIBIT 12-1 THE CONDITIONS NECESSARY FOR A SUCCESSFUL OD PROGRAM

1. *Recognition by top or other managers that the organization has problems.* Without this, it is highly unlikely that the necessary time, effort, and money will be invested in OD.
2. *Use of an outside behavioral scientist as a consultant.* Internal change agents are unlikely to have, or to be seen as having, the experience, objectivity, expertise, or freedom required to implement a major change program.
3. *Initial support and involvement of top-level managers.* Top managers play a key role in overcoming initial resistance to change. Lack of involvement and support from them would signal to lower-level managers that the activity is not considered important.

(*continued*)

[25]For discussions of efforts evaluate OD programs, see Warren R. Nielsen (Chairperson), John R. Kimberly, Larry E. Pate, Robert T. Golembiewski, Robert M. Frame, John J. Wakefield, and Richard E. Ault, "Seminar on Organization Development Assessment: Theory, Research, and Applications" *Midwest Academy of Management Proceedings*, April 1977, pp. 407–416; Jerry I. Porras and Per Olaf Berg, "Evaluation Methodology in Organization Development: An Analysis and Critique," *Journal of Applied Behavioral Science* 14, no. 2 (April–May–June 1978):151–173; and John M. Nicholas, "Evaluation Research in Organizational Change Interventions: Considerations and Some Suggestions," *Journal of Applied Behavioral Science* 15, no. 1 (January–February–March 1979):23–40.

EXAMPLE 12-1 (CONTINUED)

4. *Involvement of work group leaders.* Activities to improve the effectiveness of existing work groups are frequently an important part of OD programs. To be successful, such programs require active support and involvement by the manager of the work group.
5. *Achieving early success with the OD effort.* When the first OD changes are made and prove successful, organization members are motivated to continue the process and to attempt larger-scale changes. Early failures may destroy the credibility of the change agents and may weaken the commitment of top-level supporters.
6. *Education of organization members about OD.* People are likely to feel manipulated if they did not understand the reasons for changes and, to some extent, the theories on which OD change programs are based.
7. *Acknowledgment of managers' strengths.* Managers who are already using good management techniques are likely to resent an OD change agent who overplays the "expert" or "teacher" role. The things managers do well need to be acknowledged and reinforced.
8. *Involvement with managers of human resource departments.* The expertise and support of managers in the human resource department are essential in designing and implementing changes in such areas as employee evaluation, development, and reward policies.
9. *Development of internal OD resources.* Internal change agent expertise must be developed, and the organizations's line managers must acquire many of the change agents skills.
10. *Effective management of the OD program.* Failure by change agents and clients to coordinate and control the OD program may result in loss of impetus and isolation from the felt needs of the organization members.
11. *Measurement of results.* The success of the organization in meeting its organizational and human goals must be monitored. Data on results provide change agents and managers with important feedback on the organization's change efforts.

Source: Wendell L. French and Cecil H. Bell, Jr., *Organization Development: Behavioral Science Interventions for Organization Improvement,* 3rd ed. (Englewood Cliffs, N.J.: Prentice Hall, 1984) pp. 215–216. Adapted by permission of Prentice Hall, Inc. Englewood Cliffs, New Jersey.

ORGANIZATIONAL CULTURE

HERE'S AN EXAMPLE

Mike Quinlan, McDonald's Corporation's new CEO, pledges that McDonald's culture will remain unchanged under his quidance. There is no formal staff hierarchy; the company's annual report still lists the company's 127 officers alphabetically, and not by rank; no McDonald's employee (Quinlan included) has an office door. (*Business Week*, 5/9/88, p. 97)

QUOTATION FROM A MANAGER

Ray A. Kroc, late founder of the McDonald's Corporation, shared these axioms: On cleanliness—If you've got time to lean, you've got time to clean. On company expansion—When you're green, you grow; when you're ripe, you rot. (*Wall Street Journal*, 12/18/87, p. 1)

Culture, according to Vijay Sathe, is "the set of important understandings (often unstated) that members of a community share in common.[26] These shared understandings consist of norms, values, attitudes, and beliefs, and the community in question may be as wide as a society or industry, or as narrow as a company, department, or particular work unit. Corporate culture is an integral part of organizational life, and has important implications for managerial action.

As Table 12-4 shows, Edgar Schein has suggested that there are a number of underlying assumptions that give rise to organizational culture in whatever form we observe it.

The culture of a particular organization may be inferred from the things, sayings, doings, and feelings held in common. For example, the formality of a company's operations may be gauged by the existence of warm personal relationships within it and by its employees' style of dress. For a schematic look at such inferences for one hypothetical corporation, see Figure 12-5.

[26]Vijay Sathe, "Implications of Corporate Culture: A Manager's Guide to Action," *Organizational Dynamics* 12, no. 2 (Autumn 1983):5–23. Several books published in the early 1980s aroused great interest in corporate cultures. On the culture of Japanese organizations, see William G. Ouchi, *Theory Z: How American Business Can Meet the Japanese Challenge* (Reading, Mass.: Addison-Wesley, 1981); and Richard Tanner Pascale and Anthony G. Athos, *The Art of Japanese Management* (New York: Simon & Schuster, 1981). For discussions of successful companies and the cultures they have generated, see Thomas J. Peters and Robert H. Waterman, Jr., *In Search of Excellence* (New York: Harper & Row, 1982); and Terrence E. Deal and Allan A. Kennedy, *Corporate Cultures: The Rites and Rituals of Corporate Life* (Reading, Mass.: Addison-Wesley, 1982). Recent books exploring the concept in depth include Edgar H. Schein, *Organizational Culture and Leadership* (San Francisco: Jossey-Bass, 1985); Stanley M. Davis, *Managing Corporate Culture* (Hagerstown, Md.: Ballinger, 1985); and Ralph H. Kilman, Mary Jane Saxton, and Ray Serpa, eds., *Gaining Control of Corporate Cultures* (San Francisco: Jossey-Bass, 1985).

TABLE 12-4 BASIC UNDERLYING ASSUMPTIONS AROUND WHICH CULTURAL PARADIGMS FORM

1. *Humanity's Relationship to Nature.* At the organizational level, do the key members view the relationship of the organization to its environment as one of dominance, submission, harmonizing, finding an appropriate niche, or what?
2. *The Nature of Reality and Truth.* The linguistic and behavioral rules that define what is real and what is not, what is a "fact," how truth is ultimately to be determined, and whether truth is "revealed" or "discovered"; basic concepts of time and space.
3. *The Nature of Human Nature.* What does it mean to be "human" and what attributes are considered intrinsic or ultimate? Is human nature good, evil, or neutral? Are human beings perfectible or not?
4. *The Nature of Human Activity.* What is the "right" thing for human beings to do, on the basis of the above assumptions about reality, the environment, and human nature: to be active, passive, self-developmental, fatalistic, or what? What is work and what is play?
5. *The Nature of Human Relationships.* What is considered to be the "right" way for people to relate to each other, to distribute power and love? Is life cooperative or competitive; individualistic, group collaborative, or communal; based on traditional lineal authority, law, charisma, or what?

Source: Edgar H. Schein, *Organizational Culture and Leadership* (San Francisco: Jossey-Bass, 1985), p. 86.

FIGURE 12-5 HOW SHARED THINGS, SAYINGS, ACTIONS, AND FEELINGS SUGGEST SHARED CULTURAL UNDERSTANDINGS

Shared Things

1. Shirt sleeves.
2. One-company town.
3. Open offices.

Shared Sayings

4. "Get out there" to understand the customer. (Belief in travel)
5. "We cannot rely on systems" to meet customer needs. (Highly responsive customer service)
6. "We don't stand on rank." (No parking privileges)

Shared Actions

7. Participate in lots of meetings.
8. Make sure organization is detail-oriented to provide quality customer service.
9. Engage in personal relationships and communications.
10. Rally to meet customer needs in a crisis.
11. Expedite jobs to deliver highly responsive service.
12. Maintain close relationship with union.

Shared Feelings

13. The company is good to me.
14. We like this place.
15. We care about this company because it cares about us as individuals.

Shared Cultural Understandings

A. Provide highly responsive, quality customer service (4, 8, 11).
B. Get things done well and quickly ("expediting") (4, 7, 10, 11).
C. Operate informally (1, 6, 9, 12).
D. Perceive company as part of the family (2, 12, 13, 14, 15).
E. Encorage constructive disagreement (3, 7).

Source: Adapted from Vijay Sathe, "Implications of Corporate Culture: A Manager's Guide to Action," *Organizational Dynamics* 12, no. 2 (Autumn 1983):9.

A strong, widely recognized corporate culture is frequently cited as a reason for the success of such companies as IBM and Procter & Gamble. The ceremonies, rewards, decor, and other symbolic forms of communication found in such a company as Mary Kay Cosmetics have established a corporate culture that guides the actions of organization members. Apple Computer, a company that grew relatively quickly to eminence in its industry, worked hard to maintain the informality and personal relationships characteristic of a small company, even positioning itself in its marketing as the small-company alternative to IBM and other industry giants. Hewlett-Packard (see the Illustrative Case Study for Chapter 9) maintains a culture built on the principles of its founders, while Tandem Computers emphasizes a culture of employee-centered incentives; 3M gears its corporate culture toward innovation.

HERE'S AN EXAMPLE

The 183-page report on the status of the Federal Aviation Administration issued in 1988 says that airline executives when asked for the basis of management decisions cite "safety comes first." However, the report goes on to say that this universal answer masks wide variances in airline corporate cultures and operating procedures. (*Springfield News-Leader*, 7/28/88, p. 6B)

HERE'S AN EXAMPLE

Philip Cantelon, President of History Associates, a company devoted to writing history, says that about half of its work is writing corporate and government histories. Says Cantelon, ". . . sophisticated organizations use history for planning—to find out why some problems keep recurring." (*New York Times*, 5/29/88, p. F13)

COORDINATED RESOURCE

A good description of some of the problems encountered in changing culture can be found in "Motivate or Alienate? Firms Hire Gurus to Change Their 'Cultures,'" *Wall Street Journal*, 7/24/87, p. 19.

CLASS COMMENT

Most programs to transform corporate cultures share a common, simple goal: to increase productivity by converting worker apathy into corporate allegiance. (*Wall Street Journal*, 7/24/87, p. 19)

A company's predominant culture may change quite rapidly, or be forced by competition into change. For example, in the U.S. banking industry, pressures unleashed by deregulation have produced a marked change in attitude among established banks from what one banker called "the old bureaucratic 'your books balance at the end of the day' culture" to a culture that is more entrepreneurial, more oriented to sales and attuned to competition.[27] Peters and Waterman (see Chapter 1) make the point that companies with strong cultures that are focuses externally—that is, centered on service to the customer—may, in fact, be more sensitive to environmental changes and more quickly able to adapt to them than companies without strong cultures.[28]

As Sathe has shown, the durability and efficiency of culture is both an asset and a liability for an organization. A smart manager must learn when to stop perpetuating a culture that is unresponsive to the needs of a business. Changing corporate culture is not easy, however. Culture emerges out of the actions of organization members and the relationships which they sustain over time. In many ways, culture resembles the well-worn sports metaphor of "momentum." Many a sports announcer, especially in football, analyzes the action in terms of which team has the momentum. Momentum, however, is not a useful concept for coaches. They cannot simply order the players to "go out there and get the momentum." Rather they must prepare a detailed plan of action, spelling out a series of plays and instructing each member of the team how to maneuver on the field. The team gains the momentum by executing this plan.

In the same way, any efforts to change organizational culture must focus on what people do. If a manager can get the organization's members to behave differently, cultural change will follow. Take, for example, a company that, after a long history of minimal competition, wished to become more marketing oriented. Several years of memos, conferences, speeches, and videotapes preaching a new culture had no effect. It was only when senior executives acted, in this case simply by talking more to customers, that a new marketing orientation emerged. Programs to change the culture of an organization must be rooted in concrete behaviors and routine actions.

In Chapter 8, we briefly discussed the Seven-S approach to organizational effectiveness. This approach is often used to understand corporate culture because its focus on "superordinate goals," skills, staff, and style is one means of taking a broad look at a number of factors in organizational culture. These so-called "soft-Ss," as opposed to the "hard-Ss" of strategy, structure, and systems, provide additional levers for change. Changes in the amount of time and attention spent on certain tasks can influence the form in which cultural change will emerge. The attractiveness of the Seven-S approach lies in the fact that, because each "S" must operate in concert with the others, there are seven different ways in which to initiate a program of cultural change.

---

[27]Raoul D. Edwards et al., "Marketing in a Deregulated Environment," *U.S. Banker* 95, no. 4 (April 1984):34–36ff.

[28]Peters and Waterman, *In Search of Excellence*, pp. 77–78; Ralph H. Kilmann, Mary J. Saxton, and Roy Serpa, eds., *Gaining Control of the Corporate Culture* (San Francisco: Jossey-Bass, 1985).

ILLUSTRATIVE CASE STUDY Wrap-Up

Organizational Trauma and Triumph at AT&T

Managers at AT&T and other large companies often talk about the "culture" of the organization, and it is clear that great changes have occurred in AT&T's cultures. The shared belief of lifetime employment and stability has gone by the wayside, perhaps never to return. But in focusing on culture and change, we must also remember that every social system possesses some constants. If there are no forces for stability, then change will have no center point—no place from which to identify specific goals and the tools necessary to attain them. The challenge for Robert Allen of AT&T is to articulate clearly the future direction of AT&T and to be both patient and impatient as the company undertakes the necessary steps to develop in a controlled manner and according to the well-coordinated implementation of goal-oriented strategy. ■

SUMMARY

Organizational change is bound to occur, given the variety of forces for change that exist both within and outside of an organization. There are two constructive ways that managers can deal with change: react to it and plan for it. The former approach is appropriate for the day-to-day decisions a manager must make. The latter approach is necessary when a major part or all of the organization needs to change. An outside change agent can be particularly valuable to managers in planned change programs.

Kurt Lewin developed a three-step model of planned change: (1) ''unfreezing'' the present behavior pattern; (2) changing,'' or developing a new behavior pattern; and (3) ''refreezing'' the new behavior pattern. This model recognizes that many organizations and individuals are not ready for change. Pressures for equilibrium or stability may counteract those for change.

Resistance to change may be based on uncertainty about its causes and effects, unwillingness to give up existing benefits, and awareness of weaknesses in the proposed change. Much of the resistance can be overcome by including subordinates in change decisions.

Organizational change can involve structure, technology, and/or people. Structural changes may be made by application of classical management principles, decentralization, or changes in work flow. Technological changes may require redesign of work operations. Technostructural changes combine technological and structural elements. People changes attempt to improve the attitudes, skills, and knowledge of organization members.

Many of the efforts to change people are referred to as organizational development (OD) techniques. OD applies the principles of behavioral science to improve the effectiveness of individuals, groups, or the entire organization. Survey feedback techniques employ attitude and other surveys and systematically report the results as a basis for change. Team building is aimed at improving group effectiveness by improving task performance and relationships between team members.

Organizational culture, the shared understandings—norms, values, attitudes, and beliefs—of an organization, can foster or impede change.

REVIEW QUESTIONS

1. What are some external and internal sources of change in organizations?
2. What are some nonconstructive responses to change pressures? Can you think of some examples of these nonconstructive responses in any of our society's political, business, or not-for-profit organizations?
3. What are the two major approaches managers use to deal with change? When is each approach likely to be used?
4. What were the two major obstacles to change noted by Lewin? According to the model developed by Lewin and elaborated by Schein, what are the two mechanisms through which individuals learn new attitudes?

5. What are the three categories of resistance to change? Which type of resistance should be encouraged? How may resistance to change be overcome?
6. What are the three structural approaches to change?
7. What do technostructural approaches to change attempt to do? Why were these approaches to change developed? What are some approaches to technostructural change?
8. How does the assumption underlying the people approach to change differ from the assumption underlying the structural and technical approaches?
9. What is a good working definition of OD?
10. What assumptions about people do most OD practitioners make? Do you also hold these assumptions?
11. What are the values upon which OD is based? Which of these values do you share?
12. What are three widely used OD techniques?
13. According to French and Bell, what conditions are required for a successful OD program?
14. What is organizational culture? How does it affect an organization's ability to change?
15. How can the Seven-S model be used to understand cultural change?

CASE STUDY Undergoing Change at the Digital Equipment Corporation

From its beginning in 1957, Digital Equipment Corporation has distinguished itself as the premier manufacturer of computers that can be run by people who are not engineers. When President Kenneth Olsen, along with Harlan Anderson and Stan Olsen, started DEC in an old woolen mill in Maynard, Massachusetts, it was with a legacy of research and management ideals brought over from their experiences at the Massachusetts Institute of Technology. What they wanted to do was produce transistor computers, and they wanted to do it by following the pattern of MIT's organization: a "very generous, very trusting, and very challenging environment." Given a loan of $70,000, the three set up shop over a furniture store in the mill building, learned the necessary manufacturing processes, and did the photographic work and circuit printing themselves, regularly spilling ink into the furniture store located beneath them.

In order to overcome the academic researcher's prejudice against manufacturing, the company called itself a designer and manufacturer of computers. DEC avoided military contracts to focus on the civilian market. It also favored the development of a surplus of managers as well as the development of a large array of products, feeling that both tactics forestalled problems.

Until MIT's Jay Forrester and Bob Everett designed one, the computing world was forced to rely on IBM for the computer batch-processing of cards. DEC adopted the concept of a simpler, more easily used machine and based its strategy on that concept.

Digital's mainstay has been its VAX computers, which can talk with a variety of desktop computers and share the same software. DEC's Ethernet network allows linkage of non-DEC computers to DECs VAX minicomputers. The company has an internal communications network called Easynet, which links 341 locations in 26 countries. While some of what DEC employees communicate to one another is British cricket scores, it also allows 75,000 of DEC's 118,000 employees to contact CEO Kenneth Olsen directly, erasing convoluted lines of communication that most companies would preserve intact. But the main advantage to the network system is the time savings it affords the company, whether the savings is in manufacturing time, in ordering from the on-line catalog, or in the exchange of design work and product information. While networking has been a driving force at DEC, the firm has also agreed to address a longstanding need for a software product that links Apple's Macintosh computer with DEC's VAXes. Digital estimates that 40 percent of its customers have Macintoshes.

Until recently, Digital had the reputation of being insensitive to user needs, of being spoiled by success and arrogant. Following a rapid growth and expansion both the United States and abroad, with annual growth rates of 30 percent during its salad days, DEC's fortunes took a dive in the late 1970s, and by its twenty-fifth anniversary in 1982, Ken Olsen was acknowledging the effects of the tough times on the company's outlook and acturties.

Digital's reorganization in 1982 and 1983 resulted in a renewal program which featured a reexamination of its values and attitudes. The management discovered that the company had a good head for selling but not one for customer service. It realized that the entrepreneurial spirit with which DEC had begun had been lost. In order to go after the competition, DEC had to regain its excitement, its spirit, and its values. The company was reorganized into product lines and service groups for those lines. A sense of responsibility was engendered whereby managers—most of them moving up from the manufacturing, sales, and service departments—were given charge of their own budgets and made responsible for total product development. Profits suddenly rose in response to this decentralization. The essential conservatism of the company was matched with its resourcefulness, and the resultant galvanizing of its service mentality has been gratifying to DEC's customers as well as to its management.

Digital's salespeople are now more concerned with customer problems and not just sales; they will find another customer with a similar situation to serve as a reference. Most customers refer to the willingness to listen as the factor that distinguishes DEC's new attitude from its old one. The company that used to sell engineering solutions and technology is now bringing in applications or networking specialists as well as consultants to assist clients with problem solving.

To meet the competition coming in from small companies as well as large ones, DEC has recruited people from IBM in the hopes of altering its culture. Although President Olsen disparages such up-and-coming technical advances as reduced instruction-set computing, or RISC, it is clear that such technological changes are presenting a threat to DEC. Whether the internal "corrections" effected at DEC can meet the challenge of a rapidly changing market will be something that rival IBM and the other computer producers will be watching carefully.

Sources: Kenneth E. Olsen, *Digital Equipment Corporation: The First Twenty-Five Years* (New York: Newcomen Society in North America, 1983); and Leslie Helm with John W. Verity, Geoff Lewis, Thane Peterson, and Jonathan B. Levine, "What Next for Digital?" *Business Week,* May 16, 1988, pp. 88–92, 96. This case was written by Patricia Bennett and R. Edward Freeman.

Case Questions

1. Describe the culture at DEC. To what extent does the proliferation of networks and open network technology influence employee behavior?
2. What are the central issues of change at DEC?
3. What advice would you give to Mr. Olsen? ■

Paul Klee, *Scheidung Abends (Separated at Night)*, 1922. Watercolor. 33.5 x 23.5 cm.

13

MANAGING ORGANIZATIONAL CONFLICT AND CREATIVITY

Upon completing this chapter you should be able to:

1. Identify two views of organizational conflict.
2. Distinguish between functional and dysfunctional conflict.
3. Describe the sources of the various types of conflict.
4. Identify the consequences of organizational conflict.
5. Describe the sources of and approaches to line-staff and management-labor conflict.
6. Identify and describe methods for stimulating, reducing, and resolving conflict.
7. Describe the creative process in organizations.
8. Explain how creativity can be stimulated and encouraged in organizations.

Chapter Outline

Introduction
Conflict, Competition, and Cooperation
Changing Views of Conflict
Dynamics and Consequences of Organizational Conflict
Methods for Managing Conflict
Line and Staff Conflict
Management-Labor Conflict
Managing Organizational Creativity and Innovation

ILLUSTRATIVE CASE STUDY
Introduction

Conflict and Compromise at the Adolph Coors Company

In the mid-1970s, the Coors brewing company, located in Golden, Colorado, enjoyed a booming business. Coors Beer, "Brewed with Rocky Mountain Spring Water," was increasingly popular in the western United States, particularly among college students. Total company profits in 1977 exceeded $67 million, and the company's share of the large California market was 40 percent.

However, in April 1977 workers at the brewery struck when negotiations over union seniority rights collapsed. Following the walkout, the local union appealed to the AFL-CIO for a nationwide boycott of Coors beer as a demonstration of support for the local union. For no less than the next decade, a bitter struggle between Coors' union activists and its family owners escalated to national prominence and came to symbolize the state of management-union conflict in the United States.

The Coors workers, supported by fellow unions, claimed that Coors ownership was blatantly antiunion. The boycott sought to pressure Coors either to readmit the union as a bargaining agent for its employees or, at the very least, to remain neutral in any future organizing efforts. The support that the AFL-CIO received from other unions, notably the National Education Association, also contributed to its success. Claiming that Coors discriminated against minorities, the union was able to achieve much wider support and set off secondary boycotts, some of which are still in effect.

For its part, the company refused to promise neutrality in any union representation contest. Bill Coors, speaking for management, stated the firm's position when he announced: "If you give neutrality, you sell the farm." Coors fought hard against the threat of union activity, and in the end, the boycott hurt both the union and the company. In 1978, the company managed to have the local union decertified, and most of the striking workers were forced to return to their jobs. However, the continuing boycott hurt the company's beer sales and income—by 1987, profits fell to $44.7 million, and the company's California market share had plunged to 14 percent.

In early 1986, negotiations to end the boycott began between company management and the AFL-CIO. For two years talks continued, punctuated by long absences of parties at the bargaining table and prolonged disagreements. Finally, in August 1987, a complex settlement was reached whereby the company agreed not to conduct an antiunion campaign and accepted union contractors at a packaging facility under construction. In return, the union agreed to end the boycott. Both sides emerged from the agreement ready to move on. Peter Coors, president of the company, focused on the post-boycott marketing challenge. "We have a generation of attitudes about our company that will be hard to change," he has acknowledged since he and his brother Jeffrey took over effective control of the company from their great-grandfather, its founder, in 1985.

In some respects, the settlement between Coors and the AFL-CIO reflects changing times as much as changing attitudes on both sides. Over the 10 years of the boycott, the union movement in the United States has lost power, and some analysts speculate that union influence over labor is coming to an end. At the same time, Peter Coors represents a new generation of management. Although his father and uncle were running the company in 1977 when the problem began, Peter Coors played a major role in the negotiations that ended the struggle when sides expressed a practical willingness to compromise.

Source: Jonathan Tasini, "The Beer and the Boycott," *New York Times Magazine,* January 31, 1988, pp. 18–21, 28–29; Sandra D. Atchinson, "Will Labor's Joe Sixpack Come Back to Coors?" *Business Week,* September 7, 1987, p. 29; "Coors Beer: What Hit Us?" *Forbes,* October 16, 1978, pp. 71, 73; "Coors Undercuts Its Last Big Union," *Business Week,* July 24, 1978, pp. 47–48.

In this chapter we will discuss how conflict can be managed effectively in organizations and how innovation and creativity can be encouraged. As we discuss conflict and creativity, we will see that the two are frequently connected. Too much or too little conflict can inhibit creativity. Poorly managed conflict can do the same. But when conflict is well managed, problems can be resolved effectively, and the solutions are more likely to be fresh and innovative.

CONFLICT, COMPETITION, AND COOPERATION

The subject of conflict has been confused by different definitions and conceptions of the term. We will define conflict in a way that will allow us to discuss its constructive, functional aspects.

organizational conflict Disagreement between individuals or groups within the organization stemming from the need to share scarce resources or engage in interdependent work activities, or from differences in status, goals, or cultures. See also dysfunctional and functional conflict.

Organizational conflict is a disagreement between two or more organization members or groups arising from the fact that they must engage in interdependent work activities and/or from the fact that they have different statuses, goals, values, or perceptions. Organization members or subunits in disagreement attempt to have their own cause or point of view prevail over that of others.

This definition is intentionally broad. It does not specify how severe the disagreement is, in what manner the conflicting parties seek to prevail, how the conflict is managed, or what the outcomes are. In each case, these factors determine whether the conflict is functional or dysfunctional for the organization and to what extent.

FOR DISCUSSION

Under what conditions should a manager promote competition among employees?

One of the many semantic difficulties relating to organizational conflict is the distinction between conflict and competition. We can distinguish between these concepts on the basis of whether one party is able to keep the other from attaining its goals. **Competition** exists when the goals of the parties involved are incompatible but the parties cannot interfere with each other. For example, two production teams may compete with each other to be the first to meet a quota. (Obviously, both teams cannot come in first.) If there is no opportunity to interfere with the other party's goal attainment, a competitive situation exists; however, if the opportunity for interference exists and if that opportunity is acted upon, then the situation is one of conflict.

competition The situation in which two or more parties are striving toward mutually incompatible goals but cannot interfere with each other.

cooperation The process of working together to attain mutual objectives.

Cooperation occurs when two or more parties work together to achieve mutual goals. It is possible for conflict and cooperation to coexist. The opposite of cooperation is not conflict but lack of cooperation. For example, two parties may agree on goals but disagree strongly on how to attain those goals. When we speak of managing conflict, we mean that managers should try to find ways to balance conflict and cooperation.

CHANGING VIEWS OF CONFLICT

Attitudes toward conflict in organizations have changed considerably in the last 30 years. Stephen P. Robbins has traced this evolution, emphasizing the difference between the traditional view of conflict and the current one, which he calls the *interactionist* view.[1]

[1] Stephen P. Robbins, *Managing Organizational Conflict* (Englewood Cliffs, N.J.: Prentice Hall, 1974).

The Traditional View. The *traditional* view of conflict was that it was unnecessary and harmful. Early managers and management writers generally thought that the appearance of conflict was a clear signal that there was something wrong with the organization. They believed that conflict would develop only if managers failed to apply sound management principles in directing the organization or if managers failed to communicate to employees the common interests that bind management and employees together. If these failures were corrected, according to the traditional view, the organization should operate as a smoothly functioning, integrated whole. For example, Frederick Taylor believed that if the principles of scientific management were applied, the age-old conflict between labor and management would disappear.

FOR DISCUSSION

What common interests are held by employers and employees? What conflicting interests?

The Interactionist View. The traditional view of conflict started to change as behavioral science researchers and management writers began to identify causes of organizational conflict independent of management error and as the advantages of effectively managed conflict started to be recognized.

The current or *interactionist* view is that conflict in organizations is inevitable and even necessary, no matter how organizations are designed and operated. This view still suggests that much conflict is, in fact, dysfunctional; it can harm individuals and impede the attainment of organizational goals. But some conflict can also be functional because it may make organizations more effective. Conflict can lead to a search for solutions. Thus, it is often an instrument of organizational innovation and change. (See Table 13–1.)

From this perspective, the task of managers is not to suppress or resolve all conflict but to manage it, so as to minimize its harmful aspects and maximize its beneficial aspects.[2] Such management may even include the stimulation of conflict in situations where its absence or suppression (as in our chapter opening example) may hamper the organization's effectiveness, creativity, or innovation.

Functional and Dysfunctional Conflict

EXTRA EXERCISE

Have students think of and describe a personal situation in which conflict was a positive factor.

Conflict, as we have defined it, is inherently neither functional nor dysfunctional. It simply has the potential for improving or impairing organizational performance, depending on how it is managed. For example, managers in a company may be in conflict

[2]See M. Afzalur Rahim, "A Strategy for Managing Conflict in Complex Organizations," *Human Relations* 38, no. 1 (January 1985):81–89.

TABLE 13-1 OLD AND CURRENT VIEWS OF CONFLICT

OLD VIEW	CURRENT VIEW
Conflict is avoidable.	Conflict is inevitable.
Conflict is caused by management errors in designing and managing organizations of by troublemakers.	Conflict arises from many causes, including organizational structure, unavoidable differences in goals, differences in perceptions and values of specialized personnel, and so on.
Conflict disrupts the organization and prevents optimal performance.	Conflict contributes to and detracts from organizational performance in varying degrees.
The task of management is to eliminate conflict.	The task of management is to manage the level of conflict and its resolution for optimal organizational performance.
Optimal organizational performance requires the removal of conflict.	Optimal organizational performance requires a moderate level of conflict.

over how the annual budget is to be divided among their divisions. Properly handled, such conflict could lead to new sharing arrangements that might benefit the entire organization. For instance, more money might be allocated to the divisions in the fastest-growing markets. (In such a case, the managers who would receive less money than usual might feel that the conflict was dysfunctional, but, overall, the organization would benefit.) Other functional outcomes might be that (1) the managers find a way to use the money they receive more effectively, (2) they find a better way to cut down on expenses, or (3) they improve the whole unit's performance so that additional funds become available to all of them. It is also possible, however, that the outcome of the conflict will be dysfunctional. For example, cooperation between the managers may break down, making it difficult to coordinate the organization's activities.

The relationship between organizational conflict and performance is illustrated in Figure 13-1. There is an optimal, highly functional level of conflict at which performance is at a maximum. When the level of conflict is too low, the organization changes too slowly to meet the new demands being made upon it, and its survival is threatened. When the level of conflict is too high, chaos and disruption also endanger the organization's chances for survival.

Types of Conflict. There are six types of conflict possible in organizational life:

EXTRA EXERCISE

Have students think of examples of how an individual could be in conflict with (a) himself or herself, (b) another person, (c) another group, (d) an organization.

1. *Conflict within the individual* occurs when an individual is uncertain about what work he or she is expected to perform, when some demands of the work conflict with other demands, or when the individual is expected to do more than he or she feels capable of doing. This type of conflict often influences how an individual responds to other types of organizational conflict. (We will discuss this type of conflict in more detail in Chapter 23.)
2. *Conflict among individuals* in the same organization is frequently seen as being caused by personality differences. More often, such conflicts erupt from role-related pressures (as between managers and subordinates) or from the manner in which people personalize conflict between groups.
3. *Conflict among individuals and groups* is frequently related to the way individuals deal with the pressures for conformity imposed on them by their work group. For example, an individual may be punished by his or her work group for exceeding or falling behind the group's productivity norms.
4. *Conflict among groups in the same organization* is the type of conflict with which we will be most concerned in this chapter. Line-staff and labor-management conflicts, discussed shortly, are two common areas of intergroup conflict.

FIGURE 13-1 ORGANIZATIONAL CONFLICT AND ORGANIZATIONAL PERFORMANCE

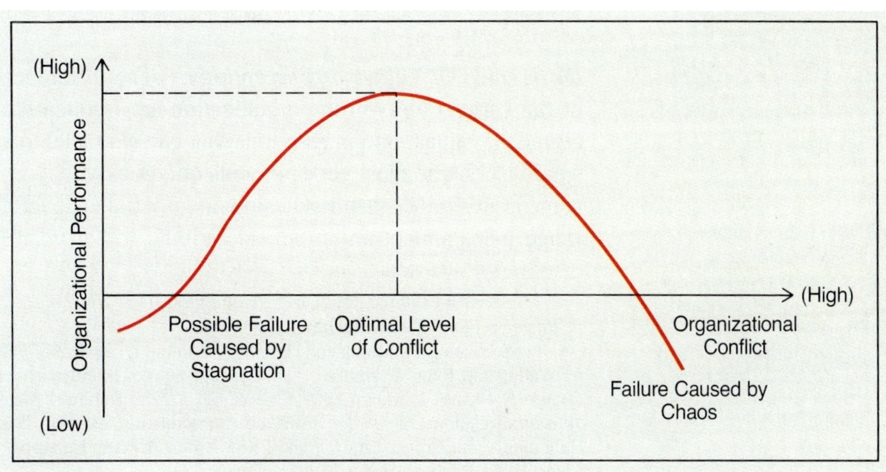

5. *Conflict among organizations* in the economic sphere has been considered an inherent and desirable form of conflict in the United States and many other countries; usually this type of conflict is called competition. Such conflict has been recognized to lead to the development of new products, technologies, and services; lower prices; and more efficient utilization of resources.[3] Government laws and regulatory agencies attempt to promote functional conflict (through antitrust legislation, for example) and manage the dysfunctional aspects of such conflict (such as false advertising and industrial espionage). One controversial trend of the 1980s has been to deregulate heavily regulated industries (airlines, banks, and railroads, for example) to spur economic competition in those industries.
6. *Conflict among individuals in different organizations* happens more and more today. Take, for example, a newspaper that regularly reports on a local company. Sooner or later, the company's public relations manager will probably come into conflict with the manager of the newspaper.

Sources of Organizational Conflict

QUOTATION FROM A MANAGER

"I've never seen one press article in my business career about a CEO who took a company through restructuring who was described as easygoing and affable."—John J. Nevin, Chairman of Firestone Tire and Rubber Company (*Fortune*, 4/25/88, p. 16)

The sources of organizational conflict discussed here are related most clearly to intergroup conflict. However, they also apply to conflict between individuals and between individuals and groups. The major sources of organizational conflict include the need to share scarce resources, differences in goals between organization units, the interdependence of work activities in the organization, and differences in values or perceptions among organization units.[4]

Shared Resources. If every unit in an organization had access to unlimited workers, money, materials, equipment, and space, the problem of how to share these resources would hardly arise. The potential for conflict exists because these vital resources are limited. They must be allocated, so some groups inevitably will get less than they want or need.

Differences in Goals. As we have seen, organization subunits tend to become specialized or differentiated as they develop dissimilar goals, tasks, and personnel. Such differentiation frequently leads to conflicts of interest or priorities, even when the overall goals of the organization are agreed upon. The sales department, for example, might want low prices to attract more customers, while the production department might want higher prices to meet manufacturing costs.

Interdependence of Work Activities. Work interdependence exists when two or more subunits depend on each other to complete their respective tasks. In such a case, the potential for a high degree of conflict or cooperation exists, depending on how the situation is managed.

HERE'S AN EXAMPLE

Ford Motor Company workers in Britain, set to strike during February of 1988, illustrate the growing assertiveness of rank-and-file workers. Union leaders, in a more conciliatory mood, had approved the company's latest offer. However, as one expert noted, "The union leaders aren't particularly in touch with their members." (*Wall Street Journal*, 2/8/88, p. 2)

Differences in Values or Perceptions. The differences in goals among the members of the various units in the organization are frequently accompanied by differences in attitudes, values, and perceptions that can also lead to conflict. For example, first-line supervisors who must get shipments out quickly may give in to union shop stewards on some issues rather than risk a slowdown. Higher-level managers, concerned with long-range management-union considerations, might want to avoid setting precedents on

[3]See, for example, William E. Rothschild, *How to Gain (and Maintain) the Competitive Advantage in Business* (New York: McGraw-Hill, 1984).

[4]See James G. March and Herbert A. Simon, *Organizations* (New York: John Wiley, 1958); Richard E. Walton and John M. Dutton, "The Management of Interdepartmental Conflict," *Administrative Science Quarterly* 14, no. 1 (March 1969):73–84; M. Afzalur Rahim, "Measurement of Organizational Conflict," *Journal of General Psychology* 109, no. 2 (October 1983):189–199; and Walter G. Stephan, "Intergroup Relations," in Gardner Lindzey and Elliot Aronson, eds., *Handbook of Social Psychology*, Vol. 2, 3rd ed. (New York: Random House, 1985), Chapter 11.

those issues and may try to restrict the flexibility of first-line supervisors. Members of the engineering department might value quality products, sophisticated design, and durability, while members of the manufacturing department might value simplicity of design and low manufacturing costs. Such incompatibility of values can lead to conflict. (''It is too expensive to do it your way.'' ''But we'll lose our reputation for quality if we do it your way.'')

Individual Styles and Organizational Ambiguities. Some individuals escalate conflicts, debates, and arguments into full-scale battles. People who are highly authoritarian, for example, or low in self-esteem may frequently anger their colleagues by overreacting to mild disagreements. Intergroup conflict is most likely when group members differ markedly in such characteristics as work attitudes, age, and education.

Intergroup conflict can also result from ambiguously defined work responsibilities and unclear goals. One manager may try to expand the role of his or her subunit; this effort will usually stimulate other managers to ''defend their turf.'' Also, if members of different groups know little about each other's jobs, they may unwittingly make unreasonable demands on each other. These demands may, in turn, trigger conflict.

Ambiguous communications can also cause intergroup conflict. In one case, when the management of a large mining corporation modernized its equipment, the union was told that no employees would lose their jobs. A few months later, when a group of former rock crushers were transferred to warehouse jobs, the union struck. It had interpreted ''job'' to mean ''task responsibility,'' whereas management had used ''job'' to mean ''employment.''

DYNAMICS AND CONSEQUENCES OF ORGANIZATIONAL CONFLICT

THOUGHT-PROVOKER

There may be an optimum level of conflict that should be permitted for the good of the organization. How can a manager define this optimum level?

Despite their diverse sources, controversies in organizations develop in remarkably similar ways. Research by Muzafer and Carolyn Sherif and their colleagues has shown how conflict affects the opposing groups. (See the Management Application on ''Intergroup Conflict at Robber's Cave.'') If the conflict is badly managed, the specific issue that led to the conflict may give way to more general issues. (''Not only do I disagree with what you propose to do in this case, but I think your entire approach is wrong.'') As the conflict intensifies, new issues often unrelated to the initial problem are brought up. Subjects that had been suppressed are brought to the surface and new issues are raised to convince those as yet uncommitted to join the fray (''While I'm at it, I might as well tell you . . . '').

Once started, a conflict can continue even after the original issue has been resolved. What begins as a disagreement on a single point may end in mutual dislike because of our tendency to seek consistency in our attitudes; we want to see people as either entirely good or entirely bad.

Once the conflict is over, there are different consequences for winners and losers.[5] Leaders of the winning group normally strengthen their hold over the group. Winners may rest on their laurels, resisting any change in their ways of doing things.[6] Conversely, defeated groups tend to split into factions as old leaders are challenged by new aspirants to leadership. Losers also become more amenable to new ways of behaving and operating. For both winners and losers, the negative stereotypes engendered by win-lose conflict can become so severe as to make future intergroup cooperation extremely difficult.

---

[5]See, for example, Robert R. Blake and Jane S. Mouton, ''Reactions to Intergroup Conflict Under Win-Lose Conditions,'' *Management Science* 7, no. 4 (July 1961):420–435.

[6]For a discussion of how the dysfunctional consequences of winning had to be overcome to create the Boston Celtics basketball ''dynasty,'' see Bill Russell and Taylor Branch, *Second Wind* (New York: Random House, 1979), pp. 119–170.

MANAGEMENT APPLICATION

INTERGROUP CONFLICT AT ROBBER'S CAVE

In a classic study of intergroup conflict, Muzafer and Carolyn Sherif and their colleagues arbitrarily divided 11- and 12-year-old boys attending a summer camp into two groups, the Rattlers and the Eagles. During the first week, the groups were kept apart while they pursued a normal round of camping activities and chose group leaders. The following week, the groups competed in a series of athletic and camping contests. As the rivalry between the two groups intensified, there were name-calling, fights, and raids.

Conflict development. After observing the boys, the researchers concluded that groups placed in a conflict situation change in predictable ways. As a rule, group members put aside former disagreements and pull together. While this cohesion may stimulate the extra effort needed to resolve problems and seize new opportunities, it may also encourage conformity at the expense of creativity and fresh approaches to problems.

Intense conflict spurs the group to give increased power to those individuals—the more aggressive, able, or articulate—who can contribute most to victory. Rivalry for leadership declines, and the group works harder to overcome the "enemy." The group also selects a strong representative to deal with the other side—someone who will not cave in to the pressure exerted by the other group.

Group perceptions are distorted. Group members believe their own skills and performance to be superior, while they rationalize or dismiss their shortcomings. At the same time, they stereotype their competitors' weaknesses. As each side belittles the other, the differences between them appear greater than they actually are. Likewise, the differences within each group appear smaller than they actually are.

The rival groups even lose their ability to think accurately about their respective positions. Strong group identification, heightened by fear of defeat or a "sell-

Less intense conflict can have a more constructive impact. New, more effective leaders may emerge. Modified goals may help the organization adjust to change. And conflict management may become institutionalized so that disagreements can be expressed without damaging the organization. In many organizations, for example, managers freely air their differences in committee meetings but abide by committee decisions once they are made.

Three Factors in Organizational Conflict

functional conflict Any conflict that has positive, constructive, and nondivisive results.

dysfunctional conflict Any conflict that results in decreased efficiency and greater factionalism within the organization.

Three factors determine whether the net result of a given dispute will be a **functional conflict,** one with positive or constructive results, or a **dysfunctional conflict,** one that increases divisiveness or decreases efficiency: the level of conflict, the organizational structure and culture, and—most importantly—the way in which the conflict is managed. We will look briefly at the first two factors and then devote the next section to the third—methods for managing conflict.

The Level of Conflict. Moderate levels of conflict have far greater potential for desirable outcomes than do high levels. With moderate conflict, the rival groups are more likely to learn to interact in constructive, problem-solving ways. As the level of conflict rises, however, so does the temptation to engage in destructive acts toward the rival group. David Mechanic describes a case in a mental hospital where ward atten-out," blinds both sides to the similarities in their proposals that could make a settlement possible.

Conflict reduction. In the third week, after the rivalry between the Rattlers and the Eagles had become disruptive, the researchers experimented with a variety of ways to restore harmony. Their first three methods proved ineffective. When they provided each group with favorable information about the other, the boys rejected it because it contradicted their own negative impressions. When they had the boys eat together and watch movies together, the rivals jostled and shoved each other and called each other names. When they asked the group leaders to negotiate, the leaders were afraid they would be dethroned if they were conciliatory. Even in adult conflicts, agreements worked out between representatives can be limited by members' suspicions that the agreements are sellouts.

The methods that worked involved setting up situations that demanded cooperation and diverted the boys' attention away from the areas of conflict. One approach was to create a superordinate, or superior, goal to take the place of the competitive goals that kept the groups apart. When the boys were told the camp could "not afford" to rent a movie requested by all, the groups joined in a fund-raising drive to pay for it.

A second approach was to unite the group to meet a common "threat" or "enemy." The researchers sabotaged the camp's water supply and disabled the camp truck to force the Rattlers and the Eagles to work together. Neither group could restore the water or tow the truck back for repairs on its own. Such common efforts eventually stimulated cooperation and friendship between the members of the two groups.

Source: Muzafer Sherif, "Experiments in Group Conflict," *Scientific American,* November 1956, pp. 54–58; Muzafer Sherif and Carolyn Sherif, *Groups in Harmony and Tension* (New York: Octagon, 1966); Andrew Tyerman and Christopher Spence, "A Critical Test of the Sherifs' Robber's Cave Experiments: Intergroup Competition and Cooperation Between Groups of Well-Acquainted Individuals," *Small Group Behavior* 14, no. 4 (November 1983):515–531.

HERE'S AN EXAMPLE

Dunlop Holdings PLC, a British tire operation bailed out by Japan's Sumitomo Rubber Industries Ltd., is succeeding under tough conditions. Sumitomo took over a 70-year-old factory with seven feisty unions. Although everything hasn't gone smoothly, Sumitomo persuaded its recalcitrant British workers to accept the needed changes. However, changes were introduced gradually and only after thorough explanation. (*Wall Street Journal,* 3/29/88, p. 26)

HERE'S AN EXAMPLE

Conflict can also occur in creative organizations. The defection of top executives of Lord Geller, a Madison Avenue advertising agency, resulted from a basic clash of its culture and that of its British parent, WPP Group PLC. (*Wall Street Journal,* 3/23/88, p. 1)

dants agreed to take on some of the administrative duties of the ward physicians in exchange for inclusion in the decision-making machinery.[7] When the physicians reneged on their part of the agreement, conflict escalated until the attendants disobeyed orders and deliberately withheld information essential to the physicians. Such high levels of conflict are almost always destructive to the organization.

Organizational Structure and Culture. Conflict can call attention to the problem areas of an organization and can lead to more effective achievement of organizational goals. However, if an organization rigidly resists change, the conflict situations may never be relieved. Tensions will continue to mount, and each new conflict will split organization subunits farther apart. In general, the more rigid the structure and culture of the organization, the less beneficial conflict is likely to be.

Unresolved conflict can also adversely affect informally structured organizations, where subunits depend a great deal on each other for information (rather than receiving most of their information from higher up). In a conflict situation, communication between subunits can break down, leaving each subunit unable to reach sound decisions.[8]

---

[7]David Mechanic, "Sources of Power of Lower Participants in Complex Organizations," *Administrative Science Quarterly* 7, no. 3 (December 1961):349–364.

[8]See Joseph A. Litterer, "Conflict in Organization: A Re-examination," *Academy of Management Journal* 9, no. 3 (September 1966):178–186; and Robert H. Miles, *Macro Organizational Behavior* (Santa Monica, Calif.: Goodyear, 1980), Chapter 5.

ILLUSTRATIVE CASE STUDY Continued

Conflict and Compromise at the Adolph Coors Company

The Coors boycott is a prime example of how conflict can be nonproductive and uncreative. Instead of illustrating the uses of the boycott as a means of negotiating a new understanding between management and labor, the management-labor conflict at Coors eventually highlighted larger issues which have always plagued such relations and which threaten to continue to do so. Organizational conflict gave way to both larger social issues and political agendas resulting in a long, drawn-out affair that was costly to both sides.

Although the issue of worker seniority may appear to be minor, it actually reflects a deep-seated difference in philosophy and values. The union saw Coors' insistence on the "right-to-work" principle as an only mildly disguised antiunion play, and Coors saw the union insistence on a union shop as antibusiness. The original issue of worker seniority got lost in the fray, and one can also detect at work in the Coors controversy many of the elements of competitiveness and conflict that Sherif discovered in her "Robber's Cave" experiments. There was a high degree of cohesion among union members—even to the point of a national boycott—and likewise solidarity on the part of the Coors family and other company executives. The conflict quickly became one of charge and countercharge, and only after extraordinary efforts was it finally resolved.

METHODS FOR MANAGING CONFLICT

In this section we discuss three forms of conflict management: (1) stimulating conflict in units or organizations whose performance is lagging because the level of conflict is too low, (2) reducing or suppressing conflict when its level is too high or counterproductive, and (3) resolving conflict.

Conflict-Stimulation Methods

At Exxon Corp., CEO Lawrence Rawl's healthy disrespect for bureaucracy and straightforward management style—along with a policy for downsizing that had eliminated almost 150,000 jobs by 1988 and redefined another 20,000—have established conflict, uncertainty, and aggressive policy implementation as key factors in the company's rapidly changing culture. Known for stating his opinions without couching them in polite terms that avoid confrontation, Rawl has also required that his top managers practice the same policy.

When Rawl arrived at his position in 1985, he assumed the leadership of a firm that preferred consensus and conciliation as decision-making measures. A self-confessed "rabble-rouser," Rawl cut back on Exxon's maze of sluggish committees that had all too often served to check and balance proposals rather than act on them. Some decision-making processes that once involved 100 people now engage the work of only 35: Rawl reasons that "with a smaller organization . . . it's pretty hard to hide." Like Rawl himself, managers forced to come out of hiding from behind anonymous decisions and reams of accompanying paperwork are apt to offend traditional sensibilities and to engage in productive conflict with other managers equally determined to perform aggressively and decisively.

Not surprisingly, morale at Exxon had dropped noticeably by 1987, but Rawl has managed to emphasize aggressive, immediate decision making by creating a climate of creative dissidence and uncertainty in which, as a corporate value, the resolution of conflict has replaced the time-consuming process of contemplating proposals until a compromise consensus of opinion has been reached. In 1987, Exxon earned profits of

"Wilson is our idea factory."
Drawing by Weber; © 1982 The New Yorker Magazine, Inc.

$4.8 billion on sales of $83 billion (second only to IBM in the U.S.), and its annual profit of $48,400 per employee was five times that of rival Mobil Corp.[9]

Upon first considering the matter, most of us would not identify *conflict* as a typical value in our culture. We have generally been taught since childhood to avoid conflict. "Stop fighting!" we are told, or "It's better to turn the other cheek," or "Why don't you be nice and give in?" However, the tendency in our culture to paper over dissension is not always productive, as Elise Boulding has demonstrated.[10] In an experiment, Boulding formed a series of groups to tackle a problem. Some groups contained a planted member prepared to challenge the majority view; some groups did not. Without fail, those groups that harbored a conflict-stimulator analyzed the problem more perceptively and came up with better solutions than did the others. Yet when the groups were instructed to drop one member, every group that had a planted dissident chose that dissident to be dropped. Such resistance to conflict, in themselves and in others, is one of the obstacles that managers like Lawrence Rawl have to overcome in stimulating productive conflict.

Situations in which conflict is too low generally involve people who are afraid to "rock the boat." Rather than trying to find new and better ways of getting things done, they passively accept things the way they are. Events, behavior, and information that could stir up people to do a better job are ignored; group members tolerate each other's weaknesses and lack of performance. Managers of such groups who become alarmed that their units seem to be drifting often find that stimulating competition and conflict can have a galvanizing effect.[11]

Suggestions for Stimulating Conflict. As we saw in the case of Exxon's Lawrence Rawl, the attitude of top managers is of critical importance in encouraging and controlling conflict. Openly stating that conflict is desirable—"I'd like to see you two take the time to fight these things out between yourselves until you reach a decision you like, rather than just smoothing things over"—will encourage organization members to bring up disagreements they might otherwise suppress. Openly stating the rules of

[9]John A. Byrne, "The Rebel Shaking up Exxon," *Business Week,* July 18, 1988, pp. 104–111; Colin Leinster, "Exxon's Axman Cometh," *Fortune,* April 14, 1988, pp. 92–96.

[10]Elise Boulding, "Further Reflections on Conflict Management," in Robert L. Kahn and Elise Boulding, eds., *Power and Conflict in Organizations* (New York: Basic Books, 1964), pp. 146–150.

[11]See Irving L. Janis, *Groupthink: Psychological Studies of Policy Decisions,* 2nd ed. (Boston: Houghton Mifflin, 1982). For an interesting analysis of how groupthink may have contributed to the *Challenger* disaster, see A. W. Kruglanski, "Freeze-Think and the Challenger," *Psychology Today,* August 1986, pp. 48–49.

conflict—"If you're completely deadlocked, call in a third party for help before you come to me"—will help keep conflict at functional levels.[12] As Exhibit 13-1 shows, the sources of conflict stimulation are numerous and varied.

EXHIBIT 13-1 CONFLICT-STIMULATION METHODS

1. *Bringing in outsiders.* A frequently used method of "shaking up" a stagnant unit or organization is to bring in managers whose backgrounds, values, and styles vary significantly from the norms. Edmund G. Brown, Jr., former governor of California, resorted to this method in 1977 when he put consumer representatives on state regulatory boards, which had long been dominated by individuals connected with the industries being regulated.
2. *Going against the book.* Excluding individuals or groups from communications that they normally receive, or adding new groups to the information network, may redistribute power and thus stimulate conflict. For example, a nursing home administrator concerned about the passivity of his patients provided them with regular information about their own conditions. They then felt more confident about disagreeing with their doctors about their treatment and took a more active role in improving their own health.
3. *Restructuring the organization.* Breaking up old work teams and departments and reorganizing them so that they have new members or responsibilities will create a period of uncertainty and readjustment. Conflict that arises during this period may lead to improved methods of operation as members adjust to new circumstances. A more open climate may also lead to conflict as organization members are encouraged to air their views.
4. *Encouraging competition.* Offering bonuses, incentive pay, and citations for outstanding performance will foster competition. If competition is maintained at a high level, it may lead to productive conflict as groups struggle to outdo each other.
5. *Selecting appropriate managers.* Authoritarian managers who do not allow opposing viewpoints to be raised often make their work groups passive. Other groups may need an active manager to shake them out of their lethargy. Finding the right manager for the particular group can encourage useful conflict where none exists.

Conflict-Reduction Methods

In the study described in the management application, the Sherifs and their colleagues reduced antagonism by diverting attention away from disagreements and by providing shared experiences of successful cooperation. In normal situations, where the conflict has not been artificially created, these conflict-reduction methods may not be as successful. It is harder to divert the groups' attention away from areas of disagreement, and the diversions do not resolve the very real sources of the conflict. Therefore, conflict-reduction methods may be unsatisfying ways of dealing with conflict in organizations. Exhibit 13-2 lists at least three of the conflict-reduction methods that the Sherif team found to be ineffective.

EXHIBIT 13-2 CONFLICT-REDUCTION METHODS

1. They provided each group with favorable information about the other group. However, this information was so at odds with the negative impressions induced by the conflict that the boys rejected it.
2. They increased pleasant social contacts between the groups by having them eat together and watch movies together. But friction increased as the rivals jostled and shoved each other and called each other names.
3. They asked the group leaders to negotiate and provide their respective groups with favorable information about the other. But the leaders felt they might be dethroned if they tried to reconcile their differences. Even in adult intergroup conflict, agreements worked out between representatives can be limited by group members' suspicions that the agreements are "sellouts."

[12]See Dean Tjosvold, "Making Conflict Productive," *Personnel Administrator* 29 (1984):121; and André Delbecq and Peter Mills, "Managerial Practices That Enhance Innovation," *Organizational Dynamics,* Summer 1985, pp. 24–34.

Conflict-Resolution Methods

COORDINATED RESOURCE

For a concise description of dealing with conflict and offering practical insights into conflict management, see *Managing Conflict at Organizational Interfaces* by L. David Brown, Addison-Wesley, 1983.

Our discussion of conflict-resolution methods will focus on actions managers can take to deal directly with the conflicting parties. Other possible methods for resolving conflict include changes in organization structure—so that, for example, conflicting members or units are separated or a grievance agency is set up. In addition, some of the coordinating mechanisms we discussed in Chapter 11—such as liaison individuals and committees—can also be used to resolve conflict.

The three conflict-resolution methods most frequently used for dominance or suppression, compromise, and integrative problem solving. These methods differ in the extent to which they yield effective and creative solutions to conflict. They also differ in the extent to which they leave parties in the conflict able to deal with future conflict situations.

Dominance and Suppression. Dominance and suppression methods usually have two things in common: (1) They repress conflict, rather than settle it, by forcing it underground; and (2) they create a win-lose situation in which the loser, forced to give way to higher authority or greater power, usually winds up disappointed and hostile. Suppression and dominance can occur in the following ways:

Forcing. When the person in authority says, in effect, ''Cut it out—I'm the boss and you've got to do it my way,'' argument is snuffed out. Such autocratic suppression may lead to indirect but nonetheless destructive expressions of conflict, such as malicious obedience. When, for example, a supervisor suggested delaying a shipment until a quality audit could identify suspected deficiencies, the production manager snapped: ''Keep your nose out of things until I tell you otherwise.'' A few mornings later, when a cutting machine broke down in the supervisor's unit, machine and operator spent an idle day before the production manager found out about it. ''Why didn't you call the maintenance crew?'' the manager asked the supervisor. ''You told me to keep my nose out of things until I heard from you,'' the subordinate shot back. Malicious obedience is merely one of many forms of conflict that can fester where conflict suppression is the rule.

Smoothing. In smoothing, a more diplomatic way of suppressing conflict, the manager minimizes the extent and importance of the disagreement and tries to talk one side into giving in. Where the manager has more information than the other parties and is making a reasonable suggestion, this method can be effective. But if the manager is seen as favoring one side or failing to understand the issue, the losing side is likely to feel resentful.

Avoidance. If quarreling groups come to a manager for a decision but the manager avoids taking a position, no one is likely to be satisfied. Pretending to be unaware that conflict exists is a frequent form of avoidance. Another form is refusal to deal with conflict by stalling and repeatedly postponing action ''until more information is available.''

Majority rule. Trying to resolve group conflict by a majority vote can be effective if members regard the procedure as fair. But if one voting block consistently outvotes the other, the losing side will feel powerless and frustrated.

Compromise. Through compromise, managers try to resolve conflict by convincing each party in the dispute to sacrifice some objectives in order to gain others. Decisions reached by compromise are not likely to leave conflicting parties feeling frustrated or hostile. From an organizational point of view, however, compromise is a weak conflict-resolution method because it does not usually lead to a solution that can best help the organization achieve its goals. Instead, the solution reached will simply be one that both parties in the conflict can life with.

Forms of compromise include *separation,* in which opposing parties are kept apart until they agree to a solution; **arbitration,** in which conflicting parties submit to the judgment of a third party (usually, but not always, the manager);[13] *settling by chance,* in which some random event such as the toss of a coin determines the outcome; *resort to rules,* in which the deadlocked rivals agree to "go by the book" and let the organization's rules decide the conflict outcome; and *bribing,* in which one party accepts some compensation in exchange for ending the conflict. None of these methods is likely to leave the parties to the conflict fully satisfied or to yield creative solutions.

arbitration A form of compromise in which opposing parties agree to submit to the decision of a third party.

Integrative Problem Solving. With this method, intergroup conflict is converted into a joint problem-solving situation that can be dealt with through problem-solving techniques. Together, parties to the conflict try to solve the problem that has arisen between them. Instead of suppressing conflict or trying to find a compromise, the parties openly try to find a solution they all can accept. Managers who give subordinates the feeling that all members and groups are working together for a common goal, who encourage the free exchange of ideas, and who stress the benefits of finding the optimum solution in a conflict situation are more likely to achieve integrative solutions.

There are three types of integrative conflict-resolution methods: consensus, confrontation, and the use of superordinate goals.

In **consensus,** the conflicting parties meet together to find the best solution to their problem, rather than trying to achieve a victory for either side. Group consensus will often yield a more effective solution than that offered by any one individual. However, it is important to prevent a premature consensus, in which the selected solution reflects the desire to end the conflict quickly instead of finding the *best* solution. The Labatt Brewing Company of Toronto hired a full-time "resident iconoclast" to generate innovation by keeping management flexible and providing ideas alien to the corporate culture.[14] (See Chapter 16 for a detailed discussion of group problem-solving processes.)

consensus A method of conflict resolution in which the parties attempt to find the best solution rather than to achieve a victory over each other.

In **confrontation,** the opposing parties state their respective views directly to each other. The reasons for the conflict are examined and methods of resolving it are sought. With skilled leadership and willingness to accept the associated stress by all sides, a rational solution can frequently be found.

confrontation A method of conflict resolution in which opposing parties, directly stating their views to one another, examine the conflict and seek means of resolving it.

We noted earlier that appeal to a higher-level goal can be an effective conflict-reduction method by distracting the attention of the parties in conflict from their separate and competing goals. The establishment of **superordinate goals** can also be a conflict-resolution method if the higher-level goal that is mutually agreed upon incorporates the conflicting parties' lower-level goals.[15] For example, two academic departments in a university had been engaged in a lengthy and destructive conflict over the relative shares of grants from a university research fund. The animosity continued for years until a group of young faculty members from each department submitted a joint proposal for a large grant from a government agency. When the proposal was accepted, the two departments started to turn their attention to increasing grants from outside agencies and reduced their competition for the university research funds. Striving for a superordinate goal (outside grants) not only resolved the major conflict between the two departments but also fostered *intergroup cohesiveness;* faculty from each discipline exchanged more information and initiated more interdepartmental projects.

superordinate goals Higher-level goals that acknowledge lower-level goals, both encompassing the guiding principles that an organization impresses upon its members and contributing toward cohesive goal-oriented activity among groups whose objectives may not coincide.

---

[13] Blair H. Sheppard, "Third Party Conflict Intervention: A Procedural Framework," in *Research in Organizational Behavior,* Vol. 6 (Greenwich, Conn.: JAI Press, 1984), pp. 141–190.

[14] Shona McKay, "A Boardroom Iconoclast," *McLeans,* September 19, 1983, p. 58. Also see Charles R. Schwenk, "Devil's Advocacy in Managerial Decision-Making," *Journal of Management Studies* 21, no. 2 (April 1984):153–168.

[15] Roy J. Lewicki and Joseph A. Litterer, *Negotiation* (Homewood, Ill.: Richard D. Irwin, 1985), pp. 279–311.

LINE AND STAFF CONFLICT

A common form of organizational conflict is the conflict between line and staff members. Because of its frequency, and because of the importance of achieving effective line-staff collaboration in modern organizations, we will discuss this type of conflict here.

Line and staff members, like members of the other differentiated units in the organization, have different time horizons, goals, interpersonal orientations, and approaches to problems. (See Chapter 9.) These differences enable line and staff members to accomplish their respective tasks effectively, but the differences also increase the potential for conflict between them.[16] (See Table 13-2.)

When Harold Geneen was CEO of ITT, line-staff conflict was actually a key component of his management philosophy: Although line managers enjoyed a high degree of autonomy with regard to operations issues, staff managers were regularly dispatched from headquarters to question performance reports and to serve as auditors. In addition, staff planners and strategists were instructed to pose difficult questions to line managers about their strategies.[17]

Some companies have become increasingly conscious of line-staff conflicts over such issues as funding for new projects and have attempted to ensure smoother operations. For example, in order to overcome the tendency of line managers to resist new ideas, Texas Instruments has established a special fund for innovative projects—virtually any employee can secure funding for an idea that meets certain criteria. By contrast, in order to prevent overly bureaucratic staff from stifling new-product ingenuity, General Electric funds innovations only out of line managers' budgets.

[16]Louis A. Allen, "The Line-Staff Relationship," *Management Record* 17, no. 9 (September 1955):346–349ff.

[17]See Harold Geneen and Alvin Moscow, *Managing* (New York: Doubleday, 1984).

TABLE 13-2 LINE AND STAFF COMPLAINTS

ISSUE	THE VIEW FROM THE LINE	THE VIEW FROM THE STAFF
Authority	Staff often oversteps its authority and intrudes on line prerogatives. Line managers, after all, bear ultimate responsibility for results.	Line gives staff too little authority. Does not support and implement staff suggestions, even though staff often has best solutions to problems in their specialities.
Making innovations	Staff does not give sound advice. Their suggestions may be impractical (because staff is cut off from day-to-day operational realities), or unrelated to the overall needs and goals of the organization (because staff has narrow perspectives).	Line is overly cautious and rigid; resists new ideas. Does not appreciate that staff is usually the first to become aware of useful innovations in their areas of expertise.
Accountability	Staff takes advantage greater access to top managers to take credit and avoid blame.	Line managers resist calling in staff, because they like to retain authority over their subunits and fear admitting they need help. They wait until the situation has completely deteriorated.

Differences in style and other characteristics often exacerbate conflicts between line and staff. For example, Melville Dalton found that staff members tend to be younger, better educated, more ambitious, more individualistic, and more concerned with their dress than are line members.[18] Alvin W. Gouldner has classified organization personnel in terms of what he called "cosmopolitans" and "locals."[19] His two categories correspond roughly to the "staff" and "line" distinction. "Cosmopolitan" staff members are committed to their work for its intrinsic qualities; they are likely to feel closer to specialists in similar activities outside the organization than to other members of their own organizaiton. "Local" line members identify themselves and their career aspirations more closely with their organizations and are less committed to specialized job skills and outside reference groups. Such differences may be seen as "lack of loyalty" by line members and "provincialism" by staff members.

Exhibit 13-3 suggests some of the means by which Edward C. Schleh and other management writers believe that the dysfunctional aspects of line-staff conflict can be reduced.[20]

EXHIBIT 13-3 SOME SUGGESTIONS FOR REDUCING LINE–STAFF CONFLICT

- *Spell out line and staff responsibilities clearly.* In general, line members should remain responsible for the operating decisions of the organization; in other words, they should be free to accept, modify, or reject staff recommendations. On the other hand, staff members should be free to give advice when they feel it is needed—not only when line members request it.
- *Integrate staff and line activities.* Staff suggestions would be more realistically based if staff members consulted line members early in the process of developing their suggestions. Such staff-line consultation would also make line members more willing to implement staff ideas.
- *Educate line to use staff properly.* Line managers will make more effective use of staff expertise when they know what the specialist can do for them. Schleh suggests that staff members describe their functions to line in conferences or brief line members individually.
- *Hold staff accountable for results.* Line members would be more amenable to staff suggestions if staff members were held liable for the failure of those suggestions. Accountability would also increase the likelihood that staff members would develop their suggestions more carefully.

MANAGEMENT-LABOR CONFLICT

HERE'S AN EXAMPLE

Machinists at Eastern Airlines, a subsidiary of Texas Air Corporation, are embroiled in bitter negotiations with the parent company. Says Phil Bakes, Eastern's president, "I suspect if we put Pope John Paul, Desmond Tutu, or Bruce Springsteen in as CEO, it would all sound the same." The machinists assert that they are bargaining in good faith and have been forced to take their case to the courts to block contract violations. (*Wall Street Journal*, 3/31/88, p. 6)

The deregulation of the airlines industry in 1978 stemmed from the belief that replacement of government regulation with the "natural" mechanism of the free market would spur competition, reduce fares, and enhance productivity. Although some of these expectations have been met, the fallout of increased competition has been far from smooth, and tension between airline management and its employees has intensified.

Perhaps hardest hit of those who have survived the transition is Eastern Airlines, part of the Texas Air empire that also includes Continental. Eastern has been losing money, posting a net loss of $181.7 million on revenues of $4.4 billion in 1987. Much of Eastern's problem has stemmed from continuing and exceedingly hostile labor-management struggles. Approximately 500 disgruntled pilots have left Eastern, relin-

---

[18]Melville Dalton, "Conflicts between Staff and Line Managerial Officers," *American Sociological Review* 15, no. 3 (June 1950):342–351.

[19]Alvin W. Gouldner, "Cosmopolitans and Locals: Toward an Analysis of Latent Social Roles—I," *Adminstrative Science Quarterly* 2, no. 3 (December 1957):281–306.

[20]Edward C. Schleh, "Using Central Staff to Boost Line Initiative," *Management Review* 65, no. 5 (May, 1976):17–23. See also Allen, "The Line-Staff Relationship," pp. 375–376. Using staff effectively is similar to using a consultant effectively. For some guidelines, see Robert R. Blake and Jane Srygley Mouton, *Solving Costly Organizational Conflicts: Achieving Intergroup Trust, Cooperation, and Teamwork* (San Francisco: Jossey-Bass, 1984), Chapters 4 and 5.

quishing hard-won seniority to start over at other airlines. By the spring of 1988, another 250 pilots had also given notice. The departure of 20 percent of its cockpit crews has caused cancellations of hundreds of Eastern flights.

Eastern's 20,000 unionized employees see themselves as suffering under management that is seemingly hostile to demands which they consider reasonable under current conditions. Present management does not hide its impatience with the union, as evidenced by wage cuts and stiffer work rules. In previous negotiations, Eastern management received big wage concessions from its pilots and flight attendants. However, the company's machinists have refused to comply with its latest demands.

Caught in the continuing battle of labor negotiations, Eastern announced in August of 1988 that it would lay off 4,000 employees and drastically cut down on the number of its routes. Eastern's final fate is still unknown. It could be merged with nonunion Continental, a large number of employees could be transferred to Continental (though not without a legal fight from the unions), or both management and unionized labor could find some grounds for agreement and cease to battle indefinitely.[21]

Obviously, the nature and course of management-labor conflict at Eastern are not new in the annals of American corporate history. Indeed, conflict between management and labor is one of the classical forms of organizational conflict. The potential for conflict here always exists, but escalates especially when a management-union labor contract is about to expire, thus requiring renegotiation.[22]

Workers and Unions

HERE'S AN EXAMPLE

The entertainment industry was bruised in 1988 by the writers' strike. In Hollywood, strikes can be costly for the entire industry superstructure. Says an industry spokesman, "If they're on strike and we don't get any scripts from them, that doesn't mean we're going to sit on our hands." (*Wall Street Journal*, 5/5/88, p. 38)

Although declining in size, unions still represent a major source of potential conflict with which managers have to deal. Approximately 22 million workers in the United States belong to unions, representing under 20 percent of the eligible, nonagricultural work force in 1984 (as opposed to 35 percent in 1950), and the percentage of eligible) unionized workers may decline still further.[23] However, although unions may be down, they are not out. For one thing, they are actively recruiting new members from nontraditional sources. Since 75 percent of the work force will be employed in service jobs by the year 2000, unions are aggressively pursuing service employees. Responding as well to changing work-force demographics, unions are directing their efforts towards women and minorities more than they have done in the past.[24]

Like their traditional counterparts, these members of the workforce are looking to unions to protect a variety of job interests they feel management does not adequately guarantee:

1. *Economic*—the right to a livable wage.
2. *Job safety*—job security, freedom from arbitrary actions by management.
3. *Social affiliation*—a need to belong and to be accepted by peers.
4. *Self-esteem*—being able to have a voice in the "system."
5. *Status and self-fulfillment*—the exercise of leadership or other abilities through union service.

---

[21]See "Is Deregulation Working?" *Business Week*, December 2, 1986, pp. 50–55; "It Wasn't Supposed to Be This Good for the Airlines," *Business Week*, August 8, 1988, pp. 24–25; and Kenneth Labitch, "The Showdown at Eastern Airlines," *Fortune*, April 11, 1988, pp. 63–66.

[22]Labor-management negotiation is just one type of bargaining that managers must be engaged in. For negotiating strategies of a more general type, see John Winkler, *Bargaining for Results* (New York: Facts on File Publications, 1984); Earl Brooks and George S. Odiorne, *Managing by Negotiations* (New York: Van Nostrand Reinhold, 1984); and Edward Levin, *Negotiating Tactics* (New York: Fawcett, 1985).

[23]The bulk of the discussion in this section on labor negotiotions is drawn from Arthur A. Sloane and Fred Witney, *Labor Relations*, 5th ed. (Englewood Cliffs, N.J.: Prentice Hall, 1985), Chapters 1, 2, and 5. For an analysis of current changes in management–labor relations, see George Strauss, "Industrial Relations: Time of Change," *Industrial Relations* 23, no. 1 (Winter 1984):1–15.

[24]See "Portfolio," *Personnel Journal* 67, no. 2 (1988):18.

ETHICS IN MANAGEMENT

NEW APPROACHES TO UNION ACTIVISM

Management-labor relations have come a long way from the fights in the streets occasioned by unrest in the automobile industry in the 1930s, and a long way from the horrid working conditions characteristic of so many business practices at the turn of the century. Although many pundits believe that unionism is on the wane in the United States, this prediction may or may not be true. It is certain only that the playing field has been changed and some of the ground rules altered.

We might do well to remember that, in 1980, when Chrysler was turned around by an historic agreement between management, unions, banks, suppliers, dealers, and other stakeholders, one key ingredient was the insistence of the United Auto Workers that it be entitled to a seat on Chrysler's Board of Directors. Unions had at long last achieved a goal of actually helping to govern—at the board level—a large company. Since 1980, there has been continued involvement of employees and their representatives not only at board-level management, but even in takeover battles to determine what company will govern a subsidiary firm.

In the airline industry for example, pilots associations from several airlines, including Eastern and United, have proposed takeovers by employees; Pan Am's unions forced out top management. A Connecticut company, Echlin, Inc., used the proxy mechanism—a strategy for collecting and making the votes of nonattendent shareholders—when contract negotiations over health and safety conditions failed. In addition, more and more unions are examining the pension fund mechanism to gain a voice in organization governance.

While picket signs and organization leaflets have not totally been replaced with calculators, three-piece suits, and sophisticated business strategies, unions are rapidly developing tactics that resemble more and more corporate governance methods than those once proposed at union rallies.

Sources: Kenneth B. Noble, "Taking the Fight to the Shareholder," *New York Times,* March 20, 1988, Sec. E., p. 4; John Hoerr, "Blue Collars in the Boardroom: Putting Business First," *Business Week,* December 14, 1987, pp. 126, 128; Charles S. Loughran, Owen F. Bieber, Daniel J. B. Mitchell, D. Quinn Mills, and Warner Woodworth, "Should Unions Have a Seat on the Board?" *Management Review,* February 1986, pp. 56–59; Tracy H. Ferguson and John Gaal, "Codetermination: A Fad or a Failure in America?" *Employee Relations Law Journal* 10, no. 2 (Autumn 1984):176–199.

Of these, safety, social affiliation, and self-esteem are the major reasons why workers join unions today. Social pressure (the urgings of unionized co-workers) and job requirements (''union shops'' requiring union membership as a condition of employment) also motivate workers to join unions.

In recent years, the intensification of price and technological competition, deregulation, and public-sector budget cutbacks has led managers to seek more efficient use of their organizations' work force. Efforts to improve efficiency frequently disrupt established work routines or threaten job security (for example, combining worker tasks, restricting overtime or weekend work, and laying off workers). Unions, in turn, have made work rule and job security issues a high priority. This situation, which is the source of conflict in many current management-labor interactions, shows no sign of abating and is likely to continue through this decade. (See the Ethics in Management box entitled ''New Approaches to Union Activism.'')

Minimizing Negotiation Conflict

Successful management-labor negotiations depends a good deal on thorough preparation. The typical union contract is far too complex to leave until the last minute. It is

COORDINATED RESOURCE

See the Lecture Extras, Chapter 13, for an anecdotal digest of the changing face of union-management relations.

now common, and necessary, to prepare for negotiations at least six months to a year before they are to commence.

In planning for negotiations, the manager first lists all the issues that have surfaced in previous negotiations, gathering information for this from past contracts, and then determines the overall priorities of these issues in terms of the company's financial, administrative, and productivity objectives. Next he or she reviews reports from line and staff on problem areas of the last contract, grievance statistics, morale problems, and any insights into the union climate and bargaining issues. Using this information, the manager can determine in advance the most and least preferable settlements on all of the bargaining issues.[25]

Traditionally, the union presents the company its proposed contractual changes to open the negotiations. The company replies with a counterproposal. Before the negotiation process, management should be clear on its stance toward the union, its objectives and priorities on each bargaining issue, and its bargaining behavior. Either or both sides may present a proposal that contains excessive demands. This may be a negotiating ploy to obtain leverage for later trade-offs, or it may be a smoke screen to conceal the bargainer's real positions. Excessive demands by unions might also reflect the pet concerns of the rank and file or of influential officials. As the negotiations progress, flexibility becomes increasingly important. Negotiators must be able to back away from their original positions, make trade-offs, and introduce alternative solutions. Exhibit 13-4 offers some guidelines for conducting negotiations.

EXHIBIT 13-4 GUIDELINES FOR CONDUCTING NEGOTIATIONS

- Have set, *clear objectives* on every bargaining item and understand the context upon which the objectives are established.
- *Do not hurry.*
- When in doubt, *caucus.*
- Be *well prepared* with firm data support for clearly defined objectives.
- Maintain *flexibility* in your position.
- *Find* out *the motivations* for what the other party wants.
- *Do not get bogged down.* If there is no progress on a certain item, move on to another and come back to it later. Build the momentum for agreement.
- Respect the importance of *face-saving* for the other party.
- Be a good *listener.*
- Build a reputation for being *fair* but *firm.*
- Control your *emotions.*
- Be sure as you make each bargaining move that you know its *relationship* to all other moves.
- *Measure each move* against your *objectives.*
- Pay close attention to the *wording* of each clause negotiated.
- Remember that negotiating is by its nature a *compromise* process.
- Learn to *understand* people—it may pay off during negotiations.
- Consider the *impact of present negotiations on future ones.*

Source: Adapted from Reed C. Richardson, *Collective Bargaining by Objectives: A Positive Approach* (Englewood Cliffs, N.J.: Prentice Hall, 1985), pp. 168–169.

In the end, it is the strike deadline that often motivates the progress of the negotiations. Management may not be able to afford a strike; the union may risk losing valuable demands if it strikes. The threat of a strike can bring both parties back to reality and grant them the opportunity to reassess their positions. Each side will make major concessions in order to avert a strike that is not in their best interests.

[25] See *The Negotiating Edge* (Palo Alto, Calif.: Human Edge Software, 1985). Another program for preparing for negotiations is *The Art of Negotiating* (Berkeley, Calif.: Experience in Software, 1985).

MANAGING ORGANIZATIONAL CREATIVITY AND INNOVATION

FOR DISCUSSION

What might be some costs to the organization of a creative climate and creative employees?

Creativity has become an important part of organizational life. When functional conflict is well managed, it enables the organization to find new and better ways—and more creative ways—of accomplishing its work. In this age of tough competition, resource scarcity, and high labor and equipment costs, anything that leads to more efficient and effective operations increases an organization's chances to survive and succeed. Creativity also enables the organization to anticipate change. This has become very important as new technologies, products, and methods of operation make old ones obsolete.

Like functional conflict, creativity flourishes best in a dynamic, tolerant atmosphere. Creative people can be bothersome; they question how things are done, they upset routine, and their ideas require checking and shaping. To encourage and manage creativity, managers must understand the creative process, know how to select people with creative ability, be able to stimulate creative behavior, and provide an organizational climate that nurtures creativity.

Creativity and Innovation

A HUMOROUS NOTE

A University of Miami management science professor, telling the Airlines Pilots Association (in jest) about 21st-century aircraft, says, "The crew will consist of one pilot and a dog. The pilot will be there to nurture and feed the dog. The dog will be there to bite the pilot if he touches anything."—Earl Wiener (*Fortune*, 9/26/88, p. 26)

Some management writers distinguish between creativity and innovation. They define *creativity* as the generation of a new idea and *innovation* as the translation of such an idea into a new product, service, or method of production. In Lawrence B. Mohr's words, creativity implies "bringing something new into being; innovation implies bringing something new into us."[26] According to Rosabeth Kanter, "innovation is the generation, acceptance, and implementation of new ideas, processes, products or services."[27]

Such distinction can be meaningful in organizational life. The skills required to generate new ideas are not the same as those required to make these ideas a reality. To make full use of its ideas, the organization may need both creative and innovative personnel. In addition, creativity alone contributes little or nothing to organizational effectiveness unless the creative ideas can in some way be used or implemented. Thus, in organizations, the creative process must include both creative and innovative elements: A new idea must indeed be created, but it must also be capable of implementation and must actually be implemented for the organization to benefit from it. Exhibit 13-5 demonstrates one convenient way of dividing the creative process into five steps.

Individual Creativity

EXTRA EXERCISE

Think of three people you consider to be creative. Compare and contrast their differences. Any comments?

Individuals differ in their ability to be creative. Highly creative people tend to be more original than less creative people. If asked to suggest possible uses for automobile tires, noncreative people might say "buoys" and "tree swings"; creative people might say such things as "eyeglass frames for an elephant" or "halos for big robots." Creative people also tend to be more flexible than noncreative people—they are able and willing to shift from one approach to another when tackling a problem. They prefer complexity to simplicity and tend to be more independent than less creative people, sticking to their guns stubbornly when their ideas are challenged. Creative people also question authority quite readily and are apt to disobey orders that make no sense to them. For this reason they may be somewhat difficult to manage in most organizations.

---

[26]Lawrence B. Mohr, "Determinants of Innovation in Organizations," *American Political Science Review* 63, no. 1 (March 1969). See also Teresa M. Amabile, "The Social Psychology of Creativity: A Componential Conceptualization," *Journal of Personality and Social Psychology* 45, no. 2 (August 1983):357–376; Roger von Oech, *A Whack on the Side of the Head* (New York: Warner Books, 1983); and Emily T. Smith, "Are You Creative?" *Business Week*, September 30, 1985, pp. 80–84.

[27]Rosabeth Moss Kanter, *The Change Masters* (New York: Simon & Schuster, 1983), p. 20.

EXHIBIT 13-5 DIVIDING THE CREATIVE PROCESS INTO FIVE STEPS

1. *Problem finding or sensing.* The individual selects a problem to work on or, more likely, becomes aware that a problem or disturbance exists. ("I'm getting bogged down in these monthly reports. Isn't there a better way to do this?")
2. *Immersion or preparation.* The individual concentrates on the problem and becomes immersed in it, recalling and collecting information that seems relevant and dreaming up hypotheses without evaluating them. ("Other companies must do this differently. Perhaps they only require bimonthly reports.")
3. *Incubation and gestation.* After assembling the available information, the individual relaxes and lets his or her subconscious mull over the material. In this little-understood but crucial step, the individual often appears to be idle or daydreaming, but his or her subconscious is in fact trying to arrange the facts into a new pattern.
4. *Insight or illumination.* Often when least expected—while eating, or falling asleep, or walking–the new, integrative idea will flash into the individual's mind. ("A preprinted checklist! That way I can give my boss the right information without wasting time.") Such inspirations must be recorded quickly, because the conscious mind may forget them in the course of other activities.
5. *Verification and application.* The individual sets out to prove by logic or experiment that the idea can solve the problem and can be implemented. Tenacity may be required at this point, since new ideas may be initially rejected as fallacious and impractical, only to be vindicated later.

Motivated more by an interesting problem than by material reward, they will work long and hard on something that intrigues them.

There are a number of tests of measuring creative ability.[28] These tests offer organizations some guidance for selecting individuals who will be most effective in situations that require creativity—new-product development, research, and advertising, for example. However, there are practical difficulties associated with administering tests for creativity, because it is hard to predict from such tests which people will actually act creatively. It is generally more practical to manage people so that their creative *actions* are increased, regardless of their initial creative *ability*, rather than attempting to select especially creative people.

Stimulating Individual and Group Creativity

The methods of stimulating creativity discussed here—brainstorming, nominal group process, synectics, and creative decision making—are designed to be used in groups. However, the principles that underlie these methods can also help individuals improve their creativity.[29]

Brainstorming. Brainstorming as a technique was developed originally by Alex F. Osborn to generate ideas for advertising campaigns.[30] It is still most often used in advertising and new-product development and to develop possible solutions for complex problems.

Brainstorming encourages the free flow of ideas without inhibition by prejudgment or criticism. In group brainstorming, group members are assembled, presented with the problem, and urged to produce as many ideas or solutions as they can. No

[28] See, for example, J. P. Guilford, "Creativity: Its Measurement and Development," in Sidney J. Parnes and Harold F. Harding, eds., *A Source Book for Creative Thinking* (New York: Scribners, 1962), pp. 151–168; and Jim G. Gillis, "Creativity, Problem-Solving, and Decision-Making," *Journal of Systems Management* 34, no. 9 (September 1983):40–42.

[29] See Charles S. Whiting, "Operational Techniques of Creative Thinking," *Advanced Management* 20, no. 10 (October 1955):24–30. See also J. Geoffrey Rawlison, *Creative Thinking and Brainstorming* (New York: Halsted Press, 1981); and Roger von Oech, *A Whack on the Side of the Head: How to Unlock Your Mind for Innovation* (New York: Warner Books, 1983).

[30] Alex F. Osborn, *Applied Imagination* (New York: Scribners, 1953).

evaluation is permitted. Quantity is preferred to quality, and rapid-fire contributions are sought. Even impractical suggestions are well received and recorded, since they may stimulate more useful recommendations. In individual brainstorming, the individual freely produces ideas, again without criticizing or evaluating them.

Donald W. Taylor, Paul C. Berry, and Clifford H. Block compared the effectiveness of groups and individuals who used the brainstorming technique. They found that individuals working alone usually developed more and better ideas than the same number of people working together in a group. The authors concluded that, despite the free atmosphere of brainstorming sessions, group members still inhibit one another's creativity and thus limit the range of ideas that are produced.[31]

The fact that brainstorming group sessions, as opposed to individual sessions, are still used in organizations may be because managers are unaware of studies like those of Taylor and his colleagues. It may also be easier for managers to arrange group sessions, which generally are fun and stimulating for the participants, than to induce individuals to brainstorm on their own. In addition, the fun of working together may provide additional advantages, such as building team spirit, mobilizing enough commitment for implementing some of the ideas, and increasing communication among members.[32]

Nominal Group Process. An extension and modification of the brainstorming approach, called the nominal group process, removes the vocal interaction that may inhibit some individuals. Group members work alone but in the same room, developing ideas. They then share their lists of ideas, one item at a time in round-robin fashion. This approach appears to yield more ideas than brainstorming, yet keeps some of the advantages of that technique.[33]

Synectics (The Gordon Technique). This technique was developed by William J. Gordon when he was a member of Arthur D. Little, Inc., a well-known research and consulting firm.[34] It was designed to help the firm invent new products for its clients. While the object of a brainstorming session is to generate as many ideas as possible, synectics aims for only one radically new idea focused on a specific problem area.

In synectics, only the group leader knows the exact nature of the problem. In this way, quick, easy solutions are avoided, and participants do not have a chance to become overly enamored of their own ideas. Group discussion is organized around a subject that is related to the problem but that does not reveal what the problem actually is. For example if the problem is to produce a new toy, the leader might suggest play or enjoyment as the discussion area. The session might open with give-and-take on the meaning of play and what types of play lead to the greatest enjoyment. Eventually,

---

[31] Donald W. Taylor, Paul C. Berry, and Clifford H. Block, "Does Group Participation When Using Brainstorming Techniques Facilitate or Inhibit Creative Thinking?" *Administrative Science Quarterly* 3, no. 1 (June 1958):23–47. See also T. Richards and B. L. Freedman, "Procedures for Managers in Idea-Deficient Situations: An Examination of Brainstorming Approaches," *Journal of Management Studies* 15, no.1 (February 1978):43–55.

[32] Some support for these possibilities can be found in the following two articles. Mark E. Comadena found that individuals who provided more new ideas in brainstorming groups preferred to work in such groups: "Brainstorming Groups: Ambiguity, Tolerance, Communication, Apprehension, Task Attraction, and Individual Productivity," *Small Group Behavior* 15, no. 2 (May 1984):251–264. Robert Kerwin, a manager at Hughes Aircraft, reports enthusiastically on the use of brainstorming techniques to achieve some of these broader objectives: "Brainstorming as a Flexible Management Tool," *Personnel Journal* 62, no. 5 (May 1983):414ff.

[33] Jeff T. Casey, Charles F. Gettys, Rebecca M. Pliske, and Tom Mehle, "A Partition of Small Group Predecision Performance into Informational and Social Components," *Organizational Behavior and Human Performance* 34, no. 1 (August 1984):112–139; and André L. Delbecq and Andrew H. Van de Ven, "A Group Process Model of Problem Identification and Program Planning," *Journal of Applied Behavioral Science* 7, no. 4 (July–August 1971):466–492.

[34] See William J. Gordon, *Synectics* (New York: Collier Books, 1968). Synectics is also described at length in Eugene Raudsepp, *How to Create New Ideas: For Fun and Profit* (Englewood Cliffs, N.J.: Prentice Hall, 1982).

under the careful direction (f the leader, the discussion might start to focus on what kinds of new toys children 'ould find most enjoyable.

Creative Group Decision Making. Creative group decision making is appropriate when there is no apparent or agreed-upon method of solving a problem. According to André L. Delbecq, creative decision-making groups should be composed of competent personnel from a variety of backgrounds and should be directed by a leader who can stimulate creative behavior.[35] The group problem-solving process is somewhat akin to brainstorming in that discussion is spontaneous, all group members participate, and the evaluation of ideas is suspended at the beginning of the session. But while brainstorming *avoids* decision making, *reaching* a decision is the aim of the creative decision-making group.

Organizational Creativity and Innovation

QUOTATION FROM A MANAGER

"If you want the best things to happen in corporate life, you have to find ways to be hospitable to the unusual person. You don't get innovation as a democratic process."—Max DePree, Chairman and CEO, Herman Miller, Inc., a furniture designer and maker (*Wall Street Journal*, 5/3/88, p. 31)

Just as individuals differ in their ability to translate their creative talents into results, organizations differ in their ability to translate the talents of their members into new products, processes, or services. To enable their organizations to use creativity most effectively, managers need to be aware of the process of innovation in organizations and to take steps to encourage this process. (See Figure 13-2 for an outline of the process of idea evaluation developed by Eastman Kodak's Office of Innovation.) The creative process in organizations involves three steps: idea generation, problem solving or idea development, and implementation.[36]

Generation of Ideas. The generation of ideas in an organization depends first and foremost on the flow of people and information between the firm and its environment. For example, the vast majority of technological innovations have been made in response to conditions in the marketplace. If organization managers are unaware that there is potential demand for a new product, or that there is dissatisfaction with already existing products, they are not likely to seek innovations.

Outside consultants and experts are important sources of information for managers, because they are frequently aware of new products, processes, or service developments in their fields. New employees may have knowledge of alternative approaches or technologies used by suppliers and competitors. Among the organization's regular members, those who constantly expose themselves to information outside their immediate work setting are valuable sources of new ideas. These people, called "technological gatekeepers" by Thomas Allen, can play a particularly important role in stimulating creativity and innovation in research and development labs.[37]

According to Kanter, the generation of ideas is more likely to promote innovation when those ideas issue from the grass-roots level of the organization. She argues that empowering the lower levels of organizations to initiate new ideas within the context of a supportive environment is a valuable means of implementing successful innovations. In addition, although many new ideas challenge a company's cultural traditions, such innovative companies as Hewlett-Packard, Wang Laboratories, and Toyota nevertheless routinely encourage employees to generate new ideas.

---

[35] André L. Delbecq distinguishes between routine decisions, compromises or negotiated decisions, and creative decisions; the decision-making approach is different for each. See "The Management of Decision-Making within the Firm: Three Strategies for Three Types of Decision-Making," *Academy of Management Journal* 10, no. 4 (December 1967):329–339.

[36] James M. Utterback, "Innovation in Industry and the Diffusion of Technology," *Science*, February 15, 1974, pp. 620–626. See also James Brian Quinn, "Managing Innovation: Controlled Chaos," *Harvard Business Review* 63 (1985):73–84.

[37] Thomas J. Allen and Stephen I. Cohen, "Information Flow in Research and Development Laboratories," *Administrative Science Quarterly* 14, no. 1 (March 1969):12–19; and Lewis A. Myers, Jr., "Information Systems in Research and Development: The Technological Gatekeeper Reconsidered," *R&D Management* 13, no. 4 (July 1983):199–206.

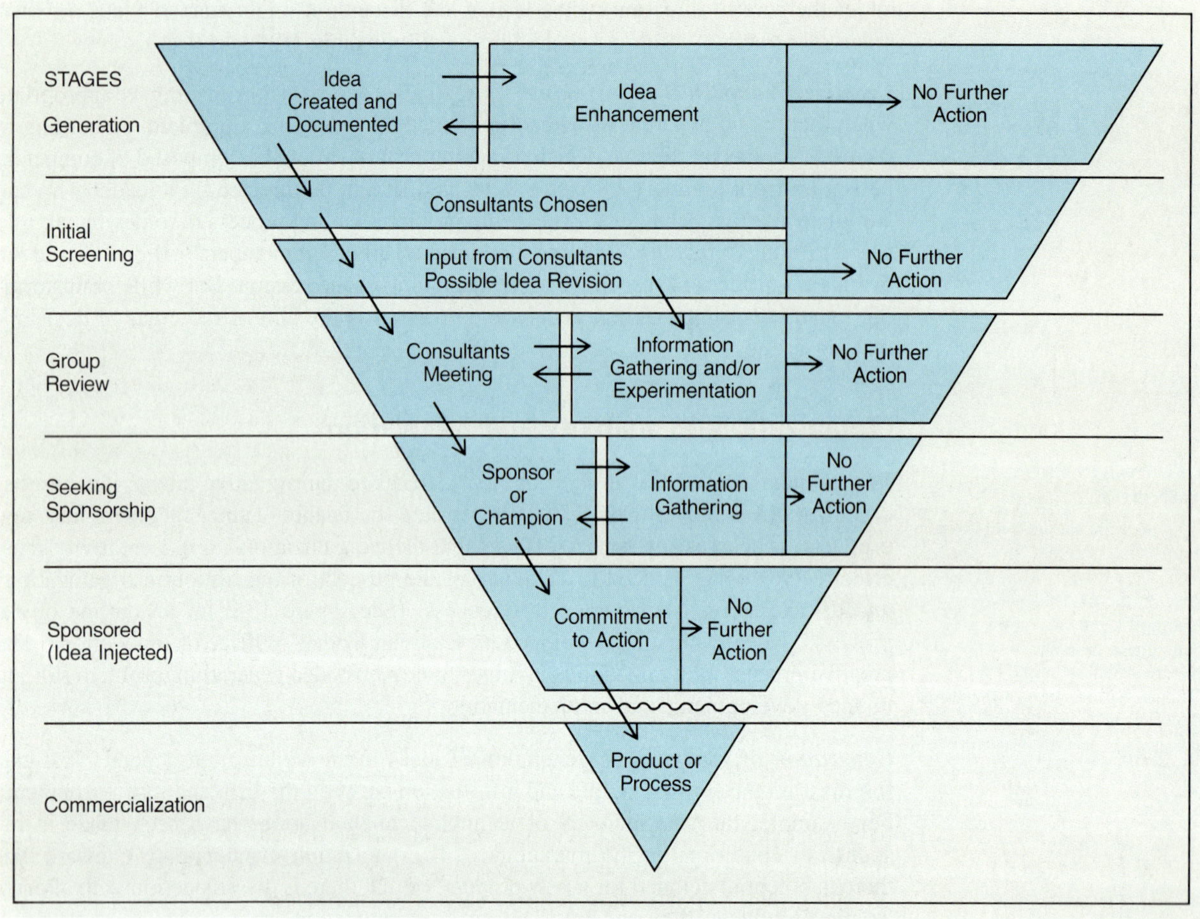

FIGURE 13-2 EASTMAN KODAK'S INNOVATION/IDEA EVALUATION SYSTEM

Idea Development. Unlike idea generation, which is greatly stimulated by external contacts, idea development is dependent on the organizational culture and processes within the organization. Organizational characteristics, values, and processes can support or inhibit the development and use of creative ideas. Commitment to the rational problem-solving approaches discussed in Chapter 6 increases the likelihood that high-quality and creative ideas will be recognized and developed fully.

The organizational structure also plays an important role. Rigidly structured organizations that inhibit communication between departments will often keep potentially helpful people from knowing that a problem exists. By creating barriers to communication, such organizations may also prevent problem solutions from reaching managers who need them. Management information systems (MISs), decision support systems (DDSs), and expert systems store and retrieve generated ideas and aid managers in idea development.[38] Recent advances in networking of such systems are especially helpful for integrative problem solving.

At Cray Research, which specializes in computer technology, new ideas are propelled through the organizational system by a variety of means, one of which is the policy of making external commitments to consumers even before a new computer product has actually been built. For example, Cray committed itself to the development

[38] Stephen G. Green, Alden S. Bean, and B Kay Snavely, "Idea Management in R&D as a Human Information Processing Analog," *Human Systems Management* 4, no. 2 (1983):98–112.

of its innovative galium arsenide circuits before implementation of the project was actually under way. In addition, Cray has fashioned an overall organizational structure that encourages creativity and performance as instigating factors in planning and development.[39]

Implementation. The implementation stage of the creative process in organizations consists of those steps that bring a solution or invention to the marketplace. For manufactured goods, these steps include engineering, tooling, manufacturing, test marketing, and promotion. While a high rate of innovation often reduces short-term profitability, it is necessary for long-term growth. For example, the Swiss watch industry, which operates by traditional practices and old-fashioned individual craftsmanship, has been in decline since the mid-1970s, when more innovative competitors introduced new products, such as digital watches, into the market.[40] When Swiss watchmakers recently introduced new products, such as the popular, inexpensive Swatch wristwatch, they were able to regain part of a market that had appeared to be lost to them.

For innovation to be successful, a high degree of integration is required among the various units of the organization. Technical specialists, responsible for the engineering side of the new product, must work with administrative and financial specialists responsible for keeping the cost of innovation within practical limits. Production managers, helping to refine the specifications of the new product, must work with marketing managers, who are responsible for test marketing, advertising, and promoting it. Proper integration of all these groups is necessary for a quality innovation to be produced on time, on budget, and for a viable market. Organizations that are too rigidly structured may have a difficult time integrating their activities. In contrast, frequent and informal communication across an organization has been shown to have positive effects on innovation.[41] For this reason, task forces (to be discussed in Chapter 16) and matrix-type organizational structures (Chapter 9), which encourage interdepartmental communication and integration, are particularly suited for generating, developing, and implementing creative ideas and approaches.

Establishing a Climate for Organizational Creativity

BACKGROUND ON CREATIVITY

Apple Computer CEO John Scully in his book *Odyssey: Pepsi to Apple* identified some general principles to help an organization reach a higher state of creativity: the safer you can make the situation, the higher you can raise the challenge; don't give people goals—tell them which way to go; encourage contrarian thinking; build emotion into the system; and encourage accountability over responsibility. (*Fortune*, 9/14/87, pp. 108–119)

As we have seen, creativity is best nurtured in a permissive climate, one that encourages the exploration of new ideas and new ways of doing things. Such a climate is difficult for many managers to accept. They may be uncomfortable with the continuing process of change, which is a necessary accompaniment of creativity. They may also be concerned that a permissive atmosphere, discipline or cost control may break down.

Rosabeth Kanter has developed a list of ten managerial attitudes—along with the appropriately counterproductive behavior—that she believes will ensure the stifling of innovative efforts. After studying attitudes and policies regarding innovation and creativity in a number of large organizations, Kanter was able to describe the means by which some managers regularly stifled innovation and prevented employees from generating new ideas. Chapter 3 of her book *The Change Masters* is entitled "Innovating Against the Grain: Ten Rules for Stifling Innovation," and her prescriptions for how *not* to encourage innovation are presented in Exhibit 13-6.

---

[39]See Steve Gross, "Breaking Out of the Shell," *Datamation*, January 1, 1987, pp. 112–113; Kenneth Labitch, "The Shootout in Supercomputers," *Fortune*, February 29, 1988, pp. 67–70; and Gross, "Cray Designs Its Future without Designer Steve Chen," *Electronic Business*, May 1, 1988, pp. 78–80.

[40]R. W. Roetheli, H. U. Balthasar, and R. R. Neiderer, "Productivity Increase and Innovation," an unpublished paper delivered at the TIMS/ORSA Conference, Dallas, October 17, 1984.

[41]Yar M. Ebadi and James M. Utterback, "The Effect of Communication on Technological Innovation," *Management Science* 30, no. 5 (May 1984):572–585.

EXHIBIT 13-6 KANTER'S "TEN RULES FOR STIFLING INNOVATION"

1. Regard any new idea from below with suspicion—because it's new, and because it's from below.
2. Insist that people who need your approval to act first go through several other levels of management to get their signatures.
3. Ask departments or individuals to challenge and criticize each other's proposals. (That saves you the job of deciding; you just pick the survivor.)
4. Express your criticisms freely, and withhold your praise. (That keeps people on their toes.) Let them know they can be fired at any time.
5. Treat identification of problems as signs of failure, to discourage people from letting you know when something in their area isn't working.
6. Control everything carefully. Make sure people count anything that can be counted, frequently.
7. Make decisions to reorganize or change policies in secret, and spring them on people unexpectedly. (That also keeps people on their toes.)
8. Make sure that requests for information are fully justified, and make sure that it is not given out to managers freely. (You don't want data to fall into the wrong hands.)
9. Assign to lower-level managers, in the name of delegation and participation, responsibility for figuring out how to cut back, lay off, move people around, or otherwise implement threatening decisions you have made. And get them to do it quickly.
10. And above all, never forget that you, the higher-ups, already know everything important about this business.

Source: Rosabeth Moss Kanter, *The Change Masters* (New York: Simon & Schuster, 1983), p. 101.

But what is the other side of the coin? How can managers accommodate their concerns about the effects of change and innovation to the increasing need to foster a climate that calls for creative participation on the part of employees at various levels of the organization? Some positive steps—some possible answers to these questions—are listed in Exhibit 13-7.

EXHIBIT 13-7 SOME PRESCRIPTIONS FOR FOSTERING ORGANIZATIONAL CREATIVITY

1. *Develop an acceptance of change.* Organization members must believe that change will benefit them and the organization. This belief is more likely to arise if members participate with their managers in making decisions and if issues like job security are carefully handled when changes are planned and implemented. (See our discussion on overcoming resistance to change in Chapter 12.)
2. *Encourage new ideas.* The managers in the organization, from top managers to lower-level supervisors, must make it clear in word and deed that they welcome new approaches. To encourage creativity, managers must be willing to listen to subordinates' suggestions, implementing promising ones or conveying them to higher-level managers.
3. *Permit more interaction.* A permissive, creative climate is fostered if individuals have the opportunity to interact with members of their own and other work groups. Such interaction encourages the exchange of useful information, the free flow of ideas, and fresh perspectives on problems.
4. *Tolerate failure.* Many new ideas prove impractical or useless. Effective managers accept and allow for the fact that time and resources will be invested in experimenting with new ideas that may not work out.
5. *Provide clear objectives and freedom to achieve them.* Organization members must have a purpose and direction for their creativity. Supplying guidelines and reasonable constraints will also give managers some control over the time and money invested in creative behavior.
6. *Offer recognition.* Creative individuals are motivated to work hard on tasks that interest them. But, like all individuals, they enjoy being rewarded for a task well done. By offering recognition in such tangible forms as bonuses and salary increases, managers demonstrate that creative behavior is valued in their organizations.

ILLUSTRATIVE CASE STUDY Wrap-Up

Conflict and Compromise at the Adolph Coors Company

It is not surprising that it was a relative outsider's view, that of the National Education Association, that led to the eventual resolution of the conflict at Coors: N.E.A. President Robert W. Cleanin began the negotiations between Coors and the AFL-CIO, the union which was seeking entry into Coors and which had devoted millions of dollars to back the boycott. In addition, it took a willingness to compromise, after many years, on both parts in order to bring about a final agreement. In fact, Coors should be a paradigm case in all of the strategies of labor-management relations. The problem with such incidents is that there are such large costs involved. Not only is there the cost of the conflict, but the cost suffered by not having a positive work environment. Conflict, however, can be productive—when it leads to resolution and to a new understanding of how two parties can mutually achieve joint needs. To a large extent, creativity is impossible without conflict; by the same token, without creativity as a goal, conflict becomes dysfunctional. ■

SUMMARY

Views of conflict have changed in the last three decades. In the traditional view, all conflict is seen as a harmful result of the failure to apply management principles. The current view is that conflict is not only inevitable but sometimes even necessary for the organization to survive.

There are various types of conflict. Conﬁct between groups in the same organization may be caused by their need to share scarce resources, by the interdependence of work activities, and by their differences in goals, values, or perceptions. Individual style differences, as well as organizational ambiguities and communication problems, may also contribute to group conflict.

Effects of conflict include a rise in group cohesion, selection of strong leaders and group representatives, and the development of distorted perceptions about one's own group and the opposing group. Whether or not these and other consequences will prove functional or dysfunctional for the organization will depend on the level of conflict, the organizational structure and culture, and how the conflict is managed.

The management of conflict may include conflict stimulation, reduction, or resolution. Conflict-simulation methods include bringing outsiders into the organization, encouraging competition, restructuring the organization, and redistributing power among the organization work groups. Conflict-reduction methods include establishing superordinate goals and uniting the conflicting groups to meet a common threat.

Undesirable or ineffective conflict-resolution methods include compromise and the suppression of conflict. Integrative problem solving, on the other hand, allows managers to resolve conflict in a way that most benefits the organization and does the least harm to conflicting individuals or groups.

Line-staff conflict and management-labor conflict are common examples of organizational conflict. Disputes between line and staff tend to derive from functional and personal differences between the two groups. Management-labor conflict tends to be more adversarial in nature. Conflict between management and unions is heightened during labor contract negotiations; successful negotiations usually require thorough preparation, the setting of clear goals and priorities, and flexibility in demands by both parties.

The management of organizational creativity requires an understanding of the creative process and how it can be stimulated. Individual or group creativity can be stimulated through brainstorming, nominal group process, synectics, and creative group decision making.

Effective organizational creativity and innovation follow a three-step procedure: idea generation, idea development, and implementation. This procedure is facilitated by an organizational structure and climate that encourage (1) the free flow of communication between the organization and its environment, (2) the free flow of communication among organization members, and (3) the integration of organizational activities.

REVIEW QUESTIONS

1. What is the difference between conflict and competition?
2. What are the traditional and interactionist views of conflict? With which view do you agree? Why?
3. What are the six types of conflict possible in organizations? Under what conditions will each type of conflict arise?
4. Why does differentiation of organization groups often lead to conflict?
5. What are the effects of organizational conflict on group attitudes and behavior? What factors determine whether these effects will be functional or dysfunctional?
6. What are the consequences of a very low level of organizational conflict? What methods of conflict stimulation can managers use?
7. In the Sherifs' conflict-reduction experiment, what two methods proved effective? Why might these methods be effective in organizations?
8. What are three types of conflict-resolution methods? In what ways can these methods be manifested? Which method is usually best? Why?
9. How do line and staff members view each other and their role in the organization? How can line and staff conflict be reduced?
10. Why do you think creativity is important in organizational life?
11. What is the difference between creativity and innovation?
12. What techniques can be used to stimulate individual or group creativity?
13. What are the three steps in the organizational creativity process? How can each step be facilitated or inhibited?
14. How can managers establish an organizational climate that encourages creativity?

CASE STUDY

Is There Creative Life After Post-it Notes?

Art Fry felt a little worried. Now that he had been branded an inventor, he felt some pressure to repeat his success; unfortunately, he was not quite sure he could do that. Where did *creativity* come from? Could you create because you were expected to? Could your surroundings contribute to the process? Certainly his employer thought so, but were 3M's expectations realistic?

Art had invented Post-it Notes—those small pads with an adhesive strip that have by now become standard equipment in every office in the country. Originally, they came only in yellow, but now they appear in a rainbow of colors and with clever sayings written on them. In the "sincerest form of flattery" there are imitations now, too. The product is definitely a success.

Art hadn't started out with the intention of fathering a revolution, even among office dwellers. He invented Post-it Notes when his bookmarks kept falling out of his hymnbook at church. In order to solve this fairly minor problem, he took an adhesive strip, an interesting but unsuccessful product of 3M research, and stuck it to the scrap of paper. It had been rejected at 3M, where Fry worked as a scientist, because it stayed put only so long as you left it alone. It was thus too easy to remove, but that was precisely the quality that is largely responsible for the success of Post-it Notes.

After concocting a design and playing with the results for a while, Art knew he had a product that people could use. However, convincing his managers at 3M was another matter—they were not sure that people would pay for adhesive-backed scrap paper. In fact, early sales results seemed to confirm their skepticism. Post-it Notes did not really start to sell until the marketing strategy was changed from a program of sending out ads and brochures to one of sending out samples of the product itself. Once people were able to play with Post-its and discover their variety of uses for themselves, sales took off. Everyone who received samples, from top-level managers to mailroom gofers, soon became a loyal user.

Obviously 3M was delighted with the success of Post-it Notes. As a company, 3M works hard to establish policies that will aid their people in creating precisely this sort of success. It sees its role as providing the tools that creative people need to turn an idea into a useful, marketable reality. An isolated individual with a "better mousetrap" may not have the expertise or the equipment to manufacture and market items like those in which 3M specializes: Even if he or she is able to do so in the early stages of the product's life, trouble commences once the competition has heated up and efficient manufacturing and lavish advertising come in to play. Therefore, 3M manages the overall process, contributing the resources and the combined talents of a large corporation.

However, in order to do this, 3M needs the original idea. Therefore, the company allows—even encourages—employees to spend company time on personal or pet projects. Post-it Notes is only one example of what can result from one of these personal endeavors. Moreover, 3M is careful to give full credit to its salaried originators, allowing them to feel responsible for their contributions to the company.

All of which returned Art to his personal dilemma. He knew 3M expected a little more out of him, now that he had proven he could come up with a good idea, champion it through the system, and create a commercial success. He also expected more out of himself as well. He had done it once, and he wanted to do it again. All he needed was a new idea, and it was precisely that, along with the drive to pursue and succeed with it, which no company could provide. Art Fry had solved the problem of fumbled unsung hymns. Now what other problem could he solve?

Source: "Lessons from a Successful Intrapreneur," *The Journal of Business Strategy* 9, no. 2 (March–April 1988):20–24.

Case Questions

1. Why was Post-it Notes successful?
2. Can creativity be managed at all?
3. Why is Art Fry worried and what can he do about it?
4. Suppose that Art Fry reported to you. What advice, as his manager, would you give him? ■

CASES ON ORGANIZING FOR STABILITY AND CHANGE

Chris Cunningham

Stover Industries was an amalgamation of four small companies in the electrical parts industry. The company was managed by its president, Elizabeth Stover, whose husband inherited one of the companies from his father. Stover, herself an engineer, elected to run the company while her husband pursued a separate career as a dental surgeon. Stover subsequently purchased the other three companies to form the present Stover Industries.

Stover was only 31 years old. She was a dynamic individual, full of ideas and drive. In the space of a year, she had transformed Stover Industries into a profitable organization known for its aggressive pursuit of sales.

Stover integrated the four companies into a unified organization by welding the individual managements into one unit. Some individuals were let go in each organization as it was purchased and became part of Stover Industries. In several other instances, executives of the newly purchased companies resigned because of difficulties in working for such a young and driving boss. The four companies continued as individual manufacturing units of the company and together employed approximately 475 production workers. Because the original companies had been competing with each other, some problems arose in integrating the individual sales staff. Consequently, the salespeople had overlapping territories. This problem was gradually being worked out, but the salespeople were permitted to keep their own old customers, making it next to impossible to assign exclusive territories to each salesperson.

Until recently, the sales staff had included 17 salespeople and the sales director. The sales director, Bill Johnson, had been with the original Stover Company as sales manager. He knew Eliabeth Stover well and was able to work as her complacent subordinate. Most of his time and energy were devoted to routine direction and coordination of the sales team. Although a trusted lieutenant of Stover, Johnson was not much more than titular head of the sales force. Stover provided the active leadership.

Approximately six months before, Stover had personally hired Chris Cunningham, a college classmate, as a salesperson for the organization. Cunningham shared some of Stover's drive and enthusiasm and, in a short time, had justified Stover's choice with a sensational sales record. In terms of sales performance, Chris Cunningham's record left little to be desired.

Nevertheless, Cunningham presented a thorny problem for Stover. The problem, as outlined by Stover, shaped up as follows:

> I hired Chris because we knew and admired each other in our college days. Chris was always a leader on campus and we had worked well together in campus affairs. Chris was just the kind of person I wanted in this organization—a lot of drive and originality, combined with tremendous loyalty. The way I operate, I need a loyal organization of people who will pitch right in on projects we develop.
>
> Chris has already proven to be a top-notch performer and will probably be our best salesperson in a year or two. Could one ask for anything better than that?
>
> Here is where the rub comes in. Chris is the sort of person who has absolutely no respect for organization. A hot order will come in, for example, and Chris will go straight to the plant with it and raise hell until that order is delivered. It doesn't make any difference that our production schedule has been knocked to pieces. The order is out, and Chris has a satisfied customer. Of course, that sort of thing gets repeat business and does show well on Chris's sales record. But, it has made running our plants a constant headache. It is not only the production people who have felt the impact of Cunningham on

the operations. Chris gets mixed up with our engineering department on new designs and has even made the purchasing department furious by needling them to hurry supplies on special orders.

You can just imagine how the rest of the organization feels about all this. The other salespeople are pretty upset that their orders get pushed aside—and are probably a bit jealous too. The production people, the engineers, the purchasing agent, and most of the rest of the staff have constantly complained to me about how Christ gets in their hair. On a personal level, the staff say they like Chris a lot but that they just cannot work with such a troublemaker in the organization.

I have talked with Chris many times about this. I have tried raising hell over the issue, pleading for change and patient, rational discussion. Chris seems like a reformed character for maybe a week after one of these sessions, everyone relaxes a bit, and then bang—off we go again in the same old pattern.

I suppose that in many ways Chris is just like me. I must admit I would probably be inclined to act in much the same way. You see, I have a lot of sympathy for Chris's point of view.

I think you can see now what my problem is. Should I fire Chris and lose a star salesperson? That does not make too much sense. In fact, Chris is probably the person who should be our sales director, if not immediately, at least in a few years. But without the ability to get along with the organization, to understand the meaning of "channels" and "procedures," Chris is not only a valuable and talented addition to the company, but a liability as well. Should I take a chance on things eventually working out and Chris getting educated to the organization? Should I put on a lot of pressure and force a change? What would that do to Chris's enthusiasm and sales record? If I just let things go, there is a real danger to my organization. My executives will think I have given Chris the green light, and they will transfer their antagonism to me. I certainly cannot afford that.

Source: This case was prepared by Todd D. Jick for the Harvard Business School, Boston, Massachusetts.

Case Questions

1. What are the problems and issues in this case?
2. What factors in successful organizational behavior are suggested in in this case? What possible weaknesses?
3. Where should the line be drawn between organizational control over personal initiative and the contribution of personal initiative to organizational effectiveness?
4. What should Stover do to deal with each of the variety of problems raised by this case? ■

The Consolidated Life Case: Caught Between Corporate Cultures

It all started so positively. Three days after graduating with his degree in business administration, Mike Wilson started his first day at a prestigious insurance company—Consolidated Life. He worked in the Policy Issue Department. The work of the department was mostly clerical and did not require a high degree of technical knowledge. Given the repetitive and mundane nature of the work, the successful worker had to be consistent and willing to grind out paperwork.

Rick Belkner was the division's vice-president, "the man in charge" at the time, an actuary by training and a technical professional described in the division as "the mirror of whomever was the strongest personality around him." It was also common knowledge that Belkner made $60,000 a year while he spent his time doing crossword puzzles.

Mike was hired as a management trainee and promised a supervisory assignment within a year. However, because of a management reorganization, it was only six weeks before he was placed in charge of an eight-person unit. The reorganization was intended to streamline workflow, upgrade and combine the clerical jobs, and make greater use of the computer system. It was a drastic departure from the old way of doing things and created a great deal of animosity and anxiety among the clerical staff.

Management realized that a flexible supervisory style was necessary to pull off the reorganization without immense turnover, so the firm gave its supervisors a free hand to run their units as they saw fit. Mike used this latitude to implement group meetings and training classes in his unit. In addition, he assured all members raises if they worked hard to attain them. By working long hours, participating in the mundane tasks with his unit, and being flexible in his management style, he was able to increase productivity, reduce errors, and reduce lost time. Things improved so dramatically that he was noticed by upper management and earned a reputation as a "superstar" despite being viewed as free-spirited and unorthodox. The feeling was that his loose, people-oriented management style could be tolerated because his results were excellent.

After a year, Mike received an offer from a different Consolidated Life division located across town. Mike was asked to manage an office in the marketing area. The pay was excellent and it offered an opportunity to turn around an office in disarray. The reorganization in his present division at Consolidated was almost complete, and most of his mentors and friends in management had moved on to other jobs. Mike decided to accept the offer. In his exit interview, he was assured that if he ever wanted to return, a position would be made for him. It was clear that he was held in high regard by management and staff alike. A huge party was thrown to send him off.

The new job was satisfying for a short time, but it became apparent to Mike that it did not have the long-term potential he was promised. After bringing on a new staff, computerizing the office, and auditing the books, he began looking for a position that would both challenge him and give him the autonomy he needed to be successful.

Eventually, word got back to Rick Belkner that Mike was looking for another job. Rick offered Mike a position with the same pay he was now receiving and control over a 14-person unit in his old division. After considering other options, Mike decided to return to his old division, feeling that he would be able to progress steadily over the next several years.

Upon his return to Consolidated Life, Mike became aware of several changes that had taken place in the six months since his departure. The most important change was the hiring of a new divisional senior vice-president, Jack Greely. Greely had been given total authority to run the division. Rick Belkner now reported to Jack.

Belkner's reputation was now that he was tough but fair. It was necessary for people in Jack's division to do things his way and "get the work out." Mike also found himself reporting to one of his former peers, Kathy Miller, who had been promoted to manager during the reorganization. Mike had always "hit it off" with Miller and foresaw no problems in working with her.

After a week, Mike realized the extent of the changes that had occurred. Gone was the loose, casual atmosphere that had marked his first tour in the division. Now, a stricter, task-oriented management doctrine was practiced. Morale of the supervisory staff had decreased to an alarming level. Jack Greely was the major topic of conversation in and around the division. People joked that MBO now meant "management by oppression."

Mike was greeted back with comments like "Welcome to prison" and "Why would you come back here? You must be desperate!" It seemed as if everyone was looking for new jobs or transfers. Their lack of desire was reflected in the poor quality of work being done.

Mike felt that a change in the management style of his boss was necessary in order to improve a frustrating situation. Realizing that it would be difficult to affect Greely's style directly, Mike requested permission from Belkner to form a Supervisors' Forum for all the managers on Mike's level in the division. Mike explained that the purpose would be to enhance the existing management-training program. The Forum would include weekly meetings, guest speakers, and discussions of topics relevant to the division and the industry. Mike thought the forum would show Greely that he was serious about both his job and improving morale in the division. Belkner gave the O.K. for an initial meeting.

The meeting took place, and ten supervisors who were Mike's peers in the company eagerly took the opportunity to "Blue Sky" it. There was a euphoric attitude about the group as they drafted their statement of intent. It read as follows:

TO: Rick Belkner
FROM: New Issue Services Supervisors
SUBJECT: Supervisors' Forum

On Thursday, June 11, the Supervisors' Forum held its first meeting. The objective of the meeting was to identify common areas of concern among us and to determine topics that we might be interested in pursuing.

The first area addressed was the void that we perceive exists in the management-training program. As a result of conditions beyond anyone's control, many of us over the past year have held supervisory duties without the benefit of formal training or proper experience. Therefore, what we propose is that we utilize the Supervisors' Forum as a vehicle with which to enhance the existing management-training program. The areas that we hope to affect with this supplemental training are: (a) morale/job satisfaction, (b) quality of work and service, (c) productivity, and (d) management expertise as it relates to the life insurance industry. With these objectives in mind, we have outlined below a list of possible activities that we would like to pursue.

1. Further utilization of the existing "in-house" training programs provided for manager trainees and supervisors, i.e., Introduction to Supervision, E.E.O., and Coaching and Counseling.
2. A series of speakers from various sections in the company. This would help expose us to the technical aspects of their departments and their managerial style.
3. Invitations to outside speakers to address the Forum on management topics such as managerial development, organizational structure and

behavior, business policy, and the insurance industry. Suggested speakers could be area college professors, consultants, and state insurance officials.

4. Outside training and visits to the field. This could include attendance at seminars concerning management theory and development relative to the insurance industry. Attached is a representative sample of a program we would like to have considered in the future.

In conclusion, we hope that this memo clearly illustrates what we are attempting to accomplish with this program. It is our hope that the above outline will be able to give the Forum credibility and establish it as an effective tool for all levels of management within New Issue. By supplementing our on-the-job training with a series of speakers and classes, we aim to develop prospective management's role in it. Also, we would like to extend an invitation to the underwriters to attend any programs at which the topic of the speaker might be of interest to them.

cc: J. Greely
Managers

The group felt the memo accurately and diplomatically stated their dissatisfaction with the current situation. However, they pondered what the results of their actions would be and what else they could have done.

Shortly after the memo had been issued, an emergency management meeting was called by Rick Belkner at Jack Greely's request to address the "union" being formed by the supervisors. Four general managers, Rick Belkner, and Jack Greely were at that meeting. During the meeting, it was suggested the Forum be disbanded to "put them in their place." However, Rick Belkner felt that if "guided" in the proper direction the Forum could die from lack of interest. His stance was adopted, but it was common knowledge that Jack Greely was strongly opposed to the group and wanted its founders dealt with. His comment was "It's not a democracy and they're not a union. If they don't like it here, then they can leave." A campaign was directed by the managers to determine who the main authors of the memo were so they could be dealt with.

About this time, Mike's unit had made a mistake on a case, which Jack Greely was embarrassed to admit to his boss. This embarrassment was more than Jack Greely cared to take from Mike Wilson. At the managers staff meeting that day, Greely stormed in and declared that the next supervisor to "screw up" was out the door. He would permit no more embarrassments of his division and repeated his earlier statement about "people leaving if they didn't like it here." It was clear to Mike and everyone else present that Mike Wilson was a marked man.

Mike had always been a loose, amiable supervisor. The major reason his units had been successful was the attention he paid to each individual and how they interacted with the group. He had a reputation for fairness, was seen as an excellent judge of personnel for new positions, and was noted for his ability to turn around people who had been in trouble. He motivated people through a dynamic, personable style and was noted for his general lack of regard for rules. He treated rules as obstacles to management and usually used his own discretion as to what was important. His office had a sign saying. "Any fool can manage by rules. It takes an uncommon man to manage without any." It was an approach that flew in the face of company policy, but it had been overlooked in the past because of his results. However, because of Mike's actions with the Supervisors' Forum, he was now regarded as a thorn in the side, not a superstar, and his oddball style only made things worse.

Faced with the fact that he was rumored to be out the door, Mike sat down to appraise the situation.

Source: This case was prepared by Joseph Weiss, Mark Wahlstrom, and Edward Marshall. See *Journal of Management Case Studies* 2 (1986):238–243.

Case Questions

1. How has the culture at Consolidated Life changed during Mike's absence?
2. Was sending the memo a good idea? What effects did it have? Why were some of them unforeseen?
3. Why is Mike now regarded as a "thorn in the side" rather than a "superstar"? What, if anything, can he do to change that perception?
4. What advice do you have for Mike? ■

Art Direction: Tyler Smith. Illustration: Anthony Russo. Client: CCS/TOYO Printing Inks, 180 Kerry Place, Norwood, Mass.

14

MOTIVATION, PERFORMANCE, AND SATISFACTION

Upon completing this chapter you should be able to:

1. Identify and describe three theoretical approaches to motivation.
2. State how views of motivation in organizations have evolved.
3. Explain the systems view of motivation in organizations.
4. Describe the contributions of various theorists on motivation and explain how their different approaches have different implications for management practice.
5. Describe two integrative approaches to motivation.
6. Discuss the implications for managers of current theories of motivation.

Chapter Outline

Introduction
The Importance of Motivation
Early Views of Motivation in Organizations
Three Types of Motivation Theories
A Systems View of Motivation in Organizations
The Impact of Past Consequences on Behavior
Integrative Approaches to Motivation
Guidelines for Effective Motivation

ILLUSTRATIVE CASE STUDY Introduction

Creating a Committed Work Force at Domino's Pizza

Why would anyone want a job delivering pizza? How did an entrepreneur become a multimillionaire in part by understanding the basics of motivating employees? What motivates Thomas Monaghan, president and CEO of Domino's Pizza, Inc.? As the head of the nation's second largest pizza chain (Pizza Hut is first), with sales in 1985 climbing 73 percent to $14.9 million, and as the proud owner of Duesenberg cars and the Detroit Tigers baseball team, Monaghan has a pretty good idea of what dreams are—and what it takes to attain them.

Monaghan's recipe for the success of Domino's is simple enough: a limited menu to hold down preparation time, guaranteed delivery within 30 minutes or a discount or a free pizza, an attitude of trust in his employees, and the provision of such performance rewards and perks as trips to the Indy 500, BMWs for top executives, and visits to his retreat in Michigan's Upper Peninsula. As well as rewarding performance, Monaghan provides the freedom for employees to try out ideas that will succeed or fail on their own merits.

Domino's Pizza has also seen its ups and downs. Due to rapid expansion in the late 1960s and an abortive attempt to take the company public, Monaghan was once faced with debts totaling $1.5 million. He refused to file for bankruptcy and instead fired everyone but his wife, who handled the payroll, and his bookkeeper. He then paid off both his creditors and the IRS. Since then, it's been back to the basics of pizza making, opening new stores, and profits. New products, such as a breakfast pizza with ham and bacon and a low-calorie pizza, are being test-marketed to expand the line; soon, it may be possible to dial a pizza on touch-tone phones. Looking to speed up delivery time, a special delivery car is being designed with projected gas mileage of 85 miles to the gallon. Domino's five-year plan includes bringing the total number of outlets to 10,000 and the annual total revenues to $10 billion. There are now Domino's outlets in Australia, Britain, Canada, Japan, and West Germany.

In terms of career development, Monaghan offers employees the chance to duplicate his own success. By starting out typically as a delivery person and moving up through the position of store manager, employees of Domino's have taken advantage of generous terms and started their own franchises. In fact, of the 600 plus franchises, 98 percent are held by former employees.

Monaghan's view of human nature reflects the belief that people work for challenges, for the rewards of their efforts, and for a sense of belonging and cooperation; that is, he believes that people are *intrinsically* motivated (or self-motivated). But he does not ignore the reality that people are motivated by factors other than the sheer challenge and sense of accomplishment that can be associated with work. He also provides *extrinsic,* or external, motivators such as monetary reward and a broad program of employee benefits. In addition to generous performance rewards, Domino's headquarters in Ann Arbor, Michigan, features an employee fitness center, a sports medicine center, a recreation lake, jogging and ski trails, and a 150-acre Domino's Farm.

The innovativeness of Domino's in meeting the competitive challenge and creating a committed work force pays tribute not only to Monaghan's blend of personal and professional ambitions in creating opportunities for others, but to his faith in people's innate capacity to be highly motivated when the organization's goals and culture are compatible with the individual's goals and comfort with that culture.

Sources: Jeffrey A. Trachtenberg, "The Dream of a Lifetime," *Forbes 400,* October 1, 1984, pp. 250, 254; Susan Ager, "An Appetite for More than Pizza," *Nation's Business,* February 1986, pp. 81–83; and Aimée Stern, "Domino's: A Unique Concept Pays Off," *Dun's Business Month,* May 1986, pp. 50–51.

TEACHING TIP

Most students seem to find motivation a fascinating topic and area of study. Motivation is *clearly important* for managers. Knowing about motivation can help job performance.

Of all management functions, leadership involves managers most directly with subordinates. Thus, leading is a central part of the manager's role, which involves working with and through others to achieve organizational goals. To a large extent, a manager's leadership ability—that is, a manager's ability to motivate, influence, direct, and communicate with subordinates—will determine the manager's effectiveness.

This chapter is concerned with how managers can motivate subordinates so that their performance and satisfaction will be increased. We start a unit on leadership with a chapter on motivation because managers cannot lead unless subordinates are motivated to follow them. In Chapter 15 we will examine the leadership styles available to managers and trends for the future. Chapter 16 discusses groups and committees and how to lead them; Chapter 17 focuses on the importance of effective communication in organizations.

THE IMPORTANCE OF MOTIVATION

motivation The factors that cause, channel, and sustain an individual's behavior.

BACKGROUND ON MOTIVATION

The word "motivation" comes from the Latin word *movere*, "to move." Understanding motivation means knowing what moves people.

Motivation those factors that cause, channel, and sustain people's behavior—has always been important for managers to understand. Managers, by definition, work with and through people, but people are complex; their motivations are not always easy to discern. Many theories exist about motivation, and most differ in what they implicitly suggest managers should do to obtain the most effective performance from their employees. Most successful managers, however, have learned by experience that people are generally very responsive to praise and encouragement—expressed not only in words but also in actions—and need to feel successful in their work to give their best effort to the organization. IBM, for example, deliberately sets its sales quotas low enough to be attainable by the majority of its salespeople. Many people are also strongly self-motivated and seek the freedom and autonomy to perform their jobs in their own way. Managers who find the key to their employees' inner motivations can tap an immense source of productive energy.[1] At the same time, Stephen Robbins speculates that, since "not more than 10 to 20 percent of North Americans are naturally high achievers, difficult goals are still recommended for the majority of workers" if employee motivation is to be successfully translated into results on a broader organizational level.[2]

---

[1]Any discussion of motivation, performance, and satisfaction in the workplace is in fact a discussion of the field known as *industrial/organizational (I/O) psychology*—the general study of organizational behavior with an emphasis on behavior in the workplace. The field of study was introduced by the German psychologist Hugo Münsterberg in 1913, with his book *Psychology and Industrial Efficiency*. See the following: A. Anastasi, *Fields of Applied Psychology*, 2nd ed. (New York: McGraw-Hill, 1979); B. M. Staw, "Organizational Behavior: A Review and Reformulation of the Field's Outcome Variables," *Annual Review of Psychology* 35 (1984):627–666; B. Schneider, "Organizational Behavior," *Annual Review of Psychology* 36 (1985):573–611; Frank J. Landy, *Psychology of Work Behavior*, 3rd ed. (Homewood, Ill.: Dorsey, 1985); T. Peters and N. Austin, *A Passion for Excellence: The Leadership Difference* (New York: Random House, 1985). The complex variety of principles established by I/O psychologists informs Thomas J. Peters and Robert H. Waterman's *In Search of Excellence* (New York: Harper & Row, 1982), pp. 55–57, 80–81.

[2]Stephen P. Robbins, *Management: Concepts and Applications*, 2nd ed. (Englewood Cliffs, N.J.: Prentice Hall, 1988), p. 346.

In the following discussion, we will cover both classical and modern theoretical perspectives in order to understand current knowledge about motivation and its relationship to work behavior and satisfaction.[3] In considering these theories, it is important to keep in mind that motivation is not the only influence on a person's performance level. Also involved are the individual's *abilities* and his or her understanding of what behaviors are necessary to achieve high performance (and high satisfaction); this factor is called **role perception.** Motivation, abilities, and role perceptions are all interrelated. Thus if *any* one factor discourages or inhibits high performance, the performance level is likely to be low, even if the other factors encourage performance.

role perception The individual's understanding of the behaviors needed to accomplish a task or perform a job.

EARLY VIEWS OF MOTIVATION IN ORGANIZATIONS

At different stages in the evolution of management thought, managers subscribed to different models or theories of motivation. We will look at three of them in the order in which they evolved: the traditional model, the human relations model, and the human resources model. As we shall see, the beliefs that managers have about motivation are important determinants of how they attempt to manage people.

The Traditional Model

TEACHING TIP

This is a good time to reemphasize how early management theory/practice contributed to the evolution of current theories and practices.

The traditional model of motivation is associated with Frederick Taylor and scientific management (see Chapter 2), which held that an important aspect of the manager's job was to make sure that workers perform repetitive tasks in the most efficient way. Managers determined how the jobs should be done and used a system of wage incentives to motivate workers—the more they produced, the more they earned.

This perspective assumed that workers were essentially lazy and that managers understood the workers' jobs better than the workers did. Workers could only be motivated by financial reward and had little to contribute beyond their labor. In many situations, this approach was effective. As efficiency improved, fewer workers were needed for a specific task. Over time, managers reduced the size of the wage incentive. Layoffs became common, and workers sought job security rather than only temporary and minor wage increases.

The Human Relations Model

Eventually, it became apparent that the traditional approach to motivation was incomplete. Elton Mayo and other human relations researchers found that the social contacts employees had at work were also important and that the boredom and repetitiveness of many tasks were themselves factors in reducing motivation. Mayo and others also believed that managers could motivate employees by acknowledging their social needs and by making them feel useful and important.

As a result, employees were given some freedom to make their own decisions on the job. Greater attention was paid to the organization's informal work groups. More information was provided to employees about managers' intentions and about the operations of the organization. The researchers also discovered that employees tended to set such group norms and acceptable behavior patterns as the rate at which group produc-

[3]For a major part of our discussion on motivation, we are deeply indebted to Richard M. Steers and Lyman W. Porter, eds., *Motivation and Work Behavior,* 3rd ed. (New York: McGraw-Hill, 1983); and to Lyman W. Porter and Raymond E. Miles, "Motivation and Management," in Joseph W. McGuire, ed., *Contemporary Management: Issues and Viewpoints* (Englewood Cliffs, N.J.: Prentice Hall, 1974), pp. 545–570.

tion would proceed. Therefore, even though management maintained formal authority to set goals and hold workers accountable for them, the workers themselves were not entirely without influence on the standards and results of the work situation. (It should be noted, however, that with the advent of automation and sophisticated techniques for monitoring performance, exerting such influence has become increasingly difficult for work groups.)

In the traditional model, workers had been expected to accept management's authority in return for high wages made possible by the efficient system designed by management and implemented by the workers. In the human relations model, workers were expected to accept management's authority because supervisors treated them with consideration and were attentive to their needs. The intent of managers, however, remained the same—to have workers accept the work situation as established by managers.

The Human Resources Model

Douglas McGregor, as well as other theorists such as Abraham Maslow, Chris Argyris, and Rensis Likert, criticized the human relations model as simply a more sophisticated approach to the manipulation of employees. These theorists suggested that employees were motivated by many factors—not only money or the desire for satisfaction, but also by the need for achievement and meaningful work. They argued that most people are already motivated to do a good job and that they do not automatically see work as undesirable. They suggested that employees are likely to derive satisfaction from good performance (rather than performing well because they have been satisfied, as in the human relations model). Thus, employees can be given far more responsibility for making decisions and carrying out their tasks.

FOR DISCUSSION

Under what conditions might Theory X assumptions be appropriate? What about Theory Y?

McGregor proposed that there are two different sets of assumptions about what motivates people. The traditional view, known as *Theory X,* contends that people have an inherent dislike of work, regard it only as necessary for survival, and will avoid it whenever possible. Most people, being lazy, prefer to be directed, want to avoid responsibility, and are relatively unambitious. They must be coerced, controlled, directed, or even threatened with punishment to get them to work towards organizational goals. Managers have to be strict and authoritarian if subordinates are to accomplish anything.

Theory Y is a much more optimistic view of human nature, assuming that the expenditure of physical and mental effort in work to be as natural as at play or rest. People will direct themselves towards objectives if their achievements are rewarded. Most people have the capacity to accept, even to seek, responsibility as well as to apply imagination, ingenuity, and creativity to organizational problems. Thus, people want and are eager to work; under the right circumstances, they derive a great deal of satisfaction from work, and they are capable of doing a good job.[4]

The problem, according to Theory Y, is that modern industrial life does not fully tap the potential of the average human being. Managers should take advantage of their subordinates' willingness and ability to work by providing a climate that will not only bring out the best in staff members but will give them room for personal improvement. *Participative management* becomes the ideal.

From a human resources perspective, then, managers should not induce workers to comply with managerial objectives by bribing them with high wages, as in the traditional model, or manipulating them with considerate treatment, as in the human relations model. Instead, managers should share responsibility for achieving organiza-

---

[4]Douglas McGregor, *The Human Side of Enterprise* (New York: McGraw-Hill, 1960); McGregor, *The Professional Manager* (New York: McGraw-Hill, 1967).

TABLE 14-1 GENERAL PATTERNS OF MANAGERIAL APPROACHES TO MOTIVATION

TRADITIONAL MODEL	HUMAN RELATIONS MODEL	HUMAN RESOURCES MODEL
	Assumptions	
1. Work is inherently distasteful to most people. 2. What they do is less important than what they earn for doing it. 3. Few want or can handle work that requires creativity, self-direction, or self-control.	1. People want to feel useful and important. 2. People want to belong and to be recognized as individuals. 3. These needs are more important than money in motivating people to work.	1. Work is not inherently distasteful. People want to contribute to meaningful goals that they have helped establish. 2. Most people can exercise far more creativity, self-direction, and self-control than their present jobs demand.
	Policies	
1. The manager should closely supervise and control subordinates. 2. He or she must break down tasks into simple, repetitive, easily learned operations. 3. He or she must establish detailed work routines and procedures, and enforce these fairly but firmly.	1. The manager should make each worker feel useful and important. 2. He or she should keep subordinates informed and listen to their objections to his or her plans. 3. The manager should allow subordinates to exercise some self-direction and self-control on routine matters.	1. The manager should make use of underutilized human resources. 2. He or she must create an environment in which all members may contribute to the limits of their ability. 3. He or she must encourage full participation in important matters, continually broadening subordinate self-direction and self-control.
	Expectations	
1. People can tolerate work if the pay is decent and the boss is fair. 2. If tasks are simple enough and people are closely controlled, they will produce up to standard.	1. Sharing information with subordinates and involving them in routine decisions will satisfy their basic needs to belong and to feel important. 2. Satisfying these needs will improve morale and reduce resistance to formal authority—subordinates will "willingly cooperate."	1. Expanding subordinate influence, self-direction, and self-control will lead to direct improvements in operating efficiency. 2. Work satisfaction may improve as a "by-product" of subordinates' making full use of their resources.

Source: Adapted from Richard M. Steers and Lyman W. Porter, eds., *Motivation and Work Behavior,* 3rd ed. (New York: McGraw-Hill, 1983), p. 14. Copyright 1983 by McGraw-Hill Book Company. Used with permission of the publisher.

tional and individual objectives, with each person contributing on the basis of his or her interests and abilities. (See Table 14-1 for a description of all three approaches.)

One study found that contemporary managers tend to believe simultaneously in two models of motivation. With their subordinates, managers tend to operate according to the human relations model: They try to reduce subordinates' resistance by improving morale and satisfaction. For themselves, however, managers prefer the human resources model: They feel their own talents are underutilized, and they seek greater responsibility from their superiors.[5]

THREE TYPES OF MOTIVATION THEORIES

TEACHING TIP

Prepare an overhead with these categories on it: content, process, and reinforcement.

It is useful to review some of the major classifications of motivation theories, since each theoretical perspective will shed light on how motivation influences work performance. Distinctions are made on the basis of *content theories,* which focus on the

[5]Raymond E. Miles, "Human Relations or Human Resources," *Harvard Business Review* 43, no. 4 (July–August 1965):148–163.

''what'' of motivation, and *process theories,* which focus on the ''how'' of motivation. *Reinforcement theories,* a third approach, emphasize the ways in which behavior is learned.

Content Theories

The content approach is associated with such names as Maslow, Alderfer, McGregor, Herzberg, Atkinson, and McClelland. Some of these are familiar to managers because these authors have strongly influenced the management field and have affected the thoughts and actions of practicing managers.

The content perspective stresses understanding the factors within individuals that cause them to act in a certain way. It attempts to answer such questions as: What needs do people try to satisfy? What impels them to action? In this view, individuals have inner needs that they are motivated to reduce or fulfill. That is, individuals will act or behave in ways that will lead to the satisfaction of their needs. (See Fig. 14-1.) For example, an employee who has a strong need to achieve may be motivated to work extra hours in order to complete a difficult task on time; an employee with a strong need for self-esteem may be motivated to work very carefully in order to produce high-quality work.

At first glance, this approach seems simple: It suggests that managers can determine subordinates' needs by observing their actions managers can predict subordinates' actions by becoming aware of their needs. In practice, however, motivation is far more complicated. There are several reasons for this complexity.

First, needs differ considerably among individuals and will change over time. Furthermore, individual differences complicate a manager's motivational task enormously. Many ambitious managers, highly motivated to achieve power and status, find it hard to understand that not all people have the same values and drives they have. As a result, such managers find that trying to motivate subordinates is a frustrating and discouraging experience.

Second, the ways in which needs are eventually translated into actions also vary considerably among individuals. Someone with a strong need for security may play it safe and avoid accepting responsibility for fear of failing and being fired. Another person with the same security need may seek out responsibility for fear of being fired for poor performance.

Third, people do not always act on their needs consistently, and the needs that motivate them may vary. While a subordinate may outperform our highest expectations

FIGURE 14-1 A CONTENT THEORY MODEL OF MOTIVATION

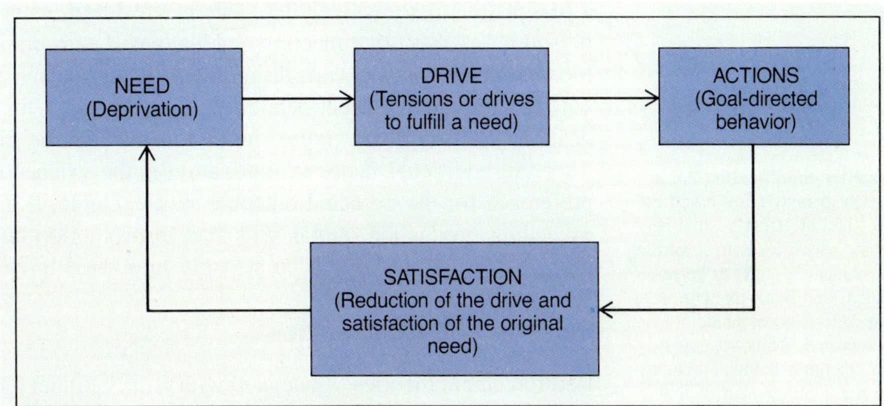

TABLE 14-2 SOURCES OF JOB SATISFACTION AND JOB DISSATISFACTION

FACTORS THAT LED TO EXTREME *SATISFACTION*	FACTORS THAT LED TO EXTREME *DISSATISFACTION*
Achievement	Company policy and administration
Recognition	Supervision Relationship with supervisor
Work itself	Work conditions Salary
Responsibility	Relationship with peers Relationship with subordinates
Advancement	Status
Growth	Security

Source: Adapted by permission of the *Harvard Business Review.* Excerpt from "One More Time: How Do You Motivate Employees?" by Frederick Herzberg, *Harvard Business Review,* Vol. 46 (January–February 1968), p. 57.

on one given day, that same subordinate may perform a similar task in a mediocre manner on another day.

Finally, the reactions of individuals to need fulfillment or lack of fulfillment will differ. Some individuals with a high security need who fail to attain their goal (say, achieving a sales objective) may become frustrated and give up trying. Others may be motivated to redouble their efforts (say, by prospecting for new customers and making additional calls on existing ones).

The more we get to know the people around us (and ourselves), the better able we will be to understand their needs and what will motivate them. However, human behavior depends on so many complexities and alternatives that we are occasionally bound to make incorrect predictions. Psychologist Frederick Herzberg and his colleagues found that there are numerous factors associated not only to job *satisfaction,* but to job *dissatisfaction* (see Table 14-2); Herzberg's *two-factor approach* is pursued in more detail later in this chapter.

Process Theories

Rather than emphasizing the content of needs and the driving nature of those needs, the process approach emphasizes how and by what goals individuals are motivated. In this view, needs are just one element in the process by which individuals decide how to behave. For example, individuals may see the strong possibility of receiving some reward (say, a salary increase) if they act in a certain way (say, by working hard). This reward will become an incentive or motive for their behavior.

Basic to process theories of motivation is the notion of expectancy—that is, what a person anticipates is likely to occur as a result of his or her behavior. For example, a person may expect that meeting deadlines will earn praise from superiors and that not meeting deadlines will earn disapproval; if that person prefers praise, then he or she will be motivated to meet deadlines. Conversely, if this person expects that meeting deadlines will not earn praise, he or she may not be motivated to do so.

An additional factor in motivation is the valence or strength of an individual's preference for the expected outcome. For example, if an individual both expects that exceeding production quotas will lead to promotion and strongly desires to be promoted, then he or she will be strongly motivated to exceed production quotas.

behavior modification An approach to motivation based on the "law of effect"—that behavior which leads to rewarding consequences tends to be repeated, and behavior with negative consequences tends not to be repeated. Thus, managers can change behavior by changing the consequences of that behavior.

Reinforcement Theories

Reinforcement theories, associated with B. F. Skinner and others, are also often called **behavior modification.** These theories do not utilize the concept of a motive or a process of motivation. Instead, they deal with how the consequences of a past action influence future actions in a cyclical learning process. In this view, people behave the way they do because they have learned through experience that certain behaviors are associated with pleasant outcomes and others with unpleasant outcomes. Because people generally prefer pleasant outcomes, they are likely to avoid behaviors with unpleasant consequences. For example, individuals may be likely to obey the law—and a manager's legitimate instructions—because they have learned at home and at school that disobedience leads to punishment.

A SYSTEMS VIEW OF MOTIVATION IN ORGANIZATIONS

EXTRA EXERCISE

Interview 3 or 4 managers and ask them to describe their approach to motivating. Bring the comments back to class and compare them to chapter concepts.

With so many different views of motivation, how can managers utilize current knowledge to improve their understanding of how individuals behave in organizations? Lyman Porter and Raymond Miles have suggested that a systems perspective toward motivation will be most useful to managers.[6] By systems perspective they mean that the entire system of forces operating on the employee must be considered before the employee's motivation and behavior can be adequately understood. By adopting a systems perspective, we can draw on the ideas put forth by content, process, and reinforcement theories. Porter and Miles believe that system consists of three sets of variables affecting motivation in organizations: individual characteristics, job characteristics, and work situation characteristics. (See Table 14-3.)

Individual characteristics are the interests, attitudes, and needs that a person brings to the work situation. Obviously, people differ in these characteristics, and their motivations will therefore differ. For example, one person may desire prestige and be motivated by a job with an impressive title; another may desire money and be motivated to earn a high salary.

Job characteristics are the attributes of the employee's tasks and include the amount of responsibility, the variety of tasks, and the extent to which the job itself has characteristics that people find satisfying. A job that is intrinsically satisfying will be more motivating for many people than a job that is not.

Work situation characteristics are factors in the work environment of the individual. Do colleagues encourage the individual to perform to a high standard or do they encourage low productivity? Do superiors reward high performance or do they ignore it? Does the organization's culture foster concern for members of the organization—or does it encourage cold and indifferent formality?

---

[6]Porter and Miles, "Motivation and Management," pp. 546–550.

TABLE 14-3 VARIABLES AFFECTING MOTIVATION IN ORGANIZATIONAL SETTINGS

INDIVIDUAL CHARACTERISTICS	JOB CHARACTERISTICS	WORK SITUATION CHARACTERISTICS
1. Interests 2. Attitudes (examples): —Toward self —Toward job —Toward aspects of the work situation 3. Needs (examples): —Security —Social —Achievement	Examples: —Types of intrinsic rewards —Degrees of autonomy —Amount of direct performance feedback —Degree of variety in tasks	1. Immediate Work Environment a. Peers b. Supervisor(s) 2. Organizational Actions a. Reward practices (1) Systemwide rewards (2) Individual rewards b. Organizational culture

Note: These lists are not intended to be exhaustive; they are meant to indicate some of the more important variables influencing employee motivation.

Source: Lyman W. Porter and Raymond E. Miles, "Motivation and Management," in Joseph W. McGuire, ed., *Contemporary Management: Issues and Viewpoints*, p. 547. © 1974. Adapted by permission of Prentice Hall, Inc., Englewood Cliffs, N.J.

Characteristics of the Individual

Each individual brings his or her own interests, attitudes, and needs to the work situation. In this section, we will discuss some contributions to our understanding of human needs and motivation.

The Hierarchy of Human Needs. Abraham Maslow's hierarchy of needs has probably received more attention from managers than any other theory of motivation, not only because it classifies human needs in a convenient way, but because it also has direct implications for managing human behavior in organizations. Maslow's is a content theory that tries to assess the individual characteristics and needs that people bring to their jobs.[7]

Maslow viewed human motivation as a hierarchy of five needs (see Fig. 14-2):

1. *Physiological*—includes the need for air, water, food, and sex.
2. *Security*—includes the need for safety, order, and freedom from fear or threat.
3. *Belongingness and love (or social needs)*—include the need for love, affection, feelings of belonging, and human contact.
4. *Esteem*—includes the need for self-respect, self-esteem, achievement, and respect from others.
5. *Self-actualization*—includes the need to grow, to feel fulfilled, and to realize one's potential.

CLASS COMMENT

Some basic concepts to understand about Maslow's theory include hierarchy of needs, prepotency, and adequate (or satisfactory) fulfillment of needs.

According to Maslow, individuals will be motivated to fulfill whichever need is *prepotent,* or most powerful, for them at a given time. The prepotency of a need depends on the individual's current situation and recent experiences. Starting with the physical needs, which are most basic, each need must be at least partially satisfied before the individual desires to satisfy a need at the next higher level.

The practical implications of this theory for motivation in organizations are many. The basic physiological needs of employees must be satisfied by a wage sufficient to feed, shelter, and protect them and their families satisfactorily, and a safe working environment must be provided before managers offer incentives designed to provide employees with esteem, feelings of belonging, or opportunities to grow. Secu-

[7]See Abraham H. Maslow, *Motivation and Personality,* 2nd ed. (New York: Harper & Row, 1970), pp. 35–58.

FIGURE 14-2 PYRAMID REPRESENTING MASLOW'S HIERARCHY OF EMOTIONS

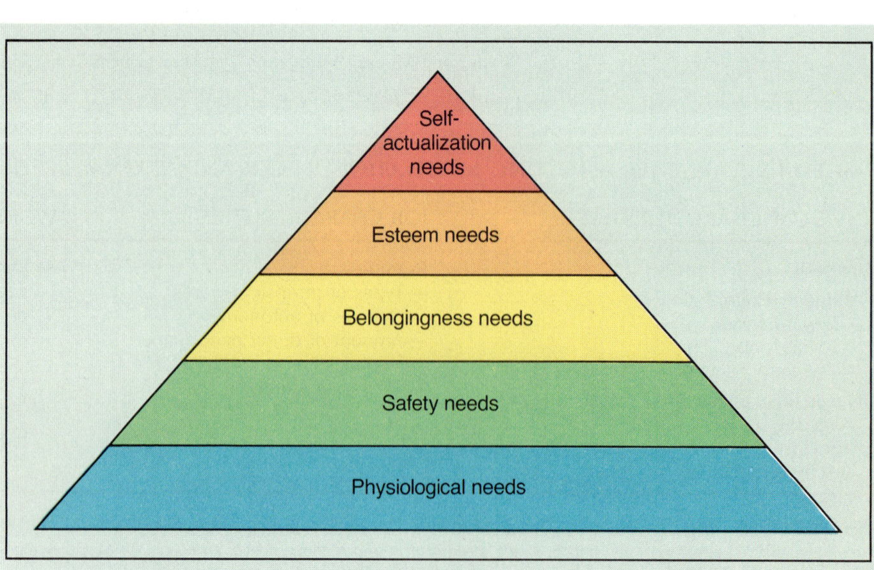

rity needs require job security, freedom from coercion or feelings of arbitrary treatment, and clearly defined regulations.

In the modern organization, both physiological and security needs are usually (but not always) met satisfactory. The need to belong and be loved, most strongly felt in relation to one's family, can also be satisfied in social contexts through friendship and being "one of the gang" at work. The work environment is a social environment, and unless employees feel that they are an integral part of the organization, they will be frustrated by an unmet need to belong and will be unlikely to respond to higher-order opportunities or incentives.

Maslow described two types of esteem needs—the desire for achievement and competence and the desire for status and recognition. In organizational terms, people want to be good at their jobs; they also want to feel that they are achieving something important when they perform their jobs. As managers, we have many ways of fulfilling both types of esteem needs in subordinates by providing challenging work assignments, performance feedback, performance recognition, and personal encouragement and by involving subordinates in goal setting and decision making. When AT&T divested itself of the Bell Operating Companies, its executives had to give careful consideration to the ways in which AT&T employees could continue to achieve important goals in their jobs. The traditional corporate value of "serving the public interest" was no longer clearly operable, and some employees began to question the worth of what they were doing as a result of their work activities.

According to Maslow, when all other needs have been adequately met, employees will become motivated by the need for self-actualization. They will look for meaning and personal growth in their work and will actively seek out new responsibilities. Maslow stresses that individual differences are greatest at this level. For some individuals, producing work of high quality may be a means for self-actualization, while for others, developing creative, useful ideas serves the same need. By being aware of the different self-actualization needs of subordinates, managers can use a variety of approaches to enable subordinates to achieve personal as well as organizational goals.[8]

ERG Theory. Psychologist Clayton Alderfer agreed that worker motivation could be gauged according to a hierarchy of needs but disagreed on a fundamental point: whereas Maslow believed that a satisfied need diminished, Alderfer stressed that when higher needs were frustrated, lower needs, although already satisfied, returned.[9]

Alderfer broke needs down into three categories: E*xistence* needs (Maslow's fundamental needs plus such factors as fringe benefits in the workplace), R*elatedness* needs (needs for interpersonal relations), and G*rowth* needs (needs for personal creativity or productive influence). The first letters of each category thus form the now-familiar acronym *ERG*. Some research indicates that workers themselves tend to categorize their needs much as Alderfer does,[10] but like Maslow, Alderfer has proposed a theory that is hard to test and, of course, difficult to evaluate in terms of its application to organizational goal setting, management practice, or personal fulfillment on the part of employees.[11] Like Maslow's, Alderfer's theory is not entirely satisfactory in accounting for the means by which human needs are translated into productive human energy.

---

[8]See Ellen L. Betz, "Two Tests of Maslow's Theory of Need Fulfillment," *Journal of Vocational Behavior* 24, no. 2 (April 1984):204–220; and Howard S. Schwartz, "Maslow and the Hierarchical Enactment of Organizational Reality," *Human Relations* 36, no. 10 (October 1983):933–956.

[9]C. P. Alderfer, "An Empirical Test of a New Theory of Human Needs," *Organizational and Human Needs* 4 (1969):142–175; and Alderfer, *Existence, Relatedness, and Growth: Human Needs in Organizational Settings* (New York: Free Press, 1972).

[10]J. Rauschenberger, N. Schmitt, and J. E. Hunter, "A Test of the Need Hierarchy Concept by a Markov Model of Change in Need Strength," *Administrative Science Quarterly* 25 (1980):654–670.

[11]J. P. Wanous and A. Zwany, "A Cross-Sectional Test of the Need Hierarchy Theory," *Organizational Behavior and Human Performance* 18 (1977):78–79.

INTERNATIONAL MANAGEMENT

QUESTIONING THE APPLICABILITY OF UNIVERSAL THEORIES OF MOTIVATION

In 1973, Geert Hofstede, a Dutch organizational consultant and scholar, studied the concepts of motivation, leadership, and organization in 72 countries to find out if American theories applied elsewhere around the globe. Using the IBM databank on international employee-attitude surveys, Hofstede was able to determine the extent to which Maslow's and other motivational theories could be applied in other nations to aid management in the motivation of its employees.

Not surprisingly, Hofstede discovered that there were many differences among cultures. He proposed that many of the differences in employee motivation, management styles, and organizational structures throughout the world could be traced to differences in the "collective mental programming" of people in different cultures.

He concluded that motivational theories such as Maslow's hierarchy of needs was by no means the description of a universal human motivational process: Rather, he concluded that it was the description of a value system—namely, the value system of the U.S. middle class to which Maslow belonged. Countries that had developed other value systems may have come to value security needs over social or self-esteem needs. For example, in Sweden, which has been quite successful in implementing participatory management styles, social needs are valued over esteem needs. In Germany, Japan, Switzerland, Italy, and Austria, security is generally valued over social and esteem needs. In France and Yugoslovia, security needs are highly valued, but so are social needs. In Canada, India, and Great Britian as well as the U.S., the general tenets of Maslow's theory applied relatively well.

Findings such as those of Hofstede prompt further speculation. The U.S., for example, is a quite heterogeneous country—a culture formed by and composed of a diverse population of individuals who have come to this country from all over the world. Moreover, that culture has experienced changes in the conformation of its diverse social structure, some leading to greater homogeneity, others to new problems in cultural diversity. Just how valuable is it to apply ostensibly universal theories of work motivation to such a culture just because it happens to be geographically identifiable?

Consider, for example, the influx of Mexican immigrants into the U.S.—some 2 million documented since the 1860s, between 4 and 7 million undocumented between the 1920s and 1980s. Recent Department of Health, Education, and Welfare statistics place the unemployment rate for Mexican-American men at 8.5 percent, compared to about 5.5 percent for non-Hispanic white males. Mexican-American workers are sharply underrepresented in sales, managerial, and professional positions, and as of the early 1980s, median family income for Mexican-American families, with one-fifth of those families subsisting below the official poverty level, was only about 70 percent of that of Anglo-American families.

In effect, then, the labor culture in the U.S., as regards not only Hispanics but blacks and Native Americans, is virtually analogous to an international labor culture, and it is not likely that the sociocultural influences on the thinking of Maslow and other classic theorists about work motivation will be directly applicable to such growing segments of the U.S. work force as its Mexican-American population.

(Exhibit 14-1 lists several of the most important demographic factors that managers and management theorists must now begin to consider. The issues raised by these statistics range from ethical to practical problems resulting from the need to rethink the application of motivational theories to a work force changing in gender, ethnicity, and age.)

Sources: Geert Hofstede, "Motivation, Leadership, and Organization: Do American Theories Apply Abroad?" *Organizational Dynamics,* Summer 1980, pp. 42–63; Hofstede and Michael Harris Bond, "The Confucius Connection: From Cultural Roots to Economic Growth," *Organizational Dynamics,* Spring 1988, pp. 5–21; Joe R. Feagin, *Racial and Ethnic Relations,* 2nd ed. (Englewood Cliffs, N.J.: Prentice Hall, 1984), Chapter 9.

EXHIBIT 14-1 MOTIVATION AND THE CHANGING DEMOGRAPHICS OF THE WORKPLACE

- Compared to 24 percent a decade ago, 37 percent of corporate managers are now women.
- In 1986, 44.6 percent of the work force consisted of white males; this figure is projected to decline to 39.2 percent by the year 2000.
- Less than 7 percent of American families now conform to the model of the traditional nuclear family, whereby the father functioned as the sole breadwinner and the mother functioning as at-home caregiver to the children.
- The baby-boom generation—people born between 1946 and 1964, are having approximately half as many children as their parents did; this same generation also tends to give high priority to family and friends and to life fulfillment within those contexts.
- America's 36 million disabled people are battling discrimination with a style and success reminiscent of that of 1960s activism.
- Constituting about 10 percent of the nation's population, gays are becoming increasingly active in lobbying for the work rights accorded other minority groups.
- The 1987 freshman class entering the University of California, Berkeley campus, was 26 percent Asian.
- Although approximately only 9 percent of American managers are currently minority-group members, it is expected that the following figures will obtain: Out of a work force of 138.8 million, 35.1 percent will be white females, 11.5 percent blacks, 4 percent Asians, and 10.2 percent Hispanics—at total of almost 61 percent of the work force.
- It is estimated that, by 1990, the average age of the work force will be 40.

Sources: Sharon Nelton, "Meet Your New Work Force," *Nation's Business* 76, no. 7 (1988):14–21; Colin Leinster, "Black Executives: How They're Doing," *Fortune,* January 18, 1988, pp. 109–120; "Corporate Women," *Business Week,* June 22, 1987, pp. 72–77; "The 'Last Minority' Fights for Its Rights," *Business Week,* June 6, 1988, pp. 140–143; "The Coming Labor Shortage," *Business Week,* August 10, 1987, pp. 48–51.

ILLUSTRATIVE CASE STUDY Continued

Creating a Committed Work Force at Domino's Pizza

At one level, Domino's is run according to a modification of Alderfer's model of work motivation. Clearly, Thomas Monaghan believes that people need to be rewarded for their efforts and that most of them, like Monaghan himself, have dreams that can be nurtured and satisfied by material wealth. Whether these dreams coincide with basic "existence needs" or the need of some people to find self-esteem through possessions is a matter of debate among psychologists. Whether they can be applied in the workplace is a question of practical managerial creativity.

He also believes that people need a sense of belonging and that they want to cooperate with others in a successful working environment. Domino's thus emphasizes teamwork. Even working at a somewhat routine and standardized job like pizza delivery, it is possible for a Domino's employee to be part of a group, a family, with the sense of belonging that families engender.

Finally, we might explain Domino's success by the fact that it challenges people to use their creativity. In a business as straightforward as pizza parlors, Domino's has found that innovation and creativity can play an important role in giving people a sense of improving the company product, in enhancing their own talents in pursuing their own opportunities, and in making the organization successful.

The Urge to Achieve and Entrepreneurial Behavior. John W. Atkinson and others hold that all healthy adults have a reservoir of potential energy. The means by which this energy is released and used depend on the strength of the individual's motivational drives and the situations and opportunities presented. An individual's striving for a particular goal results from (1) the strength of the basic motive or need involved, (2) his or her expectation of succeeding, and (3) the incentive value attached to the goal.[12]

[12]John W. Atkinson and David Birch, *An Introduction to Motivation,* rev. ed. (New York: Van Nostrand Reinhold, 1978), pp. 346–348; and John W. Atkinson, *Personality, Motivation, and Action: Selected Papers* (New York: Praeger, 1983), pp. 174–188.

Atkinson's model related behavior and performance to three basic drives, which vary significantly among individuals: the need for achievement, the need for power, and the need for affiliation or close association with others. For example, an individual might be motivated by a high need for affiliation. If he or she is in a work environment where considerable interaction with other employees takes place, the individual's potential energy for affiliation will be released, and work enjoyment might be high; on the other hand, if the work environment is unfriendly or the individual must work alone, then the individual's affiliation need will not be met in the workplace, and so motivation to come to work might be low.

David C. McClelland related these concepts directly to business drive and management. (We have already discussed, in Chapter 10, the relationship between the need for power and management success.) McClelland's research indicated that a strong need for achievement was related to how well individuals were motivated to perform their work tasks.[13]

The need for achievement can be defined as a desire to excel or to succeed in competitive situations.[14] As Exhibit 14-2 shows, McClelland found that people with a high need for achievement have several characteristics of interest to managers. Thus, those with *high achievement needs (nAch)* tend to be highly motivated by challenging and competitive work situations; conversely, people with low achievement needs tend to perform poorly in competitive or challenging work situations.[15]

EXHIBIT 14-2 McCLELLAND'S THREE-POINT DESCRIPTION OF ACHIEVEMENT MOTIVES

1. Individuals with a high need for achievement like taking responsibility for solving problems.
2. They tend to set moderately difficult goals for themselves and to take calculated risks to achieve their goals.
3. They place great importance on feedback on how well they are doing.

Source: David C. McClelland, *The Achieving Society* (Princeton, N.J.: Van Nostrand, 1961).

There is considerable evidence of the correlation between high achievement needs and high performance. McClelland found, for example, that people who succeeded in competitive occupations were well above average in achievement motivation. Successful managers, who presumably operated in one of the most competitive of all environments, had a higher achievement need than other professionals.[16] McClelland later reported considerable success in teaching adults to increase their achievement motivation and, in turn, to improve their work performance.[17] McClelland also found *the need for affiliation (nAff)* an import factor in employee satisfaction.

For managers, these findings highlight the importance of matching the individual and the job. Employees with high achievement needs thrive on work that is challeng-

[13]David C. McClelland, *The Achieving Society* (Princeton, N.J.: Van Nostrand Reinhold, 1961), and "Business Drive and National Achievement," *Harvard Business Review* 40, no. 4 (July–August 1962):99–112. Also see John G. Nicholls, "Achievement Motivation: Conceptions of Ability, Subjective Experience, Task Choice, and Performance," *Psychological Review* 91, no. 3 (July 1984):328–346.

[14]For a good discussion of achievement motivation in work situations, see Edward E. Lawler III, *Motivation in Work Organizations* (Monterey, Calif.: Brooks/Cole, 1973), pp. 20–23.

[15]Danny Miller, "The Correlates of Entrepreneurship in Three Types of Firms," *Management Science* 29, no. 7 (July 1983):770–791.

[16]See McClelland, "Business Drive and National Achievement," pp. 99–112; and Michael J. Stahl, "Achievement, Power and Managerial Motivation: Selecting Managerial Talent with the Job Choice Exercise," *Personnel Psychology* 36, no. 4 (Winter 1983):775–789.

[17]David C. McClelland, "Toward a Theory of Motive Acquisition," *American Psychologist* 20, no. 5 (May 1965):321–333. Also see the interview with David C. McClelland in "As I See It," *Forbes,* June 1, 1969, pp. 53–57.

CLASS COMMENT

To some extent, the need for achievement can be taught and learned.

ing, satisfying, stimulating, and complex; they welcome autonomy, variety, and frequent feedback from supervisors. Employees with low achievement needs prefer situations of stability, security, and predictability; they respond better to considerate than to impersonal high-pressure supervision and look to the workplace and co-workers for social satisfaction. McClelland's research also suggests that managers can, to some extent, raise the achievement need level of subordinates by creating the proper work environment—permitting their subordinates a measure of independence, increasing responsibility and autonomy, gradually making tasks more challenging, and praising and rewarding high performance. McClelland characterized this aspect of managerial motivation as a *need for power (nPow).*

High achievement needs can also be fueled by an individual's *fear of failure.*[18] Managers may be strongly motivated to take action by their fear of failing to meet personal or organizational goals and by the fear of possible public embarrassment when these failures are recognized. Conversely, for some individuals, *fear of success* can be a motive.[19] Such people fear the stress and burden of their success and the envy and dislike it may awaken in others.

Exhibit 14-3 simplifies the factors in McClelland's "three-needs" theory.

EXHIBIT 14-3 McCLELLAND'S THREE-NEEDS THEORY FOR SUCCESSFUL MANAGERIAL ACHIEVEMENT

1. **Need for achievement *(nAch)*:** the drive to excel, to achieve in relation to a set of standards, to strive to succeed
2. **Need for affiliation *(nAff)*:** the desire for friendly and close interpersonal relationships
3. **Need for power *(nPow)*:** the need to make others behave in a way that they would not otherwise

Source: David C. McClelland, *The Achieving Society* (New York: Van Nostrand, 1961); and McClelland, *Power: The Inner Experience* (New York: Irvington, 1975).

Characteristics of the Job Task

The characteristics of the job and its associated tasks, the second variable influencing motivation in organizations, is the one on which managers have the greatest potential impact. Researchers have tried to discover how a particular job will affect an individual's desire to perform that job well. Significant interest in this area developed because routine, assembly-line types of jobs were shown to reduce employee motivation and add to dissatisfaction. Understanding of the relationship between job characteristics and motivation increased when Frederick Herzberg introduced his two-factor theory. Herzberg's work generated a great deal of interest in the role of motivation in the daily operations of organizations.

FOR DISCUSSION

Think of the "best" and "worst" jobs you have had. What made them good and bad? Relate these to Herzberg's satisfiers and dissatisfiers.

A Two-Factor Approach to Work Motivation. In the late 1950s, Herzberg and his associates conducted a study of the job attitudes of two hundred engineers and accountants, asking subjects their jobs and tabulated the results. As Figure 14-3 shows, Herzberg placed responses in 1 of 16 categories: the factors on the *right* side of the figure were consistently related to job satisfaction, those on the *left* side to job dissatisfac-

[18] See Leonard H. Chusmir, "Personnel Administrators' Perception of Sex Differences in Motivation of Managers: Research-Based or Stereotyped?" *International Journal of Women's Studies* 7, no. 1 (January–February 1984):17–23; and Heinz Heckhausen, Heinz-Dieter Schmalt, and Klaus Schneider, *Achievement Motivation in Perspective* (Orlando, Fla.: Academic Press, 1985).

[19] Maureen Kearney, "A Comparison of Motivation to Avoid Success in Males and Females," *Journal of Clinical Psychology* 4, no. 4 (July 1984):1005–1007.

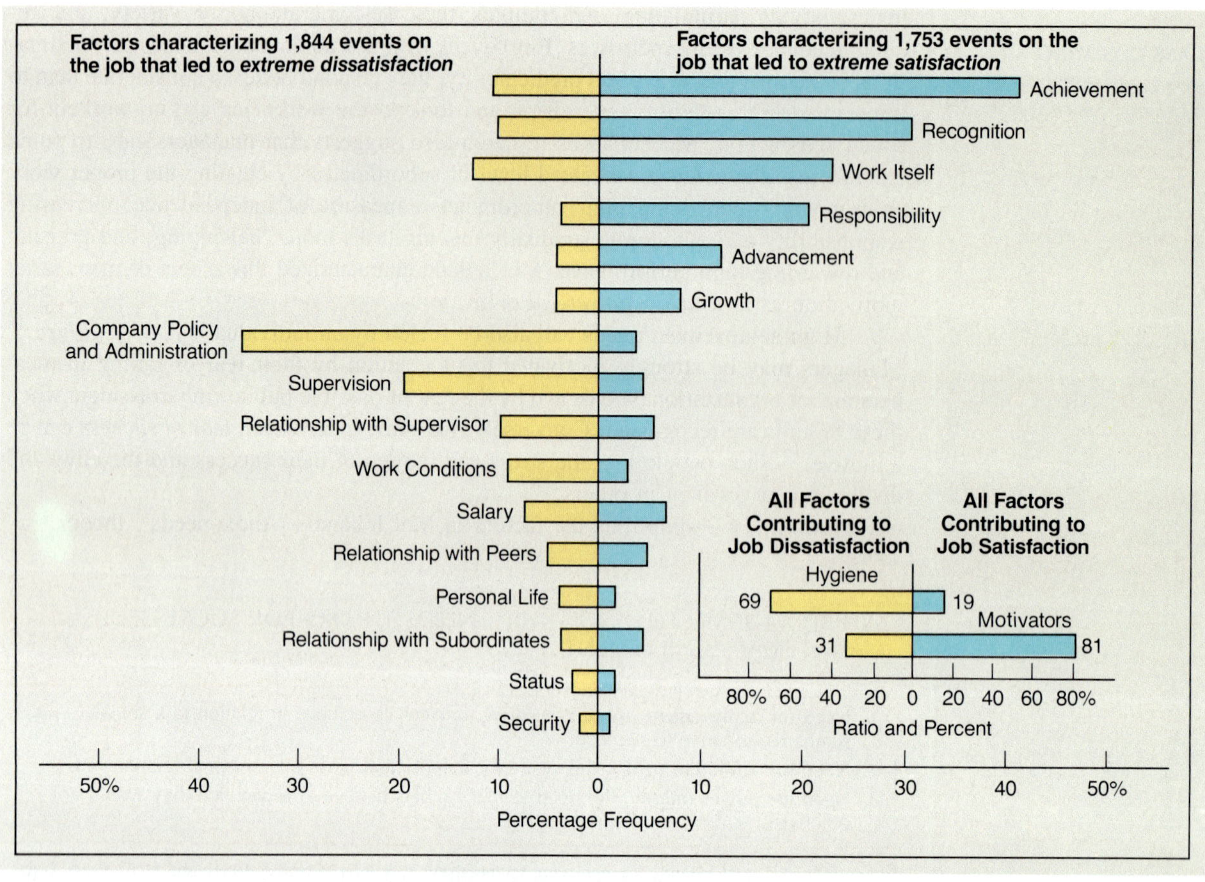

Source: Frederick Herzberg, "One More Time: How Do You Motivate Employees?" *Harvard Business Review* (January–February 1969):57. Copyright © 1969 by the President and Fellows at Harvard College; all rights reserved.

FIGURE 14-3 HERZBERG'S COMPARISON OF JOB-SATISFACTION AND JOB-DISSATISFACTION FACTORS

tion.[20] Subjects were asked to recall times when they felt exceptionally good about their jobs and times when they felt bad. From his research, Herzberg concluded that job satisfaction and job dissatisfaction come from two separate sets of factors, which he called *satisfiers* (motivating factors) and *dissatisfiers* (''hygiene'' factors).

The satisfiers included achievement, recognition, responsibility, and advancement. The satisfiers are related to the nature of the work (the job *content*) and to rewards that result directly from performance of the work tasks. The dissatisfiers included salary, working conditions, and company policy and involved the individual's relationship to the organization's environment (the job *context*) in which the work is being done. The most important of these factors is company policy, which is judged by many individuals to be a major cause of inefficiency and ineffectiveness. Positive ratings for these factors did not lead to job satisfaction but merely to the absence of dissatisfaction.

Herzberg's work has been criticized for his method of collecting data, which assumed that people will report their satisfying and dissatisfying experiences accurately.[21] Subsequent research indicates that the two-factor theory oversimplifies the

[20]Frederick Herzberg, Bernard Mausner, and Barbara Synderman, *The Motivation to Work* (New York: John Wiley, 1959). See also Frederick Herzberg, *Work and the Nature of Man* (New York: World Publishing, 1966), and ''One More Time: How Do You Motivate Employees?'' *Harvard Business Review* 46, no. 1 (January–February 1968):53–62. For a critique of this and other models, see James A. Lee, *The Gold and Garbage in Management Theories* (Athens: Ohio University Press, 1980).

[21]Victor Vroom, *Work and Motivation* (New York: John Wiley, 1964).

relationship between satisfaction and motivation, and that the identical factors may result in job satisfaction for one person and job dissatisfaction for another.[22] (See Exhibit 14-4.)

EXTRA EXERCISE

Examine one of your favorite classes. What aspects of the class could you classify as hygiene factors? As motivators?

Nevertheless, Herzberg's theory is still regarded as an important contribution to our understanding of the effects of job characteristics on satisfaction, motivation, and performance. Job enrichment programs, for example, which we discussed in Chapter 9, were strongly influenced by the work of Herzberg and his colleagues.

EXHIBIT 14-4 CRITICISMS OF HERZBERG'S TWO-FACTOR THEORY

- Since people tend to credit themselves for successful activities while blaming outside factors for unsuccessful activities, Herzberg's procedure is questionable.
- Because raters were required to make sometimes subjective interpretations, their responses are not necessarily consistent.
- Inasmuch as a person may like one part of his or her job but not another, Herzberg should have devised some scale of "overall" satisfaction of dissatisfaction.
- Unlike previous research, Herzberg's work does not take into account the variables that occur among different people in different situations.
- Although he assumed a relationship between satisfaction and productivity, Herzberg examined only satisfaction and not productivity.

Sources: Michael E. Gordon, Norman M. Pryor, and Bob V. Harris, "An Examination of Scaling Bias in Herzberg's Theory of Job Satisfaction," *Organizational Behavior and Human Performance* (February 1974):106–121; and Edwin A. Locke and Roman J. Whiting, "Sources of Satisfaction and Dissatisfaction Among Solid Waste Management Employees," *Journal of Applied Psychology* (April 1974):145–156.

Characteristics of the Work Situation

The work situation, the third set of variables that can affect job motivation, consists of two categories: the actions, policies, and culture of the organization as a whole and the immediate work environment.

Organizational Policies, Reward Systems, and Culture. The overall personnel policies of the organization, its methods for rewarding individual employees, and the organization's culture all translate into organizational actions that influence and motivate workers.

HERE'S AN EXAMPLE

Retailers are stepping up efforts to curb costly employee theft. Bloomingdale's in New York awards employees $2,500 for snitching on a dishonest co-worker. Alexander's, a New York–based discount department store chain, doubled its reward to $1,000 and has begun offering each whistle-blower a year of chances in a twice-weekly New York state lottery game. (*Wall Street Journal*, 9/17/87, p. 37)

Personnel policies, such as wage scales and employee benefits (vacations, pensions, and the like), generally have little impact on individual performance. But these policies do affect the desire of employees to remain with or leave the organization and its ability to attract new employees. For example, a no lay-off policy at IBM has long been a factor in motivating people to seek employment with the company. That policy, however, is the result in trade-offs on other matters of personnel policy. Similarly, concession bargaining between such unions as the United Auto Workers and major U.S. automobile firms has, at least temporarily, increased the motivation to improve productivity, with management working to improve employment security in exchange for payroll and benefits concessions.

CLASS COMMENT

Young workers are more likely to want performance-based incentives than fixed salaries. (*Springfield News-Leader*, 6/23/88, p. 6B)

The *reward system* of the organization guides the actions that generally have the greatest impact on the motivation and performance of individual employees. Salary increases, bonuses, and promotions can be strong motivators of individual performance—provided they are effectively administered. The reward or compensation must justify, in the employee's mind, the extra effort that improved performance requires, the reward must be directly and specifically associated with improved performance so

[22]Robert J. House and Lawrence A. Wigdor, "Herzberg's Dual-Factor Theory of Job Satisfaction and Motivation," *Personnel Psychology* 20, no. 4 (Winter 1967):369–389.

"It has come to my attention that somebody in here is only going through the motions."

Drawing by Stevenson; © 1982 The New Yorker Magazine, Inc.

that it is clear why the reward has been given, and it must be seen as fair by others in the work group so that they will not feel resentful and retaliate by lowering their own performance levels.

HERE'S AN EXAMPLE

Managers face some real problems with temporary workers. They must motivate the temps and keep quality high. At Corroon and Black Corporation, managers make sure temps get nameplates, restroom keys, and internal memos related to their work. (*Wall Street Journal*, 4/5/88, p. 39)

The organization's *culture*—the shared norms, values, and beliefs of its members—can enhance or decrease an individual's performance. Employees whose personalities do not mesh with the culture of their organization—for example, a creative, unconventional individual with low respect for authority working in a conservative accounting firm—will not be as highly motivated as employees who "fit" the culture. By the same token, a long-time employee at IBM, which is noted for its highly formal culture, might experience some difficulty in adjusting to the more informal cultures at Apple or Tandem, even though they are engaged in the same industry. In addition, certain types of cultures are likely to be more successful in motivating employees than are others. Cultures that foster respect for employees, that integrate them into the decision-making process, and that give them autonomy in planning and executing tasks encourage better performance than do highly regimented cultures. (See Chapter 12 for a fuller discussion of organizational culture.)

THOUGHT-PROVOKER

Does money motivate? Why or why not?

As managers, we want to motivate employees to high levels of performance, to loyalty and commitment to the organization, and to stability on the job. Money is the most obvious and frequently used incentive, but it is not the only means of motivating workers. In fact, assuming they perceive their compensation as fair, today's workers are responsive to such nonmonetary incentives as extra vacation days, flextime arrangements, day care for their children, recreation facilities at the workplace, and company-sponsored local transportation. Financial incentives other than salary or bonuses also have a place in an incentive system and might include pension plans with early vesting, company shareholding, company contributions to further education, and auto or home loans.

In spite of the advantages of linking pay to performance, many organizations do not attempt to use extra compensation as a motivating factor. It can be difficult to measure the performance of individuals accurately, especially when they hold jobs that are not as directly quantifiable as many production and sales jobs are. In addition, when managers do not feel capable of determining differences in individual performance, they may prefer to keep employees performing the same type of task at about the same salary level in order to avoid creating resentment about hard-to-justify pay differences.

COORDINATED RESOURCE

For a provocative view of the role of money in motivation, see "The Money Society" by M. Magnet in *Fortune*, 7/6/87, pp. 26–31.

However, according to Rosabeth Moss Kanter, the conventional "wisdom" of pay-motivation correlation is undergoing a revolution, albeit a quiet one. It is her contention that, traditionally, pay was largely reflective of input, rather than output, factors. For example, pay reflected factors such as cost to hire, with adjustment for internal equity. The real basis for pay was status or the standing of one's job in the organizational hierarchy: Jobs came with an assigned pay level that remained relatively fixed regardless of how well a job was performed or the value of that performance to the organization. But with such emerging concerns as cost, productivity, and fairness, many organizations are changing their concepts of the pay-motivation correlation. Examples include pay-for-performance policies (Bank America); dollars-for-behavior policies—that is, eliminating simple, across-the-board commissions in favor of an array of incentives for meeting performance targets (Merrill Lynch, GE); policies for entrepreneurial pay or partial employee ownership (AT&T, Sun Microsystems); gain-sharing policies—productivity bonuses on top of salaries (Preston Trucking, GM's new Saturn plant, Marine Systems Division at Honeywell, Inc.); and pay-for-skills policies, which provide individual incentives for employees to upgrade performance while creating teams that are virtually self-managed (General Foods). With this variety of new approaches to the pay-motivation correlation, new theories of motivation will no doubt be needed to explain the evolving relationship between management and employees.

The Immediate Work Environment. The immediate work environment includes attitudes and actions of peers and supervisors and the "climate" they create. Numerous studies have found that peer groups in the work situation can have an enormous influence on people's motivation and performance. Most people desire the friendship and approval of peers and will behave in accordance with the norms and values of the peer group. If the group has an "us-versus-them" approach to management and regards high producers as "rate-busters," its members will not be motivated to perform at their best level and may even be motivated to perform poorly.

QUOTATION FROM A MANAGER

In describing F. Ross Johnson, CEO of RJR-Nabisco, one manager says, "He motivates through a great combination of money and fear"—Robert J. Powelson, former president of Nabisco's U.S. Foods business. (*Business Week*, 5/23/88, p. 182)

Immediate supervisors strongly influence the motivation and performance of employees by example and instruction and through rewards and penalities ranging from praise, salary increases, and promotions to criticism, demotions, and dismissals. They also strongly affect job design and are important transmitters of the organizational culture, especially to new employees. Terrence E. Deal and Allan A. Kennedy point out that corporate "heroes" and "heroines"—managers who embody the values of the culture—provide "a pantheon of role models for managers and employees.[23] Supervisors who emulate the behavior of the organization's heroes and heroines will, in turn, transmit cultural values to their subordinates.

Changes in Work-Situation Variables. The key work-situation variables of organizational action, policy, and culture have begun to play increasingly important roles in contemporary organizational practice—especially as they have become subject to a climate of change influenced by a number of both internal and external factors. Let us consider one of these factors: the trend toward *downsizing*—the effort to reduce an organization's work force in order to make it more competitive. Such developments as downsizing are particularly interesting because they bring to light an important new

---

[23]Terrence E. Deal and Allan A. Kennedy, "Culture: A New Look Through Old Lenses," *Journal of Applied Behavioral Science* 19, no. 4 (1983):498–505.

MANAGEMENT APPLICATION

SUCCEEDING THROUGH TECHNOLOGY AND HUMAN RESOURCES AT CHAPARRAL STEEL

From 1979 to 1982, the 10 American companies known as "Big Steel" saw their employment drop from 453,000 to 247,000. At Chaparral Steel Company, owned by Co-Steel International Ltd. (the third largest Canadian steelmaker), no one has ever been laid off. Co-Steel attributes its financial and management success to its commitment to two principles: stay on the leading edge of technology and treat your people right.

Chaparral Steel can be found on the outskirts of Midlothian, Texas. Of its 935 employees, more than 75 percent have had no previous steel-making experience. New employees, who are hired by supervisors rather than personnel representative's, are given freedom to perform and are expected to be responsible for their work. In a lean company where management lines are direct, responsibility for performance remains with each employee. According to George E. Forward, president, "We expect [our employees] to act like owners."

At the same time, Chaparral has designed a number of mechanisms to motivate its employees. The company will reimburse tuition expenses if a new-hire has ambition but needs training in a specialty field, such as metalluric engineering. In addition, Chaparral sponsors a sabbatical program that provides an employee of two or three years an opportunity to visit other steel mills or customers or to perform research. Chaparral considers every employee to be a member of the sales department, and to be effective each member of the company must know, and be thoroughly challenged by the industry. Says Forward, "We all feel that most factories stifle young people, cripple them with bureaucracy. We want Chaparral to give people freedom to perform, to really tap a person's ego."

The result of Chaparral's somewhat unorthodox management technique is fierce company loyalty and a productivity rate that is increasing.

issue in motivational theory and practice—namely, the need to motivate managerial personnel as well as workers at lower levels in the organization.

COORDINATED RESOURCE

For an interesting description of factors that let well-managed companies do a good job of motivating their employees, see "Lessons from the Best Companies to Work For," by Milton Moskowitz, *California Management Review,* Winter 1985, pp. 42–47.

Many of this country's major firms have reduced the numbers of their managers and employees in the 1980s. In response to increased international competition, the mismanagement of human resources, the accelerated use of technology, disenchantment with large bureaucratic structures, and a growing espousal of the philosophy of "lean and mean," coupled with a renewed determination to focus on the organization's core business, corporations such as IBM, Xerox, Exxon, USX, and many others have begun restructuring by eliminating overlapping layers of bureaucratic activity and, as a result, laid off or fired many people.

The motivational principles of Maslow and other theorists were developed at a time when most of the major corporations practiced a paternalistic relationship with their managers. The employment contract, usually not formalized in a written document but rather as an implicit agreement about how the game would be played, was such that if the manager followed the prescribed motivational incentives within the corporate culture, the job generally brought lifetime tenure and assured employment security. In turn, the corporation demanded loyalty, dependability, and a fair day's work in exchange for a fair day's pay, a secure future, and a chance for advancement. Salary was based on one's position in the organizational hierarchy and not necessarily on performance. People tended to stay with the firm for entire careers and were expected to stay under conditions conducive to hierarchical stability.

However, during the decade of the 1980s the rules of the game changed. In the years from 1984 to 1986, an estimated 500,000 managers at more than 300 corporations lost their jobs or were eased out through early retirement or other means. Downsizing has continued as IBM, Exxon, and other major corporations continue to cut back not only on the work force but on the ranks of management. Many of once-loyal managers are now prey to distraction, disloyalty, alienation, and resentment. The outlook on advancement seems to have shifted from a faith in top management's assurances of continued employment to a commitment to the self-management of individual careers.

Some argue that the reasons for the change in the employee contract include corporate America's failure to foresee or plan for changes in the environment or management ranks swollen by the vast influx of grown-up baby boomers. Whatever the causes, the new reality is that top management must now devise new motivational strategies to cope with the fallout of downsizing—not only for those who lost their jobs but also for those who have retained their positions in a climate of continuing uncertainty. The rules of the game have changed, as has the traditional employment contract that was the basis of many classic motivational theories. Whether these theories and their application will be sufficient and appropriate for a new generation of managers is open to question. Added to the problems of how to motivate workers, the question of how to motivate managers promises to be one of the key issues in motivational theory and practice.[24]

HERE'S AN EXAMPLE

Angus Wurtele, CEO of Valspar Company, a Minneapolis-based paint company, spurs on the managers of the more-than-100 profit centers with a trio of incentives: decision-making autonomy, performance bonuses, and stock ownership. Says Wurtele, "Just one incentive won't do." (*Fortune*, 4/25/88, p. 98)

THE IMPACT OF PAST CONSEQUENCES ON BEHAVIOR

TEACHING TIP

Any discussion of "modifying behavior" generally arouses some suspicions and uneasiness from students. Use these fears and complaints as an opportunity to discuss the role of manager as a modifier of behavior.

An influential—and controversial—approach to influencing human behavior is based on the observation that the consequences of an individual's behavior in one situation can influence that individual's behavior in future, similar situations. Certain techniques, based on this principle and usually characterized as "behavior modification," have been developed to change people's behavior.[25] They may imply that individual behaviors can be predicted from a person's past experiences and present environment—a prospect sometimes disturbing to some of the individuals who strongly believe that people freely choose how to behave. However, one does not have to agree with all the underlying assumptions of these techniques to see that they are a part of daily life within and outside organizations. Rewarding a child for obedience, smiling at someone we like, frowning at something with which we disagree, grading papers, and raising the salary of a highly productive employee are familiar acts that modify behavior. We assume—and in effect predict—that the receivers of these actions will behave in the desired ways.

Work behaviors are learned. Individuals learn to be good managers or poor managers. They learn to perform a job well or poorly. They learn to be prompt, cooperative, agreeable to co-workers, and so on. Behavior modification in organizations focuses on establishing work situations—such as reward and recognition policies—that help subordinates learn work habits that are satisfying to them and that aid in the achievement of organizational goals.[26]

---

[24]Rosabeth Moss Kanter, "From Status to Contribution: Some Organizational Implications of the Changing Basis for Pay," *Personnel,* January 1987, pp. 12–37.

[25]See, for example, B. F. Skinner, *Beyond Freedom and Dignity* (New York: Alfred A. Knopf, 1971).

[26]Our discussion is based on W. Clay Hamner, "Reinforcement Theory and Contingency Management in Organizational Settings," in Henry L. Tosi and W. Clay Hamner, eds., *Organizational Behavior and Management: A Contingency Approach* (Chicago: St. Clair Press, 1974); Donald Sanzotta, *Motivational Theories and Applications for Managers* (New York: American Management Associations, 1977); and Fred Luthans and Robert Kreitner, "A Social Learning Approach to Behavioral Management: Radical Behaviorists 'Mellowing Out,'" *Organizational Dynamics* 13, no. 12 (August 1984):47–63.

Behavior Modification

The behavior modification, or learning, approach to behavior is based on the law of effect, which states that behavior that has a rewarding consequence is likely to be repeated, whereas behavior that leads to a negative, or punishing, consequence tends not to be repeated.[27] In an organization, the frequency of various behaviors can be seen as depending on the immediate consequences of those behaviors. If, for example, employees work hard to achieve organizational objectives and are directly rewarded with bonuses or privileges, they will tend to repeat their efforts when new objectives are set.

The behavior modification process may be expressed as follows:

$$\text{Stimulus} \rightarrow \text{Response} \rightarrow \text{Consequences} \rightarrow \text{Future Response}$$

That is, the individual's own voluntary behavior (response) to a situation or event (stimulus) is the cause of specific consequences. If those consequences are positive, the individual will in the future tend to have similar responses in similar situations; if those consequences are unpleasant, the individual will tend to change his or her behavior in order to avoid them.

This principle suggests that if managers wish to change the behavior of a subordinate, they must change the consequences of the behavior. A person who is frequently late, for example, might be motivated to come in on time (a behavior change) if the manager expresses strong approval for each on-time or early appearance (change of consequences), rather than shrugging the matter off. Lateness also may be stopped by expressing strong disapproval of the late arrival time. However, as we shall see, researchers believe that it is generally more effective to reward desired behavior than to punish undesired behavior.

For the consequences to influence a person's behavior, it is important that they be clearly related to that behavior. One reason managers often fail to motivate subordinates is that the reinforcements they offer are far removed from the subordinate's actions. For example, informing subordinates during the annual salary review that they have done a good job is probably less motivating than is praising them when they perform a task particularly well.

Four techniques that managers can use to modify the behavior of subordinates—positive reinforcement, avoidance learning, extinction, and punishment—are summarized in Table 14-4. In addition, certain rules for the effective application of these techniques have been proposed. A six-rule formula for the application of behavior modification, developed by W. Clay Hamner, is outlined in Exhibit 14-5. Hamner points out that although these rules conform to common sense, managers often violate them.

INTEGRATIVE APPROACHES TO MOTIVATION

The Expectancy Approach

expectancy approach A model of motivation specifying that the effort to achieve high performance is a function of the perceived likelihood that high performance can be achieved and will be rewarded if achieved and that the reward will be worth the effort expended.

Each of the approaches to motivation that we have discussed so far concentrates on one of the three sets of variables illustrated in the systems table at the beginning of the chapter (Table 14-3). Integrative approaches include two or more sets of variables in their analysis of motivation. One in particular, the **expectancy approach** (also called the expectancy/valence approach), has received considerable support from research. For this reason, and because of the generality of its applications, it has significant implications for managers. This approach attempts to overcome criticisms sometimes

[27]The original formulation of the law of effect was based on years of animal experiments by Edward L. Thorndike and appeared in *Animal Intelligence* (New York: Macmillan, 1911), p. 244.

TABLE 14-4 METHODS OF BEHAVIOR MODIFICATION

METHOD	DEFINITION	EXAMPLE
Positive Reinforcement	Encouragement of desirable behavior by means of reinforcers which are generally regarded as pleasurable and which thus promote the repetition of the behavior	Raises, promotion, and praise are all reinforcers that encourage the continuation of desirable performance
Avoidance Learning	Learning that occurs when individuals learn to avoid or escape unpleasant consequences	When an employee responds to criticism by trying to improve performance and thus avoid future criticism, he or she is practicing avoidance learning
Extinction	Absence of reinforcement following undesired behavior so that the behavior eventually no longer recurs	Refusal to reinforce activities that are disruptive of workplace practices will encourage a worker to discontinue those activities
Punishment	Application of negative consequences to correct improper behavior	Criticism, demotion, and the docking of pay are common forms of punishment in the workplace

EXHIBIT 14-5 HAMNER'S RULES FOR USING BEHAVIOR MODIFICATION TECHNIQUES

Rule 1: *Don't reward all individuals equally.* To be effective behavior reinforcers, rewards should be based on performance. Rewarding everyone equally in effect reinforces poor or average performance and ignores high performance.

Rule 2: *Be aware that failure to respond can also modify behavior.* Managers influence their subordinates by what they do not do as well as by what they do. For example, failing to praise a deserving subordinate may cause that subordinate to perform poorly the next time.

Rule 3: *Be sure to tell individuals what they can do to get reinforcement.* Setting a performance standard lets individuals know what they should do to be rewarded; they can then adjust their work pattern accordingly.

Rule 4: *Be sure to tell individuals what they are doing wrong.* If a manager withholds rewards from a subordinate without indicating why the subordinate is not being rewarded, the subordinate may be confused about what behavior the manager finds undesirable. The subordinate may also feel that he or she is being manipulated.

Rule 5: *Don't punish in front of others.* Reprimanding a subordinate might sometimes be a useful way of eliminating an undesirable behavior. Public reprimand, however, humiliates the subordinate and may cause all the members of the work group to resent the manager.

Rule 6: *Be fair.* The consequences of a behavior should be appropriate. Subordinates should be given the rewards they deserve. Failure to reward subordinates properly or overrewarding undeserving subordinates reduces the reinforcing effect of rewards.

Source: Based on W. Clay Hamner, "Reinforcement Theory and Contingency Management in Organizational Settings," in Henry L. Tosi and W. Clay Hamner, eds., *Organizational Behavior and Management: A Contingency Approach,* rev. ed. (New York: John Wiley, 1977). Copyright 1977 by John Wiley & Sons, Inc.

directed at other motivational theories, namely, that all employees are alike, that all situations are alike, and that there is one best way of motivating employees. The expectancy approach attempts to account for differences among individuals and situations.

Expectations, Outcomes, and Work Behavior. As can be seen in Exhibit 14-6, David Nadler and Edward Lawler base the expectancy approach on four assumptions about behavior in organizations. These assumptions are summarized in the so-called *expectancy model,* which has three major components: performance-outcome expectancy, valence, and effort-performance expectancy.

EXHIBIT 14-6 NADLER AND LAWLER'S FOUR BASIC ASSUMPTIONS ABOUT ORGANIZATIONAL BEHAVIOR

1. *Behavior is determined by a combination of forces in the individual and in the environment.* People have different needs and expectations, formed by past experiences, that influence their response to the work environment. Different types of work environments usually make people behave in different ways.
2. *Individuals make conscious decisions about their own behavior in organizations.* These decisions may be about (a) *membership behavior*—coming to work, staying at work, being a member of the organization—or (b) *effort behavior*—how hard to work in performing their jobs.
3. *Individuals have different needs, desires, and goals.* Individuals are satisfied or rewarded by different outcomes. Understanding individual needs leads to an understanding of how each individual can be best motivated and rewarded.
4. *Individuals decide among alternative behaviors based on their expectation that a given behavior will lead to a desired outcome.* People tend to behave in ways that they believe will lead to rewards and to avoid behavior that may lead to undesirable consequences.

Source: David A. Nadler and Edward E. Lawler III, "Motivation—A Diagnostic Approach," in J. Richard Hackman, Edward E. Lawler III, and Lyman W. Porter, eds., *Perspectives on Behavior in Organizations* (New York: McGraw-Hill, 1977), p. 27.

Performance-Outcome Expectancy. Individuals engaged in or contemplating a certain behavior expect certain consequences. For example, a worker who is thinking about doubling his or her output may expect that doubling the output will result in praise, more pay, or perhaps no reward at all; the worker may even expect hostility from other workers. Each expected outcome will affect the individual's decision on whether or not to proceed with the contemplated behavior.

valence The value of motivating strength of a reward to the individual.

Valence. The outcome of a particular behavior has a specific **valence**—a specific motivating power or value—for each specific individual. For example, the possibility of transfer to a higher-paying position in another location may have a high valence for individuals who value money or who enjoy the stimulation of a new environment; it may have a low valence for individuals who have strong ties to their neighborhood, friends, or work group. Valence is determined by the individual and is not an objective quality of the outcome itself; for a given situation, valence differs from one person to the next.

Effort-Performance Expectancy. People's expectations of how difficult it will be to perform successfully will also affect their decision on whether or not to proceed. For example, an individual may be told that increasing sales by 50 percent will lead to a much desired salary increase. Before deciding whether or not to pursue the sales increase, the individual must estimate the probability of achieving it.

Given a choice, then, an individual will tend to select the level of performance that seems to have the best chance of achieving a valued outcome. The individual asks, in effect, "Can I do it?" and "If I do it, what will it bring me?" and "Is what it will bring me worth the effort of doing it?"

The answers to these questions for the individual will depend to some extent on the types of outcomes expected. *Intrinsic* outcomes are experienced directly by the individual as a result of successful task performance. They include feelings of accomplishment, increased self-esteem, and the development of new skills. *Extrinsic* outcomes, such as bonuses, praise, or promotion, are provided by an outside agent, such as the supervisor or work group. A single level of performance may be associated with several outcomes, each having its own valence. (If I perform better, I will receive higher pay, be noticed by my supervisor, be loved more by my spouse, and feel better about myself.) Some of these outcomes may even have valence because of the individual's expectation that they will lead to other outcomes. (If my supervisor notices the quality of my work, I may get a promotion.)

Figure 14-4 illustrates the theoretical working of the expectancy model. The value of the expected reward to the individual (1) combines with the individual's perception of the effort involved in attaining the reward and the probability of achieving the reward (2) to produce a certain level of effort (3). This effort combines with the individual's abilities and traits (4) and the way he or she does the task (5) to yield a specific performance level (6). This resulting level of performance leads to intrinsic rewards (or perhaps negative consequences, if the performance level is lower than expected) which are inherent in the task accomplishment (7a) and perhaps to extrinsic rewards (7b). The wavy line in the model leading to the extrinsic rewards indicates that those rewards are not guaranteed, since they depend on how the supervisor and perhaps others assess the individual's performance and on the willingness of the organization to reward that performance. The individual has his or her own idea about the appropriateness of the total set of rewards received (8), which, when measured against the rewards actually received, results in the level of satisfaction experienced by the individual (9). The individual's experience will then be applied to his or her future assessments of the values of rewards for further task accomplishment.[28]

CLASS COMMENT

Here are some good *practical* suggestions for motivating subordinates.

Implications for Managers. The expectancy model presents managers with a number of clear implications on how to motivate subordinates. As outlined by Nadler and Lawler, these include:

[28]Lyman W. Porter and Edward E. Lawler III, *Managerial Attitudes and Performance* (Homewood, Ill.: Richard D. Irwin, 1968). See also Cynthia M. Pavett, "Evaluation of the Impact of Feedback on Performance and Motivation," *Human Relations* 36, no. 7 (July 1983):641–654; and Vida Scarpello and John P. Campbell, "Job Satisfaction and the Fit Between Individual Needs and Organizational Rewards," *Journal of Occupational Psychology* 56, no. 4 (1983):315–328.

FIGURE 14-4 THE EXPECTANCY MODEL OF MOTIVATION

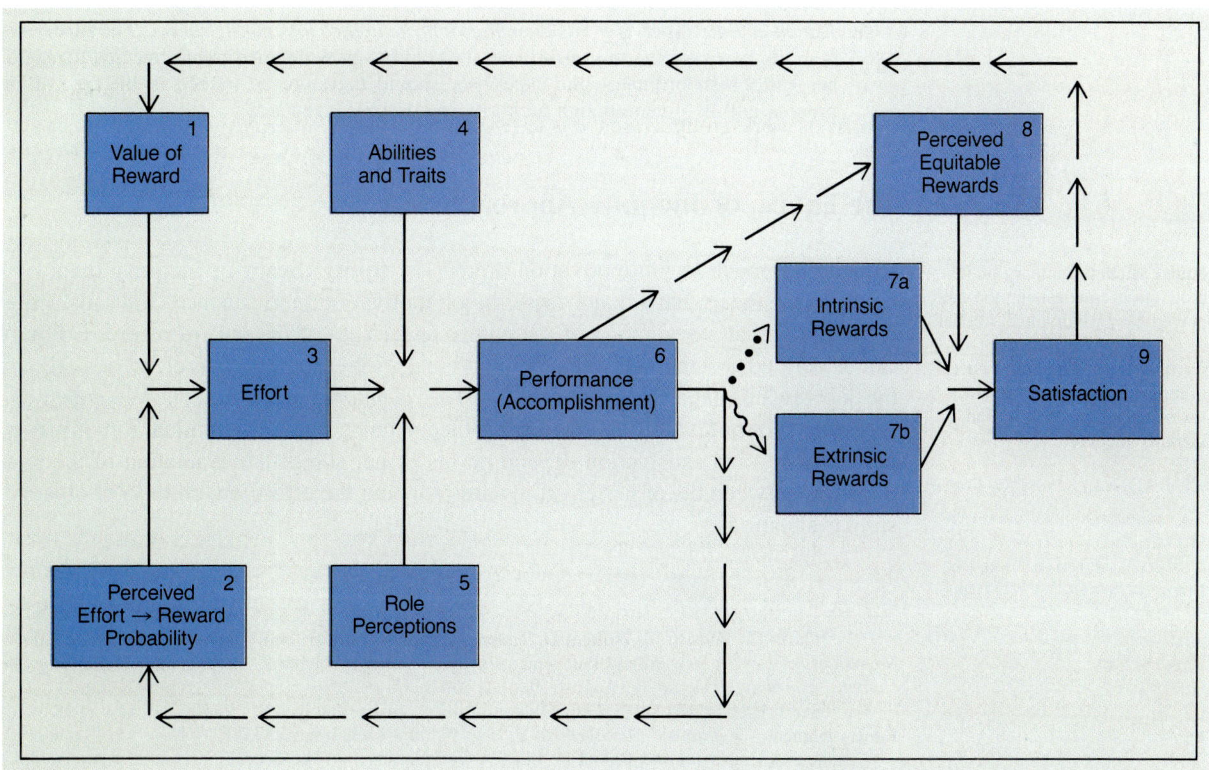

Source: Lyman W. Porter and Edward E. Lawler III, *Managerial Attitudes and Performance,* p. 165. Copyright © 1968. Used by permission of Richard D. Irwin, Inc.

1. *Determine the rewards valued by each subordinate.* If rewards are to be motivators, they must be suitable for the individual; managers can determine what rewards their subordinates seek by observing their reactions in different situations and by asking them what rewards they desire.
2. *Determine the performance you desire.* Managers must identify what performance level or behavior they want so that they can tell subordinates what they must do to be rewarded.
3. *Make the performance level attainable.* If subordinates feel that the goal they are asked to pursue is too difficult or impossible, their motivation will be low.
4. *Link rewards to performance.* To maintain motivation, the appropriate reward must be clearly associated within a short period of time with successful performance.
5. *Analyze what factors might counteract the effectiveness of the reward.* Conflicts between the manager's reward system and other influences in the work situation may require the manager to make some adjustments in the reward; for example, if the subordinate's work group favors low productivity, an above-average reward may be required to motivate a subordinate to high productivity.
6. *Make sure the reward is adequate.* Minor rewards will be minor motivators.[29]

Implications for Organizations. The expectancy model of motivation also has a number of implications for organizations. As outlined by Nadler and Lawler, these include

FOR DISCUSSION

Do you agree with these statements? Why or why not?

1. *Organizations usually get what they reward, not what they want.* The organization's reward system must be designed to motivate the behaviors desired; seniority benefits, for example, reward the duration of one's employment in the organization, not the quality of one's performance.
2. *The job itself can be made intrinsically rewarding.* If jobs are designed to fulfill some of the higher needs of employees (such as independence or creativity), they can be motivating in themselves. This implication is obviously the basis of many job enrichment programs; however, those individuals who do not desire enriched jobs should not be made to take them.[30]
3. *The immediate supervisor has an important role in the motivation process.* The supervisor is in the best position to define clear goals and to provide appropriate rewards for his or her various subordinates; the supervisor should therefore be trained in the motivation process and be given enough authority to administer rewards.[31]

The Equity or Inequity Approach

equity theory A theory of job motivation emphasizing the role played by an individual's belief in the equity or fairness of rewards and punishments in determining his or her performance and satisfaction. Also called inequity theory.

COORDINATED RESOURCE

An interesting social commentary article on "Do We Live as Well as We Used To?" can be found in *Fortune,* 9/14/87, pp. 32–46.

Another approach to job motivation, known as **equity theory** or **inequity theory**, is based on the thesis that a major factor in job motivation, performance, and satisfaction is the individual's evaluation of the equity or fairness of the reward received. Equity can be defined as a ratio between the individual's job inputs (such as effort or skill) and the job rewards (such as pay or promotion) *compared with the rewards others are receiving for similar job inputs.* Equity theory holds that an individual's motivation, performance, and satisfaction depend on his or her subjective evaluation of the relationships between his or her effort/reward ratio and the effort/reward ratio of others in similar situations.[32]

---

[29]Philip M. Podsakoff, William D. Tudor, Richard A. Grover, and Vandra L. Huber, "Situational Moderators of Leader Reward and Punishment Behaviors: Fact or Fiction?" *Organizational Behavior and Human Performance* 34, no. 1 (August 1984):21–63.

[30]See J. Richard Hackman, Greg Oldham, Robert Janson, and Kenneth Purdy," A New Strategy for Job Enrichment," *California Management Review* 17, no. 4 (Summer 1975):57–71.

[31]James C. Naylor and Daniel R. Ilgen, "Goal Settings: A Theoretical Analysis of a Motivational Technology," *Research in Organizational Behavior* 6 (1984):95–140.

[32]J. Stacey Adams, "Toward an Understanding of Inequity," *Journal of Abnormal and Social Psychology* 67, no. 5 (November 1963):422–436. See also Robert P. Vecchio, "Models of Psychological Inequity," *Organizational Behavior and Human Performance* 34, no. 2 (October 1984):266–282.

ETHICS IN MANAGEMENT

THE BUTTON EXPERIMENTS

Do people really want control over their lives or do they want to be told what to do? In Chapter 10, we looked at some experiments by Stanley Milgram that suggested that most people will do as they are told, when instructed by someone whom they perceive to represent legitimate authority; they will send 450 volts of electricity through a total stranger. In Chapter 16, we will see that, as confirmed by other experiments, they are capable of going even further.

A set of classical experiments by David Glass and Jerome Singer and their colleagues suggest that while people will do as they are told, they perform much more productively if they have some control over their situation. In one experiment, subjects were divided into two groups and told to perform a series of boring and repetitive tasks, some of which were impossible to complete. There was background noise consisting of people speaking Spanish and Armenian, machines roaring and grinding, and a clicking typewriter. One group was given a button that would shut off the noise and was told to feel free to use it—but only if the noise became too great to bear. The other group was given no button.

As expected, the group *with* the button outperformed the group *without* the button by a large margin. Members tried to solve five times the number of insoluble puzzles and had fewer errors in the repetitive tasks. But no one in the group even used the button: it was enough for them to know that they had control and could exercise it if need be. Because they perceived that they had control, the subjects performed more successfully.

In a direct application of the same experiment, every worker on the assembly line at the GM-Toyota joint-venture plant in Fremont, California, enjoys the authority to stop the line. The increase in the quality of the product and the productivity of the people has been phenomenal. It would seem that one way to motivate people is simply to give them some control over what they are asked to do.

Sources: Herbert Lefcourt, *Locus of Control: Current Trends in Theory and Research* (Hillsdale, N.J.: Erlbaum, 1976); D. C. Glass, B. Reim, and J. E. Singer, "Behavioral Consequences of Adaptation to Controllable and Uncontrollable Noise," *Journal of Experimental Social Psychology* 7 (1971):244–257; D. C. Glass, J. E. Singer, and L. N. Friedman, "Psychic Cost of Adaptation to an Environmental Stressor," *Journal of Personality and Social Psychology* 12 (1969):200–210; D. C. Glass, J. E. Singer, H. S. Leonard, D. Krantz, S. Cohen, and H. Cummings, "Perceived Control of Aversive Stimulation and the Reduction of Stress Responses," *Journal of Personality* 41 (1973):577–595; Tom Peters and Robert Waterman, *In Search of Excellence* (New York: Harper & Row, 1982).

Most discussion and research on equity theory center on money as the reward considered most significant in the workplace. People compare what they are being paid for their efforts with what others in similar situations receive for theirs. When they feel that inequity exists, a state of tension develops within them. People try to resolve this tension by appropriately adjusting their behavior. A worker who perceives that he or she is being underpaid, for example, may try to reduce the inequity by exerting less effort. Overpaid workers, on the other hand (also in a state of tension through perceived inequity), may work harder.

Recent studies have shown that an individual's reaction to inequity is dependent on the history of his or her experience of inequity. Richard A. Cosier and Dan R. Dalton point out that work relationships are not static and that inequities usually do not exist as isolated or one-time events.[33] They suggest that there is a threshold up to which an individual will tolerate a series of unfair events: Once the "straw that breaks the

[33]Richard A. Cosier and Dan R. Dalton, "Equity Theory and Time: A Reformulation," *Academy of Management Review* 8, no. 2 (April 1983):311–319.

camel's back'' is added—that is, a relatively minor injustice that pushes the individual beyond his or her limit of tolerance—an extreme and seemingly inappropriate reaction will result. For example, an outstanding worker who is denied an afternoon off for no compelling reason may suddenly become enraged if he or she has experienced a string of similar petty decisions in the past.

Individuals differ, and their methods of reducing inequity will also differ. Some will rationalize that their efforts were greater or less than they originally perceived them to be, or that the rewards are more or less valuable. For example, one person failing to receive a promotion may ''decide'' that the previously desired job actually involved too much responsibility. Others may try to make the co-workers with whom they are comparing themselves change their behavior; work team members receiving the same pay but exerting less effort, for example, may be persuaded to work harder, or high-performance workers may be discouraged from ''making the rest of us look bad.'' For managers, equity theory has several implications, the most important being that, for most individuals, rewards must be perceived as fair in order to be motivating.

Pitney-Bowes, whose core business has long been mailing equipment, is one company that devotes a good deal of energy to fostering fairness among its employees. Special ''jobholders'' meetings, chaired by a member of the Council of Personnel Relations (CPR), are held regularly. The council's sole purpose is to make employees' concerns known to management. The CPR is responsible for functioning as a ''watch-dog'' group so that employees who believe that they have been treated unfairly or inequitably can voice their concerns outside the chain of command to which they are normally subject. Unfair bonuses, benefits, and even personal matters are among the issues addressed by CPR representatives, some of whom are elected by employees.[34]

goal-setting theory A cognitive approach to the theory of work motivation which holds that workers are conscious (cognitive) creatures who strive toward goals.

HERE'S AN EXAMPLE

Outward Bound, the largest program operator of organized outdoor treks, will lead more than 2,000 executives from companies including General Electric and Pepsico on four- or five-day trips of white-water rafting, rock climbing, or sailing. Because of some recent (1987) accidents, some are questioning whether there isn't an easier way to build executive leadership and team spirit. (*Fortune*, 9/14/87, p. 6)

Goal-Setting Theory. Like equity/inequity theory, **goal-setting theory** is a *cognitive* approach to the theory of work motivation: That is, it holds that workers, as human beings, are conscious (cognitive) creatures who strive toward goals. According to psychologist Edwin Locke, the natural inclination to set and strive for goals is useful only if the individual both understands and accepts a particular goal.[35] As he and his colleagues point out in Exhibit 14-7, there are several cognitive factors influencing the intensity of worker motivation.[36]

EXHIBIT 14-7 FACTORS INFLUENCING THE INTENSITY OF WORKER MOTIVATION

- Workers are more motivated to achieve specific goals (say, a percentage of sales increases) than vague or general ones (''increased productivity'').
- Workers commit themselves more fully to difficult goals than to easy ones or to ones that simply ask them to ''get the job done.''
- Workers will not be motivated if they do not possess—and know that they possess—the abilities necessary to achieve a goal.
- Concrete rewards—for example, raises, titles, promotions—increase worker commitment.
- Feedback on performance is necessary if worker motivation is not to decline; accurate feedback usually results in properly adjusted strategy or the worker's persistence in trying to achieve the goal.

Sources: E. A. Locke, K. N. Shaw, L. M. Saari, and G. P. Latham, ''Goal Setting and Task Performance, 1969–1980,'' *Psychological Bulletin* 90 (1981):125–152; and Frank J. Landy, *Psychology of Work Behavior,* 3rd ed. (Homewood, Ill.: Dorsey Press, 1985.

[34]Robert Levering, *A Great Place to Work* (New York: Random House, 1988), pp. 68–72.

[35]E. A. Locke, ''Toward a Theory of Task Motivation and Incentives,'' *Organizational Behavior and Human Performance* 3 (1968):157–189; Locke, ''The Nature and Causes of Job Satisfaction,'' in M. D. Dunnette, ed., *The Handbook of Industrial and Organizational Psychology* (Chicago: Rand McNally, 1976).

[36]E. A. Locke, K. N. Shaw, L. M. Saari, and G. P. Latham, ''Goal Setting and Task Performance, 1969–1980,'' *Psychological Bulletin* 90 (1981):125–152.

HERE'S AN EXAMPLE

The companies identified by *Fortune* as 25 of the brightest talents in the Fortune 500 share a striking characteristic: management and members of the board of directors own significant chunks of the stock, giving them a strong voice in running the company and a stake in the outcome. (*Fortune*, 4/25/88, pp. 97–104)

When goals are specific and challenging, they function more effectively as motivating factors in both individual and group performance.[37] Research also indicates that when subordinates participate in the setting of goals rather than receive them from superiors by means of a one-way, top-down process, they are more likely to accept difficult challenges as factors in a project that it is their *intention*—not merely their task—to surmount. Thus, there are two advantages to two-way or participative goal setting: Management helps to make goals specific by communicating their relationship to organizational objectives, and subordinates are given the opportunity to appropriate those objectives into personal and group intentions to meet a goal.[38] This second advantage is particularly important because intention to reach a goal, defined here as a key aspect of *setting* that goal, is a key factor in work motivation.

Over the past 15 years, research conducted by psychologists interested in human motivation in industrial and organizational settings has tended to confirm Locke's proposition, and as we saw in Chapter 8, goal setting is an important method in the strategy known as management by objectives.

GUIDELINES FOR EFFECTIVE MOTIVATION

EXTRA EXERCISE

Have students research and write a paper on recent trends in motivation and their implications for management.

There is a discrepancy between the practice of motivating employees in most organizations and the findings of recent theories. This may be because the newer theories are unknown to many managers and ignored by others. Managers may often prefer the older theories of motivation, such as Herzberg's, because they have long been familiar with them and because these theories are easier to apply to large numbers of employees. The newer findings put a premium on understanding subordinates, carefully planning what to do, and being consistent and patient in carrying out those plans. All of these actions require some hard work and self-control.[39] In addition, increased automation and computerization may cause some managers to feel that employees can do little to improve the performance of productive systems. In Exhibit 14-8, Richard M. Steers and Lyman W. Porter suggest some implications of current theories of work motivation for managers.

EXHIBIT 14-8 STEERS AND PORTER'S SUGGESTIONS FOR IMPLEMENTING WORKER MOTIVATION STRATEGIES

1. Managers must actively and intentionally motivate their subordinates.
2. Managers should understand their own strengths and limitations before attempting to modify those of others.
3. Managers must recognize that employees have different motives and abilities.
4. Rewards should be related to performance, not to seniority or other nonmerit-based considerations.
5. Jobs should be designed to offer challenge and variety; subordinates must clearly understand what is expected of them.
6. Management should foster an organizational culture oriented to performance.
7. Managers should stay close to employees and remedy problems as they arise.
8. The active cooperation of employees should be sought in improving the organization's output; employees are, after all, also stakeholders in the organization.

Source: Richard M. Steers and Lyman W. Porter, eds., *Motivation and Work Behavior,* 3rd. ed. (New York: McGraw-Hill, 1983), pp. 642–643.

HERE'S AN EXAMPLE

Nixdorf Computer AG, a West German computer company, uses a novel strategy to compete. Says a sales manager at a large European rival, ". . . they have had impressive growth and I think the main reason is their motivation. There's a lot of spirit in that company." (*Wall Street Journal*, 3/16/88, p. 26)

[37]James C. Naylor and Daniel R. Ilgen, "Goal Setting: A Theoretical Analysis of a Motivational Technique," in *Research in Organizational Behavior*, B. M. Staw and L. L. Cummings, eds., Vol. 6 (Greenwich, Conn.: JAI Press, 1984), pp. 95–140.

[38]Miriam Erez, P. C. Early, and C. L. Hulin, "The Impact of Participation on Goal Acceptance and Performance: A Two-Step Model," *Academy of Management Journal* 28 (1985):50–66.

[39]Benjamin Schneider, "Organizational Behavior," in Mark R. Rosenzweig and Lyman W. Porter, eds., *Annual Review of Psychology* (Palo Alto, Calif.: Annual Reviews, 1985), pp. 573–611.

ILLUSTRATIVE CASE STUDY Wrap-Up

Creating a Committed Work Force at Domino's Pizza

Can Domino's sustain its success? One of the key variables may well be the degree to which employees perceive that the material rewards being handed out are equitable. Other analysts point out that Domino's must sustain its method of clearly setting goals for improvements and giving concrete rewards. It is also interesting to note that only as long as Domino's can continue to *grow* will it be possible to reward loyal and hardworking employees with the opportunity to operate their own franchises. Recall that of the 600 plus franchises, 98 percent are held by people who worked for Domino's. What happens if growth slows down? Will there still be enough major rewards to go around? If there are more chapters to be written in Domino's fabulous success story, the company may never have to answer that difficult question. Given the system that the company now uses—as well as its success under present conditions—motivation may well take care of itself. ■

SUMMARY

Motivation is very important for managers to understand, since managers must channel people's motivation in order to achieve personal and organizational goals. However, people's abilities and role perceptions are also important factors in how well they will perform.

Organizations need motivated employees to implement strategy. Theory X, which asserts that managers must be strict and authoritarian, works well for predictable tasks, but when tasks are uncertain and require problem-solving abilities, the better approach is Theory Y, which encourages participative management to tap people's natural satisfaction in their work.

Theories of motivation can be characterized as content, process, or reinforcement. Content theories stress the importance of drives or needs within the individual as motives for the individual's actions. Process theories emphasize how and by what goals individuals are motivated. Reinforcement theories focus on how the consequences of an individual's actions in the past affect his or her behavior in the future. These motivational theories have evolved from the traditional model, which suggested that people are motivated by economic necessity, through the human relations model, which emphasized job satisfaction as a motivator, to the human resources model, which suggests that high performance leads to satisfaction. According to the last model, individuals perform best when they can achieve personal as well as organizational goals.

The systems perspective on motivation identifies three variables that affect motivation in the workplace: individual characteristics, which include the interests, attitudes, and needs of the individual; job characteristics, which are the attributes inherent in the task; and work situation characteristics, which include the organization's personnel and reward policies, organizational culture, and the attitudes and actions of peers and supervisors.

Maslow theorized that individuals are motivated to fulfill a hierarchy of needs, with the need for self-actualization at the top. McClelland found that the need for achievement is closely associated with successful performance in the workplace. Herzberg developed a two-factor approach to work motivation in which job satisfaction was attributed to factors related to job content and to job context.

Characteristics of the work situation, particularly the actions of managers, have a strong impact on motivation. Proper application of behavior modification techniques has been found effective in improving employee performance and satisfaction. Behavior modification, or learning theory, suggests that behavior that is followed directly by reward is reinforced and tends to be repeated, while unrewarded or punished behavior tends not to be repeated. Managers may use a variety of reinforcement techniques, such as positive reinforcement, avoidance learning, extinction, or punishment.

Integrative approaches to motivation include the expectancy approach and equity theory. The expectancy model bases motivation, performance, and satisfaction on what the individual expects from the proposed performance, how much effort the individual expects the proposed performance will require, and the valence, or value, the anticipated rewards have for the individual. Equity theory suggests that an individual's motivation, performance, and satisfaction depend on the individual's comparison of his or her contributions and rewards with those of others in similar situations.

Many managers have not applied the findings of recent motivation theories to their own organizations; properly used, however, these theories can lead to more effective worker performance.

REVIEW QUESTIONS

1. What is motivation and why is it important? What other factors influence a person's performance?
2. How have views of motivation in organizations evolved? How might each view affect the ways in which managers behave toward subordinates?
3. What are Theory X and Theory Y? How might each theory be more applicable in different circumstances?
4. According to content theories, what motivates people? What theorists advocated this approach? Why are content theories difficult to apply?
5. What aspects of motivation do process theories emphasize? How do process theories relate the concepts of expectancy and valence to motivation?
6. How do reinforcement theories explain behavior? To what extent does the process of learning play a part in reinforcement theories?
7. In the systems perspective, what three variables affect motivation in the workplace?
8. How is Maslow's hierarchy of needs related to motivation in organizations?
9. According to Atkinson, what determines the strength of an individual's motivational drive? How did McClelland relate Atkinson's work to management? What are the implications of his findings for managers?
10. What is Herzberg's two-factor approach to job satisfaction and dissatisfaction? Why has the approach been criticized?
11. How may an organization's culture and its personnel and reward policies affect motivation?
12. Why is behavior modification controversial? What do you think of behavior modification techniques?
13. Upon what assumptions is the expectancy approach based?
14. Define performance-outcome expectancy, valence, and effort-performance expectancy. How do they affect a worker's level of performance?
15. What does equity theory suggest about the motivation, performance, and satisfaction of individuals in the organization?

CASE STUDY

Idealism, Motivation, and Community Service at the Center City YWCA

After three days of interviewing for the job of director of the Center City YWCA, Harriet Bowen was having lunch with Margaret Pierce, the retiring director. When Pierce offered her the position, Bowen hesitated.

"You still aren't sure?" Pierce asked. "Tell me what's bothering you."

"As I've told you," Bowen replied, "I'm looking for a job with a challenge. I would expect the YW to face financial difficulties—in today's economy, every nonprofit agency has these problems. But despite all the ideas and energy you have—not to mention the wide diversity of programs—the staff seems uninspired and worn out."

Pierce smiled. "That's true. You've hit on one of our biggest problems. As I've told you, the YWCA has undergone major changes in goals and programs over the past few decades. We no longer serve as a dormitory for young women when they first move to the city. Nor are we simply a place for a quick swim after work. At the National Convention, the YWs declared our major targets to be relevant programs for women, youth, and minorities. And yet our image in Center City—and even for some of our staff—is clearly that of a community recreation center, not a powerful force in the women's movement."

Bowen became animated. "I can see the types of programs you have: bilingual activities for Hispanics, creative skills classes, the Women's Center, the Rape Crisis Center, a battered wives program, youth programs, a nursery, as well as a health club for women, men, and children, and a small residence. The building is in pretty good shape. Where's the problem?"

Pierce paused. "As you know, a lot of our staff in the 1960s and 1970s started as volunteers and became paid staff when we got federal funding. But the fervor of the social movement has waned at the same time that government grants, including CETA programs, were cut back. Although the neighborhood is much safer, thanks to urban renewal, many of our traditional big contributors have moved to the suburbs. Membership has not really increased substantially. So we've had to cut some programs, lose staff, and freeze wages. As a result, we don't have enough people to maintain the building or keep up the records, let alone reach out into the community."

"But surely you must still have some idealists around," Bowen commented.

"Yes, we do. But many have left, and most of our staff does just the minimum work required, for barely adequate wages." Pierce continued, "The morale problem is more complex. In the 1970s we adopted the strong affirmative action program of the National YWCA; as a result, our staff today reflects the racial composition of Center City—half white, half minority. This wasn't easy. Qualified minority professionals are difficult to recruit. We lost some board members and long-term volunteers because of affirmative action. And some of the staff complained that less qualified people were being hired to meet quotas. Further, we lost many white members who resisted integration. Therefore, some of our programs are unintentionally segregated. But with our limited finances it's hard to create new programs and recruit really talented staff."

Bowen listened carefully as Pierce added, "It's very frustrating. We have the facilities and some good programs—but I haven't been able to communicate this to the staff or the community. I don't have time to institute better record keeping and an organized system of promotion and raises. So you see, we have a lot of the basic resources, but also a lot of problems."

Bowen smiled and sat back. "I think I understand the situation. It won't be easy to communicate my enthusiasm, but I'd like to try. I'll take the job."

"I'm very pleased," responded Pierce. "And remember, I intend to stay a member of the YW, so you can always call on me for help. Good luck."

Source: This case was written by Ellen Greenberg of the Columbia University Graduate School of Business. It is based on a real organization, but facts have been altered to enhance the teaching value of the material. Preparation of the case was supported by The Institute for Not-for-Profit Management of Columbia University. Parts of this case are adapted from an earlier case.

Case Questions

1. What are the major problems facing Harriet Bowen?
2. If you were Herzberg, how would you advise Harriet Bowen to manage the YWCA?
3. What would Nadler and Lawler tell Harriet Bowen to assist her in leading her staff?
4. How might reinforcement theory apply to this case? ■

Jean Dubuffet, *Leader in a Parade Uniform,* 1945. Oil on canvas. 36⅜ x 25⅞". Morton G. Neumann Family Collection.

15

LEADERSHIP

Upon completing this chapter you should be able to:

1. Define and explain the leadership process.
2. Describe three approaches to the study of leadership.
3. Distinguish between the two major leadership styles.
4. Describe three contingency approaches to leadership.
5. Discuss self-managed groups and self-leadership.

Chapter Outline

Introduction
Defining Leadership
Theories of Leadership
The Future of Leadership Theory

ILLUSTRATIVE CASE STUDY Introduction

New Leadership Policies at GE

Jack Welch took over as chairman of General Electric in 1981 after an extensive and well-publicized competition. Reginald Jones, chairman before Welch, managed a carefully crafted selection process which culminated in the selection of Welch, with a doctorate in chemical engineering, to run the appliance business. Chosen CEO at only age 45, Welch made sweeping changes in almost every aspect of the company, shifting its business mix and corporate culture—and its vision for the future. Welch's stated goal was to make GE number one or number two in terms of market share in every business in which it competes. He has confronted this challenge with single-minded determination.

From his years of experience at the company, Welch was convinced that GE was too bureaucratic—so fat with layer upon layer of management that it was not capable of making quick decisions, let alone implementing them. By eliminating several unnecessary layers, he began to delegate authority to the lower levels of management, where problems were first encountered and solutions were most readily available. He reduced the corporate staff from 1,700 to under 1,000 and made cuts in all parts of the company. Since 1981, GE has trimmed over 100,000 workers, and Welch has acquired the nickname "Neutron Jack" in reference to the proposed neutron bomb, which allegedly spares buildings while destroying only the enemy's human resources. Welch has also tried to instill a sense of teamwork and individual responsibility for the performance of each part of GE. He has rewarded managers who are willing to streamline, to change, and to take risks.

Always a competitor from boyhood sports to an adult career in business, Welch has spent his entire career at GE. His initial success was in increasing the revenues of the plastics division from a small piece to a major portion of GE's sales and profits. From his early days at GE, Welch had been frustrated by the company's bureaucracy, and he had spent a lot of time trying to find ways to get things done by working around the system. He had found that the key ingredients for getting things done were initiative, managerial freedom, and an intolerance for managers who could not produce. Welch still tries to apply these simple rules.

The sailing has not been smooth for Welch. Cutting 25 percent of the work force has had severe effects of morale, with the work force becoming polarized: Most employees either admire or deplore Jack Welch. According to one GE executive:

> Loyalty here is 24 hours deep. Welch has lost the dedication of a couple of hundred thousand people. He's done a remarkable job of changing the emphasis of the company. But is the price bigger than the company should be paying?

Organized labor is outspoken in its opposition to Welch's methods. Joseph F. Egan, chairman of International Union of Electronic Workers, has said, "GE has a disease—Welch-ese. It is caused by corporate greed, arrogance, and contempt for its employees."

Alternatively, Welch's admirers believe he is doing an outstanding job. They claim that his vision and the often difficult changes that he has brought to GE are exactly what the company needed. Buying RCA and Kidder, Peabody were brilliant strategic moves, say Welch's admirers, and the trimming of the work force was long overdue.

Jack Welch's impact on GE cannot yet be fully assessed. It is clear, however, that Welch has changed the direction and culture of GE. And he has produced results. And yet, while some people at GE follow Welch because they think his chosen direction is right, many others believe that they have no choice but to follow. Some say that Welch is a leader, others that he is an intimidator. Whatever the case, GE will never be the same.

Source: "Jack Welch: How Good a Manager?" *Business Week,* December 14, 1987, pp. 92–103.

THOUGHT-PROVOKER

How is leadership different from management? Or is it?

Is Jack Welch an effective leader? If so, what factors are important? If not, what may prevent Welch from being ultimately effective? Most people would probably say that effective leaders have certain desirable traits or qualities—for example, charisma, foresight, persuasiveness, and intensity. And indeed, when we think of heroic leaders such as Napoleon, Washington, Lincoln, Roosevelt, and Churchill, we recognize that such traits were natural to them and necessary for what they accomplished. However, as we shall see, hundreds of studies of leaders and leadership—some dating back to the nineteenth century—have failed to demonstrate that any trait or quality is consistently associated with effective leadership.

Although research has not yielded a set of traits possessed by effective leaders, it does seem clear that leaders play a critical role in helping groups, organizations, or societies achieve their goals. For example, it is generally accepted that England might well have lost World War II had Neville Chamberlain remained as Prime Minister. Instead, the determined and inspiring leadership of Winston Churchill probably saved England and perhaps the rest of the world as well. Managers are seldom called on to be leaders in the heroic mold of a Churchill or a Lincoln. Nevertheless, leadership abilities and skill in directing are important factors in managers' effectiveness. Many business organizations that appeared to be floundering have achieved new vigor when their presidents were replaced. If we could identify the qualities associated with leadership, our ability to select effective leaders would be increased. And if we could identify effective leadership behaviors and techniques, we would presumably be able to *learn* and *teach* these behaviors and techniques—thereby improving our personal and organizational effectiveness.

DEFINING LEADERSHIP

leadership The process of directing and inspiring workers to perform the task-related activities of the group.

In his survey of leadership theories and research, Ralph M. Stogdill has pointed out that "there are almost as many different definitions of leadership as there are persons who have attempted to define the concept."[1] We will define managerial **leadership** as the process of directing and influencing the task-related activities of group members. There are three important implications of our definition.

First, leadership must involve *other people*—subordinates or followers. By their willingness to accept directions from the leader, group members held define the leader's status and make the leadership process possible; without subordinates, all the leadership qualities of a manager would be irrelevant.

power The ability to exert influence; that is, the ability to change the attitudes or behavior of individuals or groups.

Second, leadership involves an unequal distribution of **power** among leaders and group members. Although leaders have the authority to direct some of the activities of group members who cannot similarly direct the leader's activities, certain group members will obviously affect those activities in a number of ways.

influence Any actions or examples of behavior that cause a change in attitude or behavior of another person or group.

Third, in addition to being legitimately able to give their subordinates or followers orders or directions, leaders can also **influence** subordinates in a variety of other ways.

[1]Bernard M. Bass, *Stogdill's Handbook of Leadership: A Survey of Theory and Research*, rev. ed. (New York: Free Press, 1981), p. 7.

THEORIES OF LEADERSHIP

TEACHING TIP

Here's a good opportunity to review and reinforce these concepts of power.

Why do subordinates accept direction from managers? What are the sources of a leader's power and influence? We partially answered this question in Chapter 10, when we discussed the five bases of a manager's power: *reward power, coercive power, legitimate power, referent power,* and *expert power*.[2] The greater the number of these power sources available of the manager, the greater will be his or her potential for effective leadership. It is, for example, a commonly observed fact of organizational life that managers at the same level in the organizational hierarchy may differ widely in their ability to influence, motivate, and direct the work of subordinates. Although managers at the same level may have the same legitimate powers, they are simply not equal in terms of the exercise of reward, coercive, referent, or of expert power.

In this chapter, we will attempt to extend further our understanding of leader effectiveness by discussing three major approaches to the study of leadership. The first approach views leadership as growing out of a combination of *traits;* the second approach attempts to identify the personal *behaviors* associated with effective leadership. Common to both these approaches is the assumption that individuals who possess appropriate traits or display appropriate behaviors will emerge as leaders in whatever group situations they find themselves.

However, current thinking and research lean toward a third approach—the *situational perspective on leadership*. This perspective assumes that the conditions determining leader effectiveness vary with the situation—with the tasks to be accomplished, the skills and expectations of subordinates, and so on. An individual who is an effective leader in one situation might do very poorly in another. This perspective has given rise to contingency approaches to leadership, which attempt to specify the situational factors that determine how effective a particular style will be. We examine the contributions of all these approaches in the paragraphs that follow.

---

[2]John R. P. French and Bertram Raven, "The Bases of Social Power," in Dorwin Cartwright, ed., *Studies in Social Power* (Ann Arbor: University of Michigan, 1959), pp. 150–167. See also Dennis A. Gioia and Henry P. Sims, Jr., "Perceptions of Managerial Power as a Consequence of Managerial Behavior and Reputation," *Journal of Management* 9, no. 1 (Fall 1983):7–26; and Edwin P. Hollander, "Leadership and Power," in Gardner Lindzey and Elliot Aronson, eds., *Handbook of Social Psychology,* 3rd ed. (New York: Random House, 1985), Chapter 9.

ETHICS IN MANAGEMENT

IS MORAL LEADERSHIP DIFFERENT?

Leadership is generally considered in terms of its effectiveness or ineffectiveness, but there is another aspect to leadership—namely, ethics or morality (recall from Chapter 4 that, for our purposes, the distinction between *ethics* and *morality* is negligible). How far should leaders go in trying to get others to follow them? Human history is replete with leaders who used power ruthlessly to gain and solidify support. Adolf Hitler had a special army, the SS, to terrorize opposition and innocents alike. Followers are obviously more likely to follow if the penalty for going in another direction is severe enough.

In a book entitled *Leadership,* James McGregor Burns proposes a concept called "moral leadership" as a means for evaluating the ethics of leaders. According to Burns, moral leadership goes beyond power and examines the extent to which the leader-follower relationship is based on *mutual* needs and aspirations. Moral leadership obliges leaders to do the things that they promise. For Burns charisma, cheerleading, and enforced conformity are not sufficient criteria for evaluating effective or appropriate leadership.

The Trait Approach to Leadership

HERE'S AN EXAMPLE

Frederick W. Gluck, managing director of McKinsey and Company management consulting firm, had leadership qualities even as a child. Says a person who has known him that long, "This one little kid was obviously running the whole show. He was a born leader." (*Business Week*, 6/13/88, pp. 82–84).

The first systematic effort by psychologists and other researchers to understand leadership was the attempt to identify the personal characteristics of leaders. The view that leaders are born, not made, is in fact still popular among laypersons if not professional researchers. After a lifetime of reading popular novels and viewing films and television shows, perhaps most of us believe that there are individuals who have a predisposition to leadership—that they are naturally braver, more aggressive, more decisive, and more articulate than other people.

In searching for measurable leadership traits, original researchers took two approaches: (1) They attempted to compare the traits of those who emerged as leaders with the traits of those who did not, and (2) they attempted to compare the traits of effective leaders with those of ineffective leaders.

Most studies on leadership traits fell into the first category and have largely failed to uncover any traits that clearly and consistently distinguish leaders from followers.[3] Leaders as a group have been found to be brighter, more extroverted, and more self-confident than nonleaders; they also tend to be taller. However, although millions of people have these traits, most of them obviously will never attain leadership positions. In addition, many established leaders did not and do not have these traits—Napoleon, for example, was relatively short (though not as short as he is normally purported to have been), and Abraham Lincoln was moody and introverted. It is also possible that individuals become more assertive and self-confident once they occupy a leadership position, and so even these traits may be *results* rather than the *causes* of leadership ability. Although personality measurements may one day become more exact, and certain traits may in fact become identified with leadership ability, the evidence thus

[3] Robert J. House and Mary L. Baetz, "Leadership: Some Empirical Generalizations and New Research Directions," in Barry M. Staw, ed., *Research in Organizational Behavior*, Vol. 1 (Greenwich, Conn.: JAI Press, 1979), pp. 348–354; David A. Kenny and Stephen J. Zaccaro, "An Estimate of Variance Due to Traits in Leadership," *Journal of Applied Psychology* 68, no. 4 (November 1983):678–685; Ralph M. Stogdill, "Personal Factors Associated with Leadership: A Survey of the Literature," *Journal of Psychology* 25, no. 1 (January 1948):35–71; R. D. Mann, "A Review of the Relationships Between Personality and Performance in Small Groups," *Psychological Bulletin* 56, no. 4 (July 1959):241–270; and Howard M. Weiss and Seymour Adler, "Personality and Organizational Behavior," *Research in Organizational Behavior* 6 (1984):1–50.

Moral leadership concerns values and requires that followers are provided enough knowledge of alternatives to make intelligent choices when it comes time to respond to a leader's proposal to lead. Finally, Burns says about moral leadership: "I mean the kind of leadership that can produce social change that will satisfy followers' authentic needs. I mean less the Ten Commandments than the Golden Rule. But, even the Golden Rule is inadequate, for it measures the wants and needs of others simply by our own."

Clearly, leadership has a moral dimension. Whether or not we focus entirely on moral leadership, as Burns does, is less important than is recognizing that the relationship between leader and led has a component of mortality—less important than understanding the rules that we use to interact with each other in a much broader variety of human interactions. For Burns, the leader who ignores the moral component of his position can be successful but may well go down in history as a scoundrel, or worse. A legacy of poor managerial performance will be likely be the least of his posthumous worries.

Source: James MacGregor Burns, *Leadership* (New York: Harper & Row, 1978).

far suggests that individuals who emerge as leaders possess no single constellation of traits that clearly distinguish them from nonleaders.

In addition, the issue is clouded by the question of cultural bias. For example, if being tall has long been a traditional trait associated with American leaders, this quite likely reflects an assumption about the relationship between traditional leadership traits and the inclinations of our culture to seek its leaders from among the ranks of Caucasian males. Our assumptions about leadership traits may well change as increasing numbers of women, minorities, gays, and disabled individuals assume leadership positions in greater proportion to the overall population.

QUOTATION FROM A MANAGER

"The 'hallmarks of leadership' are: Visionary skill and conceptual ability . . . a disposition toward timely action based on ingredients of instinct and judgment which prove to have a high degree of reliability . . . above-average skill in communications . . . conviction and determination in the face of endless reasons why 'it can't be done.'"—Theodore B. Palmer III, President and CEO, Yarway Corporation (*Gifted Children's Monthly*, June 1988, p. 2)

Attempts to compare the characteristics of effective and ineffective leaders—the second category of leadership trait studies—are more recent and fewer in number, but they, too, have generally failed to isolate traits strongly associated with successful leadership. One study did find that traits such as intelligence, initiative, and self-assurance were associated with high managerial levels and performance.[4] However, this study also found that the single most important factor related to managerial level and performance was the manager's supervisory ability—that is, his or her skill in using supervisory methods appropriate to the particular situation. Most other studies in this area also have found that effective leadership did not depend on a particular set of traits but rather on how well the leader's traits matched the requirements of the situation that he or she was facing.[5]

Some researchers have also found that although women are still less likely than men to emerge as leaders, they are just as effective when they do. Even though an increasing number of people believe in equality of ability and opportunity, persistent, often unconscious sexual stereotyping continues to hamper the recognition of women as potential leaders. When women do become leaders, however, they perform as well as male leaders and are generally perceived as equally effective by their subordinates.[6]

Of course, racial stereotyping remains another problem when efforts are made to identify connections between traits and leadership qualities. Although the number of blacks in the managerial ranks has been growing, very few have made it to the highest echelons in organizational hierarchies. However, such corporations as GM, AM International, Xerox, Drexel Burnham, Godfather's Pizza, IBM, and Procter & Gamble have initiated programs to enhance the placement of black men and women in leadership positions.[7]

The Behavioral Approach to Leadership

When it became evident that effective leaders did not seem to have any distinguishing traits or characteristics, researchers tried to isolate the *behaviors* characteristic of effective leaders. In other words, rather than try to figure out what effective leaders *were,* researchers tried to determine what effective leaders *did*—how they delegated tasks, how they communicated with and tried to motivate their subordinates, how they carried out their tasks, and so on. Unlike traits, behaviors can be *learned,* and so it followed that individuals trained in appropriate leadership behaviors would be able to lead more effectively.

---

[4]See Edwin E. Ghiselli, *Explorations in Managerial Talent* (Pacific Palisades, Calif.: Goodyear, 1971), pp. 39–56.

[5]See Dorwin Cartwright and Alvin Zander, eds., *Group Dynamics,* 3rd ed. (New York: Harper & Row, 1968).

[6]Natalie Porter, Florence Lindauer Geis, and Joyce Jennings, "Are Women Invisible Leaders?" *Sex Roles* 9, no. 10 (October 1983):1035–1049; Robert W. Rice, Debra Instone, and Jerome Adams, "Leader Sex, Leader Success, and Leadership Process: Two Field Studies," *Journal of Applied Psychology* 69, no. 1 (February 1984):12–31; and Susan M. Donnell and Jay Hall, "Men and Women as Managers: A Significant Case of No Significant Difference," *Organizational Dynamics* 8, no. 4 (Spring 1980):60–77.

[7]Colin Leinster, "Black Executives: How They're Doing," *Fortune,* January 18, 1988, pp. 109–120.

Research showed, nevertheless, that leadership behaviors appropriate in one situation were not necessarily appropriate in another. For example, an executive skilled at motivating creative individuals might be very successful in a consumer goods company in a highly competitive industry; such a firm may depend on flamboyant marketing techniques, and so the executive's ability to manage creative people (like artists and copywriters) would be most useful. On the other hand, in an electronics company manufacturing specialized, high-quality components, such a manager might be less useful and perhaps even counterproductive because the company's success would probably depend on its ability to maintain product quality and service rather than on its marketing approach.

Desirable leadership qualities and behaviors may also change as an organization's culture changes. For example, a genuine concern of many fast-growing computer firms such as Sun Microsystems, Apple, and others is the increasing need to adapt different managerial skills and leadership styles to organizational structures and objectives that are quite different from the entrepreneurial skills and objectives on which these companies were originally founded and originally prospered. An entrepreneur whose strong suit is technical ingenuity will not necessarily possess the leadership skills required to guide a company through an era of growth and restructuring occasioned by its entry into a new corporate environment.

HERE'S AN EXAMPLE

Ronald W. Allen, newly appointed CEO of Delta Airlines, symbolizes Delta's reawakening. He's an affable and outgoing manager who is not afraid to risk spending money on projects with less predictable payoffs. (*Business Week*, 8/1/88, p. 93)

Nevertheless, despite growing evidence that effective leadership behaviors depend at least partially on the leader's situation, some researchers have reached the conclusion that certain management behaviors are in fact more effective than others in a relatively wide variety of circumstances. These researchers have focused on two aspects of leadership behavior: **leadership functions** and **leadership styles.**

leadership functions The group-maintenance and task-related activities that must be performed by the leader, or someone else, for a group to perform effectively.

leadership styles The various patterns of behavior favored by leaders during the process of directing and influencing workers.

Leadership Functions and Styles. This first aspect of the behavioral approach to leadership shifted the focus from the individual leader to the functions that leaders performed within their groups. It appeared that in order for a group to operate effectively, *someone* had to perform two major functions: "task-related" or problem-solving functions and "group-maintenance" or social functions. Task-related functions might include suggesting solutions and offering information and opinions; group-maintenance functions may include anything that helps the group operate more smoothly—agreeing with or complimenting another group member, for example, or mediating group disagreements.

Studies in this area have found that most effective groups have some form of *shared* leadership in which one person (usually the manager or formal leader) performs the task function, while another group member performs the social function.[8] Leadership specialization may occur because a given individual has the temperament or skill to play only one role or because another might be preoccupied with one role at the expense of the other. For example, a manager focusing on the task function may present his or her ideas forcefully and encourage the group to make rapid decisions. The group-maintenance function, on the other hand, requires that the individual remain responsive to the ideas and feelings of the other group members. An individual who is able to perform *both* roles successfully would obviously be an especially effective leader.

HERE'S AN EXAMPLE

Robert M. Kavner, AT&T's Chief financial Officer, was brought in to replace Vittorio Cassoni as head of AT&T's computer division. Kavner brings a different style of leadership to his group and says he wants more attention focused on his "very able team at AT&T." (*Business Week*, 5/9/88, p. 46)

FOR DISCUSSION

How could a group effectively operate with *shared* leadership?

The second perspective on leadership behavior focuses on one of two styles that a leader may use in dealing with subordinates: a task-oriented style and an employee-oriented style. *Task-oriented* managers closely supervise subordinates to ensure that the task is performed to their satisfaction; a manager with this leadership style is more

[8]See Robert F. Bales, *Interaction Process Analysis* (Reading, Mass.: Addison-Wesley, 1951). A recent study finding contrary evidence is C. Roger Rees and Mady Wechsler Segal, "Role Differentiation in Groups: The Relationship Between Instrumental and Expressive Leadership," *Small Group Behavior* 15, no. 1 (February 1984):109–123.

concerned with getting the job done than with the development and growth of subordinates. On the other hand, *employee-oriented* managers try to motivate rather than to control subordinates; they encourage group members to perform tasks by allowing group members to participate in decisions that affect them and by forming friendly, trusting, and respectful relationships with group members.

Influences on Choice of Leadership Style. Robert Tannenbaum and Warren H. Schmidt were among the first theorists to describe various factors that they believe should influence a manager's choice of leadership style.[9] While personally favoring the employee-centered style, they acknowledge that managers need to take certain practical considerations into account before deciding how to manage. In particular, they suggest that a manager should consider three sets of "forces" before choosing a leadership style: forces in the manager, forces in subordinates, and forces in the situation.

How a manager leads will undoubtedly—and primarily—be influenced by his or her background, knowledge, values, and experience (*forces in the manager*). For example, a manager who believes that the needs of the individual must come second to the needs of the organization may take a very directive role in his or her subordinates' activities. (See Figure 15-1.)

But characteristics of *subordinates* also must be considered before managers can choose an appropriate leadership style. According to Tannenbaum and Schmidt, a manager can allow greater participation and freedom when subordinates:

- Crave independence and freedom of action.
- Want to have decision-making responsibility.

---

[9]Robert Tannenbaum and Warren H. Schmidt, "How to Choose a Leadership Pattern," *Harvard Business Review* 51, no. 3 (May–June 1973):162–164ff. (Reprint of March–April 1958 article.)

FIGURE 15-1 CONTINUUM OF LEADERSHIP BEHAVIOR

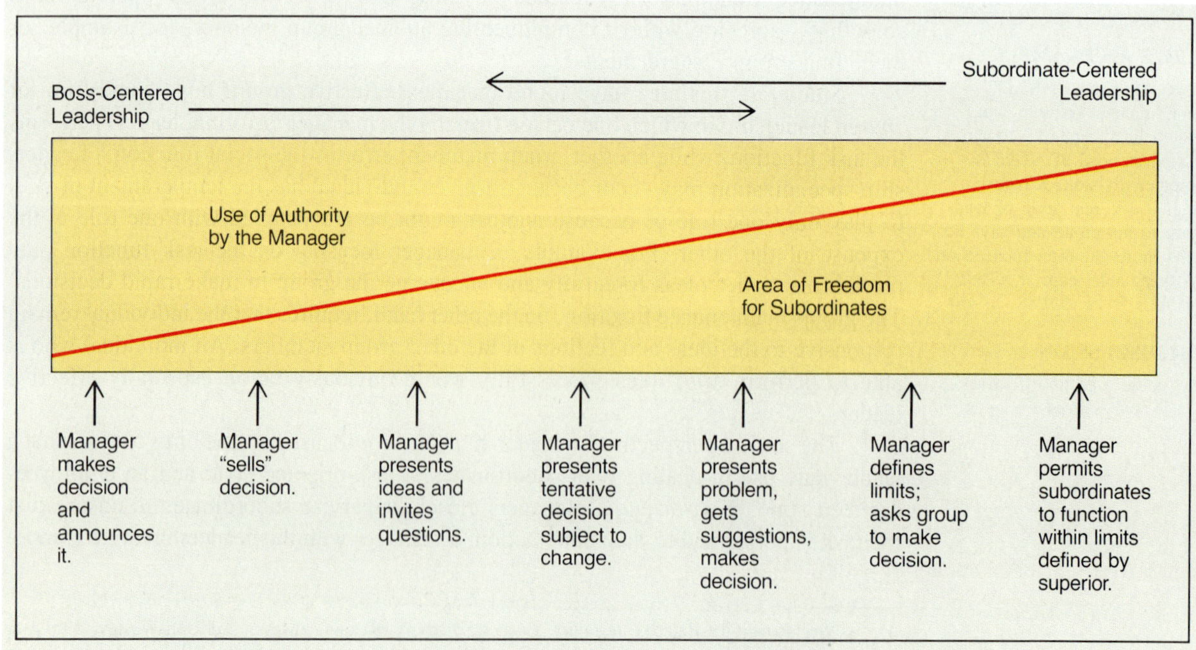

Source: Reprinted by permission of the *Harvard Business Review*: an exhibit from "How to Choose a Leadership Pattern" by Robert Tannenbaum and Warren Schmidt (May–June 1973).

INTERNATIONAL MANAGEMENT

QUESTIONING THE APPLICABILITY OF AMERICAN THEORIES OF LEADERSHIP

As we saw in Chapter 14, Dutch management scholar Geert Hofstede's study of motivation, leadership, and organization in many nations around the globe revealed that American leadership theories such as those espoused by Douglas McGregor and others do not uniformly apply to managerial practices in other countries. As Hofstede notes, American theories tend to advocate participation in the manager's decisions by subordinates—that is, participative management—as long as the initiative for participation is taken by the manager. He argues that this attitude is compatible with a particularly American view of power, analyzing the extent to which a given society accepts as a fact that power in institutions and organizations is distributed unequally.

However, in countries such as Germany, Sweden, Norway, and Israel, where power distances between people are smaller, there is a greater acceptance of management models in which initiatives are undertaken by subordinates (through forms of industrial "democracy" such as codetermination in Germany and the cooperative management style of the Scandinavian nations) and for which there is limited sympathy in the U.S. Although there have been some efforts, such as adopting the highly successful Japanese practice of quality-control circles and other attempts at participative management such as are used in Sweden and elsewhere, many of these efforts have failed to take root in a country such as ours, where there is still a fairly great distance between the power of management and that of employees. Some reports contend the failure is due to American management's typical resistance to sharing power with employees and its tendency to view the sharing of power and leadership prerogatives as a threat to its traditional role.

Hofstede concludes that leadership in any culture must by its very nature make a concession to subordinates and to the culture that has conditioned the behavior and attitudes of both managers and subordinates. He argues that leaders cannot simply choose their styles at will because what is managerially feasible depends to a large extent on the cultural conditioning of the leader's subordinates—that is, to *their* concept of power distances as well as to that of managers.

Because our work force is made up increasingly of females and members of minorities, it will be interesting to see if new internal cultures arise that alter our traditional views on the distribution of power in organizations: It is reasonable to assume that, as the conformation of the work force changes, the interrelationship between managerial and subordinate concepts of power distances will also change.

Sources: Geert Hofstede, "Motivation, Leadership, and Organization: Do American Theories Apply Abroad?" *Organizational Dynamics,* Summer 1980, pp. 42–63; Ron Zemke, "Scandanavian Management—A Look at Our Future?" *Management Reveiw* 77, no. 7 (1988):44–47.

- Identify with the organization's goals.
- Are knowledgeable and experienced enough to deal with the problem efficiently.
- Have experience with previous managers that leads them to expect participative management.

Where these conditions are lacking, managers may have to lean toward an authoritarian style. They can, however, modify their behavior once subordinates gain self-confidence in working with them.

Finally, a manager's choice of leadership style must reckon with such *situational* forces as the organization's preferred style, the specific work group, the nature of the group's work tasks, the pressures of time, and even environment factors, all of which may affect organization members' attitudes toward authority.

Most managers, for example, will move toward the leadership style favored by the organization's hierarchy. If top management emphasizes human-relations skills, the manager will incline toward an employee-centered style; if a decision, take-charge style seems favored, the managers will tend to be task- rather than employee-oriented.

The specific work group also affects the choice of style. A group that works well together may respond more to a free and open atmosphere than to close supervision; so will a group confident of its ability to solve problems as a unit. But if a work group is too large or too widely dispersed geographically, a participative management style may be difficult to use.

The Ohio State and University of Michigan Studies. Tannenbaum and Schmidt, as well as other early researchers, thought leadership style to be a "zero-sum" game: The more task-oriented a manager, the less relationship-oriented he or she could be. Subsequent research was undertaken to determine which of these two leadership styles leads to the most effective group performance.

At Ohio State University, researchers studied the effectiveness of what they called "initiating structure" (task-oriented) and "consideration" (employee-oriented) leadership behaviors. They found, as might be expected, that employee turnover rates were lowest and employee satisfaction highest under leaders who were rated high in consideration; conversely, leaders who were rated low in consideration and high in initiating structure had high grievance and turnover rates among their employees. (Figure 15-2 diagrams the leadership styles studied at Ohio State.)

The researchers also found, however, that subordinates' ratings of their leaders' effectiveness depended not so much on the particular *style* of the leader as on the *situation* in which the style was used. For example, Air Force commanders who rated high on consideration were rated as less effective than were task-oriented commanders. It is possible that the more authoritarian environment of the military, coupled with the air crews' belief that quick, hard decisions are essential in combat situations, would

FIGURE 15-2 LEADERSHIP STYLES STUDIED AT OHIO STATE

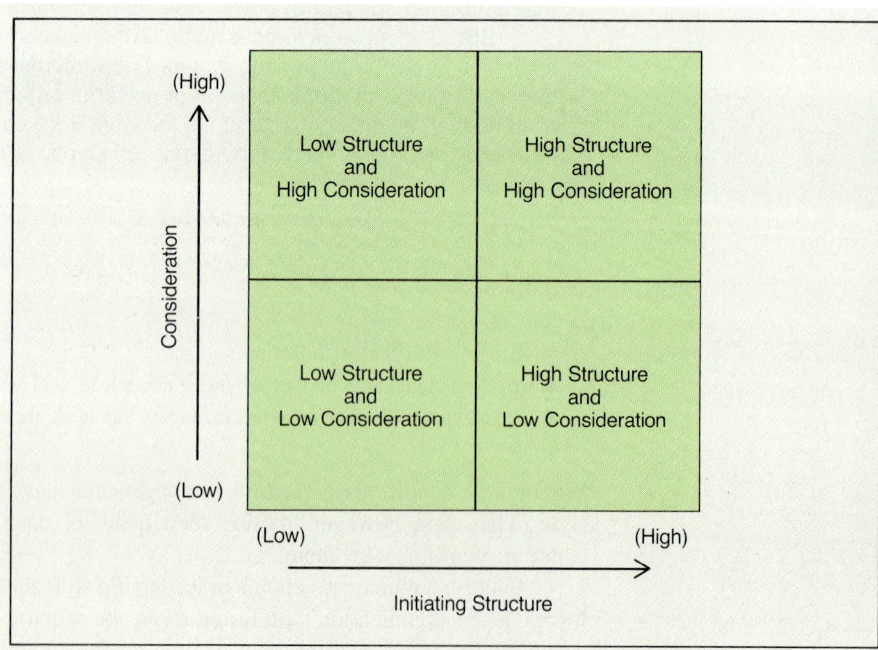

cause people-oriented leaders to be rated less effective. On the other hand, nonproduction supervisors and managers in large companies were rated more effective if they ranked high in consideration.[10]

Similarly, researchers at the University of Michigan distinguished between production-centered and employee-centered managers. Production-centered managers set rigid work standards, organized tasks down to the last detail, prescribed work methods to be followed, and closely supervised subordinates' work. On the other hand, employee-centered managers encouraged subordinate participation in goal setting and other work decisions and helped ensure high performance by inspiring trust and respect. The Michigan studies found that the most productive work groups tended to have leaders who were employee-centered rather than production-centered; they also found that the most effective leaders were those who had supportive relationships with their subordinates, tended to depend upon group rather than individual decision making, and encouraged subordinates to set and achieve high performance goals.

CLASS COMMENT

The Managerial Grid is easy to comprehend and popular as a leadership training tool. The Grid format has also been applied to other areas of management as performance improvement and management controls.

The Managerial Grid. One conclusion from the Ohio State and Michigan studies is that leadership style may well not be unidimensional: Both task orientation and employee orientation can be crucial to superior performance. The Managerial Grid, developed by Robert Blake and Jane Mouton to help measure a manager's relative concern for people and tasks, reflects just this bidimensional nature of leadership.[11]

The Managerial Grid identifies a range of management behaviors based on the various ways that task-oriented and employee-oriented styles (each expressed as a continuum on a scale of 1 to 9) can interact with each other. (See Figure 15-3.) Thus, style 1,1 management, at the lower left-hand corner of the grid, is *impoverished management*—low concern for people and low concern for tasks or production. This style is sometimes called *laissez-faire* management, because the leaders abdicates his or her leadership role.

Style 1,9 management is *country club management*—high concern for employees but low concern for production. Style 9,1 management is *task* or *authoritarian management*—high concern for production and efficiency but low concern for employees. Style 5,5 is *middle-of-the-road management*—an intermediate amount of concern for both production and employee satisfaction.

Style 9,9 management is *team* or *democratic management*—a high concern for both production and employee morale and satisfaction. Black and Mouton argue strongly that the 9,9 management style is the most effective type of leadership behavior. They believe this approach will, in almost all situations, result in improved performance, low absenteeism and turnover, and high employee satisfaction. The Blake and Mouton Managerial Grid is widely used as a training device.

QUOTATION FROM A MANAGER

"The ultimate effectiveness of a leader's intuition, vision, intelligence, energy and all other personal qualities is measured, then, not by the leader's personal triumphs, but rather by the success of the group in the achievement of its objective. This is true whether the leader is a corporate president, a general, or the dominant animal in a wolf pack."—John E. Tait, President and CEO, Penn Mutual Life Insurance Company (*Gifted Children's Monthly*, June 1988, p. 2)

Contingency Approaches to Leadership

Researchers using trait and behavioral approaches showed that effective leadership depended on *many* variables, such as organizational culture, the nature of tasks, and managerial values and experience. No *one* trait was common to all effective leaders; no *one* style was effective in all situations.

EXTRA EXERCISE

Think of persons you would call "effective" or "good" leaders. What elements can be identified in their leadership situations?

[10]See Victor H. Vroom, "Leadership," in Marvin D. Dunnette, ed., *Handbook of Industrial and Organizational Psychology* (New York: John Wiley, 1983), pp. 1527–1551.

[11]Robert R. Blake and Jane S. Mouton, *The New Managerial Grid III* (Houston: Gulf Publishing, 1984). For an early classification of leadership styles into authoritarian, *laissez-faire*, and democratic leadership, see Kurt Lewin, Ronald Lippitt, and Ralph K. White, "Patterns of Aggressive Behavior in Experimentally Created Social Climates," *Journal of Social Psychology* 10, no. 2 (May 1939):271–299.

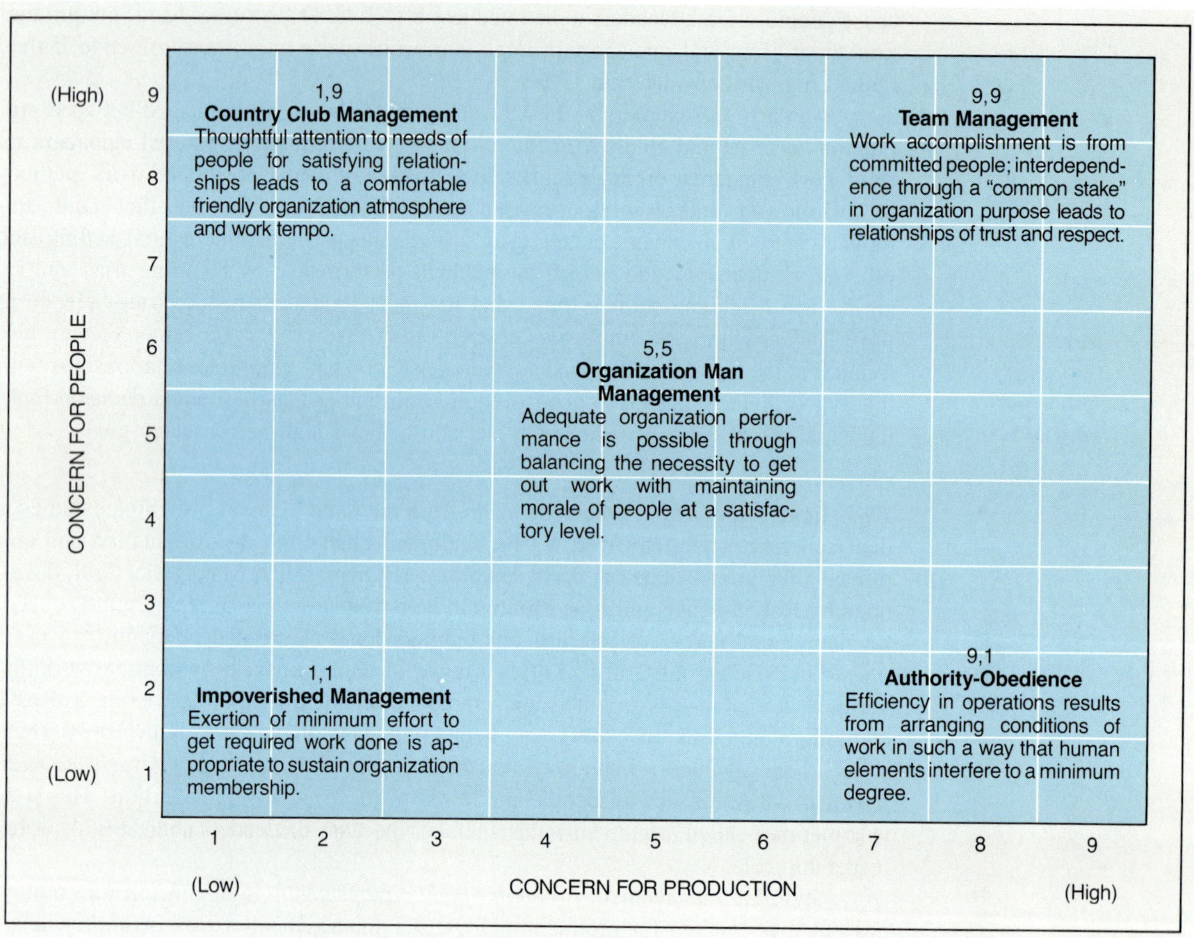

Source: The Managerial Grid figure from *The Managerial Grid III: The Key to Leadership Excellence,* by Robert R. Blake and Jane Srygley Mouton (Houston: Gulf Publishing Company). Copyright © 1985, page 12. Reproduced by permission.

FIGURE 15-3 THE MANAGERIAL GRID®

ILLUSTRATIVE CASE STUDY Continued

New Leadership Policies at GE

Part of the controversy at GE has focused on Welch's style. There is no doubt about Welch's intensity. Just by watching videotapes of his speeches, one can see the fire in his eyes and his determination to realize his vision for GE. Welch has devoted a great deal of time and energy trying to get managers at GE to confront each other, to be more open about solving conflicts. One story goes that after a bitter argument in which Welch ripped apart one manager's ideas, Welch hugged the man for openly engaging in debate and creative conflict.

Welch wants people to focus on tasks, to bring a higher level of intensity to their jobs. He believes that such intensity is one of the keys to being a successful competitor, number one or number two in every industry division in which GE is engaged. But he also knows that managing relationships are equally important—that managers accomplish tasks through people. In short, he has issued Blake and Mouton's challenge for team management as a means for GE's future success. Unfortunately, some view his radical policy of streamlining the work force as evidence that Jack Welch does not really have a concern for people in any capacity other than as a member of a team working toward Jack Welch's goals.

Therefore, researchers began trying to identify those factors in each *situation* that influenced the effectiveness of a particular leadership style. Such factors included the leader's personality, past experience, and expectations; the superior's expectations and behavior; the requirements of the task; the organizational culture and policies; and the expectations and behaviors of peers.[12] (See Figure 15-4.) Taken together, the theories resulting from this research constitute the **contingency approach** to leadership—one which focuses on the *situational factors* influencing managerial style. We will discuss each of these factors in turn.

contingency approach The view that the management technique that best contributes to the attainment of organizational goals might vary in different types of situations or circumstances.

Situational Factors in Leadership Effectiveness. *The leader's personality, past experiences, and expectations.* Naturally, a manager's values, background, experiences, and expectations affect his or her style; for example, a manager who has been successful exercising little supervision may be more prone to adopt an employee-oriented style of leadership. Evidence has also demonstrated that situations often work out the way we *expect* them to—a phenomenon often referred to as the *self-fulfilling prophecy*. One study, for instance, found that new leaders who were told that their subordinates were low performers managed in a more authoritative way than did new leaders who were told that their subordinates were high performers.[13]

---

[12]See, for example, Martin M. Chemers, "The Social, Organizational, and Cultural Context of Effective Leadership," in Barbara Kellerman, ed., *Leadership: Multidisciplinary Perspectives* (Englewood Cliffs, N.J.: Prentice Hall, 1985), pp. 91–112.

[13]George F. Farris and Francis G. Lim, Jr., "Effects of Performance on Leadership, Cohesiveness, Satisfaction, and Subsequent Performance," *Journal of Applied Psychology* 53, no. 6 (December 1969):490–497. See also Dov Eden, "Self-Fulfilling Prophecy as a Management Tool: Harnessing Pygmalion," *Academy of Management Review* 9, no. 1 (January 1984):64–73.

FIGURE 15-4 PERSONALITY AND SITUATIONAL FACTORS THAT INFLUENCE EFFECTIVE LEADERSHIP

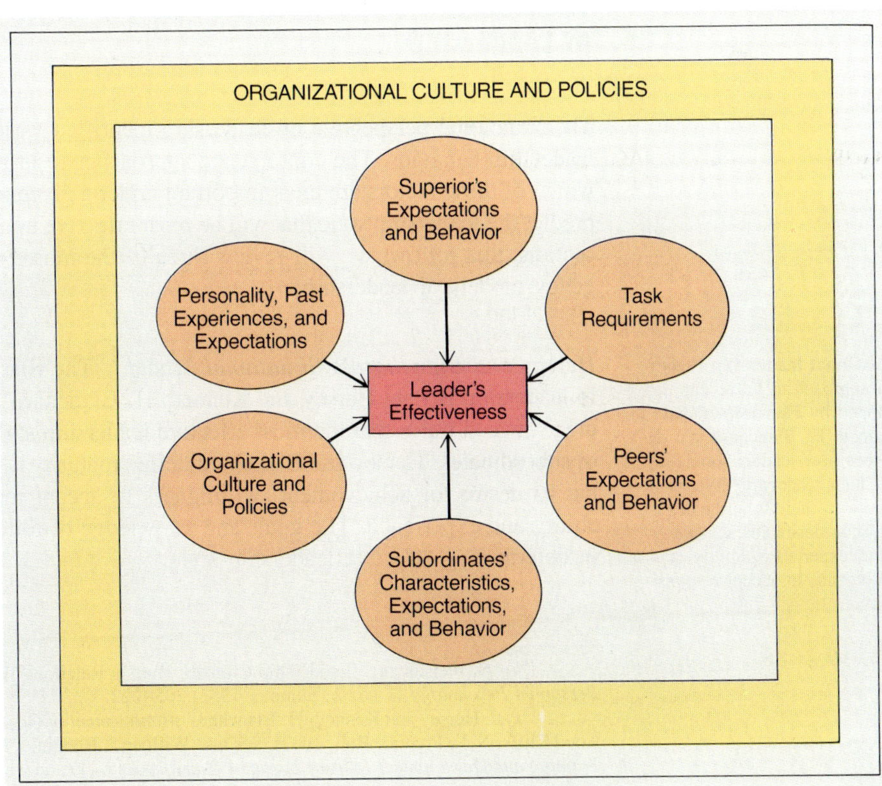

The expectations and behavior of superiors. Because of their power to dispense such organizational rewards as bonuses and promotions, superiors clearly affect the behavior of lower-level managers. In addition, lower-level managers tend to model themselves after their superiors. One study found that supervisors who learned new behaviors in a human relations training program tended to yield those behaviors quickly if they were not consistent with their immediate superior's leadership style.[14]

Subordinate's characteristics, expectations, and behaviors. The skills, training, and attitudes of subordinates also influence the manager's choice of style: highly capable employees require a less directive approach, and while some employees may prefer an authoritarian leader, others may prefer total responsibility for their own work.

Task requirements. The nature of subordinates' job responsibilities will also affect the leadership style that a manager will use. Jobs that require precise instructions (say, testing printed circuits) demand a more task-oriented style than do jobs (say, university teaching) whose operating procedures can be left largely to the individual employees.

FOR DISCUSSION

If an organization is designed and managed well, why should it need leadership?

Organizational culture and policies. The culture and policies of an organization shape the leader's behavior and the expectations of subordinates. For example, in organizations that encourage strict accountability for results, managers usually supervise subordinates quite closely.

Peers' expectations and behavior. The opinions and attitudes of a manager's peers can often affect how effectively the manager performs; hostile colleagues may harm the manager's reputation by competing for resources and behaving uncooperatively. The behavior of managers affects and influences that of their associates: whatever their own inclinations, managers tend to some extent to imitate the management style of their peers.

Theoretical Perspectives on the Contingency Approach to Leadership

The situational perspective on leadership identified various factors that can influence leadership behavior. The contingency approaches to leadership attempt (1) to identify which of these factors are most important under a given set of circumstances and (2) to predict the leadership style that will be most effective under those circumstances. In the sections that follow, we will review three of the more recent and well-known contingency models of leadership.

situational leadership theory An approach to leadership developed by Paul Hersey and Kenneth H. Blanchard that describes how leaders should adjust their leadership style in response to their subordinates' evolving desire for achievement, experience, ability, and willingness to accept responsibility.

Hersey and Blanchard's Situational Model. The first major contingency approach to leadership is Paul Hersey and Kenneth H. Blanchard's **situational leadership theory,**[15] which holds that the most effective leadership style varies with the "maturity" of subordinates. Hersey and Blanchard define maturity not as age or emotional stability but as desire for achievement, willingness to accept responsibility, and task-related ability and experience. The goals and knowledge of followers are important variables in determining effective leadership style.

---

[14] E. A. Fleishman, "Leadership Climate, Human Relations Training, and Supervisory Behavior," *Personnel Psychology* 6, no. 2 (Summer 1953):205–222.

[15] Paul Hersey and Kenneth H. Blanchard, *Management of Organizational Behavior,* 4th ed. (Englewood Cliffs, N.J.: Prentice Hall, 1982). See also William J. Reddin, "The 3-D Management Style Theory," *Training and Development Journal* 21, no. 4 (April 1967):8–17, on which Hersey and Blanchard base much of their work.

Hersey and Blanchard believe that the relationship between a manager and subordinates moves through four phases—a kind of life cycle—as subordinates develop and "mature" and that managers need to vary their leadership style with each phase. (See Figure 15-5.) In the initial phase—when subordinates first enter the organization—a high task orientation by the manager is most appropriate. Subordinates must be instructed in their tasks and familiarized with the organization's rule and procedures. At this stage, a nondirective manager causes anxiety and confusion among new employees; however, a participatory employee relationship approach would also be inappropriate at this stage because subordinates cannot yet be regarded as colleagues.

As subordinates begin to learn their tasks, task-oriented management remains essential, because subordinates are not yet willing or able to accept full responsibility. However, the manager's trust in and support of subordinates can increase as the manager becomes familiar with subordinates and wishes to encourage further efforts on their part. Thus, the manager may choose to initiate employee-oriented behaviors.

In the third phase, the subordinates' ability and achievement motivation are increased, and subordinates actively begin to seek greater responsibility. The manager will no longer need to be directive (indeed, close direction might be resented). However, the manager will continue to be supportive and considerate in order to strengthen the subordinates' resolve for greater responsibility. As subordinates gradually become more confident, self-directing, and experienced, the manager can reduce the amount of

FIGURE 15-5 THE SITUATIONAL THEORY OF LEADERSHIP

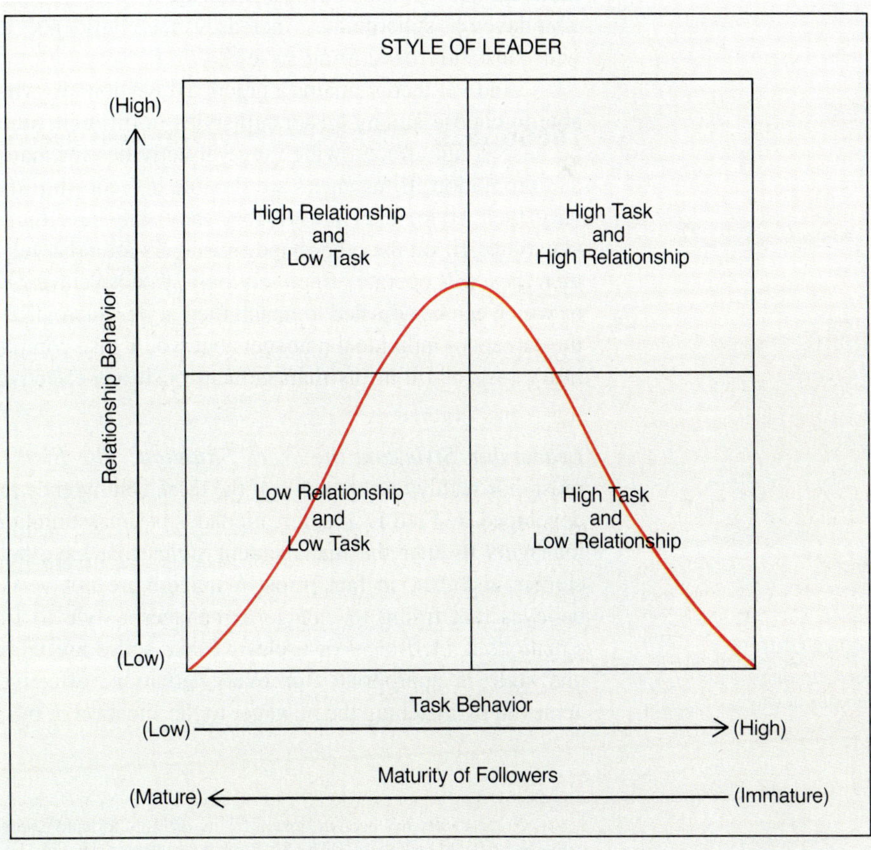

Source: Adapted from Paul Hersey and Kenneth H. Blanchard, *Management of Organizational Behavior: Utilizing Human Resources*, 4th ed., p. 152. Copyright © 1982. Reprinted by permission of Prentice-Hall, Inc., Englewood Cliffs, N.J.

"Want something that projects reason and reciprocity, quiet, confident leadership, and understated yet unmistakable power."

Drawing by D. Reilly; © 1980 The New Yorker Magazine, Inc.

support and encouragement. Subordinates are then "on their own" and no longer need or expect a directive relationship with their manager.

TEACHING TIP

Here is an opportunity once again to draw the connection between leadership and motivation.

The situational leadership theory has generated interest because it recommends a leadership type that is dynamic and flexible rather than static. The motivation, ability, and experience of subordinates must constantly be assessed in order to determine which style combination would be most appropriate under flexible and changing conditions. If the style is appropriate, according to Hersey and Blanchard, it will not only motivate subordinates but also help them move toward maturity. Thus, the manager who develops subordinates, increases their confidence, and helps them learn their work will constantly be shifting style.[16]

And yet there remains a practical question: To what extent are managers actually able to choose among leadership styles in different situations? The issue is important because it can affect a wide range of activities for management selection, placement, and promotion. If managers are flexible in leadership style, or if they can be trained to vary their style, then presumably they will be effective in a variety of leadership situations. If, on the other hand, managers are relatively inflexible in leadership style, then they will operate effectively only in those situations which best match their style or which can be adjusted to match their style. Such inflexibility would not only hamper the careers of individual managers but would also complicate enormously the organization's task of filling its management positions effectively.

Leadership Style and the Work Situation: The Fiedler Model. The second—and most thoroughly researched—of the three contingency models that we will discuss was developed by Fred E. Fiedler. Fiedler's basic assumption is that it is quite difficult for managers to alter the management styles that have helped them develop successful careers and that, in fact, most managers are not very flexible. For this reason, he believes that trying to change a manager's style to fit unpredictable or fluctuating situations is inefficient or useless. Since styles are relatively inflexible, and since no one style is appropriate for every situation, effective group performance can be achieved by matching the manager to the situation or by changing the situation to fit the

CLASS COMMENT

Change the situation or fit leaders to the situation.

[16]The theory has been criticized for its inability to handle some actual management situations logically. See Claude L. Graeff, "The Situational Leadership Theory: A Critical View," *Academy of Management Review* 8, no. 2 (April 1983):285–291. Blake and Mouton also critique the situational theory and argue for the universal superiority of the 9,9 style in "A Comparative Analysis of Situationalism and 9,9 Management by Principle," *Organizational Dynamics* 10, no. 4 (Spring 1982):20–43.

manager. For example, a comparatively authoritarian manager can be selected to fill a post that requires a directive leader; by the same token, a job can be changed to give an authoritarian manager more formal authority over subordinates.

The leadership styles that Fiedler contrasts are similar to the employee-centered and task-oriented styles discussed earlier. What differentiates his model from the others is the measuring instrument that he used. Fiedler measured leadership style on a simple scale that indicated "the degree to which a man described favorably or unfavorably his least preferred co-worker (LPC)"—the employee with whom the person could work least well. It is this measure that locates an individual on the leadership-style continuum. According to Fiedler's findings, "a person who describes his least preferred co-worker in a relatively favorable manner tends to be permissive, human relations–oriented, and considerate of the feelings of his men. But a person who describes his least preferred co-worker in an unfavorable manner—who has what we have come to call a low LPC rating—tends to be managing, task-controlling, and less concerned with the human relations aspects of the job."[17]

According to Fiedler, then, high-LPC managers want to have warm personal relations with their co-workers and will regard close ties with subordinates as important to their overall effectiveness. Low-LPC managers, on the other hand, want to get the job done; the reactions of subordinates to their leadership style is of far lower priority than is the need to maintain production. Low-LPC managers who feel that a harsh style is necessary to maintain production will not hesitate to use it.

Fiedler has identified three "leadership situations" that help determine which leadership style will be effective: leader-member relations, the task structure, and the leader's position power. Fiedler's studies did not include such other situational variables as employee motivation and the values and experiences of leaders and group members.

leader-member relations The quality of the interaction between a leader and his or her subordinates; according to Fred Fiedler, the most important influence on the manager's power.

The quality of **leader-member relations** is the most important influence on the manager's power and effectiveness: If the manager gets along well with the rest of the group, if group members respect the manager for reasons of personality, character, or ability, then the manager may not have to rely on formal rank or authority. On the other hand, a manager who is disliked or distrusted may be less able to lead informally and may have to rely on directives to accomplish group tasks.

task structure A work situation variable that, according to Fred Fiedler, helps determine a manager's power. In structured tasks, managers automatically have high power; in unstructured tasks, the manager's power is diminished.

Task structure is the second most important variable in the leadership situation. A highly structured task is one in which step-by-step procedures or instructions for the task are available; group members therefore have a very clear idea of what they are expected to do. Managers in such situations automatically have a great deal of authority: there are clear guidelines by which to measure worker performance, and the manager can back up his or her instructions by referring to a rulebook or manual—to stipulated policy. On the other hand, when tasks are unstructured, as in committee meetings, group member roles are more ambiguous, because there are no clear guidelines on how to proceed. The manager's power is diminished, since group members can more easily disagree with or question the manager's instructions.

position power The power, according to Fred Fiedler, that is inherent in the formal position the leader holds. This power may be great or small, depending upon the specific position.

The leader's **position power** is the final situational variable identified by Fiedler. Some positions, such as the presidency of a firm, carry a great deal of power and authority. The chairperson of a fund-raising drive, on the other hand, has little power over volunteer workers. Thus, high-position power simplifies a leader's task of influencing subordinates, while low-position power makes a leader's task more difficult.

[17] Fred E. Fiedler, "Engineer the Job to Fit the Manager," *Harvard Business Review* 43, no. 5 (September–October 1965):116. See also Fred E. Fiedler, "The Contingency Model," in Harold Proshansky and Bernard Seidenberg, eds., *Basic Studies in Social Psychology* (New York: Holt, Rinehart & Winston, 1965), pp. 538–551, and "Validation and Extension of the Contingency Model of Leadership Effectiveness," *Psychological Bulletin* 76, no. 2 (August 1971):128–148.

Fiedler then went on to specify eight possible combinations of these three variables in the leadership situation: Leader-member relations can be good or bad, tasks may be structured or unstructured, and position power may be strong or weak.

Using these eight categories of leadership situations and his two types of leaders—high and low LPC—Fiedler reviewed studies of over 800 groups to see which type of leader was most effective in each situation. Among the groups studied were basketball teams, executive training workshops, and Air Force and tank combat crews. A well-liked leader of a bomber crew, for example, would be in category 1 of Figure 15-6, while a disliked temporary committee chairperson would be in category 8. He found that low-LPC leaders—those who were task-oriented or authoritarian—were most effective in extreme situations—situations in which the leader either had a great deal of power and influence or had very little power and influence. High-LPC leaders—those who were employee-oriented—were most effective in situations where the leaders had moderate power and influence.

For example, the respected head of a research team would have only moderate influence over team members—influence based largely on the factor that the team respected the leader. Research tasks are relatively unstructured, and so the leader would have little influence over the way the work would be organized and performed. In addition, the leader's position power is low because team members could regard themselves as colleagues rather than subordinates (category 4). An authoritarian style would therefore be ineffective; team members would resent it, and it would encourage high performance by the group.

Fiedler's model, then, suggests that an appropriate match of the leader's style (as measured by the LPC score) and the situation (as determined by the interaction of these three variables) leads to effective managerial performance. This model has been used

FIGURE 15-6 HOW THE STYLE OF EFFECTIVE LEADERSHIP VARIES WITH THE SITUATION

High
Relationship-motivated leaders perform better
LPC
Task-motivated leaders perform better
Low

	1	2	3	4	5	6	7	8
Leader-Member Relations	Good	Good	Good	Good	Poor	Poor	Poor	Poor
Task Structure	Structured		Unstructured		Structured		Unstructured	
Leader Position Power	Strong	Weak	Strong	Weak	Strong	Weak	Strong	Weak

Source: Fred E. Fiedler and Martin M. Chemers. *Leadership and Effective Management* (Glenview, Ill.: Scott, Foresman, 1974), p. 80. Reprinted by permission of Fred E. Fiedler.

with some success as the basis of a training program in which managers are shown how to alter the situational variables to match their leadership styles rather than to modify their styles to fit the situation.[18]

Although the validity of Fiedler's model has been questioned,[19] it is widely agreed that he has made a significant contribution to our understanding of how leaders and situations can be matched for effective performance.

path-goal model A leadership theory emphasizing the leader's role in clarifying for subordinates how they can achieve high performance and its associated rewards.

A Path-Goal Approach to Leadership. Like other contingency approaches, the **path-goal models** of leadership tries to help us understand and predict leadership effectiveness in different situations. The model, formulated by Martin G. Evans[20] and Robert J. House,[21] represents a new and evolving approach.

The path-goal approach is based on the expectancy model (described in the previous chapter), which states that an individual's motivation depends on his or her expectation of reward and the valence, or attractiveness, of the reward. The path-goal approach focuses on the leader as a source of rewards and attempts to predict how different types of rewards and different leadership styles affect the motivation, performance, and satisfaction of subordinates.

Managers have at their disposal a number of ways to influence subordinates. According to Evans, the most important are the manager's ability to provide rewards and to clarify what subordinates must do to earn them. Thus, managers determine the availability of "goals" (rewards) and make clear the "paths" to be taken to reach them.

CLASS COMMENT

Managers structure the "paths" so that subordinates can achieve the goals.

Evans suggests that a manager's leadership style influences both which rewards will be available to subordinates and subordinates' perceptions of what they have to do to earn those rewards. An employee-centered manager, for example, will offer a wide range of rewards to subordinates—not only pay and promotion, but also support, encouragement, security, and respect. In addition, that manager will be sensitive to individual differences between subordinates and will tailor rewards to the individual needs and desires of subordinates. A task-oriented manager, on the other hand, will offer a narrower, less individualized set of rewards. However, according to Evans, such a manager will usually be much better at linking subordinate performance to rewards than an employee-centered manager. Subordinates of a task-oriented manager will know exactly what productivity or performance level they have to attain in order to gain bonuses, salary increases, or promotions. Evans believes that the leadership style that will most motivate subordinates will depend on the types of rewards they most desire.

House and his colleagues have also attempted to expand the path-goal theory by identifying two contingency variables that help determine the most effective leadership style: the *personal characteristics of subordinates* and the *environmental pressures and demands in the workplace* with which subordinates must cope.

The leadership style that subordinates favor will, according to House, be partially determined by their personal characteristics. He cites studies suggested that indi-

[18]Fred E. Fiedler and Linda Mahar, "A Field Experiment Validating Contingency Model Leadership Training," *Journal of Applied Psychology* 64, no. 3 (June 1979):247–254.

[19]See, for example, John E. Stinson and Lane Tracy, "The Stability and Interpretation of the LPC Score," *Proceedings of the Academy of Management* 32 (1972):182–184; George Graen, James B. Orris, and Kenneth Alvares, "Contingency Model of Leadership Effectiveness: Some Experimental Results," *Journal of Applied Psychology* 55, no. 3 (June 1971):196–201; and Walter Bungard, "Sense and Nonsense of the LPC Scale: Criticism of Fiedler's Contingency Model," *Gruppendynamik* 15, no. 1 (1984):59–74 (in German).

[20]Martin G. Evans, "Leadership and Motivation: A Core Concept," *Academy of Management Journal* 13, no. 1 (March 1970):91–102.

[21]See Robert J. House, "A Path-Goal Theory of Leader Effectiveness," *Administrative Science Quarterly* 16, no. 5 (September 1971):321–328; and Robert J. House and Terence R. Mitchell, "Path-Goal Theory of Leadership," *Journal of Contemporary Business* 3, no. 4 (Autumn 1979):81–97.

viduals who believe their behavior affects the environment favor a participatory leadership style; individuals who believe events occur because of luck or fate tend to find an authoritarian style more congenial.

Subordinates' evaluation of their own ability will also influence subordinate style preference. Those who feel highly skilled and capable may resent an overly supervisory manager, whose directives will be seen as counterproductive rather than rewarding. On the the other hand, subordinates who feel less skilled or able may prefer a manager whose more directive behavior will be seen as enabling them to carry out their tasks properly and therefore make it possible for them to earn organizational rewards. Exhibit 15-1 identifies what House describes as the three environmental factors that determine the leadership styles preferred by subordinates.

The path-goal theory of leadership is considered highly promising, especially because it attempts to explain *why* a particular leadership style is more effective in one situation than in another and because it supports the position that flexibility in responding to situatorial influences is both possible and desirable. Some research supporting the validity of path-goal theory predictions has already appeared.[22]

EXHIBIT 15-1 ENVIRONMENTAL FACTORS DETERMINING PREFERRED LEADERSHIP STYLES

1. *The nature of subordinates' tasks* will affect leadership styles in a number of ways. For example, an individual performing a structured task, such as equipment maintenance, or a repetitive task, such as truck loading, is likely to find an overly directive style redundant, since it is already clear exactly what needs to be done. Similarly, where the task itself is already highly satisfying, consideration shown by the manager will have little effect on a subordinate's motivation. If the task is unpleasant, however, a display of support by the leader may add to the subordinate's satisfaction and motivation.
2. *The organization's formal authority system* usually clarifies for subordinates which actions are likely to be met with disapproval (exceeding the budget, for example) and which are likely to lead to rewards (coming in under budget).
3. *The subordinates' work group* also affects the nature of leadership style in several ways. For groups that are not very cohesive, for example, a supportive, understanding style may be more effective. As a general rule, the leader's style will motivate subordinates to the extent that it compensates them for what they see as deficiencies in the task, authority system, or work group.

TEACHING TIP

Point out that the Vroom-Yetton and Vroom-Jago models are forms of decision trees.

Deciding When to Involve Subordinates: The Vroom-Yetton and Vroom-Jago Models. In a recent book, Victor Vroom and Arthur Jago criticize the path-goal theory as incomplete because it fails to take into account the characteristics of the decision situation within which participation must occur. They propose to extend the classic Vroom-Yetton model of situational leadership—developed in 1973 to help managers decide when and to what extent they should involve subordinates in solving a particular problem—to include a concern for both the quality of and commitment to decisions.[23]

The original Vroom-Yetton model isolated five styles of leadership that represent a continuum from authoritarian approaches (AI, AII) to consultative (CI, CII), to a fully participative one (GII). (See Exhibit 15-2 and Figure 15-7.)[24]

---

[22]Chester A. Schriesheim and Angelo S. DeNisi, "Task Dimensions as Moderators of the Effects of Instrumental Leader Behavior: A Path-Goal Approach," *Proceedings of the Academy of Management* 39 (1979):103–106.

[23]Victor H. Vroom and Arthur G. Jago, *The New Leadership: Managing Participation in Organizations* (Englewood Cliffs, N.J.: Prentice Hall, 1988).

[24]Victor H. Vroom and Philip W. Yetton, *Leadership and Decision Making* (Pittsburgh: University of Pittsburgh Press, 1973). This model has been subsequently refined by Vroom and Art Jago. We will refer to it throughout the text as the Vroom-Yetton model since this is now its standard title. Also see Victor H. Vroom, "Reflections on Leadership and Decision-Making," *Journal of General Management* 9, no. 3 (Spring 1984):18–36.

EXHIBIT 15-2 TYPES OF LEADERSHIP STYLES

AI Managers solve the problem or make the decision themselves, using information available at that time.

AII Managers obtain the necessary information from subordinate(s), then decide on the solution to the problem themselves. They may or may not tell subordinates what the problem is when they request information. The role played by subordinates in making the decision is clearly one of providing the necessary information to managers, rather than generating or evaluating alternative solutions.

CI Managers share the problem with relevant subordinates individually, getting their ideas and suggestions without bringing them together as a group. Then managers make the decision that may or may not reflect subordinates' influence.

CII Managers share the problem with subordinates as a group, collectively obtaining their ideas and suggestions. Then they make the decision that may or may not reflect subordinates' influence.

GII Managers share a problem with subordinates as a group. Managers and subordinates together generate and evaluate alternatives and attempt to reach agreement (consensus) on a solution. Managers do not try to influence the group to adopt their preferred solution, and they accept and implement any solution that has the support of the entire group.

Source: Adapted, by permission of the publisher, from "A New Look at Managerial Decision Making," by Victor H. Vroom, *Organizational Dynamics,* Summer 1973, p. 67.

The authors then suggest several questions that managers can ask themselves to help determine which style to use for the particular problem they are facing:

- Do we have enough information or skill to solve the problem on our own? If not, then AI, where we make the decision ourselves, would be inappropriate.
- Do we need to make a high-quality decision that our subordinates are likely to disagree with? If so, GII, where we seek the consensus of the group, would not be appropriate. In this case, giving up our authority to make the final decision would probably mean that the decision would not have the objective quality that the problem requires.
- Is the problem structured? That is, do we know what information we need and where to get it? If not, then CII and GII, which allow for the greatest group interaction, would be preferable. The other styles would either keep us from getting the information we need or supply us with information in an inefficient manner.
- Is the acceptance of the group critical for the success of the decision? If so, then styles AI and AII, which involve subordinates the least, might not be appropriate.
- If acceptance of the decision is important, are our subordinates likely to disagree among themselves about which is the best solution? If so, then styles CII and GII, which involve group decision making, are preferable. Only within the group can differences between subordinates be discussed openly and ultimately resolved. The other styles might leave some subordinates dissatisfied with the decision.

Depending on the nature of the problem, more than one leadership style may be suitable, or feasible. Vroom and Yetton call this suitable group the "feasible set of alternatives." (See Figure 15-7.) Where there are feasible choices, the manager may freely choose among them because both decision quality and acceptance have been taken into account. As guidance for choosing within a feasible set, Vroom and Yetton suggest two criteria:

1. When decisions must be made quickly or time must be saved, managers should choose authoritarian decision styles ("time-efficient" ones). The payoffs for these choices will occur in the short run, in the form of quicker, more efficient decisions. (Figure 15-7 indicates the approaches that may be feasible in a given problem-solving situation. The most time-efficient solutions are circled.)
2. When managers wish to develop their subordinates' knowledge and decision-making skills, the more participative styles ("time-investment") should be selected. The payoffs

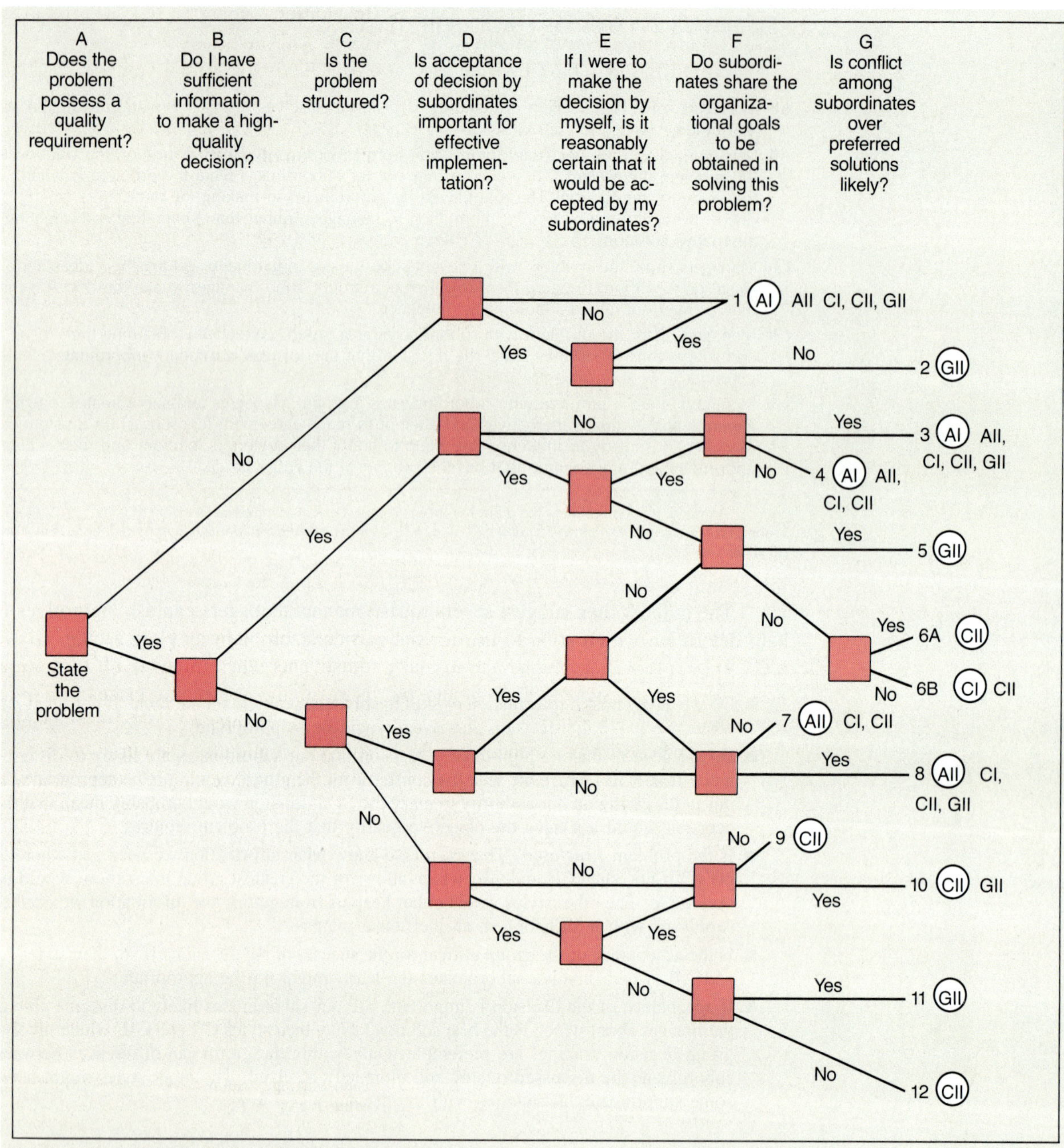

Source: Adapted, by permission of the publisher, from "A New Look at Managerial Decision Making," by Victor H. Vroom, *Organizational Dynamics*, Summer 1973, p. 70. Copyright © 1973 by AMACOM, a division of American Management Associations, New York. All rights reserved.

FIGURE 15-7 DECISION MODEL SHOWING FEASIBLE SET OF ALTERNATIVES

This model shows the preferred management styles for various types of problems. The most "time-efficient" feasible alternative for each problem is circled. (See also the box on page 477.)

for these choices will occur in the longer run, in the form of more effective subordinates and perhaps better working relationships. (In Figure 15-7, the most participative style is the last one in each feasible set.)

Vroom and others have conducted research and concluded that decisions consistent with this model tend to be successful, and those inconsistent with the model's recommendation are generally unsuccessful. In addition, subordinates appear to prefer their managers to be making decisions consistent with the model.[25]

Vroom and Jago have extended this approach by hypothesizing that the effectiveness of decisions is dependent upon the quality of the decisions, the commitment made to the decisions, and the time expended to make the decisions. In addition, they believe that the overall effectiveness of leadership is a function of *the effectiveness of decisions minus the cost of making the decisions plus the value realized in developing people's abilities by means of committed decision making*. It is possible to make a series of highly effective decisions, but if these decisions do little or nothing to develop the abilities of others—or if the decision-making process itself is cumbersome or costly—then the decisions in question will deplete the overall human capital in the organization. Thus, Vroom and Jago argue that leadership styles can be time-driven or development-driven, and as in the earlier Vroom-Yetton model, each focus may be appropriate in different circumstances.

Obviously, some people find it easier than others to adjust to different life situations. Several studies on leadership imply that managers actually do in fact have a great deal of *potential* flexibility in responding to situational influences on their leadership style.[26] No reasonably alert manager, for example, whose subordinates are clearly uncooperative and whose group's performance is declining will persist in using a specific leadership style without at least questioning its effectiveness. Thus, it is possible that individuals can learn how to diagnose a leadership situation and can, at least to some extent, alter their style, in order to make their leadership more effective. In organizations, as elsewhere in life, flexibility is desirable. It helps us respond appropriately to people and situations and to make adjustments when things don't turn out as anticipated. As managers, we should be aware of the variety of leadership styles available. Knowledge of the theories described in this chapter will help us to identify leadership behaviors as we encounter them. And we should also use our own observations to learn about leadership in actual situations. Finally, we should experiment with different approaches and learn through analysis of the results. As managers, our leadership behaviors will be learned on the job as we interact with our subordinations and their tasks.

TEACHING TIP

Emphasize the importance of these last few sentences for students learning about effective leadership.

THE FUTURE OF LEADERSHIP THEORY

FOR DISCUSSION

Why are organizations all of a sudden so interested in leadership?

Naturally, research on leadership behavior continues, and it has shown a tendency to move in diverse directions. Some research stresses the unique characteristics of partic-

[25] Vroom, "Reflections on Leadership and Decision-Making." Supporters of the model and challengers have studied it extensively. See, for example, Arthur Jago, "A Test of Spuriousness in Descriptive Models of Participative Leader Behavior," *Journal of Applied Psychology* 63, no. 3 (June 1978):383–387; R. H. Field, "A Critique of the Vroom-Yetton Contingency Model of Leadership Behavior," *Academy of Management Review* 4, no. 2 (April 1979):249–257; and Victor H. Vroom and Arthur C. Jago, "An Evaluation of Two Alternatives to the Vroom-Yetton Normative Model," *Academy of Management Journal* 23, no. 2 (June 1980):347–355. In support of the model, also see Richard M. Steers, "Individual Differences in Participative Decision-Making," *Human Relations* 30, no. 9 (September 1977):837–847.

[26] Vijay Sathe, "Implications of Corporate Culture: A Manager's Guide to Action," *Organizational Dynamics* 12, no. 2 (Autumn 1983):5–23. Several books published in the early 1980s aroused great interest in corporate cultures. On the culture of Japanese organizations, see William G. Ouchi, *Theory Z: How American Business Can Meet the Japanese Challenge* (Reading, Mass.: Addison-Wesley, 1981); and Richard Tanner Pascale and Anthony G. Athos, *The Art of Japanese Management* (New York: Simon & Schuster, 1981). For discussions of successful companies and the cultures they have generated, see Thomas J. Peters and Robert H. Waterman, Jr., *In Search of Excellence* (New York: Harper & Row, 1982); and Terrence E. Deal and Allan A. Kennedy, *Corporate Cultures: The Rites and Rituals of Corporate Life* (Reading, Mass.: Addison-Wesley, 1982). Recent books exploring the concept in depth include Edgar H. Schein, *Organizational Culture and Leadership* (San Francisco: Jossey-Bass, 1985); Stanley M. Davis, *Managing Corporate Culture* (Hagerstown, Md.: Ballinger, 1985); and Ralph H. Kilman, Mary Jane Saxton, and Ray Serpa, eds., *Gaining Control of Corporate Cultures* (San Francisco: Jossey-Bass, 1985).

ular individuals who have had significant effects on their organizations and has led to the theory of transformational or charismatic leadership. Another (and seemingly opposite) trend is in the study of self-leadership, or the impact of self-managed or autonomous groups. These groups have met with considerable success in various organizations. Still a third theory focuses not on the leaders, but rather on the followers, and examines the romantic and mysterious qualities that we tend to assign to our leaders. We will discuss each of these ideas in this section.

Transformational or Charismatic Leadership

charismatic or **transformational leaders** Leaders who, through their personal vision and energy, inspire followers and have a major impact on their organizations.

One area of growing interest focuses on individuals who have exceptional impact on their organizations. These individuals may be called **charismatic**[27] or **transformational**[28] **leaders.** The recent interest in such transformational leaders seems to stem from at least two sources. First, many large companies—including some historically very successful ones such as AT&T, IBM, and GM[29]—have recently embarked on programs involving extensive changes that must be accomplished in short periods of time. These changes are so large and pervasive that they are often called "transformations," and it has been argued that transformational leaders are necessary to bring these companies through successfully.[30]

HERE'S AN EXAMPLE

Magic leaders is the term used by David A. Nadler and Michael L. Tushman to describe corporate heroes who transform or save desperate companies. These magic leaders clearly play a central role in revitalizing companies, but sometimes the magic leader can't perform magic. Nadler and Tushman attribute this to the fact that the magic leader needs to have developed complementary leadership in the ranks below, or efforts to create change may badly disrupt the organization or even ruin it. (*Fortune*, 6/6/88, p. 261)

A second factor encouraging the growth of interest in transformational leadership is a sense that leadership theory is losing sight of the leader. As the focus of leadership theory has moved from the attempt to identify the inborn traits of leaders, to the study of the roles and behaviors of leaders and managers, to the analysis of the leadership situation, work tasks, and followers, the leader—as a person—has become a progressively less salient part of dominant theory. The public visibility of a business leader like Lee Iacocca of Chrysler or a military leader like General Douglas MacArthur reminds us that some leaders seem to have personal characteristics which do make a difference in their organizations and which are not fully appreciated or accounted for by our existing theories.

transactional leaders Leaders who determine what subordinates need to do to achieve objectives, classify those requirements, and help subordinates become confident that they can read their objectives.

In his explorations of the concept of transformational leadership, Bernard M. Bass has contrasted two types of leadership behaviors: *transactional* and *transformational*. **Transactional leaders** determine what subordinates need to do to achieve their own and organizational objectives, classify those requirements, and help subordinates become confident that they can reach their objectives by expending the necessary efforts. In contrast, transformational leaders "motivate us to do more than we originally expected to do" by raising our sense of the importance and value of our tasks, by "getting us to transcend our own self-interests for the sake of the team, organization, or larger policy," and by raising our need level to the higher-order needs, such as self-actualization.[31]

---

[27]Max Weber, *Economy and Society: An Outline of Interpretative Sociology* (New York: Bedminster Press, 1968; originally published in 1925), pp. 241–254; and Robert J. House, "A 1976 Theory of Charismatic Leadership," in James G. Hunt and Lars L. Larson, eds., *Leadership: The Cutting Edge* (Carbondale: Southern Illinois University Press, 1976), pp. 189–207.

[28]Bernard M. Bass, "Leadership: Good, Better, Best," *Organizational Dynamics* 13, no. 3 (Winter 1985):26–40; and Noel M. Tichy and David O. Ulrich, "The Leadership Challenge—A Call for the Transformational Leader," *Sloan Management Review* 26, no. 1 (Fall 1984):59–68.

[29]See Jeremy Main, Waking Up AT&T: There's Life After Culture Shock," *Fortune,* December 24, 1984, pp. 66ff.; David E. Sanger, "The Changing Image of IBM," *The New York Times Magazine,* July 7, 1985, pp. 13ff.; and Cary Reich, "The Innovator: The Creative Mind of GM Chairman Roger Smith," *The New York Times Magazine,* April 21, 1985, pp. 29ff.

[30]See Tichy and Ulrich "The Leadership Challenge." Tichy and Ulrich list the following additional companies as ones undergoing major transformations: Honeywell, Ford, Burroughs, Chase Manhattan Bank, Citibank, U.S. Steel, Union Carbide, Texas Instruments, and Control Data.

[31]Bass, "Leadership: Good, Better, Best," pp. 27–28, 31.

Much of the leadership theory that we have discussed in this chapter fits Bass's transactional category reasonable well, and Bass argues that such theory is useful and helpful, as far as it goes. However, to be fully effective—and to have a major impact on their organizations—leaders need to use their personal vision and energy to inspire their followers.

Building upon the theory of transformational leadership but with some modifications in its arguments, Richard Boyd proposes that changes in the structure and strategy of American industry have created a need for a new kind of leader who commands a range of skills different from those called for by prior management theories. He suggests that the required new leadership skills include: (1) anticipatory skills—foresight into a constantly changing environment; (2) visioning skills—a process of persuasion and example by which a person or leadership team induces a group to take action in accord with the leader's purposes or, more likely, the shared purposes of a larger group; (3) value-congruence skills—the need of corporate leaders to be in touch with employees' economic, safety, psychological, spiritual, sexual, aesthetic, and physical needs in order to engage people on the basis of shared motives, values, and goals; (4) empowerment skills—the willingness to share power and to do so effectively; and (5) self-understanding—introspective or self-understanding skills as well as frameworks within which leaders understand both their own needs and goals and those of their employees.

Having argued for this new framework, Boyd poses a question raised by most classical theories of leadership. Can these skills be *taught?* He contrasts Peter Drucker, who has argued that the essential qualities of effective leadership cannot be created or promoted, taught or learned, with Gordon Lippett, who argued that the needs, attributes, and competencies of leaders are complex but identifiable and that leaders are made, not born. As Boyd concludes, he recommends that we embrace Lippett's hypothesis if we are to develop leadership skills in U.S. corporations as well as create conditions within those organizations in which leadership can emerge. Many of the computer firms of California's Silicon Valley seem to be cognizant of the need for leaders to develop and nurture certain sets of skills in themselves and in their work forces.[32]

Although the transformational leadership concept dates back at least to Max Weber's discussions of charismatic leaders in the first decades of the century,[33] the concept has, until recently, received relatively little research attention. However, one of the more notable contributions to systematic analysis of the subject is Robert J. House's theory of charismatic leadership.[34]

In Chapter 10, we discussed the referent power that some managers possess. House's theory suggests that charismatic leaders have very high levels of referent power and that some of that power comes from the leaders' need to influence others, "extremely high levels of self-confidence, dominance, and a strong conviction in the moral righteousness of his/her beliefs"—or at least the ability to convince followers that he or she possesses such confidence and conviction.[35]

House suggests that charismatic leaders communicate a vision or higher-level ("transcendent") goal that captures the commitment and energies of followers. They are careful to create an image of success and competence and to set examples, by virtue their own behavior, of the values they espouse. They also communicate high expectations for the performance of their followers and confidence that their followers will perform up to those expectations.

---

[32]Richard E. Boyd, "Corporate Leadership Skills: A New Synthesis," *Organizational Dynamics* 16, no. 1 (1987):34–43.

[33]Weber, *Economy and Society,* pp. 241–254.

[34]House, "A 1976 Theory of Charismatic Leadership," pp. 189–207.

[35]Ibid., p. 193.

COORDINATED RESOURCE

See Lecture Extra for Chapter 15 for a more comprehensive discussion of magic leaders and what they represent.

House's theory has not yet been extensively researched, but we can expect increasing attention to be directed toward it in the near future. One aspect likely to receive careful attention is the *type* of vision transformational leaders and their followers pursue. As stirring as the names Winston Churchill, Mahatma Gandhi, and Martin Luther King are, House and others are well aware that the ability to inspire great commitment, sacrifice, and energy is no guarantee that the cause or vision is a worthwhile one. Adolf Hitler and the Reverend Jim Jones of Jonestown were also known for their charisma—and for the tragedies their leadership brought. Transformational leaders may possess great potential for revitalizing declining institutions and helping individuals find meaning and excitement in their work and lives, but they also can pose great dangers if their goals and values run counter to the basic tenets of civilized society.

Is Leadership Really Necessary?

Two recent theories, however, question the very concept of leadership as we know it. One argues that major high-technology "change agents" have changed the methods of production and operations so dramatically that previously successful methods of management are now inadequate.[36] Another theory suggests that we assign to our leaders mysterious and romantic qualities so that we can better understand our roles and perform functions in the complex systems governing our lives.[37]

self-managed work groups Work teams organized around a particular task and composed of members who possess both the skills necessary to accomplish the task and the power to determine such factors as method of operation, assignment of responsibilities, and creation of work schedules.

Self-managed Groups and Self-leadership. The deployment of a **self-managed work groups** usually includes "a relatively whole task; members who each possess a variety of skills relevant to the group task; workers with the power to determine such factors as methods of work, task schedule, and assignment of members to different tasks; and compensation and feedback about performance for the group as a whole."[38] The presence of such groups in industry means that the stress on individual strategies for completing tasks is replaced by a focus on group methods for job accomplishment.[39]

This participative approach is present in both manufacturing and nonmanufacturing organizations within the United States. For example, in Worthington Industries and Chaparral Steel, it is routine for security guards to enter orders and run ambulances, for supervisors to hire and train their own staffs, and for supervisors to determine operating procedures for new equipment. Similarly, at the GM Delco-Remy plant in Fitzgerald, Georgia, workers generally handle all quality control, track their own time, and rotate as work team leaders. At Chaparral, steel is of superb quality, and at GM Delco-Remy, the plant has exceptional records for low absenteeism, high quality, and high productivity.[40] (A simplified schematic of the Delco-Remy plant organization is presented in Figure 15-8.)

HERE'S AN EXAMPLE

Leaders come and leaders go. Donald Kingsborough, founder, chairman, and CEO of Worlds of Wonder, resigned at the request of the company's creditors. Kingsborough, described as the company's charismatic cheerleader, founded the company in 1985 and saw it instantly become a success because of its two hot-selling toys, Teddy Ruxpin and Lazer Tag. However, industry analysts and retailers soured on his overly optimistic views about Worlds of Wonder, which led to its financial problems and eventually the request for his resignation. (*Wall Street Journal*, 4/4/88, p. 23)

Manz and Sims believe that although organizations provide individual employees with certain attitudes and values, people also have their own systems of values and beliefs. They also feel that such organizational control systems as policies and operating procedures are "psychological scripts" which, intentionally or not, direct the

[36]Charles C. Manz and Henry P. Sims, Jr., "Leading Workers to Lead Themselves: The External Leadership of Self-Managing Work Teams," *Administrative Science Quarterly* 32 (1987):106–107.

[37]James R. Meindle, Sanford B. Ehrlich, and Janet M. Dukerich, "The Romance of Leadership," *Administrative Science Quarterly* 30 (1985):78–102.

[38]Thomas Cummings, "Self-Regulated Work Groups: A Socio-Technical Synthesis," *Academy of Management Review* 3 (1978):625.

[39]Charles C. Manz, "Self-Leadership: Toward an Expanded Theory of Self-Influence Processes in Organizations," *Academy of Management Review* 11 (1986):589–590.

[40]Manz, "Self-Leadership," p. 593.

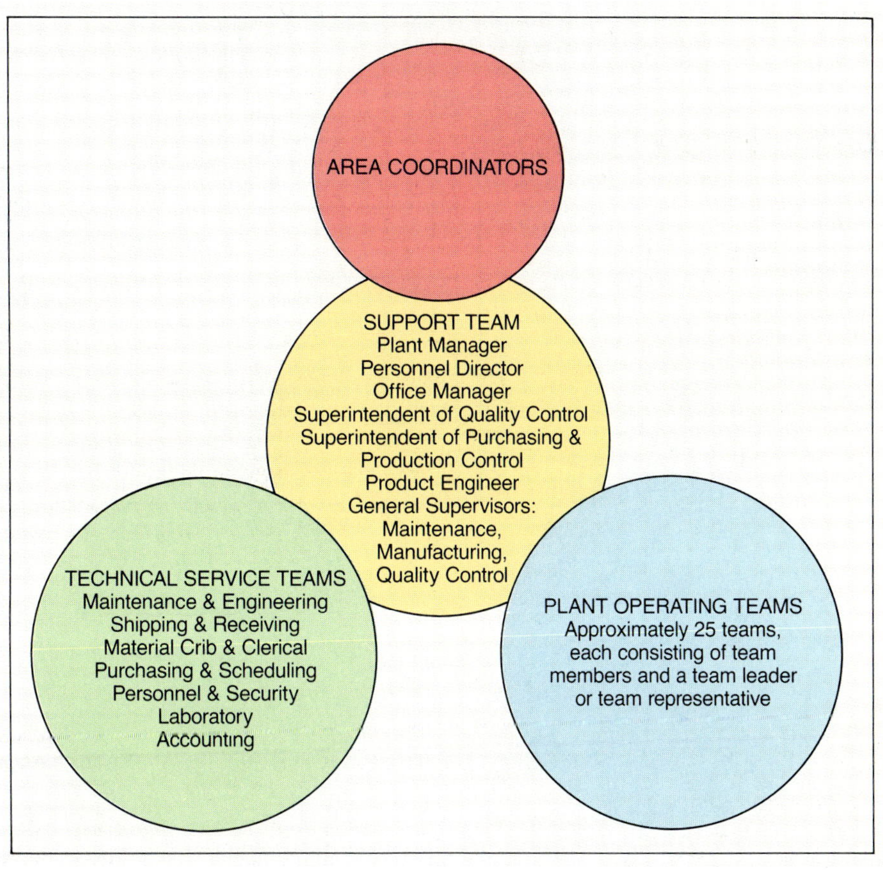

Source: From *Thriving on Chaos: Handbook for Management Revolution,* by Tom Peters. Copyright © 1987 by Excel, a California Limited Partnership. Reprinted by permission of Alfred A. Knopf, Inc.

FIGURE 15-8 ORGANIZATION CHART FOR PARTICIPATIVE OR SELF-MANAGED ORGANIZATION

behavior of individual employees. But Manz and Sims point out that, unfortunately, organizational control systems influence behaviors only *indirectly* because they can influence only the self-control systems of values and beliefs that individuals bring with them to an organization.[41] Figure 15-9 is a schematic of this process at work.

Manz and Sims suggest that the new leadership roles that emerge with these self-managed groups are more effective than are the more formal and traditional roles.[42] They call this new leadership style **self-leadership,** which they define as the ability of workers to motivate themselves to perform both tasks that are naturally appealing to them and those that are necessary but not naturally attractive. An important element of self-leadership is the choice of appealing work settings and the building of natural rewards into tasks. For example, a manager could choose to give instructions verbally rather than through written communication because he or she finds face-to-face communication more naturally rewarding.[43]

self-leadership The ability of workers to motivate themselves to perform both tasks that are naturally rewarding and those that are necessary but not appealing.

Moreover, the manager will in this instance have acknowledged the individual employee's participation in the communication process. Manz and Sims advocate a process that permits the individual's system of values and attitudes a more active role

[41]Ibid., p. 586.

[42]Manz and Sims, "Leading Workers to Lead Themselves," p. 120.

[43]Manz, "Self-Leadership," p. 593.

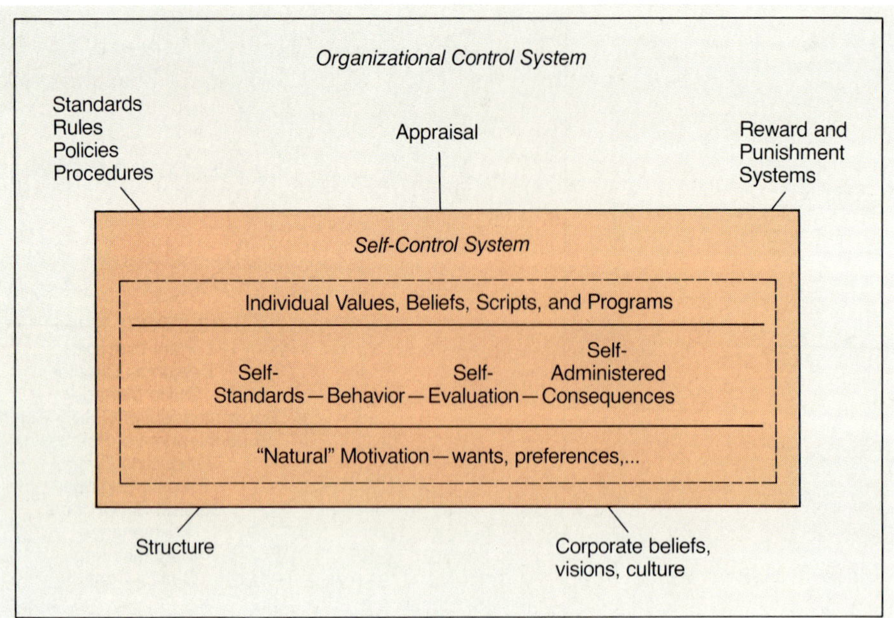

Source: Reprinted by permission of *Academy of Management Review*. A figure from "Self-leadership: Toward an Expanded Theory of Self-Influence Processes in Organizations" by Charles C. Manz (Vol. 11, No. 3, 1986). Copyright © 1986; all rights reserved.

FIGURE 15-9 THE PROCESS OF ORGANIZATIONAL AND SELF-CONTROL SYSTEMS

in implementing overall management goals—what they call "superordinate standards." In addition, they believe that when employees are allowed to invoke strategies on the basis of self-leadership and to behave on the basis of self-management, they are more likely to develop, more quickly and more consistently, behavior that does not deviate significantly from the organization's behavioral standards.[44] Conceptually, the process of this control system is schematized in Figure 15-10.

Manz and Sims studied leaders who held roles in an environment that was self-managed or self-led. They found that such leaders encouraged others to practice self-reinforcement, self-observation and evaluation; to value and act on self-expectations; to set goals for themselves; to rehearse critical procedures; and to engage in self-criticism when necessary.[45]

However, as we saw in Chapter 9 when we discussed *span of control,* the decision of such organizations as GM's Delco-Remy plant in Georgia to develop a participative approach dependent on self-managed groups would also have had significant ramification for its *quality circles*—those groups meeting periodically to consider such matters as output and quality. There are pitfalls in participative as well as traditional programs, and Exhibit 15-3 assesses those experienced by one organization.

The Romance of Leadership. Some researchers have suggested that leadership actually plays a very different role than those discussed in this chapter. They believe that we have developed romanticized views of what leaders do, what they can accomplish, and the ways in which they can affect our lives—views that have evolved because we find it hard to understand the workings of the large, complex systems within our

[44]Ibid., pp. 590–593.

[45]Manz and Sims, "Leading Workers to Lead Themselves," p. 120.

EXHIBIT 15-3 PITFALLS OF THE PARTICIPATIVE OR SELF-MANAGEMENT APPROACH

- Misunderstanding of the concept and process by upper and middle management, creating false expectations
- Resistance to the concept and process by middle managers and supervisors, often verging on outright sabotage
- Empire building by the quality circle office, substituting the illusion of immediate success for the long-term goal of institutionalizing the quality circle process
- Poor and "one-shot" training for circle members, supervisor-leaders, and managers
- Failure to prepare the organization to provide incentives for participation in quality circles
- Failure to prepare the organization to provide the information and support necessary for members to solve problems
- Failure of the organization to implement circle proposals
- Failure of the organization to measure the impact of quality circle participation—on defect rates, productivity rates, attrition rates, accident rates, scrap rates, grievance rates, lost-time rates, and so on
- Failure to develop and codify a set of process rules prior to forming the first circles
- Moving too fast—forming more circles than the quality circle office or the organization can deal with adequately

Source: From *Thriving on Chaos: Handbook for a Management Revolution,* by Tom Peters. Copyright © 1987 by Excel, a California Limited Partnership. Reprinted by permission of Alfred A. Knopf, Inc.

FIGURE 15-10 THE SELF-LEADERSHIP/SELF-MANAGEMENT CONTROL PROCESS

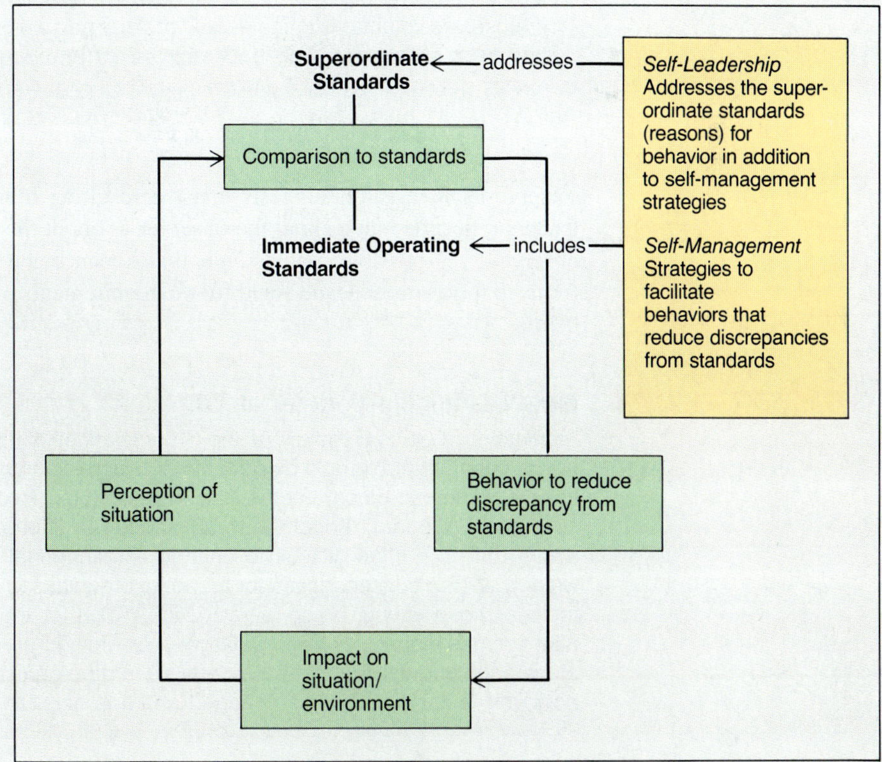

Source: Reprinted by permission of *Academy of Management Review.* A figure from "Self-leadership: Toward an Expanded Theory of Self-Influence Processes in Organizations" by Charles C. Manz (Vol. 11, No. 3, 1986). Copyright © 1986; all rights reserved.

MANAGEMENT APPLICATION

INNOVATIVE LEADERSHIP AT W. L. GORE AND ASSOCIATES

Management and leadership are different at W. L. Gore. The standard notion that people need to be motivated and led in the direction of organizational goals has largely been supplanted by a system of self-managed groups. Although W. L. Gore goes so far as to implement self-leadership, some of the company's ideas come quite close. For starters, there are no job titles at the company. There are no "workers" or "managers," only "associates." In one instance, a secretary-bookkeeper named Sarah Clifton was worried about having no business cards. She went to Bill Gore with the problem, and when he asked her what title she wanted, she replied, "Supreme Commander." Her business cards now read "Sarah Clifton, Supreme Commander." By making people feel part of the team, Gore and other companies have realized that a lot less traditional motivation and leadership is necessary than conventional wisdom would have managers believe.

Gore does not set people adrift to do their own thing—far from it. Everyone at the company has a sponsor who is responsible for seeing that its four guiding principles are followed: *fairness,* which controls destructive dissension; *freedom,* which allows associates to experience failure; *commitment,* which fuels the desire to succeed; and *discretion,* which reduces the chances for behavior that could damage the company's reputation and profitability.

Sponsors guide new members, help in their progress, take an interest in compensation, and are advocates for their associates' well-being. Of course, everything is done in teams at W. L. Gore, so individual achievement is hard to measure, but then no one is given assignments. With help from their sponsors, new employees have to find their own. By focusing on how people will commit themselves voluntarily to the pursuit of personal and organizational goals, Bill Gore has been successful. Self-leadership is not for everyone, but it can work.

Source: Tom Peters and Nancy Austin, *A Passion for Excellence* (New York: Random House, 1985).

society. Such research suggests that the resulting romantic views of leadership and leaders reflect as much about the observer as about the leader and organizations being observed.[46] A possible conclusion is that romance and mystery are necessary in order for us to follow these leaders and fill the requirements of the organizations to which we belong.[47]

ILLUSTRATIVE CASE STUDY Wrap-Up

New Leadership Policies at GE

Leadership at GE is complex. As the circumstances of the company changed from an environment characterized by government regulation and high inflation in the 1970s to one of intense global competition in the 1980s, Reginald Jones, chairman until 1981 of GE's board, thought that GE needed a different brand of leadership. Fully aware that it is often difficult to change a managerial style that is bound to have wide-sweeping consequences for an entire organization, Jones and the board nevertheless chose young, brash, smart, Jack Welch for the job. Perhaps recent media attention has made Jack Welch a larger-than-life figure—made him responsible for all of the good and evil that naturally befalls a large organization such as GE. One thing, however, is certain: GE has changed and it is not standing still. ■

[46] Meindle, Ehrlich, and Dukerich, "The Romance of Leadership," pp. 79–80.
[47] Ibid., p. 100.

SUMMARY

Leadership is an important subject for managers because of the critical role played by leaders in group and organizational effectiveness. Leadership may be defined as the process of influencing and directing the task-related activities of group members.

Three approaches to the study of leadership have been identified: the trait, behavior, and contingency approaches. The trait approach has not proved useful, since no one combination of traits consistently distinguishes leaders from nonleaders or effective leaders from ineffective leaders.

The behavior approach has focused on leadership functions and styles. Studies have found the both task-related functions and group-maintenance functions have to be performed by one or more group members in order for a group to function effectively. Studies of leadership styles have distinguished between a task-oriented, authoritarian, or initiating structure on the one hand and an employee-centered, democratic, or participative style on the other. Some studies suggest that the effectiveness of a particular style depends on the circumstances in which it is used. Tannenbaum and Schmidt, for example, maintain that a manager's choice of leadership style should be influenced by various forces in the manager, in subordinates, and in the work situation.

The difficulty of isolating universally effective leadership traits or behaviors has caused researchers to try to determine the situational variable that will cause one leadership style to be more effective than another. The major situational variables they identified include the leader's personality and past experience; the expectations and behavior of superiors; the characteristics, expectations, and behavior of subordinates; task requirements; organizational culture and policies; and the expectations and behavior of peers.

The contingency approach to leadership attempts to identify which of these situational factors is most important and to predict which leadership style will be more effective in a given situation. The Hersey-Blanchard situational theory of leadership suggests that leadership style should vary with the maturity of subordinates. The manager-subordinate relationship moves through four phases as subordinates develop achievement motivation and experience; a different leadership style is appropriate for each phase. According to the Fiedler model, leader-member relations, task structure, and the leader's position power are the most important situational variables; this model predicts which types of leaders (high LPC or low LPC) will be most effective in the eight possible combinations of these variables.

The path-goal approach formulated by Evans and House focuses on managers' abilities to dispense rewards. The leadership style a manager uses will affect the types of rewards offered and subordinates' perceptions of what they must do to earn those rewards. The personal characteristics of subordinates, as well as the environmental pressures and demands to which they are subjected, will affect which leadership style subordinates actually or potentially find rewarding.

The approach characterized by Fiedler suggests that leadership styles are relatively inflexible and that, therefore, leaders should be matched to an appropriate situation or the situation changed to match the leader. Others, however, believe that managers have a great deal of potential flexibility in their leadership styles and can therefore learn to be effective in a variety of situations.

Vroom and Yetton developed a model of situational leadership that identified five styles, ranging from authoritarian to fully participative. They also encouraged managers to seek the "feasible set of alternatives" in choosing a style to accomodate a given problem or situation. Vroom and Jago extended the Vroom-Yetton model by putting greater emphasis on the quality of the managerial decision and the nature of the manager's commitment to it. They also cautioned against otherwise good decisions that were too costly or cumbersome to implement and urged that decisions be made so as to develop the abilities of others involved in the decision.

Recent research on leadership examines the qualities of the exceptional leaders in organizations and explores the concept and operations of self-managed groups.

REVIEW QUESTIONS

1. How is leadership defined in this chapter? Discuss three implications of this definition.
2. Why was the trait approach a logical attempt to understand leadership? What two approaches did the trait researchers take? What did the leadership trait studies reveal?

3. Describe the two basic leadership functions needed for effective group performance. Must the leader perform both these functions?
4. Outline the basic idea of the Tannenbaum and Schmidt model. What factors should influence a manager's style, according to Tannenbaum and Schmidt? What are some of the practical considerations that they suggest managers must take into account in selecting a style?
5. What are the two basic leadership styles identified by the Ohio State and University of Michigan studies? Which style was thought to be more effective?
6. What is the "situational leadership theory"? How should the manager's style vary in each of the four phases?
7. Outline the basic theory of the Managerial grid. Which leadership style in the grid do Blake and Mouton feel is most effective?
8. What basic assumptions underlie the Fiedler model? What is the LPC scale? What are the basic elements in the work situation that determine which leadership style will be most effective? In what situations is a high-LPC leader effective? In what situations is a low-LPC leader effective?
9. Describe the path-goal model. On what theory of motivation is the model based? According to this model, how do managers with different leadership styles differ in their ability to influence or reward subordinates? What variables, according to this theory, help determine the most effective leadership style? Why?
10. What are the five styles of managerial decision making suggested by Vroom and Yetton? What are the most important modifications made by Vroom and Jago in the Vroom-Yetton model of leadership?

CASE STUDY Three Managerial Decisions

1. You are a manufacturing manager in a large electronics plant. At considerable expense, the company's management has recently installed new robotic assembly equipment, trimmed the work force, and put in a new simplified work system. To the surprise of everyone, however, yourself included, the expected increase in production has not materialized. In fact, production has begun to drop, overall quality has fallen off, and the number of voluntary employee separations has risen.

You do not believe there is anything wrong with the robots. Reports from other companies using them confirm this opinion, and representatives from the firm that built them have inspected them and report that they are working at peak efficiency. The robot-made assemblies are of uniform high quality.

You suspect that the new work system may be responsible for the change. But this view is not shared by your immediate subordinates, who are four first-line supervisors, each in charge of a section, and your supply manager. They variously attribute the drop in production to poor retraining of the operators, lack of adequate financial incentives, or poor morale due to fear of increasing automation. Clearly, this is an issue about which there is considerable depth of feeling among individuals and potential disagreement among your subordinates.

This morning, you received a phone call from your division manager. She had just received your production figures for the last six months and was calling to express her concern. She indicated that the problem was yours to solve as you thought best, but that she would like to know within a week what steps you plan to take.

You share your division manager's concern over the falling productivity and know that your workers do too. The problem is to decide what steps to take to rectify the situation.

2. You are a general supervisor in charge of a construction team laying a coal slurry pipeline and have to estimate your rate of progress in order to schedule materials deliveries to the next field site.

You know the nature of the terrain you will be crossing and have the historical data needed to compute the mean and variance in the rate of speed over that type of terrain. Given these two variables, it is a simple matter to calculate the earliest and latest times at which materials and support facilities will be needed at the next site. It is important that your estimate be reasonably accurate. Underestimates result in idle supervisors and workers, and overestimates result in tying up materials for a period of time before they are to be used.

Progress has been good, and your five supervisors and other members of the team stand to receive substantial bonuses if the project is completed ahead of schedule.

3. You are supervising the work of 12 chemical engineers. Their formal training and work experience are very similar, permitting you to use them interchangeably on projects. Yesterday, your manager informed you that a request had been received from a Middle Eastern affiliate for four engineers to go abroad on extended loan for a period of six to eight months. For a number of reasons, he argued and you agreed that this request should be met from your group.

All your engineers are capable of handling this assignment and, from the standpoint of present and future projects, there is no particular reason why anyone should be retained over any other. The problem is somewhat complicated by the fact that the overseas assignment is in what is generally regarded as an undesirable location.

Source: Reprinted by permission of the publisher, from "A New Look at Managerial Decision Making," by Victor H. Vroom, *Organizational Dynamics.* Summer 1973, pp. 72–73.

Case Questions

Three managerial decision-making situations have been described. Using the five decision-making styles outlined in the box on page 160, answer the following questions for each of the decision-making situations.

1. After reading the three situations, and before analyzing them, decide which of the decision-making style alternatives (AI, AII, CI, CII, GII) you would *personally* prefer to use in making each decision. Then answer the remaining questions.
2. Which is more important in the situation, quality or acceptance of the decision?
3. How critical is time in making a decision?
4. Does the manager have the information necessary to make the decision?
5. Is the decision-making situation highly structured?
6. Choose the best decision-making style (AI, AII, CI, CII, GII) and give the reason for your choice.
7. Did your choice of the "best" style in question 6 differ from the style you would personally have chosen in question 1? If so, why do you think they differed? ■

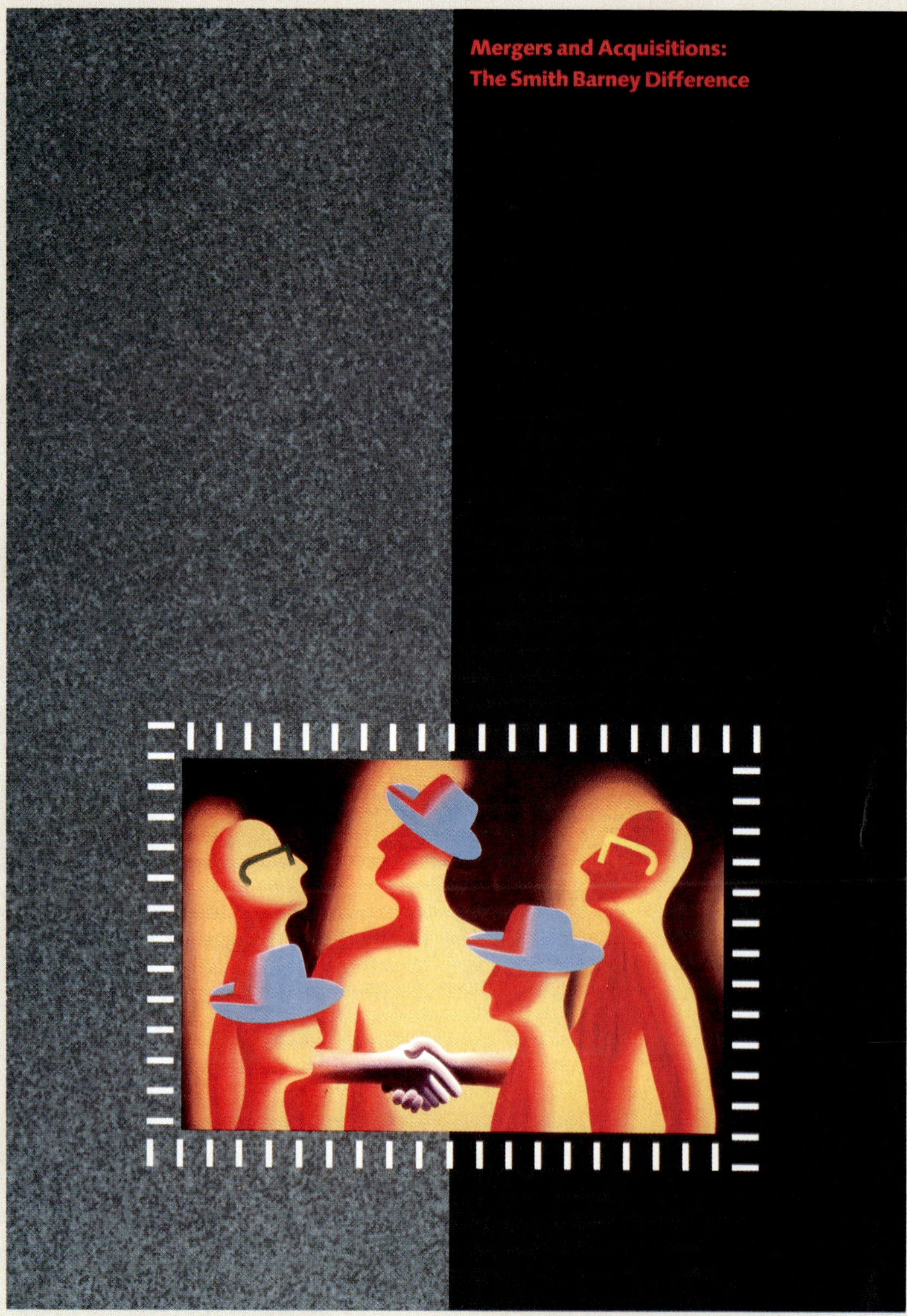

Cover of Smith Barney's Mergers & Acquisitions Brochure. Design: Carbone Smolan Associates. Artist: Mark Kostabi.

16

GROUPS AND COMMITTEES

Upon completing this chapter you should be able to:

1. Describe the characteristics of formal and informal groups.
2. State why groups are an important part of organizations.
3. Explain how group leaders, group norms, and group cohesiveness develop.
4. Identify the factors that can affect group performance.
5. Identify the assets and liabilities of group problem solving and describe how group performance can be improved.
6. State the roles of task forces and committees in organizations.
7. Explain why conflict within groups, although potentially disruptive, is also inevitable and sometimes fruitful.

Chapter Outline

Introduction
Types of Groups
Characteristics of Groups in Organizations
Problem Solving in Groups
Task Forces and Committees
Making Formal Groups Effective

ILLUSTRATIVE CASE STUDY Introduction

The Team Taurus Approach to Management at Ford

Suffering from an industry-wide decline and an increase in foreign competition, Ford Motor Company turned to a new way of managing in the early 1980s. The "Taurus" project focused on the main requirements for effective teamwork and well illustrates the need for changes in the way managers conduct business in an increasingly complex environment.

Prior to the Taurus program, American auto companies built cars sequentially—a process which the people at Ford referred to as "tossing it over the wall." Design would work on a project, "toss it over the wall" to engineering, who in turn would "toss" it to production, and so on. Needless to say no one maintained an overview of the whole project, and any sense of teamwork and interfunctional cooperation was out of the question. Naturally, coordination was difficult, and by the time a problem was discovered, it was usually too late to take efficient corrective measures—witness the enormous number of product recalls (in 1980, Ford actually recalled more cars than it built).

With the Taurus effort, Ford changed to a system known as *parallel processing.* A task force was formed under the direction of Mr. Lew Veraldi. All disciplines, from design through assembly to marketing, came on-stream in unison, interacting and contributing simultaneously from the very beginning of the project. Instead of a linear flow from one department to the next, all functional areas moved forward together, with a large number of feedback loops allowing immediate attention to problems as they arose. The risk of this approach was overlap, confusion, and duplication, but the benefits were equally clear—the total project moves faster and with fewer mistakes.

The project managers also encouraged employees to make suggestions for improvements. In the assembly plant in Atlanta, they put drawings on the wall and asked employees what changes they would like to see in the cars made in their plant. Managers wanted to know what would make the job easier and product quality higher.

During the process of collecting ideas, the Taurus team conducted a system of regular reviews and logged ideas on a computer. In every case, managers got back to the individuals who had made the suggestion—especially when the idea was not used. Thus the people who had to carry out management decisions were involved during the conceptualization stage, which had also broadened the sources of ideas—whether managers or production employees—were, as often as not, the implementors of ideas. Team spirit was high and there was a great sense of pride in the resulting product.

In addition to providing the internal structure and systems that allowed more effective group work, project managers also set tangible goals against which people could measure their performances. They picked the best cars—called "best of class"—and identified over 400 features that went on a Taurus "wish list." People were then challenged to be better than the best.

In 1986, *Motor Trend* picked the Ford Taurus as its Car of the Year, and later models have led to a healthy return to profitability for Ford. In the first half of 1988, Ford earned over $2 billion—more than its larger rival GM. The ideas behind Team Taurus, primarily ideas that involve more effective group and team work, are now sweeping the industry.

Sources: Robert Waterman, *The Renewal Factor* (New York: Bantam Books, 1987); Jim Harbour, "Ford, Where Quality Is Job 1," *Automotive Industries,* September 1986, p. 17; Lynn Adkins, "Such a Grand Design," *Business Month,* December 1987, pp. 30–31; "What's Creating an 'Industrial Miracle' at Ford," *Business Week,* July 30, 1984, pp. 80–81.

Was the secret of Ford's success simply a better understanding of groups and group processes? Working through groups is often a frustrating experience, and the idea that groups actually can be managed to outperform individuals may be difficult to accept. For example, the authors have frequently been asked by students how they could chart a management career that would avoid the inefficiency and frustration they see as inherent in group work. But such an attempt to escape group work is an unpromising approach for anyone who desires a challenging and mobile managerial career. Groups are an inevitable and useful feature of organizational life, and a considerable part of a manager's job is devoted to group and committee work. As managers, our task will be to manage organizational groups in such a way as to make them more productive and satisfying to their members.[1]

FOR DISCUSSION

Why do managers need to understand both formal and informal group behavior?

In this chapter we will describe the various types of groups that exist in organizations. We will also describe how group problem solving can be managed and improved.

TYPES OF GROUPS

TEACHING TIP

Be sure to emphasize the definition of groups, particularly the fact that group members *interact with* and *influence* each other in working toward a *common purpose*.

A *group* is defined as two or more people who interact with and influence each other toward a common purpose.[2] Three types of groups commonly exist in organizations: (1) *command groups,* composed of managers and their subordinates; (2) *committees and task forces,* formed to carry out specific organizational activities; and (3) *informal groups,* which emerge in the organization whether or not managers desire or encourage them. The first two types are *formal groups*. Managers determine their membership and direct them in order to achieve specific objectives.

Command groups will be described briefly in this chapter but are primarily dealt with elsewhere in this book, particularly in the extended discussion of leadership. In this chapter we will take a close look at committees and task forces and how they function.

reference group A group with whom individuals identify and compare themselves.

FOR DISCUSSION

Ask students to name some of their reference groups.

Managers should be aware that there are other types of groups as well. For example, **reference groups** are made up of those persons with whom specific individuals identify and compare themselves. A manager's reference group might be the other managers at his or her level within the organization or even within the industry. If the manager strongly desires promotion, his or her reference group is likely to be higher-level managers. In private life, the manager's other reference groups might include members of his or her club or community.

Such groups can affect an individual's attitudes and behavior, since people tend to model themselves after the members of their reference group. Reference groups, therefore, can be an important influence in organizational life, since the members

[1]See Dorwin Cartwright and Ronald Lippitt, "Group Dynamics and the Individual," *International Journal of Group Psychotherapy* 7, no. 1 (1957):86–102; Linda N. Jewell and H. Joseph Reitz, *Group Effectiveness in Organizations* (Glenview, Ill.: Scott, Foresman, 1983); and Deborah L. Gladstein, "Groups in Context: A Model of Task Group Effectiveness," *Administrative Science Quarterly* 29 (1984):499–517.

[2]See Marvin E. Shaw, *Group Dynamics,* 3rd ed. (New York: McGraw-Hill, 1981).

frequently adopt the performance standards and expectations of their reference groups.[3]

FOR DISCUSSION

What are the advantages and disadvantages of using groups versus individuals for getting work done?

Formal Groups

Formal groups are created deliberately by managers and charged with carrying out specific tasks to help the organization achieve its goals.[4] (Informal groups, as we shall see, may sometimes have objectives that run counter to organizational goals.)

command group A group composed of a manager and his or her subordinates who interact with each other toward a common objective.

The most prevalent type of formal group in organizations is the **command group,** which includes a manager and his or her subordinates. The formal structure of organizations consists of a series of overlapping command groups. Managers belong to command groups composed of themselves and their subordinates, and they simultaneously belong to command groups composed of their fellow managers and their own higher-level manager. In Rensis Likert's terminology, managers are the "linking pins" between the various formal work groups in their organizations. (See Figure 16-1.)

permanent formal group A long-term command group or permanent committee, such as a planning committee.

temporary formal group A group formed for a specific purpose, such as a task force or project group, that is disbanded when its purpose is accomplished.

Permanent formal groups include command groups and permanent committees. (A *planning committee* is a common example of a permanent formal group.) **Temporary formal groups** include task forces and project groups that are created to deal with a particular problem and are disbanded once the problem is solved. We will discuss task forces and committees in detail later in this chapter.

FOR DISCUSSION

Is the class you're in now a formal or informal group? Why?

Informal Groups

Informal groups emerge whenever people come together and interact regularly.[5] Such groups develop within the formal organizational structure. Members of informal groups tend to subordinate some of their individual needs to those of the group as a whole. In return, the group supports and protects them.[6] Informal groups may further the interests of the organization—Saturday morning softball games, for example, may strengthen the players' ties to the organization. They may also oppose organizational objectives, such as high performance standards, when these are considered harmful to the group. Informal groups serve essentially four major functions.[7] First, they maintain and strengthen the norms and values their members hold in common. Second, they give these members feelings of social satisfaction, status and security. In large corporations, for example, where many people feel that their employers hardly know them, informal groups enable these people to share jokes and complaints, eat together, and perhaps socialize after work. Informal groups thus satisfy the human need for friendship and support. They give their members a feeling of security based on the sharing of a common situation.

---

[3]See Dorwin Cartwright and Alvin Zander, eds., *Group Dynamics: Research and Theory,* 3rd ed. (New York: Harper & Row, 1968), p. 53; and Harold H. Kelley, "Two Functions of Reference Groups," in Guy E. Swanson, Theodore Newcomb, and Eugene J. Hartley, eds., *Readings in Social Psychology,* rev. ed. (New York: Holt, 1952), pp. 410–414.

[4]See Edgar H. Schein, *Organizational Psychology,* 3rd ed. (Englewood Cliffs, N.J.: Prentice Hall, 1980), pp. 146–153.

[5]George Homans, *The Human Group* (New York: Harcourt, 1950).

[6]John P. Wanous, Arnon E. Reichers, and S. D. Malik, "Organizational Socialization and Group Development: Toward an Integrative Perspective," *Academy of Management Review,* 9, no. 4 (1984):678–683.

[7]Keith Davis, *Human Relations at Work,* 2nd ed. (New York: McGraw-Hill, 1962), pp. 235–257, and *Human Behavior at Work: Organizational Behavior,* 6th ed. (New York: McGraw-Hill, 1981), pp. 331–332; and Schein, *Organizational Psychology,* pp. 150–152.

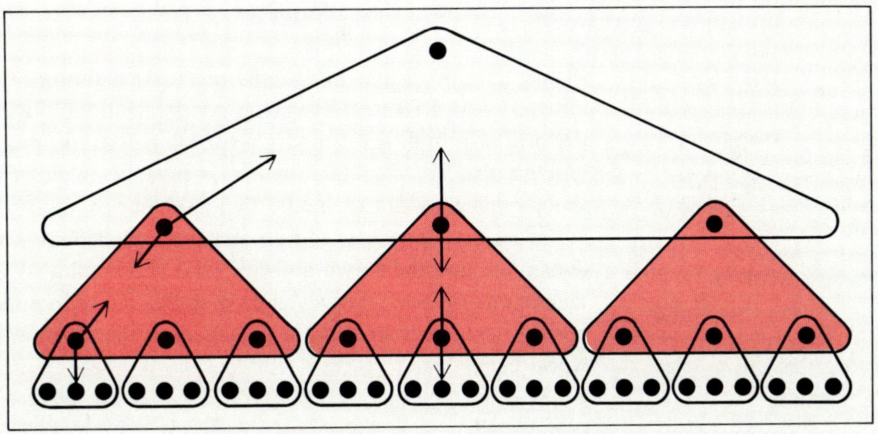

Note: The arrows indicate the linking pin function.

Source: Rensis Likert, *New Patterns of Management* (New York: McGraw-Hill, 1961), p. 113. Copyright © 1961 by McGraw-Hill, Inc. Used with permission of McGraw-Hill Book Co.

FIGURE 16-1 THE LINKING PIN

Third, informal groups help their members to communicate. Members of informal groups learn about matters that affect them by developing their own informal channels of communication that supplement more formal channels. In fact, managers often use informal networks to convey information "unofficially."

Fourth, informal groups help solve problems. They might aid a sick or tired employee or devise activities to deal with boredom. Quite often, such group problem solving helps the organization—for example, when co-workers tell nonproductive employees to "shape up." But these groups can also reduce an organization's effectiveness. A common example is the pressure placed on new employees to reduce their efforts in order that the group's normal standards not be called into question.

Informal groups may actually act as reference groups, encouraging conformity among their members. This practice may be good up to a point, because shared norms and values can improve relationships and even encourage members' creative energies. Too much conformity, however, can deter members from acting creatively or assertively (or productively).

Thus, although the social support provided by informal groups can enhance the work environment, it can also conflict with management's needs. Many people, for instance, believe that a coffee break increases productivity. However, if the informal group socializes an extension of the break for an extra 15 or 20 minutes each morning, the group's increased social satisfaction will usually be at the company's expense. In addition, each organization must learn to deal with the "grapevine"—the informal group's communication system for circulating both truth and false information about organizational activity. In particular, when employees are not informed about matters that directly affect them, they may generate information that weakens morale or leads people to make poor decisions. Finally, although the informal group's ability to uphold shared values can make the workplace more stable, it can also become a barrier to change. For example, some corporations, notably GM, have begun introducing new team-oriented approaches to improve productivity on the assembly line; conceivably, if any informal group is led to fear job losses as a result of more efficient productivity, that group could be in a position to create barriers that thwart management plans—for example, by cooperating less than fully with new directives.

CHARACTERISTICS OF GROUPS IN ORGANIZATIONS

CLASS COMMENT

Groups are important dynamic factors in all organizations. People in the organization will be members of and interact with formal and informal groups.

CLASS COMMENT

Managers must learn to effectively work in and with groups. Why?

Managers who deal with groups must (1) determine when and how groups can be utilized most effectively to achieve organizational goals, (2) manage groups so they perform at a high level, and (3) overcome the disadvantages that may be associated with groups. To do all this, managers must be aware of some special characteristics of groups that may aid or hinder them. Managers must also be cognizant of their own attitudes, both personal and professional, their own levels of understanding of group dynamics, and their own abilities (and shortcomings) in working with groups rather than in one-on-one relationships. With this factor in mind, for example, GE has developed a new program to train managers in the creation and leadership of competitive work teams.[8]

Informal Leadership

The formal leader of a group is, of course, appointed or elected to head the group. Informal leaders, on the other hand, tend to emerge gradually as group members interact. The man or woman who speaks up more than the others, who offers more and better suggestions than anyone else, or who gives direction to the group's activities usually becomes the informal leader. Even in formal groups, such self-confident, assertive individuals often develop into rivals of the formally chosen leaders, thereby weakening the leader's hold on the group members.[9]

task role The specific role within a group performed by the leader, whether formal or informal.

group building and maintenance role The group leader's specific function to fulfill the group's social needs by encouraging solidarity feelings.

As we discussed in Chapter 15, both formal and informal leaders play two basic roles. In the **task role,** the leader directs the group toward completion of the activities it is seeking to accomplish. As a sales manager, for example, our task role would include hiring and firing personnel, assigning territories, and supervising the training of new sales force members. In the **group building and maintenance role,** the leader is concerned with fulfilling the group's social needs by encouraging feelings of solidarity. For example, if as sales managers we help settle some nonwork-related dispute between salespeople, we are acting in a maintenance role. Proper exercise of this role enables the leader to keep members attached to the group over extended periods of time.

Ideally, the group leader can play both roles, enabling the group to perform with a high degree of effectiveness. In practice, however, a single leader will often be unable to perform both roles equally well; in such cases, a second person can close the gap by taking over the neglected function (usually the maintenance role).

BACKGROUND ON GROUP DYNAMICS

One of the best descriptions ever of group dynamics is "Banana Time" by Donald F. Ray in *Human Organization,* Winter 1959–60, pp. 158–168. Either summarize the account for students or have them read it. See Chapter 16 Lecture Extra for more on "Banana Time."

Group Norms and Conformity

Over time, group members form expectations about how they and the other members of the group will behave and exert pressure on one another to ensure that these expectations are met. For example, an executive who comes to work in running shoes when all the other executives are wearing dress shoes will, at the very least, be questioned about the unusual attire; perhaps he or she will even be ridiculed gently for this violation of group norms. The anticipation of rejection or acceptance by the group is usually enough to ensure that members conform to their group's expectations in advance—so it is unlikely that the executive will come to work in running shoes even once.[10]

---

[8] A. Nicholas Komanecky, "Developing New Managers at GE," *Training and Development Journal* 42, no. 6 (1988):62–64.

[9] David O. Sears, Jonathan L. Freedman, and Letitia A. Peplau, *Social Psychology,* 5th ed. (Englewood Cliffs, N.J.: Prentice Hall, 1985), pp. 367–368.

[10] Davis C. Feldman, "The Development and Enforcement of Group Norms," *Academy of Management Review* 9, no. 2 (1984):47–53; and Kenneth Bettenhausen and J. Keith Murninghan, "The Emergence of Norms in Competitive Decision-Making Groups," *Administrative Science Quarterly* 30 (1985):350–372.

When an individual does not conform to group norms, the other members of the group will initially try to persuade the deviant to conform.[11] They will try to reason with the deviant or make pointed jokes at his or her expense. If this approach fails, they are likely to escalate the pressure. If the norm being violated is considered important, they will use criticism, sarcasm, ridicule, and finally ostracism—total rejection of the individual through the "silent treatment." In some kinds of groups, where the deviant behavior touches on a truly sensitive area—as with the rate-buster who exceeds the group's output norms—the deviant may even be physically harassed. Sometimes justly, sometimes unjustly, unions, which constitute highly formal work groups, have been accused of putting pressure on individuals who deviate from work rules that the group considers to be in its own best interest. As GM, Ford, and other companies go forth with new concepts of team competition for increased productivity in traditional assembly-line settings, it will become necessary to assess the extent to which group norms, both formal and informal, will change to accommodate qualitatively different expectations of cooperation.

Enforced conformity clearly has its negative side: It may stifle initiative and innovation and reduce performance. Executives, or course, have more important matters to occupy their minds than footwear, but the conformity pressures of small, informal groups can be very powerful for important as well as trivial decisions and actions. A classic series of experiments by Solomon Asch demonstrated the power of small groups in pressuring individuals to yield to a majority opinion that could be clearly discerned as false. Asch set up his most famous experiments as if he were simply testing visual judgment. He showed people in a group a card with lines of varying lengths and asked each of them to determine which of the lines was the same length as that on a comparison card; the lines were in fact drawn so that the correct response was obvious. (See Figure 16-2.) However, one subject was always the only group member not planted by Asch, and his confederates frequently gave the wrong answer deliberately. On about 35 percent of the trials, the unwitting subject also chose to give the

[11]See Davis C. Feldman, "The Development and Enforcement of Group Norms," *Academy of Management Review* 9, no. 2 (1984):47–53.

FIGURE 16-2 CARDS SUCH AS THOSE USED IN ASCH'S SOCIAL CONFORMITY EXPERIMENT

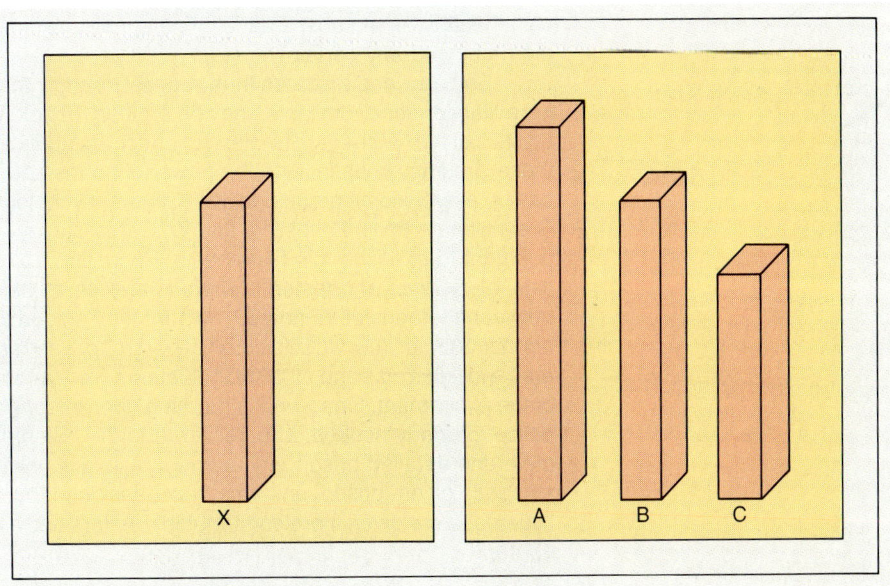

wrong answer: That is, even though the correct answer was reasonably obvious, the subject chose to *conform* to the group's judgment. See Figure 16-3: After listening to the instructions (A), the subject hears the group's unanimous decision and reexamines the cards (B); after about a dozen trials, he may still agree with the group rather than follow his own judgment (C). Asch also found that if just one of his confederates was instructed to violate the unanimous judgment of the group, the tendency of subjects to conform decreased considerably. Apparently, just one "ally" was enough to encourage independent judgment on the subject's part.[12]

You may recall from Chapter 10 that Stanley Milgram's "Yale experiments" revealed some even more unsettling possibilities about individuals' tendencies not only to *conform,* but to *obey,* under similar preplanned social circumstances. Perhaps even

---

[12]Solomon E. Asch, "Effects of Group Pressure upon the Modification and Distortions of Judgments," in H. Guetzkow, ed., *Groups, Leadership, and Men* (Pittsburgh: Carnegie Press, 1951); and Asch, "Studies of Independence and Conformity: A Minority of One Against a Unanimous Majority," *Psychological Monographs* 70, no. 9 (September 1956). Subsequent experiments have found specific factors that cause individuals to succumb to group pressure and other factors that reduce conformity. See Sarah Tanford and Steven Penrod, "Social Influence Model: A Formal Integration of Research on Majority and Minority Influence Processes," *Psychological Bulletin* 95, no. 2 (1984):189–225; and Serge Moscovici, "Social Influence and Conformity," in Gardner Lindzey and Elliot Aronson, eds., *Handbook of Social Psychology,* Vol. 2, 3rd ed. (New York: Random House, 1985), Chapter 7.

ETHICS IN MANAGEMENT

THE "AUTHORITY OF VIOLENCE"

"Torturing became a job. If the officers told you to beat, you beat. . . . You never thought you could do otherwise." Such is the recollection of a young soldier who was discharged from the army after serving a hitch as an official torturer for the Greek military regime. He had been systematically trained in the arts of obedience, desensitization, and brutality, but he had originally been selected for his job because he was judged to be psychologically and intellectually well-adjusted; by most accounts, he—and others in the elite torturer corps in which he worked—demonstrated normal, emotionally stable behavior after hours, when a day of brutalizing other human beings was done. In 1976, when psychologist Molly Harrower presented them with the psychological test results of eight Nazi war criminals and eight healthy Americans, a panel of personality assessment experts could not sort them out with any certainty.

Both fact and research thus suggest strongly that torturers, rather than being hereditary or social deviants, may be ordinary people who submit to what psychologists call the "authority of violence" under the right circumstances. At least part of these circumstances include the powerful norms and socialization processes that can be exercised by groups. In 1973, three psychologists at Stanford University—Craig Haney, Philip Zimbardo, and W. Curtis Banks—conducted an elaborate experiment to examine this hypothesis. Recruiting from newspaper ads, the scientists interviewed and tested numerous applicants before selecting 24 males—all between the ages of 17 and 30—whom they judged to be equally psychologically normal and socially well-adjusted. The group was *randomly* divided into "prisoners" and "guards," and all of the volunteers were informed as to the precise nature of the experiment. One Sunday morning, the "prisoners" were rounded up by local police, properly booked, and delivered to the "Stanford County Prison"—a complete and detailed prison environment built in a university basement. They were stripped, given prison uniforms, and assigned barren, steel-barred cells; the "guards" were given more comfortable quarters and a recreation area. (See Figure 16-4.)

FIGURE 16-3 ASCH'S SOCIAL-PRESSURE EXPERIMENT
William Vandivert

An experiment designed to last two weeks was terminated after just six days. "Prisoners," who were referred to only by ID numbers and dressed so as to be "deindividuated," had been stripped of most day-to-day civil rights, and although physical punishment had been prohibited, they soon began to show signs of dramatic emotional change, including "acute anxiety" and a passivity verging on complete servility; they became extremely distressed and even physically ill. Some of the "guards," meanwhile, seemed almost exhiliarated by the experience, reinforcing their roles with "creative cruelty and harassment"; verbal aggression—threats and insults—supplanted prohibited physical violence.

Afterward, some "guards" expressed a combination of excitement and dismay over their experience of group authority. "It was degrading," recalled one. "They abused each other because I told them to. No one questioned my authority at all." Others reflected with distress at having witnessed the darker sides of their own personalities: "When I was doing it," said one "guard," "I didn't feel regret. . . . Only afterwards . . . did it begin to dawn on me that this was a part of me I hadn't known before."

Certainly, the researchers—and the participants—learned some disturbing things about *individual* human behavior. But they also confirmed some alarming suspicions about *group* behavior. An expressly mock situation had been established between two groups. Not only did the simulated situation rapidly become socially real in the minds of both groups, totally replacing those they had known all their lives, but the members of each group readily assumed the roles expected of them as group members. Moreover, whenever any deviation from expected group norms threatened, it was quickly suppressed by escalating tactics of pressure to conform. Individual inclination and a lifetime of emotional normalcy had succumbed to the pressures of authority and conformity with alarming quickness and thoroughness.

Sources: Craig Haney, Philip Zimbardo, and W. Curtis Banks, "Interpersonal Dynamics in a Simulated Prison," *International Journal of Criminology and Penology* 1 (1973):69–97; Molly Harrower, "Were Hitler's Henchmen Mad?" *Psychology Today,* July 1976, pp. 76–80; and Janice T. Gibson and Mika Haritos-Fatouros, "The Education of a Torturer," *Psychology Today,* November 1986, pp. 50–58.

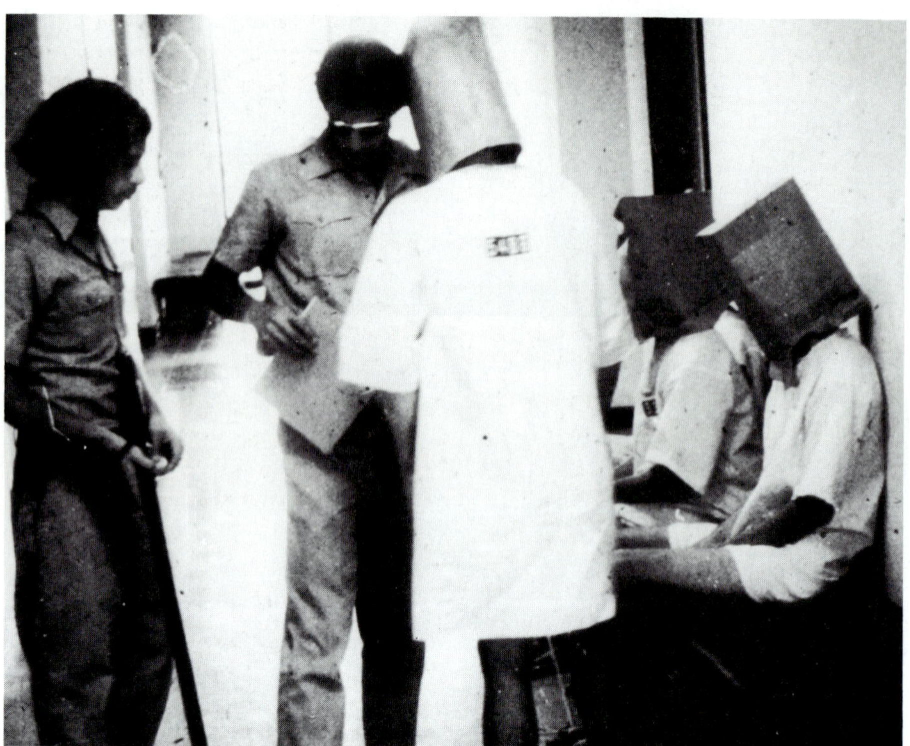

Note: See box entitled "The 'Authority of Violence.'"
P. G. Zimbardo, Inc.

FIGURE 16-4 THE STANFORD PRISON EXPERIMENT

more disturbing are the implications of the equally famous Stanford University experiments as described in the Ethics in Management box entitled "The 'Authority of Violence.'"

QUOTATION BY AN ORGANIZATION

"We believe . . . Delta must be staffed with people who are not only experienced and efficient . . . but also dedicated to the carrier's goals."—Delta Air Lines, Inc. Annual Report

So group pressures, like many other forces, have positive and negative sides. They maintain predictable patterns of work, nurture teamwork, and defend group and individual interests. But they may also suppress new ideas, restrict individual choices, and even encourage undesirable actions. For managers, the problem has never been to prevent group pressures—which are inevitable—but to channel them in constructive directions.

Group Cohesiveness

cohesiveness The degree of solidarity and positive feelings held by individuals toward their group.

The solidarity, or **cohesiveness,** of a group is an important indicator of how much influence the group has over its individual members. The more cohesive the group is—in other words, the more strongly members feel about belonging to it—the greater its influence. If the members of a group feel strongly attached to it, they are not likely to violate its norms.

Group cohesiveness thus tends to be self-perpetuating. People join groups whose members they identify with or admire. Once they join, they tend to feel and even closer sense of identification, thus increasing the group's cohesiveness. As we saw in Chapter 13, conflict with outside individuals or with other groups increases that cohesiveness still more. Highly cohesive groups often have less tension and hostility and fewer

HERE'S AN EXAMPLE

Employee involvement groups at Ford Motor Company dealerships around the country are designed to allow workers to take part in running the business. Says one dealership manager in Pompano Beach, Florida, "We have everyone working together; normally they want to stay by themselves. . . . We're like a family." (*Managing Organizational Behavior*, by Schermerhorn, Hunt, and Osborn, 1988, p. 196)

misunderstandings than do less cohesive groups.[13] Group cohesiveness can thus become a problem if it hampers communication or cooperation among different groups within a larger organization. When cooperation among groups is especially vital—for example, when an organization is involved in strategic planning—managers may have to find ways of deemphasizing the importance of disparate group membership.[14]

Management may also go out of its way to encourage group cohesiveness, sometimes by innovative or unconventional means. For example, in order to further company camaraderie and communication among people who work together, corporations such as Tandem Computers and Genetech, a biotechnology firm, hold regular beer parties to which all employees are invited. At Merle Norman Cosmetics, management sponsors Saturday night movies and serves ice cream at a 1920s-style movie emporium.[15] In Huntsville, Alabama, Goldstar of America Inc., a South Korean subsidiary of Lucky-Goldstar noted for its success in encouraging parallel production teams to compete against one another, occasionally closes down its plant early in order to accommodate volleyball games in which employees can meet one another in a spirit of camaraderie as well as good-natured competition.[16]

HERE'S AN EXAMPLE

ALMEX of Sweden produces a portable mechanical ticket machine used on public transportation. The company exports its products to more than 40 countries and has been highly profitable. It utilizes autonomous work groups who function in accordance with an agreement between management and the union. (*International Yearbook of Organizational Democracy, Vol 1: Organizational Democracy and Political Processes*, pp. 364–365)

Cohesiveness and Performance. We have already seen that the norms of a group can encourage either high or low performance by its members. Studies have found that the output of members of cohesive groups tends to be more uniform than that of members of less cohesive groups. These findings are important for managers because cohesive groups commonly set their own production standards. Groups that are hostile to management may restrict their output to levels well below management standards. This sort of restriction often occurs among factory work groups paid by piece rates because they may believe that if they reach or surpass management standards, management will establish higher standards or lower rates. Such workers may also feel that if their output stays below management levels, management will offer higher rates to increase productivity.[17]

Gregory Shea and Richard Guzzo have recently proposed that a group's effectiveness is a function of three variables: task interdependence, potency, and outcome interdependence. (See Figure 16-5.)[18] **Task interdependence** is the extent to which a group's work requires its members to interact with one another. A high level of task interdependence increases the group's **sense of potency,** "the collective belief of a group that it can be effective." **Outcome interdependence** is the degree to which the consequences of the group's work are felt by all the members.

task interdependence The extent to which a group's work requires its members to interact with each other.

sense of potency Collective belief of a group that it can be effective.

outcome interdependence The degree to which the work of a group has consequences felt by all its members.

Shea and Guzzo further explain how astute managers can create successful groups. Managers must first give each group a "character"—a clear and achievable set of objectives. A strategic-planning group, for example, might be chartered to devise a plan to a company for five years. Because groups should be given flexibility in arranging their own affairs, the manager should "concentrate on getting the charter

[13]Sears, Freedman, and Peplau, *Social Psychology*, pp. 356–357. See also Robert S. Feldman, *Social Psychology: Theories, Research, and Applications* (New York: McGraw-Hill, 1985); and Steven Penrod, *Social Psychology*, 2nd ed. (Englewood Cliffs, N.J.: Prentice Hall, 1986).

[14]John C. Whitney and Ruthu A. Smith, "Effects of Group Cohesiveness on Attitude Polarization and the Acquisition of Knowledge in a Strategic Planning Context," *Journal of Marketing Research* 20, no. 2 (1983):167–176.

[15]David L. Kirp and Douglas C. Rice, "Fast Forward—Styles of California Management," *Harvard Business Review* 66, no. 1 (1988):74–83.

[16]Henry Easton, "The Corporate Immigrants, *Nation's Business*, April 1987, pp. 12–19.

[17]Lester Coch and John R. P. French, Jr., "Overcoming Resistance to Change" *Human Relations* 1, no. 4 (1948):512–532. See also Andrew Szilagyi and Marc Wallace, *Organizational Behavior and Performance*, 3rd ed. (Glenview, Ill.: Scott, Foresman, 1983).

[18]Gregory P. Shea and Richard A. Guzzo, "Groups as Human Resources," *Research in Personnel and Human Resources Management* 5 (1987):323–356; Shea and Guzzo, "Group Effectiveness: What Really Matters," *Sloan Management Review* 27 (Spring 1987):25–31. Shea and Guzzo's model is a natural and more modern extension of the classical work of George Homans.

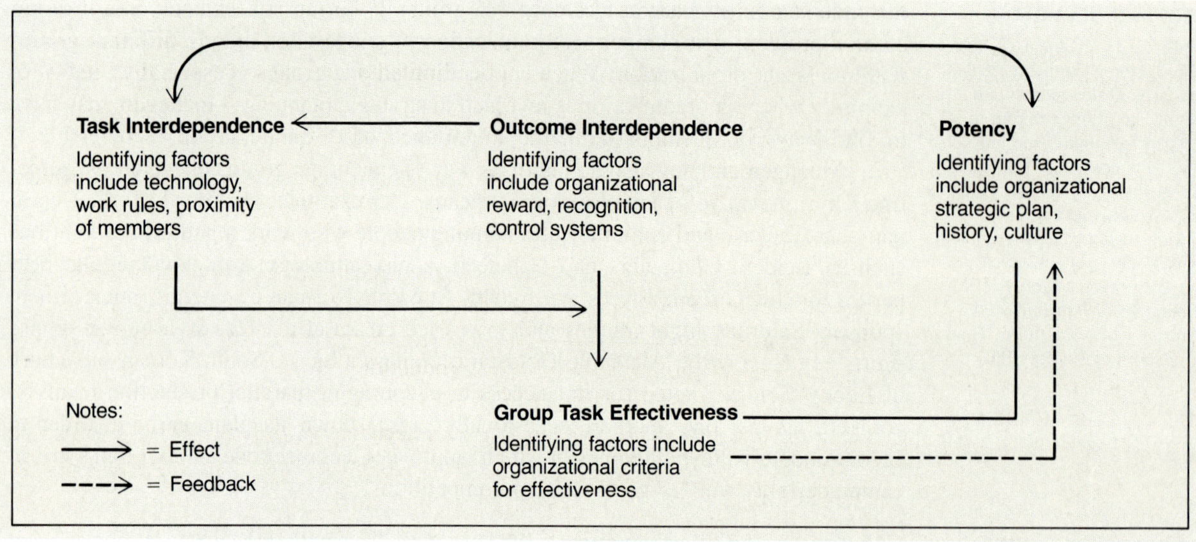

Source: Gregory P. Shea and Richard A. Guzzo, "Group Effectiveness: What Really Matters?" *Sloan Management Review* 27 (Spring 1987):26.

FIGURE 16-5 DETERMINANTS OF WORK-GROUP EFFECTIVENESS

HERE'S AN EXAMPLE

Thomas P. Vanderslice looked like the right person to take over ailing Apollo Computer, Inc. However, former Apollo executives say Vanderslice is more aloof and has a big corporation approach. "He broke the team spirit," says one former Apollo engineer. (*Business Week*, 8/8/88, p. 69)

right and not on details of how a group organizes itself." The members of the group should decide how much task interdependence their work requires.

By contrast, the manager must attempt to create a sense of outcome interdependence. If the members of a group do not share some common fate, they will have little sense of belonging. Group bonuses of peer evaluation (evaluation of the members by one another) can create a sense of shared destiny. Finally, the members of a group must feel that the organization has given them the resources—the skills, money, flexibility—that they need to fulfill the charter.

ILLUSTRATIVE CASE STUDY Continued

The Team Taurus Approach to Management at Ford

Ford used a variety of techniques in implementing Team Taurus. First of all, there were a number of types of groups at work. The union was a formal group which had clear guidelines of its own and which had to agree to the changes that Ford wanted. In addition, the Taurus group was a clear identified, formal task force with a specified leader, Mr. Veraldi. Finally, and perhaps most important, an informal group emerged during the design and production of the car itself, because Team Taurus was really all of the people who worked on the car—from factory-maintainence people to high-powered design engineers. By setting a clear task—namely, "being better than the best"—Veraldi and other Ford managers were able to keep the attention of these various groups focused on the overall goal of the project. By giving those groups clearly measurable goals, their members could see results and improvements as they were in progress. As a result, a feeling of success and satisfaction, rather than failure and uncertainty, predominated throughout the project.

PROBLEM SOLVING IN GROUPS

Every group brings both assets and liabilities to the task of problem solving. It also brings factors that can be either assets or liabilities, depending on the skills of the members and leader. Our discussion of these factors will apply to formal committees and task forces, as well as to ad hoc committees, but it will draw most heavily on research into problem solving in small ad hoc groups—small groups organized to address specific issues or pursue specific, limited goals.

EXTRA EXERCISE

An excellent experiential exercise for contrasting group and individual action is the NASA "Lost on the Moon" exercise found in "Decisions, Decisions, Decisions," by Jay Hall, *Psychology Today*, November 1971, pp. 51–54, 86, 88. (Copies of this exercise are available for a fee from the copyright holder: Teleometrics International, Inc., 2203 Timberloch Place, Suite 104, Woodlands, TX 77380)

Advantages and Disadvantages of Group Problem Solving

Group problem solving has basically four major advantages over individual problem solving. First, groups can suggest more approaches to problem solving. Generally, the more approaches that are presented, the better the chance of finding the best one.

Second, groups bring more knowledge to most problems than would any one individual. For example, a design engineer might be the best person to develop a blueprint for a new machine, but an assembly-line worker would probably have a better idea of how co-workers would use it in production.

Third, group problem solving increases the chances of successful implementation by including all concerned parties in the decision-making process. When people help to solve a problem, they see the solution as their own and have a personal stake in making it work.

Finally, people who have helped to make a decision are more likely to know and understand that decision and its outcome. When a manager makes a decision individually, it must then be relayed to those who will have to carry it out and it may become garbled in the process. When those who must execute the decision have participated in making it, the chances of communication failure are greatly reduced.

However, the group problem-solving process also has at least four major disadvantages. First, groups tend to make decisions prematurely. Their members suggest a number of solutions, and each gets both initial support and criticism. Often, the first solution to win substantial backing during the ensuing debate prevails perhaps only because it was presented skillfully or because it reflected traditional ways of thinking.[19] Once an acceptable choice has emerged, more unconventional but potentially better solutions may well be ignored.

Second, groups tend to be dominated by formal or informal leaders whose problem-solving abilities may or may not be good. Extroverted and socially assertive people tend to be more active than other participants—and thus more influential even if not always more able. Group members whose past successes or friendly relations with management have given them self-confidence may also tend to dominate the discussion.[20] Some members may simply babble on, perhaps to score points with the leader. If their monologues are not checked, others may become frustrated and "tune out"—or start playing exactly the same game.

Third, members eventually become committed to a specific plan. At this point, they frequently become more concerned with winning the debate than with finding the best solution to the problem at hand.

Finally, there is the twofold problem of commitment. Some members of a group might have a commitment to a particular solution even before the group starts to deliberate—perhaps because they think that this solution will benefit them even if not the organization. Similarly, once a decision has been made, groups tend to become and remain committed to it even if it later appears that it was a bad one. This last problem, of course, can also be a function of deficient *individual* decision making.[21]

---

[19]Hoffman, "Applying Experimental Research on Group Problem Solving to Organizations," p. 382.

[20]Ibid., pp. 377–378; Donal E. Carlston, "Effects of Pooling Order on Social Influence in Decision-Making Groups," *Sociometry* 40, no. 2 (1977):115–123; and Godfrey M. Hochbaum, "The Relation Between Group Members' Self-Confidence and Their Reactions to Group Pressures to Uniformity," *American Sociological Review* 19, no. 6 (1954):678–687.

[21]Max H. Bazerman, Toni Giuliano, and Alan Appelman, "Escalation of Commitment in Individual and Group Decision Making," *Organizational Behavior and Human Performance* 33, no. 2 (1984):141–152. See also Hoffman, "Applying Experimental Research on Group Problem Solving to Organizations," p. 378.

Key Factors in Group Decision Making: Assets or Liabilities

Generally speaking, five factors in group decision making can be *either* assets or liabilities to group effectiveness. First, the clash of ideas within a group can promote both creativity and innovation on the one hand and resentment and ill will on the other. Skillful leaders use disagreements to generate creative solutions, proposing, for example, that "Both ideas look good; how about a solution that incorporates both?"

A second factor is that group members often have different goals and perspectives. A group might, for example, be considering ways to increase profits from an unsuccessful product line. The sales manager, regarding the problem as a failure to break into specific markets, suggests more aggressive sales and promotion tactics; the controller, however, believes that costs are out of control and that sales commissions should be cut. Before solutions to the problem are proposed, the leader must get the members to agree on the essence of the problem and desired goals by citing evidence offered by both advocates. If he or she succeeds, the conflict is an asset; if the leader fails, the conflict may become a liability.

In the third place, despite popular assumptions to the contrary, groups often make riskier decisions than individuals.[22] For example, in the case of a person who must decide whether to stay in a secure job or leave it for one that is less secure but better-paying, groups are more likely than individuals to recommend the riskier choice. The group solution represents a "risky shift," as management writers put it, from the solutions that individuals are more likely to offer.[23]

---

[22]Dorwin Cartwright, "Risk Taking by Individuals and Groups: An Assessment of Research Employing Choice Dilemmas," *Journal of Personality and Social Psychology* 20, no. 3 (1971):361–378, and "Determinants of Scientific Progress: The Case of Research on the Risky Shift," *American Psychologist* 28, no. 3 (1973):222–231.

[23]See James A. F. Stoner, "A Comparison of Individual and Group Decisions Involving Risk" (Master's thesis, Massachusetts Institute of Technology, School of Industrial Management, 1961). There have been hundreds of studies published since the first "risky shifts" were demonstrated by Stoner in 1961. In spite of these extensive research efforts, the types of situations in which the phenomenon occurs and the cause and nature of the phenomenon are still unclear and remain a source of lively debate and research. See also James A. F. Stoner, "Risky and Cautious Shifts in Group Decisions: The Influence of Widely Held Values," *Journal of Experimental Social Psychology* 4, no. 4 (1968):442–459; and Russell D. Clark, "Group-Induced Shift toward Risk: A Critical Appraisal," *Psychological Bulletin* 76, no. 4 (1971):251–270.

"That's settled, then. We'll all go back to our respective divisions and act busy."

Fourth, group decisions take longer to make (and often more expensive) than decisions made by individuals. Because group decisions frequently are more sound than individual ones, some experts argue that groups use their time more effectively than do individuals. In cases where a decision must be made quickly, however, a skillful group leader will have to prevent irrelevant or uselessly prolonged discussion. Moreover, common sense reminds us of the difference between decisions made from prolonged indecision and imperfect compromise on the one hand and those made from patient deliberation on the other. The group leader must encourage the group to weigh the value of the time that they are spending.

Finally, all members of a group rarely start out supporting the same solution to a problem, so that some people must change their original positions. This can be an asset or a liability, depending on whose mind changes. If those with the most creative or practical ideas are induced to change, the group winds up with a mediocre decision, and it is the responsibility of the group leader to get the group to evaluate both the creativity and practicality of a proposal or position.

An interesting study in group decision making can be found in the Management Application box entitled "Winter Survival Test." Try it with other members of the class with whom you join in a situation that definitely demands some group decision making.

TASK FORCES AND COMMITTEES

COORDINATED RESOURCE
For an interesting description of quality circles, see "Improving the Effectiveness of Quality Circles," by Sandy J. Wayne, Ricky W. Griffin, and Thomas S. Bateman in *Personnel Administrator*, March 1986, pp. 79–88.

Comments and jokes about the time-wasting proclivities of committee work have always been popular among managers, who generally pride themselves on their individualism. Opponents of task forces and committees feel they have inflicted a crushing blow when they say something like, "No committee ever painted a Mona Lisa or sculpted a Pietà." In reality, however, a committee or task force is frequently the best means for pooling the expertise of different members of the organization and for channeling their efforts toward effective problem solving and decision making.

The need for committees has long been widely recognized in organizations. As long ago as 1960, Rollie Tillman concluded from a survey that "94 percent of the firms with more than 10,000 employees reported having formal committees."[24] It is probable that the number and types of groups active in organizations have grown considerably since that time. The greater complexity and rate of change in organizations today require the kind of information pooling and problem evaluation that committees and task forces are designed to provide.

Types of Formal Working Groups

Organizations have three main types of committees and formal task groups: task forces, standing committees, and boards or commissions.[25]

task force or **project team** A temporary group formed to address a specific problem.

Task Forces. **Task forces,** or **project teams,** are formed to deal with a specific problem or task. They continue in existence only until the task is completed or the problem solved. Task forces are usually formed to deal with complex problems or tasks that involve several organization subunits. For example, assume a computer firm de-

[24]Rollie Tillman, Jr., "Committees on Trial," *Harvard Business Review* 48, no. 4 (1960):6–7ff.

[25]A fourth type of committee is the plural executive or general management committee, a formal committee that functions as a chief executive and is responsible for the overall management of the organization in the same way that an organization president would be. See William H. Mylander, "Management by the Executive Committee," *Harvard Business Review* 33, no. 4 (1955):51–58.

MANAGEMENT APPLICATION

WINTER SURVIVAL: A TEST

You have just crash-landed in the woods of northern Minnesota and southern Manitoba. It is 11:32 A.M. in mid-January. The light plane in which you were traveling crashed on a lake. The pilot and copilot were killed. Shortly after the crash the plane sank completely into the lake with the pilot's and copilot's bodies inside. None of you who survived are seriously injured, and you are all dry.

The crash came suddenly, before the pilot had time to radio for help or inform anyone of your position. Since your pilot was trying to avoid a storm, you know the plane was considerably off course. The pilot announced shortly before the crash that you were 20 miles northwest of a small town that is the nearest known habitation.

You are in a wilderness area made up of thick woods broken by many lakes and streams. The snow depth varies from above the ankles in windswept areas to knee-deep where it has drifted. The last weather report indicated that the temperature would reach −25° in the daytime and −40° at night. There is plenty of dead wood and twigs in the immediate area. You are dressed in winter clothing appropriate for city wear—suits, pantsuits, street shoes, and overcoats.

While escaping from the plane, several members of your group salvaged 12 items. Your task is to rank these items according to their importance to your survival, starting with 1 for the most important item and ending with 12 for the least important one. You may assume that the number of passengers is the same as the number of persons in your group and that the group has agreed to stick together.

__ Ball of steel wool
__ Newspapers (one per person)
__ Compass
__ Hand ax
__ Cigarette lighter (without fluid)
__ Loaded .45-caliber pistol
__ Sectional air map made of plastic
__ Piece of heavy-duty canvas 20 by 20 feet
__ Extra shirt and pants for each survivor
__ Can of shortening
__ Quart of 100-proof whiskey
__ Family-size chocolate bars (one per person)

What do you think? In this life-and-death situation, would you and the group have a better chance to survive if you made the important decisions for the group by yourself or if you and the other survivors jointly decided what to do? For example, if all of you decided to rank the 12 items as a group, would the group's ranking be superior to your own? And how could you improve the quality of the solutions offered by your group? Try the "Winter Survival" test: Work with no more than five other students, each of whom should rank the 12 items alone, without looking at each other's answers. When you have completed your individual rankings, discuss the problem together as a group, sharing your individual solutions until you reach a consensus. Finally, check both your individual and group answers against the rankings given by survival experts—which are given in your teacher's Instructor's Manual. This exercise will show you in a practical way the relative merits of individual versus group problem solving. It may also give you some insight into the kinds of problems in human relationships that managers of groups may face.

Source: David W. Johnson and Frank P. Johnson, *Joining Together: Group Theory and Group Skills,* 3rd ed., © 1987, pp. 110–111. Reprinted by permission of Prentice Hall, Inc., Englewood Cliffs, New Jersey.

velops a new storage device that cannot be manufactured by existing facilities. A special task force may be created to determine what new manufacturing equipment will be needed, how it can be best obtained, and what changes it will require in the firm's work patterns. Task forces usually include representatives (or key decision makers)

Drawing by Ed Fisher; © 1982 The New Yorker Magazine, Inc.

from subunits, plus whatever technical experts the problem or task requires. Task forces may achieve their results in one of three ways:

1. By making recommendations to the executive to whom they are responsible.
2. By reaching decisions in the group when the appropriate executive is the formal leader.
3. By the individual representatives of the various units committing their units to take specific actions in accord with the group's conclusions.[26]

committee A formal organizational group, usually relatively long-lived, created to carry out specific organizational tasks.

Standing Committees. Standing or permanent, **committees** remain in existence to meet a continuing organizational need. Typical standing committees might be the finance committee or new-products review committee in a company or an admissions committee in a college. Usually such committees either make formal recommendations to a higher-level manager or have the authority to make their own decisions for a limited organizational activity.

board A group made up of individuals appointed or elected to manage a public or private organization.

commission Group whose members are usually appointed by government officials, charged with administrative, regulatory, or legislative tasks.

Boards and Commissions. **Boards** are made up of individuals who are appointed or elected to manage a public or private organization. School board members, for example, are elected by their community to set school policy, raise revenues, hire a principal, and perhaps even select textbooks. The board of directors of a corporation is selected by stockholders to oversee the management of the assets of the company, set company policies and goals, hire company officers to carry out those policies, and review the progress of the company toward those goals. Members of **commissions** are usually appointed by government officials to carry out administrative, legislative, or regulatory duties (the Federal Trade Commission and the Securities and Exchange Commission, for example).

Whereas the other formal groups we have discussed are concerned with the internal needs of the organization, these groups represent the interests of people outside the organization. School board members, for example, are responsible to the community; commission members are generally responsible to the public; board members are responsible to their stockholders and, increasingly, to the society of which they are a part.

---

[26]Note that in matrix organizations, discussed in Chapter 9, the project team may have its own budget and enjoy a great deal of autonomy in implementing solutions and decisions.

Key Differences between Task Forces and Committees

In many instances, committees and task forces are managed in similar ways. Some differences in procedure, however, stem from the way they are formed and the tasks they undertake. Although much of this chapter applies to both categories of formal working groups, we should note key distinctions between them. (See Table 16-1.)

Committees are generally long-lasting and perhaps permanent parts of an organization's structure. They are formed to deal with recurrent problems and decisions, to give or withhold approval, or to exchange information regularly for coordination purposes. For example, a loan approval committee in a bank might meet every week to vote on recommendations by lending officers.[27] Similarly, boards of directors usually have nominating committees and audit committees to perform the routine functions of selecting new members and reviewing the financial health of the organization.

Committees are also characterized by stability of membership. Turnover may be quite low, and there may be no formal procedure for evaluating the appropriateness and performance of committee members. Members may be chosen because of their title or position instead of individual qualifications. Committees frequently play only a passive role in task identification. Tasks are assigned through normal organizational channels, and normally only those tasks deemed appropriate for the committee reach it.

Task forces contrast with committees on each attribute just described. Because task forces are impermanent, their membership is fluid and consists of those persons best able to carry out the current part of the task. Members tend to be chosen for their skills and expertise. Task forces also tend to be more active than committees in searching out related problems and opportunities that might affect the larger task. For example, when former President Reagan appointed Hewlett-Packard CEO John Young to chair a task force on the competitiveness of American business, the task force called on a number of experts and interested parties to assemble its findings.

[27]This tendency toward permanence offers the opportunity to achieve effective, predictable, and stable committee performance. However, it also runs the danger that the committee will remain in existence after the need for it has ended. Anthony Jay has observed that "Many long-established committees are little more than memorials to dead problems." See "How to Run a Meeting," p. 43.

TABLE 16-1 SOME DIFFERENCES BETWEEN COMMITTEES AND TASK FORCES

	COMMITTEES	TASK FORCES
Duration	*Long-term:* Ends if reorganization of organization's structure terminates committee.	*Short-term:* Ends when task is completed.
Basis of Membership	*Organizational Roles and Position:* Based primarily on organizational role or hierarchical position.	*Expertise and Skills:* Role and hierarchical position are important, but particular skills and expertise may be equally or more important.
Stability of Membership	*Stable:* Members are appointed and remain on committee.	*Fluid:* Members are added and dropped as current activities require.
Identification of Tasks, Problems, and Opportunities	*Passive:* Tasks, problems, and opportunities are usually referred to committee by other parts of the organization on basis of committee's area or responsibility.	*Active:* Initial task is basis of task force formation; problem and opportunity finding are integral parts of task accomplishment.

As a rule, committee and task force membership (and the proportion of time spent working in them) is greater for managers at the top level than at the lower levels of the organization. (See Figure 16-6.) One reason for this is that only top-level managers have the authority to make policy decisions for the organization. In addition, the higher a manager's level, the larger the number of organizational subunits he or she affects. Higher-level managers, therefore, have a greater need than do lower-level managers to coordinate their own work activities with those of other subunits. This need for close coordination between higher-level managers and other subunits is often met through committees and task forces made up of individuals from the various parts of the organization.

Advantages and Disadvantages of Committees and Task Forces

Committees have some of the same advantages and disadvantages as other groups (here we will use the term "committees" to refer to all formal groups, including task forces). As we saw in our earlier discussion, the two most important advantages of group decision making are better decisions and a higher likelihood of successful implementation.

Certain advantages are specific to committees.[28] One is improved coordination. During committee discussions, members learn how the work of their own units affects that of others. This awareness often creates a new willingness and ability to coordinate the work necessary to achieve larger organizational goals.

Committees also serve as "incubators" for young executives, teaching them to free themselves from the parochial concerns of their individual units and to think about wider issues. Lower-level executives perceive and approach problems and opportunities. Higher-level managers can learn how higher-level executives perceive and approach problems and opportunities. Higher-level managers have a chance to evaluate the styles and abilities of their junior associates.

[28]The discussion is based on Ernest Dale, *Planning and Developing the Company Structure* (New York: American Management Associations, 1952), and *Organization* (New York: American Management Associations, 1967); and Hoffman, "Applying Experimental Research on Group Problem Solving to Organizations."

FIGURE 16-6 SURVEY OF EXECUTIVE COMMITTEE MEMBERSHIP

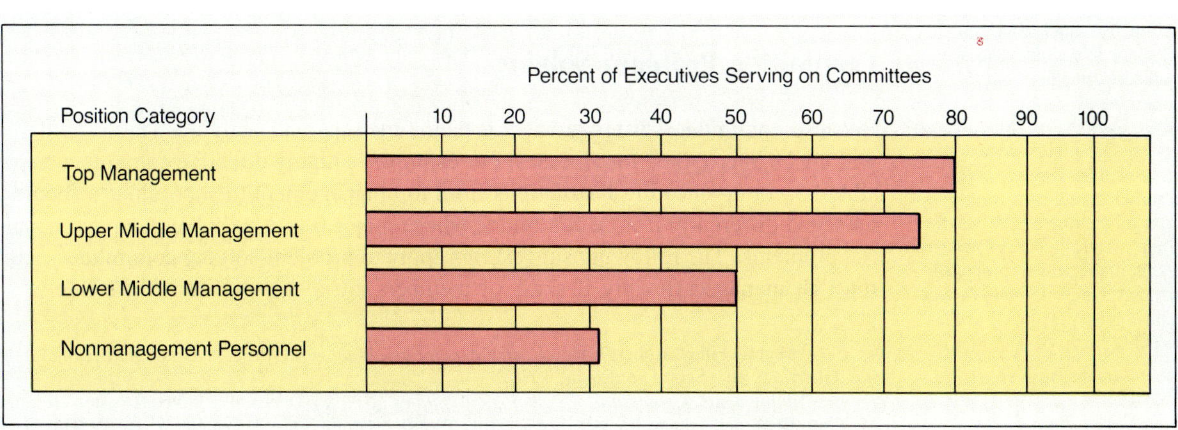

Source: Reprinted by permission of the *Harvard Business Review.* Exhibit from "Committees on Trial" by Rollie Tillman, Jr., (May–June 1960). Copyright © 1960 by the President and Fellows of Harvard College; all rights reserved.

Finally, committees help organizations avoid dangerous concentrations of power. Although certain tasks are better performed under the direction of a single authority, too much power concentrated in any one person's hands can lead to abuses, favoritism, and unwise decisions. Committees spread responsibility among their members, thus reducing the chance that any one person will have too much power. They also make it harder for people who are adversely affected by a decision to complain of favoritism, or lack of input bias, in the decision-making process.

Yet committees are not without pitfalls. As we saw in our earlier discussion of groups in general, they are often dominated by aggressive people whose suggestions might not be appropriate. Because committees are usually run by a formal leader whose rank is higher than that of the other members, the leader usually dominates. Domination, as opposed to leadership, can limit the effectiveness of a committee.[29]

In addition, members with a prior commitment to one point of view might defend it to the exclusion of others. Members with no prior commitment might accept a proposal merely because it has been made by a more powerful associate. Political pressures for compromise can be strong, whether or not the compromise really makes sense. Often, for example, executives go along with a watered-down solution to a problem they do not view as crucial so that they can gain approval for their own pet projects.

In addition to political pressures for compromise are psychological pressures. "Groupthink"—the tendency to conform uncritically to group judgments—may inhibit potential dissenters. It encourages committee members to abdicate their responsibility to think objectively and critically about all the proposals that come before them.[30] No one member is likely to feel solely responsible for a committee's ultimate decision, so members may be less careful than they would be if they had to bear individual responsibility. If a decision is hard to implement, the committee's members may feel less responsibility to help overcome the problem. Among the more recent historical decisions that many attribute to groupthink are those that went into the launching of the space shuttle *Challenger* on the morning of January 28, 1986.[31]

FOR DISCUSSION

How was this an example of "groupthink"? (You may have to lead students to news accounts following the tragedy.)

MAKING FORMAL GROUPS EFFECTIVE

HERE'S AN EXAMPLE

Workers at Musashi Semiconductor Works of Tokyo are organized into 360 groups with from eight to ten people. Membership is primarily by work station, although some self-selection is possible. Group members typically hold the same rank or position but are of mixed ages or sex. Small-group systems are highly democratic at the worker level as each group elects its own leader from its members. The small-group system generates and processes improvement proposals of many kinds. (*Sloan Management Review* 23, no. 2 (1982): 3–14)

Because formal groups are vital to successful organizations, managers must learn to use them effectively. Earlier, we discussed Shea and Guzzo's suggestions for improving group performance in general. Here, we will provide additional guidelines for committee meetings, leaders, and members.

Committee Problem Solving

Because committees differ greatly in their functions and activities, these guidelines will not be appropriate for all cases. For example, a highly directive committee responsible for communicating instructions from top management to subordinates should be managed differently from a committee whose major task is to solve complex managerial problems. The following suggestions apply to problem-solving committees, which must be managed flexibly if skills of members are to be used most effectively.

---

[29] Alan C. Filley, Robert J. House, and Steven Kerr, *Managerial Process and Organizational Behavior* (Glenview, Ill.: Scott, Foresman, 1976).

[30] Irving Janis, *Groupthink: Psychological Studies of Policy Decisions,* 2nd ed. (Boston: Houghton Mifflin, 1982); and Jeanne Longley and Dean G. Pruitt, "Groupthink: A Critique of Janis's Theory," in Ladd Wheeler, ed., *Review of Personality and Social Psychology,* Vol. 1 (Beverly Hills, Cal.: Sage Publications, 1980), pp. 74–93.

[31] A. W. Kruglanski, "Freeze-Think and the Challenger," *Psychology Today,* August 1986, pp. 48–49.

Formal Procedures. Several formal procedures are useful in helping committees operate effectively.[32]

- The committee's goals should be clearly defined, preferably in writing. This will focus the committee's activities and reduce discussion of what the committee is supposed to do.
- The committee's authority should be specified. Can the committee merely investigate, advise, and recommend, or is it authorized to implement decisions?
- The optimum size of the committee should be determined. With fewer than five members, the advantages of group work may be diminished. Potential resources increase as group size increases. While size will vary with the circumstances, the ideal number of committee members for many tasks seems to range from 5 to 10. With more than 10 to 15, a committee may become unwieldy, and it may be difficult for each member to enter and influence the work.[33]
- A chairperson should be selected on the basis of his or her ability to run an efficient meeting—that is, the ability to encourage the participation of all committee members, to keep the committee meetings from getting bogged down in irrelevancies, and to see that the necessary paperwork gets done.
- Appointing a permanent secretary to handle communications is often useful.
- The agenda and all supporting material for the meeting should be distributed before the meeting. When members can prepare in advance, they are more likely to stick to the point and to be ready with informed contributions.
- Meetings should start and end on time. The time when they will end should be announced at the outset.

Guidelines for Leaders. Committee leadership is a key factor in the successful outcome of the committee's work. The leader is responsible for the membership of the committee, for the satisfactory completion of its assigned tasks, and for his or her own leadership behavior.

The leader should control not only the size of the committee but also the qualifications of its members. Are they the right people for this committee's work? Do they have the needed skills? If not, can others be added? Are some members unnecessary? Can time be saved by removing them? In many committee situations the membership is fixed, and the chairperson may have little control over membership; even then, however, it may be possible to bring in special people with needed skills to provide assistance.

The leader must also screen the work assigned to the committee. Many committees are ineffective because they try to grapple with problems for which they do not have the expertise, organizational power, required information, or responsibility. The leader can save time and concentrate the committee's efforts be detecting inappropriate work at the outset and avoiding it.

A committee leader should be aware of the decision-making style with which he or she is most comfortable and which is most suitable for the committee's task. Leaders should make certain that the two types of leadership roles—task and maintenance—noted earlier in this chapter are provided either by themselves or by other committee members.

To manage discussions effectively, the leader should begin by making clear what the meeting should accomplish.[34] Was it called to stimulate thinking, or to draft a specific proposal? The leader should then make certain that all members understand the

---

[32]Cyril O'Donnell, "Ground Rules for Using Committees," *Management Review* 50, no. 10 (1961):63–67. See also Jay, "How to Run a Meeting."

[33]L. Richard Hoffman and M. Clark, "Participation and Influence in Problem-Solving Groups," in Hoffman, ed., *The Group Problem-Solving Process.* See also Philip Yetton and Preston Bottger, "The Relationship among Group Size, Member Ability, Social Decision Schemes, and Performance," *Organizational Behavior and Human Performance* 32, no. 2 (1983):145–149.

[34]Most of the remaining leadership guidelines in this section are taken from Jay, "How to Run a Meeting."

issue and why they are meeting to discuss it. A brief summary of the situation by the leader or another informed person is usually sufficient. As discussion proceeds, the leader should clarify misunderstandings when they occur. For example, two people may employ the same term but mean different things by it, and a third party can often spot and rectify such miscommunication. Finally, the leader should terminate the discussion at an appropriate time. This may come when agreement has been reached, when more information is needed, or whatever. The leader should recognize a logical ending point when it arrives and close the discussion swiftly.

Anthony Jay recommends that leaders follow these seven rules:[35]

1. Control the garrulous.
2. Draw out the silent.
3. Protect the weak.
4. Encourage the clash of ideas.
5. Watch out for the suggestion-squashing reflex.
6. Come to the most senior people last.
7. Close on a note of achievement.

Guidelines for Members. For Jay Hall, the group decision process has one basic aim: to resolve conflicts creatively by reaching a consensus. He defines consensus not as unanimity but as a condition in which each member accepts the group's decisions because they seem most logical and feasible. Hall offers five guidelines to help group members achieve consensus.[36]

1. State your position as clearly and logically as you can—but do not argue for it. Listen to and ponder the other members' reactions before you push your point.
2. If discussion between some members gets bogged down on any one point, do not treat it as a win-or-lose proposition. Instead, seek out the next most acceptable alternative.
3. Do not yield on any point just for the sake of harmony. Accept a solution only when it is based on sound logic.
4. Shun techniques that bypass logic for the sake of reducing conflict (such as majority vote, flipping a coin, bargaining, and averaging). When a dissenting member finally goes along with the group, don't make up for this by letting the yielder have his or her own way on some other point.
5. Root out differences of opinion and pull everyone into the discussion. Only by airing the widest possible range of opinions and drawing in all available information can the group come up with high-quality solutions.

synergy "A condition in which the whole is greater than the sum of its parts."

Working with college students and with management executives, Hall found that groups trained to apply this five-point process did consistently better in solving problems than untrained groups. A trained group frequently outperformed even its best individual member—an outcome he described as "synergy." **Synergy** may be defined as "a condition in which the whole is greater than the sum of its parts." Hall's guidelines encourage the maximum participation of group members and the search for the best possible problem solutions. They are most useful for committees working on a task that requires an ingenious or creative solution.

Special Procedures for Task Forces

Although the foregoing guidelines for committee and task force leaders and members are applicable to running a task force, formal procedures are less appropriate. Figure

[35] Ibid., pp. 56–57.

[36] Jay Hall, "Decisions, Decisions, Decisions," *Psychology Today*, November 1971, p. 54.

HERE'S AN EXAMPLE

Robert M. Bass, often called the "bashful billionaire" from Ft. Worth, Texas, relies on a group of key people to run his enterprises. Although the eight key players have functional specialties, ". . . you never know who will be the trigger point for a new deal" says one close associate. (*Business Week*, 10/3/88, pp. 96–103)

16-7 summarizes a method of task force management that emphasizes the use of task force meeting time for work planning and control.[37] Most of the work is *not* done at meetings. The group time is used to define problems and opportunities and to arrange for the right people to work on them outside the meeting.

Figure 16-7 indicates the work flow of a task force meeting. Past progress is briefly reviewed, and then the current situation is described and analyzed in terms of its problems and opportunities. Based on this analysis, new outside-the-meeting subtasks are defined. Next, the task force membership is reviewed for its appropriateness to the current roster of subtasks, and arrangements are made to add or drop members as needed. Finally, subtask responsibility is allocated among task force members, and target dates are established for subtask completion.

This task force management procedure is well suited to complex, ambiguous problems of major scale, such as reorganizing the entire sales force of a company or developing a new generation of computer terminals. There are, however, a number of other ways to manage task forces and their work.

Although many of the same skills are required for both task-force and committee management, the two groups do differ. For example, a task force that encounters new problems in pursuing its original objective is empowered to deal with them. By con-

[37] See, for example, Lawrence W. Bass, *Management by Task Forces* (Mount Airy, Md.: Lomond Books, 1975).

FIGURE 16-7 TASK FORCE WORK FLOW

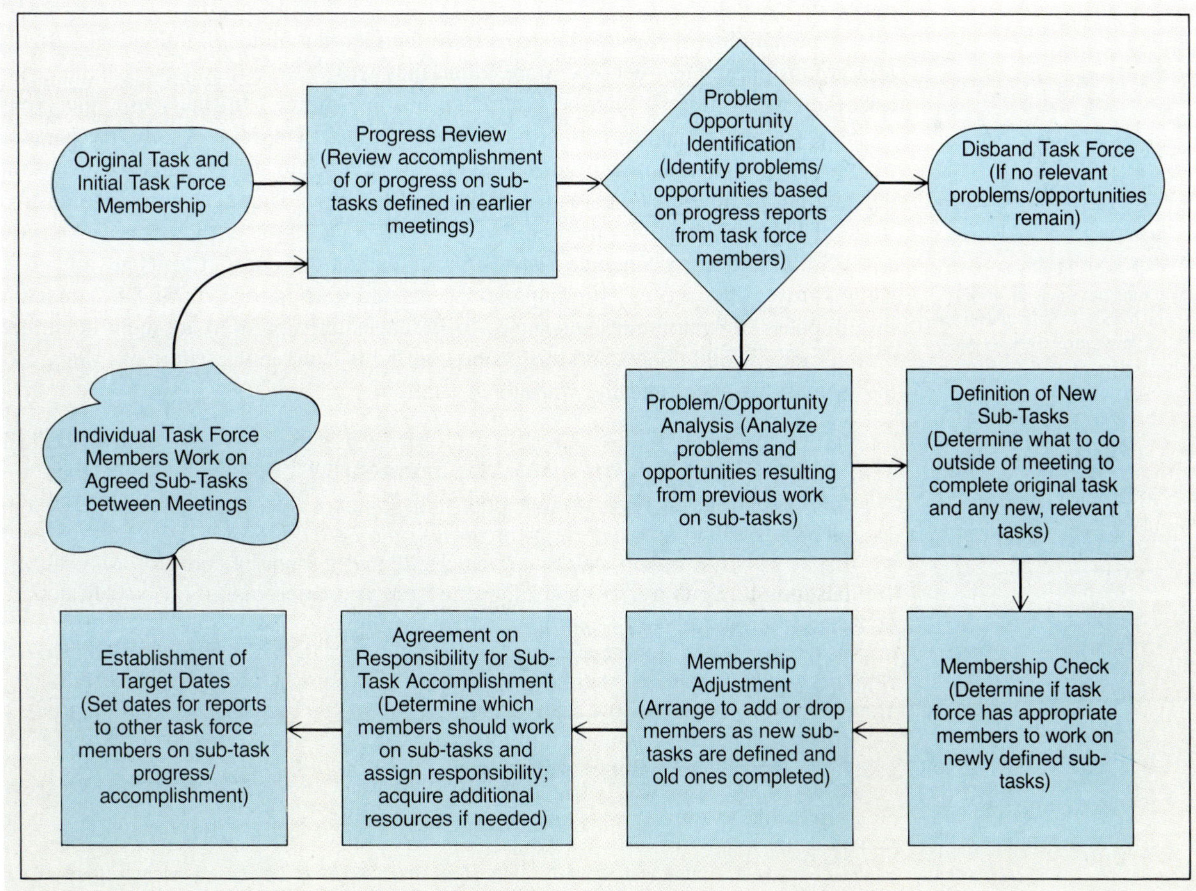

trast, a committee that encounters a new problem outside its original scope can come into conflict with other groups if it tries to bring that problem into its domain.

Conflict within Groups

Conflicts emerge not only *between* groups but also *within* them. In an important book entitled *Paradoxes of Group Life,* Kenwyn Smith and David Berg have proposed a new way to understand such intragroup (within-group) conflicts. Most people think that conflicts must be managed and resolved, but Smith and Berg suggest that such conflicts are essential to the very concept of group life. They call this insight a *paradox* and identify it according to seven aspects: identity, disclosure, trust, individuality, authority, regression, and creativity.[38]

The paradox of *identity* is that groups must unite people with different skills and outlooks precisely because they are different, while those people usually feel that the group diminishes their individuality. The paradox of *disclosure* is that although the members of a group must disclose what is on their minds if the group is to succeed, fear of rejection makes them disclose only what they think others will accept. Likewise, the paradox of *trust* is that "for trust to develop in a group, members must trust the group" in the first place; at the same time, "the group must trust its members, for it is only through trusting that trust is built."

The paradox of *individuality* means that a group can derive its strength only from the individual strengths of members who, when they participate fully in its work, might feel that their individuality has been threatened. Similarly, the paradox of *authority* is that the group derives its power from the power of its individual members, but in joining the group members diminish their individual power by putting it at the group's disposal.

The paradox of *regression* stems from the fact that although individuals usually join groups hoping to "become more" than they were before they joined, "the group asks them to be less so that the group can become more." In this sense, the group counters the individual desire to progress with pressure to regress. Finally, the paradox of *creativity* is that although groups must change in order to survive, change means the destruction of the old as well as the creation of the new. Thus, any refusal to destroy limits the groups creative potential.

EXTRA EXERCISE

Have students think of groups to which they belong and examples of how attractiveness and cohesiveness are enhanced or destroyed within these groups.

Smith and Berg conclude that if a group cannot use conflict to its advantage, it cannot grow. They write: "If group members could learn to treat conflict as a endemic to groupness, a natural consequence of 'differences attempting to act in an integrated way,'" they would understand that group conflict is "just in the nature of things, like the wetness of water and the warmth of sunlight."

ILLUSTRATIVE CASE STUDY Wrap-Up

The Team Taurus Approach to Management at Ford

The jury is still out on Ford, even though the company has been revitalized. The Taurus has experienced major repair problems, and Ford has had to carry through on its "quality is job 1" all the way to its dealers. Is this a result of "groupthink" in the Taurus design? Or is it the result of just too much change made too quickly and, perhaps, too optimistically? Can the people at Ford continue to manage the paradoxes of group life? Can managers retain their sense of individuality while identifying with the group—especially with large and diverse groups like those that comprised Team Taurus? These are just a few of the questions that managers at Ford need to ask continually as they manage and modify group processes in the interest of successful organizational enterprises. ■

[38]Kenwyn K. Smith and David N. Berg, *Paradoxes of Group Life* (San Francisco: Jossey-Bass, 1987); and Smith and Berg, "A Paradoxical Conception of Group Dynamics," *Human Relations* 40, no. 10 (1987):633–658.

INTERNATIONAL MANAGEMENT

SOME LESSONS IN SCANDINAVIAN MANAGEMENT

Although most of the focus on different management techniques that might be successfully grafted on to those typical of American companies have been devoted to Japanese management approaches and the widespread practice of work performed in groups, Japan is not the only nation that has succeeded in fashioning combinations of new and proven management attitudes and applications.

Scandinavian countries, notably Sweden, have long been known for high standards of living and political and economic stability. Part of this prosperity and stability is attributable to the Scandinavian approach to management—in particular, to the ways in which top Scandinavian management promotes firm and reliable relationships among management, employees, customers, and the community at large. For example, the practice of participative management flourishes in Sweden, where worker participation is conceived not as a temporary experiment or an ad hoc measure (as is often the case among U.S. companies). Instead, corporate accomplishments are regarded as the results of the combined creative and decision-making talents of all participants. Management applications among Scandinavian businesses tend to be based on respect for individual dignity and contribution and tend to ensure tangible rewards for individual contributions to the effectiveness of the group. Some analysts suggest that this orientation is a significant factor in the ability of such companies as Scandinavian Airline System (SAS) and Volvo to gain increasing competitive edges over their international competition.

Both SAS and Volvo are models of participatory management. The central theme of SAS's management approach is a strong belief in the ability and integrity of front-line personnel who are entrusted with a great deal of responsibility in servicing the needs of customers; the role of management is to assist the front-line people who are directly in charge of day-to-day customer relations—not to dictate top-level policy to personnel whose contact with customers is immediate and practical. Volvo, which had during the 1960s and early 1970s shared with its American counterparts problems of employee dissatisfaction and alienation on the assembly line, has developed a successful sociotechnical-system design that eliminates the assembly-line technique dating back to Henry Ford in favor of small teams of workers who rotate assignments and perform their jobs with considerable autonomy. Through this participatory approach, management and the company's unions have also come closer together in their basic values and in their ideas about how to improve overall corporate effectiveness.

Can American companies reorient themselves and successfully manage themselves according to such models? Analysts suggest that they can—if they adopt the premise that, by and large, the work force consists of intelligent people who want to do a good job. Without an acceptance of this underlying premise, they argue, American experiments in participatory management will probably continue to meet with mixed results.

Sources: Ron Zemke, "Scandinavian Management—A Look to the Future," *Management Review* 77, no. 7 (1988):44–47; "Kalmar: Ten Years Later," *Via Volvo,* Vol. 6 (1984):14–19; Pehr G. Gyllenhammar, *People at Work* (Reading, Mass.: Addison-Wesley, 1977).

SUMMARY

Groups are an inevitable part of organizational life. The manager's job is to use them effectively at appropriate times.

There are both formal and informal groups in organizations. Informal groups develop whenever people come into contact regularly. They emerge with or without the encouragement of management. Informal groups share certain values and provide social satisfaction, status, and security. They can further or frustrate the achievement of organizational objectives. Group members provide each other with support and protection. In turn, they expect each other to conform to group norms. Members who violate group norms may be subjected to a variety of pressures, ranging from attempts at persuasion to physical assault. Some level of conformity to group norms can free creative energies for more important tasks; too much conformity, however, can hamper innovation. Gregory Shea and Richard Guzzo have recently proposed that a group's effectiveness is a function of three variables: task interdependence, potency, and outcome interdependence.

Formal groups include command groups (managers and their subordinates), task forces, and committees. Task forces are formed to deal with a specific problem or task; once the task is successfully accomplished, the group is dissolved and personnel reassigned. Committees, on the other hand, remain in existence to meet continuing organizational needs. These stable groups deal with recurrent types of problems or decisions (although sometimes they outlive any useful function).

Groups are generally better at problem solving than the average individual. This is because they bring a greater amount of information and expertise to bear on a problem, generate more alternative solutions, catch mistakes, and make it more likely that the solution will be understood, accepted, and implemented. However, group problem solving is also more time-consuming and costly than is individual problem solving.

Formal groups in organizations improve coordination, develop managerial talent, and avoid excessive concentration of power in a single individual. They also run the risks of reaching decisions prematurely, discouraging individual responsibility, and being dominated by individuals who do not necessarily have the most to offer.

Managerial skill in guiding, but not dominating, group activities is an important factor in achieving success in group work. Suggestions for effective results include formal procedures for meetings, as well as guidelines for group leaders and members. Although conflicts sometimes disrupt groups, Kenwyn Smith and David Berg suggest that conflicts are normal and natural when different people attempt to act in an integrated way. Understanding this process help groups to use their conflicts creatively.

■ REVIEW QUESTIONS

1. What are the three basic types of groups in organizations? Which type of group do you think is most important? Why?
2. What are reference groups? Why is it important for managers to be aware of them? Can you identify your own reference groups?
3. Why do you think informal groups emerge in organizations? What organizational needs do they serve? What member needs do they serve?
4. How do informal leaders emerge in informal and formal work groups?
5. What are the two leadership roles of formal and informal group leaders?
6. How do group members try to enforce conformity?
7. What is the relationship between group cohesiveness and group performance? How can group cohesiveness be increased?
8. On what bases would a manager decide whether to use individual or group problem solving?
9. What are the possible advantages and disadvantages of group decision making and problem solving?
10. According to Shea and Guzzo, how can astute managers create effective groups?
11. What is a task force? What are the different types of committees and their functions?
12. What are the advantages and disadvantages of task forces and committees?
13. What formal procedures help make committees effective? How can committee leaders and members help make it effective?
14. What are the "paradoxes of group life" as seen by Smith and Berg? Why do they feel that intragroup conflict is inevitable and basically good?

CASE STUDY

The New-Products Group

Karen Smith looked at her calendar for the day. It was Thursday, and the report she had been working on was due tomorrow. That meant the group would have to meet today to hammer out its recommendations and presentation. She was not looking forward to an afternoon spend devoted to this task.

The group had been formed to design the market introduction of the company's newest product. Since the company had never marketed a retail product before, no one was quite sure what to expect. Karen and her group were expected to produce recommendations for advertising and promotion, product distribution and roll-out, and anything else they though was important. After the plan had been approved, implementation would probably fall to Karen as well, although it could be given to another member of the Marketing Department. It was a large undertaking, and Karen and four others had given it most of their time for the last few months.

Right from the start, the group had not worked well together. This fact had not surprised Karen: The personalities were strong all around, and it was clear at the outset that there would be some personality conflicts. All four group members were on the same level in the company, and no one had been specifically designated to lead the group. Therefore, the early meetings were mostly a struggle for leadership.

Karen realized very early that Ben had a deep-seated belief that women probably had no place in business—and certainly were not capable of leading men. Even then, the venom in some of his comments had come as a surprise, although other women had warned her. It was clear to Ben that he was the only one able to lead the group: After all, had he not just finished four years in the Navy? Moreover, James was only slightly more open-minded than Ben. The two of them often formed a team, and once they had come to a joint decision, it was impossible to get them to consider anyone else's recommendations. Charles was more willing to listen to the others. However, he had a tendency to come into the meetings with so much data that the group members often spent all their time trying to understand how it had been derived and not making decisions. In all, Karen was quite frustrated at both the group's slow progress and the tense atmosphere that pervaded their meetings.

They were nowhere near finished with their plan, but they would have to present their recommendations tomorrow morning. She knew that senior management was expecting a full report, and she was not very confident that she could deliver it. How would the group members ever work together well enough to get finished? The atmosphere at their meetings was already poor, and Karen could only guess what would happen when the stress of a deadline was added. She wondered if she could control the show of tempers that usually marked their gatherings, the last of which had dissolved into a shouting match between herself and Ben. She had tried, as tactfully as possible, to suggest that one of his ideas for a promotional campaign was impractical. However, he had quickly dropped the discussion and moved to a more personal level: accusing her of undermining his authority by trying to imply that she, a mere woman, knew more than he did. He had even said she could not be a true Christian, since any Christian woman would be at home raising children. Her faith was important to her, but she never considered it related to her job performance. It certainly wasn't a topic to be discussed in the group.

She sighed. It was going to be a very long day. Should she call the other group members to set the time, or should she let one of them call her? How should she act toward Ben? What could she do to keep things on track in preparation for tomorrow? All she really wanted to do was tell her boss she was sick and go home.

Source: Writer by Rebecca Villa and R. Edward Freeman, based on actual situations. Prepared especially for this book.

Case Questions

1. Why is Karen's group having problems?
2. Can you use the Shea-Guzzo model to give Karen a better idea of why the group is dysfunctional?
3. What should Karen do now? ■

Paul Rand. Poster for Advertising Typographers' Association of America. Courtesy of the Artist.

17

INTERPERSONAL AND ORGANIZATIONAL COMMUNICATION

Upon completing this chapter you should be able to:

1. Define communication and state why it is important to managers.
2. Describe a model of the communication process.
3. Distinguish between one-way and two-way communication.
4. Summarize the barriers to interpersonal communication and explain how they can be overcome.
5. Describe the factors that influence the effectiveness of communication in organizations.
6. State how the barriers to effective organizational communication can be overcome.
7. Discuss how the use of advanced information technology might affect interpersonal relations and other organizational activities.
8. Explain when more open communications are desirable and when they are not.

Chapter Outline

Introduction
The Importance of Communication
Interpersonal Communication
Barriers to Effective Communication
Communication in Organizations

ILLUSTRATIVE CASE STUDY Introduction

Communications Failures at Bhopal

All the safety features had failed—that much was abundantly clear. What Mr. Warren Anderson could not find out was *why.* As CEO of Union Carbide, he needed to know exactly what had happened in Bhopal, India, that night for a number of reasons. He knew that he would have to explain a tragic accident to employees, to government officials in both the United States and India, to the courts, and to the people. Yet, he could not get answers to his own preliminary and personal questions. When telephone contact failed to yield answers, he got on a plane and flew to India, where he was immediately placed under house arrest—unable to attend to the very business that had brought him there. His plant managers had also been arrested and were not allowed to talk to anyone. Indian government officials had closed the plant to Union Carbide management in order to prevent "tampering with evidence."

The basic facts that Anderson could not determine on December 3, 1984, were really quite simple. A runaway reaction had occurred in a storage tank of methylisocyanate (MIC), which was used to manufacture a pesticide. The valves on the tank had burst, and a cloud of poisonous gas had escaped. Climatic conditions kept the gas from dissipating, and the winds carried it to nearby shanty towns and the populous city of Bhopal, where people either died in their sleep or woke and died while fleeing. Those who survived suffered from burning eyes and lungs. Local medical facilities were not equipped for the disaster, and over the next few weeks thousands more died.

The Bhopal plant was operated by Union Carbide India, Ltd. (UCIL), with the parent company, Union Carbide, owning roughly 51 percent. After installing the plant and training its first staff, Union Carbide withdrew from the daily operation of the plant, as it was required to do by the Indian government. Union Carbide did participate in the inspections and responded to official questions and concerns, but no U.S. official of the company was on-site in Bhopal.

Meanwhile, the plant was under a great deal of pressure to cut costs. Due to production problems, it was unable to run at more than 50 percent capacity, and meeting its original profit predictions had become impossible. A number of shortcuts had thus been taken with such items as crew training, staffing patterns, and maintenance schedules. Although the plant had been virtually shut down for weeks for extensive maintenance and cleaning, a number of important safety features remained inoperable—and there remains some question as to whether they would have been adequate even had they been working.

Perhaps most importantly, the staff did not realize the importance of the situation—and even took a break for tea after the leak had been noticed, thinking they would have plenty of time to fix it. The operator in the control room did not notify his supervisor when the temperature began to rise inside the tank, and the entire situation went untended for at least an hour. The original procedures called for up to two years of training for employees in critical superintendent capacities, but these men had received about a month, using classroom materials developed in the U.S. and printed in English.

Sources: Dan Kurzman, *A Killing Wind: Inside Union Carbide and the Bhopal Catastrophe* (New York: McGraw-Hill, 1987); Arthur Sharplin, "Union Carbide of India, Ltd.," *Journal of Management Case Studies* 2 (1986):100–115; Pico Iyer, "India's Night of Death," *Time,* December 17, 1984, pp. 22–31.

Obviously, Warren Anderson had a severe communication problem. More importantly, Union Carbide had experienced a tragic episode of organizational breakdown in communication. Ultimately, not only ethical questions, but technical difficulties, cultural problems, and organizational barriers all surfaced as issues because of a massive disruption of the organization's strategy for communicating both within its own internal network and with parties outside the organization. In a critical sense, communication in the process of organizational management will also be crucial to the company's efforts to solve the problems that have already ensued in the aftermath of Bhopal.

Equally obvious is the fact that, when communication is properly regarded as the most important factor in such managerial activities as planning, organizing, motivating, and controlling, it is unquestionably the most important function not only of organizations but of individual managers as well. A glance back at the Illustrative Case Study for Chapter 1, which was carefully designed to depict "A *Typical* Day in the Life of Alison Reeves," will serve as a reminder that virtually every task performed by an individual manager—reading and writing memos and reports, meeting to devise and explain strategies, issuing directives and evaluating the implementation of plans—is a communications task.[1] It is little wonder that analysts such as Henry Mintzberg and others calculate that individual managers spend about 80 percent of their time communicating in one way or another (meetings alone can appropriate almost 60 percent of a manager's day).[2] As should be clear by now, it has been the plan of this book to describe the communications activities of managers as integral aspects of tasks—planning, decision making, coordinating, motivating, and so on—that we have organized as categories which constitute both the field of management studies and the actual tasks of management practice.

CLASS COMMENT
Communication is the thread that binds together individuals, groups, and organizations.

In this chapter, we deal with communication in organizations. First, we present a model of interpersonal communication, describe the barriers to effective interpersonal communication, and suggest ways that these barriers can be overcome. Second, we show how different types of organizational communication channels will influence such variables as group performance, leader emergence, and group-member motivation and satisfaction. We then discuss problems of communication up and down the organization's chain of command and the informal channels of communication that develop in organizations. Finally, we deal with means of overcoming organizational (rather than interpersonal) barriers to effective communication.

THE IMPORTANCE OF COMMUNICATION

FOR DISCUSSION
Why is good *writing* so important in business? How can good writing skills be developed?

As we have seen, effective communication is important for managers for two reasons. First, communication is the process by which managers accomplish the functions of planning, organizing, leading, and controlling. Second, communication is the activity to which managers devote an overwhelming proportion of their time. Rarely are managers alone at their desks thinking, planning, or contemplating alternatives. In fact, managerial time is spent largely in face-to-face, electronic, or telephone communica-

---

[1] Fred Luthans and Janet K. Larsen, "How Managers Really Communicate," *Human Relations* 39 (1986):161–178.

[2] Henry Mintzberg, *The Nature of Managerial Work* (New York: Harper & Row, 1973).

tion with subordinates, peers, supervisors, suppliers, or customers. When not conferring with others in person or on the telephone, managers may be writing or dictating memos, letters, or reports—or perhaps reading memos, letters, or reports sent to them. Even in those few periods when managers are alone, they are frequently interrupted by communications. For example, one study of middle and top managers found that they could work uninterruptedly for a half hour or more only once every two days.[3] As Exhibit 17-1 shows, Henry Mintzberg has described the manager's job in terms of three types of roles; communication plays a vital role in each.

EXHIBIT 17-1 MINTZBERG'S DEFINITION OF THE ROLE OF COMMUNICATION IN THREE MANAGERIAL ROLES

1. In their *interpersonal roles,* managers act as the figurehead and leader of their organizational unit, interacting with subordinates, customers, suppliers, and peers in the organization. Mintzberg cited studies indicating that managers spend about 45 percent of their contact time with peers, about 45 percent with people outside their units, and only about 10 percent with superiors.
2. In their *informational roles,* managers seek information from peers, subordinates, and other personal contacts about anything that may affect their job and responsibilities. They also disseminate interesting or important information in return. In addition, they provide suppliers, peers, and relevant groups outside the organization with information about their unit as a whole.
3. In their *decisional roles,* managers implement new projects, handle disturbances, and allocate resources to their unit's members and departments. Some of the decisions that managers make will be reached in private, but they will be based on information that has been communicated to the managers. The managers, in turn, will have to communicate those decisions to others.

Source: Henry Mintzberg, "The Manager's Job: Folklore and Fact," *Harvard Business Review* 53, no. 4 (July–August 1975).

Communication has been characterized as the "lifeblood" of an organization, and miscommunication has caused the equivalent of cardiovascular damage in more than one organization. Certainly, today's managers face an environment in which the issue of communications has become increasingly complex. The acceleration of technology both expedites and complicates means of communication, and an unstable environment sends rapidly changing signals reflecting shifts in social and cultural values. In addition, greater demands are being made by various "subcultures" within our larger culture, necessitating the targeting of communications to groups that respond to messages different from those to which the larger culture has traditionally responded. For example, Coca-Cola, Procter & Gamble, Anheuser-Busch, and McDonald's are among many firms that have begun budgeting larger sums of advertising dollars to communicate with a growing Hispanic market which, by 1988, was worth $130 billion and growing.[4]

Moreover, the internationalization of business has required managers to become acutely conscious of communication procedures and conventions of a diverse number of cultures. For example, Americans have been shown to be relatively direct in their style of communication, while the Japanese tend to incorporate traditional ceremonial details into their style. A renewed appreciation of languages is also required if U.S. managers are to communicate here and abroad. Although English has been termed "the" language of the planet, the first truly "global language," it is the mother tongue of only about half of the 750 million people who speak it, and people who speak other

[3] Rosemary Stewart, *Managers and Their Jobs* (London: Macmillan, 1967), pp. 72–73.
[4] "Fast Times on Avenida Madison," *Business Week,* June 6, 1988, pp. 62–67.

native tongues still value and guard their language as expressions of themselves and their cultures.

Finally, the influx of more women and minorities into our organizations and their managerial ranks also increases both the potential for miscommunication and the need to be sensitive to the nuances of linguistic messages and other forms of communication.

All in all, then, communication is a much more complex factor in our world than it was 25 years ago. Not surprisingly, the problem of defining *communication* as a subject of study has also become increasingly difficult. One researcher uncovered as many as 95 definitions, none of them entirely feasible or widely accepted.[5] For our purposes, **communication** is defined as the process by which people attempt to share meaning via the transmission of symbolic messages.

communication The process by which people attempt to share meaning via the transmission of symbolic messages.

INTERPERSONAL COMMUNICATION

Our working definition of *communication* calls attention to three essential points: (1) that communication, as we are using the term, involves *people,* and that understanding communication therefore involves trying to understand how people relate to each other; (2) that communication involves *shared meaning,* which suggests that in order for people to communicate, they must agree on the definitions of the terms they are using; and (3) that communication is *symbolic*—gestures, sounds, letters, numbers, and words can only represent or approximate the ideas they are meant to communicate.[6]

The Communication Process

John Kotter has defined communication as a process consisting of "a sender transmitting a message through media to a receiver who responds."[7] In its simplest form, this model can be schematized as follows:

Sender → Message → Receiver

This model indicates three essential elements of communication; obviously, if one of the elements is missing, no communication can take place. For example, we can send a message, but if it is not heard or received by someone, no communication has occurred.

Moreover, we must remind ourselves that although psychologists specializing in interpersonal communication continue to pursue the implications and nuances of this model, it must be regarded as a highly ideal model. For example, it assumes a hypothetical "common ground" between sender and receiver that is more easily conceptualized than precisely described.[8] Similarly, most of us are familiar with the game of "telephone," in which one person whispers a message into the ear of another. That person whispers the message to another, and so on. Inevitably, when the last person says the message out loud, it is quite different from what had first been whispered.

TEACHING TIP

You could play a game of telephone with your students. Start two different messages at opposite ends of the classroom. Have the students who receive the messages last report them. See what happened to the message!

[5]F. E. X. Dance, "The 'Concept' of Communication," *Journal of Communication* 20, no. 2 (1970):201–210.

[6]Lyman W. Porter and Karlene H. Roberts, "Communication in Organizations," in Marvin D. Dunnette, ed., *Handbook of Industrial and Occupational Psychology,* 2nd ed. (New York: John Wiley, 1983), pp. 1553–1589.

[7]John Kotter, "Power, Dependence, and Effective Management," *Harvard Business Review,* 55, no. 4 (1977):125–136.

[8]H. H. Clark, "Language Use and Language Users," in *Handbook of Social Psychology,* G. Lindzey and E. Aronson, eds., 3rd ed. (Reading, Mass.: Addison Wesley, 1984).

"Telephone" illustrates one complexity in the communication process: The sender may send a message, but the receivers may "hear" or receive a message the sender did not intend. Psychologists have also studied such complex variables as the receiver's disposition toward one-sided or two-sided arguments,[9] the receiver's response to superficial as opposed to logical aspects of a message,[10] and whether women are more easily persuaded receivers than men.[11]

Figure 17-1 illustrates a far more sophisticated model of the communication process. In the discussion that follows, we will describe each of the major elements of this model.[12]

sender The initiator of a communication.

Sender (Source). The **sender,** or source of the message, initiates the communication. In an organization, the sender will be a person with information, needs, or desires and a purpose for communicating them to one or more other people. A manager wishes to communicate information about an important production deadline for the purpose of motivating other members of the department. A production-line worker speaks to the shop supervisor for the purpose of requesting additional help with a project. Without a reason, purpose, or desire, the sender has no need to send.

encoding The translation of information into a series of symbols for communication.

Encoding. **Encoding** takes place when the sender translates the information to be transmitted into a series of symbols. Encoding is necessary because information can only be transferred from one person to another through representations or symbols. Since communication is the object of encoding, the sender attempts to establish "mutuality" of meaning with the receiver by choosing symbols, usually in the form of words and gestures, that the sender believes to have the same meaning for the receiver.

---

[9]K. Deaux and L. S. Wrightsman, *Social Psychology in the 80s,* 4th ed. (Monterey, Calif.: Brooks/Cole, 1984).

[10]R. E. Petty and J. T. Cacioppo, "The Effects of Involvement on Responses to Argument Quantity and Quality: Central and Peripheral Routes to Persuasion," *Journal of Personality and Social Psychology* 46 (1984):69–81.

[11]W. J. McGuire, "Attitudes and Attitude Change," in *Handbook of Social Psychology,* G. Lindzey and E. Aronson, eds., 3rd. ed., Vol. 2 (New York: Random House, 1985).

[12]Our discussion is based on Linda M. Micheli, Frank V. Cespedes, Donald Byker, and Thomas J. C. Raymond, *Managerial Communication* (Glenview, Ill.: Scott, Foresman, 1984), pp. 186–201; and Judson Smith and Janice Orr, *Designing and Developing Business Communications Programs That Work* (Glenview, Ill.: Scott, Foresman, 1985), pp. 4–6. See also Norman B. Sigband and Arthur H. Bell, *Communication for Management and Business* (Glenview, Ill.: Scott, Foresman, 1986); Courtland L. Bovee and John V. Thill, *Business Communications Today* (New York: Random House, 1986); and Robert W. Rasberry and Laura F. Lemoine, *Managerial Communications* (Boston: Kent, 1986).

FIGURE 17-1 A MODEL OF THE COMMUNICATION PROCESS

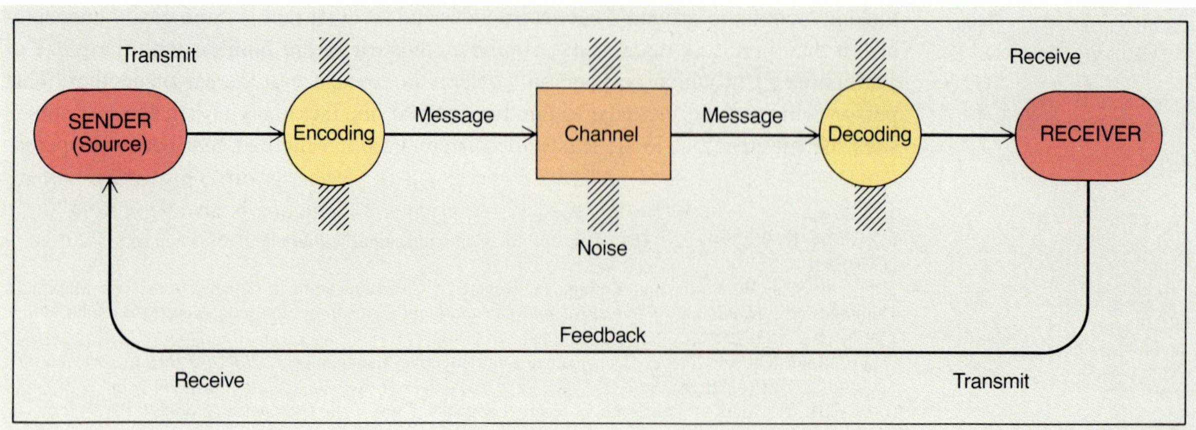

Lack of mutuality is one of the most common causes of misunderstanding or lack of communication. In Bulgaria and some parts of India, for example, "yes" is indicated with a side-to-side shake of the head, while "no" is indicated with a nod. Visiting foreigners who do not share these symbols can quickly experience or cause bewilderment when they talk with citizens of these areas. Misunderstandings may also result from subtler differences in mutuality. A manager who asks a number of subordinates to "work late" may cause a good deal of confusion as each employee decides independently what "late" means.

CLASS COMMENT

Nonverbal communication can affect the intended and interpreted meaning.

Gestures, too, may be subject to different interpretations. A worker in a noisy factory may convey to a co-worker that he wants a machine to be shut off by drawing his hand, palm down, across his neck in a "cutthroat" gesture.[13] If one walked up to a police officer and made the same gesture, a different reaction might result. Even raising one's eyebrows can have varying meanings, expressing surprise in one context and skepticism in another.

message The encoded information sent by the sender to the receiver.

Message. The **message** is the physical form into which the sender encodes the information. The message may be in any form that can be experienced and understood by one or more of the senses of the receiver. Speech may be heard; written words may be read; gestures may be seen or felt. A touch of the hand may communicate messages ranging from comfort to menace. A wave of the hand can communicate widely diverse messages depending on the number of fingers extended. Nonverbal messages are an extremely important form of communication, since they are often more honest or meaningful than oral or written messages. For example, a manager who frowns while saying "Good morning" to a late-arriving subordinate is clearly communicating something more than a polite greeting.

channel The medium of communication between a sender and a receiver.

HERE'S AN EXAMPLE

Company annual reports are a form of communication. The Smithsonian's Cooper-Hewitt Museum in New York City believes annual reports have artistic merit. Their exhibit of over 250 includes such gems as: a 1653 income statement from Mercers Company; a Pennsylvania hospital's statements printed by Benjamin Franklin in 1761; and a round 1982 annual report from Domino's Pizza that was delivered in a pizza box. (*Fortune*, 8/1/88, p. 9)

Channel. The **channel** is the method of transmission from one person to another (such as air for spoken words and paper for letters); it is often inseparable from the message. For communication to be effective and efficient, the channel must be appropriate for the message. When a phone conversation would be an unsuitable channel for transmitting a complex engineering diagram,[14] overnight express mail might be more appropriate. The needs and requirements of the receiver must also be considered in selecting a channel. An extremely complicated message, for example, should be transmitted in a channel that permits the receiver to refer to it repeatedly.

Although managers have a broad array of channels available to them, they may not always use the one that is most effective. Their choices may be guided by habit or personal preference. One person may use the telephone because he or she dislikes writing; another may continue to use handwritten memos when electronic mail would be much more efficient. Both modes are appropriate in certain circumstances, so the manager must make individual decisions for each situation.

How does one choose the best channel? Written and graphic communications, such as memos, letters, reports, and blueprints, are clear and precise and provide a permanent record. The telephone and face-to-face oral communication offer the advantage of immediate feedback. In choosing the appropriate channel, then, managers must decide whether clarity or feedback is more important. Many different factors are involved in the communication process, so no single technique is always preferable to the alternatives.[15]

---

[13] See Paul R. Timm and Christopher G. Jones, *Business Communication: Getting Results* (Englewood Cliffs, N.J.: Prentice Hall, 1983), p. 5.

[14] Larry R. Smeltzer and John L. Waltman, *Managerial Communication: A Strategic Approach* (New York: John Wiley, 1984), p. 4.

[15] Ibid., p. 41.

receiver The individual whose senses perceive the sender's message.

Receiver. The **receiver** is the person whose senses perceive the sender's message. There may be a large number of receivers, as when a memo is addressed to all the members of an organization, or there may be just one, as when one discusses something privately with a colleague. The message must be crafted with the receiver's background in mind. An engineer in a microchip manufacturing company, for example, might have to avoid using technical terms in a communication with someone in the company's advertising department; by the same token, the person in advertising might find engineers unreceptive to communications about demographics. If the message does not reach a receiver, communication has not taken place. The situation is not much improved if the message reaches a receiver but the receiver doesn't understand it.

decoding The interpretation and translation of a message into meaningful information.

Decoding. **Decoding** is the process by which the receiver interprets the message and translates it into meaningful information. It is a two-step process: The receiver must first perceive the message, then interpret it.[16] Decoding is affected by the receiver's past experience, personal assessments of the symbols and gestures used, expectations (people tend to hear what they want to hear), and mutuality of meaning with the sender. In general, *the more the receiver's decoding matches the sender's intended message, the more effective the communication has been.*

One decoding problem occurred when a manager asked a subordinate if she would like to work overtime on a weekend. There were a number of other employees available to do the work, but the supervisor thought the one he singled out would appreciate an opportunity to earn extra income. The subordinate had made special plans for Saturday, but she interpreted the manager's offer as a demand, canceled her plans, and spent the weekend working. As a result of poor communication, she interpreted the manager's message differently than he intended.[17]

noise Anything that confuses, disturbs, diminishes, or interferes with communication.

FOR DISCUSSION

What "noise" factors are there in our classroom?

Noise. **Noise** is any factor that disturbs, confuses, or otherwise interferes with communication. It may be internal (as when a receiver is not paying attention) or external (as when the message is distorted by other sounds in the environment). Noise can occur at any stage of the communication process. It may occur during passage through the channel—for example, a radio signal may be distorted by bad weather—but most interference arises in the encoding or decoding stage.[18]

The urge to make sense of a communication is so strong that a puzzling or even nonsensical communication is often decoded by the receiver into a sensible statement that may have an entirely different meaning from the originally encoded message. For example, unclear instructions on how to perform a task may cause employees to "hear" different and incorrect instructions.

Since noise can interfere with understanding, managers should attempt to restrict it to a level that permits effective communication. It can be very tiring to listen to a subordinate who speaks softly on a noisy assembly line or to try to conduct a conversation over telephone static.[19] Physical discomfort such as hunger, pain, or exhaustion can also be considered a form of noise and can interfere with effective communication. The problems are made worse, of course, by a message that is excessively complex or unclear to begin with. A clear message expressed in a straightforward fashion ("Turn off that radio!"), however, can be conveyed even in an extremely "noisy" environment.

---

[16] Ibid., p. 5.

[17] Ibid., p. 8.

[18] See James L. Gibson, John M. Ivancevich, and James H. Donnelly, Jr., *Organizations: Behavior, Structure, Processes,* 5th ed. (Dallas: Business Publications, 1985), p. 535.

[19] Smeltzer and Waltman, *Managerial Communication,* p. 189.

feedback (interpersonal) The reversal of the communication process that occurs when the receiver expresses his or her reaction to the sender's message.

Feedback. **Feedback** is a reversal of the communication process in which a reaction to the sender's communication is expressed. Since the receiver has become the sender, feedback goes through the same steps as the original communication. Organizational feedback may be in a variety of forms, ranging from direct feedback, such as a simple spoken acknowledgment that the message has been received, to indirect feedback, expressed through actions or documentation. For example, a straightforward request for a faster rate of production may be met directly with an assenting nod of the head or indirectly with record-breaking output or a union strike.

As the broken lines in Figure 17-1 suggest, feedback is optional and may exist in any degree (from minimal to complete) in any given situation. In most organizational communications, the greater the feedback, the more effective the communication process is likely to be. For example, early feedback will enable managers to know if their instructions have been understood and accepted. Without such feedback, a manager might not know (until too late) whether the instructions were accurately received and carried out.

One-Way and Two-Way Communication

one-way communication Any communication from the sender without feedback from the receiver.

two-way communication Communication that occurs when the receiver provides feedback to the sender.

As our description of the communication process implies, communication may be one-way or two-way. In **one-way communication,** the sender communicates without expecting or getting feedback from the receiver. Policy statements from top managers are usually examples of one-way communication. **Two-way communication** exists when the receiver provides feedback to the sender. Making a suggestion to a subordinate and receiving a question or countersuggestion is an example of two-way communication.

Harold Leavitt and Ronald Mueller conducted early experiments on the effects and effectiveness of one-way and two-way communication.[20] In these experiments, individuals were asked to describe an arrangement of geometric shapes to groups of listeners. They were to use words only. The listeners were asked to reproduce the diagrams from the verbal descriptions. The experiments were conducted under conditions of one-way communication and two-way communication. In the one-way communication, the sender could not see or hear the listeners. In the two-way experiment, descriptions were still limited to words, but the sender was allowed to face the listeners and the listeners could question or comment freely. The results of the experiments were as follows:

1. One-way communication takes considerably less time than two-way communication.
2. Two-way communication is more accurate than one-way communication. (That is, the diagrams were more accurately reproduced when two-way communication was used.) The feedback allows the sender to refine his or her communication for the receivers so that it becomes more precise and accurate.
3. Receivers are more sure of themselves and of their judgments when two-way communication is used. The very fact that they are permitted to ask questions probably increases the receivers' self-confidence. In addition, they can use questions to clarify any doubts they may have.
4. Senders can easily feel attacked when two-way communication is used, because receivers will call attention to the senders' ambiguities and mistakes.
5. Although it is less accurate, one-way communication appears much more orderly than two-way communication, which often appears noisy and chaotic.

[20] Harold J. Leavitt and Ronald A. H. Mueller, "Some Effects of Feedback on Communicating," *Human Relations* 4, no. 4 (1951):401–410.

As Leavitt has pointed out,[21] these results can provide guidelines for communication in organizations. If communication must be fast and accuracy is easy to achieve (as when informing employees about a minor change in the company's health plan), one-way communication is both more economical and more efficient. If orderliness is considered vital—as in a large, public meeting—one-way communication might also be more appropriate. One-way communication also has political benefits: It reduces the chance that the sender's mistakes will be publicly revealed and challenged.

COORDINATED RESOURCE

See the Lecture Extra for Chapter 17 for a discussion on how open should organizational communication be.

Where accuracy of communication is important, however (as in instructions for carrying out complex tasks), the two-way method is almost essential. Without feedback from the receiver, the sender has little basis for judging the accuracy of the communication or the degree of understanding and comprehension experienced by the receiver.

In most situations, managers will have to create the most efficient mix of one-way and two-way communication. Some categories of managerial communications, such as straightforward statements of company rules and policies, require little or no feedback to assure clarity. In many other cases, such as the formulation of organizational objectives or the implementation of a new sales strategy, two-way communication is usually essential.

BARRIERS TO EFFECTIVE COMMUNICATION

Any factor that impedes the exchange of information between a sender and a receiver is a barrier to communication.[22] Such barriers are extremely common in everyday life, and they appear in an almost unlimited variety of forms. Some are obvious problems with obvious solutions. If you are talking to a colleague and a jackhammer starts up on the sidewalk outside your window, you can wait for the jackhammer to stop or you can move to where the noise won't bother you. Other barriers are much more subtle; one must be quite perceptive even to recognize them. An older manager, for example, may feel threatened by an aggressive younger employee and as a result tend to dismiss the younger manager's most carefully thought-out suggestions, perhaps without even realizing that he or she is doing so. Although less overt, barriers of this sort have as much potential for causing problems as do the more conspicuous problems of the jackhammer variety. Indeed, one could argue that the hidden problems are likely to be more damaging because they are often related to individuals' vulnerabilities and defenses and so cannot be fixed the way a broken telephone can. Their resolution may require great tact, self-awareness, and maturity on the part of everyone involved.

Whatever their source, barriers to effective communication interfere with the receiver's understanding of the intended meaning of the sender's message. As we have already noted, managers spend most of their time communicating, and a good manager should be able to identify and understand the communication barriers that can occur in different situations—from peer to peer, subordinate to superior, superior to subordinate, and employee to customer. Understanding the general characteristics of communication barriers will help managers improve their own communications and solve communication problems with others.[23]

Communication barriers vary in their imperviousness and their significance. Rarely are they total blocks—some part of the intended message is generally able to filter through. In some cases, it is sufficient that the gist of the message be communi-

[21] Harold J. Leavitt, *Managerial Psychology*, 4th ed. (Chicago: University of Chicago Press, 1978), pp. 117–126. See also John T. Samaras, "Two-Way Communication Practices for Managers," *Personnel Journal* 59, no. 8 (1980):645–648.

[22] C. Glenn Pearce, Ross Figgins, and Steven P. Golen, *Principles of Business Communication: Theory, Application, and Technology* (New York: John Wiley, 1984), p. 516.

[23] Ibid., p. 516.

cated. A mailroom clerk who understood relatively little English might be able to function adequately most of the time if he or she clearly understood the difference between "first class" and "express mail." If the clerk failed to grasp the important part of a message and mistakenly sent a package to MIT rather than IBM, however, there might be serious consequences. Barriers often occur in groups. The clerk, for example, might avoid answering the telephone because of his or her difficulty in understanding what people were saying. He or she might consistently deliver John Jonson's mail to John Jenson. Removing one barrier—by enrolling the clerk in a program of instruction in English, perhaps—might remove a whole series of barriers to effective communication throughout the organization.

The following are some of the most common barriers to effective communication:

Differing Perceptions. One of the most common sources of communication barriers is individual variation. People who have different backgrounds of knowledge and experience often perceive the same phenomenon from different perspectives. Suppose that a new supervisor compliments an assembly-line worker for his or her efficiency and high-quality work. The supervisor genuinely appreciates the worker's efforts and at the same time wants to encourage the other employees to emulate his or her example. Others on the assembly line, however, may regard the worker's being singled out for praise as a sign that he or she has been "buttering up the boss"; they may react by teasing or being openly hostile. The event is the same, but individuals' perspectives on it differ radically.

The way a communication is perceived is influenced by the environment in which it occurs. A disagreement between colleagues during a planning session for a major project might be regarded by others as acceptable or even healthy. If the same disagreement broke out during the chief executive officer's annual address to employees, it would be regarded somewhat differently. Events that are considered appropriate in some circumstances are inappropriate in others.

Language Differences. Language differences are often closely related to differences in individual perceptions. For a message to be properly communicated, the words used must mean the same thing to sender and receiver. The same symbolic meaning must be shared. Suppose that different departments of a company receive a memo stating that a new product is to be developed in "a short time." To people in research and development, "a short time" might mean two or three years. To people in the finance department, on the other hand, "a short time" might be three to six months, whereas the sales department might think of "a short time" as a few weeks. Since many different meanings can be assigned to some words—the 500 most common English words have an average of 28 definitions *each*[24]—great care must be taken to ensure that the receiver gets the message that the sender intended.

TEACHING TIP

Re-emphasize to students that they are learning the "jargon" of management in this class. The Management Application box on corporate jargon provides some good examples of this!

Further barriers to communication may result from the use of jargon. Some corporations have their own special jargon, as the Management Application box on "Corporate Jargon" indicates. People who have special interests or knowledge, such as software designers or behavioral psychologists, are often unaware that not everyone is familiar with their specialized terms. Sometimes people use jargon to exclude others or to create an impression of superiority—both of which make communication difficult. Finally, the contemporary globalization of industry brings to light the problem of language barriers—a problem which, although not insoluble, cannot be ignored.

Noise. As we have already explained, noise is any factor that disturbs, confuses, or otherwise interferes with communication. Little communication occurs in totally noise-

[24]Ibid., p. 524.

MANAGEMENT APPLICATION

CORPORATE JARGON

"I'm really in the weeds. Please drop a red chimi on the fly. Wait! Eighty-six that. All I need is a follower."

"That looks like a bad Mickey!"

"What a dinger on a hanging hook!"

If these statements make no sense to you, don't worry. Each is an example of just how complex and inscrutable the specific jargon of a given business can get. The first example is a waitress addressing the cooking staff in a restaurant. It translates as: "I'm very busy. Please cook this food as quickly as possible. Wait! Cancel that. All I need is someone to help me carry these plates to my table." The second is a Disney employee pointing out an unsavory fact, like a cigarette butt on the sidewalk. The third is a major-league baseball player admiring a teammate's long home run off a pitcher's hanging curve ball.

Many industries, and even individual companies, develop their own languages. Sometimes, this is a play to keep others from understanding company secrets or to help insiders feel important. In other instances, it develops as a response to a need for special terms to define special items or activities.

The development of a company slang can have both positive and negative aspects. On the positive side, it may help employees feel like part of a well-defined culture. Everyone likes to feel like he or she is on the inside of a group, and corporate slang can contribute to that feeling very quickly. More importantly, an internal language can also lead to more efficiency—if the jargon has developed so that, say, 2 words take the place of 20 and are more specific at the same time. Of course, a person very new at a position may find this practice tremendously frustrating, and some companies actually publish dictionaries of organizational slang to help initiate newcomers.

However, the real meaning of a phrase can get lost if it undergoes too many variations or becomes couched in too many internal codes. When intracompany slang creeps into the telephone calls and conversations with people on the outside, communication can get quite complicated. Customers may have no idea what the person is trying to communicate. Worse, he or she may be offended by the use of a special language. To outsiders, jargon seem like an attempt to keep them on the outside rather than an effort to resolve a problem or accomplish a goal. Employees of one company trying to communicate with employees of another company can get hopelessly confused if the languages do not coincide. It can almost be as if a French person and a Chinese person were trying to hold a conversation in their native tongues. An external consultant coming into a firm may have to spend days just trying to understand what the problem *is* before trying to solve it.

Corporate slang usually develops in companies rich in history or occupying a unique position in their industry. Walt Disney, for example is almost as famous for having such internal lingo as "good" and "bad Mickeys" as for the images it creates. It is often comfortable—and efficient—nice to be able to communicate with co-workers in a special way, but employees should be aware that not everyone they meet will neither be able to speak their language nor be expected to.

Source: Adapted from Michael W. Miller, "At Many Firms, Employees Speak a Language That's All Their Own," *The Wall Street Journal,* December 29, 1987, Sec. 2, p. 17.

free environments, of course. Individuals learn to screen out many of the irrelevant messages they receive. Sometimes, however, the relevant information is also screened out. A person talking on the phone in a busy office may not hear the message her secretary is giving her from across the room. The "boy who cried wolf" was eventually correct, but his previous messages had been given so often that they had come to be dismissed as noise. Similarly, a manager who labels every order "urgent" may find that subordinates are slow to respond when a real emergency develops.

Emotionality. Emotional reactions—anger, love, defensiveness, hate, jealousy, fear, embarrassment—influence how we understand others' messages and how we influence others with our own messages. If, for example, we are in an atmosphere where we feel threatened with loss of power or prestige, we may lose the ability to gauge the meanings of the messages we receive and will respond defensively or aggressively.

Inconsistent Verbal and Nonverbal Communication. We think of language as the primary medium of communication, but the messages we send and receive are strongly influenced by such nonverbal factors as body movements, clothing, the distance we stand from the person we're talking to, our posture, gestures, facial expression, eye movements, and body contact. Even when our message is as simple as "Good morning," we can convey different intents by our nonverbal communication. A busy manager who does not want to be disturbed might respond to a subordinate's greeting without looking up from his or her work, for example.[25]

Distrust. The credibility of a message is, to a large extent, a function of the credibility of the sender in the mind of the receiver. A sender's credibility is, in turn, determined by a variety of factors. In some cases, the fact that a message comes from a manager will enhance its credibility, but it can also have the opposite effect. In negotiations between labor and management, for example, labor often regards the claims of managers with some suspicion. In this situation, as in others, the perceived character or honesty of the sender is important. In general, a manager's credibility will be high if he or she is perceived by others as knowledgeable, trustworthy, and sincerely concerned about the welfare of others.[26]

Overcoming Barriers to Interpersonal Communication

EXTRA EXERCISE

"Tune in" to your communication over the next 24-hour period. Note when barriers to communication arose and try to identify what factors or situations created the barrier. What did you do to reduce the barriers?

Overcoming barriers is a two-step process. First, one must learn to recognize the various types of barriers that can occur. Second, one must act to overcome the barriers.[27] We explain in the paragraphs that follow some of the techniques that can be used to overcome the specific barriers just described.

Overcoming Differing Perceptions. To overcome differing perceptions, the message should be explained so that it can be understood by those with different views and experiences. Whenever possible, we should learn about the background of those with whom we will be communicating. Empathizing and seeing the situation from the other person's point of view and delaying reactions until the relevant information is weighed helps to reduce ambiguous messages. When the subject is unclear, asking questions is critical.[28]

---

[25]R. Buck, *The Communication of Emotion* (New York: Guilford Press, 1984). For a discussion of how nonverbal behavior communicates such messages as sympathy, threat, or status, see A. W. Siegman and S. Feldstein, *Multichannel Integrations of Nonverbal Behavior* (Hillsdale, N.J.: Erlbaum, 1985). Nonverbal cues can also contribute to turn-taking during communication; see C. L. Kleinke, "Gaze and Eye Contact: A Research Review," *Psychological Bulletin* 100 (1986):78–100.

[26]W. Charles Redding, *The Corporate Manager's Guide to Better Communication* (Glenview, Ill.: Scott, Foresman, 1984), pp. 74–75.

[27]Pearce et al., *Principles of Business Communication,* p. 538.

[28]Ibid., pp. 522–523.

Overcoming Differences in Language. To overcome language differences, the meanings of unconventional or technical terms should be explained. Simple, direct, natural language should be used. To ensure that all important concepts have been understood, asking the receiver to confirm or restate the main points of the message is particularly helpful. In some cases, when all members of an organization or group are going to be dealing with a new terminology, it may be worthwhile to develop a training course of instruction to acquaint members with the new topic. Receivers can be encouraged to ask questions and to seek clarification of points that are unclear or may be misunderstood.[29]

It is also helpful to remain sensitive to the various alternative interpretations possible for a message. Messages can often be restated in different terms. Sometimes even a minor change can have beneficial effects. If, for example, we are replacing an unpopular sales quota system with a new system in which reaching sales objectives is only one measure of productivity, we might do well to avoid the word ''quota'' entirely because of its negative association with the old system.

Overcoming Noise. Noise is best dealt with by eliminating it. If noise from a machine makes talking difficult, turn off the machine or move to a new location. If you notice that your receiver is not listening closely, try to regain his or her attention. Avoid distracting environments. Alternately, when noise is unavoidable, increase the clarity and strength of the message.

Overcoming Emotionality. The best approach to emotions is to accept them as part of the communication process and to understand them when they cause problems. If subordinates are behaving aggressively, try to empathize. Get them to talk about their concerns, and pay careful attention to what they say. Once you understand their reactions, you may be able to improve the atmosphere by changing your own behavior. Before a crisis, try to understand your subordinates' emotional reactions and prepare yourself to deal with them. Also, think about your own moods and how they influence others.

Overcoming Inconsistent Verbal and Nonverbal Communication. The keys to eliminating inconsistencies in communication are being aware of them and not attempting to send false messages. Gestures, clothes, posture, facial expression, and other powerful nonverbal communications should agree with the message. Analyzing the nonverbal communication of other people and applying what one learns to oneself and to one's dealings with others is helpful.

CLASS COMMENT

All of these techniques have merit. However, a manager must first be aware that barriers exist and then deal with them appropriately.

Overcoming Distrust. Overcoming distrust is to a large extent the process of creating trust. Credibility is the result of a long-term process in which a person's honesty, fairmindedness, and good intentions are recognized by others. There are few shortcuts to creating a trusting atmosphere; a good rapport with the people one communicates with can only be developed through consistent performance.

redundancy Repeating or restating a message to ensure its reception or to reinforce its impact.

Redundancy. One additional approach is generally useful in getting one's message across. This is **redundancy**—repeating the message or restating it in a different form. Redundancy counteracts noise by reducing the uncertainty in the transmission of the message.[30] The optimal level of redundancy varies with the circumstances. If a message is sent in a permanent form—on paper, a tape, or a disk, for example—then little redundancy within the communication is called for. On the other hand, if the message

[29]Ibid., pp. 522, 524.

[30]David V. Gibson and Barbara E. Mendleson, ''Redundancy,'' *Journal of Business Communication* 21, no. 1 (1984):43–61, especially 52.

FOR DISCUSSION

Is redundancy used in education? How? Give examples.

is extremely complex, it may be useful to repeat key points in several different forms even in a written communication. Redundancy is also more important in oral and other "perishable" forms of communication. If someone is giving us a phone number and we don't have a pencil and paper, we are more likely to remember it if it is repeated several times.

Like other techniques, redundancy can be overused. If we hear the same message too many times, we may become bored or angry. Eventually, a receiver will come to treat such a message as noise. Furthermore, in some situations, storage of the redundant information can be a problem. Many libraries would like to have two copies of every book they buy, for example, but two copies cost twice as much, take up twice as much space, and take almost twice as long to catalog. The money, space, and time might better be devoted to another book.

ILLUSTRATIVE CASE STUDY Continued

Communications Failures at Bhopal

Clearly, Anderson and Union Carbide had a significant communication problem. First of all, there was simply a lot of confusion over the facts. Even today, no one is clear as to exactly what sequence of events led to the disaster. Each party has a different interpretation of the "facts" that have come to light, and the resulting legal battles promise to be long. Of course, there were a number of barriers to effective communication in the immediate aftermath of the event. Various parties gave voice to differing perceptions of the "facts," and the high pitch of emotion amounted to a form of noise interfering with communications channels.

In addition, Anderson had to communicate in multiple ways in the wake of the disaster—all of which were hampered by subsequent events and circumstances. The whole world was watching to see what Union Carbide would do. Anderson made the symbolic move of going to India to show his concern, but his subsequent arrest made any form of communication virtually impossible. Ultimately, he needed to have a policy of one-way communication in order to state what Union Carbide was going to do, but before that he needed to engage in multiple-party communication to determine exactly what had happened. Both channels of communication had been effectively shut down.

There also remained the little-publicized but important issue of Anderson's communication with other Union Carbide employees. After all, some of them worked in facilities very much like the one in Bhopal.

COMMUNICATION IN ORGANIZATIONS

> Because Christmas Eve falls on a Thursday, the day has been designated a Saturday for work purposes. Factories will close all day, with stores open a half day only. Friday, December 25, has been designated a Sunday, with both factories and stores open all day. Monday, December 28, will be a Wednesday for work purposes. Wednesday, December 30, will be a business Friday. Saturday, January 2, will be a Sunday, and Sunday, January 3, will be a Monday.—*From an Associated Press report on a Prague government edict.*

HERE'S AN EXAMPLE

Fortune reported the results of a product brand-name study and found that America's most powerful brands are: Coca-Cola, Campbell's, Pepsi-Cola, AT&T, McDonald's, American Express, Kellogg's, IBM, Levis, and Sears. They also reported the least powerful brand names. (*Fortune*, 7/4/88, pp. 10–12)

All the factors that we have discussed in relation to interpersonal communication also apply to communication with organizations. Effective communication in organizations, like effective communication anywhere, still involves getting an accurate message from one person to another (or perhaps to several people). As in the example above, unclear organizational communication can make a complex idea or process completely unintelligible. However, several factors unique to organizations influence the effectiveness of communication. In this section we will deal specifically with how the realities of formal organizations can affect the communication process.

"Confound it, Merriwell! Do you mean that all this time you've been talking micro while we've been talking macro?"
Drawing by Lorenz; © 1982 The New Yorker Magazine, Inc.

Factors Influencing Organizational Communication

Raymond V. Lesikar has described four factors that influence the effectiveness of organizational communication: the formal channels of communication, the organization's authority structure, job specialization, and what Lesikar calls "information ownership."[31]

EXTRA EXERCISE

Have students get a copy of a company newsletter or magazine. Describe the content and try to determine what its main purpose is. If they bring these to class, you can compare and contrast them.

Formal Channels of Communication. The *formal channels of communication* influence communication effectiveness in two ways. First, the formal channels cover an ever-widening distance as organizations develop and grow. For example, effective communication is usually far more difficult to achieve in a large retail organization with widely dispersed branches than in a small department store. Second, the formal channels of communication inhibit the free flow of information between organizational levels. An assembly-line worker, for example, will almost always communicate problems to a supervisor rather than to the plant manager. While this accepted restriction in the channels of communication has its advantages (such as keeping higher-level managers from getting bogged down in information), it also has its disadvantages (such as keeping higher-level managers from receiving information they should sometimes have). Sometimes the formal channels of communication have unexpected consequence, as the box entitled "One Memo Too Many" suggests.

Authority Structure. The organizations' *authority structure* has a similar influence on communication effectiveness. Status and power differences in the organization help determine who will communicate comfortably with whom. The content and accuracy of the communication will also be affected by authority differences among individuals. For example, conversation between a company president and a clerical worker may well be characterized by somewhat strained politeness and formality; neither party is likely to say much of importance.

[31] See Raymond V. Lesikar, "A General Semantics Approach to Communication Barriers in Organizations," in Keith Davis, ed., *Organizational Behavior: A Book of Readings,* 5th ed. (New York: McGraw-Hill, 1977), pp. 336–337.

ETHICS IN MANAGEMENT

ONE MEMO TOO MANY

For years, managers have wished that employees knew when—and *when* not—to write memos. Mostly, this complaint has come from managers weary from reading too many pieces of material suitable for "circular filing." However, recent court events have revealed a new reason for people to think twice before writing another memo: That memo can become incriminating evidence in a legal battle.

Tobacco companies, for example, have been fighting lawsuits for years. Smokers (or their relatives, or their survivors) have sought to make the cigarette manufacturers responsible for their poor health or for that of a diseased or deceased relative. Until recently, no one has succeeded with such a lawsuit, mainly because the tobacco companies have been adamant in their claims that there is no proof that cigarettes cause the cancer or lung problems alleged in the suits. Their other argument, of course, is that the smoker was free to choose to smoke and was not compelled by an addiction.

This state of affairs may change in the future. Evidence in a recent trial indicates that the tobacco companies may have been fully aware of the consequences of smoking—or at least should have been. Internal documents of the Liggett Group, Inc., indicated that its own scientists duplicated the experiments which suggested that the tar in cigarettes caused cancerous tumors to grow on mice. The documents had been in circulation as far back as 1953. Memos written by other scientists and external consultants also indicated a belief in some link between cancer and cigarette smoking.

Memos written in the early 1970s indicate that Philip Morris scientists had invented a "safer" cigarette. The company, however, killed its development, apparently because they feared the liability of suggesting their current product was less than safe. Recently, when R. J. Reynolds announced a new cigarette that produces less smoke and has fewer harmful ingredients, company lawyers wrote a memo warning management that marketing the new product could increase their vulnerability to charges that they knew conventional tobacco products to be less safe than the company had maintained. All of these memos are now being used in the courts as part of an effort to prove that the companies are fully aware of the hazards of smoking. Now that these documents have been presented, they will undoubtedly be used again and again.

Other legal cases have also used internal memos as evidence. The Beech-Nut trial in 1982 concerning the company's knowledge of the contents of its apple juice was largely decided on the strength of a memo written to warn senior management about the adulterated juice. In that case, the courts decided that Beech-Nut did know—or should have known—that the apple juice it was selling was not "pure" juice at all, but a fraudulent mix of water, sugar, and chemicals.

The memo you are about to write could thus have effects besides wearying the eyes of your manager and increasing the company's need for filing space. What you communicate and how you do it can harm and benefit, as well as affect the rights of lots of folks. Communication, too, is a matter of ethics.

Sources: Adapted from Patricia Bellew Gray, "Smoking Foes Cite New Evidence Emerging in Tobacco-Liability Suit," *The Wall Street Journal,* April 4, 1988, p. 19; and Ed Bean, "Memo Warns of Legal Risk of 'Smokeless' Cigarettes," *The Wall Street Journal,* April 13, 1988, p. 31.

job specialization The division of work into standardized, simplified tasks.

Job Specialization. **Job specialization** usually facilitates communication *within* differentiated groups. Members of the same work group are likely to share the same jargon, time horizons, goals, tasks, and personal styles. Communication *between* highly differentiated groups, however, is likely to be inhibited.

information ownership The possession by certain individuals of unique information and knowledge concerning their work.

FOR DISCUSSION

Are there times when the expense and time of a two-way communication process might not be justified? What would be some examples?

Information Ownership. The term **information ownership** means that individuals possess unique information and knowledge about their jobs. A darkroom employee, for example, may have found a particularly efficient way to develop photoprints, a department head may have a particularly effective way of handling conflict among subordinates, and a salesperson may know who the key decision makers are in his or her major accounts. Such information is a form of power for the individuals who possess it; they are able to function more effectively than their peers. Many individuals with such skills and knowledge are unwilling to share this information with others. As a result, completely open communication within the organization does not take place.

In the following sections we will discuss in some detail the effects of the organization's formal communication channels and authority structure on communication effectiveness. In addition, we will discuss the organization's informal communication system (the grapevine), which supplements the organization's formal communications network.

Communication Networks within the Organization

Some very interesting research has been carried out on communication channels in organizations and their effects on communication accuracy, task performance, and group member satisfaction. This research is particularly important because managers have some influence over how communication channels develop in their units. For example, the formal authority structure that managers establish will help determine who will interact with whom. Thus, managers can design their work units to facilitate effective communication.

communication network A set of channels within an organization or group through which communication travels.

Organizations can design their **communication networks,** or structures, in a variety of ways. Some communication networks may be rigidly designed. For example, employees can be discouraged from talking with anyone except their immediate supervisor. Such a network is usually intended to keep higher-level managers from being overburdened with unnecessary information and to maintain the higher-level managers' power and status. Other networks may be more loosely designed: Individuals may be encouraged to communicate with anyone at any level. Such networks may be used wherever a free flow of information is highly desirable, as in a research department.

To test the effect of various communication structures, a series of experiments have been performed.[32] In a representative study in this series, five subjects were seated at a table and asked to solve different types of problems. The subjects were separated by partitions and could communicate with each other to solve the problems along communication lines controlled entirely by the researchers.

COORDINATED RESOURCE

An article on ''America's Most Wanted Managers,'' in *Fortune*, 2/3/86, pp. 18–25, illustrates how important good communication skills are to success as a manager. Encourage students to read this and identify where good communication skills are noted.

Figure 17-2 illustrates four communication networks the researchers tested. In the ''circle'' network, for example, subject B could communicate (through the partitions) only with subjects A and C. To communicate with subject E, subject B would have to go through subject A or through subjects C and D. Subject C in the ''star'' pattern, on the other hand, could communicate directly with A, B, D, and E, although these subjects could not communicate directly with each other. Each of these networks can represent a real network in an organization. The ''star'' pattern, for example,

[32]See Harold J. Leavitt, ''Some Effects of Certain Communication Patterns on Group Performance,'' *Journal of Abnormal and Social Psychology* 46, no. 1 (1951):38–50. Our discussion is also based on H. Joseph Reitz, *Behavior in Organizations*, rev. ed. (Homewood, Ill.: Richard D. Irwin, 1981); Gibson et al., *Organizations: Behavior, Structure, Processes*, pp. 544–545; Leavitt, *Managerial Psychology;* and Marvin E. Shaw, ''Communication Networks,'' in Leonard Berkowitz, ed., *Advances in Experimental Social Psychology*, Vol. 1 (New York: Academic Press, 1964), pp. 111–147. See also Karlene H. Roberts and Charles O'Reilly III, ''Some Correlations of Communication Roles in Organizations,'' *Academy of Management Journal* 22, no. 1 (1979):42–57.

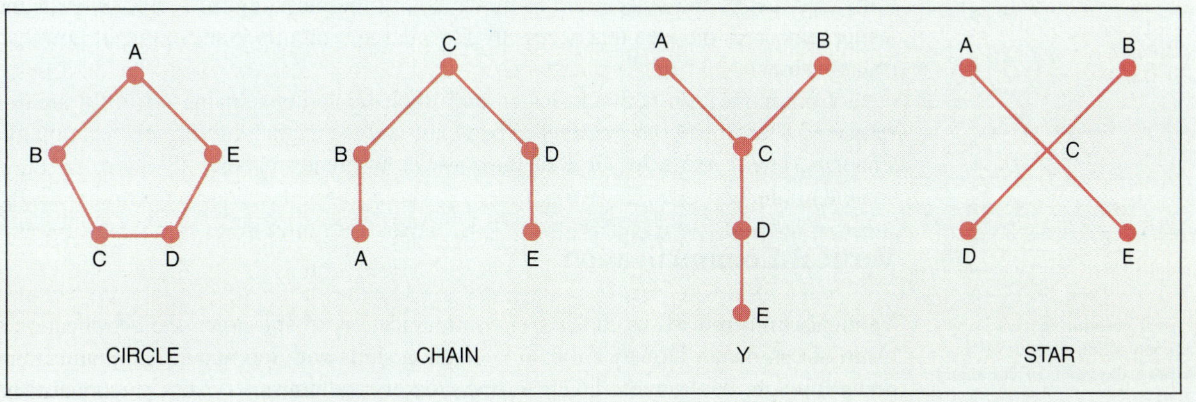

FIGURE 17-2 TYPES OF COMMUNICATION NETWORKS

might represent four salespeople (A, B, D, E) reporting to a district manager (C); the "chain" pattern might represent two subordinates (A and E) reporting to supervisors (B and D, respectively), who in turn report to the same supervisor (C).

The subjects in the experiments were given both simple and complex problems to solve. The series of studies demonstrated that network centrality was the critical feature that determined whether a particular communication network was effective and/or satisfying to its members on a particular type of task. Some networks, such as the "Y" and "star," are highly centralized, with subject C at the central position. But the "circle" and "chain" networks are decentralized, with no one member able to communicate with all the other members.

In most tests, centralized networks performed faster and more accurately than decentralized networks, *provided the tasks were comparatively simple*. For *complex* tasks, however, the decentralized networks were comparatively quicker and more accurate. The structure of communication networks is also intricately linked to larger organizational structure. Highly centralized organizational structures will inhibit the development of broad informal communications networks because most communication will be forced "through proper channels." The functioning of military units provides a good example of this principle: While a battlefield is likely to be rife with rumor, the actual deployment of troops and resources is usually centrally controlled by means of formal communications channels.

The centrality of the networks also affected leader emergence and group member satisfaction. For both simple and complex tasks, centralized groups tended to agree that person C, occupying the central position, was the leader. Obviously, C emerged as the leader in centralized networks because the other group members were so completely dependent on C for their information. In decentralized networks, however, no one position in the network emerged as the leadership position.

Group member satisfaction, on the other hand, tended to be higher in decentralized networks for all types of tasks. In fact, satisfaction was highest in the "circle," next highest in the "chain," and then in the "Y." The least satisfied group members were in the "star" network. The reason for the greater satisfaction in the decentralized networks was that members of those networks could participate in finding problem solutions. The only highly satisfied member of the centralized networks was the person at position "C," who played an active leadership role.

These experiments have many implications for the relationships between organizational structure and communication. For example, an organization with mostly routine, simple tasks would seem to work most efficiently with a formally centralized communication network, whereas more complicated tasks seem to call for decentralization. Also, the emergence of the person in the most centralized position as the leader reinforces the idea that access to information is an important source of power in organizations.

Communication-network design and implementation remains a fruitful area of research in terms of both managerial behavior and the availability of new technology. Chapter 21 will return to some of these issues in greater detail.

Vertical Communication

vertical communication Any communication that moves up or down the chain of command.

COORDINATED RESOURCE

For a good film on developing listening skills, see "Power of Listening," available from CRM McGraw-Hill, P.O. Box 641, Del Mar, California 92014.

Vertical communication consists of communication up and down the organization's chain of command. Downward communication starts with top management and flows down through management levels to line workers and nonsupervisory personnel. The major purposes of downward communication are to advise, inform, direct, instruct, and evaluate subordinates and to provide organization members with information about organizational goals and policies.

The main function of upward communication is to supply information to the upper levels about what is happening at the lower levels. This type of communication includes progress reports, suggestions, explanations, and requests for aid or decisions.[33]

Problems of Vertical Communication. Downward communication is likely to be filtered, modified, or halted at each level as managers decide what should be passed down to their subordinates. Upward communication is likely to be filtered, condensed, or altered by middle managers who see it as part of their job to protect upper management from nonessential data originating at the lower levels.[34] In addition, middle managers may keep information that would reflect unfavorably on them from reaching their superiors. Thus, vertical communication is often at least partially inaccurate or incomplete.

The importance to an organization of vertical communication was emphasized by a survey of research conducted by Lyman W. Porter and Karlene H. Roberts, who reported that two-thirds of a manager's communication takes place with superiors and subordinates.[35] The studies reviewed by Porter and Roberts also found that the accuracy of vertical communication was aided by similarities in thinking between superior and subordinate. But it was limited by status and power differences between manager and subordinate, by a subordinate's desire for upward mobility, and by a lack of trust between manager and subordinate. For example, some studies suggest that communication is likely to be less open and accurate the higher the subordinates' aspirations for upward mobility. Such subordinates are likely to be ambitious, strongly opinionated, forceful, and aggressive, and consequently are more concerned with defending their self-image than in reaching an agreement or an objectively accurate appraisal of a situation. They are also less likely to communicate reports that may be interpreted as negative comments on their performance or ability. Subordinates are also more likely to screen out problems, disagreements, or complaints when they feel that their superior has the power to punish them.

Even unambitious subordinates will be guarded in their communications if an atmosphere of trust does not exist between them and their superiors. Subordinates

[33]Kenneth N. Wexley and Gary A. Yukl, *Organizational Behavior and Personnel Psychology,* rev. ed. (Homewood, Ill.: Richard D. Irwin, 1984), pp. 80–83.

[34]Michael J. Glauser, "Upward Information Flow in Organizations: Review and Conceptual Analysis," *Human Relations* 37, no. 8 (1984):613–643.

[35]Porter and Roberts, "Communication in Organizations," pp. 1573–1574. See also Robert A. Snyder and James H. Morris, "Organizational Communication and Performance," *Journal of Applied Psychology* 69, no. 3 (1984):461–465.

conceal or distort information if they feel that their superiors cannot be trusted to be fair or that they may use the information against them. The net result of these communication problems is that higher-level managers frequently make decisions based on faulty or inadequate information.

Problems in downward communication exist when managers do not provide subordinates with the information they need to carry out their tasks effectively. Managers are often overly optimistic about the accuracy and completeness of their downward communication; in fact, they frequently fail to pass on important information (such as a higher-level change in policy) or to instruct subordinates adequately on how to perform their duties. This lack of communication is sometimes deliberate, as when managers withhold information to keep subordinates dependent on them. The net effect of incomplete downward communication is that subordinates may feel confused, uninformed, or powerless and may fail to carry out their tasks properly.

Lateral and Informal Communication

lateral communication Communication between departments of an organization that generally follows the work flow, thus providing a direct channel for coordination and problem solving.

Lateral communication usually follows the pattern of work flow in an organization, occurring between members of work groups, between one work group and another, between members of different departments, and between line and staff. The main purpose of lateral communication is to provide a direct channel for organizational coordination and problem solving. In this way, it avoids the much slower procedure of directing communications through a common superior.[36] An added benefit of lateral communication is that it enables organization members to form relationships with their peers. These relationships are an important part of employee satisfaction.[37]

A significant amount of lateral communication occurs outside the chain of command. Such lateral communication often occurs with the knowledge, approval, and encouragement of superiors who understand that lateral communication often relieves their communication burden and also reduces inaccuracy by putting relevant people in direct contact with each other.[38]

Another type of *informal communication,* not officially sanctioned, is the grapevine. The grapevine in organizations is made up of several informal communication networks that overlap and intersect at a number of points—that is, some well-informed individuals are likely to belong to more than one informal network. Grapevines show admirable disregard for rank or authority and may link organization members in any combination of directions—horizontal, vertical, and diagonal. As Keith Davis puts it, the grapevine "flows around water coolers, down hallways, through lunch rooms, and wherever people get together in groups."[39] The grapevine should not be confused with legitimate information that management seeks to transmit by word of mouth. However, when such information is transmitted by word of mouth, people at the lowest level of the organization are least likely to receive it accurately. For this reason, managers who wish to ensure that the lowest level employees receive certain information often communicate in writing.

In addition to its social and informal communication functions, the grapevine has several work-related functions as well. For example, although the grapevine is hard to

---

[36] Wexley and Yukl, *Organizational Behavior and Personnel Psychology,* pp. 82–83.

[37] See also Robert E. Kaplan, "Trade Routes: The Manager's Network of Relationships," *Organizational Dynamics* 12, no. 4 (1984):38–52; and Eric M. Eisenberg, Peter R. Monge, and Katherine I. Miller, "Involvement in Communication Networks as a Predictor of Organizational Commitment," *Human Communication Research* 10, no. 2 (1983):179–201.

[38] See Richard L. Simpson, "Vertical and Horizontal Communication in Formal Organizations," *Administrative Science Quarterly* 4, no. 2 (1959):188–196.

[39] Keith Davis, "Grapevine Communication Among Lower and Middle Managers," *Personnel Journal* 48, no. 4 (1969), pp. 269–272.

control with any revision, it is often much faster in operation than formal communication channels. Managers may use it to distribute information through planned "leaks" or judiciously placed "just-between-you-and-me" remarks.

grapevine chain The various paths through which informal communication is passed through an organization; includes the "single-strand," "gossip," "probability," and "cluster" chains.

Keith Davis, who has extensively studied grapevines in organizations, has identified four possible types of **grapevine chains.**[40] (See Figure 17-3.) In the "single-strand" chain, person A tells something to person B, who tells it to person C, and so on down the line. This chain is least accurate at passing on information. (It is the equivalent of the chain in the "telephone" game we described at the beginning of the chapter.) In the "gossip" chain, one person seeks out and tells everyone the information he or she has obtained. This chain is often used when information of an interesting but non-job-related nature is being conveyed. In the "probability" chain, individuals are indifferent about whom they offer information to; they tell people at random, and those people in turn tell others at random. This chain is likely to be used when the information is mildly interesting but insignificant. In the "cluster" chain, person A conveys the information to a few selected individuals; some of those individuals then inform a few selected others.

Davis believes that the cluster chain is the dominant grapevine pattern in organizations: Usually, only a few individuals, called "liaison individuals," pass on the information they have obtained, and they are likely to do so only to individuals they trust or from whom they would like favors. They are most likely to pass on information that is interesting to them, job-related, and, above all, timely. People do not pass on old information for fear of advertising the fact that they are uninformed.

Overcoming Organizational Barriers to Communication

In order to deal with the barriers to organizational communication, we must first recognize that communication is an inherently complex process. For one thing, the

[40]See Keith Davis, "Management Communication and the Grapevine," *Harvard Business Review* 31, no. 5 (1953):43–49; "Communication *Within* Management," *Personnel* 31, no. 3 (November 1954):212–218; and "Cut Those Rumors Down to Size," *Supervisory Management,* June 1975, pp. 2–6.

FIGURE 17-3 TYPES OF GRAPEVINE CHAINS

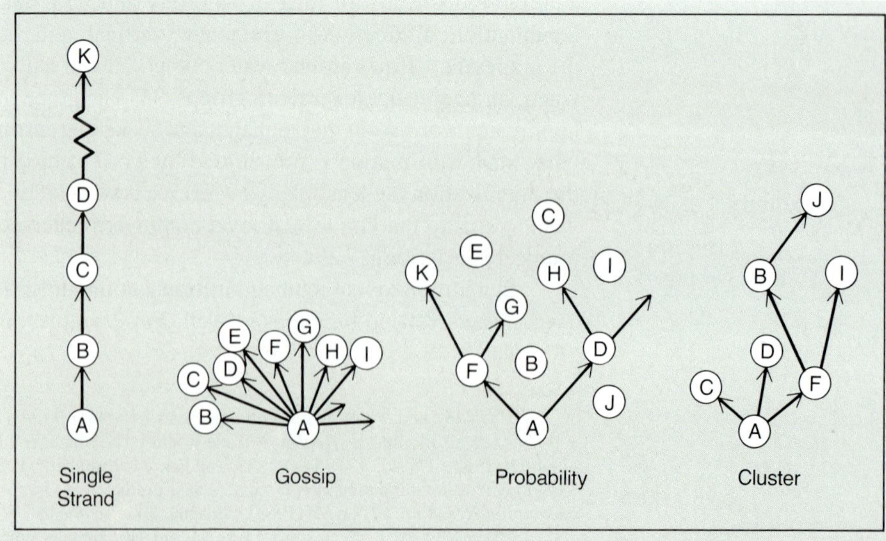

Source: Reprinted by permission of the *Harvard Business Review.* An exhibit from "Management Communication and the Grapevine" by Keith Davis (September–October 1953). Copyright © 1953 by the President and Fellows of Harvard College; all rights reserved.

HERE'S AN EXAMPLE

The Baby Bells (the seven regional telephone companies spun off from AT&T's divestiture) are having major identity problems. Says one of the advertising managers of Denver-based US West, Inc., "Becoming a household name is very tough . . . It takes a tremendous amount of dollars." (*Wall Street Journal*, 5/10/88, p. 41)

verbal and visual symbols we use to describe reality are far from precise. A simple word like "job," for example, can be applied to anything from a child's newspaper route to the presidency of the United States. Words like "achievement," "effectiveness," and "responsibility" are even more vague. This imprecision of language (and gestures) is one reason that perfect communication is difficult, if not impossible, to achieve.

Another reason that communication is inherently difficult is that human beings perceive and interpret reality based on their individual backgrounds, needs, emotions, values, and experiences. A production manager's memo to supervisors asking for figures on absenteeism will be seen as a legitimate request by one supervisor and as unnecessary meddling by another; a manager's instructions may seem coldly formal to some subordinates and appropriately polite to others; a quarterly report may be clear to one superior and confusing to another. Some writers, in fact, believe that most organizational barriers to communication are based on differences in the way people interpret the communications they receive.[41]

HERE'S AN EXAMPLE

General Motors' Saturn Unit has been searching for its "communications partners," ad agencies who will handle the new car's advertising. Prospective agencies were not judged on proposed ads but on strategic thinking, enthusiasm, and compatibility with Saturn. (*Wall Street Journal*, 5/3/88, p. 33)

Comprehending the innate barriers to communication and taking steps to minimize them are therefore the first steps toward improving a manager's ability to communicate effectively. For example, making explicit as many relevant aspects of a situation as possible will probably lead to a more effective and meaningful communication: A memo to members of the quality control department about the need to adjust inspection standards, for example, will usually be better received if it states the practical reasons for the changes (such as an increased marketing emphasis on the organization's ability to deliver high-quality products). Such a memo will sound less like an autocratic directive and more like a frank request from one person to another. Similarly, the manager should not assume that information left out of a communication will be known to the receiver. For example, a manager providing instructions should first check to see if the subordinates understand the specialized terms likely to be used. The manager should also remember that some words may have meanings to the receiver different from those the manager intends.

In recent years, the idea that the physical layout of the workplace can influence an organization's communication patterns, and in turn its culture and policies, has attracted increasing interest. An open office layout, in which everyone has direct access to everyone else, will result in one type of interpersonal interaction; linear corridors of rooms will result in a different type. Thus, the design of a company's work spaces can be used to foster or inhibit such characteristics as creativity, privacy, and direct face-to-face interactions.[42]

Communication and Advanced Information Technology

FOR DISCUSSION

How are new information technologies changing organizational communications?

The growing use of computers has dramatically altered many aspects of organizational activity. Innovations such as corporate electronic mail and teleconferencing are not yet the norm in all offices, but it appears that computer-mediated techniques will soon be used routinely for communication both within and between organizations.[43]

Increasingly, computers are used not just to gather, store, and process data but also to serve as communication centers for distributing numerical data and textual information throughout an organization.[44] In industry, a number of organizations have

---

[41]Raymond V. Lesikar, *Business Communication: Theory and Application,* 5th ed. (Homewood, Ill.: Richard D. Irwin, 1984), pp. 20–22.

[42]Fritz Steele, "The Ecology of Executive Teams: A New View of the Top," *Organizational Dynamics* 11, no. 4 (1983):65–78.

[43]See Elaine B. Kerr and Starr Roxanne Hiltz, *Computer-Mediated Communication Systems* (New York: Academic Press, 1982); and Robert Johansen and Christine Bullen, "What to Expect from Teleconferencing," *Harvard Business Review* 62, no. 2 (1984):164–174.

[44]J. F. Rockart and M. S. Scott Morton, "Implications of Changes in Information Technology for Corporate Strategy," *Interfaces* 14, no. 1 (1984):87.

INTERNATIONAL MANAGEMENT

COMMUNICATION IN AN INCREASINGLY GLOBAL ECONOMY

Here is a simple question that raises the issue of *cultural relativism*—the principle that it is unfair to judge the standards of one culture by those of another: Do the Japanese and the Chinese value teamwork equally as a managerial approach to encouraging productivity? One Chinese manager responded to this question in terms of the following parable: One Chinese worker can carry two buckets of water; two Chinese workers will carry one bucket; three Chinese workers will probably end up carrying no water at all. This answer has at least one clear implication for assessing the influence of cultural differences on worker motivation: The Chinese appear to be much more individually motivated than the Japanese, whose organizational structures reflect the highly group-oriented motivations of the culture as a whole.

Such differences, paradoxically, become both more pronounced and more important when we are reminded of the interdependence of global business activities. For example, more and more countries are investing in the U.S. economy, and Americans themselves work not only for U.S.-based multinational corporations all over the world but for a variety of foreign interests located in this country. By 1988, approximately 3 million Americans worked for foreign-owned businesses, with a concentration of these jobs in the states of California, New York, Texas, New Jersey, and Pennsylvania.

Communication difficulties, both verbal and nonverbal, become a good deal more complicated as the commercial community becomes more international in scope, and awareness of another culture's manners, language, customs, and values—and thus of its management approaches and business priorities—is essential to effective communication in a global business environment. Unfortunately, however, sociological studies show that Americans tend to be rather *ethnocentric*—that is, prone to judging the standards of other cultures by their own—in their attitudes toward foreign business cultures. Even if we do not communicate as well as we should in the practical interest of international cooperation, we do tend to communicate our penchant for ethnocentric thinking, and the result is usually the loss of both prestige and business.

electronic mail Data and text circulated through interlinked computers.

video conferencing Meetings held via telecommunications, usually by satellite television transmission, rather than by face-to-face contact.

begun to provide economic forecasts, competitive information, facts on different types of markets, and other data; as a result, managers sitting at their desks now have access to enormous amounts of information from thousands of sources around the world.[45] By using **electronic mail,** people studying the same subject on opposite sides of the country can communicate with each other. **Video conferencing** allows people who are miles (or continents) apart to be in visual contact. At Aetna, for example, a systems development group located seven miles from its users permits face-to-face communication over a two-way video-conferencing connection. Foremost McKesson, a distribution company, revolutionized its whole approach to business by the efficient use of computers to keep track of inventory and by integrating its computer system with its customers', thereby allowing them to enter orders directly and receive products more

[45]Steve Lambert, *Online: A Guide to America's Leading Information Services* (Bellevue, Wash.: Microsoft Press, 1985); and Rockart and Morton, ''Implications of Changes in Information Technology for Corporate Strategy,'' pp. 87–88.

Consider the following situation and answer the concluding question yourself before pondering the findings of the researchers who devised it:

> On an ocean voyage, you are traveling with your spouse, your child, and your mother. The ship develops problems and begins to sink. You are the only swimmer in the family and you can save only one other person. Whom would you save?

This situation was presented to a sampling of American and Asian men. Of the Americans, 60 percent said that they would save the child, and 40 percent chose the wife. No one elected to save his mother. Among the Asian men, no less than 100 percent said that they would save their mothers. Their rationale? Although you can marry again and have another child, you have just one mother.

Clearly, there are vast cultural differences at work here in the factors influencing decision making. Equally clear is the fact that the Americans would have just as much difficulty in communicating their rationale to the Asians as the Asians would in communicating theirs to the Americans. Regardless of the direction of the communication, it would certainly be difficult for sender and receiver to work out a "common ground" for reconciling their respective decisions.

The lesson here is quite simple: It is not a very wise practice to attribute similar repositories of values and attitudes to different cultures. Multiply the simple variables involved in this illustration by the vast and intricate number of variables that arise when international corporations attempt to conduct cooperative business and you will see why so many American firms have realized the need to initiate cross-cultural training programs for the growing number of employees who will be participating in cooperative international business ventures.

Sources: Brendan Boyd, "Americans Working for Foreign Interests: Where Are They?" *Global Trade Magazine,* February 1988, pp. 19–23; James A. McCaffrey and Craig R. Hafner, "When Two Cultures Collide: Doing Business Overseas," *Training and Development Journal,* October 1985, pp. 26–31; James O'Toole, "The Good Managers of Sichuan," *Harvard Business Review,* May–June 1981, pp. 28–40; and Mary Lenz, "Business Insecurity: Advisors Ease Culture Shock," *The Dallas Times-Herald,* July 9, 1984, pp. 1C, 2C.

telecommuting The use of computers to enable individuals to work at home, sending only the work (via telephone or data network) to the workplace.

quickly.[46] Already, people in some occupations are **telecommuting**—using computers connected by telephone to send and receive work that they do at home.[47]

How does the computer revolution in communications affect organizations and their managers? One consequence is that the form, content, size, and frequency of messages have changed. This has had a strong influence on how individuals and departments interact with one another. Because employees working on easy-to-use computers can complete their tasks without much help from others, they are spending less time in direct interpersonal communication. This is especially true among lower-level workers. It is now sometimes less necessary for managers or subordinates to interact with others to get information—they can call it up on their screens in seconds.

[46]Rockart and Morton, "Implications of Changes in Information Technology for Corporate Strategy," pp. 92–93.

[47]Ilan Salomon and Meira Salomon, "Telecommuting: The Employee's Perspective," *Technological Forecasting and Social Change* 25, no. 1 (1984):15–28; and Reagan M. Ramsower, *Telecommuting: The Organizational and Behavioral Effects of Working at Home* (Ann Arbor, Mich.: UMI Research Press, 1985).

This development has an important implication for supervisors: If computer workers become too isolated, the organization may lose valuable training and knowledge-sharing advantages that come from informal social contact at work. Therefore, special efforts must be made to encourage computer workers to interact with others. This can be done in several ways. Work breaks can be scheduled more frequently. Jobs can be designed so that employees do not spend all day at their terminals. Tasks can be organized so that employees must work in cooperative groups to complete them.[48] Other problems will probably arise as computers continue to proliferate in the workplace. For example, how can a supervisor manage telecommuting employees whom he or she rarely or never sees? Before introducing new technology, managers should try to understand exactly what they want it to do for their communications. They should also try to anticipate problems the new system may cause and eliminate them before they arise, rather than waiting until the system is in place and attempting to deal with them as they emerge.[49]

Openness: A Double-Edged Sword

HERE'S AN EXAMPLE

Until recently, companies have been reluctant to admit mistakes and shortcomings. Communications consultants say, however, that a virtual prerequisite to any apology is a chief executive with a strong interest in communications. (*Wall Street Journal,* 11/24/87)

HERE'S AN EXAMPLE

Industrial companies are having to cope with a new law that says that if they make or use significant quantities of any of about 300 different chemicals, they are required to notify state, local, and federal officials of the type and amount of each substance they release into the environment. Companies are trying to put the best face on bad news. Says an individual close to the situation, "It's definitely a communication challenge." (*Business Week,* 7/18/88, pp. 76–77)

Most managers and researchers like to believe that more open communication means fewer problems better communication. They assume that opening up the lines of communication within an organization can cure many of its problems. Yet Eric Eisenberg and Marsha Witten[50] suggest that openness has costs as well as benefits.

Openness, say Eisenberg and Witten, has three separate meanings in ordinary use. First, it means a willingness to reveal personal information. Some researchers believe, for example, that managers should talk honestly to subordinates about their performance on the job. Perhaps so, say Eisenberg and Witten, but in many cases this ideal may be impossible to achieve.

Managers, they state, "frequently use 'manipulative persuasion' to disguise self-interest, to distort information, and to overwhelm others." Likewise, subordinates try to conceal their own self-interest when talking to managers. These defects, say Eisenberg and Witten, cannot always be overcome, because most work relationships involve people who know each because their jobs require it, not because they choose to know each other.

A second meaning of openness involves a willingness to reveal information of an impersonal nature—next month's production schedule, for instance. As with personal information, however, complete openness may be an impossible ideal, since subordinates would at times be risking their jobs or career prospects by speaking frankly about problems on the job.

Some researchers believe that managers can use disclosures of impersonal information to make the power relations within their units more equal. Eisenberg and Witten reply that not all workers are equally able to understand or use such information. And when subordinates give work-related information to a manager, they may actually be weakening their power, which largely derives "from the highly specialized information uniquely in their possession."

The third meaning of openness has to do with the clarity of whatever information may be disclosed. Several thousand years ago a king asked a fortune teller what would happen if he invaded a neighboring country. The fortune teller replied, "A mighty

---

[48] F. Warren Benton, *Execucomp: Maximum Management with the New Computers* (New York: John Wiley, 1983), pp. 216–217.

[49] E. More and R. K. Laird, "Modern Technology and Organizational Communication Implications for Management," *Journal of Information Science* 7, nos. 4–5 (1983):182.

[50] Eric Eisenberg and Marsha Witten, "Reconsidering Openness in Organizational Communication," *Academy of Management Review* 12, no. 3 (1987):418–426.

A HUMOROUS NOTE

Oneok (one-oak), Inc., a natural gas pipeline company headquartered in Tulsa, admitted in its 1987 annual report that it had major problems during the year 1987. As the report relayed, ''As for 1987, we're glad it's over.'' A good sense of honesty and humor is always welcome!

kingdom will be destroyed.'' The king invaded and lost, finally losing his throne. The mighty kingdom that was destroyed was his own. As we can see from this example, poor communication isn't always the basic problem. In this case, the king had neither the resources to conquer his neighbor nor the wisdom to recognize his limitations. In other cases, a dispute may involve real problems so deep or sensitive that any frank and open discussion could make them worse.

Suppose, for example, that two managers are arguing about whether to give an assignment to an employee whom one of them likes and one of them detests. If the second manager tells the first, ''Fred is simply too dumb for this job,'' his opinion might be resented. Often, it makes sense to step around such problems by saying, ''I have some objections to letting Fred do this job.'' If the first manager asks, ''Isn't he smart enough?'' the second manager can avoid offense by giving another, less insulting objection.

Eisenberg and Witten conclude that managers should indeed attempt ''to create an atmosphere of mutual respect and willingness to entertain new ideas; to share feelings and sentiments when individuals so desire; and to establish . . . a climate of trust and mutual concern.'' But the two researchers also insist that a belief in ''these goals does not equal supporting openness in all circumstances.[51]

ILLUSTRATIVE CASE STUDY Wrap-Up

Communications Failures at Bhopal

The Bhopal disaster is a prime example of the necessity for the pitfalls of communication. Many managers do indeed complain of "communication problems," and as Bhopal shows, the management process is subject not only to inefficiency and frustration, but even complete breakdown, if it fails to plan for effective communication. Communication consists of more than memos, phone calls, and face-to-face meetings, and elaborate systems of "networking." It is a central feature of organizational culture: It concerns what we *say* and what we *mean,* as well as *how* we say and mean it.

As the Bhopal story continues to unfold, it will have different meanings for a variety of groups, and perhaps there can never be one conclusive story with a hard-and-fast moral to be learned from it. There are multiple lessons to be learned from the tragic story of Bhopal—lessons about planning, organizing, leading, and controlling, and the theme of communication will be among all the lessons taught in each of these management classes. (Union Carbide's disaster in Bhopal is considered in much greater detail as a failure in both reactive and programmed planning in the International Management box entitled "'The Devil's Night' in Bhopal" in Chapter 12.) ■

SUMMARY

Communication may be defined as the process by which people attempt to share meanings through symbolic messages. The process of communication is important to managers because it enables them to carry on their management functions. The activity of communication, particularly oral communication, takes up a large portion of a manager's work time.

Elements of the proposed model of communication include the sender, encoding, message, channel, receiver, decoding, noise, and feedback. Encoding is the process by which the sender converts the information to be transmitted into the appropriate symbols or gestures. Decoding is the process by which the receiver interprets the message. If the decoding matches the sender's encoding, the communication has been effective. Noise is that which interferes with the communication. Types of noise include distractions and environmental noise. Feedback is the receiver's reaction to the sender's message; thus, it repeats the communication process with the sender and receiver roles reversed.

[51] Ibid., p. 425.

Communication may be one-way or two-way. In two-way communication, unlike one-way communication, feedback is provided to the sender. One-way communication is faster than two-way and better protects the authority of the sender. Two-way communication, however, is more accurate and leads to greater receiver confidence. For complex organizational tasks, two-way communication is much preferred.

Barriers to communication include such factors as differing perceptions, language differences, noise, emotionality, inconsistent verbal and nonverbal communications, and distrust. Many of these barriers can be overcome by using simple, direct language, attempting to empathize with the receiver, avoiding distractions, being aware of one's own emotionality and nonverbal behavior, and being honest and trustworthy. Encouraging feedback and repeating one's message may also be helpful.

The effectiveness of organizational communication is influenced by the organization's formal channels of communication and authority structure, by job specialization, and by information ownership. The formal channels may be rigid and highly centralized, with individuals able to communicate with only a few persons, or they may be loose and decentralized, with individuals able to communicate with each other at any level. Experiments have found that centralized networks are faster and more accurate than are decentralized networks for simple tasks, while for complex tasks decentralized channels are quicker and more accurate. The most central person is most satisfied in centralized networks, while group members' satisfaction is higher in decentralized networks.

Vertical communication is communication that moves up and down the organization's chain of command. Status and power differences between manager and subordinates, a subordinate's desire for upward mobility, and a lack of trust between manager and subordinates interfere with accurate and complete vertical communication.

Lateral communication improves coordination and problem solving and fosters employee satisfaction. Informal communication occurs outside the organization's formal channels. A particularly quick and pervasive type of informal communication is the grapevine.

Overcoming the barriers to effective organizational communication requires that individual managers acknowledge the difficulties inherent in the communication process. Making relevant information explicit and remaining sensitive to how a particular communication will affect its receiver can minimize some of these difficulties.

The recent developments in information technology have dramatically altered many aspects of organizational activity, especially interpersonal relationships. Managers should attempt to compensate in the work environment for the isolation of those who work at computer terminals.

Managers and researchers tend to believe that more open communication would mean better communication. Yet complete openness may be an impossible ideal, and some apparent failures of communication disguise real problems that must be resolved in substance, not through more open communications. Indeed, complete openness may not even be desirable when a dispute involves problems so deep or sensitive that discussing them frankly might make them worse.

REVIEW QUESTIONS

1. Why is effective communication important to the manager?
2. List the eight elements in the expanded communication model.
3. What are some of the considerations involved in choosing the correct channel for one's message?
4. What is "noise" in a communication system?
5. Describe the common barriers to effective interpersonal communication. How may these barriers be overcome?
6. What four factors influence the effectiveness of organizational communication? How do they exert this influence?
7. What are the functions of vertical communication? How is accurate and complete vertical communication hindered?

8. What is the function of the grapevine? Why do managers sometimes use the grapevine to convey information? What are some possible grapevine chains according to Keith Davis? Which chain is most likely to be used in organizations?
9. How may the barriers to organizational communication be overcome?
10. What are some of the consequences of the use of computer communications technology in the workplace?
11. Why is complete openness on the job not always possible? Why isn't it always desirable?

CASE STUDY

The Corporate Policy Seminar

Bill McGee had a problem. As director of Human Resources at Redbird Manufacturing, a worldwide organization with several thousand managers, he had to sell the Executive Committee on the idea of continuing the Corporate Policy Seminar for a second year.

Redbird's Corporate Policy Seminar was designed to introduce the latest management thinking to Redbird's middle managers. It was one week in length, and approximately 50 managers took the seminar each week. Given the size of the company, the seminar was repeated 40 times during the year. Each week featured five or six outside speakers on various topics in management. Small-group sessions were moderated by senior executives at Redbird. Additionally, key officers and board members expressed their points of view on topics ranging from government regulation to the changing business environment, quality control, and new products.

Needless to say, this seminar was enormously expensive to run. In addition to the outside speakers' fees, Bill had to take into account the huge costs of management time expended in the seminar. However, he had begun to notice some benefits over and above those that had been expected. Because Redbird had done little if any management education before Bill had joined the company two years earlier, a great deal of excitement surrounded the seminar. Second, since Redbird was strictly functionally organized, many managers were meeting each other for the first time. Third, Redbird's many cultures from its worldwide operations were represented in the seminar room, and small-group discussions often took fascinating and quite unpredictable turns. For instance, some managers from the Swedish subsidiary had a very different view on the proper role of regulation than did their American counterparts.

As Bill began to think through his presentation to the Executive Committee, he needed a strategy. Would the committee buy the fact that this expensive seminar simply led to better communication throughout the organization? Was that argument sufficient?

Source: This case is based on a real situation, but the names and facts have been disguised. It was prepared by R. Edward Freeman solely for inclusion in this book.

Case Questions

1. What are some of the benefits that Redbird might enjoy from another round of seminars?
2. How would you structure these seminars to maximize the benefit of better communication?
3. What would Bill McGee tell the Executive Committee? How should he address the inevitable question of costs and benefits ■

CASE ON LEADING
Cookie Wars

David Liederman makes a remarkable soft-and-chewy chocolate-chip cookie. So does Debbi Fields. Some people prefer one to the other.

Cookie eaters who enjoy large chunks of chocolate in a thin, very buttery cookie with just a hint of crispiness at the edges will buy theirs at Liederman's David's Cookies stores. Connoisseurs who prefer a more traditional chip in a thicker cookie—still a bit doughy on the inside—will patronize a Mrs. Fields Chocolate Chippery store. At Mrs. Fields, you are encouraged to buy cookies still warm from the oven. At David's, they won't sell a cookie until it cools.

In 1984, American snackers will spend at least $200 million on fresh-baked, soft-and-chewy, over-the-counter cookies—twice what they spent in 1982 and half what they spent in 1985. Ever since, Liederman and Fields have both been baking big batches of business, but that is about all they have in common. For in addition to having distinctly different tastes in cookies, they have radically different notions of how to grow a cookie company.

Wheeler-dealer entrepreneurs will admire Liederman's franchising and licensing strategy. Apostles of corporate culture will applaud Field's insistence on company-owned-and-operated stores. Automation fans will marvel at David's cookie production system, while the more idiosyncratic will appreciate the flexibility that Mrs. Fields gives its employees. People who appreciate cute corporate aphorisms, such as "Good enough never is," will love Mrs. Fields. People who are embarrassed by them can take refuge at David's.

After a point, greatness in a cookie simply comes down to individual taste. Maybe that is true of cookie companies, too. Debbi Fields couldn't run David Liederman's company for a day, but neither could he run hers. Their companies, like their cookies, reflect the individuals.

Walk toward the river on East 50th Street in Manhattan to a gray, four-story townhouse. In front, double-parked, is a chauffeured Cadillac limousine. Within the house is one of midtown's rare private garages. Ring the bell, and when you have passed inspection over the hidden TV camera, walk through the garage to a two-room office area. The larger room is filled with 35-year-old David Liederman—you can recognize him by his bulk—who is likely to be shouting shorthand into a telephone that beeps more or less continuously through the day. A typical Liederman conversation might be: "What . . . Yeah. . . . No. . . . Tell him Toronto is gone. . . . Yeah."

From here Liederman presides over the growth of his cookie empire. At the moment, it consists of a management office on 42nd Street and a plant in Long Island City that manufactures and ships cookie dough to roughly 150 (and growing) David's Cookies stores. Of the 150 stores, 31 are in Manhattan and are company-owned. The rest, spread unevenly across the country, either are owned by territorial franchisees or are operated by department store employees in such places as Macy's. Four (and also growing) Japanese stores are operated by Liederman's joint-venture partner, Nissho Iwai Corporation.

There is a reason why the empire looks that way, and it reflects Liederman's view of how the business works. It has, as he sees it, two parts: First you have to make the cookie, and then you have to sell it. In both parts, you want to minimize the probability of error. In Liederman's mind, that means either minimizing the number of people involved or, when that is not practical, supervising them as closely as possible.

In part one, you make all the cookie dough in a single nearby plant where you can keep an eye on the process. Then you chill it and ship it to the stores, where all an employee must do is put the dough on a baking tray, put the tray into an automatic oven, and collect it when the finished cookies emerge 7½ minutes later.

Part two of the business—selling the freshly baked cookies—still requires lots of people, and you can't easily manage hourly counter help in Tennessee, for example, from a Manhattan townhouse. So you turn the retailing end of the business over to someone in Tennessee—a franchisee or licensee whose livelihood depends on how well he or she manages.

"Anybody who tells you that the retail business is wonderful and exciting," says Liederman, "is out of his mind. . . . The realities of the retail business in any typical urban environment are not wonderful: the external robberies, the internal robberies, the motivation. . . . A very close friend of mine is executive vice-president in charge of operations for The Horn & Hardart Company. . . . I said to him, 'Define your job for me.' He said, 'My job is to keep my employees stealing as little as possible.'

"People problems. That's why I look for guys like [Cambridge, Massachusetts, franchisee Jim] Bildner all over the country. Because if they're young and aggressive and they want to kill for the business, they'll be standing there, and that's much better than me trying to run a Cambridge cookie store out of 42nd Street, New York City.

"You have to think at the lowest common denominator. One of the reasons we do so well in the cookie business is that a chimpanzee could take cookies out of that bag and more often than not put them on the tray properly.

"One thing we talked about in Japan with my partners over there would be having a totally automatic cookie store. Do you realize there are totally automatic French-fry machines now?"

"We're a people company," chirps Debbi Fields, "and what we're really selling a customer is a feel-good feeling." Liederman would gag on the phrase.

Fields is a wasp-waisted, clear-skinned, 27-year-old, three-time mother with the kind of irrepressible California cheeriness that gives the average New Yorker—David Liederman, for example—a migraine. "That air-head," he calls her when he is especially riled. "She," Liederman maintains, "is really he. Randy Fields [Debbi's husband] runs Mrs. Fields Cookies. Debbi Fields is a nice, good-looking blonde who doesn't make any business decisions at all." Debbi Fields, for his part, wouldn't dream of calling Liederman a name—not publicly, anyway.

At Mrs. Fields's corporate offices in Park City, Utah, high in the ski country 40 minutes east of Salt Lake City, the same phrases keep popping up. "Good enough never is," a half-dozen people will say. "Having a Mrs. Fields experience" is what people there say when they mean eating a cookie. Even chief operating officer Taylor Devine, a mature, dignified New Englander, a veteran of strategic-planning consulting at Arthur D. Little in Cambridge, Massachusetts, discussed "feel-good feelings" over dinner—sober, in a public dining room. The marketing manager was the first of several Debbi Fields executives who said, "We're all high on energy here."

Even for a non-New Yorker, all this happy talk takes a little getting used to, but there is no doubt of its source. "I'm the heart and soul of the company. That's my job," explains Debbi Fields, a woman whose apparent niceness would trouble even the credulous. "Sometimes," she says, "when I'm frustrated or disappointed I think, well, maybe I haven't done enough good things. . . . So I do something nice for somebody and I snap right out of it."

"This sounds stupid," says Randy Fields, 36, a businessman who has made a lot of money in oil, venture capital, and financial consulting to *Fortune* 500 companies, "especially to a businessperson, but she succeeds because she is a good person. I've seen her stop her car and help a little old lady carry her groceries. . . . I absolutely swear that she is exactly what she appears to be."

She appears to be in charge of a company that started in 1977 with a single cookie store in Palo Alto, California, south of San Francisco, capitalized with $50,000 borrowed from Randy. In 1985, the company will by year-end have generated sales of at least $45 million from 300 cookie stores across the country and in Singapore, Australia, and Hong Kong. Each one of the stores is company-owned, and every cookie is sold by a Mrs. Field's employee.

Mrs. Fields, unlike David's, doesn't mix its cookie dough in a central plant. Instead, store employees combine ingredients (some in proportioned containers) that are shipped to the store by independent distributors under contract with the company. Nor are the store ovens automatic. Employees must put the raw dough in to bake and remember to take the finished cookies out. "I don't know how long they bake," says Colleen Clifford, who works at a Salt Lake City Mrs. Fields store. "You just *know* when they're done."

Two vice-presidents for operations at the corporate level oversee six (eventually ten) regional operations managers, each of whom is responsible for about 30 stores. Store managers, some of whom may manage two or three stores, get help from team leaders, selected from among the hourly employees. Everyone but hourly employees attends training school in Park City. Everyone in the company, even secretaries at the corporate offices, gets working experience in a cookie store, and not just at the counter. Stan Slap, one of the vice-presidents for operations, went with Debbi Fields to visit a San Francisco store soon after he joined the company. "We went in. Everything looked fine, but people were really busy, so Debbi said, 'What can I do to help?' The manager said, 'Well, the back room is a mess.' So Debbi and I spent the next two hours on our hands and knees cleaning the back room."

Before being hired by Mrs. Fields, candidates get the customary interview. In addition, they frequently get auditions before audiences of other candidates and employees. Natural hams have a leg up on competing job applicants. "We want people to be outrageous," Fields says. "We want people to be themselves. . . . We don't tell people that they have to be pleasant. We tell them that we want them to have fun. We tell them that they have to greet customers. We don't tell them how they have to greet customers." At a San Francisco Mrs. Fields, Chrissy Woodward sometimes attracts people by tossing out free cookies, then leading the assembled crowd in Mrs. Fields cheers.

Chrissy: And how MANY do you buy?
Crowd: A DOZEN!
Chrissy: Oooh-wee.
Crowd: OOOH-WEE!

A daily profit-and-loss statement is generated for every store, but store managers do not see them. "Store managers can't be profit-driven," says Randy Fields. "They have to be driven by sales and by making people happy. If they had access to the P&L, would they take the cookies off the rack after two hours?" Two hours is as long as a Mrs. Fields cookie is supposed to remain unsold. (At David's the advertised limit is 12 hours, but while Mrs. Fields promotes its warm cookies, recall that a David's cookie is a cool cookie.)

"Mrs. Fields cookies," says Debbi Fields, "is an extension of how I see the world. I believe people will do their very best, I really do, provided that they are getting proper support. . . . Sometimes I've gone into a store, and we haven't had soft-and-chewy cookies, and I've shut the store down. I'm known for doing that. They have to be perfect. There's no word at Mrs. Fields for 'it's good enough.' I'll go in and throw away $600 worth of product. I don't think about what I'm throwing away. . . . I just assume that there's been some reason why the people were not taught what the standards of the company are.

"The reason why I know when a cookie is overbaked is because I've overbaked them. I know when one is underbaked because I've underbaked them. I've been there. I understand these things. And therefore I'm there to teach [the employees]. I'm their support system. We do it together, and we start feeling good about what we're doing.

"It's a people company. That's what it's all about. . . . Mrs. Fields is in the business of selling cookies, but that's just what the customer believes. What we really do is . . . we take care of people.

"You say that people come to work for money, and I disagree with that. Money is part of a whole picture. People come to work because they need to be productive. They need to feel like they are successful in whatever they do. . . . Money is not the issue. I don't know if giving them stock in the company would change anything.

"I'm not brilliant. I am *not* brilliant. But I do understand one thing, and that is feelings, and emotion, and caring. You know, everybody likes to be made to feel special and important. They like to be acknowledged. That's my real role. To make people feel important and to create an opportunity for them. That's really my role as the cookie president, the cookie person.

"I know what I am really good at. I make great cookies; that I really do well. And I'm really good at dealing with people. So I fulfill my needs every day, because I do what I like to do. But there are some things that I am just not a whiz kid at. I am not great with numbers. And so I thought, well, understanding my limitations, I need superstars. . . . I have surrounded myself with superstars. And they know it. . . . I do rely on Randy's expertise with numbers because he's so good at it. . . . I would be foolish not to."

David's and Mrs. Fields compete, but not head-to-head—yet. The market for high-quality, premium-price, over-the-counter, hand-dropped, soft-and-chewy cookies is too big and growing too fast. "We're in a race," Liederman says, "but we're both going to win. It's comical to me that all we're both doing is selling pretty good cookies—in my case very good cookies, in her case pretty good cookies. . . .

"The problem with the cookie business is that there are four companies that are all trying to be the McDonald's. Which is not to say that Wendy's and Burger King don't make a living, but to be the clear-cut leader you have to have stores, outlets, and there's not a cookie company in the United States that has more than 160 now. By way of comparison, Baskin-Robbins has 3,200 stores. There are nine domestic ice-cream companies that have more than 300 stores. The cookie business is just starting, and we're all running around like chickens with our heads cut off picking up one location at a time. At the rate we're going, its highly conceivable that [David's] could have more stores in Japan than in the United States, which doesn't mean we won't be doing well in the United States, but it does mean that we will not have been able to get the big deal. We're talking about 7-Eleven or maybe a supermarket chain that can open up 300, 400, 500 outlets at once."

"Oh," says Debbi Fields, "you're going to ask me those questions like . . . See, that's one of the reasons I don't read those corporate-strategy books. Most people will ask me, 'Aren't cookies a fad? Isn't there a saturation point? Isn't there a product life cycle?' I think that's all baloney. My view of the market is quite simply: Are our cookies incredibly fabulous? Yes. Do they make people happy? Yes. Are they as good as homemade? In my opinion, yes. Do people love to eat them? Yes. Are they going to give up the things they love to eat? I think that's very doubtful. . . . I mean, really, if something is fresh, warm, and wonderful and it makes you feel good, are you going to stop buying cookies? You grew up with cookies. Your mom made you cookies."

Both companies are opening more stores. Each had twice as many outlets by the end of 1985 as it did in early 1984, even without Liederman's "big deal." Unlike American steel and automobiles, American cookies sell well overseas. "My Japanese partner wants the whole Far East perimeter," says Liederman. They want to buy a few franchises in Oregon, open up western Canada. 'And while we're at it,' they say, 'why not sell us a couple of stores in New York.' You don't have to be a brain surgeon to see that sooner or later I'll be learning to speak Japanese, and I'm not sure I want that right now.

"You know what? There's still no plan. The plan is I want to get hundreds of stores open . . . and to maintain controlling interest in the company. How do we get there? I don't have the answer to that. Maybe I should marry Debbi Fields."

Source: Reprinted with permission, *Inc.* magazine, July 1984. Copyright © 1984 by Inc. Publishing Company, 38 Commercial Wharf, Boston, Mass. 02110.

Case Questions

1. What are the main differences in leadership style between David Liederman and Debbi Fields?
2. What is the relationship between leadership style and organizational structure in the two companies?
3. How are employees motivated in Liederman's company? In Fields's?
4. How are interpersonal and organizational communications handled in each company?
5. Is Debbi Fields really the leader of her company? Does Liederman face threats to this business that Fields does not? Why?
6. In your opinion, which company will ultimately be more successful? ■

Stanton McDonald-Wright, *Abstraction on Spectrum (Organization 5)*. 1914–1917. Oil on canvas, 30⅛ x 24³⁄₁₆". Des Moines Art Center. Coffin Fine Arts Trust Fund. Using the basic form of the circle as representative of the color wheel, Wright imposes abstract but formal control upon a dynamic spectrum of lively shapes and colors.

18

EFFECTIVE CONTROL

Upon completing this chapter you should be able to:

1. Explain why the control function is necessary.
2. Describe the link between planning and controlling.
3. State why managers need to find the right degree of control.
4. Describe the four different types of control methods.
5. Describe the steps in the control process.
6. Summarize the issues that managers have to deal with in designing a control system.
7. Explain the importance of "key-performance areas" and "strategic-control points."
8. Describe the characteristics of effective control systems.

Chapter Outline

The Meaning of Control
The Importance of Control
Types of Control Methods
Design of the Control Process
Characteristics of Effective Control Systems

ILLUSTRATIVE CASE STUDY Introduction

An Experiment in Integrative Control at GenCorp

In the early 1970s, American managers were relatively secure in their economic worldview. American management approaches were working well, and business environments, both internal and external, were under control. However, the gradually changing business environment of the United States itself, in addition to increased competition from countries ranging from Japan to West Germany to Canada, began to promote an atmosphere in which U.S. firms, were forced to reexamine the management of their control functions. Control in most American firms had traditionally been based on a hierarchical model, according to which virtually all decisions concerning financial, personnel, marketing, customer relations, investment strategies, and other areas of business activity were almost solely the province of top management. However, turbulent changes to many companies' fortunes have caused managers to rethink the role and function of control and the means by which it could be integrated with the other management functions of leading, planning, and organizing.

In looking for new approaches to control, firms such as GenCorp, an Akron, Ohio, automotive parts manufacturer, adopted what is termed *Kaizen.* Seen by some as the single most important strategy in Japanese management, *Kaizen* literally means *improvement* and generally denotes a continuous process of improvement that involves organization members at all levels. Generally, American organizations have taken a piecemeal approach to the implementation of various Japanese techniques such as quality circles and just-in-time inventory, rather than implementing the highly integrative management approach of *Kaizen.*

For the Japanese manager and subordinate alike, *Kaizen* means improvement not just in the workplace but continuous improvement in personal life, home life, and social life. It also means that ongoing improvement involves everyone from top management to production workers. Elements of *Kaizen* can include participative-management strategies, skill-based pay plans, autonomous work teams, and a multiskilled work force. Control is integrated with the work, and the total management of the organization is shared among the total workforce, which is thus considered during virtually all aspects of planning. As a specific strategy for *control,* then, *Kaizen* is a program to integrate an organization's activities so that the pursuit of its objectives can be plotted and monitored at all levels and at all times.

Sources: Dale Feuer and Chris Lee, "The *Kaizen* Connection", *Training* 25, no. 5 (1988):23–35; Robert R. Rehder, "Japanese Transplants: A New Model for Detroit," *Business Horizons,* January–February 1988, pp. 52–61; and Masaaki Imai, *Kaizen* (New York: Random House, 1986).

THOUGHT-PROVOKER

To whom is management accountable? Who has the right to control the use of a firm's resources?

As a process of managing and monitoring the activities of the organization, the function of control has evolved over time just as have the other basic functions of management. Control originally denoted a tight hold by management on all things relevant to the operations of the firm. Decisions were made at the top and carried out below; as a rule, authority was centralized and planning was the domain of upper management. The traditional control structure was based on the bureaucratic model, which featured hierarchical control through division of labor, specialization of task, and centralized authority structures. However, several factors have prompted American management to reexamine its traditional concept of control. These factors include the advent of the information revolution, the impact of foreign competition, the evolution of the economic base from the industrial to the service, and an increasingly educated work force that has demanded greater control over its own lives within corporations as well as without. Corporations such as GenCorp are questioning the traditional approaches to control and actively seeking control processes that are more fully integrated into an organization's overall operations. Both traditional and nontraditional approaches continue to control various functions within different organizations; nevertheless, the question of *who* controls is changing.

Consider the following case. As sales manager of Data Peripherals, Inc., you must see that each division meets its sales quota. At the quarterly sales conference, Marsha Shore, regional sales manager of the Western division, reports that her division "missed our total sales objective by 8 percent but expect[s] to make that up when we surpass our objective for the next quarter." Then you hear from Bruce Conacher of the Eastern division: "Our figures for the quarter show that we exceeded our sales objective by almost 12 percent."

In evaluating the situation, you first consider the Western division. Shore has an excellent record with the company and a proven record of reliability and accuracy in predicting future performance for her division. Conacher, although new to the job, more than met his objective this time; and it seems reasonable to assume he should be able to repeat his success. You therefore decide that no special action is needed.

Sometime later, you receive the divisional profit-and-loss figures. You are more than a little surprised to find that the Western division, in spite of missing its sales objective, shows a higher contribution to profits than the Eastern division, which more than met its objective.

Naturally, you investigate. And you find the answer: In order to meet his sales objective, Conacher concentrated his division's efforts on large, established accounts, persuading them to place large orders and thereby qualify for substantial quantity discounts. Result? High sales, minimum profits.

The situation is reflected in the next quarter's results, when the Eastern division, with most of its big accounts already overstocked, falls 18 percent below its quota. The Western division, on the other hand, having spent a significant portion of its effort in the previous quarter on opening new accounts, is now reaping the benefit and, true to Shore's prediction, surpasses its objective by over 15 percent.

As in the situation just described, control factors are often key in achieving organizational effectiveness. In this part of the book, we will describe the control methods that managers can use and the ways in which the control process can be made more effective. In addition, we will examine the physical system that must be established to produce the goods or services of the enterprise effectively and efficiently. We will also discuss the role of information systems and computerized information-processing aids, such as decision-support systems and expert systems, in helping managers control their organizations.

THE MEANING OF CONTROL

Earl P. Strong and Robert D. Smith have described the need for control this way:

THOUGHT-PROVOKER

If everyone agrees on the organizational goals to be achieved, are controls necessary? Why or why not?

> There are a number of conflicting viewpoints regarding the best manner in which to manage an organization. However, theorists as well as practicing executives agree that *good management requires effective control*. A combination of well-planned objectives, strong organization, capable direction, and motivation have little probability for success unless there exists an adequate system of control.[1]

In other words, the information in the other parts of this book on planning, organizing, and leading, even if such information were effectively applied, is not likely to help managers achieve their goals unless the information on *control* is also applied effectively.

The Link between Planning and Controlling

control The process of assuring that actual activities conform to planned activities.

CLASS COMMENT

Planning and control are complementary functions that serve as cornerstones of the management process.

FOR DISCUSSION

How many of you have had experiences with plans not going right? What happened? Why? What could have been done differently?

A good definition of management **control** is "the process through which managers assure that actual activities conform to planned activities." In the planning of an organization's activities, the fundamental goals and objectives and the methods for attaining them are established. The control process measures progress toward those goals and enables managers to detect deviations from the plan in time to take corrective action.[2] Often, different individuals fulfill the planning and control roles, but they must communicate for both functions to work effectively.[3]

Our example of the situation at Data Peripherals illustrates the link between planning and controlling. The sales quotas represented the standards agreed to by upper management and the sales department; the quarterly sales conferences, during which sales managers reported on their progress toward those quotas, represented one of the company's control devices. In the example, short-term objectives were being met at the expense of long-term organizational goals. Data Peripheral's control system did not detect that trade-off—a common fault in the controls set up by many firms.[4] Additional controls might have required that a certain percentage of the sales target be made up of *new* business. Then, Conacher's concentration on *established* accounts could have been detected and corrective action taken.

Steps in the Control Process

The above definition suggests what control is intended to accomplish. It does not indicate what control *is*. Robert J. Mockler's definition of control points out the essential elements of the control process:

[1]Earl P. Strong and Robert D. Smith, *Management Control Models* (New York: Holt, Rinehart, 1968), pp. 1–2.

[2]Richard L. Daft and Norman B. Macintosh, "The Nature and Use of Formal Control Systems for Management Control and Strategy Implementation," *Journal of Management* 10, no. 1 (Fall 1984):43–66.

[3]Vijay Sathe, "The Controller's Role in Management," *Organizational Dynamics* 11, no. 3 (Winter 1983):31–48.

[4]J.H. Horovitz, "Strategic Control: A New Task for Top Management," *Long Range Planning* 12, no. 3 (June 1979):28–37.

CLASS COMMENT

Guiding behavior is the essence of control, *not* the measurements or reports.

> Management control is a systematic effort to set performance standards with planning objectives, to design information feedback systems, to compare actual performance with these predetermined standards, to determine whether there are any deviations and to measure their significance, and to take any action required to assure that all corporate resources are being used in the most effective and efficient way possible in achieving corporate objectives.[5]

Mockler's definition divides control into the four steps illustrated in Figure 18-1.

Establish Standards and Methods for Measuring Performance. For this step to be effective, the standards must be specified in meaningful terms and accepted by the individuals involved. The methods of measurement should also be accepted as accurate. An organization may set an objective to become the "leader in its field," but this standard is little more than an inspirational slogan if it is not defined and if a system for *measuring* its implementation is not established.

In service industries, standards and measurements might include waiting-time limits, the number of customers served per hour, and the speed or quality of service. For example, to obtain a franchise, prospective owner/managers of a local McDonald's might be required to ensure that no customer will wait more than five minutes for service. In an industrial enterprise, the standards and measurements could include sales and production targets, work-attendance goals, and safety records. For example, the Buick division of General Motors (GM) may be expected to manufacture 2,000 Regals every month. Those five minutes at McDonald's and 2,000 Regals at GM are *quantitative* factors and can thus be measured—that is, performance can be compared to standards.

Measure the Performance. Like all aspects of control, this is an ongoing, repetitive process, with the actual frequency of measurements being dependent on the type of activity being measured. Safe levels of gas particles in the air, for example, may be continuously monitored in a manufacturing plant, whereas progress on long-term expansion objectives may need to be reviewed by top management only once or twice a year. Similarly, the franchise owner at the local McDonald's might be required to

[5]Robert J. Mockler, *The Management Control Process* (Englewood Cliffs, N.J.: Prentice Hall, 1972), p. 2.

FIGURE 18-1 BASIC STEPS IN THE CONTROL PROCESS

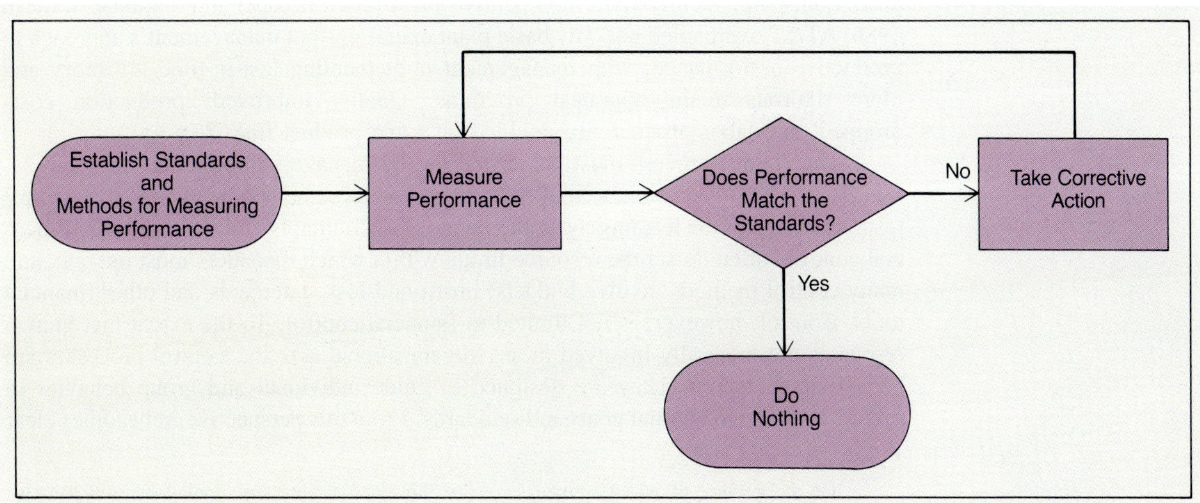

examine customer waiting time on a continuous basis. On the other hand, petitions may be put before the California Public Utility Commission only five or six times a year. Still, good managers avoid allowing extended periods to pass between performance measurements.

Determine Whether Performance Matches the Standard. In many ways, this is the easiest step in the control process. The complexities presumably have been dealt with in the first two steps; now it is a matter of comparing measured results with the established targets or standards previously set. If performance matches the standards, managers may assume that "everything is under control"; and, as Figure 18-1 shows, they do not have to intervene actively in the organization's operations.

Take Corrective Action. This step is called for if performance falls short of standards and the analysis indicates action is required. This corrective action may involve a change in one or more activities of the organization's operations, or it may involve a change in the standards originally established. For example, the franchise owner/manager may discover that more waiters are needed to meet the five-minute customer-waiting standard set by McDonald's. In other cases, controls can (and often do) reveal inappropriate (too high or too low) standards. Under these circumstances, the corrective action may involve a change in the original standards. Performance in GM's Buick division, for example, may cause management to raise the production target.

HERE'S AN EXAMPLE

"Managing success is sometimes trickier than navigating trouble." At SmithKline Beckman Corporation, the large pharmaceutical company, CEO Henry Wendt has found their new-product development lagging after scoring big with two drugs. Says Wendt, "We've been victims of our own success." (*Business Week,* 10/10/88, pp. 40–41)

Figure 18-1 also illustrates another important point—namely, that control is a dynamic process. Unless managers see the control process through to its conclusion, they are merely monitoring performance rather than exercising control. The emphasis should always be on devising constructive ways to bring performance up to standard, rather than merely identifying past failures.

For example, providing incentives has proved to be effective in improving performance and meeting standards. In several joint ventures undertaken by American and Japanese automobile manufacturers—GM-Toyota, Chrysler-Mitsubishi, Ford-Mazda—the introduction of team-management programs and the effort to adjust the social needs of employees to the technological demands made upon efficient production methods have served as effective incentives.At both its GM-Toyota plant in California and its new Saturn facility in Tennessee, GM has integrated the team-management approach as a means of restructuring its overall approach to the problem of managing performance. Similarly, AT&T has adopted the perspective that rethinking management's approach to performance standards can constitute a constructive means of both raising standards and generating appropriate performance. In setting out to make its Shreveport, Louisiana, facility more competitive on a much broader international scale in 1986, AT&T overhauled not only basic plant operations but management's approach to productive performance, with management implementing just-in-time inventory and more rigorous quality-appraisal programs. Quality improved, production costs dropped, and labor productivity doubled on some product lines.[6]

The control process must be carried out by managers throughout the organization. Because of the prominence of financial controls, some people assume that control responsibility can be left largely in the hands of accountants and comptrollers. Financial controls often do set the resource limits within which managers must operate; and many control methods involve budgets, profit-and-loss statements and other financial tools. Control, however, is not limited to financial control. To the extent that human resources are integrally involved in any organizational activity, control processes are behavioral in nature: They are designed to guide individual and group behavior in accord with organizational goals and standards. From this perspective, it becomes clear

[6]On the instance of AT&T's strategies at its Shreveport facility, see Hank Johansson and Dan McArthur, "Rediscovering the Fundamentals," *Management Review* 77, no. 1 (1988):34–37.

that *all* managers need to exercise control to carry out their activities successfully. Bill Marriott, CEO of the Marriott Corporation chain of hotels, responds personally to consumer complaints as one means of controlling customer service.[7]

The control devices that managers use are often nonfinancial in nature. For example, such factors as absenteeism, employee turnover, sales force or service-system performance, new-product development, plant safety, employee productivity, public relations, market share, and product quality—all important activities at every level of the organization—must be controlled, at least partially, through nonfinancial means. Product quality, for example, will usually be controlled through statistical quality-control methods, periodic inspections, and product testing. Technology is also becoming increasingly common in various control procedures: Computers can integrate manufacturing operations and monitor workpace, robots can be incorporated into assembly-line operations, and numerous activities can be reviewed by means of electronic surveillance.

THE IMPORTANCE OF CONTROL

EXTRA EXERCISE

What types of controls would the following businesses need to ensure they accomplish their objectives: an emergency medical clinic, college or university, automobile repair shop, a dry cleaner.

Control, then, is a very important management function. It is necessary for an organization to achieve its objectives. What factors make control important for managers and their organizations? How much control do managers need to exercise?

Organizational Factors Creating the Need for Control

There are many factors that make control a necessity in today's organizations. They include the changing environment of organizations, the increasing complexity of organizations, the fallibility of organization members, and the need for managers to delegate authority.[8]

QUOTATION FROM A BUSINESS WRITER

"GM attempted so much so fast . . . that it soon lost control of what it used to do well. . . . "—Thomas Moore (*Fortune*, 2/15/88, p. 34)

Change. Even in the most stable industries, such ideal conditions as static markets rarely exist; no manufacturer, for example, is likely to enjoy an unvarying amount of demand and cost, with one year's results largely determining the next year's production. Planning and controlling under such conditions would quickly become both automatic and, more importantly, inflexible—that is, unresponsive to unforeseen changes in the business environment. Change is an inevitable part of any organization's environment: Markets shift; new products and services emerge; new materials are discovered; new regulations are passed. Through the control function, managers detect changes that are affecting their organization's products or services. They can then move to manage effectively—that is, control—the resulting threats or opportunities these changes create.

COORDINATED RESOURCE

For a provocative discussion of who should control corporations in order to ensure they are managed in the most efficient and effective manner, see "The Battle For Corporate Control," *Business Week*, 5/18/87, pp. 102–109.

Complexity. The one-room schoolhouse and the small family business could be controlled on a relatively informal, unplanned basis. Today's vast organizations, however, require a much more formal and careful approach. Diversified product lines and services must be watched closely to ensure that quality and profitability are maintained; sales in retail outlets need to be recorded accurately and analyzed; the organization's various markets, foreign and domestic, require close monitoring.

Adding to the complexity of today's organizations is the trend in some industries toward decentralization (see Chapter 10). Many organizations now have regional sales

---

[7]Donald J. Cockburn, "Another Way of Looking at Internal Control," *CA Magazine* 117, no. 11 (November 1984):75–77.

[8]See Peter Lorange, Michael S. S. Morton, and Sumantra, *Strategic Control* (St. Paul, Minn.: West, 1986).

ETHICS IN MANAGEMENT

ETHICAL POLICY AS CONTROL AT MEAD CORP.

As we have seen throughout this book, concern about ethics has permeated much management analysis in the 1980s. The scandals on Wall Street and at the Pentagon, in addition to the exercise of questionable judgment in corporate activities ranging from advertising to human resources management, have raised many issues concerning what companies can—and should—do to ensure ethical behavior on the part of employees at all organizational levels.

Ethics can clearly be seen as a control issue. Unless employees—both managers and their subordinates—are aware of what constitutes ethical and acceptable conduct in the workplace, questionable and unethical behavior in job performance is likely to remain unchecked. Some companies have adopted an ethics code or manual and published it throughout the company, but this practice is often based on the common uncritical assumption that because people have been given the proper document to read, the company has done its corporate and social duty simply by creating an ethics policy. Instituting an ethics policy, however, is not the same thing as *enforcing* one, and unless there is active reinforcement of announced principles—reinforcement through management practice or through the corporate culture itself—such abstract codes are not likely to be effective controls of actual behavior. On the practical side, violation of such codes may also undermine organizational plans and goals.

To enforce control of the ethical behavior of all its employees—from top management to line-production personnel—management at Mead Corp. has adopted the attitude that although its primary business may be producing paper, the company does not have to be satisfied with a code of ethics routinely issued on its own Find Papers product. Top management at Mead believes that ethics should be a way of life and strives to emphasize it at every level and for everyone connected with the company.

To incorporate ethics into the total corporate culture as an effective and enforceable control for workplace behavior, Mead encourages line

and service offices, widely distributed research facilities, or geographically separated plants. Decentralization can simplify an organization's control efforts, since not all the organization's operations require control by central headquarters. IBM, for example, is experimenting increasingly with divisional control. Paradoxically, for decentralization to be effective, each decentralized unit's control activities must be especially precise. Performance against established standards has to be watched closely so that general managers can appraise the effectiveness of the unit for which they are responsible and so that corporate management can, in turn, appraise the effectiveness of the general managers.

Mistakes. If managers or their subordinates never made mistakes, managers could simply establish performance standards and note significant and unexpected changes in the environment. But organization members *do* make mistakes—wrong parts are ordered, wrong pricing decisions are made, service problems are diagnosed incorrectly. A control system allows managers to detect these mistakes *before* they become critical.

Delegation. As we discussed in Chapter 10, when managers delegate authority to subordinates, the managers' own responsibility is not diminished. The only way managers can determine if their subordinates are accomplishing delegated tasks is by implementing a system of control. Without such a system, managers are unable to check on subordinates' progress.

managers and other workers to spot potential problem areas and initiate appropriate responsive policies. For example, employees who believe that they have observed unethical behavior in a fellow employee or supervisor may make use of Project Concern, a telephone hot line maintained by the company's corporate security department. For the company's 20,000 employees nationwide, caller anonymity is assured. While a more direct approach is encouraged, Mead considers this project a viable safety valve for control on ethical behavior.

All of this is not to say that Mead's approach to ethics in management should be attributed simply to an unusually enlightened sense of social responsibility. In fact, the company's attention to ethical challenges was prompted in large part by specifically business challenges that arose when it began expanding in the 1970s by acquiring other companies. Mead thus became responsible for the ethical practices of management in those firms, and although Human Resources Vice-President Tom Schumann readily admits that "you can't really legislate ethics," he was quite cognizant of the need to synthesize the philosophy of Mead management with that of the company's new acquisitions.

For example, Mead's policies in dealing with suppliers, competitors, and customers require that the company exercise particular care in areas that could embroil it in antitrust litigation. Thus, the Mead legal department publishes an "Antitrust Compliance Guide" to outline appropriate behavior in these areas; all upper-level management and sales personnel are asked to furnish a yearly "antitrust compliance acknowledgment" detailing their relationships with suppliers and competitors. The company's "Guidelines for Proper Business Practices" incorporates policies regarding activities involving relationships not only with suppliers and employees but with government officials who have jurisdiction over the company's environmental protection and employee-safety practices. "We stay squeaky clean," acknowledges Schumann because ethical control is as much a matter of good business policy as of sound social responsibility.

Source: Barbara Jean Gray, "Taking a Stand on Ethics," *Human Resource Executive,* May 1988, pp. 34–35.

Finding the Right Degree of Control

FOR DISCUSSION

What's the difference between control of machines and control of human behavior?

The word "control" often has unpleasant connotations because it seems to threaten personal freedom and autonomy.[9] At a time when the legitimacy of authority is being sharply questioned and there is a growing movement toward greater independence and self-actualization for individuals, the concept of organizational control makes many people uncomfortable. Yet control is necessary in organizations. Today, however, organizational control methods have become more precise and sophisticated than ever, in part as a result of the widespread use of computer information systems. How can managers deal with potentially conflicting needs for personal autonomy and for organizational control?

One way is to recognize that excessive control can harm the organization and its employees. Excessively restrictive personal controls may retard motivation, inhibit creativity, and ultimately damage organizational performance. For example, in the Data Peripherals episode, Conacher's problem could be avoided by establishing a minimum new-account target. Alternatively, management might decide that the situation results mainly from Conacher's inexperience. Instead of adding another standard to the existing control system, top management might offer a more effective training program for regional sales managers.

---

[9]See Peter F. Drucker, *Management: Tasks, Practices, Responsibilities,* abridged and rev. ed. (New York: Harper & Row, 1985), Chapters 18 and 39.

The degree of control that is considered extreme or harmful will vary from one situation to another. An advertising agency, for example, may require much looser controls than a medical testing lab. The economic climate may also affect the degree of control acceptable to organization members. In a recession, most people will accept tighter controls and restrictions; when things are booming, rules and restrictions will often seem less appropriate.

Inadequate controls, of course, will also harm the organization by wasting resources and by making it more difficult to attain goals. Individuals may be harmed by inadequate controls as well; a decrease in control does not necessarily lead to an increase in personal autonomy. In fact, individuals may have even less personal freedom and autonomy because they may be unable to predict or depend on co-workers' performance. In addition, an ineffective control system might cause individual managers to supervise subordinates too closely. Under these circumstances, the freedom of subordinates will be further reduced.

FOR DISCUSSION

How do professors employ control of students?

In establishing controls, then, the task for managers is to find the proper balance between appropriate organizational control and individual freedom. With too much control, organizations become stifling, inhibiting, and unsatisfying places to work. With too little control, organizations become chaotic, inefficient, and ineffective in achieving their goals.

Because organizations, people, environments, and technology keep changing, an effective control system requires continuing review and modification. For example, if an organization's manufacturing or service divisions employ relatively unskilled individuals who are not very interested in their work, its control system might require frequent and detailed quality and productivity checks. But if the organization were to produce the same product or service in a different location with workers who are more skilled or more interested in the work, the control system might require fewer points of measurement, and the workers could be given more autonomy and more authority to monitor and correct their own performance.[10] Many firms, including, AT&T, GM, Harley-Davidson, and General Foods, have begun delegating more control functions to line employees in the workplace.

TYPES OF CONTROL METHODS

Most methods of control can be grouped into one of four basic types: pre-action controls, steering controls, screening or yes/no controls, and post-action controls.[11] The mechanisms by which each method operates are discussed here. In the next chapter, we will examine some techniques for implementing those mechanisms.

Pre-action Controls

pre-action controls (or **precontrols)** Control method ensuring that human, material, and financial resources have been budgeted.

Pre-action controls (sometimes called **precontrols**) ensure that before an action is undertaken the necessary human, material, and financial resources have been budgeted. When the time for action occurs, budgets (discussed in Chapter 19) make sure the requisite resources will be available at the times and in the types, quality, quantities, and locations needed. Budgets may call for the hiring and training of new employees, the purchase of new equipment and supplies, and the design and engineering of new materials or products. The sales budgets allocated to Shore and Conacher in the Data Peripherals illustration are examples of pre-action controls.

[10]See Giorgio Inzerilli and Michael Rosen, "Culture and Organizational Control," *Journal of Business Research* 11, no. 3 (September 1983):281–292.

[11]Our discussion is based on William H. Newman, *Constructive Control* (Englewood Cliffs, N.J.: Prentice Hall, 1975), pp. 6–9.

Steering Controls

steering controls (or **cybernetic** or **feedforward controls)** Control method designed to detect deviations from some standard goal and to permit corrective measures.

HERE'S AN EXAMPLE

Georgia-Pacific Corporation has turned around its fortunes under the direction of T. Marshall Hahn, Jr., who came on board in 1983. He used tough controls and plant modernizations as part of his strategy. (*Business Week*, 8/15/88, pp. 71–72)

Steering controls, also known as **cybernetic** or **feedforward controls,** are designed to detect deviations from some standard or goal and to allow corrections to be made before a particular sequence of actions is completed.[12] The term "steering controls" is a simple metaphor derived from the driving of an automobile—the driver steers the car to prevent it from going off the road or in the wrong direction. For example, suppose the Data Peripherals sales manager had been aware that Conacher was overloading his prime accounts to reach his sales quota. The sales manager then could have put Conacher back on track by instituting corrective action during the current quarter. Similary, if a McDonald's franchise owner/manager is able to forecast a decline in customer service, he or she could correct the deficiency before losing too much business. Steering controls are effective only if the manager can obtain timely and accurate information about changes in the environment or about progress toward the desired goal.

Yes/No or Screening Controls

yes/no controls (or **go/no go controls)** Control method for screening procedures that must be followed or conditions that must be met before operations continue.

HERE'S AN EXAMPLE

The turning point in AT&T's slide was a meeting at a Cape Cod golf resort called by the now-deceased CEO, James E. Olson. Traditionally turf-protectors, the group of 27 top executives finally settled their differences, agreeing to compromises for the common good. (*Business Week*, 1/18/88, pp. 56–62)

Yes/no control, or **go/no go control,** provides a screening process in which specific aspects of a procedure must be approved or specific conditions met before operations may continue. If Conacher had been required to have all discounts over a specified amount approved by upper management, that requirement would have been a yes/no control. Another screening control occurs in banking, when large customer withdrawals must be approved by a senior teller and one other bank officer.

Because steering controls provide a means for taking corrective action *while a program is still viable,* they are usually most important and more widely used than other types of control. Because steering controls are rarely perfect, yes/no controls become particularly useful as "double-check" devices. Where safety is a key factor, as in aircraft design, or where large expenditures are involved, as in construction programs, yes/no controls provide managers with an extra margin of security.

Post-Action Controls

post-action controls Method of control for measuring the results of a completed activity.

As the term suggests, **post-action controls** measure the results of a completed action. The causes of any deviation from the plan or standard are determined and the findings applied to similar future activities. In our Data Peripherals example, we would be exercising a form of post-action control by stipulating for our *next* quarter's objectives that 10 percent of the sales quota must come from new business. Post-action controls are also used as a basis for rewarding or encouraging service employees (for example, meeting a standard may result in a future bonus).

The flow of information and corrective action for all four types of control is shown in Figure 18-2. Speed-of-information flow is a vital factor in efficient control, since the sooner deviations are discovered, the sooner corrective action can be taken. Accuracy is also vital, since corrective actions are based on the information obtained from reports, computer printouts, and other sources. Chapter 21 will present some of the systems that have been developed to address management's need for accurate and timely information.

EXTRA EXERCISE

What types of control measures would you need to develop to accomplish getting an A in this course?

[12]See Harold Koontz and Robert W. Bradspies, "Managing through Feedforward Control," *Business Horizons* 4, no. 3 (June 1972):25–36.

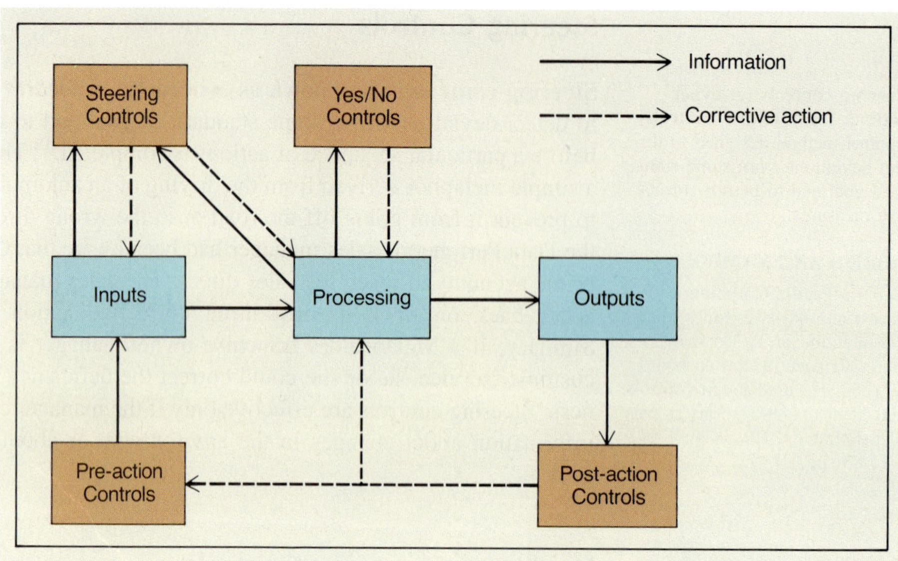

FIGURE 18-2 FLOW OF INFORMATION AND CORRECTIVE ACTION FOR THREE TYPES OF CONTROL

The Importance of Steering Controls

The four types of control we have discussed—pre-action, steering, yes/no, and post-action—are not alternatives, one being the best choice that excludes the others. Rather, they complement one another: Most organizations will use a combination of all four in attaining their goals. Steering controls are, however, particularly important. Just as outfielders cannot wait until a fly ball lands to see where they should have been standing, managers cannot afford to wait until all results are in before they begin to evaluate performance.

In addition to allowing managers to correct miscalculations, steering controls allow managers to take advantage of unexpected opportunities. Deviations from a standard or plan may, after all, take place in a positive direction; by becoming aware of these deviations before it is too late, managers can shift their organization's resources to areas where they will do the most good.

DESIGN OF THE CONTROL PROCESS

In this section, we will expand our description of the steps in the control process. Although much of our discussion will be appropriate to yes/no and post-action controls, our primary focus will be on the development of effective steering controls.

The Control Process

control system Multistep procedure applied to various types of control activities.

As Exhibit 18-1 shows, William H. Newman has provided a discussion of the procedures for establishing a **control system.** We will describe his approach in terms of five basic steps that can be applied to all types of control activities—from monitoring the frequency with which articles are published by professors at a university to checking how often a shipping department meets its delivery dates.

EXHIBIT 18-1 NEWMAN'S FIVE-STEP PROCEDURE FOR ESTABLISHING A CONTROL SYSTEM

1. Define desired results.
2. Establish predictors of results.
3. Establish standards for predictors and results.
4. Establish the information and feedback network.
5. Evaluate information and take corrective action.

Source: William H. Newman, *Constructive Control* (Englewood Cliffs, N.J.: Prentice Hall, 1975).

HERE'S AN EXAMPLE

An organization chart of a drug baron's organization, confiscated by police, looked in some ways like that of any big business. However, the financial division was not only responsible for collecting revenues and making investments, but also for laundering money. An "enforcement" division was in control of bribes, guards, and hit men. (*Fortune*, 6/20/88, pp. 27–38)

Define Desired Results. The results that managers desire to obtain (or maintain) should be defined as specifically as possible. Goals expressed in vague or general terms, such as "cut overhead costs" or "fill orders faster," are not nearly as constructive as "cut overhead by 12 percent" or "ship all orders within three working days." The latter phrasing not only provides managers with a basis for working out ways to estimate and implement necessary procedures, but it also includes a yardstick by which they can *measure* success or failure in achieving their objectives, thus incorporating one of the major steps in the overall control process.

Desired results, according to Newman, should also be linked to the responsible individual. If the objective is "reduce shipping time by 10 percent," one person (such as the manager in charge of order processing) should be given the responsibility and authority to meet that objective. If successful, that person should be given credit.

TEACHING TIP

It would help students to see the control process if you use some examples going through the various steps such as: filling catalog orders, baking loaves of bread in a bakery, getting a term paper completed, etc.

Establish Predictors of Results. The purpose of steering controls is to allow managers to correct deviations before a set of activities is completed. The deviations detected by steering controls must therefore be predictors of results—they must reliably indicate to managers whether corrective action needs to be taken. An important task of managers who are designing the control program is to find a number of reliable indicators or predictors for each of their goals.

Newman has identified several early-warning predictors that can help managers estimate whether desired results will be achieved. Among these are:

Input measurements. A change in key inputs will suggest to managers that plans should be adjusted or corrective options should be exercised. For example, incoming orders will determine the number of items to be manufactured; raw material costs will directly affect future product prices; a worsening in economic conditions will very likely cause a decline in consumer demand.

Results of early steps. If early results are better or worse than expected, reevaluation and appropriate action may be called for. The first month's sales of a new ice cream flavor, for example, may provide a useful indication of its future popularity.

Symptoms. These are conditions that seem to be associated with final results but do not directly affect those results. For example, whenever sales representatives get

"Right, Chief, you told me to go to New Jersey to inspect our plant, and I went to a revival of 'Singin' in the Rain' instead. What can I say?"

Drawing by C. Barsotti; © 1983 The New Yorker Magazine, Inc.

their sales reports in late, the sales manager may assume that quotas have not been met. The difficulty is that symptoms are susceptible to wrong or misleading interpretations.

Changes in assumed conditions. Original estimates are based on the assumption that "normal" conditions, including expected changes, will prevail. Any unexpected changes, such as new developments by competitors or material shortages, will indicate the need for a reevaluation of goals and tactics.

Managers may also use past results to help them make estimates of future performance. In this type of post-action control, performance on a previous *cycle* is used to make predictions and adjustments for the next cycle. As a general rule, the greater the number of reliable and timely predictors, the more confident the manager can be in making performance predictions.

Establish Standards for Predictors and Results. Establishing standards, or "pars," for predictors and final results is an important part of designing the control process. Without established pars, managers may overreact to minor deviations or fail to react when deviations are significant.

A par has two basic aims: (1) to motivate and (2) to serve as a benchmark against which actual performance can be compared. Obviously, a control system is most effective when it motivates people to high performance. Since most people respond to a challenge, their success in meeting a tough standard may well provide a greater sense of accomplishment than meeting an easy one. However, if a par is so tough that it seems impossible to meet, it will be more likely to discourage than to motivate effort. Standards that are too difficult may, therefore, actually cause performance to decline.

Newman has argued that very tough but potentially attainable standards should be established so that high performance will be encouraged even if the actual goals are missed. Peters and Waterman have noted that the excellently managed companies they studied tended to accomplish a similar objective by setting goals that are normally achievable and by establishing the expectation that many individuals will exceed the goals by considerable margins.[13] Both these approaches to setting standards seem to work—*provided they are well understood and accepted by everyone concerned.*[14]

Establish the Information and Feedback Network. The fourth step in the design of a control cycle is to establish the means for collecting information on the predictors and for comparing the predictors against their pars. As we shall see, the communication network works best when it flows not only upward but also downward to those who must take corrective action. In addition, it must be efficient enough to feed the relevant information back to key personnel in time for them to act on it.

management by exception Principle holding that the controlling manager be informed about operation progress only when there is a significant deviation from a plan or standard.

To focus managers' attention, control communications are often based on the **management by exception** principle. This principle suggests that the controlling manager should be informed about an operation's progress only if there is a significant deviation from the plan or standard. The manager can then concentrate fully on the problem situation.

Evaluate Information and Take Corrective Action. This final step involves comparing predictors to pars, deciding what action (if any) to take, and then taking that action. (See Figure 18-3 for the elements in a control cycle.) In the process, information about a deviation from a par must first be evaluated; as we suggested earlier, some deviations are due to local or temporary circumstances and will not really affect the final result.

---

[13]Thomas J. Peters and Robert H. Waterman, *In Search of Excellence* (New York: Harper & Row, 1982), pp. 57–59.

[14]For a discussion of the relationship between goal difficulty and performance, see Edwin A. Locke and Gary T. Latham, *Goal Setting: A Motivational Technique That Works!* (Englewood Cliffs, N.J.: Prentice Hall, 1984), especially pp. 21–26.

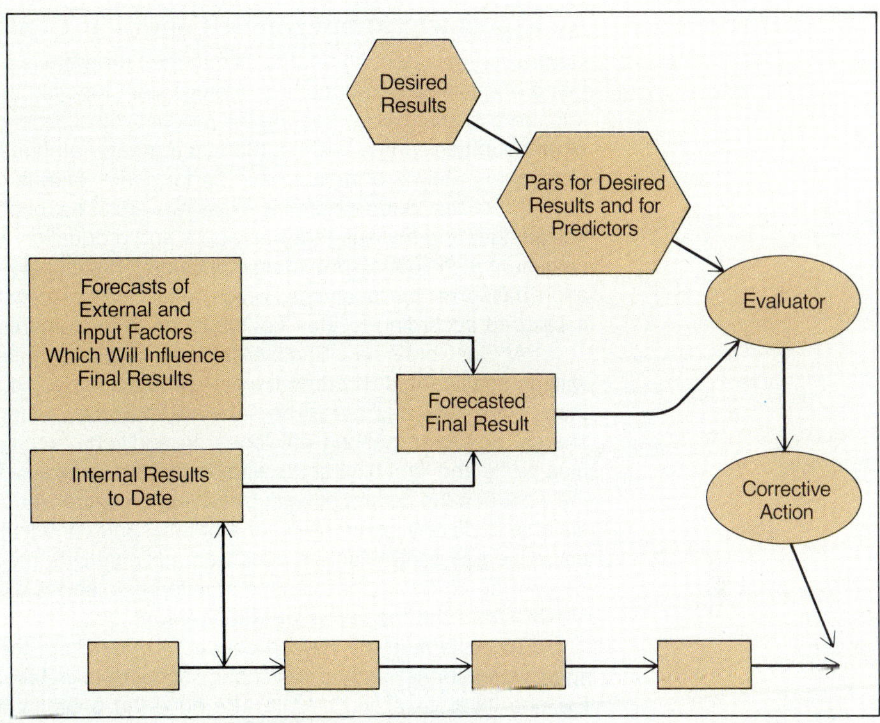

Source: William H. Newman, *Constructive Control: Design and Use of Control Systems,* p. 13. © 1975. Adapted by permission of Prentice-Hall, Inc., Englewood Cliffs, N.J.

FIGURE 18-3 ELEMENTS IN A CONTROL CYCLE

Alternative corrective actions, if they are required, are then developed, evaluated, and implemented.

Key Considerations in Establishing a Control System

Jerome E. Schnee and Thomas P. Ference have decribed a number of important considerations for establishing a control system.[15] Six of these issues will be presented in the following discussion.

FOR DISCUSSION

What are some externally imposed controls? Internally imposed controls? Why are both needed in organizations?

external standard Type of measurement derived from other organizations or other units of the same organization.

Types of Measurement. Most types of measurement are based on some form of established standards.[16] Such standards may be historical—that is, based on records and information concerning the organization's past experiences. Sales standards, for example, are often historical in nature—the salespeople are expected to increase sales by a certain amount each year. A problem with historical standards is that past performance may have been poor; in addition, circumstances may have changed.

External standards are those derived from other organizations or other units of the same organization (such as the company's various sales offices). The difficulty here is finding organizations or units that are similar enough to make the external

[15]Our discussion of these issues is based largely on Schnee and Ference's lecture notes and Newman's *Constructive Control,* supplemented by the authors' experiences; thus, it may not reflect their perspectives with complete accuracy.

[16]See Robert N. Anthony, John Dearden, and Norton M. Bedford, *Management Control Systems,* 5th ed. (Homewood, Ill.: Irwin, 1984), pp. 158–159.

ILLUSTRATIVE CASE STUDY Continued

An Experiment in Integrative Control at GenCorp

Central to implementing an effective *Kaizen* program is a systematic approach to the hiring of qualified personnel—a management function that has become increasingly important to analysts comparing the productivity of American firms with that of firms in other countries. Under *Kaizen,* there is a greater emphasis on the initial screening of personnel in terms of measurable performance than is common in many traditional hiring practices. Such emphasis examines attitudes toward work as well as the skills, knowledge, and abilities that managers and production workers bring to the job. Assessment techniques, for example, include job-simulation exercises and team evaluation based on job analyses, which reflect organizational plans and which can be measured according to their contributions to implementing those plans.

At GenCorp's new Shelbyville, Indiana, plant, those hired must be comfortable with an egalitarian environment where production people and management work as a team. All employees are to be salaried and receive identical benefits, gain-sharing shares, and even parking privileges. In addition, everyone is to wear identical dark blue pants and light blue shirts with button-down collars. The new plant will approach the work and the control of work by having an entire work force composed of individuals able to do any job in the plant. Potential and continuous learning and contribution are valued as control factors over the traditional U.S. model of centralized, hierarchical control, which emphasizes the monitoring of series of plans developed and implemented from the top levels of management.

To implement the *Kaizen* concept at GenCorp, the process of screening prospective personnel is used as a means of control that takes on increased significance. For one thing, selecting people who have the potential to adapt to the approach of increased self-control will be important for *Kaizen* to work. The first step in the selection process consists of a basic screening of applicants, which consists of a "job-fit" inventory—a questionnaire that asks applicants to agree or disagree with a series of statements such as "I find it enjoyable to be constantly learning new things about my job," "I believe it's important for hourly workers and managers to work together," and "I enjoy helping new workers." The questionnaire is designed to measure motivation as well as to present a more accurate picture of what work will be like in a participative environment. In other words, the screening process is geared to locating people who identify with team efforts—and thus to controlling the constitution of the teams that will be-responsible for implementing organizational plans.

The next step for candidates is a series of in-depth assessments, which are usually a combination of job simulations and group problem-solving exercises. At GenCorp, job candidates are asked to assemble a part according to a set of instructions while at the same time computing in their heads the average of three numbers. The next test is group-oriented, with a prospective group of employees given a real problem drawn from the company's history as a test of interpersonal skills. About half of those who go through this practical but rigorous assessment exercise fall out.

Once personnel are selected, training takes on an equally important role. GenCorp plans to invest $1.5 million just to train team leaders to train their teams. A total of $4.5 million in training is anticipated before anyone has operated a piece of production equipment. GenCorp's original team of technicians and team leaders spent two weeks in West Germany, where they helped to build, assemble, disassemble, and ship the equipment that will be used in the new plant. The group was handed $2,000 in cash, introduced to an expense sheet, and instructed on how to fill it out. Although this would be common practice for prospective engineers, it is not at all common practice in assessing and training production employees at most U.S. firms. The *Kaizen* approach is based on the idea that by the time each new employee is fully assessed and trained, he or she should be able to assume the functions of everyone else on the team—a punch-press operator, for example, should be capable of running a personnel department in another plant. After such training, its control over planning and decision making not only instills confidence in the team, but integrates a basic control function over these activities into the responsibilities of the team that is charged with the task of carrying them out.

predetermined standard Type of measurement based on careful analysis of both the organizational unit's internal and external environments.

engineered standard Type of measurement concerned with machine capacities.

assembly-line productivity standard Type of measurement to evaluate effects on efficiency and employee response to new plans.

subjective standard Type of measurement based mainly on a manager's discretion.

standards meaningful. Wherever possible, **predetermined standards** should be used. These standards are developed in the planning process; they are based on careful analysis of the organizational units' internal and external environments.

Engineered standards, concerned with machine capabilities, are often supplied by machine manufacturers. Time-and-motion studies are useful in setting **assembly-line productivity standards**—if the cost of the engineer who will perform these studies will be offset by increases in efficiency *and* if employees are willing to accept the new standards. Even professional tasks that are repetitive in nature, such as some surgical procedures or the drafting of simple wills, may have reasonable time standards set for them. For other types of tasks, **subjective standards** based on a manager's discretion may be established. Such subjective standards become more appropriate as the complexity of a task increases and the application of more elaborate, often time-consuming, often overlapping standards become unfeasible.

The Number of Measurements. The number of measurements must be limited. As the number of controls applied to an individual's work increases, the individual loses autonomy and freedom in judging how and when the work is to be performed. At some point, the individual may see the number of controls as so constraining and threatening that he or she will start thinking more in terms of self-defense rather than performance. Instead of developing new and more effective ways to get the work done or seeking new responsibilities, the individual will attempt to "look good" on those dimensions of the work that are being monitored. The resulting defensive maneuvers may well be at the expense of other aspects of the work not as subject to detailed measurement and control. Managers who do not realize this tendency may well respond to the situation by adding additional controls for the specific areas being neglected.

The problem of "overcontrol" can be tackled in three ways. First, controls should be focused on the major objectives to be achieved, rather than on minor or unimportant matters. This approach is, in part, the point Peters and Waterman make when they observe that excellently managed companies tend to have "simultaneous loose-tight properties."[17] Those companies tightly control performance on a few "core" values and allow a great deal of autonomy, independence, and innovation in seeking the objectives associated with those values. Focusing on major objectives eliminates much of the waste and unnecessary pressures of "control for the sake of control." Second, minor targets can be stated in general terms rather than quantified absolutes. For example, instead of targeting personnel turnover at some definite percentage, the criterion could be to "maintain staff at a satisfactory level." Finally, as in the excellently managed companies, organization members should be allowed considerable flexibility in achieving control objectives. Waterman argues that managers must relinquish control in order to gain control: By granting more autonomy to subordinates who are committed to stated objectives, managers are more likely to achieve those objectives. For example, managers should have the authority to train their subordinates in their own ways—so long as the desired results are achieved.

Authority for Setting Measures and Standards. Performance standards can be set with or without the participation of the people whose performance is being controlled. We have discussed the advantages of subordinate participation in the standard-setting process in a number of places throughout our text. When standards are set unilaterally by upper-level managers, there is a danger that employees will regard those standards as unreasonable or unrealistic; they may then not put forth their best efforts to meet them.

---

[17]Peters and Waterman, *In Search of Excellence,* pp. 15–16, 318–325. See also Waterman, *The Renewal Factor: How the Best Get and Keep the Competitive Edge* (New York: Bantam, 1987).

Flexibility of Standards. Managers must determine whether standards should be uniform throughout the similar units of the organization. Service territories, for example, may be considered roughly equivalent, and so the performance of service people may be measured against a uniform standard. Often, however, allowances must be made for the varied circumstances facing each organizational unit or member. For instance, when service territories are not comparable, a serviceperson's performance may be judged by the past history of his or her specific territory.

Managers must also make a similar decision about the extent to which qualitative versus quantitative measures will be used in the control system. For some tasks (such as envelope stuffing), performance may be accurately and easily measured in quantitative terms. For other tasks (such as research and development activities), both quantitative and qualitative measures will to be needed.

HERE'S AN EXAMPLE

Some companies are robbing the future and making some decisions that are not in the long-term interests of shareholders. Particularly prone are retailing and pharmaceutical companies. (*Fortune*, 7/4/88, pp. 84–89)

Frequency of Measurement. Frequency and timing of measurement depend on the nature of the task being controlled. Quality-control inspection of items coming off an assembly line often requires hourly monitoring. The use of statistical quality control (which is increasing in the United States) requires the establishment of sample size and the setting of an interval between sample testing. Product development, on the other hand, may be measured on a monthly basis, since significant changes are unlikely to take place on a daily basis.

Managers are often tempted to measure performance at a convenient time. For example, they may wish to check product quality at the end of the workday or to evaluate employees only during an annual review period. Such a temptation should be avoided, since nonrepresentative measurements may result. For example, assembly-line employees may be especially careful with the last run of items on the assembly line if they know a quality inspection will take place at the end of the day. Random inspection during the workday would probably provide more realistic measures of product quality.

Direction of Feedback. The purpose of control is to ensure that present plans are being implemented and that future plans will be developed more effectively. A well-designed control system will usually include feedback of control information to the individual or group performing the controlled activity. If the control system merely provides information for superiors to check up on their subordinates, the effectiveness of the system is lost: The people whose actions are being controlled may never find out what is necessary to perform more effectively and will view the control system as punitive. The individuals whose actions are being monitored are usually in the best position to take whatever corrective action is necessary, because they are closest to the activities being controlled.

The Management Application box on the "High-Tech Cookie" illustrates how one organization has established a system that incorporates many of the key control considerations. The box also indicates some ways in which prewritten computer packages can help managers perform the control function.[18]

Key-Performance Areas and Strategic-Control Points

key-performance or **key-result areas** Those aspects of the organization or unit that must function effectively if the whole organization or unit is to succeed in its plans.

Key-Performance Areas. To establish effective control systems, upper-level managers must first identify the key-performance areas of their organization or unit. **Key-performance** or **key-result areas** are those aspects of the unit or organization that

[18]At Frito-Lay's Muncy plant, the SAS system was the primary computer package selected to perform the quality-control information processing and analysis tasks. See *SAS/QC User's Guide, Version 5 Edition* (Cary, North Carolina: SAS Institute, 1988) for a description of the package.

MANAGEMENT APPLICATION

THE HIGH-TECH COOKIE

Frito-Lay manufactured a line of cookies in a medium-sized plant located in Muncy, Pennsylvania. High quality, as defined by moisture and ingredient-content ratios, was a primary objective of the organization. Consequently, management established a relatively sophisticated quality-control program.

First, sensoring devices were installed in the equipment used to produce the cookies. Among other things, the sensors measured the ingredient and moisture content of each manufactured batch of cookies. Data from the sensors were automatically captured and stored in a previously created computer database.

Quality-control personnel retrieved the data on a hourly basis and used a prewritten computer package to organize and summarize the information. A supervisor then analyzed the summary statistics with the aid of the same package. The analysis generated charts comparing actual hourly quality against content standards. Such standards were previously established for each plant by upper-level management at corporate headquarters after a consultation process that involved quality-control managers and supervisors throughout the company. Any deviation from a standard was immediately reported to the Muncy plant's quality-control manager.

The quality-control manager immediately informed the production manager about the nature and source of any deficiency. After evaluating the problem, the production manager took appropriate corrective action. The plant manager also was kept up to date with daily quality-control and production reports.

Source: Guisseppe A. Forgionne, "Effective Resource Allocation through Decision Support Systems," *Journal of Systems Management* 37 (December 1986):26–31.

must function effectively for the entire unit or organization to succeed. These areas usually involve major organizational activities or groups of related activities that occur throughout the organization or unit—for example, its financial transactions, its manager-subordinate relations, or its manufacturing operations. The broad controls that upper managers establish for these key-performance areas will help define the more detailed control systems and standards of lower-level managers.[19]

strategic control points Critical points in a system at which monitoring or collecting information should occur.

COORDINATED RESOURCE

See "Cutting Costs Without Cutting People" in *Fortune*, 5/25/87, pp. 26–32, for an article on some firms that are trying to achieve lower costs while minimizing personnel cuts.

Strategic-Control Points. In addition to key-performance areas, it is also important to determine the critical points in the system where monitoring or information collecting should occur. If such **strategic-control points** can be located, then the amount of information that has to be gathered and evaluated can be reduced considerably.

The most important and useful method of selecting strategic-control points is to focus on the most significant elements in a given operation. Usually, only a small percentage of the activities, events, individuals, or objects in a given operation will account for a high proportion of the expense or problems that managers will have to face. For example, 10 percent of a manufacturer's products may well yield 60 percent of its sales; 2 percent of an organization's employees may account for 80 percent of its employee grievances; and 20 percent of the police precincts in a city may account for 70 percent of the city's violent crimes.

Another useful consideration is the location of operation areas in which change occurs. For example, in an organization's system for filling customer orders, a change occurs when the purchase order becomes an invoice, when an inventory item becomes

[19]See Paul M. Stokes, *A Total Systems Approach to Management Control* (New York: American Management Association, 1968).

an item to be shipped, or when the item to be shipped becomes part of a truckload. Since errors are more likely to be made when such changes occur, monitoring change points is usually a highly effective way to control an operation.

CHARACTERISTICS OF EFFECTIVE CONTROL SYSTEMS

HERE'S AN EXAMPLE

Newly named Senior Vice-President in charge of the Software Products Group at Lotus Development Corporation is W. Frank King III. He's cracking the whip and trying to instill discipline at the notoriously laid-back company. King and Lotus may finally be getting their problems under control. (*Business Week*, 7/4/88, pp. 100–102)

Reliable and effective control systems have certain characteristics in common. The relative importance of these characteristics varies with individual circumstances, but most control systems are strengthened by their presence.[20]

1. *Accurate*. Information on performance must be accurate. Inaccurate data from a control system can cause the organization to take action that will either fail to correct a problem or create a problem where none exists. Evaluating the accuracy of the information they receive is one of the most important control tasks that managers face.
2. *Timely*. Information must be collected, routed, and evaluated quickly if action is to be taken in time to produce improvements. In our Data Peripherals example, the relevant information about sales in Conacher's division reached the sales manager too late to take action during the quarter.
3. *Objective and Comprehensible*. The information in a control system should be understandable and be seen as objective by the individuals who use it. The less subjective or ambiguous the control system is, the greater the likelihood that individuals will react knowledgeably and efficiently to the information they receive. A difficult-to-understand control system will cause unnecessary mistakes and confusion or frustration among employees.

COORDINATED RESOURCE

For an absorbing article on General Motors and the problems it faces, see "Make-or-Break Time For General Motors," *Fortune*, 2/15/88, pp. 32–42.

4. *Focused on Strategic-Control Points*. As we mentioned earlier, the control system should be focused on those areas where deviations from the standards are most likely to take place or where deviations would lead to the greatest harm. The system should also be focused on those points where corrective action can be most effectively applied. For example, it would do little good to control parts quality after the parts have already been shipped to customers. Parts quality is most logically checked while parts are being produced and immediately after they come off the assembly line.
5. *Economically Realistic*. The cost of implementing a control system should be less than, or at most equal to, the benefits derived from the control system. The best way to minimize waste or unnecessary expenditure in a control system is to do the minimum amount necessary to ensure that the monitored activity will reach the desired goal. For example, in most situations it would be wasteful for a sales manager to receive daily sales reports. Weekly or monthly sales reports are usually sufficient.
6. *Organizationally Realistic*. The control system has to be compatible with organizational realities. For example, individuals have to be able to see a relationship between performance levels they are asked to achieve and rewards that will follow. Furthermore, all standards for performance must be realistic. Status differences between individuals also have to be recognized. Individuals who must report deviations to someone they perceive as a lower-level staff member may stop taking the control system seriously.
7. *Coordinated with the Organization's Work Flow*. Control information needs to be coordinated with the flow of work through the organization for two reasons. First, each step in the work process may affect the success or failure of the entire operation. Second, the control information must get to all the people who need to receive it. For example, an appliance company that receives parts from several of its manufacturing plants and assembles them in one central location needs to be sure that all parts plants are performing up to

[20]Our discussion in this section is based on Newman, *Constructive Control;* William H. Sihler, "Toward Better Management Control Systems," *California Management Review* 14, no. 2 (Winter 1971):33–39; John R. Curley, "A Tool for Management Control," *Harvard Business Review* 29, no. 2 (March–April 1951):45–49; and Strong and Smith, *Management Control Models*, pp. 17–18. See also Peter Lorange and Declan Murphy, "Considerations in Implementing Strategic Control," *Journal of Business Strategy* 4, no. 4 (Spring 1984):27–35; and M. Lynne Markus and Jeffrey Pfeffer, "Power and the Design and Implementation of Accounting and Control Systems," *Accounting, Organizations and Society* 8, no. 2/3 (1983):205–218.

par. Plant managers also need to know when a serious problem develops in one of the other plants, since the work pace in their own plants may have to be adjusted.

8. *Flexible*. As we suggested earlier, few organizations today are in such a stable environment that they do not have to worry about the possibility of change. For almost all organizations, controls must have flexibility built into them so that the organizations can react quickly to overcome adverse changes or to take advantage of new opportunities.
9. *Prescriptive and Operational*. Effective control systems ought to indicate, upon the detection of a deviation from standards, what corrective action should be taken. The information should be in a usable form when it reaches the person responsible for taking the necessary action.
10. *Accepted by Organization Members*. For a control system to be accepted by organization members, the controls must be related to meaningful and accepted goals. Such goals must reflect the language and activities of the individuals to whom they pertain. Top managers, for example, typically are concerned with financial performance. At their level, it would be meaningful to relate at least some controls to quarterly financial results and budgets. For first-line supervisors, however, control should relate to such tangible things as hours of work, number of services rendered, percentages of rejects, downtime, and material wastage. In their eyes, controls are meaningful if they provide timely and accurate data on operational, day-to-day activities.

For a control standard to work as intended, suggests Newman, it must also be accepted by organization members as an integral and fair part of their jobs. For example, the necessity to keep costs under budget should be accepted as both normal and desirable. As you will recall from our discussion of joint goal setting in Chapters 5 and 6, when the people who must meet standards have a role in setting them, they are more likely to be committed to those standards. The control system must also be consistent with the organization's culture, or it will likely be ineffective.

HERE'S AN EXAMPLE

A new management problem for employers is the burgeoning activity of shopping-at-work. Sellers of personal products are invading the office. It's an ideal opportunity for marketers but a management problem for employers. Those who haven't decided what to do about it (forbid it, tolerate it, encourage it) will soon have to. (*Fortune*, 2/15/88, pp. 95–98)

Problems in Establishing Effective Control Systems. Most individuals experience at least some discomfort at the prospect of having their performance monitored and reported to others. As we have noted, when controls are of the "steering" kind and when progress toward goals is fed back to the individual whose actions are being controlled, resentment can often be reduced or entirely eliminated.[21] Nevertheless, a number of problems that hinder the effectiveness of control systems seem to recur.

1. Easily measured factors receive too much weight, while difficult-to-measure items are not given enough attention. This problem arises because it is quicker and easier to measure the performance of those factors that can be quantified. For example, personnel turnover figures are often carefully checked, but little or no control may be exercised over whether or not the most qualified employees are being retained. As a result, the control system may concentrate on comparatively minor matters at the expense of more important organizational goals.

2. Short-run factors may be overemphasized at the expense of long-run factors. Long-run results are more unpredictable than short-run achievements. In addition, it is often difficult, if not impossible, to design measurements that can relate long-term results to specific current actions. Customer goodwill, for example, may be an important determinant of long-term growth, but managers have a hard time fitting it into a control system. The long-term growth and survival of the organization may therefore not be given the attention they need by the control system.

3. The control system may not be adjusted to reflect shifts in importance of various activities and goals over time. No organization can afford to neglect such things as dependable quality, assured delivery, new-product development, and the control of manufacturing and selling expenses. But at various stages of the company's

[21]The problems of establishing effective control systems have many similarities to the dysfunctional reactions to budgets to be discussed in Chapter 19.

growth, a shift in emphasis may be essential as one or another of these factors assumes a higher priority in the struggle for survival. In practice, many managers accept the usefulness of existing controls, rather than adjusting them as situations change and new objectives emerge.

ILLUSTRATIVE CASE STUDY Wrap-Up

An Experiment in Integrative Control at GenCorp

GenCorp is applying the principles of *Kaizen* to integrate its approach to staffing and training into both its overall program of measured, steady growth and its commitment to controlled strategic implementation. At GenCorp, the process of ensuring that planned activities become actual activities—the process of control—has been shifted from the top of the organization to the level at which it must ultimately function: that is, to the level at which all employees, managers, and production personnel alike, assume commitment and responsibility for it. The *Kaizen* approach is not a piecemeal approach to managing and controlling people: Rather, it is an integral set of values that, ideally, permeates the total management of the organization. Rather than a specialized function delegated to a specialized, high-level staff, control becomes an overall commitment by all employees to the quality of work life throughout the organization. It has worked very well for the Japanese at home and at joint-venture plants such as GM-Toyota, Chrysler-Mitsubishi and Ford-Mazda. Success at GenCorp may show the way for other U.S.-based companies that can profit from reassessing the role and shape of control in their organizations. ■

■ SUMMARY

Control is the vitally important process through which managers assure that actual activities conform to planned activities. It involves four basic steps: (1) the establishment of standards and methods for measuring performance; (2) the measurement of performance; (3) the comparison of performance against the standards; and (4) the taking of corrective action.

The changing environment of organizations, the increasing complexity of organizations, the fact that organization members make mistakes, and the fact that managers must delegate authority are among the factors that make control necessary.

Most control methods can be grouped into four basic categories: pre-action controls, which ensure that the necessary human, material, and financial resources are available for the operation; steering controls, which detect performance deviations before a given operation is completed; yes/no or screening controls, which ensure that specific conditions are met before an operation proceeds further; and post-action controls, in which past experience is applied to future operations. While all four are important, steering controls are particularly critical since they allow corrective action to be applied early enough to prevent failure or to take advantage of unexpected opportunities.

Establishing a control system using steering controls involves (1) defining desired results; (2) establishing predictors of results; (3) establishing standards for predictors and results; (4) establishing the information and feedback network; and (5) evaluating the information and taking corrective action.

In designing a control system, managers must decide on the types and number of measurements to be used, who will set the standards, how flexible the standards will be, the frequency of measurement, and the direction that feedback will take.

For a control system to be effective, it must be accurate, timely, objective, focused on key-performance areas and strategic-control points, economically realistic, organizationally realistic, coordinated with the organization's work flow, flexible, prescriptive, and acceptable to organization members. These characteristics can be applied to controls at all levels of the organization. Moreover, effective control is equally important in service-based and industrial enterprises.

REVIEW QUESTIONS

1. What is the importance of the control function?
2. How are planning and controlling linked?
3. List the four basic steps in the control process. What are the key elements in each of these steps?
4. What organizational factors create the need for control?
5. What are the four main types of control? How is each type used? Which is most important? Why?
6. According to William Newman, what are the five steps in designing a control system? How do managers go about carrying out these steps?
7. With what six issues do Jerome Schnee and Thomas Ference suggest managers must be concerned in designing a control system? How might managers resolve these issues?
8. What are key-performance areas?
9. What is the ''management by exception'' principle?
10. What are strategic-control points? How may managers locate them?
11. What are the characteristics of effective control systems? Which of these characteristics is most important?

CASE STUDY TRN, Inc.: Electronic Monitoring in the Trucking Industry

"You just can't get on the road and run a truck anymore," Kenny Benoit, a driver for 18 years, said as he finished his run at the terminal of the Kimberly-Clark Corporation in New Milford, Connecticut.

Mr. Benoit's truck, like all 50 new tractors leased from Ryder System Inc., is equipped with electronic devices that monitor the driver. An electronic engine control system by TRW Inc. sets the top speed at 58 miles per hour and the minimum at 53, taking most control of cruising speed out of the driver's hands. Another TRW system records a vast variety of details about each trip, from the number of revolutions per minute—an important measure of fuel economy—to the length of time the truck runs at a particular speed and the duration of the unloading period.

After the 1973 fuel crisis, truck manufacturers introduced modifications that brought down the maximum speed—to 60 m.p.h., from 70 or 75—and thus improved fuel mileage. Most of the changes were mechanical, however. Now, hundreds of trucking companies are testing and installing sophisticated electronic devices capable of controlling and monitoring the driver much more closely. And they report savings well into the millions of dollars.

Besides TRW, the other major developers and manufacturers of electronic devices for trucking are Engler Instruments, Rockwell International Automotive Electronics, and Argo Instruments. Many are developing still more sophisticated devices.

"In the next three to five years there will be a lot of microcomputers put on the truck," said James R. Barr, environmental specialist at the American Trucking Association. The trend will probably be "to take more and more control away from the driver," he said.

Drivers, predictably, are unhappy with the new controls. They complain that it is often impossible to overtake cars. And when they finish their trip, they must take the device out of the cab and into the driver check-in room, where it is plugged into a computer and prints out an electronic history of the trip. "It's like someone riding with you and writing down everything you did," Mr. Benoit said.

"It bores you to death," said Gus Moffie, a driver with the Kimberly-Clark Integrated Service Corporation, a subsidiary that runs the company's fleet of 200 trucks. Mr. Moffie said that "on long stretches of road you don't have a lot to do to keep your eyes open." He added, "The other problem is that when you get in delays you can't make up the time."

But to Ralph Schatz, the fleet manager for Kimberly-Clark, which is the largest user of these devices, they have been a blessing. He said that fuel economy with the new devices, which became available to the fleet in July, has gone from an average of 5.99 miles a gallon to 7.1. He calculated that for each tenth of a mile per gallon, the company saved $85,000 a year in fuel costs.

Jerry Weeks, president of the Kimberly-Clark subsidiary, estimated that a saving of one mile per gallon represents a cut of about 22 percent in fuel costs. Thus, the company, which has an annual fuel bill of $5 million, expects to offset quickly the cost of the devices—$1,400 per tractor.

At Kimberly-Clark, the recording device has not yet been used to confront drivers whose habits may interfere with top fuel efficiency. But the company is using the information on when a truck stops and backs into a customer's loading dock as a means of charging customers who delay a driver. It has been able to collect a fee of $25 an hour for delays. Customers cannot challenge the tamper-proof recorders, Kaspar Tucci, director of United States operations for the subsidiary, said, while they would often challenge the drivers' logs.

Other companies have used the computer printouts to confront their drivers with errant driving patterns. Al Bodo, transportation manager of Royal Foods Distributors in Woodbridge, N.J., one of the Fleming Companies, said the company had set up performance parameters for drivers. After a trip, each of the company's 105 drivers brings in his cartridge, which provides a quick readout on such information as how long he idled and whether he was speeding or going over the revolutions-per-minute limit for each gear.

If a driver has far exceeded the limits, he is given counseling on his driving habits. If a driver still does not change, Mr. Bodo said, "we have taken disciplinary action." These may be warnings at first but can lead to a temporary suspension.

The system has enabled Royal Foods to get a 6 percent increase in fuel economy, from 5.4 miles a gallon last year to 5.69 this year, he said.

Trevor O. Jones, vice-president and general manager of TRW's transportation electronics group, said that the company has plans for devices that could improve the driver's comfort and safety as well as efficiency.

The technology is already here for systems that could control the climate in the cab and adjust the seat to lessen shock and vibration. A power steering assist would also allow a driver to select a steering "feel" from light to heavy, depending on preference.

Other possibilities for which the technology is in place include an engine protection system that could warn drivers to shut off the engine if it faced damage from a malfunction, a radar unit that could warn drivers if they are on a collision course with another vehicle or object, and a device that could warn drivers when they became drowsy.

All these devices, Mr. Jones said, could someday be tied into one system that could feed information continuously to a computer monitored by the fleet manager. The manager could correct inefficiencies, record road speeds, idle times, and fuel consumption, and monitor other data to improve efficiency. However, he added, the costs of such systems, which derive from aerospace technology, may delay their introduction into the trucking industry by five to 10 years.

Source: Adapted from Agis Salpukas, "Taking the Pulse of Trucking," *New York Times,* September 8, 1984, pp. 31–33.

Case Questions

1. Why has the trucking industry found it profitable to install computerized controls in its vehicles?
2. Describe the monitoring and controlling systems in terms of the four basic categories of control methods.
3. If you were a truck driver, how would you feel about such devices? Would they make the job more, or less, attractive?
4. Do you think organizations should rely on self-monitoring by employees in situations like this one? In other types of situations? Why?
5. As the manager of a trucking firm, how would you explain to your drivers why installation of devices to improve driver safety and comfort is lagging behind the use of devices to improve driver productivity?

CASE STUDY Planning and Controlling Growth at 3M

The Minnesota Mining and Manufacturing Company (3m) enjoyed consistent rapid growth during the 1960s and 1970s, and its management was widely extolled. In recent years, however, 3M's growth rate, while still respectable, has slowed. In an effort to re-energize the organization, top management has set itself some tough goals: (1) more than 10 percent annual growth in earnings per share; (2) more than a quarter of the company's annual sales from products that are less than five years old; and (3) a 35 percent reduction in manufacturing, labor, and quality-control costs over a five-year period.

In its 1986 *Annual Report,* 3M issued a statement of its "Strategies for Growth." That statement, along with two key subcategories—"Taking Advantage of Change" and "Controlling the Growth of Indirect Costs"—are reprinted here.

Strategies for Growth. For the better part of a century, 3M has achieved growth and profitability well above the average for U.S. companies. This performance has been driven by building on the company's strengths and by staying alert to opportunity, whether in technology building, product development, manufacturing, marketing, or administration. Today, in a global economy where growth is slow and competition brisk, 3M remains well-positioned for continued profitable growth. This section of the *Annual Report* examines several of the steps 3M is taking to maintain its position as one of the world's leading enterprises.

Taking Advantage of Change. Another key way 3M is driving its growth is by turning changes in the business evironment into opportunities. One of the best examples is the way 3M has capitalized on changes in the U.S. hospital-supply market. Over the past few years, this market has undergone significant changes, reflecting moves by the government and private employers to control rising health-care costs. 3M adjusted early to shifts in the marketplace. The result: 3M's medical-surgical business has grown at double the industry average, with very good profitability.

3M has responded to the market in several ways. It has combined operating units serving common customers and realized important efficiencies in product development, manufacturing, and marketing. It has capitalized on the trend toward industry capitalization. For example, the breadth of 3M's product line—more than 500 health-care products—has helped increase business with most U.S. hospital customers. Another response to industry changes: improved customer service through centralized order entry and inquiry handling. These steps are in addition to continued strong emphasis on the development of products that improve patient health while reducing costs.

3M's ability to profit from change is aided by the company's structure. 3M businesses are organized into dozens of operating units. These units operate with a great deal of autonomy, but also work closely together. This helps ensure the agility and strength needed to maneuver successfully in a business environment where changes often are swift and far-reaching.

Controlling the Growth of Indirect Costs. Keeping 3M's competitive edge depends on the continuing pursuit of efficiency and productivity in all parts of the company. That means finding ways to work smarter and to do more with less. One major effort involves the containment of indirect costs—those not involved with the making, selling, and delivering of a product. 3M is holding the growth of such costs to a rate less than the growth in sales.

Both line and staff units are participating in this effort. In one case, the seven divisions in one of 3M's largest groups—Tape, Adhesives, and Decorative Products—have consolidated their marketing communications activities. They are using one advertising agency instead of five. And they're joining with divisions outside their group in a unified effort to reach customers in such major markets as automobile manufacturing and electronics. As a result, they're getting more advertising impact for as little as half the previous cost.

Staff units also are finding better ways to do things. Data processing is a good example. 3M's Information Systems and Data Processing organization serves virtually every unit of the company. From payroll and accounting systems to the control of manufacturing processes, computer systems are increasingly important. Better management techniques have led to reduced computer downtime, more timely completion of tasks, and a significant reduction in reruns—serving internal customers better and contributing to improved profitability.

Another major effort involves streamlining the corporate organization. 3M is trying to ensure that it doesn't have more layers of management that necessary to do the job and that managers' work is focused on their units' essential tasks: satisfying customer needs. The ability and motivation of 3M's employees and the improved tools at their disposal are making it possible for some units to extend their managers' span of control by nearly 50 percent. That process will continue.

Source: Adrienne Kols and Stephen P. Robbins, *Profiles of Corporations and Managers,* 2nd ed. (Englewood Cliffs, N.J.: Prentice Hall, 1988), pp. 72, 75, 77–78, 79–80. Excerpts from 3M's 1986 *Annual Report.*

Case Questions

1. What pressures for organization-wide controls has 3M imposed on itself with its program to grow by taking advantage of changes in its complex environment?
2. Given its optimistic statement about its organizational structure, what would you expect to be 3M's advantages in imposing controls on its plans for growth?
3. Which method of control is most likely to be of the greatest value in implementing 3M's strategies for growth?
4. In which areas of its plan is 3M best prepared to implement financial controls? What steps has 3M already taken to ensure flexibility in managing its control strategy? ■

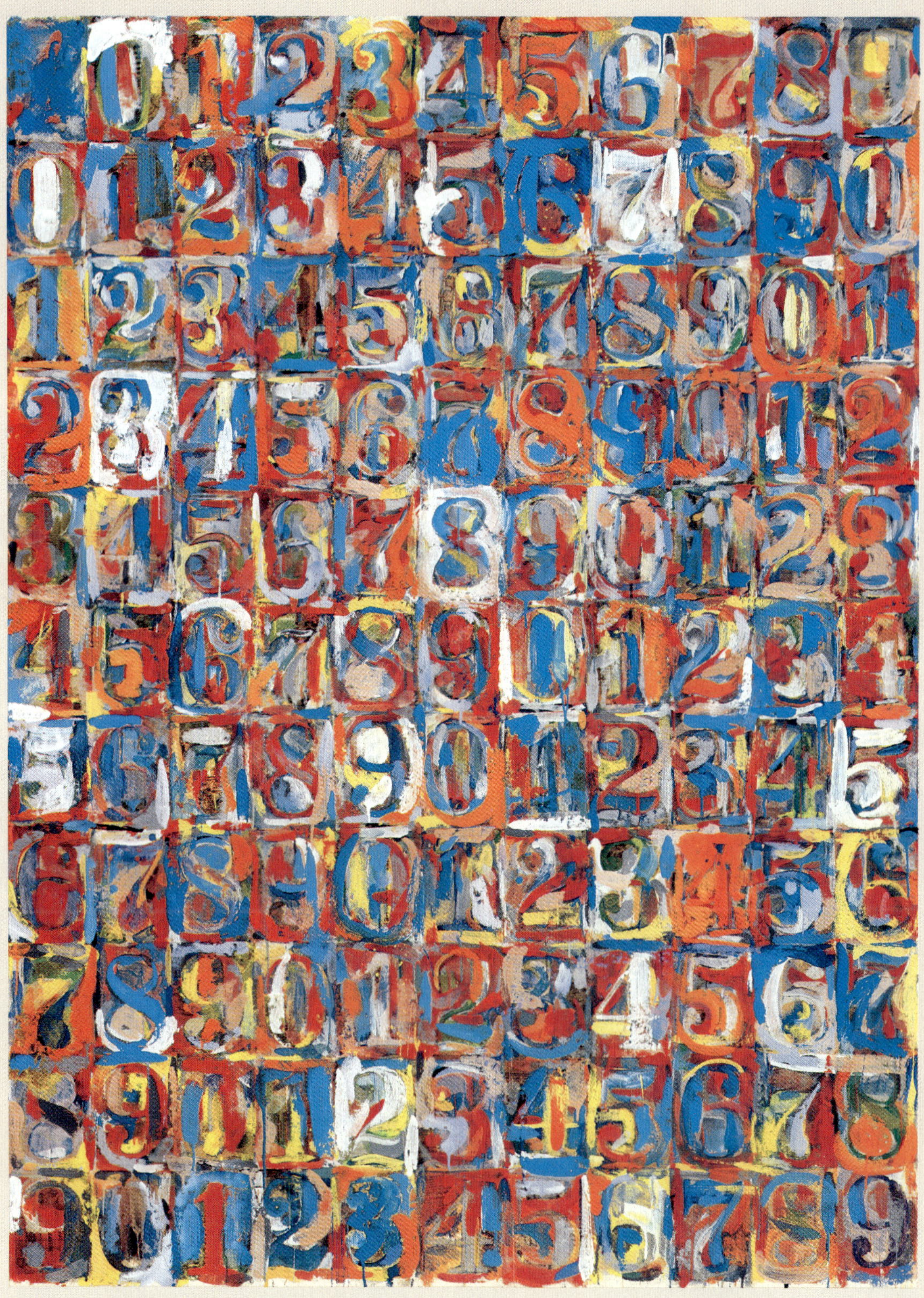

Jasper Johns, *Numbers in Color.* 1959. 66½ x 49½ inches. Encaustic and newspaper on canvas. Albright-Knox Art Gallery, Buffalo, New York. Gift of Seymour H. Knox, 1959.

19

FINANCIAL CONTROL METHODS

Upon completing this chapter you should be able to:

1. State why financial control methods are important to managers.
2. Describe various types of financial control methods, including financial statements, ratio analysis, and break-even analysis.
3. Explain why budgets are one of the most important control devices that managers use.
4. Identify the various types of budgets an organization can use.
5. Describe the potentially functional and dysfunctional aspects of budgets and how the dysfunctional aspects might be overcome.
6. Describe the two types of auditing.

Chapter Outline

Financial Controls
Budgetary Control Methods
The Budgeting Process
Types of Budgets
Auditing

ILLUSTRATIVE CASE STUDY
Introduction

Financial Resourcefulness at John Deere and Company

In the 1860's, a Vermont blacksmith named John Deere invented a plow that could turn the thick, rich soil of the vast and fertile prairies of the midwestern United States. In 1868, Deere, emphasizing a philosophy of quality products and customer service, formed a company to distribute his plows, and by 1911, the company had become a full-line manufacturer of farm equipment. In 1918, with its purchase of a gasoline engine company located in Waterloo, Iowa, Deere became one of the driving forces in the conversion of American agriculture from animal to machine power. Today, Deere is the world leader in the manufacture of farm equipment and has remained a viable concern through diversification (it is also a major supplier of construction machinery), the globalization of its enterprises (it operates facilities in Mexico, Canada, Spain, France, Australia, and elsewhere), and stable leadership (between 1928 and the present, Deere has had only three CEOs). A highly integrated manufacturer, Deere makes its own transmissions and hydraulic components and can thus count on a fairly consistent stream of potential original equipment as a source of additional sales. At its headquarters in Blackhawk, Iowa, a system of 10 minicomputers controls functions ranging from materials management to painting, and energy for the plant's operations is provided in part by its own rubbish.

Although Deere builds diesel engines for GM and works with NASA on the development of metal alloys, its core business remains agricultural equipment, an industry in which Deere controls a little over 32 percent of worldwide sales. It is no secret, however, that American agriculture has fallen on hard times, and it should come as no surprise that any company specializing in sales to agriculture will also be experiencing financial difficulties. "The economic environment surrounding our industries remains difficult and uncertain," as Deere's 1985 *Annual Report* admitted, and the figures bear out this less-than-optimistic summation. Prior to the deterioration of the farming economy beginning in 1981, Deere's sales growth averaged a steady yearly increase of 11.7 percent. Since then, it has declined at a rate of 7.1 percent per year, and profits have dropped at the rate of 41 percent per year. Since 1979, Deere's accounts receivable has risen from $1.4 billion to $2.75 billion, while equipment sales have slumped from $5 billion to $4.1 billion. Concessions on interest payments on $600 million of its accounts receivable cost Deere $50 million in interest in one year alone.

Nevertheless, with control of about 40 percent of the North American market and the lion's share of world sales (32.4 percent, compared with the 19.8 percent enjoyed by its nearest competitor, Case-International Harvester), Deere is committed to its core business of agricultural equipment. Because its external environment is so "difficult and uncertain," subject to the turbulence of commodity markets, environmental trends, and interest rates, it is clear that Deere's prosperity will depend heavily upon the company's ability to exercise control over its internal resources—namely, over the complex factors bearing upon the management of its financial resources.

Source: Peter G. Goulet and Lynda L. Goulet, " Deere and Company," in *Strategic Management: Concepts and Applications,* Samuel C. Certo and J. Paul Peter, eds. (New York: Random House, 1988), pp. 692–714.

CLASS COMMENT

A variety of tools and techniques are available for helping managers make controlling decisions.

No single, unified method of control has ever been devised for all of an organization's activities. These are simply too many kinds of activities for any one control system to be effective. Instead, managers use a series of control methods and systems to deal with the differing problems and elements of their organization. Moreover, the methods and systems can take many forms and can be intended for various groups.[1]

In this chapter, we will discuss various financial methods of control that managers can use, including budgets, financial statements, ratio analysis, break-even analysis, and audits. In varying degrees, each of these methods is vital to the success of an organization.

FINANCIAL CONTROLS

CLASS COMMENT

These financial control tools are quantitative in nature.

The financial control methods we will discuss are financial statements, ratio analysis, and break-even analysis. These methods are used to evaluate an organization's performance in dimensions that are crucial to its health and survival.

Financial Statements

financial statement Monetary analysis of the flow of goods and services to, within, and from the organization.

TEACHING TIP

For all of the methods discussed in this chapter, examples would enhance the educational process. Either obtain some from a basic accounting textbook or copies of company annual reports.

Financial statements are analyses in monetary terms of the flow of goods and services to, within, and from the organization. They are prepared by accountants and are the key summaries of the firm's accounting records. Financial statements provide a means for controlling three major conditions of an organization: its *liquidity*—the ability to convert assets into cash to meet current financial needs and obligations; its *general financial condition*—the long-term balance between debt and equity (the assets of the firm after deducting for liabilities); and its profitability—the ability to earn profits steadily and over an extended period of time.[2]

Financial statements are usually prepared *ex post* (in retrospect) to indicate what financial events *have occurred since the last statement*. Depending on the company, the period covered by a financial statement might be the previous year, the previous quarter, or the previous month. As we suggested in Chapter 18, financial statements have limited usefulness as control measures because they cover only past events and cannot, obviously, be used to influence those events. However, quarterly or monthly statements can often provide managers with useful information about trends or events in time to allow them to take corrective action during upcoming fiscal terms.

The financial statements most often used on a regular basis by organizations are balance sheets and income statements. We will describe these along with cash-flow statements and statements of the sources and uses of funds, which are also widely used.[3]

---

[1]See William H. Newman, *Constructive Control: Design and Use of Control Systems* (Englewood Cliffs, N.J.: Prentice Hall, 1975), pp. 6–9, 128–129.

[2]See Earl P. Strong and Robert D. Smith, *Management Control Models* (New York: Holt, Rinehart & Winston, 1968), pp 55.

[3]See Strong and Smith, *Management Control Models*, pp. 56–61; and J. Fred Weston and Thomas E. Copeland, *Managerial Finance*, 8th ed. (Hinsdale, Ill.: Dryden Press, 1986).

COORDINATED RESOURCE

This would be a good time to have a speaker from a local computer store talk about the availability of management software—what it is and what it does.

The use of computer software for the collection and analysis of accounting and financial data is now nearly universal. About a dozen accounting software packages have achieved national prominence. When evaluating such programs for possible purchase and implementation, financial managers should make sure that they comply with the guidelines of the IRS, the FASB (Financial Accounting Standards Board), and other regulatory agencies, and that the software vendor will continue to supply updated versions.[4]

balance sheet Description of the organization in terms of its assets, liabilities, and net worth.

CLASS COMMENT

A balance sheet is often compared to a photograph—a picture of the company at a particular point in time.

Balance Sheet. The message of a **balance sheet** is, "Here's how this organization stacks up financially *at this particular point in time.*" The point in time covered by our sample balance sheet, Figure 19-1, is indicated by the line "As of December 31, 1987."

In its simplest form, the balance sheet describes the company in terms of its *assets, liabilities,* and net worth. A company's assets range from money in the bank to the goodwill value of its name in the marketplace. The left side of the balance sheet lists these assets in descending order of liquidity. A distinction is made between current assets and fixed assets. *Current assets* cover items such as cash, accounts receivable, marketable securities and inventories—assets that could be turned into cash at a reasonably predictable value within a relatively short time period (typically, one year). *Fixed assets* show the monetary value of the company's plant, equipment, property, patents, and other items used on a continuing basis to produce its goods or services.

[4]See G. William Dauphinais and Michael A. Yesko, "Business Accounting Software Comes of Age?" *PC,* June 25, 1985, pp. 146–148; Eldon Ladd, "How to Evaluate Financial Software," *Management Acounting* 66, no. 7 (January 1985):39–42; and Erik Sandberg-Diment, "When Accounting Goes Electronic," *New York Times,* July 7, 1985, p. F17. R. McLeod, *Mangement Information Systems,* 3rd ed., (Palo Alto, Calif.: SRA, 1986), Chapter 9, discusses these prewritten accounting packages and compares them with spreadsheets.

FIGURE 19-1 THE BALANCE SHEET

CHAPNER METALS
Consolidated Balance Sheet
As of December 31, 1988

ASSETS			LIABILITIES AND NET WORTH		
Current Assets	$ 950,000		Current Liabilities	$ 600,000	
Cash		50,000	Account Payable		475,000
Marketable Securities		350,000	Accrued Expenses		
Accounts Receivable		250,000	Payable		125,000
Inventories		300,000	Long-Term Liabilities	600,000	
			Total Liabilities	1,200,000	
Fixed Assets	1,250,000				
Land		50,000	Net Worth	1,070,000	
Plant and Equipment		1,500,000	Common Stock at Par		850,000
Less Accumulated			Accumulated Retained		
Depreciation		300,000	Earnings		220,000
Other Assets					
Patents and Goodwill	70,000				
Total Assets	$2,270,000		Total Liabilities and Net Worth	$2,270,000	

Liabilities are also made up of two groups, current liabilities and long-term liabilities. *Current liabilities* are debts, such as accounts payable, short-term loans, and unpaid taxes, that will have to be paid off during the current fiscal period. *Long-term liabilities* include mortgages, bonds, and other debts that are being paid off gradually. The company's *new worth* is the residual value remaining after total liabilities have been subtracted from total assets. The widespread use of electronic spreadsheets has made the preparation of balance sheets much easier in the 1980s. In addition, prewritten computer packages have been developed specifically to process accounting transactions and prepare the resulting balance sheets and other financial statements.

income statement Summary of the organization's financial performance over a given interval of time.

Income Statement. While the balance sheet describes a company's financial condition at a given *point* in time, the **income statement** summarizes the company's financial performance over a given *interval* of time. The income statement, then, says, "Here's how much money we're making" instead of "Here's how much money we're worth."

Income statements, such as Figure 19-2, start with a figure for gross receipts or sales and then subtract all the costs involved in realizing those sales, such as the cost of goods sold, administrative expenses, taxes, interest, and other operating expenses. What is left is the net income available for stockholders' dividends or reinvestment in the business.

Cash Flow: Sources and Uses-of-Funds Statements. In addition to the standard balance sheet and income statement, many companies report financial data in the form of a statement of cash flow or a statement of sources and uses of funds. These statements show where cash or funds came from during the year (from operations, reducing accounts receivable, and sale of investments, for example) and where they were applied (purchase of equipment, payment of dividends, and reducing accounts payable, for example). They should not be confused with income statements; cash flow statements show how cash or funds were used rather than how much profit or loss was achieved.

FIGURE 19-2 THE INCOME STATEMENT

CHAPNER METALS
Statement of Income
For the Year Ended December 31, 1988

Gross Sales		$4,298,000
Less Returns	$ 798,000	
Net Sales		3,500,000
Less Cost of Sales and Operating Expenses		
Cost of Goods Sold	2,775,000	
Depreciation	100,000	
Selling and Administrative Expenses	75,000	2,950,000
Operating Profit		550,000
Other Income		15,000
Gross Income		565,000
Less Interest Expense	75,000	
Income before Taxes		490,000
Less Taxes	196,000	
Income after Taxes		$ 294,000

The federal government annually provides source- and use-of-funds statements to the general public through news releases and other documents. Sources are typically reported graphically and with tables in such general categories as asset sales, excise taxes, and income taxes. Uses-of-funds are usually for defense, federal pension plans, debt payments, and domestic services. State and local governments have similar source- and use-of-funds statements that report not only information on income and property taxes but on such revenue sources as user fees and trust funds. Use-of-fund statements on the state and local levels may include information on road construction and maintenance, social-welfare administration, and police and fire protection.

Financial statements are also used by managers, stockholders, shareholders, investment analysts, unions, and others to evaluate the organization's performance. Within the company, managers will compare the current statements of their organization with earlier statements and with those of competitors. People outside the company will use the statements to gauge the organization's strengths, weaknesses, and potential. For example, managers may go outside the company to borrow funds from bankers or to sell new stock to investors. The bankers or investors will analyze the financial statements and will be influenced by what they see in them.

FOR DISCUSSION

What *do* financial statements show? What *do* they *not* show?

However, because several types of key information for the evaluation of a firm are not provided by financial statements, the usefulness of statements is limited. For example, recent technological or scientific breakthroughs made by the company are unlikely to be reported. Likewise, financial statements may not reflect changes in the external environment—for example, abrupt shifts in the desires or real income of consumers—which may be crucial to the organization's success or failure.[5] Another factor in the external environment that may go unreported is investment on the part of foreign countries. In the late 1980's, for example, there was a rapidly escalating pattern of investment by firms headquartered in Japan, Great Britain, Italy, and elsewhere in the wake of the United States's battle with a weakened dollar. In particular, states such as California have experienced increasing foreign investment in areas ranging from agriculture to electronics. Many companies thus resort to supplementing financial statements with narratives that describe the impact of relevant internal and external factors on the organization.

Ratio Analysis

For organizations as well as for individuals, financial performance is relative. An annual salary of $30,000 will be seen as high if the average salary in the individual's field or industry is $20,000 and low if the average salary is $40,000. Similarly, company profits of $1 million might be very high for a restaurant but very low for an oil company. For the "bottom line" on a financial statement to be meaningful, it must ultimately be compared against a standard. In **ratio analysis,** key summary figures from their firm's financial statements or records are reported as percentages or fractions. Such ratios can provide quick assessments of financial performance or condition. Today, as opposed to the recent past, ratios are easily and inexpensively developed by computer from the firm's electronic records for timely use by managers.[6]

ratio analysis Reporting of key figures from the organization's financial records as percentages or fractions.

CLASS COMMENT

Ratios can also be compared to established objectives.

The ratio analysis comparisons can be made in one of two ways: (1) comparison over a time period—the present ratio compared with the same organization's ratio in the past (or with a future projection); and (2) comparison with other, similar organizations or with the industry as a whole. The first type of comparison will indicate how the organization's performance or condition has changed; the second type will suggest how well the organization is doing relative to its competitors.

---

[5]Michael H. Granof, *Financial Accounting*, 3d ed., (Englewood Cliffs, N.J.: Prentice-Hall, 1985).
[6]Weston and Copeland, *Managerial Finance*.

TEACHING TIP

Depending upon how deeply you want to cover this financial information, you could give students some sample financial statements and ask them to calculate the ratios.

There are many kinds of ratio categories and many kinds of ratios. The ratios most commonly used by organizations are profitability, liquidity, activity, and leverage; these are listed in Table 19-1. Return on investment (under profitability) is generally seen as the most important and encompassing ratio in general use; it reveals the success of the firm in employing its resources. The current ratio (under liquidity) indicates the ability of the firm to repay its present short-term debt. Inventory turnover (under activity) is often compared to industry averages and figures from previous years to assess efficiency. Debt ratios (under leverage) are computed to assess a firm's ability to meet its long-term commitments.[7]

The key to making effective *use* of ratio analysis is understanding that ratios must be *compared*. In order to compare one firm's ratios with those of a related firm or with industry-wide averages, the interested analyst thus needs reliable information. The Management Application box entitled "Where to Find Financial Ratios" identifies some readily available sources of such information.

Break-Even Analysis

Let us assume that the Biocraft Corporation makes only one product, a genetically tailored bacteria for coating plant seeds, which it sells to distributors for $20 per unit. The variable cost of producing the bacteria is $10 per unit. In addition, the company has annual fixed costs of $100,000. (See the discussion of fixed and variable costs later in this chapter.) At what precise point will the company's sales cover its costs?

break-even analysis (or **cost-volume-profit analysis**) Financial statement enabling managers to analyze the relationships among costs, sales volume, and profits.

Helping managers to find and evaluate that point is the purpose of **break-even analysis** (also called cost-volume-profit analysis). Through break-even analysis, managers can study the relationship between costs, sales volume, and profits. They can specifically determine how changes in costs and volume will affect profits.

FOR DISCUSSION

How can break-even analysis be used for planning? For controlling?

The relationship between fixed costs, variable costs, units sold, and profit can be seen in a diagram sometimes referred to as a *break-even chart* or a *profitgraph*. Figure 19-3 illustrates such a graph for our company, covering a sales period of one year. The graph shows that a net loss will result on sales of fewer than 10,000 units but that any sales above that figure will produce a profit. Our break-even point, then, is 10,000 units.

Break-even analysis gives managers a rough profit and loss estimate for different sales volumes. Managers obtain this estimate by selecting the given volume along the horizontal axis and moving up vertically to discover the projected revenue and total

[7]Granof, *Financial Accounting*. See also Gordon Shillinglaw, *Managerial Cost Accounting: Analysis and Control*, 5th ed., (Homewood, Ill.: Irwin, 1982), pp. 787–792.

TABLE 19-1 CATEGORIES OF RATIOS FOR ANALYSIS

CATEGORY	TYPICAL RATIO	CALCULATION	MEASURES
Profitability	Return on investment	Profits after taxes / Total assets	The productivity of assets
Liquidity	Current ratio	Current assets / Current liabilities	Short-term solvency
Activity	Inventory turnover	Sales / Inventory	The efficiency of inventory management
Leverage	Debt ratio	Total debt / Total assets	The proportion of financing supplied by creditors

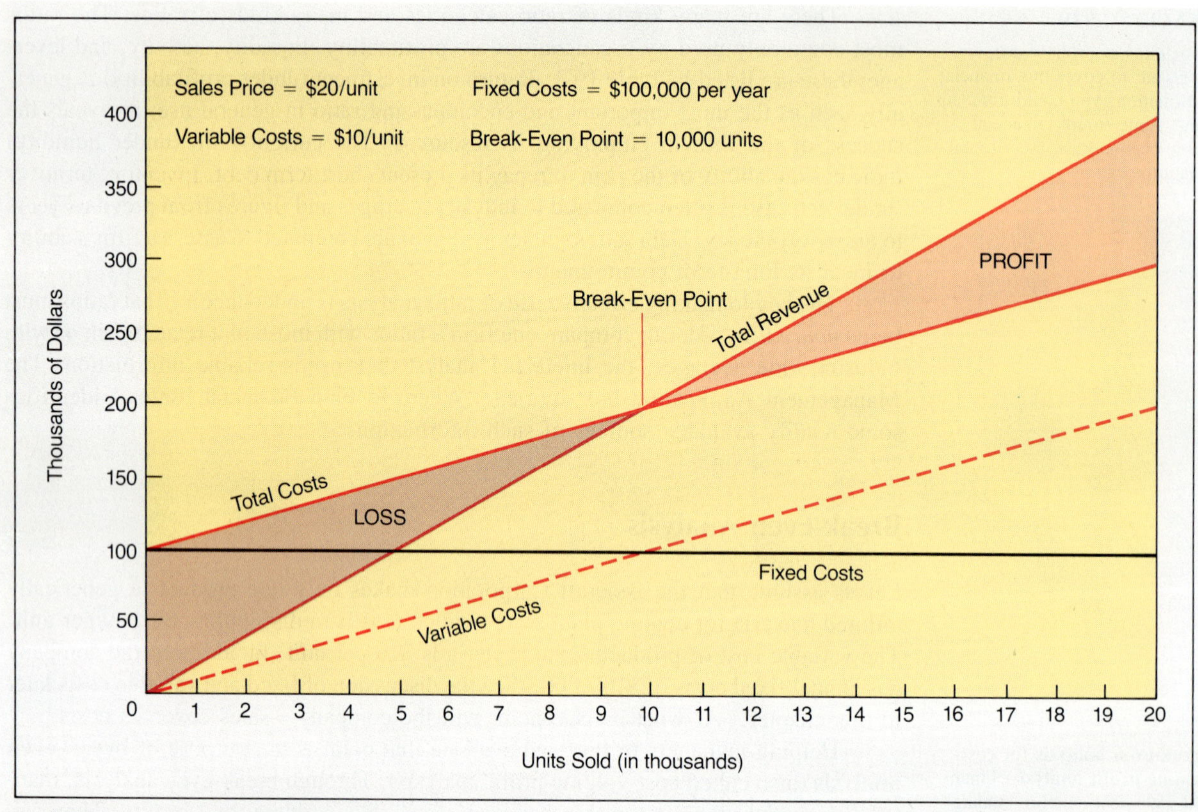

FIGURE 19-3 A PROFITGRAPH FOR BIOCRAFT CORPORATION

costs for that volume. The graph can also be used to perform a "what if" analysis—that is, to estimate the effect of changes in expenses and sales price. In our example, if fixed costs increase by $40,000, the break-even level would increase to 14,000 units. Alternatively, if the unit price of tailored bacteria drops to $15, the break-even point will move up to 20,000 units.

Break-even analysis can also be used to identify the minimum sales volume necessary to meet established profit objectives and to provide data helpful in decisions to expand capacity and to drop or add product lines.[8] As a control device, break-even analysis provides one more yardstick by which to evaluate company performance and provides a basis for corrective action to improve future performance. ("Our sales reached $5 million this month; for that sales volume, we had projected profits of $600,000, but our reported profits are only $500,000. We will need to find the causes of the difference.")

Limitations of Break-Even Analysis. One of the virtues of break-even analysis as an operational tool is its simplicity. Unfortunately, the simple assumptions upon which the above break-even analysis is based may affect the accuracy of the results. Among the more questionable assumptions are the following:

1. *That variable costs per unit are constant.* If production facilities approach capacity, bottlenecks and equipment problems may require large increases in variable labor costs to keep the equipment performing. Raw material costs may also rise because of increased production defects.

[8]R.M.S. Wilson, *Financial Control: A Systems Approach* (New York: McGraw-Hill, 1974), pp. 137–138.

MANAGEMENT APPLICATION

WHERE TO FIND FINANCIAL RATIOS

1. *Annual Statement Studies.* Published by Robert Morris Associates, this work includes 11 financial ratios computed annually for over 150 lines of business. Each line of business is divided into 4 size categories.
2. Dun and Bradstreet provides 14 ratios calculated annually for over 100 lines of business.
3. *The Almanac of Business and Industrial Financial Ratios.* This work, published by Prentice-Hall, Inc., lists industry averages for 22 financial ratios. Approximately 170 businesses and industries are listed.
4. *The Quarterly Financial Report for Manufacturing Corporations.* This work, published jointly by the Federal Trade Commission and the Securities and Exchange Commission, contains balance-sheet and income-statement information by industry groupings and by asset-size categories.
5. Trade associations and individual companies often compute ratios for their industries and make them available to analysts.

Source: James C. Van Horne, *Financial Management and Policy,* 7th ed., © 1986, pp. 767–768. Reprinted by permission of Prentice-Hall, Inc., Englewood Cliffs, New Jersey.

2. *That fixed costs are constant.* Costs that appear fixed may change in ways that are difficult to predict. For example, as volume rises, new equipment may have to be purchased to alleviate bottlenecks, additional clerical staff may be required to process orders, and additional staff people may be needed to improve coordination.
3. *That prices are constant.* Increased sales may be concentrated in a few customers who receive large-quantity discounts; or sales may be made at greater distances, with the selling company deducting the additional transportation costs from revenues.
4. *That costs can be classified as fixed or variable.* In practice, many costs are quite difficult to classify. For example, if inventories increase to support the higher production levels and an additional warehouse must be leased, is that a fixed cost, since it will not increase or decrease with subsequent volume changes, or is it a variable cost brought about by the higher volume of production?

HERE'S AN EXAMPLE

Kaypro Corporation, once a leading maker of portable computers, is losing money fast and their credit lines are drying up. Says one of their creditors, "We're simply discouraged by the company's continued losses." Immediate steps taken to save the company: hunting for another lender and a buyer for the multimillion dollar's worth of inventory, slashing advertising and research-and-development budgets, and cancelling appearances at several trade shows. (*Business Week,* 9/26/88, pp. 51–53)

In spite of its weaknesses, break-even analysis is still an important management tool. Although the information provided by an analysis like the one sketched in here may not be sufficiently precise for some instances, it is usually accurate enough for many actual decision-making and control situations. If additional accuracy is desired, management can use more advanced forms of break-even analysis. Among other things, the advanced analysis allows for nonconstant variable costs, shifting fixed expenses, and nonconstant prices. Furthermore, computer software is available that makes it easy for managers to implement break-even analysis.[9]

BUDGETARY CONTROL METHODS

budget Formal quantitative statement of resources allocated for planned activities over stipulated periods of time.

Budgets are formal quantitative statements of the resources set aside for carrying out planned activities over given periods of time. They are the most widely used means for planning and controlling activities at every level of an organization. A budget indicates

[9]For an article on how to set up break-even charts using *Lotus 1-2-3* and *Symphony* software, see Charles W. Kidd, "Using the Power of Break-even Analysis," *Lotus 1,* no. 2 (June 1985):29–30ff. P. Gray, *Guide to IFPS,* 2nd ed., (New York: McGraw-Hill, 1987), Chapter 6, suggests how the fourth-generation computer language IFPS could be used to perform break-even analysis.

the expenditures, revenues, or profits planned for some future date. The planned figures become the standard by which future performance is measured.

Budgetary Control

EXTRA EXERCISE

Have students develop a personal budget for the remainder of the semester. They should think about estimated "revenues" and "expenses." After they have done this, ask them how they felt about the "budgeting process." Was it easy? Hard? Why?

Budgets are a fundamental part of organizations' control programs.[10] They are widely used because they are stated in monetary terms. Dollar figures are easily used as a common denominator for a wide variety of organizational activities—hiring and training personnel, purchasing equipment, manufacturing, advertising, and selling—and so they can be used by the organization's existing accounting system to cover all departments. In addition, the monetary aspect of budgets means that they can directly convey information on a key organizational resource—capital—and on a key organizational goal—profit. They are, therefore, heavily favored by profit oriented companies.

Another reason why budgets are the most widely used control tool is that they establish clear and unambiguous standards of performance. Budgets cover a set time period—usually a year. At stated intervals during that time period, actual performance will be compared directly with the budget. Frequently, deviations can quickly be detected and acted upon.

In addition to being a major control device, budgets are also one of the major means of coordinating the activities of the organization. The interaction between managers and subordinates that takes place during the budget development process will help define and integrate the activities of organization members.

In this section we will describe the role of budgets in a control system, the budgeting process itself, the types of budgets that managers have available, the benefits and drawbacks of budgets, and how those drawbacks can be overcome.

HERE'S AN EXAMPLE

Control Data Corporation, a large computer company, is facing some slow times. At virtually every one of CDC's high-technology businesses, earnings are hurting because of soft markets or intense price competition. Says one analyst, "You've got a company that's out of balance." It's got too many businesses it can't support." (*Business Week*, 10/10/88, p. 43)

Responsibility Centers

Control systems can be devised to monitor organizational *functions* or organizational *projects*. Controlling a function involves making sure that a specified activity (such as production or sales) is properly carried out. Controlling a project involves making sure that a specified end result is achieved (such as the development of a new product or the completion of a building). Budgets can be used for both types of systems; our discussion will emphasize the use of budgets to control functions as such a system is illustrated in Figure 19-4.

responsibility center Any organizational function or unit whose manager is responsible for all of its activities.

Any organizational or functional unit headed by a manager who is responsible for the activities of that unit is called a **responsibility center.** All responsibility centers use resources (inputs or costs) to produce something (outputs or revenues). Typically, responsibility is assigned to a revenue, expense, profit, and/or investment center. (See Fig. 19-4.) The decision usually will depend on the activity performed by the organizational unit and on the manner in which inputs and outputs are measured by the control system. We will describe such centers briefly here. Later, we will more fully examine the kinds of budgets used in these centers.

revenue center Organizational unit in which outputs measured in monetary terms are not directly compared to input costs.

Revenue Centers. **Revenue centers** are those organizational units in which outputs are measured in monetary terms but are not directly compared to input costs. A sales department is an example of such a unit. The effectiveness of the center is not judged by how much revenue (in the form of sales) exceeds the cost of the center (in salaries or

[10]This discussion of budgets is based on Robert N. Anthony, John Dearden, and Norton M. Bedford, *Management Control Systems*, 5th ed. (Homewood, Ill.: Irwin, 1984), especially Chapters 5, 6, and 7.

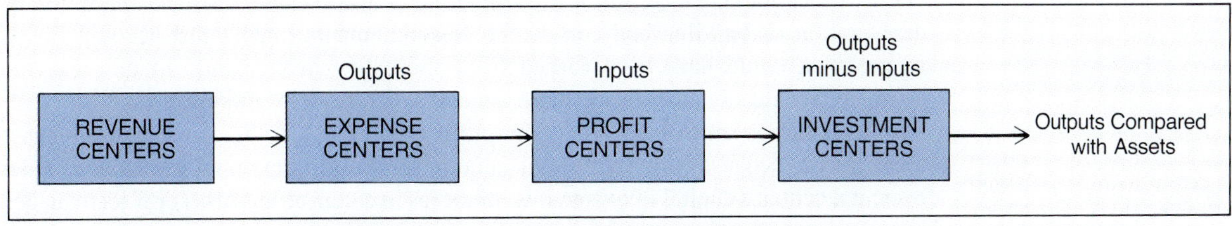

FIGURE 19-4 BUDGETING SYSTEM FOR CONTROLLING FUNCTIONS

rent, for example). Rather, budgets (in the form of sales quotas) are prepared for the revenue center and the figures compared with sales orders or actual sales. In this way, a useful picture of the effectiveness of individual salespeople or of the center itself can be determined.

expense center Commonly, administrative, service, and research departments where inputs are measured in monetary terms, although outputs are not.

Expense Centers. In **expense centers,** inputs are measured by the control system in monetary terms, but outputs are not. So budgets will be devised only for the input portion of these centers' operations. Organizational units commonly considered expense centers include administrative, service, and research departments.

There are two categories of expense centers: engineered and discretionary. *Engineered expenses* are those for which costs can be calculated or estimated with high reliability—for example, the costs of direct labor or raw materials. *Discretionary expenses* are those for which costs cannot be reliably estimated beforehand (research costs, for example) and must depend to a large extent on the manager's discretion. At review time, actual input expenses will be measured against budgeted input expenses. Moreover, accounting and computer services will generate both engineered and discretionary expenses at the center.

profit center Organizational unit where performance is measured by numerical differences between revenues and expenditures.

HERE'S AN EXAMPLE

Hicks and Haas, a leveraged buyout firm based in Dallas, controls one-third of the noncola market and is the third largest soda seller after Coca Cola and PepsiCo. Their brands: Dr Pepper, Seven-Up, and A&W Root Beer. Through savvy management and marketing, the firm has the three soft drink companies recharged and sparkling. The value of the companies has clearly increased but returns on the holdings cannot be realized until they are sold. (*Fortune,* 2/15/88, pp. 68–82)

Profit Centers. In a **profit center,** performance is measured by the numerical difference between revenues (outputs) and expenditures (inputs). Such a measure is used to determine how well the center is doing economically and how well the manager in charge of the center is performing.

A profit center is created whenever an organizational unit is given responsibility for earning a profit. In a divisionalized organization, in which each of a number of divisions is completely responsible for its own product line, the separate divisions are considered profit centers. The expenditures of all a division's subunits are totaled and then subtracted from the revenues derived from that division's products or services. The net result is the measure of that division's profitability.

In nondivisionalized organizations, or *within* a division, individual departments may also be made into profit centers by crediting them for revenues and charging them for expenses. A manufacturing department, for example, would normally be considered an expense center. Allowing the manufacturing department to "sell" its products at an agreed-upon price (called a *transfer price*) to the sales department would be one way to turn that department into a profit center. The difference between the transfer price and the manufacturing cost per unit would represent the manufacturing department's "profit."

investment center Organizational unit that not only measures the monetary value of inputs and outputs, but also compares outputs with assets used in producing them.

Investment Centers. In an **investment center,** the control system again measures the monetary value of inputs and outputs, but it also assesses how those outputs compare with the assets employed in producing them. Assume, for example, that a new hospital requires a capital investment of $20 million in property, buildings, equipment, and working capital. In its first year, the hospital has $2 million in labor and other input expenses and $4 million in revenue. For two reasons the hospital would *not* be consid-

HERE'S AN EXAMPLE

New CEO of Pillsbury Company, Philip L. Smith, has the formidable task of whipping Pillsbury back into shape. Most of Pillsbury's operations, especially Burger King, are suffering from weak financial performance and a host of apparently aimless management shuffles. He has his work cut out for him! (*Business Week,* 8/8/88, p. 23)

ered to have earned a $2 million profit. First, an allowance must be made for the depreciation of building and equipment. Second, management must account for the interest that could have been earned from alternative investments. In this way, the company would obtain a much more accurate picture of profitability.

It is important to realize that any profit center can also be considered an investment center, because its activities will require some form of capital investment. However, if a center's capital investment is minor (as in a consulting firm) or if its managers have no control over capital investment, it may be more appropriately treated as a profit center.

THE BUDGETING PROCESS

In this section, we will focus on four key areas of the budgeting process: (1) the ways in which budgets are drawn up and approved, (2) the role played by the budget department and budget committees, (3) the ways in which budgets are revised, and (4) problems that commonly occur when budgets are being developed.[11]

How Budgets Are Drawn Up and Approved

The budgeting process usually begins when managers receive top management's economic forecasts and sales and profit objectives for the coming year. The information will usually be accompanied by a timetable stating when budgets must be completed. The forecasts and objectives provided by top management represent guidelines within which other managers' budgets will be developed.

FOR DISCUSSION

When would each of these types of budgeting be best? What situational (external, organizational, individual) factors would influence the choice?

In a few organizations, the preference process is known as "top-down" budgeting: Budgets are imposed by top managers with little or no consultation with lower-level managers.[12] Most companies, however, prefer the process of "bottom-down" budgeting: Budgets are prepared, at least initially, by those who must implement them. The budgets are then sent up for approval by superiors.

"Bottom-up" budgeting has many advantages for many organizations. Supervisors and lower-level department heads have a more intimate view of their needs than do managers at the top, and they can provide more realistic breakdowns to support their proposals. They are also less likely to overlook some vital ingredient or hidden flaw that might subsequently impede implementation efforts. Managers will also be more strongly motivated to accept and meet budgets that they have had a hand in shaping. Finally, morale and satisfaction are usually higher when individuals participate actively in making decisions that affect them. Table 19-2 lists the best aspects of top-down and bottom-up budgeting.

The process by which lower-level managers participate in developing budgets is similar to the multilevel planning process described in Chapter 5. Supervisors prepare their budget proposals using the guidelines drawn up by upper management. The lower-level budgets are reviewed, finalized, and used by department heads to draw up department budgets. These budgets are then submitted to higher-level managers for approval. The process continues until all budgets are completed, assembled by the

---

[11]See Shillinglaw, *Managerial Cost Accounting,* pp. 209–234; Anthony, Dearden, and Bedford, *Management Control Systems,* p. 444; and Jeremy Bacon, *Managing the Budget Function* (New York: National Industrial Conference Board, 1970).

[12]For a good description of this budget process, see Chris Argyris, "Human Problems with Budgets," *Harvard Business Review* 31, no. 1 (January 1953):97–110. See also Peter Brownell, "Leadership Style, Budgetary Participation and Managerial Behavior," *Accounting, Organizations and Society* 8, no. 4 (1983):307–321.

TABLE 19-2 TOP-DOWN AND BOTTOM-UP BUDGETING

WHAT TOP-DOWN BUDGETING INCORPORATES BEST:	WHAT BOTTOM-UP BUDGETING INCORPORATES BEST:
Economic industry projections ↓	↑ Operational plans
Company planning parameters	Information on competition, products, and markets
Corporate goals	Alternative courses of action
Overall resource availability	Specific resource requirements

Source: Reprinted by permission of the *Harvard Business Review.* An exhibit from "Budget Choice: Planning vs. Control" by Neil C. Churchill (July–August 1984). Copyright © 1984 by the President and Fellows of Harvard College; all rights reserved.

controller or budget director, and submitted to the budget committee for further review. Management then will need capital budgeting techniques, such as the standard formulas presented in Table 19-3, to help evaluate the budget requests. Finally, the master budget is sent to top management (the president, chief executive officer, or board of directors) for approval.

The Role of Budget Personnel

CLASS COMMENT

Repeat: Developing budgets is the *responsibility* of line managers. Why is this so?

Developing budgets is the responsibility of line managers. They may receive information and technical assistance from the staff of a planning group or budget department. (Managers of staff departments will, of course, be responsible for their own department budgets; the distinctions between line and staff positions are detailed in Chapter 10.) Many organizations have formal budget departments and committees. These groups are likely to exist in large, divisionalized organizations in which the division budget plays a key role in planning, coordinating, and controlling activities.[13]

The *budget department,* which generally reports to the corporate controller, provides budget information and assistance to organizational units, designs budget systems and forms, integrates the various departmental proposals into a master budget for the organization as a whole, and reports on actual performance relative to the budget.

The *budget committee,* made up of senior executives from all functional areas, reviews the individual budgets, reconciles divergent views, alerts or approves the budget proposals, and then refers the integrated package to the board of directors. Later, when the plans have been put into practice, the committee reviews the control reports that monitor progress. In most cases, the budget committee must approve any revisions made during the budget period.

[13]Kenneth A. Merchant, "Influence on Departmental Budgeting: An Empirical Examination of a Contingency Model," *Accounting, Organizations and Society* 9, nos. 3/4 (1984):291–307.

TABLE 19-3 CAPITAL BUDGETING TECHNIQUES

TECHNIQUE	FORMULA	INFORMATION
Payback	Investment/cash flow	Time to recoup the investment
Present value	Investment—sum or discounted cash flows	Net worth of the future cash flows generated by the investment
Internal rate of return	Present value of cash outflow = present value of cash inflow	Percentage return on the investment

"At the moment, there's $413,874,691.03 in the kitty."
Drawing by Weber; © 1982 The New Yorker Magazine, Inc.

How Budgets Are Revised

HERE'S AN EXAMPLE

Unocal Corporation, an oil products company, is selling off assets to avoid becoming a target for corporate raiders who want to sell off the assets for their own gain. Says the newly named CEO, Richard J. Stegemeier, "We have profit goals for everything. If it makes more sense to sell it than run it, that's what we're going to do." (*Business Week,* 10/10/88, p. 80)

Budgets cannot be revised whenever managers please. Nevertheless, because budgets are based on forecasts that can be rapidly invalidated by changing circumstances, provision should be made for necessary revisions. In cases where the budget is used primarily as a planning tool, formal updating periods may be established at stated intervals. Where the budget is a main part of the control and evaluation mechanism, revisions are limited to cases where deviations have become so great as to make the approved budget unrealistic. The aim is to build reasonable stability and firmness into the budget without being excessively rigid.[14]

Comparisons of actual performance with budgets are known as reviews or *audits,* and are now often done electronically. To be effective, audits depend on a regular, accurate flow of data from organizational units. Unit managers will regularly submit monthly or weekly progress reports that are audited on a monthly basis by those individuals with control responsibility or automatically by computer. If deviations are detected, the appropriate managers will be asked to explain them and to specify the corrective planned action. Serious deviations may require that the budget be revised.[15]

For example, the U.S. Department of Defense annually buys a variety of weapons systems for the armed services. Frequently, audits of defense contractors reveal significant cost overruns that can be explained partially by inflation in material costs, partially by delays in development, and even partially by ineffective management. These overruns usually require Pentagon officials to revise the corresponding weapons budgets. In the late 1980s, a major scandal over procurement procedures rocked the Pentagon, resulting in widespread allegations that both financial and ethical controls were lax and subject to abuse. Congress, the Administration, and the military were all

[14]Paul J. Carruth and Thurrell O. McClendon, "How Supervisors React to 'Meeting the Budget' Pressure," *Management Accounting* 66, no. 5 (November 1984):50–54.

[15]Jerry A. Viscione, "Small Company Budgets: Targets Are Key," *Harvard Business Review* 62, no. 3 (May–June 1984):42–50.

accused—and accused one another—of being unable to keep the Pentagon's massive procurement apparatus under control, and debate still rages over what measures will be necessary to implement effective control over such a complex system.

Some Problems in Budget Development

During the budget development process, the organization's limited resources are allocated, and managers may fear that they will not be given their fair share. Tension will heighten as competition with other managers increases. Anxieties may also arise because managers know they will be judged by their ability to meet or beat budgeted standards. Hence, they are concerned about what those standards will be. Conversely, their superiors are concerned with establishing aggressive budget objectives. As a result, the superiors will often try to trim their subordinates' expenditure requests or raise their revenue targets. In Exhibit 19-1, Henry L. Tosi describes four important reactions to these budget-development anxieties.

EXHIBIT 19-1 TOSI'S FOUR IMPORTANT REACTIONS TO BUDGET ANXIETIES

1. *Political Behavior.* Political activity may increase sharply as managers try to influence resource allocations. Managers may withhold information until the last minute in order to magnify its importance, ingratiate themselves with superiors, or attempt to gain influence in other ways.
2. *Dysfunctional Reactions to Budget Units.* Supervisors who are unhappy with resource allocations are not really in a position to vent their anger on their superiors. Instead, they will usually take out their hostility on the staff personnel who compile the budget data and assemble the final budget figures.
3. *Overstatement of Needs.* Slack is often built into budgets as a legitimate hedge against unforeseen events and inflation. Some managers, however, pad their budget estimates to protect themselves in the struggle for resources and to compensate for the fact that cuts are often made in requested amounts. Managers who submit requests based only on their actual needs will then suffer if their requests are automatically cut along with those of other managers.
4. *Covert Information Systems.* When budgets are kept secret, managers will often try to find out how their allocations compare with others by developing covert or informal information sources–secretaries, budget staff members, or colleagues. The danger for the organization lies in the possibility that inaccurate information will be spread through the grapevine, unnecessarily increasing the rivalry and tension between organizational units.

Source: Henry L. Tosi, Jr., "The Human Effects of Budgeting Systems on Management," *MSU Business Topics* 22, no. 4 (Autumn 1974).

Organization-wide participation in the budgeting process, as in the examples provided earlier, often minimizes these types of anxiety reactions. When all managers are involved in budget development, they are more likely to be satisfied with their resource allocations.[16]

TYPES OF BUDGETS

operating budget Budget indicating the goods and services the organization expects to consume in a budget period.

Organization budgets are of two kinds: operating budgets and financial budgets. The **operating budgets** indicate the goods and services the organization expects to consume in the budget period; they usually list both physical quantities (such as barrels of

[16]For a discussion of the successful use of a rational budget decision-making model by Stanford University, see Ellen Earle Chaffee, "The Role of Rationality in University Budgeting," *Research in Higher Education* 19, no. 4 (1983):387–406.

financial budget Budget detailing the money expected to be spent during the budget period and indicating its sources.

TEACHING TIP

Be sure that students *understand* the differences here. If you have access to some examples (check annual reports, local companies, your school's budget, etc.), show them.

oil) and cost figures. The **financial budgets** spell out in detail the money the organization intends to spend in the same period and where that money will come from. Figure 19-5 shows the operating and financial components of a manufacturing firm's comprehensive budget. Each rectangle in the diagram represents one or more of the types of budgets we describe below. These different types of budgets make up the firm's overall budgetary plan.[17]

Operating Budgets

The most common types of operating budgets parallel three of the responsibility centers discussed earlier—expense, revenue, and profit.[18]

Expense Budgets. As mentioned earlier, there are two types of expense budgets, one for each of the two types of expense centers—engineered cost budgets and discretionary cost budgets.

engineered cost budget Budget describing material and labor costs of each item produced, including estimated overhead costs.

Engineered cost budgets are typically used in manufacturing plants but can be used by any organizational unit in which output can be accurately measured. These budgets usually describe the material and labor costs involved in each production item, as well as the estimated overhead costs.[19] Hewlett-Packard, for example, has an annual

[17]See Shillinglaw, *Managerial Cost Accounting,* pp. 209–210.

[18]Anthony, Dearden, and Bedford, *Management Control Systems,* pp. 198–202, 443–448.

[19]For a discussion of the use of one such budgeting technique in military acquisitions, see H. W. Lanford and T. M. McCann, ''Effective Planning and Control of Large Projects—Using Work Breakdown Structure,'' *Long Range Planning* 16, no. 2 (April 1983):38–50.

FIGURE 19-5 BUDGET COMPONENTS

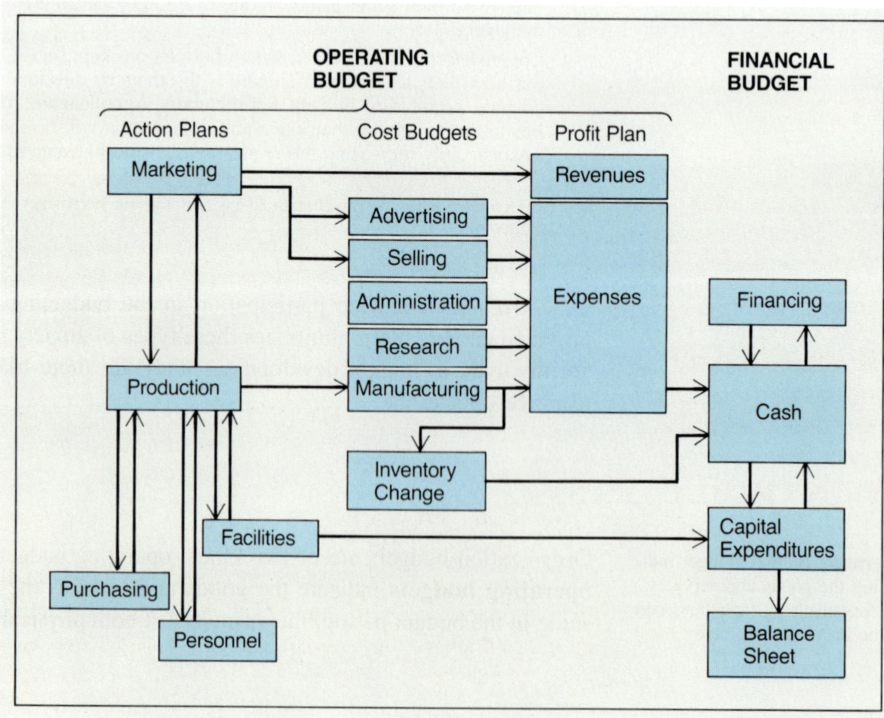

Source: Gordon Shillinglaw, *Managerial Cost Accounting,* 5th ed., p. 210. Copyright © 1982. Reproduced with permission of Richard D. Irwin, Inc.

budget that describes the labor, material, and overhead expenses involved in manufacturing its computer peripherals (printers, plotters, and boards). Such an engineered cost budget is designed to measure efficiency: Exceeding the budget will mean that operating costs were higher than they should have been.

discretionary cost budget Budget used for departments in which output cannot be accurately measured.

Discretionary cost budgets are typically used for administrative, legal, accounting, research, and other such departments in which output cannot be accurately measured. Discretionary cost budgets are not used to assess efficiency, because performance standards for discretionary expenses are difficult to devise. For example, if Procter & Gamble's research and development department exceeds its budget, it will often be difficult for managers to determine how that department's work could have been performed more efficiently.

revenue budget Budget measuring marketing and sales effectiveness by multiplying the unit price of each product by the predicted sales quantity.

Revenue Budgets. **Revenue budgets** are meant to measure marketing and sales effectiveness. They consist of the expected quantity of sales multiplied by the expected unit selling price of each product. The revenue budget is the most critical part of a profit budget, yet it is also one of the most uncertain, because it is based on projected future sales. Companies with a large volume of back orders, like Volvo, or those whose sales volume is limited only by the companies' productive capacity can make firmer revenue forecasts than can companies that must reckon with the fluctuations of an unstable or unpredictable market—for example, Exxon. However, marketing and sales managers of even these latter companies can control the quality and quantity of their advertising, service, personnel training, and other factors that affect sales. This control gives them some influence over sales volume and frequently enables them to make reasonably accurate sales estimates.

profit budget (or **master budget**) Budget combining cost and revenue budgets in one unit.

Profit Budgets. A **profit budget** combines cost and revenue budgets in one statement. It is used by managers who have responsibility for both the expenses and revenues of their units. Such managers frequently head an entire division or company, like R. S. Reynolds' food products subsidiary. Profit budgets, sometimes called *master budgets,* consist of a set of projected financial statements and schedules for the coming year. Thus, they serve as annual profit plans. As Exhibit 19-2 indicates, profit budgets have three main uses.

EXHIBIT 19-2 THE MAIN USES OF PROFIT BUDGETS

1. They plan and coordinate overall corporate activities. For example, they make it possible to integrate the use of manufacturing facilities with sales forecasts.
2. They provide benchmarks that are useful in judging the adequacy of expense budgets. For example, if the budget indicates that profits will be low, the expense budget might be revised downward.
3. They help assign responsibility to each manager for his or her share of the overall organization's performance.

Financial Budgets

The *capital expenditure, cash, financing,* and *balance sheet budgets* integrate the financial planning of the organization with its operational planning. These budgets, prepared with information developed from the revenue, expense, and operating budgets, serve three major purposes. First, they verify the viability of the operating budgets ("Will we generate enough cash to do what we are planning to do?"). Second, their preparation reveals financial actions that the organization must take to make execution of its operating budgets possible ("If events conform to plans, we'll be short of cash in October and November; we'd better talk to our bankers this month about a line of credit to cover that period''). Third, they indicate how the organization's operating plans will affect its future financial actions. If these actions will be difficult or undesirable, appropriate changes in the operating plans may be required. (''In order to make our planned capital expenditures, we will have to arrange major borrowings in the capital markets in the next 12 months. But our economists say that will be poor timing; we had better rethink the expansion of our unit in Texas.'') Recent research has found that industry is adopting increasingly sophisticated financial budgeting techniques. Most of these have been developed by academics.[20]

capital-expenditure budget Budget indicating future investments to be made in buildings, equipment, and other physical assets of the organization.

Capital-Expenditure Budgets. **Capital-expenditure budgets** indicate the future investments in new buildings, property, equipment, and other physical assets the organization is planning to renew and expand its productive capacity. For example, Dow Chemical annually budgets funds for innovative or additional processing plants, handling devices, and transportation equipment.

Formulation of the capital-expenditure budget reveals important projects the organization will undertake and significant cash requirements the organization will face in the future. Because of the long useful life of buildings and equipment and their relative inflexibility, the choices made on new capital expenditures are not easily altered. Thus, the decisions in the capital-expenditure budget are frequently among the more important for the organization.

cash budget Budget combining estimates for revenues, expenses, and new capital expenditures.

Cash Budgets. **Cash budgets** bring together the organization's budgeted estimates for revenues, expenses and new capital expenditures. The development of the cash budget will frequently reveal information about the *level* of funds flowing through the organization and about the *pattern* of cash disbursements and receipts. For example, preparation of the cash budget may show that the firm will be generating a great deal more cash than it will be using during the next year. This information may encourage management to move more aggressively on its capital expenditure program or even to consider additional areas of investment.

financing budget Budget which assures the organization of available funds to meet shortfalls of revenues when compared to expenses and which schedules potential borrowing needs.

Financing Budgets. **Financing budgets** are developed to assure the organization of the availability of funds to meet the shortfalls of revenues relative to expenses in the short run and to schedule medium- and longer-term borrowing or financing. These budgets are developed in conjunction with the cash budget to provide the organization with the funds it needs at the times it needs them. A local florist, for example, may establish a yearly financial budget that shows monthly revenues, cash inflows from debts, labor, material, overhead, and loan-payment expenses involved in operating the business.

balance-sheet budget (or **pro forma balance sheet**) Budget combining all other budgets to project the balance sheet at the end of the budgeting period.

TEACHING TIP

There's a lot of different terms here. Help students see the variations by looking at what each type of budget is designed to do (show).

Balance-Sheet Budgets. The **balance-sheet budget** brings together all of the other budgets to project how the balance sheet will look at the end of the period if actual results conform to planned results. This budget, also called a *pro forma balance sheet,* can be thought of as a final check on the organization's planned programs and activities. Analysis of the balance-sheet budget may suggest problems or opportunities that will require managers to alter some of the other budgets. For example, the balance-sheet budget may indicate that the company has planned to borrow more heavily than is prudent. This information might lead to a reduction in planned borrowing and reduced capital expenditures or—alternatively—to issue additional stock to obtain some of the desired financing.

---

[20]Thomas P. Klammer and Michael C. Walker, ''The Continuing Increase in the Use of Sophisiticated Capital Budgeting Techniques,'' *California Management Review* 27, no. 1 (Fall 1984):137–148.

Variable versus Fixed Budgets

One difficulty with budgets is that they are often inflexible. Thus, they may be seen as inappropriate for situations that change in ways beyond the control of those responsible for achieving the budgeted objectives. For example, an expense budget based on annual sales of $12 million may be completely off track if sales of $15 million are achieved. The expense of manufacturing will almost always increase if more items are produced to meet the larger demand. It would therefore be unreasonable to expect managers to keep to the original expense budget.

To deal with this difficulty, many managers resort to a *variable* budget. (This type of budget also is referred to as a flexible budget, sliding-scale budget, and step budget.) Whereas *fixed* budgets express what individual costs should be at *one* specified volume, variable budgets are cost *schedules* that show how each costs should vary as the level of activity or output varies. Variable budgets are, therefore, useful in identifying in a far and realistic manner how costs are affected by the amount of work being done.

There are three types of costs that must be considered when developing variable budgets: fixed, variable, and semi-variable costs.[21] The fixed and variable cost components are illustrated in Figure 19-6.

fixed costs Those unaffected by the amount of work accumulated in the responsibility center.

Fixed Costs. **Fixed costs** are those that are unaffected by the amount of work being done in the responsibility center. These costs accumulate only with the passage of time. For example, for many organizational units, monthly salaries, insurance payments, rent, and research expenditures will not vary significantly for moderate ranges of activity.

[21] We are indebted to Glenn A. Welsch, *Budgeting: Profit Planning and Control,* 4th ed. (Englewood Cliffs, N.J.: Prentice Hall, 1976), for our treatment of this topic.

FIGURE 19-6 THE VARIABLE AND FIXED COMPONENTS OF TOTAL COST

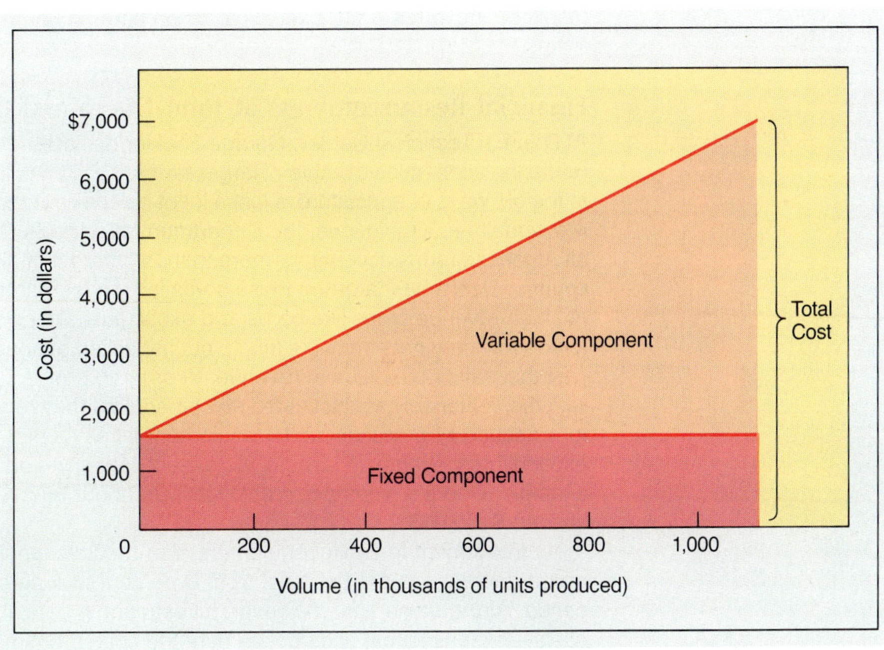

variable costs Expenses varying directly with the amount of work being performed.

Variable Costs. **Variable costs** are expenses that vary directly with the quantity of work being performed. An example is raw materials—the more goods produced, the greater the quantity (and cost) of raw materials required.

semivariable costs Those, like short-term labor costs, varying with the amount of work performed but not in a proportional way.

Semivariable Costs. **Semivariable costs** are those that vary with the volume of work performed but *not* in a directly proportional way. Semivariable costs often represent a major part of an organization's expenses. For example, short-term labor costs are usually semivariable—the number of personnel hired (or laid off) will rarely be based directly on day-to-day changes in production. Similarly, the cost of the total sales effort often does not vary directly with the number of products sold.

In devising their budgets, managers must try to break down their total costs into fixed and variable elements. The result will be more accurate and useful budgets. The problem in devising variable budgets is that cost variability is often difficult to determine. (The problems and methods of devising variable budgets are discussed in Exhibit 19-3.)

EXHIBIT 19-3 DEVISING VARIABLE BUDGETS

1. *Direct estimates.* Managers estimate which components of their expenses are variable, either by exercising their judgment based on experience or by relying on studies performed by industrial engineers.
2. *High and low point method.* Two budgets are developed—one for maximum assumed output and one for minimum assumed output. The difference in cost between these two budgets divided by the difference in volume will yield the variable rate.
3. *Correlation method.* Monthly data on the organization's past output and cost variability are assembled. Projections based on these data and on conditions in the present are made to estimate future cost variability.

Variable budgets are used most appropriately in responsibility centers, where operations are repetitive, where there are a large number of different expenses, and where these expenses can be accurately estimated. Large-scale expense centers, such as the manufacturing facilities in the steel and toy industries, are particularly well-suited for the variable budget approach. The main disadvantage of variable budgets is that they are often quite expensive to prepare.

ILLUSTRATIVE CASE STUDY Continued

Financial Resourcefulness at John Deere and Company

At Deere's Technical Center, George Stickler declares, "We've never found a way to refute the economies of scale of larger farms. . . . I think the whole idea of going back to the old ways of agriculture is just a lot of baloney." Although statistics on the matter are sometimes ambiguous, the Department of Agriculture reports that 0.4 percent of all American farms account for more than 20 percent of all agricultural revenue in this country. Deere has targeted these so-called, "super farms," which often raise costly but high-revenue crops like herbs and exotic nuts. An error of one foot in the width of a crop row may not seem like much, but multiplied over several hundred acres, it can cost thousands of dollars in revenue. In order to provide such agricultural operations with the immensely sophisticated machinery that they require, Deere committed itself to a decade of massive capital equipment investments. Initially costly, such capital expenditures eventually create increased capacity—and productivity. In 1976, for example, Deere's sales per employee was about $57,000; by 1985, that figure exceeded $100,000.

Investment in capital equipment also reduces labor costs—at Deere, the gain was a decrease in per-unit cost from 8 percent to 4 percent over the same 10-year period. At the same time, however, investment in capital equipment increases *fixed costs*—expenses that accumulate over the course of time and are unaffected by the numerical difference between revenues and expenditures. Thus, the company's *break-even point* rises, whereby losses must be incurred or prices hiked. Since neither option is desirable, Deere was forced to lower its break-even point by cutting costs elsewhere: Scheduling efficiency, for example, had to be improved, and the white-collar work force had to be reduced.

In addition, Deere reorganized four major divisions—its foundry, hydraulics-production, drive train-production, and several machined-parts operations—into a Component Works division that produced a total of 70 percent of the finished parts needed for its heavy equipment. Under the new system, each of the four units became "factories within a factory" designed to focus on a narrower line of products and to exercise a great deal more autonomy, efficiency, and flexibility. As a result, each unit is now capable of producing not only the components required for a finished product (a John Deere tractor or combine) but related, salable products which, in effect, are in excess of required capacity. The cost per unit for the parent organization is thus reduced. In 1986, the Component Works division was able to set a goal of reducing its break-even point by 33 percent—to the point at which 22 percent of capacity would be sufficient for the division to break even!

It is important to remember, however, that this financial strategy will succeed only as long as the company also continues to succeed in cutting fixed costs. In all likelihood, Deere will have to follow some of its competitors in closing older plants and consolidating the operations of its facilities.

Zero-Base Budgeting

In the normal budgeting process, the previous year's level of expenditure is often assumed to have been appropriate. The task of individuals preparing the budget is to decide what activities and funds should be dropped and, more often, what activities and funds should be added. Such a process builds into an organization a bias toward continuing the same activities year after year—well after their relevance and usefulness may have been lost because of environmental changes or changes in the organization's objectives.

zero-base budgeting (ZBB) A budgeting approach in which all of the organization's activities, existing and proposed, are considered on an equal footing in resource-allocation decisions, rather than using the previous year's budget as a starting point.

Zero-base budgeting (ZBB), in contrast, enables the organization to look at its activities and priorities afresh. The previous year's resource allocations are not automatically considered the basis of this year's resource allocations. Instead, each managers has to justify anew his or her entire budget request.

ZBB involves allocating an organization's funds on the basis of a cost-benefit analysis of each of the organization's major activities.[22] Exhibit 19-4 discusses the three major steps in zero-base budgeting.

EXHIBIT 19-4 THE MAJOR STEPS IN ZERO-BASE BUDGETING

1. *Break down each of an organization's activities into "decision packages."* A decision package includes all the information about an activity that managers need to evaluate that activity and compare its costs and benefits to other activities, *plus* the consequences expected if the activity is not approved, and the alternative activities that are available to meet the same purpose.
2. *Evaluate the various activities and rank them in order of decreasing benefit to the organization.* Usually each manager will rank the activities for which he or she is responsible. Rankings for all organizational activities are reviewed and selected by top managers.
3. *Allocate resources.* The organization's resources are budgeted according to the final ranking that has been established.

[22]See Peter A. Pyhrr, "Zero-Base Budgeting," *Harvard Busines Review* 48, no. 6 (November-December 1970):111–121.

FOR DISCUSSION

Does ZBB encourage short-term thinking by managers? Why or why not?

ZBB includes these benefits: Managers must quantify each alternative and thereby provide the measures needed for comparisons; low-priority programs can be cut or eliminated with more confidence; and alternative programs and their advantages are presented with greater clarity for periodic review. However, the approach does have some drawbacks as well. One major problem is that managers are often quite reluctant to submit their programs to such intense scrutiny. Or they may inflate the importance of the activities they control. In addition, managers often inadequately understand the aims, strengths, and weaknesses of ZBB. Further, their lack of understanding may prevent them from marshaling appropriate data for its implementation.[23] A less critical problem, but one that must be considered, is the increased information processing required by ZBB.[24] These problems can be overcome, however, through proper training of managers and farsighted administration of the entire program.[25]

Functional and Dysfunctional Aspects of Budget Systems

FOR DISCUSSION

Why is acceptability so important?

Like other control methods, budgets have the potential to help organizations and their members reach their goals. How useful budgets are in practice depends on how effectively they are conceived and implemented. It is particularly important that the budgeting process, like other types of control, be clear and acceptable to the people whose activities it controls.

Potentially Functional Aspects of Budgets. V. Bruce Irvine has described some of the potentially functional aspects of budgets.[26]

1. *Budgets can have a positive impact on motivation and morale.* Most individuals need to achieve things they are committed to and desire to be accepted by groups to which they belong. Budgets can activate these motivational factors by creating common goals and the feeling that everyone is working toward them.

2. *Budgets make it possible to coordinate the work of the entire organization.* Since a comprehensive budget is a blueprint of all the firm's plans for the coming year, top management can tie together the activities of every unit.

3. *Budgets can be used as a warning device for taking corrective action.* One of the main purposes of any control system is to alert the appropriate organization members that a standard has been violated. If, for example, actual expenses exceed the budget by a significant margin, then mangers know that some corrective action is probably needed.

4. *The budget system helps people learn from experience.* Once the budget period is over, managers can analyze what occurred, isolate errors and their causes, and take steps to avoid those errors in the next budget period.

5. *Budgets improve resource allocation.* In the budgeting process, all requests for resources should be clarified and logically supported. The need to quantify their plans forces managers to examine their available resources more carefully when considering how to allocate them. Furthermore, it encourages the department head or

---

[23]Stanton C. Lindquist and K. Bryant Mills, "Whatever Happened to Zero-Base Budgeting?" *Managerial Planning* 28, no. 4 (January-February 1981):31–35.

[24]Lawrence A. Gordon, Susan Haka, and Allen G. Schick, "Strategies for Information Systems Implementation: The Case of Zero Base Budgeting," *Accounting, Organizations and Society* 9, no. 2 (1984):111–123.

[25]For a recent book on the use of ZBB in data processing departments, see Thomas J. Francl, W. Thomas Lin, and Miklos A. Vasarhelyi, *Planning, Budgeting, and Control for Data Processing: How to Make Zero Base Budgeting Work for You* (New York: Van Nostrand Reinhold, 1984).

[26]V. Bruce Irvine, "Budgeting: Functional Analysis and Behavioral Implications," *Cost and Management* 44, no. 2 (March–April 1970):6–16.

ETHICS IN MANAGEMENT

THE JIMMY CARTER YEARS

As an aspiring public servant in Georgia, Jimmy Carter was exposed to long-standing patronage and systems "empire building" tactics employed by some politicians and was outraged by practices that he perceived as at least borderline unethical. Drawing on his experience as an engineer and businessman, Carter formulated some ideas to help avoid such practices.

In Carter's view, public programs should exist only if they continued to serve a useful function. According to him, advocates should be required to justify the program's relevance and value. Moreover, the justification must include objective evidence.

When Carter became governor of Georgia, he seized the chance to implement some of his ideas. In particular, prior resource allocations for questionable state programs no longer constituted an automatic base for future budgeting. Instead, administrators were asked to explain each year why the programs were still needed and to justify the levels of funding requested.

Naturally, the approach caused a great deal of controversy, especially among the politicians affected. The experience also identified some refinements required to make the approach viable. When Carter became President of the United States, he used his Georgia experience and the insight of many experts to implement a modified, and more detailed, version of his original idea. Today, the implementation and the concept are still used by many public, and a few private, enterprises.

Sources: Victor Lasky, Jimmy Carter: *The Man and the Myth* (New York: Richard Marek, 1979), pp. 99–120; 313–342; Jack R. Meredith and Samuel J. Mantel, *Project Management: A Managerial Approach* (New York: Wiley, 1984), pp. 183–185.

supervisor to study the manner in which resources are converted into productive activity. Such a study, which will be discussed more fully in Chapter 20, can also reveal unproductive activities, including employee waste and pilferage.

6. *Budgets improve communication.* A plan cannot be put into effect unless it is communicated to those who must carry it out. In the process of developing the budget with those responsible for its implementation, managers can communicate their own objectives and plans more effectively. Suppose, for example, that waste and pilferage are adversely affecting profitability. Budgets will enable managers to demonstrate how such employee behavior can ultimately affect the ability of the firm to pay acceptable wages and avoid layoffs.

HERE'S AN EXAMPLE

MasterCard International, Inc. is facing stiff competition, which is cutting profit margins. Says Arthur B. Ziegler, Chairman of MasterCard, Inc., "MasterCard needs to pull its act together." (*Business Week,* 10/10/88, p. 123)

7. *Budgets help lower-level managers see where they fit in the organization.* The budget gives these managers goals around which to organize their activities. In addition, it indicates what organizational resources will be made available to them.

8. *Budgets let new people see where the organization is going.* This aspect of budgets can enhance the morale of junior managers because it helps them become acclimated to the organization's goals and priorities.

9. *Budgets serve as means of evaluation.* Performance can more easily (and often more fairly) be measured against previously approved benchmarks.

Potentially Dysfunctional Aspects of Budgets. Managers often find that unintended and unanticipated consequences arise from their budget systems. These dysfunctional aspects of their budget systems may interfere with the attainment of the organization's goals.[27] In this section we will describe some of the dysfunctional aspects of the budgeting process that commonly develop.

1. *Differing perceptions of budgets by organization members*. Irvine identified a number of reasons why budgets are often perceived as dysfunctional. Supervisors may view budgets as unfair because others use them to evaluate results without investigating the reasons for success or failure. Budgets would be considered more fair if reasons for budget deviations and mitigating circumstances were taken into account. Supervisors may also find budgets unhelpful in handling immediate problems. Finally, because managers sometimes find it difficult to understand the jargon and specialized formats of performance reports prepared by the budget department, they often cannot adequately respond to the criticism the reports may contain.

2. *Mechanical considerations*. Certain potentially negative effects of budgets can be traced to the mechanics of budgets and the budgeting process. For instance, there are expenses involved in installing and operating a budget system; if these costs outweigh the benefits obtained by the system, the organization's goals are not being effectively achieved.

3. *Communication and budgets*. Often, employees whose performance is being controlled may not know whether they have conformed to the budget until their superiors call them in about a problem or perhaps not even until a performance appraisal takes place. In addition, deviations may not be communicated to them until the budget period is over; as a result, employees never get the opportunity to learn from their mistakes and to initiate corrective action. As a result, budgets may be regarded as a rating tool or as a device for catching mistakes.

However, as Figure 19-7 illustrates, when actual results are communicated immediately and directly, employees affected can then act to correct errors or at least avoid repeating mistakes in the future. In addition, they can rely more confidently on the budget for guidance in their daily activities.

---

[27]Our discussion is based on Irvine, "Budgeting: Functional Analysis and Behavioral Implications," and Argyris, "Human Problems with Budgets."

FIGURE 19-7 THE IMPORTANCE OF THE COMMUNICATION FACTOR WHEN USING BUDGETS TO CONTROL AND MOTIVATE EMPLOYEES

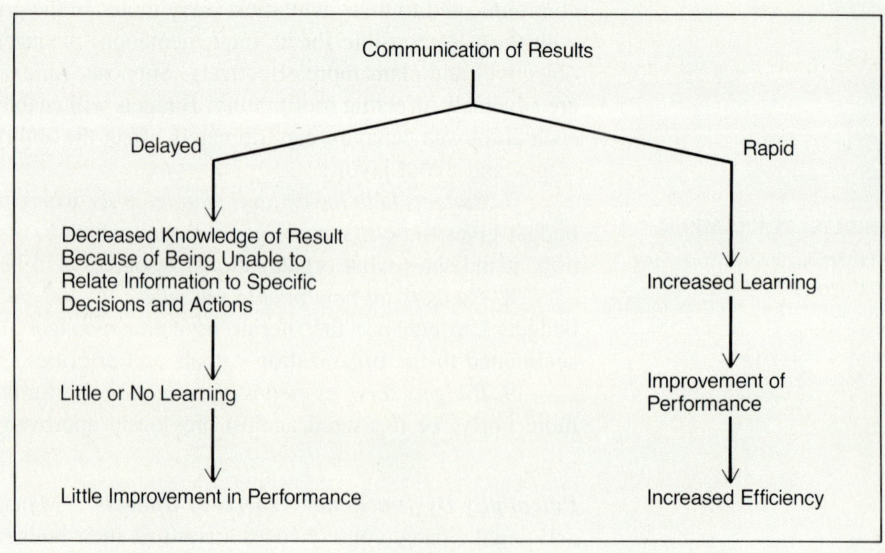

Source: Reprinted from an article appearing in *Cost and Management* by V. B. Irvine, March/April 1970 issue, by permission of The Society of Management Accountants of Canada.

4. *The motivational impact of budgets*. Most managers believe budgets are effective motivational devices. When budgeted standards are not met, it is assumed that people will be motivated to work harder next time around. When high standards are set and made known to employees, most managers believe the employees will be more motivated to attain those standards.

In Kurt Lewin's *force field* concept,[28] which is discussed in Chapter 12, behavior is seen as the result of an equilibrium between opposing *driving* and *restraining* forces. Managers often try to motivate employees to high performance by promising more rewards or applying verbal pressure. The budgeting process also increases the pressure on employees. As Irvine has noted, managers will use budgets to raise their subordinates' performance in a number of specific ways, including budget pep talks, red circles around poor showings, production and sales drives built around the budget, threats of reprimand, and inducing feelings of failure if budgets are not met.

These pressures for increased efficiency are generally felt by employees, who may begin to resist and resent them and find ways to minimize their growing work load and protect themselves from censure. Interdepartmental strife may increase, with every supervisor trying to blame budget deviations on someone else. Scapegoating may increase, as line people blame staff members for budget deviations or production department members blame salespeople for a poor sales record.

To blunt the dysfunctional impact on motivation, Irvine suggests that management would do better if it reduced the forces that decrease performance rather than increasing the pressures for greater performance. For example, the resentment that budget pressures generate can often be reduced when managers and subordinates meet, develop, and agree on budget standards together. Meetings can also be held to discuss any problems that employees anticipate with a particular budget and ways the budget can be improved. The budgets can also be used more openly as a positive rating device; budget staff members should be encouraged to credit publicly individuals who are coming in under budget, instead of just publicizing poor showings. As Peters and Waterman have noted, excellently managed companies tend to be particularly good at celebrating success in meeting the objectives that are frequently included in budgets.

5. *Goal difficulty and goal achievement*. Much of what management writers have noted about negative reactions to budgets is related to two common perceptions. The first is that budget goals may be seen as too high. For example, a very high sales or production level may have been set. Second, the amount of resources allocated to attain the budgeted goals may be perceived as inadequate. For example, the expense budget may be too restrictive for the goals to be accomplished.

HERE'S AN EXAMPLE

Unisys Corporation (company formed with the combination of Burroughs and Sperry) is enjoying a healthy post-merger. Gross margins have improved by over a third during 1988, and net profits in 1988 should rise 30 percent. (*Business Week*, 10/3/88, pp. 123–126)

One generally accepted guideline for effective budgeting is to establish goals that are difficult but attainable. If such goals are set, as Peters and Waterman and other researchers have observed, employees will often be challenged and inspired to improve their performance and meet or exceed the budgeted goals.[29]

Roger Dunbar has analyzed some of the research on goal setting.[30] He suggests that setting high goals will improve performance up to a certain point; eventually, however, the goals become unacceptable to employees, and their performance drops off sharply. Also, there is a point at which even increased performance becomes less profitable for the organization—as goals become more difficult to attain and are con-

[28]Kurt Lewin, "Group Decision and Social Change," in Eleanor E. Maccoby, Theodore M. Newcomb, and Eugene L. Hartley, eds., *Readings in Social Psychology,* 3d ed. (New York: Holt, Rinehart & Winston, 1958), pp. 197–211. See also Edgar F. Huse and Thomas G. Cummings, *Organization Development,* 3d ed. (St. Paul, Minn.: West Publishing, 1985), pp. 72–73.

[29]See Neil C. Churchill, "Budget Choice: Planning vs. Control," *Harvard Business Review* 62, no. 4 (July–August 1984):150–166.

[30]Roger L. M. Dunbar, "Budgeting for Control," *Administrative Science Quarterly 16,* no. 1 (March 1971):88–96.

sistently missed, the cost of coordination increases. When the added cost of coordination nullifies the benefits achieved by higher performance, says Dunbar, then that higher performance is no longer profitable for the organization.

AUDITING

To much of the general public, the term *auditing* conjures up scenes of stern-faced individuals scrutinizing a company's books in order to find out who is cheating the company, how they are juggling the figures to cover it up, and how much they have already embezzled. Although the discovery of fraud is, in fact, one important facet of auditing, it is far from the only one. Auditing has many important uses, from validating the honesty and fairness of financial statements to providing a critical basis for management decisions. In this section, we will discuss two types of auditing: *external auditing* and *internal auditing*.[31]

External Auditing

external audit Verification process involving the independent appraisal of financial accounts and statements.

The traditional **external audit** is largely a verification process involving the independent appraisal of the organization's financial accounts and statements. Assets and liabilities are verified, and financial reports are checked for completeness and accuracy. The audit is conducted by accounting personnel employed by an outside CPA firm, such as Coopers and Lybrand or Booz, Allen, and Hamilton, or by chartered accountants. The auditors' purpose is *not* to prepare the company's financial reports; their job is to verify that the company, in preparing its own financial statements and valuing its assets and liabilities, has followed generally accepted accounting principles and applied them correctly.

The external audit plays a significant role in encouraging honesty not only in the preparation of statements but also in the actual operation of the organization. It is, in fact, a major systematic check against fraud within the organization. For people outside the organization, such as bankers and potential investors, the external audit provides the major assurance that publicly available financial statements are accurate.

The external audit takes place after the organization's operating period is finished and its financial statements are completed. For this reason, and also because it generally focuses on a comparatively limited set of financial statements and transactions, the external audit does not usually make a major contribution to control of the ongoing operations of the organization. However, knowing that the audit will inevitably occur is a strong deterrent against actions that may lead to embarrassment (or an uncomfortable prison term) if they are discovered during or after the audit. Failure to act on the warnings of external auditors can be costly. In June 1985, officials of New York's Transit Authority announced that they would have to write off $100 million of government reimbursement funds because of haphazard documentation of expenses. They had been made aware of the problem by the accounting firm of Ernst & Whitney in 1982, but no action was taken.[32]

Internal Auditing

internal audit Audit performed by the organization to ensure that its assets are properly safeguarded and its financial records reliably kept.

The **internal audit** is carried out by members of the organization. Its objectives are to provide reasonable assurance that the assets of the organization are being properly safeguarded and that financial records are being kept reliably and accurately enough for

[31] See Wayne S. Boutell, *Contemporary Auditing* (Belmont, Calif: Dickenson Publishing, 1970); and Arthur W. Holmes and Wayne S. Overmyer, *Basic Auditing,* 5th ed. (Homewood, Ill.: Irwin, 1976).

[32] Suzanne Daley, "Billing Errors Cost Transit Authority Millions," *New York Times,* June 20, 1985, pp. Al, B16.

the preparation of financial statements. Internal audits also assist managers in appraising the organization's operational efficiency.

The internal audit will evaluate how adequately the organization's control system is working toward realizing organizational objectives. It will evaluate several of the organization's reports for accuracy and usefulness and will lead to recommendations for improvements in the control system. Because of the concentration on the operations of the organization, this process is also known as "operational auditing."

The internal audit may be carried out as a separate project by assigned members of the financial department or, in larger organizations, by a full-time internal auditing staff. The range and depth of the audit will also vary greatly, depending on company size and policy, from a relatively narrow survey to a broad, comprehensive analysis. This more complete internal audit will provide an appraisal not only of the organization's control system but also of its policies, procedures, and use of authority. It may also evaluate the quality and effectiveness of the managerial methods being used.

Although the internal audit does provide management with useful information, it does have some limitations:

1. *Cost.* Internal audits can be expensive, particularly if they are carried out in depth.
2. *Skill.* Internal auditing involves more than simply gathering facts. Well-trained personnel are needed if the results are to be useful to managers.
3. *Tact.* Even if the auditors are skilled, many employees may still regard auditing as a form of "snooping" or "checking up." If the auditors are not tactful and experienced in interpersonal communication, the audit may even have a negative effect on the employees' motivation.

ILLUSTRATIVE CASE STUDY Wrap-Up

Financial Resourcefulness at John Deere and Company

Obviously, Deere's internal financial strategy hinges upon its ability to generate revenue through sales of its products. In turn, its sales strategy hinges upon the success of its network of dealerships—"our greatest assets," according to the company's Marketing Policy Manual. "If they do not succeed, any success we have is bound to be short-lived."

However, it is precisely Deere's relatively strong dealership network that has suffered most from the crunch on the American agricultural economy. Sophisticated tractors and combines retail at roughly $100,000, and dealers usually have to finance inventories running into millions of dollars. The National Farm and Power Equipment Association reports that, between 1980 and 1985, it lost about 20 percent of its membership. How do Deere's dealers hang on in a depressed agricultural economy? There are about 3,500 of them, and they depend heavily on revenue from servicing the machines that they have sold and providing parts for them.

In addition, the parent organization offers generous interest concessions to its dealers, primarily through the John Deere Credit Company, which finances the purchase of both farm and industrial equipment, the latter including bulldozers, snowblowers, riding movers, and other small lawn-and-garden implements. As we have seen, Deere's interest concessions to its dealers have, over the last seven years, cost the company considerable sums of money. In 1984, however, Deere took a major step in consolidating its financial-services capacity by purchasing a company called Farm Plan—a firm that coordinates financial activities with banks in 23 states to loan farmers money for the purchase of everything from heavy equipment to fertilizer. Deere also maintains an insurance division that currently holds 3.7 billion in assets that go a long way toward offsetting operating losses elsewhere. Deere's 1985 financial statement refers politely to "other income" of over $200 million—half of which comes from its financial subsidiaries.

Contemplating food prices is not a favorite pastime for most American consumers, but the fact remains that farm capacity in this country is about 25 percent more than it needs to be. However, for reasons that range from the political to the emotional, American farmers will continue producing—at a rate, according to most analysts, with which its industrial-service sector will be hard-pressed to match. If the farm-machinery business in which John Deere is a major player successfully deploys both its capacity and technological know-how, it should grow in real terms at the rate of about 3 percent per year. ■

SUMMARY

Financial control methods include budgets, financial statements, ratio analysis, break-even analysis, and audits. Commonly used financial statements are balance sheets, income statements, and cash flow and sources and uses of funds statements. These statements are used by managers to control their organization's activities and by individuals outside the organization to evaluate its effectiveness. Common types of ratio analysis are profitability, liquidity, activity, and leverage. These ratios may be used to compare the organization's performance against that of competitors or against its own performance in the past. Break-even analysis is designed to reveal the relationship between costs, sales volume, and profits.

Budgets are among the most widely used devices for controlling and coordinating the activities of an organization. The four major types of responsibility centers that budgets may control are revenue, expense, profit, and investment centers. The budgeting process begins when top management sets the strategies and goals for the organization. The budgeting process begins when top management sets the strategies and goals for the organization. The creation of the budget involves many levels of management, with the budget's final approval coming from the board of directors.

The budget development process typically arouses anxiety among managers, who may react with behavior adverse to the best interests of the organization. Effective participation in the budgeting process usually reduces these reactions.

Overall organizational budgets may be operating or financial. Specific types of budgets include expense (engineered and discretionary), revenue, profit, cash, capital expenditure, and balance sheet budgets. Budgets may also be fixed, variable, or semivariable. Zero-base budgeting is a special budgeting approach that attempts to base resource allocations on current rather than historical needs.

Budgets have potentially functional and dysfunctional aspects. Potentially functional aspects include improved coordination and communication, higher motivation and morale, and increased learning by lower-level managers. Potentially dysfunctional aspects include differing perceptions by line and staff members, mechanical problems, and unnecessary and harmful pressures on organization members. Some of these pressures may be reduced if high but attainable budget goals are set.

Auditing serves many important functions in the organization, from validating the accuracy of financial statements and uncovering fraud to providing a critical basis for management decisions. External auditing is an independent appraisal of a firm's financial accounts and statements. Internal audits are carried out within the organization to assure proper safeguards that exist for company assets, to confirm that records are being accurately kept, and to seek ways of improving organizational efficiency.

Auditing, like other financial functions, is now being computerized. Today's managers can make use of specialized software for preparing everything from financial statements to budgets.

REVIEW QUESTIONS

1. Financial statements are used to control what three major conditions of an organization?
2. What are the major types of financial statements? What information does each type provide?
3. What is ratio analysis? How may comparisons of ratios be made? What are the major types of ratios used by organizations? What information is each type expected to provide?

4. What is the purpose of break-even analysis? What are the steps involved in creating a profitgraph? What is the break-even point? What are the advantages and disadvantages of break-even analysis?
5. Why are budgets so widely used in organizations?
6. What are four major types of responsibility centers? What original units are commonly considered as belonging to each type of center? How is the performance of each center measured?
7. How are budgets prepared, approved, and revised? What are the advantages of lower-level participation in the budgeting process?
8. What four reactions has Henry Tosi described concerning the anxieties of budget development?
9. What types of budgets are used for three of the responsibility centers described in the chapter? Describe each budget. What is the purpose of each budget?
10. What are cash, expenditure, and balance sheet budgets? Why are they used?
11. What are variable budgets? What types of costs must managers consider when devising variable budgets? Why? How may variable costs be determined?
12. What are the basic steps in zero-base budgeting? What are some benefits as well as problems to this approach?
13. What are the potentially functional and dysfunctional aspects of budgets?
14. What are the two basic types of audits? What is the purpose of each type?
15. How has computerization affected financial control?

CASE STUDY The Audit Report

Jay O'Malley was supervisor of general accounting for Mitan Mines in Butte, Montana. One of his responsibilities was to make monthly estimates of the firm's workers' compensation costs. Jay handled the estimate in a standardized manner. Every six months, Mitan Mines would get a billing from the state's Workers' Compensation Commission for costs charged against Mitan during the previous six months. Jay would take this figure, divide it by six, and charge this amount against each of the next six months. In this way, Mitan hoped to accrue the approximate amount to pay the next semiannual bill.

The bill for the last half of 1983 arrived in February 1984. To the surprise of Jay, his boss, the mine's controller, and the mine's general manager, the bill was for nearly double the amount Jay had set aside. Mitan had been charged with several large compensation cases during the latter half of 1983, resulting in a bill for 487,000. Jay had accrued only $264,000.

Standard accounting practices required Jay to charge the underaccrual—$223,000—to February 1984s operations. Jay made the appropriate entry. Jay's boss concurred. But when the preliminary February figures were worked out, the mine's forecasted profit of approximately $150,000 became a $75,000 loss. When the general manager was advised why February's profit had disappeared, he exploded: "No way, I've told head office that we'll make money this month. I understand what the accounting rules are, but I've got to placate my bosses at head office. Adjust the entry you've made. Take the $223,000, and spread it out over three months!"

Jay and the controller explained to the general manager that this was an improper practice and would certainly be uncovered when the internal auditors eventually reviewed the records. The general manager was unmoved. "Just do it the way I tell you. Remember, you work for me, not the accounting profession!"

In July 1984, the company's internal audit group arrived at the plant, unannounced. The four-person team spent three weeks reviewing the mine's financial status and operating practices. Upon completion of their work, they submitted an audit report to the mine's general manager. Copies were also sent to the company's corporate controller, vice-president of mining operations, director of corporate auditing, and chairman of the board. Among the comments made by the audit group was that the mine's controller had disregarded proper accounting practices by not charging the $223,000 workers' compensation underaccrual to the mine's operation in February of 1984. The findings of the audit report resulted in letters from the vice-president of mining operations to the mine's general manager and from the corporate controller to the mine's controller. In effect, the letters said Mitan mines personnel should follow standard accounting practices and refrain from future financial manipulations.

Source: Stephen P. Robbins, *Management: Concepts and Practices,* © 1984, pp. 469–471. Reprinted by permission of Prentice-Hall, Inc., Englewood Cliffs, New Jersey.

Case Questions

1. Who is at fault here?
2. Do you think the audit and resulting letters will achieve their purpose?
3. How would you have handled this situation if you had been the mine's controller.
4. How would you have handled this situation if you were the vice-president for mining operations? ■

Gerald Murphy, *Watch*, 1925. Oil on Canvas. 78½ x 78⅞". Dallas Museum of Art, Foundation for the Arts Collection, gift of the Artist.

20

PRODUCTIVITY AND OPERATIONAL CONTROL*

Upon completing this chapter you should be able to:

1. Explain why production/operations management is important to society, the organization, and the individual.
2. Explain the significance of productivity and describe the way in which it is commonly expressed.
3. Identify factors that affect productivity on the national level and in individual organizations.
4. Discuss the international productivity challenge and how individual companies are competing on the basis of competitive priorities and improved operational control.
5. Describe the major features of an operations system.
6. Identify the six decision areas that go into the design of an operations system.
7. Name the three key objectives of operational planning and control and explain why it is important to strike a balance among them.

Chapter Outline

Introduction
Changing Views of Production and Operations
Productivity
Competitive Priorities for Business
Characteristics of Production/Operations Systems
Designing Production/Operations Systems
Operational Planning and Control Decisions

*This chapter is based in part on information and research provided by James K. Weeks, University of North Carolina at Greensboro.

ILLUSTRATIVE CASE STUDY
Introduction

At Ford, Quality Is Job One

Between 1980 and 1987, Ford Motor Company's market share rose 3 points to 20 percent. Meanwhile, the market share of General Motors, Ford's biggest and most powerful domestic rival, shriveled 9 points to 37 percent. In the first nine months of 1987, Ford earned more money than GM and Chrysler combined. The company's profits for the year totaled $3.3 billion, compared with GM's $2.9 billion. It was the first time that Ford had surpassed GM in profits since 1924. Clearly, Ford was moving forward while GM was spinning its wheels: Ford's 1986 sales were roughly the same as GM's 1981 sales. "If you look at where we are now," muses Ford CEO Donald Petersen, "it's where they were just a few years ago."

Ford has become the comeback player of the decade in the automotive industry—after having lost over $3 billion during the early 1980s. How did such a dramatic turnaround come about? In order to answer this question, we must look at a little history. During the late 1970s and early 1980s, American automobile manufacturers increasingly lost sales to foreign competition. According to most industry analysts, the reason was relatively simple: the inferior quality of American-made cars. The symptoms were especially prominent at Ford when, in 1980, Henry Ford II stepped down as chairman of the company. Philip Caldwell took over as chairman, Petersen as president, and, together, they undertook one of the most dramatic restructuring programs in the annals of American corporate history. For one thing, cost cutting became a top priority: In the early 1980s, Caldwell and Petersen initiated a plan to trim Ford's worldwide labor force of 380,000 by some 50,000 jobs. In so doing, they sent out a clear message to the organization. Cooperation with the new culture at Ford was necessary for everyone who wished to participate in the company's rebirth. By the same token, new avenues for active participation were opened up: A firm believer in participative management, Petersen opened himself to input from individuals at every level of the organization, from vice-presidents to assembly-line workers. "I want you to remember one thing," he is proud of saying. "The credit goes here to my team, not me."

Second, Ford embarked upon an unprecedented program of quality control that went hand-in-hand with its new policy of participative management. "We stopped shipping products," recalls Caldwell, now a senior director at Shearson Lehman Brothers, "if an employee on the floor said they weren't right, and we stopped penalizing people if they didn't make their quotas because of worries about quality. That was a radical departure for Ford." Having concurred with industry-wide analysis that *quality* was the key to rejuvenation, management at Ford undertook an ambitious program to improve its quality-control procedures. The company's extensively advertised slogan became: "At Ford, Quality Is Job One."

Sources: Robert E. Petersen, "How Ford Became #1," *Motor Trend* 39, no. 12 (1987):4, 6–7; Petersen and H.A. Poling, "The U.S.: Team at the Top of No. 2," *Fortune,* November 9, 1987, p. 82; J. S. Treece, "Donald Petersen," *Business Week,* April 15, 1988, pp. 131–134; and Brian Dumaine, "A Humble Hero Drives Ford to the Top," *Fortune,* January 4, 1988, 22–24.

Systems for the production and delivery of goods and services have always been an essential part of civilization. They have existed, in various degrees of sophistication, from the days when our prehistoric ancestors went out on hunting and gathering trips through every stage of history up to and including the establishment of today's tribal meeting place, the suburban shopping mall.

In every modern society, resources are limited. Efficient utilization of resources is necessary if we are to meet educational, health care, and other service and material needs and demands. In addition, the survival of any individual organization depends on how efficiently it produces its goods and/or services. The quality and cost of a product are determined largely by the effectiveness and efficiency of the system used to produce it. And finally, our standard of living and work satisfaction are determined in no small part by the nature of the production systems of our society.[1]

CHANGING VIEWS OF PRODUCTION AND OPERATIONS

Since the industrial revolution, a substantial body of knowledge has accumulated on the use of mathematics, computers, industrial engineering, and behavioral science techniques in manufacturing environments. Successful use of these methods in the first half of the twentieth century helped make the U.S. economy the most productive in the world. From the early 1950s until recently, however, the importance of maintaining leadership in productive activities was largely ignored by American managers in their quest for dynamic marketing approaches and ever more sophisticated financial arrangements. Today, manufacturing systems in the United States need revitalization to remain competitive in the international environment. Production systems, the majority of which were developed several decades ago, also require adaptation to the most recent social, economic, and technological changes.

HERE'S AN EXAMPLE

The trimming and reshaping of U.S. corporations has put unprecedented demands on top executives and on the dwindling number of middle managers. Motivating the remaining employees can mean the difference between being leaner and more competitive or just leaner. (*Fortune*, 5/23/88, pp. 42–52)

However, the U.S. is currently facing a paradox. American manufacturers have typically boosted productivity not by employing new human resources or innovative financial techniques, but by relying on such traditional approaches as plant closings (Chrysler, GM, IBM, Levi Strauss), downsizing (IBM, Xerox), laying off production workers (USX, Chrysler), and selling off failing or unwanted businesses (Exxon, Alcoa, Xerox). As a result, however, the United States currently lags behind Japan, South Korea, Great Britain, Norway, West Germany, Sweden, France, Canada, and other countries in productivity growth.

It has been argued that the problem lies in the fact that American firms focus on capital investment as a means to reduce labor and consequently ignore the huge benefits to be gained from improved quality, reduced inventories, and the more timely introduction of new products. In so doing, America has been shortchanging itself on its own human capital, pouring hundreds of billions of dollars into capital equipment rather than retaining and retraining its valuable human capital and gearing its efforts to improve productivity to new approaches to the relationship between work and productivity. Recently, some companies, such as GM, have begun to balance their capital and human investments as parts of programs to improve overall productivity. Xerox has gone so far as to train the employees of its suppliers in product quality.

---

[1]John O. McClain and L. Joseph Thomas, *Operations Management: Production of Goods and Services*, 2nd ed. (Englewood Cliffs, N.J.: Prentice-Hall, 1985), p. 6.

COORDINATED RESOURCE

A descriptive reading on the strategic importance of manufacturing is "Competing Through Manufacturing," by Steven C. Wheelwright and Robert H. Hayes in *Harvard Business Review*, January–February 1985, pp. 99–109.

Other companies, such as Rockwell, Calcorp, Parker Hannifin Corp., and a few others, are approaching the problem by developing a "new math" formula for productivity, tossing out traditional cost-accounting methods and making capital-investment decisions in new and novel ways. For example, instead of automating to cut costs, they invest in automated capital equipment to cut lead times, boost quality, reduce inventories, and increase flexibility. At Calcorp Inc., a maker of graphic plotters, management surveyed the shop and actually decided to *de-automate* by eliminating the traditional assembly line and using carts to push work around. The new system takes a fraction of the former space and output has tripled. Although not yet a widespread approach, it appears that the "new math" of productivity can add up to new benefits from both structural changes and innovative approaches to technology.[2]

operations The production activities of an organization.

Because of the need to revitalize production systems, the management of *production* and **operations** has reemerged as an exciting and challenging aspect of organizational life. As Exhibit 20-1 demonstrates, three trends are becoming evident in the field of operations.

EXHIBIT 20-1 THREE TRENDS EMERGING IN THE OPERATIONS FIELD

1. Greater worker involvement and participation at all levels of the organization.
2. Significant changes in production process design. For example, increasingly effective methods for integrating design with production requirements have great potential for improving both quality and manufacturability.
3. A growing recognition that a focus on high quality is often associated with high productivity. Productivity and quality are, in fact, now seen as complementary rather than competing goals.

These trends acquire a revolutionary character when contrasted with the traditional view that production/operations management was limited to manufacturing. It was, in fact, originally known as *manufacturing management,* and was oriented primarily toward the production of physical goods in large quantities at the lowest possible cost. However, service organizations also have a production/operations system. H & R Block, for example, produces completed tax returns. Similarly, your local car wash produces clean automobiles. Hence, the newer term, **operations management,** is now used in place of manufacturing management.

operations management Complex management activity that includes planning production, organizing resources, directing operations and personnel, and monitoring system performance.

Operations management typically entails: (1) planning the production/operations system; (2) organizing the necessary human and capital resources; (3) directing operations and personnel; and (4) monitoring the system's performance to be sure it meets organizational objectives. In recent decades, operations management has received particular attention in such areas as retailing, health, transportation, and government.[3]

This chapter will examine the ways in which organizations are improving their productivity in order to remain competitive in today's global markets, the ways in which organizations are managing and controlling their operations systems, the ways in which these systems can be designed and improved, and the ways in which managers can increase the overall productivity of their organizations. In the process, we shall convey some information about new developments in operations management—developments that may go a long way toward rejuvenating U.S. industry.

CLASS COMMENT

Competitive challenges facing U.S. industries are stimulating major investments in new technology.

[2]"The Productivity Paradox," *Business Week,* June 6, 1988, pp. 100–114; "Needed: Human Capital," *Business Week,* September 19, 1988, pp. 100–103.

[3]This discussion is based on Everett E. Adam, Jr., and Ronald J. Ebert, *Production and Operations Management: Concepts, Models, and Behavior,* 5th ed. (Englewood Cliffs, N.J.: Prentice Hall, 1981), pp. 17, 28; and James B. Dilworth, *Production and Operations Management: Manufacturing and Nonmanufacturing,* 2nd ed. (New York: Random House, 1983), p. 14.

PRODUCTIVITY

''The chief means whereby humankind can raise itself out of poverty to a condition of relative material affluence is by increasing productivity.''[4] This should be obvious: The main way to increase output *per capita* (which normally translates directly into the standard of living) is by increasing productivity.

productivity Measure of how well an operations system functions and indicator of the efficiency and competitiveness of a single firm or department.

Productivity is the measure of how well an operations system functions. Individual organizations must be productive to survive. For the individual manager, productivity is an indicator of the efficiency and competitiveness of his or her firm or department.

TEACHING TIP

Emphasize the ratio of outputs to inputs—trying to produce more outputs with less inputs.

Productivity also is important to the economic well-being of the nation. The level of productivity—and changes in this level—can affect inflation, economic growth, and the balance of payments. For example, productivity increases help reduce inflation by counteracting the escalating costs of labor, materials, energy, and other expenses. By increasing productivity, firms also can save scarce resources. In addition, productivity improvements strengthen the competitive position of a firm—or a country—in the international market.

What Is Productivity?

John Kenderick defines productivity as ''the relationship between output of goods and services (O) and the inputs (I) of resources, human and nonhuman, used in the production process; the relationship is usually expressed in ratio form O/I.'' That is, productivity is the ratio of output to input. The higher the numerical value of this ratio, the greater the productivity.

For example, assume that a legal clinic with eight lawyers (the input) produces output consisting of 100 client consultation per day. Productivity would equal 100/8 or 12.50. Assume that a second legal clinic next door has 15 lawyers handling 125 consultations per day. The productivity ratio would be 125/15 or 8.33. The smaller firm has a higher productivity ratio on a quantitative basis. (Whether this is due to the greater skill or experience of its associates or to their lower standards of performance is reflected in the *quality* of their output, an issue that is not factored into this productivity ratio.)

Both productivity ratio for a given period and the comparison with other ratios over time are important measures. The ratio at any given time measures the efficiency of the operations at that time. Comparisons of the ratios over time measure the gain or loss in productivity.

There are two types of productivity ratios:[5]

- *Total productivity* relates all output to all input with the ratio Total Output/Total Input.
- *Partial productivity* relates all output to major categories of input with the ratio Total Output/Partial Input.

COORDINATED RESOURCE

Point out the figures (indicators) given weekly in the *Business Week* Index.

One familiar example of a partial productivity ratio is the labor productivity index or output per work-hour ratio. (The legal clinic example above was such a partial productivity ratio.) Most productivity measures quoted by economists and business executives are, in fact, labor productivity indexes. This partial productivity measure

[4]The following discussion is drawn from John W. Kendrick, *Understanding Productivity: An Introduction to the Dynamics of Productivity Change* (Baltimore: Johns Hopkins, 1977), pp. 1, 14.

[5]Charles E. Craig and R. Clark Harris, ''Total Productivity Measurement at the Firm Level,'' *Sloan Management Review* 14, no. 3 (Sprint 1973):13–29.

may be appropriate for the national economy, but its use is questionable in gauging the productivity of an individual organization.[6]

Improving Productivity in Organizations

Today, much management attention is devoted to measuring and increasing productivity. Such attention has revealed several ways to improve productivity in an organization. Some of the ways include:[7]

1. The introduction of decision support systems
2. Opening a central warehouse with automatic storage and retrieval
3. Smoothing work flow to cut down on the number of employees needed at peak times
4. Providing computer facilities in user areas
5. Training
6. Incentive programs based on increases in long-term productivity

Attempts to increase productivity have been classified by Jon English and Anthony R. Marchione as either *big bang approaches* or *incremental approaches*.[8]

Subscribers to the "big bang" method attempt to boost productivity by large one-time investments in capital equipment. Although this approach is often effective, improvements in technology and equipment do not automatically lead to higher productivity. As English and Marchione have noted, for example, the airline industry learned a painful lesson when it invested in jumbo jets in 1966. Productivity was hardly improved by operating scores of high-priced planes with more empty seats than passengers.

The incremental approach seeks to improve productivity by making small changes in equipment, training, and procedures. This approach recognizes that, no matter how new or technologically advanced its equipment, an organization cannot be truly efficient unless its people, processes, and structure are efficiently coordinated.

HERE'S AN EXAMPLE

Some service companies are finding that computers don't always improve productivity. Many reasons are given such as: not changing existing practices to exploit technology, preoccupation with marketing maneuvers, and data overload. Says a retired Xerox Corporation computer executive in response to these problems, "There are no computer problems. There are only management problems." (*Wall Street Journal*, 4/19/88, p. 37)

One type of business that has been relatively successful in improving productivity is the retail clothing store. The average annual improvement in the productivity of labor in retail stores over the past 16 years has been 2.9 percent in retail clothing, compared with 1.2 percent for all nonfarm businesses.[9]

There are several apparent reasons for this success. One is the increase in the ratio of chain stores to unaffiliated independents. This large ratio results in an overall increase in productivity for the industry because chain stores have greater sales per employee than the independents. The latter emphasize personal service and are consequently far more labor-intensive. Another contributing factor is the proliferation of discount clothing stores. These stores employ such features as self-selection and central checkout, which raise the productivity levels.[10]

Technological advances have greatly contributed to the increased efficiency of retail stores in general. Point-of-sale computers have facilitated the monitoring of stock

---

[6]Donald J. Wait, "Productivity Measurement: A Management Accounting Challenge," *Management Accounting* 16, no. 11 (May 1980):25.

[7]For these and other examples, see K. L. Brookfield, "Dimensions of Productivity Improvement," *Journal of Systems Management* 34, no. 12 (December 1983):26–29; and Robert C. Holland, "Strategic Planning: Some New Directions," *Journal of Accountancy* 156, no. 3 (September 1983):132.

[8]Jon English and Anthony R. Marchione, "Productivity: A New Perspective," *California Management Review* 25, no. 2 (January 1983):58.

[9]Brian Friedman, "Apparel Stores Display Above-Average Productivity," *Monthly Labor Review* 107, no. 10 (October 1984):37.

[10]Shoppers who desire personal attention from salespeople might argue that some of these "productivity" improvements are overstated because the decrease of quality implicit in decreased personal service has not been taken into account.

levels and made for speedier reordering. The computerization of customer billing and accounts payable has reduced the amount of time spent on bookkeeping. More effective security and antishoplifting systems have contributed by lowering theft costs.

Because of investment cost, computerization had been largely confined to chain stores until recently. As the price of microcomputers and specialized retailing software continues to fall, however, more and more small independent retail shops are taking advantage of that technology to narrow the productivity gap between themselves and chain stores. Some managers are now calling on computers for help in analyzing various staffing patterns and their associated costs. For example, a manager might devise alternative staffing plans based on his or her own experience, and then use a spreadsheet program to determine the comparative costs of each approach.[11]

Productivity through People

COORDINATED RESOURCE

For a provocative and disturbing report on the state of the U.S. labor force, see "Human Capital: The Decline of America's Work Force," *Business Week*, 9/19/88, pp. 100–141.

Workers' attitudes have an important influence on productivity. In recent years, much concern has been expressed about the apparent decline of the vaunted U.S. work ethic—the American commitment to hard work and personal achievement. A study by Daniel Yankelovich and John Immerwahr for the Public Agenda Foundation[12] has demonstrated the alarming lack of commitment of many Americans to their jobs, but does not attribute that lack of commitment to the loss of the old work ethic. This study found that the work ethic was still alive and healthy; yet only 23 percent of workers surveyed reported that they are performing at full capacity, almost half (44 percent) said they do not put a great deal of effort into their jobs over and above what is required, and 62 percent of workers, managers, and labor union leaders believed people are not working as hard as they used to. Yankelovich and Immerwahr attribute much of this lack of job effort to management's failure to reward hard work and high performance. For example, almost one-half of the managers surveyed said there was no relationship between how good a job people do and how much people are paid.

Faced with the task of improving productivity, many managers concentrate on updating equipment rather than on developing employees. Experience has shown this approach to be limited in effectiveness. According to one set of estimates since 1929 less than one-fifth of American productivity improvement has been due to increasing the amount of capital per worker. More than 75 percent has been due to improving worker training and knowledge, health care, and the allocation of tasks.[13]

Peters and Waterman (see Chapter 1) revealed that the excellently managed companies they studied see the average employee "as the root source of quality and productivity gain." Such companies do not look to "capital investment as the fundamental source of efficiency improvement." Instead, employees are considered the source of ideas for improvement. Keys to the excellent companies' success in achieving high productivity are having high expectations for their employees' performance, "respecting them as individuals," trusting them, and "treating them as adults."[14]

In a subsequent book, *Thriving on Chaos* (1987), Peters has gone further in arguing that there are *no* excellent companies based on traditional hierarchical management and organizational structures. He sets forth new criteria for contemporary excel-

---

[11]F. Warren Benton, EXECUCOMP—*Maximum Management with the New Computers* (New York: Wiley, 1983), p. 167.

[12]Daniel Yankelovich and John Immerwahr, *Putting the Work Ethic to Work: A Public Agenda Report on Restoring America's Competitive Vitality* (New York: Public Agenda Foundation, 1983).

[13]Thomas R. Horton, "Training: A Key to Productivity Growth," *Management Review* 72, no. 9 (September 1983):2.

[14]Thomas J. Peters and Robert H. Waterman, Jr., *In Search of Excellence: Lessons from America's Best-Run Companies* (New York: Warner Books, 1982), pp. 14–15, 260–277.

lence, such as world-class quality, enhanced responsiveness through increased flexibility, and commitment to continuous innovation and improvement. Peters stresses the need to empower people and argues that the emergence of a genuinely global marketplace creates the need for new approaches not simply to managing employees but to restructuring whole organizations in the interest of flexibility, adaptability, and creative agility as necessary measures for surviving an increasingly turbulent environment. He argues that the organization of the future will demand that all employees, including and especially management, ignore traditional, hidebound formal boundaries so that everyone will be prepared for timely decision making and responsive action.[15] In *The Renewal Factor* (1987), Waterman stresses the integral importance of *people's* engagement in the workplace. He argues for the increased empowerment of employees and stresses the values of teamwork, trust in the organization's work force, and a commitment from management that all of the organization's human resources will contribute to its mission.[16]

Several studies have delved into the particulars of the relationship between human-resource motivation and productivity. Don Nightingale, for example, has concluded that *profit sharing* has led to productivity improvement in thousands of firms.[17] Company-wide profit-sharing plans can be particularly effective in situations where supervising and evaluating individual performance is not viable. Additionally, profit sharing can lower internal resistance to technological change and foster teamwork between employees.

HERE'S AN EXAMPLE

General Motor's new compensation plan reflects a general trend toward tying pay to performance. Says Roy S. Roberts, Vice-President for Corporate Personnel, "If you are a poor performer, we're going to work with you to try and make you a better performer. If you cannot do that over time, we'll have to ask you to leave the team." (*Wall Street Journal*, 1/26/88, p. 39)

The use of *financial incentives* to motivate performance had been a part of management theory of quite some time. For example, Frederick W. Taylor (see Chapter 2) wrote in 1911 that "the best type of management in ordinary use . . . [is] the management of 'initiative and incentive.'[18] (The use of rewards is discussed more thoroughly in Chapter 14.)

HERE'S AN EXAMPLE

Maytag Company's nonsupervisory personnel turned in 6,346 suggestions (an average of 3 per employee) during 1987. More than 2,700 of these ideas were actually implemented. Employee awards, which ranged up to $7,500, totaled $200,322. (*Wall Street Journal*, 3/15/88, p. 1)

Many companies are finding that offering financial or merchandise awards to employees for productivity improvement ideas can pay off quite effectively. Employees of Stanley Air Tools, which implemented a program offering prizes such as video recorders, generated 18,000 ideas, of which 4,000 were found to be usable.[19] The amount that companies award for successful ideas is generally related to the value of the suggestions. For example, a company might give a certain percentage of the amount saved by implementing a suggestion or offer a set dollar amount for ideas leading to less measurable improvements, such as increased safety or worker attendance.

The concept of *white-collar productivity* is growing in importance as the ratio of white-collar to blue-collar workers continues to rise. The need for improvement in this area is accentuated by the estimates of some experts that most office employees waste 45 percent of the day.[20] Furthermore, some predict that, by the turn of the century, the percentage of all wage earners represented by white-collar workers might rise from the current number of slightly more than half to as much as 90 percent.[21]

---

[15] Peters, *Thriving on Chaos: Handbook for a Management Revolution* (New York: Alfred A. Knopf, 1987).

[16] Robert H. Waterman, Jr., *The Renewal Factor: How the Best Get and Keep the Competitive Edge* (New York: Bantam, 1987).

[17] Don Nightingale, "Profit Sharing: New Nectar for the Worker Bees," *Canadian Business Review* 11, no. 1 (Spring 1984):11.

[18] Frederick W. Taylor, *The Principles of Scientific Management* (New York: Norton, 1947; originally published in 1911), p. 34.

[19] Bruce A. Jacobs, "Prizes for Productivity Ideas," *Industry Week*, July 11, 1983, p. 66.

[20] Merrill Douglass and Donna Douglass, "Improve White-Collar Productivity," *Personnel Administrator* 27, no. 2 (December 1982):12.

[21] Edmund Fitzgerald, "Telecommunications Seen as the Missing Link in the Productivity of Managers," *Communications News* 20 no. 12 (December 1983):100–101.

Factors Influencing Productivity

The role of management in influencing productivity gains is clear. However, many other interrelated factors also affect productivity. Their complexity is clear when we look at the following considerations.

QUOTATION FROM A MANAGER

"This business is so competitive we need everybody pulling their weight." —Roy S. Roberts, Vice-President for Corporate Personnel, General Motors Corporation (*Wall Street Journal*, 1/26/88, p. 39)

Work Force. The makeup of the work force is very important to productivity. For example, many countries with basically homogeneous cultures—including South Korea, Norway, France, West Germany, Canada, Belgium, Denmark, Great Britain, the Netherlands, Japan, and Sweden—enjoyed a 2 to 3 percent growth rate in output per worker between 1981 and 1985, while the United States with an increasingly heterogenous population, experienced only a 1 percent growth rate. The diversity of the United States work force may eventually contribute to enormous gains over the long run, but the initial problems entailed in integrating thousands of people from numerous different cultures, may of them less (or differently) educated than their American counterparts and unfamiliar with American rules of the organizational game, remain a constant challenge to the United States in its ongoing efforts to increase worker productivity in an economy that is as complex as its work force is heterogeneous.[22]

Energy Costs. The costs of oil, gas, and electricity have a significant effect on productivity. Spiraling energy costs and shortages were regarded by many observers as the biggest factors in slowing productivity growth during the 1970s.

Condition of Facilities and Investment in New Plants and Equipment. Other nations, starting from a nonindustrial base or rebuilding after wartime destruction, have modern, efficient production facilities. On the other hand, U.S. industry, especially heavy industries such as steel, has been hampered by old facilities and outdated equipment.

HERE'S AN EXAMPLE

Innovating—creating new products, new services, new ways of producing—has become the most urgent concern of corporations everywhere. Who are the innovators: Procter & Gamble, Corning Glass Works, General Electric, Monsanto, etc. (*Fortune*, 6/6/88, pp. 51–64)

Level of Research and Development Spending. The 1980s have seen a significant improvement in industry support for basic research at universities.[23] This improvement follows a decade or so of reduced investment in research and development by both government and private industry. The research on manufacturing that was carried out during the 1970s tended to concentrate on saving energy and reducing pollution rather than focusing on improving worker performance and productivity processes. The result was that, in many cases, productivity improvement lagged.

Growth of the Less Productive Service Sector. In 1970, 20 million people were employed in the service sector; by 1983, however, the figure had increased to 31 million. Much of the increase was in jobs that pay below-average wages, such as fast-food-chain attendants and nursing-home aides. At the same time, those employed in manufacturing have decreased slightly, from 20.7 million in 1970 to 19.9 million in 1983, and agricultural workers have remained about the same.[24]

Changes in Family Structure. With over half of married women at work, the increased divorce rate, the attraction of alternative life-styles, and the increase in single-

[22]Thomas Rollins and Jerold R. Bratkovich, "Productivity's People Factor," *Personnel Administrator*, February 1988, pp. 50–57.

[23]Donald R. Fowler, "University-Industry Research Relationships," *Research Management* 27, no. 1 (January–February 1984):35.

[24]*Statistical Abstract of the United States:* 1985, 105th ed. (Washington, D.C.: Bureau of the Census, 1984), p. 404.

parent families, added financial and emotional pressure on many workers may produce negative effects on work performance.

Increased Use of Alcohol and Drugs. This is a difficult factor to evaluate, but alcohol and drug abuse, more frequent now than a few decades ago, is now estimated to cost U.S. businesses nearly $50 billion annually. The loss of dollars, as well as the tragic impact of substance abuse on individuals, has prompted the establishment by many companies of Employee Assistance Programs (EAPs) to help employees and their families overcome their problems and resume their places as productive members of their organizations.[25]

A Shift in Workers' Attitudes and Motivation. As we noted earlier, some employers and social critics contend that workers today no longer have the traditional work ethic: that is, that they no longer work as hard as they used to. Other observers believe the work ethic is strong but that management practices discourage workers from doing their best on the job.

Cost to Industry of Government Regulation. Many industries must comply with strict government regulations concerning pollution control and other measures to improve health and safety on the job. Productivity is affected because the cost of the equipment and paperwork involved has to be absorbed by the business organizations affected. The 1980s have seen a decrease of regulation in some areas.

Financial Pressures. In recent years inflation has been minimal. When it is high, however, it may affect productivity growth by making it difficult to anticipate and control production costs and by discouraging additional investment. However, the late 1980s saw an increase in the inflationary trend that combined with such fiscal problems as a weak dollar, a volatile stock market, an enormous federal deficit, and balance-of-trade concerns, to have significant effects on investment and productivity patterns in the United States.

Tax Policies. Outdated tax laws have frequently penalized new investment by ignoring inflation. Deductions for depreciation have been spread over too long a period to provide for replacement costs of outdated equipment, and rising prices can create illusory profits on which real taxes must still be paid.

The impact of the factors just discussed (as well as others) upon future productivity growth is varied. Some factors may be temporary and their effects already absorbed by the economy. For example, the work force expansion during the 1970s has slowed down and is not likely to retard future productivity gains. The 1981 tax bill was designed to encourage business investment, and tax reform in 1987 has had a variety of effects. Other factors, such as drug abuse and changes in family structure, are social problems affecting all levels of national life. But some must be addressed by managers if productivity gains—necessary to counter inflation and improve the quality of life for all—are to be realized. In this latter category are such factors as new facility investment and research and development programs. Figure 20-1 shows that, despite many factors adversely affecting U.S. productivity, sales per employee have grown in several key industries over the last decade.

---

[25]Philip Hunsaker and Cynthia Pavett, "Drug Abuse in the Brokerage Industry," *Personnel,* July 1988, pp. 54–58.

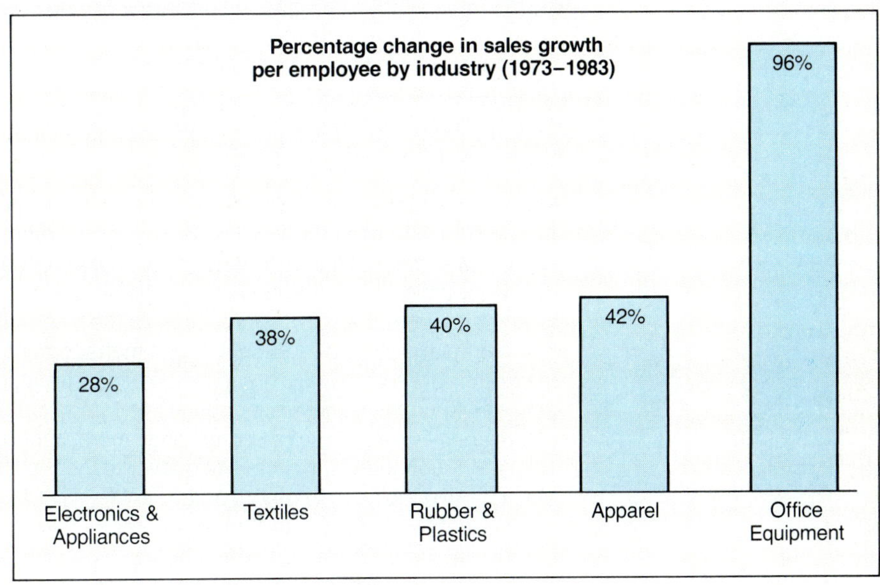

Source: Peter Nulty, "The Princes of Productivity," *Fortune,* April 30, 1983, p. 254. Used by permission.

FIGURE 20-1 PRODUCTIVITY GROWTH IN CERTAIN INDUSTRIES

Productivity Management

HERE'S AN EXAMPLE

A union-management committee at General Motor's seat-cover plant in Grand Rapids, Michigan, has agreed to these changes to boost productivity: just-in-time deliveries, "focused factory" structure, working with suppliers to eliminate shortages, finding ways to do tasks now done by outside contractors. (*Business Week,* 8/8/88, pp. 46–47)

In an attempt to improve productivity, some organizations have set up systematic and coordinated productivity improvement programs.[26] Chase and Aquilano observe that methods to improve productivity fall into four general categories:

1. Product and process improvements
2. Work and job improvements
3. Employee motivation methods
4. Organizational change

We have explored aspects of these topics in many of the preceding chapters of this book. Work and job improvements are discussed in Chapter 9, the need for change and ways to effect it in Chapters 12 and 13, and employee motivation in Chapter 14. Chapters 18, 19, and 21 examine ways that managers can keep abreast of productivity in their organizations, and Chapter 24 discusses productivity in the light of international management practices.

COORDINATED RESOURCE

An interesting article on companies who are doing a good job of innovating is "The Innovators" in *Fortune,* 6/6/88, pp. 51–64.

Manufacturing companies seem to be doing a better job in controlling and improving some of the principle factors of low productivity, as evidenced by a mid-1980s resurgence in basic manufacturing, with manufacturing companies maintaining 3 percent growth and a 2.2 percent productivity improvement since 1979. Forced by foreign competition to slash its labor force and close obsolete plants, the U.S. manufacturing sector has managed an impressive comeback. General Electric's commitment of $11.6 billion over the past six years is one example of a company attacking a poor capital-labor ratio; for the present, the modernization of the company's major appliance divi-

[26]For a survey of the emerging productivity management staff function, see Mart Mooney, *Organizing for Productivity* (New York: Conference Board, 1981).

INTERNATIONAL MANAGEMENT

THE *MAQUILA* INDUSTRY: THE U.S. SEARCHES FOR IMPROVED PRODUCTIVITY IN MEXICO

Much has been written lately about the production woes of the American industrial sector. Reasons cited for decreased productivity range from very real increases in international competition to theories about the deterioration of the traditional American work ethic. Whatever the actual factors involved, American firms have begun to employ numerous new approaches to the improvement of productivity—from new workplace strategies such as team management and increased on-line automation to more ambitious organization-wide strategies such as moving a firm's activities to countries where it hopes to find improved productivity through greater commitment to work opportunities and, more importantly, cheaper labor costs.

Although many firms have relocated to the Far East, others, such as General Motors, have looked across the border to Mexico. Of particular interest to growing number of U.S. firms are two cities—Laredo, Texas, and her sister city of Nuevo Laredo, Mexico. These two cities, home to more than 500,000 people, are currently enjoying a tremendous industrial boom that shows few signs of abating in the near future. Many American and foreign companies seeking cheaper labor, lower operating costs, fewer governmental restrictions, and more strategically located stations from which to ship products across the U.S. have settled in the Laredo-Nuevo Laredo area over the last 20 years.

The resultant industry is known as the "*maquila* industry," after the term *maquiladora,* which refers to "production sharing" factories located along the 2,000-mile border, and the very term *maquiladora* has become for many people an almost magical word denoting prosperity for workers on both sides of the border. At present, there are about 1,400 facilities on the U.S.-Mexico border; 90 percent are U.S.-operated, and they employ approximately 390,000 workers. By 1990, there should be about 1,550 plants in the area with a work force of almost 450,000 people.

However, not everyone agrees with the assessment that the *maquiladora* program is a key solution to American productivity and economic problems. For example, in Flint, Michigan, home to GM, employment by the company has dropped from 80,000 in 1978 to less than 48,000 a decade later; by the mid-1990s, the figure could be less than 35,000. "It's unfair," says one 20-year veteran of the GM assembly line in Flint. "The Mexican people are not the ones who buy those cars. At least the Japanese are moving into this country and creating jobs for Americans." And certain figures would seem to bear out this assessment. For

sion appears to have scared off potential Japanese competition. Westinghouse focuses its efforts on the quality of work life by creating work teams that are responsible for their own supervision and for inspecting their own work for quality problems. This approach is similar to the concept of Quality Circles, discussed later in this chapter.[27]

What else can American firms do to continue their remarkable comeback? Most companies develop competitive problems when they lose sight of production's reason for being: to produce quality products that the consumer wants and for which he or she is willing to pay a reasonable price. Companies need to rediscover an operations focus—a plan whereby more time, effort, and commitment is devoted to the efficient

THOUGHT-PROVOKER

How did U.S. companies get away from an operations focus?

[27]For an evaluation of American companies' experience with quality circles, see Robert Wood, Frank Hull, and Koya Azumi, "Evaluating Quality Circles: The American Application," *California Management Review* 26, no. 1 (Fall 1983):37–52.

example, Sony Corp., having established a television plant in San Diego, California, in 1972, opened another in nearby Tijuana, Mexico, in 1987. Currently, Sony employs 1,500 workers in San Diego, 800 in Tijuana. All Sony televisions sold in the United States originate in one of these two plants, and Sony purchases 70 percent of its supplies from American firms—each of which thus requires a work force to keep up with Sony's demands. Nevertheless, many people—particularly union members in the United States—see the *maquilodora* program as a systematic, large-scale depletion of American jobs. Other critics have leveled charges of exploitation, pointing to the large number of Mexican female laborers who often make only $4 a day while continuing to subsist in deplorable living conditions (on a trip to GM's Juarez plant, William H. Bywater, president of the Union of Electronic, Electrical, Technical, Salaried & Machine Workers, observed that many of the company's *maquiladora* workers had set up housekeeping in nearby caves). Proponents of the *maquila* program counter the argument by pointing out that *maquiladora* facilities use U.S. parts and provide work for thousands on both sides of the border, allow the United States to be more competitive in work markets, and help Mexico to pay its foreign debt and stabilize a fragile economy in an area of the world of obvious strategic importance to the United States.

The debate is not likely to disappear, especially as the *maquila* program is continuing to grow and to show results in productivity. Many of the newer *maquilas* involve massive investment in equipment, use the latest manufacturing techniques (such as statistical-control methods), and stress employee involvement, often sharing information on costs, quality, and waste usage with workers. The overall productivity in many of the plants is quite high and appears to be improving at a steady rate. For example, GM's Delco Electronic Corp. plant at Matamoros, Mexico, assembles auto radios and other electronic equipment: The quality of the finished product ranks near the top for the corporation as a whole, with low costs permitting a higher percentage of GM cars to be equipped with Delco-made radios instead of cheaper imported radios. Among the consequences of this improvement in productivity is the retention of jobs at Delco plants in the United States.

Both the impact of the *maquiladoras* on the U.S. economy and the program's productivity rate are well worth watching not only because they focus attention on the issues of productivity and economic progress, but because of the international and domestic social, political, and economic issues that have been raised in the debate between supporters and opponents of the *maquiladora* system.

Sources: Gary Jacobson, "The Boom on Mexico's Border," *Management Review,* July 1988, pp. 21–24; Thomas M. Rohan, "Mexico Border Boom: Salvation or Slavery?" *Industry Week,* August 15, 1988, pp. 46–49.

production of goods. This operations focus entails lowering production costs, cutting down on excessive overhead costs, and reducing quality problems. Of course, there are other considerations. Does the customer want highly reliable or dependable products? Does the customer want a flexible product—one that is capable of being used for many different types of problems? Does the consumer want speedy and reliable customer service? IBM has developed the reputation as the leader in computers by hiring a huge work force of salespeople and customer-service representatives who all are responsive to the needs and desires of the consumer.

COMPETITIVE PRIORITIES FOR BUSINESS

The IBM commitment to service is an illustration of a manufacturer of goods providing the ultimate in service response to a customer—extreme flexibility. The IBM approach demands that customer-service personnel be prepared to answer such questions as How can my company serve you best? and What type of products will satisfy your particular needs? The IBM customer-service representative may not know the answers to all the relevant questions, and the company may not even have a product to meet that specific need, but the company still receives high marks in the mind of the customer because it tries to accommodate that customer's needs and desires. A manufacturer of products can do the same thing: provide flexibility in its product line so that it can react very quickly to specific customer needs.

Unfortunately, "providing flexibility" may not be as easy as it sounds—and may be cost-prohibitive. Producers of products and deliverers of services select certain criteria on which to excel in offering their goods and compete with other companies for customers. Generally, customers will buy products based on how well the products measure up to their standards for certain criteria. For instance, McDonald's offers a product line of hamburgers which are fairly cheap, have a consistent quality, and are highly "standardized." If a customer were more interested in a "special" hamburger ("Hold the ketchup!") to fit his or her individual needs, Wendy's might be a better fast-food restaurant for this individual since Wendy's is set up to handle special requests—although at a slightly higher price.

CLASS COMMENT

All of these are competitive opportunities.

competitive priorities Four major criteria, including pricing, quality levels, quality reliability, and flexibility, on which products are evaluated.

The different criteria on which products are evaluated are called **competitive priorities.** The four major competitive priorities include cost to the consumer (or pricing), quality level, quality reliability, and flexibility.

"We could never have done it without him."

Pricing. Lowering prices squeezes unit-profit margins, but higher sales volumes may follow. For example, Earl Scheib, Inc., of Beverly Hills operates 275 car-repair shops that offer cheap, ''no-frills,'' face-lifts. Unit-profit margins are protected by careful cost accounting, and Scheib's low prices have increased sales at an annual rate of 15 percent and earnings at almost 50 percent per year.

Quality Level. Quality level has two components—namely, high-performance design and fast delivery time. Characteristics of high-performance design are superior features, close tolerances, and greater durability of the product or service. An example is Maytag washers and dryers. In an industry marked by highly competitive products and prices, Maytag has been able to charge premium prices because customers believe in the superior capability of the product and the expected longer life of the washer and dryer. Customers also expect efficient repair schedules if anything happens to malfunction, since the company's advertising depicts the Maytag repairman as an extremely lonely and idle person.

Fast delivery time is also exemplified by fast-food wizard Donald Smith. He has recently taken a top position with Xian, a new Chicago-based Chinese restaurant chain. Smith believes that the maximum waiting time for food served at the service counter must be cut down from 80 seconds to no more than 30 in order for Xian to succeed. In addition, this speedup in service must be accomplished without compromising the high quality of the product.

HERE'S AN EXAMPLE

Alcoa, Inc. knows about quality now. In the early 1980s, Japanese producers of aluminum sheets for beverage cans began to cut into its market. The Japanese were exporting higher-quality aluminum sheets that worked better in high-speed can-making machines. Alcoa responded by building a state-of-the-art facility and launching an ambitious quality-improvement program. The investment is paying off as Alcoa is regaining lost market share and is beginning to export to Japan. (*Wall Street Journal*, 1/11/88, p. 1)

Quality Reliability. Quality reliability is consistent quality and on-time delivery. Consistent quality measures the frequency with which the design specifications are met; McDonald's restaurants are world-renowned for uniformly achieving their design specifications. Although you may not experience the same delights as those offered at five-star restaurants, you can expect the same quality standards whether you eat at a McDonald's in Charlotte, New York, or Paris. Toyota's small cars are not noted for the ability to compete with Cadillacs on quality *level* (consequently the Toyota's price is much lower), but they are world-renowned for their quality *reliability*—they are highly consistent in quality from one individual car to another.

HERE'S AN EXAMPLE

McDonald's Corporation is one of the epitomes of corporate success. Says CEO Mike Quinlan about the ideals instilled by Ray Kroc, late founder of McDonald's, ''. . . standards of excellence. Don't compromise. Use the best ingredients. The best equipment. . . .'' (*Fortune*, 7/4/88, pp. 112–116)

Flexibility. Flexibility refers to both product and volume flexibility. Product flexibility means that product designs are in a state of flux and that the firm places an emphasis on specialization—that is, products are customized to individual preference. The level of output for an individual product is low because the firm competes primarily on its ability to produce difficult, one-of-a-kind products. This is the exact opposite of mass production, where standardization of the product has occurred and the producer makes large quantities of one item. Product flexibility is illustrated by National Semiconductor Corporation's decision to enter the growing market for custom-designed computer chips when the company was hit by a slump in the mass-production sector of the semiconductor industry. It made quick design changes and introduced new products quickly in order to take advantage of an inadequate supply of custom-designed chips. Some of its custom chips sell for as much as $1 million apiece.

HERE'S AN EXAMPLE

A new stage in the modernization of American manufacturing is occurring. It's referred to as computer-enabled enterprise (CEE) and it requires a total change in the way companies are managed. In CEE, the emphasis is on flexibility. Allen Bradley, a manufacturing company based in Milwaukee, reflects the potential of CEE. The company makes over 300,000 different items, but its number of manufacturing employees is only about 2,500 (down from 8,000 ten years ago). (*Wall Street Journal*, 4/19/88, p. 35)

Volume flexibility is the ability to quickly accelerate or decelerate the rate of production as the demand for a firm's product changes. McDonald's is a good example, as it increases or decreases its work force from hour to hour in order to meet changes in customer demands. McDonalds uses a certain number of employees for an eight-hour shift and supplements it by adding part-time employees at noon and 6 P.M. These part-time employees are usually housewives or elderly citizens supplementing Social Security benefits by working a few hours each week.

The primary problem with the criteria of competitive priorities is the fact that they are often conflicting in nature. As a rule, for example, a product that is very flexible is one that is also very costly. If you think about the highest-quality car in the world, you will remember that the Rolls Royce also carries a premium price to offset the expense of that quality. Compaq's line of personal computers includes options allowing the user to run computer programs very fast, to have telecommunications capability, and to have enormous amounts of internal memory; obviously, these options increase the price substantially above the price of a "standard" personal computer. But the key to improved market competitiveness is the ability of a firm to meet all types of consumer demands for a certain product line—a key factor of which the Japanese are quite cognizant, much to the misfortune of many American firms.

CHARACTERISTICS OF PRODUCTION/OPERATIONS SYSTEMS

operations system Production/operations system denoting both manufacturing and service systems.

TEACHING TIP

This would be an excellent time to review basic systems concepts.

In this section we will describe how production/operations systems work. For simplicity's sake, we will use the term **operations system** to denote both manufacturing and service systems.

An organization that produces goods and/or services may be viewed as a *system,* a set of related and interacting components that perform functions and have goals pertaining to the whole. (See Chapter 2.) These related components are called subsystems, and operations is one of them. Decisions made regarding one subsystem usually affect the other subsystems. If, for example, the personnel subsystem declares a 6-month moratorium on hiring, the operations subsystem will certainly feel the effects when terminated employees are not replaced.

The Operations System: A Model

CLASS COMMENT

Inputs Process Outputs—converting inputs into outputs.

The operations subsystem can be defined as a "set of components whose function is to transfer a set of inputs into some desired output."[28] Figure 20-2 provides a conceptual model of this subsystem. As the diagram shows, the input (workers, equipment, and technical knowledge) provides the resources and energies needed to produce the output. Output includes the desired goods and/or services of the organization as well as undesirable by-products, such as atmospheric pollution or toxic waste.[29]

The process of transformation or conversion from input to output are varied. *Physical* transformations occur in manufacturing, *locational* in transportation, and *exchange* in retailing. In warehousing the transformation is merely *storage,* while in a legal firm it is *informational,* in medicine *physiological,* and in entertainment the transformation results in *gratification.*

The external environment includes such factors as government regulations, inflation, economic policies, labor supply and negotiations, weather, international relations, suppliers, vendors, or any other influence on resources and operations. (See Chapter 3.) The feedback loop in Figure 20-2 reflects the information gained during the entire process. This information makes it possible to decide whether changes are required. Exhibit 20-2 demonstrates how this model might be applied to certain components of a hospital's operations.

Operations management activities include both decisions related to the design of the operations system and decisions related to the operation and control of the system. In the first category are decisions on product design, process design, job design,

[28]Richard B. Chase and Nicholas J. Aquilano, *Production and Operations Management: A Life Cycle Approach,* 4th ed. (Homewood, Ill.: Irwin, 1985), p. 10. Many other discussions in this chapter are based on this text.

[29]This description of the model is based on Elwood S. Buffa, *Modern Production/Operations Management,* 6th ed. (New York: Wiley, 1980), pp. 4, 8–9. See also L. J. Krajewski and L. P. Ritzman, *Operations Management: Strategy and Analysis,* (Reading, Massachusetts: Addison-Wesley, 1987), pp. 3–4, 169–208.

capacity planning, layout planning, and site selection. These are long-term, strategic decisions. Operation and control decisions affect such matters as production and inventory planning and control, purchasing, and quality control. Decisions in these areas have to be made frequently and continually to keep the system going.

EXHIBIT 20-2 AN EXAMPLE OF THE FEEDBACK LOOP IN THE OPERATION OF A HOSPITAL

- *Input:* nurses, doctors, medical supplies, equipment
- *Transformation:* health-care treatment
- *Output:* treated patients
- *Feedback:* hospital costs, number of patients treated, quality of care
- *Environment:* government regulations, insurance charges, inflation, labor problems, accidents

Source: Richard B. Chase and Nicholas J. Aquilano, *Production and Operations Management: A Life Cycle Approach*, 4th ed. (Homewood, Ill.: Richard D. Irwin, 1985).

PREDICTION FROM A MANAGER

By the year 2000, four out of five technological breakthroughs are likely to originate outside the United States.—Simon Ramo, an expert on U.S. high tech (*Fortune*, 5/9/88, p. 124)

Operations Management and Strategic Planning. Because the effectiveness of the operations system is so important to the success of the organization, it should be designed to be compatible with the strategies of the organization. (See Chapter 7.) Conversely, existing and future operations systems capabilities should be considered in formulating organizational strategy. The hazards of failing to view operations as an important component of strategy development have been emphasized by U.S. companies' recent competitive problems in worldwide manufacturing industries such as automobiles, machine tools, and consumer electronics.

The operations system operates within the larger framework of organizational strategy. The strategic plan of the organization should serve as a clear, consistent guide to operations policies. Figure 20-3 charts the path of decisions involved in developing a typical operations strategy.

The demands placed upon the operations system to meet organizational strategy should be consistent with the design and operating policies of the operations system.

FIGURE 20-2 CONCEPTUAL MODEL OF AN OPERATIONS SYSTEM

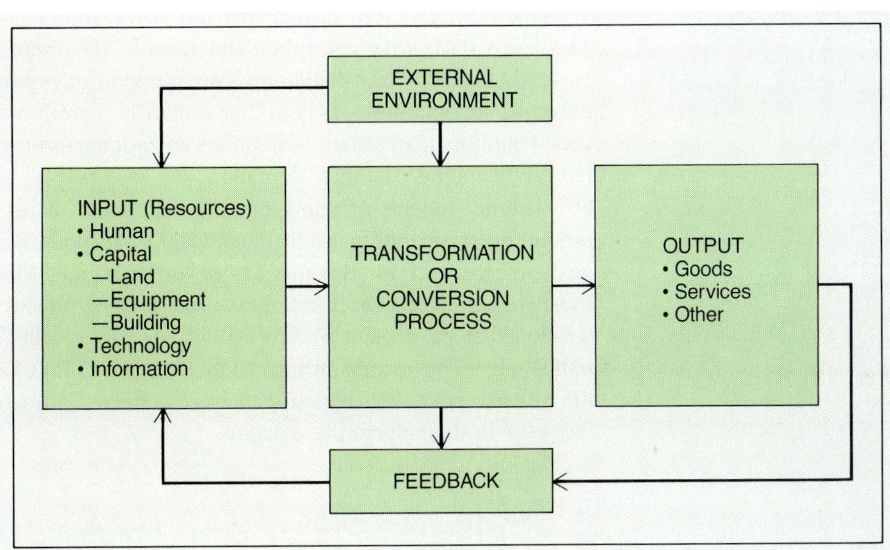

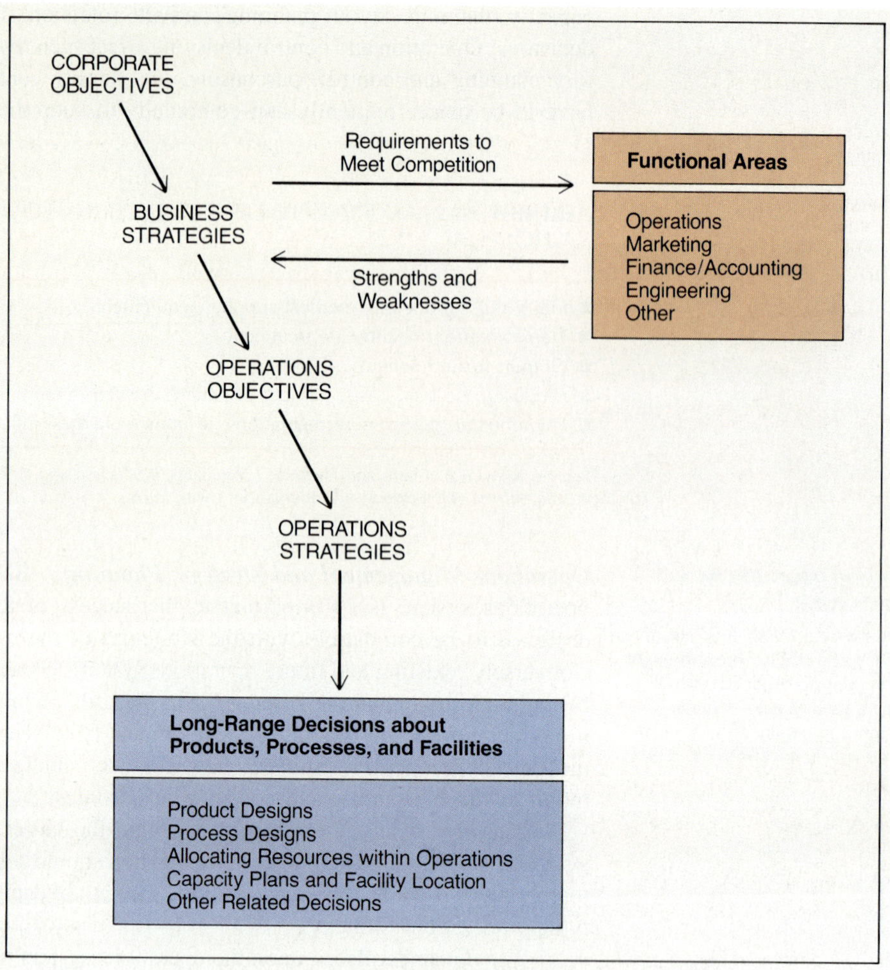

Source: From *Production and Operations Management,* Second Edition, by Norman Gaither. Copyright © 1984 by the Dryden Press. Reprinted by permission of the publisher.

FIGURE 20-3 DECISIONS INVOLVED IN OPERATIONS STRATEGY

Wickham Skinner has termed this top-down approach a "manufacturing focus."[30] This focus starts with an explicit statement of the organization's objectives and strategies, which is then translated into a set of operations system decisions and policies. For example, an operations system that cannot be readily modified to produce new products would be inconsistent with an organizational strategy of a firm that is adapting to rapidly changing customer demand.

Some students of management—and some managers—have tended to look on production or operations as the backwater of corporate activity, removed from the real challenge and action. But this has never been true. Many organizations have in fact prospered precisely because they used their production capabilities as a strategic weapon that gave them a competitive edge over other firms that did not share this philosophy. The success of many Japanese firms, for example, can be traced in part to the effectiveness with which they have achieved attractive design, high quality, and low cost in their operating systems.

[30]Wickham Skinner, *Manufacturing in the Corporate Strategy* (New York: Wiley, 1978), p. 406.

Continuous and Assembly-Line Production and Job-Shop Production. Operations systems can be categorized using a scale that has *continuous and assembly-line production* at one end and *job-shop production* at the other.[31] **Continuous and assembly-line systems** produce standardized output of their own design, frequently in large volumes. Examples are oil refineries, automobile assembly lines, and fast-food chains. In contrast, **job-shop systems** make small amounts of custom-tailored products to satisfy specific contracts. A custom-furniture maker is an example of a job shop, as is an automotive-repair center or a computer software-development firm.

continuous and assembly-line system System producing standardized output of its own design, usually in large volume.

job-shop system System for making small amounts of custom-tailored products, usually to fulfill a contract.

In planning, the type of system selected—continuous or job shop—should be consistent with the nature of the organization's product or service and with the organization's strategic goals. And since products have life cycles, it is necessary for an organization to plan new products from time to time to continue meeting its objectives of growth and efficiency.

ILLUSTRATIVE CASE STUDY Continued

At Ford, Quality Is Job One

During the initial stages of its program to improve quality control, Ford managers discovered that many of the company's materials and component parts were of inferior quality. As a result, many assembled vehicles had to be reworked in order to satisfy factory-inspection standards. Not surprisingly, the process of reworking slowed down the production process considerably. Even after more stringent quality-control measures were imposed, Ford encountered additional problems. Although plant layouts were generally well-designed, there was still poor coordination of work effort. Frequently, materials or assemblies failed to arrive at designated work centers when they were needed to keep the overall production process at levels of full activity. In addition, despite heavy expenditures on market research designed to forecast consumer demand, Ford often found itself with large stockpiles of finished cars sitting in storage areas and awaiting delivery to franchise operators. Moreover, franchise dealerships across the country continued to report a high incidence of consumer complaints and repairs having to be made during warranty periods.

In order to overcome such problems, Ford management made preventive quality control a high priority throughout the organization. Materials and parts were procured only from reliable suppliers, inspected upon delivery, and placed in service only when deemed acceptable to the company. Millions of dollars were also invested in robots and other specialized equipment designed to ensure precision assembly. Perhaps most importantly, in keeping with Petersen's philosophy of participative management, the company formed employee groups that directly incorporated workers into the quality-control effort. An extensive system was established to monitor operations on a continuing basis, with the resultant data used to compare system performance against production input, processing, and output standards. New statistical techniques were adopted throughout the process.

In order to alleviate coordination problems in both manufacturing and production, management took several steps. First, it turned to consumer forecasts to establish the production and shipping schedules needed to accommodate realistic demand. Second, it identified how much material and how many parts and assemblies would be required to meet a variety of production and shipping schedules. Third, a computer system determined the purchase and inventory policies required to provide the materials, parts, and assemblies and specified the times when they would be needed.

---

[31] Dilworth, *Production and Operations Management,* pp. 10–11.

DESIGNING PRODUCTION/OPERATIONS SYSTEMS

Designing a production/operations system involves making decisions about *what, how many, how, where,* and *who*. This section will deal with each of those decisions in turn. For simplicity's sake, we will continue to use the term *operations system* to denote both manufacturing and service systems.

Product/Service Planning and Design

The first design decision affecting the operations system is planning *what* output is to be produced. This decision influences, and is in turn influenced by, the technology available and the operations structure within the organization.

HERE'S AN EXAMPLE
Xerox Corporation, in response to competitive advances, had to slash its traditional four- to five-year product development cycle or be overrun by competitors. Xerox made a sweeping reorganization and invested millions of dollars and can now produce new copiers in approximately two years. (*Wall Street Journal,* 2/23/88, pp. 1ff)

Planning products and services is a strategic task involving marketing, finance, human resources, and operations. After some preliminary analysis of potential products and services has been carried out by marketing and engineering, the operations manager often becomes involved in this design decision.

The product/service design process consists of three basic steps:

1. *Research:* Generate the product/service ideas.
2. *Selection:* From among the research-generated ideas, choose those that are technologically feasible, marketable, and compatible with organizational strategy.
3. *Design:* Develop design specifications for the product/service. Final specifications should be optimal in terms of reliability, quality, and cost (which can be kept low by such means as component compatibility, interchangeability, and design simplicity).

computer-aided design (CAD) Design and drafting performed interactively on a computer.

CAD. Technological advances have recently made it possible for product design and drafting to be performed interactively on a computer, a process known as **computer-aided design (CAD).**[32] For example, General Motors now uses CAD to design the metal-stamping dies for its new cars. Car bodies are made from sheet metal that is stamped in large presses into the correct shape. Different dies are inserted into the press to give each stamping (a hood or fender) its form; the dies must be carefully designed to prevent wrinkling or tearing the sheet metal during the process. With CAD, GM designers can create computer models of proposed stamping forms early in the designing procedure and avoid later manufacturing difficulties. Previously, it took about 27 months to create the tooling for new car models. GM officials estimate that the use of CAD could reduce that time by up to 7 months.[33]

Once decided upon, the product or service design becomes a key source of information for planning the required input and the transformation process of the operations system.

Capacity Planning

The second decision in designing the operations system is *how many* products—or *how much* service—is to be produced. This is called **capacity planning.**

capacity planning Operations decision concerned with the quantity of goods or services to be produced.

''Capacity'' refers to ''the maximum theoretical rate of productive or conversion capability for an existing product mix of an organization's operations.'' The complex planning complex known as ''capacity'' is summed up in Exhibit 20-3.

---

[32]James R. Evans, David R. Anderson, Dennis J. Sweeney, and Thomas A. Williams, *Applied Production and Operations Management,* 2nd ed. (St. Paul, Minn.: West Publishing, 1987), pp. 106–109. See also Stan Kolodziej, ''Micro-Based CAD Systems—From Plain Vanilla to Thirty Flavors,'' *Computerworld Focus,* June 19, 1985, pp. 39–40.

[33]John Holusha, ''Metal Forming By Computer,'' *New York Times,* November 22, 1984, p. D2.

EXHIBIT 20-3 THE COMPLEX PROCESS OF CAPACITY

- Predicting future demand, including, insofar as possible, the likely impact of technology, competition, and other events.
- Translating these predictions into actual physical capacity requirements.
- Generating alternative capacity plans to meet the requirements.
- Analyzing and comparing the economic effects of the alternative plans.
- Identifying and comparing the risks and strategic effects of the alternative plans.

Sources: Everett E. Adam, Jr., and Ronald J. Ebert, *Production and Operations Management: Concepts, Models, and Behavior,* 5th ed. (Englewood Cliffs, N.J.: Prentice Hall, 1986); E. S. Buffa, *Modern Production/Operations Management,* 6th ed. (New York: Wiley, 1980).

FOR DISCUSSION

Can these production and operations management topics be applied to service sector organizations? How?

Long-range technological forecasting—which can extend 5 or 10 years into the future—may be needed to anticipate or predict future capacity demands. Unforeseeable events—new technological discoveries, wars, recessions, embargoes, and the effects of an unknown inflation rate—cannot always be factored into forecasting equations. Although planning demand well into the future is complicated and risky, organizations often properly expend considerable effort in doing so. (See Chapter 5).

Completed forecasts must then be translated into capacity requirements. This implies that existing capacity must be measured. In some cases, measuring capacity is easy enough; for example, gauging the number of tons of steel produced by a steel mill. For a system with a diverse and less readily classified product or service—such as a legal office—measuring capacity is less straightforward. Input measures are generally used for such systems; that is, capacity may be defined as the number of lawyers in the legal office.

The forecasted physical capacity requirements may compel the organization to change its operations system to meet the future demand. Capacity changes may be brought about by short-run and/or long-run modifications. *Short-run capacity changes* include overtime work, shifting existing personnel, subcontracting, and using inventories or back orders. *Long-run capacity changes* involve adding or removing capacity by physical facility expansion (more press hammers, more lawyers) or contraction (fewer press hammers, fewer lawyers).

Alternative capacity plans, each of which fits the required demand but through different means (more press hammers, subcontracting), should be analyzed. The costs of each and all of their strategic effects should be weighed and compared. The alternative with the lowest cost could turn out to result in lost sales and market-share losses, which may (or may not) be inconsistent with organizational strategy. (A subcontracting slowdown may cause delays in delivery and thus loss of market to a competitor.) Costs, risks, and strategic effects must be thoughtfully weighed by managers.

Process Selection

Process selection, the third design decision, determines *how* the product or service will be produced. According to Richard Chase and Nicholas Aquilano, process selection involves four technological decisions.[34]

Major Technological Choice. Does technology exist to produce the product? Are there competing technologies among which we should choose? Should innovations be licensed from elsewhere, such as foreign countries, or should an internal effort be

[34]Chase and Aquilano, *Production and Operations Management,* p. 34. Our discussion of process selection is based in part on their discussion, pp. 34–42.

made to develop the needed technology.[35] The importance of the major technological choice phase is highlighted by such recent developments as microchips and gene splicing. Although the major technical choice is largely the province of engineers, chemists, biogeneticists, and other technical specialists, top managers should comprehend as fully as possible the technology, its likely evolution, and the alternatives.

Minor Technological Choice. What transformation processes will be used? Once the major technological choice is made, there may be a number of minor technological *process alternatives* available. The operations manager should be involved in evaluating alternatives for costs and for consistency with the desired product and capacity plans. Should the process be continuous? A continuous process, which is carried out 24 hours a day to avoid expensive startups and shutdowns, is used by the steel and chemical industries, among others. An assembly-line process, on the other hand, follows the same series of steps to mass-produce each item but need not run 24 hours a day; examples are the automobile and ready-to-wear clothing industries. Job-shop processes produce items in small lots, perhaps custom-made for a given market or customer; examples are lumber yards and aircraft manufacturers.

Even if the continuous job-shop choice can be easily made, the alternatives do not end there. For example, in a factory, the fabrication, joining together, and finishing of two pieces of metal may represent only a minuscule part of creating a finished product. As Table 20-1 illustrates, there may be numerous ways of casting and molding, several ways of cutting, forming, assembling, and finishing. A simple hardware operation could thus involve choices among 46 process alternatives and numerous combinations. Deciding on the best combination of processes in terms of costs and the total operations process can be difficult.

Specific-Component Choice. What types of equipment (and degree of automation) should be used? Should the equipment be specific-purpose (tying it to this product), or general-purpose (leaving open the possibility of using the equipment to make other products)? To what degree should machines be used to replace humans in performing and automatically controlling the work? **Computer-aided manufacturing (CAM)** and industrial robots are being used increasingly in many manufacturing systems.

computer-aided manufacturing (CAM) Use of machines to perform and control required work.

CAM involves the use of a computer to help monitor and control processing equipment through the various phases of production. When CAD and CAM are linked

TABLE 20-1 PROCESS CHOICES: BASIC HARDWARE MANUFACTURING PROCESSES

CASTING AND MOLDING	MACHINING	METAL WORKING	ASSEMBLY	FINISHING
Sand casting	Turning	Forging	Soldering	Cleaning
Shell casting	Drilling	Extruding	Brazing	Blasting
Investment casting	Milling	Punching	Welding	Deburring
Die casting	Shaping	Trimming	Mechanical fastening	Painting
Permanent mold casting	Cutting	Drawing	Gluing	Plating
Powered metal molding	Broaching	Rolling	Press fitting	Buffing
Compression molding	Grinding	Forming	Shrink fitting	Heat treating
Transfer	Honing	Coining		Buffing
Extrusion	Etching	Swaging		Polishing
Injection molding		Spinning		Hardening
Laminating				

Source: Adapted from Donald F. Eary and Gerald E. Johnson, *Process Engineering for Manufacturing* (Englewood Cliffs, N.J.: Prentice Hall, 1962), p. 3. Adapted by permission of Prentice Hall.

[35]For a detailed analysis of this subject, see Bela Gold, ''Managerial Considerations in Evaluating the Role of Licensing in Technological Development Strategies,'' *Managerial and Decision Economics* 3, no. 4 (1982):213–217.

computer-integrated manufacturing (CIM) The use of machines to link computer-aided design and computer-aided manufacturing systems so that new product designs can be manufactured automatically in the factory.

in **computer-integrated manufacturing (CIM)**—which is also called CAD/CAM—new product designs can be manufactured immediately and automatically in the factory. Computers in the plant retool production machinery and initiate assembly operations according to instructions provided by the CAD system; in turn, the CAD system works within the limits of the CAM's retooling and production capabilities. Such totally integrated design and manufacturing facilities are currently being developed and tested (see Fig. 20-4). Many manufactured-housing companies, such as Techno Craft, Miles, and Ryland, already use the technology to custom-design and build—within their own factories—residential, commercial, and industrial buildings that match customer specifications.

HERE'S AN EXAMPLE

Robots are moving into services much like their human counterparts. They can do jobs that are dangerous or boring, such as cleaning up nuclear plants, picking oranges, or guarding commercial buildings. (*Fortune*, 9/14/87, pp. 81–88)

Most industrial robots are basically computer-controlled mechanical arms that can be equipped with grippers, tools, or vacuum cups. More sophisticated robots may also be equipped with video imaging systems that allow them to "see" their work and with built-in computers that allow them to independently sort items or perform other complicated tasks. In some industries, notably automotive manufacturing, paper making, and textile spinning, robots are already performing simple assemblies. They are automated, flexible, and more reliable than humans—though, of course, far more limited—and are especially suited for use in dangerous environments.

Process-Flow Choice. How should the product or service flow through the operations system? The final process-selection step determines how materials and products will move through the system. Assembly drawings, assembly charts, route sheets, and flow process charts are used to analyze process flow. Analysis may lead to resequenc-

FIGURE 20-4 THE CAD/CAM MARKET

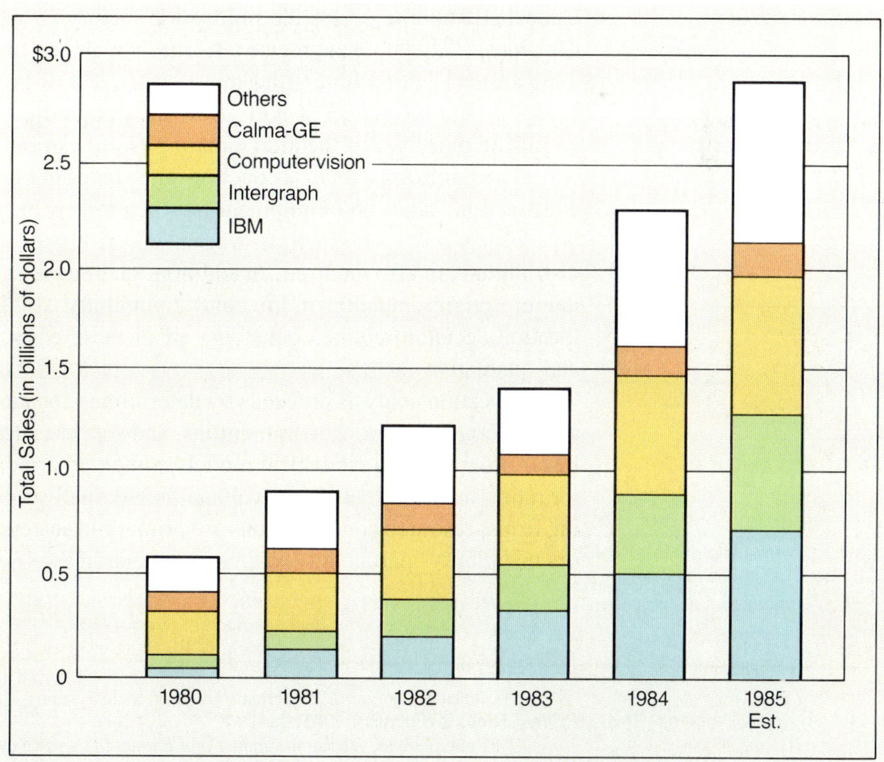

Total sales of major CAD/CAM systems manufacturers in billions of dollars.

Source: Eric N. Berg, "CAD/CAM's Pioneer Bets It All," *New York Times,* March 24, 1985, p. F4. Copyright © 1985 by The New York Times Company. Reprinted by permission.

ing, combining, or eliminating operations to reduce materials handling and storage costs. In general, the less storage and delay involved in the process, the better.

In recent years, increasing use has been made of Automated Guided Vehicle Systems (AGVS). These systems employ driverless battery-operated vehicles that move back and forth between pickup and delivery points. Currently, this is achieved by placing a wire guide path in the floor that can be sensed by the vehicles' antennas. Research is now in process to do away with the wire and to combine AGVS with robotics to create mobile robots.[36]

The four phases of process selection are closely interrelated. In each phase, choices should be made to minimize the process operations costs.

FOR DISCUSSION

Can you think of some examples where companies have shifted part of their work to you? (Examples: pumping gas, ATM's at banks, bagging groceries, assembling toys and furniture.)

In service systems, process selection depends on the nature of the system. Service systems with low customer contact, such as the check-clearing operation of a bank, can carry out process selection by following the four phases outlined above. In systems with high customer contact, such as retail establishments, the processes or procedures for interacting with the customer must also be selected. For a standardized service, these processes can be specific and allow for little variability—for example, the cash-dispensing function of an automated teller machine (ATM) at a bank. For customized services, variable procedures must be designed—for example, the evaluation of a personal loan application at the same bank. There are specialized computer systems designed to assist bank, department store, and other service industry managers in performing customized evaluations.[37] Large banks, like the Bank of America and Chase Manhattan, use such systems to assist their officers in evaluating loan applications from traders and companies dealing in lesser developed countries.

Facility-Location Planning

EXTRA EXERCISE

Interview some local managers. Ask them why they located their businesses where they did. As a class, discuss and compare the responses.

Choosing where to locate the production facility is one of the most important design decisions. "The more aggregate a facility's planning mistake—for example, a factory, a department, a machine—the more costly it will be, the less likely that it will be changed, and the longer it will affect the operation."[38]

The objective of location planning is to position the capacity of the system in a way that minimizes total production and distribution costs. *Fixed capital costs* for construction, land, and equipment are incurred for new or additional facilities. *Variable operations costs* such as wages, taxes, energy and materials acquisition, and distribution are also incurred. In addition, qualitative factors such as labor availability, union, activity, quality of life, and community attitudes should be evaluated. The location decision requires balancing all of these costs, effects on potential revenues, and qualitative factors.

Location analysis proceeds by determining location requirements and then evaluating alternative regions, communities, and specific sites. Traditional financial models, linear programming, statistical models,computer simulation models, and location factor rating models are used to evaluate the alternative locations. For many manufacturing firms, resource considerations are primary in selecting a location. For many service organizations—particularly convenience services—nearness to the customer often

[36]Gunnar K. Lofgren, "Automatic Guide Vehicle Systems," *Production and Inventory Management Review* 3, no. 2 (February 1983):28–29.

[37]Efraim Turban, *Decision Support and Expert Systems* (New York: Macmillan, 1988), Chapters 3 and 7, provides a description and some applications of such systems.

[38]Philip E. Hicks and Areen M. Kumtha, "One Way to Tighten Up Plant Location Decisions," *Industrial Engineering* 3, no. 4 (April 1971):19–23.

dominates the selection process because the location strongly affects demand and revenue.[39]

Layout Planning

EXTRA EXERCISE

Visit some different businesses-such as a video rental store, fastfood restaurant, large grocery store, factory (if one is nearby) and observe their operations flow. Diagram it. How does it work? Could it be better? How?

Layout planning involves decisions about *how* to arrange the physical facilities spatially. This is the integrative phase of designing the operations system. In layout planning, and process and equipment decisions are translated into physical arrangements for production.

Space must be provided for:

- *Productive facilities,* such as work stations and materials-handling equipment.
- *Nonproductive facilities,* such as storage areas and maintenance facilities.
- *Support facilities,* such as offices, restrooms, waiting rooms, cafeterias, and parking lots.

Space must also be provided for materials and additional capacity. Any location-related requirements, such as docking facilities or heating units, must also be planned.

A good layout minimizes materials handling, maximizes worker and equipment efficiency, and satisfies a host of other factors. Exhibit 20-4 outlines the characteristics of a good layout. Layouts can be characterized by work flow or by function of the operations system.

work-flow layout Layout planning concerned with product layouts (for the sequential steps in production), process layouts (for arranging production according to task), and fixed-position layouts (for handling such large or heavy products as ships).

Work-flow layouts include:

- *Product layouts,* arranged for the sequential steps in producing the product or rendering the service. Such a layout is appropriate for continuous or repetitive operations, such as mass-producing air conditioners or serving food in a cafeteria. (Figure 20-5 depicts a simple product layout in a small factory.)
- *Process layouts,* arranged according to task. Such a layout is appropriate for job-shop operations systems, such as universities and automotive repair shops, where there is no one route through the system for all products or services.
- *Fixed-position layouts,* where a large or heavy production itself—such as a ship—stays in one location, with people, tools, materials and equipment moved to the product as needed.

function layout Layout planning concerned with storage layouts (for minimizing inventory and storage costs), marketing layouts (for maximizing product exposure and sales), and project layouts (for building such one-of-a-kind products as a dam).

Function layouts include:

- *Storage layouts,* designed to minimize inventory and storage costs, as in warehouses.
- *Marketing layouts,* designed to maximize product exposure and sales. Supermarkets are an example.
- *Project layouts,* established to build projects or one-of-a-kind products, such as dams or buildings. This differs from the fixed-position layout described earlier in that the latter is designed to turn out more than one unit of a large product.

In practice, most operations systems use a combination of layouts appropriate to the needs of different stages of product or service creation.

Job Design

CLASS COMMENT

Relate this information to the information in Chapter 10 on job design.

The final decision in designing the operations system concerns the structure of individual jobs—*how* will the work be done and *who* wili do it? Job design specifies the

[39]For a survey of the current state of the art of retail store location selection, see C. Samuel Craig, Avijit Ghosh, and Sara McLafferty, "Models of the Retail Location Process: a Review," *Journal of Retailing* 60, no. 1 (Spring 1984):5–36.

EXHIBIT 20-4 THE MARKS OF A GOOD PLANT LAYOUT

1. Planned activity interrelationships
2. Planned materials flow pattern
3. Straight-line flow
4. Minimum backtracking
5. Auxiliary flow lines
6. Straight aisles
7. Minimum handling between operations
8. Planned materials-handling methods
9. Minimum handling distances
10. Processing combined with materials handling
11. Movement progresses from receiving toward shipping
12. First operations near receiving
13. Last operations near shipping
14. Point-of-use storage where appropriate
15. Layout adaptable to changing conditions
16. Planned for orderly expansion
17. Minimum goods in process
18. Minimum materials in process
19. Maximum use of all plant levels
20. Adequate storage space
21. Adequate spacing between facilities
22. Building constructed around planned layout
23. Materials delivered to employees and removed from work areas
24. Minimum walking by production operators
25. Proper locations of production and employee service facilities
26. Mechanical handling installed where practicable
27. Adequate employee service functions
28. Planned control of noise, dirt, fumes, dust, humidity, etc.
29. Maximum processing time to overall production time
30. Minimum manual handling
31. Minimum re-handling
32. Partitions don't impeded material flow
33. Minimum handling by direct labor
34. Planned scrap removal
35. Receiving and shipping in logical locations

Source: James M. Apple, *Plant Layout and Materials Handling,* 3d ed., pp. 18–19, Copyright © 1977 by John Wiley & Sons, Inc. Used by permission.

content and methods of work by individuals and groups in the operations system. Because job design is reflected in labor expense, it affects the ultimate cost of the product or service.

Job design consists of three activities: specifying individual work tasks, specifying the method of performing the work tasks, and combining work tasks into jobs for assignment to individuals (job content). (Considerations in the design of jobs are discussed in Chapter 10).

Work methods analysis attempts to find the best way of performing the tasks in a given job. Time and motion studies, principles of motion economy, and other industrial engineering tools have been applied to determine optimal work arrangements. These techniques are used to study such factors as the rhythm of work, the use of the hands and tools, and ways to avoid fatigue on the job. Such environmental factors as temperature, air flow, humidity, noise, and lighting levels should be controlled to ease task performance and increase job satisfaction. Job design must also take into account health and safety requirements and regulations as set forth in the Occupations Safety and Health Act of 1970 (OSHA) and subsequent federal, state, and local regulations. The box entitled "The Traveling Circus Show" illustrates why it is important for management to consider such health and safety requirements/regulations.

FIGURE 20-5 A SIMPLE PRODUCT LAYOUT

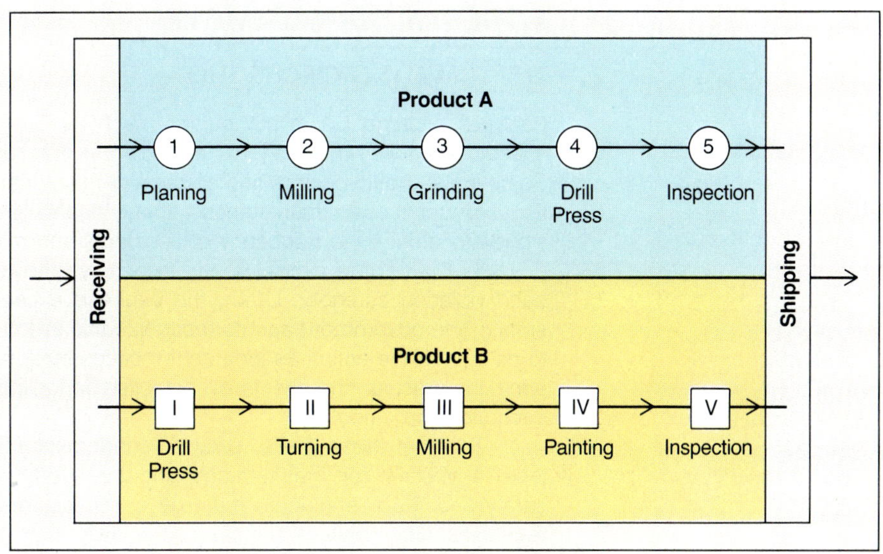

Source: Production and Operations Management, Third Edition, by Arthur C. Laufer. Published by South-Western Publishing Co., Cincinnati, Ohio.

Once design has been completed, job production standards are then developed using work measurement techniques. Such standards are established as a basis for comparison when measuring and judging output. A standard can be established for various product attributes, such as quantity, quality, or cost. Production standards indicate what an average worker or group of workers can produce under average job conditions. They are usually developed using a combination of informal rules of thumb, historical performance studies, stopwatch studies, predetermined time studies, and statistical approaches to work sampling.

Standards form the basis for comparison to be used in planning and controlling the operations system—the subject of the next section.

OPERATIONAL PLANNING AND CONTROL DECISIONS

Even when the operations system has been successfully designed and placed into actual operation, much of the managerial challenge still remains. That is because decisions on a shorter-term basis—month to month, day to day, and even hour to hour—must be made as to how the system will be operated and controlled. As Figure 20-6 illustrates, operational planning and control decisions involve scheduling and control of labor, materials, and capital input to produce the desired quantity and quality of output most efficiently.

CLASS COMMENT

Flexibility and adaptability are important.

Operational planning and control are based on forecasts of future demand for the output of the system. Even with the best possible forecasting and the most finely tuned operations system, however, demand cannot always be met with existing system capacity in a given time period. Unexpected market trends, new-product developments, or competitors' actions can throw the forecasts off, and problems in the operations system can reduce capacity. Ultimately shorter-term managerial decisions must be made to allocate system capacity to meet demands in a given time period.

ETHICS IN MANAGEMENT

THE TRAVELING CIRCUS SHOW

Facilities of large circus companies, such as Circus USA, are periodically inspected by government agents enforcing OSHA regulations and requirements. Sometimes, the inspectors find equipment-maintenance and fire-inspection violations. Under these circumstances, these agents propose safety guidelines designed to reduce the frequency of accidents and mishap-cost per person.

It will cost the circus money to achieve the relevant compliance levels in each violation category. Often, the expense exceeds the budget available for safety. The government agents recognize this dilemma and are frequently willing to delay punitive action as long as the circus makes progress toward full compliance. In particular, the agents will establish periodic goals for the circus to meet in each violation category.

To meet these goals, circus management must typically redesign circus jobs, especially for maintenance and transportation personnel. Occasionally, safety and traffic engineers must be consulted to assist management with the redesigns. Nevertheless, the circus is usually more than willing to incur the additional expense.

There are several reasons for the attitude adopted by the circuses. First, protecting customer safety is their ethical responsibility. Second, accidents can lead to substantial lawsuits. Third, failure to comply may force the government to close down the circus.

Source: Guiseppe A. Forgionne, *Quantitative Decision Making* (Belmont, Calif.: Wadsworth, 1986), pp. 456–457.

Operations Planning and Control

TEACHING TIP

You could invite a guest speaker from a local business to talk about some of these operations planning and control techniques.

Operations managers typically formulate plans that range from daily or weekly to yearly in outlook. The objectives of operations planning and control are to maximize customer service, minimize inventory investment, and maximize system operating efficiency. Often these three objectives conflict, and plans must be made to obtain the best balance. For example, if operations managers focus too rigidly on minimizing inventory investment, a sudden increase in sales will make it difficult to meet customer service requirements.

To some extent, completely meeting any one of the objectives means sacrificing the other two. A system may operate with the greatest efficiency when it is put into operation only after sufficient orders have been received to require a large batch of output. In meeting the third objective, then, management will definitely have failed to meet the first, since customers must wait for some time for service. The second objective has also been slighted because our large-batch philosophy demands a large available stock of input materials in inventory. By keeping enough output in inventory to satisfy some orders, management could achieve a higher degree of customer service and still maintain operating efficiency. However, the policy would require a larger inventory investment than the large-batch philosophy.

And so it goes. In this "what if" manner, the trade-off calculations are endless. Achieving a balance in operations objectives is one of the most delicate jobs within an organization.

Production Plans. Production plans are based on forecasts. First, overall plans are made for a 6- to 18-month period. These aggregate production plans specify how operations system capacity will be used to meet anticipated output demands. The variables in the operations system that can be controlled are aggregate production rates, employment levels, and inventory levels. Next, the aggregate operations plans must be translated into master production schedules that specify the quantity and short-term timing of specific end products.[40]

Detailed Scheduling. Detailed or short-term scheduling specifies the quantity and type of items to be produced and how, when, and where they should be produced for the next day or week. Detailed scheduling involves the following processes:

[40]Jay Heizer and Barry Render, *Production and Operations Management: Strategies and Tactics* (Boston: Allyn and Bacon, 1988), part four, discuss some of the appropriate methodologies. Barry Render and R. M. Starr, *Micro-computer Software for Management Science and Operations Management* (Boston: Allyn and Bacon, 1986), present a relevant computer system.

FIGURE 20-6 MODEL OF OPERATIONS PLANNING AND CONTROL SYSTEM

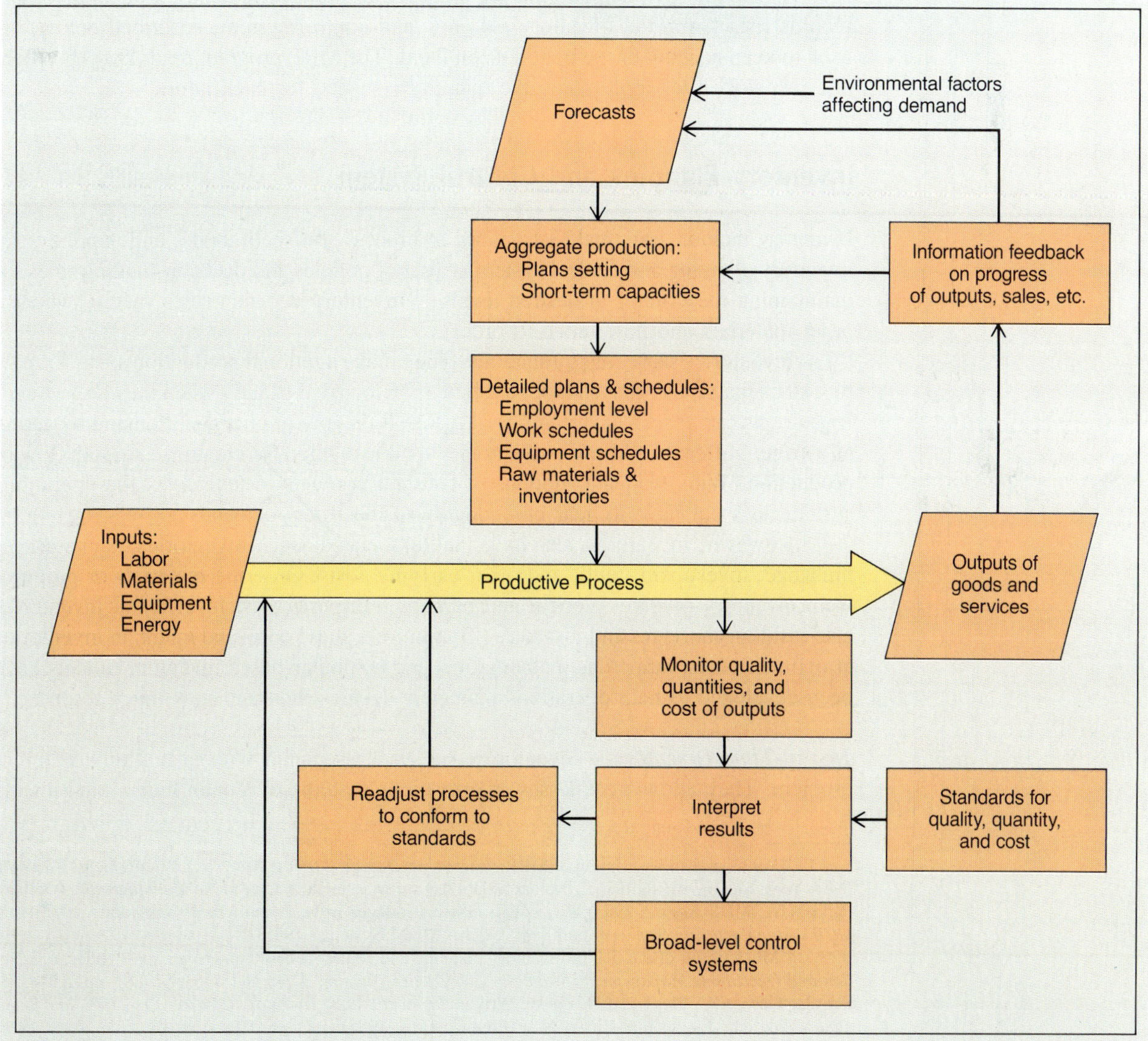

Source: Adapted from Elwood S. Buffa, *Modern Production/Operations Management,* 6th ed., p. 159. Copyright © 1980 by John Wiley & Sons. Used by permission.

- Allocating orders, equipment, and labor to work centers
- Establishing a sequence for the work
- Developing work schedules
- Initiating work performance
- Updating the status of the work
- Revising schedules

materials-requirements planning Operational planning system whereby end products are analyzed to determine the materials needed to produce them.

Materials-Requirements Planning. The master production schedule is the basis of the **materials-requirements planning (MRP)** system. End products are analyzed or "exploded" to determine the materials and parts needed to produce the product. The required quantity is then adjusted for materials and parts already on hand. Order time for the materials and parts still needed is calculated, incorporating the lead time necessary to order the materials and receive them in ample time before production begins.

Since the proliferation of microcomputers in the corporate world, many managers have come to rely on decision support systems (see chapter 6) for MRP. Product design specifications in the form of *bills of materials (BOM)* are supplied on an input file. This BOM file identifies the parts needed to produce the end product. Inventory records files (from the inventory planning and control system, described below) are used to keep account of the materials on hand. The MRP program reads both the BOM and inventory files to compute the quantities needed for each item.[41]

Inventory Planning and Control System

Inventory includes raw materials, work in process, finished goods, and supplies. An inventory planning and control system is a set of policies and decision-making rules for maintaining these items at desired levels.[42] Inventory decision rules specify when to order materials and how much to order.

Inventories serve many functions. They make a rational production system possible, since materials often cannot be relied upon to arrive exactly when they are needed. Inventories can absorb uncertainties in materials supply or customer demand by acting as a safety buffer. In addition, inventories are one method for creating a smooth flow of production. With adequate supplies of finished products in inventory, the operations system does not have to gear up suddenly to meet new demands.

However, inventories also have their associated costs. Inventories incur storage, breakage, investment, theft, and other carrying costs. Ordering materials or products from inventory involves clerical and perhaps transport costs. Insufficient inventories also result in shortages and lost sales. To minimize these costs and maintain inventories at optimal levels, numerous mathematical and computer-based inventory models have been developed to help operations managers decide when and how much to order.[43]

Just-in-Time Inventory. Inventories are also associated with an entirely different problem: They allow weaknesses in operations systems to remain hidden and uncor-

---

[41] For a detailed description of MRP systems, see Joseph Orlicky, *Materials Requirements Planning* (New York: McGraw-Hill, 1975). Typical MRP DSS software include *Myte Myke Manufacturing* (Orchard Park, N.Y.: MDS Assoc., 1985); *Twin Oaks mrp 2* (Cottage Grove, Minn.: Twin Oaks, Inc., 1985); and *MCBA Manufacturing System* (Southfield, Mich.: MDM Systems, 1985).

[42] Much of our discussion of inventory planning and control is based on Herzer and Render, *Production and Operations Management: Strategies and Tactics* (Boston: Allyn and Bacon, 1988), pp. 530–540. See also George W. Plossl and Oliver W. Wright, *Production and Inventory Control: Principles and Techniques*, 2nd ed. (Englewood Cliffs, N.J.: Prentice Hall, 1985).

[43] For a brief but excellent discussion of the innovative approach to minimizing inventories used by some Japanese companies, see Robert H. Hayes, "Why Japanese Factories Work," *Harvard Business Review* 59, no. 4 (July–August 1981):59.

just-in-time inventory system Inventory system in which production quantities are ideally equal to delivery quantities, with materials purchased and finished goods delivered "just in time."

COORDINATED RESOURCE

For a good overview of lessons we can learn from the Japanese, see "Japanese Manufacturing Techniques: Their Importance to U.S. Manufacturers," by Kiyoshi Suzaki, *Journal of Business Strategy*, Winter 1985, pp.10–19.

rected. In the mid 1970s, the world began to take notice of the Japanese *kanban*, or **just-in-time inventory system.** *Kanban* strives toward an ideal state in which production quantities are equal to delivery quantities. In other words, carrying costs are minimized by eliminating as much as possible the amount of inactive inventory kept on hand. Materials are bought more frequently and in smaller amounts, "just in time" to be used, and finished goods are produced and delivered "just in time" to be sold.[44] In striving toward ever smaller inventories of work in process, problems in the operations system are revealed. Correcting the problems can improve productivity and quality dramatically.

The possibility of improving *both* productivity *and* quality is one of the more exciting aspects of just-in-time and other modern approaches to operations management. In its 1985 annual report, Intel Corporation—a leading manufacturer of microprocessors—reported improvements in both quality and productivity from installing just-in-time and related systems. For example, as Figure 20-7 shows, defects per million parts on a microcomputer product dropped by more than tenfold in a three-year period, and the rework rate in an assembly operation showed similar improvements. Not only are these types of improvements leading managers to rethink the quality/productivity trade-offs long taken for granted, but they are also raising questions about the need to sacrifice one or more of the operations planning and control objectives of maximizing customer service, minimizing inventory investment, and maximizing system operating efficiency.

In its dishwasher assembly factory in Louisville, Kentucky, GE has achieved similar results by combining the just-in-time method with a "use a part, make a part" system, in which machines manufacture parts right next to the assembly line.[45] (See the chapter case for a fuller discussion of GE's productivity experiment.)

[44]For an excellent discussion of JIT systems, see Richard J. Schonberger, *Japanese Manufacturing Techniques: Nine Hidden Lessons in Simplicity* (New York: Free Press, 1982)

[45]Gene Bylinsky, "America's Best-Managed Factories," *Fortune*, May 28, 1984, p. 23.

FIGURE 20-7 IMPACTS OF MODERN OPERATIONS METHODS AT THE INTEL CORPORATION

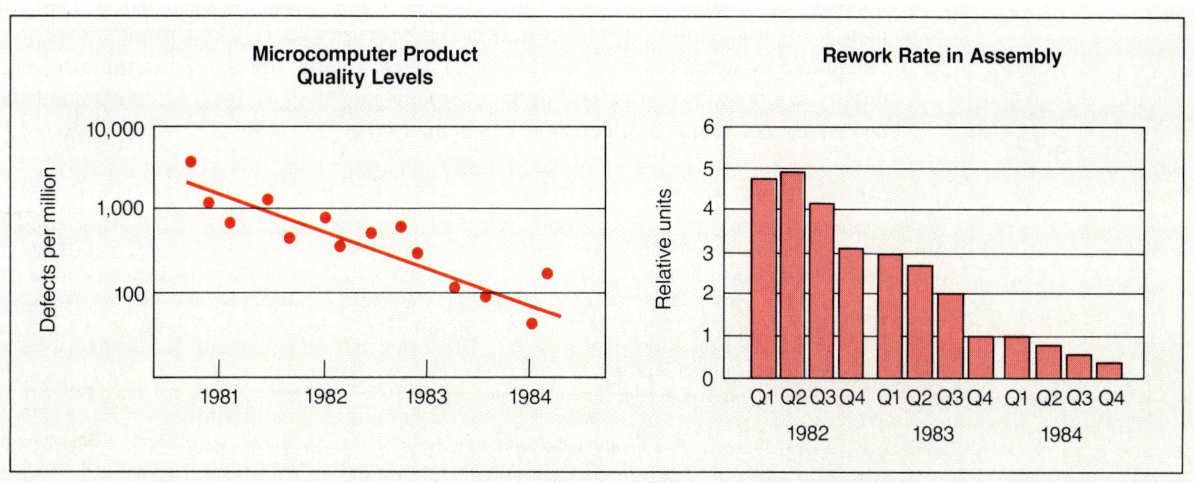

Note: Q1, Q2, Q3, and Q4 represent the first quarter, second quarter, third quarter, and fourth quarter, respectively.

Source: Intel Corporation—First Quarter Report, March 30, 1985, and *Annual Stockholders Meeting Report,* March 26, 1985. Courtesy Intel Corporation.

quality control Strategy for managing each stage of production so that early corrections can be made instead of reworking the product after end-of-line inspection.

FOR DISCUSSION

Why is quality such a popular topic now?

HERE'S AN EXAMPLE

The major reason cited in a 1986 study by Cambridge Reports of 1,500 people of what's responsible for the quality decline in U.S. products was, "Managers care more about profits." For other the responses, see *Wall Street Journal*, 1/11/88, p. 1.

COORDINATED RESOURCE

An interesting article excerpted from a book written by a well-respected computer expert is "How to Revive U.S. High Tech," *Fortune*, 5/9/88, pp. 124–133.

Quality Control. According to David Garvin of Harvard University, "quality is the competitive issue of the '80s."[46] With Americans no longer seeing **quality control** as a mere inspection task, it is now being viewed as an integral part of company strategy. One result is that quality control is being practiced increasingly at each stage of the manufacturing process, making early corrections possible, instead of coming into play only at an end-of-line inspection where faulty products are discarded or reworked.

Changes are also apparent in the practices companies are adopting to improve product quality. Many recent quality-improvement efforts encourage worker involvement and management participation that cut across functions and levels.[47]

Recognizing that the trade-off between productivity and quality, once thought of as inevitable, does not seem necessary in many cases, Lee Iacocca turned the phrase "quality and productivity—they go together" into one of his reform measures when he assumed the helm of the troubled Chrysler Corporation in 1978.[48] He foresaw that improving quality meant lower repair, inspection, scrap, and product warranty costs. More reliable automobiles also meant greater customer loyalty and increased sales. (See the part case.)

Managers make two kinds of quality-control decisions: strategic decisions and tactical decisions.[49] Strategic decisions set the level of quality for the output of the organization. They influence product design, training of personnel, selection and maintenance programs for equipment, reward systems, and so on. Tactical, day-to-day decisions on quality control are concerned with such matters as when output should be inspected, how much of the output should be inspected, what should cause output to be rejected, and when corrective actions should be taken regarding the production process or personnel.

Strategic-quality decisions primarily involve quality planning and taking steps to improve quality in order to maintain a competitive position in today's markets. Quality can be promoted among both customers and employees: Customers want quality products and employees at all organizational levels like to be associated with a winner. From an economic perspective, when quality is emphasized and subsequently improved, waste is decreased or eliminated at the same time that operations costs are reduced. Labor hours are saved because less reworking of products is needed and material is not thrown away. At the same time, customers receive products and services that are "fit" for use and do not fail frequently or incur high warranty costs. As a result, product prices can be lowered to share this productivity gain with customers, or the higher-quality product (as compared with competitors' product offerings) can command a premium price and a more secure market niche. The impact on the company is twofold: Employees have increased job security because of a sound competitive position, and stockholders benefit through higher overall profits. To summarize, high quality can make everyone within the company a winner—a message that some firms and managers seem to understand better than others.

---

[46]Quoted in Sandra Blakeslee, "Restoring Quality in Quality Control," *New York Times* Careers '85 Special Supplement, October 14, 1985, p. 34. See also Bradley T. Gale and Richard Klavans, "Formulating a Quality Improvement Strategy," *Journal of Business Strategy* 5, no. 3 (Winter 1985):21–32; and Madhev H. Sinha, *Essentials of Quality Assurance Management* (New York: Wiley, 1986).

[47]Frank S. Leonard and W. Earl Sasser, "The Incline of Quaiity," *Harvard Business Review* 60, no. 5 (September–October 1982):168.

[48]Al Fleming, "Chrysler Quality & Productivity VP George Butts," *Automotive News*, February 28, 1983, p. E10.

[49]For an analysis of the advantages of strategic-operations decisions, see Steven C. Wheelwright, "Japan—Where Operations Really Are Strategic," *Harvard Business Review* 59, no. 4 (July–August 1981):67–74; and Robert H. Hayes and Steven Wheelwright, *Restoring Our Competitive Edge: Competing through Manufacturing* (New York: Wiley, 1984).

Analysis of quality planning has revolved around the work of two management consultants, J. M. Juran and W. E. Deming. They have worked extensively with the Japanese during the past several decades to enhance product quality through statistical methods. Both individuals emphasize data collection and analysis as a basis for improved managerial decision making about the quality of the product. Juran's approach has the basic intent of achieving productivity gains through an emphasis on quality, and he specifies goals for management and lays the blame for poor quality and low levels of productivity on management rather than on workers. He has also promoted this position as a consultant for American firms such as Caterpillar Tractor and Texas Instruments.

COORDINATED RESOURCE
The videotape "The Kyocera Experiment" illustrates how a Japanese company is trying to instill its Japanese concepts and work methods in an American subsidiary. This videotape is from the Enterprise series and is available from: LCA, 108 Wilmont Road, Deerfield, IL 60015-9990, or call 1-800-621-2131.

Deming (see the Management Application box, "From the Land of Opportunity to the Land of the Rising Sun," in Chapter 1) is perhaps the most widely recognized American in Japanese manufacturing circles, and he has emphasized statistical analysis as the basis for controlling and improving the production process and achieving higher quality levels. Successful U.S. applications of Deming's approach have taken place at the Nashua Corporation and Ford Motor Company. Quality assurance executives at Ford have seen this as their primary focus in the 1980s. Ford has utilized management consultants such as Deming to stimulate the commitment required among its employees. Top executives have diligently stressed quality, and quality education has become a major activity at all levels within Ford. Suppliers have also become a part of the quality emphasis. Ford provides conferences, schools, and manuals to teach suppliers what is expected of them and how to achieve these expectations. Ford's approach was first to improve quality and then to capitalize on this improvement in its marketing campaign. Company advertisements promote Ford products as the best-made American products.[50]

acceptance-sampling procedure Quality-control procedure to determine if the finished product conforms to design specifications.

process-control procedure Quality-control procedure for monitoring quality during production of the product or rendering of the service.

Today, statistical quality-control procedures are used extensively in the decision-making process. In general, these procedures can be placed into two categories. **Acceptance-sampling procedures** determine if the completed product conforms to design specifications. (Does it work as it should?) **Process-control procedures** monitor quality while the product is actually being produced or while the service is actually being rendered. (Are design specifications being met?) Process control also can detect shifts at some point in the process that may signal future quality problems.

The "control" part of quality control takes place when output that does not conform to specifications is identified and corrective action is taken: A new supplier might be located, a worn machine overhauled, or an incompetent worker retrained or replaced.

In some Japanese companies statistical quality control has been used very successfully to motivate workers to produce high-quality products. This approach has also been used successfully by some U.S. firms, such as Motorola.[51] One of the mechanisms used is the *quality circle,* which consists of a group of labor and management personnel belonging to a single department that meets at regular intervals to solve quality-control problems. Quality circles provide a future-oriented approach, seeking high-quality products in the current production run and in the future.

EXTRA EXERCISE
Write a short paper on what you think factories of the future will look like.

---

[50] W. Edwards Deming, Paper presented at the TIMS meeting at Gold Coast City, Australia, July 1986.

[51] See Francesca Lunzer, "Does Your Car Have a Fan Belt?" *Forbes,* December 3, 1984, p. 222. See also J. M. Juran, *Quality Control Handbook* (New York: McGraw-Hill, 1974).

ILLUSTRATIVE CASE STUDY Wrap-Up

At Ford, Quality Is Job One

As a result of its renewed quality-control efforts, Ford is recognized today as a quality leader among American automobile manufacturers: By and large, consumers perceive Ford-built vehicles to be well-designed, well-engineered machines that provide reliable service.

Ford's "Quality Is Job One" program was a direct and concerted response to foreign competition. Indeed, such changes in a firm's environment often motivate its management to take action such as that which we have just described on the part of one of America's most well-known firms. The case of Ford also reminds us that, in today's environment, managers cannot afford to focus exclusively on the adjustment of financial and marketing policies. Today's managers now recognize that organizational goals can be achieved by attending to their companies' production and operations systems.

However, neither Ford nor any other U.S. automaker is out of the woods, particularly as regards foreign competition. Donald Petersen himself, for example, wants the quota of Japanese cars entering the United States to be cut by 600,000 units per year, and he figures that by 1990, there will be only three buyers for every four vehicles produced by American manufacturers. During the stock market crash of October 1987, Ford stock plummeted from $93 to $75 per share, and its 1988 profits dipped by 20 percent. Nevertheless, Petersen hopes to weather hard times with an available cash reserve of over $9 billion, and he retains his commitment to quality as the key to Ford's continued revival: "The principles by which we will live and die," he has announced, "is that once we can do something well, we have to figure out how to do it even better." ■

■ SUMMARY

Production management or operations management is a key job in an organization and is important as well to our society and to us as individuals. How well production systems function is closely tied both to organizational health and to our standard of living. Once thought of solely as manufacturing management, production management is now recognized as a necessity for service industries also, and hence this chapter uses the newer term ''operations management.'' Recently, operations management has been undergoing major changes, with greater worker involvement, improvements in production process design, and achievement of both high quality and high productivity being the most important aspects.

Operations systems can be studied as a ''set of components whose function is to transform a set of inputs into some desired output.'' The input—workers, technology, know-how—is transformed by means of a particular process into output—the finished products or services. Operations managers have a twofold job: supervising design of the operations system and supervising the performance of the system. Both functions should be carried out in a manner that implements organizational strategy; and conversely, an organization's strategy should be formulated with its operations system in mind.

Design of an operations system means deciding upon (1) the product or service to produce; (2) the quantity or amount of it to produce—capacity planning; (3) the processes to employ to produce it; (4) the location at which to produce it; (5) the layout of facilities; and (6) how the jobs will be structured and assigned.

The second operations management function—supervising the performance of the system—becomes important once the system has been designed. Ultimately, managerial operations decisions are made month by month, day by day, and even hour by hour. Managers must strike a balance among three key objectives: to maximize customer service, minimize inventory investment, and maximize system operating efficiency. Various types of specialized planning and control techniques play key roles in operations management, such as materials requirements planning, inventory planning and control, detailed scheduling, and quality control.

The measure of how well an operations system functions is called productivity. Productivity is measured as the ratio of output to input. Productivity figures, imprecise at best, indicate an improving or deteriorating competitive situation when compared over time. On a national scale, productivity influences the standard of living, inflation, economic growth, and balance of payments. At the level of the individual firm, it is one of the keys to survival.

Much attention has been paid recently to increasing productivity. Improvements have focused on changes in capital equipment, employee policies, and organizational procedures and structure. Although new technologies like CIM (CAD/CAM) systems play important roles in increasing productivity in some industries, many observers still see the key to the way people are treated and managed as the key to productivity gains.

REVIEW QUESTIONS

1. What do the terms *production management* and *operations management* mean?
2. How do the authors define the operations subsystem within the organization?
3. What are the five elements of a system as the authors define them?
4. The authors further define operations systems as continuous and assembly-line systems or job-shop systems. Discuss the characteristics and give an example of each.
5. Discuss the basic steps in the product/service design process.
6. What is meant by capacity planning?
7. The third major decision in design is process selection, or how the product or service will be produced. Chase and Aquilano suggest that this is a four-part decision. What are those parts?
8. Distinguish between facility location planning and layout planning.
9. The final decision in designing an operations system is the structure of individual jobs, or job design. Specifically what is meant by the term *job design?*
10. What are the objectives of operations planning and control, and how are they related?
11. What do the acronyms MRP and BOM mean?
12. Inventories are an integral or important part of many production systems. What are the major opposing costs associated with inventories?
13. What is a productivity ratio, and what does it measure?
14. Describe the just-in-time concept of inventory control.
15. What is the difference between a ''big bang'' approach and an incremental approach to improving productivity?
16. What changes have recently occurred in the way managers view quality control?
17. What benefits does computerization offer to the manager of a retail store?
18. Discuss how companies can compete on different product characteristics, or competitive priorities.

CASE STUDY GE Turns Old into New in Kentucky

"In this plant," says Ray Rissler, "we have proved that it is possible to take a 30-year old facility and transform it into a competitive new unit; and we have also shown that you can take a labor force with a strong union that resisted change and convince it that change is necessary."

Rissler is manager of the modernization project at General Electric's dishwasher plant in Louisville, Kentucky. All around him, one of the showpieces of modern-day U.S. factory engineering is humming away to the smooth rhythms of a largely automated production line. It is a rhythm that is currently tapping out dollars in abundance for GE, as the combination of increased market share and an expanding domestic economy bring back memories of the industry's peak year in 1973.

Like several other U.S. factories that have recently arisen on the foundations of mature old manufacturing industries, the plant represents a renaissance in U.S. methods and productivity. Its startup has been accompanied by a quantum leap in productivity and what amounts to a revolution in quality. With the same number of workers as before the changeover, the plant now produces 25 percent more units in a year, giving GE about 30 percent of the market. As far as quality is concerned, Rissler says the plant has delivered virtually a tenfold improvement as measured by customer complaints in the first year of warranty.

The change in the plant goes back to 1979, when GE, faced with intense pressure on profit margins generally in household appliances, was asking itself if it wanted to continue at all in that sector. Unlike Westinghouse, however, GE decided to stay. "Our name on household appliances is a pervasive reminder of the company in virtually every household in America," says Rissler. GE also saw that to survive as an effective force it had to improve both quality and productivity. These objectives were partly prompted by the market environment, which had become steadily tougher. But they also derived indirectly from the threat of Japanese competition. The market had been educated by Japanese products to demand better quality; and GE had good reason to believe that after the highly successful foray of the Japanese electrical companies into television and audio, they were lining up kitchen products as well.

Because the dishwasher division is a relatively small one, it was able to go for a radical—and risky— method of reorganizing, involving the production workers in the design of the product line and the production process. The reorganization got off to a good start when the normally militant work force came into the discussions early and threw its weight behind the plan. The project has thus been much less bothered by disputes than others in the past—strikes at the entire Louisville complex, which embraces a variety of products, have fallen from 400,000 people-hours a year to less than 50,000.

On the production side, engineers solved a problem that had baffled them for two decades. Because of the large range of machines manufactured by the company, the assembly process was necessarily complex and required a degree of dexterity apparently beyond the reach of automation. The solution occurred in a flash one day when a GE team was visiting a plant in Japan and noticed that all the manufacturing processes that introduced elements—usually decorative trim and electronic controls—to differentiate products from one another had been pushed to the end of the line. Using this principle, GE was able to go back and redesign the entire plant and the whole product range so than only in the last few steps is individualized assembly needed on each washer.

The revamp was helped by the use of a GE-developed weight-bearing plastic, Permatuf, that virtually did away with steel and porcelain in the construction of the central washing tub and provided the base for the new dishwasher design. It also created a concept around which to organize the plant, since it led the GE engineers toward standardization of the basic washtub. By simplifying the design at this point, the company was able to automate a major part of the manufacturing process.

As a result, manufacturing has been enormously accelerated. The tubs are manufactured at the beginning of the three-mile-long production line, then meander around the plant on robotized assembly lines to emerge as finished machines on an average of 18 hours. Before the change, the machines were much heavier, were made of more parts, and took six days to make. In addition, virtually all plastic and metal parts are now made at the point of use, reducing inventory costs from around $9.5 million to $3.9 million despite the higher rate of output.

GE uses a variety of computerized optical devices, including laser bar-code readers, to track units on the production line and automatically divert washers in need of repair or testing to a special holding area. An optical alignment system installs the dishwasher doors to tolerances of a few thousandths of an inch.

GE admits that the impressive results of these changes have not been exposed to the criteria of Japanese competition, now regarded as the iron test of U.S. technology. But GE's next step will be a $200 million investment in the refrigeration business, where its ability will be directly measured against the Japanese. Sanyo has established a plant in California, and GE believes that the Japanese company has sufficient experience in the Japanese refrigerator market to make it a tough competitor. "In dishwashers we did what we had to do to remain ahead even though we did not absolutely need to do it," says Roger Schipke, senior vice-president. "But in refrigerators we know that we have to be competitive on a world-class basis because the Japanese competitors market their products worldwide. We believe at the moment that we can go into the lead."

Source: Adapted from Terry Dodsworth, "Turning the Old into the Dynamic New." *Financial Times,* September 10,1984, p. 19.

Case Questions

1. Why did GE revamp its dishwasher plant?
2. What changes were made, and how did they increase productivity?
3. How has Japanese competition influenced GE's operations strategy in household appliances?
4. In your opinion, are foreign-made goods of higher quality than American-made goods? Support your opinion with specific examples. ■

Stuart Davis, *Blips and Ifs*. Oil on canvas. 1963–1964. 71⅛ x 53⅛″. Amon Carter Museum, Fort Worth, Texas.

21

INFORMATION SYSTEMS AND CONTROL

Upon completing this chapter you should be able to:

1. State why an information system is an important part of management planning, decision making, and control.
2. Describe how managers can evaluate the value and cost of information.
3. Explain why managers at different levels of the organization have different information needs.
4. Describe how a management information system (MIS) can be implemented effectively.
5. Identify the problems that can develop when a computer-based MIS is being implemented and state the ways these problems can be overcome.
6. Describe the different types of management information and decision systems—MISs, decision-support systems (DSSs), and artificial-intelligence (AI) applications.
7. Describe the uses and impacts of decision-support and expert systems on managers and organizations.

Chapter Outline

Introduction
Information and Control
Management Information Systems
Designing a Computer-Based MIS
Implementing a Computer-Based MIS
End-User Computing
The Impact of Computers and MIS on Managers and Organizations

ILLUSTRATIVE CASE STUDY
Introduction

Using Technology at Sears for Strategic Advantage

"Attention, shoppers, today we have a number of clothing specials that can be found under the revolving blue light" is the sort of announcement that can be heard daily in retail stores throughout the country. As Carl Johnson makes a dash for the special display in his local Sears store, he tries to remember how much credit he has left on his Sears charge account. His shopping companion, Bill Calkins, is trying hard to keep up, but the store is jammed with merchandise, and it is difficult to squeeze through the aisles. Carl turns to Bill and says, "I hope they have my size—I've been waiting for this sale on summer suits for weeks." The year is 1965, and retailing is just beginning to discover the benefits of computerization.

Carl finds several items to purchase and brings them to the sales counter. "Will this be cash or charge?" asks the sales clerk. "Charge it to my Sears account," responds Carl. The clerk rings up the merchandise, picks up the charge card, and phones the credit office. After checking a printout, the credit office approves the charge purchase, and Carl is on his way. As they are leaving the store, Carl turns to Bill and says, "Why don't you get a Sears charge so you can take advantage of the sales whenever you want? It beats running all over town to find a power drill or a sports coat." The scene, from a television commercial, ends with the announcer reminding viewers how easy it is to qualify for a Sears charge account.

Sears has been a leader in using computers to support its retail operations, and Charles Carlson, vice-president of information systems and data processing for the $40 billion retailing giant, smiles as he reruns the film of the above episode. He is reviewing advertising copy from the past 25 years to get a sense of how important computers have been in the success of the Sears retail operations. In 1965, computers were being used for back-room functions such as accounts receivable, but they had very little impact on the rest of retailing operations. Carlson found it hard to believe that Sears could gain a strategic advantage from as simple an application as computerized credit. In the days of large, cumbersome mainframe computers operating in a centralized environment, Sears had enjoyed the resources to develop the system and get a jump on the competition.

Sources: Catherine L. Harris, "Information Power," *Business Week,* October 14, 1985, pp. 107–114; Glenn Rifkin, "Computers in Retailing: Shopping for Strategic Advantage" *Computerworld,* November 24, 1986, pp. 39, 42, 47–48, 51, 54–55; Rifkin, "Large, Small Stores Seek High-Tech Edge," *Computerworld,* November 24, 1986, pp. 42, 44; Peter Cohen, "Retail Cashes in on PCs," *Computerworld,* November 24, 1986, pp. 50–51.

CLASS COMMENT

Information is the lifeblood of any system—particularly organizations.

All the managerial functions—planning, organizing, leading, and controlling—are necessary for successful organizational performance. To support these functions, especially planning and controlling, systems for supplying information to managers are of special importance. Only with accurate and timely information can managers monitor progress toward their goals and turn plans into reality. If managers cannot stay "on track," anticipating potential corrections, developing the skills to recognize when corrections are necessary, and then making appropriate corrections or adjustments as they progress, their work may be both fruitless and costly.

Over the last two decades, Americans have become virtually accustomed to the news of recalls of products ranging from atuomotive transmissions to IUDs. A general concern has arisen about the ability of American firms to control effectively the overall quality of products that are competing directly with those of foreign suppliers who do not seem to be experiencing the same difficulties. Such concern has focused greater attention not only on on the need to provide better training for human resources but on the need to find technological solutions to problems posed by the demands of improved quality control.

If you were to look at a new Toyota car in a showroom, you would find that Toyota has a computer-generated sticker attached to the window to display the pricing and EPA information. The Toyota dealer probably has a computerized inventory system to tell you if he has a car with the options that you want—perhaps even the color that you have dreamed about. Finally, should you need financing, the bank computer can quickly check your credit and help the salesperson close the sale. From the largest corporation to the modest home-town auto dealer, the computer plays a vital part in the control of business operations.

management information system (MIS) Computer-based information system for more effective planning, decision making, and control.

COORDINATED RESOURCE

See "Information Power," *Business Week*, 10/14/85, pp. 108–114. The Lecture Extra for Chapter 21 has a brief synopsis of this article.

Managers at all levels are finding that computer-based information systems provide the information necessary for effective operation. These **management information systems (MIS)** are rapidly becoming indispensable for planning, decision making, and control. How quickly and accurately managers receive information about what is going right and what is going wrong—how well the information system functions—determines, to a large extent, how effective the control system will be.[1] In addition, organizational information and decision-support systems (DSS) are undergoing major changes as a result of dramatic increases in computer capabilities and use. For example, as we discuss later in this chapter, in less than a decade MIS has evolved into DSS, and DSS in turn has begun to evolve toward artificial-intelligence applications. Computer-based information systems offer managers ever-increasing opportunities for improving their control systems. Thus, it has become crucial for managers to understand how these systems should be designed, implemented, and managed.

INFORMATION AND CONTROL

To appreciate the central role played by information in making control effective, consider a modest-sized manufacturer of automobile replacement parts with annual sales

[1]Information systems are also important for effective planning. See Kweku Ewusi-Mensah, "Information Systems for Planning," *Long Range Planning* 17, no. 5 (October 1984):111–117. See also Niv Ahituv and Seev Neumann, *Principles of Information Systems for Management*, 2nd ed. (Dubuque, Iowa: William C. Brown, 1986).

of $10 million. Every year, the firm's 350 employees service 20,000 customer orders. These orders must be processed, billed, assembled, packed, and shipped—adding up to some 400,000 transactions that must be controlled.

And that is only the beginning. The firm writes 25,000 checks annually. Half of these cover wages; most of the others pay for the 5,000 purchase orders issued every year. Costs are assembled from 17,000 time cards, 6,000 job orders, and 20,000 materials requisitions. Each year, that small $10 million firm is processing almost a million pieces of information related to its activities—and that figure does not include all the other pieces of control information being processed, such as those related to inventory and quality control.

The Computer Revolution

HERE'S AN EXAMPLE

Keeping track of business at Kraft, Inc., Grocery Products Group, used to be a nightmare. The top executives used to get stacks of paper with the previous day's sales results at 3:00 each afternoon. Now with PC's, they get the same information as early as 8:30 A.M., organized geographically and by product line. Says Vice-President Jack A. Peterson, "We conduct our work lives differently." (*Business Week*, 6/27/88, pp. 84–86)

Before the widespread use of computers, managers could not effectively make use of large amounts of valuable information about an organization's activities. The information either reached managers too late or was simply too expensive to gather in usable form.[2] Today, managers have at their command a wide range of data-processing and information tools. In place of a few financial controls, managers can draw on computer-based information systems to control activities in every area of their organization. On any number of performance measures, the information provided by these systems helps managers compare standards with actual results, detect deviations, and take corrective action before it is too late to make changes.

The introduction of computerized information systems has sharply changed management control in many organizations. Even a neighborhood retailer may now use computers to control inventory, sales, billing, and other activities. In large organizations, complex electronic data-processing (EDP) systems monitor entire projects and sets of operations. Increasingly, information will be recognized as an important business resource, perhaps even indispensable to the effective management of a business enterprise in the 1990s.[3]

HERE'S AN EXAMPLE

About 15 years ago, Mexican authorities using computerized information found that the Cancun location, because of its sand, climate, and accessibility, was ideal for developers to build a resort city. The phenomenal popularity of this vacation spot attests to the correctness of this information.

Contemporary managers need to be effective at, and comfortable with, using computers, since managerial dependence on them is growing rapidly. By 1990, 51 percent of American managers will be using some sort of electronic work station[4] and the U.S. Commerce Department projects the population of personal computers worldwide to be 100 million. Because computers provide managers with quick and easy access to information, they should understand how computerized information systems work; how they are developed; their applications capabilities, limitations, and costs; and the manner in which information systems may be used.[5]

The Value and Cost of Information

In designing or improving an information system for management, one of the issues that managers need to consider is whether the benefits of the proposed system justify

---

[2]Earl P. Strong and Robert D. Smith, *Management Control Models* (New York: Holt, Rinehart & Winston, 1968), pp. 119–120.

[3]Paul L. Tom, *Managing Information as a Corporate Resource* (Glenview, Ill.: Scott, Foresman, 1987), p. 4.

[4]Peggy Schmidt, "What's New in Computer Psychology," *New York Times*, January 20, 1985, p. F15.

[5]For a description of 12 computer-related competence standards for managers, see F. Warren Benton, *Execucomp: Maximum Management with the New Computers*, (New York: John Wiley, 1983), pp. 9–16.

FOR DISCUSSION

What gives information value? How can the value of information be measured?

the cost. Another is whether the proposed system fits the plan for the organization's overall information needs.[6] Cost-effectiveness of an information system can be difficult to determine, because the value of the information is difficult to quantify.[7] Robert H. Gregory and Richard L. Van Horn have suggested that the value of information depends on four factors: its quality, timeliness, quantity, and relevance to management's ability to take action.[8]

Information quality. The more accurate the information, the higher its quality and the more securely managers can rely on it when making decisions. In general, however, the cost of obtaining information increases as the quality of the desired information becomes higher. If information of a higher quality does not add materially to a manager's decision-making capability, it is not worth the added cost.

Information timeliness. For effective control, corrective action must be applied before too great a deviation from the plan or standard has taken place. Thus, the information provided by an information system must be available to the right person at the right time for the appropriate action to be taken.

Information quantity. Managers can hardly make accurate and timely decisions without sufficient information. However, managers are often inundated with irrelevant and useless information. If they receive more information than they can productively use, they may overlook information on serious problems.

Information relevance. Similarly, the information that managers receive must have relevance to their responsibilities and tasks. The personnel manager does not need to know inventory levels—and the manager in charge of reordering inventory does not need to know about the status of staff members in other departments.

TEACHING TIP

Be sure to emphasize the subtle differences in these terms since we often use the terms interchangeably (and wrongly).

information Technically, processed data that supplies information about a specific situation or process.

management information Information representing relevant and important features about a situation so that a manager can take specific action.

Finally, in deciding what information a given manager needs, it is helpful to distinguish among data, information, and management information. *Data* are raw, unanalyzed facts, figures, and events from which information *can* be developed—for example, the number of cars sitting on the lot of an automobile dealership in Lubbock or the inventory records for welding rods at a factory in Spokane. **Information** is analyzed or processed data that informs a recipient about a situation—whether the number of cars sold in Lubbock by the 15th of August this year compares favorably or unfavorably with sales during the same period last year or the inventory of welding rods at the Spokane plant is above or below the desired minimum inventory. **Management information** is information that has action implications; that is, because it is accurate, timely, and relevant and because it represents the key features of a situation, managers can determine from it what they must do about the situation. As different as their operations and objectives may be, both the Lubbock and Spokane organizations require accurate, timely, relevant information if they are to be managed effectively. Management information systems are exceedingly useful tools for maintaining and tracking this essential information. Some of the new ways in which information is gathered and used are described in the Management Application box entitled "Information Power."

---

[6]Robert Behling, *Computers and Information Processing* (Boston: Kent Publishing, 1986), pp. 500–502.

[7]Gilbert W. Fairholm, "A Reality Basis for Management Information System Decisions," *Public Administration Review* 39, no. 2 (March–April 1979):176–179; and Fred R. McFadden and James D. Suver, "Costs and Benefits of a Data Base System," *Harvard Business Review* 56, no. 1 (January–February 1978):131–139.

[8]Robert H. Gregory and Richard L. Van Horn, "Value and Cost of Information," in J. Daniel Couger and Robert W. Knapp, *Systems Analysis Techniques* (New York: Wiley, 1974), pp. 473–489. See also Barry J. Epstein and William R. King, "An Experimental Study of the Value of Information," *Omega* 10, no. 3 (1982):249–258.

MANAGEMENT APPLICATION

INFORMATION POWER—HOW COMPANIES ARE USING NEW TECHNOLOGIES TO GAIN A COMPETITIVE EDGE

The ability to use computers creatively to collect, organize, distribute, and control information is spelling the difference between success and mediocrity in industries ranging from airlines to autobody repair. Computers are changing the way that we do business, fast becoming indispensable allies in marketing, customer service, product development, human resource management, and even strategic planning. Consider the following:

> Merrill Lynch & Co. uses computers to combine information on a customer's checking, savings, credit card, and securities accounts to help identify idle funds that are "swept" into interest-bearing money market accounts. Since introduction of the Cash Management Account in 1978, Merrill Lynch has lured billions of dollars of assets from other financial institutions.
>
> Security Pacific Automation Co., a subsidiary of Security Pacific Bank, sells its services both to Security Pacific and to other banks. Banking requires an immense investment in technology and considers the application of computers a competitive weapon. By putting terminals into car dealerships to link them with Security Pacific Credit Corp., the bank can provide credit-checking services and calculate loan payments immediately, helping dealers to close the sale much more efficiently. The company also generates lending business for the bank.

MANAGEMENT INFORMATION SYSTEMS

HERE'S AN EXAMPLE

Phillips 66 Company, a division of Phillips Petroleum Company, eliminated 40 percent of its management jobs and developed an electronics information system to help track data. Says President Robert G. Wallace, "We needed a more meaningful way of managing business information." (*Business Week*, 6/27/88, pp. 84–86)

THOUGHT-PROVOKER

Do formal information systems pose any dangers to organizations? Why or why not?

One of the difficulties associated with discussing management information systems is the fact that there are many definitions of them.[9] For our purposes, we will define an MIS as *a formal method of making available to management the accurate and timely information necessary to facilitate the decision-making process and enable the organization's planning, control, and operational functions to be carried out effectively*. The system provides information on the past, present, and projected future and on relevant events inside and outside the organization.[10]

The use of the word "formal" in our definition is not intended to negate the importance of the informal communication network in the organization's control mechanisms. In fact, managers often detect problems *before* they show up in formal control reports because they are tuned in to the grapevine. The ability of managers to maintain effective informal communication channels, to sense the implications of the information those channels transmit, and to evaluate, decide, and act quickly on such information extends enormously the usefulness of the MIS.

---

[9]John Dearden, in "MIS Is a Mirage," *Harvard Business Review* 50, no. 1 (January–February 1972):90, even suggested that the concept of MIS "is embedded in a mishmash of fuzzy thinking and incomprehensible jargon." Since then, however, managers have become more comfortable with the concept, and there is greater agreement about it; see Paul H. Cheney and Norman R. Lyons, "MIS Update," *Data Management* 19, no. 10 (October 1980):26–32.

[10]See Walter J. Kennevan, "Management Information Systems," *Data Management* 8, no. 9 (September 1970):62–64.

American Airlines, through its Sabre reservation system, lists the flight schedules of every major airline in the world for over 10,000 automated travel agents throughout the country. American gains in two ways: It obtains increased airline travel business because it has control over the display of flight information (American can list its flights first), and it charges agents $1.75 for every reservation made through the system.

Akzo, a billion-dollar Dutch chemical company, has perfected a computer system that permits an autobody shop technician to punch in a description of a car and the parts and repair work needed. The system then displays a parts-and-labor calculation obtained from processing a data file of spare parts, repair procedures, and labor-hour guidelines. The goal of the system is to provide everything the technician needs to know about the repair, including paint coatings required for the repair work, creating increased markets for Akzo's paint products.

As computers, telecommunications, and video technology become more entwined, the potentials of each multiply. With the computer in mind, business is beginning to reconfigure things from the ground up. This process leads to entirely different approaches to existing markets and whole new product lines that did not previously seem a logical extension of business. Technology is changing the way that we do business by providing better customer service, market intelligence, and better financial and cash management.

Source: Based on Catherine L. Harris, "Information Power: How Companies Are Using New Technologies to Gain a Competitive Edge," *Business Week,* October 14, 1985.

The Evolution of MIS

BACKGROUND ON INFORMATION TECHNOLOGY

Information technology is bringing about change in all aspects of business. For an interesting description of the development of information technology, see "Computers and Managerial Choice" by G. W. P. Keen, in *Organizational Dynamics,* Autumn 1985, pp. 35–49.

Organizations have always had some kind of management information system, even if it was not recognized as such.[11] In the past, these systems were of a highly informal nature in their setup and utilization. Not until the advent of computers, with their ability to process and condense large quantities of data, did the design of management information systems become a formal process and field of study. Attempts to use computers effectively led to the identification and study of information systems and to the planning, implementation, and review of new ones.

electronic data processing (EDP) Computerized data processing and information management, including report standardization for operating managers.

EDP. When computers were first introduced into organizations, they were used mainly to process data for a few organizational functions—usually accounting and billing. Because of the specialized skills required to operate the expensive, complex, and sometimes temperamental equipment, computers were located in **electronic data processing (EDP)** departments. As the speed and ease of processing data grew, other data-processing and information-management tasks were computerized. To cope with these new tasks, EDP departments developed standardized reports for the use of operating managers.

MIS. The growth of EDP departments spurred managers to focus more on planning their organizations' information systems. These efforts led to the emergence of the

[11]This discussion is drawn, in part, from Michael S. Scott Morton and John F. Rockart, "Implications of Changes in Information Technology for Corporate Strategy," *Interfaces* 14, no. 1 (January–February 1984):84–95.

computer-based information system (CBIS) (or computer-based MIS) Information system that goes beyond the mere standardization of data to aid in the planning process.

concept of **computer-based information systems (CBIS),** which became better known as computer-based MIS—or simply MIS. As the EDP departments' functions expanded beyond routine processing of masses of standardized data, they began to be called MIS departments.

DSS. Recent advances in computer hardware and software have made it possible for managers to gain "on-line" or "real-time" access to the data bases in CBISs. The widespread use of microcomputers has enabled managers to create their own data bases and electronically manipulate information as needed rather than waiting for reports to be issued by the EDP/MIS department. While MIS reports are still necessary for monitoring ongoing operations, DSS permits less structured use of data bases as special decision needs arise.[12]

Artificial Intelligence. One of the fastest-growing areas of information technology, artificial intelligence uses the computer to simulate some of the characteristics of human thought.[13] Expert systems use artificial-intelligence techniques to diagnose problems, recommend strategies to avert or solve these problems and to offer a rationale for these recommendations. In effect, the expert system acts like a human "expert" in analyzing unstructured situations. (We discuss artificial intelligence and expert systems in more detail later in this chapter.)

Differing Information for Different Management Levels

G. Anthony Gorry and M. S. Scott Morton have pointed out that an organization's information system must provide information to managers with three levels of responsibilities: operational control, management control, and strategic planning.[14] We can think of these three categories in terms of the activities that take place at different levels of the managerial hierarchy (first-line, middle, and top). The design of the MIS must take into account the information needs of the various managerial levels, as well as meeting the routine transaction-processing needs of the total organization. For example, as shown in Table 21-1, the information sources for operational control are based largely within the organization, while the information sources for strategic planning tend to be outside the organization.

Operational Control. An MIS for operational control must provide highly accurate and detailed information on a daily or weekly basis. A production supervisor has to know if materials wastage is excessive, if costly overruns are about to occur, or if the machine time for a job has expired. The MIS must provide a high volume of timely and detailed information derived from daily operations.

Middle Management. Middle-level managers, such as division heads, will be concerned with the current and future performance of their units. They will therefore need information on important matters that will affect those units—large-scale problems

[12]For further discussion of the differences between and evolution of MIS and DSS, see Ralph H. Sprague, Jr., "A Framework for the Development of Decision Support Systems," in Hugh J. Watson and Archie B. Carroll, eds., *Computers for Business* (Plano, Texas: Business Publications, 1984), pp. 197–226.

[13]Barry Shore, *Introduction to Computer Information Systems* (New York: Holt, Rinehart & Winston, 1988), pp. 304–313.

[14]G. Anthony Gorry and Michael S. Scott Morton, "A Framework for Management Information Systems," *Sloan Management Review* 13, no. 1 (Fall 1971):55–70. Gorry and Scott Morton based their framework on the three-part division of managerial activities described by Robert N. Anthony in *Planning and Control Systems* (Boston: Harvard University Graduate School of Business Administration, 1965), pp. 15–21.

with suppliers, abrupt sales declines, or increased consumer demand for a particular product line. Thus, the type of information middle-level managers will require consists of aggregate (summarized) data from within the organization as well as from sources outside the organization.

Top Management. For top managers, the MIS must provide information for strategic planning and management control. For strategic planning, the external sources of information—on economic conditions, technological developments, the actions of competitors—assume paramount importance.[15] This information is difficult to computerize because the supporting data are generally beyond the control of the organization.

For the *management control* functions of top managers, however, the sources of information must be both internal and external. Top managers are typically concerned about the overall financial performance of their organizations. They therefore need information on quarterly sales and profits, on the other relevant indicators of financial performance (such as stock value), as well as on the performance of competitors. Internal control reports for top managers come in at monthly, quarterly, and sometimes even annual intervals. At the headquarters of Mrs. Field's Cookies, computer-based reports are reviewed hour by hour.

How may the various needs of different managerial levels be translated into a management information system? One major company designed the manufacturing component of its MIS this way: *Supervisors* receive daily reports on direct and indirect labor, materials usage, scrap, production counts, and machine downtime; *superintendents* and *department heads* receive weekly departmental cost summaries and product-cost reports; *plant managers* receive weekly and monthly financial statements and analyses, analyses of important costs, and summarized product-cost reports; *divisional managers* receive monthly plant comparisons, financial planning reports, product-cost summaries, and plant-cost control reports; and, finally, *top managers* receive overall monthly and quarterly financial reviews, financial analyses, and summarized comparisons of divisional performance.

EXTRA EXERCISE

How might each of these managerial positions need and use an MIS: personnel director for General Electric Corporation, night-shift manager at your local McDonald's, president of your university.

[15] Charles R. Litecky, "Corporate Strategy and MIS Planning," *Journal of Systems Management* 32, no. 1 (January 1981):36–39.

TABLE 21-1 INFORMATION REQUIREMENTS BY DECISION CATEGORY

CHARACTERISTICS OF INFORMATION	OPERATIONAL CONTROL (FIRST LINE)	MANAGEMENT CONTROL (TOP AND MIDDLE LEVEL)	STRATEGIC PLANNING (TOP LEVEL)
Source	Largely internal	⟷	Largely external
Scope	Well defined, narrow	⟷	Very wide
Level of Aggregation	Detailed	⟷	Aggregate
Time Horizon	Historical	⟷	Future
Currency	Highly current	⟷	Fairly old
Required Accuracy	High	⟷	Low
Frequency of Use	Very frequent	⟷	Infrequent

Source: Adapted from G. Anthony Garry and Michael S. Scott Morton, "A Framework for Management Information Systems," *Sloan Management Review* 13, no. 1 (Fall 1971):59.

ILLUSTRATIVE CASE STUDY Continued

Using Technology at Sears for Strategic Advantage

Carl Johnson stands under the revolving blue light, with an arm full of clothing bargains. "Come on, Bill," he says, "let's check out so we can get home in time to catch the rest of the game." The clerk smiles as he runs a light pen over the specially prepared pricing tag on each garment, waiting for the point-of-sale (POS) terminal to search the mainframe computer, ring up the sale price, and record the transaction details for later reporting to management. Sears has had POS for several years now, and individual store systems are linked with both headquarters and regional distribution centers to gain processing power and save on paperwork.

Carl hands his charge card to the clerk, watches him key the account number into the POS terminal, and in a few seconds his credit approval is stamped on the sales ticket. The clerk packs the purchases, and Bill are Carl are on their way out the door. Bill still does not have a Sears charge, but he is thinking about getting one. "Carl," he muses, "it's amazing how much change there has been in the Sears store this past ten years. Here we are in 1975, in the age of computers, and the clerk doesn't even have to know the price of the item to ring it up. The POS terminal does it all. Will wonders never cease?"

Charles Carlson is still viewing films that Sears used for various advertising campaigns and remembers well the first stores that installed POS systems. Managers fell in love with them. "We were able to manage credit, gather merchandise information, calculate our inventory, and monitor staffing requirements through this single system," recalls Carlson. "It revolutionized the retailing business." It would seem that in most markets, Sears was able to keep a competitive advantage by applying advanced computer technology to address a variety of retailing problems.

DESIGNING A COMPUTER-BASED MIS

Many articles and books have described the systematic steps that should be followed in designing and implementing an MIS.[16] Robert G. Murdick reviewed a number of these sources and adapted them to form his own model of how an MIS should be developed.[17] (See Fig. 21-1.) This flowchart indicates the complexity and amount of work required for MIS development. For the sake of simplicity, Exhibit 21-1 breaks down Murdick's model into four stages.

EXHIBIT 21-1 MURDOCK'S FOUR-STAGE MODEL OF MIS DEVELOPMENT

1. *A preliminary survey and problem definition stage.* With the formation of a task force charged with the design of an MIS, there should be a thorough assessment of the organization's capabilities and strategic goals, as well as an assessment of any external factors relevant to the organization's functions. From this assessment, a definition of the information system the organization needs can be decided upon, and the determination of informational, operational, and functional objectives can be accomplished.
2. *A conceptual design stage.* Through an analysis of the current information system, alternative MIS designs with specific performance requirements can be developed. These alternatives are then weighed against organization objectives, capabilities, and needs. This examination leads to an initial selected project plan. At this point, tasks are delegated, information on the task force's study communicated to employees, and the plan for a training program conceived.

(continued)

[16]See, for example, John C. Carter and Fred N. Silverman, "Establishing an MIS," *Journal of Systems Management* 31, no. 1 (January 1980):15–21; and W. L. Harrison, *Computers and Information Processing* (St. Paul: West, 1986).

[17]Robert G. Murdick, "MIS Development Procedures," *Journal of Systems Management* 21, no. 12 (December 1970):22–26.

EXHIBIT 21-1 (CONTINUED)

3. *A detailed design stage.* Once the conceptual plan is decided upon, performance specifications of the new MIS can be established. Components, programming, flowcharting, and data bases (including specifications for personnel interaction with the system) can be designed. A model of the system is created, tested, refined, and reviewed until it meets the specified level of performance.
4. *A final implementation stage.* The formal requirements for the new MIS are determined. The logistics of space allocations, equipment additions, and forms design are worked out and enacted. The training program commences. Design and testing of software for the MIS are completed, and the organization's data bases are entered into the system. After a series of final checks, the MIS is ready for implementation.

It should be emphasized that creation of an MIS is a long-term task that requires the skills of a variety of specialists. In fact, the design and implementation of an MIS such as that shown in Murdick's model might well require a major team effort by managers and information systems analysts over a period of two or three years.

Guidelines for Effective Design

How can these steps in the MIS development process be carried out effectively? For our purposes, we can focus on six guidelines for effective MIS design: (1) make users part of the design team; (2) carefully consider the costs of the system; (3) consider alternatives to in-house software development; (4) favor relevance and selectivity of information over sheer quantity; (5) pretest the system before installation; and (6) train the operators and users of the system carefully.

FOR DISCUSSION

How might organizational culture affect the choice of a MIS?

1. *Include users on the design team.* It is widely agreed that cooperation between the operating managers (who use the information) and systems designers is not only desirable but necessary. Users know what information they need, when it is needed, and how it will be used for managerial action and decision making. Unless operating managers have a decisive voice in the design of the MIS, the information system may fail to provide needed information while simultaneously overloading them with useless information.[18]

2. *Weigh the money and time costs of the system.* To keep the MIS on track and on budget, designers need to specify how the system will be developed—and this includes schedules of time required for different steps, milestones to be reached, and budgeted costs. If managers justify the design and installation of a new system on a cost-benefit basis, cost overruns are less likely to occur. It should be noted that the greater portion of MIS operating costs go for the maintenance of existing software.[19]

3. *Consider alternatives to in-house software development.* The high cost of software development has led management to look for ways to reduce costs and for developing and implementing new systems. In some situations, organizations may find their data-processing requirements are very similar to the needs of other businesses, and suitable software is available from hardware manufacturers or software suppliers. In recent years, the wide acceptance of commercial software by both large and small organizations has brought the costs down and has increased the availability.

FOR DISCUSSION

Is quality of information important? Why? How would you ensure high-quality information?

4. *Favor relevance and selectivity over sheer quantity.* As we have seen, a manager needs enough information for an informed decision; more information is not

[18]See Arnold Barnett, "Preparing Management for MIS," *Journal of Systems Management* 23, no. 1 (January 1972):40–43.

[19]Michael Potter and Robin McNeill, "The New Programmer—The Next Wave of Computer Innovation in North American Business," *Business Quarterly* 48, no. 4 (Winter 1983):132–134.

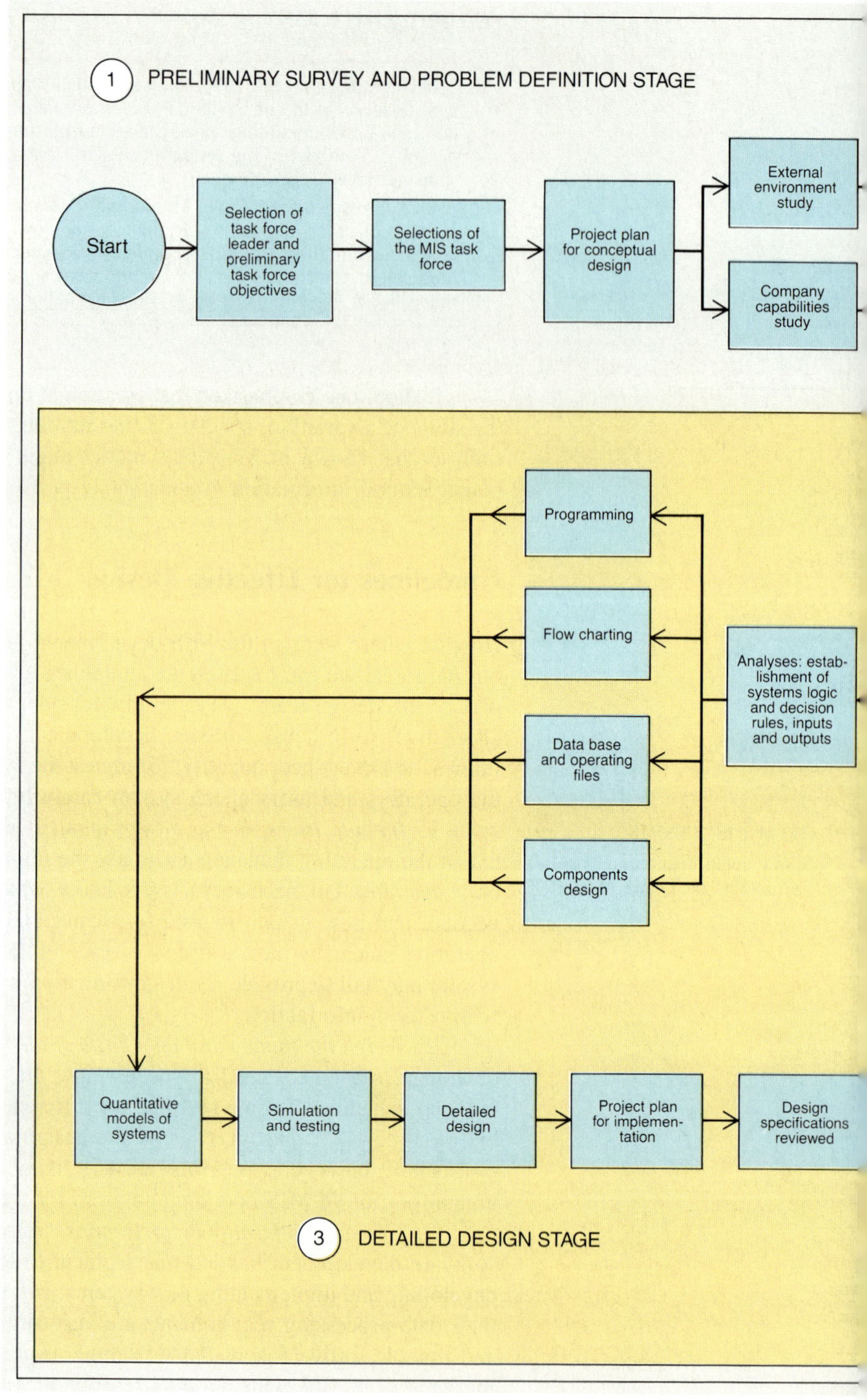

FIGURE 21-1 MIS DEVELOPMENT

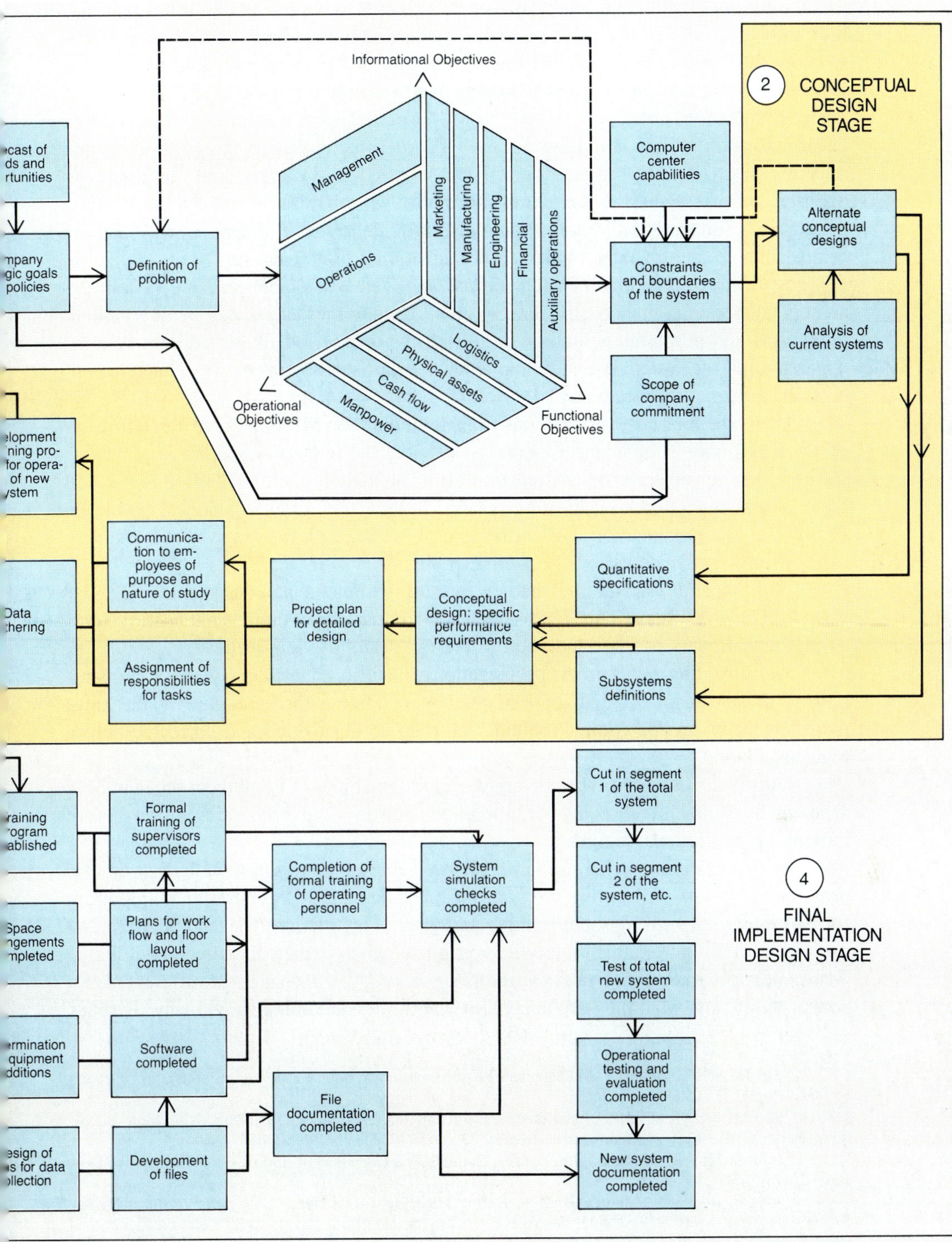

Source: Adapted from Robert G. Murdick, "MIS Development Procedures," *Journal of Systems Management* 21, no. 12 (December 1970):24–25. Reprinted by permission.

necessarily better, although many managers prefer to have too much rather than too little information.[20] In one study, decision makers who perceived themselves as experiencing information overload had lower performance levels but a higher satisfaction level than those decision makers who perceived information underload.[21] A properly designed MIS does not supply middle- or top-level managers with the routine details of an organization's daily activities.[22] The MIS *filters* or evaluates information so that only the most relevant information will be supplied to the appropriate manager. In addition, the effective MIS *condenses* information, so what is relevant can be absorbed quickly. The information system should also provide top-level managers with data on critical factors and changes related to organizational effectiveness.[23]

5. *Pretest the system before installation.* Even when managers and system designers cooperate in the system's development, important factors may be overlooked. Omissions and problems will show up during the test period. If they do not become apparent until the system is finally implemented, costly problems may arise and expensive changes may be necessary.

There are four basic approaches to installing a new MIS that have some bearing on the length and extensiveness of the pretest stage.[24] In *crash* or *direct installation,* the new system replaces the old one entirely. The switch is effected all at once, and there is total dependence on the new system. In this case, extensive pretest should be done, since the organization will not be able to fall back on the old system if the new system fails or reveals major operational problems.[25]

With *parallel installation,* the new system is implemented and operated side by side with the old system. This approach allows comparison of outputs between systems so that adjustments can be made before the old system is removed.

Pilot installation offers the organization the ability to test the new MIS in operation as it is used by a small part of the organization—for example, by the sales management of one division. Problems can then be discovered and corrected before total installation.

Phased installation offers the organization the ability to implement the new MIS segment by segment, allowing for operational testing and problem solution before moving on to the next segment.

6. *Provide adequate training and written documentation for the operators and users of the system.* A training program for managers and MIS operators is important for two major reasons. Without training and written instructions for the operation and use of the MIS, the organization will be at a loss when experienced personnel leave. Also, operators must understand the information needs of managers at different levels so that they know what they are doing, for whom they are doing it, and why. Perhaps

---

[20] See Russell L. Ackoff, "Management Misinformation Systems," *Management Science,* December 1967, pp. 147–156.

[21] Charles A. O'Reilly III, "Individuals and Information Overload in Organizations: Is More Necessarily Better?" *Academy of Management Journal* 23, no. 4 (December 1980):684–696.

[22] John P. Murray, *Managing Information Systems as a Corporate Resource* (Homewood, Ill.: Dow Jones-Irwin, 1984).

[23] John F. Rockart, "Chief Executives Define Their Own Data Needs," *Harvard Business Review* 57, no. 2 (March–April 1979):81–93, describes a process for determining the factors CEOs consider critical for their organizations' success ("critical success factors").

[24] See H. L. Capron and Brian K. Williams, *Computers and Data Processing,* 2nd ed. (Menlo Park, Calif.: Benjamin/Cummings Publishing, 1984), Chapter 9; and Steven L. Mandell, *Computers and Data Processing: Concepts and Applications,* 2nd ed. (St. Paul, Minn.: West Publishing, 1982), p. 34.

[25] A case study from the Harvard Business School, "First National City Bank Operating Group (A), 474–165, 1975, and (B), 474–166, 1975," describes the direct installation approach used by John Reed—currently CEO of Citicorp—to mechanize the "back office" operations (routine check and other paper processing) of Citibank when he was senior vice-president of the Operating Group in 1970. This mechanization effort was not a purely MIS installation. However, it is an example of the direct approach to a complex operations systems conversion that used computers and related equipment and that contained facets of Citibank's MIS.

"Here's the story, gentlemen. Sometime last night, an 11-year-old kid in Akron, Ohio, got into our computer and transferred all our assets to a bank in Zurich."
Drawing by Stevenson; © 1983 The New Yorker Magazine, Inc.

most important, managers need to understand how the MIS operates so they can control it, rather than letting it control them.

Even with great care in design and implementation, an MIS may not fit the needs of users as closely as desired, either because it is difficult to use (not sufficiently user-friendly) or because it does not supply all the information asked for. As systems are developed, it should be made plain how the new MIS will change the organizational structure and task responsibilities and how the job of each employee will be affected by the new MIS.[26]

IMPLEMENTING A COMPUTER-BASED MIS

QUOTATION FROM A MANAGER

"The difference between now and five years ago is that [information] technology had limited function. You weren't betting your company on it. Now you are."—William H. Gruber, President of Research and Planning, Inc. (*Business Week,* 10/14/85, p. 108)

Use of computers as a means of addressing many organizational concerns has grown rapidly, despite the problems involved in implementing a computerized MIS. Managers should be aware of the systems and technological problems of systems design and installation, although these are, strictly speaking, the concern of information system and data-processing personnel and are obviously beyond the scope of an introductory management text. Our discussion, therefore, focuses on the "people concerns," which are more important for most managers to understand, are at least as difficult to address, and are no less likely to inhibit successful implementation of a computerized information system. The primary responsibility for addressing such concerns will fall upon managers.[27]

---

[26]Benton, *Execucomp,* p. 238.

[27]Our discussion in this section is based on G. W. Dickson and John K. Simmons, "The Behavioral Side of MIS," *Business Horizons* 13, no. 4 (August 1970):59–71.

Problems in Implementing a Computer-Based MIS

Organizational Resistance. In Exhibit 21-2, G. W. Dickson and John K. Simmons indicate five major factors that determine whether and to what extent the implementation of a new MIS will be resisted.

EXHIBIT 21-2 DICKSON AND SIMMONS'S FIVE FACTORS LEADING TO THE RESISTANCE OF A NEW MIS SYSTEM

1. *Disruption of established departmental boundaries.* The establishment of a new MIS often results in changes in several organizational units. For example, inventory and purchasing departments may be merged to make use of the MIS more efficient. Such changes may be resisted by department members, who may resent having to change the way they do things or the people with whom they work.
2. *Disruption of the informal system.* The informal communication network may be disrupted as a new MIS alters communication patterns. If organization members prefer some of the earlier, informal mechanisms for gathering and distributing information, they may resist the more formal channels set up for the new system.
3. *Specific individual characteristics.* People with many years of service with the organization have "learned the ropes" and know how to get things done in the existing system. They may tend to resist change more tenaciously than newer people who have been with the organization for a comparatively short period of time and who do not have as large an investment in organizational know-how and relationships.
4. *The organizational culture.* If top management maintains open communication, deals with grievances, and, in general, establishes a culture with high trust throughout the organization, there is likely to be less resistance to the installation of a new MIS. However, if top managers are isolated or aloof from other organization members, or if the organizational culture supports inflexible behavior, then effective implementation of the MIS is likely to be hindered.
5. *How the change is implemented.* As we have seen repeatedly in earlier chapters, the manner in which changes are designed and implemented affects the amount of resistance the changes will encounter. In general, when managers and subordinates make change decisions together, there is greater likelihood that the changes will be accepted.

Source: G. W. Dickson and John K. Simmons, "The Behavioral Side of MIS," *Business Horizons* 13, no. 4 (August 1970):59–71.

Dickson and Simmons have observed that the frustrations associated with the implementation of a new MIS can manifest themselves in three ways:

- *Aggression* is manifested when individuals hit back at the object (or person) frustrating them. Aggression against a computer-based MIS has gone as far as sabotage—by using equipment incorrectly, by putting incomplete or inadequate information into the system, or by actual destruction of hardware or software.
- *Projection* is the psychological mechanism of blaming difficulties on someone or something else. When managers (or other individuals) blame the computer system for problems caused by human error or other factors unrelated to the system itself, projection is taking place.
- *Avoidance* is manifested when individuals defend themselves by withdrawing from or avoiding a frustrating situation. Managers may exhibit avoidance behavior when they ignore the output of an MIS in favor of their own information sources.

Because people at different levels of the organization are affected by a computer-based MIS in different ways, the frequency with which each type of behavior is manifested will depend on the hierarchical level of the individuals and managers affected by the MIS change. (See Table 21-2.) Among lower-level nonclerical personnel, for example, the installation of a new MIS may cause an increase in job complexity. Clerical workers (like data-entry operators) who will be working directly with the new system are less likely to manifest aggression toward it unless there is a perceived fear that the

TABLE 21-2 WORK GROUPS, THEIR RELATION TO MIS, AND THEIR POSSIBLE DYSFUNCTIONAL BEHAVIORS

ORGANIZATIONAL SUBGROUP	RELATION TO MIS	DYSFUNCTIONAL BEHAVIOR
Top Management	Generally unaffected and unconcerned with systems	Avoidance
Technical Staff	Systems designers and agents of systems change	None
Operating Management	Controlled from above by systems; job content and context modified by new systems	Aggression, avoidance, and projection
Operating Personnel: Clerical	Particularly affected by clerical systems; jobs eliminated; job patterns changed	Projection
Nonclerical	Provide system inputs	Aggression

Source: Adapted from G. W. Dickson and John K. Simmons, "The Behavioral Side of MIS," *Business Horizons* 13, no. 4 (August 1970):63.

introduction of the new system will reduce the total number of available jobs: The MIS represents a major part of their job. They may, however, resist changes in the system through projection—for example, by making remarks about the new system's failings and inadequacies relative to the old system.

Operating management—including both first-line and middle managers—generally experiences the greatest impact from a new MIS. The information supplied by the MIS to top managers will, after all, help determine how the operating managers are evaluated. The problem for operating managers is that they have less control over how and when this information is filtered, interpreted, and presented to their superiors; instead of supplying it directly to top managers, they supply it to the MIS, which is operated by staff specialists. This loss of control can be a source of anxiety to operating managers.

QUOTATION FROM A PROFESSOR

"Before they [computers] really have an impact, a lot of work styles and organizational structures are going to have to change."—Warren G. Briggs, Professor at Suffolk University School of Management (*Business Week*, 6/27/88, p. 86)

Other sources of anxiety for managers include the fact that a computerized MIS tends to allow more centralized decision making, which makes it easier for top managers to increase their control over operating managers. In addition, there is always the possibility that a computer-based MIS will eliminate or substantially alter some first-line and middle-management jobs. Thus, the resistance of operating managers to the MIS may encompass all three types of psychological reactions: They may fight the system (aggression); they may ignore it, sticking to their old communication channels (avoidance); or they may blame the system for failures caused by other factors (projection). Table 21-3 illustrates the reasons why operating managers are especially likely to resist a computer-based MIS.

The top management in many organizations is, in the main, unaffected by the implementation of an MIS. Top managers require extensive external information and find that the MIS will meet only a portion of their needs. If the MIS has been oversold to top management, it will lead to significant unrealized expectations, which in turn will become disappointments once the MIS is operational.

The design of the MIS takes place within the political system of the organization, and nonrational considerations of MIS designers and subgroups of users can have an impact on the eventual design, implementation, use, and organizational reaction and behavior toward the new MIS.[28] For example, divisional requirements for information by middle management might differ from the overall organizational requirements for

[28]Daniel Robey and M. Lynne Markus, "Rituals in Information System Design," *MIS Quarterly* 8, no. 1 (March 1984):5–15.

TABLE 21-3 REASONS FOR RESISTANCE TO MIS (BY WORKING GROUP)

	TOP MANAGEMENT	OPERATING MANAGEMENT	OPERATING (CLERICAL)	OPERATING (NONCLERICAL)
Threats to economic security		X	X	
Threats to status or power		X	X*	
Increased job complexity	X		X	X
Uncertainty or unfamiliarity	X	X	X	X
Changed interpersonal relations or work patterns		X*	X	
Changed superior-subordinate relationships		X*	X	
Increased rigidity or time pressure	X	X	X	
Role ambiguity		X	X*	X
Feelings of insecurity		X	X*	X*

X = The reason is possibly the cause of resistance to MIS development.
X* = The reason has a strong possibility of being the cause of resistance.

Source: G. W. Dickson and John K. Simmons, "The Behavioral Side of MIS," *Business Horizons* 13, no. 4 (August 1970):68. Copyright © 1970 by the Foundation for the School of Business at Indiana University. Reprinted by permission.

FOR DISCUSSION

Are there any management situations in which a formal MIS might not be helpful? Describe.

information by top management. The information most useful to top managers might also facilitate the evaluation of divisional performance; this might be perceived by middle managers as a threat to their security. Both groups may jockey for position and try to protect their interests. After the design is completed, winners and losers of the political battle may take different stances toward the new MIS.

COORDINATED RESOURCE

See "Is Your Computer Secure," *Business Week,* 8/1/88, pp. 64–72.

Security. Security of the new system is a control issue that must be addressed in design and implementation stages—for example, by placing equipment in safe and supervised areas and by the construction of password and read-only files. Table 21-4 outlines some important security concerns and the degree of risk associated with two major MIS configurations—mainframe computers and micro- or personal computers. While the protection of mainframe configurations is usually adequate, security for microcomputer systems is sorely lacking in many organizations, which tend to be ignorant of the risks involved and often neglect appropriate security measures.[29]

Organizations using microcomputer-based information systems have experienced increased control problems, such as theft and vandalism, the destruction or alteration of data, and the unauthorized dissemination of restricted or sensitive information.[30] Problems with theft and vandalism can be limited by placing equipment in secure areas or by making existing facilities more secure. Software or program piracy can be prevented by copyguarding important programs and by securely storing authorized originals and backup copies. Data can be protected by making alterations to on-line data files possible only with the correct password or by making backup copies of disks to preserve originals from intentional or accidental erasure. (However, duplicating software and data files creates more copies to be stolen.) Those managers who need the data files on a timely basis can each be issued a disk copy under tight reporting procedures and schedules. The Ethics in Management box entitled "Security Issues and the Computer" explores additional dimensions of the security of control systems.

TEACHING TIP

You might want to bring in an outside speaker to address this intriguing topic. Check with a local computer store, the head of your university computing system, or even a police officer.

Overcoming Implementation Problems

No single approach will overcome all the implementation problems we have identified. Each situation must be separately diagnosed and its own individual "cure" prescribed.

[29]Edwin B. Opliger, "Identifying Microcomputer Concerns," *EDP Journal,* no. 1 (1985):42–67.

[30]Paul E. Dascher and W. Ken Harmon, "The Dark Side of Small Business Computers," *Management Account 65,* no. 11 (May 1984):62–67.

TABLE 21-4 COMPUTER SECURITY CONCERNS

CONCERN	MAINFRAME COMPUTERS	MICROCOMPUTERS
Physical Security	Greater exposure per occurrence because of cost factors.	Possibility of more frequent occurrence because of the working environment.
Fire damage		
Water damage		
Deliberate destruction		
Wind damage		
Theft of computer	Not a concern due to size of the central processing unit (CPU).	Greater concern due to size and locations.
Theft of terminals, other peripherals	Size, location, general building security, and other factors are similar for both.	
Loss or destruction of storage media	Maximum exposure, but mitigated by hardware/software controls, better storage facilities, tighter security.	Maximum exposure due to physical characteristics of media (floppy disk) and physical location of computers, lack of secure storage areas.
Software Security		
Theft of licensed software	Some exposure, but less likely due to limited market for material.	Significant exposure due to open market for pirated material.
Programs Written In-house		
Accuracy of new programs	Considerable exposure, but mitigated by quality of data processing personnel and by testing requirements.	Greater exposure because: Users are not programmers. Testing and review are incomplete.
Program changes	Considerable exposure in either case, but there are generally tighter controls in large installations. Micro users are not subject to the same constraints.	
Program loss or destruction	Exposure mitigated by software controls and by backup/recovery procedures generally in place.	Greater exposure for some configurations: may not have adequate facilities for making backup copies.
Inability to continue processing due to lack of documentation	Minimal exposure; runs generally not dependent upon documentation. Also, mitigated by quality assurance reviews and turnover requirements.	Greater exposure (if the person running the job leaves, the job may have to be reprogrammed) due to user independence, lack of documentation requirements.
Data security (integrity)	Moderate exposure, but mitigated by run-to-run balancing capabilities, machine/software checks.	Greater exposure to loss due to ease of erasing files. If data are down-loaded from mainframe, some may not be received. Also, if similar data are down-loaded to various micros and processed independently, the data can lose integrity.
Release of privileged data	Considerable exposure, but mitigated by locking devices and/or password protection, personnel controls.	Greater exposure due to lack of separation of duties, user-controlled security.
Inappropriate Use of Corporate Assets		
Initial justification for installation	Minor exposure due to required review and approval procedures.	Greater exposure, cost not considered substantial.
Processing data not required by business (game playing, use of facilities for moonlighting, duplication of effort, and so on)	Some exposure, but mitigated by console logs, review capabilities, and monitoring by management. Chargeback systems also tend to reduce exposure.	Greater exposure due to lack of the controls listed under Mainframe heading.

Source: Adapted from Edwin B. Opliger, "Identifying Microcomputer Concerns," *EDP Journal* (1985):43–44.

However, some implementation problems can be mitigated if the MIS design process follows the guidelines we mentioned above. Dickson and Simmons have described a number of factors that they consider important in helping managers overcome implementation problems:

1. *User orientation.* Perhaps the most critical step in overcoming implementation problems is to ensure that the MIS is user-oriented in both design and implementation.

ETHICS IN MANAGEMENT

SECURITY ISSUES AND THE COMPUTER

To say that the financial community has become dependent on the computer is an understatement. With more than $500 billion transferred daily, most of it by electronic signals generated and collected by computers, it is little surprise that bank robbers no longer fit the stereotype of a Bonnie and Clyde. A terminal has replaced a gun, coaxial cable serves as a tunnel or ladder, and the combination to the safe is a just few simple passwords keyed into the computer system. Moreover, when the computer criminal is caught, banks are often hesitant to prosecute and publicly reveal how vulnerable they are, judges are reluctant to put white-collar criminals in jail with murderers and armed robbers, and lately bank management has begun to fear personal liability for letting the crime take place. Besides, we all know that the bank is insured and nobody really gets hurt!

As an instrument for mischief, the computer is a most seductive toy—part of a game to be played by those clever enough to master its subtleties and outwit their opponents. The film *War Games* provides a good illustration of how fun often crosses the boundary into something much more serious. Computers are used in all sorts of illegal and unethical capers. Teen-age "hackers" broke into medical records at the Sloane-Kettering Cancer Center in New York and "mucked around" with the data. Fortunately, no serious injury resulted for any of the patients, but invaluable medical research data were lost. Any company or organization that utilizes telecommunications and remote terminals is exposed to this kind of mischief.

It is worth the trouble to try to appreciate how seductive is this temptress, the computer. For starters, the sense of anonymity and secrecy in manipulating the computer—through terminals, personal computers, or other means—undermines the fear of getting caught—which, for many of us, is unfortunately the most powerful deterrent to misbehaving. Besides, the corporate victim of a computer crime is often thought of as being greedy, careless, and even deserving of its fate. The crime may begin as a small manipulation, often by a trusted employee, just "to see if it works." The company may even be inviting computer crime by providing limited safeguards, lax policies, and easy access to the computer. When the company fails to provide effective security, some people feel they deserve to be taken—"the unlocked door asks to be opened," as the saying goes. Also, both the public and the media often applaud the computer criminal's ingenuity in "cracking the system."

Perhaps the most publicly acceptable unethical behavior is the copying of proprietary (copyrighted) software. It is estimated that for every legal copy of software, there are between five and ten illegal copies floating around. Most of this copying has come about since the introduction of personal computers with soft-

If the system's output fails to meet the users' needs, users will stick firmly, and logically, to their own systems, thereby reducing the chances that the MIS will eventually become useful to them. MIS design staff should be rewarded for fulfilling user needs as well as for meeting project deadlines.[31]

2. *Participation*. Many implementation problems can be overcome (or avoided) if future users are made members of the MIS team. Operating managers in particular should have a major say in the items to be included, the disposition of information, and

[31]Michael Newman, "User Involvement—Does It Exist, Is It Enough?" *Journal of Systems Management* 35, no. 5 (1984):34–38.

ware that can be physically carried on a diskette from one machine to another. Software developers insist that a purchaser acquires only the right to use the software and does not have the right to make duplicate copies for sharing with others. However, enforcement of software ownership rights is very difficult, and in only a few cases have we seen software developers go after those who use bootleg copies of their products. Lotus Development Co., marketing its spreadsheet package *Lotus 1-2-3,* has been the most aggressive in rooting out illegal copies and calling offending organizations to task.

The laws relevant to computer use are still somewhat unclear and misunderstood. The Computer Fraud and Abuse Act of 1986 and the Electronic Communications Privacy Act of 1986 have added some teeth to the laws and provided the courts with some basic guidelines. For example, since 1968 it has been illegal to intercept telephone conversations without court authorization (wiretap), but until recently no laws prohibited the interception of electronic digital signals such as computers use to send messages to terminals and to each other. Because many organizations have computers at different sites that communicate directly with one another, potentially vital data are being transmitted constantly. Until 1986, a competitor could literally steal all of the business information being transmitted without fear of legal recourse. Today, with the new laws, such interception is no longer legally possible. However, federal legislation is generally limited to interstate activities, leaving states to deal with their internal problems as best they can. At the state level, we do not even have agreement on how to define computer crime, and only 35 states have any significant legislation enacted to make various computer activities criminal offenses. In addition, many of the statutes conflict in terms of definition and the severity of the penalties they impose, and others have legislation that was written to cover only one specific instance of computer crime.

The emergence of computer crime may be a reflection of the value system in our society, and we may not even care if the computer criminal is able to get away with his or her scheme so long as it does not hurt us. An activity that may help the company (saving money by illegal software copying) may be condoned by management even though they recognize that they may be in violation of the law. E. F. Hutton recently pleaded guilty to wire fraud after systematically causing bank overdrafts and having the interest-free use of the money. In an effort to manage its surplus cash carefully, Hutton used computers to create float in its accounts. Eventually, these tactics tarnished the company's reputation by pushing legality to the limit. The branch managers were simply taking full advantage of what was available to them—of what they thought the law and the banks would permit. In the end, they admitted that management was concerned only with results and that no one really thought about breaking the law or getting caught.

Source: Based on William P. Haas, "The Temptress Computer," *Olean State Business,* July 6, 1987.

possible job modifications. If the entire design and implementation process is taken over by technologists, serious line–staff conflicts may develop.[32]

3. *Communication*. The aims and characteristics of the system should be clearly defined and communicated to all members of the MIS team as well as to users. This task is particularly difficult because the character of an MIS evolves as it is being designed and implemented, and therefore the final nature of the MIS cannot be known

[32]Blake Ives and Margrethe H. Olson, "User Involvement and MIS Success: A Review of Research," *Management Science* 30, no. 5 (May 1984):586–603. Ives and Olson note the lack of research demonstrating the benefits of user participation, but they do suggest that participation is useful for unstructured situations and also for situations where user acceptance is important for MIS success.

with precision at the outset. But without a clear understanding of the system's basic objectives and characteristics, team members and users will have constant differences of opinion, and the installed MIS is unlikely to satisfy the needs of users.

4. *Redefinition of performance measurements.* A new MIS may modify a manager's job to the point where old methods of performance evaluation no longer apply. For this reason, an MIS that calls for new evaluation procedures and/or criteria must be accompanied by incentives to encourage both high performance and acceptance of the system. The new methods must also be clearly explained so that managers will know how their accomplishments will be measured and rewarded.

5. *New challenges.* The notion that a computer can do many of the things that a manager can do—and do them faster and perhaps more thoroughly—has a lot to do with the feelings of insecurity a computer-based MIS may arouse. One way to reduce this sense of insecurity is to publicize the challenges made possible by the computer system. A new MIS may liberate middle managers from many boring and routine tasks and may also give them the opportunity to use information provided by the system in more creative and productive ways.

END-USER COMPUTING

COORDINATED RESOURCE

See "Management's Newest Star: Meet the Chief Information Officer," *Business Week,* 10/13/86, pp. 160–172.

end-user computing The creative use of computers by those who are not experts in data processing.

For the past decade or more, organizations have experienced a pent-up demand for computing and information resources, coupled with long lead times for MIS systems development, testing, and installation.[33] At the same time, information technology has advanced to the point at which computer support permeates all of the functional units, and users are becoming more responsible and accountable for the information systems in their organizations.[34] With the development of problem-solving software that can be easily learned and used, **end-user computing**—the creative use of computers by employees who are not data-processing experts—is growing at the rate of 50–90 percent per year.[35]

The information center has evolved as a means for assisting end-users throughout the organization with educational and operational services related to acquiring and using computers. In many cases, information centers are becoming partners with traditional system-development staffs.[36] To remain vital and viable, an information-center staff must be capable of introducing new technology and tools to the organization, and they must be able to guide and support end-users who will learn to use and apply these tools.[37]

Decision-support systems and artificial-intelligence techniques are becoming more useful to managers. As with MIS, DSS and artificial intelligence offer managers the ability to receive filtered, condensed, and analyzed information that can enhance their job performance and, in the case of artificial intelligence, provide managers with an information system that can keep pace with their own knowledge and sophistication.

Decision-Support Systems

decision-support system (DSS) Computer system accessible to nonspecialists to assist in planning and decision making.

A **decision-support system (DSS)** is an interactive computer system that is easily accessible to, and operated by, noncomputer specialists to assist them in planning and

[33]John F. Rockart and Lauren S. Flannery, "The Management of End-User Computing," *Communications of the ACM* 26, no. 10 (October 1983):776–784.

[34]Thomas E. Gallo, *Strategic Information Management Planning* (Englewood Cliffs, N.J.: Prentice Hall, 1988), p. 18.

[35]Rockhart and Flannery, "The Management of End-User Computing."

[36]Ralph H. Sprague, Jr., and Barbara C. McNurlin, *Information Systems Management in Practice* (Englewood Cliffs, N.J.: Prentice Hall, 1986), pp. 311–333.

[37]John N. Oglesby, "How to Shop for Your Information Center," *Datamation* 33, no. 11 (June 1, 1987):70–76.

decision-making functions. While DSSs may differ in their emphases on data-access and modeling functions, there is an overriding emphasis in all such systems on user accessibility to data for decision making.[38] This decision-making applicability permits managers to simulate problems using formal mathematical models and to test the outcomes of various alternatives for reaching the best possible decisions.[39]

Differences between DSS and MIS. Since the DSS is an outgrowth of the MIS, there are basic similarities between them: They are both computer-based and designed to supply information to managers. However, there are some important advantages to a DSS. First of all, a DSS is geared to information *manipulation* and not essentially to data storage and retrieval, as are many MISs.[40] A DSS is operated directly by its users; when they need access to information, they can immediately consult their own on-line system without having to wait days or weeks for results from the MIS department. Once managers call up the required data through a DSS, they can manipulate it directly, asking questions and reformatting the data to meet their specific needs without having to explain what they want to EDP/MIS staff.[41] Managers can thus be certain that they will get the information they need when they need it. In addition, direct manipulation of data has the advantage of greater security for sensitive information.

Another key difference between an MIS and a DSS is that a DSS helps managers make nonroutine decisions in unstructured situations.[42] An MIS, on the other hand, emphasizes standard, periodical reports and cannot respond well to nonroutine, unstructured, or ad hoc situations.[43] MIS departments may be unfamiliar with the decisions made in such situations; because they often have a tremendous backlog of requests for data, they may be unable to respond quickly to additional special requests. Conversely, some managers who have no difficulty manipulating the data themselves may have difficulty explaining their information requirements to MIS staff.

The ability of DSS users to access data directly and perform some of their own data-management chores has reduced one kind of intraorganizational conflict. In the early stages of computer-based MIS development, conflicts and stresses between MIS users—managers and others—and EDP/MIS department personnel arose from a variety of issues. These included the dependence of users on DP experts; the differing personal styles, backgrounds, values, and objectives of users and experts; and the evolving nature of information systems as new technologies and concepts appeared almost overnight.[44] The introduction of DSSs and on-line access to data has led to a reduction in friction between individuals from various organizational subcultures and EDP/MIS staff, who often constitute a subculture of their own.

Using DSS. At Pet Foods in St. Louis, the sales-forecasting department performs a large percentage of its own data-processing tasks. Using readily available DSS applica-

---

[38]Steven Alter, in "A Taxonomy of Decision Support Systems," *Sloan Management Review* 19, no. 1 (Fall 1977):39–59, describes seven different types of DSS from systems that are heavily data-oriented to those that are heavily model-oriented. His taxonomy is based on the extent to which the system's outputs bear on decision making.

[39]Bernard C. Reinmann and Allan D. Waren, "User-Oriented Criteria for the Selection of DSS Software," *Communications of the ACM* 28, no. 2 (February 1985):166–179. See also Reinmann, "Decision Support Systems: Strategic Management Tools for the Eighties," *Business Horizons,* September–October, 1985, pp. 71–77.

[40]"Fourth-Generation Languages Make DSS Feasible for All Managers," *Management Review* 73, no. 4 (April 1984):4–5.

[41]Donald R. Wood, "The Personal Computer: How It Can Increase Management Productivity," *Financial Executive* 52, no. 2 (February 1984):15.

[42]Andrew T. Masland, "Integrators and Decision Support System Success in Higher Education," *Research in Higher Education* 20, no. 2 (1984):211–233.

[43]Hugh J. Watson and Marianne M. Hill, "Decision Support Systems or What Didn't Happen with MIS," *Interfaces* 13, no. 5 (October 1983):81–88.

[44]These initial conflicts and stresses are described in Chris Argyris, "Management Information Systems: The Challenge to Rationality and Emotionality," *Management Science* 17, no. 6 (February 1971):B275–292.

tions software, users can project sales demand by units per territory and region and translate that information into a financial forecast. Through this process, the department can determine the effects of closing a particular warehouse in a matter of days where the same task might take the MIS department weeks or months.[45] This is but one example of the successful application of DSS.

The ideal DSS solicits input data needed from the user and then prompts the user to consider all key-decision points.[46] Many software applications on the market can perform these functions. Among the more popular DSS applications software are spreadsheet packages such as *Lotus 1-2-3,* data-management packages such as *dBase III* and *Powerbase,* project-management software such as *Total Project Manager,* integrated software packages such as *Symphony, Framework,* and *Jazz* and assorted financial analysis and planning packages. DSS software can support such organizational functions as marketing, production, and finance as well as many other decision-making areas.[47]

EXTRA EXERCISE

Have students find out the characteristics of the following general types of computers: supercomputer, mainframe computer, minicomputer, microcomputer, or desktop computer.

DSS vs. EDP/MIS. The proliferation of microcomputers, off-the-shelf DSS software, and fourth-generation programming languages that boost programmer productivity has reduced the demand for MIS programmers, who generally specialize in the writing of programs for minicomputers and mainframes.[48] User-MIS department conflicts, which were reduced through the introduction of a DSS, may be replaced by the fears of EDP/MIS staff that their influence and control over information resources will be reduced. Companies still need the massive data-processing and storage capacities of mainframe computers, and mainframes require EDP MIS staff to operate and maintain them. Organizations are best served by an information system that integrates both DSS and MIS functions and activities.[49]

Another concern of EDP/MIS staff is that with every manager using his or her own DSS, there will be a proliferation of unauthorized and incompatible private files.[50] Some MIS staff may fear that data will become an individual resource rather than an organizational one—data becoming the proprietary concern of individuals who might hold it for "ransom"—or that confusion will be created as to which data files are correct. However, this possible problem is more than compensated for by the real advantages of a DSS, which are, on the whole, advantages to the organization as well. The extra cost and duplication of computing resources and the lack of control over data in DSSs are outweighed by the more effective decisions that they make possible.[51] Centralized control of data, the aim of an MIS, should be supplanted by decentralized controls for the sharing of accurate DSS data.[52]

Expert Systems and Artificial Intelligence

Even though DSSs are currently being widely adopted, expert systems (ESs) may well take their place in the near future as tools for improving organizational decision making and control.[53] Expert systems are also called "knowledge-based" systems since they

---

[45]Jennifer E. Beaver, "Bend or Be Broken," *Computer Decisions* 16, no. 6 (1984):43.

[46]Andrew P. Sage, Bernard Galing, and Adolpho Langomasi, "The Methodologies for Determination of Information Requirements for Decision Support Systems," *Large Scale Systems* 5, no. 2 (October 1983):158.

[47]"What's Happening with DSS?" *EDP Analyzer* 22, no. 7 (July 1984):1–16.

[48]Potter and McNeill, "The New Programmer—The Next Wave of Computer Innovation in North American Business," p. 132.

[49]See Harry Katzan, Jr., *Management Support Systems: A Pragmatic Approach* (New York: Van Nostrand Reinhold, 1984), pp. 2–3.

[50]Beaver, "Bend or Be Broken," p. 132.

[51]"What's Happening with DSS?" *EDP Analyzer,* pp. 1–16.

[52]Wood, "The Personal Computer: How It Can Increase Management Productivity," pp. 17–18.

[53]"What's Happening with DSS?" *EDP Analyzer.*

artificial intelligence (AI) Development of computational approaches to simulate intelligent human thought or behavior.

expert system Application of artificial intelligence denoting the technology entailed by the development of computational approaches to human functioning.

THOUGHT-PROVOKER

Will artificial intelligence or expert systems ever replace people? Why or why not?

are built on a framework of known facts and responses to situations. They may also be called **artificial intelligence (AI).**[54] Artificial intelligence refers to the use of the computer to simulate characteristics of human thought by developing computational approaches to intelligent behavior. Although the exact terminology for this new technology has not been totally agreed upon, we have used the term **expert systems** in our discussion to differentiate such systems from AI, of which they are more appropriately considered an application.[55] The other application of AI is natural-language processing.[56]

The potential importance to managers of artificial-intelligence research—the effort to make machines smarter—cannot be overstated. According to Patrick H. Winston and Karen A. Prendergast, "Some people believe artificial intelligence is the most exciting scientific and commercial enterprise of the century."[57] Sales of AI technology exceeded $700 million in 1985, an increase of 60 percent over 1984. Projected sales for 1990 are $3-12 billion and $50-120 billion by the year 2000. Hundreds of small companies, many bankrolled by industrial giants such as Lockheed, GM, and Control Data, are entering the field with specialized AI software and expert systems.[58] Expert systems are designed to apply the fruits of AI research to scientific, technological, and business problems by emulating the abilities and judgments of human experts and making the experts' point of view available to a nonexpert. Typically, a human expert has specialized knowledge that he or she uses to solve specific problems.

Expert systems perform similarly to human experts; they can diagnose problems, recommend alternative solutions and strategies, offer rationales for their diagnoses and recommendations, and in some instances learn from previous experiences by adding information developed in solving problems to their current base of knowledge.[59] The expert systems developed in the 1980s now function productively in diverse areas, such as medical diagnosis, mineral and oil exploration, and equipment-fault locating.[60]

An expert system guides users through problems by asking them an orderly set of questions about the situation and drawing conclusions based on the answers it has been given. Its problem-solving abilities are guided by a set of programmed rules modeled on the actual reasoning processes of human experts in the field.[61] They are particularly relevant for inferring and deducing from problems involving unstructured aspects and are more tolerant of errors and imperfect knowledge than are conventional programs.[62]

Because of their advanced capabilities, expert systems may supplant many kinds of DSSs. Users will no longer have to develop alternatives from information supplied

---

[54]The discussion of expert systems is drawn mainly from Robert W. Blanning, "Knowledge Acquisition and System Validation in Expert Systems for Management," *Human Systems Management* 4, no. 4 (Autumn 1984):280–285; Robert W. Blanning, "Expert Systems for Management: Possible Application Areas," *Institute for Advancement of Decision Support Systems DSS-84 Transactions* (1984):69–77; and Robert W. Blanning, "Issues in the Design for Expert Systems for Management," *Proceedings of the National Computer Conference* (1984):489–495.

[55]Walter Reitman, "Artificial Intelligence Applications for Business: Getting Acquainted," in Walter Reitman, ed., *Artificial Intelligence Applications for Business* (Norwood, N.J.: Ablex Publishing, 1984), pp. 1–9. For an excellent discussion of AI, see Jeffrey Rothfelder, *Minds Over Matter: A New Look at Artificial Intelligence* (New York: Simon & Schuster, 1985). See also Karl W. Wiig, "AI: Management's Newest Tool," *Management Review*, August 1986, pp. 24–28; and R. Kurzweil, "What Is Artificial Intelligence Anyway?" *American Scientist* 73 (1985):258–264.

[56]Shore, *Introduction to Computer Information Systems*, pp. 304–313.

[57]Patrick H. Winston and Karen A. Prendergast, eds., *The AI Business: The Commercial Uses of Artificial Intelligence* (Cambridge, Mass.: MIT Press, 1985), preface.

[58]See Emily T. Smith, "A High-Tech Market That's Not Feeling the Pinch," *Business Week*, July 1, 1985, p. 78.

[59]Michael W. Davis, "Anatomy of Decision Support," *Datamation*, June 15, 1985, pp. 201ff.

[60]Kenneth Fordyce, Peter Norden, and Gerald Sullivan, "Review of Expert Systems for the Management Science Practitioner," *Interfaces* 17, no. 2 (March–April 1987):64–77.

[61]Robert C. Schank with Peter G. Childers, *The Cognitive Computer: On Language, Learning, and Artificial Intelligence* (Reading, Mass.: Addision-Wesley, 1985), p. 33.

[62]Jay Liebowitz, *Introduction to Expert Systems* (Santa Cruz, Calif.: Mitchell Publishing, 1988), pp. 3–21.

INTERNATIONAL MANAGEMENT

INFORMATION-SYSTEM STRATEGIES

A few years ago when Toyota was a pioneer among Japanese companies with its expansion efforts in the United States, it had some lessons to learn about managing information American-style. Just what makes the American style of information management so different? First, American companies purchase packaged software rather than develop each application from scratch. The Japanese style is typically to search for a best solution and then to develop software to accomplish the processing necessary to meet the best solution requirements. Almost as important are the hardware and software standards maintained by American companies. By contrast, Japanese firms allow their work groups to acquire the hardware that they believe will be best for their processing needs with no thought to what other work groups are doing. Finally, American companies develop voice- and data-communications expertise within the organization rather than relying on outside support, as Japanese firms generally do. It is interesting to note that many Japanese companies with American operations are standardizing their equipment by purchasing U.S.-made hardware rather than by importing NEC, Fujitsu, and other Japanese-made equipment. This practice provides compatibility with much of the American business environment—a fact that would not be the case with imported hardware.

Business has been good and Toyota has been increasing investment in its U.S. operations, adding both manufacturing and distribution capabilities. Toyota has brought with it the Japanese management style, which is a management-by-consensus system, requiring a great deal of management participation in all decision making. This system calls for increasingly complex communications, especially between the American operations and the headquarters in Japan. Toyota solved this problem by implementing a private satellite-based network called Toyonet. The need for communications expertise within the organization now becomes very clear, as this communication network is critical to the success of Toyota's U.S. operations.

Hitachi is another Japanese firm that found out the hard way that the traditional Japanese management system does not work especially well in its U.S. operations. The company organization had been based on individual profit cen-

by a DSS, but instead will be readily able to evaluate the alternatives and explanations offered by expert systems. Expert systems can provide expertise when human experts are not available and in many cases reach conclusions more rapidly even when they are. Human experts may find expert systems useful when making decisions involving complex, interdependent elements.

Uses of Expert Systems. The implementation of the first expert systems occurred at the end of the 1970s. One of the first business applications of expert systems was developed by Schlumberger Ltd.; its system evaluates potential oil sites by using an amount of data far exceeding that which human experts could interpret in a timely fashion.[63]

A task is generally more suitable for an expert system when there is a large discrepancy between the best and worst performers of the task. Whether ESs are far enough along in development to bring most organizations strategic benefits remains

---

[63]Howard Austin, "Market Trends in Artificial Intelligence," in Reitman, ed., *Artificial Intelligence Applications for Business,* pp. 267–286.

ters, with each division having a high degree of autonomy. This setup meant that each division was free to acquire hardware and software that it thought would address its specific needs, without regard for what other divisions were doing. With 14 divisions in its U.S. operations, Hitachi ended up with several incompatible systems, including some of its own Hydac systems shipped in from Japan. The problem surfaced when the president of the company wanted to track certain large customers through several divisions of the company. Because of hardware and software incompatibilities, he was told that this was not possible.

Developing custom-computer programs presents an especially difficult problem for Japanese companies. Hiring American programmers to meet their needs has proven to be very expensive, and the shortage of technical personnel makes it almost impossible to find enough staff. The Americans whom they do hire often find it frustrating to work within the Japanese management style, which requires waiting for a consensus and exercising a great deal of patience while decisions are being made. With U.S. work visas in limited supply, Japanese software engineers and programmers cannot be relocated to America in sufficient numbers to meet system-development requirements, so Japanese companies are looking more to packaged software to satisfy their processing needs.

Although they are often slow to embrace American information systems or techniques, many Japanese firms have shown that they are willing to learn. Although still maintaining the long-term, pragmatic view, they are able to incorporate American standards and conventions into their information-systems operations. Their hope is that the lessons they learn will make them more competitive on both sides of the Pacific. With the Department of Commerce reporting Japanese investment in the U.S. to be $23.4 billion for 1986, in addition to an investment increase of 142 percent from 1984 to 1986, it is clear that large Japanese companies intend to make major commitments to their U.S. operations. A merging of Japanese and American information-system styles seems to be working for many of them. This would not be the first time that the Japanese have learned something from American business and then improved upon it.

Source: Based on Jeff Moad, "Japanese Pledge Allegiance to U.S. Information Systems Strategies," *Datamation,* February 15, 1988.

open to question. About half the *Fortune* 500 companies are developing ESs, yet few success stories have come to the attention of the business community.[64] Managers must be careful to avoid unrealistic expectations with this new technology, and must separate the reality from the hype of expert systems. Exhibit 21-3 summarizes four broad categories of management-information tasks to which expert systems are not being applied and will continue to be applied in the near future.

Some business-oriented expert-system software is already available. Odyssey is a scheduling system that permits users to resolve any conflicts in scheduling business trips. Nudge helps users schedule business meetings. And Omega performs personnel-assignment functions by matching job requirements to personnel characteristics.[65]

[64]Hugh J. Watson, Archie B. Carroll, and Robert I. Mann, *Information Systems for Management* (Plano, Texas: Business Publications, 1987), pp. 170–181.

[65]Blanning, "Knowledge Acquisition and System Validation in Expert Systems for Management," p. 282. See also Fred L. Luconi, Thomas W. Malone, and Michael S. Morton, "Expert Systems: The Next Challenge for Managers," *Sloan Managment Review,* Summer 1986, pp. 3–14; and Efraim Turban and Paul R. Watkins, "Integrating Expert Systems and Decision Support Systems," *MIS Quarterly* 10 (1986):121–138.

EXHIBIT 21-3 FOUR BROAD CATEGORIES OF MANAGEMENT-INFORMATION TASKS APPLYING EXPERT SYSTEMS

1. *Resource allocation.* Expert systems are used for such tasks as portfolio management and capital budgeting.
2. *Problem diagnosis.* Financial statements, accounts receivable reports, and other kinds of reports can be reviewed for possible problems, divergences, and inconsistencies.
3. *Scheduling and assignment.* Expert systems can, for example, be applied to office scheduling and personnel assignment tasks.
4. *Information management.* Information sources contained in data files and produced by decision modeling can be managed through expert systems. For example, an expert system might make recommendations on information fed to it on proposed financial or operating decisions such as closing a particular plant or developing a new product line.

Design and Implementation of Expert Systems. Robert W. Blanning has identified five characteristics of managerial decision making that may have implications in expert-system design, implementation, acceptance, and use:[66]

1. The majority of management problems are unstructured.
2. A manager's time and attention are limited resources.
3. Managers have different problem-solving styles.
4. Managers frequently work in groups on both formal and informal bases.
5. Many managers already have access to an array of computer-based tools.

Given these characteristics, it can be seen that imparting managerial knowledge to an expert system is no mean task; many problems are open-ended and unstructured, and managers solve them in very different ways. Also, because expert systems tolerate imperfect knowledge and use heuristics (rules of thumb) as the basis for problem solving, the user cannot be assured that the results are always accurate. Regardless of the application, expert systems consist of the three basic building blocks summarized in Exhibit 21-4.[67]

EXHIBIT 21-4 THE THREE BASIC BUILDING BLOCKS OF THE EXPERT SYSTEM

1. *Dialogue structure.* It is recognized that interactions between human and machine are critical factors in the success of expert systems. One study found that 4.4 percent of the ES code (instructions) was for the user input and output routines. Ease of use and good documentation are particularly important, as self-training is the dominant form of end-user training.*
2. *Inference engine.* This is the program that allows a hypothesis to be generated from the knowledge base to provide the strategies to draw inferences and produce solutions. The inference engine can work from facts to conclusions, when basic ideas are the starting point (data-driven reasoning), or it can use a hypothesis as the starting point, working from conclusions to facts (goal-driven reasoning).
3. *Knowledge base.* Knowledge of a particular application area (domain knowledge) which includes facts and rules of thumb based upon experience. The knowledge can be represented by if-then logical rules, mathematical formulas, and frames or scripts that are expressed in natural language.

*R. Ryan Nelson and Paul H. Cheney, "Training Today's User," *Datamation* 33, no. 10 (May 15, 1987):121–122.

Expert systems can be classified as problem-specific, shells, or custom-designed. *Problem-specific systems* are fully developed by a vendor to focus on a

[66]Blanning, "Issues in the Design of Expert Systems for Management," p. 493.
[67]Liebowitz, *Introduction to Expert Systems,* p. 95.

particular problem, and are sold for turn-key operation. A *shell* contains a generalized dialog structure and inference engine and acts as a tool for building expert systems for which a knowledge base can be developed. *Custom-expert systems* require development of all three components using AI languages (LISP, PROLOG) and are extremely time-consuming and expensive to develop.

natural-language processing Use of everyday language instead of special codes or instructions to communicate with a computer system.

Natural-Language Processing. Communicating with a computer has been a tedious and difficult task, requiring special codes and structure for instructions to be understood. **Natural-language processing** uses everyday language to communicate with the computer system and eliminates the need for technical training for the end-user. Current systems have limited vocabularies, but they are able to deal with many of the ambiguities inherent in the English language.

Another benefit with natural-language processing is that the end-user can eliminate the user of a keyboard. Voice-recognition systems are being marketed that utilize AI techniques to allow all communication with the computer to be routed through a microphone. The user has only to speak clearly and slowly for applications as wide ranging as word processing and circuit design. This leaves hands free to manipulate other equipment, such as a mouse, or provides communication capability for those that may not have the full use of their hands.

The Future of Expert Systems. American organizations are currently investing much effort and resources in the development of artificial intelligence for expert systems and other applications.[68] The Japanese are also devoting a great deal of energy to AI in their "fifth-generation" computer project: The expectation is that a qualitative advantage in computer technology will translate into a national economic advantage.[69] Along with limited computer hardware capabilities, a principal challenge for ES designers is the effective filtering out of knowledge-base biases that are imparted by the particular, unique views and values of the experts who are the sources of the knowledge that constitutes the knowledge base.[70] New expert systems will be developed rapidly as a result of these efforts, although these systems may be very expensive for some time to come.[71]

Managing End-User Computing

FOR DISCUSSION

What are some of the opportunities? What are some of the risks?

End-user computing presents opportunities for improved performance, but it also entails risks for the organization. A critical starting point for effective management is the development of a strategy for end-user computing. It is important to have a vision of how end-user computing will contribute to the competitive positioning of the firm. This view will lead to enhanced productivity of white-collar workers, and by having the user initiate and control his or her own processing requests, it may help to overcome the shortage of information-system professionals experienced by most organizations. If we were to investigate a purchasing department that has moved from transaction processing to end-user computing and followed a machine tool order through the system, we would find that using the computer to access vendor and price information is only the starting point. Instead of being just a processor of the purchase request, the purchasing agent can check the data base and determine if the organization has existing

---

[68]"What's Happening with DSS?" *EDP Analyzer*.

[69]Winston and Prendergast, eds., *The AI Business*. For discussions of Japanese and American efforts in AI, see also Edward A. Feigenbaum and Pamela McCorduck, *The Fifth Generation: Artificial Intelligence and Japan's Computer Challenge to the World* (New York: New American Library, 1984); and Frank Rose, *Into the Heart of the Mind: An American Quest for Artificial Intelligence* (New York: Harper & Row, 1984).

[70]Liebowitz, *Introduction to Expert Systems*, pp. 131–137.

[71]Beaver, "Bend or Be Broken," p. 138.

machine tools similar to the one being requested. If one or more is found, the data base can be interrogated to determine if excess capacity exists, and if so, the agent can recommend that the requestor use the installed equipment.[72]

The risks associated with end-user computing include increased exposure of both data and software, leading to threats of data security and integrity. In conjunction with this problem, we also find that the end-user often does not show adequate concern for data validation and quality assurance. In the MIS, the systems professional is responsible for the entire process and can control data collection and entry activities. End-users have also been accused of ineffective use of resources, a failure to properly document their software, and overanalysis.[73]

Software concerns include the responsibility for development and continued ownership of the software. Without some central control, there is sure to be duplication of effort throughout the organization. Once the end-user has a system operating, the responsibility for compatibility with other systems throughout the organization (for file sharing and networking) is often more than the end-user is willing to assume. Also, if the user leaves the organization, who has ownership of any systems he or she developed while an employee? Management must establish policies to address these issues. When purchased software is used, such as *Lotus 1-2-3* or *dBase III+*, software piracy becomes a concern. Making copies of software to share with others in the organization is illegal in most instances, and organizations can be held liable for their copying activities.

THE IMPACT OF COMPUTERS AND MIS ON MANAGERS AND ORGANIZATIONS

EXTRA EXERCISE

Have students interview managers for how they obtain and use information.

FOR DISCUSSION

How is information technology changing the education process at your school?

The application of computer technology to management information and decision-support systems has certainly had an effect on how managers perform their tasks and on how organizations behave. An early study of the impact of computerization suggested that there would be an increased structuring of middle management, increased status for some middle-management positions, more differences between top and middle management, and a recentralization of the organization.[74]

The chief effect of computerization has been the ability of organizations to process (and create) paperwork with ever greater accuracy and speed; there has been little effect on the roles of managers and the structure of organizations.[75] The segregation of middle managers into "functionary" and "programmer" roles has not taken place. In fact, Paul Attewell and James Rule cite evidence that computerization may lead to an increase in the number of management levels.[76] They have also found that access to information can strengthen the positions of subordinates.

The formation of an elite and aloof top level of management has also not come to pass. The amount of use that top managers make of computer-based information and computers themselves varies from organization to organization and is a matter of contention among management authors.[77] And top management is not necessarily in

---

[72]Sprague and McNurlin, *Information Systems Management in Practice,* p. 307.

[73]Rockart and Flannery, "The Management of End-User Computing."

[74]Harold J. Leavitt and Thomas L. Whisler, "Management in the 1980's," *Harvard Business Review* 36, no. 6 (November–December 1958):41–48. See also Jerome Kanter, *Management Information Systems* (Englewood Cliffs, N.J.: Prentice-Hall, 1984), pp. 289–316.

[75]Scott Morton and Rockart, "Implications of Changes in Information Technology for Corporate Strategy," pp. 84–95.

[76]Paul Attewell and James Rule, "Computing and Organizations: What We Know and What We Don't Know," *Communications of the ACM* 27, no. 12 (December 1984):1184–1192.

[77]For a lively debate on the use and impact of computers on top management, see John Dearden, "Will the Computer Change the Job of Top Management?" *Sloan Management Review* 25, no. 1 (Fall 1983):57–60; and David Davis, "Computers and Top Management," *Sloan Management Review* 25, no. 3 (Spring 1984):63–67.

control of the computerization of the organization. For example, individual departments can often purchase microcomputers and powerful DSS software directly without having a corporate EDP/MIS decision on its purchase.[78] In this way, middle managers are determining their information and systems needs for themselves and not having systems imposed on them from above. At the same time, information-systems departments in organizations are undergoing changes. Many organizations are considering combining office automation, data processing, and information-communication functions into one department.[79] What the effects of this change will be remains to be seen.

The results on the recentralization of organizations are not conclusive. In their review of the literature on the effects of computers, Attewell and Rule found that computer-based information systems either do not greatly affect organizational structure or, at most, reinforce existing structures.[80] On the one hand, they found that computerization increased ''top-down'' communication and top-level monitoring of operational activities—steps toward centralization. However, they also noted that the effective use of MIS data by middle managers may lead to decentralization. In cases where changes did occur, centralization occurred more often than decentralization. Other studies claim that intraorganizational networking and use of DSSs can lead to greater delegation and decentralization.[81]

---

[78]Erik Sandberg-Diment, ''Macintosh Marketing Overcomes Its Drawbacks,'' *The New York Times*, March 26, 1985, p. C4.

[79]Scott Morton and Rockart, ''Implications of Changes in Information Technology for Corporate Strategy,'' pp. 84–95.

[80]Attewell and Rule, ''Computing and Organizations,'' pp. 1188–1189.

[81]John Child, ''New Technology and Developments in Management Organization,'' *Omega* 12 no. 3 (1984):220.

FIGURE 21-2 WHAT PACKING MORE POWER ON A CHIP WILL BRING

	1980	1985	1987	1990	1995
Circuit Size:	4 Microns	2 Microns	1 Micron	0.5 Micron	0.25 Micron
Memory Capacity:	64K	256K	1,024K	4,096K	16,384K
Power Range:	Desktop Microcomputer	Minicomputer	Mainframe Computer	Supercomputer	Ultracomputer
Applications:	Digital watches, video games, personal computers	Lap computers, engineering work stations, programmable appliances	Pocket computers, electronic map-navigators, high-resolution TVs	Robot that can see, freeze-frame TVs, computers that recognize and use natural languages	Star Wars systems, personal robots, computers with humanlike logic

Source: Reprinted from the June 10, 1985 issue of *Business Week* by special permission. Copyright ©1985 by McGraw-Hill, Inc.

The Continuing Computer Revolution

COORDINATED RESOURCE

See *In The Age of the Smart Machine: The Future of Work and Power* by Shoshana Zuboff (Basic Books), 1988.

To say that we are rapidly moving from an industrial-based society to an information-based one is not an overstatement. For the foreseeable future, managers will have to keep abreast of, and anticipate, further advancements and applications from the continuing computer revolution. In addition, managers will need to evaluate new developments and determine their effects on their organizations.

The expansion of computer capabilities and further developments in artificial intelligence may prompt major adjustments in the way managers work and in the way organizations act. Figure 21-2 shows the projected increase in memory for microprocessor chips and illustrates a few of the applications that will be possible with the more powerful circuits becoming available. In the near future, it might not be unusual to see, for example, a manager carrying on a dialog with a pocket computer that can organize messages, schedule meetings, and offer business advice. Robots and robot-vision systems for manufacturing control will become normal parts of the production process. One day, we may truly create an information-based society whose members will have the leisure time to enjoy the fruits of its key industries: knowledge, communications, and computer-based consumer products.[82]

THOUGHT-PROVOKER

How will advanced information technologies change our society?

ILLUSTRATIVE CASE STUDY Wrap-Up

Using Technology at Sears for Strategic Advantage

Charles Carlson is reviewing the 1987 year-end financial statements for Sears. He is surprised that the estimated value of computer systems is listed at $270 million. Sears has come a long way since the 1960s, when a few centralized locations processed back-room operations. Carlson then attends a meeting at which he briefs management on his information-system plans for the coming year.

"Staff," he begins, "you can count on improved computer support for merchandise planning. With reduced margins on much of our merchandise, we plan to install a decision-support system that will recap your last year's store results and model future sales so you can decide where adjustments need to be made. Also, we will be providing additional information services by establishing another system that will monitor data from outside Sears and blend it with your current reports."

"Just a minute, Charlie," interjects one top management official. "In our last briefing, you told us to expect artificial intelligence applications to be developed by this year." Ken Fougere wanted to know what had happened to the application of this state-of-the-art technology he has been reading about in *The Wall Street Journal.* "Are we close to having a system that we can use to help eliminate the tedium of merchandise planning and buying?"

"Ken," replies Carlson, "we are still struggling with trying to capture the knowledge necessary to run an expert system successfully for the buying function. We have several buyers who always seem to make the right selections of merchandise, sizes, colors, and styles. Our problem has been to ask enough of the right questions to complete our knowledge base. The expert system shell is in pretty good shape, so once we have the knowledge base in place, we will be off and running. We have Wendy Weaver, our top analyst, working on the problem." When questioned about how long this process would take, Carlson was not able to give any dates. He was, however, able to assure management about prospects for the future as long as the implementation process was handled carefully and patiently: "I know you are all anxious for this system, but we want to be sure it will work properly before we make it available to our store managers. What you don't need is a computer-created disaster. Please be patient, we are doing the best we can." ■

---

[82]Marvin R. Gore and John W. Stubbe, *Computers and Information Systems,* 2nd ed. (New York: McGraw-Hill, 1984), pp. 386–387.

SUMMARY

Effective planning, decision making, and control are based on the effective management of information. All organizations have both an informal and a formal information system: Today, a formal information system is usually computer-based. There are three forms of computer-based information systems—management information systems. MIS decision-support systems (DSS), and expert systems. Over the years, MIS has been evolving into DSS and from there to expert systems.

An MIS may be defined as a formal method for providing managers with the information they need to carry out their tasks effectively. The value of information supplied by an MIS depends on the information's quality, quantity, timeliness, and relevance to management action. The cost of obtaining the information must be balanced against the information's benefits.

The information needs of managers differ with their hierarchical level. Top managers require information on strategic planning. Thus, their information sources will be largely external. Middle-level managers require information sources that will be both external and internal. In addition, they will require a more rapid information flow. Lower-level managers, who are concerned with operational control, will require frequent, highly detailed, and accurate information—predominantly from internal sources.

Guidelines for an effective MIS include: (1) making users part of the design team; (2) carefully considering the costs of the system; (3) favoring relevance and selectivity over sheer quantity; (4) pretesting the system before installation; and (5) training the operators and users of the system carefully.

There are a number of people problems that can arise when a computer-based MIS is being implemented. These problems are likely to develop if the MIS disrupts established departmental boundaries, if it disrupts the informal communication system, if individuals resist the system, if the organizational culture is not supportive, and if the change is implemented without manager-subordinate participation. The reactions of organization members to a computer-based MIS may include aggression, projection, and avoidance, depending on their organizational level and how the MIS will affect them.

A DSS is a direct user-access information system that permits managers to manipulate data and create models in order to assist them in making unstructured decisions. A DSS differs from an MIS because it involves the direct interaction of users with data.

Artificial intelligence refers to the use of the computer to simulate characteristics of human thought. Expert systems are a form of artificial intelligence that exhibit many features of human experts. These systems are distinctly user-oriented and, through prompting and questioning the user, can diagnose problems, recommend solutions, and offer explanations for their diagnoses. Expert systems are currently being applied to resource allocations, problem diagnosis, scheduling and personnel assignments, and information management. Natural-language processing uses everyday language to communicate with the computer, eliminating the need for the end-user to have extensive technical training.

The application of computer technology to management information and decision-support systems has allowed organizations to process paperwork with greater accuracy and speed; there has been little effect on the roles of managers and the structure of organizations. But AI applications show promise and may yet bring fundamental changes to managing.

REVIEW QUESTIONS

1. Why is an effective information system a key part of effective managerial planning, decision making, and control?
2. On what four factors does the value of information depend? How do managers weigh these factors against the cost of a management information system (MIS)?
3. How might MIS be defined?
4. What are the differences between data information and management information? Which is most desirable for managers? Why?
5. What are the differing information needs at different management levels? How may an MIS be designed to meet these different needs?

6. What are the four major stages in developing an MIS? How may these stages be carried out effectively?
7. According to Dickson and Simmons, what five factors determine whether and to what extent the implementation of a new MIS will be resisted?
8. What are the major security concerns associated with computer-based information systems? How may they be solved?
9. In what three ways may individuals show the frustrations associated with the implementation of a computer-based MIS?
10. What is a decision support system (DSS)? How does it differ from an MIS?
11. How can a DSS be used?
12. What is artificial intelligence? How is it applied in problem solving?
13. What is an expert system? How does it differ from an MIS and a DSS?
14. To what kinds of tasks can expert systems be applied?
15. What are the building blocks of an expert system?
16. What are the opportunities and risks associated with end-user computing.
17. How will future developments in computer technology have an impact on managers, organizations, and their use of information?

CASE STUDY The Human Edge in Software: Electronic Advisors

Gary Chapman ordinarily suffers fools patiently, if not gladly. But today, when a fellow employee at EEV, Inc., an electronic parts manufacturer in Elmsford, New York, pokes his head into Chapman's office, interrupting the sales manager's telephone conversation for the third time, Chapman says firmly, "I'm busy. I'm on the phone."

The tactic works. His colleague retreats—once and for all.

Chapman is both surprised and delighted by the outcome. To learn how best to handle his nettlesome co-worker, he sought advice from neither friend, how-to book, consultant, nor shrink. Instead he turned to *The Management Edge,* a software package from Human Edge Software Corporation in Palo Alto, California, a new company whose computer programs promise frazzled managers sound advice on handling subordinates, superiors, customers—indeed, anyone they might encounter during the business day.

Although using the computer to juggle people—rather than words or numbers—may have the ring of Orwellian fantasy, the concept is catching on among software developers. Resource 1, Inc., in San Diego, for example, is introducing computer programs based on the work of noted management experts and best-selling authors, such as Alec Mackenzie (*The Time Trap*) and Kenneth Blanchard and Robert Lorber (*Putting the One Minute Manager to Work,* their sequel to *The One Minute Manager*). The software, claims Mona Williams, a company spokeswoman, will help managers change their behavior while simultaneously teaching them computer skills.

Human Edge's business-strategy software is by far the most sophisticated attempt yet to tackle the vagaries of human behavior. Founded by psychologist Jim Johnson, who also started Psych Systems, Inc., developer and seller of the first online automated psychological testing service, the company has five products—*The Sales Edge, The Management Edge, The Negotiation Edge, The Communications Edge,* and *The Leadership Edge*—that are all expert, or knowledge-based, systems, a type of artificial intelligence.

Writing this kind of software requires collecting a number of "rules" that are culled either from experts or from the existing research on a subject. Using the rules, a computer can then figure out what the best course of action is in any given situation. To develop *The Sales Edge,* for example, Johnson and his staff went through stacks of sales-oriented business literature, gleaning, he says, "every piece of advice that any expert has ever offered." Then they structured the recommendations according to their appropriateness for individual personality types.

All the programs work similarly: First you agree or disagree with 70 to 100 statements, such as, "I often have trouble going to sleep because of worries about the job," "I like to attend parties related to my job," and "A good manager has total control." From your responses the computer develops a personality profile.

Then, whenever you need tips on dealing with a specific individual, you assess his or her character by checking off adjectives: "self-protecting," "simple-minded," "smart," or "prestige-oriented," for instance. (With *The Management Edge* you also describe the work environment; *The Negotiation Edge,* which used decision-making theory based on mathematical formulas, requires that you enter your expectations.)

With the profiles loaded, the computer will search through its huge store of information—the packages contain 300,000 to 400,000 words of text on two or three disks—and produce a report giving you specific pointers on how to act most effectively with the targeted individual. *The Sales Edge,* which walks you through preparation, presentation, and opening and closing ploys, tells you what to expect from your quarry and how to succeed. *The Management Edge* covers such areas as motivating employees, finding the right niche for a worker, firing, and improving communications.

When Gary Chapman plugged in *The Management Edge,* he was told that his co-worker, whose irritating habits he had chalked up to overenthusiasm, belongs to that troublesome class of individuals who don't recognize other people's responsibilities and obligations. And, the report admonished Chapman, "you too easily forgive those things." On the second or third occasion, point your view out to him, the report continued, then go about your business—advice which Chapman followed with good effect.

Chapman has also tried *The Management Edge* with customers and managers of the corporation's parent company in England. As a technical person, he says, he tends to be "very meticulous about numbers" and usually gets "right down to the details." But the computer informed him that several of his frequent business contacts become overwhelmed by too many specifics. So Chapman forced himself to concentrate on the larger picture by putting a big sign on his desk that read, "No details." "It was fantastic," he says. "People were more receptive to the things I wanted to do."

"I hope nobody else gets [*The Management Edge*]," Chapman adds, "because it's like a secret weapon, like being able to hear somebody's dreams. You can plan the whole strategy before you go see [anyone], and you know you're right."

Although some users consider the programs the next best thing to an ever-vigilant personal consultant, detractors argue that this type of software is, by its nature, limited. "It's a nice game, and it might be reasonably accurate," says Murray Weiner, a consultant with Rohrer, Hibler & Replogle, Inc., an international industrial psychology and management consulting firm. "But it can't possibly get into all of the conceivable interactions."

Even Johnson admits that strategy software isn't a total solution to life's tribulations. When Johnson wanted to fire an employee of his Palo Alto firm who had become a morale problem, he ran the outplacement section of *The Management Edge* on him. Proceed with caution, the report advised, this employee tends to be litigious. So Johnson hired a labor lawyer to ensure that the procedure was carried out in strict accordance with California law. "Sure enough," says Johnson, "he sued."

Source: Reprinted with permission. *Inc.* magazine, March 1984. Copyright © 1984 by Inc. Publishing Company, 38 Commercial Wharf, Boston, Mass. 02110.

Case Questions

1. How is Gary Chapman using *The Management Edge* to make decisions?
2. What are the limitations of the program? What are the advantages?
3. Do you agree with Murray Weiner that *The Management Edge* and other such programs are no more than "games"?
4. In your opinion, will most managers be using an information system like *The Management Edge* in the future? Explain. Would you be comfortable with such a system? Discuss why or why not.

CASE STUDY Using Decision-Support Systems at General Motors

General Motors, one of the largest corporations in the world, markets more than eight million vehicles each year with a value in excess of $80 billion. The Delco Electronics Division of GM produces electronic control modules, radios, speakers, heater controls, and a variety of small plastic parts and sensors that are used on all GM vehicles. The Delco plants in Milwaukee, Wisconsin, and Matamoros, Mexico, ship finished goods to the Kokomo, Indiana, facility for product consolidation before order filling and shipping by truck directly to about 30 GM assembly plants throughout the country. As a part of a campaign to reduce its product cost, Delco is focusing both on controlling and reducing inventory costs at the plants and at the warehouse in Kokomo and on reducing inventory costs due to material handling time and transit time.

Jim Schneider, manager of material control for Delco, was given the job of finding the means of reducing inventory costs. Jim began by analyzing the flow of materials and looking at ways of reducing the logistics costs associated with the product-shipping network. He knew that he might be able to reduce inventory costs by shipping directly from the Delco plants to each GM assembly facility, thus avoiding the costs associated with the Kokomo component-consolidation and warehousing functions. He also realized that this system would substantially increase the shipping costs for the components because he would ship less than full loads on an irregular schedule. Jim quickly decided that before he could make any shipping decisions, he would need to understand the trade-offs in the transportation and inventory costs. He began to recognize that his objective was more than just controlling inventory costs: It was to minimize the combined costs of inventory and transportation for all Delco products shipped to the GM assembly plants.

Jim sought the aid of GM management scientists to help him develop a model of the trade-off between transportation and inventory costs, with the transportation cost-decision variables identified as shipment size, shipment frequencies, and shipping routes. He found that shipping large loads infrequently over a specified route reduced transportation costs per item but also increased the inventory cost per item. As might be expected, he also found that shipping smaller loads more frequently reduced the inventory costs but resulted in increased transportation costs. In addition, the route selected for each load often impacted the total costs, because there could be additional handling and increased transport time.

Michael Frick, one of the management scientists assigned to the project, developed some mathematical equations to reflect the structure of freight charges, load mixes, truck capacities, and total system inventory. To simplify the model, freight costs were estimated based on distance traveled rather than following the tariff charts. A computer program was then written and tested. Once Michael had the model operating, he performed sensitivity analysis to see how the total cost changed with various shipping options. This allowed Jim to study the cost impact of demand fluctuations, and the team found that minimizing cost requires simultaneously determining optimal routes and shipment sizes. Because an enormous number of routing options exists, this level of analysis would not have been possible without computer support. Michael had the beginning of a decision-support system. The development team soon found the software could be run on a microcomputer and christened it TRANSPART. Pilot testing and the development of user-friendly interfaces polished TRANSPART so that it could be easily used by management.

Because the model focused on trade-offs and used graphics to illustrate solutions, various strategies could be easily evaluated. Jim could now answer questions regarding trade-offs between transportation and inventory costs, costs associated with alternative shipping strategies, and the sensitivity of total costs to changes in such key variables as fluctuations in interest rates (which would impact inventory carrying costs) and freight tariffs. Jim was now able to see at a glance that transportation and inventory costs must be managed together. Testing for sensitivity to changes in key parameters (such as warehouse material handling time and inventory-carrying costs) was no longer a burden because the computer did all of the formula computations and calculations.

After a number of runs, Jim was ready to present his findings to management. He was first able to show that by using optimal shipment sizes from the warehouse the firm could show immediate savings. By selecting alternative shipping strategies—that is, by shipping some components from the warehouse and some directly from the Delco plant to the GM assembly facility—it could reduce warehouse congestion and save even more on transportation and handling costs. Jim was given the go-ahead to implement the changes shown by the model to provide the optimum shipping strategies and in the first year has been able to reduce Delco product-shipping costs by more than $2 million. His decision-support system has been a resounding success!

A side benefit of developing TRANSPART is that Delco and GM now have a tool that can be applied throughout the organization, as all facets of the automobile manufacturing industry have inventory and shipping requirements. In the first year of use, Jeff Abbott reports that GM of Canada saved hundreds of thousands of dollars by using TRANSPART for freight carrier selections. Larry Lamon of the GM Truck and Bus Operations feels that it is hopeless to try to come up with an optimum strategy for transportation and inventory without the aid of a computer and found that TRANSPART handled the complex situation for him. Savings after using TRANSPART to analyze in-plant inventory for Pontiac Motor Division were over $35,000 for the first year. In addition to the immediate cost savings obtained with using TRANSPART, the system will help various divisions of GM to understand the implications of just-in-time manufacturing on freight and transportation costs. The Japanese have been using this technique for several years, and it is currently attracting a great deal of attention from American industry. TRANSPART will provide some hard data that will help management determine of the usefulness of this methodology for the various GM operations.

Source: Based on Dennis E. Blumenfeld et al., "Reducing Logistics Costs at General Motors," *Interfaces*, January–February 1987.

1. Why would shipping large loads infrequently over a specified route reduce transportation costs? Why would inventory costs be increased using the large load approach?
2. Why has General Motors waited until now to develop a decision support system to evaluate transportation and inventory costs?
3. What input data would be needed to operate the model for analyzing the transportation and inventory cost trade-offs to determine the minimum cost solution?
4. Why would TRANSPART be useful in assessing just-in-time management strategies?
5. What other manufacturing functions lend themselves to decision support systems such as the one developed by General Motors?
6. How useful is a decision support system such as TRANSPART in the decision-making activities of small business? Can these tools be used by a manager that has little or no computer experience? ■

CASE ON CONTROLLING

Osborne Computer: Trying for Rapid Growth Without Controls

Only rarely may a new firm hit the jackpot: a meteoric rise surpassing even the most optimistic expectations of founders and investors. In the heady excitement of great growth, anything seems possible. It is tantalizing to think that such an enterprise is invincible to competition. Alas, such stars can sometimes come tumbling back to earth. Perhaps no better example can be found in modern business annals than the almost vertical rise and collapse of Osborne Computer Corporation. Founded in 1981, the business was booming at a $100 million clip—in barely 18 months. But on September 14, 1983, the company sought protection from creditors under Chapter 11 of the Bankruptcy Code.

Adam Osborne was born in Thailand, the son of a British professor, and spent his earliest years in India. His parents were disciples of a maharishi, although he was educated in Catholic schools. He was later sent to Britain for schooling, and in 1961, at the age of 22, he moved to the United States. He obtained a Ph.D. in chemical engineering at the University of Delaware and then worked for Shell Development Company in California.

Osborne and Shell soon parted company, the bureaucratic structure frustrating him. He became interested in computers, and in 1970 he set up his own computer consulting company. The market for personal computers had begun to mushroom in the mid-1970s, and he emerged as a guru. He had a computer column, "From the Fountainhead," for *Interface Age,* and he began making speeches and building a reputation. He wrote a book, *Introduction to Microcomputers,* geared to the mass market. But it was turned down by a publisher. So Osborne published it himself, and it sold 300,000 copies. By 1975, his publishing company had put out some forty books on microcomputers, nearly a dozen of which he had written himself. In 1979, he sold his publishing company to McGraw-Hill but agreed to stay as a consultant through May 1982.

Osborne was thus in a position to take full advantage of the growth of the microcomputer industry. But he had also angered many in the industry by his stinging criticisms and bold assertions. In particular, he spoke out sharply against the pricing strategies of the personal computer manufacturers, contending that they were ignoring the mass market by constantly raising prices with every new feature added.

Osborne himself came to be the subject of some of the most colorful copy of the industry. Tall and energetic, he possessed a strong British accent to go along with his volubility, his charm, and his supreme confidence. He seemed to epitomize the new breed of entrepreneurs drawn to the epicenter of the new high-tech industry, the so-called Silicon Valley in California.

Early in 1981, Osborne put his criticisms and assertions to the test. To a chorus of skeptics he announced plans to manufacture and market a new personal computer, one priced well below the competition. His first machines were ready for shipping by that July, and before long the skeptics were running for the hills. Now Osborne could prove that he was a doer, and not merely a talker.

In the early 1970s, computers ranged from small units to the very large, with prices reaching limits only affordable by well-heeled firms. The industry was dominated by one company, IBM, which held 70 percent of the market. All the other firms in the industry were scrambling for small shares. IBM seemed to have an unassailable advantage, because it had the resources for the heaviest marketing expenditures in the industry as well as the best research and development. The firm with the masterful lead in a rapidly growing industry has ever-increasing resources over its lesser competitors, who can hardly hope to catch up and, it seems, must be content to chip away at the periphery of the total market.

The computer industry had been characterized by rapid technological changes since the early 1960s. By the early 1970s, however, the new technology being introduced generally involved peripheral accessories, and not further major changes in main units.

Before the advent of microelectronics technology, which makes smaller parts possible, computers were very costly and complicated. It was not economically feasible for one person to interact with one computer. The processing power at that time existed only in a central data processing installion, and, for those who could not afford to have their own computer, time-sharing services were available.

The minicomputer industry began in 1974, when a few small firms began using memory chips to produce do-it-yourself-kit computer systems for as little as $400. These proved to be popular, and other companies began to build microcomputers designed for the affluent hobbyist and small-business owner.

In 1975, microcomputer and small-business computer shipments went over the $1 billion mark. As the mainframe market began to mature, the microcomputer industry was starting its rocketing ascent. In 1975, the first personal computer reached the market.

Personal computers can be defined as easy-to-use desktop machines that are microprocessor based, have their own power supply, and are priced below $10,000. With various software packages, these computers can be customized to serve the needs of businesses and a variety of professionals such as accountants, financial analysts, scientists, and educators, as well as sophisticated individuals at home. It should be noted that the minicomputer had grown up without IBM, the company that had dominated mainframe computers and had accounted for two-thirds of all computer revenues in the mid-1970s. And one of the great success stories of the century had occurred with personal computers. Apple Computer had been started in a family garage on $1,300 in capital in 1976. By 1982, sales had reached $583 million, and Steven Jobs, a college dropout who was the co-founder at age 21, had become one of the richest people in America with a net worth exceeding $225 million.

Portable computers are a subset of personal computers, being, as the name implies, lightweight and relatively easy to carry. Actually, three categories of portable computers are recognized by the industry: (1) handheld; (2) portable, which have a small display screen, limited memory, and weigh between 10 and 20 pounds; and (3) transportable, which have bigger screens and memories, and weigh more than 20 pounds. Osborne Computer was in the third group.

Osborne had discerned a significant niche in the portable computer market: "I saw a truck-size hole in the industry, and I plugged it," he said. He hired Lee Felsenstein, a former Berkeley radical, to design a powerful unit that weighed only 24 pounds and could be placed in a briefcase small enough to fit under an airline seat. It was the first portable business computer (other portable computers were far less sophisticated). And it sold for $1,795, which was hundreds of dollars less than other business-oriented computers and half the price of an Apple. Osborne was able to sell for this price because he ran a low-overhead operation. For example, he hired Georgette Psaris, then 25, and made her vice president of sales and marketing. But her office was in a chilly former warehouse. He was able to achieve economies of scale and also capitalized on the declining prices of semiconductor parts. The computers were assembled from standard industry components. The display screen was small, only five inches across, and there was no color graphics capability. Osborne himself admitted, "The Osborne 1 had no technology of consequence. We made the purchasing decision convenient by bundling hardware and needed software in one price."

To cut costs on software, Osborne employed no programmers, a drastic departure from the practice of other personal computer makers. Instead, he relied entirely on independent software companies to provide programs written in the popular programming languages. To reduce software costs still further, Osborne gave some software suppliers equity in the company. The result was that Osborne was able to provide almost $1,500 worth of software packages as part of the $1,795 system price.

Osborne also had a flair for showmanship. One of his first triumphs was at the 1981 West Coast Computer Fair in San Francisco. In place of the rather ordinary booths and displays of the other computer makers, he spent a substantial part of his venture capital to build a plexiglas booth that towered toward the ceiling. The Osborne company logo, the "Flying O," dominated the show.

He believed that mass distribution was a key to success. By 1982, he had signed an agreement with Computerland, the largest computer retailer. This extended Osborne's distribution by doubling in one swoop the number of retail stores carrying his computer. The Osborne 1 was proving to be a hot item, with sales hitting $10 million by the end of 1981, the first year of operation, although the first computer had not even been shipped until July. By the end of 1982, after only 18 months of operation, annual sales were soaring to $100 million. Predictions were that "most of the Osborne management team would be millionaires by the time they're 40 or even 30." And the bare-bones operating style had been forsaken.

By 1983, some 750 retail outlets were stocking the company's portables: the Computerland chain, Xerox's retail stores, Sears's business centers, and department stores such as Macy's. And early in 1983, 150 office equipment dealers with experience in selling the most advanced copiers were also added, enabling Osborne to reach small- and medium-sized businesses.

In summary, Osborne was certainly not the originator of the portable computer, but he was the first to sell such computers in mass quantities. And he expanded the market greatly: Every key person in a data-processing department and every manager behind a desk became a sales target.

By early 1983, Osborne, under pressure from his investors, began to loosen his grip on the company. It was felt that the growing operation—it already had 800 employees—required professional managers, which Osborne and his early hirees were not. Osborne was an entrepreneur, not an administrator, and the two abilities were quite different. To protect the company's front-running position (estimated at an 80 to 90 percent market share), Robert Jaunich, II, president of Consolidated Foods, was hired to head up Osborne Computer as president and chief executive officer. Adam Osborne moved up to chairman. Jaunich had turned down offers from Apple and Atari because he felt that these firms would not give him enough control. He also sacrificed a $1 million incentive to remain at Consolidated Foods. So he must have felt strongly that the opportunities and the potential of Osborne far surpassed those of his other options.

Jaunich moved quickly to decentralize the management structure. Georgette Psaris, vice president of marketing, was moved into a newly created position as vice president of strategic planning. She was replaced by Joseph Roebuck, lured from Apple Computer, where he had been marketing director. Fred Brown, the director of sales for Osborne, was elevated to vice president of sales; and David Lorenzen, a consultant for Osborne, was made director of marketing services, with responsibility for dealer-support programs.

The distribution strategy which Adam Osborne believed to be one of the strengths of the venture was refined. The computer store outlets were continued, but some alternative channels were instituted. A major addition was an affiliation with Harris Corporation's computer systems division, which would act as a national distributor for contacting major firms. Harris was a $1.7 billion minicomputer firm that had in its computer systems division some 70 salespeople and 1,200 support personnel, including systems analysts. To protect Osborne's smaller clients, Harris agreed to handle only large orders of 50 units and over.

Brown, vice-president of sales, targeted United Press International (UPI), the news service, in order to sell Osborne portables as personal workstations to its 1,000-subscriber newspapers. He also began to explore other distribution possibilities, including independent sales organizations, airlines, and hotel chains.

As competitors started to enter the portable market and offer cheaper and fancier machines than the Osborne 1, the firm began readying itself to broaden its product line. An even cheaper version of the Osborne 1, the Vixen, was prepared. And an Executive 1 was unveiled in the spring of 1983, with an Executive 2 planned for late summer, these offering more storage capacity and larger screens than Osborne 1. The Executive 1 could serve as a terminal to communicate with a mainframe, enabling users to work with larger data bases and handle more complicated jobs. This was to have a $2,495 price tag with some $2,000 worth of software, including word processing, an electronic spreadsheet, and data base management. The Executive 2, at $3,195, was to be promoted as compatible with IBM's hot-selling personal computer, the IBM PC.

In 1982, Osborne spent $3.5 million on advertising. This included $1.5 million in consumer magazines, $500,000 on television spots, and $1.5 million in business publications. Plans were laid to continue heavy advertising to reinforce product differentiation. The sales force was also being expanded to keep pace with the growing firm. An eight-person sales force was to be expanded to 30 or 40, permitting more specialized selling. Instead of selling to all types of customers, sales specialists would concentrate either on retail or nonretail accounts. Brown explained this rationale: "Retailers . . . need help on such things as point-of-sale displays to stimulate the guy who comes in off the street. Dealers call on purchasing and data-processing departments and need advice on direct-mail campaigns.

The sky seemed to be the limit. Osborne was predicting revenues of $300 million for 1983. And, when he made one of his frequent trips abroad, he was received by ambassadors and prime ministers, most of whom wanted stock in his company. He was the head of the fastest-growing company Silicon Valley had ever seen—even faster than Apple.

The first premonition of trouble came to Adam Osborne on April 26, 1983. He was giving a seminar in Colorado, when he received a call. "Over the weekend considerable losses were discovered," he was told. "That's not possible," he is reported to have said.

The news that earlier profit figures had been in error was particularly ominous because of its timing. A public stock offering had been planned on April 29. This was designed to raise about $50 million, and would make the top executives of Osborne rich. How would news of losses instead of profits affect the stock offering? Adam Osborne had to wonder.

Actually, in the few days Adam had been away from the office, the bad news had been building up. In the first two months of the fourth fiscal quarter (the fiscal year ended in February 1983), pretax profits had been reported to be running $300,000 ahead of company projections; and in February, the company had racked up an all-time high in shipments—all these with supposedly very high profit margins. Projections had been that profits in February would be in the neighborhood of $750,000 for that month alone, and the future had seemed remarkably bright.

But the heady optimism was to disappear emphatically. By late March, the results for February showed, instead of the profit, a loss of more than $600,000, reflecting charges against new facilities as well as very heavy promotional spending. For the entire fiscal year, a loss of $1.5 million was incurred, despite revenues of slightly more than $100 million.

The worst was yet to come. On April 21, Jaunich, the CEO, had learned that later data showed that the company would have a $1.5 million loss for the February quarter and a $4 million loss for the full year. The chief reasons seemed to be excessive inventories of old stock that the company did not even realize it had, liabilities in software contracts, and the need for greater bad-debt and warranty reserves. Jaunich still planned to file for the stock offering, although the attractiveness of the company's stock was rapidly diminishing.

Unbelievably, worse was to come. On April 24, Jaunich was informed that the losses would be even greater: $5 million for the quarter and $8 million for the year, owing to further unrecorded liabilities and more inventory problems.

That same day, Jaunich decided to scrap the offering, despite heavy pressure to find another underwriter to bring the stock to market. Now every report blackened the situation further. The final report for the year showed a loss of more than $12 million. Heavy losses continued over the next months, as further adjustments in inventories and reserves became necessary. Adam Osborne's house of cards was on the verge of collapse.

Osborne had had no trouble attracting seed money from venture capitalists before—indeed, venture capital firms had been clamoring to participate. But now that the company's earnings problems had come to light, such funding was drying up. A few investors still had hopes, and Osborne found another $11 million in June. But an additional $20 million, which the company considered necessary to speed a needed competitive product from drawing board to market, could not be found.

Sporadic employee layoffs had been occurring since late spring as the company desperately tried to improve its cash flow. But the climax came on Friday, September 16. On the previous Tuesday, the company had filed for protection from creditor lawsuits under Chapter 11 of the Federal Bankruptcy Code. The company filed its petition after three creditors had filed two lawsuits saying Osborne owed them a total of $4.7 million. Osborne's petition stated that it owed secured and unsecured creditors about $45 million, while its assets were $40 million.

Osborne's employees had to expect the worst when a meeting was abruptly called in the company cafeteria. They soberly listened as top management announced that more than 300, about 80 percent of the company staff still remaining, were to be immediately "furloughed." Final paychecks were issued, and the workers were given two hours to empty their desks and vacate the company offices.

News of the company's Chapter 11 filing and near-total shutdown shocked the industry, although Osborne's recently sagging sales and the consequent need for cash were well known. The company had made strenuous efforts to raise money, especially after July shipments had turned soft, and the banks were pressing it to improve its shrinking capital base. But venture capitalists were fleeing the industry as a serious shakeout got underway not only for Osborne, but for other personal computer firms as well. The market was just not able to support some 150 microcomputer companies.

Adam Osborne was an entrepreneur, not a professional manager. Perhaps this accounted for most of the problems that befell his company. The entrepreneur is often incompatible with the manager, who must necessarily be engrossed with the nitty-gritty of details and day-to-day controls over operations. Osborne had never managed more than 50 people, but the organization had grown 20 times larger. He had operated according to a "fire-fighting" perspective: He never planned in advance and dealt with problems as they arose. "I had no professional training whatsoever in finance or business management," Osborne admitted.

Osborne's board of directors and the venture capitalists who had contributed mightily to the fledgling enterprise exerted sufficient pressure to persuade Adam Osborne to step aside and turn over operating responsibilities to a professional manager, Robert Jaunich, early in 1983. But this was apparently too late to rectify the damage that had already been done. It is tempting to speculate on what might have happened if such measures had been taken six months earlier.

Some of the mistakes are inexcusable from the standpoint of any prudently run operation. But perhaps they can be explained as a result of the heady excitement that can accompany geometrically rising sales and the euphoria that clouds rational judgments and expectations. Other mistakes can be credited as much to simple miscalculations—of which any firm could be guilty—as to the impact of competitors of all kinds, and particularly the rapidity with which the awesome IBM entered the market and dominated it.

Lack of controls was the most obvious failing of the company. It had no efficient means of monitoring inventories of finished products. Consequently, managers did not know how much inventory they had. They did not know how much they were spending or needed to spend. Information management was sorely lacking—and this in a company whose product was primarily geared to aiding information management. Although rapid growth can be accompanied by growing pains and difficulty in keeping abreast of booming operations, in Osborne's case the lack was abysmal and accounted for supposed profits suddenly being revealed as devastating losses. Other examples of incompetence were: unrecorded liabilities, with some bills never handed over to the accounting department; no reserves established for the shutdown of a New Jersey plant that was producing computers with a 40 percent failure rate; insufficient funds set aside to pay for a new European headquarters on Lake Geneva in Switzerland.

Lack of controls permitted expenses to run rampant. "Everybody was trying to buy anything they wanted," said one former Osborne employee. When Jaunich finally took over the managerial reins, he clamped down hard on expenses, but it was too late.

By spring of 1983, miscalculations had reduced cash flow to a trickle. Osborne had planned to introduce a new computer, the Executive, but he made the grievous mistake of announcing it too soon. Although the Executive was not supposed to compete against the original Osborne 1, many dealers saw it as doing just that. Upon learning of the new machine in April, many canceled their orders for the Osborne 1. This in itself necessitated heavy inventory write-offs, as the Osborne was not planned to be phased out. Compounding the problems, the Executive was delayed and not ready for initial shipments until May. Consequently, April was a month with practically no sales.

Another major mistake was failing to realize just how quickly competitors could react and counter a successful strategy in this volatile industry, how quickly a competitive advantage—the low price, portability, and bundling of software—could be matched by competitors and even improved upon.

Other companies, notably Kaypro and Compaq, entered the market with low-priced computers and at least as much bundled software. But the biggest impact was that of IBM. Its personal computer was introduced in late 1981, and it quickly became the industry standard against which other competitors were judged. And Osborne turned out to be slow in adopting IBM's state-of-the-art technology. Furthermore, Osborne was slow to come up with a model that was compatible with the IBM personal computer at home or in the office. Scores of other computer companies jumped to produce IBM-compatible computers while Osborne lagged. Suddenly, its product was not selling; hardly a year after coming to market, the formerly popular Osborne computer with its tiny screen was practically obsolete.

One new product developed by Osborne was in fact obsolete even before it was introduced. The Vixen was originally scheduled to be introduced in December 1982. It was a cheaper version of the Osborne 1 and ten pounds lighter. But a poorly designed circuitboard caused production delays, and the project was finally scrapped as company resources were at last redirected to the Executive model, an IBM-compatible unit with a larger screen. But the Osborne production delays and the speed with which IBM took over the personal computer market were tough to cope with.

The environment for personal computer makers was rapidly becoming unhealthy by 1983. A major shakeout for the more than 150 small manufacturers in this industry had been inevitable. A major reason for the proliferation of firms had been a tidal wave of venture capital. Early winners like Apple Computer had dazzled investors and led to the perception of a "can't lose" industry. It became almost too easy to start a new computer company. "As a result, a whole series of 'me-too' companies have been started. They are developing products that do not have a unique feature or competitive advantage. They don't stand a chance," one venture capitalist said. Only the strongest firms were likely to survive. And yet, because of its size and its head start, Osborne should have been one of the survivors.

As demand by businesses and consumers alike for small computers was rapidly increasing, so was cutthroat competition. Price cutting and shrinking profit margins were inevitable. And certainly, dealers' shelves could hardly accommodate more than a few brands.

The first presentiment of worsening problems for the industry came early in 1983, when three big manufacturers of low-priced home computers, Atari, Texas Instruments, and Mattel, reported first-half losses totaling more than half a billion dollars. Makers of higher-priced computers tried to dissociate themselves from this low-end calamitous environment. But other well-known companies such as Victor Technologies, Fortune Systems, and Vector Graphics all reported shocking losses for the second quarter. Even Apple Computer saw its stock price sink nearly 34 points between June and September of 1983.

Indicative of the price cutting going on, Texas Instruments' (TI) 99/4A home computer, which sold for $525 when introduced in 1981, was retailing for $100 by early 1983. Yet each 99/4A cost about $80 in parts and labor, to which TI's overhead expenses, dealer profits, and marketing costs had to be added.

Other computer makers were struggling desperately to revamp their production and marketing efforts. For example, Vector Graphic, after losing $1.7 million in the second quarter of 1983, obtained a new $7 million line of credit to help it tailor its computers to specialty markets such as accounting systems for farmers.

Now the problems of the industry had dried up venture capital. Osborne was partly the victim of an external situation over which it had no control. The external factors were unforgiving of its internal mistakes.

Source: Adapted from Robert F. Hartley, *Management Mistakes*, 2nd ed. (John Wiley & Sons, 1986), pp. 215–28.

Case Questions

1. What factors accounted for the surge of competition in the portable computer field? Should these have been anticipated by a prudent executive?
2. In what ways does this case reveal the importance of the linkage between planning and control?
3. What kind of controls would you have advised Osborne to set up to prevent its debacle?
4. Did Osborne Computer have any unique strengths that could have enabled it to survive in this hotly competitive industry?
5. If you had been called in as a consultant to Osborne Computer in March of 1983, what advice would you have given Jaunich? ■

Ad for Peerless Motor Car Co. from LIFE, October 21, 1909. (Hank Ehlbeck). Courtesy Jones, Brakeley & Rockwell, Inc.

22

ENTREPRENEURSHIP

Upon completing this chapter you should be able to:

1. Define the specific function of entrepreneurs in the productive process.
2. Explain the economic and noneconomic roots of entrepreneurship.
3. Understand the importance of entrepreneurship to economic growth, productivity, and economic change.
4. Sketch the psychological and sociological factors behind entrepreneurship.
5. Outline the entrepreneurial process.
6. Show how entrepreneurs go about choosing a line of business and a specific type of business organization.
7. Outline three strategies for entrepreneurs.
8. Describe the relationship between large organizations and entrepreneurial ventures.
9. Explain the policies and practices that older, more established companies must adopt to encourage entrepreneurship.
10. Distinguish between ''entrepreneurial'' and ''administrative'' corporate cultures.
11. Indicate the barriers to and problems for entrepreneurship.
12. Discuss the ''dark side of entrepreneurship.''

Chapter Outline

Introduction
The Meaning of Entrepreneurship
The Importance of Entrepreneurship
The Entrepreneur
The Entrepreneurial Process
Entrepreneurial Organizations
Barriers and Problems

ILLUSTRATIVE CASE STUDY Introduction

Start-Up Pains at Nova Pharmaceutical Corporation

It takes courage and conviction to break into the pharmaceutical industry, which is dominated by such giants as Eli Lilly, Merck, and Pfizer. Brand-name recognition and huge capital requirements pose significant barriers for a start-up entrepreneur wanting to join the big league. Moreover, the research-intensive nature of the business necessitates a large, steady infusion of capital, while the returns from these investments—which depend on the success of the firm's products—remain highly uncertain.

On the other hand, rewards from a successful product can be very attractive, catapulting a small, struggling start-up into multimillion-dollar fame and fortune. This prospect was a sufficiently strong incentive for Donald J. Stark, a one-time high school principal who left his lucrative job as president of Sterling Drug's Pharmaceutical Group to become CEO of Nova. Stark had observed one key fact about this industry—namely, that because of regulatory constraints and the tendency of major firms to emphasize growth over research, there was a dearth of new products in the drug industry.

Nova was founded in 1982 around the talents of three men. David Blech had been a stockbroker, his brother Isaac a public relations executive. As they watched some biotechnology companies do well, they decided to quit their jobs and play the start-up game. In search of a scientific star to complete their team, the Blechs found Dr. Solomon Snyder, a biochemistry pioneer in research into how the human body senses pain. The trio hit it off well; the Blech brothers provided the management expertise needed with investors, government, and other key external stakeholders, while Snyder provided the medical expertise.

All of the senior managers, such as Donald Stark, were recruited from major drug companies. Each understood the risks of competing with the giants of the industry, but each believed that Nova had a competitive advantage that would help it succeed.

The substantial commitments in time and money to work in the laboratory were difficult barriers for Nova, which based its research on a complex theory of receptor-cell behavior in the pain-response system of the human body. The key principle holds that critical processes taking place in the body—from the initial perception of pain to the production of antibodies that fight disease—are orchestrated by chemical messengers that match corresponding receptors on nerve cells; drugs often work because they can turn these receptors on or, alternatively, block their action. Nova assumed that the breakthroughs in receptor pharmacology would increase its ability to tailor drugs to specific receptor sites and that such breakthroughs would ultimately determine the pace of evolution of new-drug development.

However, scientific breakthroughs cannot be ordered like room service. By 1986, Nova was nurturing 15 research projects but had no guarantees that any would grow into the success needed to start a family of recognizable products. In addition, there are dangers at every step in the process. Each stage of testing along the way to commercialization is closely monitored by a very cautious Food and Drug Administration, which must approve any final product. The slightest complication or side effect can ruin a product's chances of success without its ever meeting its first commercial test.

Sources: William H. Miller, "Can Don Stark Mix Up a Winner?" *Industry Week,* September 30, 1985, pp. 76–77; "Dreams of Future Profits," *Financial World,* September 4–17, 1985, pp. 51–52; Emily T. Smith, "This Company Could Lead a Revolution in Drugs," *Business Week,* March 24, 1986, p. 100; "Celanese and Nova Form Joint Venture," *C&EN,* July 7, 1986, p. 8; Gene G. Marcial, "Pain Relief May Make Nova Feel Good Again," *Business Week,* June 1, 1987, p. 114.

The functions of most of the people who participate in the process of producing goods and services are fairly self-evident. Inventors get the idea for new products or services. Capitalists provide the funds needed to produce them. Specialized workers provide whatever services are needed to turn an idea into a product or service for sale to the public. Managers direct the workers from day to day. You might think we have already listed every role in the productive process. We have not. One role is left over: that of the entrepreneur. It is the hardest to understand, as well as one of the most controversial.

Some inventors have a natural talent for business, but many more of them have been people who liked to make and discover things but did not know what to do when they succeeded. Capitalists may also be business executives, but their specific function is to provide the financial resources for an enterprise, and many are content to do only that. And some specialized employees sometimes do go into business—but only by ceasing to be specialized employees. Managers obviously are in business, but a manager who takes over an existing operation is usually very different from a manager who starts one up. Steven Jobs, for example, is a genius at computers and applied his knowledge to the founding of Apple Computers. After the company began realizing its tremendous growth potential, Jobs brought in a professional manager, John Scully, to oversee the company's growth in a more structured manner. Many start-up firms find themselves with problems if the founding entrepreneur lacks the combination of skills necessary to be both "idea person" and manager (or fails to perceive the vital distinction between the two). The landscape of entrepreneurism, from food-service to biotechnology firms, is littered with the remains of companies whose founders could not function as managers or failed to enlist the services of managers when they became needed.

THE MEANING OF ENTREPRENEURSHIP

entrepreneur Either the originator of a new business venture or a manager who tries to improve an organizational unit by initiating productive changes.

COORDINATED RESOURCE

Two videotapes from the Enterprise series that illustrate the pleasures and problems of entrepreneurship are "Chef's Special" (about the start-up of a new restaurant) and "Cash on The Vine" (about the start-up of a new California winery). Available from LCA, 108 Wilmont Road, Deerfield, Il 60015-9990, or call 1-800-621-2131.

The function that is specific to **entrepreneurs** is the ability to take the factors of production—land, labor, and capital—and use them to produce new goods or services. The entrepreneur perceives opportunities that other business executives do not see or do not care about.

Some entrepreneurs use information that is generally available to produce something new. Henry Ford, for example, invented neither the automobile nor the division of labor, but he applied the division of labor to the production of automobiles in a new way: the assembly line. Other entrepreneurs see new business opportunities. For example, Akio Morita, the president of Sony, the Japanese consumer electronics giant, saw that his company's existing products could be adapted to create a new one: the Walkman personal stereo. "Basically, the entrepreneur sees a need and then brings together the manpower, materials, and capital required to meet that need."[1]

[1] Jules Backman, ed., *Entrepreneurship and the Outlook for America* (New York: Free Press, 1983), p. 3.

Entrepreneurial Roles

entrepreneurship As opposed to management, the seemingly discontinuous process of combining resources to produce changes in production.

Entrepreneurship is different from management. As Paul H. Wilken notes,

> Entrepreneurship . . . involves combining *to initiate changes* in production where [management] involves combining *to produce*. Management therefore refers to the *ongoing coordination* of the production process, which can be visualized as a continual combining of the factors of production. But entrepreneurship is a discontinuous phenomenon, appearing to initiate changes in the production process . . . and then disappearing until it reappears to initiate another change.[2]

As this definition suggests, even undoubted entrepreneurs do not always function in the entrepreneurial role. Entrepreneurs often play other roles, especially those of capitalist and manager, while people who primarily act as capitalists or managers may at times become entrepreneurs. Many people who want above all to be entrepreneurs find that they must eventually leave the new ventures they create because they do not have the proper state of mind to run an established business. Others, like Steven Jobs, leave to continue new entrepreneurial pursuits. Jobs left Apple in 1985 and, with a few friends and $20 million in capital from Texas businessman H. Ross Perot, started a new company called Next Inc., where he plans to produce a ''fourth-wave microcomputer'' that he promises to be 10 times more powerful than the most popular IBM and Apple personal computers.[3]

CLASS COMMENT

Entrepreneurs tend to be company starters rather than company builders.

Entrepreneurship is above all about change. (In Exhibit 22-1, Wilken categorizes five key types of changes initiated by entrepreneurs.) ''Entrepreneurs see change as the norm and as healthy. Usually, they do not bring about the change themselves [that is, they are usually not inventors]. But—and this defines entrepreneur and entrepreneurship—*the entrepreneur always searches for change, responds to it, and exploits it as an opportunity*.''[4]

EXHIBIT 22-1 TYPES OF CHANGES INITIATED BY ENTREPRENEURS

1. Initial expansion—original production of goods
2. Subsequent expansion—subsequent change in the amount of goods produced
3. Factor innovation—increase in supply or productivity of factors
   a. Financial—procurement of capital from new source or in new form
   b. Labor—procurement of labor from new source or of new type; upgrading of existing labor
   c. Material—procurement of old material from new source or use of a new material
4. Production innovations—changes in the production process
   a. Technological—use of new production technique
   b. Organizational—change of form of structure of relationships among people
5. Market innovations—changes in the size or composition of the market
   a. Product—production of new good or change in quality or cost of existing good
   b. Market—discovery of a new market

Source: Paul H. Wilken, *Entrepreneurship: A Comparative and Historical Study* (Norwood, N.J.: Ablex Publishing Corporation, 1979).

FOR DISCUSSION

What does it mean to be an entrepreneur?

These words were written by Peter Drucker, a well-known contemporary management writer, but they might just as easily have come from the pen of Joseph Schumpeter (1883–1950), the Austrian economist who assigned the term ''entrepre-

[2]Paul H. Wilken, *Entrepreneurship: A Comparative and Historical Study* (Norwood, N.J.: Ablex Publishing, 1979), p. 60.

[3]Steve Jobs Tries to Do It Again,'' *Fortune,* May 23, 1988, pp. 83–86.

[4]Peter F. Drucker, *Innovation and Entrepreneurship* (New York: Harper & Row, 1986), pp. 27–28.

neurship." For Schumpeter, indeed, the whole process of economic change hung ultimately on the person who makes it happen—the entrepreneur.[5]

Factors Affecting Entrepreneurship

Some societies—notably in the United States, South Korea, and many Southeast Asian countries like Thailand, Indonesia, Malaysia, and Singapore—abound with entrepreneurs. Others, like the Soviet Union and mainland China, have far fewer entrepreneurs, although those countries recently changed their laws to encourage entrepreneurship. Countries like England, where many companies such as airlines and automobile manufacturers have been operated by the government, have in recent years begun to turn these firms over to private industry, encouraging entrepreneurship through new opportunities in private ownership. Other nations, such as Japan, that have been bound by strong traditions of business-government cooperation have not characteristically encouraged entrepreneurial ventures (although there is evidence of increasing sentiment in favor of entrepreneurship in Japan itself). Both economic and noneconomic conditions can affect the level of entrepreneurship within any society.

Economic Factors. Since entrepreneurship is essentially the promotion of economic change, "the same factors that promote economic growth and development account for the emergence of entrepreneurship."[6] There are two kinds of economic factors. The first consists of market incentives: new social needs the entrepreneur can attempt to satisfy in new ways. The other economic factor is, first, the existence of a sufficient stock of capital to fund new enterprises and, second, institutions (like banks) that direct capital to people who wish to use it for entrepreneurial projects. To some extent, old wealth is a precondition for new wealth. At any rate, societies that have lacked economic vitality are likely to have neither the market opportunities nor the capital to fund entrepreneurs. Some nations that lack their own capital—like Mexico—invite partnerships with foreign firms as a measure for increasing the flow of capital into their economies.

HERE'S AN EXAMPLE
The Small Business Climate Index compiled by American Express Company has declined for a full year. It appears that business conditions for smaller companies are deteriorating. (*Business Week*, 8/8/88, p. 73)

Noneconomic Factors. The Soviet Union is a poorer society than the United States is today but more wealthy than the United States was in the nineteenth century. Nonetheless, the Soviet Union has few entrepreneurs, while the United States, both now and then, has had many of them. The reason lies in the cultural and social differences between the two countries.

Above all, the reason is that in the United States, entrepreneurs and entrepreneurial behavior enjoy a legitimacy they do not have in the Soviet Union. Upon coming to power in the mid-1980s, Mikhail Gorbachev sought to change Soviet law to legalize and even encourage entrepreneurship, particularly by worker-owned cooperatives. Yet in early 1988, Gorbachev himself attacked co-ops that "take advantage of shortages" to raise their prices.[7] But a shortage, of course, is one of the things that most entrepreneurs imbued with the values of a capitalist society would regard as a market opportunity. It is easier to change the law than to change norms and values. In the United States, whole political and economic ideologies have been built around the values central to entrepreneurship. Moreover, our legal structure, which is based on the values of free enterprise, protects the rights of individuals much more than does its Soviet counterpart, which is based on a socialist economic-legal structure.

---

[5]Wilken, *Entrepreneurship*, p. 57.
[6]Ibid., p. 7.
[7]Daniel Ford, "Rebirth of a Nation," *The New Yorker*, March 28, 1988, p. 78.

Another factor that affects entrepreneurship is social mobility. In India, for example, most people are born into castes, social divisions that perform specific economic functions, such as fishing or farming. Although the caste structure is by no means so rigid as it used to be, it is still fairly strict, especially in rural areas. As a result, it is harder for a child of an Indian carpenter, let's say, to become an entrepreneur in some other field than it would be for a carpenter's child in the United States. Yet Indians who live in the United States are even more prone to engage in entrepreneurial activity than other Americans are. The reason is that caste boundaries are much weaker for Indians who live here than for Indians who stayed at home, where entrepreneurship is discouraged by heavy corporate and personal income taxes as well as personal-wealth and excise taxes. Currently, however, the Indian government is pursuing reforms that would permit more economic flexibility, this encouraging not only entrepreneurial ventures but both increased domestic and foreign investment.[8]

Moreover, the Indians who live in the United States, like many entrepreneurs throughout the world, are "marginal." That is, they do not belong to any of the groups that make up the historical core of our population: white Protestants of British and European descent. Because the Indians are marginal, they can see certain opportunities more clearly than members of the core groups, who are likely to take the facts of our society more for granted.

THE IMPORTANCE OF ENTREPRENEURSHIP

HERE'S AN EXAMPLE
Business schools are having a tough time finding professors to teach courses in entrepreneurship. The number of qualified professors is short, but demand for the courses keeps rising. (*New York Times*, 4/17/88, pp. 3ff.)

Entrepreneurship is currently a very popular topic among students of management and economics. It was not always so. Before 1960, most economists understood its importance, but during the next decade, they tended to underrate it. To begin with, the attention then devoted to big companies obscured the fact that most new jobs are created by newer, smaller ones. Moreover, the function of the entrepreneur—organizing new productive resources to expand supply—seemed less important. In those days, the dominant school of economics was chiefly interested in managing consumer *demand*.

In the 1970s, the mood changed again. Economics concerned primarily with consumer demand failed to prevent the constant inflation of that decade. Economists began to worry about the fact our productivity was increasing much less rapidly than it had earlier—from 2 percent to 3 percent annually, in the good years of the 1950s and 1960s, to almost nothing. This made economists more interested in the *supply* of goods and services—the entrepreneur's sphere—and less interested in managing demand for them.

start-up Business founded by individuals intending to change the environment of a given industry either by the introduction of a new product or production process.

Slower growth called attention to those sectors of the economy that were still growing quickly: medical services, electronics, robotics, genetic engineering, and a few others. These are all high-tech industries in which many companies are small **start-ups** founded by people who wanted to change the business world—by entrepreneurs, in other words. What George Gilder calls the "heroic creativity of entrepreneurs"[9] came to seem more and more essential.

Economic Growth

One reason economists started paying more attention to small new firms is that they seem to provide most of the new jobs in our economy. In an important U.S. industry,

[8]William A. Stoever, "India: The Long, Slow Road to Liberalization," *Business Horizons*, January–February 1988, pp. 42–46.

[9]George Gilder, *Wealth and Poverty* (New York: Basic Books, 1981).

HERE'S AN EXAMPLE

A survey of hiring intentions conducted by Dun & Bradstreet Corporation finds that businesses with fewer than 100 employees will generate about 51 percent of the 2.4 million new U.S. jobs expected in 1988. This is down from an estimated 59 percent in 1987, however. (*Business Week*, 4/11/88, p. 91)

electronics, a trade association study showed that companies which have survived for 5 to 10 years hire more than 50 times as many people as do companies that have been around for more than 20 years.[10]

Moreover, one researcher, David Birch, has estimated that in the United States more than four-fifths of all new employment openings come from small businesses. Of these openings, upwards of 30 percent are provided by companies that are less than 5 years old.

But Birch adds, "Not all small businesses are job creators. The job creators are the relatively few younger ones that start up and expand rapidly in their youth, outgrowing the 'small' designation in the process."[11] Birch has also found that new companies—and therefore the jobs they create—are increasingly found in the service sector of the economy rather than the manufacturing sector.[12]

HERE'S AN EXAMPLE

Some critics say that entrepreneurs are hurting U.S. competitiveness. Says one of these critics, "It is simply unlikely that more than 800 relatively small manufacturers can survive against 15 or 20 giants in Japan." (*New York Times*, 6/14/88, pp. D1ff.)

Productivity

We saw earlier that *productivity*—the ability to produce more goods and services with less labor and other inputs—increased much less rapidly in the United States during the 1970s than it had in the 1950s and 1960s. Many economists concluded, and still believe, that falling rates in the increase of productivity were the most fundamental problem of our economy. One reason for the greater interest in entrepreneurship has been the growing recognition of its role in raising productivity.

Higher productivity is chiefly a matter of improving production techniques, and this task, according to John Kendrick, is "the entrepreneurial function par excellence." Two of the keys to higher productivity are **research and development (R&D)** on the one hand, investment in new plant and machinery on the other. According to Kendrick, "there is a close link between R&D and investment programs, with a high entrepreneurial input into both."[13]

research and development (R&D) Entrepreneurial function devoting organizational assets to the design, testing, and production of new products.

R&D is not the sole influence on productivity growth. Government regulation and **macroeconomic policy**—that is, taxation, spending, and money creation—are important, too. Many economists believe that innovation—the essential precondition for high productivity growth—was (as Kendrick put it) "dampened by the developments of the past decade [the 1970s], especially by accelerating inflation and its consequences and by increasing governmental interventions in the business economy."[14] In this respect, entrepreneurs are important, says Kendrick, because they "help contain the negative impacts of regulations."[15]

macroeconomic policy Decisions considering such factors as taxation, development costs, regulatory control, and other external factors that might affect the development of a new product.

HERE'S AN EXAMPLE

Donald E. Hoffman, owner of Creative Playthings, Ltd. has branched into providing a swing set for different price ranges. His company, which he formed in 1976 after failing to find a decent swing set for his son, now sells half of all wooden sets made in the U.S. (*Business Week*, 8/8/88, p. 73)

New Technologies, Products, and Services

Another consequence of the association between entrepreneurship and change is the role that entrepreneurs play in promoting innovative technologies, products, and services. Many people who have developed new technologies, products, and services—Gore-Tex fabric, for example, as well as microprocessors and personal computers—were employees of large corporations that refused to use them, forcing the inventors to

[10]Karl H. Vesper, *Entrepreneurship and Public Policy* (Pittsburgh: Carnegie-Mellon University, The Graduate School of Industrial Administration, 1983), p. 14.

[11]David Birch, "Who Creates Jobs," *The Public Interest* 65 (Fall 1981).

[12]David Birch, *The Job Creation Process* (Cambridge, Mass.: MIT Program on Neighborhood and Regional Change, 1979), in Sue Birley, "The Role of New Firms: Births, Deaths and Job Generation," *Strategic Management Journal* 7 (1986):363.

[13]Backman, *Entrepreneurship and the Outlook for America*, p. 17.

[14]Ibid., p. 9.

[15]Ibid., p. 18.

ETHICS IN MANAGEMENT

"COMPETING WITH THE BIGGIES"

Battlelines have been drawn in a modern version of David and Goliath: Ben & Jerry's Homemade and Häagen-Dazs are battling over the market for super-premium ice cream, which has become big business. Over the last 10 years, Americans have consumed the high-fat, low-air treat in ever-increasing amounts. Not surprisingly, this boom in demand has resulted in the introduction of numerous brands and fierce competition for market shares.

In the beginning, there was Häagen-Dazs, begun by a Brooklyn immigrant who sold his company to Pillsbury as the market was expanding. Before long, other brands emerged on the scene, including Ben & Jerry's, which was originally developed by Ben Cohen and Jerry Greenfield to cater to the college population in Vermont. Although there are several other brands on the market, these two are now the major competitors in one of the business world's fiercest battles for consumers.

As a subsidiary of a large company, Häagen-Dazs enjoys national distribution. Ben & Jerry's is currently distributed in 35 states. However, much of their distribution has been threatened by a Häagen-Dazs move to create exclusive distributionships: Häagen-Dazs would like to require that distributors and retailers who handle its product handle no other ice cream in the super-premium class. The practice is widespread in some segments of the food market—for example, Coke and Pepsi each require that its bottlers handle only one of the two. However, in market segments where there are only a few competitors this practice can severely affect the competition and effectively lock the smaller company out of the market.

become entrepreneurs. (When Gore-Tex had actually been developed, no established garment manufacturer wanted to use it, and it was ignored until a struggling smaller one decided to experiment with the product.) In California's Silicon Valley, one study showed that as many as four-fifths of all companies had been started by exiles from larger companies. Table 22-1 provides an interesting list of inventions, ranging from the zipper to titanium, that have resulted from the innovative efforts of entrepreneurs over the past several decades.

Other innovations—for example, Henry Ford's mass-production line—were pioneered by people who opted for independent product supply from the start. Yet as Ford's example shows, start-ups may eventually become so successful that they cease to be entrepreneurial either in spirit or ownership.

Sometimes, one entrepreneurial innovation will give rise to many others. The most famous and important case comes from the very start of the Industrial Revolution during the second half of the eighteenth century. Early in the century, imported cotton fabric from India gave some British entrepreneurs the idea of producing it in Britain. At first, the raw cotton (mostly from the American South) was spun into yarn by hand-operated machines and then woven, also by hand-operated machines, into fabric. But a problem arose: The machines that did the spinning worked too slowly to produce enough yarn to keep all the weaving machines fully occupied. Spinning, therefore, was a bottleneck, and before long, inventors were working to unjam it. In the mid-1760s, James Hargreaves invented the spinning jenny, a machine that could produce up to 11 threads of cotton simultaneously. Later in the century, the spinning jenny was linked to the steam engine, so that it no longer had to be worked by the operator's foot. The overall effect of these innovations was to increase the amount of cotton thread still further: Now there was too much thread and not enough weaving capacity—exactly the

In this case, the maneuver can also be interpreted as a violation of the Sherman-Clayton Act, which mandates fair trade.

As Ben & Jerry's began to move from local sales in Vermont to distribution throughout New England, Häagen-Dazs sent letters to the independent dealers who sold its product stating that they could not sell both Häagen-Dazs and Ben & Jerry's. Ben & Jerry's believed this ploy denied them the chance to compete and were ready to take Pillsbury to court to prove it. They also took their complaint to the public, distributing ads that told the story and printing bumperstickers that asked "What's the doughboy afraid of?" Eventually, Pillsbury and Ben & Jerry's reached an out-of-court settlement which prohibited exclusive dealerships for two years in any new market into which Ben & Jerry's chose to venture.

Soon, Ben & Jerry's ice cream was sweeping not only through New England, but other areas of the country as well. The two companies are very different and have pursued different strategies for promoting their products to slightly different consumers. Häagen-Dazs spends large sums on national advertising campaigns designed by a prominent ad agency. Ben & Jerry's latest ads were developed by an in-house staff and produced using local talent. Both brands cater to an upscale market, but Häagen-Dazs presents a product with a continental flair, while Ben & Jerry's capitalizes on its home-grown appeal.

So, these two companies, with their different cultures, different strategies, and different flavors, continue to battle for consumer loyalty. Who will win the next round? No one can be certain, but the ethics of competition will continue to an issue in the battle for the sweet tooth.

Sources: Keith H. Hammonds, "Is Häagen Dazs Trying to Freeze Out Ben & Jerry's?" *Business Week,* December 7, 1987, p. 65; "Davids Reject Goliath-Like Path," *Advertising Age,* October 12, 1987, pp. S3–S4, S6, S8–S9; Calvin Trillin, "Competitors," *The New Yorker,* July 8, 1985, 31–32, 35–38, 41, 43–45.

opposite of the old problem. Again, inventors went to work. In 1785, an English clergyman invented the power loom, a weaving machine powered by a steam engine. Innovation had come full circle.

Much as one invention often begets another, one company often begets another company. Figure 22-1 depicts all the many off spring of California's Fairchild Semiconductors, itself an offshoot of another company, Shockley Transistor Laboratories.

THE ENTREPRENEUR

COORDINATED RESOURCE
Money magazine presented a quiz on whether a person has entrepreneurial attitudes in "Do You Have What It Takes?" March 1978, pp. 1–4.

What kinds of people are entrepreneurs? What skills and attitudes must they have? Can we all be entrepreneurs? Can the business culture take steps to promote their emergence? These are important questions, and much recent research has been devoted to them.

Psychological and Sociological Factors

First, let's consider the personal qualities of entrepreneurs and the social environments that tend to produce them. Psychological and sociological factors are not always easy to distinguish, so we will consider them together.

The Theory of Need-Achievement. As we saw in Chapter 14, perhaps the first, and certainly the most important, theory of entrepreneurship's psychological roots was put forward in the early 1960s by David McClelland, who found that certain kinds of

TABLE 22-1 SOME CONTRIBUTORS OF INDEPENDENT INVESTORS AND SMALL ORGANIZATIONS

INVENTIONS	INVENTORS
Digital Computers	Eckert, Mauchly
Xerography	Carlson
Laser	Townes
Insulin	Banting
Turbojet Engine	Whittle, Von Ohain
Magnetic Recording	Camras
Oxygen Steelmaking Process	Schwartz, Miles, Burrer
Gyrocompass	Kaempfe, Sperry, Brown
Rocketry	Goddard
Shell Molding	Croning
Shrink Proof Knitwear	Walton
Zipper	Judson, Sundback
Self-Winding Wristwatch	Harwood
Continuous Hot-Strip Steel	Tytus
Helicopter	Cierva, Focke, Sikorsky
Air Conditioning	Carrier
Ball Point Pen	Biro, Biro
Tungsten Carbide	Schroeter
Velcro	de Mestral
Fiberglass Surfboards	Simmons
String Trimmers	Ballas
Magnetic Core Memory	Wang
Flexible Soda Straws	Friedman
Vacuum Tube	DeForest
FM Radio	Armstrong
Penicillin	Fleming
Petroleum Catalytic Cracking	Houdry
Fiber Optics	Kapany
Heterodyne Radio	Fessenden
Streptomycin	Waksman
Cyclotron	Lawrence
Titanium	Kroll
Cotton Picker	Rust, Rust
Dacron Polyester Fiber	Winfield, Dickson
Automatic Transmission	Hobbs
Mercury Dry Cell	Ruben
Power Steering	Davis
Color Photography	Mannes, Godowsky
Polaroid Camera	Land
Cellophane	Brandenberger
Bakelite	Bakeland
Hovercraft	Cockerell
Metal Laminated Skies	Head
Fiberglass Snow Skis	Kirschner
Prince Tennis Racquet	Head
Geodesic Domes	Fuller

Sources: Adapted from Jacob Rabinow, National Bureau of Standards. Reprinted from Karl H. Vesper, *Entrepreneurship and National Policy* (1983). Walter E. Heller International Corporation Institute for Small Business.

need-achievement According to McClelland, a social motive to excel that tends to characterize successful entrepreneurs, especially when reinforced by cultural factors.

people, including and especially those who become entrepreneurs, have a high need for achievement, or **need-achievement.** Some societies, moreover, tend to produce a larger percentage of people with high need-achievement than other societies do. But McClelland was interested in more than the *psychological* factors involved in achieve-

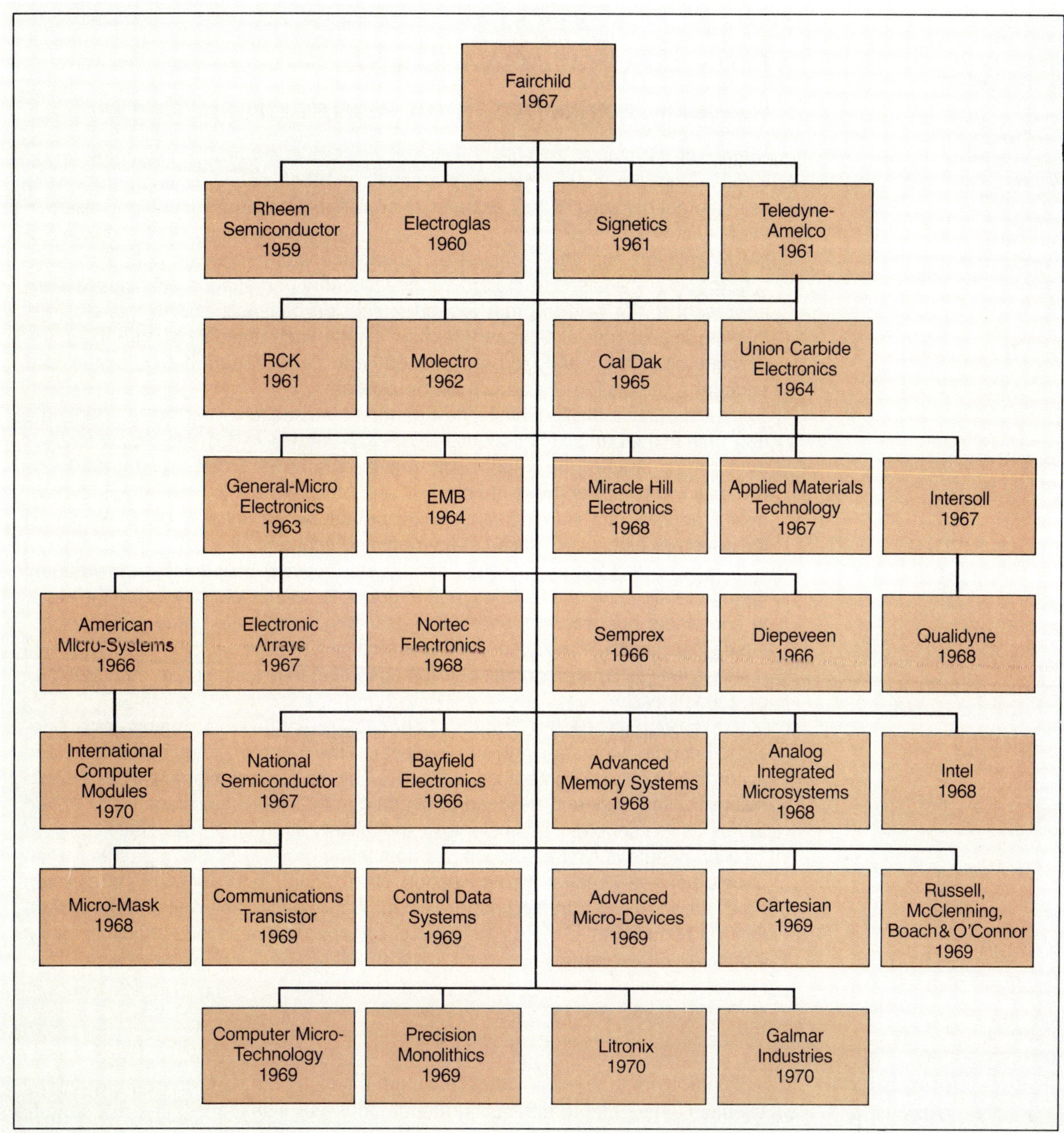

Source: Kirk P. Drahem, "Factors Influencing the Formation of Technical Companies," in Cooper and Komives, 1972. With permission. Reprinted from Karl H. Vesper, *Entrepreneurship and National Policy* (1983). Walter E. Heller International Corporation Institute for Small Business.

FIGURE 22-1 WHAT FAIRCHILD BEGAT

ment-oriented behavior. He also sought *sociological* factors—chose things that might account for differences among *societies* as well as individuals. In effect, as Paul Wilken has said, "entrepreneurship becomes the link . . . between need-achievement and economic growth," the latter of which is a specifically social phenomenon.[16]

[16]Wilken, *Entrepreneurship*, p. 17.

INTERNATIONAL MANAGEMENT

ECONOMIC EXPERIMENTS IN THE PEOPLE'S REPUBLIC OF CHINA

During the "Cultural Revolution" initiated by Mao Tse-tung, the economy of the world's most populous nation was a strictly *planned economy.* Managers were selected not because of their experience or skills but because of their dedication to the Maoist program for change and development. In fact, during the heady days of the Revolution, the very concept of "sound management" was condemned as "bourgeois revisionism"; scholars and practitioners of management science were often sent to the field in order to work alongside peasants and to reorient their thinking in properly revolutionary terms. Despite such antimanagement bias, the Chinese economy managed between 1950 and 1976 to feed, house, clothe, and educate a population of nearly 1 billion people.

After Mao's death, China's new generation of leaders eventually proposed a new path to the pursuit of economic prosperity—that is, to economic growth rather than simply meeting the most basic needs of a huge population. In 1980, the National People's Congress announced economic reforms to be introduced, however gradually, into virtually all of China's state-owned enterprises. In modifying the country's highly centralized state-managed economy, the reforms actually encouraged entrepreneurship within certain state-owned businesses, encouraging them to retain reinvest profits, to market goods to consumers other than the state, to coordinate budgets with operational planning, to allocate some profits as bonuses to productive employees, to encourage participative decision making, and to manage the task of personnel selection according to grounds other than ideological faithfulness.

Through the 1980s, China continued to accelerate its reform program, hoping to become an increasingly viable player in the game of global economics, and according to an assessment issued in 1987 by the Congressional Office of Technology, China is indeed destined to become increasingly important to the United States as its economic, technological, and military strength grows. There are over 1 billion people in China, and with its population growing at the rate of 14 million people per year, such firms as Reebok, Nike, Squib, Ingersoll-Rand, and others have already been attracted not only to market opportunities on the other side of the "Bamboo Curtain," but to the productive capacities of an industrious, if not yet industrialized economy.

COORDINATED RESOURCE

See "The New Independents," *Fortune*, 4/25/88, pp. 66–80.

People with high need-achievement are distinctive in several ways, according to McClelland. They like to take risks, though only reasonable ones, and risk stimulates them to greater effort. What sort of society produces people of this kind? McClelland's views have evolved. In *The Achieving Society* (1961), his emphasis was psychological, placing emphasis on the role of parents, especially on the kind of mother who is most likely to nurture an aspiring entrepreneur and who expects her son to be masterful and self-reliant. However, in a later book, *Motivating Economic Achievement* (1971), McClelland and co-author D. Winter put less emphasis on the parent-child relationship as a cause of high need-achievement and more on social and cultural factors, replacing the parent as the object of the individual's needs for approval with an entire culture that will reward achievement with influence and power.

It is perhaps interesting to note that Henry Ford, one of the wealthiest and most famous men in America in 1918, lost a bid for a U.S. Senate seat that year. William Randolph Hearst, whose publishing empire made him one of the country's most influential individuals, successively failed to become mayor of New York City, governor of New York, and the Democratic nominee for president between 1903 and 1907. On the

However, the course of change has not always run smoothly for the People's Republic of China, either for its state-operated enterprises or for its joint-venture enterprises. Like Mao himself, China's current leaders are faced with the task of changing a predominantly peasant culture into one whose economy can reap the benefits of twentieth-century technology and innovation. At the same time, however, China's new leaders are attempting to *modify*—not *discard*—a planned or command economy (see the International Management box entitled "Planning in the USSR," Chapter 5). Although the traumatic consequences of the "Cultural Revolution" have apparently rendered Chinese bureaucrats more open to experimentation than their Soviet counterparts, they must still manage an economy which, if it should expand too quickly, will experience the predictable effects of inflation—namely, upward-spiraling wages and prices and a law of supply and demand that is being violated by a centralized planning system unresponsive to changing market requirements.

Nevertheless, today's China is the locus of unique economic experimentation—a country in which an ideological disposition toward centralized planning is now trying to coexist with the idiosyncrasies of the open market. Today, many of China's leaders are arguing for the establishment of profitable enterprises, greater response to the demands of an open and flexible market, and the utility of foreign technolgy and investment. China now allows some state-owned firms to issue shares, is experimenting with a system of stocks and bonds, and permits some businesses to experiment in restructuring even if such a policy should result in the loss of hundreds of jobs. In an effort to compete with the other industrialized economies of Eastern Asia (notably Japan, Korea, and Taiwan), China has encouraged genuine entrepeneurial activities in the production of items ranging from candles to watches.

No one knows for certain whether or not a "new" entrepreneurial China will emerge from the current wave of changes, but it does seem obvious that today's China will ultimately offer a unique array of management opportunities not only for its own people but for foreign industries, located in the United States or elsewhere, looking toward joint venture as a means of international expansion.

Sources: James O'Toole, "The Good Managers of Sichuan," *Harvard Business Review,* May–June 1981, pp. 28–40; "China's Reformers Say: Let a Thousand Businesses Bloom," *Business Week,* April 1988, pp. 70–72; "The Next 'Asian Miracle' May Be Underway—In China," *Business Week,* November 2, 1988, pp. 144–145; and Susan Leshnover, "China's Opportunities," *Management Review* 77, no. 7 (1988):48–51.

other hand, Joseph Kennedy, who had made a fortune in banking and shipbuilding by the 1930s, took time out to serve as head of both the Securities and Exchange Commission and the U.S. Maritime Commission before becoming ambassador to Great Britain. In 1921, Andrew Mellon resigned as president of the immensely powerful Mellon National Bank to serve three presidents as Secretary of the Treasury before he, too, was appointed ambassador to Great Britain. Mellon also provided $10 million to found the Mellon Institute of Industrial Research and donated his art collection to make possible the National Gallery of Art. The vast philanthropic activities of other legendary American entrepreneurs, such as Andrew Carnegie and John D. Rockefeller, may offer some support for McClelland's theory that the needs of "born" entrepreneurs are conditioned as much by social as psychological reinforcement.

Psychosocial Theories. McClelland is not the only researcher trying to understand the psychological and sociological roots of entrepreneurship. Everett Hagen stresses the psychological consequences of social change. At some point, notes Hagen, many social groups experience a radical loss of status. In predominantly Catholic France, for example, Protestants were tolerated in the seventeenth century but found themselves increasingly subject to legal and social persecution in the eighteenth century. There are many ways of responding to such a loss of status, including Hagen's five categories of *retreatism, ritualism, innovation, reformism,* and *rebellion.*

HERE'S AN EXAMPLE

An emerging phenomenon on the corporate scene: new independents—individuals who are graduates of the best business schools and who have often seen big corporations up close. They don't like what they've seen and so started their own business. But not like the traditional entrepreneurs but because they wanted independence. (*Fortune,* 4/25/88, pp. 66–80)

Retreatism is the most important in promoting entrepreneurship. At first, the men of such groups may respond to the loss of status with confusion or weakness, but if they do, their achievements will not intimidate the men of future generations. If the women of such groups continue to hold high expectations for their sons, they may grow up with high need-achievement. Since the law or social attitudes may prevent them from seeking the usual forms of achievement, such as holding political office or owning land, the sons of disenfranchised groups must seek other outlets for their abilities—notably business, as did the Protestants of eighteenth-century France. Perhaps the most notable example is the Rothschild family, overseers of an immensely wealthy and powerful banking concern throughout Europe from the eighteenth to the twentieth century.

Other psychosocial theories of entrepreneurship stress the entrepreneur's motives or goals. Cole, for example, thinks that besides wealth, entrepreneurs seek power, prestige, security, and service to society. Stepanek points particularly to nonmonetary goals, such as independence, personal self-esteem, power, and the regard of the community. Evans distinguishes by motive among three kinds of entrepreneurs: managing entrepreneurs, whose chief goal is security; innovating entrepreneurs, who crave excitement; and controlling entrepreneurs, who above all want power. Finally, Rostow has examined intergenerational changes in the families of entrepreneurs. He believes that the first generation seeks wealth, the second prestige, and the third art and beauty in general.[17]

In the mid-1980s, Thomas Begley and David P. Boyd studied the literature[18] on the psychological roots of entrepreneurship.[19] They tried to find out how the founders of small businesses—entrepreneurs, in other words—differ from people who manage existing small businesses. In addition, Begley and Boyd wanted to know how entrepreneurial attitudes affect the bottom lines of small companies.

They considered five dimensions. First came need-achievement as described by McClelland. "Most studies," Begley and Boyd discovered, "support the prevalence of high n ach [need-achievement] among practicing entrepreneurs." Furthermore, in "studies of successful entrepreneurs, a high achievement orientation seems invariably present."[20]

The second dimension is what Begley and Boyd, following the psychologist Julian B. Rotter, call "locus of control"—the idea that people can control their own lives, as distinguished from a belief in luck, fate, and a variety of external forces. As the two researchers see it, need-achievement logically implies that people can control their own lives and that the exercise of need-achievement is difficult to imagine with-

[17]This discussion is drawn from Wilken, *Entrepreneurship,* p. 20.

[18]For example, Thomas Begley and David P. Boyd, "The Relationship of the Jenkins Activity Survey to Type A Behavior Among Business Executives," *Journal of Vocational Behavior* 27(1987):316–328; C. Borland, "Locus of Control, Need for Achievement, and Entrepreneurship," unpublished doctoral dissertation (Austin: University of Texas, 1974); David P. Boyd, "Type A Behavior, Financial Growth, and Organizational Growth in Small Business Firms," *Journal of Occupational Psychology* 57:137–140; J. A. Hornaday and J. Abboud, "Characteristics of Successful Entrepreneurs," *Personnel Psychology* 24:141–153; P. R. Liles, *New Business Ventures and the Entrepreneur* (Homewood, Ill.: Richard D. Irwin, 1974); J. A. Timmons, "Characteristics and Role Demands of Entrepreneurship," *American Journal of Small Business* 3(1987):5–17; J. A. Welsh and J. P. White, "Converging Characteristics of Entrepreneurs," in K. H. Vesper, ed., *Frontiers of Entrepreneurship Research* (Wellesley, Mass.: Babson Center for Entrepreneurial Studies, 1981), pp. 504–515.

[19]Thomas Begley and David P. Boyd, "Psychological Characteristics Associated with Performance in Entrepreneurial Firms and Smaller Businesses, *Journal of Business Venturing* 2 (1987):79–93.

[20]Ibid., p. 81.

Drawing by Ed Fisher; © 1988 The New Yorker Magazine, Inc.

out the influence of that conviction. Both founders and managers tend to think that they are pulling their own strings.

The third dimension that Begley and Boyd studied is the willingness to take risks. The two found that entrepreneurs who are willing to take moderate risks seem, on average, to earn higher returns on assets than both entrepreneurs who, on the one hand, take no risks or, on the other, those who take what may be extravagant risks.

Tolerance for ambiguity is the fourth dimension of Begley and Boyd's study. Very few decisions are made with complete information, and the outcome of most decisions is hardly ever obvious before they have been made. All business executives must have a certain amount of tolerance for ambiguity (and thus error), but some studies suggest that entrepreneurs have more than managers on other levels.

Finally, there is what psychologists call ''Type A'' behavior—''a chronic, incessant struggle to achieve more and more in less and less time, and if required to do so, against the opposing efforts of other things or other persons.''[21] Both founders and managers of small businesses have much higher rates of Type A behavior than do other business executives.

Competence

Attitudes do not in themselves make an entrepreneur. As Karl Vesper observes, in the mid-1970s, when Steve Wozniak and Steve Jobs were creating Apple Computers Incorporated, there may have been many other people who wanted to be entrepreneurs

[21] M. Friedman and R. H. Rosenman, *Type A Behavior and Your Heart* (Greenwich, Conn.: Fawcett, 1974).

QUOTATION FROM AN ENTREPRENEUR

"For all I know, if I succeed at making money, I'll decide that making money is a lot of fun and I should try to make lots more. Although probably I won't. I don't have much to spend it on other than interesting projects."—Stephen Wolfram, genius physicist and budding entrepreneur (*Fortune*, 4/11/88, p. 93)

distinctive competence Entrepreneurial desire to start a business coupled with the ability or experience to compete effectively once the enterprise is initiated.

even more than they did.[22] Besides desire, Wozniak and Jobs had a profitable business idea—"just the right product suited to a big market that others were not prepared to serve."[23]

The two friends also had the electronics and marketing skills to exploit their idea, as well as the modesty to reach out to executives with skills and experience that they did not have. Would-be entrepreneurs, says Vesper, must also have access to capital and other production assets, personal contacts, and enough time to create a firm from scratch.

To date, there have been few studies into why there are so many people who want to start up businesses and so few who do. Attendance at seminars conducted by government agencies, university programs, and private promoters is reasonably high, but there are probably two reasons for the scarcity of profitable business start-ups by the attendees. First, there is certainly no one-to-one correspondence between attendance figures and reasonably profitable ideas. Second, there appears to be a lack among many entrepreneurial aspirants of what some analysts call **distinctive competence.** In particular, as Figure 22-2 shows, there is a great deal of difference between desiring to

[22]Vesper, *Entrepreneurship and Public Policy*, p. 42.
[23]Ibid., p. 43.

FIGURE 22-2 ENTREPRENEURIAL DESIRE VERSUS CAPABILITY

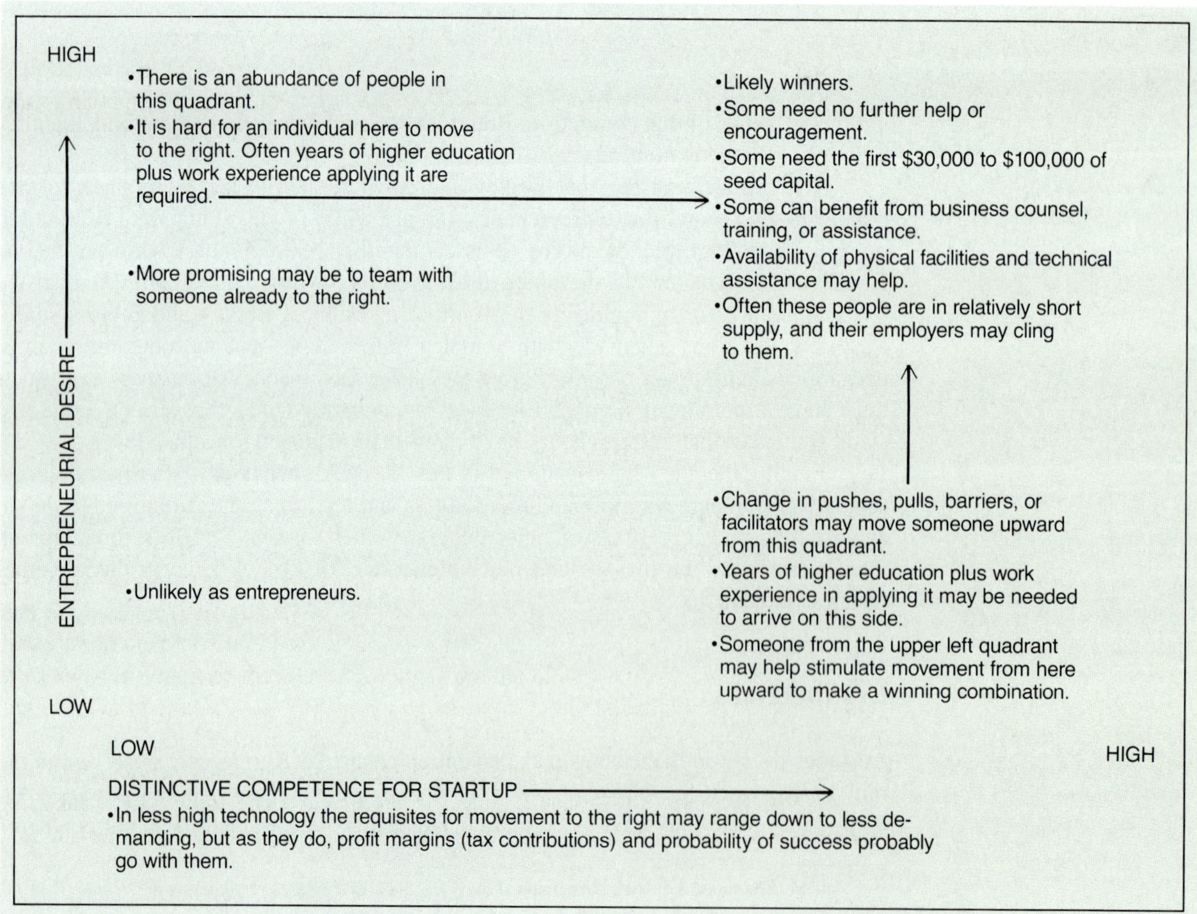

Source: Karl H. Vesper, *Entrepreneurship and National Policy* (1983). Walter E. Heller International Corporation Institute for Small Business.

start a business (even with a feasible idea) and the competence to *compete* effectively. Of course, Wozniak and Jobs had the right idea at the right time, but their "distinctive competence" included an insightful analysis of the market and the management that they would need to perform against their competitors.

ILLUSTRATIVE CASE STUDY Continued

Start-Up Pains at Nova Pharmaceutical Corporation

Nova has marshaled some entrepreneurial spirit in a lot of people who risked their careers simply to create a company that will make their lives and their industry better. Intentions aside, Nova has had severe problems with financing, as continuing research efforts demand more and more ongoing resources. In order to keep up its momentum, Nova thus had to seek outside help: It signed research contracts with Celanese, GAF, and Marion Laboratories in return for much-needed capital and marketing expertise.

Paradoxically, then, although Nova began as an idea—a vision of an opportunity that had become foreclosed to large firms—it has grown to depend for its survival on the same kinds of capital input that have sustained its outsized competitors. Entrepreneurship is more than vision and ideas. Naturally, it requires hard work and superb management skills—and solid, dependable financing. So far, Nova is still in the game.

THE ENTREPRENEURIAL PROCESS

THOUGHT-PROVOKER
Can the entrepreneurial process be taught?

An organization is a living thing that is born, grows, ages, and, sooner or later, dies. Entrepreneurs are a part of that process—that is, part of the organizational life cycle (see Chapter 9). They are present at the creation and the act of entrepreneurship—the creation and nurturing of a firm—unfolds in a process comprising several distinct stages.[24]

Stages in the Entrepreneurial Process

The first stage in the entrepreneurial process is some change in the real world. A war, for example, may destroy a country's manufacturing facilities but spare its trained work force; in another country, a large number of births takes place within a certain span of years; in a third, the traditional commercial aristocracy is supplanted by small businesspeople and professional men and women. Changes like these would lead to changes in every aspect of life in each country.

Some of these changes create needs for new services or goods. The destruction of Japan's prewar industry, at the end of World War II, allowed the country to rebuild its industry from scratch. A phenomenon like the American "baby boom" of the late 1940s and 1950s created a huge age-specific market for goods and services that has been experienced in the 1970s and 1980s and will be felt well into the next decade and even the next century. And traditional aristocracies have needs that are very different from those of the middle class, so that an economy that is designed chiefly to serve the needs of a small number of privileged consumers is very different from the kind of economy found in societies that have mass markets for goods and services.

The second stage in the entrepreneurial process is "The Idea." Let's take the personal computer as a case in point. Microprocessors, the personal computer's brain,

[24]This discussion is based upon Joshua Ronen, "Some Insights into the Entrepreneurial Process," in Joshua Ronen, ed., *Entrepreneurship* (Lexington, Mass.: D. C. Heath, 1983), pp. 152–154.

had been on the market since the early 1970s and made the personal computer possible. One would think that the chairman of Hewlett-Packard, Steve Wozniak's employer when he got the idea for the Apple, would have gotten down on his knees and begged Wozniak to invent something just like this. That did not happen. *Instead, Wozniak could not talk his company into developing the product!*

Remember, too, that the idea of a personal computer was not even Wozniak's. A company called Altair had already put out a computer that was so personal that you had to put it together yourself. Yet it was Apple Computers, not Altair, that entered the ranks of the *Fortune* 500. Wozniak and Jobs perceived something that Altair had not—namely, that the personal computer market was potentially a lot bigger than the clique of hobbyists it was currently serving and that most consumers would care neither to put the thing together nor to write software in an assembly language (or even write software at all).

Some discoveries furnish substitutes for things that already exist. The need for such substitutes is often pretty obvious. Other discoveries, like personal computers, involve new needs. Yet before personal computers actually existed, it was almost impossible to persuade anybody that he or she needed one.

HERE'S AN EXAMPLE

An entrepreneurship program in St. Louis allows 25 minority youth to learn to be entrepreneurs. Says one sponsor of the program, "Fundamentally, what we have to preach is ownership. That's what's important for these kids to know because that's what this society is all about . . . ." (*Wall Street Journal*, 5/10/88, p. 16)

Choosing a Business

In many ways, jobs are like schools—except that they pay.[25] A lot of people start up a company in a certain line of business after working in it for someone else. Those who start businesses in the early stages of expanding industries can acquire market share more cheaply, but also more speculatively, than entrepreneurs who look for opportunities in established industries. An entrepreneur might even buy an existing company if that were the cheapest way of getting the needed resources.

franchising Entrepreneurial system whereby an individual runs a business based on the right to market a good or service granted by a manufacturer or other organization.

As Table 22-2 illustrates, there are many different *types* of businesses that the would-be entrepreneur must also consider. **Franchising,** which has become much more common during the last several decades, includes both buying an existing business and starting a new one. Whoever buys a franchise buys a brand name that enjoys name recognition among potential customers. Yet at the same time, franchise operators own their own businesses and are their own bosses. Of course, they cannot run their businesses just as they please; they usually have to conform to the standards of the franchise, and sometimes they must buy the franchiser's goods or services. But it is precisely the popularity of a franchiser's good or services that induces people to get a franchise in the first place.

Entrepreneurs have to make other decisions about the form that their enterprises will take: the ownership of a single person, partnerships, or private or public corporate ownership. Joint ventures became much more common during the mid-1980s, as American firms, especially in the automobile industry, sought out Japanese partners.

No matter what organizational form an entrepreneur may choose, the management process discussed in this book is relevant. Planning, organizing, leading, and controlling occur in all organizations, however new or old, big or small.

ENTREPRENEURIAL ORGANIZATIONS

We saw earlier that entrepreneurs are all agents of change who add new possibilities to an economy by mixing together new and old information, new and old resources. We tend to think of entrepreneurs as characteristic of small, new companies, but the truth is

[25]This section is based on Melvin J. Stanford, *New Enterprise Management* (Reston, Va.: Reston Publishing, 1982).

TABLE 22-2 BASIC FORMS OF BUSINESS

BUSINESS FORM	FEATURE				
	Liability	Continuity	Transferability	Management	Equity Investment
Proprietorship	Personal, unlimited	Ends with death or decision of owner	Free to sell at any time	Personal, unrestricted	Personal
Partnership–General	Personal and unlimited, joint and several	Ends with death or decision of any partner	Individual interest can be sold with consent of all partners	Unrestricted or depending upon partnership agreement	Personal by partner(s)
Partnership–Limited*	For limited partners only invested capital. For general as above	Limited partners do not affect. As above for general partners	Limited free to sell. General as above	Limited may not participate, dependent upon agreement.	Personal by partner(s)
Corporation	Capital invested	As stated in charter, perpetual or specified period of years	Stock may be sold or traded without affecting other stock	Under control of Board of Directors, which is selected by stockholders	Purchase of stock

*Limited partnerships consist of both general and limited partners, with different rules for each.

Source: Melvin J. Stanford, *New Enterprise Management,* © 1982, p. 50. Reprinted by permission of Prentice-Hall, Inc., Englewood Cliffs, N.J.

intrapreneuring Corporate entrepreneurship, whereby an organization seeks to expand by exploring new opportunities through new combinations of its existing resources.

that big established ones have much more information and many more resources of all kinds. So the entrepreneurial role can be played in any kind of company, of any size or age. Corporate entrepreneurship, sometimes called **intrapreneuring,**[26] is the process of "extending the firm's domain of competence and corresponding opportunity set through internally generated new resource combinations."[27]

Planning and Strategy

EXTRA EXERCISE

Write a short paper on the role of women in developing new businesses.

There are several ways of trying to be an entrepreneur.[28] One strategy, as Peter Drucker puts it, is to be there "fustest with the mostest." In this case, the entrepreneur tries to take the lead in a new line of business from the start. One rather interesting case of a company that followed this strategy, both as a small firm and then as an established one, is Hofmann-LaRoche, a leading drugmaker based in Switzerland.

Hofmann-LaRoche started small. In the 1920s, it put all its resources into producing and marketing vitamins, which older drug companies, along with medical opinion, still regarded with skepticism. Even now, the company still supplies almost half of the world's gigantic demand for vitamins.

Hofmann-LaRoche bet its money against the medical establishment again during the 1930s, when, as Drucker says, it "went into the new sulfa drugs—even though most scientists of the time 'knew' that systemic drugs could not be effective against infections; and then, 20 years later, it went into the muscle-relaxing tranquilizers

[26]Gifford Pinchot III, *Intrapreneuring* (New York: Harper & Row, 1985).

[27]Robert A. Burgelman, "Designs for Corporate Entrepreneurship in Established Firms," *California Management Review* 26, no. 3 (Spring 1984):154.

[28]This section is based upon Peter Drucker, "Entrepreneurial Strategies," *California Management Review* 27, no. 2 (Winter 1985):9–25.

Librium and Valium—which at that time were equally 'heretical' and incompatible with what 'every scientist knew.'''[29]

TEACHING TIP

If there are any small business ''entrepreneurs'' in your town, invite them in to speak to the class.

This is a successful case, but naturally there are many unsuccessful ones, too. If at first you don't succeed by using the ''fustest with the mostest'' strategy, you may not succeed at all because you may have bet the whole company and lost.

Drucker calls another strategy ''creative imitation.'' Over the years, its most striking practitioner has been International Business Machines Corporation. In the 1930s, the last decade before the emergence of computers, IBM was the biggest firm in the adding machine business and had even designed what might be called the first real computer, which was finished in 1945. Yet IBM shelved it and started to build machines based upon a rival computer, ENIAC, designed at the University of Pennsylvania.

Moreover, the first company to market a business computer was Sperry, with its Univac. IBM beat out Sperry in the long run because IBM understood the nature of the computer business better than anyone else. Computers, in the early 1950s, were rare and wonderful things. Hardly anyone had ever had anything to do with them, or even quite knew what they were. They had to be programmed by direct instructions to the computer hardware, consisting of thousands upon thousands of vacuum tubes.

Sperry and other companies either in the business or thinking about entering it assumed that these conditions would endure forever. IBM knew it was wrong. The firm understood that the market for computers was huge and that computers would have to be designed with this huge market in mind—the same insight that the founders of Apple Computer were to have in the mid-1970s. So we see that the idea of ''creative imitation,'' though a paradox, is not absurd.

Drucker illustrates the meaning of his third and final category of entrepreneurial strategies, ''entrepreneurial judo,'' by telling the story of the transistor.[30] What was then the AT&T Bell Telephone Company announced its discovery in 1947. Bell had developed the transistor specifically to replace old-fashioned vacuum tubes, which burned out at frequent and unpredictable intervals in the company's switching equipment. Tubes were also used in a great many other products—computers, radios, hi-fis, and televisions, for example. It should have been obvious that transistors would replace tubes in each and every one of them.

In fact, it was obvious, and many companies had plans to convert to transistors with all deliberate speed—by 1970 or thereabouts. It did not happen that way because Sony's Akio Morita paid $25,000 for a license to incorporate transistors into his company's products. In the mid-1950s, Sony came out with a cheap transistor radio and proceeded to transistorize all of its consumer electronics products, winning a market lead that it has never relinquished.

However, companies can be downed by entrepreneurial judo, says Drucker, because they are prone to certain vices. For example, there is the *NIH (''not invented here'') syndrome*—the ''arrogance that leads a company or an industry to believe that something new cannot be any good unless they themselves thought of it.'' Another vice is what Drucker calls the ''tendency to *'cream'* a market, that is, to get the high-profit part of it.''[31] Many companies, in other words, gravitate toward the high end of a business, ignoring markets below it that may be much larger.

Drucker illustrates a third vice by pointing to the delusions of American radio manufacturers, who believed that their vacuum-tube radios were better than Sony's transistorized models because the U.S. companies ''had put 30 years of effort into making radio sets bigger, more complicated, and more expensive.'' The public preferred the small transistorized sets, and the public is always right in matters of this sort.

---

[29]Ibid., p. 10.
[30]Ibid., p. 19.
[31]Ibid., p. 21.

A fourth vice is succumbing to the temptation to charge a premium price, which "is always an invitation to the competitor."[32] A fifth bad habit is the tendency to "maximize rather than optimize"—in other words, to take a basic product and adapt it to different needs or many different applications. In this way, the product generally becomes too complex and not exactly suited to any of them. A company with such a product is always liable to be brought down by a competitor with products designed for specific applications.

Organizing

As we have already seen, the entrepreneurial role can be played within organizations of any size. Robert A. Burgelman has studied the relationship between large organizations and entrepreneurial ventures.[33]

COORDINATED RESOURCE

See Lecture Extra for Chapter 22 for information on research for small businesses.

Much, thinks Burgelman, depends upon the entrepreneurial project's importance to the company that sponsors it. If it is very important but not related to a company's core business, it should be spun off as a special business unit. If it is partly related, it should be assigned to a new-product department. If the entrepreneurial project is strongly related to a company's core business, it should be directly integrated into existing business units.

Should a project be unimportant, Burgelman recommends different alternatives. Projects that are not related to a company's core activities should be spun off into separate businesses. Partly related projects should be contracted out. Strongly related projects should be performed by subcontractors who receive some nurturing from the contracting company.

If a project's importance is uncertain and unrelated to the company's main line of business, Burgelman says that it should be implemented by an independent business unit. If it is partly related, the company should consider setting up a new-venture division. If the project is of uncertain importance but strongly related to the core activities of the company, it should establish what Burgelman calls "a micro new-ventures department."

In such a department, managers are "allowed to develop a strategy within budget and time constraints but should otherwise not be limited by current divisional or even corporate-level strategies. Operational linkages should be strong, to take advantage of the existing capabilities and skills and to facilitate transferring back newly developed ones."[34] (In Figure 22-3, Burgelman illustrates nine alternatives for the design of administrative and operational linkages between an organization's new and existing businesses.)

Leading

Older, larger organizations that want to innovate, says Peter Drucker, must recognize first of all that it is always easier to continue doing things as they have been done before.[35] They must get used to the idea that change always looks hard before it is undertaken. Such organizations should also require their subunits to justify their existence every few years. They should follow "a systematic policy of abandoning what-

---

[32]Ibid., p. 22.

[33]Burgelman, "Designs for Corporate Entrepreneurship in Established Firms," pp. 154–166.

[34]Ibid., p. 162.

[35]This section is based upon Chapter 13, "The Entrepreneurial Business," of Peter Drucker's *Innovation and Entrepreneurship*, pp. 147–176.

Operational Relatedness	Strongly Related	Partly Related	Unrelated
Strategic Importance: Very Important	1. Direct Integration	2. New Product/ Business Department	3. Special Business Units
Uncertain	4. Micro New Ventures Department	5. New Venture Division	6. Independent Business Units
Not Important	7. Nurturing and Contracting	8. Contracting	9. Complete Spin Off

Source: Robert A. Burgelman, "Designs for Corporate Entrepreneurship in Established Firms," *California Management Review* 26, no. 3 (Spring 1984). Copyright © 1984 by the Regents of the University of California. Reprinted by permission of The Regents.

FIGURE 22-3 ORGANIZATION DESIGNS FOR CORPORATE ENTREPRENEURSHIP

ever is outworn, obsolete, no longer productive, as well as the mistakes, failures, and misdirections of effort."[36]

Why, for example, did companies which knew that transistors would sooner or later transform the whole electronics business fail to apply transistors themselves? Why was the actual breakthrough left to a small Japanese company? Because the managers of American electronics firms thought only about the problems of their existing business—not, says Drucker, about the opportunities it presented.

For starters, attitudes must change. In entrepreneurial companies, the entrepreneurs become role models: "Entrepreneurial companies always look for the people and units that do better and do differently. They single them out, feature them, and constantly ask them: 'What are you doing that explains your success? What are you doing that the rest of us aren't doing, and what are you not doing that the rest of us are?'"

Drucker has a very definite view of how entrepreneurial ventures should be structured within larger companies, and it is radically different from Burgelman's. Says Drucker: "The entrepreneurial, the new, has to be organized separately from the old and existing. Whenever we have tried to make an existing unit the carrier of the entrepreneurial project, we have failed."[37] Drucker believes this axiom is applicable to businesses of any size. (Proctor & Gamble, Johnson & Johnson, and 3M follow Drucker's strategy in their own well-known entrepreneurial ventures. (See the Management Application box entitled "The Care and Flourishing of Entrepreneurs at 3M.") Finally, someone in the larger organization—perhaps the CEO—should be responsible for promoting innovation within it.

A HUMOROUS NOTE

But not for the people profiled in "Great Fortunes Lost," *Fortune*, 7/18/88, pp. 75–84.

Besides these "do's," there are several "don'ts." Companies should not innovate outside of their area of expertise. New ventures should not be required to show high short-term returns on investment. Finally, it is almost impossible for companies to buy their way into entrepreneurship by purchasing entrepreneurial firms. The people who worked for them as independent businesses almost always get out when they are bought by larger ones, and the acquiring company rarely has people who can take over after the original group leaves.

---

[36]Ibid., p. 151.

[37]Ibid., pp. 161–162.

MANAGEMENT APPLICATION

THE CARE AND FLOURISHING OF ENTREPRENEURS AT 3M

The development of entrepreneurs boils down to a principle that is fairly simple: Human beings are endowed with the urge to create—to bring into being something that has either never existed or worked so well before. Although that drive to create is stronger in some people than in others, it exists to some degree in just about everyone.

It follows, then, that the process of developing entrepreneurs can be enhanced by nurturing and respecting a certain dimension of human nature and honoring it within the context of a profit-making enterprise. At bottom, then, it is a process not simply of encouraging innovation as an end in itself, but rather of encouraging the conversion of innovation into the rewards of success and profit.

How can a company accomplish this process of conversion? It all comes back to a respect for people and their natural urge to create: There must be an invitation to new ideas, and ideally it should be an open invitation. Once a good idea emerges, there must be support from management, including the resources necessary to help the innovator realize this idea.

Opportunity gets the innovator started, but somewhere along the line, there must be a proper reward.

But there's another side to the coin. If innovators like to think of a reward waiting for them at the end of a project, they must also be concerned with what happens if they fail. In point of fact, most innovators *do*—at least once in their careers and probably a lot more often than that. At 3M, chairman and CEO Lewis Lehr has a saying: "You have to kiss a lot of frogs to find a prince."

There is probably no company anywhere which does not profess to be concerned about innovation these days. But what happens when judgment day rolls around each year and managers are forced to defend their results? Does the manager who has spent money backing a few risky projects suffer in comparison with a manager who has milked his cash cow for one more year? If so, then managers and their people will be able to read the company's real priorities very clearly.

At 3M, Lehr tries to meet this problem head-on by setting a clear innovation target for each of his divisions. Basically, they are expected to generate 25 percent of their sales each year from products new to the company's line within the last five years. 3M managers are judged not only on their ability to make existing product lines grow, but also on their knack for bringing innovative new products to market.

Source: Adapted from Lewis Lehr, "The Care and Flourishing of Entrepreneurs at 3M," *Directors and Boards* (Winter 1986):18–20.

Controlling the Entrepreneurial Culture

entrepreneurial culture According to Stevenson and Gumpert, corporate culture focusing on the emergence of new opportunities, the means of capitalizing on them, and the creation of the structure appropriate for pursuing them.

administrative culture According to Stevenson and Gumpert, corporate culture focusing on existing opportunities, organizational structures, and control procedures.

Since companies may contain both entrepreneurial and established units, they must often embody two different and even conflicting corporate cultures (see Chapter 3). Howard H. Stevenson and David E. Gumpert call them **entrepreneurial cultures** and the **administrative cultures.**[38] These are ideal types—that is, collections of traits that make sense together and may be found, to a greater or lesser extent, in particular cases.

Stevenson and Gumpert say, for example, that an ideal administrator would ask such questions as "What resources do I control? What structure determines our organi-

[38] Howard H. Stevenson and David E. Gumpert, "The Heart of Entrepreneurship," *Harvard Business Review* 63 (March–April 1985):85–94.

HERE'S AN EXAMPLE

Some suggestions for helping those managing their own small business: set goals; be flexible; don't be afraid to take chances; keep meticulous, organized records; enlist a good accountant; communicate with your employees; and get all the information you can. (*Joplin Globe*, Joplin, Missouri, February 1988)

zation's relationship to its market? How can I minimize the impact of others on my ability to perform? What opportunity is appropriate?''[39]

By contrast, an ideal entrepreneur would ask very different questions: ''Where is the opportunity? How do I capitalize on it? What resources do I need? How do I gain control over them? What structure is best?''[40]

Table 22-3 lists certain dimensions of the entrepreneurial and administrative psychologies. In the first dimension, strategic orientation, the most entrepreneurial kind of managers will be driven by ''perception of opportunity.'' The pressures they experience include diminishing opportunities as they age and changes in consumer economics, political rules, social values, or technology they cannot understand.

At the other extreme, the strategic orientations of those managers with the most administrative kinds of personalities are driven by ''controlled resources''—the amount of a company's money, skills, and other assets that they can command. The pressures upon them include social contracts with colleagues and subordinates, as well as performance-measurement criteria and planning systems and cycles. Stevenson and Gumpert also list certain characteristics of each orientation and believe that other orientations can be properly described as falling between these two extremes.

BARRIERS AND PROBLEMS

FOR DISCUSSION

What are the similarities of managing a small business and a large business? Differences?

Karl Vesper, whose work on the preconditions of entrepreneurship has already been mentioned, also studied the barriers to it.[41] Why do many entrepreneurs fail? The most common reason, says Vesper, is ''lack of a viable concept.'' Another common one is a lack of market knowledge. Sometimes, it is hard to attract the people with the best information because they already have attractive jobs, because they are chained to their present employers by ''golden handcuffs,'' or because they are complacent and feel no need to do first-rate or important work. Even a lack of technical skills can be a problem, says Vesper.

Then too there is the difficulty of finding the $25,000 to $100,000 a start-up typically needs. Once it gets going, a certain number of entrepreneurs fail because they lack general business know-how. Certain people might be deterred from entering certain lines of work—for example, housecleaning—by what they see as a social stigma. Others are discouraged by the monopolies controlling certain professions, notably medicine and the law.

In Figure 22-4, Vesper summarizes various kinds of start-up businesses and the barriers they typically encounter. In Figure 22-5, he lists 12 common barriers; the arrows indicate how certain environmental ''helps'' can act to reduce the effect of barriers.

The Dark Side of Entrepreneurship

FOR DISCUSSION

If you were starting your own business, what steps could you take to insure its success?

If entrepreneurs have a recognizable personality type, it is not all sweetness and light. As Manfred Kets de Vries points out in an article called ''The Dark Side of Entrepreneurship,'' some entrepreneurs ''have personality quirks that make them hard people to work with.''[42] Entreprereurs, argues de Vries, have a need for control, and at times

[39]Ibid., p. 86.

[40]Ibid., p. 87.

[41]Vesper, *Entrepreneurship and Public Policy,* pp. 59–68.

[42]Manfred Kets de Vries, ''The Dark Side of Entrepreneurship,'' *Harvard Business Review* 63 (November–December 1985):160–167.

TABLE 22-3 THE ENTREPRENEURIAL CULTURE VS. THE ADMINISTRATIVE CULTURE

	← ENTREPRENEURIAL FOCUS		ADMINISTRATIVE FOCUS →	
	Characteristics	Pressures	Characteristics	Pressures
A Strategic orientation	Driven by perception of opportunity	Diminishing opportunities Rapidly changing technology, consumer economics, social values, and political rules	Driven by controlled resources	Social contracts Performance measurement criteria Planning systems and cycles
B Commitment to seize opportunities	Revolutionary, with short duration	Action orientation Narrow decision windows Acceptance of reasonable risks Few decision constituencies	Evolutionary, with long duration	Acknowledgment of multiple constituencies Negotiation about strategic course Risk reduction Coordination with existing resource base
C Commitment of resources	Many stages, with minimal exposure at each stage	Lack of predictable resource needs Lack of control over the environment Social demands for appropriate use of resources Foreign competition Demands for more efficient resource use	A single stage, with complete commitment out of decision	Need to reduce risk Incentive compensation Turnover in managers Capital budgeting systems Formal planning systems
D Control of resources	Episodic use or rent of required resources	Increased resource specialization Long resource life compared with need Risk of obsolescence Risk inherent in the identified opportunity Inflexibility of permanent commitment to resources	Ownership or employment of required resources	Power, status, and financial rewards Coordination of activity Efficiency measures Inertia and cost of change Industry structures
E Management structure	Flat, with multiple informal networks	Coordination of key noncontrolled resources Challenge to hierarchy Employees' desire for independence	Hierarchy	Need for clearly defined authority and responsibility Organizational culture Reward systems Management theory

Source: Howard H. Stevenson and David E. Gumpert, "The Heart of Entrepreneurship," *Harvard Business Review* (March–April 1985).

"their preoccupation with control affects their ability to take direction or give it appropriately."[43] Indeed, "many entrepreneurs are misfits who need to create their own environment." They tend to distrust others, and the whole world as well, often thinking of themselves always victims of convention-bound thinking or bureaucratic inertia.

[43] Ibid., p. 161.

PRINCIPAL BARRIERS / TYPE OF START-UP	A. Lack of a Viable Concept	B. Lack of Market Knowledge	C. Lack of Technical Skills	D. Lack of Seed Capital	E. Lack of Business Knowhow	F. Complacency: Lack of Motivation	G. Social Stigma	H. Job "Lock-ins" "Golden Handcuffs"	I. Time Pressures, Distractions	J. Legal Constraints, Regulations	K. Monopoly, Protectionism	L. Inhibitions Relating to Patents
WHOLESALE TRADE		✓			✓	✓			✓			
RETAIL TRADE	✓				✓	✓	✓		✓			
SERVICE	✓				✓	✓	✓		✓	✓	✓	
HIGH TECHNOLOGY	✓	✓	✓	✓	✓	✓		✓	✓			✓
PROPRIETARY (OTHER) MFG.	✓	✓	✓	✓	✓	✓			✓			✓
NONPROPRIETARY (OTHER) MFG.			✓			✓		✓	✓			
CONSTRUCTION						✓			✓	✓	✓	

Source: Karl H. Vesper, *Entrepreneurship and National Policy* (1983). Walter E. Heller International Corporation Institute for Small Business.

FIGURE 22-4 BARRIERS AND TYPES OF START-UPS THEY TEND TO INHIBIT MOSTLY

They tend to need reinforcement—a need "to show others that they amount to something, that they cannot be ignored."[44]

ILLUSTRATIVE CASE STUDY Wrap-Up

Start-Up Pains at Nova Pharmaceutical Corporation

Managers at Nova must plan, organize, lead, and control just like their counterparts in large organizations. The management process can be easier, on the one hand, since there are fewer long-standing organizational barriers in place; on the other hand, managerial efficiency suffers from a lack of organizational experience. Operations that are routine at large organizations must be constantly reinvented or modified at smaller ones. In order to hasten the influx of experienced management personnel, Nova's founders have cleverly resorted to recruiting managerial talent from the same companies with which they hope to compete. Too often, entrepreneurs fail to pay sufficient attention to the managerial process, hoping that innovation and technical ingenuity will carry the day. Such a route is littered with failures.

Will Nova be the IBM or Genentech or Apple Computer of the 1990s? It is too early to tell. But by paying attention to *both* scientific and managerial fundamental principles, Nova clearly intends to take advantage of its opportunity. ■

[44]Ibid., p. 163.

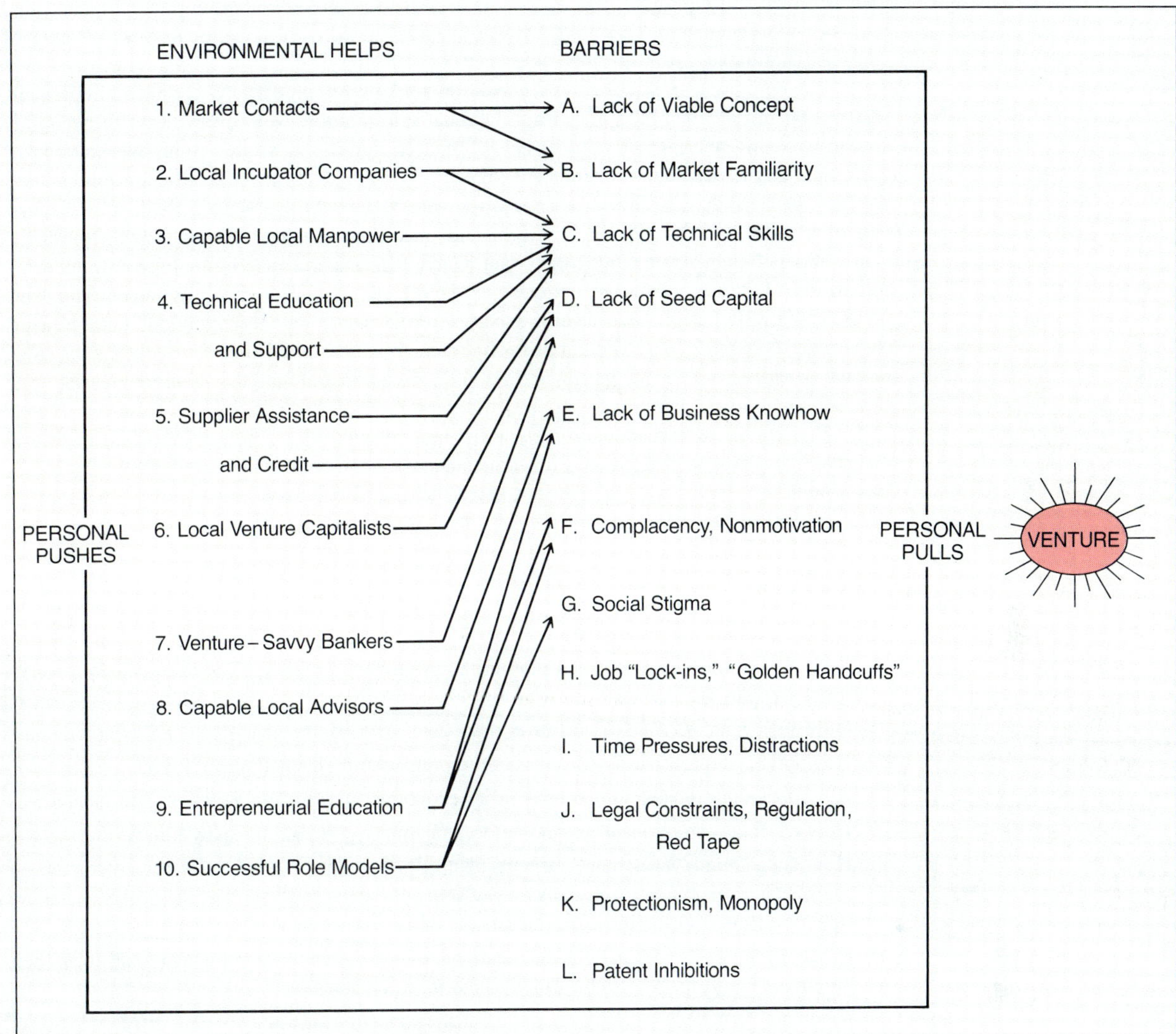

Source: Karl H. Vesper, *Entrepreneurship and National Policy* (1983). Walter E. Heller International Institute for Small Business.

FIGURE 22-5 BARRIERS TO ENTREPRENEURSHIP

SUMMARY

The function specific to entrepreneurs is the ability to take factors of production and use them to produce new goods or services. Entrepreneurs often play other roles, especially those of capitalists and managers. Economic and noneconomic conditions can affect a society's level of entrepreneurship. The economic factors include market incentives and a sufficient stock of capital, as well as the disposition of banks. Noneconomic conditions include cultural values and legal protections for individual rights.

During the 1960s, economists tended to underrate entrepreneurship. In the 1970s, however, the mood changed as economists became more interested in the supply of goods and services—the entrepreneur's sphere. One reason economists changed their minds is that small new firms provide most new jobs. Another is the growing recognition of entrepreneurship's role in raising productivity and promoting economic innovation.

The most important theory of entrepreneurship's psychosocial roots was put forward by McClelland. He found that certain kinds of people, especially those who become entrepreneurs, have a high need for achievement and that some societies produce more people with this need than do others. In the mid-1980s, Begley and Boyd studied the literature on the psychosocial roots of entrepreneurship, finding that it was also associated with such dimensions as "locus of control," willingness to take risks, tolerance for ambiguity, and Type A behavior.

The entrepreneurial role can be played in any kind of company. Corporate entrepreneurship is sometimes called intrapreneuring. Drucker says that there are several ways of becoming an entrepreneur: entering a line of business "fustest with the mostest," "creative imitation," and "entrepreneurial judo." Companies do not take advantage of obvious opportunities, says Drucker, because they are prone to certain vices: the NIH syndrome, getting involved in the high end of a business, charging high prices, and maximizing rather than optimizing products.

Older, larger organizations that want to innovate must change by making entrepreneurs role models. Drucker believes that companies should not mix managerial units and entrepreneurial ones, innovate outside their area of expertise, or attempt to buy their way into entrepreneurship. Since companies may contain both entrepreneurial and established units, they must often embody what Howard H. Stevenson and David E. Gumpert call both the "entrepreneurial" and the "administrative" cultures.

Barriers to entrepreneurship include the lack of good ideas, market knowledge, general business know-how, and the money to start a business. Entrepreneurs have a definite personality type, including "personality quirks that make them hard people to work with." They have a need for control, and at times this prevents them from working effectively with others.

REVIEW QUESTIONS

1. What function do entrepreneurs play in the productive process? How does this role sometimes overlap with others?
2. How do societies sometimes differ in the extent to which they encourage entrepreneurship?
3. How have scholarly attitudes toward entrepreneurship changed since 1960?
4. How does entrepreneurship contribute to economic growth, productivity, and change?
5. How can one entrepreneurial innovation sometimes give rise to many others.
6. How does David McClelland's theory of need-achievement account for the emergence of individual entrepreneurs? How have McClelland's ideas evolved over the years? What are other psychosocial theories of entrepreneurship?
7. What are the decisions that entrepreneurs have to make about the organizational form their ventures should have? How do they make these decisions?
8. What are Drucker's entrepreneurial strategies and the advantages and disadvantages of each?
9. Why does Drucker, unlike Burgelman, think that entrepreneurial ventures must always be kept separate from a company's conventional units?
10. How do the "entrepreneurial" and the "administrative" corporate cultures differ?
11. What problems, both internal and external, do entrepreneurs face?

CASE STUDY Space Saving and Cost Cutting at Associated Video Hut, Inc.

For Todd W. LeRoy and Michael L. Atkinson, success working for others in the financial-services industry on Wall Street did not dampen the entrepreneurial spirit they had grown up with. In 1986, while actively brainstorming for ideas that would help them launch a new venture, the duo came up with a novel way of conducting the video-rental business.

In a market which appeared to be saturated with thousands of independent mom-and-pop and franchised outlets—and in which price competition put a good amount of pressure on profit margins—it was difficult to believe that one more chain could distinguish itself on the industry. The two decided, however, that there was a lot of fat in the operations of existing video stores. For example, a trade association survey reported that the average video store in 1986 covered 2,089 square feet and stocked 3,478 tapes. On average, the tapes included 2,417 different titles, but rented just 12 percent of those every day, with the remaining 88 percent of the inventory sitting on the shelves.

LeRoy and Atkins realized that conventional stores paid huge overhead to house tapes that they did not rent very often and, also, that the majority of videophiles wanted new releases rather than movies that had gone out of fashion. They thus conceived the idea of small, inexpensive video stores that carried 10 to 25 copies each of current hot titles and formed a new company—Associated Video Hut, Inc., d/b/a Video's 1st—to franchise a national chain of drive-through, video-rental kiosks specializing in hit movies. *Video's 1st*—the trade name of the operating company—would hand over a turn-key kiosk, complete with training, initial inventory, grand opening, and adequate working capital on the franchisee's site. Each kiosk would be a Fotomat-type prefabricated 48-square-foot portable housing that could be moved to some other place if the first location turned out to be poor.

The founders expected about 40 percent of the roughly 300-tape inventory to be rented daily at $2.95 per day, giving each kiosk an astounding 24 percent profit before taxes on an annual revenues of $139,317 in the second year of operations. These figures, however, were based on an important assumption: People would pay more for convenience and selection. Price, according to LeRoy and Atkinson, would not be a critical issue.

However, crucial to the success of this venture was cash flow: If their pricing theory failed, the profit margin was likely to vanish. Moreover, it would take nine months from the time a contract was signed with a franchisee to the time that cash from that transaction flowed in. Putting additional strain on the finances of the start-up would be the investment in headquarter staff for support services to the kiosk owners.

Success of the venture also depended on operational issues like inventory management and service. Keeping only the recent hits in the stores meant replenishing the inventory every two or three months. Even if there were a big demand in the marketplace for new releases, maintaining the high inventory turn would need efficient service to customers. However, with only one employee per kiosk, and with most of the business crammed into a few peak hours on the weekends, there was a danger of loosing business from people unwilling to wait in lines like those at their drive-through banks.

These factors, while important, could be overcome with some imaginative execution of the basic concept. What worried most industry analysts was the absence of any significant barrier to entry. If these guys can do it, why couldn't anybody else? After all, as far as LeRoy and Atkinson were concerned, successful entrepreneurship required only a cheap prefabricated kiosk and a few tapes of hit movies.

Source: Based on Tom Richman, "Anatomy of a Start-Up: Drive-In Movies," *Inc.*, February 1988, pp. 42–48.

Case Questions

1. What are the risks to Associated Video Hut, Inc.?
2. How would Peter Drucker characterize the company's entrepreneurial strategy?
3. How does Associated Video Hut, Inc., create value for customers? Suppliers? Employees? Communities where stores are located? The owners?
4. How might LeRoy and Atkinson overcome potential problems?

CASE STUDY

Pro-Line Corporation Puts a New Face on an Old Industry

With $600 and a borrowed typewriter, Comer Cottrell entered the beauty business 17 years ago, marketing his own hair-care formula and building a company whose rapid growth once almost threatened its survival.

From a shoestring start in Los Angeles, Cottrell's Pro-Line Corporation has expanded into a $26 million company that has 175 employees. With its headquarters now located in Dallas, Pro-Line has become the largest black-owned firm in the Southwest. It was ranked 39th in *Black Enterprise* magazine's 1987 list of the top 100 black businesses in the United States.

Pro-Line's beauty products sell well not only in the United States but also in the Caribbean, Europe, Africa, Saudi Arabia, and the Orient.

Comer Cottrell at 55 runs an empire of creams and gels that has become the major success in his career. Nonetheless, some of his ventures over the years turned into disappointments. He struck out with a Chinese restaurant in a black section of Los Angeles, for example. And he sold his stable of race horses after he decided that the sport of kings was not for him. Cottrell has succeeded, as he puts it, in "selling hope—that's all the beauty business is."

Cottrell's decision to get into the beauty business grew out of a discovery he made some years go.

"I managed an Air Force base exchange and noticed that there were no hair products for blacks," he says. "Twenty percent of the people on the base were black. I talked to the authorities, and they told me there was no need for such products." Cottrell then asked various chemical companies if their scientists could come up with products for the care of the then-popular "Afro" hairstyle. A successful formula was developed eight months later.

Since he could not afford to pay a company in advance to make the first batch of his new product, Cottrell persuaded a small manufacturing firm to gamble on him. The company made him a quantity of what he named Pro-Line Oil Sheen hair spray. He peddled his new product to black beauticians and barbers, and he paid off the manufacturer within 20 days.

In 1975, with Pro-Line then five years old, Cottrell opened a distribution center in Birmingham, Ala., but he found it hard to obtain shelf space in area stores. The Chicago-based Johnson Products Company, the market leader for black cosmetics, had all the displays.

It turned out that the Johnson company's hard-working area manager was Isabell Paulding, who was a former Miss Black Alabama and a onetime runner-up for the Miss Black America title—and who would become Cottrell's wife a year after they met.

In an interview in the *Dallas Morning News* in 1984, Cottrell said: "I got in touch with her and asked her to tell me how she did it. She wouldn't tell me anything. I couldn't hire her, so the only alternative was to marry her."

By 1980, Pro-Line was running out of space for expansion of its Los Angeles plant. Cottrell looked eastward, where his major markets had been developed. He decided to move the company to Dallas—a move that he says nearly killed Pro-Line.

As production lines were being shut down in Los Angeles, Pro-Line came out with its Curly Kit Home Permanent. Sales jumped $11 million in 10 months.

"Here we were moving our equipment from California to Texas, and we couldn't keep up with the orders," says Cottrell. "Competitors jumped in with similar products."

When the new $4 million, 127,000-square-foot Texas facility went into operation, Pro-Line fought back to keep its market share. It is now the fourth-largest ethnic beauty concern in the United States.

Strong competition from both general and ethnic firms has led Pro-Line to advertise on prime-time television shows such as "Dynasty" and ABC's "Monday Night Football." Pro-Line purchased time in 20 of the latter show's markets around the country, says Rene Brown, the company's marketing director, in order to advertise a new product for black men. It is a comb-through hair relaxer for those with short hairstyles.

Cottrell has a group of scientists working on new products as well as assuring the quality of those he is producing now. He is cautious, however, about expanding too fast. "We make about 18 percent profit," he says. "We're working on a five-year plan. We want steady growth."

Source: Michael Whittaker, *Nation's Business,* January 1988, p. 24. Reprinted by permission.

Case Questions

1. How would you characterize Pro-Line's strategy?
2. What have been the key factors in its success so far?
3. What are some potential problems? Do you think there is a worldwide market for Pro-Line's products?
4. What are the key factors of a five-year plan?
5. How can Mr. Cottrell ensure that the entrepreneurial spirit of Pro-Line stays alive? ■

James McMullan. Poster from the musical *Working*. Courtesy of the Artist.

23

ORGANIZATIONAL CAREERS AND INDIVIDUAL DEVELOPMENT

Upon completing this chapter you should be able to:

1. Describe early career experiences and dilemmas that can influence adjustment to an organization and later career success.
2. Discuss some causes of stress in organizations and explain how stress can be managed.
3. Explain the relationship between the life cycle and the evolution of careers over time.
4. Explain what is meant by the terms "career concepts" and "career anchors."
5. Describe how an individual's position within the organization can change over time.
6. Explain what is meant by a "career plateau."
7. Discuss the various strategies and techniques that can be used to manage one's career.
8. Discuss mentoring and the special problems faced by dual-career couples and women in management.

Chapter Outline

Introduction
Early Organizational Career Experiences
Early Career Dilemmas
Careers over Time
Individual Career Management

ILLUSTRATIVE CASE STUDY Introduction

Selina Proctor: Parent and Professional

When Elizabeth screamed, Selina Proctor bolted out of bed and grabbed her bathrobe. She glanced at the clock—it was 3:30 A.M.—and at her sleeping husband, Kenneth, who had not been awakened by the piercing wail of the 18-month-old child. Elizabeth continued to cry as Selina held her closely and tried to comfort her. Selina guessed that Elizabeth was suffering from yet another ear infection—the fourth of the winter.

As she stood there gazing at the whimpering child, Selina's thoughts turned abruptly to practicalities. She knew that she would have to get Elizabeth to the doctor first thing in the morning, but she also had an important meeting scheduled for 9:00 A.M. Selina and a senior partner in her law firm were to represent one of the firm's clients in discussions about the terms of a $20 million lawsuit brought against the client and five other defendants. Because of the number of defendants, the meeting has been difficult to arrange. At last, after delays of several weeks, it was set. Selina had prepared memoranda for the senior partner in charge and was to make a presentation to all the defendants concerning the costs if a prompt settlement were not reached.

Selina realized that she could not possibly take Elizabeth to the doctor and get to work in time for the meeting. The doctor's office wouldn't open until 8:00 A.M., and the earliest possible appointment was at 9:00 A.M.—and in all likelihood, that appointment would not be available.

As a lawyer, Selina could generally set her own schedule. She felt that the difficulties she faced while the children were young could be somewhat eased if her husband were more flexible about his work and committed more energy to child care and household tasks. She couldn't tell whether his job was really as demanding as he claimed, but she suspected it wasn't. Kenneth believed women as fully as capable as men in every aspect of the modern workaday world, but in Selina's view, he didn't fully appreciate the demands of parenthood.

Selina had never missed an appointment or meeting because of child-care responsibilities. She had always been able to work things out to accommodate her clients, her employer, and her children. She was both amused and disgusted by the lawyers who worried that part-timers were likely to miss important meetings. Busy lawyers were always missing important meetings—you can only be in one place at a time, and busy lawyers have numerous clients constantly clamoring for their attention. Scheduling seemed to become a controversial issue only if children were involved. Sometimes, it seemed as if tennis matches and dental appointments received more respect that a child's needs when offered as a scheduling constraint.

Nevertheless, Selina did not want to have to miss tomorrow's meeting. She hoped that Kenneth would be able to stay home in the morning to take Elizabeth to the doctor. If he couldn't, what would she do? She didn't want to challenge Kenneth about which commitment—his or hers—was more important. A confrontation would only lead to bigger questions: Whose career was more important? Whose contribution to the family was more valuable?

It was half past five, and Elizabeth had dozed off. Selina was starting to grow weary of her own thoughts—she had been through them so many times before. Maybe she should just quit her job.

Source: Adapted from Lynda Sharp Paine, a case prepared for the Center for the Study of Applied Ethics, The Colgate Darden Graduate School of Business Administration, University of Virginia, 1984.

Working mothers face especially difficult dilemmas in career management. Most adults, however, have to make a series of tough decisions about work throughout their careers. They must select an employer, satisfy supervisors, handle stress on the job, compete for promotions, decide when to change jobs, balance their work and home lives, and so on. Many of these events and problems are predictable, so that it is possible to prepare for them ahead of time. A growing body of research on career development has given us a better understanding of how careers evolve and how career problems can be managed.[1]

CLASS COMMENT
Managing careers is a challenge for individuals as well as businesses.

In the other chapters of this book (particularly Chapter 11), we have been concerned with how individuals manage *other people's* careers or the organization's resources. In this chapter, the emphasis is on the *individual's* own career. We will describe the influence of early organizational experiences on the individual's future performance and satisfaction; the early career dilemmas a young manager is likely to encounter; the stages through which careers evolve; and, finally, how individuals can take an active role in managing their careers so that they can realize their career goals.

EARLY ORGANIZATIONAL CAREER EXPERIENCES

The Formation of Expectations

THOUGHT-PROVOKER
Why are careers important?

Many young and re-entry people, particularly women who have never worked in a formal organizational setting, are challenged and excited by their first weeks on a new job. For others, this early period is frustrating and disappointing. Some difficulties may be due to the individual's lack of information and preparation. Often, unpleasant surprises result from the unrealistic expectations aroused during the recruiting process. (See Chapter 11.) Recruiters and interviewers inflate the attractiveness of a job to secure a sufficient number of candidates in the applicant pool. Applicants overstate their abilities and understate their needs to improve their chances of getting the job. In addition, they may fail to research the organization to which they are applying. Thus, each side offers an assortment of truths, half truths, and concealments—all likely to create problems when those hired begin to work. New employees may soon learn that the initial job is not as challenging as they had expected, that their treatment will not be special after all, and that their ability to affect the organization is nowhere near what they had been led to believe. There is, of course, the other side of the coin. Organizations like IBM recruit with the utmost care, expending time, resources, and energy to screen and select potential employees. Other firms have gone out of their way to attract women and minorities as candidates for middle-management positions. Among others, they include IBM, American Express, General Mills, GTE, Hallmark, Levi-Strauss, Hewlett-Packard, Lotus, and Simon & Schuster.

The problem of inflated expectations can exist for anyone, but it may be especially severe for those young MBAs who have done particularly well in their studies and/or have graduated from prestigious business schools. They have become accustomed to fast, regular (and usually favorable) feedback on their performance and to the

[1]Robert B. Slaney and Joyce E. A. Russell, "Perspectives on Vocational Behavior, 1986: A Review," *Journal of Vocational Behavior* 31 (1987):111–173.

challenging atmosphere of the university. They expect to find the same conditions on their new job. But once on the job, they perceive themselves as just additional cogs in a wheel—their skills and abilities unused and unsought.[2]

An individual whose expectations are inconsistent with the realities of a new job is not likely to develop an effective and satisfying work role in the organization. Edgar Schein found that almost 75 percent of one sample of MBA graduates changed jobs at least once over a five-year period.[3] He also found that within five years most companies lose over half of the college graduates they hire. Schein attributes this high turnover to the clash between the graduates' expectations and the realities of the organization. Similarly, in their study of a small group of American business school graduates working in South America, John D. Aram and James A. F. Stoner found that job continuation and satisfaction were related to how closely the graduates' initial expectations matched the realities of their jobs.[4]

The Reality Shock Syndrome. Apparently, for many individuals the disparity between initial job expectations and the hard realities of the job can be unpleasant and disconcerting. This clash between high expectations and frustrating on-the-job experiences has been characterized by Douglas T. Hall as "reality shock."[5] As Exhibit 23-1 shows, Hall suggests that reality shock produces a **syndrome of unused potential,** or **reality shock syndrome,** in new job recruits.

syndrome of unused potential, or **reality shock syndrome** According to Hall, an individual's reaction to the difference between high job expectations and the frustrating day-to-day realities of the workplace.

A particularly powerful cause of the reality shock syndrome is the realization by new employees that they must conform to the established procedures and practices of the organization far more than they had anticipated. Each organization attempts to "socialize" its new employees to its values, norms, and behavior patterns—that is, to its *culture*. A conservative organization, for example, may have fairly strict dress codes, an aggressively managed organization may have comparatively high sales quotas, a rigidly structured organization may limit the amount of communication between departments. To get ahead in the organization, or even to fit comfortably within it, new employees soon discover they must conform to these previously established patterns. New entrants may also discover that many of their ideas and innovations are strongly resisted. Organizations are usually much slower to change than new recruits expect, and even good suggestions are frequently ignored. Given these realities, it is hardly surprising that so many newcomers leave their first jobs a few months or a few years after they have been hired.[6]

FOR DISCUSSION

Ask students if they have had any of these experiences. Would they be willing to share it with the class? If you have had any of these experiences, share it.

The Realistic Job Preview. To create more realistic expectations, some organizations give applicants and new employees a **realistic job preview (RJP),** which describes positive *and* negative aspects of the position. For example, recruits might be told that they will be supervised quite closely in their first job, rather than being given a large amount of independence, or that some aspects of their jobs will be boring. James A. Breaugh's four criteria for improving RJPs are listed in Exhibit 23-2.

realistic job preview (RJP) Description provided by the organization to applicants and new employees that summarizes both the positive and negative aspects of the job.

---

[2]See Lyman W. Porter, Edward E. Lawler III, and J. Richard Hackman, *Behavior in Organizations* (New York: McGraw-Hill, 1975), pp. 131–136, 172–178.

[3]Edgar H. Schein, "The First Job Dilemma," *Psychology Today,* March 1968, pp. 22–37.

[4]John D. Aram and James A. F. Stoner, "Development of an Organizational Change Role," *Journal of Applied Behavioral Science* 8, no. 4 (October–November–December 1972):438–449. See also John Paul Kotter, "The Psychological Contract: Managing the Joining-Up Process," *California Management Review* 15, no. 3 (Spring 1973):91–99. For a thorough discussion of the process of entering an organization, see John P. Wanous, *Organizational Entry: Recruitment, Selection, and Socialization of Newcomers* (Reading, Mass.: Addison-Wesley, 1980).

[5]For a recent set of articles by the leading thinkers on career development, see Douglas Hall and Associates, *Career Development in Organizations* (San Francisco: Jossey/Bass, 1986).

[6]John Van Maanen and Edgar H. Schein, "Toward a Theory of Organizational Socialization," in Barry M. Staw, ed., *Research in Organizational Behavior,* vol. 1 (Greenwich, Conn.: JAI Press, 1979), pp. 209–264; and Wanous, *Organizational Entry,* pp. 167–198.

EXHIBIT 23-1 HALL'S SIX FACTORS IN "REALITY SHOCK SYNDROME"

1. *Low initial challenge.* Recruiters often overstate the promise and challenge of the first job in order to attract the most promising candidates. Most organizations, however, start new employees on comparatively easy projects and only gradually increase the difficulty of the projects as the recruits gain training and experience.'
2. *Low self-actualization satisfaction.* The recruiter may promise growth and self-fulfillment on the job. Often, however, the organization rewards conformity to its customs and ways of doing things. Recruits who desire more independence may choose to look for another opportunity soon.
3. *Lack of performance appraisal.* Most organizations promise new recruits regular feedback on their performance. Most managers favor such feedback and believe that performance appraisal is necessary to motivate and train new employees. However, many managers perform the appraisal task poorly or neglect it entirely. Young recruits are left in a state of confusion about how well they are doing and what they need to do to improve.
4. *Unrealistically high aspirations.* New college graduates and MBAs begin work eager to apply the modern skills and techniques they have been taught. Many such graduates believe that they already have the ability to perform at managerial levels well above their entry position. In fact, they are generally unskilled in the practical applications of the techniques they have learned in school, and their high aspirations and "classroom theories" are often resented by others in the organization. Superiors will generally not appreciate learning that a skill they have been using is outdated. The fact that others do not rate them quite as highly as they rate themselves comes as a rude awakening to many young employees.
5. *Inability to create challenge.* When experienced individuals are given unchallenging jobs, they can often create challenge for themselves—by doing the job in a new and better way, for example, or by asking for additional assignments. Recent graduates, however, accustomed to having challenging assignments presented to them, may have little or no experience in creating challenge on their own; they may therefore accept dull assignments passively.
6. *Threats to superiors.* Often, newcomers fresh out of college or graduate school bring more technical expertise to a job than their superiors possess and may also be entering the organization at a much higher salary than the superior initially received. For these reasons, the young recruits may be regarded as threats, and the relationship between superiors and the new employees can become somewhat strained.

Source: Douglas. T. Hall, *Careers in Organizations* (Pacific Palisades, Calif.: Goodyear, 1976).

EXHIBIT 23-2 BREAUGH'S FOUR-POINT CRITERIA FOR IMPROVING RJPs

1. By creating more realistic expectations, RJPs reduce the chances that employees will later be disappointed.
2. By letting candidates know what types of problems are expected, RJPs may improve their ability to resolve the problems.
3. By creating an atmosphere of honesty, RJPs may improve employees' commitment to the organization because they feel that they made informed decisions, rather than being tricked or misled.
4. By describing jobs realistically, RJPs increase the chances that inappropriate candidates will turn down jobs that would not meet their needs.

Source: James A. Breaugh, "Realistic Job Previews: A Critical Appraisal and Future Research Directions," *Academy of Management Review* 8, no. 4 (October 1983).

Studies of the effectiveness of RJPs have yielded mixed results. Some indicate that RJPs produce more realistic job expectations and decreased job turnover,[7] while others find that they have no significant impact.[8] This lack of clarity results in part

---

[7]See, for example, John P. Wanous, "Effects of a Realistic Job Review on Job Acceptance, Job Attitudes, and Job Survival," *Journal of Applied Psychology* 58, no. 3 (December 1973):327–337; Wanous, *Organizational Entry*, pp. 37–84; and Bernard L. Dugoni and Daniel R. Ilgen, "Realistic Job Previews and the Adjustment of New Employees," *Academy of Management Journal* 24, no. 3 (September 1981):579–591.

[8]See Donald P. Schwab, "Review of Wanous, *Organizational Entry*," *Personnel Psychology* 34 no. 1 (Spring 1981):167–170; and Breaugh, "Realistic Job Previews," p. 612.

from the difficulty of conducting such research on organizational setting and also from variations in the ways RJPs are actually conducted. Whether or not formal previews produce the benefits claimed in some research, it is probably desirable for recruiters and interviewers to try to give a balanced picture of the job and the organization when they are negotiating with potential recruits.

Early Job Experiences

COORDINATED RESOURCE

See "Love, Don't Lose the Newly Hired," *Fortune*, 6/6/88, pp. 271–274.

Three aspects of the individuals's early job experiences seem especially relevant to subsequent career success: the amount of challenge in the first assignment, the actions of the first supervisor, and how well the individual fits into the organizational culture.

Initial Job Assignment. The importance of the initial job assignment has been affirmed by a number of research studies. One study of 1,000 recent college graduates hired by a large manufacturing company found that about half had left the company within a three-year period. Those graduates who had left the company, as well as those who had remained, cited the lack of job challenge as the major cause of disenchantment with the firm.[9] In the study discussed in Chapter 11, David E. Berlew and Douglas T. Hall followed the careers of 62 junior executives over the first five years of employment.[10] The researchers found that the degree of challenge the junior executives were given in their first jobs correlated closely with how successfully they performed subsequent assignments and with how rapidly their careers advanced.

Berlew and Hall suggest that the successful accomplishment of challenging tasks causes individuals to internalize high performance standards, which are then applied to future work tasks. In addition, successful task accomplishment causes the organization's expectations to increase so that individuals are given more difficult and challenging assignments. Those who are given unchallenging jobs, on the other hand, neither internalize high standards nor receive as much recognition for their work. Yet, despite the evident importance of challenging job assignments, many organizations continue to provide their new employees with relatively routine initial assignments.

Actions of the First Supervisor. The influence of the first supervisor on a new employee's subsequent performance has also been noted by a number of researchers.[11] For the newcomer, the first supervisor embodies the virtues and defects of the organization itself. If the supervisor is found wanting by the new employee, the organization may be regarded as an undesirable place to work. Nevertheless, many companies often entrust the handling of incoming graduates to men and women who have not trained for the task and who are not especially good managers. Other companies—including Merck Pharmaceuticals and Philip Morris—have been noted for their willingness and ability to recruit, develop, and retain new employees through programs designed to assist managers in the integration of newcomers.

Special training, patience, and insight are required by supervisors of new employees for a number of reasons. First, new employees are likely to make a higher-than-average number of mistakes; impatient supervisors may overreact to these mis-

---

[9]Marvin D. Dunnette, Richard D. Arvey, and Paul A. Banas, "Why Do They Leave?" *Personnel* 50, no. 3 (May–June 1973):25–39.

[10]David E. Berlew and Douglas T. Hall, "The Socialization of Managers: Effects of Expectations on Performance," *Administrative Science Quarterly* 11, no. 2 (September 1966):207–223.

[11]See, for example, Schein, "The First Job Dilemma"; J. Sterling Livingston, "Pygmalion in Management," *Harvard Business Review* 47, no. 4 (July–August 1969):81–89; and Douglas W. Bray, Richard J. Campbell, and Donald Grant, *Formative Years in Business* (New York: Wiley, 1974), p. 73.

ETHICS IN MANAGEMENT

THE ART OF WRITING A RÉSUMÉ

You are beginning a job search. Perhaps you are frustrated with your present job, or maybe you are just graduating from school and seeking a new and exciting position. One of your first tasks is to write a résumé. There are shelves of books available to help you, as well as services that will advise you, do your typing, and even print out your final copy. In the end, however, the responsibility for the content of the résumé rests with you. What will you say? How will you present your qualifications?

Regardless of the source, much of the professional advice you get will be virtually identical. Everyone says, "Use action verbs" and "Present accomplishments, not just duties." People tell you to "Use numbers to back up your assertions" and "Show a progression of responsibility." Nevertheless, such advice is generally solid, and it will quickly become apparent that you are not simply cataloging your qualifications. The process of writing a résumé is not as easy as it may first appear.

Your résumé is important: This single page can make or break your search for a new career. If it does not make a good impression, you probably won't even get invited for an interview. Employers use the résumé to screen hundreds of prospective employees and pare the list down to the 10 or 20 they want to interview. During this process, the average résumé is only examined for about 30 seconds—a very short time in which to make your presentation and convince someone who does not know you that you are worthy of further consideration. Small wonder, then, that writing that résumé is an important and high-pressure start on a career.

Applicants must search for just the right words to describe their experience and education, trying to find the key to passing the first screen. Given the importance of the document, it is not surprising that some candidates go beyond "dressing up" résumés with over-embellished prose to inserting complete falsehoods. Degrees from colleges attended only briefly, if at all, and positions never held appear more frequently than most people realize. To combat this, many employers now use certification services to check the accuracy of the résumés they receive. Obviously, an inaccurate résumé normally precludes further consideration, and even if it lands you the job, eventual discovery can result in charges of fraud.

But what about the vast gray area between complete honesty and blatant lies? When do action verbs and embellished accomplishments distort the real picture? How much difference is there between "*contributed to* the budget report" and "*wrote* the budget report"? Between "*part of a team* to establish a new program to . . ." and "*established* a new program to . . ."? Just when does the process—not to mention the natural inclination and practical necessity—of presenting yourself in the best possible light become dishonest?

Source: William Bryant Logan, "Detective Story," *Venture,* September 1987, p. 124; "Certified Résumés Eliminate Hiring Fears," *Chain Store Age Executive,* June 1987, p. 68.

takes and weaken the new employees' self-image and enthusiasm. Second, insecure supervisors often control new employees too closely—either to keep them from making mistakes or to keep them from appearing too successful or knowledgeable. The result is that the employees are not permitted to learn from their mistakes and may not achieve recognition for their successes.

Finally, and most important, the expectations of supervisors affect new employee's attitudes and performance, since the employees will tend to fulfill those expectations regardless of their actual ability.[12] If, for example, the supervisor looks upon the newcomers as potentially outstanding performers, he or she will treat them accordingly, thereby motivating them to do their best—and the supervisor's expectation will tend to be confirmed. Conversely, a supervisor who expects newcomers to perform poorly will communicate these expectations directly or indirectly, thereby triggering the indifferent performance that fulfills the negative expectation.

HERE'S AN EXAMPLE

Should you take a chance on a job in a family-owned company? If you do decide, be aware of the potential pitfalls. Get deals in writing, be flexible and diplomatic, don't be a mediator in family squabbles, etc. (*Business Week,* 7/11/88, p. 109)

How Individuals Fit in the Organizational Culture. As noted in earlier chapters, every organization has a culture—a set of shared understandings that determine the organization's style of work, attitude toward employees, and approach to how tasks should be accomplished. In one job, a newcomer may feel comfortable from the outset. He or she speaks the same language co-workers do and gets good responses to early efforts and initiatives. In another job, a clash of styles is evident from the beginning or soon emerges. The congruence between individual style and an organization's culture has an early impact that may color the individual's whole experience with the organization. It helps determine how well employees are likely to perform, how much they will enjoy working in the organization, and whether they are likely to want to stay.

A fit that is initially less than perfect does not necessarily mean that a person is in the wrong job. The individual will make adjustments as he or she is socialized into the organization's practices. Indeed, adjustments of this sort are likely even when the employee and the organization are very compatible. If the initial fit is good, these adjustments will tend to be small and painless for both the individual and his or her co-workers. On the other hand, attempts to make major changes can be traumatic and are relatively unlikely to be successful. Of course, the organization may also make adjustments to accommodate the individual, but such adjustments are normally small in magnitude and slow in coming.[13]

EARLY CAREER DILEMMAS

HERE'S AN EXAMPLE

This poem was written by a sales clerk in H. J. Heinz, the food processing company, in its Australian subsidiary:

Whither
I am still waiting . . .
What for—I don't know;
So, how will anybody else.
However,
I guess
It will soon be over
Then, I'll start waiting again.
Wondering
What I'll be doing
Whom I'll be with
to share the uncertainty,
Expounding the myth—
And continue wondering . . .
Where am I headed?

(''Career Development Is for Everyone,'' by Abbe Brown, *Personnel Administrator,* March 1986, p. 47)

Based on a review of the literature and on an analysis of his own interviews with hundreds of young managers, Ross A. Webber has pinpointed three classes of career problems that typically plague managers early in their working lives: political insensitivity and passivity, loyalty dilemmas, and personal anxiety.[14] Webber suggests that awareness of these problems may keep their potentially damaging consequences to a minimum.

Political Insensitivity and Passivity

As we saw in Chapter 10, the struggle for and exercise of power are inevitable and probably essential parts of organizational life. Managers *seek* power because with power they can more easily achieve personal and organizational goals. Managers *exercise* power in order to influence their subordinates to perform effectively and in order to protect the integrity of their units.

---

[12]The powerful impact of expectations on performance has been demonstrated experimentally in research review by Robert Rosenthal and Donald B. Rubin, ''Interpersonal Expectancy Effects: The First 345 Studies,'' *Behavioral and Brain Sciences* 1, no. 3 (September 1978):377–415. See also Dov Eden, ''Self-Fulfilling Prophecy as a Management Tool: Harnessing Pygmalion,'' *Academy of Management Review* 9, no. 1 (January 1984):64–73.

[13]For an exercise that simulates how one might assess one's fit with an organization, see James G. Clawson, John P. Kotter, Victor A. Faux, and Charles C. McArthur, *Self-Assessment and Career Development,* 2nd ed. (Englewood Cliffs, N.J.: Prentice Hall, 1985), pp. 277–287,

[14]Ross A. Webber, ''The Three Dilemmas of Career Growth,'' *MBA* 9, no. 5 (May 1975):41–48.

Forming political alliances is also an integral part of organizational life. Managers who "play politics" well—that is, who skillfully gain the cooperation of their peers and superiors and who utilize that cooperation to achieve organizational objectives—help their units and the total organization perform well. People who belong to powerful political alliances can focus their energies and make decisions more effectively. A politically allied manager, for example, can get information quickly from the informal network of colleagues and can speed up the decision-making process.

Like other sources of power, however, political alliances can be used destructively. Forming a political alliance to gain dominance over another person and thereby diminish his or her influence is unlikely to benefit the manager or the organization in the long run. Using people as pawns is self-defeating because it produces resistance or passivity.[15]

When used appropriately, organizational politics produces benefits and should not be avoided. But young business school graduates are often insensitive to this aspect of the organization. They may not distinguish between healthy organizational politics and the unhealthy manipulation of power. Furthermore, the texts, lectures, and case studies on which their education is based often create the impression that organizational problems are always solved *rationally*—that objectively sound solutions, for example, are always accepted on the basis of their merits. In reality, supervisors may ignore the suggestions of newcomers because they have not had time to gain confidence in the subordinate's judgment or because they see such suggestions as threats to their position.

Confronted with these realities, according to Webber, new employees frequently become passive or withdrawn. Instead of seeking to understand their surroundings, forming their own political connections, and beginning to build a power base, young managers often concentrate on their narrow specialties and permit their careers to drift.

As new employees begin to develop their political awareness and contacts, they should build effective working relationships with a broad base of people who will help them do their jobs, rather than commit themselves to a single alliance or powerful individual. Young managers who learn to accept organizational realities as they are, says Webber, can adapt more quickly to the organization and begin to manage their own careers early.

Loyalty Dilemmas

QUOTATION FROM A MANAGER

Says an industry leader about Sam Skaggs, President of American Stores, Inc., "Any real good businessman has a streak of barracuda in him, and so does Sam. But no more than anybody else." (*Wall Street Journal,* 3/28/88, p. 23)

When new employees enter the organization, they are confronted with various demands on their loyalty from their superiors. Demands for loyalty are legitimate, because a certain amount of compliance is necessary to keep the organization functioning. However, definitions of loyalty differ and loyalty demands often conflict with reality as perceived by a young subordinate. Moreover, if taken to an extreme, meeting some definitions of loyalty can damage both the subordinate and the organization. Webber describes five common ways that loyalty can be defined by a superior:

1. *"Obey me."* Managers have a right to expect that their legitimate directives will be carried out. Disobedience if carried too far will prevent the organization from reaching its objectives. However, unquestioning obedience on the part of subordinates can lead to ineffective actions. Subordinates who know, for example, that a superior's instructions are inappropriate but who proceed to obey them out of loyalty are doing their superior and organization more harm than good. Sometimes, loyalty may even call for disobedience of an order that is unethical, or made in haste or anger. Recall our discussion of Stanley Milgram's obedience experiment in Chapter 10.

---

[15]David C. McClelland, "The Two Faces of Power," *Journal of International Affairs* 24, no. 1 (1970):29–47.

2. *''Protect me and don't make me look bad.''* Managers are responsible for and ultimately judged by the actions of their subordinates. They therefore have a right to expect that subordinates consider their superiors' reputation as they carry out their work activities and interact with those outside their organizational units. Sometimes, however, this loyalty demand leads subordinates to avoid taking necessary risks or to cover up mistakes.

3. *''Work hard.''* In the eyes of many managers, the best proof of loyalty to the organization is the willingness to work long and hard. However, if unrealistic standards of performance are demanded, morale may drop and subordinates may feel overburdened.

4. *''Be successful.''* ''Get the job done no matter what'' and ''I don't care what you do as long as the bottom line shows a profit'' are often implicit (if not explicit) in managers' instructions to their subordinates. This may cause subordinates to feel a conflict between organizational loyalty and their own ethical codes. If they disobey instructions, their careers might suffer; if they violate their ethics (or the law), guilt or scandal might result.

5. *''Tell me the truth.''* It is obviously important for superiors to be told about problems in their units—not only so they can take steps to deal with the problems, but also so they can prepare to deal with their own superiors. All too often, however, reporting a problem—especially when it is in the subordinate's area of responsibility—may cause the subordinate to be blamed or punished. In such situations, newcomers often learn to apply their loyalty selectively, putting self-protection before the needs of their superiors or the organization. As a consequence, failures may not be reported until it is too late to minimize their consequences.

Personal Anxiety

HERE'S AN EXAMPLE

A new study by Opinion Research of Princeton, New Jersey, found that one-third of the 3,000 managers surveyed reported increasing work pressure. This figure is up from 22 percent in 1980. (*Fortune*, 6/20/88, pp. 78–84)

As their assignments grow more challenging, and salary increases and promotions signal recognition of their efforts, young managers derive greater satisfaction from their jobs. Webber suggests that, paradoxically, they also begin to feel anxiety about their growing commitment to the organization. The independence and integrity they valued as students and young managers sometimes conflict with the increasing demands made on them in higher-level positions. The manner in which they resolve this conflict will play an important role in determining how their careers unfold.

Edgar Schein has described three ways in which an individual can respond to the organization's efforts to enforce compliance with its values and expectations:[16]

1. *Conformity:* The individual completely accepts all the organization's norms and values. Total conformity represents a loss for both the individual and the organization. The individual loses his or her sense of identity and initiative, while the organization loses access to the diversity of opinion and ideas that its long-term health requires.

2. *Rebellion:* The individual completely rejects the organization's values and expectations. The rebellious, extremely individualistic person either causes the organization to change or, more likely, voluntarily leaves the organization or is dismissed.

HERE'S AN EXAMPLE

Even the fast track eventually comes to an end. A lot of fast-track executives are finding themselves on a ''high golden plateau.'' Learning to cope with this or to make changes requires some inner soul-searching. (*Fortune*, 8/1/88, pp. 229–233)

3. *Creative Individualism:* The individual accepts the organization's important, constructive values and neglects those that are trivial or inappropriate. Obviously, this distinction is difficult to make. The individual's decision about which norms are important may not be accurate, and the individual may be criticized for violating even unimportant norms. Moreover, with each lateral transfer or promotion, new norms come into play while others lose their relevance. (The values of one's superior in a

---

[16]Edgar H. Schein, ''Organizational Socialization and the Profession of Management,'' *Industrial Management Review* 9, no. 2 (Winter 1968):1–16.

research department, for example, are likely to be somewhat different from those of one's superior in the sales department.) An individual will therefore have to make many choices about which values to accept over the course of his or her career. Nevertheless, the benefits of creative individualism are high: The individual maintains his or her integrity, independence, and personal sense of satisfaction, and the organization has access to the fresh ideas and objective viewpoints it needs.

Role Conflict

role conflict According to Katz and Kahn, situation in which an individual is confronted by two or more incompatible demands.

Daniel Katz and Robert L. Kahn have discussed the **role conflict** individuals experience when they are confronted with two or more incompatible demands. Katz and Kahn have identified six types of role conflict that they believe are fairly common in organizations:[17]

TEACHING TIP

Try to give your students examples of each of these. Or ask them to give examples from jobs they've had.

1. *Intrasender conflict* occurs when a single supervisor presents a subordinate with a set of incompatible orders or expectations. For example, a division manager orders a purchasing agent to buy materials immediately at a price that requires prior home office authorization and then warns the agent not to violate the rulebook regulations.
2. *Intersender conflict* arises when orders or expectations from one person or group clash with the expectations or orders from other persons or groups—for example, when a superior orders a supervisor to speed up production, and the work crew makes clear that any attempt to comply with this order will lead to serious trouble in the ranks.
3. *Person-role conflict* occurs when on-the-job role requirements run counter to the individual's needs or values. An executive ordered to bribe a domestic or foreign official, for example, might find the assignment completely unethical. Yet his or her desire for career success might make it difficult to refuse to carry out the order.
4. *In role overload conflict,* the individual is confronted with orders and expectation from a number of sources that cannot be completed within the given time and quality limits. Should quality be sacrificed in the interests of time? Should some tasks be carried out and others ignored? If so, which tasks should get priority? Dilemmas like these are a constant part of the manager's job.
5. *Role ambiguity* occurs when the individual is provided with insufficient or unclear information about his or her responsibilities. The individual is therefore uncertain about what he or she is supposed to do. Role ambiguity is often experienced by new managers who are given a set of duties and responsibilities without being told exactly how to carry them out.
6. *Inter-role conflict* occurs when the different roles played by the same person give rise to conflicting demands. The relationship between work and family, for example, has become an increasing source of tension, especially in two-career families.[18] Workers must somehow reconcile their roles as managers and as parents and spouses. The problem is that the demands of the job may leave individuals with little time for family responsibilities. This kind of role conflict can affect a worker's sense of personal and family well-being as well as his or her job performance. Jeffrey H. Greenhaus, Arthur G. Bedeian, and Kevin W. Mossholder have found that role conflict, along with other factors such as the time committed to work and the perceived supportiveness and equity of the work environment, influences the relationship between job performance and well-being.[19]

---

[17]Daniel Katz and Robert L. Kahn, *The Social Psychology of Organizations,* 2nd ed. (New York: Wiley, 1978). See also Robert L. Kahn, D. M. Wolfe, R. P. Quinn, J. D. Snock, and R. A. Rosenthal, *Organizational Stress: Studies in Role Conflict and Ambiguity* (New York: Wiley, 1964); and Andrew J. DuBrin, *Fundamental of Organizational behavior: An Applied Perspective,* 2nd ed. (Elmsford, N.Y.: Pergamon Press, 1978), Chapter 4.

[18]Francine Hall and Douglas T. Hall, *The Two-Career Couple* (Reading, Mass.: Addison-Wesley, 1978).

[19]Jeffrey H. Greenhaus, Arthur G. Bedeian, and Kevin W. Mossholder, "Work Experiences, Job Performance, and Feelings of Personal and Family Well-Being," *Journal of Vocational Behavior* 31 (1987):200–215.

FOR DISCUSSION

Why study stress?

stress The tension and pressure that result when an individual views a situation as presenting a demand that threatens to exceed his or her capabilities or resources.

FOR DISCUSSION

Why should employers be concerned with helping employees cope with stress? What can they do to make the workplace less stressful?

stressor Source of pressure and tension that creates stress.

quantitative overloading Situation that occurs when an individual is given more tasks than he or she can accomplish in a given time.

qualitative overloading Situation occurring when an individual lacks the abilities or resources necessary for the satisfactory completion of a task.

underloading Stress, resulting in boredom and monotony, produced when an individual has insufficient work to do.

Stress

Stress is created for many organization members by the conflicts they feel between their independence and their commitment to the organization, organizational pressures for conformity, day-to-day demands of the workplace, and various forms of role conflict. Young managers may be particularly at risk—some evidence indicates that young people in general are more vulnerable to stress than older employees.[20] For everyone, however, stress is simply a fact of organizational life. Fortunately, many of the causes and effects of stress are subject to change when they are appropriately managed.[21]

Causes of Stress. What exactly do we mean by *stress?* One widely accepted definition is offered by Joseph E. McGrath: ". . . there is a potential for stress when an environmental situation is perceived as presenting a demand which threatens to exceed the person's capabilities and resources for meeting it."[22] The sources of pressure and tension that cause stress are known as **stressors.**

Different jobs vary greatly in the amount of stress they generate. Physicians, office managers, and supervisors, for example, must endure a good deal of stress. Craft workers, farm laborers, and college professors, on the other hand, face relatively little stress.[23] People also differ in what causes them to experience stress, how severely they feel it, and how they react to it. Before a major exam, many students feel some stress, but some feel virtually none. Of those who feel stress, some will feel it only slightly, whereas others may be nearly incapacitated by it. Of those who feel it severely, some will be able to calm themselves using various kinds of relaxation techniques, but others will be unable to control it.

When most of us imagine a stressful environment, we envision a harried office worker, the in-box overflowing with work to be done, trying simultaneously to answer the phone, explain to the boss why everything is late, and write a report. This picture is not inaccurate—role overload is a major cause of stress at work. There are two kinds of overload. **Quantitative overloading** occurs when a person has more work than he or she can complete in a given time. **Qualitative overloading** occurs when the employee lacks the skills or abilities needed to complete the job satisfactorily. **Underloading** can also be a problem—a person who does not have enough to do faces boredom and monotony, which are also quite stressful.

In addition to role conflicts and over- and underloading, a variety of aspects of the work environment can cause stress. These include:

- *Responsibility for others.* Those who must work with other people, motivate them, and make decisions that will affect their careers experience more stress than those who do not have such responsibilities.
- *Lack of participation in decisions.* People who feel that they are not involved in decisions that influence their jobs experience relatively high levels of stress.
- *Performance evaluations or appraisals.* Having one's performance evaluated can be very stressful, especially when it affects one's job and income.

[20] Saroj Parasuraman and Joseph A. Alutto, "Sources and Outcomes of Stress in Organizational Settings: Toward the Development of a Structural Model," *Academy of Management Journal* 27, no. 2 (June 1984):330–350.

[21] Our discussion is based largely on Robert A. Baron, *Understanding Human Relations: A Practical Guide to People at Work* (Boston: Allyn & Bacon, 1985), pp. 272–302. Other general sources on stress are Leonard Moss, *Management Stress* (Reading, Mass.: Addison-Wesley, 1981); James C. Quick and Jonathan D. Quick, *Organizational Stress and Preventive Management* (New York: McGraw-Hill, 1984); and Jere E. Yates, *Managing Stress: A Businessperson's Guide* (New York: AMACOM, 1979).

[22] Joseph E. McGrath, "Stress and Behavior in Organizations," in Marvin D. Dunnette, ed., *Handbook of Industrial and Organizational Psychology* (New York: Wiley, 1983), p. 1352.

[23] Based on information gathered by the National Institute for Occupational Safety and Health, U.S. Department of Health, Education, and Welfare, 1978. See Baron, *Understanding Human Relations,* p. 301.

HERE'S AN EXAMPLE

Smoking is costly for the employer, too. A study by William Weis of the Albers School of Business in Seattle puts the annual cost of a smoker at $4,611 more than a nonsmoking employee. *(Springfield News-Leader)*

- *Working conditions*. Crowded, noisy, or otherwise uncomfortable working conditions can be a source of stress.
- *Change within an organization*. Stress can result from any major change within an organization—an alteration in company policy, a reorganization, or a change in leadership, for example.

Effects of Stress. Stress can have serious consequences for both our health and our work performance. In terms of health, the current belief among many medical practitioners is that 50 to 70 percent of all physical illnesses are related to stress. The link between stress and heart disease is well known. High levels of stress are also associated with diabetes, ulcers, high blood pressure, and arteriosclerosis. Stress can cause depression, irritation, anxiety, fatigue, lowered self-esteem, and reduced job satisfaction. Sustained over a long enough period, stress can lead to attempts to escape through the use of drugs or alcohol. It may also lead to **burnout,** which has been defined as a state of mind resulting from prolonged exposure to intense emotional stress and involving three major components: physical, emotional, and mental exhaustion.[24]

burnout State of emotional, mental, and physical exhaustion that results from continued exposure to high stress.

Salvatore R. Maddi and Suzanne C. Kobasa have investigated the factors causing some people to be exhausted and drained by stressful events and others to be stimulated and challenged by them. The ability to handle stress, they found, was a function of the four characteristics listed in Exhibit 23-3.

HERE'S AN EXAMPLE

The busiest people in business, CEOs, have both a strategy and tactics for making the most of their time. Read about their tricks. (*Fortune*, 1/18/88, pp. 88–97)

COORDINATED RESOURCE

See "Stress on the Job," *Newsweek*, 4/25/88, pp. 40–45. An anecdotal description of this article appears in the Lecture Extra for Chapter 23.

EXHIBIT 23-3 MADDI AND KOBASA'S FOUR CHARACTERISTICS OF STRESS MANAGEMENT

- Personal style and personality (how one tended to perceive, interpret, and respond to stressful events).
- Social supports (the extent to which family, friends, co-workers, and others provided encouragement and emotional support during stressful events).
- Constitutional predisposition (how robust and healthy one's body seemed to be in terms of inborn physical construction).
- Health practices (the extent to which one stayed in good physical condition through exercise and avoiding destructive behaviors like smoking).

Source: Salvatore R. Maddi and Suzanne C. Kobasa, *The Hardy Executive: Health and Stress* (Homewood, Ill.: Dow Jones-Irwin, 1984).

EXTRA EXERCISE

Identify some high-stress jobs. Some low-stress jobs. Now, interview some people who have these types of jobs. Talk to them about their jobs—how they cope with pressures, what satisfactions they get, how they would change the job if they could, etc.

In their research, the most important factor by far was a personality dimension they called "hardiness." Individuals high in hardiness were *committed* to their work and life rather than being alienated from them, had a sense of control rather than powerlessness when confronted with problems, and interpreted change and problems as challenges rather than as threats.

These three characteristics of commitment, control, and challenge led the individuals high in hardiness to think about stressful events in optimistic ways and to act decisively toward them—thus changing them in a less stressful direction. This **transformational coping** process served them well in managing their organizations and at the same time reduced the likelihood of illness in both the short and long run. Individuals low in hardiness, on the other hand, tended to think pessimistically about stressful events and took evasive action to avoid contact with them. In doing so, they were less effective managerially and much more likely to experience health problems.

transformational coping According to Maddi and Kobasa, the process whereby commitment to work values, a sense of control over work variables, and the view of problems as challenges can turn stressful situations in less stressful directions.

Managing Stress. Stress is inevitable in modern organizations, especially given the changing times that we discussed in Chapter 3. If individuals are to grow and prosper in organizations, then they must include stress management as a normal port of career

[24] A. M. Pines, E. Aronson, and D. Kafrey, *Burnout: From Tedium to Personal Growth* (New York: Free Press, 1981).

QUOTATION FROM A RESEARCHER

"I'd like to tell CEOs that they have to help these people or they will die."—Barr Taylor, associate professor of psychiatry at Stanford University (*Fortune*, 6/20/88, p. 78)

development. Perhaps the single best way to prevent stress is to pay more attention to the fit between the individual and the organization when selecting a job. Thus, career management itself can be a primary method of reducing stress.

Individuals can also actively manage their jobs to eliminate some of the overloading that causes stress. They can delegate work to their subordinates, pass some tasks on to other units of the organization, and plan carefully for periods of peak workload. There are several ways by which upper-level managers can reduce stress throughout the organization. See Exhibit 23-4.

EXHIBIT 23-4 REDUCING STRESS THROUGHOUT THE ORGANIZATION

- Decentralizing authority in order to reduce feelings of helplessness among employees
- Adjusting reward systems so that performance appraisals are viewed as fair and reasonable
- Allowing employees to participate in making decisions that will affect them*
- Improving and broadening lines of communication
- Enlarging jobs so that they include more varied activities
- Enriching jobs by giving employees more responsibility for planning and directing their own

*Susan E. Jackson, "Participation in Decision Making as a Strategy for Reducing Job-Related Strain," *Journal of Applied Psychology* 68, no. 1 (1983).

COORDINATED RESOURCE

An excellent book covering all the important theories of stress on the job is *Stress and Work* by John M. Ivancevich and Michael T. Matteson (Scott, Foresman, 1980)

coping skills training Programs teaching people to recognize and cope with situations in which they feel helpless.

Some stress is unavoidable. One of the best ways to cope is to develop the habit of viewing problems optimistically and acting decisively toward them—experiencing commitment, control, and challenge rather than alienation, powerlessness, and threat. Although Maddi and Kobasa refer to hardiness as a "personality" characteristic—and personality is notoriously difficult to change—they are optimistic about people's ability to increase their hardiness and offer some specific suggestions for doing so. Similar approaches are used in **coping skills training,** programs in which people learn to recognize and cope with situations that cause them to feel helpless.[25]

Improving physical fitness is one step in handling stress. People who exercise and strengthen their cardiovascular systems and increase their endurance are less susceptible to illnesses caused by stress.

relaxation training Popular methods including meditation and biofeedback, by which individuals learn to control muscle tension and ease the experience of stress.

FOR DISCUSSION

What can you be doing to lessen the stresses in your life now? How about when you begin your career?

Training in relaxation techniques can also diminish the effects of stress. **Relaxation training** is a popular method in which people learn how to relax their muscles—for example, starting with the feet and working toward the head. Deep breathing can also lower tension. Another technique is *meditation,* in which individuals assume a comfortable position, close their eyes, and attempt to clear all disturbing thoughts from their minds. Finally, *biofeedback* techniques help people learn how to detect and control physical changes (such as high blood pressure) that may be linked to stress. Occupational stress management programs using techniques such as these hold a good deal of promise for helping people handle stress on the job.

CAREERS OVER TIME

In this section we will help readers look ahead to future events in their careers. For at least two reasons, students and managers are often intrigued by theories, books, and

[25] Lawrence R. Murphy, "Occupational Stress Management: A Review and Appraisal," *Journal of Occupational Psychology* 57, no. 1 (1984):1–15. See also Addison W. Somerville, Agnes R. Allen, Barbara A. Noble, and D. L. Sedgwick, "Effect of a Stress Management Class: One Year Later," *Teaching of Psychology* 11, no. 2 (April 1984):82–85.

ILLUSTRATIVE CASE STUDY Continued

Selina Proctor: Parent and Professional

Selina Proctor is experiencing a number of early career dilemmas, not the least of which is a small child with a chronic health problem. Although Selina works only part-time, she is a professional who no doubt has the same high expectations as some of her full-time co-workers. Moreover, it is difficult to manage the expectations of others in a professional setting—meetings must occur when the schedule has been worked out. Given her part-time schedule, Selina had thought a great deal about her place and role in the law firm. Ignoring such warnings as fatigue, conflicting schedules, and late paperwork, she may have come to believe that she had made the culture of the firm work for her rather than against her.

Part of Selina's problem can be explained as role conflict. Being a mother, spouse, and professional is a difficult balancing act under any circumstances, and when there is a complex crisis including an important meeting, a sick baby, and a spouse who is not as helpful as possible, the inevitable results are anxiety and stress. If Selina is to continue her success, she will have to find ways of managing the stress factors in her life: As a rule, they do not simply go away.

FOR DISCUSSION

What are the consequences of inadequate career planning?

COORDINATED RESOURCE

See *Career Management* by Jeffrey H. Greenhous (Dryden Press), 1987.

articles on the evolution of careers over time. First, each of us has a career, and we can place ourselves at some stage or point in the various career models. We can consider how well the particular model describes our past experiences and behaviors and contemplate what the model implies for our future. If we accept the model, we can use it as a tool in planning our future. If we reject it, we can use it as a springboard for creating our own perspective, one that better corresponds to our own past experiences and our view of ourselves and the world. Second, the models can help us to understand others in our lives—bosses, co-workers, subordinates, parents, siblings, spouses, friends, and so on—and to manage our relationships with them.

In this section, we consider first how lives and careers evolve over time. We focus on the predictable live and career events experienced by most (but not all) individuals. Then we examine the themes and patterns that may emerge in our careers and that can help us manage our working lives. Finally, we consider the career-related roles and events that occur within organizations.[26]

Careers and the Life Cycle

The Erikson Model. Many theorists base their analysis of career events on psychoanalyst Erik Erikson's famous theory of life stages.[27] Erikson has divided the individual's life into eight stages, four in childhood and four in adulthood. In each stage the individual must successfully complete a ''developmental task'' before going on to the next stage.

Erikson's four adult stages are adolescence, young adulthood, adulthood, and maturity. (The childhood stages are not important for our discussion.) In *adolescence,* the individual's developmental task is to achieve an ego identity. The individual tries to reconcile the differences between his or her self-perception and how he or she is perceived by others. Also, the individual attempts to select an occupation in which his or her skills and interests can be utilized. In *young adulthood,* the individual attempts to develop satisfactory relationships or intimacy with others. This intimacy may involve a mate, a work group, or members of a common cause. In *adulthood,* the individual is concerned with what Erikson calls generativity—the guiding of the next

---

[26]Much of our discussion is based on Hall, *Careers in Organizations,* pp. 47–64.

[27]See Erik H. Erikson, *Childhood and Society,* 2nd ed. (New York: Norton, 1963), pp. 247–274.

"Welcome aboard, Mr. Ryker. For a while you'll be a little frog in a big pond, but we need little frogs."
Drawing by Weber; © 1981 The New Yorker Magazine, Inc.

generation. For example, the person passes on his or her knowledge and values to children or students, or sponsors younger colleagues in the workplace. Finally, in *maturity,* the person attempts to achieve ego integrity—the feeling that life has been satisfying and meaningful.[28]

The Levinson Model. An especially interesting perspective on the evolution of careers has been provided by Daniel Levinson and his colleagues.[29] Levinson studied a group of 40 men in four occupational groups (hourly workers in industry, business executives, university biologists, and novelists) between the ages of 35 and 45. He suggests that adult life involves a series of personal and career-related crises or transitions that occur in a fairly predictable sequence every five to seven years. (See Fig. 23-1.)

- *Age 17–22: Early Adult Transition.* The individual must successfully manage to break away from family ties and become his or her own person. Individuals in this stage may still be at least partially dependent financially and emotionally on their parents. Those who gradually assert their independence can embark on their careers with some measure

[28]Donald Super and his colleagues have divided vocational life into five stages: *growth* (birth–14), *exploration* (15–24), *establishment* (25–44), *maintenance* (45–64), and *decline* (65 and older). See Donald E. Super, John O. Crites, Raymond C. Hummel, Helen P. Moser, Phoebe L. Overstreet, and Charles F. Warnath, *Vocational Development: A Framework for Research* (New York: Teachers College Press, 1957), pp. 40–41.

[29]Daniel J. Levinson, Charlotte N. Darrow, Edward B. Kein, Maria H. Levinson, and Braxton McKee, *The Seasons of a Man's Life* (New York: Knopf, 1978). This discussion and many other parts of this chapter have benefited greatly from a review by James G. Claswon. See Clawson et al., *Self-Assessment and Career Development,* pp. 386–387; Gail Sheehy, *Passages* (New York: Dutton, 1976); and Roger L. Gould, *Transformations: Growth and Change in Adult Life* (New York: Simon & Schuster, 1978).

of self-sufficiency and confidence. Those who prolong parental ties, according to Levinson, often underperform in their careers.

- *Age 22–28: Entering the Adult World.* The individual has completed his or her education and begins to make commitments for the future. A life-style and career are selected. The individual becomes preoccupied, in Levinson's terms, with getting into the adult world. For those who are uncertain about the course they wish to follow, these years may be characterized by a dogged search for satisfactory career goals.

FIGURE 23-1 CAREERS AND THE LIFE CYCLE

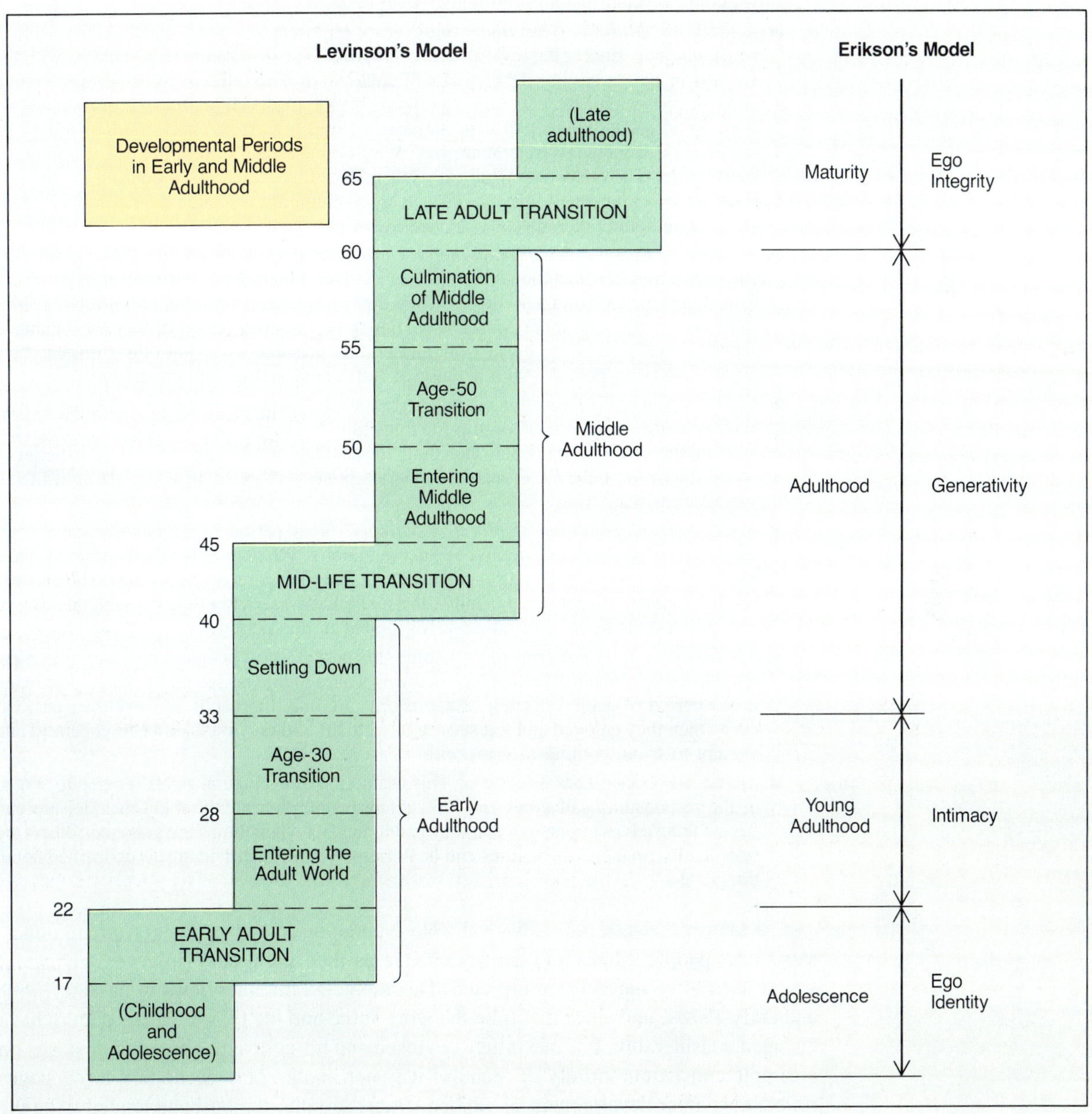

Sources: Levinson's Model from *The Seasons of a Man's Life*, by Daniel J. Levinson. Copyright © 1978 by Daniel J. Levinson. Reprinted by permission of Sterling Lord Literistic, Inc. Erikson's Model adapted from Erik H. Erikson, *Childhood and Society*, 2nd ed. (New York: Norton, 1963).

- *Age 28–33: Age-30 Transition.* Sometime during this period the individual reviews his or her progress toward previously established personal and career goals. If progress has been satisfactory, the individual may continue on the same track. If not, radical changes and turmoil may result. Moves to a new geographic location, job or career changes, or divorces are comparatively common during this stage. Even seemingly successful individuals may feel that they have only one last chance to break out of their established pattern and to do what they really want to do with their lives.
- *Age 33–40: Settling Down.* In these years, everything else is subordinated to job and career advancement. The individual strives toward becoming his or her own person. Social contacts and friendships are cut or minimized to enable the individual to concentrate on getting ahead on the job. In place of friends, a young manager may seek a ''sponsor'' in the company who will help steer him or her toward the top. Those individuals who are uncomfortable with authority figures may have a particularly difficult time searching for and relating to a higher-level sponsor.
- *Age 40–45: Mid-life Transition.* These years represent a second transitional period in which the individual again reviews career progress. The manager who is satisfied with the way his or her career has developed will continue to work effectively. In fact, a certain pride in one's achievements and experience begins to develop. But if progress has not lived up to early dreams and expectations, a ''mid-life crisis'' may result. Feelings of resentment, sadness, or frustration may cause an individual to lose his or her emotional equilibrium. The crisis may manifest itself in excessive drinking, in quitting the job and possibly wrecking one's managerial career, in flaunting a ''middle-aged hippie'' life-style, or in some other spectacular break with past behavior.
- *Age 45–50: Entering Middle Adulthood.* During this period, the reassessments conducted during the mid-life transition are consolidated. Individuals settle into their new or reconfirmed perspectives on their careers. They devote increased attention to old relationships and develop new one more consciously. For some, this is a period of increased concern about decline and constraints at work and in their personal lives. For others this can be a highly satisfying period—with a sense of fulfillment and mature creativity.
- *Age 50–55: Age-50 Transition.* In this period, issues and tasks that were not satisfactorily handled in the earlier age-30 or mid-life transitions come up. Individuals who changed too little in the mid-life transition and built unsatisfactory life structures may experience crises. Levinson believes at least a moderate crisis will occur in either the mid-life or age-50 transition.
- *Age 55–60: Culmination of Middle Adulthood.* This period is a relatively stable one, similar to the settling down period of early adulthood. Whether or not their ambitions have been satisfied, individuals must accept the fact that their careers are coming to an end and begin to prepare for retirement. Individuals who have been able to rejuvenate themselves and enrich their lives can find great fulfillment in this period.
- *Age 60–65: Late Adult Transition.* During this period, most people retire, and retirement often has a significant effect on how one views oneself and is viewed by others. For many it is a period of deep reflection. Some people are only too happy to leave their careers, even when they enjoyed and felt successful in them. Others find the transition painful and attempt to avoid coming to grips with it.
- *Age 65 and Older: Late Adulthood.* This is a period of evaluation and summing up. Freed of the responsibility of going to work, many people thoroughly enjoy their leisure and devote themselves to pursuits that they had to neglect when they were younger. Others are troubled by financial difficulties and health problems. Much remains to be learned about this period.

Levinson's work provides a valuable foundation for subsequent efforts to understand how people's lives and careers change as they get older. However, his career stages need to be carefully interpreted. He conducted his interviews in the late 1960s and early 1970s, and since that time the work force and the typical career pattern have changed considerably. For one thing, Levinson and his colleagues based their stages on a sample consisting entirely of men, so it is not known how accurately these stages reflect the career development of women. In his sample, the husband tended to be the sole breadwinner and the wife was a full-time homemaker and child-raiser. Therefore, it is not clear how well the career and life stages will fit even men in the future—as progressively more of them become members of dual-career couples. Future research may show that the career patterns of men and women in dual-career couples will more closely resemble each other than they will those of men or women in one-earner families.

Career Patterns and Themes

Levinson's work presents a model of the career and life tasks to be addressed in different chronological periods in one's life. Michael J. Driver[30] and Edgar H. Schein[31] have suggested that careers can also be looked at in terms of broad *themes* or *patterns* that emerge over time. Their perspectives are concerned with how individuals' abilities, interests, and desires influence their subsequent career patterns.

Driver's Career Concepts. Many of us share certain assumptions about the nature of careers. We assume, first, that careers involve working in an organization; second, that an individual will attempt to move up in the organization, acquiring more influence and a larger income; and third, that the person's ultimate goal is to head the organization.

This stereotypical view does not encompass all of the career patterns that people follow. Many people—even many people who have undergraduate and graduate degrees in management—do not want to become presidents of their organizations. Some do not wish to be promoted, and some wish to avoid working for an organization altogether. Driver's **career concepts,** illustrated in Figure 23-2 along with two other patterns, offer several alternative ways people may perceive their careers.

The first, or **linear career concept,** most closely resembles the stereotypical view of careers we have just discussed. The individual chooses a field early in life, develops a plan for upward movement in the field, and executes it. The movement may be up an organization hierarchy, within a professional association, or within some similar reference group.

A person who has a **steady-state career concept** also selects a job or field early in life and stays with it. Although the person may continue to improve professional skills and seek a higher income, he or she does not attempt to move up the organizational hierarchy.

Driver believes that individuals with linear career concepts are motivated by the need for achievement—"to move up and score according to established 'rules of the game'"—and steady starters are motivated by security.[32] **Spiral career concept** individuals, on the other hand, are motivated by the desire for personal growth. They tend to plunge into a new job or field, work hard, and frequently perform very well—moving up in status and rank. Then, after about five to seven years, they move into another type of work or an entirely new field that offers new challenges and opportunities to grow.

The last group, those with a **transitory career concept,** drift with no particular pattern from one job to another, never choosing a particular field and only occasionally and temporarily moving up in an organization. Driver suggests that they are driven by the need for independence and perhaps by the fear of commitment.

career concepts According to Driver, four basic career patterns—linear, steady state, spiral, and transitory—by which people perceive their careers.

linear career concept According to Driver, career concept by which an individual chooses a field, develops a plan for advancement, and executes it.

steady-state career concept According to Driver, career concept by which an individual chooses a field but, even though improving professionally and financially, does not seek to move up the organizational hierarchy.

spiral career concept According to Driver, career concept by which individuals motivated by personal growth perform well enough to advance in status and rank.

transitory career concept According to Driver, career concept by which an individual moves from one job to another with no apparent pattern or progress.

[30] Michael J. Driver, "Career Concepts—A New Approach to Career Research," in Ralph Katz, ed., *Career Issues in Human Resource Management* (Englewood Cliffs, N.J.: Prentice Hall, 1982), pp. 23–32; and "Career Concepts and Career Management in Organizations," in Cary L. Cooper, ed., *Behavioral Problems in Organizations* (Englewood Cliffs, N.J.: Prentice Hall, 1979), pp. 79–139.

[31] Edgar H. Schein, *Career Dynamics: Matching Individual and Organizational Needs* (Reading, Mass.: Addison-Wesley, 1978), pp. 124–171. For a summary of these concepts, see Thomas J. DeLong, "The Career Orientations of MBA Alumni: A Multidimensional Model," in Katz, *Career Issues,* pp. 50–64.

[32] Driver, "Career Concepts—A New Approach to Career Research," p. 27.

FIGURE 23-2 CAREER CONCEPTS AND PATTERNS

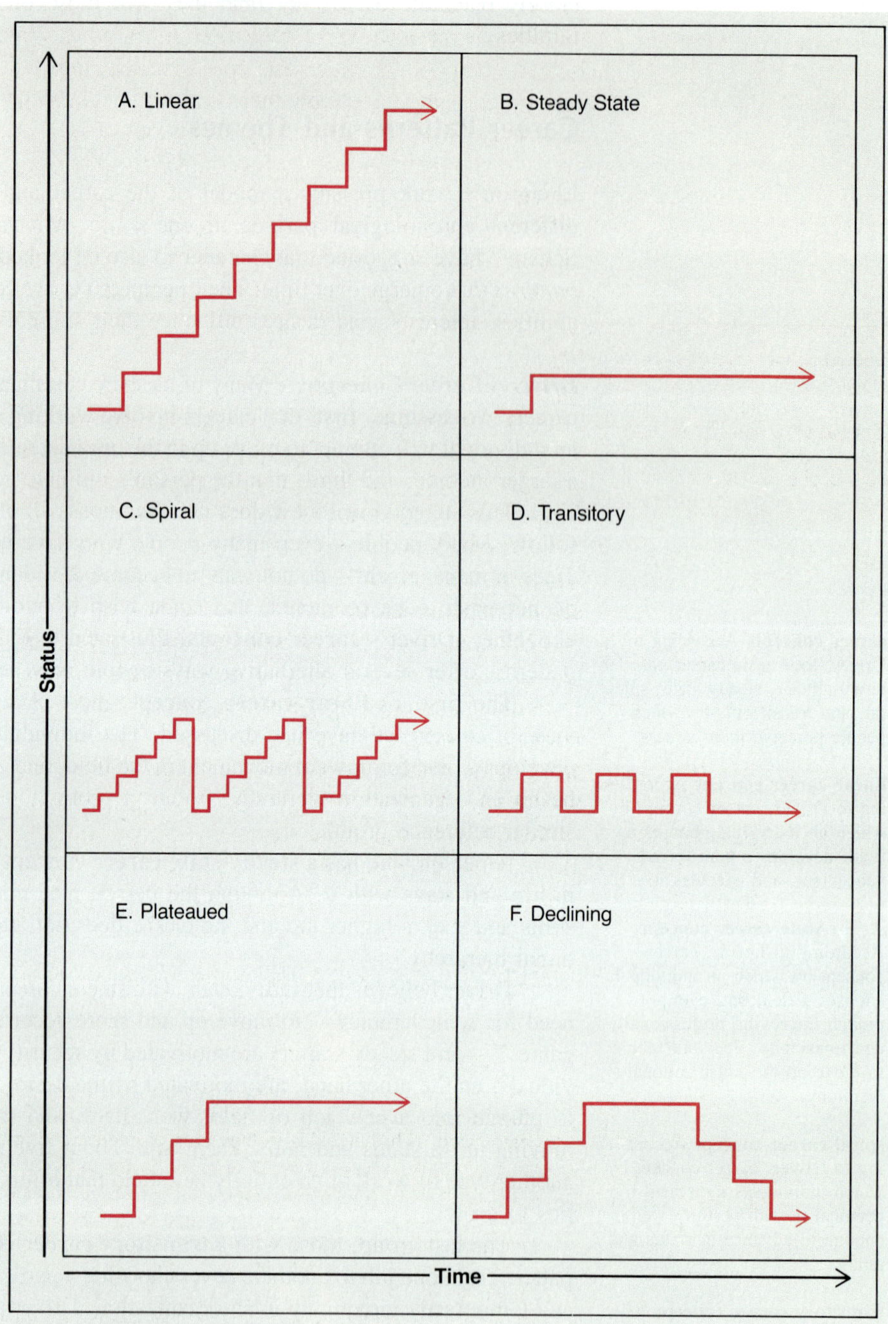

Source: Adapted from James G. Clawson, John P. Kotter, Victor A. Faux, and Charles C. McArthur, *Self-Assessment and Career Development,* 2nd ed. (Englewood Cliffs, N.J.: Prentice Hall, 1985), p. 166.

Although there is no necessary connection between a person's chosen field and a particular career concept, certain fields may tend to be associated with a certain concept. Semiskilled laborers and actors, for example, may tend to follow the transitory concept, seeking work where they can find it but rarely rising to higher levels. The steady-state career concept seems to be most common in the established professions (for example, medicine) and skilled trades (for example, carpentry). Individuals in these fields, after completing training, may become better at what they do and receive higher fees, but their day-to-day work changes relatively little. The linear concept may be most common for corporate managers and professors, among others; they begin at the bottom rung of the organization and gradually acquire more responsibility and higher status and income. The spiral concept might predominate among consultants and writers, who may apply their skills in one area and then in another. Of course, in all of these fields, there are many exceptions to the single most common career pattern.

In addition to Driver's four career concepts, two other patterns are common in careers. A *plateaued* individual has risen to a certain level and then remains at that level (this pattern is discussed later in the chapter). In a *declining* career, a person rises to a certain level, remains there for a time, and then begins a descent back to lower levels. These two patterns are also illustrated in Figure 23-2.

career anchor According to Schein, an occupational self-concept—and individual's sense of the kind of work he or she seeks to pursue and what that work implies about the individual.

Schein's Career Anchors. A **career anchor** is an occupational self-concept—a personal sense of the type of work an individual wants to pursue and what that work implies about the individual. According to Schein, people's career anchors begin to develop early in their careers, when they are going through a period of mutual discovery with their organizations. New employees gradually come to understand how they fit into the organization and how they contribute to it. They also come to understand how the organization meets their needs, interacts with them, and gives them feedback. As employees go through this process of adaptation, they develop an occupational self-concept. Schein sees this self-concept as having three components: (1) self-perception of talents and abilities based on one's performance in a variety of work settings; (2) self-perceived motives and needs based on both self-diagnosis and on feedback from others; and (3) self-perceived attitudes and values based on interactions with the norms and values implicit in the organization and the work setting. People need to work in an organization for a few years, Schein says, before they can develop an accurate sense of what they really want and where it can be achieved. On the basis of his research, he concluded that many people were motivated by one of the five factors categorized in Exhibit 23-5.

EXHIBIT 23-5 SCHEIN'S FIVE FACTORS IN CAREER MOTIVATION

1. *Technical/Functional Competence.* Some individuals "fall in love" with a particular field or function. They want to be outstanding financial analysts or first-rate market researchers. Although they may become managers, they are attracted and challenged by their field or the functional area of their work, not by the process of managing per se. Their self-concepts are associated with their skills in their area of interest and training.
2. *Managerial Competence.* Some individuals simply want to manage—and the larger the operation to be managed, the more attractive it is to them. They believe their abilities lie in the area of analyzing problems, making decisions, remaining emotionally stable, and being interpersonally competent. Their early career experiences indicate to them that they will be able to rise in the management hierarchy.
3. *Security.* Some individuals seek a secure work environment and career by tying themselves to a particular organization or geographic location. If their commitment is to a particular organization, they accept the organization's values, norms, and definition of their career path—for example, moving geographically if they are transferred or promoted. If their commitment is to a specific geographic location, they will change employers rather than move away from the preferred location.
4. *Creativity.* Some individuals want to create something new. Their fundamental need is to start something and make it a success. They tend to take leadership roles on new projects and to become entrepreneurs.
5. *Autonomy.* Some individuals simply do not want to be in an organization. They find organizational life unpleasant or difficult in some way, and they are primarily concerned with maintaining their freedom. They seek work in realms where there will be few restrictions on their ability to pursue their interests.

Source: Edgar H. Schein, *Career Dynamics: Matching Individual and Organizational Needs* (Reading, Mass.: Addison-Wesley, 1978).

Individuals with security, technical/functional, or managerial career anchors are likely to have a comfortable relationship with the organization they work for. However, those with autonomy anchors, and some with creativity anchors, are likely to be uncomfortable in any organization.

Although many individuals seem to feel that one or perhaps two of the career anchors fit their own self-perception fairly accurately, the five career anchors should not be considered a definitive list. Schein developed his concepts by studying the careers of 44 graduate management school alumni, and he and other researchers have described other possible career anchors.[33]

Careers Within Organizations

HERE'S AN EXAMPLE

Malcolm Bricklin, who is bailing out of Global Motors because of its struggling sales, has been through several failed ventures, the most memorable of which was his effort in the mid-1970s to build a gull-winged sports car called (of course) the Bricklin. Says one close individual, ". . . while he may have been short on implementation, Mr. Bricklin was long on ideas." (*Wall Street Journal*, 4/19/88, p. 42)

In this section we focus on how careers may develop *within* organizations. We will consider two perspectives, Edgar Schein's conical model and the sequential roles and relationships model of Gene W. Dalton, Paul H. Thompson, and Raymond L. Price.

Schein's Conical Model. Schein has offered a distinctive perspective on careers, emphasizing not only how the individual's behavior changes in the course of a career but also how the individual's positions and relationships within the organization change over time.[34] Schein focuses particularly on how individuals' movements through the various parts of the organization affect their actions and the way they are perceived by the organization.

According to Schein, the organization can be viewed more usefully as a cone, rather than as the traditional hierarchical triangle. (See Fig. 23-3.) The three dimensions of the cone represent the ways an individual can move through the various parts of the organization. **Vertical movement** is hierarchical change in one's formal rank or management level. **Radial movement** is movement toward or away from the organization's "central core" or "inner circle" of power. **Circumferential movement** is a transfer to a different division, function, or department.

vertical movement According to Schein, hierarchical change in one's formal rank or management level.

radial movement According to Schein, movement either toward or away from an organization's central "core" of power.

circumferential movement According to Schein, transfer from one division, function, or department to another.

Each type of movement, according to Schein, involves passage through appropriate boundaries. *Hierarchical* boundaries separate one management level from another, *inclusion* boundaries separate groups closer to the center of power from those farther away, and *circumferential* boundaries separate one division or department from another. A central concept in this model is that for individuals to cross these boundaries, they must first be accepted by the members of the group they are trying to join.

Schein describes how different individuals within the organization might move through the organization in one or all of the three possible directions. An outstanding scientist, for example, might be promoted to ever higher levels (to keep him or her from leaving for a better job) without ever coming an inch closer to the core of administrative power. Conversely, a supervisor of long standing who has moved radially toward the center of power by building good relationships with the production manager and other important managers may wield more influence within the organization than the higher-ranking scientist. Those destined for the upper levels of management may first move across a number of functional boundaries (such as production, sales, and finance) to acquire a generalist's background before they are promoted to a higher rank and allowed greater influence. Continued circumferential movement, without an upward passage through the boundaries of rank, may be the mark of an individual who is needed by the organization but who is not considered suitable for promotion.

---

[33] DeLong, "The Career Orientations of MBA Alumni," in Katz, *Career Issues*, p. 53. DeLong has noted three plausible possibilities: *identity*, the anchor for those who seek the status of belonging to certain companies and organizations; *service*, the anchor for those who want to use their skills to help others; and *variety*, the anchor for those who seek novelty and freshness in their work projects.

[34] Edgar H. Schein, "The Individual, the Organization, and the Career: A Conceptual Scheme," *Journal of Applied Behavioral Science* 7, no. 4 (October–November–December 1971):401–426.

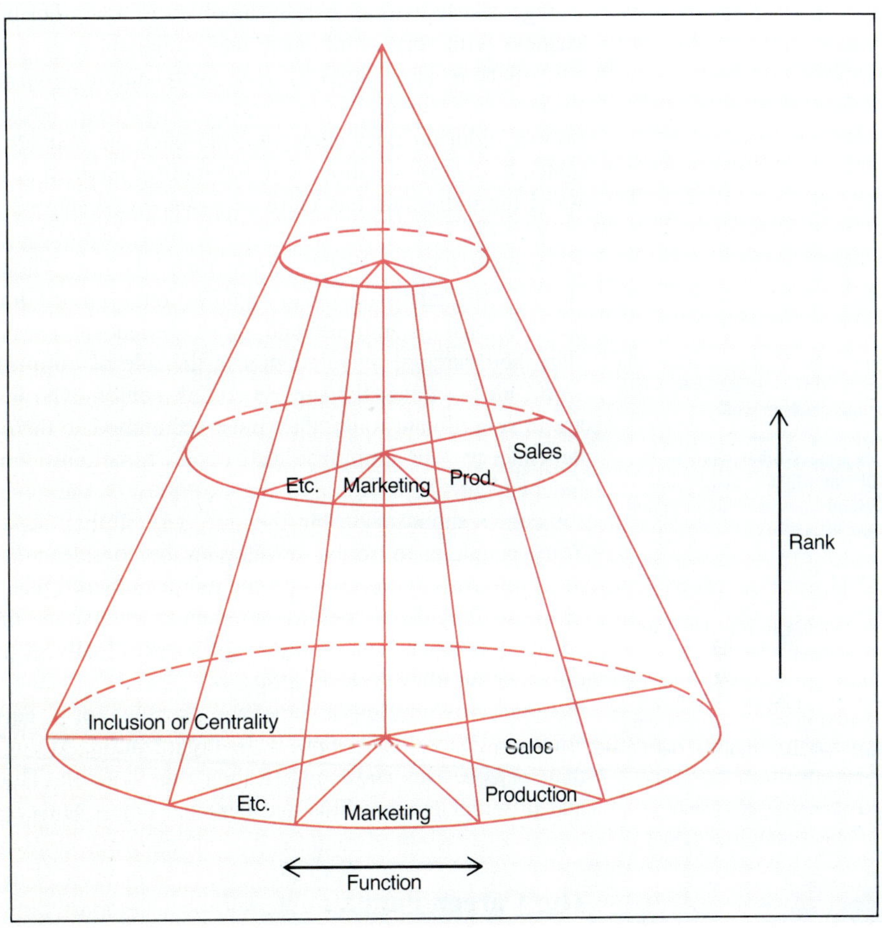

Source: Adapted with permission from NTL Institute, "The Individual, the Organization, and the Career": A Conceptual Scheme by Edgar H. Schein, p. 404, *The Journal of Applied Behavioral Science,* Vol. 7, No. 4. Copyright 1971.

FIGURE 23-3 A THREE-DIMENSIONAL MODEL OF AN ORGANIZATION

To Schein, a person's career within the organization involves a series of passages of steps from one position in the cone to another. With each passage, the organization will attempt to influence the individual, and the individual will attempt to influence the organization in return. If, for example, the individual moves radially or vertically, the members of the individuals's new department or power alliance will attempt to *socialize* the individual to their way of doing things. Acquiring the proper values and attitudes is considered an important part of a more to a higher level or a more powerful position. If the individual moves circumferentially, members of the new division or department will emphasize the *training* of the individual. Such a move requires that the individual be taught new skills more than new attitudes and values. Successful socialization or training will cause the individual to become accepted and prepared for a move to the next position.

The individual's attempt to influence the organization is termed *innovation* by Schein. Innovation, Schein believes, will most likely occur when the individual is in the middle of a given career stage, rather than having just entered or preparing to leave that stage. New arrivals, obviously, have still not become fully accepted, so they therefore are comparatively powerless to induce change. People who are about to move to another position have lame duck status and therefore less influence. At the middle of a stage, the individual is fully involved in his or her present job and can recommend changes with some confidence and authority.

Schein also suggests that socialization, training, and innovation continue throughout a career. He believes, however, that socialization and training are more prevalent during early career stages, when the individual has not yet been fully acclimated to the organization, and that innovation is more prevalent at later career stages, when the individual has more experience and status.

Four Career Roles and Relationships. Dalton, Thompson, and Price have emphasized a different dimension of organizational activity, focusing on the sequence of roles and relationships an individual may experience.[35] (See Table 23-1.) When individuals start their careers, they function in the role of **apprentices.** They do mostly routine work, ideally under the supervision of mentors who will help them learn. Since they are in subordinate roles, they must accommodate themselves to a certain measure of dependence. The employee next comes to be considered a **colleague** who makes an independent contribution to the activities of the organization. Colleagues are still someone's subordinate, but they rely less on their superiors for advice and direction. Some people have trouble developing the confidence necessary for independence. At the third level, employees become **mentors** themselves. Mentors function in a number of roles. They develop ideas and manage others, and they must learn to assume some responsibility for their subordinates' work. Finally, if they continue to progress in the organization, they become **sponsors,** upper-level managers who define the direction of the entire organization or some major segment of it. Part of their influence lies in their ability to choose key people in the organization. At this level, managers must broaden their perspectives and lengthen their time horizon. Thus, at each stage, tasks change and different relationships and personal adjustments are required.[36]

apprentice Starting worker who usually does routine work under a supervisor or mentor.

colleague Worker who, while still subordinate, makes independent contributions to organizational activities.

mentor Employee who develops ideas, supervises others, and assumes responsibility for the work of subordinates.

sponsor Upper-level manager involved in the major decision-making activities of the organization.

The Career Plateau

career plateau Career stage in which the likelihood of additional hierarchical promotion is very low.

The **career plateau** may be defined as "the point in a career where the likelihood of additional hierarchical promotion is very low."[37] The term has a negative connotation, because it seems to imply that the individual is no longer promotable because of lack of ability or some other flaw. This negative connotation, however, is derived in part from the widespread acceptance of the *linear* career concept as the only model for a successful career.

Rather than always being a sign of a personal shortcoming, reaching a career plateau is a normal organizational occurrence—it happens to just about everyone. Lack of ability, lack of skill in organizational politics, or inaccurate assessment by a superior is sometimes responsible. Usually, however, individuals reach a plateau simply because there are far more candidates for higher-level positions than there are positions available. Since job openings become progressively more scarce as one ascends the

---

[35] Gene W. Dalton, Paul H. Thompson, and Raymond L. Price, "The Four Stages of Professional Careers—A New Look at Performance by Professionals," *Organizational Dynamics* 6, no. 1 (Summer 1977):19–42.

[36] The relationship of professional and private lives of managers is dealt with by Paul Evans and Fernando Bartolomé in *Must Success Cost So Much?* (New York: Basic Books, 1980), pp. 27–41.

[37] Thomas P. Ference, James A. F. Stoner, and E. Kirby Warren, "Managing the Career Plateau," *Academy of Management Review* 2, no. 4 (October 1977):602–612. Our discussion is based on these sources: Stoner, Ference, Warren, and H. Kurt Christensen, *Managerial Career Plateaus—An Exploratory Study* (New York: Center for Research in Career Development, Columbia University, 1980); and Warren, Ference, and Stoner, "Case of the Plateaued Performer," *Harvard Business Review* 53, no. 1 (January–February 1975):30–38ff. See also John W. Slocum, Jr., William L. Cron, Richard W. Hansen, and Sallie Rawlings, "Business Strategy and the Management of Plateaued Employees," *Academy of Management Journal* 28, no. 1 (March 1985):133–154.

TABLE 23-1 BASIC STAGES, POSITIONS, AND PROCESSES INVOLVED IN A CAREER

BASIC STAGES AND TRANSITIONS	STATUSES OR POSITIONS	PSYCHOLOGICAL AND ORGANIZATIONAL PROCESSES: TRANSACTIONS BETWEEN INDIVIDUAL AND ORGANIZATION
1. Pre-entry	Aspirant, applicant, rushee	Preparation, education, anticipatory socialization
Entry (transition)	Entrant, postulant, recruit	Recruitment, rushing, testing, screening, selection, acceptance ("hiring"); passage through external inclusion boundary; rites of entry; induction and orientation
2. Basic training, novitiate	Trainee, novice, pledge	Training, indoctrination, socialization, testing of the person by the organization, tentative acceptance into group
Initiation, first vows (transition)	Initiate, graduate	Passage through first inner inclusion boundary, acceptance as member and conferring of organizational status, rite of passage and acceptance
3. First regular assignment	New member	First testing by the person of his or her own capacity to function; granting or real responsibility (playing for keeps); passage through functional boundary with assignment to specific job or department
Substages a. Learning the job b. Maximum performance c. Becoming obsolete d. Learning new skills, etc.		Indoctrination and testing of person by immediate work group leading to acceptance or rejection; if accepted, further education and socialization (learning the ropes); preparation for higher status through coaching, seeking visibility, finding sponsors
Promotion or leveling off (transition)		Preparation, testing, passage through hierarchical boundary, rite of passage; may involve passage through functional boundary as well (rotation)
4. Second assignment	Legitimate member (fully accepted)	Repetition of processes under no. 3
5. Granting of tenure	Permanent member	Passage through another inner inclusion boundary
Termination and exit (transition)	Old-timer, senior citizen	Preparation for exit . . . rites of exit (testimonial dinners and so on)
6. Post-exit	Alumnus, emeritus, retired	Granting of peripheral status, consultant or senior adviser

Source: Adapted with permission from NTL Institute, "The Individual, the Organization, and the Career: A Conceptual Scheme, by Edgar H. Schein, pp. 415–416, *The Journal of Applied Behavioral Science,* Vol. 7, No. 4. Copyright 1971.

organizational hierarchy, even highly successful managers eventually reach a career plateau.

In recent years, organizational growth has slowed, but the number of management candidates has increased. At the same time, mandatory retirement laws have been repealed, forcing organizations to retain plateaued workers for a longer time. This has caused more attention to be given to the problems faced by individuals and their organizations when a career plateau is reached. Before we discuss these problems, we should note that for the individual manager a career plateau is frequently reached at the same time as a mid-life crisis.[38] For the organization, the way in which career plateaus are managed is likely to have a strong influence on how well the organization functions.

---

[38]See Harry Levinson, "On Being a Middle-Aged Manager," *Harvard Business Review* 47, no. 4 (July–August 1969):51–60.

Management Career States. Two variables are useful in defining an individual's current career state: the organization's evaluation of how promotable the individual is and the organization's perception of how well the individual is performing at present. Based on these variables, four basic stages in management careers can be identified (see Fig. 23-4):

1. *Learners or comers*. These individuals, considered to have advancement potential, are not performing up to par at present. Not many individuals are likely to be in this category, but members of training programs and recently promoted managers who have not yet fully learned their new jobs could be included in it.
2. *Stars*. These individuals are seen as doing high-quality work and are considered to have high advancement potential. There are sometimes placed on "fast-track" career paths and usually receive the greatest exposure to management development activities.
3. *Solid citizens*. These managers, seen as doing good or even outstanding work, have for one reason or another little, if any, chance for further advancement. They may constitute the largest group of managers in most organizations and accomplish most of their organization's work.
4. *Deadwood*. These individuals are seen as having little or no chance for advancement, and their current performance is seen as marginal or inadequate. Often they are shunted aside to minor, dead-end posts and then forgotten, but sometimes attempts are made to rehabilitate them so that they become solid citizens once again.

The solid citizens and deadwood have reached career plateaus, while the comers and stars are still on an upward track. Since the solid citizens are effective, it might

FIGURE 23-4 A MODEL OF MANAGERIAL CAREER STATES

CURRENT PERFORMANCE	LIKELIHOOD OF FUTURE PROMOTION (Low)	LIKELIHOOD OF FUTURE PROMOTION (High)
(High)	Solid Citizens (effective "plateauees") Organizationally "Plateaued" / Personally "Plateaued"	Stars
(Low)	Deadwood (ineffective "plateauees")	Learners (comers)

Source: Thomas P. Ference, James A. F. Stoner, and E. Kirby Warren, "Managing the Career Plateau," *Academy of Management Review*, 2, no. 4 (October 1977). Used by permission.

seem that the only problems for management are how to speed up the development of the learners and how to "turn around" the deadwood. And the learners do receive additional training help while deadwood frequently receive special attention as candidates for rehabilitation or outright dismissal. Yet the solid citizens present management with a greater challenge than is usually recognized. Once they realize they have reached a career plateau, the solid citizens may lose motivation and gradually drift into the deadwood category—unless management takes steps to prevent this decline. The dangers of lost motivation may be particularly great for individuals who think of their careers in *linear* terms or whose career anchor is *managerial competence*.

As our discussion implies, these career stages change over time. Newcomers usually enter the organization as learners. If they perform well, they move into the "star" category and become active candidates for promotions. With each promotion they temporarily move again into the "learner" category; as they take command in their new jobs, they again become "stars." As the years pass, however, increasing numbers of individuals reach career plateaus. This may happen for *organizational* reasons—fewer job openings exist at higher levels; younger or more qualified candidates may be sought by the organization for the higher-level jobs available; or the individuals may be regarded as too valuable in their present positions to be promoted. Individuals may also reach plateaus for *personal* reasons—they may lack the technical or career skills needed to move to a higher position, or they may simply lack the desire for further promotion. Regardless of the reason for reaching a plateau, they now become "solid citizens."

Solid citizens can be productive and successful for many years, maintaining a sense of growth and achievement by seeking new challenges or by obtaining transfers to other jobs at the same organizational level. Eventually, however, age, lack of motivation, or lack of new training may cause their performance to decline.[39] In a study of middle managers at a British financial organization, Evans and Gilbert traced the decline in job satisfaction and motivation to age rather than to the person's having reached a career plateau.[40] Older managers had lower expectations of their future rewards (pay, benefits, and advancement) from the organization than younger managers—regardless of whether either had plateaued. Older managers were more interested in mentoring, a potentially beneficial but relatively unappreciated activity.

Options at the Career Plateau. When a career plateau becomes unsatisfying, managers do have some options. For instance, they can get additional training to qualify themselves for another job or promotion, or they can move to another organization with greater opportunities. Early retirement has also become more common as large organizations have come under pressure to "downsize" and "restructure." Corporations such as AT&T and IBM have begun to offer lucrative early retirement options to employees in order to cut back the size of their work forces. Thus age may no longer by the primary ground for a retirement decision. One employee of a large *Fortune* 500 company, for example, took early retirement at 34 and used the incentive package to fund an entrepreneurial business. This trend to start second careers after "retirement" adds a whole new dimension to career management.

It is important to remember that one's bosses, co-workers, and subordinates will also be passing through the various career states. Understanding the process by which careers develop and plateaus are reached is useful in helping others deal with the experience.

---

[39]See Laurence J. Peter and Raymond Hull, *The Peter Principle* (New York: Morrow, 1969). Peter and Hull suggest that the managerial career cycle ends when managers are promoted to their "level of incompetence": a job beyond their ability. This certainly does happen, but managers probably reach plateaus more frequently while they are still performing effectively and when they then can still develop and grow.

[40]Martin G. Evans and Elizabeth Gilbert, "Plateaued Managers: Their Need Gratifications and Their Effort-Performance Expectations," *Journal of Management Studies* 21, no. 1 (1984):99–110.

INDIVIDUAL CAREER MANAGEMENT

THOUGHT-PROVOKER
What's your definition of career success?

While organizations can help individuals manage their careers,[41] career management is ultimately the individual's responsibility. Conscious career management by the individual can have many advantages. Like organizations, individuals who develop plans for the future are more likely to achieve their goals. They can focus their energies on the career goals they have selected, rather than drifting from job to job. In addition, they are less vulnerable to chance events and to having undesirable career decisions made for them by others. Finally, individuals who are competent in managing their own careers and who have well-thought-out goals and plans for reaching them tend to be more motivated and purposeful then others. Thus, they are often more useful to their organizations and more likely to be successful within them.

Individual Career Planning

EXTRA EXERCISE
Know thyself! What do you want to be? What are your strengths and weaknesses? Your interests? What are you happiest doing?

The starting point for individual career planning is to understand what one wants from one's work, career, and life. (Various career planning approaches offer assistance in gaining insight into these matters.) To many people, career planning means developing a program for moving toward the top of the organization. As we explained in our discussion of Driver's career concepts and Schein's career anchors, however, planning for a linear career of this sort is inappropriate for many other individuals.

FOR DISCUSSION
What are the dangers in choosing a career goal that is not compatible with one's own goals or desires?

Realistic Career Strategies. Individual career planning can be approached like any other type of planning, although it resembles strategic planning most closely.[42] Alan N. Schoonmaker has offered a nine-step career strategy that includes systematic career planning.[43] Some of his steps sound rather harsh—in the first two steps, for example, he reminds us of certain unpleasant facts about organizational careers. Nevertheless, his strategy is basically realistic. The steps are:

1. *Accept the fact that there are some inescapable and irreconcilable conflicts between you and your organization.* In short, what is good for the organization is not always good for you. So, being careful not to be disloyal, you must always recognize the need to look out for your own interests.

2. *Accept the fact that your superiors are essentially indifferent to your career ambitions.* Your superiors are ultimately responsible only for themselves and their units; you should assume they will help you only if doing so helps them achieve their own objectives. As Schoonmaker has noted, the responsibility of your superiors to themselves and the organization would make any other attitude improper for them.

---

[41]Many organizations have developed programs to assist individuals in managing their careers. For example, under the guidance of Walter D. Storey, General Electric has developed career planning programs and a manual entitled *Career Action Planning*. Arthur D. Little uses a manual entitled *Effective Career Management*. The point at which organizations should work with individuals to develop and manage their careers is discussed thoroughly by Manuel L. London and Stephen A. Stumpf in *Managing Careers* (Reading, Mass.: Addison-Wesley, 1982).

[42]For information on developing individual career plans, see Alan N. Schoonmaker, *Executive Career Strategy* (New York: American Management Associations, 1971); Andrew H. Souerwine, *Career Strategies: Planning for Personal Achievement* (New York: AMACOM, 1978); Richard Nelson Bolles, *What Color Is Your Parachute?* [revised annually] (Berkeley, Calif.: Ten Speed Press, 1986); and Nicholas N. Weiler, *Reality and Career Planning: A Guide to Personal Growth* (Reading, Mass.: Addison-Wesley, 1977). Detailed guidance on individual career planning can be found in London and Stumpf, *Managing Careers*. The Clawson et al. text (*Self-Assessment and Career Development*) provides detailed guidance on developing a career strategy that is especially appropriate for MBA students, but many other students have also found it useful. In addition, a growing number of college and graduate schools of business offer full-credit courses in career planning and development for their management students. Schools that have offered such courses for a number of years include the Harvard Business School, Fordham Graduate School of Business Administration, and Northeastern University.

[43]Schoonmaker, *Executive Career Strategy*, pp. 6–11.

Realizing this will help you avoid being manipulated by false promises and unrealistic expectations.

3. *Analyze your own goals.* Many people act to fulfill goals they have been taught should be important to them rather than those that really are. They therefore may spend their entire lives searching for an unattainable satisfaction. To get what you want, you first have to *know* what you want. Career management does not mean simply charting a series of promotions that end in an executive suit—it means planning to achieve *any* career goal that is meaningful to *you*.

4. *Analyze your assets and liabilities.* It is unrealistic to pursue goals that require abilities you do not have; it is foolish not to take advantage of those abilities you do have. Your career goals should allow you to maximize your assets and minimize your liabilities.

5. *Analyze your opportunities.* Determine what your options are inside and outside of the organization. Systematically assess the positions available in your own and other firms. Personal observations, tips from colleagues, and published information may be useful in this process.

6. *Learn the rules for company politics.* Note what your company values and rewards and how those who are rewarded behave. Learn which people are the most crucial in accomplishing various kinds of tasks. (''Keep up a good relationship with the parts department manager and he'll help you meet your production schedule.'')

7. *Plan your career.* A goal without a plan is no better than a daydream. Many managers select goals without any idea of how they are going to reach them; often, they fail to attain those goals because they drift indecisively from job to job or stay too long in one position. Planning will help you to make better decisions at each step of your career.

8. *Carry out your plan.* The best plan is useless if it is not carried out. If your plan calls for you to ask for a raise, request a transfer, find another job, or turn down a job offer—*do it!*

9. *Chart your progress.* Very rarely does a career progress without a hitch—a sponsor takes early retirement, the job market changes, a new colleague in the same department proves to be a ''star.'' Your goals are also likely to change somewhat over time—a new opportunity, for example, may not seem attractive if you are highly satisfied in your present job. Like organizational plans, career plans have to be revised periodically to keep up with current realities.

COORDINATED RESOURCE

For a provocative look at what's going on in corporate life, see ''Caught In The Middle,'' *Business Week*, 9/12/88, pp. 80–88.

Managing the Work Situation. Once you have developed a career plan and have a job in your field, you can use a number of tactics to further your career. First and most important, you can *do excellent work*.[44] The better you are at helping your organization meet its goals, the more likely the organization is to reward you. But doing good work produces more personal benefits as well. It is more satisfying to do good work than to do mediocre work. To keep doing excellent work, you must keep learning and growing. Superior work usually garners more acknowledgment, respect, and support from bosses, peers, and subordinates. It leads to more exciting and challenging opportunities within and outside the organization. Furthermore, those who have proved their ability to do first-rate work are likely to be given more autonomy. This list could be extended almost indefinitely. Of course, excellent work alone does not *inevitably* lead to career success—your efforts may be ignored, or they may arouse the jealousy of your colleagues—but as a general rule, it is the best possible basis for attempts to realize your career ambitions.

First-rate work cannot be done in isolation. A person who performs brilliantly in some areas but doesn't get along with colleagues is unlikely to go very far. This

[44]This section is based in part on Schoonmaker, *Executive Career Strategy*, and DuBrin, *Fundamentals of Organizational Behavior*, Chapter 5.

suggests two other tactics for succeeding in the organization: *develop good working relationships* and *help your boss succeed*. It is difficult to imagine how one could truly be doing excellent work without being effective in these two areas.

Developing good working relationships is crucial to success because organizations are by their nature cooperative efforts. Ronald J. Burke notes that it's *both* what you know *and* who you know that counts.[45] To accomplish tasks, you must establish a network of co-workers—superiors, peers, and subordinates—who are able and willing to help you meet your objectives. It is easier to do excellent work if you are part of such a network (and it is easier to become part of such a network if you do excellent work). Building good relationships begins early in your career. At times it may be tempting to disagree publicly with your boss, go over your supervisor's head to a superior, engage in personal criticism, hold grudges, express hostility, or seek revenge, but such actions do not advance careers. Every bad working relationship is a lost opportunity.

Helping your boss succeed is a good way to help yourself succeed. The more you help your boss—by doing good work, suggesting new approaches to problems, and keeping him or her informed—the more valuable to your boss you will be. In fact, becoming indispensable to an upwardly mobile boss can help you become part of an "advancement sandwich," in which your boss, you, and the subordinate that you train move up in the organization together. Other bosses are also likely to find you an attractive subordinate if you have helped your superior become more successful.[46] Other techniques may be less important than those we have just described but can still be useful. See Exhibit 23-6.

Handling Specific Career Issues

FOR DISCUSSION

How can organizations help employees cope with some of these career issues?

We have been discussing general strategies for meeting career goals. Three additional topics are also of interest to new managers in considering their own lives and careers. First, many new managers will be members of dual-career couples. Such couples must cooperatively plan their careers and their personal relationship more carefully than either single people or spouses in traditional marriages. Second, managers need to understand mentoring relationships. Third, women's careers in management may require especially careful planning because women have often faced special barriers in managerial situations, and the events of their lives make some career issues more acute for them than for men.

HERE'S AN EXAMPLE

More and more kids are accompanying their parents on business trips. The kids and the parents all seem to benefit from this arrangement. Says one traveling mom, "If we want to spend time with our children, we have to take them along." (*Business Week*, 11/30/87, pp. 79–82)

Dual-Career Couples. Couples in which both partners are employed full time must work hard to integrate and balance the demands and opportunities of two separate careers. Mutual accommodation is constantly necessary on small matters. When both partners return from work tired, who will make dinner? Who stays home to take care of a child with an upset stomach? Major conflicts also arise. Suppose that one partner receives a very attractive job offer in another part of the country and the other partner is reluctant to leave his or her current job. Which one gives in? Flexibility and willingness to compromise are imperative for both the career and the relationship. Despite the extra problems faced by dual-career married couples, however, E. A. House has found that neither their marital satisfaction nor their sex-role orientations differ from that of single provider couples.[47]

As Exhibit 23-7 shows, Francine Hall and Douglas T. Hall have identified four general styles of effectively managing two careers. Each is based on the spouses' differing (or similar) degree of commitment to home or to career.

---

[45]Ronald J. Burke, "Relationships in and Around Organizations: It's *Both* Who You Know and What You Know That Counts," *Psychological Reports* 55, no. 1 (August 1984):293–307.

[46]See John J. Gabarro and John P. Kotter, "Managing Your Boss," *Harvard Business Review* 58, no. 1 (January–February 1980):92–100; and Lloyd Baird and Kathy Kram, "Career Dynamics: Managing the Superior/Subordinate Relationship," *Organizational Dynamics* 11, no. 4 (Spring 1983):46–64.

[47]Hall and Hall, *The Two-Career Couple*, pp. 232–235.

EXHIBIT 23-6 ADDITIONAL TECHNIQUES FOR MANAGING THE WORK SITUATION

- *Be mobile.* For those who aspire to top management, movement within the organization is highly desirable. Experience across the functional lines of an organization for example, will help you develop the variety of skills you will need as a general manager. Experience at different geographic locations will give you an understanding of the organization as a whole and may bring you to the attention of those at the very top. You should be aware, however, that high geographic mobility usually costs a great deal in terms of one's social and family relationships. You must weigh the sacrifices that repeated moves require against the growth potential they may afford.*

  If you are growing as much and as fast as you desire and are being appropriately recognized, then movement outside your organization is not an effective strategy. Joining another organization normally will require a whole new set of alliances and relationships. But if you are not gaining the experience and training necessary for advancement, if you have been placed in a dead-end job, or if you are not progressing as fast in the responsibility and recognition as you desire, then leaving for a more challenging opportunity elsewhere is usually a better idea than waiting for things to improve where you are.
- *Find a sponsor.* A higher-level sponsor is an organizational ally who can pass on the knowledge he or she has gained to younger employees. Later in this chapter we discuss this topic at some length.
- *Become visible.* It can be very frustrating to know you are doing good work but not being rewarded for it. To receive recognition for your performance, you have to make sure your superiors are aware of it. This can be done in a number of tactful ways. These include sending memos to a superior when projects have been completed, submitting short progress reports, and seeking evaluation and advice directly from a superior or from colleagues. Making it known that you have received and rejected another job offer is, according to Schoonmaker, a particularly effective way of getting noticed.
- *Present the right image.* When you become visible, it is important to give the right impression. Hardworking individuals who appear slow or uncertain may be perceived as lazy or indifferent, regardless of actual performance. Individuals who are eager to "belong" to the organization but dress or behave in ways that are contrary to the organization's "style" may be regarded as nonconformists or outsiders. Clothing, posture, tone of voice, and demeanor all contribute to how individuals are perceived. Some people find it phony and distasteful to try to fit the mold of the organization. However, if you select an organization whose norms and values are compatible with yours, you should have relatively few problems adjusting to its style.†

*See John F. Viega, "The Mobile Manager at Mid-Career," *Harvard Business Review* 51, no. 1 (January–February 1973):115–119; Viega, "Do Managers on the Move Get Anywhere?" *Harvard Business Review* 59, no. 2 (March–April 1981).
†Alan N. Schoonmaker, *Executive Career Strategy* (New York: American Management Association, 1971).

EXHIBIT 23-7 HALL AND HALL'S FOUR STYLES OF MANAGING TWO CAREERS

- *Accommodators.* Couples of this type most closely resemble the traditional family. One spouse assumes major (but not total) responsibility for career roles and the other assumes major responsibility for family roles.
- *Adversaries.* This type occurs when both spouses are highly involved in their careers but also value having someone take responsibility for home-related roles. There are likely to be conflicts because neither is willing or able to make the career sacrifices necessary to maintain the home.
- *Allies.* In this type, the two spouses are both highly involved in either their career or home roles and place little emphasis on the other area. If both are highly involved in their career roles, for example, they are likely to forgo having children and devote little attention to maintaining a well-ordered home.
- *Acrobats.* Couples of this sort are highly involved in all their roles. They give equal weight to both family and career, but rather than attempting to get their spouses to take over, they attempt to perform both roles themselves.

Source: Francine Hall and Douglas T. Hall, *The Two-Career Couple* (Reading, Mass.: Addison-Wesley, 1978).

As dual-career couples have become more common, organizations have become more responsive to their special needs. This may involve such changes as providing flexible work environments, revising transfer policies, offering couples career management assistance, and providing local support services, such as day care and after-school centers for children.[48]

HERE'S AN EXAMPLE

The 1988 nominees for the U.S. Business Hall of Fame have very diverse accomplishments. The nominees who are profiled include: William R. Hewlett, David Packard, H. Ross Perot, Estee Lauder, Milton S. Hershey, King C. Gillette, and Benjamin Graham. (*Fortune*, 3/14/88, pp. 142–147)

Mentors and Mentoring Relationships. As recounted by Homor in *The Odyssey,* Mentor was the servant of Odysseus entrusted with a wide range of responsibilities in the care and training of Odysseus's son, Telemachus.[49] Today, as we mentioned in the section on finding a sponsor, mentors are still seen as older, more experienced individuals who pass on the benefits of their experience to younger persons. Some observers believe that mentor relationships play a key role in assisting those who have successful careers. Others contend that they are less important and that the relationships are more complex than Homer suggests.

According to Kathy E. Kram,[50] the interactions that occur in a mentoring relationship can certainly be helpful in a person's career. She divides the functions of mentoring into two broad categories: career functions and psychosocial functions. *Career functions* are the aspects of the relationship that help the younger person learn the ropes and prepare for advancement. Included in this realm are such activities as sponsoring the younger person's career through public support, helping the junior person gain exposure and visibility in the organization, coaching the younger colleague in specific strategies, protecting him or her from negative contacts, and seeing that he or she is assigned challenging, constructive work.

psychosocial function According to Kram, aspect of a professional relationship that improves one's sense of competence, identity, and effectiveness.

Psychosocial functions are the aspects of the relationship that "enhance a sense of competence, clarity of identity, and effectiveness in a professional role."[51] The mentor's attitudes, values, and behavior provide a model for the younger person to emulate. The older person also provides support and encouragement for the younger colleague and helps him or her explore personal concerns that may interfere with productivity at work. Finally, the two colleagues are often friends who like and understand each other and enjoy each other's company.

HERE'S AN EXAMPLE

Tomorrow's CEOs are apt to be quite different from their own bosses. They have learned to operate in a business world that has seen massive changes and are the most worldly U.S. executives poised to run some of the nation's largest corporations. Some of these executives are profiled in *Fortune,* 5/9/88, pp. 30–42.

Kram's studies indicate that the mentor relationship is not one-sided. In addition to the satisfaction of passing on the benefits of experience, the mentor receives technical and psychological support from a loyal subordinate and recognized by others as effectively developing talent. The relationship can also take a number of different forms—it is not restricted to a single older person dispensing wisdom to a younger colleague. Mentor roles can be filled by a number of persons, both within the organization and outside it—one's boss, other individuals higher in the organization, co-workers, friends outside work, a spouse, and even subordinates. Attempts to identify a single individual and form a mentor relationship with him or her are frequently misdirected and unsuccessful. If one happens to find a single person with whom one feels compatible and who fulfills a variety of mentoring roles, so much the better. However, Kram says it is more important to develop a *network* of mutually supportive relationships in which a number of individuals provide a variety of mentoring functions.[52]

---

[48]E. A. House, "Sex Role Orientation and Marital Satisfaction in Dual- and One-Provider Couples," *Sex Roles* 14 (1986):245–259.

[49]We were reminded of this fact by James G. Clawson, "Is Mentoring Necessary?" *Training and Development Journal* 39, no. 4 (April 1985):36.

[50]Kathy E. Kram, *Mentoring at Work: Developmental Relationships in Organizational Life* (Glenview, Ill.: Scott, Foresman, 1985), Chapters 2 and 3. Also see Kathy Kram, "Mentoring in the Workplace," in Douglas T. Hall and Associates, *Career Development in Organizations* (San Francisco: Jossey/Bass, 1986), pp. 160–201.

[51]Kram, *Mentoring at Work,* p. 22.

[52]See also Kathy E. Kram and Lynn A. Isabella, "Mentoring Alternatives: The Role of Peer Relationships in Career Development," *Academy of Management Journal* 28, no. 1 (March 1985):110–132.

FOR DISCUSSION

Will prospects for women improve as more enter executive positions? Why or why not?

Women's Careers in Management. Women managers must confront the same challenges and issues as men in management, and they must deal with additional issues as well. According to Yount, the division of labor along gender lines has led to sex role stereotypes and to self-images that correspond to those stereotypes.[53] Part-time work, for example, is viewed as a sign of inadequacy in a man, since he is supposed to be a breadwinner. It is seen as appropriate for a woman, however, since her primary concerns are supposed to be home and family.[54] In practice, discrimination, sexual stereotyping, the conflicting demands of marriage and work life, and increased social isolation and loneliness are more likely to affect managerial women than men.[55] These factors can prevent women from entering management and may make it harder for them to do their best work when they do become managers. The problems women may face in pursuing managerial careers stem from at least three sources: (1) the woman's attitudes toward herself and her career, (2) the attitudes of the men and women with whom she works, and (3) broad organizational policies and procedures. Each source may create barriers to women's career progress and success. Circumstances in all three areas are changing, however, and in general the trend is for barriers to be reduced.

HERE'S AN EXAMPLE

Some women have beat the corporate game. They have learned to pattern their lives on those of career men and keep the top job in sight. They succeed, however, by being themselves, not guys in dresses. (*Fortune*, 9/12/88, pp. 128–138)

Women's Attitudes. Until recently, most females who were old enough to consider becoming managers had not been socialized to see themselves in managerial roles. This factor, in combination with organizational and societal barriers to professional and managerial careers, led many women to choose other alternatives. The changes in this area have been dramatic. In 1972 and 1973, for example, less than 5 percent of all MBA graduates were female; by 1981 and 1982, the figure had risen to approximately 30 percent.[56] By 1987, 33 percent of graduating MBA students were women, and the total of women in management and administrative roles had risen to 37 percent.[57]

Nevertheless, many women's expectations remain relatively low. A study of Stanford MBAs found that women graduates had lower ultimate salary hopes and expectations. In fact, on the average, women's peak salary expectations were less than 40 percent of men's.[58] Another study of educated women of all ages found that though women did not fear success, many wondered whether their achievements were worth the price.[59] These doubts and low expectations may be realistic: Women's careers often do demand sacrifices at home, and childbearing, organizational barriers, and other factors may hinder their careers. However, lower expectations may also function as a self-fulfilling prophecy, discouraging women from progressing as far as they might in their careers.

Attitudes of Co-workers. It has long been recognized that some workers are prejudiced against female professionals and managers. This prejudice is not based on the performance of women managers and professions as a group. Research shows that men and women managers are very similar in terms of attitudes, behavior, and perfor-

---

[53]K. R. Yount, "A Theory of Productive Activity: The Relationships Among Self-Concept, Gender, Sex Role Stereotypes, and Work-Emergent Traits," *Psychology of Women Quarterly* 10 (1986):63–88.

[54]A. H. Eagly and V. J. Steffen, "Gender Stereotypes, Occupational Roles, and Beliefs About Part-Time Employees," *Psychology of Women Quarterly* 10 (1986):252–262.

[55]Debra L. Nelson and James C. Quick, "Professional Women: Are Distress and Disease Inevitable?" *Academy of Management Review* 10, no. 2 (April 1985):206–218. See also Cary L. Cooper and Marilyn J. Davidson, "The High Cost of Stress on Women Managers," *Organizational Dynamics* 10, no. 4 (Spring 1982):44–53. An excellent collection of articles on the role of women in organizations is Lynda L. Moore, ed., *Not as Far as You Think: The Realities of Working Women* (Lexington, Mass.: Lexington Books, 1986).

[56]Ruth B. Ekstrom, "Women in Management: Factors Affecting Career Entrance and Advancement," *Selection* 2, no. 1 (Spring 1985):29–32.

[57]"Corporate Women," *Business Week,* June 22, 1987, pp. 72–77.

[58]Ekstrom, "Women in Management," p. 30.

[59]M. A. Paludi and J. Fankell-Hauser, "An Idiographic Approach to the Study of Women's Achievement Striving," *Psychology of Women Quarterly* 10 (1986):89–100.

mance.[60] Other research indicates that the biases against women found in earlier studies are diminishing. Hazel F. Ezell, Charles A. Odewahn, and J. Daniel Sherman, for example, report that men who have been subordinates of women managers are more favorably disposed toward them than are men who have not.[61] As women become more common at all levels of management, we can expect further changes and greater acceptance.

Organizational Policies and Procedures. Although the Reagan administration was not as aggressive as some previous administrations in enforcing legislation for equal opportunity and affirmative action for women and minorities, there have still been dramatic reductions in the barriers to women and minorities in education and organizational careers since the passage of the 1964 Civil Rights Act.

Just as some men face special career barriers and members of minorities face even greater barriers, many women managers will face gender-related barriers. This is not to say that such barriers cannot be overcome with creativity and persistence—some can and some cannot. Nor is it true that being a women is never advantageous—in some circumstances it is. However, many women have to devote time and energy to dealing with issues, problems, and barriers that most men never encounter, and dealing with these issues detracts from "getting the job done."

Since the situation is changing so rapidly, it seems likely that models of women's careers and career success based on even recent experiences may prove to be poor predictors of the future. How, then, can a woman manage her own career most effectively? If we assume that most career tasks are reasonably similar for men and women but that a few are quite different, the most fruitful approach may be to work hard at doing the best possible job with the many "general" issues and use the existing models and guidelines for handling gender-related tasks.[62]

Fortunately, more and more female success models are coming to the fore, as women begin to break through the so-called "glass ceiling" of top management. They include: Ellen Hancock, 40, head of IBM's $5.5 billion communications-business division (compensation, $250,000); Diana Harris, 44, Vice-President of Corporate Development, Bausch & Lomb ($175,000); Ellen Marram, 40, President, Grocery Division, Nabisco ($250,000); Roxanne Decyk, 34, Senior Vice-President of Administration, Navistar ($200,000); and Ellen Monahan, 41, Vice-President of Planning, RJR Reynolds ($150,000).[63]

ILLUSTRATIVE CASE STUDY Wrap-Up

Selina Proctor: Parent and Professional

From the case of Selina Proctor we can infer that our subject has entered a transitional phase of her career—one in which she is thinking about what she has to do to become a partner in the law firm and in which she must balance this goal with others. Perhaps Selina has a linear view of her career, and part of her problem may be that by working only part-time, her career goals are not entirely reasonable. Alternatively, Selina suffers from adhering to the fairly traditional male-female roles that she and her partner have adopted, however consciously or unconsciously. Even though she is working at a demanding job, she is still regarded as mother and primary care-provider

[60]Susan M. Donnell and Jay Hall, "Men and Women as Managers: A Significant Case of No Significant Difference," *Organizational Dynamics* 8, no. 4 (Spring 1980):60–77.

[61]See, for example, Hazel F. Ezell, Charles A. Olewahn, and J. Daniel Sherman, "Women Entering Management: Differences in Perceptions of Factors Influencing Integration," *Group and Organizational Studies* 7, no. 2 (June 1982):243–253.

[62]See Eliza G. C. Collins, *"Dearest Amanda . . ." An Executive's Advice to Her Daughter* (New York: Harper & Row, 1984); and Betty Lehan Harragan, *Games Mother Never Taught You: Corporate Gamesmanship for Women* (New York: Rawson, 1977).

[63]"Corporate Women," pp. 75–76; "Big Changes at Big Blue," *Business Week*, February 15, 1988, pp. 92–98.

for her child. Unless she begins to modify some of her role expectations, she may well find herself asking whether working was worth it or whether she gave up too much of her professional ambition for the personal goals entailed by motherhood—especially as she herself conceives them. Each of these questions is complex in itself, and obviously neither becomes simpler when they must both be confronted simultaneously.

The case of Selina Proctor illustrates both the difficulties of careérs in organizations and the need to manage them. The problem and the issues that it raises are especially acute for women and dual-career families, because today these roles and family configurations are coming more and more to characterize a changing society. ■

SUMMARY

Certain events occur with relative predictability over the course of a persons's career. Understanding these events enables us to prepare for them and to take an active role in managing our own careers.

Early career experiences commonly include the formation of unrealistic expectations and reality shock when these expectations clash with frustrating on-the-job experiences. Low initial challenge, low self-actualization satisfaction, and lack of performance appraisal are some organizational factors that contribute to reality shock. Realistic job previews may help prevent reality shock, but research has yielded inconsistent results on this point.

The amount of challenge in the initial job assignment, the actions of one's first supervisor, and the new employee's fit with the organizational culture are particularly important career influences. Dilemmas that arise early in one's career relate to political insensitivity and passivity, loyalty demands, and personal anxiety about one's growing commitment to the organization. The latter can sometimes be resolved through "creative individualism," which permits the individual to accept only the most important values of the organization.

Stress is part of organizational life. It is often caused by overload.There are two kinds of overloading: quantitative, in which a person has more work than he or she has time for, and qualitative, in which the person lacks the skills to do a job. Underloading may also be a problem. Stress can have serious health consequences. A variety of techniques can be used to reduce stressful factors in the environment and to help people deal with the stress that does occur.

Several models of the career stages through which many individuals must pass have been developed. Levinson and his colleagues, for example, have devised a model that describes adult life as a series of predictable events that occur every five or seven years. The stages are called the early adult transition, entering the adult world, the age-30 transition, settling down, the mid-life transition, the beginning of middle adulthood, the age-50 transition, the second middle adult structure, the late adult transition, and the late adult era.

Driver and Schein have developed two perspectives on the patterns that careers follow. Driven has suggested that most careers follow one of four basic career concepts: transitory, steady state, linear, or spiral. Schein developed the concept of the career anchor, a form of self-concept that develops through one's experiences in the workplace and that functions as a guide for one's entire career. Schein described five career anchors—security, technical or functional competence, managerial competence, creativity, and autonomy.

Schein has also devised a model that describes how the individual's positions within the organization change over time. The organization appears as a cone in which vertical, radial, and circumferential movement can take place across various boundaries. With each movement, the individual is socialized or trained to fit into the new position. Schein believes individuals are most likely to be innovative at the midpoint of their tenure in a position.

Individuals reach a career plateau when they are no longer candidates for promotion. Stars and learners are considered eligible for promotion; solid citizens and deadwood, however, are considered no longer promotable. Almost everyone in an organization eventually reaches a plateau, frequently because of the scarcity of positions available at higher levels of the hierarchy.

The starting point for individual career planning is to understand what one wants from one's work, career, and life. Schoonmaker has offered a nine-step career strategy that involves systematic career planning. Once one has mounted a successful job campaign and gotten a job in one's chosen field, much can be done to manage the work situation to one's advantage. The most important tasks are to do excellent work, develop good working relationships, and help your boss succeed.

Dual-career couples must work hard to integrate and balance the demands and opportunities of two separate careers. Mentors serve a variety of functions, some of them directly related to one's career, others more psychosocial in nature. Mentor roles can be filled by a variety of persons within and outside the organization; the employee need not attempt to form a relationship with a single individual.

Women face a number of barriers to successful careers. Three major sources of barriers are women's attitudes toward themselves and their careers, the attitudes of co-workers, and organizational policies and procedures. Although barriers have been reduced in recent years and will probably diminish further, women in management will face greater pressures than men for some time.

REVIEW QUESTIONS

1. Why do you think individuals develop unrealistic expectations about their first jobs? Why is this tendency especially severe among business school graduates?
2. What is reality shock? What factors contribute to it?
3. What three factors in an individual's early job experiences have an especially strong influence on subsequent job success? Why are these factors so influential?
4. Why are young business school graduates often insensitive to the political dimension of organizational life? What is the proper function of political alliances in an organization?
5. Webber describes five common ways by which loyalty may be defined by a superior. What are these five ways? What ethical and other conflicts arise sometimes for subordinates in applying these directives?
6. In what three ways can people respond to the organization's efforts to enforce compliance with its expectations? Which way do you think is best? Why?
7. What are the six types of role conflict identified by Katz and Kahn?
8. What are the most common causes of stress? How can stress affect health? Describe the various procedures that can be used to reduce stress and help people deal with it.
9. What are the ten stages in Levinson's model of adult development?
10. Compare Driver's career concepts notion with Schein's idea of career anchors.
11. Identify individuals you know who work for organizations and try to fit them into the career stages or states of the various models presented in the chapter. Can they be accurately placed?
12. According to Schein, what three types of movement are possible within organizations? What three types of organizational boundaries exist? How does the organization attempt to influence the individual who is making a position change? How can the individual most effectively influence the organization?
13. List the nine steps in Schoonmaker's career strategy. How reasonable do they sound to you?
14. What are three most important steps one can take in the work situation to further one's career?
15. What are the special issues that must be confronted by dual-career couples? Discuss the four general styles of managing two careers.
16. According to Kram, what are the two categories of functions served by mentors? Should one assume that it is imperative to find an individual to serve as one's mentor? Why or why not?
17. What are some of the special problems faced by women in management?

CASE STUDY Andrew Krieger's Career Decision at Soros Fund

The last year had been a busy one, especially in terms of career moves, for Andrew Krieger. The year before, he had been a currency trader at Bankers Trust. As such, he had bought (and sold) foreign currency, betting that its value would increase (or decrease) relative to the dollar. It was a high-pressure job that demanded an ability to take huge risks in stride. His bets were usually correct, and he had done very well, earning the bank more than $300 million and a $3 million bonus for himself. Not bad for a 31-year-old who had been out of business school just five years.

However, high volume of trading created interpersonal problems on the job. Some of his co-workers were annoyed because his activities occasionally affected theirs: He worked in such large amounts of currency that the entire market would often respond to one of his trades—a fact which could catch his co-workers by surprise, frustrating their own bets on the behavior of the market. The risks he took in order to achieve his spectacular returns also worried his employer. Although his trades usually resulted in millions of dollars in profits, Krieger regularly risked many millions in the process. His superiors tried to exert a little more control over Krieger, seeking to minimize the risk-taking impulse and to build a solid team out of the department rather than relying on a single star.

So Krieger had decided he would be happier if he left Bankers Trust, hoping to find more time for himself and a more personally rewarding job. Since Soros Fund Management was smaller, it offered him more freedom, and so he had chosen to work there. But the change was not working out as he had envisioned it. When he exercised his freedom, he worried his current employer even more than he had worried Bankers Trust. In order to make the largest possible returns, he invested all the money he could find. Unfortunately, this practice often left other parts of the firm short of capital for their investments in the stock market—a fact which tended to leave a lot of people unhappy. Nor did George Soros, the president of the Soros Fund, see eye-to-eye with Krieger on strategic matters. The big-risk/big-reward strategy he favored not only concerned Soros but generated publicity that Soros did not appreciate.

So, it looked as if Krieger had made a mistake. Several private investors had asked him if he would oversee their investments, and he was seriously considering going into business for himself. Maybe that way he would have the freedom he craved without having to worry about conflicts with co-workers and employers. And maybe working with an individual's money rather than an institution's would give him a greater feeling of satisfaction. However, it was a risk. He would have less capital to bet with and would be hard-pressed to take the occasionally inevitable losses.

Should he leave Soros? Should he give it more time, in hopes that the problems he was encountering would go away? Would he really by any happier anywhere else? Krieger could not be sure of any of the answers.

Sources: Adapted from Charles W. Stevens, "Andrew Krieger Made $3 Million Last Year; Why Isn't He Happy?" *The Wall Street Journal,* March 24, 1988, pp. 1, 16; Stevens and George Anders, "Options Trading Whiz Krieger Quits Again—This Time from Soros Fund," *The Wall Street Journal,* June 7, 1988, p. 28.

Case Questions

1. In what stage of his career is Mr. Krieger?
2. What are the factors that are causing stress in Mr. Krieger's life?
3. What can he do to manage this stress?
4. Should Mr. Krieger leave Soros? What advice would you give him. ■

Raoul Dufy, *Street Decked with Flags, Le Havre*. 1906. Oil on canvas 31⅞ x 25⅞". Musee National d'Art Moderne, Paris. Courtesy of the Granger Collection.

24

INTERNATIONAL MANAGEMENT

Upon completing this chapter you should be able to:

1. Describe the process by which a company goes international.
2. Define a multinational enterprise (MNE).
3. Discuss the positive and negative impacts that MNEs have on their home and host countries.
4. List and discuss the managerial challenges of operating in the international environment.
5. Describe the managerial approaches MNEs may select to apply abroad.

Chapter Outline

Introduction
The Increasing Internationalization of the World Economy
The Multinational Enterprise
The Challenges of Multinational Management
Selecting a Managerial Approach

ILLUSTRATIVE CASE STUDY Introduction

Sumitomo: The Thrust Toward International Banking

Widely regarded as Japan's most efficient, aggressive, and innovative bank, Sumitomo has long been the most profitable. In 1986, it had the lowest ratio of operating expenses to operating income, the highest net profit and deposits per employee, and, except for the Bank of Tokyo, the highest number of loans and deposits per branch. Boosting Sumitomo's flexibility and efficiency—and illustrating its innovativeness—was its early commitment to state-of-the-art electronic banking. In 1967, it was the first Japanese bank to put all customer accounts on-line. In 1969, it installed the country's first cash dispenser, and in 1974, it launched automatic banking. The bank cut staff by 10 percent in the first half of the 1980s—a key ingredient in the quadrupling of net income per employee in the same period. By 1985, Sumitomo had committed another $208 million to enhance its information systems.

While tight operations and emphasis on profits gave Sumitomo the capability to compete in world markets, the real reason for the bank's accelerating international thrust was perhaps probably the dynamics in the domestic banking environment in Japan. Domestic business had become less attractive, as demand for loans from traditionally highly leveraged Japanese companies declined with the slowing down of the country's economic growth and as companies started shifting from debt to equity or to cheaper convertibles on Euromarkets in order to fund most of their capital needs. In addition, a gradual program of deregulation launched by the Finance Ministry in 1982 intensified domestic competition and put more pressure on the profit margins.

To keep the lending business profitable, Sumitomo identified two methods—efficiency in operations and diversification into new, fee-generating fields. The fee-generating activity—basically, all non-lending activity—had traditionally been tightly regulated in Japan, and the banks' role was generally very limited. But gradual deregulation by the Finance Ministry opened up such activities to both domestic and foreign banks. To exploit the new opportunities, domestic banks had to learn the new businesses, and the best place was to do that overseas.

In 1986, Sumitomo made a large and aggressive aquisition—12.5 percent of Goldman, Sachs & Company, a N.Y. investment bank. Many bankers are intrigued by this deal because Sumitomo's role is strictly limited by the Federal Reserve Board, which expressed concern that the arrangement might put more cracks in the Glass-Steagall Act, which separates commercial banks from investment banks. As a result, the Japanese bank cannot increase its stake in new acquisition, cannot have any management role, and may not engage in joint venture.

However, as a Swiss banker notes, " . . . Sumitomo is not thinking of the next quarterly returns but far beyond that—ten years, twenty, thirty." The bank is going to bide its time until it is prepared to incorporate Goldman more fully into its corporate philosophy in order to become a major force in global merchant banking.

Still, only about 25 percent of the bank's profits come from international operations. Now, top Sumitomo officials talk in terms of getting 40 percent of their profits from abroad. And the company's president, Koh Komatsu, makes no secret of his desire to make Sumitomo into "Japan's Citibank."

Sources: Takashi Ikahata, "Quality and Quantity Mark Sumitomo Bank's History," *Business Japan,* October 1986, pp. 30–36; Robert Neff, "Leading Japan's Overseas Banking Drive," *International Management,* March 1985, pp. 52–53, 55; Joel Dreyfuss, "A Japanese Survivor Leads the Charge on World Banking," *Fortune,* January 5, 1987, pp. 60–61; Kevin Rafferty, "Probing the Sumitomo Culture," *The Institutional Investor,* November 1986, pp. 297–301, 303; Sarah Bartlett with Stan Crock, "U.S. Bankers Try to Capitalize on Sumitomo's Deal," *Business Week,* October 13, 1986, p. 50.

CLASS COMMENT

Managers must learn about operating effectively in an international environment.

Before we look at the characteristics of international business, we must understand how and why the economies of all nations have become more and more interdependent. And it is not only business that has become increasingly multinational; so too have many other kinds of activities. Foreign students have been very common at our colleges for several decades. Tourist trips that cross international borders have become more common, too, along with outerspace ventures involving people and equipment from several countries. Telecommunications links make exchanges among the countries of the world vastly easier, cheaper, and faster than they have ever been.

In addition, countries once closed to Western political and economic ideas, particularly the USSR and the People's Republic of China, are becoming more receptive to the principles of the open market. Joint ventures between American firms and those headquartered in European and Asian nations are becoming much more common. More and more foreign countries are not only investing in the U.S. stock and bond markets, but are purchasing American companies and establishing their own facilities in the U.S.

THE INCREASING INTERNATIONALIZATION OF THE WORLD ECONOMY

A Brief History

portfolio investment Investment in foreign assets whereby a company purchases shares in companies that own those assets.

direct investment Investment in foreign assets whereby a company purchases assets that it manages directly.

multinational companies Those which operate in more than one country, including investment in foreign manufacturing facilities.

Companies and individuals can own foreign assets in two fundamental ways. On the one hand, they can purchase shares in the companies that own those assets. Foreign **portfolio investment** of this sort gives those companies and individuals a claim on profits, but not the right to participate in management. By contrast, companies and individuals can also set up or purchase assets and then manage them actively. This kind of foreign **direct investment** is what concerns us here.[1]

Multinational companies, which operate in more than one country, have been around for hundreds of years. But they were great rarities until the late nineteenth century. By then, U.S. companies like General Electric, International Telephone and Telegraph, and Singer Sewing Machine Company had started to invest in overseas manufacturing facilities. So too had West European companies like Ciba, Imperial Chemicals, Nestlé, Siemens, and Unilever.

Even in the nineteenth century, multinational companies were not at all common. The internationalization of business firms did not get seriously under way until the end of World War II, in 1945. At that point, the United States was the only major country that had not been devastated. Quite the contrary, in fact: The size of our economy had almost doubled since we had entered the war, at the end of 1941. We dominated the world's economic, political, and military affairs. In this climate, many U.S. firms started making substantial direct investments in foreign primary industries, such as mining and petroleum, which provided raw materials for our economy.

From the mid-1950s onward, U.S. companies started to make substantial direct investments in foreign manufacturing facilities. In the 1960s, it was American service

[1]This section is based upon William A. Dymsza, "Trends in Multinational Business and Global Environments: A Perspective," *Journal of International Business Studies* (Winter 1984); 25–46.

HERE'S AN EXAMPLE
A recent McKinsey and Company survey of mid-sized companies doing business abroad shows that they expect their international sales to jump 15 to 20 percent a year for at least the next five years. (*Fortune*, 6/6/88, p. 87)

firms—banks, insurance companies, marketing consultants, and the like—that expanded overseas. U.S. companies were so aggressive and successful that a well-known French journalist, Jacques Servan-Schrieber, wrote a book called *The American Challenge,* in which he warned that Europe might not succeed in maintaining its economic independence from the United States.

Western Europe's firms—particularly in such industries as chemicals, electrical gear, pharmaceuticals, and tires—started to counterattack in the late 1960s by setting up and acquiring U.S. affiliates. So did the gigantic Japanese trading companies—particularly during the 1980s, when they were trying to stave off protectionist U.S. legislation that would cut their access to the American market. To lower their manufacturing costs, Japanese and U.S. companies also started to invest in facilities in less well-developed nations. In fact, even Third World companies started to sink their money into overseas facilities, usually to evade limits on the amount of goods they could export to the United States from their home bases.

Why Companies Go International

CLASS COMMENT
Competitive global markets are a reality facing U.S. firms.

Direct foreign investment by business firms represents a form of capital movement.[2] Early theories of capital movement suggested that money moves "from areas where returns on capital are lower to those where they are higher."[3] This seems to make intuitive sense. Yet in 1959, Steven Hymer showed that it does not account for all direct foreign investment.

Hymer argued that most companies that make such investments are "oligopolistic"; in other words, they enjoy a very large share of the market for the goods or services they provide. Usually, they dominate their markets either because they reap economies of scale beyond the reach of smaller companies or because they have "some sort of 'superior' proprietary knowledge" that gives them "a more desirable product" than their rivals offer.[4]

Hymer's theory does not in itself explain why such companies often chose to produce their goods or services overseas, instead of exporting from their home bases. Reasons do, however, suggest themselves. Perhaps, for example, these companies wish to avoid tariffs or import quotas levied by the importing countries.

product-cycle theory According to Vernon, the process whereby products originally developed for home markets earn enough foreign demand to justify direct foreign investment in their production.

Raymond Vernon put forward another theory of foreign direct investment in the late 1960s. Vernon's **product-cycle theory** attempts to explain why U.S. firms have been responsible for most foreign direct investment. Companies that develop attractive new products sell them first in their home markets, Vernon noted. Sooner or later, foreigners may learn about these products. At this stage, most companies would export the product or service rather than produce it abroad. But as foreign demand grows, the economics of foreign production change. Eventually, the foreign market becomes large enough to justify foreign direct investment.

U.S. companies are responsible for most foreign direct investment, thought Vernon, because during much of the present century they generated most new consumer products and production techniques. As a result, many of the products and services that have crossed international borders were U.S. products and services, and they eventually won markets large enough to justify overseas production.

H. Levy and M. Sarrat propose yet another theory of foreign direct investment. They compare companies that acquire foreign production facilities to investors who

[2]This section is based upon Chapter 2, "Foreign Direct Investment and Multinational Firms," in Yoshi Tsurumi, *Multinational Management: Business Strategy and Government Policy* (Cambridge, Mass.: Ballinger Publishing, 1977), pp. 73–127.

[3]Ibid., p. 76.

[4]Ibid., p. 76.

diversify their portfolio of investments. Much as such an investment portfolio is usually designed to protect its owner from fluctuations in the value or return of any single asset, so direct foreign investment lets a company "construct a 'portfolio' which has more optimal risk/return characteristics than one which contains income streams from one nation only."[5]

FOR DISCUSSION

What environmental forces are leading to the increasing internationalization of business?

Reasons for going abroad may also vary by industry. Petroleum and mining companies often go international to get a reliable or cheaper source of raw materials. Some manufacturing companies, by contrast, have often ventured overseas to protect old markets or to seek new ones. Recently, they have looked in foreign lands for cheap sources of labor, although as workers in countries such as South Korea demand higher wages and more of the benefits to be reaped from economies that are beginning to prosper, the search for cheaper labor has become politically unpredictable and often quite risky.

The nationality of a company may affect its motives for going international. Companies based outside the United States may choose to come here to find political stability, but American companies have never ventured abroad for that reason, since few countries have as much political stability as the United States does. Likewise it has been much more common for foreign companies to come to the United States to get technology and managerial know-how than vice versa. More recently, American companies have started looking to Japan for new technological and managerial perspectives. However, as the box on Japanese manufacturing in America indicates, often there are problems.

How Companies Go International

COORDINATED RESOURCE

See "The Globalization of Markets" by Theodore Leavitt, *Harvard Business Review*, May–June 1983, pp. 92–102.

Few organizations are multinational to start. More commonly, they proceed through several stages of internationalization. Christopher Korth has broken this process down into four stages, or degrees (see Table 24-1), which apply both to manufacturing and to services. Not all companies reach the fourth and last stage, and some companies that do reach it later recede, as Chrysler did in the early 1980s, when it sold much its overseas manufacturing capacity.

[5]Ibid., p. 82.

TABLE 24-1 FOUR DEGREES OF INTERNATIONALIZATION

	FIRST-DEGREE INTERNATIONALIZATION	SECOND-DEGREE INTERNATIONALIZATION	THIRD-DEGREE INTERNATIONALIZATION	FOURTH-DEGREE INTERNATIONALIZATION
Nature of contact with foreign markets	Indirect, passive	Direct, active	Direct, active	Direct, active
Locus of international operations	Domestic	Domestic	Domestic and international	Domestic and international
Orientation of company	Domestic	Domestic	Primarily domestic	Multinational (domestic operations viewed as part of the whole)
Type of international activity	Foreign trade of goods and services	Foreign trade of goods and services	Foreign trade, foreign assistance contracts, foreign direct investment	Foreign trade, foreign assistance contracts, foreign direct investment
Organizational structure	Traditional domestic	International department	International division	Global structure

Source: Christopher M. Korth, *International Business, Environment and Management*, 2nd ed., p. 7. Copyright 1985. Reprinted by permission of PrenticeHall, Inc., Englewood Cliffs, N.J.

ETHICS IN MANAGEMENT

JAPANESE MANUFACTURERS IN AMERICA

From 1981 to 1987, the number of manufacturing plants owned by Japanese companies in the United States has more than doubled. Many large companies, especially car makers, have established plants here not only in order to avoid import quotas and tariffs, but to better supply the American appetite for Japanese goods. The weakening dollar makes such investments look very attractive, and the trend will probably continue. However, the Japanese companies that run factories in the U.S. have not been bestowed with unmitigated blessings. Although the majority of these Japanese ventures are successful, a number of plants are experiencing severe problems.

Most of the successful ventures have been newly built and newly staffed plants and are usually equipped with the latest technology. By employing fresh labor forces, they avoid having to deal with unions and have more freedom to establish policies that suit Japanese management style. In addition, they are frequently located in small towns where the local population is grateful for the job opportunities and capital influx. The Honda plant in Maryville, Ohio, is a good example of such a success story. It recently began shipping cars made in the United States back to Japan.

The plant's top management is Japanese, and the plant itself runs on largely according to Japanese management style. Workers participate in "quality circles" to find improvements in manufacturing techniques and cost control. Most workers had little experience in building cars when they were hired, but extensive training has made them extremely productive. Since opening the Maryville plant, Honda has expanded its capacity by 50 percent and built two additional plants.

Unfortunately, the Sanyo factory in Forrest City, Arkansas, has not experienced the same sort of success. Sanyo bought the factory from American owners—and inherited its problems at the same time. Principal among these was a heavily unionized work force that has refused to adapt to the Japanese way of doing things. Quality circles have failed here, as has the practice of consensus management. Part of the problem may have been that few of the Japanese managers spoke fluent English, and communication headaches were common. Plant production has been severely cut, and many local employees expect that it will soon cease altogether.

Another problem that all Japanese companies face is unhappiness among its own management personnel. Japanese managers sent to oversee American plants find the transition difficult, and their families often fare worse. Language and cultural barriers make integration into a community difficult, especially in larger cities where altruistic behavior toward foreigners is not an everyday activity. Those families located in small towns often fare better, thanks to helpful neighbors. The difference between Japanese and American schools also worries Japanese parents, since a good education is essential for success in Japan. The stress faced by these managers often makes them less effective simply by distracting their attention.

As Americans continue to demand Japanese goods, and as American property continues to be a good investment, Japanese companies will continue to open factories and businesses here. Some of them will find success where others will not. The keys seem to be a cooperative labor force, helpful local populations, and Japanese managers able to find the compromises necessary to overcome cultural differences.

Sources: Ernest Beazley, "Battered Image: In Spite of Mystique, Japanese Plants in U.S. Find Problems Abound," *Wall Street Journal,* June 22, 1988, pp. 1, 17; Stewart Toy with Neil Gross and James B. Treece, "The Americanization of Honda," *Business Week,* April 25, 1988, pp. 90–96; John Schwartz with Jeanne Gordon and Mark Veverka, "The 'Salarymen' Blues," *Newsweek,* May 9, 1988, pp. 51–52.

HERE'S AN EXAMPLE

U.S. companies have followed a five-stage evolution of expansion abroad: kept everything in U.S. and used foreign distribution; established own sales company abroad; local production and sales and service in key countries; established full-fledged autonomous businesses with all major functions (this is the stage many U.S. multinationals are in now); and worldwide personnel, R&D, and financing strategies (the stage some of the most successful and advanced multinationals are in). (*Wall Street Journal*, 4/25/88, p. 26)

Companies at the first stage of internationalization have only passive dealings with foreign individuals and organizations. At this point, for example, a company might content itself with filling overseas orders that had come in without any serious selling effort on its part. International contacts might be handled by an existing department. Third parties, such as agents and brokers, often act as go-betweens for companies at the first stage of internationalization.

By the second stage, companies deal directly with their overseas interests, though they may continue to use third parties also. At this point, most companies do not have employees based abroad, but domestic employees would regularly travel abroad on business. The company might decide to set up an import or export department.

In the third stage, a company's international interests shape its overall makeup in an important way. Although still essentially domestic in nature, the company has a direct hand in importing, exporting, and perhaps producing its goods and services abroad. In the final step, the company sees its activities as essentially multinational as opposed to domestic.

ethnocentric management Attitude that the home country's management practices are superior to those of other countries and can be exported along with the organization's goods and services.

polycentric management Attitude that since a foreign country's management policies are best understood by its own management personnel, the home organization should rely on foreign offices.

geocentric management Attitude that accepts both similarities and differences between domestic and foreign management policies and so attempts to strike a balance between those that are most effective.

Managerial Attitudes Toward Internationalization

A company's main resource is its people. Their attitudes guide its internationalization, or prevent it. Howard Perlmutter has identified three primary attitudes among the managers of international companies: ethnocentric, polycentric, and geocentric.

Ethnocentric managers see foreign countries and their people as inferior to those of the home country. These managers believe that the practices of the home country can be exported along with its goods and services. A **polycentric manager** sees all countries as different and as hard to understand. Believing that a company's foreign offices are likely to understand their needs, such managers leave them alone. **Geocentric managers** recognize similarities as well as differences among countries. Such managers attempt to draw on the most effective techniques and practices, wherever they originate.

Firms with foreign interests are likely to have managers with each of these perspectives. Perlmutter believes that polycentric attitudes are the most suitable kind for managers of multinational companies, but they are also the hardest to learn and accept.

THE MULTINATIONAL ENTERPRISE

multinational enterprise (MNE) Large corporation with operations and divisions spread over several countries but controlled by a central headquarters.

Although it does not necessarily follow that a company will progress through all four degrees once it begins the process of internationalization, some companies do grow to the point where they become **multinational enterprises (MNEs).** The study of such companies is relatively new, and there is a lack of consensus as to the exact definition of an MNE. We will define an MNE as a cluster of corporations controlled by one headquarters but with operations spread over many countries.[6]

In this section we will examine the growth of MNEs both in size and in number and discuss their spread both geographically and in the types of activities in which they are involved. We will also examine the economic and noneconomic impacts that MNEs have on their home countries (where they originate) and their host countries (where they operate).

[6]Stefan H. Robock and Kenneth Simmonds, *International Business and Multinational Enterprises*, 3rd ed. (Homewood, Ill.: Irwin, 1983), p. 7. See also Yair Aharoni, "The Issue of Defining Transnational Corporations," in *Transnational Corporations in World Development: A Re-examination* (New York: United Nations, 1978), pp. 158–161, and "On the Definition of a Multinational Corporation," *Quarterly Review of Economics and Business* 11, no. 3 (Autumn 1971):27–37.

The Rise and Spread of Multinational Enterprises

COORDINATED RESOURCE

For a current listing of the 50 leading U.S. exporters, see *Fortune,* 7/18/88, p. 71.

HERE'S AN EXAMPLE

Some aggressive U.S. companies are storming foreign markets. For example: Guild Wineries and Distilleries of Woodbridge, California is succeeding at selling basic medium-priced table wines in Denmark; Amway Corporation, the privately held manufacturer of cosmetics, soaps, and vitamins has seen sales increase over 100 percent a year since 1979 in Japan; POM of Russellville, Arkansas, tiny manufacturer of parking meters, has their meters in places such as Malaysia, Chile, Ontario, and Holland; etc. (*Fortune,* 6/6/88, pp. 87–102)

International business has existed in some sense since prehistory, when such products as flint blanks and ceramics were traded across great distances. At the time of the Roman Empire, it was possible in many lands to buy the goods of distant foreign producers. The first American company to operate a foreign production plant successfully was the Singer Sewing Machine Company, whose Scottish factory opened in 1868.[7]

In the last two decades, many studies of the multinational firm have been undertaken. This research interest is primarily a result of the tremendous growth that has occurred in the last 25 years in both the size and the number of MNEs. An obvious companion to this growth has been an increase in the influence of MNEs, accompanied by much debate, concern, and study on the part of governments and organizations such as the United Nations.

Table 24-2 gives an idea of just how large some multinational firms have grown. It shows the 1984 ranking of the world's nations and MNEs, according to gross national product or total sales, respectively. Although the United States, with monoliths like Exxon, General Motors, ITT, IBM, and Union Carbide, accounts for more than half of the world's direct foreign investment, it does not have a monopoly on the world's largest MNEs.[8] Many of them are European, such as the Royal Dutch/Shell group, British Petroleum, and ENI (Italy). They are being joined by an increasing number of Japanese firms, including Mitsubishi, Toyota, and Hitachi.

The Impact of MNE Operations

Some studies of the impact of MNEs on host or home countries have shown the overall impact to be solidly favorable, but others have reached the opposite conclusion.[9] It is fair to say that most studies indicate the effects are *relatively* favorable. However, these studies are usually heavily dependent on key assumptions made by the researchers. And, because there may be a mix of positive and negative effects, how the effects are weighted can influence the overall conclusion. For example, if an MNE had only two sources of influence—creating jobs and bribing government officials—its overall effect would be favorable if we care a great deal about jobs and don't mind bribery. Its effect is negative if our preferences (weighting) are reversed.

HERE'S AN EXAMPLE

IBM has changed its approach to handling Japanese customers by exhibiting a new openness to customer needs. IBM made the move to halt the erosion of its market share there. Some experts, though, say that Japanese companies are already a step ahead of IBM's marketing moves and as long as Japanese companies lavish more attention on customers than IBM, Japanese users aren't likely to switch. (*Wall Street Journal,* 4/4/88, p. 6)

The Impact of MNEs on Host Countries. Christopher Korth has identified some of the potential benefits and costs that the operations of an MNE may have on a host country.[10] Note that these benefits and costs, listed below, are only potential. Whether they actually occur in a specific situation depends on the environment, including government actions, and the actual behavior of the MNE involved. Some of the major potential benefits are:

- Transfer of capital, technology, and enterpreneurship to the host country
- Improvement of the host country's balance of payments

---

[7]Myra Wilkens, *The Emergence of Multinational Enterprise* (Cambridge, Mass.: Harvard University Press, 1970)

[8]Reed Moyer, ed., *International Business: Issues and Concepts* (New York: Wiley, 1984), p. 137.

[9]See, for example, Richard J. Barnet and Ronald E. Müller, *Global Reach: The Power of the Multinational Corporations* (New York: Simon & Schuster, 1974) for a popular critique of MNEs, widely cited by critics of MNEs in the 1970s. See also Joseph S. Nye, Jr., "Multinational Corporations in World Politics," *Foreign Affairs* 53, no. 1 (October 1974):153–175; and Peter F. Drucker, "Multinationals and Developing Countries: Myths and Realities," *Foreign Affairs* 43, no. 1 (October 1974):121–143 (both reprinted in Moyer, *International Business*).

[10]This discussion is based on Christopher M. Korth, *International Business, Environment, and Management,* 2nd ed. (Englewood Cliffs, N.J.: Prentice Hall, 1985), pp. 277–297, 308–326.

TABLE 24-2 RANKING OF MNES AND NATIONS ACCORDING TO GNP OR TOTAL SALES

RANKING	NATION OR FIRM	GNP OR TOTAL SALES FOR 1982 ($ BILLIONS)
22	Belgium	$106.5
23	*Exxon*	97.2
24	Indonesia	88.5
25	*Shell*	83.8
26	South Africa	81.2
27	Nigeria	77.9
28	Austria	75.1
28	South Korea	75.1
30	Argentina	71.6
31	Hungary	69.1
31	Venezuela	69.1
33	Turkey	63.7
34	Denmark	63.6
35	Yugoslavia	63.3
36	*General Motors*	60.0
37	*Mobil Oil*	59.9
38	Norway	58.5
39	Romania	57.6
40	Finland	52.2
41	*British Petroleum*	51.3
42	Taiwan	48.9
43	*Texaco*	47.0
44	Algeria	46.8
45	Greece	42.0
46	Philippines	41.6
47	Colombia	39.4
48	Thailand	38.3
49	Bulgaria	37.5
50	*Ford*	37.1
51	*IBM*	34.4
51	*Standard Oil of California*	34.4
53	*Du Pont*	33.3
54	Pakistan	33.1
55	Kuwait	31.8
56	Egypt	30.5
57	*Gulf Oil*	28.4
58	*Standard Oil (Indiana)*	28.1
59	Hong Kong	27.8
60	*ENI (Italy)*	27.5
61	Malaysia	27.0
62	*General Electric*	26.5
62	*Atlantic Richfield*	26.5
64	United Arab Emirates	26.1

Note: Belgium is ranked 22 because it is 22nd in GNP among nations; the United States is ranked number 1.

Sources: World Bank, *World Development Report, 1984* (Washington, D.C., 1984), and "International 500," *Fortune,* August 22, 1983, p. 170. Eastern bloc and Taiwan data are from *Handbook of Economic Statistics, 1983,* published by the Central Intelligence Agency, September 1983.

- Creation of local job and career opportunities
- Improved competition in the local economy
- Greater availability of products for local consumers

These benefits may occur in any given situation, and many MNE managers and some analysts believe that they usually do. It is possible, though, that in each area of potential benefit the opposite can in fact occur. For example, the MNE may use local financing, thereby absorbing capital that might have financed indigenous companies. Or a few well-advertised, standardized consumer products may drive many locally produced products from the market, thereby reducing consumer choice.

Not all costs have analogous benefits, however. Generally, the potential negative effects, which are very emotional issues with some observers, can be placed into three broad categories:

- Political interference on the part of the MNE
- Social-cultural disruptions and changes (which are bound to have both advocates and opponents)
- Local economic dependence on decisions made outside of the country

There have clearly been abuses on the part of some MNEs in the past. United Fruit, for example, is generally acknowledged to have engaged in extensive political and economic interference in Latin America between the two world wars. More recently, officials of ITT have been accused of conspiring with the CIA to prevent the election of Salvador Allende Gossens, a Marxist, to the presidency of Chile.[11] And the Japanese electronics giant, Hitachi, has admitted stealing proprietary technology from IBM.

Generally, however, the ethics of MNEs are kept on a par with or above those of local companies. Today, MNEs have high political visibility and, despite their size and power, are vulnerable to punitive actions by local governments. Under such conditions, few companies are likely to risk even the appearance of unethical behavior.

It is worth noting that although MNEs are viewed with caution and suspicion by some host country government officials, they are actively courted by most countries rather than denied entry.

FOR DISCUSSION

In what ways do products of MNEs touch our lives?

The Impact of MNEs on Home Countries. The debate over the benefits and costs of MNEs to their home countries is less intense than is that over the effects on host countries. This is probably due to the absence of highly charged emotional issues, such as political interference, cultural disruption, and economic dependence. Exhibit 24-1 lists some of the benefits that a nation might gain from MNEs.[12]

EXHIBIT 24-1 HOME-COUNTRY BENEFITS FROM MNES

- The acquisition of raw materials from abroad, often from a steadier supply and at lower prices than can be found domestically
- Technology and management expertise acquired from competing in foreign markets
- The export of components and finished goods for assembly or distribution in foreign markets
- An inflow of income from overseas profits (dividends), licensing fees, and management contracts
- Job and career opportunities at home and abroad in connection with overseas operations

One potential negative effect on home countries that MNE critics point to is a weakening in the national balance of payments, caused by the outflow of capital from investments made overseas and a reduction in exports as products are manufactured overseas rather than at home. In the long run, these losses may be more than compensated for by the flow of income from dividends, licensing fees, royalties, and sales of components for foreign assembly. Another risk, however, is the chance that the home country could suffer the lessening or loss of technological advantage.[13]

---

[11]Robock and Simmonds, *International Business and Multinational Enterprises*, p. 233 (originally from "Dollar Diplomacy, 1972 Style," *Newsweek*, April 10, 1972).

[12]Korth, *International Business, Environment, and Management*, pp. 297–301.

[13]Lawrence G. Franko, "Foreign Direct Investment in Less Developed Countries; Impact on Home Countries," *Journal of International Business Studies* 9, no. 2 (Winter 1978):55–65; and Robert G. Hawkins and Bertram Finn, "Regulation of Multinational Firms' Foreign Activities: Home Country Policies and Concerns," *Journal of Contemporary Business* 6, no. 4 (Autumn 1977):14–30 (both reprinted in Moyer, *International Business*).

The most volatile issue on the home front is whether foreign investment (most obviously in manufacturing) by an MNE causes the loss of domestic jobs. If a company's factory production is moved overseas, on the surface it would certainly seem to cause job loss at home. Some observers feel that this job displacement is inevitable whether or not MNEs decide to invest overseas. They contend that even if one organization ignores the possible cost benefits of moving its production overseas, some of its competitors will take advantage of the opportunity. This will put the stay-at-home company at a competitive disadvantage with a consequent loss of business and reduction of work force. Hence, the job loss will take place anyway.[14] Other observers note, however, that such a conclusion is heavily dependent on assumptions about what would happen if all local companies were prohibited from investing in overseas manufacturing. Those observers go on to note that many government tax, political, and insurance policies and programs actually encourage companies to manufacture abroad rather than at home.

The actions of MNEs abroad may also have possible political effects on their home countries. Examples would be the continuing protests by some segments of U.S. society over the involvement and investment in South African business by American MNEs and the move to effect more governmental regulation of the American chemical industry following the Bhopal disaster of 1984.

ILLUSTRATIVE CASE STUDY Continued

Sumitomo: The Thrust Toward International Banking

Obviously, Sumitomo is an example of foreign *direct* investment in the case of the Banca del Gottardo acquisition. By contrast, its stake in Goldman, Sachs is an example of *indirect* foreign investment because Sumitomo is prevented from having any management role. However, the latter acquisition also represents one of the many different forms of impact that a foreign company can have on its host. Regulators became concerned about the further erosion of the "wall" established between the lending activities of commercial banks and the dealmaking and securities activities of investment banks. What better symbol of Japanese business success than the even partial acquisition of one of the most respected names on Wall Street—Goldman, Sachs?

The managers at Sumitomo clearly envision a future in accord with Korth's fourth stage of development. The very analogy with Citibank, a worldwide multinational, is telling. However, the challenges to develop the proper managerial attitudes at Sumitomo will be difficult. Managers, at some level in the company, must learn to handle a host of differing conditions, people, and cultures.

THE CHALLENGES OF MULTINATIONAL MANAGEMENT

EXTRA EXERCISE

Find a local company that is doing business on an international level. Interview them about the opportunities and problems.

Managing in a multinational environment forces managers to deal with unique challenges. In this section, we shall examine the social, economic, political, legal, and technical aspects of the international environment and ways of dealing with them. We will also find out how the tasks, problems, and opportunities of the international business environment shape the managerial function in multinational companies. Finally, we will return to a topic already broached in Chapter 2: the evolution of management thought.

[14]Moyer, *International Business,* p. 138. For a discussion of the types of jobs U.S. MNEs might move overseas and the impacts of doing so on the U.S. economy and work force, see Robert A. Reich, *The New American Frontier* (New York: Times Books, 1983).

Managing in a Multinational Environment

COORDINATED RESOURCE

Good descriptions of strategic concerns in international management are found in "Strategic Planning for Global Competition" by David C. Shanks, *Journal of Business Strategy*, Winter 1985, pp. 80–89; and "The International Challenge to U.S. Business" by David C. Garfield, *Journal of Business Strategy*, Spring 1985, pp. 26–29.

Monitoring problems is more difficult in the international environment than it is domestically, and so too is dealing with them. Each foreign country is different from the home country and also from all other countries where a firm might do business. As a multinational company enters more and more national markets, it may lose its ability to attend to any one problem. Managers may have difficulty adjusting to the increased complexity. Some managers never do.

Large domestic companies focus on those elements of their business environment that may change. Over the long run, so do multinational companies. Yet when a company is first getting established in a foreign country, it is the environment's current state that gets most attention. When a firm plants the flag in a new country, it has to learn local laws, customs, languages, and so forth—the enduring aspects of a culture, not the rapidly changing ones. Sometimes this isn't so easy, as the International Management box entitled "Becoming an International Business" shows.

HERE'S AN EXAMPLE

The "open-door" policy in China has allowed some U.S. companies a crack at the huge consumer market there. But many of the old problems of operating in China remain: getting hard currency for repatriating profits, getting raw materials, dealing with the multilevel state-run sales bureaucracy, etc. (*Business Week*, 8/8/88, p. 40)

Multinational companies must learn to deal with foreign patterns of economic growth, investment, and inflation. They must also concern themselves with various aspects of international trade, such as the value of a country's currency relative to other currencies (the foreign-exchange rate) and its balance of payments, as well as the extent of controls on imports and exports, on foreign investors, and on the repatriation of foreign earnings to the multinational's home country.

Firms that wish to expand into a foreign country must also assess its political stability; the business attitudes of its government, ruling party, and opposition (legal and illegal); and the effectiveness of its government bureaucracy. Both a country's internal and foreign policies can powerfully influence the business environment.

A multinational company must adjust to a multinational legal environment, which includes laws and regulations dealing with taxes, tariffs, quotas, copyright laws,

"It doesn't look good. Some of our nationals are at war with some of our other nationals."

Drawing by S. Harris; © 1983 The New Yorker Magazine, Inc.

INTERNATIONAL MANAGEMENT

BECOMING AN INTERNATIONAL BUSINESS

A company that wants continued growth but has already mastered its home market often turns an eye toward business in the international arena. Many companies find that the market in another country is even richer than that at home. The opening of an international branch or the venture into international sales is often a very promising avenue for future growth. Unfortunately, its often not as easy as it seems: There are a host of problems which accompany a move into foreign sales, and even more problems appear when *manufacturing* on foreign soil is considered.

You might think that an American company which wants to do business in England would have a fairly easy time of it. After all, there are no language barriers, and the cultures are not appreciably different. However, even the small differences which do exist make it a move which must be carefully planned and executed. Is there a true demand for one country's product in another? If it is a product new to the foreign culture, will people be willing to change their way of doing things? Will they accept a product made in a foreign country? What seems like a necessity in America might strike a Britisher as completely useless. Will the American name and packaging be appealing to another country's people? What we consider common may even be offensive in another country. Finally, the laws surrounding import and distribution must be studied and mastered.

Obviously, America to Britain is a relatively easy transition to make. But what about America to Japan? Currently, the U.S. government is trying to encourage export to Japan in order to close the trade deficit between the two countries. Some companies that have been willing to participate have found it very difficult. Japan has a very different system for distributing goods to retailers that is difficult for foreigners to understand and break into. The Japanese reliance on long-term relationships and personal trust makes it very difficult for a new company, even a domestic one, to be successful. A foreign firm faces this difficulty with the additional handicaps of language and cultural differences. Our way of doing business quickly and without ceremony often offends Japanese customers.

Trade between the United States and the Soviet Union, once considered unthinkable, is another example of the difficulties encountered in international business relations. The differences in culture and bureaucracy have been nearly impossible to overcome. However, the changes that now appear to be occurring in the Soviet Union have made things easier, and increased trade between the two countries seems more feasible. Business executives are beginning to understand what will be necessary for this project to succeed—an understanding which is clearly the first step toward making things happen. There have been some joint ventures started recently; if these succeed, then others are sure to follow. The Soviets are eager to acquire American products—and the technology to produce them—and we are interested in opening a vast new market.

The manufacture and sale of products in a foreign country takes a significant amount of time and work. First, the culture must be studied so that a company knows what can be sold and how to sell it. Laws must be understood—and sometimes changed. Most of all, however, the host country must be as interested in receiving the products as the manufacturer is in selling them, both on popular and official levels.

Sources: Peter Gumbel, "An American in Moscow: James Giffen Helps U.S. Firms Get a Foot in the Door," *Wall Street Journal,* May 3, 1988, p. 27; Kevin Kelley, "Going Global? You'll Need Lawyers, Lobbyists—and Luck," *Business Week,* March 21, 1988, p. 146; Geoffrey Jones, "Foundations of Foreign Success," *Management Today,* June 1987, pp. 86–88, 92, 130.

and currency exchange.[15] Home-country laws may also affect overseas operations. For example, the Foreign Corrupt Practices Act of 1977 makes it illegal for U.S. firms to bribe foreign political decision makers, an accepted practice in many countries. Critics charge that the act hampers U.S. business unduly, since ours is the only nation that has passed such a law.

FOR DISCUSSION

How does culture affect international management?

To succeed in a foreign country, business managers must know and adapt to the nature of those societies where they do business. Different cultures have different concepts of formality and courtesy, even different ideas about when a 10 A.M. meeting should start.[16] (See the box that has excerpted information for people about to encounter the United States for the first time.) It is especially important to understand a nation's social structure: separate subgroups based upon religion, ethnicity, language, sex, age, and class.

Multinational executives must adapt to the fact that levels of technology vary among countries. Production technologies that work well in the United States, with its fairly high technological level, might not work well in Ecuador. Moreover, the Ecuadorians and their government might resent being forced to adapt to new technology, a change that is often traumatic. Any technological change is difficult, and the support of the host government may be nearly essential.

Handling the Differences

COORDINATED RESOURCE

For a good videotape on international management, see "The Colonel Comes to Japan," an Enterprise series videotape available from LCA, 108 Wilmont Road, Deerfield, IL 60015-9990, or call 1-800-621-2131.

Managers pay particular attention to national peculiarities when they are deciding whether to enter or stay in a particular country and are considering ways of reducing the risks of their ventures. National peculiarities are also important in day-to-day operations. Sometimes these differences are difficult to see, but in other instances outsiders can spot opportunities in cultures that take factors in their own business environment for granted. Recently, Japanese stock traders have begun a process known as "dividend capture," which involves trading large blocks almost instantaneously to capture available dividends. The policy is perfectly legal but rarely practiced on such a large scale by American traders. The Japanese will buy a large block of stock and then sell it in seconds—merely to go on record as having owned it and to capture some of the dividends that the company pays.

Multinational companies must forecast economic conditions in the countries they operate in, sell to, or purchase from. Large companies have their own staffs of economists; smaller ones tend to rely on the general knowledge of nonspecialized line managers and on forecasts supplied by private companies, governments, and banks.

One of the most important things a multinational company must know about any country where it does business is the exchange rate between its currency and the currencies of other nations. When a company enters into a transaction with overseas customers or suppliers and it is not paid immediately, it is in effect gambling on the currency in which it will be paid. Say that a U.S. firm agrees to buy 100,000 francs' worth of raw materials for its Swiss factory from a French supplier. The terms of the agreement state that the U.S. firm will pay within 90 days in French francs. If the exchange rate shifts from 10 francs to the dollar at the time of the sale to 9 francs to the dollar 90 days later, the U.S. company will have to pay $11,111 for its 100,000 francs, not the $10,000 they would have cost at the time of the sale. A shift in the other direction would make the U.S. company's payment cheaper.

---

[15]Donald A. Ball and Wendell H. McCulloch, *International Business: Introduction and Emotion*, 2nd ed. (Plano, Texas: Business Publications Essentials, 1985), pp. 242–267.

[16]For an interesting early book that called managers' attention to these kinds of differences, see Edward T. Hall, *The Silent Language* (New York: Doubleday, 1959).

When millions of dollars change hands, such fluctuations can be significant. As a result, many multinational companies "hedge" and "cover" their international financial transactions. (These terms refer to methods of protecting investors from possible fluctuations in currency exchange rates.[17]) Companies can try to cover themselves against losses by negotiating contracts that specify which currency will be used in payment, as well as by taking out and making loans in foreign currencies. Foreign-exchange-rate forecasting, hedging, and covering methods have become very sophisticated.

political risk Possibility that political changes, either in the short or long run, can affect the activities of an organization doing business in foreign countries.

FOR DISCUSSION

What problems could arise from hiring local people as managers?

Political risk forecasting has become quite sophisticated, too. **Political risk** is the possibility that political changes, either in the short or the long run, will affect the activities of a company that does business abroad.[18] When companies, especially Japanese companies, expand overseas, they attract resentment. One way of defusing it is to hire local people, particularly well-connected ones, to staff local offices.

The use of local nationals in key management positions can also ease political, social, and cultural friction. And increasing numbers of companies have tried to prepare the managers they send overseas more thoroughly than they used to. These managers are encouraged to interest themselves in the host country's history, culture, and, especially, language, the straight road to the heart of any culture. (Exhibit 24-2 contains excerpts from a pamphlet for people about to encounter Americans for the first time.)

EXHIBIT 24-2 WHAT AMERICANS ARE LIKE

- Citizens of the United States call themselves "Americans." Other "Americans"—citizens of Mexico, Central and South America—often find the term inappropriate. However, Americans have been calling themselves "Americans" for the more than 200 years of their brief history, and you will hear the term often.
- Americans are very informal. They like to dress informally, entertain informally, and they treat each other in a very informal way, even when there is a great difference in age or social standing. Foreign students may consider this informality disrespectful, even rude, but it is a part of U.S. culture.
- Americans are generally competitive. The American style of friendly joking or banter, of "getting the last word in," and the quick witty reply are subtle forms of competition. Although such behavior is natural to Americans, you may find it overbearing or disagreeable.
- Americans are achievers. They are obsessed with records of achievement in sports and they keep business achievement charts on their office walls and sports awards displayed in their homes.
- Americans ask a lot of questions, some of which may to you seem pointless, uninformed, or elementary. You may be asked very personal questions by someone you have just met. No impertinence is intended; the questions usually grow out of genuine interest.
- Americans value punctuality. They keep appointment calendars and live according to schedules. To foreign students, Americans seem "always in a hurry," and this often makes them appear brusque. Americans are generally efficient and get a great many things done, simply by rushing around.
- Silence makes Americans nervous. They would rather talk about the weather than deal with silence in a conversation.

Source: Excerpts from Margo Ernest, ed., *Predeparture Orientation Handbook: For Foreign Students and Scholars Planning to Study in the United States* (Washington, D.C.: U.S. Information Agency, Bureau of Educational and Cultural Affairs, 1984), pp. 103–105, as cited in "What Americans Are Like," *New York Times*, April 16, 1985.

Some experts argue that most multinational companies have failed to adjust their production methods to suit the varying levels of technological sophistication found

[17]See Carl R. Beidleman, John J. Hilley, and James Greenleaf, "Alternatives in Hedging Long-Date Contractual Foreign Exchange Exposure," *Sloan Management Review* 24, no. 4 (Summer 1983):45–54.

[18]Robock and Simmonds, *International Business and Multinational Enterprises*, p. 342.

throughout the world. Introducing automated production techniques to a culture whose technology depends on extensive manual labor may be neither appropriate nor successful. Yet other observers praise multinational companies for using high technology in less-developed countries, which thereby gain experience with it.

Adjusting the Management Process

Operating in the international environment also affects the ways in which the basic management functions of planning, organizing, leading, and controlling are carried out. Our focus here, as in the previous discussion, will be on management actions at the "macro" level: What special steps are needed in the planning and control systems of MNEs? Should organizations be structured and coordinated differently in different countries? Should performance appraisal and reward systems differ among countries? In addition, there are decisions to be made on the "micro" level: How should one individual interact with another from a different country? Should people in one country be managed differently from people in another?

The discussion that follows covers some of the differences between purely domestic and international management processes, but obviously not all of them.

Planning. In Chapter 5, we noted some of the reasons that companies were likely to engage in strategic planning: the increasing rate of technological change, the growing complexity of both the managerial job and the external environment, and the longer lead time between current decisions and their future results. When a company is multinational, there are at least three additional factors that make strategic planning essential:[19]

1. The scope of the multinational management task—the many and varied tasks required to run a global organization.
2. The increase in the internationalization of the company—the greater distances between the firm's subsidiaries, the differences between their environments, and their complex interrelationships.
3. The necessity of greater efficiency due to increased and more varied competition. This desire for efficiency has led many organizations to institute worldwide marketing and production standards in an effort to reduce costs.

Rather than merely supplementing their domestic strategy with a separate international one, MNEs are likely to adopt a *global* strategic plan that incorporates both areas—often a difficult task given the firm's complex structure, multiple environments, and so on. One of the most difficult tasks of multinational strategic planning is balancing the autonomy and initiative of individual subsidiaries against the consistency and predictability of the total system.

The strategic planning process for an MNE goes beyond merely developing a strategy. It also places emphasis on improving the management practices of the organization. One study on the long-term planning of U.S. and Australian companies with significant international operations showed that three of the four activities that received relatively high effort were: (1) aiding corporate management in the formulation of strategy, goals, and objectives; (2) integrating operational and strategic planning; and (3) improving the quality of thinking of corporate management.[20] Another study, an

---

[19]Ball and McCulloch, *International Business,* pp. 611–612. See also David C. Shanks, "Strategic Planning for Global Competition," *Journal of Business Strategy* 5, no. 3 (Winter 1985):80–89.

[20]The fourth high-effort activity was associated with the mechanics of basic planning: defining guidelines, formats, and timetables. See Noel Capon, Chris Christodoulou, John U. Farley, and James Hulbert, "A Comparison of Corporate Planning Practice in American and Australian Manufacturing Companies," *Journal of International Business Studies* 15, no. 2 (Winter 1984):41–54.

informal inquiry conducted by Jacques Horovitz in the early 1980s, produced similar results. He found that large European MNEs were focusing their attention on improving the strategic thinking of their managers.[21] Thus, companies appear to be putting a high priority on learning to behave more strategically.

Organizing. Like any other company, an MNE must accomplish the basic organizing functions we discussed in Chapter 9. It is especially important for MNEs to strike an optimum balance between two basic organizational tasks that tend to inhibit one another. The first of these tasks is finding the most efficient manner to combine work into units (departmentalization). This must be balanced against the second tasks, the coordination of the work so that the organization's overall objectives can be met.[22]

Most MNEs have moved in an evolutionary manner from being domestic, to being somewhat international, to being fully multinational. As Table 24-3 shows, many of them create an international division early on. (The table uses the term "MNC"—multinational corporation—instead of MNE.) Later, however, they downgrade this division and start opting for global thinking, in which no distinction is made

[21]Jacques Horovitz, "New Perspectives on Strategic Management," *Journal of Business Strategy* 4, no. 3 (Winter 1984):19–33.

[22]Ball and McCulloch, *International Business*, p. 613.

TABLE 24-3 EVOLUTION OF MULTINATIONAL CORPORATION ORGANIZATIONAL FORM

MNC ENVIRONMENT	MNCs' ORGANIZATIONAL RESPONSE	TYPICAL PROBLEMS
I. Primarily domestic; Overseas business not significant.	Export department, International Divison.	Inability to integrate overseas operations with domestic operations.
II. Overseas operations and opportunities significant—sales, investment, returns.	Global organization—worldwide product groups or area groups.	Missed opportunities due to a simple dominant orientation.
III. Business environment complex—simultaneous need for sensitivity to diversity in markets and ability to achieve economies.	Global matrix structure.	Inability to get strategic focus for businesses.
	Use of relative power for strategic focus.	Need for very sophisticated managerial behavior and systems.
	Use of corporate functional groups for strategic coordination. Use of corporate planning teams.	
IV. Host government's interest in containing strategic freedom of salient businesses.	Response contingent upon the relative bargaining strengths of host government and the firm.	Judging the relative bargaining strengths.
V. Host government's desire to contain the strategic freedom of all MNCs operating within its territory	Opt out or adapt.	Businesses that the subsidiary is involved in do not reflect parents' strengths. Tacit host government—subsidiary coalition.

Source: Anant R. Negandhi, *Functioning of the Multinational Corporation: A Global Comparative Study* (New York: Pergamon Press, 1980). Reproduced by permission.

between domestic and international business. This process involves frequent reorganization and experimentation with different organizational structures as the company seeks to balance the requirements of changing strategies, capabilities, and environments.[23]

EXTRA EXERCISE

You are the manager in charge of selecting employees to be sent on international assignment. What qualities, experience, and characteristics would you look for in prospective employees?

Even when the company has achieved a global orientation, its operations in many different environments make it difficult to decide which departmentalization method will work the best. Most commonly, operations are partitioned according to either products or geography. Less frequently, departments will be created according to types of customers or organizational function (production, finance, personnel, marketing, and so on). No matter which form is chosen, there are going to be tough trade-offs.

Because of these trade-offs, many MNEs adopt some form of matrix structure (see Chapter 9). Although matrix structures may be necessary in these cases, substantial managerial skill is required to make them work well and to be able to work within them. Furthermore, they are viewed as problematic by those who subscribe to Peters and Waterman's observations about the desirability of simple form (see Chapter 1).[24]

Companies that decide to go international have a further organizational choice: to join forces with a foreign firm or perhaps even with several. They may do so to exploit opportunities in the other firm's country, in a third country, or in both. Indeed Howard V. Perlmutter and David A. Heenan, who have studied international cooperation,[25] argue that a true **global strategic partnership** among companies must be international, "extending beyond a few developed countries," to include newly industrializing, less-developed, and socialist nations.[26] Firms that forge these strategic alliances will try either to assume "leadership as low-cost suppliers" or to come forward with the best possible product or service, or both.

global strategic partnership Alliance formed by an organization with one or more foreign countries, generally with an eye toward exploiting the other countries' opportunities and toward assuming leadership in either supply or production.

Consider, for example, the strategic alliances forged by Philips of the Netherlands, Europe's largest electronics company. Philips wanted to strengthen itself in two other markets: the United States and the Far East. In the United States, Philips allied itself with AT&T, the communications giant, which is giving the Dutch company access to its electronic components in return for Philips' global marketing expertise. In Japan, Philips joined forces with Matsushita. And "every Philips alliance has cost leadership and/or differentiated product superiority in at least one national market as its objective."[27]

To be successful, think Perlmutter and Heenan, global strategic partnerships must meet six conditions. First, "each partner must believe the other has something it needs."[28] The partners must choose a strategy before they start to do business, not afterward. They must share the same attitudes toward control of the new business. U.S. companies, say the two researchers, have traditionally felt that "power, not parity, should govern collaborative ventures," whereas Japanese and European companies "subscribe to management by consensus."[29]

What Perlmutter and Heenan regard as the "most important factor in the endurance of a global alliance is chemistry"—operating styles, corporate cultures, and moral values.[30] Such joint ventures must also agree to discard whatever organizational forms do not work. Finally, there must be some ultimate decision maker and some way

[23]For suggestions on how excessive reorganizations have been avoided by such companies as Corning, Timken, and Eli Lilly, see Christopher A. Bartlett, "MNCs: Get Off the Reorganization Merry-Go-Round," *Harvard Business Review* 61, no. 2 (March–April 1983):138–146, and "How Multinational Organizations Evolve," *Journal of Business Strategy* 3, no. 1 (Summer 1983):20–32.

[24]Ball and McCulloch, *International Business*, pp. 613–623.

[25]This section on global strategic partnerships is based upon their article, "Cooperate to Compete Globally," *Harvard Business Review* 64 (March–April 1986):136–152."

[26]Ibid., p. 137.

[27]Ibid., p. 137.

[28]Ibid., p. 145.

[29]Ibid., p. 146.

[30]Ibid., p. 146.

of making decisions stick. Otherwise, "the new venture suffers from unclear lines of authority, poor communication, and slow decision making."[31]

Staffing. With regard to staffing, there are both advantages and disadvantages to being a multinational firm. On the one hand, finding the right people for organizational positions is often more difficult for MNEs than for domestic companies. Talented employees are often unwilling to relocate to another country. On the other hand, an MNE literally has a whole world of talent to draw on.

Of particular importance to MNEs is effective selection and training of any personnel who will have a high level of international involvement, either by being stationed abroad or by interacting frequently with managers and other individuals from overseas. Rosalie Tung has reported that Japanese MNEs have better success rates with managers they send overseas than do U.S. MNEs. She attributes this success to more effective selection and training of managers and offers several recommendations to American MNEs seeking to improve their performance in this area. These include sponsoring training programs for managers and their families going abroad and developing a longer-term orientation toward overseas operations. This longer-term orientation would involve longer tenures abroad for managers and more consistent support for them from corporate headquarters.[32]

Many men (and some women) used to assume that women were unsuitable for or uninterested in international jobs, particularly in countries with patriarchal social structures. The fallacy of this viewpoint is now generally recognized, although even today less than 3 percent of all international managers are women.[33]

International compensation is frequently a tricky area for MNEs. Often there are conflicts within the organization between attempts to adapt to differences among countries and pressures to maintain uniform compensation policies and procedures throughout the organization as a whole. If an organization adopts inconsistent salary scales, it will probably have difficulty in moving managers from high-paying countries to low-paying ones. In addition, jealousy may arise among managers who receive different compensation for comparable jobs. Yet if company-wide uniform pay scales are decided on, the MNE may find itself paying well above the market level in some countries, which can be considered an unnecessary expense. In other countries, its salary scales may be below the country's norm, and the MNE may have trouble attracting and retaining skilled managers. One solution that many companies have adopted is to pay a similar base salary and then add on various bonuses and allowances according to individual situations.[34]

Although executive-compensation practices have always varied widely from nation to nation, being dependent upon such factors as tax policies and economic conditions, it is now possible to identify a few trends in international practice. First, as more and more managers and executives become needed, the pressure to recruit and retain capable individuals has become stronger. Second, as their services become more valuable, talented managerial and executive personnel are demanding greater compensation. Third, corporate policy in the U.S. and other countries has influenced international compensation practices: For example, many American MNEs have developed new compensation programs at home that are designed to be extended to operations abroad. Fourth, local tax and other compensation-related laws such as top marginal income rate must, as always, be considered. Some specific national trends include the following: In Germany, individuals at lower-management levels are being granted

[31]Ibid., p. 150.

[32]Rosalie L. Tung, "Human Resource Planning in Japanese Multinationals: A Model for U.S. Firms?" *Journal of International Business Studies* 15, no. 2 (Fall 1984):139–149.

[33]Nancy J. Adler, "Women in International Management: Where Are They?" *California Management Review* 26, no. 4 (Summer 1984):81.

[34]Ball and McCulloch, *International Business*, p. 644; *Worldwide Executive Compensation: New Problems and Solutions* (New York: Business International Corp., 1974).

participation in performance-based incentive plans; French managers are realizing benefits from more long-term incentive plans and are receiving larger annual bonuses; Japanese companies are gradually increasing the rate of incentive compensation through performance bonuses; from 1979 to 1985, British firms offering executive stock-option plans climbed from 10 percent to 96 percent, with executive bonus plans rising from a participation rate of 8 percent to 67 percent during the same period.[35]

An organization composed of individuals with a wide variety of backgrounds, nationalities, and cultures obviously offers many possibilities for conflict and disagreement. Based on the theories of conflict management and its relationship to creativity discussed in Chapter 14, an MNE has a great opportunity to capitalize on its diversity. Although poor resolution of conflict will hurt organizational performance, effective resolution has the potential to open up higher levels of creativity and performance.

Leading. The topic of leading in an MNE is currently a source of much debate. Because of its importance, we will devote special attention to it in the section on Selecting a Managerial Approach.

Controlling. Theoretically, an MNE could centralize all aspects of control and organizational decision making at its headquarters. As we saw in our discussion of delegation (Chapter 11), however, this would be extremely inefficient and impractical. The same can be said of allowing all decisions to be made at the business-unit level.

Generally, the decision-making and control processes are distributed between the company headquarters and its subsidiaries in each nation. As Exhibit 24-3 shows, there are five factors that influence where decisions will be made.

EXHIBIT 24-3 FIVE FACTORS INFLUENCING CONTROL DECISIONS IN AN MNE

1. Trade-offs between the benefits of standardization and the tailoring of products and equipment to local conditions.
2. The proficiency of overseas business unit management and the degree of reliance on that management at corporate headquarters.
3. The size of the MNE and the length of time it has been an MNE.
4. The need for individual units to make sacrifices for the benefit of the international enterprise as a whole.
5. The need to motivate unit management through involvement in the decision-making process.

Source: Donald A. Ball and Wendell H. McCulloch, Jr., *International Business: Introduction and Essentials,* 2nd ed. (Plano, Tex.: Business Publications, 1985).

bureaucratic control Method of control that employs strict regulations to ensure desired behavior by organizational units—often used by multinational enterprises to control subsidiaries.

culture control Method of control, often associated with large Japanese companies, that emphasizes implicit and informal direction based on a broad company culture.

The two prevaling control models used by MNEs today are bureaucratic control and culture control. **Bureaucratic control** employs explicit rules and regulations that outline desired output and behavior. **Culture control,** which is characteristic of many large Japanese firms, utilizes implicit and informal direction based on a broad company culture.[36] Bureaucratic companies usually spell out operational procedures for their foreign managers in the form of manuals and keep close tabs on those managers' actions. Culture control firms, on the other hand, tend to train their managers extensively before they send them overseas and then give them more authority and autonomy and require fewer formal reports.

---

[35]Brian J. Brooks, "Trends in International Executive Compensation," *Personnel* 64, no. 5 (1987):67–70.

[36]B. R. Baliga and Alfred M. Jaeger, "Multinational Corporations: Control Systems and Delegation Issues," *Journal of International Business Studies* 15, no. 2 (Fall 1984):26–28. See also Alfred M. Jaeger, "The Transfer of Organizational Culture Overseas: An Approach to Control in the Multinational Corporation," *Journal of International Business Studies* 14, no. 2 (Fall 1983):101.

All MNEs need to have their affiliates report regularly on new technology, market developments, and competitors' actions. These and other reports can aid headquarters in the vital task of developing and implementing an effective management evaluation system. The tasks of tracking events in the international environment and developing effective systems for evaluating local management can be quite complex due to the variety of circumstances under which each subsidiary and its management operate.

SELECTING A MANAGERIAL APPROACH

FOR DISCUSSION

How can a prospective manager best prepare for a career that will increasingly require international activity?

As was mentioned above, the issue of leadership in MNEs is currently the focus of lively inquiry and debate. The issues involved go beyond the question of which managerial approach should be favored by top management for the total system and for each host country operation. Also raised is the question of which managerial approach is likely to work best in the *home* country.

Our discussion will be built on three possibilities:

1. The possibility that no single approach to management—including the Western or Japanese ones—will be effective and appropriate in all the world's diverse societies.
2. The possibility that Japanese management procedures offer some insights and broad guidelines for effective management in general—even if they are not the universally best way to manage in all environments.
3. The possibility that a new synthesis of management theories may be emerging, building on the earlier successes of U.S./Western management approaches in the 1950s and 1960s and the present success of many companies like the ones studied by Peters and Waterman—companies with some practices quite similar to those of well-managed Japanese companies.

Applying U.S. Approaches Abroad

FOR DISCUSSION

Ask your students who have traveled abroad to share their impressions and experiences.

How well do U.S. approaches work abroad? There are at least two ways to view this question. Plainly, on the one hand, U.S. companies have a long record of successful overseas operations following the types of practices supported by U.S./Western-based theory. It was not too long ago, in fact, that some writers feared that U.S. MNEs would completely dominate world business.[37] And their management skills were seen as their key competitive advantage.

On the other hand, management theory states that what works managerially in a given situation depends on a number of factors. (Recall the contingency theories of leadership that were presented in Chapter 15 and the various influences that can enter into motivation as explained in Chapter 14.) Therefore, it is logical to assume that, in the international arena, what works with some people won't work with others. An organization needs to plan wherever it has operations but the best way to go about planning might be quite different in India and in the United States.

The Hofstede Studies. As we saw in Chapter 14, the Dutch management scholar Geert Hofstede conducted studies in 40 countries in order to draw some conclusions about the relationship between national chatacter and motivational propensities among employees.[38] He concluded that not only do people vary a lot, but those variations

[37] See, for example, Jean-Jacques Servan-Schreiber, *The American Challenge* (New York: Atheneum, 1968).

[38] Geert Hofstede, "The Cultural Relativity of Organizational Practices and Theories," *Journal of International Business Studies* 14, no. 1 (Fall 1983):78–85, and *Culture's Consequences: International Differences in Work-Related Values* (Beverly Hills, Calif.: Sage Publications, 1980). For a rich debate on the applicability of Western management in other cultures, see Geert Hofstede, "Motivation, Leadership, and Organization: Do American Theories Apply Abroad?" *Organizational Dynamics* 9, no. 1 (Summer 1980):42–63, and "Do American Theories Apply Abroad? A Reply to Goodstein and Hunt," *Organizational Dynamics* 10, no. 1 (Summer 1981):63–68; and John W. Hunt, "Applying American Behavioral Science: Some Cross-Cultural Problems," *Organizational Dynamics* 10, no. 1 (Summer 1981):55–62.

seriously challenge the rules of effective managerial practice based on Western theories and peoples. As can be seen in Exhibit 24-4, Hofstede cites four dimensions that he feels describe important aspects of a national culture.

EXHIBIT 24-4 HOFSTEDE'S FOUR IMPORTANT DIMENSIONS OF A NATIONAL CULTURE

1. The first dimension he calls *individualism versus collectivism*. This measures an individual's relationship with other people and the degree to which the desire for personal freedom is played off against the need for social ties.
2. The dimension called power *distance* evaluates the way a particular society handles the inequality among people. On one end of the scale are countries and peoples that try to play down inequality as much as possible. At the other end are cultures that accept and support large imbalances in power, status, and wealth.
3. The *uncertainty avoidance* dimension measures how a society deals with the uncertainty of the future. A weak-uncertainty-avoidance society is one that does not feel threatened by this uncertainty and is generally tolerant and secure about the future. Strong uncertainty-avoidance cultures, on the other hand, try to overcome future uncertainties by developing institutions that create security and avoid risk. These include legal, technological, and religious institutions.
4. The last dimension Hofstede calls *masculinity versus feminity*. Hofstede defines a society as masculine if there are extensive divisions of social roles by sex and as feminine if these divisions are relatively small.

Sources: Geert Hofstede, "The Cultural Relativity of Organizational Practices and Theories," *Journal of International Business Studies* 14, no. 1 (Fall 1983); *Culture's Consequences: International Differences in Work-Related Values* (Beverly Hills, Calif.: Sage Publications, 1980).

HERE'S AN EXAMPLE

McDonald's Corporation opened its first hamburger bar in Eastern Europe in Belgrade, Yugoslavia. The Belgrade McDonald's is a joint venture with Yugoslavia's biggest general trading concern, Genex. Says a senior McDonald's executive, "We plan to move step by step, one restaurant at a time, one country at a time." (*Financial Times*, 3/29/88)

In light of the differences between nations that he found in these dimensions, Hofstede feels that it is unrealistic to expect any single management approach to be applicable worldwide. For example, he notes that U.S. theories on leadership are appropriate for leading people in a culture that is extremely high in individualism. Applying these theories to countries that are collectivist in nature—most Third World nations, for example—is likely to yield an ineffective employer-employee relationship.

Western theories of motivation, he feels, are likewise flawed by a high individualism bias. In the United States, the strongest form of motivation is regarded as an internal need to gain self-respect or achieve personal goals. In collectivist societies, motivation is more externally directed. People feel obligations to the groups to which they belong, such as their family, enterprise, or country, and are driven to seek more "status" within these groups than to gain self-realization.

Hofstede sees organizational structure and policies as ways to distribute power and avoid uncertainty. As such, it is affected by power distance and uncertainty avoidance. The United States placed very close to the middle of the scale in both these aspects in Hofstede's studies. This fact may account for some of the success of U.S. MNEs—organizational practices favored by U.S. managers may be reasonably acceptable to people from cultures at other ends of the scale.

HERE'S AN EXAMPLE

In order to avoid likely U.S. trade sanctions, Japan agreed to allow U.S. construction companies the right to bid on 14 major public works projects. These projects include a new airport near Osaka, the Tokyo Bay Bridge, and others. (*Wall Street Journal*, 3/30/88, p. 3)

Applying Japanese Approaches Abroad and Synthesizing Differing Approaches

Although Hofstede has expressed serious doubts about the applicability of American/Western management practices in other countries, some observers have become very excited about the effectiveness of Japanese practices. The study of Japanese management has become such a fad, in fact, that stories like the following have been heard in many a boardroom:

> A Frenchman, a Japanese, and an American are to be executed by a firing squad. As the executioner leads them into the courtyard, he offers each the traditional last request. ''I wish,'' responds the Frenchman, ''to sing La Marseillaise one last time.'' ''Granted,'' replies the executioner. ''I would like to give a lecture on Japanese management one last time,'' says the Japanese. ''Granted,'' says the executioner, who then looks at the American. ''Please,'' implores the American, ''shoot me first so I won't have to listen to any more lectures on Japanese management!''

It should be noted that what most people refer to as ''Japanese management practices'' are drawn from a select group of companies, responsible for perhaps as little as one-third of employment within Japan.

William G. Ouchi (see Chapter 2) is among those who have studied Japanese business with the hope that it might provide solutions to some American problems.[39] Table 24-4 lists some of the characteristics noted by Ouchi that distinguish Japanese organizations from American ones.

TABLE 24-4 CHARACTERISTICS OF JAPANESE AND AMERICAN ORGANIZATIONS

JAPANESE ORGANIZATIONS	AMERICAN ORGANIZATIONS
Lifetime Employment	Short-Term Employment
Slow Evaluation and Promotion	Rapid Evaluation and Promotion
Non-Specialized Career Paths	Specialized Career Paths
Implicit Control Mechanisms	Explicit Control Mechanisms
Collective Decision Making	Individual Decision Making
Collective Responsibility	Individual Responsibility
Wholistic Concern	Segmented Concern

Source: William G. Ouchi, *Theory Z: How American Business Can Meet the Japanese Challenge* (Reading, Mass.: Addison-Wesley, 1981), p. 58.

HERE'S AN EXAMPLE

In the United States, Honda Motor Company now sells more cars than any foreign company. Their future is inextricably tied to the U.S. market. Says the company's CEO and president, Tadashi Kume, ''In the future, I expect America to take on a more important position in our total business.'' (*Business Week*, 4/25/88, pp. 90–96)

These differences in organizational characteristics are associated with differences in managerial behavior. Naturally, there are wide variations in how individual Japanese managers act, as is the case in all countries. Yet, there are a number of ways in which Japanese managers *appear*, on the average, to differ from American managers. Overall, Japanese managers appear to be more concerned with the longer-term implications of decisions and actions and more willing to make current sacrifices for future benefits. They are more likely to encourage subordinates to participate in decision making and to welcome and acknowledge suggestions from subordinates. Partly because of this participation, they are also less likely to make quick, unilateral decisions; communication between managers and subordinates is also more indirect and subtle. Managers try hard to avoid embarrassing co-workers in public or in private. They get to know their co-workers well as individuals and show concern for their welfare, even helping to resolve personal problems outside the workplace.

There is much controversy over Japanese management style. Some observers doubt that management is the key to the success of ''Japan, Inc.'' Others challenge the ''one big happy family'' image of Japanese companies and argue that employee fear of punishment is a major factor in Japanese success. They also point out the restricted

[39]William G. Ouchi, *Theory Z: How American Business Can Meet the Japanese Challenge* (Reading, Mass.: Addison-Wesley, 1981). Other studies of note are Richard Pascale and Anthony Athos, *The Art of Japanese Management* (New York: Simon & Schuster, 1981); and N. Hatvany and V. Pucik, ''An Integrated Management System: Lessons from the Japanese Experience,'' *Academy of Management Review* 6, no. 3 (July 1981):469–480.

nature of some of the supposed employee benefits in Japanese firms. For example, "lifetime employment" is essentially restricted to males, since it is assumed that women will work for a few years, get married, and then leave the company. In addition, guaranteed lifetime employment terminates at age 55. Most individuals are then forced to seek other, lower-paying jobs because of relatively modest pension benefits.[40]

HERE'S AN EXAMPLE

Japanese corporations have been awarding multimillion dollar grants to universities across the United States and have emerged as the largest foreign source of university research funding. The money is to foster goodwill but is also a modest investment to gain access to America's brightest talents. (*Business Week*, 7/11/88, pp. 70–72)

In the overall analysis, however, Japanese companies do seem to do many things well. Several studies offer evidence that Japanese management practices work well for Japanese subsidiaries operating in the United States and the United Kingdom.[41] In fact, Pascale and Athos, among other observers, have noted that there is much similarity between well-managed Japanese firms and well-managed U.S. firms.[42]

This similarity between well-managed Japanese and U.S. firms should not come as too much of a surprise. And it contains a unique irony. When they studied American management theories during the 1950s, the Japanese accepted them as genuine practices of American companies, not realizing that in actuality few U.S. companies followed them.[43] When American managers were interviewed by those visitors from overseas, they frequently described what they felt they should be doing rather than what they were doing. In addition, the Japanese listened carefully to some American experts who were largely ignored at home, like W. Edwards Deming, whose concepts of quality control profoundly influenced the Japanese drive to move from a country known for shoddy products to a world leader in manufacturing quality.[44] These theories and apparent management practices were then adapted to the Japanese situation and put into practice. A high commitment was made to refining and improving them over time according to feedback gathered from their usage. Honda is one example of a Japanese company that used this approach successfully in designing its products for the U.S. market.[45]

QUOTATION FROM A BUSINESS RESEARCHER

"Fully 95 percent of the planet's population lies outside the United States and it is growing 70 percent faster. Much of it is also getting rich in a hurry."—Christopher Knowlton, *Fortune* writer (*Fortune*, 6/6/88, p. 87)

The same "try it, find out what happens, try to improve it, and try again" approach may well be the "secret" to management excellence in any country or organization in the future. Fayol's perspective that organizations require planning, organizing, leading, and controlling is likely to remain valid, but how this general framework will be best applied in any given country will depend on many contingencies. As managers "try, observe, adjust, and try again," the resulting practices around the world should acquire similarities to each other, and the differences may look like "commonsense" differences once they are uncovered. And those practices that do work will continue to change and evolve over time.[46]

---

[40] S. Prakash Sethi, Nobuaki Namiki, and Carl L. Swanson, *The Attack on Theory Z: The False Promise of the Japanese Miracle* (Marshfield, Mass.: Pitman, 1984).

[41] See Martin K. Starr and Nancy E. Bloom, *The Performance of Japanese-Owned Firms in America: Survey Report* (New York: Center for Operations, Graduate School of Business, Columbia University, 1985); Malcolm Trevor, "Does Japanese Management Work in Britain?" *Journal of General Management* 8, no. 4 (Summer 1983):28–43; and Satoshi Kamata, *Japan in the Passing Lane: An Insider's Account of Life in a Japanese Auto Factory* (New York: Pantheon, 1983). For a discussion of the extent to which some Japanese companies have introduced these techniques in U.S. subsidiaries, see Richard D. Robinson, *The Japan Syndrome: Is There One?* (Atlantic: Georgia State University, 1985).

[42] See also Pascale and Athos, *The Art of Japanese Management;* and J. Bernard Keys and Thomas R. Miller, "The Japanese Management Theory Jungle," *Academy of Management Review* 9, no. 2 (April 1984):345–346.

[43] Raymond G. Hunt, "Taking Mayo and McGregor Seriously," *California Management Review* 27, no. 1 (Fall 1984):173–176; and Ryuji Fukada, *Managerial Engineering: Techniques for Improving Quality and Productivity in the Workplace* (Stamford, Conn.: Productivity, 1983).

[44] W. Edwards Deming, "The Roots of Quality Control," *Pacific Basin Quaterly,* no. 12 (Spring–Summer 1985):1–4.

[45] Richard T. Pascale, "Perspectives on Strategy: The Real Story Behind Honda's Success," *California Management Review* 26, no. 3 (Spring 1984):47–72.

[46] Modesto A. Maidique, "Point of View: The New Management Thinkers," *California Management Review* 26, no. 1 (Fall 1983):151–161.

ILLUSTRATIVE CASE STUDY Wrap-Up

Sumitomo: The Thrust Toward International Banking

Sumitomo's activities suggest strongly its belief that competitiveness and the separation of business and government will endure as a part of American business culture. The Japanese bank is clearly betting that, in the future, the restrictions imposed on investment and commercial banks will be lifted and that competition will heighten. It has also decided that as Europe moves toward becoming an essentially unified economic community, it is important for the bank to establish a presence in that community.

The success of Sumitomo depends on whether the bank can continue to plan, organize, lead, and control in a more globally competitive environment. Most Japanese companies have shown a remarkable ability to do just that, and Sumitomo is no exception. ■

SUMMARY

The economies of all nations have become more interdependent. Companies and individuals can own foreign assets either by purchasing shares in other companies, which own the assets, or by going multinational and managing assets directly.

Steven Hymer argued that most multinational companies are ''oligopolistic.'' Raymond Vernon suggested that U.S. companies go multinational more often than foreign ones do because during much of the present century, Americans generated most new consumer products and production techniques. H. Levy and M. Sarrat compare companies that acquire foreign production facilities to prudent investors who diversify their investment portfolios.

The internationalization of business firms didn't get seriously under way until the end of World War II. The extent of a company's internationalization is defined by such factors as the directness of the company's international involvement, the company's organizational structure, and the importance of the company's international concerns relative to its domestic ones. The way an organization's management perceives the international realm can generally be categorized as either ethnocentric, polycentric, or geocentric.

On balance, it would seem that multinational enterprises (MNEs) do have a positive effect on their host countries. Potential benefits would include technology and capital transfer, improvement of the host country's balance of payments, and the creation of local job and career opportunities. The most debated issue surrounding the effect of MNEs on their home countries is whether foreign investment, particularly in manufacturing, causes the loss of domestic jobs.

A manager dealing in the international environment faces a unique set of challenges and problems. For one thing, international managers must cope with a variety of environments that are all quite different from one another. In addition, there are often conflicts within an MNE between attempts to adapt to differences among countries and pressures to maintain uniform policies throughout the MNE as a whole.

There is currently much debate over selecting a managerial approach for an MNE. Although U.S. firms have attained a fair amount of success operating abroad, Geert Hofstede's research indicates that any single approach is likely to be ineffective in many of the diverse societies around the world. The success of Japanese companies, however, suggests that Japanese management practices may offer some guidelines toward effective management in general.

REVIEW QUESTIONS

1. Why do companies become internationalized?
2. Describe the four degrees of corporate internationalization identified by Christopher Korth.
3. What are some international activities in which a company might engage?
4. List the three attitudes toward internationalization that managers may adopt.
5. Define a multinational enterprise (MNE).

6. What are the possible impacts of MNEs on their host countries? On their home countries?
7. What aspects of the international environment must managers be aware of?
8. How can familiarity with and responsiveness to foreign sociocultural characteristics aid international managers.
9. How should managers adjust management practices when planning for the international environment?
10. What special problems do the managers of MNEs face when organizing international operations?
11. According to Rosalie Tung, how can the managers of American MNEs learn from the human resource management practices of Japanese MNEs?
12. Discuss Hofstede's findings on variations in national character. How might these be relevant to managers?
13. How does Japanese management style differ from U.S. management style?

CASE STUDY Lucky-Goldstar: Management, Korean Style

When Japanese companies first began manufacturing in the United States, many people smiled at certain of their corporate oddities, such as prework exercise, but analysts were also struck with the efficiency of the Japanese management style. Now, the Koreans are coming, setting up their own factories and bringing their version of management "harmony."

Dozens of South Korean corporations have already opened offices in the United States, and two have begun manufacturing operations. The Lucky-Goldstar Group opened a color television factory in Huntsville, Alabama, two and a half years ago and is now bustling with expansion plans. Last fall the Samsung Group also began producing color televisions, at a factory in Roxbury Township, N.J.

In gambling that they can manufacture profitably in America, just when American manufacturers are bitterly complaining and even going abroad because of foreign competition, the Koreans are counting on a blend of their own traditional management style with American business methods.

The Korean style is similar to the much better known Japanese approach, although experts say the Koreans are often more willing to blend their techniques with American methods. Korean management aims to foster a family atmosphere, in which employees interact freely with executives and share a strong commitment to the company's success.

Acting more as a gentle patriarch than as president of the Gold Star of America plant, P. W. Suh has taken charge of the delicate task of grafting Korean management principles onto Dixie. Mr. Suh concedes that there have been awkward moments—such as the reluctance of some American workers to wear uniforms—but in general employees and management alike appear to appreciate the result.

"You wouldn't believe what Gold Star does for us," said Rachel Cothren, pausing from her job on the assembly line. "My husband was in the hospital for major surgery, and some of the management came and sat with me through that. Mr. Suh came and stayed with me in intensive care, and brought books and magazines."

This carefully cultivated image of a friendly, caring company of one happy family typifies the Korean management style. But the friendship is not for nothing. It is intended to keep unions at bay and to foster a loyalty and enthusiasm in the work force that will generate more televisions per hour than American management can. One measure of its success is a daily absenteeism rate at Gold Star that averages 1 percent, compared with 5 percent in American companies.

The idea is to import not Korean televisions but Korean management methods. These methods are associated with an economic miracle that produced even faster economic growth in South Korea over the last 25 years than in Japan. The Korean growth was three times faster than that in the United States.

The principal weapon in the Korean armory is its management philosophy, what the Koreans call *inhwa,* or harmony. Even in South Korea, Lucky-Goldstar is an exemplar of this philosophy.

"If we are in a hurry, we may ask employees for special consideration to do things differently," said D. H. Koo, president of overseas operations for the Lucky-Goldstar Group, explaining the Korean approach. "And they will oblige. But in the United States maybe they do not care that there is a hurry."

Mr. Koo and his colleagues in the Lucky-Goldstar boardrooms want employees at the Huntsville plant to care, and so they are trying to transplant *inhwa.* "I expect dedication and loyalty in the future, if we help our family," Mr. Suh said, using "family" to refer to his work force.

Telling employees about company goals, and even asking for help, are cardinal principles of Gold Star. "Family meetings," for all of the staff, are held monthly, and quality discussions are scheduled for every two weeks. In addition, bonuses are used to build enthusiasm. About three days a week, workers get a bonus—an hour of overtime pay—if their assembly line has increased output while maintaining quality levels. Employees also get $50 in cash if they do not miss a day of work for three months.

Similar management methods are used at the other Korean manufacturing plant in the United States, Samsung's in Roxbury Township. The employees are also called a family, and interaction between workers and executives is stressed.

Like the Japanese, the Koreans are coming to the United States largely because of fear that protectionist rules could keep out their exports. In February 1984, the Commerce Department ruled that Korean electronics companies were dumping—or selling for less than fair value—color television sets in the United States. Gold Star is now required to post cash deposits of 7.4 percent of the value of its shipments, although the final assessments may vary from that.

But in coming to America, the Koreans are also facing tough price competition. Although 1983 and 1984 were boom years for color televisions, with about 16 million units sold last year, price competition has been severe.

Although imports have been a major reason for the price competition, three out of four television sets sold in the United States are still made in this country. About two dozen manufacturers continue to produce sets in the United States.

Charles K. Ryan, an analyst at Merrill Lynch & Company, has said that Korean companies operating in South Korea and in the United States might come to dominate the lower level of the color television market—namely, that for 13-inch and low-priced 19-inch models—while more established companies would continue to produce larger, more complex televisions whose mark-up is higher.

One frustration for Gold Star is that because it lacks name recognition and a reputation, it has to sell at lower prices than its competition. Gold Star sells its televisions under its own name and under private brand names like Montgomery Ward, General Electric, and K mart.

Notwithstanding the competition, Gold Star seems to be happy with its American experience. Since opening the factory in Huntsville, Gold Star has doubled its capacity and plans soon to manufacture microwave ovens, computers, and videocassette recorders. Gold Star executives are buoyed by the finding that televisions produced in Huntsville can compete in price with sets produced in South Korea.

The basic wage in the Huntsville plant is $4.56 an hour, although bonuses and benefits add significantly to that. The comparable South Korean wage is $1.30. But mechanization has reduced the role of labor in the Alabama plant, so that it costs only about $7 more to produce a television set in Huntsville than to build it in South Korea and ship it to the United States. The anti-dumping duty on Korean sets more than makes up that gap, Gold Star said.

Source: Nicholas D. Kristof, "Management, Korean Style," *New York Times,* April 11, 1985, pp. Diff.

Case Questions

1. Describe the Korean method of management. What advantages and disadvantages does it have over U.S. methods? How has it borrowed from U.S. methods?
2. Why are Korean manufacturers setting up manufacturing operations in the United States?
3. In your opinion, will the entry of foreign electronics manufacturers have a positive or negative impact on the domestic electronics industry? Explain.
4. Can the recent success of Japanese and Korean MNEs be best explained by political, economic, or cultural factors?

CASE STUDY

The Colonel Goes to Japan

For successful American companies, operating overseas often means reevaluation of the way they do business. While the science of management remains more or less the same despite national borders, the art of exploiting productive resources is almost totally dependent on sensitivity to the cultural peculiarities of the target country.

This truism was effectively put into practice by Kentucky Fried Chicken when it entered the Japanese restaurant industry in 1970. The success of this venture reflects a clever mix of modern management techniques with centuries-old traditions.

Realizing that the Japanese business environment stressed relationship management more than cold economic rationality, the company made a joint-venture agreement with the Mitsubishi trading company. Not only would this partner provide substantial capital to finance a chain of stores, but it would also provide KFC with access into [sometimes xenophobic] Japanese business community.

KFC hired Loy Weston—an IBM executive—to head its Japanese operations. One of the first things that Weston did upon taking charge was to get himself a local deputy. He felt that the young entrepreneur, who had approached him to sell cardboard boxes on his own initiative, had extraordinary leadership qualities in combination with a good feel for business culture and practice in Japan, and would be a valuable asset in a foreign environment.

The duo then began the process of adapting the American concept of fried chicken to local conditions. Capitalizing on the "hire for life" norm in Japan, Weston decided that he should make an extensive investment in the training of employees. This strategy would help not only in providing good service when the business went on-stream, but would also encourage employee involvement in the whole marketing and sales process—a key element of Japanese management philosophy.

Simultaneously, Weston carefully developed trusting relationships with the individual store owners. He was quick to recognize that a firm handshake provided stronger ties than a formal written contract. With a gregarious personality—and a sensitivity for local traditions and societal hierarchies—he was able to strike good rapport with the store owners.

In addition to managing a matrix of relationships around him, Weston was also quite open to adapting operational variables to local business conditions. Instead of enforcing American standards down Japanese throats, he modified the store layout to accommodate crowded population centers and changed the menu to suit the Japanese palate.

Marketing and advertising, too, were adapted to the Japanese mind. Because the customers liked to see what they ordered from the menu, samples made out of wax and silicon were displayed in front of every store. Television commercials emphasized the Americanness of the product and suggested an air of aristocratic elegance around the food.

Before a new store went on-stream, employees of the company made a courtesy tour of the neighborhood to distribute gifts of smoked chicken and to solicit good wishes. All the businesses in the area, including the competition, were presented with a token gift and an invitation (with a discount coupon) to visit the new KFC outlet. Then on the day of inauguration, a religious ceremony was performed by a priest to solicit the cooperation of otherworldly forces!

By 1981, KFC had successfully established itself in the $65 billion Japanese food market. It had 324 stores across the nation, of which 125 were company-owned, with the remaining being franchises.

Source: PBS videocassette entitled "Enterprise: The Colonel Comes to Japan."

Case Questions

1. How did Kentucky Fried Chicken overcome the so-called "trade barriers" to American companies doing business in Japan?
2. Describe planning, organizing, leading, and controlling at KFC-Japan.
3. What barriers might exist to the continued success of KFC in Japan?
4. What lessons can be learned for other organizations doing business in Japan? In other cultures? ■

CASE ON EMERGING CONCEPTS IN MANAGEMENT

Career and Ethics: Active or Passive Management?

Rick Montrose contemplated the situation in which he now found himself. Hired as an organizational consultant two months ago for a small but growing plastics firm, the day of his final report and recommendations was drawing near. He realized that the facts that he had learned in the preceding eight weeks had to be weighed carefully and that he must also consider his own aspirations and career.

Having graduated from college two years before, Rick had gone the corporate route immediately out of school because of the advancement potential and the financial rewards. Starting from a staff engineering position, he had risen rapidly to a middle-management line position, but various factors had caused Rick to leave the corporate life and strike out on his own.

After finishing up a successful production consulting assignment, Rick had taken advantage of his loose schedule to travel to Midvale, his old college town, to visit some friends. While out one night, he had run into an old college flame, Robin Furnall, and had been invited to stay at her apartment while he was in town. This unlikely romantic rendezvous actually paved the way for a second consulting job—at the firm where Robin was employed as the personal secretary to the president, Jim Larton.

When Robin learned of Rick's background and expertise, she informed her boss. The resulting interview showed the firm to be in need of policy guidelines, operating procedures, organizational restructuring, and day-to-day leadership. After the customary reference checks, Robin came home one day and informed Rick that he was to be offered the job on a two-month contract with a renewal clause for another two months if needed. After confirmation of the offer from Larton, Rick had rented an apartment in town, despite Robin's generous offer to move in as her roommate for two months. Rick wanted the job and experience too much to risk losing it on account of Robin (or any woman).

The company, PlasTech, Inc., now almost three years old, had grown from a basement operation to a present sales volume of $2 million. Using shrewd long-term contracts, Larton had succeeded in profiting from the plastics-market shortage situation the last two years. PlasTech was now both nationally and internationally recognized as an innovative researcher and reliable distributor of specialty plastics. Jim Larton not only relied on luck to prosper, but was also a brilliant inventor and strategist who always was one step ahead of his competitors in marketing techniques and product introductions.

The next stage of expansion lay in the production of consumer plastic goods. Larton's tenth patent had just been approved, and he was awaiting only capital and manufacturing facilities to move these inventions from the drawing board into production. He had just completed arrangements for the construction of a $500,000 factory and office complex to be located on the outskirts of Midvale and financed by an SBA loan. He had also taken an option on 800 acres of land in Arizona on which to eventually build a western research and warehousing facility when the Midvale plant was operational. Larton both understood the market potential in the Western states for his new products and personally wanted to move his wife and three children "out of this cold, flat land."

The constant attention by Larton to the planning and design details of expansion had taken its toll on the day-to-day operations of the firm. The possibility of on-site problem solving or problem solving by lower-level managers had been largely short-circuited. There was a general lack of guidance, supervision, and direction, resulting in some customer complaints, lost accounts, and severe internal problems. The inability and lack of interest to cope with these problems had been bothering Larton for some time. When Robin had come to work one Monday with the news that she had met a consultant whom she knew personally, he knew that this was what the firm needed—two weeks later, Rick Montrose was hired.

After about three weeks, Rick became very interested in the amount of innovation and excitement present in this small firm and in the dynamic, young industry. PlasTech employed 54 people (43 females) with an average age of 23. The formal organization, as in most rapidly growing firms, was structured so that all department heads were reporting to Mr. Larton. Although he found several problem areas, which were to be expected in such a rapidly growing firm (for example, procedure documentation, policy formation), the functioning of the work force was being affected by something other than the present operating systems.

There seemed to be an underlying motivation and morale problem impairing the accomplishment of even the most trivial tasks. In order to get to the heart of the matter, Rick had decided to interview all the employees during the fourth and fifth week to find out their individual views of the firm. Quite a few of those interviewed placed many confidences in Rick—revelations that revealed the true nature of the power structure within the firm.

The subject of the majority of complaints and the source of most of the morale problem was Mr. Larton's secretary—Robin. Although probably the hardest-working person in the firm, she had been using her position as Mr. Larton's secretary as a lever to gain power and to influence his decisions concerning internal affairs. In Mr. Larton's absence, she had continually taken charge and made decisions that other department heads should clearly have made.

Because of his involvement with external problems, Larton himself had come to rely on Robin for advice on the functioning of the company. More than once Rick had heard, "You have to be on Robin's good side in order to get any place in this company." The employees' complaints to Larton seemed to have fallen on deaf ears, and the influence of Robin had been the cause for several resignations. Several employees had confided in Rick that Robin had probably got a previous accountant fired because she disliked him and felt her power base was being threatened.

The singularly most discomforting allegation was that Robin and Larton seemed to have more than just a business relationship, many out-of-town trips and late nights at work serving interests more prurient than plastics. Robin had recently bragged at a party (while under the influence of alcohol) that Mr. Larton paid her a salary that was third highest in the whole organization—behind only one design engineer and Larton himself. Their intimate relationship was common knowledge to the employees, and this created a general atmosphere of mistrust and insecurity. The only apparent way to a promotion or raise was through Robin, and the establishment of oneself on her good side was a prime concern to everyone. Relative competence and reliability were considered minimal factors in advancement.

In the beginning of Rick Montrose's sixth week at PlasTech, Larton had called him in for a conference. After the usual informalities, Larton got straight to the point. He had checked on Rick's previous accomplishments, which, when combined with his outstanding performance to date, indicated to him that Rick had much potential in this industry. He was very impressed with Rick's grasp of the business, and he wanted him to consider taking charge of the operation as general manager so that Larton could devote himself more fully to research work.

Larton wanted to move out West as soon as the new plant was completed in Midvale and would leave Rick in charge of all Eastern and Central operations. He assured Rick of complete autonomy in any decision making plus absolute control of all phases of the firm from staffing to financing. In addition to a handsome starting salary and a bonus program, Rick was offered a stock-option plan that would make him the second majority shareholder in five years (local businessmen, relatives, and employees owned 40 percent, Larton 60 percent of the stock outstanding).

Larton wanted Rick to take some time to think about the offer and to give him an answer when the consulting project was finished. Rick left Mr. Larton's office, walking past a glaring Robin. He was overwhelmed by the magnitude of the offer but overjoyed at the possibility to launch himself into a new and interesting career.

The two weeks after Larton's offer only served to complicate Rick's situation. On Friday of that week, Rick had arrived at work to find a memo from Mr. Larton leaving him in charge of things until Robin and he got back in one week from an extended, urgent trip East. The eighth week of work, in the extended absence of both Larton and Robin, went very smoothly. On Thursday, Robin called from the Baltimore airport saying that the trip would be lengthened until next Monday and that Mr. Larton wanted the final consulting recommendations and an answer to the job offer on his desk by Tuesday. On the Friday of Rick's final week of consulting, following Robin's call, a call from Mrs. Larton was transferred to him. She wondered if he had heard from her husband and if he was still expected in that evening. Rick had to tell her that Mr. Larton rarely informed anyone of his whereabouts or schedule, preferring to call in to check on things.

That afternoon, Rick completed the first part of his consulting report but was stumped as to how far to go on the final part of it. He was completely undecided whether to mention all the details about Robin or just some, to recommend her termination, to have her moved to another position (where?), or to ignore her completely. Further, he did not know whether Mr. Larton knew that he himself had spent ten days with Robin before taking the job.

Robin and Rick's friendship had completely disintegrated since his coming to PlasTech, partly due to his moving out and his refusal to date her, partly because of his increasing influence with the employees at her workplace. She had recently refused to talk to him and had even ignored an official request for some data from Mr. Larton's files.

Rick had learned enough about Mr. Larton to realize that his affair with Robin was a tremendous ego boost to the 43-year-old man and that he not only enjoyed the sexual conquest but the envious remarks from his business cronies as to the "fine-looking office decorations" and "my wife would never let met get away with something like *that*."

Rick enjoyed the work at PlasTech and liked the idea of becoming general manager. The financial benefits would probably surpass his uncertain consulting fees and would allow him to pay off some of the bills left over from his consulting start. With 5 to 10 years of experience as general manager of PlasTech, Rick knew that he would be groomed for the top management of any of several multinational chemical or plastic companies. However, despite the handsome benefits of this job, he also had to weigh the costs inherent in any such small, tightly held firm. Not only were there the personal problems evident in Robin and Larton's relationship, but there was also the possibility that the firm could fail—in which case, the mark on his record would be far from impressive. Based on the newness of the venture, the aggressiveness of Larton himself, and the increasing competition that was developing in the industry, Rick considered the chance of the firm failing as approximately one in five.

Another perplexing problem was that Rick did not know where Larton drew the line between the firm and his "fun." Being the majority shareholder and the president, Larton was entitled to run the company any way he felt, but Rick wondered exactly where the personal involvement ended and rationality began. Would Larton's conduct spill over into Rick's area of control and affect his effectiveness in a period of change?

With these things in mind, Rick pondered the courses of action that were available to him and just how he should word his final report. He knew that the exact wording would have a definite effect on his ability to accept the job and on his working relationship with Larton, should he opt to accept the job. The final decision had to be weighed as to his own personal feelings, his career aspirations, and his ethical sense of what was "right" to do in the situation as a professional and as a consultant.

Source: This case was prepared by Frank S. Leonard under the direction of Professor Jeffrey A. Barach as a basis for class discussion rather than to illustrate effective or ineffective administrative practices. Adapted and reprinted with permission.

Case Questions

1. What would you advise Rick Montrose to say in the rest of his report? Be as specific and practical as possible—put yourself in his shoes.
2. Write any additions to Rick Montrose's report that you feel are appropriate (try limiting yourself to less than 200 words). Be prepared to defend your position and the decision you are going to give Mr. Larton.
3. If Rick takes the job as general manager, what strategies should he follow to assure himself a successful career? What specific actions should he take (or not take), and why?
4. How has Rick managed his career so far? What are his strong points and successes? What are his shortcomings and mistakes? What should he concentrate on in the future? ■

GLOSSARY

acceptance-sampling procedure Quality-control procedure to determine if the finished product conforms to design specifications.

action research The method through with organizational-development change agents learn what improvements are needed and how the organization can best be aided in making improvements.

administration Setting aside individual goals in favor of larger organizational goals.

administrative culture According to Stevenson and Gumpert, corporate culture focusing on existing opportunities, organizational structures, and control procedures.

apprentice Starting worker who usually does routine work under a supervisor or mentor.

arbitration A form of compromise in which opposing parties agree to submit to the decision of a third party.

artificial intelligence (AI) Development of computational approaches to simulate intelligent human thought or behavior.

assembly-line productivity standard Type of measurement to evaluate effects on efficiency and employee response to new plans.

balance sheet Description of the organization in terms of its assets, liabilities, and net worth.

balance-sheet budget (or **pro forma balance sheet**) Budget combining all other budgets to project the balance sheet at the end of the budgeting period.

behavioral school A group of management scholars trained in sociology, psychology, and related fields who use their diverse knowledge to understand and improve the way organizations are managed.

behavior modification An approach to motivation based on the "law of effect"—that behavior which leads to rewarding consequences tends to be repeated, and behavior with negative consequences tends not to be repeated. Thus, managers can change behavior by changing the consequences of that behavior.

board A group made up of individuals appointed or elected to manage a public or private organization.

boundary-spanning roles Jobs in which individuals act as liaisons between departments or organizations that are in frequent contact.

bounded rationality The concept that managers make the most logical decisions they can within the constraints of limited information and ability.

break-even analysis (or **cost-volume-profit analysis**) Financial statement enabling managers to analyze the relationships among costs, sales volume, and profits.

budget Formal quantitative statement of resources allocated for planned activities over stipulated periods of time.

budgeting Process for providing formal quantitative statements of the resources allocated to specific programs or projects for a given period.

budgets Formal quantitative statements of the resources allocated to specific programs or projects for a given period.

bureaucracy Organization with a legalized formal and hierarchical structure.

bureaucratic control Method of control that employs strict regulations to ensure desired behavior by organizational units—often used by multinational enterprises to control subsidiaries.

burnout State of emotional, mental, and physical exhaustion that results from continued exposure to high stress.

capacity planning Operations decision concerned with the quantity of goods or services to be produced.

capital-expenditure budget Budget indicating future investments to be made in buildings, equipment, and other physical assets of the organization.

career anchor According to Schein, an occupational self-concept—and individual's sense of the kind of work he or she seeks to pursue and what that work implies about the individual.

career concepts According to Driver, four basic career patterns—linear, steady state, spiral, and transitory—by which people perceive their careers.

career plateau Career stage in which the likelihood of additional hierarchical promotion is very low.

cash budget Budget combining estimates for revenues, expenses, and new capital expenditures.

centralization The extent to which authority is concentrated at the top of the organization.

change agent The individual leading or guiding the process of a change in an organizational situation.

channel The medium of communication between a sender and a receiver.

charismatic or **transformational leaders** Leaders who, through their personal vision and energy, inspire followers and have a major impact on their organizations.

charity principle Doctrine of social responsibility requiring more fortunate individuals to assist less fortunate members of society.

circumferential movement According to Schein, transfer from one division, function, or department to another.

classical organization theory An early attempt, pioneered by Henri Fayol, to identify principles and skills that underlie effective management.

client system The individual, group, or organization that is the target of a planned change.

closed system A system that does not interact with its environment.

coercive power The negative side of reward power, based on the influencer's ability to punish the influencee.

cohesiveness The degree of solidarity and positive feelings held by individuals toward their group.

collaborative management Management through power sharing and subordinate participation; the opposite of hierarchical imposition of authority.

colleague Worker who, while still subordinate, makes independent contributions to organizational activities.

collective bargaining The process of negotiating and administering agreements between labor and management concerning wages, working conditions, and other aspects of the work environment.

command group Group composed of a manager and his or her subordinates who interact with each other toward a common objective.

commission Group whose members are usually appointed by government officials, charged with administrative, regulatory, or legislative tasks.

committee A formal organizational group, usually relatively long-lived, created to carry out specific organizational tasks.

common morality The body of rules covering ordinary ethical problems.

communication The process by which people attempt to share meaning via the transmission of symbolic messages.

communication network A set of channels within an organization or group through which communication travels.

comparable worth The principle that jobs requiring comparable skills and knowledge merit equal compensation even if the nature of the work activity is different.

competition The situation in which two or more parties are striving toward mutually incompatible goals but cannot interfere with each other.

competitive priorities Four major criteria, including pricing, quality levels, quality reliability, and flexibility, on which products are evaluated.

computer-aided design (CAD) Design and drafting performed interactively on a computer.

computer-aided manufacturing (CAM) Use of machines to perform and control required work.

computer-assisted instruction (CAI) A training technique in which computers are used to lessen the time necessary for training by instructors and to provide additional help to individual trainees.

computer-based information system (CBIS) (or **computer-based MIS**) Information system that goes beyond the mere standardization of data to aid in the planning process.

computer-integrated manufacturing (CIM) The use of machines to link computer-aided design and computer-aided manufacturing systems so that new product designs can be manufactured automatically in the factory.

confrontation A method of conflict resolution in which opposing parties, directly stating their views to one another, examine the conflict and seek means of resolving it.

consensus A method of conflict resolution in which the parties attempt to find the best solution rather than to achieve a victory over each other.

contingency approach The view that the management technique that best contributes to the attainment of organizational goals might vary in different types of situations or circumstances.

continuous and assembly-line system System producing standardized output of its own design, usually in large volume.

control The process of assuring that actual activities conform to planned activities.

controlling The process of monitoring actual organizational activities to see that they conform to planned activities and correcting flaws or deviations.

control system Multistep procedure applied to various types of control activities.

cooperation The process of working together to attain mutual objectives.

coordination The integration of the activities of the separate parts of an organization to accomplish organizational goals.

coping skills training Programs teaching people to recognize and cope with situations in which they feel helpless.

corporate social performance A single theory of corporate social action encompassing social principles, processes and policies.

corporate social responsiveness The second theory of corporate social responsibility, a more pragmatic, action-oriented view than the philosophical concepts of the charity or stewardship principles.

critical path method (CPM) A network analysis technique used to schedule and control work on projects for which the time required to complete tasks is known fairly precisely.

cultural relativism The idea that morality is relative to a particular culture, society, or community.

culture control Method of control, often associated with large Japanese companies, that emphasizes implicit and informal direction based on a broad company culture.

decentralization The delegation of power and authority from higher to lower levels of the organization, often accomplished by the creation of small, self-contained organizational units.

decision making The process of identifying and selecting a course of action to solve a specific problem.

decision-support system (DSS) Computer system accessible to nonspecialists to assist in planning and decision making.

decoding The interpretation and translation of a message into meaningful information.

delegation The act of assigning formal authority and responsibility for completion of specific activities to a subordinate.

departmentalization The grouping into departments of work activities that are similar and logically connected.

dependence According to Hannan and Freeman, the theoretical problem faced by an organization because of its need for vital resources from outside sources.

development program A process designed to develop skills necessary for future work activities.

dialectical inquiry method A method of analysis in which a decision maker determines and negates his or her assumptions, and then creates "counter solutions" based on the negative assumptions.

differential rate system Frederick W. Taylor's compensation system involving the payment of higher wages to more efficient workers.

direct-action elements Elements of the environment that directly influence an organization's activities.

direct contact Simplest form of lateral relationship, communication between individuals who must deal with the same situation or problem.

direct investment Investment in foreign assets whereby a company purchases assets that it manages directly.

discretionary cost budget Budget used for departments in which output cannot be accurately measured.

distinctive competence Entrepreneurial desire to start a business coupled with the ability or experience to compete effectively once the enterprise is initiated.

division of work The breakdown of a complex task into components so that individuals are responsible for a limited set of activities instead of the task as a whole.

duties Obligations to take specific steps or obey the law.

dysfunctional conflict Any conflict that results in decreased efficiency and greater factionalism within the organization.

economic variables General economic conditions and trends that may be factors in an organization's activities.

effectiveness The ability to determine appropriate objectives: "doing the right things."

efficiency The ability to minimize the use of resources in achieving organizational objectives: "doing things right."

electronic data processing (EDP) Computerized data processing and information management, including report standardization for operating managers.

electronic mail Data and text circulated through interlinked computers.

empowerment The act of delegating power and authority 'o a subordinate so that the goals of the manager can be accomplished.

encoding The translation of information into a series of symbols for communication.

end-user computing The creative use of computers by those who are not experts in data processing.

engineered cost budget Budget describing material and labor costs of each item produced, including estimated overhead costs.

engineered standard Type of measurement concerned with machine capacities.

entrepreneur Either the originator of a new business venture or a manager who tries to improve an organizational unit by initiating productive changes.

entrepreneurial culture According to Stevenson and Gumpert, corporate culture focusing on the emergence of new opportunities, the means of capitalizing on them, and the creation of the structure appropriate for pursuing them.

entrepreneurship As opposed to management, the seemingly discontinuous process of combining resources to produce changes in production.

equity theory A theory of job motivation emphasizing the role played by an individual's belief in the equity or fairness of rewards and punishments in determining his or her performance and satisfaction. Also called inequity theory.

ethics The concept and the study of the concept of who is—and should be—benefited or harmed by any action.

ethnocentric management Attitude that the home country's management practices are superior to those of other countries and can be exported along with the organization's goods and services.

expectancy approach A model of motivation specifying that the effort to achieve high performance is a function of the perceived likelihood that high performance can be achieved and will be rewarded if achieved and that the reward will be worth the effort expended.

expense center Commonly, administrative, service, and research departments where inputs are measured in monetary terms, although outputs are not.

expert power Power based on the belief or understanding that the influencer has specific knowledge or relevant expertise which the influencee does not.

expert system Application of artificial intelligence denoting the technology entailed by the development of computational approaches to human functioning.

external audit Verification process involving the independent appraisal of financial accounts and statements.

external stakeholders Groups or individuals that affect an organization's activities from its external environment.

external standard Type of measurement derived from other organizations or other units of the same organization.

feedback (interpersonal) The reversal of the communication process that occurs when the receiver expresses his or her reaction to the sender's message.

feedback (job-based) The part of system control in which the results of actions are returned to the individual, allowing work procedures to be analyzed and corrected.

financial budget Budget detailing the money expected to be spent during the budget period and indicating its sources.

financial statement Monetary analysis of the flow of goods and services to, within, and from the organization.

financing budget Budget which assures the organization of available funds to meet shortfalls of revenues when compared to expenses and which schedules potential borrowing needs.

first-line (or first-level) managers Managers who are responsible for the work of operating employees only and do not supervise other managers; they are the "first" or lowest level of managers in the organizational hierarchy.

fixed costs Those unaffected by the amount of work accumulated in the responsibility center.

flextime A system that permits employees to arrange their work hours to suit their personal needs.

flows Components such as information, material, and energy that enter and leave a system.

forecasting The attempt, using specific techniques, to predict outcomes and project future trends.

formal authority Power rooted in the general understanding that specific individuals or groups have the right to exert influence within certain limits by virtue of their position within the organization. Also called legitimate power.

formal or systematic appraisal A formalized appraisal process for rating current subordinate performance, identifying subordinates deserving raises or promotions, and identifying subordinates in need of further training.

franchising Entrepreneurial system whereby an individual runs a business based on the right to market a good or service granted by a manufacturer or other organization.

functional authority The authority of staff-department members to control the activities of other departments that are related to specific staff responsibilities.

functional conflict Any conflict that has positive, constructive, and nondivisive results.

functional manager A manager responsible for just one organizational activity, such as finance or human resource management.

functional organization A form of departmentalization in which everyone engaged in one functional activity, such as marketing or finance, is grouped into one unit.

functional strategy Implementation strategy providing the details necessary to put organizational strategy into action.

function layout Layout planning concerned with storage layouts (for minimizing inventory and storage costs), marketing layouts (for maximizing product exposure and sales), and project layouts (for building such one-of-a-kind products as a dam).

Gantt chart A graphic method of planning and control that allows a manager to view the starting and ending dates for various tasks.

general manager The individual responsible for all activities, such as production, sales, marketing, and finance, for an organization like a company or subsidiary.

geocentric management Attitude that accepts both similarities and differences between domestic and foreign management policies and so attempts to strike a balance between those that are most effective.

global strategic partnership Alliance formed by an organization with one or more foreign countries, generally with an eye toward exploiting the other countries' opportunities and toward assuming leadership in either supply or production.

goal-setting theory A cognitive approach to the theory of work motivation which holds that workers are conscious (cognitive) creatures who strive toward goals.

grapevine chain The various paths through which informal communication is passed through an organization; includes the "single-strand," "gossip," "probability," and "cluster" chains.

group building and maintenance role The group leader's specific function to fulfill the group's social needs by encouraging solidarity feelings.

Hawthorne effect The possibility that workers who receive special attention will perform better simply because they received that attention: one interpretation of Elton Mayo and his colleagues' studies.

heuristic principles A method of decision making that proceeds along empirical lines, using rules of thumb, to find solutions or answers.

human resource audit The analysis and appraisal of the organization's current human resources.

human resource management (HRM) The management function that deals with recruitment, placement, training, and development of organization members.

human resource planning Planning for the future personnel needs of an organization, taking into account both internal activities and factors in the external environment.

income statement Summary of the organization's financial performance over a given interval of time.

incremental adjustment A method of managerial problem solving in which each successive action represents only a small change from activities.

indirect-action elements Elements of the external environment which affect the climate in which an organization's activities take place, including economic and political situations, but which do not affect the organization directly.

influence Any actions or examples of behavior that cause a change in attitude or behavior of another person or group.

informal organization The undocumented and officially unrecognized relationships between members of an organization that inevitably emerge out of the personal and group needs of employees.

informal performance appraisal The process of continuously feeding back to subordinate information regarding their work performance.

information Technically, processed data that supplies information about a specific situation or process.

information ownership The possession by certain individuals of unique information and knowledge concerning their work.

initial strategy approach According to Alfred D. Chandler, "The determination of the basic long-term goals and objectives of an enterprise, and the adoption of courses of action and the allocation of resources necessary for carrying out these goals."

inputs Resources from the environment, such as raw materials and labor, that may enter any organizational system.

integrating roles Roles that are established when a specific product, service, or project spans several departments and requires coordination and attention from a single individual not in the departments in question.

integration Degree to which employees of various departments work together in a unified way.

internal audit Audit performed by the organization to ensure that its assets are properly safeguarded and its financial records reliably kept.

internal stakeholders Groups or individuals, such as employees, which are not strictly part of an organization's environment but for whom an individual manager remains responsible.

intrapreneuring Corporate entrepreneurship, whereby an organization seeks to expand by exploring new opportunities through new combinations of its existing resources.

investment center Organizational unit that not only measures the monetary value of inputs and outputs, but also compares outputs with assets used in producing them.

job design The division of an organization's work among its employees.

job enlargement The combining of various operations at a similar level into one job to provide more variety for workers and thus increase motivation and satisfaction. An increase in job scope.

job enrichment The combining of several activities from a vertical cross section of the organization into one job to provide the worker with more autonomy and responsibility. An increase in job depth.

job-shop system System for making small amounts of custom-tailored products, usually to fulfill a contract.

job specialization The division of work into standardized, simplified tasks.

just-in-time inventory system Inventory system in which production quantities are ideally equal to delivery quantities, with materials purchased and finished goods delivered "just in time."

key-performance or key-result areas Those aspects of the organization or unit that must function effectively if the whole organization or unit is to succeed in its plans.

lateral communication Communication between departments of an organization that generally follows the work flow, thus providing a direct channel for coordination and problem solving.

lateral relationship A relationship that cuts

across the chain of command, allowing direct contact between members of different departments. Examples include some committees, liaison roles, and integrating roles.

leader-member relations The quality of the interaction between a leader and his or her subordinates; according to Fred Fiedler, the most important influence on the manager's power.

leadership The process of directing and inspiring workers to perform the task-related activities of the group.

leadership functions The group-maintenance and task-related activities that must be performed by the leader, or someone else, for a group to perform effectively.

leadership styles The various patterns of behavior favored by leaders during the process of directing and influencing workers.

legitimate power Power that exists when a subordinate or influencee acknowledges that the influencer has a "right" or is lawfully entitled to exert influence—within certain bounds. Also called formal authority.

linear career concept According to Driver, career concept by which an individual chooses a field, develops a plan for advancement, and executes it.

line authority The authority of those managers directly responsible, throughout the organization's chain of command, for achieving organizational goals.

macroeconomic policy Decisions considering such factors as taxation, development costs, regulatory control, and other external factors that might affect the development of a new product.

management The process of planning, organizing, leading, and controlling the work of organization members and of using all available organizational resources to reach stated organizational goals.

management by exception Principle holding that the controlling manager be informed about operation progress only when there is a significant deviation from a plan or standard.

management by objectives (MBO) A formal set of procedures that establishes and reviews progress toward common goals for managers and subordinates.

management information Information representing relevant and important features about a situation so that a manager can take specific action.

management information system (MIS) Computer-based information system for more effective planning, decision making, and control.

management science (MS) Mathematical techniques for modeling, analysis, and solution of management problems. Also called operations research.

managerial linking role A role that may be required if an integrating position does not coordinate a particular task effectively.

managerial performance The measure of how efficient and effective a manager is—how well he or she determines and achieves appropriate objectives.

materials-requirements planning Operational planning system whereby end products are analyzed to determine the materials needed to produce them.

matrix organization An organizational structure in which each employee reports to both a functional or division manager and to a project or group manager.

mature matrix Organizational in which both dimensions of structure are permanent and balanced, with power held equally by both a functional and project manager.

mentor Employee who develops ideas, supervises others, and assumes responsibility for the work of subordinates.

message The encoded information sent by the sender to the receiver.

middle managers Managers in the midrange of the organizational hierarchy; they are responsible for other managers and sometimes for some operating employees.

milestone scheduling A technique that adds detail and precision to the Gantt chart by marking particular dates by which the various phases of the entire project are to be completed.

moral rules Rules for behavior that often become internalized as moral values.

motivation The factors that cause, channel, and sustain an individual's behavior.

multidivisional firm An organization that has expanded into different industries and diversified its products.

multinational companies Those which operate in more than one country, including investment in foreign manufacturing facilities.

multinational enterprise (MNE) Large corporation with operations and divisions spread over several countries but controlled by a central headquarters.

naive relativism The idea that all human beings are themselves the standard by which their actions should be judged.

natural-language processing Use of everyday language instead of special codes or instructions to communicate with a computer.

need-achievement According to McClelland, a social motive to excel that tends to characterize successful entrepreneurs, especially when reinforced by cultural factors.

network analysis A technique used for scheduling complex projects that contain interrelationships between activities or events.

noise Anything that confuses, disturbs, diminishes, or interferes with communication.

nonprogrammed decisions Specific solutions created through an unstructured process to deal with non-routine problems.

one-way communication Any communication from the sender without feedback from the receiver.

open system A system that interacts with its environment.

operating budget Budget indicating the goods and services the organization expects to consume in a budget period.

operational strategy Organizational strategy spelling out facility locations and including marketing and financial strategies.

operations The production activities of an organization.

operations management Complex management activity that includes planning production, organizing resources, directing operations and personnel, and monitoring system performance.

operations system Production/operations system denoting both manufacturing and service systems.

organizational conflict Disagreement between individuals or groups within the organization stemming from the need to share scarce resources or engage in interdependent work activities, or from differences in status, goals, or cultures. See also dysfunctional and functional conflict.

organizational culture The set of important understandings, such as norms, values, attitudes, and beliefs, shared by organization members.

organizational design The determination of the organizational structure that is most appropriate for the strategy, people, technology, and tasks of the organization.

organizational development (OD) A long-range effort supported by top management to increase an organization's problem-solving and renewal processes through effective management of organizational culture.

organizational structure The arrangement and interrelationships of the various component parts and position of a company.

organization chart A diagram of an organization's structure, showing the functions, departments, or positions of the organization and how they are related.

organizing The process of arranging an organization's structure and coordinating its managerial practices and use of resources to achieve its goals.

orientation or **socialization** A program designed to help employees fit smoothly into an organization.

outcome interdependence The degree to which the work of a group has consequences felt by all its members.

outputs Transformed inputs that are returned to the external environment as products or services.

path-goal model A leadership theory emphasizing the leader's role in clarifying for subordinates how they can achieve high performance and its associated rewards.

performance gaps The difference between the objectives established in the goal formation process and the results likely to be achieved if the existing strategy is continued.

permanent formal group A long-term command group or permanent committee, such as a planning committee.

permanent overlay Organizational structure in which project teams are continued for ongoing purposes.

planning The process of establishing objectives and suitable courses of action before taking action.

policy A standing plan that establishes general guidelines for decision making.

policy-formulation approach The concept of implementing day-to-day rules that puts boundaries around what a functional area can and cannot do.

political risk Possibility that political changes, either in the short or long run, can affect the activities of an organization doing business in foreign countries.

political variables Factors that may influence an organization's activities as a result of the political process or climate.

polycentric management Attitude that since a foreign country's management policies are best understood by its own management personnel, the home organization should rely on foreign offices.

portfolio framework An approach to corporate-level strategy advocated by the Boston Consulting Group.

portfolio investment Investment in foreign assets whereby a company purchases shares in companies that own those assets.

position power The power, according to Fred Fiedler, that is inherent in the formal position the leader holds. This power may be great or small, depending upon the specific position.

post-action controls Method of control for measuring the results of a completed activity.

power The ability to exert influence; that is, the ability to change the attitudes or behavior of individuals or groups.

pre-action controls (or **precontrols**) Control method ensuring that human, material, and financial resources have been budgeted.

predetermined standard Type of measurement based on careful analysis of both the organizational unit's internal and external environments.

premises The basic assumptions upon which planning and decision making are based.

primary relations Interaction between a business and market-oriented groups, such as customers, employees, shareholders and creditors.

procedure A standing plan of detailed guidelines for handling organizational actions that occur regularly.

process consultation A technique by which consultants help organization members understand and change the ways they work together.

process-control procedure Quality-control procedure for monitoring quality during production of the product or rendering of the service.

product-cycle theory According to Vernon, the process whereby products originally developed for home markets earn enough foreign demand to justify direct foreign investment in their production.

productivity Measure of how well an operations system functions and indicator of the efficiency and competitiveness of a single firm or department.

product or **market organizational structure** The organization of a company by divisions that brings together all those involved with a certain type of product or customer.

profit budget (or **master budget**) Budget combining cost and revenue budgets in one unit.

profit center Organizational unit where performance is measured by numerical differences between revenues and expenditures.

program A single-use plan that covers a relatively large set of organizational activities and specifies major steps, their order and timing, and unit responsible for each step.

program evaluation and review technique (PERT) A network analysis technique, using estimates of the time required to complete tasks, which is used to schedule and control projects for which task completion times cannot be predicted fairly precisely.

programmed decisions Solutions to routine problems determined by rule, procedure, or habit.

project The smaller and separate portions of the programs.

psychosocial function According to Kram, aspect of a professional relationship that improves one's sense of competence, identity, and effectiveness.

qualitative forecasting A judgment-based forecasting technique used when hard data are scarce or difficult to use.

qualitative overloading Situation occurring when an individual lacks the abilities or resources necessary for the satisfactory completion of a task.

quality control Strategy for managing each stage of production so that early corrections can be made instead of reworking the product after end-of-line inspection.

quantitative forecasting Forecasting techniques used when enough hard data exist to specify relationships between variables.

quantitative overloading Situation that occurs when an individual is given more tasks than he or she can accomplish in a given time.

radial movement According to Schein, movement either toward or away from an organization's central "core" of power.

ratio analysis Reporting of key figures from the organization's financial records as percentages or fractions.

realistic job preview (RJP) A description provided by the organization to applicants and new employees that gives both the positive and negative aspects of a job.

receiver The individual whose senses perceive the sender's message.

recruitment The development of a pool of job candidates in accordance with a human resource plan.

redundancy Repeating or restating a message to ensure its reception or to reinforce its impact.

reference group A group with whom individuals identify and compare themselves.

referent power Power based on the desire of the influencee to be like or identify with the influencer.

refreezing Transforming a new behavioral pattern into the norm through reinforcement and supporting mechanisms.

relaxation training Popular methods including meditation and biofeedback, by which individuals learn to control muscle tension and ease the experience of stress.

reorientation situation Strategy situation in which poor performance despite sound strategy calls for change to be implemented by outsiders.

replacement chart A chart that diagrams an organization's positions, showing the incumbents, likely future candidates, and readiness of candidates to enter those positions.

research and development (R&D) Entrepreneurial function devoting organizational assets to the design, testing, and production of new products.

responsibility center Any organizational function or unit whose manager is responsible for all of its activities.

revenue budget Budget measuring marketing and sales effectiveness by multiplying the unit price of each product by the predicted sales quantity.

revenue center Organizational unit in which outputs measured in monetary terms are not directly compared to input costs.

reward power Power derived from the fact that one person, known as an influencer, has the ability to reward another person, known as an influencee, for carrying out orders, which may be expressed or implied.

rights Claims that entitle a person to take a particular action.

role conflict According to Katz and Kahn, situation in which an individual is confronted by two or more incompatible demands.

role perception The individual's understanding of the behaviors needed to accomplish a task or perform a job.

rules Standing plans that detail specific actions to be taken in a given situation.

scalar principle The concept that a clear line of authority through the organization must exist if delegation is to work successfully.

scientific management A management approach, formulated by Frederick W. Taylor and others between 1890 and 1930, that sought to determine scientifically the best methods for performing any task, and for selecting, training, and motivating workers.

secondary relations Interaction between a business and nonmarket-oriented segments of society, such as the law and moral forces.

selection The mutual process whereby the organization decides whether or not to make a job offer and the candidate decides on the acceptability of the offer.

selective blend situation Strategy situation entailing major changes in organizational strategy that blend both outsiders and insiders to perform corrective measures.

self-leadership The ability of workers to motivate themselves to perform both tasks that are naturally rewarding and those that are necessary but not appealing.

self-managed work groups Work teams organized around a particular task and composed of members who possess both the skills necessary to accomplish the task and the power to determine such factors as method of operation, assignment of responsibilities, and creation of work schedules.

semivariable costs Those, like short-term labor costs, varying with the amount of work performed but not in a proportional way.

sender The initiator of a communication.

sense of potency Collective belief of a group that it can be effective.

sensitivity training An early personal growth technique, at one time fairly widespread in organizational development efforts, that emphasizes increased sensitivity in interpersonal relationships.

Seven-S model According to Waterman and others, framework for change identifying seven key factors than can adversely affect successful change in an organization.

single-use plans Detailed courses of action used once or only occasionally to solve problems that do not occur repeatedly.

situational leadership theory An approach to leadership developed by Paul Hersey and Kenneth H. Blanchard that describes how leaders should adjust their leadership style in response to their subordinates' evolving desire for achievement, experience, ability, and willingness to accept responsibility.

social variables Factors, such as demographics and social values, that may influence an organization from its external environment.

span of management The number of subordinates reporting directly to a given manager.

spiral career concept According to Driver, career concept by which individuals motivated by personal growth perform well enough to advance in status and rank.

sponsor Upper-level manager involved in the major decision-making activities of the organization.

stability situation Strategy situation in which good past performance and the minor nature of needed changes make insiders the best choice for implementing.

staff authority The authority of those groups of individuals who provide line managers with advice and services.

stakeholders Those groups or individuals who are directly or indirectly affected by an organization's pursuit of its goals.

standing plans An established set of decisions used by managers to deal with recurring or organizational activities; major types are policies, procedures, and rules.

start-up Business founded by individuals intending to change the environment of a given industry either by the introduction of a new product or production process.

steady-state career concept According to Driver, career concept by which an individual chooses a field but, even though improving professionally and financially, does not seek to move up the organizational hierarchy.

steering controls (or **cybernetic** or **feed-forward controls**) Control method designed to detect deviations from some standard goal and to permit corrective measures.

stewardship principle Biblical doctrine that requires businesses and wealthy individuals to see themselves as stewards, or caretakers, holding their property in trust for the benefit of society as a whole.

strategic business-unit (SBU) planning Grouping business activities within a multibusiness corporation because they generate closely related products or services.

strategic control The process of checking strategy implementation progress against the strategic plan at periodic or critical intervals to determine if the corporation is moving toward its strategic objectives.

strategic control points Critical points in a system at which monitoring or collecting information should occur.

strategic management approach A pattern based on the principle that the overall design of the organization can be described only if the attainment of objectives is added to policy and strategy as one of the key factors in management's operation of the organization's activities.

strategy The broad program for defining and achieving an organization's objectives; the organization's response to its environment over time.

strategy-formulation task A model of strategy formulation that must take into account the organization's goals and its strategy.

strategy implementation The fifth task in the strategy management process that is a basically administrative task.

stress The tension and pressure that result when an individual views a situation as presenting a demand that threatens to exceed his or her capabilities or resources.

stressor Source of pressure and tension that creates stress.

subjective standard Type of measurement based mainly on a manager's discretion.

subsystems Those parts comprising the whole system.

superordinate goals Higher-level goals that acknowledge lower-level goals, both encompassing the guiding principles that an organization impresses upon its members and contributing toward cohesive goal-oriented activity among groups whose objectives may not coincide.

syndrome of unused potential, or **reality shock syndrome** According to Hall, an individual's reaction to the difference between high job expectations and the frustrating day-to-day realities of the workplace.

synergy The situation in which the whole is greater than its parts. In organizational terms, the fact that departments that interact cooperatively can be more productive than if they operate in isolation.

system boundary The boundary that separates each system from its environment. It is rigid in a closed system, flexible in an open system.

System 4 Ideal organizational structure where there is extensive group participation in supervision and decision making.

System 1 Traditional organizational structure where power and authority are distributed according to the manager-subordinate relationship.

systems approach View of the organization as a unified, directed system of interrelated parts.

Systems 2 and 3 Intermediate stages between traditional structure and ideal structure.

task force or **project team** A temporary group formed to address a specific problem.

task interdependence The extent to which a group's work requires its members to interact with each other.

task role The specific role within a group performed by the leader, whether formal or informal.

task structure A work situation variable that, according to Fred Fiedler, helps determine a manager's power. In structured tasks, managers automatically have high power; in unstructured tasks, the manager's power is diminished.

team building A method of improving organizational effectiveness at the team level by diagnosing barriers to team performance and improving interteam relationships and task accomplishment.

technological variables New developments in products or processes, as well as advances in science, which may affect an organization's activities.

telecommuting The use of computers to enable individuals to work at home, sending only the work (via telephone or data network) to the workplace.

temporary formal group A group formed for a specific purpose, such as a task force or project group, that is disbanded when its purpose is accomplished.

temporary overlay A short-term structure in which project teams are created only for special needs.

theory Principle or set of principles designed to explain the relationship between two or more observable facts.

top management Managers responsible for the overall management of the organization. They establish operating policies and guide the organization's interactions with its environment.

traditional pyramid The most common type of organizational structure, in which command is unified at the top level.

training program A process designed to maintain or improve current job performance.

transactional leaders Leaders who determine what subordinates need to do to achieve objectives, classify those requirements, and help subordinates become confident that they can read their objectives.

transaction analysis An approach to improving interpersonal effectiveness, sometimes used in organizational development efforts, that concentrates on the styles and content of communication.

transformational coping According to Maddi and Kobasa, the process whereby commitment to work values, a sense of control over work variables, and the view of problems as challenges can turn stressful situations in less stressful directions.

transitory career concept According to Driver, career concept by which an individual moves from one job to another with no apparent pattern or progress.

turnover situation Strategy situation in which poor performanace entails major changes that can be handled by insiders.

two-way communication Communication that occurs when the receiver provides feedback to the sender.

uncertainty According to Hannan and Freeman, the theoretical problem posed to an organization by lack of information.

underloading Stress, resulting in boredom and monotony, produced when an individual has insufficient work to do.

unfreezing Making the need for change so obvious that the individual, group, or organization can readily see and accept that change must occur.

unity of command principle A guideline for delegation that states that each individual in an organization should report to only one superior.

valence The value of motivating strength of a reward to the individual.

values Relatively permanent desires that seem to be good in themselves.

variable costs Expenses varying directly with the amount of work being performed.

vertical communication Any communication that moves up or down the chain of command.

vertical information system Means through which data are transmitted up and down the managerial hierarchy.

vertical integration Broadening the scope of an organization's operations while retaining the original single product.

vertical movement According to Schein, hierarchical change in one's formal rank or management level.

video conferencing Meetings held via telecommunications, usually by satellite television transmission, rather than by face-to-face contact.

work-flow layout Layout planning concerned with product layouts (for the sequential steps in production), process layouts (for arranging production according to task), and fixed-position layouts (for handling such large or heavy products as ships).

yes/no controls (or **go/no go controls**) Control method for screening procedures that must be followed or conditions that must be met before operations continue.

zero-base budgeting (ZBB) A budgeting approach in which all of the organization's activities, existing and proposed, are considered on an equal footing in resource-allocation decisions, rather than using the previous year's budget as a starting point.

"zone of indifference" or **"area of acceptance"** According to Barnard and Simon, respectively, inclinations conditioning individuals to accept orders that fall within a familiar range of responsibility or activity.

COMPANY INDEX

Adolph Coors Company, 235, 390, 398
Ajax, Ltd. (Great Britain), 130
Akzo Company (Netherlands), 657
Alcoa, Inc., 364, 615, 627
Alexander's, 439
Allen Bradley Company, 627
Allied/Signal Corporation, 245
ALMEX (Sweden), 501
Altair Company, 712
American Airlines, 79, 339, 657
American Brands, 229
American Express Company, 79, 334, 699, 729
American Tobacco Company, 338
Amgen Company, 93
AM International, 462
Amtrak, Inc. 79
Amway Corporation, 772
Anheuser Busch Company, 174–75, 522
Apollo Computer, Inc., 502
Apple Computer, Inc., 147, 148, 246, 280, 384, 689, 692, 712
Argo Instruments, 576
Arrow Electronics, 245
Arthur Anderson Company, 348
Arthur D. Little, Inc., 410, 754*n*
Arthur D. Little and Company, 90*n*
Asahi Chemical and Kowa Company (Japan), 93
Associated Video Hut, Inc., 722–23
AT&T Company, 78, 95, 102, 120–21, 146, 204, 213–14, 273, 323, 331, 335, 362, 374, 385, 433, 441, 463, 480, 558, 562, 563, 714, 753, 782
Atari Computer, 692
Atex Company, 100
Atlantic Richfield Company, 773

Bank of America, 441, 636
Bausch & Lomb Company, 213
Baxter Travenol Company, 93
Beatrice Foods, 270
Bechtel Corporation, 18
Beech-Nut Corporation, 107, 109, 251–52, 535
Bell Telephone Laboratories, Inc., 89, 232, 273
Bendix Corporation, 169
Ben & Jerry's Homemade Ice Cream Company, 702–3
Bethlehem Steel Company, 36, 46
Biogen Company, 93
Bio-Response Company, 93
Biotech General Company, 93
Bloomingdale's, 439
Boehringer Company (Germany), 93
Boeing Corporation, 18
Booz, Allen & Hamilton, 154, 606
Boston Consulting Group, 206–7
British Petroleum Company, Ltd., 772, 773
Burlington Industries, 182

Calcorp, Inc., 616
Canon USA, Inc., 91, 97, 98
Carnegie Steel Company, 110
Cell Technology Company, 93
Chaparral Steel Company, 442, 482
Chase Manhattan Bank, 636
Chemical Bank, 106–7, 115, 128
Chiron Company, 93
Chrysler Corporation, 69, 93–94, 138–39, 145, 158, 244, 245, 287, 300, 406, 558, 615, 644
Circus USA, 640
Citibank, 664*n*, 775
Club Med, 293
Coca-Cola Company, 213, 522
Colgate-Palmolive Company, 69–71
Combustion Engineering Corporation, 213
Compaq Computers, 628
Consolidated Automobile Manufacturers, Inc., 64
Consolidated Life Insurance Company, 419–21
Control Data Corporation, 590
Coopers & Lybrand, 606
Corning Glass Works, 244, 782*n*
Corroon and Black Corporation, 440
Cray Research, 253, 412–13
Creative Playthings, Ltd., 701
Crown, Cork and Seal Company, 209–10

Daiichi/Toray Company (Japan), 93
Damon Clinical Laboratories, Inc., 93
Dana Corporation, 148, 245
Dashman Company, 160–61
David's Cookies, 548–51
Dayton-Hudson Corporation, 111
Delta Air Lines, Inc., 247, 463, 500
Digital Equipment Corporation (DEC), 348, 386–87
Diversified Conglomerate Incorporated (DCI), 219–20
Domino's Pizza, Inc., 424, 435, 452, 525
Dow-Corning Company, 271, 272
Dresser Industries, 125
Drexel Burnham Lambert, Inc., 462
Dun & Bradstreet Corporation, 701
Dunlop Holdings PLC (Great Britain), 397
Du Pont de Nemours, E. I., and Company, 93, 154, 227, 232, 339, 773
Duquesne Light Company, 150

Eastern Airlines, 79, 338, 404–5, 406
Eastman Kodak Company, 18, 68, 71, 72, 91, 97–100, 109, 208, 232, 247, 323, 339, 412
Echlin, Inc., 406
Eikonix Corporation, 97, 98
Eli Lilly & Company, 782*n*
El Sahd Construction Company (Kuwait), 130
Emery Air Freight Corporation, 74
Engler Instruments, 576
ENI Company (Italy), 772, 773
Ernst and Whitney, 606
Exxon Corporation, 79, 398–99, 442, 597, 615, 772, 773

Fairchild Semiconductor, 703
Federal Express, 192, 202, 211, 218
Federated-Allied Stores, 465
Fleetwood Company, 235
Ford Motor Company, 32–33, 41, 46, 62,

Ford Motor Company *(continued)* 111, 287, 313, 394, 492, 501, 502, 514, 558, 614, 631, 645, 646
Foremost McKesson Company, 542–43
Fortune Systems, 692
Fox Photo Inc., 97
Frito-Lay Companies, 18, 570*n*, 571
Fuji Photofilm USA, Inc., 68, 91

Gannett Company, 359
GenCorp, 554, 568, 574
General Electric Company, 91, 141, 240, 241, 244, 313, 322, 323, 332, 339, 348, 350–51, 403, 441, 458, 468, 486, 496, 623–24, 643, 648–49, 754*n*, 767, 773
General Foods Corporation, 144–45, 182, 313, 335, 441, 562
General Mills Corporation, 729
General Motors Corporation, 32, 62, 80, 93, 147, 158, 227, 231, 263, 267, 268, 280, 287, 313, 364, 369, 441, 462, 480, 482, 495, 541, 558, 562, 572, 614, 615, 620, 623, 624, 625, 632, 686–87, 772, 773
Genetech Compnay, 93, 501
Genetics Institute, 92, 93
Georgia-Pacific Corporation, 563
Getty Oil Company, 164, 169
Godfather's Pizza, 462
Goldman, Sachs & Company, 766, 775
Goldstar of America, Inc., 501, 790–91
Gore, W. R., and Associates, 486
Green Cross Company (Japan), 93
Greyhound Corporation, 365
GTE, 729
Guild Wineries and Distilleries, 772
Gulf Oil Corporation, 773
Gulf & Western Corporation, 2–3

Haagen-Dazs Company, 702–3
Hallmark Company, 334, 729
Hanes Corporation, 235
Harley-Davidson Company, 562
Harris Corporation, 690
Hawley & Hazel Chemical Company, 70–71
Hertz Rent A Car, 266
Hewlett-Packard Company, 227–28, 232, 260, 275, 291, 334, 384, 411, 596–97, 729
Hicks and Haas, 591
History Associates, 384
Hitachi, Ltd., 676–77, 772, 774
Hoechst Company (Germany), 93
Hofmann-LaRoche Company (Switzerland), 713–14
Holiday Inns, 348
Honda Motor Company, Ltd., 93, 287, 770, 787, 788
Honeywell, Inc., 334, 380–81, 441
Huffy Corporation, 317, 318
Human Edge Software Corporation, 684–85
Hyundai Corporation, 287

IBM Corporation, 18, 91, 117, 147, 201, 232, 236, 245–47, 298, 315, 324, 335, 339, 346, 348, 372, 384, 425, 439, 440, 442, 443, 462, 480, 560, 615, 625–26, 688, 692, 714, 729, 753, 772, 773
ICN Pharmaceuticals, 98
Imperial Chemical Industries (Great Britain), 294–95
Ingersoll-Rand Corporation, 706
Integrated Genetics Company, 93
Intel Corporation, 643
Interferon Sciences, Inc., 93
Interleaf, Inc., 97
ITT Corporation, 232, 403, 767, 772, 774

John Deere and Company, 582, 600–601, 607–8
Johnson & Johnson, 93, 109, 121–22, 213, 716
Johnson Products Company, 724

Kabivitrum Company (Sweden), 93
Kentucky Fried Chicken, 213, 792–93
Kimberly-Clark Corporation, 576
Konica Corporation, 91
Kyowa Company (Japan), 93

Labatt Brewing Company, 402
Levi Strauss and Company, 19, 615, 729
Liggett Group, Inc., 535
Liggett & Myers, 229
Lilly Company, 93
Limited, The, 148, 323
Lockheed Missile and Space Company, 154
Lord Geller, 397
Lotus Development Corporation, 572, 671, 729
Lucky-Goldstar Group (Korea), 790–91

Marathon Oil Company, 82–83
Martin Marietta Corporation, 169
Mary Kay Cosmetics, 384
MasterCard International, Inc., 603
Mattel Corporation, 692
Maytag Company, 620, 627
Mazda Corporation, 558
McDonald's Corporation, 18, 382, 522, 626, 627
MCI Corporation, 192, 202
McKinsey & Company, 230–32, 768
Mead Corporation, 560–61
Meiji Company (Japan), 93
Meiji Milk Company (Japan), 93
Memorex Corporation, 91
Mercers Company, 525
Merck & Company, 224, 232–33, 244, 250, 334, 732
Merle Norman Cosmetics, 501
Merrill Lynch & Company, 441, 656
Minolta Corporation, 68, 91
Mitan Mines, 610
Mitsubishi Corporation, 93, 94, 558, 772, 792
Mobil Oil Corporation, 79, 773
Monsanto (Searle) Corporation, 93
Morton Thiokol Company, 236
Mrs. Field's Cookies, 548–51, 659
Musashi Semiconductor Works (Japan), 510

Nashua Corporation, 645
National Football League, 210
National Semiconductor Corporation, 627
Nestlé Company, Inc., 252
New Jersey Bell Telephone Company, 47
Next, Inc., 698
Nike, Inc., 706
Nikon, Inc., 68, 91
Nissan Corporation, 93, 287
Nixdorf Computer AG (West Germany), 451
Nordisk Company (Denmark), 93
Nova Pharmaceutical Corporation, 696, 720

Occidental Petroleum Corporation, 150, 213
Oneok, Inc., 545
Osborne Computer Corporation, 688–92

Pacific Mutual Corporation, 368
Pan American Airlines, 406
Parker Hannifin Corporation, 616
Penn Central Corporation, 281
Penney, J. C., Company, Inc., 117, 118
Penzoil Corporation, 169, 186
PepsiCo, 213, 334
Philip Morris Company, 334, 535, 732
Philips Company (Netherlands), 213, 782
Piedmont Airlines, 79
Pillsbury Company, 592, 702, 703
Pitney-Bowes Company, 450
PlasTech, Inc., 794–96
Polaroid Corporation, 68, 97, 99, 208
POM Company, 772
Precision Machine Tool Company, 133–35
Preston Trucking, 441
Procter & Gamble Company, 18, 78, 109, 114, 213, 232, 335, 384, 462, 522, 716
Pro-Line Corporation, 724–25
Prudential-Bache Securities, 93
Purex Corporation, 240

RCA Corporation, 91, 348
Reebok International Corporation, 20–21, 706
Reliance Group Holdings, 287
Reynolds, R. J., Company, 229, 535
RJR Nabisco, Inc., 213
Robert Morris Associates, 589
Rockwell International Corporation, 576, 616
Rohm and Haas Company, 92
Rolls Royce Company, 628
Royal Dutch/Shell Group, 772
Royal Foods Distributors, 577

Samsung Group (Korea), 790, 791
Sanyo Corporation, 770
Scandinavian Airline System (SAS), 515
Seagram Company, 213
Searle, G. D., Company, 21
Sears, Roebuck, and Company, 110, 197, 228, 652, 660, 681–82
Security Pacific Automation Company, 656
Serono Labs, 93
Servus Rubber Company, 194
Shell Oil Company, 773
Shionogi Company (Japan), 93
Simonds Rolling Machine Company, 36
Simon & Schuster, Inc., 729
Singer Sewing Machine Company, 767, 772
SmithKline Beckman Corporation, 93, 558
Sony Corporation, 91, 328, 348, 357, 625, 714–15

Southwestern Bell, 380–81
Sperry Corporation, 714
Squibb Corporation, 706
Standard Oil Companies, 44, 227, 773
Stanley Air Tools Company, 620
Stover Industries, 418–19
Sumitomo Bank, 766, 775, 789
Sumitomo Chemical Company (Japan), 93
Sumitomo Rubber Industries, Ltd. (Japan), 397
Sun Microsystems, 97, 98, 441

Tandem Computers, 147, 384, 501
Texaco, Inc., 79, 164, 169, 186
Texas Instruments, Inc., 692
3M Corporation, 18, 91, 232, 384, 417, 578–79, 716, 717
Timken Company, 782*n*
Toshiba America, Inc., 91
Toyota Motor Corporation, 93, 263, 287, 411, 558, 627, 676, 772
Tri-State Telephone Company, 102
TRW, Inc., 271, 576–77
TWA, Inc., 79

Union Carbide Corporation, 78, 364–65, 520, 533, 545, 772
Unisys Corporation, 605
United Airlines, 406
United Parcel Service (UPS), 192, 218, 373
United States Football League, 210
Unocal Corporation, 594
U.S. Steel Corporation, 110, 322
USX Corporation, 442, 615

Valspar Company, 443
Vector Graphics, 692
Victor Technologies, 692
Volkswagen of America, Inc., 93, 95
Volvo AB, 515, 597

Wal-Mart, 148
Walt Disney Company, 214
Wang Laboratories, Inc., 411
Weirton Steel Company, 366
Wellcome PLC Company (Great Britain), 93
Wendy's Old Fashion Hamburgers, 246, 626
Western Electric Company, 48
Westinghouse Corporation, 322, 348, 624
Wilkie, Farr & Gallagher, 286
Winnebago Corporation, 235
Worlds of Wonder, 482
Worthington Industries, 482
WPP Group PLC (Great Britain), 397

Xerox Corporation, 79, 91, 348, 442, 462, 615, 632
Xian Restaurants, 627

Yamanouchi Company (Japan), 93

NAME INDEX

Aaker, David A., 218*n*
Abbey, Augustus, 414*n*
Abbot, Jeff, 687
Abboud, J., 708*n*
Abernathy, William, 21–22
Ackerman, Robert, 112–13, 199*n*
Ackoff, Russell L., 664*n*
Adair, John G., 50*n*
Adam, Everett E., Jr., 155*n*, 616*n*, 633*n*
Adams, J. Stacy, 448*n*
Adams, Jerome, 462*n*
Adams, John R., 313*n*
Adams, Samuel Hopkins, 45
Adelman, Leonard, 54*n*
Adkins, Lynn, 492
Adler, Nancy, J., 783*n*
Adler, Seymour, 461*n*
Agee, William, 169
Ager, Susan, 424
Agnew, Neil M., 177*n*
Agor, W. H., 171*n*
Aharoni, Yair, 771*n*
Ahituv, Niv, 653*n*
Akers, John, 298, 315
Al-Bazzaz, Shawki, 214*n*
Albert, Michael, 4*n*
Albrecht, Maryann H., 331*n*, 337, 338*n*
Alderfer, Clayton, 429, 433
Aldrich, H. E., 95*n*, 96*n*
Alexander, Larry D., 344*n*
Alexander, Tom, 253
Allen, Agnes R., 740*n*
Allen, Louis A., 309*n*, 403*n*
Allen Robert, 245, 362, 385
Allen, Ronald W., 463
Allen, Thomas J., 274*n*, 411
Alter, Steven, 673*n*
Alutto, Joseph A., 738*n*
Alvares, Kenneth, 475*n*
Amabile, Teresa M., 408*n*
Anastasi, A., 425*n*
Anders, George, 763
Anderson, David R., 156*n*, 157, 632*n*
Anderson, Gavin, 70, 71
Anderson, Harlan, 386
Anderson, Warren, 107, 364, 520, 533
Andrews, Kenneth R., 198, 211*n*, 212
Ansoff, H. Igor, 72–73, 198
Anthony, Robert N., 567*n*, 590*n*, 592*n*, 596*n*, 658*n*
Apple, James M., 638
Aquilano, Nicholas J., 623, 628*n*, 629, 633
Aram, John D., 345*n*, 730
Archer, Ernest R., 166*n*
Archer, Stephen A., 175*n*
Argyris, Chris, 51, 283–84, 426, 592*n*, 673*n*
Armstrong, J. Scott, 151*n*, 152, 195, 239*n*
Aronson, D., 739*n*
Aronson, Elliot, 368*n*, 394*n*, 460*n*, 498*n*, 523*n*, 524*n*
Arp, Jean, 222
Arvey, Richard D., 352*n*, 732*n*
Asch, Solomon, 497–99
Asplind, Jan, 346*n*
Astley, W. Graham, 7*n*, 82*n*, 307*n*
Atchison, Sandra D., 390
Athos, Anthony G., 214, 382*n*, 479*n*, 787*n*, 788
Atkinson, John W., 429, 435–36
Atkinson, Michael L., 722–23
Attewell, Paul, 680, 681
Ault, Richard E., 381*n*
Aupperle, Kenneth E., 114*n*
Austin, Howard, 676*n*
Austin, Larry M., 54*n*
Austin, Nancy, 18*n*, 195*n*, 425*n*, 486
Avery, Tom, 134–35
Axelrod, Robert, 184
Axumi, Koya, 624*n*

Babbage, Charles, 35
Backman, Jules, 697*n*, 701*n*
Bacon, Jeremy, 592*n*
Baetz, Mary L., 461*n*
Baier, K., 86*n*
Baird, Lloyd, 756*n*
Baker, Kenneth R., 54*n*
Baker, Phil, 404
Bales, Robert F., 463*n*
Baliga, B. R., 784*n*
Ball, Donald A., 778*n*, 780*n*, 781*n*, 782*n*, 783*n*
Balthasar, H. U., 413*n*
Bamforth, K. W., 373*n*
Banas, Paul A., 732*n*
Banks, W. Curtis, 498–99
Barnard, Chester I., 46–48, 274–75, 301
Barnes, Zane E., 381
Barnet, Richard J., 772*n*
Barnett, Arnold, 661*n*
Barnhill, J. Allison, 165*n*
Baron, Robert A., 738*n*
Bartlett, C. A., 230*n*
Bartlett, Sara, 766
Bartolome, Fernando, 750*n*
Bass, Bernard M., 459, 480–81
Bass, Lawrence W., 513*n*
Bass, Robert E., 56*n*
Bass, Robert M., 513
Bateman, Thomas S., 505
Bazerman, Max H., 178, 179, 503*n*
Bean, Alden S., 412*n*
Bean, Ed, 535
Beauchamp, Tom L., 82*n*
Beaver, Jennifer E., 674*n*, 679*n*
Beazley, Ernest, 770
Beckhard, Richard, 375, 378*n*
Bedeian, Arthur G., 264*n*, 737
Bedford, Norton M., 567*n*, 590*n*, 592*n*, 596*n*
Beer, Michael, 354, 355
Begley, Thomas, 708–9
Behling, Robert, 655*n*
Behrendtz, Hakan, 346*n*
Beidleman, Carl R., 779*n*
Belkner, Rick, 419–21
Bell, Arthur H., 524*n*
Bell, Cecil H., Jr., 371*n*, 375, 376, 378, 379, 381–82
Bennett, Amanda, 245
Bennis, Warren G., 366
Benoit, Kenny, 576
Benton, F. Warren, 544*n*, 619*n*, 654*n*, 665*n*
Berenbeim, Ronald, 118, 121*n*, 123
Berg, David, 514
Berg, Eric N., 635*n*
Berg, Per Olaf, 381*n*
Berkman, Barbara, 253
Berlew, David E., 345*n*, 732
Berne, Eric, 377*n*
Berry, Paul C., 410
Bertalanffy, Ludwig von, 56*n*
Bettenhausen, Kenneth, 496*n*
Betz, Ellen L., 433*n*
Bieber, Owen F., 406
Bildner, Jom, 549
Binzen, Peter, 281*n*
Birch, David, 435*n*, 701
Blake, Robert R., 395*n*, 404*n* 467, 468, 472*n*
Blakeslee, Sandra, 644*n*
Blanchard, Kenneth H., 185*n*, 470–72, 684
Blanning, Robert W., 675*n*, 677*n*, 678
Blech, David, 696
Blech, Isaac, 696
Blicker, Alan, 266
Block, Clifford H., 410
Blood, Milton, 320
Bloom, Nancy E., 788*n*
Bluedorn, Allen C., 37*n*
Blumenfeld, Dennis E., 687
Bock, Gordon, 224

Bodo, Al, 577
Bok, Edward, 45
Bolles, Richard Nelson, 754*n*
Bond, Michael Harris, 434
Bondanella, Peter, 53
Borland, C., 708*n*
Boseman, Glenn, 211*n*
Bottger, Preston, 511*n*
Boulding, Elise, 399
Boulding, Kenneth E., 56*n*
Bourgeois, L. J., 226*n*
Boutell, Wayne S., 606*n*
Bovee, Courtland L., 524*n*
Bowen, Harriet, 454–55
Bowen, H. R., 111
Bowie, Norman E., 82*n*
Boyd, Brendan, 543
Boyd, David P., 708–9
Boyd, Richard, 481
Bradspies, Robert W., 563*n*
Brady, J. V., 379*n*
Bramel, Dana, 49*n*
Branch, Taylor, 395*n*
Brandenberg, Richard G., 34*n*
Bratkovich, Jerold R., 621*n*
Bray, Douglas W., 344*n*, 732*n*
Breaugh, James A., 731
Brewster, Tom, 28–29
Bricklin, Malcolm, 748
Bridges, Fancis J., 165*n*
Brookfield, K. L., 618*n*
Brooks, Brian J., 784*n*
Brooks, Earl, 50*n*
Brown, Charles, 120–21
Brown, Edmund G., 400
Brown, Fred, 690
Brown, John L., 177*n*
Brown, L. David, 401
Brown, L. M., 273*n*
Browne, Paul C., 285*n*
Brownell, Peter, 592*n*
Buck, R., 531*n*
Buell, Barbara, 68
Buffa, Elwood S., 628*n*, 641
Bullen, Christine, 541*n*
Bungard, Walter, 475*n*
Burack, Elmer H., 331*n*, 332*n*
Burgelman, Robert A., 713*n*, 715, 716
Burke, James, 122
Burke, Ronald J., 756
Burnham, David H., 24*n*, 305
Burns, James McGregor, 460–61
Burns, James R., 54*n*
Bush, Donald H., 23*n*
Bush, George, 144
Byars, Lloyd L., 148*n*, 235*n*
Byker, Donald, 524*n*
Bylinsky, Gene, 643*n*
Byrne, John A., 224, 399*n*
Bywater, William H., 625

Cacioppo, J. T. 524*n*
Caldwell, Philip, 614
Campbell, Richard J., 344*n*, 732*n*
Campion, Michael A., 316*n*, 320
Cannon, Hugh, 338*n*
Cantelon, Philip, 384
Capon, Noel, 780*n*
Cappy, Michael, 194
Capron, H. L., 664*n*
Carey, Alex, 49*n*
Carlisle, Howard M., 281*n*
Carlson, Charles, 652, 660, 681–82
Carlson, Robert E., 342*n*
Carlson, Sue, 15*n*
Carlston, Donald E., 503*n*
Carnegie, Andrew, 40, 110, 116, 707
Carr, Albert R., 340
Carroll, Archie B., 114, 658*n*, 677*n*
Carroll, Lewis, 200
Carroll, Paul B., 298
Carroll, Stephen J., 12*n*, 239*n*, 240–42
Carruth, Paul J., 594*n*
Carter, Jimmy, 603
Carter John C., 660*n*
Carter, Nancy M., 37*n*
Cartwright, Dorwin, 460*n*, 462*n*, 493*n*, 494*n*, 504*n*
Casey, Jeff T., 410*n*
Cassoni, Vittorio, 213
Castro, Janice, 138
Certo, Samuel C., 582
Cespedes, Frank V., 524*n*
Chacko, Thomas I., 242*n*
Chaffee, Ellen Earle, 595*n*
Chakravarty, Subrata N., 68
Chammah, Albert, 184
Champion, John M., 65*n*
Chandler, Alfred D., 197*n*, 198, 227, 228, 230, 322
Chandler, Colby H., 97, 99, 100
Channon, D., 229*n*
Chapman, Carl, 91
Chapman, Gary, 684–85
Chapple, Eliot D., 373*n*
Chase, Richard B., 623, 628*n*, 629, 633
Chemers, Martin M., 469*n*, 474
Chen, Stephen, 253
Cheney, Paul H., 656*n*, 678
Cheng, Joseph L. C., 275*n*
Child, John, 681*n*
Childers, Peter G., 675*n*
Christensen, H. Kurt, 750*n*
Christenson, C. Roland, 198*n*, 256
Christodoulou, Chris, 780*n*
Churchill, Neil C., 144*n*, 593, 506*n*
Chusmir, Leonard H., 437*n*
Clark, H. H., 523*n*
Clark, M., 511*n*
Clark, Russell D., 504*n*
Clawson, James G., 734*n*, 742*n*, 746, 754*n*, 758*n*
Cleanin, Robert W., 415
Cleland, David I., 267*n*, 273*n*, 313*n*
Clifford, Colleen, 549
Clifton, Sara, 486
Cobb, Anthony T., 307*n*
Coch, Lester, 501*n*
Cochran, Philip L., 111*n*, 114*n*
Cockburn, Donald J., 559*n*
Cohen, Ben, 702
Cohen, J. Kalman, 211*n*
Cohen, Peter, 652
Cohen, S., 449
Cohen, Stephen I., 411*n*
Coll, Steve, 164
Collins, Eliza, 363*n*, 760*n*
Collins, Paul D., 289*n*
Conlon, Edward J., 10*n*
Connolly, Terry, 10*n*
Coolidge, Calvin, 88
Cooper, Cary L., 745*n*, 759*n*
Cooper, Joel, 368*n*
Cooper, W. W., 371*n*
Coors, Bill, 390
Coors, Jeffrey, 390
Coors, Peter, 390
Copeland, Thomas E., 583*n*, 586*n*
Cosier, Richard A., 172*n*, 449
Costas, John, 338*n*
Cothren, Rachel, 790
Cottrell, Comer, 724–25
Cougar, Daniel J., 655*n*
Craig, C. Samuel, 637*n*
Craig, Charles E., 617*n*
Crawford, B., 125*n*
Crino, Michael D., 285*n*
Crites, John O., 742*n*
Crock, Stan, 766
Cron, William L., 750*n*
Croyle, Robert T., 368*n*
Cummings, H., 449
Cummings, L. L., 352*n*, 451*n*
Cummings, Thomas G., 367, 368*n*, 482*n*, 605*n*
Cunningham, Chris, 418–19
Curley, John R., 572*n*
Cyert, Richard M., 211*n*

Daft, Richard L., 278*n*, 556*n*
Dale, Ernest, 262, 265*n*, 322*n*, 509*n*
Daley, Suzanne, 606*n*
Dalton, Dan R., 449
Dalton, Gene W., 750
Dalton, Melville, 404
Dance, F. E. X., 523*n*
Daniels, John R., 267*n*
Darrow, Charlotte N., 742*n*
Dascher, Paul E., 668*n*
Daughen, Joseph R., 281*n*
Dauphinais, G. William, 584*n*
Davidson, Marilyn J., 759*n*
Davis, David, 680*n*
Davis, Keith, 109, 494*n*, 534*n*, 539
Davis, Michael W., 675*n*
Davis, Peter S., 208*n*
Davis, Stanley M., 271*n*, 272–73, 382*n*, 479*n*
Day, Diane L., 207*n*
Deal, Terence E., 382*n*, 441, 479*n*
Dearborn, De Witt C., 170
Dearden, John, 567*n*, 590*n*, 592*n*, 596*n*, 656*n*, 680*n*
Deaux, K., 524*n*
Decyk, Roxanne, 760
Delbecq, Andre, 400*n*, 410*n*, 411
DeLong, Thomas J., 745*n*, 748*n*
Deming, W. Edwards, 9, 60–61, 645, 788
Demmings, Dara, 70, 71
DeNisi, Angelo S., 476*n*
DePree, Max, 411
Dess, Gregory G., 208*n*
Deutsch, Claudia H., 247*n*
Deutsch, Stuart Jay, 10*n*
Devanna, M. A., 244*n*
Devine, Taylor, 549
Dewey, John, 166*n*
Dickinson, E. E., 286
Dickson, G. W., 665*n*, 666–69
Dickson, John W., 414*n*
Dickson, William J., 49, 274*n*
Dilworth, James B., 154*n*, 616*n*, 631*n*
Dobrzynski, Judith H., 236
Donnell, Susan M., 462*n*, 760*n*
Donnelly, James H., Jr., 526*n*
Dossett, Dennis L., 346*n*
Douglass, Donna, 620*n*
Douglass, Merrill, 620*n*
Doz, Y. L., 230*n*
Drahem, Kirk B., 705
Dreyfuss, Joel, 766
Driver, Michael J., 745–47
Drucker, Peter F., 8*n*, 10, 15*n*, 60, 139, 166*n*, 170, 172, 204, 238–39, 481, 561*n*, 698, 713–16, 772*n*
Dubno, Peter, 338*n*
DuBrin, Andrew J., 737*n*, 755*n*
Dufy, Raoul, 764
Dugoni, Bernard L., 731*n*
Dukakis, Michael, 144, 300
Dukerich, Janet M., 482*n*, 486*n*
Dulewicz, Victor, 344*n*
Dumaine, Brian, 614
Dunbar, Roger, 605–6
Duncan, Robert, 285*n*, 286, 288*n*
Dunnette, Marvin D., 732*n*, 738*n*
Durant, William, 62
Dutton, John M., 394*n*
Dutton, Richard E., 414*n*
Dyer, William G., 378*n*
Dymsza, William A., 767*n*

Eagly, A. H., 759*n*
Earley, P. C., 241*n*, 451*n*
Eary, Donald F., 634
Eason, Henry, 76*n*
Eastman, George, 97
Easton, Henry, 501*n*
Ebadi, Yar M., 413*n*
Ebert, Ronald J., 155*n*, 616*n*, 633*n*
Eden, Dov, 469*n*, 734*n*
Edwards, Raoul D., 384*n*
Egan, Joseph F., 458
Ehlbeck, Hank, 694
Ehrlich, Sanford B., 482*n*, 486*n*
Einhorn, H. J., 181*n*
Eisenberg, Eric M., 539*n*, 544–45
Ekstrom, Ruth B., 759*n*

Elbing, Alvar O., 70*n*
Ely, Paul, Jr., 260
Emerson, Harrington, 39*n*
Emery, Fred E., 71–72, 285*n*
Emin, Hussein, 338*n*
Emurian, H. H., 379*n*
English, Jon, 618
Ephlin, Donald, 364
Epstein, Barry J., 655*n*
Epstein, E., 76*n*
Epstein, Edwin M., 113*n*, 114*n*
Erez, Miriam, 241*n*, 451*n*
Erikson, Erik H., 741–43
Ernest, Margo, 779
Estes, Ralph, W., 168*n*
Evan, William M., 82*n*
Evans, James R., 632*n*
Evans, Martin G., 475, 753
Evans, Paul, 750*n*
Evered, Roger, 193*n*
Everest, Larry, 365
Everett, Bob, 386
Ewusi-Mensah, Kweku, 653*n*
Ezell, Hazel F., 760

Fahey, Liam, 83, 86, 87*n*, 215*n*
Fahrmann, V. L., 273*n*
Fairholm, Gilbert W., 655*n*
Falbe, Cecilia M., 83*n*, 108*n*
Farley, John U., 780*n*
Farris, George F., 469*n*
Faux, Victor A., 734*n*, 746
Fayol, Henri, 41–43, 58, 59, 60, 281–82
Feagin, Joe R., 434
Fearon, Harold E., 154*n*
Feigenbaum, Edward A., 679*n*
Feldman, David C., 496*n*, 497*n*
Feldman, Howard, 54*n*
Feldman, J. M., 181*n*, 192
Feldstein, S., 531*n*
Ference, Thomas P., 171*n*, 567, 750*n*, 752
Feuer, Dale, 554
Fiedler, Fred E., 472–75
Field, Ann R., 298
Field, Hubert S., 337*n*, 338*n*
Field, R. H., 479*n*
Fields, Debbi, 548–51
Fields, Randy, 549, 550
Figgins, Ross, 528*n*
Filley, Alan C., 510*n*
Finger, Phyllis A., 172*n*
Finn, Bertram, 774*n*
Finn, David, 260
Fisch, Gerald G., 307*n*, 311, 315
Fischer, David W., 140*n*
Fischoff, B., 181*n*
Fiske, Edward B., 348*n*
Fitzgerald, Edmund, 620*n*
Fitzgerald, Michael, 320*n*
Flanders, Walter, 40
Flannery, Lauren S., 672*n*, 680*n*
Fleishman, E. A., 470*n*
Fleming, Al, 644*n*
Fletcher, Clive A., 344*n*
Flippo, Edwin B., 53*n*
Follett, Mary Parker, 3, 46–47
Fombrun, Charles J., 82*n*, 350, 351*n*
Foote, Susan B., 109*n*
Ford, Daniel, 699*n*
Ford, Henry, 32, 33, 40–41, 62, 706
Ford, Robert N., 317*n*
Fordyce, Kenneth, 675*n*
Forgionne, Guisseppe A., 571, 640
Forrester, Jay, 54*n*, 386
Forward, George E., 442
Fowler, Donald R., 621*n*
Frame, Robert M., 381*n*
Francl, Thomas J., 602*n*
Frankell-Hauser, J., 759*n*
Franko, L., 230*n*, 774*n*
Frederick, William C., 110*n*, 113*n*, 115*n*
Frederickson, James W., 193*n*
Freedman, B. L., 410*n*
Freedman, David H., 192
Freedman, Jonathan L., 496*n*, 501*n*
Freeman, J. H., 95, 96
Freeman, R. Edward, 69*n*, 77, 82*n*, 83*n*, 102, 108*n*, 116*n*, 127, 133, 196*n*, 204, 210*n*, 220, 325
French, John R. P., 241*n*, 302, 350*n*, 460*n*, 501*n*
French, Wendell L., 341*n*, 371*n*, 375, 376, 378, 379, 381–82
Frick, Michael, 686
Friedman, Brian, 618*n*
Friedman, L. N., 449
Friedman, M., 709*n*
Friedman, Milton, 108–9, 115
Friedman, Rose, 109*n*
Friend, Ronald, 49*n*
Fritz, Carol J., 189*n*
Frombrun, C. J., 244*n*
Fry, Art, 417
Fukada, Ryuji, 788*n*
Fulmer, Robert M., 196*n*
Furnall, Robin, 794–96

Gabarro, John J., 25*n*, 756*n*
Gaither, Norman, 630
Galbraith, Jay R., 196*n*, 228, 228*n*, 243, 271*n*, 277*n*, 279, 281*n*
Gale, Bradley T., 644*n*
Galing, Bernard, 674*n*
Gallo, Thomas E., 672*n*
Gantt, Henry L., 37, 46, 153
Garfield, David C., 776
Garner, John, 133–35
Garvin, David, 644
Gavin, Alexander, 130
Geis, Florence Lindauer, 462*n*
Gellerman, Saul, 28
Geneen, Harold, 403
Geoffrion, A. M., 54*n*
George, Claude S., Jr., 34*n*
Gerald, Allen, 206*n*
Getty, Gordon, 164
Gettys, Charles F., 410*n*
Ghiselli, Edwin E., 462*n*
Ghosh, Avijit, 637*n*
Gibson, David V., 532*n*
Gibson, James L., 526*n*
Gibson, Janice T., 499
Gibson, T. A., 273*n*
Gilbert, Daniel J., 196*n*, 204, 220
Gilbert, Daniel R., Jr., 83*n*, 108*n*
Gilbert, Elizabeth, 753
Gilbreth, Frank B., 37–38
Gilbreth, Lillian M., 37–38
Gilder, George, 700
Gillen, Dennis J., 12*n*
Gillette, King C., 758
Gillis, Jim G., 409*n*
Gimbel, Bernard, 465
Ginsberg, Ari, 193*n*
Gioia, Dennis A., 460*n*
Girly, Joe, 255
Glaberson, William G., 68
Glass, David, 449
Glassman, James K., 138
Glauser, Michael J., 538*n*
Gleicher, David B., 171
Gluck, Frederick W., 461
Glueck, William F., 346*n*
Goggins, William C., 272
Gold, Bela, 634*n*
Goldman, Marshall, 143
Goldstein, Irwin L., 341
Golembiewski, Robert T., 381*n*
Golen, Steven P., 528*n*
Golper, John B., 337*n*
Gomersall, Earl R., 345*n*
Gooding, Judson, 39*n*
Gorbachev, Mikhail, 95, 143, 699
Gordon, Jeanne, 770
Gordon, Lawrence A., 602*n*
Gordon, Michael E., 439
Gordon, William J., 410
Gore, Bill, 486
Gore, Marvin R., 681*n*
Gorry, G. Anthony, 658, 659
Gossen, Martyn E., 274*n*
Gould, Lewis J., 44*n*
Gould, Roger L., 742*n*
Gouldner, Alvin W., 404
Goulet, Lynda L., 582
Goulet, Peter G., 582
Graeff, Claude L., 472*n*
Graen, George, 475*n*
Graham, Benjamin, 758
Graham, Robert J., 170*n*, 171*n*
Grandori, Anna, 172
Granger, Charles H., 213*n*
Granof, Michael H., 586*n*
Grant, Donald, 344*n*, 732*n*
Grantges, R. F., 273*n*
Gray, P., 589*n*
Gray, Patricia Bellew, 535
Greely, Jack, 420–21
Green, Stephen G., 412*n*
Greene, Harold, 102
Greenfield, Jerry, 702
Greenhaus, Jeffrey H., 737, 741
Greenleaf, James, 779*n*
Greenwood, William T., 56
Gregory, Robert H., 655
Greiner, Larry E., 375*n*
Griffin, Ricky W., 505
Griffith, Samuel B., 53
Grinyear, Peter, 214*n*
Gross, Neil, 770
Gross, Steve, 253, 413*n*
Grosse, Richard A., 154*n*
Grover, Richard A., 448*n*
Guetzkow, H., 498
Guilford, J. P., 409*n*
Gulick, Luther, 263*n*
Gumbel, Peter, 777
Gumpert, David E., 717–19
Gupta, A., 244*n*
Gustafson, Stanley, 245
Guterel, Fred, 201*n*
Guteri, Fred V., 253
Guth, William D., 170, 198*n*
Guzzo, Richard, 501–2
Gyllenhammar, Pehr G., 515

Haas, William P., 671
Hackman, J. Richard, 316*n*, 320, 375*n*, 448*n*
Hafner, Craig R., 543
Hagedorn, Ann, 71
Hagen, Everett, 707–8
Hahn, T. Marshall, 563
Hajner, Katie, 192
Haka, Susan, 602*n*
Halberstam, David, 32*n*
Halcon, Allan, 331*n*
Hales, Colin P., 15*n*
Hall, Carol, 252
Hall, Douglas T., 345*n*, 730–32, 737*n*, 741*n*, 756, 757
Hall, Edward T., 778*n*
Hall, Francine S., 337, 338*n*, 737*n*, 756, 757
Hall, Jay, 462*n*, 503, 512, 760*n*
Hambrick, Donald C., 207*n*, 229*n*
Hammonds, Keith H., 703
Hamner, W. Clay, 443*n*, 444, 445
Hancock, Ellen, 760
Haney, Craig, 498–99
Hannan, M. T., 95, 96
Hansen, Richard W., 750*n*
Harding, Harold F., 409*n*
Haritos-Fatouros, Mika, 499
Harmon, W. Ken, 668*n*
Harragan, Betty Lehan, 760*n*
Harris, Bob V., 439
Harris, Catherine L., 652, 657
Harris, Diana, 760
Harris, Louis, 108
Harris, Marilyn A., 68
Harris, R. Clark, 617*n*
Harris, Robert G., 22
Harrison, W. L., 660*n*
Harrower, Molly, 498, 499
Hart, Ann Weaver, 336*n*
Hartley, Edward J., 494*n*
Hartley, Eugene L., 605*n*
Hartley, Robert F., 692
Hartman, Edwin, 196*n*
Harvey, Donald F., 227*n*
Harvey-Jones, John, 294–95
Haspeslagh, Phillipe, 207*n*
Hatfield, John D., 114*n*

Hatvaay, N., 787*n*
Hawkins, Katherine, 185*n*
Hawkins, Robert G., 774*n*
Hax, Arnoldo C., 207
Hayes, Robert H., 21–22, 193, 194, 203, 616, 642*n*, 644*n*
Hearst, William Randolph, 706
Heath, Charles O., 153*n*, 155*n*, 157*n*
Heck, William C., 346*n*
Heckhausen, Heinz, 437*n*
Hedley, Barry, 207*n*
Heenan, David A., 782
Heizer, Jay, 641*n*, 642*n*
Helm, Leslie, 68, 387
Hempel, Carl G., 56*n*
Heneman, Herbert G., III, 342*n*
Hennessy, Edward L., Jr., 82*n*
Herbert, Theodore T., 168*n*
Herden, Richard, 172*n*
Herman, Stanley N., 376
Herold, David M., 196*n*
Hersey, Paul, 470–72
Hershey, Milton S., 758
Hershey, Robert, 341
Herzberg, Frederick, 429, 430, 437–39
Hewitt, Tommy, 194
Hewlett, William, 227, 758
Hicks, Philip E., 636*n*
Hickson, David J., 290*n*
Hill, Marianne M., 673*n*
Hilley, John J., 779*n*
Hiltz, Starr Roxanne, 541*n*
Hirschman, A., 76
Hirshhorn, Larry, 378*n*
Hochbaum, Godfrey M., 503*n*
Hoerr, John, 406
Hofer, Charles W., 193, 197–99, 200*n*, 201, 206*n*, 211*n*, 212, 215*n*, 216, 217, 281*n*
Hoffman, L. Richard, 503*n*, 509*n*, 511*n*
Hofstede, Geert, 434, 465, 785–86
Hogarth, R. M., 181*n*
Holland, Robert C., 618*n*
Hollander, Edwin P., 460*n*
Holley, William H., Jr., 337*n*, 338*n*
Holmes, Arthur W., 606*n*
Holmes, Sandra L., 112*n*
Holton, Richard H., 95*n*
Holusha, John, 632*n*
Homans, George C., 49*n*, 494*n*
Hornaday, J. A., 708*n*
Horniman, Alexander, 116*n*
Horovitz, Jacques, 781
Horovitz, J. H., 556*n*
Horton, Thomas R., 619*n*
Hougland, James G., Jr., 58*n*
House, E. A., 756, 758*n*
House, Robert J., 195, 439*n*, 461, 475–76, 480*n*, 481–82, 510*n*
Hrebiniak, Lawrence G., 196*n*, 225, 226, 242*n*
Huber, George P., 185*n*
Huber, Vandra L., 448*n*
Hudson, Richard L., 80*n*
Hughes, Charles Evans, 44
Hulbert, James, 780*n*
Hulin, Charles L., 241*n*, 320, 451*n*
Hull, Frank, 289*n*, 624*n*
Hull, Raymond, 349*n*, 753*n*
Hulvershorn, Patti R., 346*n*
Hummel, Raymond C., 742*n*
Hunsaker, Philip, 622*n*
Hunt, James G., 480*n*
Hunt, Raymond G., 788*n*
Hunter, J. E., 433*n*
Hurlock, James, 68
Huse, Edgar F., 367, 368*n*, 605*n*
Hyatt, Joshua, 194*n*
Hymer, Steven, 768

Iacocca, Lee J., 138–39, 145, 158, 244, 245, 300, 480, 644
Ikihata, Takashi, 766
Ilgen, Daniel R., 448*n*, 451*n*, 731*n*
Imai, Masaaki, 554
Immerwahr, John, 619
Instone, Debra, 462*n*
Inzerilli, Giorgio, 562*n*
Irvine, V. Bruce, 602, 604, 605
Isaack, Thomas S., 171*n*
Isabella, Lynn A., 758*n*
Ivancevich, John M., 241*n*, 526*n*, 740
Ives, Blake, 671*n*
Iyer, Pico, 520

Jackson, Jesse, 300
Jackson, Susan E., 740
Jacobs, Bruce A., 620*n*
Jacobson, Gary, 625
Jaeger, Alfred M., 784*n*
Jago, Arthur C., 476–79
James, John H., 65*n*
Janis, Irving L., 182, 399*n*, 510*n*
Jaunich, Robert, 690, 691
Jay, Anthony, 508*n*, 511*n*, 512
Jennings, Joyce, 462*n*
Jerkovsky, William, 273*n*
Jernberg, Frank, 346*n*
Jewell, Linda N., 493*n*
Jick, Todd D., 419
Jobs, Steve, 148, 689, 698, 709–11
Johansen, Robert, 541*n*
Johansson, Hank, 558*n*
Johns, Jaspar, 580
Johnson, Bill, 418
Johnson, David W., 506
Johnson, F. Ross, 441
Johnson, Frank P., 506
Johnson, Gerald E., 634
Johnson, Jim, 684
Johnson, Kirk, 341
Johnson, Robert Wood, 122
Johnson, Spencer, 185*n*
Jonas, Hans, 56*n*
Jones, Allen P., 352*n*
Jones, Bob, 2
Jones, Christopher G., 525*n*
Jones, Gareth R., 263*n*, 345*n*
Jones, Geoffrey, 777
Jones, Patricia E., 216
Jones, Reginald, 332, 458
Jones, Trevor O., 577
Joyce, William F., 225, 226, 242*n*, 372
Juran, J. M., 645

Kafrey, D., 739*n*
Kahn, Robert L., 375*n*, 399*n*, 737
Kahneman, Daniel, 177, 180*n*
Kamata, Satoshi, 788*n*
Kane, Larry, 64
Kanter, Jerome, 680*n*
Kanter, Rosabeth M., 7*n*, 60*n*, 195*n*, 305–6, 408, 411, 413, 414, 441, 443*n*
Kaplan, Robert E., 168*n*, 539*n*
Karger, Delmar W., 196*n*
Kast, Fremont E., 57*n*
Katz, Daniel, 737
Katz, Marsha, 337*n*
Katz, Ralph, 274*n*, 745*n*
Katz, Robert L., 14, 23, 24
Katzan, Harry, Jr., 674*n*
Kaufman, Herbert, 368*n*
Kavner, Robert M., 463
Kay, Emmanuel, 241*n*, 350*n*
Kazanjian, Robert K., 227*n*, 228, 243
Kearney, Maureen, 437*n*
Kedia, Ben L., 285*n*
Keen, G. W. P., 657
Kein, Edward B., 742*n*
Keller, John J., 192, 298, 362
Kellerman, Barbara, 469*n*
Kelley, Harold H., 494*n*
Kelley, Kevin, 777
Kendrick, John W., 617, 701
Kennedy, Allan A., 382*n*, 441, 479*n*
Kennedy, John F., 76
Kennedy, Joseph, 707
Kennevan, Walter J., 656*n*
Kenny, David A., 461*n*
Keon, Thomas L., 37*n*
Kepner, Charles H., 166*n*, 168*n*
Kerpit, L., 95*n*
Kerr, Elaine B., 541*n*
Kerr, Peter, 286*n*
Kerr, Steven, 510*n*
Kerwin, Robert, 410*n*
Kerzner, Harold, 273*n*
Kets de Vries, Manfred F. R., 25*n*, 718–20
Keys, J. Bernard, 788*n*
Khedouri, Franklin, 4*n*
Kidd, Charles W., 589*n*
Kiefer, Charles, 375*n*
Kieser, Alfred, 309*n*
Kiesler, Sara, 171
Kilgore, Sheldon, 21
Kilmann, Ralph H., 382*n*, 384*n*, 479*n*
Kim, Jay S., 241*n*
Kimberly, John R., 381*n*
Kindel, Stephen, 370
Kindleberger, Charles, 57
King, R. W., 365
King, W. Frank, III, 572
King, William R., 655*n*
Kingsborough, Donald, 482
Kirchof, Nicki S., 267*n*, 313*n*
Kirkland, R. I., 365
Kirkpatrick, Donald L., 351*n*
Kirp, David L., 501*n*
Klammer, Thomas P., 598*n*
Klavans, Richard, 644*n*
Klee, Paul, 258, 296
Klein, Harold E., 199*n*, 215*n*
Kleinfeld, Sonny, 138
Klimoski, Richard, 344*n*
Knapp, Robert W., 655*n*
Knight, F. H., 175*n*
Kobasa, Suzanne C., 739
Kolb, David A., 141*n*
Kolodney, Harvey F., 271*n*
Kolodziej, Stan, 632*n*
Kols, Adrienne, 579
Komanecky, Nicholas, 496*n*
Komatsu, Koh, 766
Koo, D. H., 791
Koontz, Harold, 56, 563*n*
Koriat, A., 181*n*
Korth, Christopher, 769, 772, 774*n*
Kostabi, Mark, 490
Kotter, John P., 16*n*, 25*n*, 306, 368*n*, 370, 523, 734*n*, 746, 756*n*
Krajewski, L. J., 628*n*
Kram, Kathy, 756*n*, 758
Krantz, D., 449
Krantz, James, 378*n*
Kraus, William A., 373*n*
Kreitner, Robert, 443*n*
Krieger, Andrew, 763
Kristof, Nicholas D., 791
Kroc, Ray A., 382, 627
Kroop, Dean H., 54*n*
Kruglanski, A. W., 399*n*, 510*n*
Kuhn, Thomas S., 34*n*
Kume, Tadashi, 787
Kumtha, Areen M., 636*n*
Kurland, Mark A., 215*n*
Kurzman, Dan, 520
Kurzweil, R., 675*n*

Labich, Kenneth, 253
Labitch, Kenneth, 405*n*, 413*n*
LaBonte, Joseph, 20
Ladd, Eldon, 584*n*
Laird, R. K., 544*n*
Lambert, Steve, 542*n*
Lamon, Larry, 687
Land, Edwin, 97
Landsberger, Henry A., 49*n*
Landy, Frank J., 425*n*, 450
Lanford, H. W., 157*n*, 596*n*
Lange, David R., 280*n*
Langley, Monica, 353
Langomasi, Adolpho, 674*n*
Larsen, Janet K., 520*n*
Larson, Lars L., 480*n*
Larton, Jim, 794–96
Lasky, Victor, 603
Latham, Gary P., 241*n*, 450, 566*n*
Laud, Robert L., 350, 351*n*
Lauder, Estee, 758
Laufer, Arthur C., 638

Lavan, Helen, 337*n*
Lawler, Edward E., 50, 316*n*, 349*n*, 351, 375*n*, 436*n*, 445–48, 730*n*
Lawrence, M. J., 151*n*
Lawrence, Paul R., 59*n*, 271*n*, 272, 276, 288, 354, 355, 368*n*
Leap, Terry L., 337*n*, 338*n*
Learned, Edmund P., 198*n*
Leavitt, Harold J., 34*n*, 299*n*, 371, 372, 527–28, 536*n*, 680*n*, 769
Lee, Chris, 554
Lee, James A., 53*n*, 438*n*
Lee, Sang M., 55*n*, 92*n*
Lefcourt, Herbert, 449
Lehr, Lewis, 717
Leinster, Colin, 399*n*, 435, 462*n*
Lemoine, Laura F., 524*n*
Lengel, Robert H., 278*n*
Lenway, S., 125*n*
Lenz, Mary, 543
Leonard, Frank S., 644*n*
Leonard, H. S., 449
Leonard-Barton, Dorothy, 373*n*
Leone, Robert A., 76*n*
Leontiades, Milton, 206*n*
LeRoy, Todd W., 722–23
Leshnover, Susan, 707
Lesikar, Raymond V., 534, 541*n*
Levering, Robert, 450*n*
Levine, Jonathan B., 260, 387
Levinson, Daniel, 742–44
Levinson, Harry, 751*n*
Levinson, Maria H., 742*n*
Levitt, Theodore, 73*n*, 90*n*, 204
Levy, H., 768–69
Lewicki, Roy J., 402*n*
Lewin, Kurt, 367, 368, 467*n*, 605
Lewis, Arthur M., 192
Lewis, Geoff, 298, 362, 387
Lewis, W. Walker, 11*n*
LiCari, Jerome, 251–52
Licata, Betty Jo, 23*n*
Lichtenstein, S., 180*n*, 181*n*
Lieberman, Morton A., 377*n*
Liebowitz, Jay, 675*n*, 678*n*, 679*n*
Liederman, David, 548–51
Likert, Jane Gibson, 283*n*
Likert, Rensis, 283–85, 426, 494, 495
Liles, P. R., 708*n*
Lim, Francis G., Jr., 469*n*
Lin, W. Thomas, 602*n*
Linblom, Charles E., 183*n*
Lindquist, Stanton C., 602*n*
Lindzey, Gardner, 368*n*, 394*n*, 460*n*, 498*n*, 523*n*, 524*n*
Linneman, Robert E., 199*n*
Lippett, Gordon, 481
Lippitt, Ronald, 467*n*, 493*n*
Litecky, Charles R., 659*n*
Litterer, Joseph A., 397*n*, 402*n*
Livingston, J. Sterling, 23, 172*n*, 732*n*
Lober, Brian, 320*n*
Locke, Edwin A., 37*n*, 241*n*, 242*n*, 439, 450, 566*n*
Lofgren, Gunnar K., 636*n*
Logan, William Bryant, 733
Lohr, Steve, 8*n*
London, Manuel L., 754*n*
Longenecker, Justin G., 58*n*
Longley, Jeanne, 510*n*
Lorange, Peter, 144*n*, 200, 242*n*, 248–49, 559*n*, 572
Lorber, Robert, 684
Lorenzen, David, 690
Lorsch, Jay W., 53*n*, 58*n*, 59, 276, 288
Loughran, Charles S., 406
Lovenheim, Barbara, 344*n*
Luconi, Fred L., 677*n*
Lunzer, Francesca, 645*n*
Luthans, Fred, 55*n*, 58*n*, 443*n*, 521*n*
Lyles, Marjorie A., 171
Lyons, Norman R., 656*n*

MacArthur, Douglas, 480
Maccoby, Eleanor E., 605*n*
Machiavelli, Niccolo, 52, 53
Macintosh, Norman B., 556*n*
Mackenzie, Alec, 684
MacMillan, Ian C., 207*n*, 215, 216, 332*n*
Maddi, Salvatore R., 739
Magnusen, Karl O., 289*n*
Mahar, Linda, 475*n*
Mahmoud, Essam, 151*n*
Maidique, Modesto A., 788*n*
Maier, Norman R. F., 182, 185
Main, Jeremy, 214*n*, 480*n*
Majluf, Nicolas S., 207
Makridakis, Spyros, 151*n*
Malik, S. D., 494*n*
Malik, Zafar A., 196*n*
Malinowski, Frank, 343*n*
Malloy, Maura, 337*n*
Malone, Thomas W., 677*n*
Mandell, Steven L., 664*n*
Mann, Leon, 182
Mann, R. D., 461*n*
Mann, Robert I., 677*n*
Mantel, Samuel J., 603
Manz, Charles C., 482*n*, 483–85
Mao Tse-Tung, 53
March, James G., 177*n*, 306*n*, 394*n*
Marchione, Anthony R., 618
Marcial, Gene G., 696
Margulies, Newton, 366*n*, 380*n*
Marino, Kenneth E., 280*n*
Mark, Reuben, 71
Markus, M. Lynne, 572*n*, 667*n*
Marram, Ellen, 760
Marriott, Bill, 559
Martino, Joseph P., 151*n*
Marx, Karl, 263
Masland, Andrew T., 673*n*
Maslow, Abraham H., 51, 426, 429, 432–33, 434
Mason, F. R., 263*n*
Mason, Todd, 362
Matteson, Michael T., 740
Mauriel, John, 196*n*
Mayo, Elton, 49–51, 426
McAfee, R. Bruce, 350*n*
McArthur, Charles C., 734*n*, 746
McArthur, Dan, 558*n*
McCaffrey, James A., 543
McCall, Morgan W., Jr., 168*n*
McCann, T. M., 157*n*, 596*n*
McCaskey, Michael B., 214*n*
McClain, John O., 615*n*
McClelland, David, 24*n*, 305–6, 428, 436–37, 703–4, 735
McClendon, Thurrell O., 594*n*
McConkey, Dale D., 239*n*
McCorduck, Pamela, 679*n*
McCulloch, Wendell H., 778*n*, 780*n*, 781*n*, 782*n*, 783*n*
McDonald-Wright, Stanton, 552
McFadden, Fred R., 655*n*
McGill, Arclu, 374
McGoldrick, C. C., 181*n*
McGrath, Joseph E., 738
McGregor, Douglas M., 51, 283, 350*n*, 427, 428
McGuire, Joseph W., 53*n*, 70, 70*n*, 109*n*, 368*n*, 426*n*, 431, 524*n*
McIntyre, James M., 141*n*
McKay, Shona, 402*n*
McKee, Braxton, 742*n*
McKenzie, Richard B., 353
McKinley, John, 164, 169, 186
McLafferty, Sara, 637*n*
McLeod, R., 584*n*
McMullan, James, 726
McNeill, Robin, 661*n*, 674*n*
McNichols, Thomas J., 199*n*
McNurlin, Barbara C., 672*n*, 680*n*
McPartland, Matthew, 106–7, 115, 128
McQueen, Jennifer, 332*n*
Meadows, Dennis H., 54*n*
Mechanic, David, 396–97
Mee, John F., 271*n*
Mehle, Tom, 410*n*
Meindle, James R., 482*n*, 486*n*
Melloan, George, 82*n*
Mellon, Andrew, 40, 707
Mellon, Craig, 339*n*
Mendleson, Barbara E., 532*n*
Merchant, Kenneth A., 593*n*
Meredith, Jack R., 603
Merwin, John, 192
Mesarovic, Mihajlo, 54*n*
Mescon, Michael H., 4*n*
Metcalf, Henry C., 46*n*
Meyer, Herbert H., 241*n*, 350
Meyerhoff, J. L., 379*n*
Micheli, Linda M., 524*n*
Miesing, Paul, 202*n*
Miles, Matthew B., 377*n*
Miles, Raymond E., 229, 332*n*, 426*n*, 428*n*, 431
Miles, Robert H., 264*n*, 397*n*
Milgram, Stanley, 304, 305
Milkovitch, George T., 346*n*
Miller, Danny, 436*n*
Miller, Edwin L., 331*n*
Miller, James R., 54*n*
Miller, Katherine I., 420, 539*n*
Miller, Michael W., 298, 530
Miller, P., 242*n*
Miller, Robert W., 154*n*, 155*n*
Miller, Thomas R., 788*n*
Miller, Walter B., 299*n*
Miller, William H., 696
Mills, D. Quinn, 354, 406
Mills, K. Bryant, 602*n*
Mills, Peter, 400
Mindlin, S., 95*n*
Miner, John B., 24*n*, 333*n*
Miner, Mary G., 333*n*
Mintzberg, Henry A., 15–18, 23, 26, 172, 199*n*, 521*n*, 522
Mirvis, P., 50
Mitchell, Daniel J. B., 406
Mitchell, Russell, 362
Mitchell, Terence R., 475*n*
Mitroff, Ian J., 171
Moad, Jeff, 677
Mockler, Robert J., 557
Moeller, Nancy L., 320*n*
Moffie, Gus, 576
Mohr, Lawrence B., 408
Mohrman, Allan M., Jr., 349*n*, 351
Monaghan, Thomas, 424, 435
Monahan, Ellen, 760
Monge, Peter R., 539*n*
Montrose, Rick, 794–96
Mooney, James D., 275*n*, 311*n*
Mooney, Mart, 623*n*
Moore, Lynda L., 759*n*
Moore, Thomas, 559
More, E., 544*n*
Morgan, Gareth, 285*n*
Morgan, Marilyn A., 285*n*
Morita, Akio, 328, 697, 714
Morosky, Robert, 465
Morris, James H., 538*n*
Morse, John W., 288
Morton, Dean, 260
Morton, Michael S. Scott, 541*n*, 542*n*, 543*n*, 559*n*, 657*n*, 658, 659, 677*n*, 680*n*, 681*n*
Moscovici, Serge, 498*n*
Moscow, Alvin, 403*n*
Moscowitz, Milton, 442
Moser, Helen P., 742*n*
Moss, Leonard, 738*n*
Mossberg, Walter, 353
Mossholder, Kevin W., 737
Mougey, E. H., 379*n*
Mouton, Jane S., 395*n*, 404*n*, 467, 468, 472*n*
Moyer, Reed, 772*n*, 774*n*, 775*n*
Muchinsky, P. M., 405
Muczyk, Jan P., 240*n*
Mueller, J. A., 89*n*
Mueller, Ronald, 527
Muller, Ronald E., 772*n*
Mulligan, Thomas, 21, 23
Munsterberg, Hugo, 425*n*
Murdick, Robert G., 660, 663
Murningham, J. Keith, 496*n*
Murphy, Declan, 144*n*, 572*n*
Murphy, Gerald, 612

Murphy, Lawrence R., 740*n*
Murray, John P., 664*n*
Murray, Thomas J., 253
Musa, Mark, 53
Myers, Lewis A., Jr., 411*n*
Myers, M. Scott, 345*n*
Mylander, William L., 505*n*

Nader, Ralph, 76, 80
Nadler, David A., 277*n*, 371*n*, 445–48, 480
Namiki, Nobuaki, 788*n*
Narayanan, V. K., 83, 86, 87*n*, 215*n*
Nash, Laura L., 120, 122
Nashimura, Hajime, 92
Nathanson, Daniel A., 196*n*, 281*n*
Naumes, William, 199*n*
Naylor, James C., 451*n*
Neff, Robert, 766
Negandhi, Anant R., 781
Nehrbass, Richard, 342
Neiderer, R. R., 413*n*
Nelson, Debra L., 759*n*
Nelson, R. Ryan, 678
Nelton, Sharon, 306*n*, 331*n*, 435
Neuharth, Allan, 359
Neumann, Seev, 653*n*
Nevin, John J., 394
Newcomb, Theodore M., 494*n*, 605*n*
Newman, Michael, 670*n*
Newman, William H., 145*n*, 315*n*, 562*n*, 564–65, 567, 583*n*
Nicholas, John M., 381*n*
Nicholls, John G., 436*n*
Nickerson, R. S., 181*n*
Niehoff, Marilee S., 344*n*
Nielsen, Warren R., 381*n*
Nightingale, Don, 620
Nixon, Richard, 266
Noble, Barbara A., 740*n*
Noble, Kenneth B., 406
Noe, Raymond, 320*n*
Norburn, D., 242*n*
Norden, Peter, 675*n*
Norman, James R., 68
Norwood, Janet L., 336
Nossiter, Vivien, 307*n*
Novak, William, 138
Nulty, Peter, 623
Nutt, Paul C., 369*n*
Nye, Joseph S., Jr., 772*n*

Odewahn, Charles A., 760
Odiorne, George S., 239*n*, 405*n*
O'Donnell, Cyril, 300*n*, 511*n*
Oech, Roger von, 408*n*, 409*n*
Oglesby, John N., 672*n*
Olian, Judy D., 332*n*
Olm, Kenneth W., 165*n*
Olsen, Kenneth, 386–87
Olsen, Stan, 386
Olson, David L., 55*n*
Olson, Frank, 266
Olson, James, 245, 362, 563
Olson, Margrethe H., 671*n*
O'Malley, Jay, 610
O'Neill, Paul, 364
Opliger, Edwin B., 668*n*, 669
O'Reilly, Charles, III, 536*n*, 664*n*
Orlicky, Joseph, 642*n*
O'Rourke, J. Tracy, 373
Orris, James B., 475*n*
Osborn, Alex F., 409
Osborne, Adam, 688–92
O'Toole, James, 543, 707
Ottaway, Richard N., 366*n*
Ouchi, William G., 60–61, 382*n*, 479*n*, 787
Overmyer, Wayne S., 606*n*
Overstreet, Phoebe L., 742*n*
Owen, Robert, 35, 37, 49

Packard, David, 227, 758
Paine, Frank T., 199*n*
Paine, Lynda Sharp, 106, 728
Palmer, Russell E., 90*n*
Palmer, Theodore B., 462
Paludi, M. A., 759*n*
Parasuraman, Saroj, 738*n*
Parker, L. D., 46*n*, 47
Parnes, Sidney J., 409*n*
Parry, Charles, 364
Pascale, Richard Tanner, 214, 382*n*, 479*n*, 787*n*, 788
Pastin, Mark, 117
Pate, Larry E., 381*n*
Paul, Karen, 338*n*
Pavett, Cynthia, 622*n*
Pearce, C. Glenn, 528*n*, 531*n*
Pearce, John A., II, 233*n*, 235*n*, 237*n*, 238, 245, 246
Penrod, Steven, 498*n*, 501*n*
Peplau, Letitia A., 496*n*, 501*n*
Perlmutter, Howard, 771, 782
Perot, H. Ross, 698, 758
Perrow, Charles, 289*n*, 316*n*
Pestel, Eduard, 54*n*
Peter, J. Paul, 582
Peter, Lawrence J., 349*n*, 753*n*
Peters, Thomas J., 8, 18–20, 60–61, 80*n*, 140*n*, 195*n*, 214, 226, 230*n*, 231, 247*n*, 382*n*, 384, 425*n*, 449, 479*n*, 483, 485, 486, 566, 569, 605, 619–20
Petersen, Donald, 143, 614, 646
Petersen, Robert E., 614
Peterson, Thane, 362, 387
Petty, R. E., 524*n*
Pfeffer, Jeffrey, 8*n*, 305*n*, 321, 572*n*
Phatak, Arvind, 211*n*
Pheysey, Diana C., 290*n*
Phillips, David Graham, 44
Phillips, Julien R., 230*n*, 231
Phillips, L. D., 181*n*
Pierce, Margaret, 454
Pinchot, Gifford, III, 713*n*
Pines, A. M., 739*n*
Pitts, Robert A., 267*n*
Pitz, G. F., 181*n*
Pitzer, Mary J., 253
Pliske, Rebecca M., 410*n*
Plossl, George W., 642*n*
Podsakoff, Philip M., 448*n*
Poling, H. A., 614
Pollack, Andres, 155*n*
Pondy, Louis R., 299*n*
Poor, Riva, 318*n*
Porras, Jerry I., 381*n*
Porter, Lyman W., 375*n*, 426*n*, 428, 431, 447*n*, 451, 523*n*, 538, 730*n*
Porter, Michael E., 96*n*, 205, 208–11
Porter, Natalie, 462*n*
Post, James, 113
Potter, Michael, 661*n*, 674*n*
Pounds, William, 23*n*, 170–71
Powelson, Robert J., 441
Prahalad, C. K., 230*n*
Premack, S. L., 342*n*
Prendergast, Karen A., 675, 679*n*
Preston, Lee E., 110*n*, 113
Price, Raymond L., 750
Pringle, Charles D., 58*n*
Proctor, Selina, 728, 741, 760–61
Proshansky, Harold, 473*n*
Pruitt, Dean G., 510*n*
Pryor, Norman M., 439
Psaris, Georgette, 690
Pucik, V., 787*n*
Pugh, D. S., 290*n*
Pyhrr, Peter A., 601*n*

Quick, James C., 738*n*, 759*n*
Quick, Jonathan D., 738*n*
Quinlan, Mike, 382, 627
Quinn, James B., 89*n*, 411*n*
Quinn, R. P., 737*n*

Rabinow, Jacob, 704
Rafferty, Kevin, 766
Rahim, M. Afzalur, 392*n*, 394*n*
Raia, Anthony P., 366*n*, 380*n*
Raisingham, Duru, 172
Ramaprasad, Arkalgud, 57*n*
Ramo, Simon, 629
Ramsower, Reagan M., 543*n*
Rappaport, Alfred, 196*n*, 242*n*
Rappoport, Anatol, 184
Rasberry, Robert W., 524*n*
Raub, S. Avery, 311*n*
Raudsepp, Eugene, 410*n*
Rauschenberger, N. Schmitt, 433*n*
Raven, Bertram, 302, 460*n*
Rawl, Lawrence, 398
Rawlings, Sallie, 750*n*
Rawlison, J. Geoffrey, 409*n*
Ray, Donald F., 496
Ray, R. L., 379*n*
Raymond, J. C., 524*n*
Reagan, Ronald, 94, 108, 353, 508
Reck, Ross R., 154*n*
Reddin, William J., 470*n*
Reddin, W. J., 239*n*
Redding, W. Charles, 531*n*
Reed, John, 664*n*
Reed, M. I., 22*n*
Rees, C. Roger, 463*n*
Reeves, Allison, 2–3, 8, 26
Rehder, Robert R., 554
Reibstein, Larry, 192, 298
Reich, Cary, 480*n*
Reich, Robert A., 775*n*
Reichers, Arnon E., 494*n*
Reiley, Alan C., 311*n*
Reim, B., 449
Reinmann, Bernard C., 673*n*
Reitman, Walter, 675*n*
Reitz, H. Joseph, 414*n*, 493*n*, 536*n*
Render, Barry, 641, 642*n*
Renier, James J., 381
Rescher, N., 86, 86*n*
Resnick, Susan M., 349*n*, 351
Reuter, Vincent G., 154*n*
Reynolds, Jeff, 28
Rhyne, Lawrence C., 196*n*
Rice, Berkeley, 50*n*
Rice, Douglas C., 501*n*
Rice, Robert W., 462*n*
Richards, Max, 211*n*
Richards, T., 410*n*
Richman, Tom, 723
Ricklefs, Roger, 108*n*
Rifkin, Glenn, 652
Riggs, James L., 153*n*, 155*n*, 157*n*
Rissler, Ray, 648
Ritzer, George, 337*n*
Ritzman, L. P., 628*n*
Robbins, Stephen P., 391, 425*n*, 579, 610
Roberts, Johnie L., 359
Roberts, Karlene H., 523*n*, 536*n*, 537
Roberts, Roy S., 620, 621
Robey, Daniel, 281*n*, 667*n*
Robinson, Richard B., Jr., 195*n*, 233*n*, 235*n*, 237*n*, 238, 245, 246
Robinson, Richard D., 788*n*
Robock, Stefan H., 771*n*, 774*n*, 779*n*
Rockart, John F., 541*n*, 542*n*, 543*n*, 657*n*, 664*n*, 672*n*, 680*n*, 681*n*
Rockefeller, John D., 40, 44, 707
Roebuck, Joseph, 690
Roetheli, R. W., 413*n*
Roethlisberger, Fritz J., 49, 274*n*
Rollins, Thomas, 621*n*
Rollwagen, John, 253
Roman, Daniel D., 151*n*
Ronen, Joshua, 711*n*
Roosevelt, Franklin D., 107
Roosevelt, Theodore, 40, 45
Roseenman, R. H., 709*n*
Rosen, Michael, 562*n*
Rosenberg, Larry J., 197*n*
Rosenbloom, David H., 78*n*
Rosenblum, John W., 116*n*, 199*n*
Rosenstein, Eliezer, 277*n*
Rosenthal, Robert, 734*n*, 737*n*
Rosenzweig, James E., 57*n*
Rosenzweig, Mark R., 451*n*
Rothschild, William E., 394*n*
Rotter, John Paul, 730*n*

Rotter, Julian B., 708
Rubin, Donald B., 734n
Rubin, Irwin M., 141n, 345n
Ruch, William A., 154n
Rue, Leslie W., 196n
Rule, James, 680, 681
Rumelt, Richard P., 197n, 217, 229
Russell, Bill, 395n
Russell, George, 220
Russell, Joyce E. A., 729n
Ryan, Charles K., 791
Rynes, Sara L., 332n

Saari, L. M., 450
Sachdeva, Paramjit S., 7n, 307n
Sage, Andrew P., 674n
Salancik, Gerald R., 8n, 321
Salazar, Ruben, 92
Salomon, Ilan, 543n
Salomon, Meira, 543n
Salpukas, Agis, 577
Salter, M., 242n
Samaras, John T., 528n
Sammon, William L., 215n
Samper, J. Philip, 97
Sandberg-Diment, Erik, 584n, 681n
Sanger, David E., 480n
Sanzotta, Donald, 443n
Saporito, Bill, 313n
Sarrat, M., 768–69
Sashkin, Marshall, 86n
Sasser, W. Earl, 644n
Sathe, Vijay, 145n, 382, 383, 384, 479n, 556n
Saxton, Mary Jane, 382n, 384n, 479n
Sayles, Leonard R., 373n
Schank, Robert C., 675n
Schatz, Ralph, 576
Schein, Edgar H., 39n, 53n, 368, 378n, 382n, 383, 479n, 494n, 730, 732n, 736, 745, 747–50
Schellenberger, Robert, 211n
Schendel, Dan E., 193n, 197–99, 200n, 201, 206n, 211n, 215n, 217, 281n
Schewe, Charles D., 197n
Schick, Allen G., 602n
Schleh, Edward C., 404
Schlesinger, Leonard A., 368n, 370
Schmalt, Heinz-Dieter, 437n
Schmidt, Peggy, 654n
Schmidt, Warren H., 464
Schnee, Jerome E., 567
Schneider, Benjamin, 451n
Schneider, Jim, 686–87
Schneider, Klaus, 437n
Schonberger, Richard J., 155n, 643n
Schoonmaker, Alan N., 754–55
Schriesheim, Chester A., 476n
Schuler, Randall S., 332n
Schultz, Ellen, 334n
Schumach, Murray, 175n
Schumpeter, Joseph, 698–99
Schwab, Donald P., 342n, 731n
Schwade, Stephen, 346n
Schwartz, Howard S., 433n
Schwartz, John, 770
Schwartz, Michael, 138
Schweiger, David M., 172n
Schweiger, E. M., 242n
Schwenk, Charles R., 402n
Scott, B. R., 229n
Sculley, John, 148, 413
Sears, David O., 496n, 501n
Sedgwick, D. L., 740n
Segal, Mady Wechsler, 463n
Seidenberg, Bernard, 473n
Serpa, Ray, 349n, 382n, 384n, 479n
Serrin, William, 336n
Servan-Schrieber, Jacques, 768
Sethi, S. Prakash, 83n, 108n, 788n
Shafritz, Jay M., 78n
Shanks, David C., 776, 780n
Sharplin, Arthur, 520
Shaw, Barry M., 352n
Shaw, K. N., 450n
Shaw, Marvin E., 493n, 536n
Shea, Gregory, 501–2
Sheehy, Gail, 742n
Shelly, M. W., II, 371n
Shenon, Philip, 338n
Shepard, Jon M., 49n, 58n
Sheppard, Blair H., 402n
Sherif, Carolyn, 395–97, 400
Sherif, Muzafer, 395–97, 400
Sherman, J. Daniel, 760
Sherwood, John J., 378n
Shetty, Y. K., 281n
Shillinglaw, Gordon, 587, 592n, 596n
Shore, Barry, 658n, 675n
Siegman, A. W., 531n
Sigband, Norman B., 524n
Sihler, William H., 572n
Silverman, Fred N., 660n
Simmonds, Kenneth, 771n, 774n, 779n
Simmons, John K., 665n, 666–69
Simon, Herbert A., 170, 174n, 176–77, 274, 301, 394n
Simon, Mary E., 274n
Simon, Ruth, 68
Simpson, Richard L., 539n
Sims, Henry P., Jr., 460n, 482n, 483–84
Sinclair, Upton, 44, 45n
Singer, Jerome, 449
Sinha, Madhev H., 644n
Skaggs, Sam, 735
Skinner, B. F., 430, 443n
Skinner, Wickham, 630
Slaney, Robert B., 729n
Slap, Stan, 549
Sloane, Arthur A., 78n, 405n
Slocum, John W., Jr., 58n, 750n
Slovic, P., 180n
Smeltzer, Larry R., 525n, 526n
Smith, Adam, 262–63
Smith, Donald, 627
Smith, Emily T., 408n, 675n, 696
Smith, Kenwyn, 514
Smith, Nick, 28–29
Smith, Philip L., 592
Smith, Robert D., 556, 583n, 654n
Smith, Ruthu A., 501n
Smith, Timothy, 71
Smythe, Jessica, 187–89
Snavely, B. Kay, 412n
Snock, J. D., 737n
Snow, Charles C., 196n, 229, 332n
Snyder, Robert A., 538n
Snyder, Solomon, 696
Somerville, Addison W., 740n
Sorensen, Charles, 40
Souerwine, Andrew H., 754n
Spector, Bert, 354, 355
Spence, Christopher, 397
Spitalnic, Robert, 215n
Sprague, Ralph H., Jr., 658n, 672n, 680n
Sproull, Lee, 171
Stahl, Michael J., 436n
Stalker, G. M., 22–23, 59n, 287–88
Stanford, Melvin J., 712n, 713
Stark, Donald J., 696
Starr, Martin K., 56, 788n
Starr, R. M., 641
Staw, Barry M., 242n, 425n, 451n, 461n
Stead, Bette Ann, 338n
Steele, Fritz, 541n
Steele, Timothy P., 241n
Steers, Richard M., 426n, 428, 451, 479n
Steffen, V. J., 759n
Stegemeier, Richard J., 594
Steinberg, Saul, 287
Steiner, George A., 149n
Stephan, Walter G., 394n
Stern, Aimee, 424
Stevens, Charles W., 763
Stevenson, Howard H., 717–19
Stewart, Rosemary, 15n, 99n, 522n
Stewart, Todd I., 58n
Stickler, George, 600
Stieglitz, Harold, 265n, 308n
Stinson, John E., 475n
Stoever, William A., 700n
Stogdill, Ralph M., 459, 461n
Stokes, Paul M., 571n
Stoner, James A. F., 345n, 504n, 513, 730, 750n, 72
Stonich, P. J., 242n
Stopford, J., 230n
Storey, Walter D., 754n
Strand, R., 114
Strauss, George, 405n
Strickland, A. J., 200n, 202, 207n, 268
Stroh, Peter, 375n
Strong, Earl P., 556, 583n, 654n
Strong, William, 64
Stubbe, John W., 681n
Stumpf, Stephen A., 754n
Suh, P. W., 790
Sullivan, George, 338n
Sullivan, Gerald, 675n
Sullivan, John, 219–20
Sullivan, Leon, 127
Sullivan, Mark, 45
Summers, Lynn S., 346n
Sun Tzu, 53
Super, Donald, 742n
Sussman, Lyle, 172n
Suttle, J. Lloyd, 316n
Suver, James D., 655n
Suzuki, Y., 230n
Swanson, Carl L., 788n
Swanson, Guy E., 494n
Sward, Keith, 40
Sweeney, Dennis J., 156n, 632n
Szilagyi, Andrew, 501n

Taber, Tom, 302n
Tagiuri, Renato, 170
Tait, John E., 467
Tanford, Sara, 498n
Tannenbaum, Robert, 464
Tarbell, Ida, 44
Tasini, Jonathan, 390
Taylor, Alexander L., III, 68, 138
Taylor, Bart, 740
Taylor, Donald W., 410
Taylor, Frank, 86n
Taylor, Frederick W., 33, 35–37, 39–41, 46, 48, 281–82, 316, 373, 392, 620
Teets, John W., 365
Terrenberry, Shirley, 285n
Thayer, Paul W., 316n, 320
Theoret, Andre, 172
Thierauf, Robert J., 54n, 154n
Thill, John V., 524n
Thomas, John M., 366
Thomas, L. Joseph, 615
Thompson, Arthur A., 200n, 202, 207n, 268
Thompson, James D., 275n, 289n
Thompson, Paul H., 750
Thompson, Victor A., 282
Thorndike, Edward L., 444n
Thune, Stanley S., 195
Thurow, Lester, 91
Tichey, Noel M., 244n, 480n
Tilles, Seymour, 56n
Tillman, Rollie, 505, 509
Timm, Paul R., 525n
Timmons, J. A., 708n
Tjosvold, Dean, 400n
Tolchin, Martin, 76n
Tolchin, Susan J., 76n
Tom, Paul L., 654n
Tomlinson, J., 22n
Tosi, Henry L., Jr., 58n, 239n, 240–42, 443n, 445, 595
Townsend, Robert, 265
Toy, Stewart, 770
Trachtenberg, Jeffrey A., 424n
Tracy, Lane, 475n
Treece, James B., 770
Treece, J. S., 614
Tregoe, Benjamin B., 166n, 168n
Trevor, Malcolm, 788n

Trigano, Gilbert, 293
Trillin, Calvin, 703
Trist, Eric L., 71–72, 285*n*, 373*n*
Trost, Cathy, 340
Trowbridge, Charles L., 97
Tsurumi, Yoshi, 768*n*
Tubbs, Mark E., 241*n*
Tucci, Kaspar, 576
Tudor, William D., 448*n*
Tuller, David, 341
Tulloch, Henry W., 106
Tung, Rosalie, 783
Turban, Efraim, 636*n*, 677*n*
Turla, Peter, 185*n*
Tushman, Michael L., 277, 480
Tutu, Desmond, 127
Tversky, Amos, 177, 180*n*
Twomey, David P., 337*n*
Tyerman, Andrew, 397

Ueberroth, Peter, 91
Ulrich, David O., 480*n*
Ulschak, F. L., 346*n*
Urwick, Lyndall, 46*n*, 263*n*
Utterback, James M., 215, 411*n*, 413*n*
Uyterhoeven, Hugo, 199*n*

Vagelos, Roy, 224, 232, 244, 250
Valente, Judith, 236
Vanderslice, Thomas P., 502
Van de Ven, Andrew H., 410*n*
Vandivert, William, 499
Van Fleet, David, 264*n*
Van Horn, Richard L., 655
Van Horne, James C., 589
Van Maanen, John, 730*n*
Vasarhelyi, Miklos A., 602*n*
Vecchio, Robert P., 448*n*
Veraldi, Lew, 492
Verity, John W., 298, 387
Vernon, Raymond, 768
Vesper, Karl H., 701*n*, 709–10, 718, 721
Veverka, Mark, 770
Viega, John C., 757
Viscione, Jerry A., 594*n*
Vogel, David, 80*n*
Vroom, Victor H., 183, 438*n*, 467*n*, 476–79, 489

Wagner, Abe, 377*n*
Wait, Donald J., 618*n*
Wakefield, John J., 381*n*
Walczak, David, 337*n*
Walker, Michael C., 598*n*
Wallace, Mark, 501*n*
Waltman, John L., 525*n*, 526*n*
Walton, Richard E., 354, 355, 394*n*
Wang, Ako, 133, 134
Wankel, Charles, 338*n*
Wanous, John P., 333*n*, 342*n*, 433*n*, 494*n*, 730*n*, 731*n*
Waren, Allan D., 673*n*
Warnath, Charles F., 742*n*
Warren, E. Kirby, 91, 750*n*, 752
Wartick, Steven L., 111*n*, 114*n*
Wason, P. C., 181*n*
Waterman, Robert H., 18–20, 195*n*, 214, 226, 230*n*, 231, 247*n*, 382*n*, 384, 425*n*, 449, 479*n*, 492, 566, 569, 605, 619, 620
Watkins, Paul R., 677*n*
Watson, Hugh J., 658*n*, 673*n*, 677*n*
Wayne, Sandy J., 505
Webber, Ross A., 285*n*, 734
Weber, Max, 42–43, 281–82, 300*n*, 480*n*, 481*n*
Weeks, James K., 613
Weeks, Jeremy, 576
Weigle, Charles B., 256
Weiler, Nicholas N., 754*n*
Weiner, Murray, 685
Weis, William, 739
Weiss, Howard M., 461*n*
Welch, Jack, 141, 332, 458, 468
Welles, Chris, 252
Wells, L., 230*n*
Welsch, Glenn A., 599*n*
Welsh, J. A., 708*n*
Wendt, Henry, 558
Wenzel, Burckhardt, 331*n*
Weston, J. Fred, 583*n*, 586*n*
Weston, Loy, 792
Wexley, Kenneth N., 281*n*, 332*n*, 538*n*, 539
Wheeler, Ladd, 510*n*
Wheelwright, Steven C., 151*n*, 193, 194, 203, 205, 214*n*, 616, 644*n*
Whisler, Thomas L., 680*n*
White, J. P., 708*n*
White, Karol K., 265*n*
White, Michael C., 285*n*
White, Ralph K., 467*n*
Whiting, Charles S., 409*n*
Whiting, Roman J., 439
Whitmore, Kay, 99
Whitney, John C., 501*n*
Whittaker, Michael, 725
Wiegner, Kathleen K., 260
Wiener, Earl, 408
Wieters, C. David, 154*n*
Wigdor, Lawrence A., 439*n*
Wiig, Karl W., 675*n*
Wikstrom, Walter S., 333
Wilken, Paul H., 698, 705*n*
Wilkens, Myra, 772*n*
Williams, Brian K., 664*n*
Williams, Mona, 684
Williams, Thomas A., 156*n*, 632*n*
Willis, Rod, 284
Willmott, Hugh C., 15*n*
Wilson, G., 76*n*
Wilson, John W., 192
Wilson, Lyn S., 79*n*
Wilson, Mike, 419–21
Wilson, R. M. S., 588*n*
Winfare, Sam, 64
Winkler, John, 405*n*
Winston, Patrick H., 675, 679*n*
Winter, D., 706
Winter, Ralph E., 318
Witney, Fred, 78*n*, 405*n*
Witten, Marsha, 544–45
Wolfe, D. M., 737*n*
Wolfe, Joseph, 202*n*
Wolfram, Stephen, 710, 712
Wood, D. Robley, Jr., 196*n*
Wood, Donald R., 673*n*
Wood, Donna J., 45
Wood, Robert, 110, 197, 624
Woodman, Richard W., 378*n*
Woodward, Chrissy, 550
Woodward, Joan, 59, 289–91
Woodward, Susan, 106
Woodworth, Warner, 406
Worthy, J. C., 110*n*
Wozniak, Stephen, 148, 709–12
Wren, Daniel A., 34*n*
Wright, Oliver W., 642*n*
Wrightsman, L. S., 524*n*
Wrigley, L., 228–29
Wrong, Dennis H., 299*n*
Wurtele, Angus, 443
Wysocki, Bernard, Jr., 92*n*

Yager, Ed, 351*n*
Yago, Glenn, 138
Yalom, Irvin D., 377*n*
Yankelovich, Daniel, 619
Yasai-Ardekani, Masoud, 214*n*
Yates, Jere E., 738*n*
Yesko, Michael A., 584*n*
Yetton, Philip W., 476*n*, 511*n*
Yoo, Sangjin, 92*n*
Young, John A., 94, 260, 508
Yount, K. R., 759
Yukl, Gary A., 341*n*, 281*n*, 302*n*, 538*n*, 539
Yunker, Gary, 50*n*

Zaccaro, Stephen J., 461*n*
Zander, Alvin, 462*n*, 494*n*
Zaragoza, C. E., 242*n*
Zemke, Ron, 465, 515
Ziegler, Arthur B., 603
Zimbardo, Philip, 498–99
Zwany, A., 433*n*

SUBJECT INDEX

Acceptance-sampling procedures, 645
Acceptance view of formal authority, 301, 302
Access discrimination, 338
Achievement needs, 435–37
Achieving Society, The (McClelland), 706
Action research, 376
Adjustment, decision making and, 178–80, 183
Adjustment bias, 180
Administration, 199–200
Administrative culture, 717–19
Advertising, 208–9
Affiliation needs, 436–37
Affirmative action, 336–37, 339
Age Discrimination in Employment Act of 1967, 337
Aggression, management information system implementation and, 666–67
Aging of the population, 84–85
Alcohol use, productivity and, 622
Alternative solutions
  development of, 167
  evaluation of, 167–68, 217–18
  identification of, 217
  selection of, 168, 217–18
Ambiguity, tolerance for, 709
American Management Association, 347
Amnesty International, 20, 21
Analysis, as function of managers, 7
Anchoring, decision making and, 178–79
Annual objectives, 237–38
Anxiety, 736–37
Appalachian Regional Commission, 75
Apprenticeship, 346, 750
Arbitration, 402
Area of acceptance, 301
Artificial intelligence, 658, 675–79
Art of War, The (Sun Tzu), 53
Aspirations, unrealistic, 731
Assembly-line productivity standards, 569
Assessment centers, 343–44
Assets, 584
Attention, 20, 49
Attitudes
  as barrier to effective strategy implementation, 248
  of co-workers toward women, 759–60
  of managers toward internationalization, 771
Auditing, 594, 606–7, 610
Authoritarian management style, 467, 468, 477
Authority
  classical principle of, 43, 45
  of committees, 511
  communication effectiveness and, 534
  decentralization of (*see* Decentralization)
  delegation of, 310–15
  formal (*see* Formal authority)
  functional, 309–10
  job design and, 315–21
  line, 307–8
  obedience/conscience conflict, 304, 305
  for setting measures and standards, 569
  staff, 308–9
  of violence, 498–500
Automated Guided Vehicle Systems (AGVS), 636
Automation, 39
Autonomy, 317, 569, 747
Availability, decision making and, 177
Avoidance
  as barrier to problem solving, 182, 183
  as conflict-resolution method, 401
  management information system implementation and, 666
Avoidance learning, 445

Background investigation, 341
Balance sheet, 584–85
Balance-sheet budgets, 598
Bar codes, 89
Bargaining power of customers and suppliers, 208, 210
Base technologies, 89
BCG Matrix, 206–7
Behavioral approach to leadership, 462–67
Behaviorally experienced training, 346
Behavioral model of control, 46–47
Behavioral rating, 350
Behavioral school
  behavioral science approach, 51–53, 55
  defined, 48
  human relations management (*see* Human relations management)
Behavioral science approach, 51–53, 55
Behavior modification, 430–31, 443–45
Belongingness needs, 432
Biases
  in decision making, 179–81, 185
  in performance appraisal, 351
Big-bang productivity improvement method, 618
Bills of materials (BOM), 642
Biological job design, 319, 320
Board for International Broadcasting, 75
Boards
  defined, 507
  of directors, 82, 507
Bona fide occupation qualifications (BFOQs), 338
Bottom-up budgeting, 592, 593
Boundary-spanning roles, 278
Bounded rationality, 176–77
Brainstorming, 152, 409–10
Break-even analysis, 587–89
Break-even chart, 587, 588
Budget committee, 593
Budget department, 593
Budgeting process, 592–95
Budgeting system, 591
Budgets, 589–606
  approval of, 593
  as control tool, 590
  defined, 144–47, 589
  development of, 592–93
  financial, 596–98
  as link between planning and control, 144
  operating, 595–97
  potentially dysfunctional aspects of, 603–6
  potentially functional aspects of, 602–3

problems in development of, 595
responsibility centers and, 590–92
revision of, 594–95
role of personnel, 593
variable vs. fixed, 599–600
zero-base, 601–2
Bureaucracy, 42–43, 282
Bureaucratic control, 784
Bureaucratic management, Weber's model of, 42–43
Burnout, 739
Business-unit strategy, 203, 211–18

Capacity planning, 632–33
Capital budgeting techniques, 593
Capital-expenditure budgets, 598
Capital requirements, 209
Career anchors, 747–48
Career concepts, 745–47
Career functions, 758
Career plateau, 750–53
Careers, 728–62
case studies, 728, 741, 760–61, 763, 794–95
dual-career couples, 756–58
early job experiences, 732–34
formation of expectations, 729–32
individual planning, 754–56
life cycle and, 741–45
loyalty dilemmas, 735–36
within organizations, 748–50
organizations as providers of, 6
patterns and themes, 745–48
personal anxiety and, 736–37
political insensitivity and passivity and, 734–35
role conflict and, 737
stress and, 738–40
Career states, 752–53
Cash budgets, 598
Cash cow category, in BCG matrix, 206, 207
Cash flow statements, 585
Catch-up strategy, 236
Causes, diagnosis of, 167
Central Intelligence Agency (CIA), 75
Centralization, 43, 321, 323, 681
Certainty, 175
Chairpersons, 511
Challenge
in initial job assignments, 732
lack of, and reality shock syndrome, 731
stress management and, 739
Change (*see* Environmental Change; Organizational change)
Change agent, 366
Change Masters, The (Kanter), 413–14
Changing environment (*see* Environmental change)
Channels of communication, 525, 534
Charismatic leadership, 480–82
Charity principle, 62, 110, 111
Chief executive officers, 244, 249
Circumferential movement, 748
Civil Rights Act of 1964, 335–38
Classical organization theory, 41–46
authority and, 300–302, 310–13
contributions of, 43–44
delegation and, 311–13
limitations of, 44–45
organization design and, 281–82, 372
Classical school, 34–46
classical organization theory (*see* Classical organization theory)
evolution of, 55
scientific management, 35–39, 426
Classroom instruction, 346, 347
Client system, 366
Closed system, 57
Coaching, 347
Coalitions, 82–83
Coercive power, 302
Cohesiveness, group, 500–502
Collaborative management, 375
Colleagues, 750
Collective bargaining, 78
Combination strategy, 236
Command economies, 144
Command groups, 494
Commanding, in classical organization theory, 42
Command unit, classical principle of, 43, 45
Commissions, 507
Commitment
anxiety about, 736–37
in four C's model for human resources, 356
group, 503
renewal of corporate success and, 20
stress management and, 739
Committees, 278, 507–12
Commodity Futures Trading Commission, 75
Common morality, 119
Communication, 520–46
barriers to, 528–33
budgets and, 603, 604
case studies, 520, 533, 545, 547
defined, 523
importance of, 521–23
management information system implementation and, 671–72
one-way and two-way, 527–28
organizational (*see* Organizational communication)
process of, 523–27
Communication networks, 536–38
Comparable worth, 336–37, 339
Compensation
incentive, 242–43
international, 783–84
Competence
career motivation and, 747
entrepreneurship and, 709–11
in four C's model for human resources, 356
Competition
international, 79–80, 90–94
vs. organizational conflict, 391
role of, 79–80
Competitive priorities, 625–28
Competitor performance, problem solving and, 171
Complex environments, 288, 289
Complex interventions, 226
Complex projects, planning, 152–57
Compromise, 401–2
Computer-aided design (CAD), 632
Computer-aided manufacturing (CAM), 634–35
Computer-aided instruction (CAI), 346
Computer-based information systems (CBIS), 658
Computer-integrated manufacturing (CIM), 635
Computers
communications and, 541–44
impact of, 680–81
information systems and (*see* End-user computing; Management information systems)
retail store efficiency and, 618–19, 652, 660
security and, 668–71
Conceptual skill, 14–15
Conceptual thinking, 7
Confidence, lack of, 142
Confirmation trap, 181
Conflict
intragroup, 514
organizational (*see* Organizational conflict)
role, 737
Conflict-reduction methods, 400
Conflict-resolution methods, 401–2
Conflict-stimulation methods, 398–400
Conformity, 496–500, 736
Confrontation meetings, 378
Confrontation method of conflict resolution, 402
Congruence, 356
Conical career model, 748–50
Conscience/obedience conflict, 304, 305
Consensus, 402, 512
Consolidated Edison Company of New York v. *Public Service Commission of New York* (1980), 88
Consumer advocates, 76–78
Consumer Product Safety Commission, 75
Content theories of motivation, 428–29
Contingency approach to leadership
defined, 469
Fiedler model, 472–76
path-goal model, 475–76
situational leadership model, 470–72
Vroom-Yetton and Vroom-Jago models, 476–79
Contingency approach to management, 57–59
Continuous and assembly-line systems, 631, 634
Control, 554–692
behavioral model of, 46–47
budgeting (*see* Budgeting)
case studies, 554, 568, 574, 576–79, 688–92
in classical organization theory, 42
defined, 54, 144, 556
degree of, 561–62
financial (*see* Financial control)
holistic model of, 47
importance of, 559–62
information and, 653–56 (*See also* End-user computing; Management information systems)
link between planning and, 144–45, 556
in management process model, 13
methods, 562–64
in multinational enterprises, 784–85
need for, 556, 559–60

Control (*continued*)
operations (*see* Operations planning and control; Operations systems)
process design, 564–72
steps in process, 556–59
Control systems
defined, 564
design of, 564–72
effective, characteristics of, 572–74
Cooperation, 391
Coordination, 275–80
achievement of, 277–80
case study, 260, 275
in classical organization theory, 42
defined, 261, 275
problems in achieving, 276–77
Coping skills training, 740
Corporate day care, 340
Corporate-level strategy, 202–3
Corporate portfolio strategies, 205–7
Corporate responsibility (*see* Social responsibility)
Corporate social performance, 114
Corporate social-policy-process model, 114*n*
Corporate social responsibility (*see* Social responsibility, corporate)
Corporate social responsiveness, 112–15
Corrective action, 558, 602
Cost disadvantages, 209
Cost-effectiveness, 356
Cost schedules, 599–600
Cost-volume-profit analysis, 587–89
Country club management style, 467, 468
Course of action, development of, 144
CPM (critical path method), 154–57
Creative group decision making, 411
Creative individualism, 736–37
Creativity, 408–15
career motivation and, 747
case study, 417
group, 409–11, 504
individual, 408–11
vs. innovation, 408
organizational, 411–15
stimulation of, 409–11
Critical incidents, 347
Cultural relativism, 125–26, 130
Culture
motivation and, 434
national, 786
organizational (*see* Organizational culture)
Culture control, 784
Current assets, 584
Current liabilities, 585
Current ratio, 587
Current situation, definition of, 142–43
Customers
bargaining power of, 208, 210
division by, 269
role of, 73
Custom-expert systems, 679
Cybernetic controls, 563
Cyclical economic changes, 87–88

Day care, corporate, 340
Deadwood career state, 752–53
Debt ratio, 587
Decentralization, 321–24
advantages of, 321
case study, 298, 315, 324
defined, 321
factors influencing, 322–23
as planned change, 372
trends in, 323
Decisional roles, 522
Decision implementation, 168–69
Decision making, 8, 164–87
biases in, 179–81, 185
bounded rationality and, 176–77
case studies, 164, 169, 186, 187–89
certainty and, 175
creative group, 411
criteria for engaging in, 172–73
defined, 140, 165
delegation and, 314
heuristics in, 177–79, 181, 185
improving effectiveness of, 182–86
nonprogrammed decisions, 175
opportunity finding and, 171–72
problem finding and, 169–71
problem-solving process, 165–69
programmed decisions, 174–75
rational, 176, 184, 185
risk and, 175–76, 504
social practice and, 22–23
strategic, 217–18
uncertainty and, 175–76
Decision-making roles, 15–18
Decision monitoring, 169
Decision-support systems (DSS)
case studies, 684–87
defined, 672–73
vs. electronic data processing, 674
vs. management information systems, 673
use of, 673–74
Declining career, 747
Decoding, 526
Delegation, 310–15, 560
Democratic management style, 467, 468
Demographics, 83–86
Demotions, 352
Departmentalization, 261
Dependence, 95–96
Detailed scheduling, 641–42
Development, organizational, 375–82
Development programs, 330, 345–48
"Devil's Advocate Method, The," 172
Dialectical inquiry method, 172
Differential rate system, 35–36
Diplomatic skills, 7
Direct-action environment, 70–84, 98
Direct contact, 278
Direct investment, 767–69
Direction unity, classical principle of, 43
Discipline
classical principle of, 43
defined, 352
Discourses, The (Machiavelli), 52
Discretionary expenses, 591
Discrimination, 335–39
Disseminator role, 16, 17
Distinctive competence, 710–11
Distribution channels, access to, 209
Distrust, 531, 532
Disturbance-handler role, 16, 18
Diversification marketing, 235
Divisional organization structure, 269–71, 321
Division managers, social responsiveness and, 112–13
Division of labor, classical principle of, 43, 45
Division of work, 261–64, 276
Dog category, in BCG matrix, 206, 207
Dominance methods, 401
Downsizing, 284, 369, 441–43, 753
Driving forces, 367
Drug testing, 338–39
Drug use, productivity and, 622
Dual-career couples, 756–58
Duties, 119
Dynamic environments, 288, 289
Dysfunctional conflict, 396

Econometric methods, 152
Economic growth, entrepreneurship and, 700–701
Economic indicators, 87
Economic information, forecasting for, 151
Economic needs, 39
Economic variables, 87–88
Economies of scale, 209
Effectiveness
defined, 139
as managerial performance criterion, 10
Efficiency
defined, 139
as managerial performance criterion, 10
Efficiency techniques, 38–39
Effort-performance expectancy, 446
Ego needs, 51
Electronic data processing (EDP), 654, 657, 674
Electronic mail, 542
Emotionality, 531, 532
Empathy, capacity for, 23
Employee Assistance Programs (EAPs), 339
Employee-oriented managers, 464, 467, 475
Employees
management of (*see* Human resource management)
participation in planning, 144–45, 240–42
role of, 80
Employment rights, 335–39
Empowerment, 19, 317
Encoding, 524–25
End-user computing, 672–80
decision-support systems (*see* Decision-support systems)
defined, 672
expert systems, 674–79
management of, 679–80
Energy costs, productivity and, 621
Engineered cost budgets, 596–97
Engineered expenses, 591
Engineered standards, 569
Enterprise Strategies, 204
Entrepreneurial culture, 717–19
Entrepreneurs
defined, 697
psychological and sociological characteristics of, 703–9
types of change initiated by, 698
Entrepreneurship, 696–722
barriers to, 718–21

case studies, 696, 711, 720, 722–25
corporate, 712–19
defined, 698
factors affecting, 699–700
importance of, 700–703
process of, 711–12
Environmental analysis, 215
Environmental change, 69
defined, 286–87
human resource management and, 331, 354–55
need for control and, 559
organizational change and, 363
strategy implementation and, 229–32
Environmental constraints on strategy implementation, 248–49
Environmental evolution, 71–73
Environmentalists, 76, 78
Environmental Protection Agency (EPA), 75, 78
Environmental variables, 83–90
Equal employment opportunity, 335–39, 760
Equal Employment Opportunity Commission (EEOC), 75, 336, 339
Equal Pay Act of 1963, 335–36
Equipment
process selection and, 634–35
Equipment, productivity and, 621
Equity, classical principle of, 43
Equity theory of motivation, 448–50
ERG theory, 433
Esprit de corps, classical principle of, 43
Essay rating, 350
Esteem needs, 432, 433
Ethics, 116–23
active or passive management, 794–95
application of, 120–21
authority of violence, 498–500
case studies, 20–21, 106, 115, 128
common morality, 119
computer security, 670–71
as control issue, 560–61
corporate day care, 340
customer safety, 640
defined, 116
ethnicity and, 70–71
exclusive distributorships, 702–3
institutionalization of, 121–23
language of, 118–19
leadership and, 460–61
levels of, 116–17
memo writing and, 535
muckraking and, 44–45
obedience/conscience conflict, 304, 305
organizational development and, 377
planning and, 150
public view of, 108
résumé writing, 733
strategic planning and, 204
top management responsibility, 266
union activism, 406
whistleblowing, 236, 251–52
Ethnocentric managers, 771
Evolutionary interventions, 225, 226
Excellence in management, factors in, 18–20
Exchange rates, 778
Exclusive distributorships, 702–3
Executive obsolescence, as barrier to strategy implementation, 249
Existence needs, 433
Expectancy approach to motivation, 444–48
Expectancy model, 445–48
Expectations
career, 729–32
leadership effectiveness and, 469, 470
of supervisors, 733–34
Expense budgets, 596–97
Expense centers, 591
Expert power, 302–3
Expert systems, 674–79
External auditing, 606
External environment, 68–100
case studies, 68, 91, 97–100, 102
change and (*see* Environmental change)
components of, 70–71
direct-action, 70–84, 98
human resource management and, 331
indirect-action, 70–72, 83–90, 98
international, 90–95
management of, 96, 98–99
operations systems and, 628, 629
organizational change and, 363
organizational design and, 285–89
strategic planning and, 195
theories of, 95–96
External stakeholders, 73–80
External standards, 567, 569
Extinction, 445
Extraordinary activities, acquisition of power with, 307
Extrinsic outcomes, 446

Failure, fear of, 141, 142
Family group, 379
Family-location planning, 636–37
Family structure, productivity and, 621–22
Farm Credit Administration, 75
Federal Communications Commission (FCC), 74, 75
Federal Deposit Insurance Corporation (FDIC), 75
Federal Labor Relations Authority (FLRA), 75
Federal Reserve System, 75
Federal Trade Commission (FTC), 75
Feedback, 35
in communication process, 527
in control system, 566, 570
defined, 57
delegation and, 314
informal performance appraisal, 349
job design and, 317
management by objectives and, 241
survey, 378–79
Feedforward controls, 563
Fiedler contingency leadership model, 472–75
Figurehead role, 16, 17
Finance strategies, 234, 235
Financial budgets, 596–98
Financial control, 19, 582–608
auditing, 594, 606–7, 610
break-even analysis, 587–89
budgets (*see* Budgets)
case studies, 582, 600–601, 607–8, 610
financial statements, 583–86
ratio analysis, 586–87, 589
Financial incentives, 620
Financial institutions, role of, 79
Financial pressures, productivity and, 622
Financial statements, 583–86
Financing budgets, 598
First-line managers
defined, 10
management information systems and, 658
planning by, 12
skills needed, 15
Fixed assets, 584
Fixed budgets, 599–600
Fixed capital costs, 636
Fixed costs, 599
Fixed-position layouts, 637
Flexibility, product and volume, 627–28
Flextime, 319
Flows, 57
Forced distribution systems, 350
Force-field theory, 367
Forcing, 401
Forecasting, 149–52
in capacity planning, 633
for economic and sales information, 151, 152
human resource, 332
indirect-action environment and, 98
Formal authority, 299–302
basis of, 300–302
defined, 299–300
delegation of, 310–15
leadership style and, 476
Formal channels of communication, 534
Formal groups, 494
Formal organizational structure, 267–74
Formal performance appraisal, 349–50
Four C's Model for human resources, 355–56
Franchising, 712
Functional authority, 309–10
Functional competence, 747
Functional conflict, 396
Functional layouts, 637
Functional-level strategy, 203–5
Functional managers, 11
Functional organization, 228, 267–68, 289
Functional strategy development, 233–36

Gantt charts, 37, 152, 153
General Accounting Office (GAO), 75
General financial condition, 583
General managers, 11
General recruiting, 332–33
General Services Administration (GSA), 75
Geocentric managers, 771
Geography, division by, 269
Global strategic partnership, 782
Goals
budgetary, 605–6
of committees, 511
current, identification of, 214
differences in, as source of conflict, 394
group, 305, 504
organizational, 12
organizational achievement of, 5
prioritization of, 7
selection of, 12
setting, 141–42, 212–14, 241, 605–6
superordinate, 232, 402

Goals (*continued*)
(*See also* Objectives)
Goal-setting theory of motivation, 450–51
Gordon Technique, The (synectics), 410–11
Gospel of Wealth, The (Carnegie), 110
Government
international competition and, 94–95
role of, 74–76
social responsibility and, 109
Government agencies, 75
Government policy, 209
Government regulation, productivity and, 622, 701
Grapevine, 539–40
Grapevine chain, 540
Graphic rating, 350
Group building and maintenance role, 496
Group creativity, 409–11
Group maintenance leadership functions, 463
Groups, 492–516
boards, 507
case studies, 492, 502, 514, 517
cohesiveness of, 500–502
commissions, 507
committees, 278, 507–12
defined, 493
informal leaders of, 496
norms and conformity in, 496–500
problem solving in, 502–5
task forces, 278–79, 413, 505–10, 512–14
types of, 493–95
Groupthink, 510
Growth needs, 433

Halo effect, 351
Harvard Business School, 354–56
Hawthorne effect, 49
Hawthorne experiments, 48–49
Heuristics principles, 177–79, 181, 185
Hierarchy
classical principle of, 43
managerial, 278
of needs, 51–52, 432–33
Hindsight bias, 181
Hiring (*see* Recruitment; Selection)
Hiring specification, 334
Historical standards, 567
History of Standard Oil (Tarbell), 44
Holistic model of control, 47
Human relations management, 48–51
contributions of, 49–50
Hawthorne experiments, 48–49
limitations of, 50–51
motivation and, 426–28
organizational design and, 283–85
Human resource audit, 332
Human resource management of, 236, 328–58
case studies, 328, 348, 357, 359
defined, 329
demotions, 352
development programs, 330, 345–48
discipline, 352
human resource planning, 329–32
international, 783–84
performance appraisal, 345, 348–51
planned change and, 373, 374
process of, 329–30
promotions, 38, 335, 352
recruitment (*see* Recruitment)
selection (*see* Selection)
separations, 352–54
socialization, 330, 344–45
strategic planning and, 331, 354–56
training (*see* Training)
Human resource planning, 329–32
Human resources model of motivation, 427–28
Human resources surveys, 345
Human skill, 14, 15

Idea development, 412–13
Idea generation, 411
Immediate work environment, 441
Impoverished management style, 467, 468
In-basket exercise, 344
Incentive compensation, 242–43
Income statement, 585
Incremental adjustment, 183
Incremental productivity improvement method, 618
Independent units, 280
Indirect-action environment, 70–72, 83–90, 98
Individual characteristics, 431–33, 435–37
Individual creativity, 408–11
Individualism, creative, 736–37
Inequity theory of motivation, 448–50
Inflexibility, as barrier to effective strategy implementation, 249
Influence
defined, 300, 459
(*See also* Power)
Informal communication, 539–40
Informal group leaders, 496, 503
Informal groups, 494–95
Informal organizational structure, 274–75
Informal performance appraisal, 349
Information
control and, 653–56
defined, 655
management, 655 (*See also* End-user computing; Management information systems)
Informational roles, 15–17, 522
Information ownership, 536
Information processing, 277
Information quality, 655
Information quantity, 655
Information relevance, 185, 655
Information systems (*see* End-user computing; Management information systems)
Information technology, advanced, 541–44
Information timeliness, 655
Informed opportunism, 19
Initial job assignment, 732
Initial strategy approach, 198
Initiative, classical principle of, 43
Innovation
conical career model and, 749–50
vs. creativity, 408
entrepreneurship and, 701–5
organizational, 413–15
Innovative strategy, 235–36
Input measurements, 565
Inputs, 57, 70
In Search of Excellence (Peters and Waterman), 61
Institutionalizing strategy, 244–47
Integrating roles, 279
Integration, 276
Integrative approaches
to management theory, 59–61
to motivation, 444–51
Integrative problem solving, 402
Interactionist view of conflict, 391, 392
Internal auditing, 606–7
Internal constraints on strategy implementation, 249
Internal environment
human resource management and, 331
organizational change and, 363–64
organizational design and, 286
Internal-policy level of moral questions, 117
Internal stakeholders, 80, 82
International competition, 79–80, 90–94
International environment, 90–95
Internationalization, 767–71
International management, 766–89
case studies, 766, 775, 789, 790–93
challenges of, 775–85
communication and, 522–23, 542–43
cultural relativism and, 125–27, 130
internationalization, 767–71
managerial approach selection, 785–88
multinational enterprises, 771–75, 780–85
strategic partnerships, 213
Internship, 346
Interpersonal communication, 523–28
Interpersonal roles, 15–17, 522
Inter-role conflict, 737
Intersender conflict, 737
Interstate Commerce Commission (ICC), 75
Interviews, selection, 341, 342
Intrapreneurship, 713
Intrasender conflict, 737
Intrinsic outcomes, 446
Inventory planning and control, 642–45
Inventory turnover, 587
Investment centers, 591–92

Japanese firms
characteristics of, 787
competition with U.S. firms, 91–93
cultural differences, 777
managerial approaches of, 61, 786–88
manufacturers in the U.S., 770
manufacturing quality improvement, 9
stock traders, 778
training of multinational enterprise managers, 783
Jargon, 529, 530
Job applications, 341
Job assignment, initial, 732
Job characteristics, 431, 437–39
Job descriptions, 334
Job design, 315–21, 637, 639
Job dissatisfaction, 430, 437–39
Job enlargement, 263, 317, 373
Job enrichment, 263, 317, 373
Job experiences, early, 732–34
Job requirements analysis, 345
Job rotation, 346, 347
Job satisfaction, 39, 50–51

job design and, 319–21
two-factor approach to, 430, 437–39
Job-shop systems, 631, 634
Job specialization, 262–63, 535
Job titles, 339
Jungle, The (Sinclair), 44–45
Just-in-time inventories, 642–43

Key-performance areas, 570–71
Key technologies, 89–90
Knowledge
of environment, lack of, 142
organizational, lack of, 141
organizational preservation of, 6
Knowledge-based systems, 674–79
Korean firms, 92
Korean management style, 790–91

Labor force, women in, 86
Labor-management conflict, 404–7
Labor market, 334
Labor unions
conflict with management, 405–7
role of, 78
Laissez-faire management style, 467, 468
Language differences, 522–23, 529, 532
Large-batch production, 290
Lateral communication, 539
Lateral relationship, 278
Layout planning, 637, 638
Leaderless group discussion exercise, 344
Leader-member relations, 473, 474
Leader role, 16, 17
Leadership, 424–546
case studies, 458, 468, 486, 488–89, 548–51
defined, 4, 459
entrepreneurial, 715–16
of groups (*see* Groups)
influence and, 459
in management process model, 13
motivation (*see* Motivation)
power and, 459, 460
theories of (*see* Leadership theories)
Leadership functions, 463–64
Leadership specialization, 463
Leadership style
in behavioral approach, 463–68
in contingency approach, 470–79
Leadership theories, 460–85
behavioral approach, 462–67
contingency approach (*see* Contingency approach to leadership)
romance of leadership, 484, 486
self-leadership, 483–84
self-managed groups, 482–83
situational factors, 469–70
trait approach, 461–62
transformational (or charismatic) leadership, 480–82
Learner career state, 752–53
Least-preferred co-worker (LPC) measure, 474–75
Legal environment, multinational, 776, 778
Legitimate power, 302
Liabilities, 584–85
Liason role, 16, 17
Library of Congress, 75
Life cycle
career, 741–45
technological, 89–90
Life expectancy, 85
Lifestyle changes, 83, 86
Linear career concept, 745–47
Line authority, 307–8
Line-staff conflict, 403–4
Liquidity, 583
Long-run capacity changes, 633
Long-term liabilities, 585
Love needs, 432
Loyalty dilemmas, 735–36

Macroeconomic policy, 701
Majority rule, 401
Management, defined, 3–4
Management by exception, 566
Management by objectives (MBO), 238–42, 347, 350
Management development programs, 330, 346–48
Management Edge, The (software), 684–85
Management information, defined, 655
Management information systems (MIS), 278, 412, 656–72
case studies, 652, 660, 681–82
vs. decision support systems, 673
defined, 653, 656
design of, 660–65
evolution of, 657–58
impact of computers on, 680–81
implementation of, 665–72
management level and, 658–59
Management-labor conflict, 404–7
Management learning, 24–25
Management level
defined, 10–11
management information systems and, 658–59
management skills and, 14–15
planning and, 12
Management process
case studies, 2, 8, 26
model of, 11–14
(*See also* Control; Leadership; Organizing; Planning)
Management science school, 54, 55
Management theory, 32–62
behavioral school (*see* Behavioral school)
case studies, 32, 40–41, 62, 64–65
classical school (*see* Classical school)
evolution of, 55–61
integrative approach to, 59–61
management science school, 54, 55
neo-human relations approach, 59–61
recent approaches (*see* Contingency approach; Systems approach)
theory, defined, 33
transitional theories, 46–48
Manager-centered development programs, 346
Managerial attitudes toward internationalization, 771
Managerial competence, 747
Managerial Grid, 467, 468
Managerial hierarchy, 278
Managerial integrating roles, 279
Managerial interventions, 225, 226
Managerial performance, defined, 8
Managerial roles, 82
communication and, 522
coordination enhancing, 278–79
group building and maintenance, 496
task, 496
types of, 15–18
Managerial style
as barrier to effective strategy implementation, 249
human relations approach and, 49–50
organizational effectiveness and, 232
Managers
attributes of, 6–8
matching strategies with, 243–44
roles of (*see* Roles)
selection of, 342–43
types of, 10–11. (*See also* First-line managers; Middle managers; Top managers)
Maquila industry, 624–25
Market development, 235
Market entry barriers, 209
Marketing layouts, 637
Marketing strategies, 234, 235
Market organization, 267–71
Market penetration, 235
Mass production, 290
Master budgets, 597
Materials-requirements planning, 642
Matrix organization, 267, 271–74, 279, 289, 413
Mature matrix organization structure, 272–73
Measurement, in control process, 565, 567, 569, 570
Mechanistic job design, 316, 319, 320
Mechanistic organizational system, 287, 288
Media, role of, 78
Mediation, 7
Memo writing, 535
Mentoring relationships, 758
Mentors, 750, 758
Message, 525
Middle managers
defined, 11
management information systems and, 658–59
planning by, 12
skills needed, 15
Middle-of-the-road management style, 467, 468
Milestone scheduling, 153–54
Mistakes, need for control and, 560
Models
defined, 11
management process, 11–14
Monitoring role, 16, 17
Moral relativism, 123–27
Moral rules, 119
Moral theory
relativism, 123–27
(*See also* Ethics; Social responsibility, corporate)
Motivating Economic Achievement (McClelland and Winter), 706
Motivation, 424–53
behavioral science approach, 51–52
budgets and, 602, 604
career, 747

Motivation (*continued*)
case studies, 424, 435, 452, 454–55
content theories of, 428–29
culture and, 434
defined, 425
equity (or inequity) theory of, 448–50
expectancy approach to, 444–48
goal-setting theory of, 450–51
guidelines for, 451
human relations model of, 426–28
importance of, 425–26
individual characteristics and, 431–33, 435–37
integrative approaches to, 444–51
job characteristics and, 431, 437–39
past consequences and, 443–44
process theories of, 429, 430
productivity and, 619–20, 622
reinforcement theories of, 429–31
systems view of, 431–43
traditional model of, 426, 428
Western theories of, 786
work situation characteristics and, 431, 439–43
Motivational job design, 316–17, 319, 320
Muckraking, 44–45
Multidivisional firm, 228
Multinational enterprises (MNEs), 771–75, 780–85
Multinational firms, 230, 767–71
Mutual aid, 119

Naive relativism, 124–25
National Aeronautics and Space Administration (NASA), 75, 89
National Labor Relations Board (NLRB), 75
National Transportation Safety Board, 75
Natural-language processing, 679
Natural selection, 96
Need-achievement theory, 703–9
Needs
for achievement, 435–37
for affiliation, 436–37
in Barnard management theory, 47–48
in content theory of motivation, 429–30
ERG theory of, 433
hierarchy of, 51–52, 432–33
in human relations approach, 49
for power, 436, 437
in scientific management theory, 39
Needs analysis, 346
Negotiations, management-labor, 406–7
Negotiator role, 16, 18
Neoclassical approach to organizational design, 283–85
Neo-human relations approach, 59–61
Network-based scheduling, 154–57
Networks
communication, 536–38
stakeholder, 82–83
Net worth, 585
Noise, 526, 529–32
Nominal group process, 410
Nonmalevolence, 119
Nonprogrammed decisions, 175
Nonverbal communication, 531, 532
Norms, group, 496–500
Nuclear Regulatory Commission, 75

Obedience/conscience conflict, 304, 305
Objective-based performance appraisal, 350
Objectives
annual, 237–38
decision, identification of, 167
management by, 238–42, 347, 350
(*See also* Goals)
Occupational Safety and Health Administration (OSHA), 74, 75
Occupations Safety and Health Act of 1970, 639
Off-the-job development, 347–48
Off-the-job training, 346
Ohio State University, 466–67
One-way communication, 527–28
On-the-job development, 347
On-the-job training, 346
Open system, 57
Openness, 544–45
Operating budgets, 595–97
Operational control, 639
Operationalizing strategy, 233–44
annual objectives, 237–38
defined, 233
functional strategy, 233–36
management by objectives, 238–42
matching managers and strategies, 243–44
reward systems, 242–43
Operational strategy, 233
Operations
defined, 616
trends in, 616
(*See also* Operations management; Operations systems)
Operations management
defined, 616
operations system design, 632–39
planning and control (*see* Operations planning and control)
strategic planning and, 629–30
Operations planning and control, 639–45
defined, 639
detailed scheduling, 641–42
inventory, 642–45
materials-requirements, 642
objectives of, 640
production plans, 640–41
Operations research, 53–54
Operations strategies, 235
Operations systems, 614–46
capacity planning, 632–33
case studies, 614, 631, 646–48
changing views of, 615–16
characteristics of, 628–31
defined, 628
family-location planning, 636–37
job design, 315–21, 637, 639
layout planning, 637, 638
process selection, 633–36
productivity and (*see* Productivity)
product/service planning and design, 632
Opportunity finding, 23, 171–72
Order, classical principle of, 43
Organic organizational system, 287, 288
Organizational analysis, 345
Organizational change, 363–85
case studies, 362, 374, 385–87
forces for, 363–64
managerial responses to pressures for, 365–66
models of process, 366–68
organizational culture and (*see* Organizational culture)
organizational development, 375–82
planned, 365–67, 370–74
resistance to, 142, 368–70
strategic planning and, 197, 215–17
stress and, 739
technological, 151, 371, 373
(*See also* Creativity)
Organizational communication, 533–45
advanced information technology, 541–44
barriers to, 540–541
factors influencing, 534–36
informal, 539–40
lateral, 539
networks, 536–38
openness, 544–45
vertical, 538–39
Organizational complexity, need for control and, 559–60
Organizational conflict, 390–407
case study, 390, 398, 415
changing views of, 391–92
vs. competition, 391
defined, 391
dynamics and consequences of, 395–97
line-staff, 403–4
management-labor, 404–7
management of, 398–402
nature of, 392–93
sources of, 394–95
types of, 393–94
Organizational creativity, 411–15
Organizational culture, 247, 382–84
centralization and, 323
change in, 383
defined, 375
early job experience and, 734
entrepreneurial, 717–19
importance of, 383
leadership style and, 470
management information systems and, 666
motivation and, 440
organizational conflict and, 397
reality shock syndrome and, 730
underlying structure, 383
Organizational design, 280–91
classical approach, 281–82, 372
early approaches, 281
environment and, 285–89
neoclassical approach, 283–85
task-technology relationship and, 289–91
Organizational development (OD), 375–82
Organizational form, 712
Organizational goals, 12
Organizational performance, 8, 10
Organizational size, decentralization and, 322–23
Organizational structure
adjustment to external environment with, 99
authority (*see* Authority)

case studies, 260, 275, 291, 293–95
change of, 371–73, 372–73
coordination (*see* Coordination)
decentralization (*see* Decentralization)
defined, 264
departmentalization, 261
divisional, 269–71, 321
division of work, 261–64, 276
entrepreneurial role and, 715
formal, 267–74
functional, 228, 267–68, 289
informal, 274–75
international management and, 781–83
major aspects of, 265
management information systems and, 680–81
matrix, 267, 271–74, 279, 289, 413
organizational conflict and, 397
organizational design (*see* Organizational design)
organization chart, 265–67
product/market organization, 267–71
strategy implementation and, 226–32
Organization chart, 265–67
Organizations, functions of, 5–6
Organizing, 260–421
case studies, 418–21
in classical organization theory, 42
conflict (*see* Organizational conflict)
creativity (*see* Creativity)
defined, 4, 264
human resource management (*see* Human resource management)
in management process model, 13
organizational change and (*see* Organizational change)
organizational structure (*see* Organizational structure)
Orientation, 344–45
Outcome interdependence, 501
Outplacement services, 353
Outputs, 57, 70
Outside recruitment, 334–35
Overconfidence bias, 181

Panic, as barrier to problem solving, 183
Paradoxes of Life (Smith and Berg), 514
Parallel installation, 664
Parochialism, as barrier to strategy implementation, 249
Partial productivity ratio, 617–18
Participative management, 427–28, 477–78
Past consequences, motivation and, 443–44
Past experience
deviation from, problem solving and, 170
leadership effectiveness and, 469
Path-goal model, 475–76
Peers
leadership style and, 470
ratings by, 349
People's Republic of China, 95, 125, 140, 706–7, 776
Perceptions, differing, 529, 531, 541, 604
Perceptual/motor job design, 319, 320
Performance appraisal, 345, 348–51, 738
Performance gaps, 216–17
Performance measurement, 557–58, 672
Performance-outcome expectancy, 446
Permanent formal groups, 494
Permanent overlay organization structure, 272
Personality, leadership effectiveness and, 469
Personal level of moral questions, 117
Personnel policies, 439
Person-role conflict, 737
PERT (program evaluation and review technique), 154–57
Phased installation, 664
Physical examination, 341
Physical needs, 39, 51
Physiological needs, 432
Pilot installation, 664
Planned change, 365–67, 370–74
Planned work activities, 347
Planning, 138–206
adjustment to external environment with, 99
case study, 138, 145, 158
in classical organization theory, 42
complex projects, 152–57
decision making and (*see* Decision making)
defined, 4, 139, 165
entrepreneurial, 713–14
forecasting (*see* Forecasting)
link between controlling and, 144–45, 556
in management process model, 12
need for, 139
operational, 145–48, 205–6
operations (*see* Operations planning and control)
problem solving and (*see* Problem solving)
steps in, 141–44
strategic (*see* Strategic planning)
Plant-closing notification, 353
Plants, productivity and, 621
Plateaued individual, 747
Policies, defined, 147
Policy-formulation approach, 197–98
Political insensitivity and passivity, 734–35
Political risk, 779
Political skills, 7
Political variables, 88
Politics, 20
as barrier to effective strategy implementation, 248
international management and, 776
Polycentric managers, 771
Portfolio framework for strategy formulation, 206–7
Portfolio investment, 767–69
Position descriptions, 334
Position power, 473, 474
Positive reinforcement, 445
Post-action controls, 563
Postal Rate Commission, 75
Potency, sense of, 501
Power, 20
authority (*see* Authority; Formal authority)
as barrier to effective strategy implementation, 249
communication effectiveness and, 534
defined, 300, 459
leadership and, 459, 460
need for, 23, 436, 437
in organizations, 303, 305–7
position, 473, 474
sources of, 302–3
Power shifts, as barrier to strategy implementation, 248
Practice of Management, The (Drucker), 239
Pre-action controls (precontrols), 562
Predetermined standards, 569
Pregnancy Discrimination Act of 1978, 337–38
Premises, 149
Pricing, 627
Primary relations, 113
Principles of Scientific Management, The (Taylor), 37
Priority setting, 184–85
Prior probability bias, 180
Privacy, right to, 338–39
Problem definition, 166
Problem finding, 23, 169–71, 409
Problem solving
committee, 510–512
group, 502–5
improving effectiveness of, 182–85
integrative, 402
process of, 165–69
(*See also* Decision making)
Problem-specific systems, 678–79
Procedures, 278
Process consultation, 377–78
Process flow, 635–36
Process layouts, 637
Process production, 290
Process selection, 633–36
Process theories of motivation, 429, 430
Product, division by, 269
Product-cycle theory, 768
Product differentiation, 209
Production plans, 640–41
Production strategies, 234, 235
Production systems (*see* Operations systems)
Productivity, 617–25
competitive priorities and, 625–28
defined, 617
division of work and, 262–63
entrepreneurship and, 701
factors influencing, 621–22
group cohesiveness and, 50–52
improvement of, 618–19, 623–25
macroeconomic policy and, 701
management theories of (*see* Management theory)
planned change and, 371–74
research and development and, 621, 701
worker motivation and, 619–20, 622
Productivity management, 623–25
Productivity ratios, 617–18
Product layouts, 637, 638
Product organization, 267–71
Product planning and design, 632
Profit budgets, 597
Profit centers, 591
Profitgraph, 587, 588

Profit sharing, 620
Pro forma balance sheet, 598
Programmed decisions, 174–75
Programs, defined, 146
Projection, management information system implementation and, 666, 667
Project layouts, 637
Project management, 152–57
Projects, defined, 146
Project teams (*see* Task forces)
Promise keeping, 119
Promotions, 38, 335, 352
Protective strategy, 236
Psychological characteristics of entrepreneurs, 703–9
Psychology of Management (Gilbreth), 38
Psychosocial functions, 758
Psychosocial theories of entrepreneurship, 707–9
Public view of business, 108
Punishment, 445

Qualitative overloading, 738
Qualititative forecasting, 151, 152
Quality circle, 645
Quality control, 9, 644–45
Quality level, 627
Quality reliability, 627
Quantitative forecasting, 151, 152
Quantitative overloading, 738
Quantitative school
  management science (*see* Management science school)
  operations research, 53–54
Question mark category, in BCG matrix, 206, 207
Questionnaires, 378

Radial movement, 748
Railroad Retirement Board, 75
Random event bias, 180
Ratio analysis, 586–87, 589
Rational decision making, 176, 184–85
Realistic job preview (RJP), 342, 730–32
Reality shock syndrome, 730, 731
Rebellion, 736
Recall bias, 180
Receiver, 526
Recruitment, 332–39
  affirmative action, 336–37, 339
  defined, 329, 332
  equal employment opportunity, 335–39, 760
  general, 332–33
  job descriptions, 334
  position descriptions, 334
  sources for, 334–35
  specialized, 333
Redundancy, 532–33
Reference groups, 493–94
Referent power, 303
Reform, 35
Refreezing, 368
Regional population, 85–86
Reinforcement theories, 429–31
Relatedness needs, 433
Relativism, moral, 123–27
Relaxation training, 740
Relevance, acquisition of power with, 307
Remuneration
  classical principle of, 43
  (*See also* Compensation)
Renewal Factor, The: How the Best Companies Get and Keep the Competitive Edge (Waterman), 226, 620
Reorientation situation, 246
Replacement chart, 332, 333
Representativeness, decision making and, 178
Research and development, 235–36, 621, 701
Resource allocation, 602–3
Resource-allocator role, 16, 18
Resource analysis, 215–16
Resource dependence, 96
Respect for persons and property, 119
Responsibility, 6–7
  delegation of, 310–12
  social (*see* Social responsibility, corporate)
  stress and, 738
Responsibility centers, 590–92
Restraining forces, 367
Résumé writing, 733
Retreatism, 708
Return on investment, 587
Revenue budgets, 597
Revenue centers, 590–91
Reward power, 302
Rewards
  in behavior modification, 443–45
  in equity theory, 448–50
  in expectancy theory, 446–48
  in path-goal approach to leadership, 475
  systems of, 242–43
Rights, 118–19
Risk
  decision making and, 175–76, 504
  political, 779
Risk taking, 709
Robots, 39
Role ambiguity, 737
Role conflict, 737
Role-overload conflict, 737
Role perception, 426
Role playing, 346
Roles
  of managers (*see* Managerial roles)
  of stakeholders, 71–83
Romance of leadership, 484, 486
Rules, 148, 278

Safety needs, 51, 432–33
Sales information, forecasting for, 151
Sample size bias, 180
Satisficing, 176–77, 438
Scalar principle, 312
Scarcity, as barrier to effective strategy implementation, 248
Scenario construction, 152
Scheduling
  milestone, 153–54
  network-based, 154–57
  operations, 641–42
Scientific management, 35–39, 426
Scientific selection and development, 39
Screening controls, 563
Search strategy bias, 180
Secondary relations, 113
Securities and Exchange Commission (SEC), 75
Security
  career motivation and, 747
  management information systems and, 668–71
Security needs, 432–33
Segmentable environments, 289
Segmentation methods, 152
Selection, 339, 341–44
  assessment centers, 343–44
  defined, 329, 339
  of managers, 342–43
  of multinational enterprise managers, 783
  steps in, 341–42
Selective blend situation, 245–46
Selective Service System, 75
Self-actualizing man concept, 51–52
Self-actualizing needs, 51–52, 432, 433, 731
Self-fulfilling prophecy, 469
Self-leadership, 483–85
Self-managed work groups, 482–83, 485
Semivariable costs, 600
Sender, 524
Sensitivity training, 377
Separation method of conflict resolution, 492
Separations (termination), 352–54
Sequential interventions, 226
Service planning and design, 632
Service sector growth, productivity and, 621
Seven-S model, 230–32
Sexual harassment, 337
Shared resources, as source of conflict, 394
Shareholders, role of, 80, 82
Shop Management (Taylor), 37
Short-run capacity changes, 633
Simple environments, 288–89
Single-use plans, 146–47
Situational approach (*see* Contingency approach)
Situational leadership model, 470–72
Skills
  management level and, 14–15
  organizational effectiveness and, 232
Skill variety, 317
Slack resources, 280
Small-batch production, 290
Small Business Administration (SBA), 75
Smoothing, 401
Social audits, 121
Socialization, 330, 344–45, 749, 750
Social man concept, 49, 51
Social needs, 39, 49, 432
Social performance, corporate, 114
Social responsibility, corporate, 106–15
  case studies, 20–21, 106, 115, 128
  changing concept of, 107–8
  corporate social responsiveness and, 112–15
  history of, 110–12
  planning and, 150
  profit maximization view, 108–9
  (*See also* Ethics)
Social responsiveness, corporate, 112–15
Social values, 83, 86–87
Social variables, 83–87

Societal functions of organizations, 5
Societal-level moral questions, 116
Sociological characteristics of entrepreneurs, 703–9
Solid citizen career state, 752–53
Solution finding, 167
Source of message, 524
Sources-and-uses-of-funds statements, 585–86
South Africa, 125–27
Span of management, 263–64
Special group, 379
Special interest groups, 76–78, 88
Specialized recruiting, 333
Spiral career concept, 745–47
Spokesperson role, 16, 17
Sponsors, 307, 750
Stability situation, 246
Stable environment, 286, 287
Staff
  organizational effectiveness and, 232
  (*See also* Human resource management)
Staff authority, 308–9
Staff-line conflict, 403–4
Staff specialists, social responsiveness and, 112–13
Staff stability, classical principle of, 43
Stakeholders
  defined, 69
  ethics and, 116–17
  roles of, 73–83
  strategic anticipation of reactions of, 215
Standards
  flexibility of, 570
  setting, 557, 566, 569
  shifting, 351
  types of, 567, 569
Standing committees, 507–10
Standing plans, 147–48
Standing procedures, 148
Stanford University, 498–500
Star career state, 752, 753
Star category, in BCG matrix, 206, 207
Start-ups, 700
Static environments, 288–89
Steady-state career concept, 745, 746
Steering controls, 563–65
Stewardship principle, 110–11
Storage layouts, 637
Strategic business unit (SBU) planning, 203, 211–18
Strategic control, 218
Strategic-control points, 571–72
Strategic management approach, 198–200
Strategic partnerships, 213
Strategic planning, 192–219
  business-unit strategy, 203, 211–18
  case studies, 192, 202, 211, 218–20
  decentralization and, 322
  defined, 193
  effectiveness of, 195–96
  entrepreneurial, 713–15
  evolution of concept, 196–201
  frameworks for, 206–11
  vs. general types of planning, 194
  human resource management and, 331, 354–56
  importance of, 193–96
  international management and, 780–81
  levels of, 202–6
  vs. operational planning, 205–6
  operations management and, 629–30
  strategic implementation (*see* Strategic implementation)
Strategic-quality decisions, 644
Strategy control, 200
Strategy-formulation task, 199
Strategy implementation, 218, 224–51
  case studies, 224, 232–33, 250–53
  defined, 199
  effective, barriers to, 248–49
  institutionalizing strategy, 244–47
  operationalizing strategy (*see* Operationalizing strategy)
  organizational structure and, 226–32
  typology of, 225–26
Stress, 738–40
Stressors, 738
Structural economic changes, 87
Style (*see* Leadership style; Managerial style)
Subjective standards, 569
Subordinates
  as influence on leadership style, 464–65, 470, 475–77
  ratings of bosses by, 349–50
  in situational leadership theory, 471–72
Substitute products, 208, 210
Subsystems, defined, 56–57
Succession plans, 245
Superior's ratings of subordinates, 349
Superordinate goals, 232, 402
Suppliers
  bargaining power of, 208, 210
  role of, 73–74
Suppression methods, 401
Survey feedback, 378–79
Surveys of opinions, 152
Symbolic role of managers, 7–8
Syndrome of unused potential, 730, 731
Synectics (The Gordon Technique), 410–411
Synergy, 57, 512
System 1, 2, 3, and 4 organizations, 284–85
Systematic performance appraisal, 349–50
System boundary, 57
Systems approach, 56–57
Systems view of motivation, 431–43

Task forces, 278–79, 413, 505–510, 512–14
Task identity, 317
Task interdependence, 501
Task management style, 467, 468
Task-oriented managers, 463–64, 466–67, 475
Task-related leadership functions, 463
Task requirements, leadership style and, 470
Task role, 496
Task significance, 317
Task structure, 473, 474
Task-technology relationship, 289–91
Tax policies, productivity and, 622, 701
Team building, 378–80
Team management style, 467, 468
Teamwork, 20
Technical competence, 747
Technical skill, 14, 15
Technological change, 151, 371, 373
Technological variables, 88–90
Technology
  as barrier to effective strategy implementation, 248–49
  entrepreneurship and, 701–5
  international environment and, 90
  organizational structure and, 289–91
  process selection and, 633–34
  productivity improvement and, 618–19
  (*See also* Computers)
Technostructural change, 373
Telecommuting, 543
Temporary formal groups, 494
Temporary overlay organization structure, 272
Termination policy, 353–54
Theory
  defined, 33
  (*See also* Management theory)
Theory X, 427
Theory Y, 427
Three-position plan of promotion, 38
Thriving on Chaos: Handbook for Management Revolution (Peters), 18–19, 61, 226, 619–20
Top-down budgeting, 592, 593
Top managers
  defined, 11
  management information systems and, 659, 667, 668, 680–81
  planning by, 12
  responsibility for subordinates issue, 266
  skills needed, 15
  social responsiveness of, 112–13
  strategy implementation and, 244–46
  style of, 232
Total productivity ratio, 617
Traditional model of motivation, 426, 428
Traditional pyramid organization structure, 272
Traditional view of conflict, 392
Traditions, as barrier to effective strategy implementation, 249
Training
  conical career model and, 749, 750
  coping skills, 740
  criticism of, 21–24
  defined, 330
  human relations approach and, 50
  management information system operator, 664–65
  multinational enterprise manager, 783
  relaxation, 740
Training positions, 347
Training programs, 345–48
Trait approach to leadership, 461–62
Transactional leaders, 480–81
Transaction analysis (TA), 377
Transfer price, 591
Transfers, 352
Transformational coping, 739
Transformational leadership, 480–82
Transitional theories, 46–48
Transitory career concept, 745, 746
Transportation costs, 90, 91
Treatment discrimination, 338
Trust, 20
Turbulent environment, 287
Turnover situation, 245
Two-way communication, 527–28
Type A behavior, 709

Uncertainty, 95–96, 175–76
Underloading, 738
Unfreezing, 368
Uniform Guidelines on Employee Selection Procedures, 338
Union of Soviet Socialist Republics, 95, 140, 144, 230, 777
United States Arms Control & Disarmament Agency, 75
United States Chambers of Commerce, 75
United States International Trade Commission, 75
United States Postal Service, 75
Unit production, 289–90
Unity of command, 312, 313
University of Michigan, 467
University-sponsored management development programs, 347–48
Unused potential, syndrome of, 730, 731

Valence, 446
Values
  as barrier to effective strategy implementation, 249
  defined, 118
  differences in, as source of conflict, 394–95
  social, 83, 86–87
Values-based strategies, 205
Variable budgets, 599
Variable costs, 600
Variable operations costs, 636
Vendors, role of, 74
Vertical communication, 538–39
Vertical information system, 278
Vertical integration, 228
Vertical movement, 748
Vestibule training, 346
Veterans Administration (VA), 75
Video conferencing, 542
Vietnam-Era Veterans' Readjustment Act of 1974, 337
Violence, authority of, 498–500
Visibility, acquisition of power with, 307
Vocational Rehabilitation Act of 1973, 337
Vroom-Jago leadership model, 479
Vroom-Yetton leadership model, 476–77

Wealth of Nations (Smith), 262
Whistleblowing, 236, 251–52
White-collar productivity, 620
Women
  attitudes of co-workers toward, 759–60
  career expectations, 729, 759
  equal employment opportunity, 336–39, 760
  in labor force, 86
Work, division of, 261–64
Work activities, planned, 347
Work design, 39
Work ethic, 619
Work flow, 373, 572–73
Work flow layouts, 637
Work force, productivity and, 621
Work groups, self-managed, 482–83, 485
Working conditions, stress and, 739
Work methods analysis, 639
Workplace layout, 541
Work schedules, alternative, 318–19
Work situation
  characteristics of, 431, 439–43
  management of, 755–57

Yale experiments, 304, 305, 498
Yes/no controls, 563

Zero-base budgeting, 601–2
Zone of indifference, 301

HOW TO USE YOUR AIE

Thought-Provokers—questions designed to get students to think about the complexity and dynamics of the management process.

THOUGHT-PROVOKER

What were the economic, cultural, and political forces like at this time? How would these have contributed to the development of this scientific management approach?

By 1893, Taylor decided he could best put his ideas into effect as a private consulting management engineer. He was soon able to report impressive improvements in productivity, quality, worker morale, and wages while working with one client, Simonds Rolling Machine Company. In one operation, Simonds employed 120 women to inspect bicycle ball bearings. The work was tedious, the hours were long, and there seemed little reason to believe improvements could be made. Taylor proved otherwise. First, he studied and timed the movements of the best workers. Then he trained the rest in the methods of their more effective co-workers and transferred or laid off the poorest performers. He also introduced rest periods during the workday, along with his differential pay rate system and other improvements. The results were impressive: Expenses went down while productivity, quality, earnings, and worker morale went up. (See Exhibit 2-1.)

EXHIBIT 2-1 IMPROVEMENTS IN PRODUCTIVITY AT THE SIMONDS ROLLING MACHINE COMPANY.

Task:	Inspection of the balls used in bicycle ball bearings. An established operation employing 120 workers who were "old hands" and skilled at their jobs.
Major Changes Made:	Additional training based on study of higher-performing workers. Selection on the basis of appropriate skills, laying off or transferring lower performers. Workday shortened from 10½ to 8½ hours. Rest periods introduced. Efficiency of control system increased (but with no change in inspection standards).
Results Reported:	Thirty-five inspectors did work formerly done by 120. Accuracy improved by two-thirds. Wages received rose by 80 to 100 percent. Apparent improvements in worker morale.

Coordinated Resources—reference practical resources such as videotapes, films, books and periodicals with a given chapter. (See the Supplements Guide for complete integration of all supplements in this text's package.)

THE TOOLS OF ETHICS

COORDINATED RESOURCE

A recently completed landmark study on business ethics entitled, "Corporate Ethics: A Prime Business Asset" is available from The Business Roundtable, 200 Park Avenue, New York, NY 10166, or call (212) 682-6370. An excerpt from this document on Johnson & Johnson's Credo is found in the box on Ethics in Management. In addition, see the Lecture Extras Supplement for an anecdotal digest of the contents of the report.

We engage in some kind of ethical reasoning every day of our lives, but in order to improve it, we must analyze it explicitly as well as practice it casually. Business will not overcome the moral uncertainties that now plague it until it addresses ethical issues in ethical terms.

Ethical Language

Some companies, such as IBM, have an open-door policy to encourage employees to speak about problems. Others, such as J. C. Penney, have spelled out policies about conflict of interest. (See the Management Application box entitled "A Code of Conduct at J. C. Penney.")